OpenGL°

SUPERBIBLE
Fourth Edition

OpenGL®

SUPERBIBLE

Fourth Edition

Comprehensive Tutorial and Reference

Richard S. Wright, Jr.
Benjamin Lipchak
Nicholas Haemel

Addison-Wesley

Upper Saddle River, NJ • Boston • Indianapolis • San Francisco
New York • Toronto • Montreal • London • Munich • Paris • Madrid
Cape Town • Sydney • Tokyo • Singapore • Mexico City

The publisher offers excellent discounts on this book when ordered in quantity for bulk purchases or special sales, which may include electronic versions and/or custom covers and content particular to your business, training goals, marketing focus, and branding interests. For more information, please contact:

U.S. Corporate and Government Sales
(800) 382-3419
corpsales@pearsontechgroup.com

For sales outside the United States please contact:

International Sales
international@pearsoned.com

This Book Is Safari Enabled

 The Safari® Enabled icon on the cover of your favorite technology book means the book is available through Safari Bookshelf. When you buy this book, you get free access to the online edition for 45 days.

Safari Bookshelf is an electronic reference library that lets you easily search thousands of technical books, find code samples, download chapters, and access technical information whenever and wherever you need it.

To gain 45-day Safari Enabled access to this book:

- Go to http://www.awprofessional.com/safarienabled
- Complete the brief registration form
- Enter the coupon code RHH3-KFJH-A29I-4BHP-8T3W

If you have difficulty registering on Safari Bookshelf or accessing the online edition, please e-mail customer-service@safaribooksonline.com.

Visit us on the Web: www.informit.com\aw

Library of Congress Cataloging-in-Publication Data:

Wright, Richard S., 1965-
  OpenGL superbible : comprehensive tutorial and reference / Richard S. Wright, Jr., Benjamin Lipchak, Nicholas Haemel. — 4th ed.
       p. cm.
  Includes bibliographical references.
  ISBN 0-321-49882-8 (pbk. : alk. paper) 1. Computer graphics. 2. OpenGL. I. Lipchak, Benjamin. II. Haemel, Nicholas. III. Title.
  T385.W728 2007
  006.6'6—dc22

                                                            2007012602

ISBN-13: 978-0-321-49882-3
ISBN-10: 0-321-49882-8

Text printed in the United States on recycled paper at Edwards Brothers, Ann Arbor, Michigan
Third printing, January 2009

Editor-in-Chief
Mark Taub

Acquisitions Editor
Debra Williams-Cauley

Development Editor
Songlin Qiu

Technical Reviewers
Paul Martz
Brian Collins

Managing Editor
Gina Kanouse

Senior Project Editor
Lori Lyons

Copy Editor
Cheri Clark

Indexer
Erika Millen

Proofreader
Williams Woods
Publishing

Publishing Coordinator
Kim Boedigheimer

Interior Designer
Gary Adair

Cover Designer
Alan Clements

Composition
Gloria Schurick

Contents at a Glance

Table of Contents

Preface

My career has been built on a long history of making "stupid" choices and accidentally being right. First, I went to Microsoft's DOS, instead of the wildly popular CP/M. Later, I recall, friends counseled me that Windows was dead, and too hard to program for, and that OS/2 was the future (you couldn't lose by sticking with IBM, they'd say).

Just got lucky, I guess.

There were a few other minor wrong turns that just happened to fortunately have me pointed away from some other collapsing industry segment, but my next really big stupid decision was writing the first edition of this book. I had already built a nice comfortable career out of fixing SQL database problems, and was making the transition to large-scale enterprise IT solutions in the healthcare industry. A book on OpenGL? I had no idea what I was doing. The first time I read the official OpenGL specification, I had to all but breathe in a paper bag, my first co-author quit in disgust, and the whole project was very nearly canceled before the book was half-finished.

As soon as the book came out, I had some meager credibility outside my normal field of expertise. I was offered a job at Lockheed-Martin/Real3D doing "real" OpenGL work. My then-current boss (God bless you, David, wherever you are!) tried really hard to talk me out of throwing my career away. Everybody knows, he insisted, that whatever Microsoft does is going to be the way the industry goes, and Microsoft's Talisman graphics platform was going to bury OpenGL into obscurity. Besides, there was only one other book on OpenGL in existence; how big a thing could it possibly be?

Eleven years have passed, and as I finish yet the fourth edition of this book (and looking at a shelf full of OpenGL books), the number of people reading this who remember the short-lived hype of Talisman would probably fit in the back of my minivan. An OpenGL engineer I used to know at IBM had in her e-mail signature: "OpenGL. It's everywhere. Do the math." This has never been truer than it is today.

OpenGL today is the industry-leading standard graphics API on nearly every conceivable platform. This includes not only desktop Windows PCs and Macs, but UNIX workstations, location-based entertainment systems, major game consoles (all but one), hand-held gaming devices, cellphones, and a myriad of other embedded systems such as avionic and vehicle instrumentation.

Across platforms, OpenGL is the undisputed champion of 3D content creation applications, 3D games, visualization, simulation, scientific modeling, and even 2D image and video editing. OpenGL's widespread success can be attributed to its elegance and ease of use, its power and flexibility, and the overwhelming support it has received from the developer and IHV communities. OpenGL can be extended as well, providing all the benefits of an open standard, as well as giving vendors the ability to add their own proprietary added value to implementations.

You have probably heard that programmable hardware is the future of 3D graphics programming, and of graphics APIs. This is no longer true. Programmable hardware is no longer in the future; it is here now, today, even on the lowest cost motherboard embedded 3D chipsets. It is not a fluke that this edition follows the last at the closest interval of the series. The pace of evolving graphics technology is simply staggering, and this edition brings you up-to-date on the now-latest OpenGL version 2.1.

We have reinforced the chapters on fixed-pipeline programming, which is not going away anytime soon, and have affectionately deemed them "The Old Testament;" still relevant, illustrative, and the foundation on which the "New Testament" of programmable hardware is based. I find the analogy quite appropriate, and I would refute anyone who thinks the fixed pipeline is completely dead and irrelevant. The rank and file of application developers (not necessarily cutting-edge game developers) would, I'm sure, agree.

That said, we have still trimmed some dead weight. Color Index mode is ignored as much as possible, some old paletted rendering material from the Windows chapter has been pruned, and we have eliminated all the old low-level assembly-style shader material to make room for updated and expanded coverage of the high-level shading language (GLSL). You'll also find a whole new chapter on OpenGL on hand-held systems, totally rewritten Mac OS X and Linux chapters, and a really great new chapter on advanced buffer techniques such as offscreen rendering, and floating-point textures.

Another big change some readers will notice is that the OpenGL SuperBible has been acquired and adopted into the Addison-Wesley Professional OpenGL series. I can't begin to express how grateful I am and humbled I feel by this honor. I myself have worn out the covers on at least one edition of every volume in this series.

One of the reasons, I think, for the longevity of this book has been the unique approach it takes among OpenGL books. As much as possible, we look at things through the eyes of someone who is excited by 3D graphics but knows very little about the topic. The purpose of a tutorial is to get you started, not teach you everything you will ever need to know. Every professional knows that you never reach this place. I do occasionally get some criticism for glossing over things too much, or not explaining things according to the strictest engineering accuracy. These almost never come from those for whom this book was intended. We hope for a great many of you that this will be your first book on OpenGL and 3D graphics. We hope for none of you that it will be your last.

Well, I did make one really "smart" decision about my career once. Once upon a time in the early 1980s, I was a student looking at a computer in an electronics store. The salesman approached and began making his pitch. I told him I was just learning to program and was considering an Amiga over his model. I was briskly informed that I needed to get serious with a computer that the rest of the world was using. An Amiga, he told me, was not good for anything but "making pretty pictures." No one, he assured me, could make a living making pretty pictures on his computer. Unfortunately, I listened to this "smart" advice and regretted it for over ten years. Thank God I finally got stupid.

As for making a living "making pretty pictures?" Do the math.

Oh, and my latest stupid decision? I've left Windows and switched to the Mac. Time will tell if my luck holds out.

—Richard S. Wright Jr.

Preface to the Previous, Third Edition

I have a confession to make. The first time I ever heard of OpenGL was at the 1992 Win32 Developers Conference in San Francisco. Windows NT 3.1 was in early beta (or late alpha), and many vendors were present, pledging their future support for this exciting new graphics technology. Among them was a company called Silicon Graphics, Inc. (SGI). The SGI representatives were showing off their graphics workstations and playing video demos of special effects from some popular movies. Their primary purpose in this booth, however, was to promote a new 3D graphics standard called OpenGL. It was based on SGI's proprietary IRIS GL and was fresh out of the box as a graphics standard. Significantly, Microsoft was pledging future support for OpenGL in Windows NT.

I had to wait until the beta release of NT 3.5 before I got my first personal taste of OpenGL. Those first OpenGL-based screensavers only scratched the surface of what was possible with this graphics API. Like many other people, I struggled through the Microsoft help files and bought a copy of the *OpenGL Programming Guide* (now called simply "The Red Book" by most). The Red Book was not a primer, however, and it assumed a lot of knowledge that I just didn't have.

Now for that confession I promised. How did I learn OpenGL? I learned it by writing a book about it. That's right, the first edition of the *OpenGL SuperBible* was me learning how to do 3D graphics myself...with a deadline! Somehow I pulled it off, and in 1996 the first edition of the book you are holding was born. Teaching myself OpenGL from scratch enabled me somehow to better explain the API to others in a manner that a lot of people seemed to like. The whole project was nearly canceled when Waite Group Press was acquired by another publisher halfway through the publishing process. Mitchell Waite stuck to his guns and insisted that OpenGL was going to be "the next big thing" in computer graphics. Vindication arrived when an emergency reprint was required because the first run of the book sold out before ever making it to the warehouse.

That was a long time ago, and in what seems like a galaxy far, far away...

Only three years later 3D accelerated graphics were a staple for even the most stripped-down PCs. The "API Wars," a political battle between Microsoft and SGI, had come and gone; OpenGL was firmly established in the PC world; and 3D hardware acceleration was as common as CD-ROMs and sound cards. I had even managed to turn my career more toward an OpenGL orientation and had the privilege of contributing in some small ways to the OpenGL specification for version 1.2 while working at Lockheed-Martin/Real3D. The second edition of this book, released at the end of 1999, was significantly expanded and corrected. We even made some modest initial attempts to ensure that all the sample programs were more friendly in non-Windows platforms by using the GLUT framework.

Now, nearly five years later (eight since the first edition!), we bring you yet again another edition, the third, of this book. OpenGL is now without question the premier cross-platform real-time 3D graphics API. Excellent OpenGL stability and performance are available on even the most stripped-down bargain PC today. OpenGL is also the standard for UNIX and Linux operating systems, and Apple has made OpenGL a core fundamental technology for the new Mac OS X operating system. OpenGL is even making inroads via a new specification, OpenGL ES, into embedded and mobile spaces. Who would have thought five years ago that we would see Quake running on a cellphone?

It is exciting that, today, even laptops have 3D acceleration, and OpenGL is truly everywhere and on every mainstream computing platform. Even more exciting, however, is the continuing evolution of computer graphics hardware. Today, most graphics hardware is programmable, and OpenGL even has its own shading language, which can produce stunningly realistic graphics that were undreamed of on commodity hardware back in the last century (I just had to squeeze that in someplace!).

With this third edition, I am pleased that we have added Benjamin Lipchak as a co-author. Benj is primarily responsible for the chapters that deal with OpenGL shader programs; and coming from the ARB groups responsible for this aspect of OpenGL, he is one of the most qualified authors on this topic in the world.

We have also fully left behind the "Microsoft Specific" characteristics of the first edition and have embraced a more multiplatform approach. All the programming examples in this book have been tested on Windows, Mac OS X, and at least one version of Linux. There is even one chapter apiece on these operating systems, with information about using OpenGL with native applications.

—Richard S. Wright Jr.

Acknowledgments

First, I have to thank God for somehow turning an innumerable amount of seemingly bad decisions into gold. Including against all "good advice" to get into computer graphics and OpenGL in particular. Second, I have to thank my wife LeeAnne. There was no way I could take on the fourth edition of this book, and I initially decided not to take this project on. She pretty much made me do it—and without complaining or whimpering shouldered all Boy Scout meetings, Girl Scout meetings, music lessons, school meetings, parent orientations, bake sales, fund raisers, soccer practices (NO I did not miss any games!), trips to the doctor, shopping trips, grocery runs, friends birthday parties, social engagements of every size and shape, and pretty much all of Christmas. Many late nighters were also made possible by a thermos of "Mamma's Magic Mojo"; Starbuck's, eat your heart out! All three of my brilliant children, Sara, Stephen, and Alex, thanks so much for letting Daddy hide out every night after dinner—and not giving me too much grief over missed movies and camping trips.

Thank you Benjamin Lipchak and Nick Haemel for being first-class coauthors. Your contributions to the book have had a lot to do with its recent longevity. Special thanks because you were both crazy enough to do this twice! Thanks to AMD/ATI for letting these guys out of the box, and for the use of some really cool sample shaders. The editors and staff at Addison Wesley have also been fantastic. Debra Williams-Cauley was especially patient and somewhat creative when it came to getting this project off the ground. Working with Songlin Qiu has been a great pleasure, and I especially appreciated her frequent encouragement just when I felt like this project would never end. Cheri Clark, thanks for making me look like I didn't sleep through high school English! Thank you, Lori Lyons, for being persistent about those pesky deadlines. I am also honored to have had Dave Shreiner, Paul Martz, and Brian Collins involved in this edition. Paul and Brian's review of the chapters has without a doubt increased the caliber of this edition substantially over my past efforts.

Many thanks also go out to Apple—in particular Kent Miller for some help on the Mac chapter—but also to everyone on the Apple OpenGL mailing list for many questions answered, and tips just picked up by trolling! NVIDIA also chipped in, with thanks in particular to Brian Harvey and Cass Everitt for being responsive to questions, and especially thanks to Michael Gold and Barthold Lichtenbelt for a conference call getting me up to speed on the OpenGL situation in Windows Vista. Thanks, too, to Robert Kennett at AMD/ATI for updating some code for me in the Windows chapter.

Many thanks to Full Sail for their support over the past few years by allowing me the privilege of teaching OpenGL on a part-time basis. I come in for a few hours, I get to talk about what I really love to talk about, and the audience has to act as though they enjoy it and pay attention. I even get paid. How on earth I keep getting away with this is beyond me!

Thank you, Rob Catto, for covering for me and looking the other way from time to time. Ed Womack, you are a scholar and a gentleman, and your F-16 model rocks. I'm sorry I defaced it with an OpenGL logo[el] but I couldn't help myself. Thanks also to my lab specialist Chris Baptiste, for a great attitude and for teaching my class from time to time so that I could get some other work done. Finally, I'd like to thank Software Bisque for this contractors dream "day job" of making great astronomy software, and getting paid to use OpenGL on a daily basis. Steve, Tom, Daniel, and Matt, you are all a class act. Working with you guys is an honor and privilege, not to mention a total blast!

—Richard S. Wright Jr.

I'd like to begin by acknowledging my colleagues at AMD who have unselfishly given their valuable time and advice reviewing my chapters, and leaving me to take all the credit. These folks are the masters of the OpenGL universe, and I am fortunate to work side by side with (or sometimes hundreds of miles away from) this caliber of individual on a daily basis. In particular, I'd like to thank Dan Ginsburg, Rick Hammerstone, Evan Hart (now at NVIDIA), Bill Licea-Kane, Glenn Ortner, and Jeremy Sandmel (now at Apple). Thanks to technical editors Paul Martz and Brian Collins for their depth and breadth of knowledge and for unleashing it mercilessly. And most of all, thanks to Richard Wright for the opportunity to work with you again on this project.

Thanks to the team of editors and other support staff at Addison-Wesley for transforming my lowly text into something I'm proud of. Your eagle eyes spared me from sweating the details, making writing hundreds of pages much less strenuous.

Thanks to WPI professors Mike Gennert, Karen Lemone, John Trimbur, Susan Vick, Matt Ward, Norm Wittels, and others for the solid foundation I lean on every day. A shout out to all my friends at GweepNet for distracting me with PC game LAN parties when I was burnt out from too much writing. To my entire extended family, including Beth, Tim, Alicia, Matt, Jen, and Corey, thanks for tolerating my surgically attached laptop during the winter months. To Mom and Dad, for providing me with top-quality genetic material and for letting me bang away on the TRS-80 when I should have been outside banging sticks against trees, I am forever grateful. To brother Paul, your success in everything you do provides me with nonstop healthy competition. To sister Maggie, you redefine success in my eyes every time I see you. You both make me proud to have you as siblings. Last, but not least, I'd like to thank my wife, Jessica, for the science project she's been assembling in her belly while I funnel all my attention into a laptop computer. It's time for our project now.

—Benjamin Lipchak

First, I would like to thank Richard and Benj for allowing me the opportunity to collaborate on this project. You guys have been great and very supportive for a new author. Thanks for putting up with all my silly questions. Also, thanks to ATI. What a great stomping ground for someone to get started in graphics! A special thanks to all of my friends and mentors at ATI—you all have been a great help and resource, and the best in the field!

I would also like to acknowledge the editors and staff at Addison Wesley. You have been incredibly helpful throughout the entire process. Thanks for all your hard work in polishing our text and keeping us on track.

Last, and certainly not least, I would like to thank my wife Anna, and all of my family for putting up with my distraction through this whole process. You graciously have been patient, even through the holidays, as I struggled with my deadlines. Anna, your dedication to medicine and your own publications has given me the strength to finish this project. Thank you for all your support and encouraging words, despite being even busier than I.

—Nicholas Haemel

About the Authors

Richard S. Wright, Jr. has been using OpenGL for more than 12 years, since it first became available on the Windows platform, and teaches OpenGL programming in the game design degree program at Full Sail in Orlando, Florida. Currently, Richard is the president of Starstone Software Systems, Inc., where he develops third-party multimedia simulation software for the PC and Macintosh platforms using OpenGL.

Previously with Real 3D/Lockheed Martin, Richard was a regular OpenGL ARB attendee and contributed to the OpenGL 1.2 specification and conformance tests. Since then, Richard has worked in multidimensional database visualization, game development, medical diagnostic visualization, and astronomical space simulation.

Richard first learned to program in the eighth grade in 1978 on a paper terminal. At age 16, his parents let him buy a computer with his grass-cutting money instead of a car, and he sold his first computer program less than a year later (and it was a graphics program!). When he graduated from high school, his first job was teaching programming and computer literacy for a local consumer education company. He studied electrical engineering and computer science at the University of Louisville's Speed Scientific School and made it half way through his senior year before his career got the best of him and took him to Florida. A native of Louisville, Kentucky, he now lives with his wife and three children in Lake Mary, Florida. When not programming or dodging hurricanes, Richard is an avid amateur astronomer and an Adult Sunday School teacher.

Benjamin Lipchak graduated from Worcester Polytechnic Institute with a double major in technical writing and computer science. "Why would anyone with a CS degree want to become a writer?" That was the question asked of him one fateful morning when Benj was interviewing for a tech writing job at Digital Equipment Corporation. Benj's interview took longer than scheduled, and he left that day with job offer in hand to work on the software team responsible for DEC's AlphaStation OpenGL drivers.

Benj's participation in the OpenGL Architecture Review Board began when he chaired the working group that generated the GL_ARB_fragment_program extension spec. While chairing the Khronos OpenGL Ecosystem Technical SubGroup, he established the OpenGL SDK and created the OpenGL Pipeline newsletter, of which he remains editor.

Benj will now participate in the Khronos OpenGL ES Working Group. After 12 years of OpenGL driver development and driver team management at DEC, Compaq, and ATI, he is headed for smaller pastures. Benj recently became manager of AMD's handheld software team. Although the API is familiar, the new challenges of size and power consumption make for a great change of scenery. In his fleeting spare time, Benj tries to get outdoors for some hiking or kayaking. He also operates an independent record label, Wachusett Records, specializing in solo piano music.

Nicholas Haemel, developer at AMD in the Graphics Products Group, was technical reviewer for *OpenGL SuperBible, Third Edition*, and contributed the chapters on GLX and OpenGL ES.

Introduction

Welcome to the fourth edition of the *OpenGL SuperBible*. For more than ten years, we have striven to provide the world's best introduction to not only OpenGL, but 3D graphics programming in general. This book is both a comprehensive reference of the entire OpenGL API and a tutorial that will teach you how to use this powerful API to create stunning 3D visualizations, games, and other graphics of all kinds. Starting with basic 3D terminology and concepts, we take you through basic primitive assembly, transformations, lighting, texturing, and eventually bring you into the full power of the programmable graphics pipeline with the OpenGL Shading Language.

Regardless of whether you are programming on Windows, Mac OS X, Linux, or a hand-held gaming device, this book is a great place to start learning OpenGL, and how to make the most of it on your specific platform. The majority of the book is highly portable C++ code hosted by the GLUT or FreeGLUT toolkit. You will also find OS-specific chapters that show how to wire OpenGL into your native window systems. Throughout the book, we try to make few assumptions about how much previous knowledge the reader has of 3D graphics programming topics. This yields a tutorial that is accessible by both the beginning programmer and the experienced programmer beginning OpenGL.

What's New in This Edition

Readers of the previous editions will notice right away that the reference material has been reorganized. Instead of attempting to place individual functions with chapters that use them, we now have Appendix C, which contains the complete OpenGL API reference for the GL function. This is a much more appropriate and useful organizational structure for this material. These reference pages are also now based on the "official" OpenGL man pages, which means there will be no more incomplete or missing function calls. Detailed function entries will also be more concise and complete.

The Mac OS X and Linux chapters in this edition have been totally rewritten from the ground up. Sometimes a revision is not sufficient, and the best thing to do is just start over. We think readers will like these two newly rewritten chapters, which will be useful to anyone needing an introduction to the specifics of getting OpenGL up and running on their particular platform. Also, on the platform topic, the Windows chapter has been updated and pruned of some older and obsolete topics. Of note is the fact that OpenGL's widely rumored demise on Vista has, in fact, NOT occurred.

We have also added two completely new chapters. In this edition, we bring you full coverage of the latest OpenGL ES specification. We also provide a very exciting chapter on advanced OpenGL buffer usage, including off screen rendering, floating point buffers and textures, and pixel buffer objects. Throughout all the chapters, coverage has been touched up to include OpenGL 2.1 functionality, and to focus more on current OpenGL programming techniques. (Chapter 11, for example, deals with geometry submission and was modified heavily for this purpose.)

Finally, you'll find a Color insert with a gallery of images for which black and white just does not do adequate justice. A book on graphics programming is certainly more useful with color images. Some techniques, for example, are impossible to demonstrate on the printed page without the use of color. Other images are provided because the black-and-white versions simply do not convey the same information about how a particular image should look.

How This Book Is Organized

The *OpenGL SuperBible* is divided into three parts: The Old Testament, The New Testament, and the Apocrypha. Each section covers a particular personality of OpenGL—namely, the fixed pipeline, programmable hardware, and finally some platform-specific bindings. We certainly would not equate our humble work with anyone's sacred texts. However, the informed reader will certainly see how strong and irresistible this metaphor actually is.

Part I: The Old Testament

You'll learn how to construct a program that uses OpenGL, how to set up your 3D-rendering environment, and how to create basic objects and light and shade them. Then we'll delve deeper into using OpenGL and some of its advanced features and different special effects. These chapters are a good way to introduce yourself to 3D graphics programming with OpenGL and provide the conceptual foundation on which the more advanced capabilities later in the book are based.

Chapter 1—Introduction to 3D Graphics and OpenGL. This introductory chapter is for newcomers to 3D graphics. It introduces fundamental concepts and some common vocabulary.

Chapter 2—Using OpenGL. In this chapter, we provide you with a working knowledge of what OpenGL is, where it came from, and where it is going. You will write your first program using OpenGL, find out what headers and libraries you need to use, learn how to set up your environment, and discover how some common conventions can help you remember OpenGL function calls. We also introduce the OpenGL state machine and error-handling mechanism.

Chapter 3—Drawing in Space: Geometric Primitives and Buffers. Here, we present the building blocks of 3D graphics programming. You'll basically find out how to tell a computer to create a three-dimensional object with OpenGL. You'll also learn the basics of hidden surface removal and ways to use the stencil buffer.

Chapter 4—Geometric Transformations: The Pipeline. Now that you're creating three-dimensional shapes in a virtual world, how do you move them around? How do you move yourself around? These are the things you'll learn here.

Chapter 5—Color, Materials, and Lighting: The Basics. In this chapter, you'll take your three-dimensional "outlines" and give them color. You'll learn how to apply material effects and lights to your graphics to make them look real.

Chapter 6—More on Colors and Materials. Now it's time to learn about blending objects with the background to make transparent (see-through) objects. You'll also learn some special effects with fog and the accumulation buffer.

Chapter 7—Imaging with OpenGL. This chapter is all about manipulating image data within OpenGL. This information includes reading a TGA file and displaying it in an OpenGL window. You'll also learn some powerful OpenGL image-processing capabilities.

Chapter 8—Texture Mapping: The Basics. Texture mapping is one of the most useful features of any 3D graphics toolkit. You'll learn how to wrap images onto polygons and how to load and manage multiple textures at once.

Chapter 9—Texture Mapping: Beyond the Basics. In this chapter, you'll learn how to generate texture coordinates automatically, use advanced filtering modes, and use built-in hardware support for texture compression. You'll also learn about OpenGL's support for point sprites.

Chapter 10—Curves and Surfaces. The simple triangle is a powerful building block. This chapter gives you some tools for manipulating the mighty triangle. You'll learn about some of OpenGL's built-in quadric surface generation functions and ways to use automatic tessellation to break complex shapes into smaller, more digestible pieces. You'll also explore the utility functions that evaluate Bézier and NURBS curves and surfaces. You can use these functions to create complex shapes with an amazingly small amount of code.

Chapter 11—It's All About the Pipeline: Faster Geometry Throughput. For this chapter, we introduce OpenGL display lists, vertex arrays, and vertex buffer objects for improving performance and organizing your models. You'll also learn how to create a detailed analysis showing how to best represent large, complex models.

Chapter 12—Interactive Graphics. This chapter explains two OpenGL features: selection and feedback. These groups of functions make it possible for the user to interact with objects in the scene. You can also get rendering details about any single object in the scene.

Chapter 13—Occlusion Queries: Why Do More Work Than You Need To? Here, you'll learn about the OpenGL occlusion query mechanism. This feature effectively lets you perform an inexpensive test-render of objects in your scene to find out whether they will be hidden behind other objects, in which case you can save time by not drawing the actual full-detail version.

Chapter 14—Depth Textures and Shadows. This chapter covers OpenGL's depth textures and shadow comparisons. You'll learn how to introduce real-time shadow effects to your scene, regardless of the geometry's complexity.

Part II: The New Testament

In the second part of the book, you'll find chapters on the new features in OpenGL supporting programmable hardware, in particular the OpenGL Shading Language (GLSL). These chapters don't represent just the newest OpenGL features, they cover the fundamental shift that has occurred in graphics programming—a shift that is fundamentally different, yet complementary, and descended from the old fixed-pipeline-based hardware.

Chapter 15—Programmable Pipeline: This Isn't Your Father's OpenGL. Out with the old, in with the new. This chapter revisits the conventional fixed-functionality pipeline before introducing the new programmable vertex and fragment pipeline stages. Programmability via the OpenGL Shading Language allows you to customize your rendering in ways never before possible.

Chapter 16—Vertex Shading: Do-It-Yourself Transform, Lighting, and Texgen. This chapter illustrates the usage of vertex shaders by surveying a handful of examples, including lighting, fog, squash and stretch, and skinning.

Chapter 17—Fragment Shading: Empower Your Pixel Processing. You learn by example—with a variety of fragment shaders. Examples include per-pixel lighting, color conversion, image processing, bump mapping, and procedural texturing. Some of these examples also use vertex shaders; these examples are representative of real-world usage, where you often find vertex and fragment shaders paired together.

Chapter 18—Advanced Buffers. Here, we discuss some of the latest and most exciting features in OpenGL, including offscreen accelerated rendering, faster ways to copy pixel data asynchronously, and floating-point color data for textures and color buffers.

Part III: The Apocrypha

Where do we put material that does not belong in the OpenGL canon? The Apocrypha! The third and last part of the book is less about OpenGL than about how different operating systems interface with and make use of OpenGL. Here we wander outside the "official" OpenGL specification to see how OpenGL is supported and interfaced with on Windows, Mac OS X, Linux, and hand-held devices.

Chapter 19—Wiggle: OpenGL on Windows. Here, you'll learn how to write real Windows (message-based) programs that use OpenGL. You'll learn about Microsoft's "wiggle" functions that glue OpenGL rendering code to Windows device contexts. You'll also learn how to respond to Windows messages for clean, well-behaved OpenGL applications. Yes, we also talk about OpenGL on Vista.

Chapter 20—OpenGL on Mac OS X. In this chapter, you'll learn how to use OpenGL in native Mac OS X applications. Sample programs show you how to start working with GLUT, Carbon, or Cocoa using the Xcode development environment.

Chapter 21—GLX: OpenGL on Linux. This chapter discusses GLX, the OpenGL extension used to support OpenGL applications through the X Window System on UNIX and Linux. You'll learn how to create and manage OpenGL contexts as well as how to create OpenGL drawing areas.

Chapter 22—OpenGL ES: OpenGL on the Small. This chapter is all about how OpenGL is pared down to fit on hand-held and embedded devices. We cover what's gone, what's new, and how to get going even with an emulated environment.

Conventions Used in This Book

The following typographic conventions are used in this book:

- Code lines, commands, statements, variables, and any text you type or see onscreen appear in a `computer` typeface.

- Placeholders in syntax descriptions appear in an *`italic computer`* typeface. You should replace the placeholder with the actual filename, parameter, or whatever element it represents.

- *Italics* highlight technical terms when they first appear in the text and are being defined.

About the Companion Web Site

This is the first time this book has shipped without a CD-ROM. Welcome to the age of the Internet! Instead, all our source code is available online at our support Web site:

www.opengl.org/superbible

Here you'll find the source code to all the sample programs in the book, as well as prebuilt projects for Developers Studio (Windows), and Xcode (Mac OS X). For Linux users we'll have make files for command-line building of the projects as well. We even plan to post a few tutorials, so check back from time to time, even after you've downloaded all the source code.

PART I
The Old Testament

The first 14 chapters of this "Super Book" (*Bible* is from the Greek word for *book*) are about the beginnings of hardware-accelerated 3D graphics. Today, we refer to this body of functionality as *fixed-pipeline* rendering. Although it is certainly true that most of the recent press and excitement in the 3D graphics world revolves around the New Testament of computer graphics, *shaders*, the historical fixed-pipeline functionality of OpenGL is still quite pertinent, and useful.

For many, the fixed pipeline is completely adequate for their rendering needs, and they will find this part of the book instructive, and helpful for learning to use OpenGL. The true promise of hardware rendering for many, however, will be held in the second part of this book. Still, for those, the fixed pipeline is the foundation on which shaders are built. An understanding of the fixed pipeline is arguably even *necessary* before one can appreciate the power, flexibility, and freedom afforded by programmable hardware.

CHAPTER 1

Introduction to 3D Graphics and OpenGL

by Richard S. Wright Jr.

WHAT YOU'LL LEARN IN THIS CHAPTER:

- A brief overview of the history of computer graphics

- How we make 3D graphics on a 2D screen

- About the basic 3D effects and terminology

- How a 3D coordinate system and the viewport works

- What vertices are, and how we use them

- About the different kinds of 3D projections

This book is about OpenGL, a programming interface for creating real-time 3D graphics. Before we begin talking about what OpenGL is and how it works, you should have at least a high-level understanding of real-time 3D graphics in general. Perhaps you picked up this book because you want to learn to use OpenGL, but you already have a good grasp of real-time 3D principles. If so, great: Skip directly to Chapter 2, "Using OpenGL." If you bought this book because the pictures look cool and you want to learn how to do this on your PC...you should probably start here.

A Brief History of Computer Graphics

The first computers consisted of rows and rows of switches and lights. Technicians and engineers worked for hours, days, or even weeks to program these machines and read the results of their calculations. Patterns of illuminated bulbs conveyed useful information to the computer users, or some crude printout was provided. You might say that the first form of computer graphics was a panel of blinking lights. (This idea is supported by stories of early programmers writing programs that served no useful purpose other than creating patterns of blinking and chasing lights!)

Times have changed. From those first "thinking machines," as some called them, sprang fully programmable devices that printed on rolls of paper using a mechanism similar to a teletype machine. Data could be stored efficiently on magnetic tape, on disk, or even on rows of hole-punched paper or stacks of paper-punch cards. The "hobby" of computer graphics was born the day computers first started printing. Because each character in the alphabet had a fixed size and shape, creative programmers in the 1970s took delight in creating artistic patterns and images made up of nothing more than asterisks (*).

Going Electric

Paper as an output medium for computers is useful and persists today. Laser printers and color inkjet printers have replaced crude ASCII art with crisp presentation quality and photographic reproductions of artwork. Paper and ink, however, can be expensive to replace on a regular basis, and using them consistently is wasteful of our natural resources, especially because most of the time we don't really need hard-copy output of calculations or database queries.

The cathode ray tube (CRT) was a tremendously useful addition to the computer. The original computer monitors, CRTs were initially just video terminals that displayed ASCII text just like the first paper terminals—but CRTs were perfectly capable of drawing points and lines as well as alphabetic characters. Soon, other symbols and graphics began to supplement the character terminal. Programmers used computers and their monitors to create graphics that supplemented textual or tabular output. The first algorithms for creating lines and curves were developed and published; computer graphics became a science rather than a pastime.

The first computer graphics displayed on these terminals were *two-dimensional,* or *2D.* These flat lines, circles, and polygons were used to create graphics for a variety of purposes. Graphs and plots could display scientific or statistical data in a way that tables and figures could not. More adventurous programmers even created simple arcade games such as *Lunar Lander* and *Pong* using simple graphics consisting of little more than line drawings that were refreshed (redrawn) several times a second.

The term *real-time* was first applied to computer graphics that were animated. A broader use of the word in computer science simply means that the computer can process input as fast as or faster than the input is being supplied. For example, talking on the phone is a real-time activity in which humans participate. You speak and the listener hears your communication immediately and responds, allowing you to hear immediately and respond again, and so on. In reality, there is some delay involved due to the electronics, but the delay is usually imperceptible to those having the conversation. In contrast, writing a letter is not a real-time activity.

Applying the term *real-time* to computer graphics means that the computer is producing an animation or a sequence of images directly in response to some input, such as joystick movement or keyboard strokes. Real-time computer graphics can display a wave form being measured by electronic equipment, numerical readouts, or interactive games and visual simulations.

Going 3D

The term *three-dimensional,* or *3D,* means that an object being described or displayed has three dimensions of measurement: width, height, and depth. An example of a two-dimensional object is a piece of paper on your desk with a drawing or writing on it, having no perceptible depth. A three-dimensional object is the can of soda next to it. The soft drink can is round (width and depth) and tall (height). Depending on your perspective, you can alter which side of the can is the width or height, but the fact remains that the can has three dimensions. Figure 1.1 shows how we might measure the dimensions of the can and piece of paper.

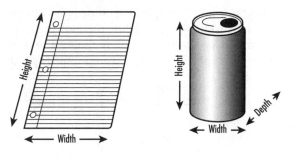

FIGURE 1.1   Measuring two- and three-dimensional objects.

For centuries, artists have known how to make a painting appear to have real depth. A painting is inherently a two-dimensional object because it is nothing more than canvas with paint applied. Similarly, 3D computer graphics are actually two-dimensional images on a flat computer screen that provide an illusion of depth, or a third dimension.

2D + Perspective = 3D

The first computer graphics no doubt appeared similar to what's shown in Figure 1.2, where you can see a simple three-dimensional cube drawn with 12 line segments. What makes the cube look three-dimensional is *perspective,* or the angles between the lines that lend the illusion of depth.

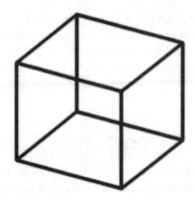

FIGURE 1.2   A simple wireframe 3D cube.

To truly see in 3D, you need to actually view an object with both eyes or supply each eye with separate and unique images of the object. Look at Figure 1.3. Each eye receives a two-dimensional image that is much like a temporary photograph displayed on each retina (the back part of your eye). These two images are slightly different because they are received at two different angles. (Your eyes are spaced apart on purpose.) The brain then combines these slightly different images to produce a single, composite 3D picture in your head.

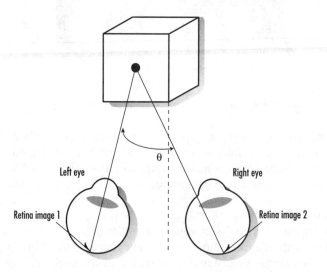

FIGURE 1.3   How you see three dimensions.

In Figure 1.3, the angle between the images becomes smaller as the object goes farther away. You can amplify this 3D effect by increasing the angle between the two images. View-Master (those hand-held stereoscopic viewers you probably had as a kid) and 3D movies capitalize on this effect by placing each of your eyes on a separate lens or by providing color-filtered glasses that separate two superimposed images. These images are usually overenhanced for dramatic or cinematic purposes. Of late this effect has become more popular on the PC as well. Shutter glasses that work with your graphics card and software will switch between one eye and the other, with a changing perspective displayed onscreen to each eye, thus giving a "true" stereo 3D experience. Unfortunately, many people complain that this effect gives them a headache or makes them dizzy!

A computer screen is one flat image on a flat surface, not two images from different perspectives falling on each eye. As it turns out, most of what is considered to be 3D computer graphics is actually an approximation of true 3D. This approximation is achieved in the same way that artists have rendered drawings with apparent depth for years, using the same tricks that nature provides for people with one eye.

You might have noticed at some time in your life that if you cover one eye, the world does not suddenly fall flat. What happens when you cover one eye? You might think you are still seeing in 3D, but try this experiment: Place a glass or some other object just out of arm's reach, off to your left side. (If it is close, this trick won't work.) Cover your right eye with your right hand and reach for the glass. (Maybe you should use an empty plastic one!) Most people will have a more difficult time estimating how much farther they need to reach (if at all) before touching the glass. Now, uncover your right eye and reach for the glass, and you can easily discern how far you need to lean to reach the glass. You now know why people with one eye often have difficulty with distance perception.

Perspective alone is enough to create the appearance of three dimensions. Note the cube shown previously in Figure 1.2. Even without coloring or shading, the cube still has the appearance of a three-dimensional object. Stare at the cube for long enough, however, and the front and back of the cube switch places. Your brain is confused by the lack of any surface coloration in the drawing. Figure 1.4 shows the output from the sample program BLOCK from this chapter's subdirectory in the source distribution. Run this program as we progress toward a more and more realistic-appearing cube. We see here that the cube resting on a plane has an exaggerated perspective but still can produce the "popping" effect when you stare at it. By pressing the spacebar, you will progress toward a more and more believable image.

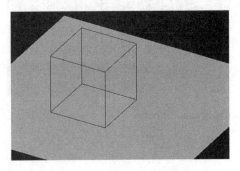

FIGURE 1.4   A line-drawn three-dimensional cube.

3D Artifacts

The reason the world doesn't suddenly look flat when you cover one eye is that many of the 3D world's effects are still present when viewed two-dimensionally. The effects are just enough to trigger your brain's ability to discern depth. The most obvious cue is that nearby objects appear larger than distant objects. This perspective effect is called *foreshortening*. This effect and color changes, textures, lighting, shading, and variations of color intensities (due to lighting) together add up to our perception of a three-dimensional image. In the next section, we take a survey of these tricks.

A Survey of 3D Effects

Now you have some idea that the illusion of 3D is created on a flat computer screen by means of a bag full of perspective and artistic tricks. Let's review some of these effects so we can refer to them later in the book, and you'll know what we are talking about.

The first term you should know is *render*. Rendering is the act of taking a geometric description of a three-dimensional object and turning it into an image of that object onscreen. All the following 3D effects are applied when the objects or scene are rendered.

Perspective

Perspective refers to the angles between lines that lend the illusion of three dimensions. Figure 1.4 shows a three-dimensional cube drawn with lines. This is a powerful illusion, but it can still cause perception problems as we mentioned earlier. (Just stare at this cube for a while, and it starts popping in and out.) In Figure 1.5, on the other hand, the brain is given more clues as to the true orientation of the cube because of hidden line removal. You expect the front of an object to obscure the back of the object from view. For solid surfaces, we call this *hidden surface removal*.

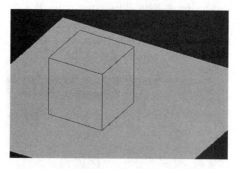

FIGURE 1.5   A more convincing solid cube.

Color and Shading

If we stare at the cube in Figure 1.5 long enough, we can convince ourselves that we are looking at a recessed image, and not the outward surfaces of a cube. To further our perception, we must move beyond line drawing and add color to create solid objects. Figure 1.6 shows what happens when we naively add red to the color of the cube. It doesn't look like a cube anymore. By applying different colors to each side, as shown in Figure 1.7, we regain our perception of a solid object.

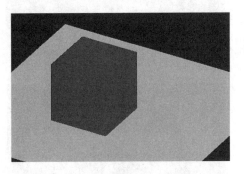

FIGURE 1.6   Adding color alone can create further confusion.

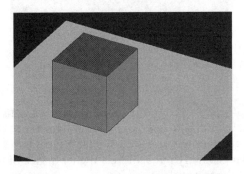

FIGURE 1.7   Adding different colors increases the illusion of three dimensions.

Light and Shadows

Making each side of the cube a different color helps your eye pick out the different sides of the object. By shading each side appropriately, we can give the cube the appearance of being one solid color (or material) but also show that it is illuminated by a light at an angle, as shown in Figure 1.8. Figure 1.9 goes a step further by adding a shadow behind the cube. Now we are simulating the effects of light on one or more objects and their interactions. Our illusion at this point is very convincing.

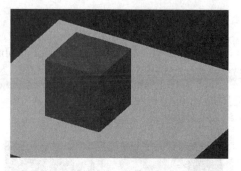

FIGURE 1.8   Proper shading creates the illusion of illumination.

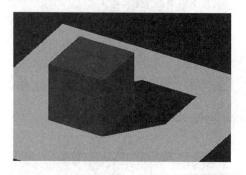

FIGURE 1.9   Adding a shadow to further increase realism.

Texture Mapping

Achieving a high level of realism with nothing but thousands or millions of tiny lit and shaded polygons is a matter of brute force and a lot of hard work. Unfortunately, the more geometry you throw at graphics hardware, the longer it takes to render. A clever technique allows you to use simpler geometry but achieve a higher degree of realism. This technique takes an image, such as a photograph of a real surface or detail, and then applies that image to the surface of a polygon.

Instead of plain-colored materials, you can have wood grains, cloth, bricks, and so on. This technique of applying an image to a polygon to supply additional detail is called *texture mapping*. The image you supply is called a *texture*, and the individual elements of the texture are called *texels*. Finally, the process of stretching or compressing the texels over the surface of an object is called *filtering*. Figure 1.10 shows the now-familiar cube example with textures applied to each polygon.

FIGURE 1.10   Texture mapping adds detail without adding additional geometry.

Fog

Most of us know what fog is. Fog is an atmospheric effect that adds haziness to objects in a scene, which is usually a relation of how far away the objects in the scene are from the viewer and how thick the fog is. Objects very far away (or nearby if the fog is thick) might even be totally obscured.

Figure 1.11 shows the skyfly GLUT demo (included with most GLUT distributions) with fog enabled. Despite the crudeness of the canyon walls, note how the fog lends substantially to the believability of the scene.

FIGURE 1.11   Fog effects provide a convincing illusion for wide-open spaces.

Blending and Transparency

Blending is the combination of colors or objects on the screen. This is similar to the effect you get with double-exposure photography, where two images are superimposed. You can use the blending effect for a variety of purposes. By varying the amount each object is blended with the scene, you can make objects look transparent such that you see the object and what is behind it (such as glass or a ghost image).

You can also use blending to achieve an illusion of reflection, as shown in Figure 1.12. You see a textured cube rendered twice. First, the cube is rendered upside down below the floor level. The marble floor is then blended with the scene, allowing the cube to show through. Finally, the cube is drawn again right side up and floating over the floor. The result is the appearance of a reflection in a shiny marble surface.

FIGURE 1.12   Blending used to achieve a reflection effect.

Antialiasing

Aliasing is an effect that is visible onscreen due to the fact that an image consists of discrete pixels. In Figure 1.13, you can see that the lines that make up the cube on the left have jagged edges (sometimes called *jaggies*). By carefully blending the lines with the background color, you can eliminate the jagged edges and give the lines a smooth appearance, as shown in the cube on the right. This blending technique is called *antialiasing*. You can also apply antialiasing to polygon edges, making an object or a scene look more realistic and natural.

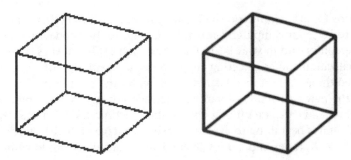

FIGURE 1.13   Cube with jagged lines versus cube with smooth lines.

Common Uses for 3D Graphics

Three-dimensional graphics have many uses in modern computer applications. Applications for real-time 3D graphics range from interactive games and simulations to data visualization for scientific, medical, or business uses. Higher-end 3D graphics find their way into movies and technical and educational publications as well.

Real-Time 3D

As defined earlier, real-time 3D graphics are animated and interactive with the user. One of the earliest uses for real-time 3D graphics was in military flight simulators. Even today, flight simulators are a popular diversion for the home enthusiast. Figure 1.14 shows a screenshot from a popular flight simulator that uses OpenGL for 3D rendering (www.flightgear.org).

FIGURE 1.14   A popular OpenGL-based flight simulator from Flight Gear.

The applications for 3D graphics on the PC are almost limitless. Perhaps the most common use today is for computer gaming. Hardly a title ships today that does not require a 3D graphics card in your PC to play. Although 3D has always been popular for scientific visualization and engineering applications, the explosion of cheap 3D hardware has empowered these applications like never before. Business applications are also taking advantage of the new availability of hardware to incorporate more and more complex business graphics and database mining visualization techniques. Even the modern GUI is being affected, and is beginning to evolve to take advantage of 3D hardware capabilities. The Macintosh OS X, for example, uses OpenGL to render all its windows and controls for a powerful and eye-popping visual interface.

Figures 1.15 through 1.19 show some of the myriad applications of real-time 3D graphics on the modern PC. All these images were rendered using OpenGL.

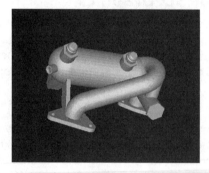

FIGURE 1.15   3D graphics used for computer-aided design (CAD).

FIGURE 1.16   3D graphics used for architectural or civil planning (image courtesy of Real 3D, Inc.).

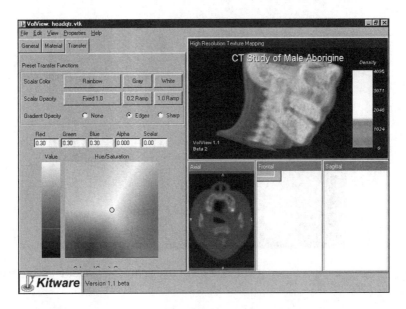

FIGURE 1.17   3D graphics used for medical imaging applications (VolView by Kitware).

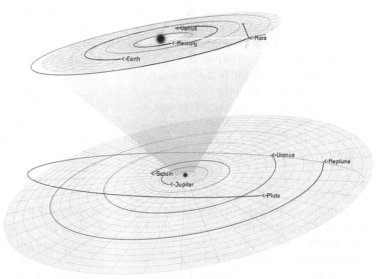

FIGURE 1.18   3D graphics used for scientific visualization (image courtesy of Software Bisque, Inc.).

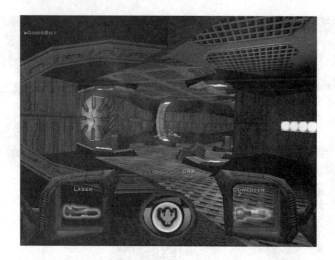

FIGURE 1.19   3D graphics used for entertainment (Descent 3 from Outrage Entertainment, Inc.).

Non–Real-Time 3D

Some compromise is required for real-time 3D applications. Given more processing time, you can generate higher quality 3D graphics. Typically, you design models and scenes, and a ray tracer processes the definition to produce a high-quality 3D image. The typical process is that some modeling application uses real-time 3D graphics to interact with the artist to create the content. Then the frames are sent to another application (the ray tracer) or subroutine, which renders the image. Rendering a single frame for a movie such as *Toy Story* or *Shrek* could take hours on a very fast computer, for example. The process of rendering and saving many thousands of frames generates an animated sequence for playback. Although the playback might appear real-time, the content is not interactive, so it is not considered real-time, but rather pre-rendered.

Shaders

The current state of the art in real-time computer graphics is *programmable shading*. Today's graphics cards are no longer dumb rendering chips, but highly programmable rendering computers in their own right. Like the term CPU (central processing unit), the term GPU has been coined, meaning graphics processing unit, referring to the programmable chips on today's graphics cards. These are highly parallelized and very, very fast. Just as important, the programmer can reconfigure how the card works to achieve virtually any special effect imaginable.

Every year, shader-based graphics hardware gains ground on tasks traditionally done by the high-end ray tracing and software rendering tools mentioned previously. Figure 1.20 shows an image of the earth in Software Bisque's *Seeker* solar system simulator. This application uses a custom OpenGL shader to generate a realistic and animated view of the earth over 60 times a second. This includes atmospheric effects, the sun's reflection in the water, and even the stars in the background. A color version of this figure is shown in Color Plate 2 in the Color insert.

FIGURE 1.20   Shaders allow for unprecedented real-time realism (image courtesy of Software Bisque, Inc.).

Basic 3D Programming Principles

Now, you have a pretty good idea of the basics of real-time 3D. We've covered some terminology and some sample applications on the PC. How do you actually create these images on your PC? Well, that's what the rest of this book is about! You still need a little more introduction to the basics, which we present here.

Immediate Mode and Retained Mode

There are two different approaches to low-level programming APIs for real-time 3D graphics—both of which are well supported by OpenGL. The first approach is called *retained mode*. In retained mode, you provide the API or toolkit with higher level geometric descriptions of your objects in the scene. These blocks of geometry data can be transferred quickly to the graphics hardware, or even stored directly in the hardware's local memory for faster access.

The second approach to 3D rendering is called *immediate mode*. In immediate mode, you procedurally build up geometric objects one piece at a time. Although flexible, this suffers performance-wise. We will discuss why this happens and ways to get around it in Chapter 11, "It's All About the Pipeline: Faster Geometry Throughput."

With both immediate mode and retained mode, new commands have no effect on rendering commands that have already been executed. This gives you a great deal of low-level control. For example, you can render a series of textured unlit polygons to represent the sky. Then you issue a command to turn off texturing, followed by a command to turn on lighting. Thereafter, all geometry (probably drawn on the ground) that you render is affected by the light but is not textured with the sky image.

Coordinate Systems

Let's consider now how we describe objects in three dimensions. Before you can specify an object's location and size, you need a frame of reference to measure and locate against. When you draw lines or plot points on a simple flat computer screen, you specify a position in terms of a row and column. For example, a standard VGA screen has 640 pixels from left to right and 480 pixels from top to bottom. To specify a point in the middle of the screen, you specify that a point should be plotted at (320,240)—that is, 320 pixels from the left of the screen and 240 pixels down from the top of the screen.

In OpenGL, or almost any 3D API, when you create a window to draw in, you must also specify the *coordinate system* you want to use and how to map the specified coordinates into physical screen pixels. Let's first see how this applies to two-dimensional drawing and then extend the principle to three dimensions.

2D Cartesian Coordinates

The most common coordinate system for two-dimensional plotting is the Cartesian coordinate system. Cartesian coordinates are specified by an x coordinate and a y coordinate. The x coordinate is a measure of position in the horizontal direction, and y is a measure of position in the vertical direction.

The *origin* of the Cartesian system is at x=0, y=0. Cartesian coordinates are written as coordinate pairs in parentheses, with the x coordinate first and the y coordinate second, separated by a comma. For example, the origin is written as (0,0). Figure 1.21 depicts the Cartesian coordinate system in two dimensions. The x and y lines with tick marks are called the *axes* and can extend from negative to positive infinity. This figure represents the true Cartesian coordinate system pretty much as you used it in grade school. Today, differing window mapping modes can cause the coordinates you specify when drawing to be interpreted differently. Later in the book, you'll see how to map this true coordinate space to window coordinates in different ways.

The x-axis and y-axis are perpendicular (intersecting at a right angle) and together define the xy plane. A *plane* is, most simply put, a flat surface. In any coordinate system, two axes (or two lines) that intersect at right angles define a plane. In a system with only two axes, there is naturally only one plane to draw on.

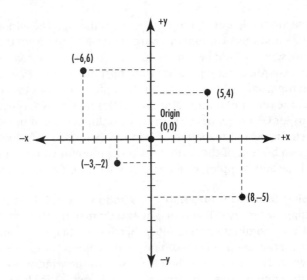

FIGURE 1.21   The Cartesian plane.

Coordinate Clipping

A window is measured physically in terms of pixels. Before you can start plotting points, lines, and shapes in a window, you must tell OpenGL how to translate specified coordinate pairs into screen coordinates. You do this by specifying the region of Cartesian space that occupies the window; this region is known as the clipping region. In two-dimensional space, the clipping region is the minimum and maximum x and y values that are inside the window. Another way of looking at this is specifying the origin's location in relation to the window. Figure 1.22 shows two common clipping regions.

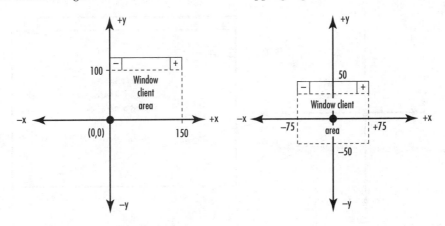

FIGURE 1.22   Two clipping regions.

In the first example, on the left of Figure 1.22, x coordinates in the window range left to right from 0 to +150, and the y coordinates range bottom to top from 0 to +100. A point in the middle of the screen would be represented as (75,50). The second example shows a clipping area with x coordinates ranging left to right from –75 to +75 and y coordinates ranging bottom to top from –50 to +50. In this example, a point in the middle of the screen would be at the origin (0,0). It is also possible using OpenGL functions (or ordinary Windows functions for GDI drawing) to turn the coordinate system upside down or flip it right to left. In fact, the default mapping for Windows windows is for positive y to move down from the top to bottom of the window. Although useful when drawing text from top to bottom, this default mapping is not as convenient for drawing graphics.

Viewports: Mapping Drawing Coordinates to Window Coordinates

Rarely will your clipping area width and height exactly match the width and height of the window in pixels. The coordinate system must therefore be mapped from logical Cartesian coordinates to physical screen pixel coordinates. This mapping is specified by a setting known as the *viewport*. The viewport is the region within the window's client area that is used for drawing the clipping area. The viewport simply maps the clipping area to a region of the window. Usually, the viewport is defined as the entire window, but this is not strictly necessary; for instance, you might want to draw only in the lower half of the window.

Figure 1.23 shows a large window measuring 300×200 pixels with the viewport defined as the entire client area. If the clipping area for this window were set to 0 to 150 along the x-axis and 0 to 100 along the y-axis, the logical coordinates would be mapped to a larger screen coordinate system in the viewing window. Each increment in the logical coordinate system would be matched by two increments in the physical coordinate system (pixels) of the window.

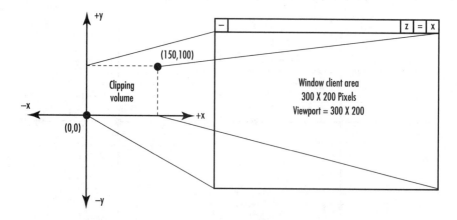

FIGURE 1.23   A viewport defined as twice the size of the clipping area.

In contrast, Figure 1.24 shows a viewport that matches the clipping area. The viewing window is still 300×200 pixels, however, and this causes the viewing area to occupy the lower-left side of the window.

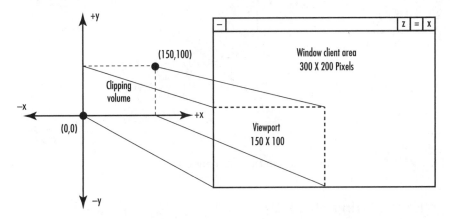

FIGURE 1.24   A viewport defined as the same dimensions as the clipping area.

You can use viewports to shrink or enlarge the image inside the window and to display only a portion of the clipping area by setting the viewport to be larger than the window's client area.

The Vertex—A Position in Space

In both 2D and 3D, when you draw an object, you actually compose it with several smaller shapes called *primitives*. Primitives are one- or two-dimensional entities or surfaces such as points, lines, and polygons (a flat, multisided shape) that are assembled in 3D space to create 3D objects. For example, a three-dimensional cube consists of six two-dimensional squares, each placed on a separate face. Each corner of the square (or of any primitive) is called a *vertex*. These vertices are then specified to occupy a particular coordinate in 3D space. A vertex is nothing more than a coordinate in 2D or 3D space. Creating solid 3D geometry is little more than a game of *connect-the-dots*! You'll learn about all the OpenGL primitives and how to use them in Chapter 3, "Drawing in Space: Geometric Primitives and Buffers."

3D Cartesian Coordinates

Now, we extend our two-dimensional coordinate system into the third dimension and add a depth component. Figure 1.25 shows the Cartesian coordinate system with a new axis, z. The z-axis is perpendicular to both the x- and y-axes. It represents a line drawn perpendicularly from the center of the screen heading toward the viewer. (We have rotated our view of the coordinate system from Figure 1.21 to the left with respect to the y-axis and down and back with respect to the x-axis. If we hadn't, the z-axis would come straight out at you, and you wouldn't see it.) Now, we specify a position in three-dimensional space with three coordinates: x, y, and z. Figure 1.25 shows the point (–4,4,4) for clarification.

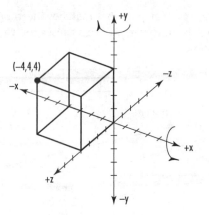

FIGURE 1.25   Cartesian coordinates in three dimensions.

Projections: Getting 3D to 2D

You've seen how to specify a position in 3D space using Cartesian coordinates. No matter how we might convince your eye, however, pixels on a screen have only two dimensions. How does OpenGL translate these Cartesian coordinates into two-dimensional coordinates that can be plotted on a screen? The short answer is "trigonometry and simple matrix manipulation." Simple? Well, not really; we could actually go on for many pages explaining this "simple" technique and lose most of our readers who didn't take or don't remember their linear algebra from college. You'll learn more about it in Chapter 4, "Geometric Transformations: The Pipeline," and for a deeper discussion, you can check out the references in Appendix A, "Further Reading/References." Fortunately, you don't need a deep understanding of the math to use OpenGL to create graphics. You might, however, discover that the deeper your understanding goes, the more powerful a tool OpenGL becomes!

The first concept you really need to understand is called *projection*. The 3D coordinates you use to create geometry are flattened or *projected* onto a 2D surface (the window background). It's like tracing the outlines of some object behind a piece of glass with a black marker. When the object is gone or you move the glass, you can still see the outline of the object with its angular edges. In Figure 1.26, a house in the background is traced onto a flat piece of glass. By specifying the projection, you specify the *viewing volume* that you want displayed in your window and how it should be transformed.

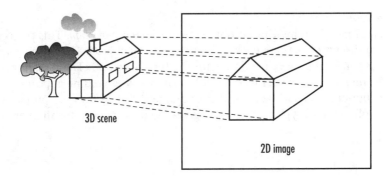

FIGURE 1.26   A 3D image projected onto a 2D surface.

Orthographic Projections

You are mostly concerned with two main types of projections in OpenGL. The first is called an *orthographic,* or parallel, projection. You use this projection by specifying a square or rectangular viewing volume. Anything outside this volume is not drawn. Furthermore, all objects that have the same dimensions appear the same size, regardless of whether they are far away or nearby. This type of projection (shown in Figure 1.27) is most often used in architectural design, computer-aided design (CAD), or 2D graphs. Frequently, you will also use an orthographic projection to add text or 2D overlays on top of your 3D graphic scenes.

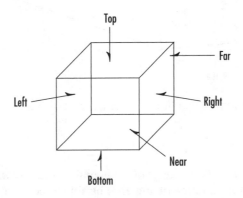

FIGURE 1.27   The clipping volume for an orthographic projection.

You specify the viewing volume in an orthographic projection by specifying the far, near, left, right, top, and bottom clipping planes. Objects and figures that you place within this viewing volume are then projected (taking into account their orientation) to a 2D image that appears on your screen.

Perspective Projections

The second and more common projection is the *perspective projection*. This projection adds the effect that distant objects appear smaller than nearby objects. The viewing volume (see Figure 1.28) is something like a pyramid with the top shaved off. The remaining shape is called the *frustum*. Objects nearer to the front of the viewing volume appear close to their original size, but objects near the back of the volume shrink as they are projected to the front of the volume. This type of projection gives the most realism for simulation and 3D animation.

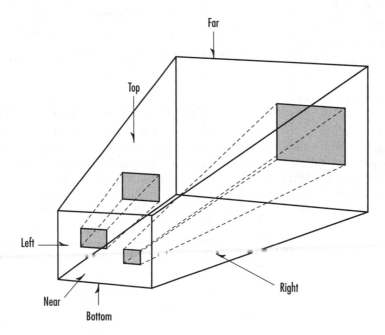

FIGURE 1.28   The clipping volume (frustum) for a perspective projection.

Summary

In this chapter, we introduced the basics of 3D graphics. You saw why you actually need two images of an object from different angles to be able to perceive true three-dimensional space. You also saw the illusion of depth created in a 2D drawing by means of perspective, hidden line removal, coloring, shading, and other techniques. The Cartesian coordinate system was introduced for 2D and 3D drawing, and you learned about two methods used by OpenGL to project three-dimensional drawings onto a two-dimensional screen.

We purposely left out the details of how these effects are actually created by OpenGL. In the chapters that follow, you will find out how to employ these techniques and take maximum advantage of OpenGL's power. In the sample code distribution, you'll find one program for this chapter that demonstrates some of the 3D effects covered here. In this program, BLOCK, pressing the spacebar advances you from a wireframe cube to a fully lit and textured block complete with shadow. You won't understand the code at this point, but it makes a powerful demonstration of what is to come. By the time you finish this book, you will be able to revisit this example and improve on it yourself, or even be able to write it from scratch.

Using OpenGL

by Richard S. Wright Jr.

WHAT YOU'LL LEARN IN THIS CHAPTER:

- Where OpenGL came from and where it's going

- Which headers need to be included in your project

- How to use GLUT with OpenGL to create a window and draw in it

- How to set colors using RGB (red, green, blue) components

- How viewports and viewing volumes affect image dimensions

- How to perform a simple animation using double buffering

- How the OpenGL state machine works

- How to check for OpenGL errors

- How to make use of OpenGL extensions

Now that you have had an introduction to the basic terminology and the ideas behind 3D graphics, it's time to get down to business. Before using OpenGL, we will need to talk about what OpenGL is and what it is not so that you have an understanding of both and the power and the limits of this API. This chapter is about the "Big Picture" of how OpenGL operates and how to set up the rendering framework for your 3D masterpieces.

What Is OpenGL?

OpenGL is strictly defined as "a software interface to graphics hardware." In essence, it is a 3D graphics and modeling library that is highly portable and very fast. Using OpenGL, you can create elegant and beautiful 3D graphics with exceptional visual quality. The greatest advantage to using OpenGL is that it is orders of magnitude faster than a ray tracer or software rendering engine. Initially, it used algorithms carefully developed and optimized by Silicon Graphics, Inc. (SGI), an acknowledged world leader in computer graphics and animation. Over time, OpenGL has evolved as other vendors have contributed their expertise and intellectual property to develop high-performance implementations of their own.

OpenGL is not a programming language like C or C++. It is more like the C runtime library, which provides some prepackaged functionality. There really is no such thing as an "OpenGL program" (okay, maybe with shaders there is, but that comes much later in this book!) but rather a program the developer wrote that "happens" to use OpenGL as one of its Application Programming Interfaces (APIs). You might use the C runtime library to access a file or the Internet, and you might use OpenGL to create real-time 3D graphics.

OpenGL is intended for use with computer hardware that is designed and optimized for the display and manipulation of 3D graphics. Software-only implementations of OpenGL are also possible, and the older Microsoft implementations, and Mesa3D (www.mesa3d.org) fall into this category. Apple also makes a software implementation available on OS X. With these software-only implementations, rendering may not be performed as quickly, and some advanced special effects may not be available at all. However, using a software implementation means that your program can potentially run on a wider variety of computer systems that may not have a 3D accelerated graphics card installed.

OpenGL is used for various purposes, from CAD engineering and architectural applications to modeling programs used to create computer-generated monsters in blockbuster movies. The introduction of an industry-standard 3D API to mass-market operating systems such as Microsoft Windows and the Macintosh OS X has some exciting repercussions. With hardware acceleration and fast PC microprocessors becoming commonplace, 3D graphics are now typical components of consumer and business applications, not only of games and scientific applications.

Evolution of a Standard

The forerunner of OpenGL was IRIS GL from Silicon Graphics. Originally a 2D graphics library, it evolved into the 3D programming API for that company's high-end IRIS graphics workstations. These computers were more than just general-purpose computers; they had specialized hardware optimized for the display of sophisticated graphics. The hardware provided ultra-fast matrix transformations (a prerequisite for 3D graphics), hardware support for depth buffering, and other features.

Sometimes, however, the evolution of technology is hampered by the need to support legacy systems. IRIS GL had not been designed from the onset to have a vertex-style geometry processing interface, and it became apparent that to move forward SGI needed to make a clean break.

OpenGL is the result of SGI's efforts to evolve and improve IRIS GL's portability. The new graphics API would offer the power of GL but would be an "open" standard, with input from other graphics hardware vendors, and would allow for easier adaptability to other hardware platforms and operating systems. OpenGL would be designed from the ground up for 3D geometry processing.

The OpenGL ARB

An open standard is not really open if only one vendor controls it. SGI's business at the time was high-end computer graphics. Once you're at the top, you find that the opportunities for growth are somewhat limited. SGI realized that it would also be good for the company to do something good for the industry to help grow the market for high-end computer graphics hardware. A truly open standard embraced by a number of vendors would make it easier for programmers to create applications and content that is available for a wider variety of platforms. Software is what really sells computers, and if SGI wanted to sell more computers, it needed more software that would run on its computers. Other vendors realized this, too, and the OpenGL Architecture Review Board (ARB) was born.

Although SGI originally controlled licensing of the OpenGL API, the founding members of the OpenGL ARB were SGI, Digital Equipment Corporation, IBM, Intel, and Microsoft. On July 1, 1992, version 1.0 of the OpenGL specification was introduced. Over time, the ARB grew to consist of many more members, many from the PC hardware community, and it met four times a year to maintain and enhance the specification and to make plans to promote the OpenGL standard.

Over time, SGI's business fortunes declined for reasons well beyond the scope of this book. In 2006, an essentially bankrupt SGI transferred control of the OpenGL standard from the ARB to a new working group at The Khronos Group (www.khronos.org). The Khronos Group is a member-funded industry consortium focused on the creation and maintenance of open media standards. Most ARB members were already members of Khronos, and the transition was essentially painless. Today, the Khronos Group continues to evolve and promote OpenGL and its sibling API, OpenGL ES, which is covered in Chapter 22, "OpenGL ES—OpenGL on the Small."

OpenGL exists in two forms. The industry standard is codified in the *OpenGL Specification*. The specification describes OpenGL in very complete and specific (the similarity in words here is not an accident!) terms. The API is completely defined, as is the entire state machine, and how various features work and operate together. Hardware vendors such as ATI, NVIDIA, or Apple then take this specification and implement it. This *implementation*, then, is the embodiment of OpenGL in a form that software developers and customers can use to generate real-time graphics. For example, a software driver and a graphics card in your PC together make up an OpenGL implementation.

Licensing and Conformance

An implementation of OpenGL is either a software library that creates three-dimensional images in response to the OpenGL function calls or a driver for a hardware device (usually a display card) that does the same. Hardware implementations are many times faster than software implementations and are now common even on inexpensive PCs.

A vendor who wants to create and market an OpenGL implementation must first license OpenGL from The Khronos Group. They provide the licensee with a sample implementation (entirely in software) and a device driver kit if the licensee is a PC hardware vendor. The vendor then uses this to create its own optimized implementation and can add value with its own extensions. Competition among vendors typically is based on performance, image quality, and driver stability.

In addition, the vendor's implementation must pass the OpenGL conformance tests. These tests are designed to ensure that an implementation is complete (it contains all the necessary function calls) and produces 3D rendered output that is reasonably acceptable for a given set of functions.

Software developers do not need to license OpenGL or pay any fees to make use of OpenGL drivers. OpenGL is natively supported by most operating systems, and licensed drivers are provided by the hardware vendors themselves.

The API Wars

Standards are good for everyone, except for vendors who think that they should be the only vendors customers can choose from because they know best what customers need. We have a special legal word for vendors who manage to achieve this status: *monopoly.* Most companies recognize that competition is good for everyone in the long run and will endorse, support, and even contribute to industry standards. An interesting diversion from this ideal occurred during OpenGL's youth on the Windows platform.

When low-cost 3D graphics accelerators began to become available for the PC, many hardware vendors and game developers were attracted to OpenGL for its ease of use compared to Microsoft's Direct 3D. Microsoft provided a driver kit that made it very easy to make an OpenGL driver for Windows 98. This kit saved literally years of effort in creating a robust OpenGL driver for Windows NT and Windows 98. Microsoft discouraged vendors from using a more rigorous driver model, and every PC graphics card vendor had created OpenGL drivers ready to ship with Windows 98.

This attention to OpenGL by game developers created quite a political stir at the 1997 SigGraph and Game Developers conferences. Just before Windows 98 was released, Microsoft announced that it would not extend the OpenGL driver code license beyond the Windows 98 beta period, and that hardware vendors were forbidden to release their drivers.

Virtually every PC hardware vendor had a robust and fast OpenGL driver ready to roll for consumer PCs, but couldn't ship them. To further complicate things, shortly thereafter a struggling SGI announced a new Windows NT–based workstation. SGI simultaneously pledged to discontinue promoting OpenGL for consumer applications, and to work with Microsoft on a new API called Fahrenheit. OpenGL was as good as dead.

The Future of OpenGL

A funny thing happened on the way to oblivion, and even without SGI, OpenGL began to take on a life of its own. Hardware vendors with some help from SGI (pre-Fahrenheit) continued to support OpenGL with new drivers. Games aren't the only application that OpenGL was well suited for, and most developers wanted their Windows NT software to be able to run on the consumer version of Windows, too. When OpenGL was again widely available on consumer hardware, developers didn't really need SGI or anyone else touting the virtues of OpenGL. OpenGL was easy to use and had been around for years. This meant there was an abundance of documentation (including the first edition of this book), sample programs, SigGraph papers, and so on. OpenGL began to flourish.

As more developers began to use OpenGL, it became clear who was really in charge of the industry: the developers. The more applications that shipped with OpenGL support, the more pressure mounted on hardware vendors to produce better OpenGL hardware and high-quality drivers. Consumers don't really care about API technology. They just want software that works, and they will buy whatever graphics card runs their favorite game or application the best. Developers care about time to market, portability, and code reuse. (Go ahead. Try to recompile that old Direct3D 4.0 program. I dare you!) Using OpenGL enabled many developers to meet customer demand better, and in the end it's the customers who pay the bills.

As time passed, Fahrenheit fell solely into Microsoft's hands and was eventually discontinued altogether. Direct3D has evolved further to include more and more OpenGL features, functionality, and ease of use. Ten years later, today's Direct3D bears little resemblance to the tortured API it once was. OpenGL's popularity, however, has continued to grow as an alternative to Windows-specific rendering technology and is now widely supported across all major operating systems and hardware devices. Even cellphones with 3D graphics technology support a subset of OpenGL, called OpenGL ES. Today, all new 3D accelerated graphics cards for the PC ship with both OpenGL and Direct3D drivers. This is largely due to the fact that many developers continue to prefer OpenGL for new development. OpenGL today is widely recognized and accepted as *the* industry-standard API for real-time 3D and 2D graphics. Yes, even 2D! The OpenGL imaging subset and fragment processing programmability has made it the darling of hardware accelerated image and video processing applications as well.

This momentum will carry OpenGL into the foreseeable future as the API of choice for a wide range of applications and hardware platforms. All this also makes OpenGL well positioned to take advantage of future 3D graphics innovations. Because of OpenGL's extension mechanism, vendors can expose new hardware features without waiting on Microsoft or some industry committee, and cutting-edge developers can exploit them as soon as updated drivers are available. With the addition of the OpenGL shading language (see Part II, "The New Testament"), OpenGL has shown its continuing adaptability to meet the challenge of an evolving 3D graphics programming pipeline. Finally, OpenGL is a specification that has shown that it can be applied to a wide variety of programming paradigms. From C/C++ to Java and Visual Basic, even newer languages such as C# are now being used to create PC games and applications using OpenGL. OpenGL is here to stay.

How Does OpenGL Work?

OpenGL is a procedural rather than a descriptive graphics API. Instead of describing the scene and how it should appear, the programmer actually prescribes the steps necessary to achieve a certain appearance or effect. These "steps" involve calls to the many OpenGL commands. These commands are used to draw graphics primitives such as points, lines, and polygons in three dimensions. In addition, OpenGL supports lighting and shading, texture mapping, blending, transparency, animation, and many other special effects and capabilities.

OpenGL does not include any functions for window management, user interaction, or file I/O. Each host environment (such as Mac OS X or Microsoft Windows) has its own functions for this purpose and is responsible for implementing some means of handing over to OpenGL the drawing control of a window.

There is no "OpenGL file format" for models or virtual environments. Programmers construct these environments to suit their own high-level needs and then carefully program them using the lower-level OpenGL commands.

Generic Implementations

As mentioned previously, a generic implementation is a software implementation. Hardware implementations are created for a specific hardware device, such as a graphics card or game console. A generic implementation can technically run just about anywhere as long as the system can display the generated graphics image.

Figure 2.1 shows the typical place that OpenGL and a generic implementation occupy when a Windows application is running. The typical program calls many functions, some of which the programmer creates and some of which are provided by the operating system or the programming language's runtime library. Windows applications wanting to create output onscreen usually call a Windows API called the *graphics device interface (GDI)*. The GDI contains methods that allow you to write text in a window, draw simple 2D lines, and so on.

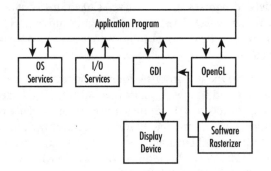

FIGURE 2.1   OpenGL's place in a typical application program.

Usually, graphics-card vendors supply a hardware driver that the operating system interfaces with to create output on your monitor. A software implementation of OpenGL takes graphics requests from an application and constructs (rasterizes) a color image of the 3D graphics. It then supplies this image for display on the monitor. On other operating systems, the process is reasonably equivalent, but you replace the GDI with that operating system's native display services.

OpenGL has a couple of common generic implementations. Microsoft has shipped its software implementation with every version of Windows NT since version 3.5 and Windows 95 (Service Release 2 and later). Windows 2000 and XP also contain support for a generic implementation of OpenGL. These versions of OpenGL are typically slow, and only support OpenGL functionality up to version 1.1. This by no means limits the capabilities or efficiency of native vendor-provided OpenGL drivers. We'll discuss this in more detail in Chapter 19, "Wiggle: OpenGL on Windows."

During the height of the so-called "API Wars," SGI released a software implementation of OpenGL for Windows that greatly outperformed Microsoft's implementation. This implementation is not officially supported but is still occasionally used by a few developers in niche markets. MESA 3D is another "unofficial" OpenGL software implementation that is widely supported in the open-source community. Mesa 3D is not an OpenGL license, so it is an "OpenGL work-alike" rather than an official implementation. In any respect other than legal, you can essentially consider it to be an OpenGL implementation nonetheless. The Mesa contributors even make a good attempt to pass the OpenGL conformance tests.

Hardware Implementations

A hardware implementation of OpenGL usually takes the form of a graphics card driver. Figure 2.2 shows its relationship to the application much as Figure 2.1 did for software implementations. Note that OpenGL API calls are passed to a hardware driver. This driver does not pass its output to the Windows GDI for display; the driver interfaces directly with the graphics display hardware.

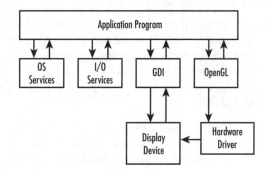

FIGURE 2.2   Hardware-accelerated OpenGL's place in a typical application program.

A hardware implementation is often referred to as an *accelerated implementation* because hardware-assisted 3D graphics usually far outperform software-only implementations. What isn't shown in Figure 2.2 is that sometimes part of the OpenGL functionality is still implemented in software as part of the driver, and other features and functionality can be passed directly to the hardware. This idea brings us to our next topic: the OpenGL pipeline.

The Pipeline

The word *pipeline* is used to describe a process that can take two or more distinct stages or steps. Figure 2.3 shows a simplified version of the OpenGL pipeline. As an application makes OpenGL API function calls, the commands are placed in a command buffer. This buffer eventually fills with commands, vertex data, texture data, and so on. When the buffer is flushed, either programmatically or by the driver's design, the commands and data are passed to the next stage in the pipeline.

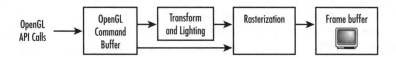

FIGURE 2.3   A simplified version of the OpenGL pipeline.

Vertex data is usually transformed and lit initially. In subsequent chapters, you'll find out more about what this means. For now, you can consider "transform and lighting" to be a mathematically intensive stage where points used to describe an object's geometry are recalculated for the given object's location and orientation. Lighting calculations are performed as well to indicate how bright the colors should be at each vertex.

When this stage is complete, the data is fed to the rasterization portion of the pipeline. The rasterizer actually creates the color image from the geometric, color, and texture data. The image is then placed in the *frame buffer.* The frame buffer is the memory of the graphics display device, which means the image is displayed on your screen.

This diagram provides a simplistic view of the OpenGL pipeline, but it is sufficient for your current understanding of 3D graphics rendering. At a high level, this view is accurate, so we aren't compromising your understanding, but at a low level, many more boxes appear inside each box shown here. There are also some exceptions, such as the arrow in the figure indicating that some commands skip the transform and lighting stage altogether (such as displaying raw image data on the screen).

Early OpenGL hardware accelerators were nothing more than fast rasterizers. They accelerated only the rasterization portion of the pipeline. The host system's CPU did transform and lighting in a software implementation of that portion of the pipeline. Higher-end (more expensive) accelerators had transform and lighting on the graphics accelerator. This arrangement put more of the OpenGL pipeline in hardware and thus provided for higher performance.

Even most low-end consumer hardware today has the transform and lighting stage in hardware. The net effect of this arrangement is that higher detailed models and more complex graphics are possible at real-time rendering rates on inexpensive consumer hardware. Games and applications developers can capitalize on this effect, yielding far more detailed and visually rich environments.

OpenGL: An API, Not a Language

For the most part, OpenGL is not a programming language; it is an application programming interface (API). Whenever we say that a program is OpenGL-based or an OpenGL application, we mean that it was written in some programming language (such as C or C++) that makes calls to one or more of the OpenGL libraries. We are not saying that the program uses OpenGL exclusively to do drawing. It might combine the best features of two different graphics packages. Or it might use OpenGL for only a few specific tasks and environment-specific graphics (such as the Windows GDI) for others. The only exception to this rule of thumb is, of course, the *OpenGL Shading Language,* which is covered in Part II.

As an API, the OpenGL library follows the C calling convention. As it turns out, this choice of calling convention makes it possible to easily call OpenGL directly from most other languages as well. In this book, the sample programs are written in C++. C++ programs can easily access C functions and APIs in the same manner as C, with only some minor considerations. C++ is the modern language of choice for most performance-minded applications. Very basic C++ classes can dramatically simplify most programming tasks as well. We promise to keep the object usage to a minimum, no STL/Template/Operator Overloaded/Meta blah blah...we promise!

Other programming languages—such as Visual Basic—that can call functions in C libraries can also make use of OpenGL, and OpenGL bindings are available for many other programming languages. Using OpenGL from these other languages is, however, outside the scope of this book and can be somewhat tedious to explain. To keep things simple and easily portable, we'll stick with C++ for our examples.

Standard Libraries and Headers

Although OpenGL is a "standard" programming library, this library has many implementations and versions. On Microsoft Windows, for example, the actual Microsoft software implementation is in the opengl32.dll dynamic link library, located in the Windows system directory. On most platforms, the OpenGL library is accompanied by the OpenGL utility library (GLU), which on Windows is in glu32.dll, also located in the system directory. The utility library is a set of utility functions that perform common (but sometimes complex) tasks, such as special matrix calculations, or provide support for common types of curves and surfaces. On Mac OS X, OpenGL and the GLU libraries are both included in the OpenGL Framework. Frameworks on OS X are similar in many respects to Windows DLLs.

The steps for setting up your compiler tools to use the correct OpenGL headers and to link to the correct OpenGL libraries vary from tool to tool and from platform to platform. They also change over time as newer versions of these tools are released. It is *usually* safe to assume that if you are reading a book on programming 3D graphics, you already know how to actually compile programs with your preferred development environment. Note the italics on the word *usually*! For this reason, in the source code distribution, you'll find preconfigured projects for Visual Studio on Windows, XCode on Mac OS X, and some generic "make" files for Linux. On our Web site (www.opengl.org/superbible) you'll find some more detailed tutorials to walk you through this if necessary.

On all platforms, the prototypes for all OpenGL functions, types, and macros are contained (by convention) in the header file gl.h. The utility library functions are proto-typed in a different file, glu.h. These files are usually located in a special directory in your *include* path, set up automatically when you install your development tools. For example, the following code shows the initial header inclusions for a basic Windows program that uses OpenGL:

```
#include<windows.h>
#include<gl/gl.h>
#include<gl/glu.h>
```

On an Apple OS X system, your include files might look more like this:

```
#include <Carbon/Carbon.h>
#include <OpenGL/gl.h>
#include <OpenGL/glu.h>
```

Some Header Customizations

To keep things from getting too complicated, all the examples in the book (with the exception being those in Part III, "The Apocrypha," all on platform-specific code) include one header file that takes care of all the platform-specific variations:

```
#include "../../shared/gltools.h"      // OpenGL toolkit
```

This file is in the /shared folder, and all the sample programs have the same relative position to this folder. If you look in this header, near the top, you'll find the platform-specific code broken out like this:

```
// Windows
#ifdef WIN32
#include <windows.h>           // Must have for Windows platform builds
#include "glee.h"              // OpenGL Extension "autoloader"
#include <gl\gl.h>             // Microsoft OpenGL headers (version 1.1 by themselves)
```

```
#include <gl\glu.h>            // OpenGL Utilities
#include "glut.h"              // Glut (Free-Glut on Windows)
#endif

// Mac OS X
#ifdef __APPLE__
#include <Carbon/Carbon.h>     // Brings in most Apple specific stuff
#include "glee.h"              // OpenGL Extension "autoloader"
#include <OpenGL/gl.h>         // Apple OpenGL shaders (version depends on
                               // OS X SDK version)
#include <OpenGL/glu.h>        // OpenGL Utilities
#include <Glut/glut.h>         // Apples Implementation of GLUT
#endif
```

You'll also notice a few other headers we haven't discussed yet. The first is glee.h. This header belongs to the GLEE library, which stands for OpenGL Easy Extension library. This library (or accompanying glee.c source file in our examples) transparently adds OpenGL extensions to your projects. The basic Microsoft headers include only OpenGL 1.1 functionality, and GLEE adds the rest of the API to your project. Apple keeps their headers more up-to-date, but still there may be some extensions or later functions you may need. GLEE works almost like magic!

Finally you'll see glut.h. We'll explain what GLUT is soon (all our samples use it). GLUT is natively supported on OS X and is supplied by Apple with their development tools. On Windows, we have used *freeglut,* which is an open-source implementation of the GLUT library. In addition to this header, on Windows builds, you need to add freeglut_static.lib. On Mac OS X with XCode, you add the GLUT Framework, and on Linux, GLUT is included in the library list in the make files.

If you look in the /examples/src/shared folder where gltools.h is located, you'll also find gltools.cpp. This source file is also added to many of the sample projects. This contains a collection of useful and frequently used functions written and used regularly by the authors in their own OpenGL-based work. A few other headers contain some simple C++ classes as well, and we'll discuss these in more detail as they come up.

API Specifics

OpenGL was designed by some clever people who had a lot of experience designing graphics programming APIs. They applied some standard rules to the way functions were named and variables were declared. The API is simple and clean and easy for vendors to extend. OpenGL tries to avoid as much *policy* as possible. Policy refers to assumptions that the designers make about how programmers will use the API. Examples of policies include assuming that you always specify vertex data as floating-point values, assuming that fog is always enabled before any rendering occurs, or assuming that all objects in a scene are affected by the same lighting parameters. Making these kinds of assumptions would eliminate many of the popular rendering techniques that have developed over time.

This philosophy has contributed to the longevity and evolution of OpenGL. Still, as time marches on, unanticipated advances in hardware capabilities, and the creativity of developers and hardware vendors, has taken its toll on OpenGL as it has progressed through the years. Despite this, OpenGL's basic API has shown surprising resilience to new unanticipated features. The ability to compile ten-year-old source code with little to no changes is a substantial advantage to application developers, and OpenGL has managed for years to add new features with as little impact on old code as possible. Future versions of OpenGL are in the works with "lean and mean" profiles, where some older features and models may eventually be dropped.

Data Types

To make it easier to port OpenGL code from one platform to another, OpenGL defines its own data types. These data types map to normal C/C++ data types that you can use instead, if you want. The various compilers and environments, however, have their own rules for the size and memory layout of various variable types. By using the OpenGL defined variable types, you can insulate your code from these types of changes.

Table 2.1 lists the OpenGL data types, their corresponding C/C++ data types under most 32-bit environments (Win32/OS X, etc.), and the appropriate suffix for literals. In this book, we use the suffixes for all literal values. You will see later that these suffixes are also used in many (but not all) OpenGL function names. The internal representation is the same on all platforms (even 64-bit OSs), regardless of machine size or compiler used (provided you have an appropriate SDK!).

TABLE 2.1   OpenGL Variable Types' Corresponding C Data Types

OpenGL Data Type	Internal Representation	Defined as C Type	C Literal Suffix
GLbyte	8-bit integer	signed char	b
GLshort	16-bit integer	short	s
GLint, GLsizei	32-bit integer	long	l
GLfloat, GLclampf	32-bit floating point	float	f
GLdouble, GLclampd	64-bit floating point	double	d
GLubyte, GLboolean	8-bit unsigned integer	unsigned char	ub
GLushort	16-bit unsigned integer	unsigned short	us
GLuint, GLenum, GLbitfield	32-bit unsigned integer	unsigned long	ui

TABLE 2.1 Continued

OpenGL Data Type	Internal Representation	Defined as C Type	C Literal Suffix
GLchar	8-bit character	char	None
GLsizeiptr,			
GLintptr	native pointer	ptrdiff_t	None

All data types start with a GL to denote OpenGL. Most are followed by their corresponding C data types (byte, short, int, float, and so on). Some have a u first to denote an unsigned data type, such as ubyte to denote an unsigned byte. For some uses, a more descriptive name is given, such as size to denote a value of length or depth. For example, GLsizei is an OpenGL variable denoting a size parameter that is represented by an integer. The clamp designation is a hint that the value is expected to be "clamped" to the range 0.0–1.0. The GLboolean variables are used to indicate true and false conditions; GLenum, for enumerated variables; and GLbitfield, for variables that contain binary bit fields.

Pointers and arrays are not given any special consideration. An array of 10 GLshort variables is simply declared as

```
GLshort shorts[10];
```

and an array of 10 pointers to GLdouble variables is declared with

```
GLdouble *doubles[10];
```

Some other pointer object types are used for NURBS and quadrics. They require more explanation and are covered in later chapters.

Function-Naming Conventions

Most OpenGL functions follow a naming convention that tells you which library the function is from and often how many and what types of arguments the function takes. All functions have a root that represents the function's corresponding OpenGL command. For example, glColor3f has the root Color. The gl prefix represents the gl library, and the 3f suffix means the function takes three floating-point arguments. All OpenGL functions take the following format:

<Library prefix><Root command><Optional argument count><Optional argument type>

Figure 2.4 illustrates the parts of an OpenGL function. This sample function with the suffix 3f takes three floating-point arguments. Other variations take three integers (glColor3i), three doubles (glColor3d), and so forth. This convention of adding the number and types of arguments (see Table 2.1) to the end of OpenGL functions makes it easy to remember the argument list without having to look it up. Some versions of glColor take four arguments to specify an alpha component (transparency) as well.

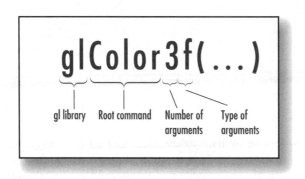

FIGURE 2.4   A dissected OpenGL function.

In the reference section (Appendix C) of this book, these "families" of functions are listed by their library prefix and root. All the variations of glColor (glColor3f, glColor4f, glColor3i, and so on) are listed under a single entry—glColor.

Any conformant C/C++ compiler will assume that any floating-point literal value is of type double unless explicitly told otherwise via the suffix mechanism. When you're using literals for floating-point arguments, if you don't specify that these arguments are of type float instead of double, many compilers will issue a warning while compiling because it detects that you are passing a double to a function defined to accept only floats, resulting in a possible loss of precision, not to mention a costly runtime conversion from double to float. As OpenGL programs grow, these warnings quickly number in the hundreds and make it difficult to find any real syntax errors. You can turn off these warnings using the appropriate compiler options, but we advise against doing so. It's better to write clean, portable code the first time. So clean up those warning messages by cleaning up the code (in this case, by explicitly using the float type)—not by disabling potentially useful warnings.

Additionally, you might be tempted to use the functions that accept double-precision floating-point arguments rather than go to all the bother of specifying your literals as floats. However, OpenGL uses floats internally, and using anything other than the single-precision floating-point functions adds a performance bottleneck because the values are converted to floats anyhow before being processed by OpenGL—not to mention that every double takes up twice as much memory as a float. For a program with a lot of numbers "floating" around, these performance hits can add up pretty fast!

Platform Independence

OpenGL is a powerful and sophisticated API for creating 3D graphics, with more than 300 commands that cover everything from setting material colors and reflective properties to doing rotations and complex coordinate transformations. You might be surprised that OpenGL does not have a single function or command relating to window or screen management. In addition, there are no functions for keyboard input or mouse interaction. Consider, however, that one of the OpenGL designers' primary goals was for OpenGL to be a platform independent abstraction of graphics hardware. Creating and managing windows and polling for user input are inherently operating system related tasks. You do not ask your graphics card if the user has pressed the enter key! There are, of course, some other very good platform independent abstractions of this sort, too, but these tasks fall outside the scope of graphics rendering. Remember the first sentence of this chapter, "OpenGL is a software interface to graphics hardware."

Using GLUT

In the beginning, there was AUX, the OpenGL auxiliary library. The AUX library was created to facilitate the learning and writing of OpenGL programs without the programmer being distracted by the minutiae of any particular environment, be it UNIX, Windows, or whatever. You wouldn't write "final" code when using AUX; it was more of a preliminary staging ground for testing your ideas. A lack of basic GUI features limited the library's use for building useful applications.

AUX has since been replaced by the GLUT library for cross-platform programming examples and demonstrations. GLUT stands for *OpenGL utility toolkit* (not to be confused with the standard GLU—OpenGL utility library). Mark Kilgard, while at SGI, wrote GLUT as a more capable replacement for the AUX library and included some GUI features to at least make sample programs more usable under X Windows. This replacement includes using pop-up menus, managing other windows, and even providing joystick support. GLUT is not public domain, but it is free and free to redistribute. GLUT is widely available on most UNIX distributions (including Linux), and is natively supported by Mac OS X, where Apple maintains and extends the library. On Windows, GLUT development has been discontinued. Since GLUT was originally not licensed as open source, a new GLUT implementation, *freeglut,* has sprung up to take its place. All the Windows GLUT-based samples in this book make use of the freeglut library, which is also available on our Web site.

For most of this book, we use GLUT as our program framework. This decision serves two purposes. The first is that it makes most of the book accessible to a wider audience. With a little effort, experienced Windows, Linux, or Mac programmers should be able to set up GLUT for their programming environments and follow most of the examples in this book.

The second point is that using GLUT eliminates the need to know and understand basic GUI programming on any specific platform. Although we explain the general concepts, we do not claim to write a book about GUI programming, but rather about OpenGL. Using GLUT for the basic coverage of the API, we make life a bit easier for Windows/Mac/Linux novices as well.

It's unlikely that all the functionality of a commercial application will be embodied entirely in the code used to draw in 3D. Although GLUT does have some limited GUI functionality, it is very simple and abbreviated as far as GUI toolkits go. Thus you can't rely entirely on the GLUT library for everything. Nevertheless, the GLUT library excels in its role for learning and demonstration exercises, and hiding all the platform specific details of window creation and OpenGL context initialization. Even for an experienced programmer, it is still easier to employ the GLUT library to iron out 3D graphics code before integrating it into a complete application.

Your First Program

To understand the GLUT library better, look at possibly the world's shortest OpenGL program, which was written using the GLUT library. Listing 2.1 presents the SIMPLE program. Its output is shown in Figure 2.5. You'll also learn just a few things about OpenGL along the way!

LISTING 2.1   Source Code for SIMPLE: A Very Simple OpenGL Program

```
#include "../../shared/gltools.h"      // OpenGL toolkit


/////////////////////////////////////////////////////////
// Called to draw scene
void RenderScene(void)
    {
    // Clear the window with current clearing color
    glClear(GL_COLOR_BUFFER_BIT);

    // Flush drawing commands
    glFlush();
    }


/////////////////////////////////////////////////////////
// Set up the rendering state
void SetupRC(void)
    {
    glClearColor(0.0f, 0.0f, 1.0f, 1.0f);
    }


/////////////////////////////////////////////////////////
// Main program entry point
void main(void)
int main(int argc, char* argv[])
    {
    glutInit(&argc, argv);
    glutInitDisplayMode(GLUT_SINGLE | GLUT_RGBA);
    glutCreateWindow("Simple");
    glutDisplayFunc(RenderScene);
```

LISTING 2.1   Continued

```
    SetupRC();

    glutMainLoop();

    return 0;
    }
```

FIGURE 2.5   Output from the SIMPLE program.

The SIMPLE program doesn't do much. When run from the command line (or development environment), it creates a standard GUI window with the caption `Simple` and a clear blue background. If you are running Visual C++, when you terminate the program, you see the message `Press any key to continue` in the console window. You need to press a key to terminate the program. This standard feature of the Microsoft IDE for running a console application ensures that you can see whatever output your program places onscreen (the console window) before the window vanishes. If you run the program from the command line, you don't get this behavior. If you double-click on the program file from Explorer, you see the console window, but it vanishes when the program terminates.

This simple program contains four GLUT library functions (prefixed with `glut`) and three "real" OpenGL functions (prefixed with `gl`). Let's examine the program line by line, after which we will introduce some more functions and substantially improve on the first example.

The Header
Listing 2.1 contains only one include file:

```
#include "../../shared/gltools.h"      // OpenGL toolkit
```

This file, which we mentioned earlier, includes the `gl.h` and `glut.h` headers, which bring in the function prototypes used by the program.

The Body

Next, we skip down to the entry point of all C programs:

```
int main(int argc, char* argv[])
    {
    glutInit(&argc, argv);
```

Console-mode C and C++ programs always start execution with the function `main`. If you are an experienced Windows nerd, you might wonder where `WinMain` is in this example. It's not there because we start with a console-mode application, so we don't have to start with window creation and a message loop. With Win32, you can create graphical windows from console applications, just as you can create console windows from GUI applications. These details are buried within the GLUT library. (Remember, the GLUT library is designed to hide just these kinds of platform details.)

The first line of code in `main` is a call to `glutInit`, which simply passes along the command-line parameters and initializes the GLUT library.

Display Mode: Single Buffered

Next we must tell the GLUT library what type of display mode to use when creating the window:

```
glutInitDisplayMode(GLUT_SINGLE | GLUT_RGBA);
```

The flags here tell it to use a single-buffered window (GLUT_SINGLE) and to use RGBA color mode (GLUT_RGBA). A single-buffered window means that all drawing commands are performed on the window displayed. An alternative is a double-buffered window, where the drawing commands are actually executed on an offscreen buffer and then quickly swapped into view on the window. This method is often used to produce animation effects and is demonstrated later in this chapter. In fact, we use double-buffered mode for the rest of the book. RGBA color mode means that you specify colors by supplying separate intensities of red, green, blue, and alpha components. The alternative is color index mode, which is now largely obsolete, in which you specify colors by using an index into a color palette.

Creating the OpenGL Window

The next call to the GLUT library actually creates the window on the screen. The following code creates the window and sets the caption to `Simple`:

```
glutCreateWindow("Simple");
```

The single argument to `glutCreateWindow` is the caption for the window's title bar.

Displaying Callback

The next line of GLUT-specific code is

```
glutDisplayFunc(RenderScene);
```

This line establishes the previously defined function RenderScene as the display callback function. This means that GLUT calls the function pointed to here whenever the window needs to be drawn. This call occurs when the window is first displayed or when the window is resized or uncovered, for example. This is the place where we put our OpenGL rendering function calls.

Set Up the Context and Go!

The next line is neither GLUT- nor OpenGL-specific but is a convention that we follow throughout the book:

```
SetupRC();
```

In this function, we do any OpenGL initialization that should be performed before rendering. Many of the OpenGL states need to be set only once and do not need to be reset every time you render a frame (a screen full of graphics).

The last GLUT function call comes at the end of the program:

```
glutMainLoop();
```

This function starts the GLUT framework running. After you define callbacks for screen display and other functions (coming up), you turn GLUT loose. glutMainLoop never returns after it is called until the main window is closed, and needs to be called only once from an application. This function processes all the operating system–specific messages, keystrokes, and so on until you terminate the program.

OpenGL Graphics Calls

The SetupRC function contains a single OpenGL function call:

```
glClearColor(0.0f, 0.0f, 1.0f, 1.0f);
```

This function sets the color used for clearing the window. The prototype for this function is

```
void glClearColor(GLclampf red, GLclampf green, GLclampf blue, GLclampf alpha);
```

GLclampf is defined as a float under most implementations of OpenGL. In OpenGL, a single color is represented as a mixture of red, green, and blue components. The range for each component can vary from 0.0 to 1.0. This is similar to the Windows specification of colors using the RGB macro to create a COLORREF value. The difference is that in Windows each color component in a COLORREF can range from 0 to 255, giving a total of

256×256×256—or more than 16 million colors. With OpenGL, the values for each component can be any valid floating-point value between 0 and 1, thus yielding a virtually infinite number of potential colors. Practically speaking, color output is limited on most devices to 24 bits (16 million colors) total.

Naturally, OpenGL takes this color value and converts it internally to the nearest possible exact match with the available video hardware. Table 2.2 lists some common colors and their component values. You can use these values with any of the OpenGL color-related functions.

TABLE 2.2   Some Common Composite Colors

Composite Color	Red Component	Green Component	Blue Component
Black	0.0	0.0	0.0
Red	1.0	0.0	0.0
Green	0.0	1.0	0.0
Yellow	1.0	1.0	0.0
Blue	0.0	0.0	1.0
Magenta	1.0	0.0	1.0
Cyan	0.0	1.0	1.0
Dark gray	0.25	0.25	0.25
Light gray	0.75	0.75	0.75
Brown	0.60	0.40	0.12
Pumpkin orange	0.98	0.625	0.12
Pastel pink	0.98	0.04	0.7
Barney purple	0.60	0.40	0.70
White	1.0	1.0	1.0

The last argument to glClearColor is the alpha component, which is used for blending and special effects such as transparency. Transparency refers to an object's capability to allow light to pass through it. Suppose you would like to create a piece of red stained glass, and a blue light happens to be shining behind it. The blue light affects the appearance of the red in the glass (blue + red = purple). You can use the alpha component value to generate a red color that is semitransparent so that it works like a sheet of glass—an object behind it shows through. There is more to this type of effect than just using the alpha value, and in Chapter 6, "More on Colors and Materials," you'll learn more about this topic; until then, you should leave the alpha value as 1.

Clearing the Color Buffer
All we have done at this point is set OpenGL to use blue for the clearing color. In our RenderScene function, we need an instruction to do the actual clearing:

```
glClear(GL_COLOR_BUFFER_BIT);
```

The `glClear` function clears a particular buffer or combination of buffers. A buffer is a storage area for image information. The red, green, and blue components of a drawing are usually collectively referred to as the *color buffer* or *pixel buffer.*

More than one kind of buffer (color, depth, stencil, and accumulation) is available in OpenGL, and these buffers are covered in more detail later in the book. For the next several chapters, all you really need to understand is that the color buffer is the place where the displayed image is stored internally and that clearing the buffer with `glClear` removes the last drawing from the window. You will also see the term *framebuffer*, which refers to all these buffers collectively since they work in tandem.

Flushing That Queue

The final OpenGL function call comes last:

```
glFlush();
```

This line causes any unexecuted OpenGL commands to be executed. We have one at this point: `glClear`.

Internally, OpenGL uses a rendering pipeline that processes commands sequentially. OpenGL commands and statements often are queued up until the OpenGL driver processes several "commands" at once. This setup improves performance because communication with hardware is inherently slow. Making one trip to the hardware with a truckload of data is much faster than making several smaller trips for each command or instruction. We'll discuss this feature of OpenGL's operation further in Chapter 11, "It's All About the Pipeline: Faster Geometry Throughput." In the short program in Listing 2.1, the `glFlush` function simply tells OpenGL that it should proceed with the drawing instructions supplied thus far before waiting for any more drawing commands.

SIMPLE might not be the most interesting OpenGL program in existence, but it demonstrates the basics of getting a window up using the GLUT library, and it shows how to specify a color and clear the window. Next, we want to spruce up our program by adding some more GLUT library and OpenGL functions.

Drawing Shapes with OpenGL

The SIMPLE program made an empty window with a blue background. Now, let's do some drawing in the window. In addition, we want to be able to move and resize the window and have our rendering code respond appropriately. In Listing 2.2, you can see the modifications. Figure 2.6 shows the output of this program (GLRect).

LISTING 2.2   Drawing a Centered Rectangle with OpenGL

```
#include "../../shared/gltools.h"      // OpenGL toolkit


///////////////////////////////////////////////////////////
// Called to draw scene
```

LISTING 2.2   Continued

```
void RenderScene(void)
    {
    // Clear the window with current clearing color
    glClear(GL_COLOR_BUFFER_BIT);

    // Set current drawing color to red
    //          R     G     B
    glColor3f(1.0f, 0.0f, 0.0f);

    // Draw a filled rectangle with current color
    glRectf(-25.0f, 25.0f, 25.0f, -25.0f);

    // Flush drawing commands
    glFlush();
    }


//////////////////////////////////////////////////////////
// Set up the rendering state
void SetupRC(void)
    {
    // Set clear color to blue
    glClearColor(0.0f, 0.0f, 1.0f, 1.0f);
    }


//////////////////////////////////////////////////////////
// Called by GLUT library when the window has chanaged size
void ChangeSize(GLsizei w, GLsizei h)
    {
    GLfloat aspectRatio;

    // Prevent a divide by zero
    if(h == 0)
        h = 1;

    // Set Viewport to window dimensions
    glViewport(0, 0, w, h);

    // Reset coordinate system
    glMatrixMode(GL_PROJECTION);
    glLoadIdentity();
```

LISTING 2.2   Continued

```
    // Establish clipping volume (left, right, bottom, top, near, far)
    aspectRatio = (GLfloat)w / (GLfloat)h;
    if (w <= h)
        glOrtho (-100.0, 100.0, -100 / aspectRatio, 100.0 / aspectRatio,
                1.0, -1.0);
    else
        glOrtho (-100.0 * aspectRatio, 100.0 * aspectRatio,
                -100.0, 100.0, 1.0, -1.0);

    glMatrixMode(GL_MODELVIEW);
    glLoadIdentity();
    }


///////////////////////////////////////////////////////////
// Main program entry point
void main(void)
int main(int argc, char* argv[])
    {
    glutInit(&argc, argv);
    glutInitDisplayMode(GLUT_SINGLE | GLUT_RGB);
    glutCreateWindow("GLRect");
    glutDisplayFunc(RenderScene);
    glutReshapeFunc(ChangeSize);
    SetupRC();

    glutMainLoop();

    return 0;
    }
```

FIGURE 2.6   Output from the GLRect program.

Drawing a Rectangle

Previously, all our program did was clear the screen. We've now added the following lines of drawing code:

```
// Set current drawing color to red
//          R    G    B
glColor3f(1.0f, 0.0f, 0.0f);

// Draw a filled rectangle with current color
glRectf(-25.0f, 25.0f, 25.0f, -25.0f);
```

These lines set the color used for future drawing operations (lines and filling) with the call to glColor3f. Then glRectf draws a filled rectangle.

The glColor3f function selects a color in the same manner as glClearColor, but no alpha translucency component needs to be specified (the default value for alpha is 1.0 for completely opaque):

```
void glColor3f(GLfloat red, GLfloat green, GLfloat blue);
```

The glRectf function takes floating-point arguments, as denoted by the trailing f. The number of arguments is not used in the function name because all glRect variations take four arguments. The four arguments of glRectf, shown here, represent two coordinate pairs, (x1, y1) and (x2, y2):

```
void glRectf(GLfloat x1, GLfloat y1, GLfloat x2, GLfloat y2);
```

The first pair represents the upper-left corner of the rectangle, and the second pair represents the lower-right corner.

How does OpenGL map these coordinates to actual window positions? This is done in the callback function ChangeSize. This function is set as the callback function for whenever the window changes size (when it is stretched, maximized, and so on). This is set by the glutReshapeFunc in the same way that the display callback function is set:

```
glutReshapeFunc(ChangeSize);
```

Any time the window size or dimensions change, you need to reset the coordinate system.

Scaling to the Window

In nearly all windowing environments, the user can at any time change the size and dimensions of the window. Even if you are writing a game that always runs in full-screen mode, the window is still considered to change size once—when it is created. When this happens, the window usually responds by redrawing its contents, taking into consideration the window's new dimensions. Sometimes, you might want to simply clip the drawing for smaller windows or display the entire drawing at its original size in a larger window. For our purposes, we usually want to scale the drawing to fit within the window, regardless of the size of the drawing or window. Thus, a very small window would have a complete but very small drawing, and a larger window would have a similar but larger drawing. You see this effect in most drawing programs when you stretch a window as opposed to enlarging the drawing. Stretching a window usually doesn't change the drawing size, but magnifying the image makes it grow.

Setting the Viewport and Clipping Volume

In Chapter 1 we discussed how the viewport and viewing volume affect the coordinate range and scaling of 2D and 3D drawings in a 2D window on the computer screen. Now, we examine the setting of viewport and clipping volume coordinates in OpenGL.

Although our drawing is a 2D flat rectangle, we are actually drawing in a 3D coordinate space. The glRectf function draws the rectangle in the xy plane at z = 0. Your perspective is along the positive z-axis to see the square rectangle at z = 0. (If you're feeling lost here, review this material in Chapter 1, "Introduction to 3D Graphics and OpenGL.")

Whenever the window size changes, the viewport and clipping volume must be redefined for the new window dimensions. Otherwise, you see an effect like the one shown in Figure 2.7, where the mapping of the coordinate system to screen coordinates stays the same regardless of the window size.

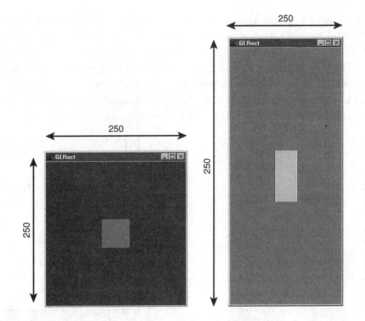

FIGURE 2.7   The effects of changing the window size but not the coordinate system.

Because window size changes are detected and handled differently under various environments, the GLUT library provides the function glutReshapeFunc, which registers a callback that the GLUT library will call whenever the window dimensions change. The function you pass to glutReshapeFunc is prototyped like this:

```
void ChangeSize(GLsizei w, GLsizei h);
```

We have chosen ChangeSize as a descriptive name for this function, and we will use that name for our future examples.

The ChangeSize function receives the new width and height whenever the window size changes. We can use this information to modify the mapping of our desired coordinate system to real screen coordinates, with the help of two OpenGL functions: glViewport and glOrtho.

Defining the Viewport

To understand how the viewport definition is achieved, let's look more carefully at the ChangeSize function. It first calls glViewport with the new width and height of the window. The glViewport function is defined as

```
void glViewport(GLint x, GLint y, GLsizei width, GLsizei height);
```

The *x* and *y* parameters specify the lower-left corner of the viewport within the window, and the *width* and *height* parameters specify these dimensions in pixels. Usually, *x* and *y* are both 0, but you can use viewports to render more than one drawing in different areas of a window. The viewport defines the area within the window in actual screen coordinates that OpenGL can use to draw in (see Figure 2.8). The current clipping volume is then mapped to the new viewport. If you specify a viewport that is smaller than the window coordinates, the rendering is scaled smaller, as you see in Figure 2.8.

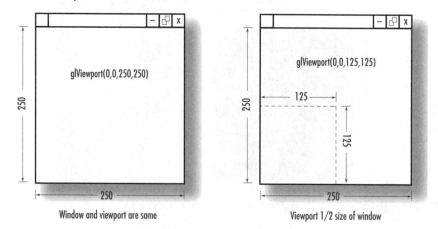

FIGURE 2.8   Viewport-to-window mapping.

Defining the Clipped Viewing Volume

The last requirement of our `ChangeSize` function is to redefine the clipping volume so that the aspect ratio remains square. The aspect ratio is the ratio of the number of pixels along a unit of length in the vertical direction to the number of pixels along the same unit of length in the horizontal direction. In English, this just means the width of the window divided by the height. An aspect ratio of 1.0 defines a square aspect ratio. An aspect ratio of 0.5 specifies that for every two pixels in the horizontal direction for a unit of length, there is one pixel in the vertical direction for the same unit of length.

If you specify a viewport that is not square and it is mapped to a square clipping volume, the image will be distorted. For example, a viewport matching the window size and dimensions but mapped to a square clipping volume would cause images to appear tall and thin in tall and thin windows and wide and short in wide and short windows. In this case, our square would appear square only when the window was sized to be a square.

In our example, an orthographic projection is used for the clipping volume. The OpenGL command to create this projection is `glOrtho`:

```
void glOrtho(GLdouble left, GLdouble right, GLdouble bottom,
             GLdouble top, GLdouble near, GLdouble far );
```

In 3D Cartesian space, the `left` and `right` values specify the minimum and maximum coordinate value displayed along the x-axis; `bottom` and `top` are for the y-axis. The `near` and `far` parameters are for the z-axis, generally with negative values extending away from the viewer (see Figure 2.9). Many drawing and graphics libraries use window coordinates (pixels) for drawing commands. Using a real floating-point (and seemingly arbitrary) coordinate system for rendering is one of the hardest things for many beginners to get used to. After you work through a few programs, though, it quickly becomes second nature.

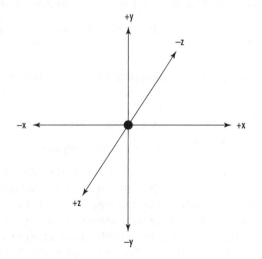

FIGURE 2.9   Cartesian space.

Just before the code using glOrtho, notice these two function calls:

```
// Reset coordinate system
glMatrixMode(GL_PROJECTION);
glLoadIdentity();
```

The subject of matrices and the OpenGL matrix stacks comes up in Chapter 4, "Geometric Transformations: The Pipeline," where we discuss this topic in more detail. The projection matrix is the place where you actually define your viewing volume. The single call to glLoadIdentity is needed because glOrtho doesn't really establish the clipping volume, but rather modifies the existing clipping volume. It multiplies the matrix that describes the current clipping volume by the matrix that describes the clipping volume described in its arguments. For now, you just need to know that glLoadIdentity serves to "reset" the coordinate system before any matrix manipulations are performed. Without this "reset," every time glOrtho is called, each successive call to glOrtho could result in a further corruption of the intended clipping volume, which might not even display the rectangle.

The last two lines of code, shown here, tell OpenGL that all future transformations will affect our models (what we draw):

```
glMatrixMode(GL_MODELVIEW);
glLoadIdentity();
```

We purposely do not cover model transformation until Chapter 4. You do need to know now, however, how to set up these things with their default values. Otherwise, if you become adventurous and start experimenting, your output might not match what you expect.

Keeping a Square Square

The following code does the actual work of keeping our square square:

```
// Establish clipping volume (left, right, bottom, top, near, far)
aspectRatio = (GLfloat)w / (GLfloat)h;
if (w <= h)
    glOrtho (-100.0, 100.0, -100 / aspectRatio, 100.0 / aspectRatio,
            1.0, -1.0);
else
    glOrtho (-100.0 * aspectRatio, 100.0 * aspectRatio,
            -100.0, 100.0, 1.0, -1.0);
```

Our clipping volume (visible coordinate space) is modified so that the left side is always at $x = -100$ and the right side extends to 100 unless the window is wider than it is tall. In that case, the horizontal extent is scaled by the aspect ratio of the window. In the same manner, the bottom is always at $y = -100$ and extends upward to 100 unless the window is taller than it is wide. In that case, the upper coordinate is scaled by the inverse of the aspect ratio. This serves to keep a square coordinate region 200×200 available (with 0,0 in the center) regardless of the shape of the window. Figure 2.10 shows how this works.

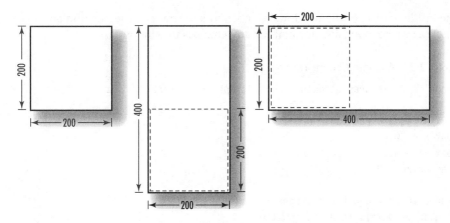

FIGURE 2.10 The clipping region for three different windows.

Animation with OpenGL and GLUT

So far, we've discussed the basics of using the GLUT library for creating a window and using OpenGL commands for the actual drawing. You will often want to move or rotate your images and scenes, creating an animated effect. Let's take the previous example, which draws a square, and make the square bounce off the sides of the window. You could create a loop that continually changes your object's coordinates before calling the RenderScene function. This would cause the square to appear to move around within the window.

The GLUT library enables you to register a callback function that makes it easier to set up a simple animated sequence. This function, glutTimerFunc, takes the name of a function to call and the amount of time to wait before calling the function:

```
void glutTimerFunc(unsigned int msecs, void (*func)(int value), int value);
```

This code sets up GLUT to wait *msecs* milliseconds before calling the function func. You can pass a user-defined value in the *value* parameter. The function called by the timer has the following prototype:

```
void TimerFunction(int value);
```

When the time expires, this function is fired only once. To effect a continuous animation, you must reset the timer again in the timer function.

In our GLRect program, we can change the hard-coded values for the location of our rectangle to variables and then constantly modify those variables in the timer function. This causes the rectangle to appear to move across the window. Let's look at an example of this kind of animation. In Listing 2.3, we modify Listing 2.2 to bounce around the square off the inside borders of the window. We need to keep track of the position and size of the rectangle as we go along and account for any changes in window size.

LISTING 2.3   Animated Bouncing Square

```
#include "../../shared/gltools.h"      // OpenGL toolkit

// Initial square position and size
GLfloat x1 = 0.0f;
GLfloat y1 = 0.0f;
GLfloat rsize = 25;

// Step size in x and y directions
// (number of pixels to move each time)
GLfloat xstep = 1.0f;
GLfloat ystep = 1.0f;

// Keep track of windows changing width and height
GLfloat windowWidth;
GLfloat windowHeight;

///////////////////////////////////////////////////////////
// Called to draw scene
void RenderScene(void)
    {
    // Clear the window with current clearing color
    glClear(GL_COLOR_BUFFER_BIT);

        // Set current drawing color to red
    //          R     G     B
    glColor3f(1.0f, 0.0f, 0.0f);

    // Draw a filled rectangle with current color
    glRectf(x1, y1, x1 + rsize, y1 - rsize);

    // Flush drawing commands and swap
    glutSwapBuffers();
    }

///////////////////////////////////////////////////////////
// Called by GLUT library when idle (window not being
// resized or moved)
void TimerFunction(int value)
    {
```

LISTING 2.3   Continued

```
// Reverse direction when you reach left or right edge
if(x1 > windowWidth-rsize || x1 < -windowWidth)
    xstep = -xstep;

// Reverse direction when you reach top or bottom edge
if(y1 > windowHeight || y1 < -windowHeight + rsize)
    ystep = -ystep;

// Actually move the square
x1 += xstep;
y1 += ystep;


// Check bounds. This is in case the window is made
// smaller while the rectangle is bouncing and the
// rectangle suddenly finds itself outside the new
// clipping volume
if(x1 > (windowWidth-rsize + xstep))
    x1 = windowWidth-rsize-1;
else if(x1 < -(windowWidth + xstep))
x1 = - windowsWidth -1;

if(y1 > (windowHeight + ystep))
    y1 = windowHeight-1;
else if(y1 < -(windowHeight - rsize + ystep))
y1 = -windowHeight + rsize -1;


  // Redraw the scene with new coordinates
glutPostRedisplay();
glutTimerFunc(33,TimerFunction, 1);
}


/////////////////////////////////////////////////////////
// Main program entry point
int main(int argc, char* argv[])
    {
glutInit(&argc, argv);
glutInitDisplayMode(GLUT_DOUBLE | GLUT_RGB);
glutInitWindowSize(800,600);
glutCreateWindow("Bounce");
```

LISTING 2.3   Continued

```
    glutDisplayFunc(RenderScene);
    glutReshapeFunc(ChangeSize);
    glutTimerFunc(33, TimerFunction, 1);

    SetupRC();
    glutMainLoop();

    return 0;
}
```

Double Buffering

One of the most important features of any graphics package is support for *double buffering*. This feature allows you to execute your drawing code while rendering to an offscreen buffer. Then a swap command places your drawing onscreen instantly.

Double buffering can serve two purposes. The first is that some complex drawings might take a long time to draw, and you might not want each step of the image composition to be visible. Using double buffering, you can compose an image and display it only after it is complete. The user never sees a partial image; only after the entire image is ready is it shown onscreen.

A second use for double buffering is animation. Each frame is drawn in the offscreen buffer and then swapped quickly to the screen when ready. The GLUT library supports double-buffered windows. In Listing 2.3 note the following line:

```
glutInitDisplayMode(GLUT_DOUBLE | GLUT_RGBA);
```

We have changed GLUT_SINGLE to GLUT_DOUBLE. This change causes all the drawing code to render in an offscreen buffer.

Next, we also changed the end of the RenderScene function:

```
    . . .
    // Flush drawing commands and swap
    glutSwapBuffers();
    }
```

No longer are we calling glFlush. This function is no longer needed because when we perform a buffer swap, we are implicitly performing a flush operation.

These changes cause a smoothly animated bouncing rectangle, shown in Figure 2.11. The function glutSwapBuffers still performs the flush, even if you are running in single-buffered mode. Simply change GLUT_DOUBLE back to GLUT_SINGLE in the bounce sample to see the animation without double buffering. As you'll see, the rectangle constantly blinks and stutters, a very unpleasant and poor animation with single buffering.

FIGURE 2.11   Follow the bouncing square.

The GLUT library is a reasonably complete framework for creating sophisticated sample programs and perhaps even full-fledged commercial applications (assuming you do not need to use OS-specific or GUI features). It is not the purpose of this book to explore GLUT in all its glory and splendor, however. Here and in the reference section to come, we restrict ourselves to the small subset of GLUT needed to demonstrate the various features of OpenGL.

The OpenGL State Machine

Drawing 3D graphics is a complicated affair. In the chapters ahead, we will cover many OpenGL functions. For a given piece of geometry, many things can affect how it is drawn. Is a light shining on it? What are the properties of the light? What are the properties of the material? Which, if any, texture should be applied? The list could go on and on.

We call this collection of variables the *state* of the pipeline. A state machine is an abstract model of a collection of state variables, all of which can have various values, be turned on or off, and so on. It simply is not practical to specify all the state variables whenever we try to draw something in OpenGL. Instead, OpenGL employs a state model, or state machine, to keep track of all the OpenGL state variables. When a state value is set, it remains set until some other function changes it. Many states are simply on or off. Lighting, for example (see Chapter 5, "Color, Materials, and Lighting: The Basics"), is either turned on or turned off. Geometry drawn without lighting is drawn without any lighting calculations being applied to the colors set for the geometry. Any geometry drawn *after* lighting is turned back on is then drawn with the lighting calculations applied.

To turn these types of state variables on and off, you use the following OpenGL function:

```
void glEnable(GLenum capability);
```

You turn the variable back off with the corresponding function:

```
void glDisable(GLenum capability);
```

For the case of lighting, for instance, you can turn it on by using the following:

```
glEnable(GL_LIGHTING);
```

And you turn it back off with this function:

```
glDisable(GL_LIGHTING);
```

If you want to test a state variable to see whether it is enabled, OpenGL again has a convenient mechanism:

```
Glboolean glIsEnabled(GLenum capability);
```

Not all state variables, however, are simply on or off. Many of the OpenGL functions yet to come set up values that "stick" until changed. You can query what these values are at any time as well. A set of query functions allows you to query the values of Booleans, integers, floats, and double variables. These four functions are prototyped thus:

```
void glGetBooleanv(GLenum pname, GLboolean *params);
void glGetDoublev(GLenum pname, GLdouble *params);
void glGetFloatv(GLenum pname, GLfloat *params);
void glGetIntegerv(GLenum pname, GLint *params);
```

Each function returns a single value or a whole array of values, storing the results at the address you supply. The various parameters are documented in the reference section in Appendix C, "API Reference" (there are a lot of them!). Most may not make much sense to you right away, but as you progress through the book, you will begin to appreciate the power and simplicity of the OpenGL state machine.

Saving and Restoring States

OpenGL also has a convenient mechanism for saving a whole range of state values and restoring them later. The *stack* is a convenient data structure that allows values to be *pushed* on the stack (saved) and *popped* off the stack later to retrieve them. Items are popped off in the opposite order in which they were pushed on the stack. We call this a Last In First Out (*LIFO*) data structure. It's an easy way to just say, "Hey, please save this" (push it on the stack), and then a little later say, "Give me what I just saved" (pop it off the stack). You'll see that the concept of the stack plays a very important role in matrix manipulation when you get to Chapter 4.

A single OpenGL state value or a whole range of related state values can be pushed on the attribute stack with the following command:

```
void glPushAttrib(GLbitfield mask);
```

Values are correspondingly restored with this command:

```
void glPopAttrib(GLbitfield mask);
```

Note that the argument to these functions is a bit field. This means that you use a bitwise mask, which allows you to perform a bitwise OR (in C using the ¦ operator) of multiple state values with a single function call. For example, you could save the lighting and texturing state with a single call like this:

```
glPushAttrib(GL_TEXTURE_BIT ¦ GL_LIGHTING_BIT);
```

A complete list of all the OpenGL state values that can be saved and restored with these functions is located in the reference section in Appendix C, for the glPushAttrib function listing.

OpenGL Errors

In any project, you want to write robust and well-behaved programs that respond politely to their users and have some amount of flexibility. Graphical programs that use OpenGL are no exception, and if you want your programs to run smoothly, you need to account for errors and unexpected circumstances. OpenGL provides a useful mechanism for you to perform an occasional sanity check in your code. This capability can be important because, from the code's standpoint, it's not really possible to tell whether the output was the Space Station Freedom or the Space Station Melted Crayons!

When Bad Things Happen to Good Code

Internally, OpenGL maintains a set of six error flags. Each flag represents a different type of error. Whenever one of these errors occurs, the corresponding flag is set. To see whether any of these flags is set, call glGetError:

```
Glenum glGetError(void);
```

The glGetError function returns one of the values listed in Table 2.3. The GLU library defines three errors of its own, but these errors map exactly to two flags already present. If more than one of these flags is set, glGetError still returns only one distinct value. This value is then cleared when glGetError is called, and glGetError again will return either another error flag or GL_NO_ERROR. Usually, you want to call glGetError in a loop that continues checking for error flags until the return value is GL_NO_ERROR.

You can use another function in the GLU library, gluErrorString, to get a string describing the error flag:

```
const GLubyte* gluErrorString(GLenum errorCode);
```

This function takes as its only argument the error flag (returned from `glGetError`) and returns a static string describing that error. For example, the error flag `GL_INVALID_ENUM` returns this string:

```
invalid enumerant
```

TABLE 2.3   OpenGL Error Codes

Error Code	Description
GL_INVALID_ENUM	The enum argument is out of range.
GL_INVALID_VALUE	The numeric argument is out of range.
GL_INVALID_OPERATION	The operation is illegal in its current state.
GL_STACK_OVERFLOW	The command would cause a stack overflow.
GL_STACK_UNDERFLOW	The command would cause a stack underflow.
GL_OUT_OF_MEMORY	Not enough memory is left to execute the command.
GL_TABLE_TOO_LARGE	The specified table is too large.
GL_NO_ERROR	No error has occurred.

You can take some peace of mind from the assurance that if an error is caused by an invalid call to OpenGL, the command or function call is ignored. The only exceptions to this are any OpenGL functions that take pointers to memory (that may cause a program to crash if the pointer is invalid).

Identifying the Version

As mentioned previously, sometimes you want to take advantage of a known behavior in a particular implementation. If you know for a fact that you are running on a particular vendor's graphics card, you may rely on some known performance characteristics to enhance your program. You may also want to enforce some minimum version number for particular vendors' drivers. What you need is a way to query OpenGL for the vendor and version number of the rendering engine (the OpenGL driver). Both the GL library and the GLU library can return version- and vendor-specific information about themselves.

For the GL library, you can call `glGetString`:

```
const GLubyte *glGetString(GLenum name);
```

This function returns a static string describing the requested aspect of the GL library. The valid parameter values are listed under `glGetString` in Appendix C, along with the aspect of the GL library they represent.

The GLU library has a corresponding function, `gluGetString`:

```
const GLubyte *gluGetString(GLenum name);
```

It returns a string describing the requested aspect of the GLU library.

Getting a Clue with `glHint`

There is more than one way to skin a cat; so goes the old saying. The same is true with 3D graphics algorithms. Often a trade-off must be made for the sake of performance, or perhaps if visual fidelity is the most important issue, performance is less of a consideration. Often an OpenGL implementation may contain two ways of performing a given task—a fast way that compromises quality slightly and a slower way that improves visual quality. The function `glHint` allows you to specify certain preferences of quality or speed for different types of operations. The function is defined as follows:

```
void glHint(GLenum target, GLenum mode);
```

The *target* parameter allows you to specify types of behavior you want to modify. These values, listed under `glHint` in Appendix C, include hints for fog quality, antialiasing accuracy, and so on. The *mode* parameter tells OpenGL what you care most about—faster render time and nicest output, for instance—or that you don't care (the only way to get back to the default behavior). Be warned, however, that all implementations are not required to honor calls into `glHint`; it's the only function in OpenGL whose behavior is intended to be entirely vendor-specific.

Using Extensions

With OpenGL being a "standard" API, you might think that hardware vendors are able to compete only on the basis of performance and perhaps visual quality. However, the field of 3D graphics is very competitive, and hardware vendors are constantly innovating, not just in the areas of performance and quality, but in graphics methodologies and special effects. OpenGL allows vendor innovation through its extension mechanism. This mechanism works in two ways. First, vendors can add new functions to the OpenGL API that developers can use. Second, new tokens or enumerants can be added that will be recognized by existing OpenGL functions such as `glEnable`.

Making use of new enumerants or tokens is simply a matter of adding a vendor-supplied header file to your project. Vendors must register their extensions with the OpenGL Working Group (a subset of the Khronos Group), thus keeping one vendor from using a value used by someone else. Conveniently, there is a standard header file `glext.h` that includes the most common extensions.

Checking for an Extension

Gone are the days when games would be recompiled for a specific graphics card. You have already seen that you can check for a string identifying the vendor and version of the

OpenGL driver. You can also get a string that contains identifiers for all OpenGL extensions supported by the driver. One line of code returns a character array of extension names:

```
const char *szExtensions = glGetString(GL_EXTENSIONS);
```

This string contains the space-delimited names of all extensions supported by the driver. You can then search this string for the identifier of the extension you want to use. For example, you might do a quick search for a Windows-specific extension like this:

```
if (strstr(extensions, "WGL_EXT_swap_control" != NULL))
    {
    wglSwapIntervalEXT =
            (PFNWGLSWAPINTERVALEXTPROC)wglGetProcAddress("wglSwapIntervalEXT");

    if(wglSwapIntervalEXT != NULL)
        wglSwapIntervalEXT(1);
    }
```

If you use this method, you should also make sure that the character following the name of the extension is either a space or a NULL. What if, for example, this extension is superceded by the WGL_EXT_swap_control2 extension? In this case, the C runtime function strstr would still find the first string, but you may not be able to assume that the second extension behaves exactly like the first. A more robust toolkit function is included in the file gltools.cpp in the source distribution from our Web site:

```
int gltIsExtSupported(const char *extension);
```

This function returns 1 if the named extension is supported or 0 if it is not. The examples/src/shared directory contains a whole set of helper and utility functions for use with OpenGL, and many are used throughout this book. All the functions are prototyped in the file gltools.h.

This example also shows how to get a pointer to a new OpenGL function under Windows. The windows function wglGetProcAddress returns a pointer to an OpenGL function (extension) name. Getting a pointer to an extension varies from OS to OS; this topic is dealt with in more detail in Part III of this book. Fortunately, 99% of the time you can just use the GLEE library as we have and you "auto-magically" get extension function pointers for whatever functionality is supported by the driver.

The Windows-specific extension and the typedef (PFNWGLSWAPINTERVALEXTPROC) for the function type is located in the wglext.h header file, also included in the examples/src/shared directory. We also discuss this particular important extension in Chapter 19, "Wiggle: OpenGL on Windows."

In the meantime, again the gltools library comes to the rescue with the following function:

```
void *gltGetExtensionPointer(const char *szExtensionName);
```

This function provides a platform-independent wrapper that returns a pointer to the named OpenGL extension.

Whose Extension Is This?

Using OpenGL extensions, you can provide code paths in your code to improve rendering performance and visual quality or even add special effects that are supported only by a particular vendor's hardware. But who owns an extension? That is, which vendor created and supports a given extension? You can usually tell just by looking at the extension name. Each extension has a three-letter prefix that identifies the source of the extension. Table 2.4 provides a sampling of extension identifiers.

TABLE 2.4 A Sampling of OpenGL Extension Prefixes

Prefix	Vendor
SGI_	Silicon Graphics
ATI_	ATI Technologies
NV_	NVIDIA
IBM_	IBM
WGL_	Microsoft
EXT_	Cross-Vendor
ARB_	ARB Approved

It is not uncommon for one vendor to support another vendor's extension. For example, some NVIDIA extensions are widely popular and supported on ATI hardware. When this happens, the competing vendor must follow the original vendor's specification (details on how the extension is supposed to work). Frequently, everyone agrees that the extension is a good thing to have, and the extension has an EXT_ prefix to show that it is (supposed) to be vendor neutral and widely supported across implementations.

Finally, we also have ARB-approved extensions. The specification for these extensions has been reviewed (and argued about) by the OpenGL ARB. These extensions usually signal the final step before some new technique or function finds its way into the core OpenGL specification.

Summary

We covered a lot of ground in this chapter. We introduced you to OpenGL, told you a little bit about its history, introduced the OpenGL utility toolkit (GLUT), and presented the fundamentals of writing a program that uses OpenGL. Using GLUT, we showed you the easiest possible way to create a window and draw in it using OpenGL commands. You learned to use the GLUT library to create windows that can be resized, as well as create a simple animation. You were also introduced to the process of using OpenGL for drawing—composing and selecting colors, clearing the screen, drawing a rectangle, and setting the viewport and clipping volume to scale images to match the window size. We discussed the various OpenGL data types and the headers required to build programs that use OpenGL.

With a little coding finally under your belt, you are ready to dive into some other ideas you need to be familiar with before you move forward. The OpenGL state machine underlies almost everything you do from here on out, and the extension mechanism will make sure you can access all the OpenGL features supported by your hardware driver, regardless of your development tool. You also learned how to check for OpenGL errors along the way to make sure you aren't making any illegal state changes or rendering commands. With this foundation, you can move forward to the chapters ahead.

CHAPTER 3

Drawing in Space:
Geometric Primitives and Buffers

by Richard S. Wright Jr.

WHAT YOU'LL LEARN IN THIS CHAPTER:

How To	Functions You'll Use
Draw points, lines, and shapes	`glBegin/glEnd/glVertex`
Set shape outlines to wireframe or solid objects	`glPolygonMode`
Set point sizes for drawing	`glPointSize`
Set line drawing width	`glLineWidth`
Perform hidden surface removal	`glCullFace/glClear`
Set patterns for broken lines	`glLineStipple`
Set polygon fill patterns	`glPolygonStipple`
Use the OpenGL Scissor box	`glScissor`
Use the stencil buffer	`glStencilFunc/glStencilMask/glStencilOp`

If you've ever had a chemistry class (and probably even if you haven't), you know that all matter consists of atoms and that all atoms consist of only three things: protons, neutrons, and electrons. All the materials and substances you have ever come into contact with—from the petals of a rose to the sand on the beach—are just different arrangements of these three fundamental building blocks. Although this explanation is a little oversimplified for almost anyone beyond the third or fourth grade, it demonstrates a powerful principle: With just a few simple building blocks, you can create highly complex and beautiful structures.

The connection is fairly obvious. Objects and scenes that you create with OpenGL also consist of smaller, simpler shapes, arranged and combined in various and unique ways. This chapter explores these building blocks of 3D objects, called *primitives*. All primitives in OpenGL are one-, two-, or three-dimensional objects, ranging from single points to lines and complex polygons. In this chapter, you learn everything you need to know to draw objects in three dimensions from these simpler shapes.

Drawing Points in 3D

When you first learned to draw any kind of graphics on any computer system, you probably started with pixels. A pixel is the smallest element on your computer monitor, and on color systems that pixel can be any one of many available colors. This is computer graphics at its simplest: Draw a point somewhere on the screen, and make it a specific color. Then build on this simple concept, using your favorite computer language to produce lines, polygons, circles, and other shapes and graphics. Perhaps even a GUI...

With OpenGL, however, drawing on the computer screen is fundamentally different. You're not concerned with physical screen coordinates and pixels, but rather positional coordinates in your viewing volume. You let OpenGL worry about how to get your points, lines, and everything else projected from your established 3D space to the 2D image made by your computer screen.

This chapter and the next cover the most fundamental concepts of OpenGL or any 3D graphics toolkit. In the upcoming chapter, we provide substantial detail about how this transformation from 3D space to the 2D landscape of your computer monitor takes place, as well as how to transform (rotate, translate, and scale) your objects. For now, we take this capability for granted to focus on plotting and drawing in a 3D coordinate system. This approach might seem backward, but if you first know how to draw something and then worry about all the ways to manipulate your drawings, the material in Chapter 4, "Geometric Transformations: The Pipeline," is more interesting and easier to learn. When you have a solid understanding of graphics primitives and coordinate transformations, you will be able to quickly master any 3D graphics language or API.

Setting Up a 3D Canvas

Figure 3.1 shows a simple viewing volume that we use for the examples in this chapter. The area enclosed by this volume is a Cartesian coordinate space that ranges from –100 to +100 on all three axes—x, y, and z. (For a review of Cartesian coordinates, see Chapter 1, "Introduction to 3D Graphics and OpenGL.") Think of this viewing volume as your three-dimensional canvas on which you draw with OpenGL commands and functions.

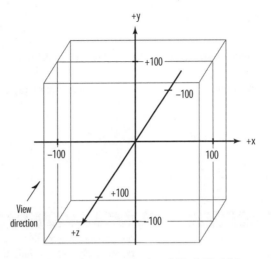

FIGURE 3.1   A Cartesian viewing volume measuring 100×100×100.

We established this volume with a call to glOrtho, much as we did for others in the preceding chapter. Listing 3.1 shows the code for the ChangeSize function that is called when the window is sized (including when it is first created). This code looks a little different from that in the preceding chapter, and you'll notice some unfamiliar functions (glMatrixMode, glLoadIdentity). We'll spend more time on these functions in Chapter 4, exploring their operation in more detail.

LISTING 3.1   Code to Establish the Viewing Volume in Figure 3.1

```
// Change viewing volume and viewport.  Called when window is resized
void ChangeSize(GLsizei w, GLsizei h)
    {
    GLfloat nRange = 100.0f;

    // Prevent a divide by zero
    if(h == 0)
        h = 1;

    // Set Viewport to window dimensions
    glViewport(0, 0, w, h);

    // Reset projection matrix stack
    glMatrixMode(GL_PROJECTION);
    glLoadIdentity();

    // Establish clipping volume (left, right, bottom, top, near, far)
```

LISTING 3.1   Continued

```
    if (w <= h)
        glOrtho (-nRange, nRange, -nRange*h/w, nRange*h/w, -nRange, nRange);
    else
        glOrtho (-nRange*w/h, nRange*w/h, -nRange, nRange, -nRange, nRange);

// Reset Model view matrix stack
glMatrixMode(GL_MODELVIEW);
glLoadIdentity();
    }
```

WHY THE CART BEFORE THE HORSE?

Look at any of the source code in this chapter, and you'll notice some new functions in the RenderScene functions: glRotate, glPushMatrix, and glPopMatrix. Although they're covered in more detail in Chapter 4, we're introducing them now. They implement some important features that we want you to have as soon as possible. These functions let you plot and draw in 3D and help you easily visualize your drawing from different angles. All this chapter's sample programs employ the arrow keys for rotating the drawing around the x- and y-axes. Look at any 3D drawing dead-on (straight down the z-axis), and it might still look two-dimensional. But when you can spin the drawings around in space, it's much easier to see the 3D effects of what you're drawing.

There is a lot to learn about drawing in 3D, and in this chapter we want you to focus on that. By changing only the drawing code for any of the examples that follow, you can start experimenting right away with 3D drawing and still get interesting results. Later, you'll learn how to manipulate drawings using the other functions.

A 3D Point: The Vertex

To specify a drawing point in this 3D "palette," we use the OpenGL function glVertex—without a doubt one of the most used functions in all the OpenGL API. This is the "lowest common denominator" of all the OpenGL primitives: a single point in space. The glVertex function can take from one (a pointer) to four parameters of any numerical type, from bytes to doubles, subject to the naming conventions discussed in Chapter 2, "Using OpenGL."

The following single line of code specifies a point in our coordinate system located 50 units along the x-axis, 50 units along the y-axis, and 0 units along the z-axis:

```
glVertex3f(50.0f, 50.0f, 0.0f);
```

Figure 3.2 illustrates this point. Here, we chose to represent the coordinates as floating-point values, as we do for the remainder of the book. Also, the form of glVertex that we use takes three arguments for the x, y, and z coordinate values, respectively.

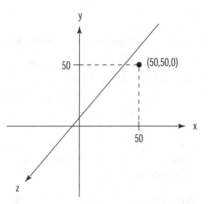

FIGURE 3.2   The point (50,50,0) as specified by `glVertex3f(50.0f, 50.0f, 0.0f)`.

Two other forms of `glVertex` take two and four arguments, respectively. We can represent the same point in Figure 3.2 with this code:

```
glVertex2f(50.0f, 50.0f);
```

This form of `glVertex` takes only two arguments, specifying the x and y values, and assumes the z coordinate to be 0.0 always.

The form of `glVertex` taking four arguments, `glVertex4`, uses a fourth coordinate value, w (set to 1.0 by default when not specified) for scaling purposes. You will learn more about this coordinate in Chapter 4 when we spend more time exploring coordinate transformations.

Draw Something!

Now, we have a way of specifying a point in space to OpenGL. What can we make of it, and how do we tell OpenGL what to do with it? Is this vertex a point that should just be plotted? Is it the endpoint of a line or the corner of a cube? The geometric definition of a vertex is not just a point in space, but rather the point at which an intersection of two lines or curves occurs. This is the essence of primitives.

A primitive is simply the interpretation of a set or list of vertices into some shape drawn on the screen. There are 10 primitives in OpenGL, from a simple point drawn in space to a closed polygon of any number of sides. One way to draw primitives is to use the `glBegin` command to tell OpenGL to begin interpreting a list of vertices as a particular primitive. You then end the list of vertices for that primitive with the `glEnd` command. Kind of intuitive, don't you think?

Drawing Points

Let's begin with the first and simplest of primitives: points. Look at the following code:

```
glBegin(GL_POINTS);                 // Select points as the primitive
    glVertex3f(0.0f, 0.0f, 0.0f);       // Specify a point
    glVertex3f(50.0f, 50.0f, 50.0f);    // Specify another point
glEnd();                            // Done drawing points
```

The argument to glBegin, GL_POINTS tells OpenGL that the following vertices are to be interpreted and drawn as points. Two vertices are listed here, which translates to two specific points, both of which would be drawn.

This example brings up an important point about glBegin and glEnd: You can list multiple primitives between calls as long as they are for the same primitive type. In this way, with a single glBegin/glEnd sequence, you can include as many primitives as you like. This next code segment is wasteful and will execute more slowly than the preceding code:

```
glBegin(GL_POINTS);         // Specify point drawing
    glVertex3f(0.0f, 0.0f, 0.0f);
glEnd();

glBegin(GL_POINTS);         // Specify another point
    glVertex3f(50.0f, 50.0f, 50.0f);
glEnd()
```

INDENTING YOUR CODE

In the foregoing examples, did you notice the indenting style used for the calls to glVertex? Most OpenGL programmers use this convention to make the code easier to read. It is not required, but it does make finding where primitives start and stop easier.

Our First Example

The code in Listing 3.2 draws some points in our 3D environment. It uses some simple trigonometry to draw a series of points that form a corkscrew path up the z-axis. This code is from the POINTS program, which is in the source distribution for this chapter. All the sample programs use the framework we established in Chapter 2. Notice that in the SetupRC function, we are setting the current drawing color to green.

LISTING 3.2   Rendering Code to Produce a Spring-Shaped Path of Points

```
// Define a constant for the value of PI
#define GL_PI 3.1415f

// This function does any needed initialization on the rendering
```

LISTING 3.2 Continued

```
// context.
void SetupRC()
    {
    // Black background
    glClearColor(0.0f, 0.0f, 0.0f, 1.0f );

    // Set drawing color to green
    glColor3f(0.0f, 1.0f, 0.0f);
    }


// Called to draw scene
void RenderScene(void)
    {
    GLfloat x,y,z,angle; // Storage for coordinates and angles

    // Clear the window with current clearing color
    glClear(GL_COLOR_BUFFER_BIT);

    // Save matrix state and do the rotation
    glPushMatrix();
    glRotatef(xRot, 1.0f, 0.0f, 0.0f);
    glRotatef(yRot, 0.0f, 1.0f, 0.0f);

    // Call only once for all remaining points
    glBegin(GL_POINTS);

    z = -50.0f;
    for(angle = 0.0f; angle <= (2.0f*GL_PI)*3.0f; angle += 0.1f)
        {
        x = 50.0f*sin(angle);
        y = 50.0f*cos(angle);

        // Specify the point and move the Z value up a little
        glVertex3f(x, y, z);
        z += 0.5f;
        }

    // Done drawing points
    glEnd();

    // Restore transformations
```

LISTING 3.2   Continued

```
glPopMatrix();

// Flush drawing commands
glutSwapBuffers();
}
```

Only the code between calls to `glBegin` and `glEnd` is important for our purpose in this and the other examples for this chapter. This code calculates the x and y coordinates for an angle that spins between 0° and 360° three times. We express this programmatically in radians rather than degrees; if you don't know trigonometry, you can take our word for it. If you're interested, see the box "The Trigonometry of Radians/Degrees." Each time a point is drawn, the z value is increased slightly. When this program is run, all you see is a circle of points because you are initially looking directly down the z-axis. To see the effect, use the arrow keys to spin the drawing around the x- and y-axes. The effect is illustrated in Figure 3.3.

FIGURE 3.3   Output from the POINTS sample program.

ONE THING AT A TIME

Again, don't get too distracted by the functions in this example that we haven't covered yet (`glPushMatrix`, `glPopMatrix`, and `glRotate`). These functions are used to rotate the image around so you can better see the positioning of the points as they are drawn in 3D space. We cover these functions in some detail in Chapter 4. If we hadn't used these features now, you wouldn't be able to see the effects of your 3D drawings, and this and the following sample programs wouldn't be very interesting to look at. For the rest of the sample code in this chapter, we show only the code that includes the `glBegin` and `glEnd` statements.

THE TRIGONOMETRY OF RADIANS/DEGREES

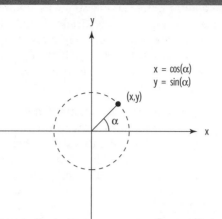

The figure in this box shows a circle drawn in the xy plane. A line segment from the origin (0,0) to any point on the circle makes an angle (a) with the x-axis. For any given angle, the trigonometric functions sine and cosine return the x and y values of the point on the circle. By stepping a variable that represents the angle all the way around the origin, we can calculate all the points on the circle. Note that the C runtime functions `sin()` and `cos()` accept angle values measured in radians instead of degrees. There are 2*PI radians in a circle, where PI is a nonrational number that is approximately 3.1415. (*Nonrational* means it is a repeating decimal number that cannot be represented as a fraction.)

Setting the Point Size

When you draw a single point, the size of the point is one pixel by default. You can change this size with the function glPointSize:

```
void glPointSize(GLfloat size);
```

The glPointSize function takes a single parameter that specifies the approximate diameter in pixels of the point drawn. Not all point sizes are supported, however, and you should make sure the point size you specify is available. Use the following code to get the range of point sizes and the smallest interval between them:

```
GLfloat sizes[2];      // Store supported point size range
GLfloat step;          // Store supported point size increments

// Get supported point size range and step size
glGetFloatv(GL_POINT_SIZE_RANGE,sizes);
glGetFloatv(GL_POINT_SIZE_GRANULARITY,&step);
```

Here, the `sizes` array will contain two elements that contain the smallest and largest valid value for `glPointsize`. In addition, the variable step will hold the smallest step size allowable between the point sizes. The OpenGL specification requires only that one point size, 1.0, be supported. The Microsoft software implementation of OpenGL, for example, allows for point sizes from 0.5 to 10.0, with 0.125 the smallest step size. Specifying a size out of range is not interpreted as an error. Instead, the largest or smallest supported size is used, whichever is closest to the value specified.

By default, points, unlike other geometry, are not affected by the perspective division. That is, they do not become smaller when they are further from the viewpoint, and they do not become larger as they move closer. Points are also always square pixels, even if you use glPointSize to increase the size of the points. You just get bigger squares! To get round points, you must draw them antialiased (coming up in Chapter 6, "More on Colors and Materials").

OPENGL STATE VARIABLES

As we discussed in Chapter 2, OpenGL maintains the state of many of its internal variables and settings. This collection of settings is called the *OpenGL State Machine.* You can query the State Machine to determine the state of any of its variables and settings. Any feature or capability you enable or disable with glEnable/glDisable, as well as numeric settings set with glSet, can be queried with the many variations of glGet.

Let's look at a sample that uses these new functions. The code in Listing 3.3 produces the same spiral shape as our first example, but this time, the point sizes are gradually increased from the smallest valid size to the largest valid size. This example is from the program POINTSZ in source distribution for this chapter. The output from POINTSZ shown in Figure 3.4 was run on Microsoft's software implementation of OpenGL. Figure 3.5 shows the same program run on a hardware accelerator that supports much larger point sizes.

FIGURE 3.4 Output from the POINTSZ program.

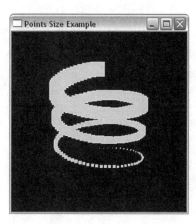

FIGURE 3.5   Output from POINTSZ on hardware supporting much larger point sizes.

LISTING 3.3   Code from POINTSZ That Produces a Spiral with Gradually Increasing Point
Sizes

```
// Define a constant for the value of PI
#define GL_PI 3.1415f

// Called to draw scene
void RenderScene(void)
    {
    GLfloat x,y,z,angle;    // Storage for coordinates and angles
    GLfloat sizes[2];       // Store supported point size range
    GLfloat step;           // Store supported point size increments
    GLfloat curSize;        // Store current point size
    ...
    ...


    // Get supported point size range and step size
    glGetFloatv(GL_POINT_SIZE_RANGE,sizes);
    glGetFloatv(GL_POINT_SIZE_GRANULARITY,&step);

    // Set the initial point size
    curSize = sizes[0];

    // Set beginning z coordinate
    z = -50.0f;

    // Loop around in a circle three times
    for(angle = 0.0f; angle <= (2.0f*GL_PI)*3.0f; angle += 0.1f)
```

LISTING 3.3   Continued

```
    {
    // Calculate x and y values on the circle
    x = 50.0f*sin(angle);
    y = 50.0f*cos(angle);

    // Specify the point size before the primitive is specified
    glPointSize(curSize);

    // Draw the point
    glBegin(GL_POINTS);
        glVertex3f(x, y, z);
    glEnd();

    // Bump up the z value and the point size
    z += 0.5f;
    curSize += step;
    }
...
...
}
```

This example demonstrates a couple of important things. For starters, notice that glPointSize must be called outside the glBegin/glEnd statements. Not all OpenGL functions are valid between these function calls. Although glPointSize affects all points drawn after it, you don't begin drawing points until you call glBegin(GL_POINTS). For a complete list of valid functions that you can call within a glBegin/glEnd sequence, see the reference section in Appendix C.

If you specify a point size larger than what is returned in the size variable, you also may notice (depending on your hardware) that OpenGL uses the largest available point size but does not keep growing. This is a general observation about OpenGL function parameters that have a valid range. Values outside the range are *clamped* to the range. Values too low are made the lowest valid value, and values too high are made the highest valid value.

The most obvious thing you probably noticed about the POINTSZ excerpt is that the larger point sizes are represented simply by larger cubes. This is the default behavior, but it typically is undesirable for many applications. Also, you might wonder why you can increase the point size by a value less than one. If a value of 1.0 represents one pixel, how do you draw less than a pixel, or, say, 2.5 pixels?

The answer is that the point size specified in `glPointSize` isn't the exact point size in pixels, but the approximate diameter of a circle containing all the pixels that are used to draw the point. You can get OpenGL to draw the points as better points (that is, small filled circles) by enabling point smoothing. Together with line smoothing, point smoothing falls under the topic of *antialiasing*. Antialiasing is a technique used to smooth out jagged edges and round out corners; it is covered in more detail in Chapter 6.

Points can also be made to grow and shrink with the perspective projection, but this is not the default behavior. A feature called *point parameters* makes this possible, and is a bit deep for this early in the book. We will discuss point parameters along with another interesting point texturing feature called point sprites in Chapter 9, "Texture Mapping: Beyond the Basics."

Drawing Lines in 3D

The `GL_POINTS` primitive we have been using thus far is reasonably straightforward; for each vertex specified, it draws a point. The next logical step is to specify two vertices and draw a line between them. This is exactly what the next primitive, `GL_LINES`, does. The following short section of code draws a single line between two points (0,0,0) and (50,50,50):

```
glBegin(GL_LINES);
    glVertex3f(0.0f, 0.0f, 0.0f);
    glVertex3f(50.0f, 50.0f, 50.0f);
glEnd();
```

Note here that two vertices specify a single primitive. For every two vertices specified, a single line is drawn. If you specify an odd number of vertices for `GL_LINES`, the last vertex is just ignored. Listing 3.4, from the LINES sample program, shows a more complex sample that draws a series of lines fanned around in a circle. Each point specified in this sample is paired with a point on the opposite side of a circle. The output from this program is shown in Figure 3.6.

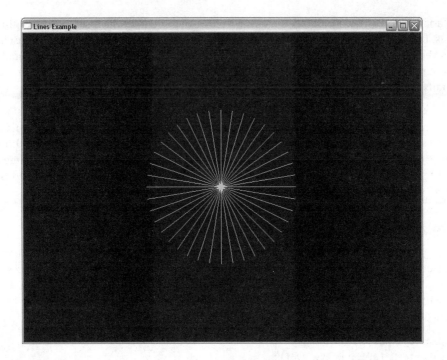

FIGURE 3.6 Output from the LINES sample program.

LISTING 3.4 Code from the Sample Program LINES That Displays a Series of Lines Fanned in a Circle

```
// Call only once for all remaining points
glBegin(GL_LINES);

// All lines lie in the xy plane.
z = 0.0f;
for(angle = 0.0f; angle <= GL_PI; angle += (GL_PI/20.0f))
    {
    // Top half of the circle
    x = 50.0f*sin(angle);
    y = 50.0f*cos(angle);
    glVertex3f(x, y, z);          // First endpoint of line

    // Bottom half of the circle
    x = 50.0f*sin(angle + GL_PI);
    y = 50.0f*cos(angle + GL_PI);
    glVertex3f(x, y, z);          // Second endpoint of line
```

LISTING 3.4 Continued

```
    }

// Done drawing points
glEnd();
```

Line Strips and Loops

The next two OpenGL primitives build on GL_LINES by allowing you to specify a list of vertices through which a line is drawn. When you specify GL_LINE_STRIP, a line is drawn from one vertex to the next in a continuous segment. The following code draws two lines in the xy plane that are specified by three vertices. Figure 3.7 shows an example.

```
glBegin(GL_LINE_STRIP);
    glVertex3f(0.0f, 0.0f, 0.0f);      // V0
    glVertex3f(50.0f, 50.0f, 0.0f);    // V1
    glVertex3f(50.0f, 100.0f, 0.0f);   // V2
glEnd();
```

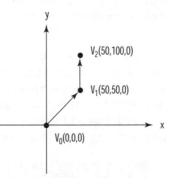

FIGURE 3.7 An example of a GL_LINE_STRIP specified by three vertices.

The last line-based primitive is GL_LINE_LOOP. This primitive behaves just like GL_LINE_STRIP, but one final line is drawn between the last vertex specified and the first one specified. This is an easy way to draw a closed-line figure. Figure 3.8 shows a GL_LINE_LOOP drawn using the same vertices as for the GL_LINE_STRIP in Figure 3.7.

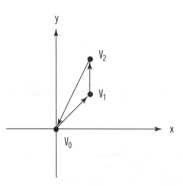

FIGURE 3.8   The same vertices from Figure 3.7 used by a GL_LINE_LOOP primitive.

Approximating Curves with Straight Lines

The POINTS sample program, shown earlier in Figure 3.3, showed you how to plot points along a spring-shaped path. You might have been tempted to push the points closer and closer together (by setting smaller values for the angle increment) to create a smooth spring-shaped curve instead of the broken points that only approximated the shape. This perfectly valid operation can move quite slowly for larger and more complex curves with thousands of points.

A better way of approximating a curve is to use GL_LINE_STRIP to play connect-the-dots. As the dots move closer together, a smoother curve materializes without you having to specify all those points. Listing 3.5 shows the code from Listing 3.2, with GL_POINTS replaced by GL_LINE_STRIP. The output from this new program, LSTRIPS, is shown in Figure 3.9. As you can see, the approximation of the curve is quite good. You will find this handy technique almost ubiquitous among OpenGL programs.

FIGURE 3.9   Output from the LSTRIPS program approximating a smooth curve.

LISTING 3.5   Code from the Sample Program LSTRIPS, Demonstrating Line Strips

```
// Call only once for all remaining points
glBegin(GL_LINE_STRIP);

z = -50.0f;
for(angle = 0.0f; angle <= (2.0f*GL_PI)*3.0f; angle += 0.1f)
    {
    x = 50.0f*sin(angle);
    y = 50.0f*cos(angle);

    // Specify the point and move the z value up a little
    glVertex3f(x, y, z);
    z += 0.5f;
    }

// Done drawing points
glEnd();
```

Setting the Line Width

Just as you can set different point sizes, you can also specify various line widths when drawing lines by using the glLineWidth function:

```
void glLineWidth(GLfloat width);
```

The glLineWidth function takes a single parameter that specifies the approximate width, in pixels, of the line drawn. Just as with point sizes, not all line widths are supported, and you should make sure that the line width you want to specify is available. Use the following code to get the range of line widths and the smallest interval between them:

```
GLfloat sizes[2];      // Store supported line width range
GLfloat step;          // Store supported line width increments

// Get supported line width range and step size
glGetFloatv(GL_LINE_WIDTH_RANGE,sizes);
glGetFloatv(GL_LINE_WIDTH_GRANULARITY,&step);
```

Here, the sizes array will contain two elements that contain the smallest and largest valid value for glLineWidth. In addition, the variable step will hold the smallest step size allowable between the line widths. The OpenGL specification requires only that one line width, 1.0, be supported. The Microsoft implementation of OpenGL allows for line widths from 0.5 to 10.0, with 0.125 the smallest step size.

Listing 3.6 shows code for a more substantial example of `glLineWidth`. It's from the program LINESW and draws 10 lines of varying widths. It starts at the bottom of the window at –90 on the y-axis and climbs the y-axis 20 units for each new line. Every time it draws a new line, it increases the line width by 1. Figure 3.10 shows the output for this program.

FIGURE 3.10   A demonstration of `glLineWidth` from the LINESW program.

LISTING 3.6   Drawing Lines of Various Widths

```
// Called to draw scene
void RenderScene(void)
    {
    GLfloat y;                  // Storage for varying Y coordinate
    GLfloat fSizes[2];          // Line width range metrics
    GLfloat fCurrSize;          // Save current size
    ...
    ...
    ...


    // Get line size metrics and save the smallest value
    glGetFloatv(GL_LINE_WIDTH_RANGE,fSizes);
    fCurrSize = fSizes[0];

    // Step up y axis 20 units at a time
    for(y = -90.0f; y < 90.0f; y += 20.0f)
        {
        // Set the line width
        glLineWidth(fCurrSize);

        // Draw the line
        glBegin(GL_LINES);
            glVertex2f(-80.0f, y);
```

LISTING 3.6   Continued

```
        glVertex2f(80.0f, y);
    glEnd();

    // Increase the line width
    fCurrSize += 1.0f;
    }
...
...
}
```

Notice that we used `glVertex2f` this time instead of `glVertex3f` to specify the coordinates for the lines. As mentioned, using this technique is only a convenience because we are drawing in the xy plane, with a z value of 0. To see that you are still drawing lines in three dimensions, simply use the arrow keys to spin your lines around. You easily see that all the lines lie on a single plane.

Line Stippling

In addition to changing line widths, you can create lines with a dotted or dashed pattern, called *stippling*. To use line stippling, you must first enable stippling with a call to

```
glEnable(GL_LINE_STIPPLE);
```

Then the function `glLineStipple` establishes the pattern that the lines use for drawing:

```
void glLineStipple(GLint factor, GLushort pattern);
```

> **REMINDER**
>
> Any feature or capability that is enabled by a call to `glEnable` can be disabled by a call to `glDisable`.

The *pattern* parameter is a 16-bit value that specifies a pattern to use when drawing the lines. Each bit represents a section of the line segment that is either on or off. By default, each bit corresponds to a single pixel, but the *factor* parameter serves as a multiplier to increase the width of the pattern. For example, setting *factor* to 5 causes each bit in the pattern to represent five pixels in a row that are either on or off. Furthermore, bit 0 (the least significant bit) of the pattern is used first to specify the line. Figure 3.11 illustrates a sample bit pattern applied to a line segment.

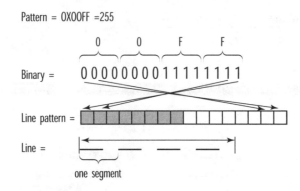

FIGURE 3.11   A stipple pattern is used to construct a line segment.

WHY ARE THESE PATTERNS BACKWARD?

You might wonder why the bit pattern for stippling is used in reverse when the line is drawn. Internally, it's much faster for OpenGL to shift this pattern to the left one place each time it needs to get the next mask value. OpenGL was designed for high-performance graphics and frequently employs similar tricks elsewhere.

Listing 3.7 shows a sample of using a stippling pattern that is just a series of alternating on and off bits (0101010101010101). This code is taken from the LSTIPPLE program, which draws 10 lines from the bottom of the window up the y-axis to the top. Each line is stippled with the pattern 0x5555, but for each new line, the pattern multiplier is increased by 1. You can clearly see the effects of the widened stipple pattern in Figure 3.12.

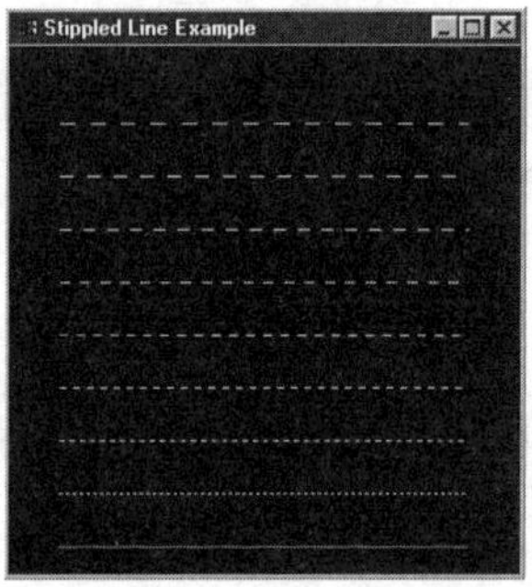

FIGURE 3.12   Output from the LSTIPPLE program.

LISTING 3.7   Code from LSTIPPLE That Demonstrates the Effect of `factor` on the Bit Pattern

```
// Called to draw scene
void RenderScene(void)
    {
    GLfloat y;              // Storage for varying y coordinate
    GLint factor = 1;       // Stippling factor
    GLushort pattern = 0x5555;    // Stipple pattern
...

...
    // Enable Stippling
    glEnable(GL_LINE_STIPPLE);

    // Step up Y axis 20 units at a time
    for(y = -90.0f; y < 90.0f; y += 20.0f)
        {
        // Reset the repeat factor and pattern
        glLineStipple(factor,pattern);

        // Draw the line
        glBegin(GL_LINES);
            glVertex2f(-80.0f, y);
            glVertex2f(80.0f, y);
        glEnd();

        factor++;
        }
    ...
    ...
    }
```

Just the ability to draw points and lines in 3D gives you a significant set of tools for creating your own 3D masterpiece. Figure 3.13 shows a 3D weather mapping program with an OpenGL-rendered map that is rendered entirely of solid and stippled line strips.

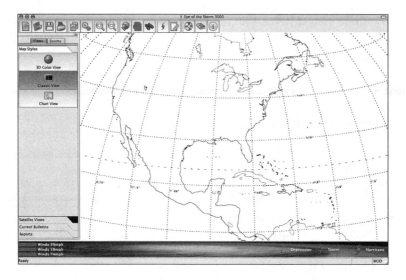

FIGURE 3.13   A 3D map rendered with solid and stippled lines.

Drawing Triangles in 3D

You've seen how to draw points and lines and even how to draw some enclosed polygons with GL_LINE_LOOP. With just these primitives, you could easily draw any shape possible in three dimensions. You could, for example, draw six squares and arrange them so they form the sides of a cube.

You might have noticed, however, that any shapes you create with these primitives are not filled with any color; after all, you are drawing only lines. In fact, arranging six squares produces just a wireframe cube, not a solid cube. To draw a solid surface, you need more than just points and lines; you need polygons. A polygon is a closed shape that may or may not be filled with the currently selected color, and it is the basis of all solid-object composition in OpenGL.

Triangles: Your First Polygon

The simplest polygon possible is the triangle, with only three sides. The GL_TRIANGLES primitive draws triangles by connecting three vertices together. The following code draws two triangles using three vertices each, as shown in Figure 3.14:

```
glBegin(GL_TRIANGLES);
    glVertex2f(0.0f, 0.0f);              // V0
    glVertex2f(25.0f, 25.0f);            // V1
    glVertex2f(50.0f, 0.0f);             // V2

    glVertex2f(-50.0f, 0.0f);            // V3
```

```
      glVertex2f(-75.0f, 50.0f);        // V4
      glVertex2f(-25.0f, 0.0f);         // V5
glEnd();
```

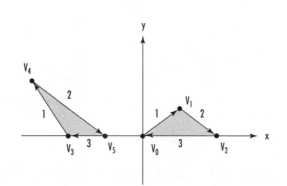

FIGURE 3.14   Two triangles drawn using GL_TRIANGLES.

NOTE

The triangles will be filled with the currently selected drawing color. If you don't specify a
drawing color yourself at some point, you will get the default, which is white.

Winding

An important characteristic of any polygonal primitive is illustrated in Figure 3.14. Notice
the arrows on the lines that connect the vertices. When the first triangle is drawn, the
lines are drawn from V0 to V1, then to V2, and finally back to V0 to close the triangle.
This path is in the order in which the vertices are specified, and for this example, that
order is clockwise from your point of view. The same directional characteristic is present
for the second triangle as well.

The combination of order and direction in which the vertices are specified is called
winding. The triangles in Figure 3.14 are said to have *clockwise winding* because they are
literally wound in the clockwise direction. If we reverse the positions of V4 and V5 on the
triangle on the left, we get *counterclockwise winding*. Figure 3.15 shows two triangles, each
with opposite windings.

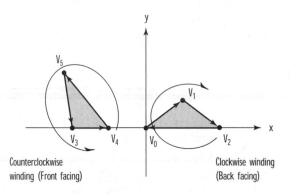

FIGURE 3.15   Two triangles with different windings.

OpenGL, by default, considers polygons that have counterclockwise winding to be front facing. This means that the triangle on the left in Figure 3.15 shows the front of the triangle, and the one on the right shows the back of the triangle.

Why is this issue important? As you will soon see, you will often want to give the front and back of a polygon different physical characteristics. You can hide the back of a polygon altogether or give it a different color and reflective property (see Chapter 5, "Color, Materials, and Lighting: The Basics"). It's important to keep the winding of all polygons in a scene consistent, using front-facing polygons to draw the outside surface of any solid objects. In the upcoming section on solid objects, we demonstrate this principle using some models that are more complex.

If you need to reverse the default behavior of OpenGL, you can do so by calling the following function:

```
glFrontFace(GL_CW);
```

The GL_CW parameter tells OpenGL that clockwise-wound polygons are to be considered front facing. To change back to counterclockwise winding for the front face, use GL_CCW.

Triangle Strips

For many surfaces and shapes, you need to draw several connected triangles. You can save a lot of time by drawing a strip of connected triangles with the GL_TRIANGLE_STRIP primitive. Figure 3.16 shows the progression of a strip of three triangles specified by a set of five vertices numbered V0 through V4. Here, you see that the vertices are not necessarily traversed in the same order in which they were specified. The reason for this is to preserve the winding (counterclockwise) of each triangle. The pattern is V0, V1, V2; then V2, V1, V3; then V2, V3, V4; and so on.

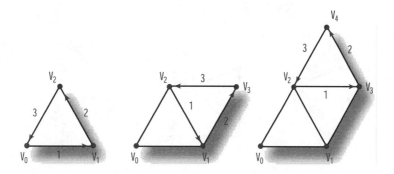

FIGURE 3.16   The progression of a `GL_TRIANGLE_STRIP`.

For the rest of the discussion of polygonal primitives, we don't show any more code fragments to demonstrate the vertices and the `glBegin` statements. You should have the swing of things by now. Later, when we have a real sample program to work with, we'll resume the examples.

There are two advantages to using a strip of triangles instead of specifying each triangle separately. First, after specifying the first three vertices for the initial triangle, you need to specify only a single point for each additional triangle. This saves a lot of program or data storage space when you have many triangles to draw. The second advantage is mathematical performance and bandwidth savings. Fewer vertices means a faster transfer from your computer's memory to your graphics card and fewer vertex transformations (see Chapter 4).

> **TIP**
>
> Another advantage to composing large flat surfaces out of several smaller triangles is that when lighting effects are applied to the scene, OpenGL can better reproduce the simulated effects. You'll learn more about lighting in Chapter 5.

Triangle Fans

In addition to triangle strips, you can use `GL_TRIANGLE_FAN` to produce a group of connected triangles that fan around a central point. Figure 3.17 shows a fan of three triangles produced by specifying four vertices. The first vertex, V0, forms the origin of the fan. After the first three vertices are used to draw the initial triangle, all subsequent vertices are used with the origin (V0) and the vertex immediately preceding it (Vn–1) to form the next triangle.

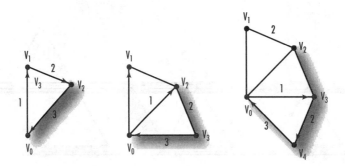

FIGURE 3.17   The progression of `GL_TRIANGLE_FAN`.

Building Solid Objects

Composing a solid object out of triangles (or any other polygon) involves more than assembling a series of vertices in a 3D coordinate space. Let's examine the sample program TRIANGLE, which uses two triangle fans to create a cone in our viewing volume. The first fan produces the cone shape, using the first vertex as the point of the cone and the remaining vertices as points along a circle farther down the z-axis. The second fan forms a circle and lies entirely in the xy plane, making up the bottom surface of the cone.

The output from TRIANGLE is shown in Figure 3.18. Here, you are looking directly down the z-axis and can see only a circle composed of a fan of triangles. The individual triangles are emphasized by coloring them alternately green and red.

FIGURE 3.18   Initial output from the TRIANGLE sample program.

The code for the `SetupRC` and `RenderScene` functions is shown in Listing 3.8. (This listing contains some unfamiliar variables and specifiers that are explained shortly.) This program demonstrates several aspects of composing 3D objects. Right-click in the window, and you will notice an Effects menu; it will be used to enable and disable some 3D drawing features so that we can explore some of the characteristics of 3D object creation. We'll describe these features as we progress.

LISTING 3.8   SetupRC and RenderScene Code for the TRIANGLE Sample Program

```
// This function does any needed initialization on the rendering
// context.
void SetupRC()
    {
    // Black background
    glClearColor(0.0f, 0.0f, 0.0f, 1.0f );

    // Set drawing color to green
    glColor3f(0.0f, 1.0f, 0.0f);

    // Set color shading model to flat
    glShadeModel(GL_FLAT);

    // Clockwise-wound polygons are front facing; this is reversed
    // because we are using triangle fans
    glFrontFace(GL_CW);
    }



// Called to draw scene
void RenderScene(void)
    {
    GLfloat x,y,angle;          // Storage for coordinates and angles
    int iPivot = 1;             // Used to flag alternating colors

    // Clear the window and the depth buffer
    glClear(GL_COLOR_BUFFER_BIT | GL_DEPTH_BUFFER_BIT);

    // Turn culling on if flag is set
    if(bCull)
        glEnable(GL_CULL_FACE);
    else
        glDisable(GL_CULL_FACE);

    // Enable depth testing if flag is set
    if(bDepth)
        glEnable(GL_DEPTH_TEST);
    else
        glDisable(GL_DEPTH_TEST);

    // Draw the back side as a wireframe only, if flag is set
```

LISTING 3.8   Continued

```
if(bOutline)
    glPolygonMode(GL_BACK,GL_LINE);
else
    glPolygonMode(GL_BACK,GL_FILL);


// Save matrix state and do the rotation
glPushMatrix();
glRotatef(xRot, 1.0f, 0.0f, 0.0f);
glRotatef(yRot, 0.0f, 1.0f, 0.0f);


// Begin a triangle fan
glBegin(GL_TRIANGLE_FAN);

// Pinnacle of cone is shared vertex for fan, moved up z-axis
// to produce a cone instead of a circle
glVertex3f(0.0f, 0.0f, 75.0f);

// Loop around in a circle and specify even points along the circle
// as the vertices of the triangle fan
for(angle = 0.0f; angle < (2.0f*GL_PI); angle += (GL_PI/8.0f))
    {
    // Calculate x and y position of the next vertex
    x = 50.0f*sin(angle);
    y = 50.0f*cos(angle);

    // Alternate color between red and green
    if((iPivot %2) == 0)
        glColor3f(0.0f, 1.0f, 0.0f);
    else
        glColor3f(1.0f, 0.0f, 0.0f);

    // Increment pivot to change color next time
    iPivot++;

    // Specify the next vertex for the triangle fan
    glVertex2f(x, y);
    }
```

LISTING 3.8 Continued

```
// Done drawing fan for cone
glEnd();


// Begin a new triangle fan to cover the bottom
glBegin(GL_TRIANGLE_FAN);

// Center of fan is at the origin
glVertex2f(0.0f, 0.0f);
for(angle = 0.0f; angle < (2.0f*GL_PI); angle += (GL_PI/8.0f))
    {
    // Calculate x and y position of the next vertex
    x = 50.0f*sin(angle);
    y = 50.0f*cos(angle);

    // Alternate color between red and green
    if((iPivot %2) == 0)
        glColor3f(0.0f, 1.0f, 0.0f);
    else
        glColor3f(1.0f, 0.0f, 0.0f);

    // Increment pivot to change color next time
    iPivot++;

    // Specify the next vertex for the triangle fan
    glVertex2f(x, y);
    }

// Done drawing the fan that covers the bottom
glEnd();

// Restore transformations
glPopMatrix();

glutSwapBuffers ();
}
```

Setting Polygon Colors

Until now, we have set the current color only once and drawn only a single shape. Now, with multiple polygons, things get slightly more interesting. We want to use different colors so we can see our work more easily. Colors are actually specified per vertex, not per polygon. The shading model affects whether the polygon is solidly colored (using the current color selected when the last vertex was specified) or smoothly shaded between the colors specified for each vertex.

The line

```
glShadeModel(GL_FLAT);
```

tells OpenGL to fill the polygons with the solid color that was current when the polygon's last vertex was specified. This is why we can simply change the current color to red or green before specifying the next vertex in our triangle fan. On the other hand, the line

```
glShadeModel(GL_SMOOTH);
```

would tell OpenGL to shade the triangles smoothly from each vertex, attempting to interpolate the colors between those specified for each vertex. You'll learn much more about color and shading in Chapter 5.

Hidden Surface Removal

Hold down one of the arrow keys to spin the cone around, and don't select anything from the Effects menu yet. You'll notice something unsettling: The cone appears to be swinging back and forth plus and minus 180°, with the bottom of the cone always facing you, but not rotating a full 360°. Figure 3.19 shows this effect more clearly.

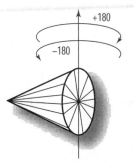

FIGURE 3.19   The rotating cone appears to be wobbling back and forth.

This wobbling happens because the bottom of the cone is drawn after the sides of the cone are drawn. No matter how the cone is oriented, the bottom is drawn on top of it, producing the "wobbling" illusion. This effect is not limited to the various sides and parts of an object. If more than one object is drawn and one is in front of the other (from the viewer's perspective), the last object drawn still appears over the previously drawn object.

You can correct this peculiarity with a simple feature called *depth testing*. Depth testing is an effective technique for hidden surface removal, and OpenGL has functions that do this for you behind the scenes. The concept is simple: When a pixel is drawn, it is assigned a value (called the z value) that denotes its distance from the viewer's perspective. Later, when another pixel needs to be drawn to that screen location, the new pixel's z value is compared to that of the pixel that is already stored there. If the new pixel's z value is higher, it is closer to the viewer and thus in front of the previous pixel, so the previous pixel is obscured by the new pixel. If the new pixel's z value is lower, it must be behind the existing pixel and thus is not obscured. This maneuver is accomplished internally by a depth buffer with storage for a depth value for every pixel on the screen. Almost all the samples in this book use depth testing.

You should request a depth buffer when you set up your OpenGL window with GLUT. For example, you can request a color and a depth buffer like this:

```
glutInitDisplayMode(GLUT_DOUBLE | GLUT_RGBA | GLUT_DEPTH);
```

To enable depth testing, simply call

```
glEnable(GL_DEPTH_TEST);
```

If you do not have a depth buffer, then enabling depth testing will just be ignored. Depth testing is enabled in Listing 3.8 when the bDepth variable is set to True, and it is disabled if bDepth is False:

```
// Enable depth testing if flag is set
if(bDepth)
    glEnable(GL_DEPTH_TEST);
else
    glDisable(GL_DEPTH_TEST);
```

The bDepth variable is set when you select Depth Test from the Effects menu. In addition, the depth buffer must be cleared each time the scene is rendered. The depth buffer is analogous to the color buffer in that it contains information about the distance of the pixels from the observer. This information is used to determine whether any pixels are hidden by pixels closer to the observer:

```
// Clear the window and the depth buffer
glClear(GL_COLOR_BUFFER_BIT | GL_DEPTH_BUFFER_BIT);
```

A right-click with the mouse opens a pop-up menu that allows you to toggle depth testing on and off. Figure 3.20 shows the TRIANGLE program with depth testing enabled. It also shows the cone with the bottom correctly hidden behind the sides. You can see that depth testing is practically a prerequisite for creating 3D objects out of solid polygons.

FIGURE 3.20   The bottom of the cone is now correctly placed behind the sides for this orientation.

Culling: Hiding Surfaces for Performance

You can see that there are obvious visual advantages to not drawing a surface that is obstructed by another. Even so, you pay some performance overhead because every pixel drawn must be compared with the previous pixel's z value. Sometimes, however, you know that a surface will never be drawn anyway, so why specify it? *Culling* is the term used to describe the technique of eliminating geometry that we know will never be seen. By not sending this geometry to your OpenGL driver and hardware, you can make significant performance improvements. One culling technique is backface culling, which eliminates the backsides of a surface.

In our working example, the cone is a closed surface, and we never see the inside. OpenGL is actually (internally) drawing the back sides of the far side of the cone and then the front sides of the polygons facing us. Then, by a comparison of z buffer values, the far side of the cone is either overwritten or ignored. Figures 3.21a and 3.21b show our cone at a particular orientation with depth testing turned on (a) and off (b). Notice that the green and red triangles that make up the cone sides change when depth testing is enabled. Without depth testing, the sides of the triangles at the far side of the cone show through.

FIGURE 3.21A   With depth testing.

FIGURE 3.21B   Without depth testing.

Earlier in the chapter, we explained how OpenGL uses winding to determine the front and back sides of polygons and that it is important to keep the polygons that define the outside of our objects wound in a consistent direction. This consistency is what allows us to tell OpenGL to render only the front, only the back, or both sides of polygons. By eliminating the back sides of the polygons, we can drastically reduce the amount of processing necessary to render the image. Even though depth testing will eliminate the appearance of the inside of objects, internally OpenGL must take them into account unless we explicitly tell it not to.

Backface culling is enabled or disabled for our program via the following code from Listing 3.8:

```
// Clockwise-wound polygons are front facing; this is reversed
// because we are using triangle fans
glFrontFace(GL_CW);
...
...


// Turn culling on if flag is set
if(bCull)
    glEnable(GL_CULL_FACE);
else
    glDisable(GL_CULL_FACE);
```

Note that we first changed the definition of front-facing polygons to assume clockwise winding (because our triangle fans are all wound clockwise).

Figure 3.22 demonstrates that the bottom of the cone is gone when culling is enabled. The reason is that we didn't follow our own rule about all the surface polygons having the same winding. The triangle fan that makes up the bottom of the cone is wound clockwise, like the fan that makes up the sides of the cone, but the front side of the cone's bottom section is then facing the inside (see Figure 3.23).

FIGURE 3.22   The bottom of the cone is culled because the front-facing triangles are inside.

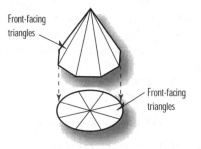

FIGURE 3.23   How the cone was assembled from two triangle fans.

We could have corrected this problem by changing the winding rule, by calling

```
glFrontFace(GL_CCW);
```

just before we drew the second triangle fan. But in this example, we wanted to make it easy for you to see culling in action, as well as set up for our next demonstration of polygon tweaking.

WHY DO WE NEED BACKFACE CULLING?

You might wonder, "If backface culling is so desirable, why do we need the ability to turn it on and off?" Backface culling is useful for drawing closed objects or solids, but you won't always be rendering these types of geometry. Some flat objects (such as paper) can still be seen from both sides. If the cone we are drawing here were made of glass or plastic, you would actually be able to see the front and the back sides of the geometry. (See Chapter 6 for a discussion of drawing transparent objects.)

Polygon Modes

Polygons don't have to be filled with the current color. By default, polygons are drawn solid, but you can change this behavior by specifying that polygons are to be drawn as outlines or just points (only the vertices are plotted). The function glPolygonMode allows polygons to be rendered as filled solids, as outlines, or as points only. In addition, you can apply this rendering mode to both sides of the polygons or only to the front or back. The following code from Listing 3.8 shows the polygon mode being set to outlines or solid, depending on the state of the Boolean variable bOutline:

```
// Draw back side as a polygon only, if flag is set
if(bOutline)
    glPolygonMode(GL_BACK,GL_LINE);
else
    glPolygonMode(GL_BACK,GL_FILL);
```

Figure 3.24 shows the back sides of all polygons rendered as outlines. (We had to disable culling to produce this image; otherwise, the inside would be eliminated and you would get no outlines.) Notice that the bottom of the cone is now wireframe instead of solid, and you can see up inside the cone where the inside walls are also drawn as wireframe triangles.

FIGURE 3.24   Using glPolygonMode to render one side of the triangles as outlines.

Other Primitives

Triangles are the preferred primitive for object composition because most OpenGL hardware specifically accelerates triangles, but they are not the only primitives available. Some hardware provides for acceleration of other shapes as well, and programmatically, using a general-purpose graphics primitive might be simpler. The remaining OpenGL primitives provide for rapid specification of a quadrilateral or quadrilateral strip, as well as a general-purpose polygon.

Four-Sided Polygons: Quads

If you add one more side to a triangle, you get a quadrilateral, or a four-sided figure. OpenGL's GL_QUADS primitive draws a four-sided polygon. In Figure 3.25, a quad is drawn from four vertices. Note also that these quads have clockwise winding. One important rule to bear in mind when you use quads is that all four corners of the quadrilateral must lie in a plane (no bent quads!).

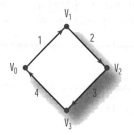

FIGURE 3.25   An example of GL_QUADS.

Quad Strips

As you can for triangle strips, you can specify a strip of connected quadrilaterals with the GL_QUAD_STRIP primitive. Figure 3.26 shows the progression of a quad strip specified by six vertices. Note that these quad strips maintain a clockwise winding.

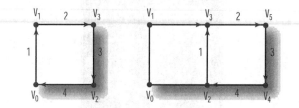

FIGURE 3.26   The progression of GL_QUAD_STRIP.

General Polygons

The final OpenGL primitive is the GL_POLYGON, which you can use to draw a polygon having any number of sides. Figure 3.27 shows a polygon consisting of five vertices. Polygons, like quads, must have all vertices on the same plane. An easy way around this rule is to substitute GL_TRIANGLE_FAN for GL_POLYGON!

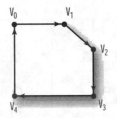

FIGURE 3.27   The progression of GL_POLYGON.

WHAT ABOUT RECTANGLES?

All 10 of the OpenGL primitives are used with glBegin/glEnd to draw general-purpose polygonal shapes. Although in Chapter 2 we used the function glRect as an easy and convenient mechanism for specifying 2D rectangles, henceforth we will resort to using GL_QUADS.

Filling Polygons, or Stippling Revisited

There are two methods for applying a pattern to solid polygons. The customary method is texture mapping, in which an image is mapped to the surface of a polygon, and this is covered in Chapter 8, "Texture Mapping: The Basics." Another way is to specify a stippling pattern, as we did for lines. A polygon stipple pattern is nothing more than a 32×32 monochrome bitmap that is used for the fill pattern.

To enable polygon stippling, call

```
glEnable(GL_POLYGON_STIPPLE);
```

and then call

```
glPolygonStipple(pBitmap);
```

pBitmap is a pointer to a data area containing the stipple pattern. Hereafter, all polygons are filled using the pattern specified by pBitmap (GLubyte *). This pattern is similar to that used by line stippling, except the buffer is large enough to hold a 32-by-32-bit pattern. Also, the bits are read with the most significant bit (MSB) first, which is just the opposite of line stipple patterns. Figure 3.28 shows a bit pattern for a campfire that we use for a stipple pattern.

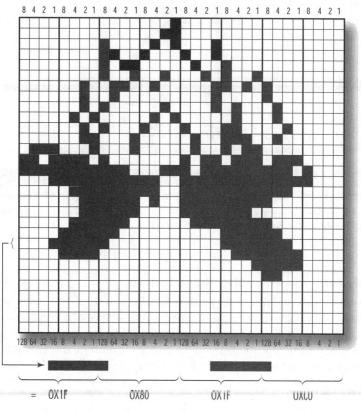

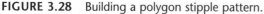

FIGURE 3.28   Building a polygon stipple pattern.

PIXEL STORAGE

As you will learn in Chapter 7, "Imaging with OpenGL," you can modify the way pixels for stipple patterns are interpreted by using the `glPixelStore` function. For now, however, we stick to the simple default polygon stippling.

To construct a mask to represent this pattern, we store one row at a time from the bottom up. Fortunately, unlike line stipple patterns, the data is, by default, interpreted just as it is stored, with the most significant bit read first. Each byte can then be read from left to right and stored in an array of GLubyte large enough to hold 32 rows of 4 bytes apiece.

Listing 3.9 shows the code used to store this pattern. Each row of the array represents a row from Figure 3.28. The first row in the array is the last row of the figure, and so on, up to the last row of the array and the first row of the figure.

LISTING 3.9   Mask Definition for the Campfire in Figure 3.28

```
// Bitmap of campfire
GLubyte fire[] = { 0x00, 0x00, 0x00, 0x00, 0x00, 0x00, 0x00, 0x00,
                   0x00, 0x00, 0x00, 0x00, 0x00, 0x00, 0x00, 0x00,
                   0x00, 0x00, 0x00, 0x00, 0x00, 0x00, 0x00, 0x00,
                   0x00, 0x00, 0x00, 0xc0, 0x00, 0x00, 0x01, 0xf0,
                   0x00, 0x00, 0x07, 0xf0, 0x0f, 0x00, 0x1f, 0xe0,
                   0x1f, 0x80, 0x1f, 0xc0, 0x0f, 0xc0, 0x3f, 0x80,
                   0x07, 0xe0, 0x7e, 0x00, 0x03, 0xf0, 0xff, 0x80,
                   0x03, 0xf5, 0xff, 0xe0, 0x07, 0xfd, 0xff, 0xf8,
                   0x1f, 0xfc, 0xff, 0xe8, 0xff, 0xe3, 0xbf, 0x70,
                   0xde, 0x80, 0xb7, 0x00, 0x71, 0x10, 0x4a, 0x80,
                   0x03, 0x10, 0x4e, 0x40, 0x02, 0x88, 0x8c, 0x20,
                   0x05, 0x05, 0x04, 0x40, 0x02, 0x82, 0x14, 0x40,
                   0x02, 0x40, 0x10, 0x80, 0x02, 0x64, 0x1a, 0x80,
                   0x00, 0x92, 0x29, 0x00, 0x00, 0xb0, 0x48, 0x00,
                   0x00, 0xc8, 0x90, 0x00, 0x00, 0x85, 0x10, 0x00,
                   0x00, 0x03, 0x00, 0x00, 0x00, 0x00, 0x10, 0x00 };
```

To make use of this stipple pattern, we must first enable polygon stippling and then specify this pattern as the stipple pattern. The PSTIPPLE sample program does this and then draws an octagon using the stipple pattern. Listing 3.10 shows the pertinent code, and Figure 3.29 shows the output from PSTIPPLE.

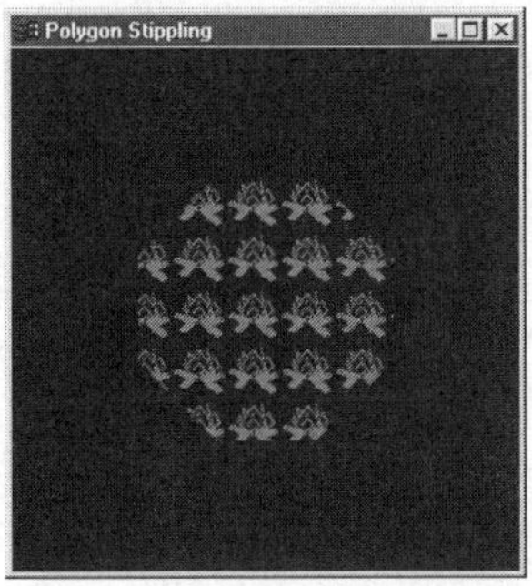

FIGURE 3.29   Output from the PSTIPPLE program.

LISTING 3.10   Code from PSTIPPLE That Draws a Stippled Octagon

```
// This function does any needed initialization on the rendering
// context.
void SetupRC()
    {
    // Black background
    glClearColor(0.0f, 0.0f, 0.0f, 1.0f );

    // Set drawing color to red
    glColor3f(1.0f, 0.0f, 0.0f);

    // Enable polygon stippling
    glEnable(GL_POLYGON_STIPPLE);

    // Specify a specific stipple pattern
    glPolygonStipple(fire);
    }


// Called to draw scene
void RenderScene(void)
    {
    // Clear the window
    glClear(GL_COLOR_BUFFER_BIT);
    ...
    ...
    // Begin the stop sign shape,
    // use a standard polygon for simplicity
    glBegin(GL_POLYGON);
        glVertex2f(-20.0f, 50.0f);
        glVertex2f(20.0f, 50.0f);
        glVertex2f(50.0f, 20.0f);
        glVertex2f(50.0f, -20.0f);
        glVertex2f(20.0f, -50.0f);
        glVertex2f(-20.0f, -50.0f);
        glVertex2f(-50.0f, -20.0f);
        glVertex2f(-50.0f, 20.0f);
    glEnd();
    ...
    ...
    glutSwapBuffers ();
    }
```

Figure 3.30 shows the octagon rotated somewhat. Notice that the stipple pattern is still used, but the pattern is not rotated with the polygon. The stipple pattern is used only for simple polygon filling onscreen. If you need to map an image to a polygon so that it mimics the polygon's surface, you must use texture mapping (see Chapter 8).

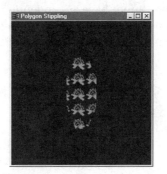

FIGURE 3.30   PSTIPPLE output with the polygon rotated, showing that the stipple pattern is not rotated.

Polygon Construction Rules

When you are using many polygons to construct a complex surface, you need to remember two important rules.

The first rule is that all polygons must be planar. That is, all the vertices of the polygon must lie in a single plane, as illustrated in Figure 3.31. The polygon cannot twist or bend in space.

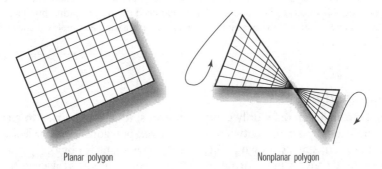

Planar polygon   Nonplanar polygon

FIGURE 3.31   Planar versus nonplanar polygons.

Here is yet another good reason to use triangles. No triangle can ever be twisted so that all three points do not line up in a plane because mathematically it takes only three points to define a plane. (If you can plot an invalid triangle, aside from winding it in the wrong direction, the Nobel Prize committee might be looking for you! No cheating! Three points in a straight line do not count!)

The second rule of polygon construction is that the polygon's edges must not intersect, and the polygon must be convex. A polygon intersects itself if any two of its lines cross. *Convex* means that the polygon cannot have any indentions. A more rigorous test of a convex polygon is to draw some lines through it. If any given line enters and leaves the polygon more than once, the polygon is not convex. Figure 3.32 gives examples of good and bad polygons.

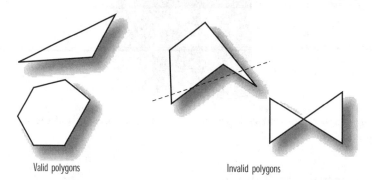

Valid polygons   Invalid polygons

FIGURE 3.32   Some valid and invalid primitive polygons.

WHY THE LIMITATIONS ON POLYGONS?

You might wonder why OpenGL places the restrictions on polygon construction. Handling polygons can become quite complex, and OpenGL's restrictions allow it to use very fast algorithms for rendering these polygons. We predict that you'll not find these restrictions burdensome and that you'll be able to build any shapes or objects you need using the existing primitives. Chapter 10, "Curves and Surfaces," discusses some techniques for breaking a complex shape into smaller triangles.

Subdivision and Edges

Even though OpenGL can draw only convex polygons, there's still a way to create a nonconvex polygon: by arranging two or more convex polygons together. For example, let's take a four-point star, as shown in Figure 3.33. This shape is obviously not convex and thus violates OpenGL's rules for simple polygon construction. However, the star on the right is composed of six separate triangles, which are legal polygons.

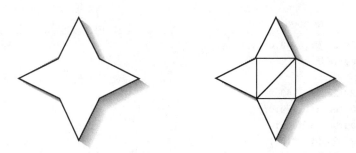

FIGURE 3.33 A nonconvex four-point star made up of six triangles.

When the polygons are filled, you won't be able to see any edges and the figure will seem to be a single shape onscreen. However, if you use glPolygonMode to switch to an outline drawing, it is distracting to see all those little triangles making up some larger surface area.

OpenGL provides a special flag called an *edge flag* to address those distracting edges. By setting and clearing the edge flag as you specify a list of vertices, you inform OpenGL which line segments are considered border lines (lines that go around the border of your shape) and which ones are not (internal lines that shouldn't be visible). The glEdgeFlag function takes a single parameter that sets the edge flag to True or False. When the function is set to True, any vertices that follow mark the beginning of a boundary line segment. Listing 3.11 shows an example of this from the STAR sample program.

LISTING 3.11   Sample Usage of glEdgeFlag from the STAR Program

```
// Begin the triangles
glBegin(GL_TRIANGLES);

    glEdgeFlag(bEdgeFlag);
    glVertex2f(-20.0f, 0.0f);
    glEdgeFlag(TRUE);
    glVertex2f(20.0f, 0.0f);
    glVertex2f(0.0f, 40.0f);

    glVertex2f(-20.0f,0.0f);
    glVertex2f(-60.0f,-20.0f);
    glEdgeFlag(bEdgeFlag);
    glVertex2f(-20.0f,-40.0f);
    glEdgeFlag(TRUE);

    glVertex2f(-20.0f,-40.0f);
    glVertex2f(0.0f, -80.0f);
    glEdgeFlag(bEdgeFlag);
```

LISTING 3.11   Continued

```
      glVertex2f(20.0f, -40.0f);
      glEdgeFlag(TRUE);

      glVertex2f(20.0f, -40.0f);
      glVertex2f(60.0f, -20.0f);
      glEdgeFlag(bEdgeFlag);
      glVertex2f(20.0f, 0.0f);
      glEdgeFlag(TRUE);

      // Center square as two triangles
      glEdgeFlag(bEdgeFlag);
      glVertex2f(-20.0f, 0.0f);
      glVertex2f(-20.0f,-40.0f);
      glVertex2f(20.0f, 0.0f);

      glVertex2f(-20.0f,-40.0f);
      glVertex2f(20.0f, -40.0f);
      glVertex2f(20.0f, 0.0f);
      glEdgeFlag(TRUE);

// Done drawing triangles
glEnd();
```

The Boolean variable bEdgeFlag is toggled on and off by a menu option to make the edges appear and disappear. If this flag is True, all edges are considered boundary edges and appear when the polygon mode is set to GL_LINES. In Figure 3.34, you can see the output from STAR, showing the wireframe star with and without edges.

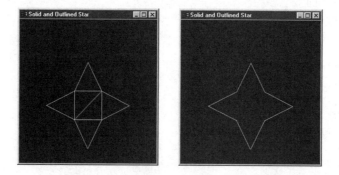

FIGURE 3.34   The STAR program with edges enabled (left) and without edges enabled (right).

Other Buffer Tricks

You learned from Chapter 2 that OpenGL does not render (draw) these primitives directly on the screen. Instead, rendering is done in a buffer, which is later swapped to the screen. We refer to these two buffers as the front (the screen) and back color buffers. By default, OpenGL commands are rendered into the back buffer, and when you call `glutSwapBuffers` (or your operating system–specific buffer swap function), the front and back buffers are swapped so that you can see the rendering results. You can, however, render directly into the front buffer if you want. This capability can be useful for displaying a series of drawing commands so that you can see some object or shape actually being drawn. There are two ways to do this; both are discussed in the following section.

Using Buffer Targets

The first way to render directly into the front buffer is to just tell OpenGL that you want drawing to be done there. You do this by calling the following function:

```
void glDrawBuffer(Glenum mode);
```

Specifying `GL_FRONT` causes OpenGL to render to the front buffer, and `GL_BACK` moves rendering back to the back buffer. OpenGL implementations can support more than just a single front and back buffer for rendering, such as left and right buffers for stereo rendering, and auxiliary buffers. These other buffers are documented further in Appendix C, "API Reference."

The second way to render to the front buffer is to simply not request double-buffered rendering when OpenGL is initialized. OpenGL is initialized differently on each OS platform, but with GLUT, we initialize our display mode for RGB color and double-buffered rendering with the following line of code:

```
glutInitDisplayMode(GLUT_DOUBLE | GLUT_RGB);
```

To get single-buffered rendering, you simply omit the bit flag `GLUT_DOUBLE`, as shown here:

```
glutInitDisplayMode(GLUT_RGB);
```

When you do single-buffered rendering, it is important to call either `glFlush` or `glFinish` whenever you want to see the results actually drawn to screen. A buffer swap implicitly performs a flush of the pipeline and waits for rendering to complete before the swap actually occurs. We'll discuss the mechanics of this process in more detail in Chapter 11, "It's All About the Pipeline: Faster Geometry Throughput."

Listing 3.12 shows the drawing code for the sample program SINGLE. This example uses a single rendering buffer to draw a series of points spiraling out from the center of the window. The `RenderScene` function is called repeatedly and uses static variables to cycle through a simple animation. The output of the SINGLE sample program is shown in Figure 3.35.

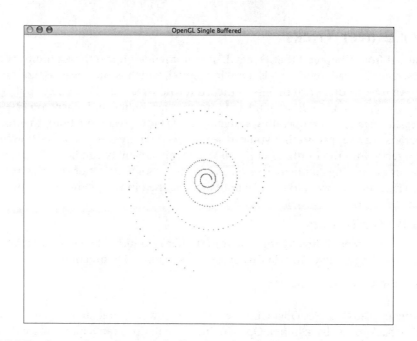

FIGURE 3.35   Output from the single-buffered rendering example.

LISTING 3.12   Drawing Code for the SINGLE Sample

```
///////////////////////////////////////////////////////////
// Called to draw scene
void RenderScene(void)
        {
        static GLdouble dRadius = 0.1;
        static GLdouble dAngle = 0.0;

        // Clear blue window
        glClearColor(0.0f, 0.0f, 1.0f, 0.0f);

        if(dAngle == 0.0)
            glClear(GL_COLOR_BUFFER_BIT);

        glBegin(GL_POINTS);
            glVertex2d(dRadius * cos(dAngle), dRadius * sin(dAngle));
        glEnd();

        dRadius *= 1.01;
        dAngle += 0.1;
```

LISTING 3.12   Continued

```
    if(dAngle > 30.0)
        {
        dRadius = 0.1;
        dAngle = 0.0;
        }

    glFlush();
    }
```

Manipulating the Depth Buffer

The color buffers are not the only buffers that OpenGL renders into. In the preceding chapter, we mentioned other buffer targets, including the depth buffer. However, the depth buffer is filled with depth values instead of color values. Requesting a depth buffer with GLUT is as simple as adding the GLUT_DEPTH bit flag when initializing the display mode:

```
glutInitDisplayMode(GLUT_RGB | GLUT_DOUBLE | GLUT_DEPTH);
```

You've already seen that enabling the use of the depth buffer for depth testing is as easy as calling the following:

```
glEnable(GL_DEPTH_TEST);
```

Even when depth testing is not enabled, if a depth buffer is created, OpenGL will write corresponding depth values for all color fragments that go into the color buffer. Sometimes, though, you may want to temporarily turn off writing values to the depth buffer as well as depth testing. You can do this with the function glDepthMask:

```
void glDepthMask(GLboolean mask);
```

Setting the mask to GL_FALSE disables writes to the depth buffer but does not disable depth testing from being performed using any values that have already been written to the depth buffer. Calling this function with GL_TRUE re-enables writing to the depth buffer, which is the default state. Masking color writes is also possible but is a bit more involved; it's mentioned in Chapter 6.

Cutting It Out with Scissors

One way to improve rendering performance is to update only the portion of the screen that has changed. You may also need to restrict OpenGL rendering to a smaller rectangular region inside the window. OpenGL allows you to specify a scissor rectangle within your window where rendering can take place. By default, the scissor rectangle is the size of the window, and no scissor test takes place. You turn on the scissor test with the ubiquitous glEnable function:

glEnable(GL_SCISSOR_TEST);

You can, of course, turn off the scissor test again with the corresponding glDisable function call. The rectangle within the window where rendering is performed, called the *scissor box,* is specified in window coordinates (pixels) with the following function:

void glScissor(GLint *x*, GLint *y*, GLsizei *width*, GLsizei *height*);

The *x* and *y* parameters specify the lower-left corner of the scissor box, with *width* and *height* being the corresponding dimensions of the scissor box. Listing 3.13 shows the rendering code for the sample program SCISSOR. This program clears the color buffer three times, each time with a smaller scissor box specified before the clear. The result is a set of overlapping colored rectangles, as shown in Figure 3.36.

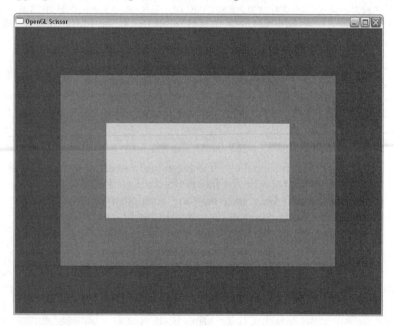

FIGURE 3.36   Shrinking scissor boxes.

LISTING 3.13   Using the Scissor Box to Render a Series of Rectangles

```
void RenderScene(void)
    {
    // Clear blue window
```

LISTING 3.13 Continued

```
glClearColor(0.0f, 0.0f, 1.0f, 0.0f);
glClear(GL_COLOR_BUFFER_BIT);

// Now set scissor to smaller red sub region
glClearColor(1.0f, 0.0f, 0.0f, 0.0f);
glScissor(100, 100, 600, 400);
glEnable(GL_SCISSOR_TEST);
glClear(GL_COLOR_BUFFER_BIT);

// Finally, an even smaller green rectangle
glClearColor(0.0f, 1.0f, 0.0f, 0.0f);
glScissor(200, 200, 400, 200);
glClear(GL_COLOR_BUFFER_BIT);

// Turn scissor back off for next render
glDisable(GL_SCISSOR_TEST);

glutSwapBuffers();
}
```

Using the Stencil Buffer

Using the OpenGL scissor box is a great way to restrict rendering to a rectangle within the window. Frequently, however, we want to mask out an irregularly shaped area using a stencil pattern. In the real world, a stencil is a flat piece of cardboard or other material that has a pattern cut out of it. Painters use the stencil to apply paint to a surface using the pattern in the stencil. Figure 3.37 shows how this process works.

FIGURE 3.37 Using a stencil to paint a surface in the real world.

In the OpenGL world, we have the *stencil buffer* instead. The stencil buffer provides a similar capability but is far more powerful because we can create the stencil pattern ourselves with rendering commands. To use OpenGL stenciling, we must first request a stencil buffer using the platform-specific OpenGL setup procedures. When using GLUT, we request one when we initialize the display mode. For example, the following line of code sets up a double-buffered RGB color buffer with stencil:

```
glutInitDisplayMode(GLUT_RGB ¦ GLUT_DOUBLE ¦ GLUT_STENCIL);
```

The stencil operation is relatively fast on modern hardware-accelerated OpenGL implementations. It can also be turned on and off with `glEnable/glDisable`. For example, we turn on the stencil test with the following line of code:

```
glEnable(GL_STENCIL_TEST);
```

With the stencil test enabled, drawing occurs only at locations that pass the stencil test. You set up the stencil test that you want to use with this function:

```
void glStencilFunc(GLenum func, GLint ref, GLuint mask);
```

The stencil function that you want to use, *func*, can be any one of these values: GL_NEVER, GL_ALWAYS, GL_LESS, GL_LEQUAL, GL_EQUAL, GL_GEQUAL, GL_GREATER, and GL_NOTEQUAL. These values tell OpenGL how to compare the value already stored in the stencil buffer with the value you specify in *ref*. These values correspond to never or always passing, passing if the reference value is less than, less than or equal, greater than or equal, greater than, and not equal to the value already stored in the stencil buffer, respectively. In addition, you can specify a mask value that is bitwise ANDed with both the reference value and the value from the stencil buffer before the comparison takes place.

STENCIL BITS

You need to realize that the stencil buffer may be of limited precision. Stencil buffers are typically only between 1 and 8 bits deep. Each OpenGL implementation may have its own limits on the available bit depth of the stencil buffer, and each operating system or environment has its own methods of querying and setting this value. In GLUT, you just get the most stencil bits available, but for finer-grained control, you need to refer to the operating system–specific chapters later in the book. Values passed to *ref* and *mask* that exceed the available bit depth of the stencil buffer are simply truncated, and only the maximum number of least significant bits is used.

Creating the Stencil Pattern

You now know how the stencil test is performed, but how are values put into the stencil buffer to begin with? First, we must make sure that the stencil buffer is cleared before we start any drawing operations. We do this in the same way that we clear the color and depth buffers with `glClear`—using the bit mask `GL_STENCIL_BUFFER_BIT`. For example, the following line of code clears the color, depth, and stencil buffers simultaneously:

```
glClear(GL_COLOR_BUFFER_BIT ¦ GL_DEPTH_BUFFER_BIT ¦ GL_STENCIL_BUFFER_BIT);
```

The value used in the clear operation is set previously with a call to

```
glClearStencil(GLint s);
```

When the stencil test is enabled, rendering commands are tested against the value in the stencil buffer using the glStencilFunc parameters we just discussed. Fragments (color values placed in the color buffer) are either written or discarded based on the outcome of that stencil test. The stencil buffer itself is also modified during this test, and what goes into the stencil buffer depends on how you've called the glStencilOp function:

```
void glStencilOp(GLenum fail, GLenum zfail, GLenum zpass);
```

These values tell OpenGL how to change the value of the stencil buffer if the stencil test fails (*fail*), and even if the stencil test passes, you can modify the stencil buffer if the depth test fails (*zfail*) or passes (*zpass*). The valid values for these arguments are GL_KEEP, GL_ZERO, GL_REPLACE, GL_INCR, GL_DECR, GL_INVERT, GL_INCR_WRAP, and GL_DECR_WRAP. These values correspond to keeping the current value, setting it to zero, replacing with the reference value (from glStencilFunc), incrementing or decrementing the value, inverting it, and incrementing/decrementing with wrap, respectively. Both GL_INCR and GL_DECR increment and decrement the stencil value but are clamped to the minimum and maximum value that can be represented in the stencil buffer for a given bit depth. GL_INCR_WRAP and likewise GL_DECR_WRAP simply wrap the values around when they exceed the upper and lower limits of a given bit representation.

In the sample program STENCIL, we create a spiral line pattern in the stencil buffer, but not in the color buffer. The bouncing rectangle from Chapter 2 comes back for a visit, but this time, the stencil test prevents drawing of the red rectangle anywhere the stencil buffer contains a 0x1 value. Listing 3.14 shows the relevant drawing code.

LISTING 3.14   Rendering Code for the STENCIL Sample

```
void RenderScene(void)
    {
    GLdouble dRadius = 0.1; // Initial radius of spiral
    GLdouble dAngle;        // Looping variable

    // Clear blue window
    glClearColor(0.0f, 0.0f, 1.0f, 0.0f);

    // Use 0 for clear stencil, enable stencil test
    glClearStencil(0.0f);
    glEnable(GL_STENCIL_TEST);
```

LISTING 3.14   Continued

```
// Clear color and stencil buffer
glClear(GL_COLOR_BUFFER_BIT | GL_STENCIL_BUFFER_BIT);

// All drawing commands fail the stencil test, and are not
// drawn, but increment the value in the stencil buffer.
glStencilFunc(GL_NEVER, 0x0, 0x0);
glStencilOp(GL_INCR, GL_INCR, GL_INCR);

// Spiral pattern will create stencil pattern
// Draw the spiral pattern with white lines. We
// make the lines white to demonstrate that the
// stencil function prevents them from being drawn
glColor3f(1.0f, 1.0f, 1.0f);
glBegin(GL_LINE_STRIP);
    for(dAngle = 0; dAngle < 400.0; dAngle += 0.1)
        {
        glVertex2d(dRadius * cos(dAngle), dRadius * sin(dAngle));
        dRadius *= 1.002;
        }
glEnd();

// Now, allow drawing, except where the stencil pattern is 0x1
// and do not make any further changes to the stencil buffer
glStencilFunc(GL_NOTEQUAL, 0x1, 0x1);
glStencilOp(GL_KEEP, GL_KEEP, GL_KEEP);

// Now draw red bouncing square
// (x and y) are modified by a timer function
glColor3f(1.0f, 0.0f, 0.0f);
glRectf(x, y, x + rsize, y - rsize);

// All done, do the buffer swap
glutSwapBuffers();
    }
```

The following two lines cause all fragments to fail the stencil test. The values of *ref* and *mask* are irrelevant in this case and are not used.

```
glStencilFunc(GL_NEVER, 0x0, 0x0);
glStencilOp(GL_INCR, GL_INCR, GL_INCR);
```

The arguments to glStencilOp, however, cause the value in the stencil buffer to be written (incremented actually), regardless of whether anything is seen on the screen. Following these lines, a white spiral line is drawn, and even though the color of the line is white so you can see it against the blue background, it is not drawn in the color buffer because it always fails the stencil test (GL_NEVER). You are essentially rendering only to the stencil buffer!

Next, we change the stencil operation with these lines:

```
glStencilFunc(GL_NOTEQUAL, 0x1, 0x1);
glStencilOp(GL_KEEP, GL_KEEP, GL_KEEP);
```

Now, drawing will occur anywhere the stencil buffer is not equal (GL_NOTEQUAL) to 0x1, which is anywhere onscreen that the spiral line is not drawn. The subsequent call to glStencilOp is optional for this example, but it tells OpenGL to leave the stencil buffer alone for all future drawing operations. Although this sample is best seen in action, Figure 3.38 shows an image of what the bounding red square looks like as it is "stenciled out."

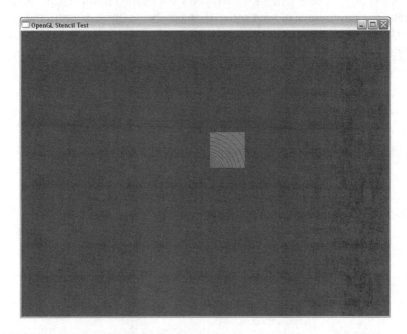

FIGURE 3.38   The bouncing red square with masking stencil pattern.

Just as with the depth buffer, you can also mask out writes to the stencil buffer by using the function glStencilMask:

```
void glStencilMask(GLboolean mask);
```

Setting the mask to `false` does not disable stencil test operations but does prevent any operation from writing values into the stencil buffer.

Summary

We covered a lot of ground in this chapter. At this point, you can create your 3D space for rendering, and you know how to draw everything from points and lines to complex polygons. We also showed you how to assemble these two-dimensional primitives as the surface of three-dimensional objects.

You also learned about some of the other buffers that OpenGL renders into besides the color buffer. As we move forward throughout the book, we will use the depth and stencil buffers for many other techniques and special effects. In Chapter 6, you will learn about yet another OpenGL buffer, the Accumulation buffer. You'll see later that all these buffers working together can create some outstanding and very realistic 3D graphics.

We encourage you to experiment with what you have learned in this chapter. Use your imagination and create some of your own 3D objects before moving on to the rest of the book. You'll then have some personal samples to work with and enhance as you learn and explore new techniques throughout the book.

CHAPTER 4

Geometric Transformations: The Pipeline

by Richard S. Wright Jr.

WHAT YOU'LL LEARN IN THIS CHAPTER:

How To	Functions You'll Use
Establish your position in the scene	gluLookAt
Position objects within the scene	glTranslate/glRotate
Scale objects	glScale
Establish a perspective transformation	gluPerspective
Perform your own matrix transformations	glLoadMatrix/glMultMatrix
Use a camera to move around in a scene	gluLookAt

In Chapter 3, "Drawing in Space: Geometric Primitives and Buffers," you learned how to draw points, lines, and various primitives in 3D. To turn a collection of shapes into a coherent scene, you must arrange them in relation to one another and to the viewer. In this chapter, you start moving shapes and objects around in your coordinate system. (Actually, you don't move the objects, but rather shift the coordinate system to create the view you want.) The ability to place and orient your objects in a scene is a crucial tool for any 3D graphics programmer. As you will see, it is actually convenient to describe your objects' dimensions around the origin and then *transform* the objects into the desired position.

Is This the Dreaded Math Chapter?

In most books on 3D graphics programming, yes, this would be the dreaded math chapter. However, you can relax; we take a more moderate approach to these principles than some texts.

The keys to object and coordinate transformations are two matrices maintained by OpenGL. To familiarize you with these matrices, this chapter strikes a compromise between two extremes in computer graphics philosophy. On the one hand, we could warn you, "Please review a textbook on linear algebra before reading this chapter." On the other hand, we could perpetuate the deceptive reassurance that you can "learn to do 3D graphics without all those complex mathematical formulas." But we don't agree with either camp.

In reality, you can get along just fine without understanding the finer mathematics of 3D graphics, just as you can drive your car every day without having to know anything at all about automotive mechanics and the internal combustion engine. But you had better know enough about your car to realize that you need an oil change every so often, that you have to fill the tank with gas regularly, and that you must change the tires when they get bald. This knowledge makes you a responsible (and safe!) automobile owner. If you want to be a responsible and capable OpenGL programmer, the same standards apply. You need to understand at least the basics so you know what can be done and what tools best suit the job. If you are a beginner, you will find that, with some practice, matrix math and vectors will gradually make more and more sense, and you will develop a more intuitive (and powerful) ability to make full use of the concepts we introduce in this chapter.

So even if you don't already have the ability to multiply two matrices in your head, you need to know what matrices are and that they are the means to OpenGL's 3D magic. But before you go dusting off that old linear algebra textbook (doesn't everyone have one?), have no fear: OpenGL does all the math for you. Think of using OpenGL as using a calculator to do long division when you don't know how to do it on paper. Although you don't have to do it yourself, you still know what it is and how to apply it. See—you can eat your cake and have it too!

Understanding Transformations

If you think about it, most 3D graphics aren't really 3D. We use 3D concepts and terminology to describe what something looks like; then this 3D data is "squished" onto a 2D computer screen. We call the process of squishing 3D data down into 2D data *projection*, and we introduced both orthographic and perspective projections back in Chapter 1, "Introduction to 3D Graphics and OpenGL." We refer to the projection whenever we want to describe the type of transformation (orthographic or perspective) that occurs during projection, but projection is only one of the types of transformations that occur in OpenGL. Transformations also allow you to rotate objects around; move them about; and even stretch, shrink, and warp them.

Three types of geometric transformations occur between the time you specify your vertices and the time they appear on the screen: viewing, modeling, and projection. In this section, we examine the principles of each type of transformation, which are summarized in Table 4.1.

TABLE 4.1   Summary of the OpenGL Transformation Terminology

Transformation	Use
Viewing	Specifies the location of the viewer or camera
Modeling	Moves objects around the scene
Modelview	Describes the duality of viewing and modeling transformations
Projection	Sizes and reshapes the viewing volume.
Viewport	A pseudo-transformation that scales the final output to the window

Eye Coordinates

An important concept throughout this chapter is that of *eye coordinates*. Eye coordinates are from the viewpoint of the observer, regardless of any transformations that may occur; you can think of them as "absolute" screen coordinates. Thus, eye coordinates represent a virtual fixed coordinate system that is used as a common frame of reference. All the transformations discussed in this chapter are described in terms of their effects relative to the eye coordinate system.

Figure 4.1 shows the eye coordinate system from two viewpoints. On the left (a), the eye coordinates are represented as seen by the observer of the scene (that is, perpendicular to the monitor). On the right (b), the eye coordinate system is rotated slightly so you can better see the relation of the z-axis. Positive x and y are pointed right and up, respectively, from the viewer's perspective. Positive z travels away from the origin toward the user, and negative z values travel farther away from the viewpoint into the screen.

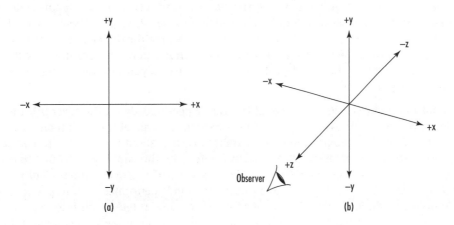

FIGURE 4.1   Two perspectives of eye coordinates.

When you draw in 3D with OpenGL, you use the Cartesian coordinate system. In the absence of any transformations, the system in use is identical to the eye coordinate system just described.

Viewing Transformations

The viewing transformation is the first to be applied to your scene. It is used to determine the vantage point of the scene. By default, the point of observation in a perspective projection is at the origin (0,0,0) looking down the negative z-axis ("into" the monitor screen). This point of observation is moved relative to the eye coordinate system to provide a specific vantage point. When the point of observation is located at the origin, as in a perspective projection, objects drawn with positive z values are behind the observer. In an orthographic projection, however, the viewer is assumed to be infinitely far away on the positive Z axis, and can see everything within the viewing volume.

The viewing transformation allows you to place the point of observation anywhere you want and look in any direction. Determining the viewing transformation is like placing and pointing a camera at the scene.

In the grand scheme of things, you must specify the viewing transformation before any other modeling transformations. The reason is that it appears to move the current working coordinate system in respect to the eye coordinate system. All subsequent transformations then occur based on the newly modified coordinate system. Later, you'll see more easily how this works, when we actually start looking at how to make these transformations.

Modeling Transformations

Modeling transformations are used to manipulate your model and the particular objects within it. These transformations move objects into place, rotate them, and scale them. Figure 4.2 illustrates three of the most common modeling transformations that you will apply to your objects. Figure 4.2a shows translation, in which an object is moved along a given axis. Figure 4.2b shows a rotation, in which an object is rotated about one of the axes. Finally, Figure 4.2c shows the effects of scaling, where the dimensions of the object are increased or decreased by a specified amount. Scaling can occur nonuniformly (the various dimensions can be scaled by different amounts), so you can use scaling to stretch and shrink objects.

The final appearance of your scene or object can depend greatly on the order in which the modeling transformations are applied. This is particularly true of translation and rotation. Figure 4.3a shows the progression of a square rotated first about the z-axis and then translated down the newly transformed x-axis. In Figure 4.3b, the same square is first translated down the x-axis and then rotated around the z-axis. The difference in the final dispositions of the square occurs because each transformation is performed with respect to the last transformation performed. In Figure 4.3a, the square is rotated with respect to the origin first. In 4.3b, after the square is translated, the rotation is performed around the newly translated origin.

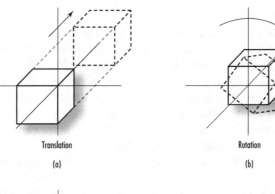

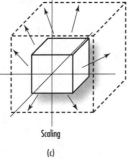

FIGURE 4.2   The modeling transformations.

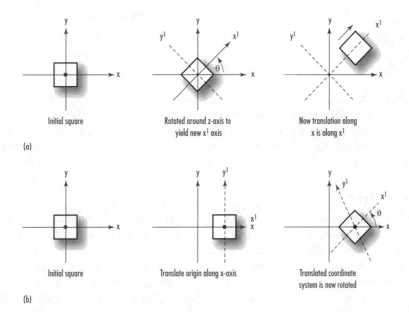

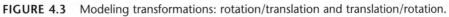

FIGURE 4.3   Modeling transformations: rotation/translation and translation/rotation.

The Modelview Duality

The viewing and modeling transformations are, in fact, the same in terms of their internal effects as well as their effects on the final appearance of the scene. The distinction between the two is made purely as a convenience for the programmer. There is no real difference visually between moving an object backward and moving the reference system forward; as shown in Figure 4.4, the net effect is the same. (You experience this effect firsthand when you're sitting in your car at an intersection and you see the car next to you roll forward; it might seem to you that your own car is rolling backward.) The viewing transformation is simply a modeling-like transformation that is applied to the entire scene, where objects in your scene will often each have their own individual model transformation, applied after the viewing transformation. The term *modelview* indicates that these two transformations are combined in the transformation pipeline into a single matrix—the modelview matrix.

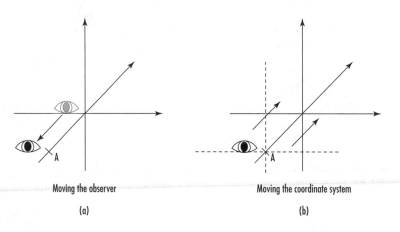

Moving the observer

(a)

Moving the coordinate system

(b)

FIGURE 4.4   Two ways of looking at the viewing transformation.

The viewing transformation, therefore, is essentially nothing but a modeling transformation that you apply to a virtual object (the viewer) before drawing objects. As you will soon see, new transformations are repeatedly specified as you place more objects in the scene. By convention, the initial transformation provides a reference from which all other transformations are based.

Projection Transformations

The projection transformation is applied to your vertices after the modelview transformation. This projection actually defines the viewing volume and establishes clipping planes. The clipping planes are plane equations in 3D space that OpenGL uses to determine whether geometry can be seen by the viewer. More specifically, the projection transformation specifies how a finished scene (after all the modeling is done) is projected to the final image on the screen. You'll learn about two types of projections in this chapter: orthographic and perspective.

In an *orthographic*, or parallel, projection, all the polygons are drawn onscreen with exactly the relative dimensions specified. Lines and polygons are mapped directly to the 2D screen using parallel lines, which means no matter how far away something is, it is still drawn the same size, just flattened against the screen. This type of projection is typically used for rendering two-dimensional images such as blueprints or two-dimensional graphics such as text or onscreen menus.

A *perspective* projection shows scenes more as they appear in real life instead of as a blueprint. The trademark of perspective projections is *foreshortening*, which makes distant objects appear smaller than nearby objects of the same size. Lines in 3D space that might be parallel do not always appear parallel to the viewer. With a railroad track, for instance, the rails are parallel, but using perspective projection, they appear to converge at some distant point.

The benefit of perspective projection is that you don't have to figure out where lines converge or how much smaller distant objects are. All you need to do is specify the scene using the modelview transformations and then apply the perspective projection. OpenGL works all the magic for you. Figure 4.5 compares orthographic and perspective projections on two different scenes.

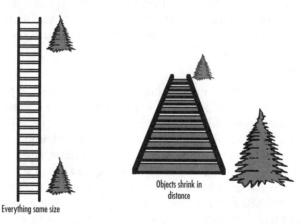

FIGURE 4.5   A side-by-side example of an orthographic versus perspective projection.

Orthographic projections are used most often for 2D drawing purposes where you want an exact correspondence between pixels and drawing units. You might use them for a schematic layout, text, or perhaps a 2D graphing application. You also can use an orthographic projection for 3D renderings when the depth of the rendering has a very small depth in comparison to the distance from the viewpoint. Perspective projections are used for rendering scenes that contain wide-open spaces or objects that need to have the foreshortening applied. For the most part, perspective projections are typical for 3D graphics. In fact, looking at a 3D object with an orthographic projection can be somewhat unsettling.

Viewport Transformations

When all is said and done, you end up with a two-dimensional projection of your scene that will be mapped to a window somewhere on your screen. This mapping to physical window coordinates is the last transformation that is done, and it is called the *viewport* transformation. Usually, a one-to-one correspondence exists between the color buffer and window pixels, but this is not always strictly the case. In some circumstances, the viewport transformation remaps what are called "normalized" device coordinates to window coordinates. Fortunately, this is something you don't need to worry about.

The Matrix: Mathematical Currency for 3D Graphics

Now that you're armed with some basic vocabulary and definitions of transformations, you're ready for some simple matrix mathematics. Let's examine how OpenGL performs these transformations and get to know the functions you call to achieve the desired effects.

The mathematics behind these transformations are greatly simplified by the mathematical notation of the matrix. You can achieve each of the transformations we have discussed by multiplying a matrix that contains the vertices (usually, this is a simple vector) by a matrix that describes the transformation. Thus, all the transformations achievable with OpenGL can be described as the product of two or more matrix multiplications.

What Is a Matrix?

The Matrix is not just a Hollywood movie trilogy, but an exceptionally powerful mathematical tool that greatly simplifies the process of solving one or more equations with variables that have complex relationships to each other. One common example of this, near and dear to the hearts of graphics programmers, is coordinate transformations. For example, if you have a point in space represented by x, y, and z coordinates, and you need to know where that point is if you rotate it some number of degrees around some arbitrary point and orientation, you would use a matrix. Why? Because the new x coordinate depends not only on the old x coordinate and the other rotation parameters, but also on what the y and z coordinates were as well. This kind of dependency between the variables and solution is just the sort of problem that matrices excel at. For fans of the *Matrix* movies who have a mathematical inclination, the term *matrix* is indeed an appropriate title.

Mathematically, a matrix is nothing more than a set of numbers arranged in uniform rows and columns—in programming terms, a two-dimensional array. A matrix doesn't have to be square, but each row or column must have the same number of elements as every other row or column in the matrix. Figure 4.6 presents some examples of matrices. They don't represent anything in particular, but serve only to demonstrate matrix structure. Note that it is also valid for a matrix to have a single column or row. A single row or column of numbers is also more simply called a *vector,* and vectors also have some interesting and useful applications all their own.

$$\begin{bmatrix} 1 & 4 & 7 \\ 2 & 5 & 8 \\ 3 & 6 & 9 \end{bmatrix} \begin{bmatrix} 0 & 42 \\ 1.5 & 0.877 \\ 2 & 14 \end{bmatrix} \begin{bmatrix} 1 \\ 2 \\ 3 \\ 4 \end{bmatrix}$$

FIGURE 4.6   Three examples of matrices.

Matrix and *vector* are two important terms that you will see often in 3D graphics programming literature. When dealing with these quantities, you will also see the term *scalar*. A scalar is just an ordinary single number used to represent magnitude or a specific quantity (you know—a regular old, plain, simple number…like before you cared or had all this jargon added to your vocabulary).

Matrices can be multiplied and added together, but they can also be multiplied by vectors and scalar values. Multiplying a point (a vector) by a matrix (a transformation) yields a new transformed point (a vector). Matrix transformations are actually not too difficult to understand but can be intimidating at first. Because an understanding of matrix transformations is fundamental to many 3D tasks, you should still make an attempt to become familiar with them. Fortunately, only a little understanding is enough to get you going and doing some pretty incredible things with OpenGL. Over time, and with a little more practice and study (see Appendix A, "Further Reading/References"), you will master this mathematical tool yourself.

In the meantime, you can find a number of useful matrix and vector functions and features available, with source code, in the files `math3d.h` and `math3d.cpp` in the `/shared` folder. This 3d math library (referred to for now on simply as math3d) will greatly simplify many tasks in this chapter and the ones to come. One "useful" feature of this library is that it lacks incredibly clever and highly optimized code! This makes the library highly portable and very easy to understand. You'll also find it has a very OpenGL-like API.

The Transformation Pipeline

To effect the types of transformations described in this chapter, you modify two matrices in particular: the modelview matrix and the projection matrix. Don't worry; OpenGL provides some high-level functions that you can call for these transformations. After you've mastered the basics of the OpenGL API, you will undoubtedly start trying some of the more advanced 3D rendering techniques. Only then will you need to call the lower-level functions that actually set the values contained in the matrices.

The road from raw vertex data to screen coordinates is a long one. Figure 4.7 provides a flowchart of this process. First, your vertex is converted to a 1×4 matrix in which the first three values are the x, y, and z coordinates. The fourth number is a scaling factor that you can apply manually by using the vertex functions that take four values. This is the w coordinate, usually 1.0 by default. You will seldom modify this value directly.

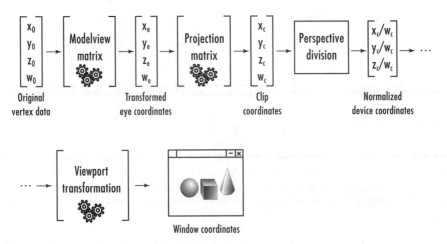

FIGURE 4.7   The vertex transformation pipeline.

The vertex is then multiplied by the modelview matrix, which yields the transformed eye coordinates. The eye coordinates are then multiplied by the projection matrix to yield clip coordinates. OpenGL effectively eliminates all data outside this clipping space. The clip coordinates are then divided by the w coordinate to yield normalized device coordinates. The w value may have been modified by the projection matrix or the modelview matrix, depending on the transformations that occurred. Again, OpenGL and the high-level matrix functions hide this process from you.

Finally, your coordinate triplet is mapped to a 2D plane by the viewport transformation. This is also represented by a matrix, but not one that you specify or modify directly. OpenGL sets it up internally depending on the values you specified to glViewport.

The Modelview Matrix

The modelview matrix is a 4×4 matrix that represents the transformed coordinate system you are using to place and orient your objects. The vertices you provide for your primitives are used as a single-column matrix and multiplied by the modelview matrix to yield new transformed coordinates in relation to the eye coordinate system.

In Figure 4.8, a matrix containing data for a single vertex is multiplied by the modelview matrix to yield new eye coordinates. The vertex data is actually four elements with an extra value, w, that represents a scaling factor. This value is set by default to 1.0, and rarely will you change it yourself.

$$\begin{bmatrix} X \\ Y \\ Z \\ W \end{bmatrix} \begin{bmatrix} 4 \times 4 \\ M \end{bmatrix} = \begin{bmatrix} X_e \\ Y_e \\ Z_e \\ W_e \end{bmatrix}$$

FIGURE 4.8   A matrix equation that applies the modelview transformation to a single vertex.

Translation

Let's consider an example that modifies the modelview matrix. Say you want to draw a cube using the GLUT library's `glutWireCube` function. You simply call

```
glutWireCube(10.0f);
```

A cube that measures 10 units on a side is then centered at the origin. To move the cube up the y-axis by 10 units before drawing it, you multiply the modelview matrix by a matrix that describes a translation of 10 units up the y-axis and then do your drawing. In skeleton form, the code looks like this:

```
// Construct a translation matrix for positive 10 Y
...

// Multiply it by the modelview matrix
...

// Draw the cube
glutWireCube(10.0f);
```

Actually, such a matrix is fairly easy to construct, but it requires quite a few lines of code. Fortunately, OpenGL provides a high-level function that performs this task for you:

```
void glTranslatef(GLfloat x, GLfloat y, GLfloat z);
```

This function takes as parameters the amount to translate along the x, y, and z directions. It then constructs an appropriate matrix and multiplies it onto the current matrix stack. The pseudocode looks like the following, and the effect is illustrated in Figure 4.9:

```
// Translate up the y-axis 10 units
glTranslatef(0.0f, 10.0f, 0.0f);

// Draw the cube
glutWireCube(10.0f);
```

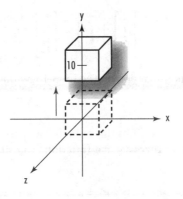

FIGURE 4.9   A cube translated 10 units in the positive y direction.

IS TRANSLATION ALWAYS A MATRIX OPERATION?

The studious reader may note that translations do not always require a full matrix multiplication, but can be simplified with a simple scalar addition to the vertex position. However, for more complex transformations that include combined simultaneous operations, it is correct to describe translation as a matrix operation. Fortunately, if you let OpenGL do the heavy lifting for you, as we have done here, the implementation can usually figure out the optimum method to use.

Rotation

To rotate an object about one of the three coordinate axes, or indeed any arbitrary vector, you have to devise a rotation matrix. Again, a high-level function comes to the rescue:

```
glRotatef(GLfloat angle, GLfloat x, GLfloat y, GLfloat z);
```

Here, we perform a rotation around the vector specified by the *x*, *y*, and *z* arguments. The angle of rotation is in the counterclockwise direction measured in degrees and specified by the argument *angle*. In the simplest of cases, the rotation is around only one of the coordinate systems cardinal axes (X, Y, or Z).

You can also perform a rotation around an arbitrary axis by specifying x, y, and z values for that vector. To see the axis of rotation, you can just draw a line from the origin to the point represented by (x,y,z). The following code rotates the cube by 45° around an arbitrary axis specified by (1,1,1), as illustrated in Figure 4.10:

```
// Perform the transformation
glRotatef(45.0f, 1.0f, 1.0f, 1.0f);

// Draw the cube
glutWireCube(10.0f);
```

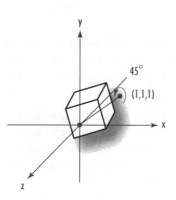

FIGURE 4.10   A cube rotated about an arbitrary axis.

Scaling

A scaling transformation changes the size of your object by expanding or contracting all the vertices along the three axes by the factors specified. The function

```
glScalef(GLfloat x, GLfloat y, GLfloat z);
```

multiplies the *x*, *y*, and *z* values by the scaling factors specified.

Scaling does not have to be uniform, and you can use it to both stretch and squeeze objects along different directions. For example, the following code produces a cube that is twice as large along the x- and z-axes as the cubes discussed in the previous examples, but still the same along the y-axis. The result is shown in Figure 4.11.

```
// Perform the scaling transformation
glScalef(2.0f, 1.0f, 2.0f);

// Draw the cube
glutWireCube(10.0f);
```

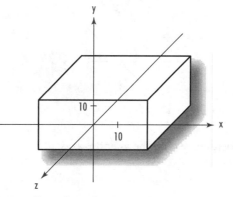

FIGURE 4.11   A nonuniform scaling of a cube.

The Identity Matrix

About now, you might be wondering why we had to bother with all this matrix stuff in the first place. Can't we just call these transformation functions to move our objects around and be done with it? Do we really need to know that it is the modelview matrix that is modified?

The answer is yes and no (but it's no only if you are drawing a single object in your scene). The reason is that the effects of these functions are cumulative. Each time you call one, the appropriate matrix is constructed and multiplied by the current modelview matrix. The new matrix then becomes the current modelview matrix, which is then multiplied by the next transformation, and so on.

Suppose you want to draw two spheres—one 10 units up the positive y-axis and one 10 units out the positive x-axis, as shown in Figure 4.12. You might be tempted to write code that looks something like this:

```
// Go 10 units up the y-axis
glTranslatef(0.0f, 10.0f, 0.0f);

// Draw the first sphere
glutSolidSphere(1.0f,15,15);

// Go 10 units out the x-axis
glTranslatef(10.0f, 0.0f, 0.0f);

// Draw the second sphere
glutSolidSphere(1.0f);
```

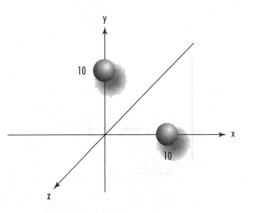

FIGURE 4.12   Two spheres drawn on the y- and x-axes.

Consider, however, that each call to glTranslate is cumulative on the modelview matrix, so the second call translates 10 units in the positive x direction from the previous translation in the y direction. This yields the results shown in Figure 4.13.

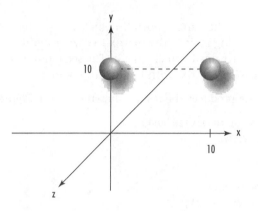

FIGURE 4.13 The result of two consecutive translations.

You can make an extra call to glTranslate to back down the y-axis 10 units in the negative direction, but this makes some complex scenes difficult to code and debug—not to mention that you throw extra transformation math at the CPU or GPU. A simpler method is to reset the modelview matrix to a known state—in this case, centered at the origin of the eye coordinate system.

You reset the origin by loading the modelview matrix with the *identity matrix*. The identity matrix specifies that no transformation is to occur, in effect saying that all the coordinates you specify when drawing are in eye coordinates. An identity matrix contains all 0s, with the exception of a diagonal row of 1s. When this matrix is multiplied by any vertex matrix, the result is that the vertex matrix is unchanged. Figure 4.14 shows this equation. Later in the chapter, we discuss in more detail why these numbers are where they are.

$$\begin{bmatrix} 8.0 \\ 4.5 \\ -2.0 \\ 1.0 \end{bmatrix} \begin{bmatrix} 1.0 & 0 & 0 & 0 \\ 0 & 1.0 & 0 & 0 \\ 0 & 0 & 1.0 & 0 \\ 0 & 0 & 0 & 1.0 \end{bmatrix} = \begin{bmatrix} 8.0 \\ 4.5 \\ -2.0 \\ 1.0 \end{bmatrix}$$

FIGURE 4.14 Multiplying a vertex by the identity matrix yields the same vertex matrix.

As we've already stated, the details of performing matrix multiplication are outside the scope of this book. For now, just remember this: Loading the identity matrix means that no transformations are performed on the vertices. In essence, you are resetting the modelview matrix to the origin.

The following two lines load the identity matrix into the modelview matrix:

```
glMatrixMode(GL_MODELVIEW);
glLoadIdentity();
```

The first line specifies that the current operating matrix is the modelview matrix. After you set the current operating matrix (the matrix that your matrix functions are affecting), it remains the active matrix until you change it. The second line loads the current matrix (in this case, the modelview matrix) with the identity matrix.

Now, the following code produces the results shown earlier in Figure 4.12:

```
// Set current matrix to modelview and reset
glMatrixMode(GL_MODELVIEW);
glLoadIdentity();

// Go 10 units up the y-axis
glTranslatef(0.0f, 10.0f, 0.0f);

// Draw the first sphere
glutSolidSphere(1.0f, 15, 15);

// Reset modelview matrix again
glLoadIdentity();

// Go 10 units out the x-axis
glTranslatef(10.0f, 0.0f, 0.0f);

// Draw the second sphere
glutSolidSphere(1.0f, 15, 15);
```

The Matrix Stacks

Resetting the modelview matrix to identity before placing every object is not always desirable. Often, you want to save the current transformation state and then restore it after some objects have been placed. This approach is most convenient when you have initially transformed the modelview matrix as your viewing transformation (and thus are no longer located at the origin).

To facilitate this procedure, OpenGL maintains a *matrix stack* for both the modelview and projection matrices. A matrix stack works just like an ordinary program stack. You can push the current matrix onto the stack with `glPushMatrix` to save it and then make your changes to the current matrix. Popping the matrix off the stack with `glPopMatrix` then restores it. Figure 4.15 shows the stack principle in action.

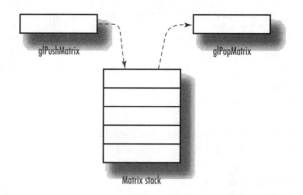

FIGURE 4.15   The matrix stack in action.

TEXTURE MATRIX STACK

The texture stack is another matrix stack available to you. You use it to transform texture coordinates. Chapter 8, "Texture Mapping: The Basics," examines texture mapping and texture coordinates and contains a discussion of the texture matrix stack.

The stack depth can reach a maximum value that you can retrieve with a call to either

```
glGet(GL_MAX_MODELVIEW_STACK_DEPTH);
```

or

```
glGet(GL_MAX_PROJECTION_STACK_DEPTH);
```

If you exceed the stack depth, you get a GL_STACK_OVERFLOW error; if you try to pop a matrix value off the stack when there is none, you generate a GL_STACK_UNDERFLOW error. The stack depth is implementation dependent. For the Microsoft software implementation, the values are 32 for the modelview and 2 for the projection stack.

A Nuclear Example

Let's put to use what we have learned. In the next example, we build a crude, animated model of an atom. This atom has a single sphere at the center to represent the nucleus and three electrons in orbit about the atom. We use an orthographic projection, as we have in all the examples so far in this book.

Our ATOM program uses the GLUT timer callback mechanism (discussed in Chapter 2, "Using OpenGL") to redraw the scene about 10 times per second. Each time the RenderScene function is called, the angle of revolution about the nucleus is incremented. Also, each electron lies in a different plane. Listing 4.1 shows the RenderScene function for this example, and the output from the ATOM program is shown in Figure 4.16.

LISTING 4.1   RenderScene Function from ATOM Sample Program

```
// Called to draw scene
void RenderScene(void)
{
    // Angle of revolution around the nucleus
    static GLfloat fElect1 = 0.0f;

    // Clear the window with current clearing color
    glClear(GL_COLOR_BUFFER_BIT | GL_DEPTH_BUFFER_BIT);

    // Reset the modelview matrix
    glMatrixMode(GL_MODELVIEW);
    glLoadIdentity();


    // Translate the whole scene out and into view
    // This is the initial viewing transformation
    glTranslatef(0.0f, 0.0f, -100.0f);

    // Red Nucleus

    glColor3ub(255, 0, 0);
    glutSolidSphere(10.0f, 15, 15);

    // Yellow Electrons

    glColor3ub(255,255,0);

    // First Electron Orbit
    // Save viewing transformation
    glPushMatrix();

    // Rotate by angle of revolution
    glRotatef(fElect1, 0.0f, 1.0f, 0.0f);

    // Translate out from origin to orbit distance
    glTranslatef(90.0f, 0.0f, 0.0f);

    // Draw the electron
    glutSolidSphere(6.0f, 15, 15);

    // Restore the viewing transformation
    glPopMatrix();
```

LISTING 4.1   Continued

```
// Second Electron Orbit
glPushMatrix();
glRotatef(45.0f, 0.0f, 0.0f, 1.0f);
glRotatef(fElect1, 0.0f, 1.0f, 0.0f);
glTranslatef(-70.0f, 0.0f, 0.0f);
glutSolidSphere(6.0f, 15, 15);
glPopMatrix();


// Third Electron Orbit
glPushMatrix();
glRotatef(360.0f, -45.0f, 0.0f, 0.0f, 1.0f);
glRotatef(fElect1, 0.0f, 1.0f, 0.0f);
glTranslatef(0.0f, 0.0f, 60.0f);
glutSolidSphere(6.0f, 15, 15);
glPopMatrix();


// Increment the angle of revolution
fElect1 += 10.0f;
if(fElect1 > 360.0f)
    fElect1 = 0.0f;

// Show the image
glutSwapBuffers();
}
```

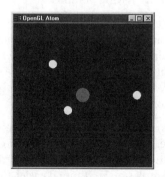

FIGURE 4.16   Output from the ATOM sample program.

Let's examine the code for placing one of the electrons, a couple of lines at a time. The first line saves the current modelview matrix by pushing the current transformation on the stack:

```
// First Electron Orbit
// Save viewing transformation
glPushMatrix();
```

Now the coordinate system appears to be rotated around the y-axis by an angle, `fElect1`:

```
// Rotate by angle of revolution
glRotatef(fElect1, 0.0f, 1.0f, 0.0f);
```

The electron is drawn by translating down the newly rotated coordinate system:

```
// Translate out from origin to orbit distance
    glTranslatef(90.0f, 0.0f, 0.0f);
```

Then the electron is drawn (as a solid sphere), and we restore the modelview matrix by popping it off the matrix stack:

```
// Draw the electron
    glutSolidSphere(6.0f, 15, 15);

    // Restore the viewing transformation
    glPopMatrix();
```

The other electrons are placed similarly.

Using Projections

In our examples so far, we have used the modelview matrix to position our vantage point of the viewing volume and to place our objects therein. The projection matrix actually specifies the size and shape of our viewing volume.

Thus far in this book, we have created a simple parallel viewing volume using the function `glOrtho`, setting the near and far, left and right, and top and bottom clipping coordinates. In OpenGL, when the projection matrix is loaded with the identity matrix, the diagonal line of 1s specifies that the clipping planes extend from the origin to +1 or –1 in all directions. The projection matrix by itself does no scaling or perspective adjustments unless you load a perspective projection matrix.

The next two sample programs, ORTHO and PERSPECT, are not covered in detail from the standpoint of their source code. These examples use lighting and shading that we haven't covered yet to help highlight the differences between an orthographic and a perspective projection. These interactive samples make it much easier for you to see firsthand how the projection can distort the appearance of an object. If possible, you should run these examples while reading the next two sections.

Orthographic Projections

The orthographic projection that we have used for most of this book so far is square on all sides. The logical width is equal at the front, back, top, bottom, left, and right sides. This produces a parallel projection, which is useful for drawings of specific objects that do not have any foreshortening when viewed from a distance. This is good for 2D graphics such as text, or architectural drawings for which you want to represent the exact dimensions and measurements onscreen.

Figure 4.17 shows the output from the sample program ORTHO in this chapter's subdirectory in the source distribution. To produce this hollow, tubelike box, we used an orthographic projection just as we did for all our previous examples. Figure 4.18 shows the same box rotated more to the side so you can see how long it actually is.

FIGURE 4.17   A hollow square tube shown with an orthographic projection.

FIGURE 4.18   A side view showing the length of the square tube.

In Figure 4.19, you're looking directly down the barrel of the tube. Because the tube does not converge in the distance, this is not an entirely accurate view of how such a tube appears in real life. To add some perspective, we must use a perspective projection.

FIGURE 4.19   Looking down the barrel of the tube.

Perspective Projections

A perspective projection performs perspective division to shorten and shrink objects that are farther away from the viewer. The width of the back of the viewing volume does not have the same measurements as the front of the viewing volume after being projected to the screen. Thus, an object of the same logical dimensions appears larger at the front of the viewing volume than if it were drawn at the back of the viewing volume.

The picture in our next example is of a geometric shape called a *frustum*. A frustum is a truncated section of a pyramid viewed from the narrow end to the broad end. Figure 4.20 shows the frustum, with the observer in place.

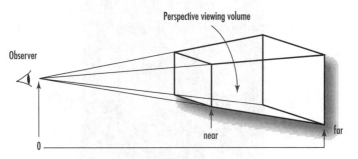

FIGURE 4.20   A perspective projection defined by a frustum.

You can define a frustum with the function glFrustum. Its parameters are the coordinates and distances between the front and back clipping planes. However, glFrustum is not as intuitive about setting up your projection to get the desired effects, and is typically used for more specialized purposes (for example, stereo, tiles, asymmetric view volumes). The utility function gluPerspective is easier to use and somewhat more intuitive for most purposes:

```
void gluPerspective(GLdouble fovy, GLdouble aspect,
                    GLdouble zNear, GLdouble zFar);
```

Parameters for the gluPerspective function are a field-of-view angle in the vertical direction, the aspect ratio of the width to height, and the distances to the near and far clipping planes (see Figure 4.21). You find the aspect ratio by dividing the width (w) by the height (h) of the window or viewport.

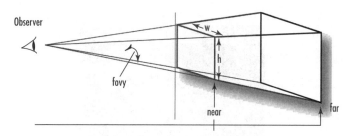

FIGURE 4.21   The frustum as defined by gluPerspective.

Listing 4.2 shows how we change our orthographic projection from the previous examples to use a perspective projection. Foreshortening adds realism to our earlier orthographic projections of the square tube (see Figures 4.22, 4.23, and 4.24). The only substantial change we made for our typical projection code in Listing 4.2 was substituting the call to gluOrtho2D with gluPerspective.

FIGURE 4.22   The square tube with a perspective projection.

FIGURE 4.23 A side view with foreshortening.

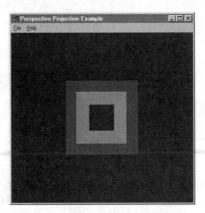

FIGURE 4.24 Looking down the barrel of the tube with perspective added.

LISTING 4.2 Setting Up the Perspective Projection for the PERSPECT Sample Program

```
// Change viewing volume and viewport.  Called when window is resized
void ChangeSize(GLsizei w, GLsizei h)
    {
    GLfloat fAspect;

    // Prevent a divide by zero
    if(h == 0)
        h = 1;

    // Set viewport to window dimensions
    glViewport(0, 0, w, h);
```

LISTING 4.2   Continued

```
fAspect = (GLfloat)w/(GLfloat)h;

// Reset coordinate system
glMatrixMode(GL_PROJECTION);
glLoadIdentity();

// Produce the perspective projection
gluPerspective(60.0f, fAspect, 1.0, 400.0);

glMatrixMode(GL_MODELVIEW);
glLoadIdentity();
}
```

We made the same changes to the ATOM example in ATOM2 to add perspective. Run the two side by side, and you see how the electrons appear to be smaller as they swing far away behind the nucleus.

A Far-Out Example

For a more complete example showing modelview manipulation and perspective projections, we have modeled the sun and the earth/moon system in revolution in the SOLAR sample program. This is a classic example of nested transformations with objects being transformed relative to one another using the matrix stack. We have enabled some lighting and shading for drama so that you can more easily see the effects of our operations. You'll learn about shading and lighting in the next two chapters.

In our model, the earth moves around the sun, and the moon revolves around the earth. A light source is placed at the center of the sun, which is drawn without lighting to make it appear to be the glowing light source. This powerful example shows how easily you can produce sophisticated effects with OpenGL.

Listing 4.3 shows the code that sets up the projection and the rendering code that keeps the system in motion. A timer elsewhere in the program triggers a window redraw 10 times a second to keep the RenderScene function in action. Notice in Figures 4.25 and 4.26 that when the earth appears larger, it's on the near side of the sun; on the far side, it appears smaller.

LISTING 4.3   Code That Produces the Sun/Earth/Moon System

```
// Change viewing volume and viewport.  Called when window is resized
void ChangeSize(GLsizei w, GLsizei h)
    {
    GLfloat fAspect;
```

LISTING 4.3   Continued

```
    // Prevent a divide by zero
    if(h == 0)
        h = 1;

    // Set viewport to window dimensions
    glViewport(0, 0, w, h);

    // Calculate aspect ratio of the window
    fAspect = (GLfloat)w/(GLfloat)h;

    // Set the perspective coordinate system
    glMatrixMode(GL_PROJECTION);
    glLoadIdentity();

    // Field of view of 45 degrees, near and far planes 1.0 and 425
    gluPerspective(45.0f, fAspect, 1.0, 425.0);

    // Modelview matrix reset
    glMatrixMode(GL_MODELVIEW);
    glLoadIdentity();
    }

// Called to draw scene
void RenderScene(void)
    {
    // Earth and moon angle of revolution
    static float fMoonRot = 0.0f;
    static float fEarthRot = 0.0f;

    // Clear the window with current clearing color
    glClear(GL_COLOR_BUFFER_BIT | GL_DEPTH_BUFFER_BIT);

    // Save the matrix state and do the rotations
    glMatrixMode(GL_MODELVIEW);
    glPushMatrix();

    // Translate the whole scene out and into view
    glTranslatef(0.0f, 0.0f, -300.0f);

    // Set material color, to yellow
    // Sun
    glColor3ub(255, 255, 0);
```

LISTING 4.3 Continued

```
glDisable(GL_LIGHTING);
glutSolidSphere(15.0f, 15, 15);
glEnable(GL_LIGHTING);

// Position the light after we draw the Sun!
glLightfv(GL_LIGHT0,GL_POSITION,lightPos);

// Rotate coordinate system
glRotatef(fEarthRot, 0.0f, 1.0f, 0.0f);

// Draw the earth
glColor3ub(0,0,255);
glTranslatef(105.0f,0.0f,0.0f);
glutSolidSphere(15.0f, 15, 15);


// Rotate from Earth-based coordinates and draw moon
glColor3ub(200,200,200);
glRotatef(fMoonRot,0.0f, 1.0f, 0.0f);
glTranslatef(30.0f, 0.0f, 0.0f);
fMoonRot+= 15.0f;
if(fMoonRot > 360.0f)
    fMoonRot = 0.0f;

glutSolidSphere(6.0f, 15, 15);


// Restore the matrix state
glPopMatrix();     // Modelview matrix


// Step Earth orbit 5 degrees
fEarthRot += 5.0f;
if(fEarthRot > 360.0f)
    fEarthRot = 0.0f;

// Show the image
glutSwapBuffers();
}
```

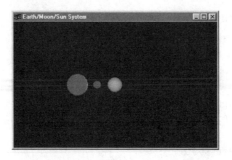

FIGURE 4.25   The sun/earth/moon system with the earth on the near side.

FIGURE 4.26   The sun/earth/moon system with the earth on the far side.

Advanced Matrix Manipulation

These higher-level "canned" transformations (for rotation, scaling, and translation) are great for many simple transformation problems. Real power and flexibility, however, are afforded to those who take the time to understand using matrices directly. Doing so is not as hard as it sounds, but first you need to understand the magic behind those 16 numbers that make up a 4×4 transformation matrix.

OpenGL represents a 4×4 matrix not as a two-dimensional array of floating-point values, but as a single array of 16 floating-point values. This approach is different from many math libraries, which do take the two-dimensional array approach. For example, OpenGL prefers the first of these two examples:

```
GLfloat matrix[16];        // Nice OpenGL friendly matrix
GLfloat matrix[4][4];      // Popular, but not as efficient for OpenGL
```

OpenGL can use the second variation, but the first is a more efficient representation. The reason for this will become clear in a moment. These 16 elements represent the 4×4 matrix, as shown in Figure 4.27. When the array elements traverse down the matrix columns one by one, we call this *column-major matrix ordering*. In memory, the 4×4 approach of the two-dimensional array (the second option in the preceding code) is laid out in a *row-major order*. In math terms, the two orientations are the *transpose* of one another.

$$\begin{bmatrix} a_0 & a_4 & a_8 & a_{12} \\ a_1 & a_5 & a_9 & a_{13} \\ a_2 & a_6 & a_{10} & a_{14} \\ a_3 & a_7 & a_{11} & a_{15} \end{bmatrix}$$

FIGURE 4.27   Column-major matrix ordering.

The real magic lies in the fact that these 16 values represent a particular position in space and an orientation of the three axes with respect to the eye coordinate system (remember that fixed, unchanging coordinate system we talked about earlier). Interpreting these numbers is not hard at all. The four columns each represent a four-element vector. To keep things simple for this book, we focus our attention on just the first three elements of these vectors. The fourth column vector contains the x, y, and z values of the transformed coordinate system's origin. When you call glTranslate on the identity matrix, all it does is put your values for x, y, and z in the 12th, 13th, and 14th position of the matrix.

The first three elements of the first three columns are just directional vectors that represent the orientation (vectors here are used to represent a direction) of the x-, y-, and z-axes in space. For most purposes, these three vectors are always at 90° angles from each other, and are usually each of unit length (unless you are also applying a scale or shear). The mathematical term for this (in case you want to impress your friends) is *orthonormal* when the vectors are unit length, and *orthogonal* when they are not. Figure 4.28 shows the 4×4 transformation matrix with the column vectors highlighted. Notice that the last row of the matrix is all 0s with the exception of the very last element, which is 1.

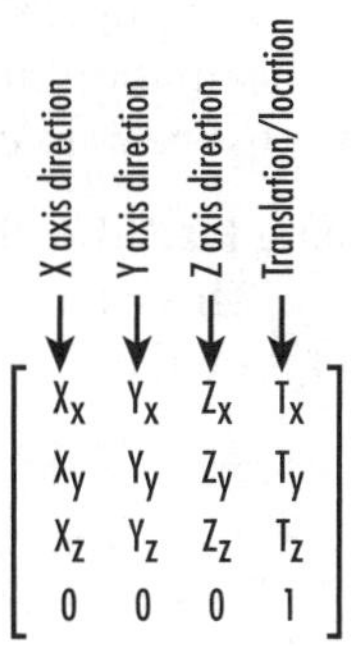

$$\begin{array}{cccc} \text{X axis direction} & \text{Y axis direction} & \text{Z axis direction} & \text{Translation/location} \\ \downarrow & \downarrow & \downarrow & \downarrow \end{array}$$

$$\begin{bmatrix} X_x & Y_x & Z_x & T_x \\ X_y & Y_y & Z_y & T_y \\ X_z & Y_z & Z_z & T_z \\ 0 & 0 & 0 & 1 \end{bmatrix}$$

FIGURE 4.28   How a 4×4 matrix represents a position and orientation in 3D space.

The most amazing thing is that if you have a 4×4 matrix that contains the position and orientation of a different coordinate system, and you multiply a vertex (as a column matrix or vector) by this matrix, the result is a new vertex that has been transformed to the new coordinate system. This means that any position in space and any desired orientation can be uniquely defined by a 4×4 matrix, and if you multiply all of an object's vertices by this matrix, you transform the entire object to the given location and orientation in space!

HARDWARE TRANSFORMATIONS

Most OpenGL implementations have what is called *hardware transform and lighting*. This means that the transformation matrix multiplies many thousands of vertices on special graphics hardware that performs this operation very, very fast. (Intel and AMD can eat their hearts out!) However, functions such as `glRotate` and `glScale`, which create transformation matrices for you, are usually not hardware accelerated because typically they represent an exceedingly small fraction of the enormous amount of matrix math that must be done to draw a scene.

Loading a Matrix

After you have a handle on the way the 4×4 matrix represents a given location and orientation, you may to want to compose and load your own transformation matrices. You can load an arbitrary column-major matrix into the projection, modelview, or texture matrix stacks by using the following function:

```
glLoadMatrixf(GLfloat m);
```

or

```
glLoadMatrixd(GLfloat m);
```

Most OpenGL implementations store and manipulate pipeline data as floats and not doubles; consequently, using the second variation may incur some performance penalty because 16 double-precision numbers must be converted into single-precision floats.

The following code shows an array being loaded with the identity matrix and then being loaded into the modelview matrix stack. This example is equivalent to calling `glLoadIdentity` using the higher-level functions:

```
// Load an identity matrix
GLfloat m[] = { 1.0f, 0.0f, 0.0f, 0.0f,      // X Column
                0.0f, 1.0f, 0.0f, 0.0f,      // Y Column
                0.0f, 0.0f, 1.0f, 0.0f,      // Z Column
                0.0f, 0.0f, 0.0f, 1.0f };    // Translation

glMatrixMode(GL_MODELVIEW);
glLoadMatrixf(m);
```

Although OpenGL implementations use column-major ordering, OpenGL (versions 1.2 and later) does provide functions to load a matrix in row-major ordering. The following two functions perform the transpose operation on the matrix when loading it on the matrix stack:

```
void glLoadTransposeMatrixf(Glfloat* m);
```

and

```
void glLoadTransposeMatrixd(Gldouble* m);
```

Performing Your Own Transformations

Let's look at an example now that shows how to create and load your own transformation matrix—the hard way! In the sample program TRANSFORM, we draw a *torus* (a doughnut-shaped object) in front of our viewing location and make it rotate in place. The function DrawTorus does the necessary math to generate the torus's geometry and takes as an argument a 4×4 transformation matrix to be applied to the vertices. We create the matrix and apply the transformation manually to each vertex to transform the torus. Let's start with the main rendering function in Listing 4.4.

LISTING 4.4   Code to Set Up the Transformation Matrix While Drawing

```
void RenderScene(void)
    {
    M3DMatrix44f    transformationMatrix;   // Storage for rotation matrix
    static GLfloat yRot = 0.0f;          // Rotation angle for animation
    yRot += 0.5f;

    // Clear the window with current clearing color
    glClear(GL_COLOR_BUFFER_BIT | GL_DEPTH_BUFFER_BIT);

    // Build a rotation matrix
    m3dRotationMatrix44(transformationMatrix, m3dDegToRad(yRot),
                                        0.0f, 1.0f, 0.0f);
    transformationMatrix[12] = 0.0f;
    transformationMatrix[13] = 0.0f;
    transformationMatrix[14] = -2.5f;

    DrawTorus(transformationMatrix);

    // Do the buffer Swap
    glutSwapBuffers();
    }
```

We begin by declaring storage for the matrix here:

```
M3DMatrix44f    transformationMatrix;    // Storage for rotation matrix
```

The data type `M3DMatrix44f` is of our own design and is simply a `typedef` declared in `math3d.h` for a floating-point array 16 elements long:

```
typedef GLfloat M3DMatrix44f[16];       // A column major 4x4 matrix of type GLfloat
```

The animation in this sample works by continually incrementing the variable `yRot` that represents the rotation around the y-axis. After clearing the color and depth buffer, we compose our transformation matrix as follows:

```
m3dRotationMatrix44(transformationMatrix, m3dDegToRad(yRot), 0.0f, 1.0f, 0.0f);
transformationMatrix[12] = 0.0f;
transformationMatrix[13] = 0.0f;
transformationMatrix[14] = -2.5f;
```

Here, the first line contains a call to another `math3d` function, `m3dRotationMatrix44`. This function takes a rotation angle in radians (for more efficient calculations) and three arguments specifying a vector around which you want the rotation to occur. The macro function `m3dDegToRad` does an in-place conversion from degrees to radians. With the exception of the angle being in radians instead of degrees, this is almost exactly like the OpenGL function `glRotate`. The first argument is a matrix into which you want to store the resulting rotation matrix.

As you saw in Figure 4.28, the last column of the matrix represents the translation of the transformation. Rather than do a full matrix multiplication, we can simply inject the desired translation directly into the matrix. Now the resulting matrix represents both a translation in space (a location to place the torus) and then a rotation of the object's coordinate system applied at that location.

Next, we pass this transformation matrix to the `DrawTorus` function. We do not need to list the entire function to create a torus here, but focus your attention to these lines:

```
objectVertex[0] = x0*r;
objectVertex[1] = y0*r;
objectVertex[2] = z;
m3dTransformVector3(transformedVertex, objectVertex, mTransform);
glVertex3fv(transformedVertex);
```

The three components of the vertex are loaded into an array and passed to the function `m3dTransformVector3`. This `math3d` function performs the multiplication of the vertex against the matrix and returns the transformed vertex in the array `transformedVertex`. We then use the vector version of `glVertex` and send the vertex data down to OpenGL. The result is a spinning torus, as shown in Figure 4.29.

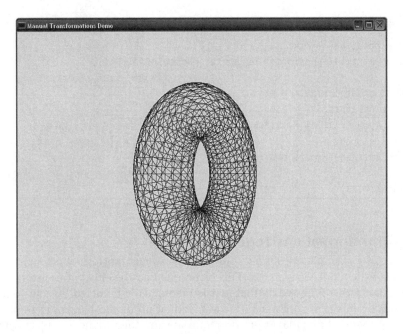

FIGURE 4.29   The spinning torus, doing our own transformations.

It is important that you see at least once the real mechanics of how vertices are transformed by a matrix using such a drawn-out example. As you progress as an OpenGL programmer, you will find that the need to transform points manually will arise for tasks that are not specifically related to rendering operations, such as collision detection (bumping into objects), frustum culling (throwing away and not drawing things you can't see), and some other special effects algorithms.

For geometry processing, however, the TRANSFORM sample program is very inefficient, despite its instructional value. We are letting the CPU do all the matrix math instead of letting OpenGL's dedicated hardware do the work for us (which is much faster than the CPU!). In addition, because OpenGL has the modelview matrix, all our transformed points are being multiplied yet again by the identity matrix. This does not change the value of our transformed vertices, but it is still a wasted operation.

For the sake of completeness, we provide an improved example, TRANSFORMGL, that instead uses our transformation matrix but hands it over to OpenGL using the function `glLoadMatrixf`. We eliminate our `DrawTorus` function with its dedicated transformation code and use a more general-purpose torus drawing function, `gltDrawTorus`, from the glTools library. The relevant code is shown in Listing 4.5.

LISTING 4.5   Loading the Transformation Matrix Directly into OpenGL

```
// Build a rotation matrix
m3dRotationMatrix44(transformationMatrix, m3dDegToRad(yRot),
                                          0.0f, 1.0f, 0.0f);

transformationMatrix[12] = 0.0f;
transformationMatrix[13] = 0.0f;
transformationMatrix[14] = -2.5f;


glLoadMatrixf(transformationMatrix);


gltDrawTorus(0.35, 0.15, 40, 20);
```

Adding Transformations Together

In the preceding example, we simply constructed a single transformation matrix and loaded it into the modelview matrix. This technique had the effect of transforming any and all geometry that followed by that matrix before being rendered. As you've seen in the previous examples, we often add one transformation to another. For example, we used glTranslate followed by glRotate to first translate and then rotate an object before being drawn. Behind the scenes, when you call multiple transformation functions, OpenGL performs a matrix multiplication between the existing transformation matrix and the one you are adding or appending to it. For example, in the TRANSFORMGL example, we might replace the code in Listing 4.5 with something like the following:

```
glPushMatrix();
        glTranslatef(0.0f, 0.0f, -2.5f);
        glRotatef(yRot, 0.0f, 1.0f, 0.0f);

        gltDrawTorus(0.35, 0.15, 40, 20);
glPopMatrix();
```

Using this approach has the effect of saving the current identity matrix, multiplying the translation matrix, multiplying the rotation matrix, and then transforming the torus by the result. You can do these multiplications yourself by using the math3d function m3dMatrixMultiply, as shown here:

```
M3DMatrix44f rotationMatrix, translationMatrix, transformationMatrix;
...
m3dRotationMatrix44(rotationMatrix, m3dDegToRad(yRot), 0.0f, 1.0f, 0.0f);
m3dTranslationMatrix44(translationMatrix, 0.0f, 0.0f, -2.5f);
m3dMatrixMultiply44(transformationMatrix, translationMatrix, rotationMatrix);
glLoadMatrixf(transformationMatrix);

gltDrawTorus(0.35f, 0.15f, 40, 20);
```

OpenGL also has its own matrix multiplication function, glMultMatrix, that takes a matrix and multiplies it by the currently loaded matrix and stores the result at the top of the matrix stack. In our final code fragment, we once again show code equivalent to the preceding, but this time we let OpenGL do the actual multiplication:

```
M3DMatrix44f rotationMatrix, translationMatrix, transformationMatrix;
...
glPushMatrix();
    m3dRotationMatrix44(rotationMatrix, m3dDegToRad(yRot), 0.0f, 1.0f, 0.0f);
    gltTranslationMatrix44(translationMatrix, 0.0f, 0.0f, -2.5f);

    glMultMatrixf(translationMatrix);
    glMultMatirxf(rotationMatrix);

    gltDrawTorus(0.35f, 0.15f, 40, 20);
glPopMatrix();
```

As you can see, there is considerable flexibility in how you handle model transformations. Using the OpenGL functions allows you to offload as much as possible to the graphics hardware. Using your own functions gives you ultimate control over any intermediate steps. The freedom to mix and match approaches as needed is another reason OpenGL is an extremely powerful and flexible API for doing 3D graphics.

Moving Around in OpenGL Using Cameras and Actors

To represent a location and orientation of any object in your 3D scene, you can use a single 4×4 matrix that represents its transform. Working with matrices directly, however, can still be somewhat awkward, so programmers have always sought ways to represent a position and orientation in space more succinctly. Fixed objects such as terrain are often untransformed, and their vertices usually specify exactly where the geometry should be drawn in space. Objects that move about in the scene are often called *actors*, paralleling the idea of actors on a stage.

Actors have their own transformations, and often other actors are transformed not only with respect to the world coordinate system (eye coordinates), but also with respect to other actors. Each actor with its own transformation is said to have its own frame of reference, or local object coordinate system. It is often useful to translate between local and world coordinate systems and back again for many nonrendering-related geometric tests.

An Actor Frame

A simple and flexible way to represent a frame of reference is to use a data structure (or class in C++) that contains a position in space, a vector that points forward, and a vector that points upward. Using these quantities, you can uniquely identify a given position and orientation in space. The following class, GLFrame, makes use of the math3d library, and stores this information all in one place:

```
class GLFrame
    {
    protected:
        M3DVector3f vLocation;
        M3DVector3f vUp;
        M3DVector3f vForward;

    public:
    . . .
    };
```

Using a frame of reference such as this to represent an object's position and orientation is a very powerful mechanism. To begin with, you can use this data directly to create a 4×4 transformation matrix. Referring to Figure 4.28, the up vector becomes the y column of the matrix, whereas the forward-looking vector becomes the z column vector and the position is the translation column vector. This leaves only the x column vector, and because we know that all three axes are unit length and perpendicular to one another (orthonormal), we can calculate the x column vector by performing the cross product of the y and z vectors. Listing 4.6 shows the GLFrame method GetMatrix, which does exactly that.

LISTING 4.6   Code to Derive a 4×4 Matrix from a Frame

```
/////////////////////////////////////////////////////////////////////
// Derives a 4x4 transformation matrix from a frame of reference
void GLFrame::GetMatrix(M3DTMatrix44f mMatrix, bool bRotationOnly = false)
    {
    // Calculate the right side (x) vector, drop it right into the matrix
    M3DVector3f vXAxis;
    m3dCrossProduct(vXAxis, vUp, vForward);

    // Set matrix column does not fill in the fourth value...
    m3dSetMatrixColumn44(matrix, vXAxis, 0);
    matrix[3] = 0.0f;

    // Y Column
    m3dSetMatrixColumn44(matrix, vUp, 1);
    matrix[7] = 0.0f;

    // Z Column
    m3dSetMatrixColumn44(matrix, vForward, 2);
    matrix[11] = 0.0f;
```

LISTING 4.6   Continued

```
// Translation (already done)
if(bRotationOnly == true)
    {
    matrix[12] = 0.0f;
    matrix[13] = 0.0f;
    matrix[14] = 0.0f;
    }
else
    m3dSetMatrixColumn44(matrix, vOrigin, 3);

matrix[15] = 1.0f;
    }
```

Applying an actor's transform is as simple as calling `glMultMatrixf` with the resulting matrix.

Euler Angles: "Use the Frame, Luke!"

Many graphics programming books recommend an even simpler mechanism for storing an object's position and orientation: Euler angles. Euler angles require less space because you essentially store an object's position and then just three angles—representing a rotation around the x-, y-, and z-axes—sometimes called *yaw, pitch, and roll.* A structure like this might represent an airplane's location and orientation:

```
struct EULER {
    M3DVector3f  vPosition;
    GLfloat      fRoll;
    GLfloat      fPitch;
    GLfloat      fYaw;
    };
```

Euler angles are a bit slippery and are sometimes called "oily angles" by some in the industry. The first problem is that a given position and orientation can be represented by more than one set of Euler angles. Having multiple sets of angles can lead to problems as you try to figure out how to smoothly move from one orientation to another. Occasionally, a second problem called "gimbal lock" comes up; this problem makes it impossible to achieve a rotation around one of the axes. Lastly, Euler angles make it more tedious to calculate new coordinates for simply moving forward along your line of sight or trying to figure out new Euler angles if you want to rotate around one of your own local axes.

Some literature today tries to solve the problems of Euler angles by using a mathematical tool called *quaternions*. Quaternions, which can be difficult to understand, really don't solve any problems with Euler angles that you can't solve on your own by just using the frame of reference method covered previously. We already promised that this book would not get too heavy on the math, so we will not debate the merits of each system here. But we should say that the quaternion versus linear algebra (matrix) debate is more than 100 years old and by far predates their application to computer graphics!

Camera Management

There is really no such thing as a camera transformation in OpenGL. We use the camera as a useful metaphor to help us manage our point of view in some sort of immersive 3D environment. If we envision a camera as an object that has some position in space and some given orientation, we find that our current frame of reference system can represent both actors and our camera in a 3D environment.

To apply a camera transformation, we take the camera's actor transform and flip it so that moving the camera backward is equivalent to moving the whole world forward. Similarly, turning to the left is equivalent to rotating the whole world to the right. To render a given scene, we usually take the approach outlined in Figure 4.30.

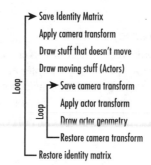

FIGURE 4.30   Typical rendering loop for a 3D environment.

The OpenGL utility library contains a function that uses the same data we stored in our frame structure to create our camera transformation:

```
void gluLookAt(GLdouble eyex, GLdouble eyey, GLdouble eyez,
        GLdouble centerx, GLdouble centery, GLdouble centerz,
        GLdouble upx, GLdouble upy, GLdouble upz);
```

This function takes the position of the eye point, a point directly in front of the eye point, and the direction of the up vector. The `GLFrame` class also contains a shortcut function that performs the equivalent action using its internal frame of reference:

```
void GLFrame::ApplyCameraTransform(bool bRotOnly = false);
```

The GLFrame class has the added flexibility that you can apply the camera's rotation transform only. The C++ default parameter shown here allows you to ignore this unless you have some special need for this feature.

Bringing It All Together

Now let's work through one final example for this chapter to bring together all the concepts we have discussed so far. In the sample program SPHEREWORLD, we create a world populated by a number of spheres (Sphere World) placed at random locations on the ground. Each sphere is represented by an individual GLFrame class instance for its location and orientation. We also use the frame to represent a camera that can be moved about Sphere World using the keyboard arrow keys. In the middle of Sphere World, we use the simpler high-level transformation routines to draw a spinning torus with another sphere in orbit around it.

This example combines all the ideas we have discussed thus far and shows them working together. In addition to the main source file sphereworld.cpp, the project also includes the gltools.cpp, math3d.cpp, and glframe.h modules from the \shared folder. We do not provide the entire listing here because it uses the same GLUT framework as all the other samples, but the important functions are shown in Listing 4.7.

LISTING 4.7   Main Functions for the SPHEREWORLD Sample

```
#define NUM_SPHERES       50
GLFrame     spheres[NUM_SPHERES];
GLFrame     frameCamera;


/////////////////////////////////////////////////////////////////
// This function does any needed initialization on the rendering
// context.
void SetupRC()
    {
    int iSphere;

    // Bluish background
    glClearColor(0.0f, 0.0f, .50f, 1.0f );

    // Draw everything as wire frame
    glPolygonMode(GL_FRONT_AND_BACK, GL_LINE);

    // Randomly place the sphere inhabitants
    for(iSphere = 0; iSphere < NUM_SPHERES; iSphere++)
        {
        // Pick a random location between -20 and 20 at .1 increments
        float x = ((float)((rand() % 400) - 200) * 0.1f);
```

LISTING 4.7   Continued

```
            float z = (float)((rand() % 400) - 200) * 0.1f;
            spheres[iSphere].SetOrigin(x, 0.0f, z);
            }
        }


///////////////////////////////////////////////////////////
// Draw a gridded ground
void DrawGround(void)
    {
    GLfloat fExtent = 20.0f;
    GLfloat fStep = 1.0f;
    GLfloat y = -0.4f;
    GLint iLine;

    glBegin(GL_LINES);
        for(iLine = -fExtent; iLine <= fExtent; iLine += fStep)
            {
            glVertex3f(iLine, y, fExtent);     // Draw Z lines
            glVertex3f(iLine, y, -fExtent);

            glVertex3f(fExtent, y, iLine);
            glVertex3f(-fExtent, y, iLine);
            }

    glEnd();
    }


// Called to draw scene
void RenderScene(void)
    {
    int i;
    static GLfloat yRot = 0.0f;          // Rotation angle for animation
    yRot += 0.5f;

    // Clear the window with current clearing color
    glClear(GL_COLOR_BUFFER_BIT | GL_DEPTH_BUFFER_BIT);

    glPushMatrix();
        frameCamera.ApplyCameraTransform();
```

LISTING 4.7   Continued

```
        // Draw the ground
        DrawGround();

        // Draw the randomly located spheres
        for(i = 0; i < NUM_SPHERES; i++)
            {
            glPushMatrix();
            spheres[i].ApplyActorTransform();
            glutSolidSphere(0.1f, 13, 26);
            glPopMatrix();
            }

        glPushMatrix();
            glTranslatef(0.0f, 0.0f, -2.5f);

            glPushMatrix();
                glRotatef(-yRot * 2.0f, 0.0f, 1.0f, 0.0f);
                glTranslatef(1.0f, 0.0f, 0.0f);
                glutSolidSphere(0.1f, 13, 26);
            glPopMatrix();

            glRotatef(yRot, 0.0f, 1.0f, 0.0f);
            gltDrawTorus(0.35, 0.15, 40, 20);
        glPopMatrix();
    glPopMatrix();

    // Do the buffer Swap
    glutSwapBuffers();
    }




// Respond to arrow keys by moving the camera frame of reference
void SpecialKeys(int key, int x, int y)
    {
    if(key == GLUT_KEY_UP)
        frameCamera.MoveForward(0.1f);

    if(key == GLUT_KEY_DOWN)
        frameCamera.MoveForward(-0.1f);

    if(key == GLUT_KEY_LEFT)
```

LISTING 4.7   Continued

```
        frameCamera.RotateLocalY(0.1f);

    if(key == GLUT_KEY_RIGHT)
        frameCamera.RotateLocalY(-0.1f);

    // Refresh the Window
    glutPostRedisplay();
    }
```

The first few lines contain a macro to define the number of spherical inhabitants as 50. Then we declare an array of frames and another frame to represent the camera:

```
#define NUM_SPHERES      50
GLFrame     spheres[NUM_SPHERES];
GLFrame     frameCamera;
```

The GLFrame class has a constructor that initializes the camera or actor as being at the origin and pointing down the negative z-axis (the OpenGL default viewing orientation).

The SetupRC function contains a loop that initializes the array of sphere frames and selects a random x and z location for their positions:

```
// Randomly place the sphere inhabitants
for(iSphere = 0; iSphere < NUM_SPHERES; iSphere++)
    {
    // Pick a random location between -20 and 20 at .1 increments
    float x = ((float)((rand() % 400) - 200) * 0.1f);
    float z = (float)((rand() % 400) - 200) * 0.1f;
    spheres[iSphere].SetOrigin(x, 0.0f, z);
    }
```

The DrawGround function then draws the ground as a series of crisscross grids using a series of GL_LINE segments:

```
///////////////////////////////////////////////////////////
// Draw a gridded ground
void DrawGround(void)
    {
    GLfloat fExtent = 20.0f;
    GLfloat fStep = 1.0f;
    GLfloat y = -0.4f;
    GLint iLine;
```

```
glBegin(GL_LINES);
    for(iLine = -fExtent; iLine <= fExtent; iLine += fStep)
        {
        glVertex3f(iLine, y, fExtent);      // Draw Z lines
        glVertex3f(iLine, y, -fExtent);

        glVertex3f(fExtent, y, iLine);
        glVertex3f(-fExtent, y, iLine);
        }

glEnd();
    }
```

The RenderScene function draws the world from our point of view. Note that we first save the identity matrix and then apply the camera transformation using the GLFrame member function ApplyCameraTransform. The ground is static and is transformed by the camera only to appear that you are moving over it:

```
glPushMatrix();
    frameCamera.ApplyCameraTransform();

        // Draw the ground
        DrawGround();
```

Then we draw each of the randomly located spheres. The ApplyActorTransform member function creates a transformation matrix from the frame of reference and multiplies it by the current matrix (which is the camera matrix). Each sphere must have its own transform relative to the camera, so the camera is saved each time with a call to glPushMatrix and restored again with glPopMatrix to get ready for the next sphere or transformation:

```
// Draw the randomly located spheres
for(i = 0; i < NUM_SPHERES; i++)
    {
    glPushMatrix();
    spheres[i].ApplyActorTransform();
    glutSolidSphere(0.1f, 13, 26);
    glPopMatrix();
    }
```

Now for some fancy footwork! First, we move the coordinate system a little farther down the z-axis so that we can see what we are going to draw next. We save this location and then perform a rotation, followed by a translation and the drawing of a sphere. This effect makes the sphere appear to revolve around the origin in front of us. We then restore our transformation matrix, but only so that the location of the origin is z = –2.5. Then another rotation is performed before the torus is drawn. This has the effect of making a torus that spins in place:

```
glPushMatrix();
    glTranslatef(0.0f, 0.0f, -2.5f);

    glPushMatrix();
        glRotatef(-yRot * 2.0f, 0.0f, 1.0f, 0.0f);
        glTranslatef(1.0f, 0.0f, 0.0f);
        glutSolidSphere(0.1f, 13, 26);
    glPopMatrix();

    glRotatef(yRot, 0.0f, 1.0f, 0.0f);
    gltDrawTorus(0.35, 0.15, 40, 20);
glPopMatrix();
glPopMatrix();
```

The total effect is that we see a grid on the ground with many spheres scattered about at random locations. Out in front, we see a spinning torus, with a sphere moving rapidly in orbit around it. Figure 4.31 shows the result.

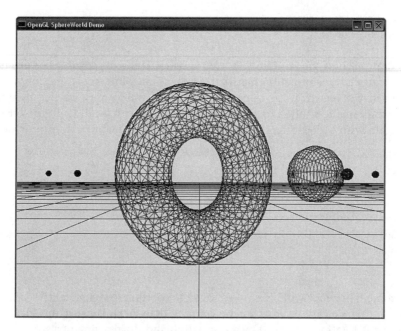

FIGURE 4.31   The output from the SPHEREWORLD program.

Finally, the `SpecialKeys` function is called whenever one of the arrow keys is pressed. The up- and down-arrow keys call the `glTools` function `gltMoveFrameForward`, which simply moves the frame forward along its line of sight. The `gltRotateFrameLocalY` function rotates a frame of reference around its local y-axis (regardless of orientation) in response to the left- and right-arrow keys:

```
void SpecialKeys(int key, int x, int y)
    {
    if(key == GLUT_KEY_UP)
        frameCamera.MoveForward(0.1f);

    if(key == GLUT_KEY_DOWN)
        frameCamera.MoveForward(-0.1f);

    if(key == GLUT_KEY_LEFT)
        frameCamera.RotateLocalY(0.1f);

    if(key == GLUT_KEY_RIGHT)
        frameCamera.RotateLocalY(-0.1f);

    // Refresh the Window
    glutPostRedisplay();
    }
```

A NOTE ON KEYBOARD POLLING

Moving the camera in response to keystroke messages can sometimes result in less than the smoothest possible animation. The reason is that the keyboard repeat rate is usually no more than about 20 times per second. For best results, you should render at least 30 frames per second (with 60 being more optimal) and poll the keyboard once for each frame of animation. Doing this with a portability library like GLUT is somewhat tricky, but in the OS-specific chapters later in this book, we will cover ways to achieve the smoothest possible animation and methods to best create time-based animation instead of the frame-based animation (moving by a fixed amount each time the scene is redrawn) done here.

Summary

In this chapter, you learned concepts crucial to using OpenGL for creation of 3D scenes. Even if you can't juggle matrices in your head, you now know what matrices are and how they are used to perform the various transformations. You also learned how to manipulate the modelview and projection matrix stacks to place your objects in the scene and to determine how they are viewed onscreen.

We also showed you the functions needed to perform your own matrix magic, if you are so inclined. These functions allow you to create your own matrices and load them onto the matrix stack or multiply them by the current matrix first. The chapter also introduced the powerful concept of a frame of reference, and you saw how easy it is to manipulate frames and convert them into transformations.

Finally, we began to make more use of the glTools and math3d libraries that accompany this book. These libraries are written entirely in portable C++ and provide you with a handy toolkit of miscellaneous math and helper routines that can be used along with OpenGL.

CHAPTER 5

Color, Materials, and Lighting: The Basics

by Richard S. Wright Jr.

WHAT YOU'LL LEARN IN THIS CHAPTER:

How To	Functions You'll Use
Specify a color in terms of RGB components	glColor
Set the shading model	glShadeModel
Set the lighting model	glLightModel
Set lighting parameters	glLight
Set material reflective properties	glColorMaterial/glMaterial
Use surface normals	glNormal

This is the chapter where 3D graphics really start to look interesting (unless you really dig wireframe models!), and it only gets better from here. You've been learning OpenGL from the ground up—how to put programs together and then how to assemble objects from primitives and manipulate them in 3D space. Until now, we've been laying the foundation, and you still can't tell what the house is going to look like! To recoin a phrase, "Where's the beef?"

To put it succinctly, the beef starts here. For most of the rest of this book, science takes a back seat and magic rules. According to Arthur C. Clarke, "Any sufficiently advanced technology is indistinguishable from magic." Of course, there is no real magic involved in color and lighting, but it sure can seem that way at times. If you want to dig into the "sufficiently advanced technology" (mathematics), see Appendix A, "Further Reading/References."

Another name for this chapter might be "Adding Realism to Your Scenes." You see, there is more to an object's color in the real world than just what color we might tell OpenGL to make it. In addition to having a color, objects can appear shiny or dull or can even glow with their own light. An object's apparent color varies with bright or dim lighting, and even the color of the light hitting an object makes a difference. An illuminated object can even be shaded across its surface when lit or viewed from an angle.

What Is Color?

First, let's talk a little bit about color itself. How is a color made in nature, and how do we see colors? Understanding color theory and how the human eye sees a color scene will lend some insight into how you create a color programmatically. (If color theory is old hat to you, you can probably skip this section.)

Light as a Wave

Color is simply a wavelength of light that is visible to the human eye. If you had any physics classes in school, you might remember something about light being both a wave and a particle. It is modeled as a wave that travels through space much like a ripple through a pond, and it is modeled as a particle, such as a raindrop falling to the ground. If this concept seems confusing, you know why most people don't study quantum mechanics!

The light you see from nearly any given source is actually a mixture of many different kinds of light. These kinds of light are identified by their wavelengths. The wavelength of light is measured as the distance between the peaks of the light wave, as illustrated in Figure 5.1.

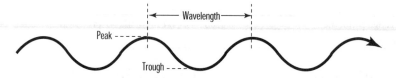

FIGURE 5.1   How a wavelength of light is measured.

Wavelengths of visible light range from 390 nanometers (one billionth of a meter) for violet light to 720 nanometers for red light; this range is commonly called the *visible spectrum*. You've undoubtedly heard the terms *ultraviolet* and *infrared*; they represent light not visible to the naked eye, lying beyond the ends of the spectrum. You will recognize the spectrum as containing all the colors of the rainbow (see Figure 5.2).

FIGURE 5.2   The spectrum of visible light.

Light as a Particle

"Okay, Mr. Smart Brain," you might ask. "If color is a wavelength of light and the only visible light is in this 'rainbow' thing, where is the brown for my Fig Newtons or the black for my coffee or even the white of this page?" We begin answering that question by telling you that black is not a color, nor is white. Actually, black is the absence of color, and white is an even combination of all the colors at once. That is, a white object reflects all wavelengths of colors evenly, and a black object absorbs all wavelengths evenly.

As for the brown of those fig bars and the many other colors that you see, they are indeed colors. Actually, at the physical level, they are composite colors. They are made of varying amounts of the "pure" colors found in the spectrum. To understand how this concept works, think of light as a particle. Any given object when illuminated by a light source is struck by "billions and billions" (my apologies to the late Carl Sagan) of photons, or tiny light particles. Remembering our physics mumbo jumbo, each of these photons is also a wave, which has a wavelength and thus a specific color in the spectrum.

All physical objects consist of atoms. The reflection of photons from an object depends on the kinds of atoms, the number of each kind, and the arrangement of atoms (and their electrons) in the object. Some photons are reflected and some are absorbed (the absorbed photons are usually converted to heat), and any given material or mixture of materials (such as your fig bar) reflects more of some wavelengths than others. Figure 5.3 illustrates this principle.

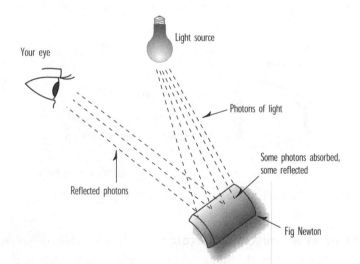

FIGURE 5.3   An object reflects some photons and absorbs others.

Your Personal Photon Detector

The reflected light from your fig bar, when seen by your eye, is interpreted as color. The billions of photons enter your eye and are focused onto the back of your eye, where your retina acts as sort of a photographic plate. The retina's millions of cone cells are excited when struck by the photons, and this causes neural energy to travel to your brain, which interprets the information as light and color. The more photons that strike the cone cells, the more excited they get. This level of excitation is interpreted by your brain as the brightness of the light, which makes sense; the brighter the light, the more photons there are to strike the cone cells.

The eye has three kinds of cone cells. All of them respond to photons, but each kind responds most to a particular wavelength. One is more excited by photons that have reddish wavelengths; one, by green wavelengths; and one, by blue wavelengths. Thus, light that is composed mostly of red wavelengths excites red-sensitive cone cells more than the other cells, and your brain receives the signal that the light you are seeing is mostly reddish. You do the math: A combination of different wavelengths of various intensities will, of course, yield a mix of colors. All wavelengths equally represented thus are perceived as white, and no light of any wavelength is black.

You can see that any "color" that your eye perceives actually consists of light all over the visible spectrum. The "hardware" in your eye detects what it sees in terms of the relative concentrations and strengths of red, green, and blue light. Figure 5.4 shows how brown is composed of a photon mix of 60% red photons, 40% green photons, and 10% blue photons.

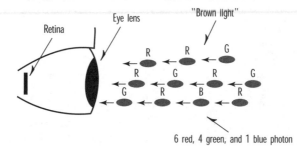

FIGURE 5.4   How the "color" brown is perceived by the eye.

The Computer as a Photon Generator

Now that you understand how the human eye discerns colors, it makes sense that when you want to generate a color with a computer, you do so by specifying separate intensities for the red, green, and blue components of the light. It so happens that color computer monitors are designed to produce three kinds of light (can you guess which three?), each with varying degrees of intensity. For years the CRT (Cathode Ray Tube) reigned supreme. In the back of these computer monitors is an electron gun that shoots electrons at the back of the screen. This screen contains phosphors that emit red, green, and blue light when struck by the electrons. The intensity of the light emitted varies with the intensity of the electron beam. These three color phosphors are packed closely together to make up a single physical dot on the screen (see Figure 5.5).

A few hold-outs still prefer the CRT technology over LCD (Liquid Crystal Display) for various reasons, such as higher refresh rate. LCDs work in a similar way by combining three colors of light, except they are solid state. Each pixel on your LCD screen has a light behind it and three very small computer-controlled polarized (red, green, and blue) filters. Basic LCD technology is based on the polarization of light, and blocking that light with the LCD material electronically. A huge technological achievement to be sure, but it still all boils down to very crowded tiny dots emitting red, green, and blue light.

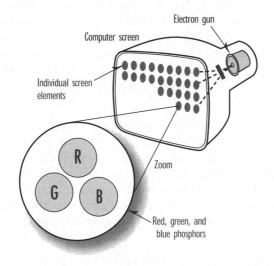

FIGURE 5.5   How a computer monitor generates colors.

You might recall that in Chapter 2, "Using OpenGL," we explained how OpenGL defines a color exactly as intensities of red, green, and blue, with the glColor command.

PC Color Hardware

There once was a time (actually, 1982) when state-of-the-art PC graphics hardware meant the Hercules graphics card. This card could produce bitmapped images with a resolution of 720×348, and crisper text than the original IBM Monochrome Display Adapter (MDA) developed for the original IBM PC. The drawback was that each pixel had only two states: on and off. At that time, bitmapped graphics of any kind on a PC were a big deal, and you could produce some great monochrome graphics—even 3D!

Actually predating the Hercules card by one year was the Color Graphics Adapter (CGA) card. Also introduced with the first IBM PC, this card could support resolutions of 320×200 pixels and could place any 4 of 16 colors on the screen at once. A higher resolution (640×200) with 2 colors was also possible but wasn't as effective or cost conscious as the Hercules card. (Color monitors = $$$.) CGA was puny by today's standards; it was even outmatched by the graphics capabilities of a $200 Commodore 64 or Atari home computer at the time. Lacking adequate resolution for business graphics or even modest modeling, CGA was used primarily for simple PC games or business applications that could benefit from colored text. Generally, it was hard to make a good business justification for this more expensive hardware.

The next big breakthrough for PC graphics came in 1984 when IBM introduced the Enhanced Graphics Adapter (EGA) card. This one could do more than 25 lines of colored text in new text modes, and for graphics, it could support 640×350-pixel bitmapped graphics in 16 colors! Other technical improvements eliminated some flickering problems of the CGA ancestor and provided for better and smoother animation. Now arcade-style games, real business graphics, and even simple 3D graphics became not only possible but even reasonable on the PC. This advance was a giant move beyond CGA, but still PC graphics were in their infancy.

The last mainstream PC graphics standard set by IBM was the VGA card (which stood for Video Graphics Array rather than the commonly held Video Graphics Adapter), introduced in 1987. This card was significantly faster than the EGA; it could support 16 colors at a higher resolution (640×480) and 256 colors at a lower resolution of 320×200. These 256 colors were selected from a palette of more than 16 million possible colors. That's when the floodgates opened for PC graphics. Near photo-realistic graphics became possible on PCs. Ray tracers, 3D games, and photo-editing software began to pop up in the PC market.

IBM, as well, had a high-end graphics card—the 8514—, introduced in 1987 for its "workstations." This card could do 1,024×768 graphics at 256 colors, and came with a whopping one megabyte of memory! IBM thought this card would be used only by CAD and scientific applications! But one thing is certain about consumers: They always want more. It was this short-sightedness that cost IBM its role as standard setter in the PC graphics market. Other vendors began to ship "Super-VGA" cards that could display higher and higher resolutions, with more and more colors. First, we saw 800×600, then 1,024×768 and even higher, with first 256 colors, and then 32,000, and 65,000. Today, 32-bit color cards can display 16 million colors at resolutions far greater than 1,024×768. Even entry-level Windows PCs sold today can support at least 16 million colors at resolutions of 1,024×768 or more.

All this power makes for some really cool possibilities—photo-realistic 3D graphics, to name just one. When Microsoft ported OpenGL to the Windows platform, that move enabled creation of high-end graphics applications for PCs. Combine today's fast

PC Display Modes   179

processors with 3D-graphics accelerated graphics cards, and you can get the kind of performance possible only a few years ago on $100,000 graphics workstations—for the cost of a Wal-Mart Christmas special! Today's typical home machines are capable of sophisticated simulations, games, and more. Already the term *virtual reality* has become as antiquated as those old Buck Rogers rocket ships as we begin to take advanced 3D graphics for granted.

PC Display Modes

Microsoft Windows and the Apple Macintosh revolutionized the world of PC graphics in two respects. First, they created mainstream graphical operating environments that were adopted by the business world at large and, soon thereafter, the consumer market. Second, they made PC graphics significantly easier for programmers to do. The graphics hardware was "virtualized" by display device drivers. Instead of having to write instructions directly to the video hardware, programmers today can write to a single API (such as OpenGL), and the operating system handles the specifics of talking to the hardware.

Screen Resolution

Screen resolution for today's computers can vary from 640×480 pixels up to 1,600×1,200 or more. The lower resolutions of, say, 640×480 are considered adequate for some graphics display tasks; people with eye problems often run at the lower resolutions, but on a large monitor or display. You must always take into account the size of the window with the clipping volume and viewport settings (see Chapter 2). By scaling the size of the drawing to the size of the window, you can easily account for the various resolutions and window size combinations that can occur. Well-written graphics applications display the same approximate image regardless of screen resolution. The user should automatically be able to see more and sharper details as the resolution increases.

Color Depth

If an increase in screen resolution or in the number of available drawing pixels in turn increases the detail and sharpness of the image, so too should an increase in available colors improve the clarity of the resulting image. An image displayed on a computer that can display millions of colors should look remarkably better than the same image displayed with only 16 colors.

Bang the Rocks Together!

The most primitive display modes you may ever encounter are the 4-bit (16-color) and 8-bit (256-color) modes. These modes do rarely show up, but only as the base display mode when you first install an operating system without any specific graphics card drivers. At one time, these depths were the "new hotness," but these modes are useless by today's standards for graphics applications and can be safely ignored.

Going Deeper

Typical consumer graphics hardware today comes in three flavors: 16, 24, and 32 bits per pixel. The 16-bit display modes are available on many shipping graphics cards today, but are rarely used on purpose. This mode supports 65,536 different colors, and consumes less memory for the color buffer than the higher bit depth modes. Many graphics applications have very noticeable visual artifacts (usually in color gradations) at this color depth. The 24- and 32-bit display modes support 8 bits of color per color component, allowing more than 16 million colors onscreen at a time.

Nearly all 3D graphics hardware today supports 32-bit color mode. This allows for 8 bits per RGBA color channel. Visually, there is no real difference between 24- and 32-bit display modes. A graphics card that reserves 32 bits per pixel does so for one of two reasons. First, most memory architectures perform faster with each pixel occupying exactly 4 bytes instead of 3. Second, the extra 8 bits per pixel can be used to store an alpha value in the color buffer. This alpha value can be used for some graphics operations. You'll learn more about uses for alpha in the next chapter.

In Chapter 18, "Advanced Buffers," you'll learn about OpenGL's support for the most cutting-edge color technology: floating-point color buffers.

Using Color in OpenGL

You now know that OpenGL specifies an exact color as separate intensities of red, green, and blue components. You also know that modern PC hardware might be able to display nearly all these combinations or only a very few. How, then, do we specify a desired color in terms of these red, green, and blue components?

The Color Cube

Because a color is specified by three positive color values, we can model the available colors as a volume that we call the *RGB colorspace*. Figure 5.6 shows what this colorspace looks like at the origin with red, green, and blue as the axes. The red, green, and blue coordinates are specified just like x, y, and z coordinates. At the origin (0,0,0), the relative intensity of each component is zero, and the resulting color is black. The maximum available on the PC for storage information is 24 bits, so with 8 bits for each component, let's say that a value of 255 along the axis represents full saturation of that component. We then end up with a cube measuring 255 on each side. The corner directly opposite black, where the concentrations are (0,0,0), is white, with relative concentrations of (255,255,255). At full saturation (255) from the origin along each axis lie the pure colors of red, green, and blue.

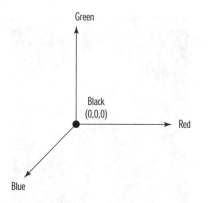

FIGURE 5.6   The origin of RGB colorspace.

This "color cube" (see Figure 5.7) contains all the possible colors, either on the surface of the cube or within the interior of the cube. For example, all possible shades of gray between black and white lie internally on the diagonal line between the corner at (0,0,0) and the corner at (255,255,255).

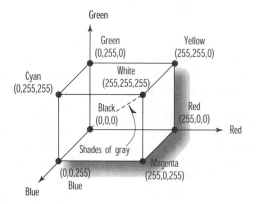

FIGURE 5.7   The RGB colorspace.

Figure 5.8 shows the smoothly shaded color cube produced by a sample program from this chapter, CCUBE. The surface of this cube shows the color variations from black on one corner to white on the opposite corner. Red, green, and blue are present on their corners 255 units from black. Additionally, the colors yellow, cyan, and magenta have corners showing the combination of the other three primary colors. You can also spin the color cube around to examine all its sides by pressing the arrow keys.

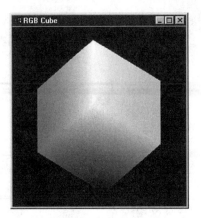

FIGURE 5.8   The output from CCUBE is this color cube.

Setting the Drawing Color

Let's briefly review the glColor function. It is prototyped as follows:

```
void glColor<x><t>(red, green, blue, alpha);
```

In the function name, the *<x>* represents the number of arguments; it might be 3 for three arguments of red, green, and blue or 4 for four arguments to include the alpha component. The alpha component specifies the translucency of the color and is covered in more detail in the next chapter. For now, just use a three-argument version of the function.

The *<t>* in the function name specifies the argument's data type and can be b, d, f, i, s, ub, ui, or us, for byte, double, float, integer, short, unsigned byte, unsigned integer, and unsigned short data types, respectively. Another version of the function has a v appended to the end; this version takes an array that contains the arguments (the v stands for vectored). In Appendix C, "API Reference," you will find an entry with more details on the glColor function.

Most OpenGL programs that you'll see use glColor3f and specify the intensity of each component as 0.0 for none or 1.0 for full intensity. However, it might be easier, if you have Windows programming experience, to use the glColor3ub version of the function. This version takes three unsigned bytes, from 0 to 255, to specify the intensities of red, green, and blue. Using this version of the function is like using the Windows RGB macro to specify a color:

```
glColor3ub(0,255,128) = RGB(0,255,128)
```

In fact, this approach might make it easier for you to match your OpenGL colors to existing RGB colors used by your program for other non-OpenGL drawing tasks. However, we should say that, internally, OpenGL represents color values as floating-point values, and you may incur some performance penalties due to the constant conversion to floats that must take place at runtime. It is also possible that in the future, higher resolution color buffers may evolve (in fact, floating-point color buffers are already starting to appear), and your color values specified as floats will be more faithfully represented by the color hardware.

Shading

Our previous working definition for glColor was that this function sets the current drawing color, and all objects drawn after this command have the last color specified. After discussing the OpenGL drawing primitives in a preceding chapter, we can now expand this definition as follows: The glColor function sets the current color that is used for all vertices drawn after the command. So far, all our examples have drawn wireframe objects or solid objects with each face a different solid color. If we specify a different color for each vertex of a primitive (point, line, or polygon), what color is the interior?

Let's answer this question first regarding points. A point has only one vertex, and whatever color you specify for that vertex is the resulting color for that point. Easy enough.

A line, however, has two vertices, and each can be set to a different color. The color of the line depends on the shading model. Shading is simply defined as the smooth transition from one color to the next. Any two points in the RGB colorspace (refer to Figure 5.7) can be connected by a straight line.

Smooth shading causes the colors along the line to vary as they do through the color cube from one color point to the other. Figure 5.9 shows the color cube with the black and white corners identified. Below it is a line with two vertices, one black and one white. The colors selected along the length of the line match the colors along the straight line in the color cube, from the black to the white corners. This results in a line that progresses from black through lighter shades of gray and eventually to white.

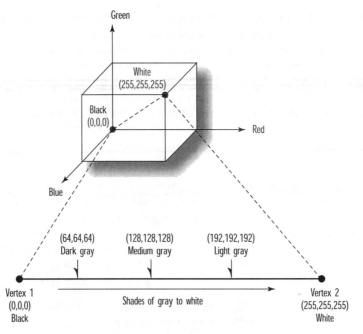

FIGURE 5.9   How a line is shaded from black to white.

You can do shading mathematically by finding the equation of the line connecting two points in the three-dimensional RGB colorspace. Then you can simply loop through from one end of the line to the other, retrieving coordinates along the way to provide the color of each pixel on the screen. Many good books on computer graphics explain the algorithm to accomplish this effect, scale your color line to the physical line on the screen, and so on. Fortunately, OpenGL does all this work for you!

The shading exercise becomes slightly more complex for polygons. A triangle, for instance, can also be represented as a plane within the color cube. Figure 5.10 shows a triangle with each vertex at full saturation for the red, green, and blue color components. The code to display this triangle is shown in Listing 5.1 and in the sample program titled TRIANGLE.

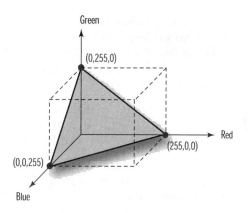

FIGURE 5.10   A triangle in RGB colorspace.

LISTING 5.1   Drawing a Smooth-Shaded Triangle with Red, Green, and Blue Corners

```
// Enable smooth shading
glShadeModel(GL_SMOOTH);

// Draw the triangle
glBegin(GL_TRIANGLES);
    // Red Apex
    glColor3ub((GLubyte)255,(GLubyte)0,(GLubyte)0);
    glVertex3f(0.0f,200.0f,0.0f);

    // Green on the right bottom corner
    glColor3ub((GLubyte)0,(GLubyte)255,(GLubyte)0);
    glVertex3f(200.0f,-70.0f,0.0f);

    // Blue on the left bottom corner
    glColor3ub((GLubyte)0,(GLubyte)0,(GLubyte)255);
    glVertex3f(-200.0f, -70.0f, 0.0f);
glEnd();
```

Setting the Shading Model

The first line of Listing 5.1 actually sets the shading model OpenGL uses to do smooth shading—the model we have been discussing. This is the default shading model, but it's a good idea to call this function anyway to ensure that your program is operating the way you intended.

The other shading model that can be specified with `glShadeModel` is `GL_FLAT` for flat shading. *Flat shading* means that no shading calculations are performed on the interior of primitives. Generally, with flat shading, the color of the primitive's interior is the color that was specified for the last vertex. The only exception is for a `GL_POLYGON` primitive, in which case the color is that of the first vertex.

Next, the code in Listing 5.1 sets the top of the triangle to be pure red, the lower-right corner to be green, and the remaining lower-left corner to be blue. Because smooth shading is specified, the interior of the triangle is shaded to provide a smooth transition between each corner.

The output from the TRIANGLE program is shown in Figure 5.11. This output represents the plane shown graphically in Figure 5.10.

FIGURE 5.11   The output from the TRIANGLE program.

Polygons, more complex than triangles, can also have different colors specified for each vertex. In these instances, the underlying logic for shading can become more intricate. Fortunately, you never have to worry about it with OpenGL. No matter how complex your polygon, OpenGL successfully shades the interior points between each vertex.

Color in the Real World

Real objects don't appear in a solid or shaded color based solely on their RGB values. Figure 5.12 shows the output from the program titled JET from the sample code for this chapter. It's a simple jet airplane, hand plotted with triangles using only the methods covered so far in this book. As usual, JET and the other example programs in this chapter allow you to spin the object around by using the arrow keys to better see the effects.

FIGURE 5.12   A simple jet built by setting a different color for each triangle.

The selection of colors is meant to highlight the three-dimensional structure of the jet. Aside from the crude assemblage of triangles, however, you can see that the jet looks hardly anything like a real object. Suppose you constructed a model of this airplane and painted each flat surface the colors represented. The model would still appear glossy or flat depending on the kind of paint used, and the color of each flat surface would vary with the angle of your view and any sources of light.

OpenGL does a reasonably good job of approximating the real world in terms of lighting conditions. To do so, it uses a simple and intuitive lighting model that isn't necessarily based on the physics of real world light. In the OpenGL lighting model, unless an object emits its own light, it is illuminated by three kinds of light: ambient, diffuse, and specular. In the real world, there is of course no such thing. However, for our abstraction of lighting, these three kinds of light allow us to simulate and control the three main kinds of effects that light has when shining on materials.

Ambient Light

Ambient light doesn't come from any particular direction. It has an original source somewhere, but the rays of light have bounced around the room or scene and become directionless. Objects illuminated by ambient light are evenly lit on all surfaces in all directions. You can think of all previous examples in this book as being lit by a bright ambient light because the objects were always visible and evenly colored (or shaded) regardless of their rotation or viewing angle. Figure 5.13 shows an object illuminated by ambient light. You can think of ambient light as a global "brightening" factor applied per light source. In OpenGL, this lighting component really approximates scattered light in the environment that originates from the light source.

FIGURE 5.13   An object illuminated purely by ambient light.

Diffuse Light

The diffuse part of an OpenGL light is the directional component that appears to come from a particular direction and is reflected off a surface with an intensity proportional to the angle at which the light rays strike the surface. Thus, the object surface is brighter if the light is pointed directly at the surface than if the light grazes the surface from a greater angle. Good examples of diffuse light sources include a lamp, candle, or sunlight streaming in a side window at noon. Essentially, it is the diffuse component of a light source that produces the shading (or change in color) across a lit object's surface. In Figure 5.14, the object is illuminated by a diffuse light source.

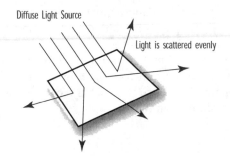
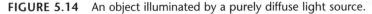

Diffuse Light Source

Light is scattered evenly

FIGURE 5.14   An object illuminated by a purely diffuse light source.

Specular Light

Like diffuse light, specular light is a highly directional property, but it interacts more sharply with the surface and in a particular direction. A highly specular light (really a material property in the real world) tends to cause a bright spot on the surface it shines on, which is called the *specular highlight.* Because of its highly directional nature, it is even possible that depending on a viewer's position, the specular highlight may not even be visible. A spotlight and the sun are good examples of sources that produce strong specular highlights. Figure 5.15 shows an object illuminated by a purely specular light source.

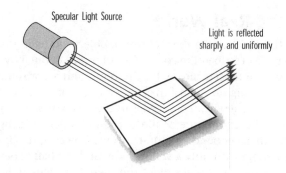

Specular Light Source

Light is reflected
sharply and uniformly

FIGURE 5.15   An object illuminated by a purely specular light source.

Putting It All Together

No single light source is composed entirely of any of the three types of light just described. Rather, it is made up of varying intensities of each. For example, a red laser beam in a lab is composed of almost a pure-red specular component producing a very bright spot where it strikes any object. However, smoke or dust particles scatter the beam all over the room, giving it a very small ambient component. This would produce a slight red hue on other objects in the room. If the beam strikes a surface at a glancing blow, a very small diffuse shading component may be seen across the surface it illuminates (although in this case it would be largely overpowered by the specular highlight).

Thus, a light source in a scene is said to be composed of three lighting components: ambient, diffuse, and specular. Just like the components of a color, each lighting component is defined with an RGBA value that describes the relative intensities of red, green, and blue light that make up that component (for the purposes of light color, the alpha value is ignored). For example, our red laser light might be described by the component values in Table 5.1.

TABLE 5.1   Color and Light Distribution for a Red Laser Light Source

	Red	Green	Blue	Alpha
Specular	0.99	0.0	0.0	1.0
Diffuse	0.10	0.0	0.0	1.0
Ambient	0.05	0.0	0.0	1.0

Note that the red laser beam has no green or blue light. Also, note that specular, diffuse, and ambient light can each range in intensity from 0.0 to 1.0. You could interpret this table as saying that the red laser light in some scenes has a very high specular component, a small diffuse component, and a very small ambient component. Wherever it shines, you are probably going to see a reddish spot. Also, because of conditions in the room, the ambient component—likely due to smoke or dust particles in the air—scatters a tiny bit of light all about the room.

Materials in the Real World

Light is only part of the equation. In the real world, objects do have a color of their own. Earlier in this chapter, we described the color of an object as defined by its reflected wavelengths of light. A blue ball reflects mostly blue photons and absorbs most others. This assumes that the light shining on the ball has blue photons in it to be reflected and detected by the observer. Generally, most scenes in the real world are illuminated by a white light containing an even mixture of all the colors. Under white light, therefore, most objects appear in their proper or "natural" colors. However, this is not always so; put the blue ball in a dark room with only a yellow light, and the ball appears black to the viewer because all the yellow light is absorbed and there is no blue to be reflected.

Material Properties

When we use lighting, we do not describe polygons as having a particular color, but rather as consisting of materials that have certain reflective properties. Instead of saying that a polygon is red, we say that the polygon is made of a material that reflects mostly red light. We are still saying that the surface is red, but now we must also specify the material's reflective properties for ambient, diffuse, and specular light sources. A material might be shiny and reflect specular light very well, while absorbing most of the ambient or diffuse light. Conversely, a flat colored object might absorb all specular light and not look shiny under any circumstances. Another property to be specified is the emission property for objects that emit their own light, such as taillights or glow-in-the-dark watches.

Adding Light to Materials

Setting lighting and material properties to achieve the desired effect takes some practice. There are no color cubes or rules of thumb to give you quick and easy answers. This is the point at which analysis gives way to art, and science yields to magic. When drawing an object, OpenGL decides which color to use for each pixel in the object. That object has reflective "colors," and the light source has "colors" of its own. How does OpenGL determine which colors to use? Understanding these principles is not difficult, but it does take some simple grade-school multiplication. (See, that teacher told you you'd need it one day!)

Each vertex of your primitives is assigned an RGB color value based on the net effect of the ambient, diffuse, and specular illumination multiplied by the ambient, diffuse, and specular reflectance of the material properties. Because you make use of smooth shading between the vertices, the illusion of illumination is achieved.

Calculating Ambient Light Effects

To calculate ambient light effects, you first need to put away the notion of color and instead think only in terms of red, green, and blue intensities. For an ambient light source of half-intensity red, green, and blue components, you have an RGB value for that source of (0.5, 0.5, 0.5). If this ambient light illuminates an object with ambient reflective properties specified in RGB terms of (0.5, 1.0, 0.5), the net "color" component from the ambient light is

(0.5 * 0.5, 0.5 * 1.0, 0.5 * 0.5) = (0.25, 0.5, 0.25)

This is the result of multiplying each of the ambient light source terms by each of the ambient material property terms (see Figure 5.16).

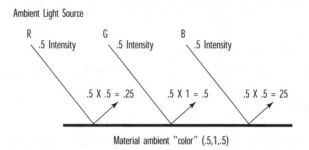

Ambient Light Source

R .5 Intensity   G .5 Intensity   B .5 Intensity

.5 X .5 = .25   .5 X 1 = .5   .5 X .5 = 25

Material ambient "color" (.5,1,.5)

FIGURE 5.16 Calculating the ambient color component of an object.

Thus, the material color components actually determine the percentage of incident light that is reflected. In our example, the ambient light had a red component that was at one-half intensity, and the material ambient property of 0.5 specified that one-half of that one-half intensity light was reflected. Half of a half is a fourth, or 0.25.

Diffuse and Specular Effects

Calculating ambient light is as simple as it gets. Diffuse light also has RGB intensities that interact in the same way with material properties. However, diffuse light is directional, and the intensity at the surface of the object varies depending on the angle between the surface and the light source, the distance to the light source, any attenuation factors (whether it is foggy between the light and the surface), and so on. The same goes for specular light sources and intensities. The net effect in terms of RGB values is figured the same way as for ambient light, with the intensity of the light source (adjusted for the angle of incidence) being multiplied by the material reflectance. Finally, all three RGB terms are added to yield a final color for the object. If any single color component is greater than 1.0, it is clamped to that value. (You can't get more intense than full intensity!)

Generally, the ambient and diffuse components of light sources and materials are the same and have the greatest effect in determining the color of the object. Specular light and material properties tend to be light gray or white. The specular component depends significantly on the angle of incidence, and specular highlights on an object are usually set to white.

Adding Light to a Scene

This text might seem like a lot of theory to digest all of a sudden. Let's slow down and start exploring some examples of the OpenGL code needed for lighting; this exploration will also help reinforce what you've just learned. We demonstrate some additional features and requirements of lighting in OpenGL. The next few examples build on our JET program. The initial version contains no lighting code and just draws triangles with hidden surface elimination (depth testing) enabled. When we're done, the jet's metallic surface will glisten in the sunlight as you rotate it with the arrow keys.

Enabling the Lighting

To tell OpenGL to use lighting calculations, call glEnable with the GL_LIGHTING parameter:

```
glEnable(GL_LIGHTING);
```

This call alone tells OpenGL to use material properties and lighting parameters in determining the color for each vertex in your scene. However, without any specified material properties or lighting parameters, your object remains dark and unlit, as shown in Figure 5.17. Look at the code for any of the JET-based sample programs, and you can see that we have called the function SetupRC right after creating the rendering context. This is the place where we do any initialization of lighting parameters.

FIGURE 5.17   An unlit jet reflects no light.

Setting Up Cosmic Background Radiation

There is a global light source in OpenGL that emits only ambient light. I call this the Cosmic Background Radiation—a term borrowed from the Big Bang theory—because it's a light source that shines evenly in all directions. This global ambient illumination is a zero-cost way to add a simple offset to the results of OpenGL lighting calculations. This can be useful, for example, to illuminate the back sides of objects that are not being illuminated directly by a light source. If your lit scene appears too dark, you can monkey with this ambient light until you get the levels you want.

This global ambient light is set in the OpenGL light model, which can be modified with the glLightModel function.

The first lighting parameter used in our next example (the AMBIENT program) is GL_LIGHT_MODEL_AMBIENT. It lets you specify a global ambient light that illuminates all objects evenly from all sides. The following code specifies a bright white light:

```
// Bright white light - full intensity RGB values
    GLfloat ambientLight[] = { 1.0f, 1.0f, 1.0f, 1.0f };

    // Enable lighting
    glEnable(GL_LIGHTING);

    // Set light model to use ambient light specified by ambientLight[]
    glLightModelfv(GL_LIGHT_MODEL_AMBIENT,ambientLight);
```

The variation of glLightModel shown here, glLightModelfv, takes as its first parameter the lighting model parameter being modified or set and then an array of the RGBA values that make up the light. The default RGBA values of this global ambient light are (0.2, 0.2, 0.2, 1.0), which is fairly dim. Other lighting model parameters allow you to determine whether the front, back, or both sides of polygons are illuminated and how the calculation of specular lighting angles is performed. See the reference section in Appendix C for more information on these parameters.

Setting Material Properties

Now that we have an ambient light source, we need to set some material properties so that our polygons reflect light and we can see our jet. There are two ways to set material properties. The first is to use the function glMaterial before specifying each polygon or set of polygons. Examine the following code fragment:

```
Glfloat gray[] = { 0.75f, 0.75f, 0.75f, 1.0f };
...
...
glMaterialfv(GL_FRONT, GL_AMBIENT_AND_DIFFUSE, gray);

glBegin(GL_TRIANGLES);
    glVertex3f(-15.0f,0.0f,30.0f);
    glVertex3f(0.0f, 15.0f, 30.0f);
    glVertex3f(0.0f, 0.0f, -56.0f);
glEnd();
```

The first parameter to glMaterialfv specifies whether the front, back, or both (GL_FRONT, GL_BACK, or GL_FRONT_AND_BACK) take on the material properties specified. The second parameter tells which properties are being set; in this instance, both the ambient and diffuse reflectances are set to the same values. The final parameter is an array containing the RGBA values that make up these properties. All primitives specified after the glMaterial call are affected by the last values set, until another call to glMaterial is made.

Under most circumstances, the ambient and diffuse components are the same, and unless you want specular highlights (sparkling, shiny spots), you don't need to define specular reflective properties. Even so, it would still be quite tedious if we had to define an array for every color in our object and call glMaterial before each polygon or group of polygons.

Now we are ready for the second and preferred way of setting material properties, called *color tracking*. With color tracking, you can tell OpenGL to set material properties by only calling glColor. To enable color tracking, call glEnable with the GL_COLOR_MATERIAL parameter:

```
glEnable(GL_COLOR_MATERIAL);
```

Then the function glColorMaterial specifies the material parameters that follow the values set by glColor. For example, to set the ambient and diffuse properties of the fronts of polygons to track the colors set by glColor, call

```
glColorMaterial(GL_FRONT,GL_AMBIENT_AND_DIFFUSE);
```

The earlier code fragment setting material properties would then be as follows. This approach looks like more code, but it actually saves many lines of code and executes faster as the number of different colored polygons grows:

```
// Enable color tracking
glEnable(GL_COLOR_MATERIAL);

// Front material ambient and diffuse colors track glColor
glColorMaterial(GL_FRONT,GL_AMBIENT_AND_DIFFUSE);

...
...
glcolor3f(0.75f, 0.75f, 0.75f);
glBegin(GL_TRIANGLES);
    glVertex3f(-15.0f,0.0f,30.0f);
    glVertex3f(0.0f, 15.0f, 30.0f);
    glVertex3f(0.0f, 0.0f, -56.0f);
glEnd();
```

Listing 5.2 contains the code we add with the SetupRC function to our jet example to set up a bright ambient light source and to set the material properties that allow the object to reflect light and be seen. We have also changed the colors of the jet so that each section rather than each polygon is a different color. The final output, shown in Figure 5.18, is not much different from the image before we had lighting. However, if we reduce the ambient light by half, we get the image shown in Figure 5.19. To reduce it by half, we set the ambient light RGBA values to the following:

```
GLfloat ambientLight[] = { 0.5f, 0.5f, 0.5f, 1.0f };
```

You can see how we might reduce the ambient light in a scene to produce a dimmer image. This capability is useful for simulations in which dusk approaches gradually or when a more direct light source is blocked, as when an object is in the shadow of another, larger object.

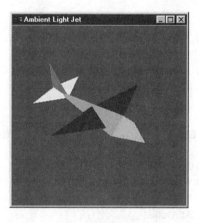

FIGURE 5.18   The output from the completed AMBIENT sample program.

FIGURE 5.19   The output from the AMBIENT program when the light source is cut in half.

LISTING 5.2   Setup for Ambient Lighting Conditions

```
// This function does any needed initialization on the rendering
// context.  Here it sets up and initializes the lighting for
// the scene.
void SetupRC()
    {
    // Light values
    // Bright white light
    GLfloat ambientLight[] = { 1.0f, 1.0f, 1.0f, 1.0f };

    glEnable(GL_DEPTH_TEST);    // Hidden surface removal
    glEnable(GL_CULL_FACE);      // Do not calculate inside of jet
    glFrontFace(GL_CCW);        // Counterclockwise polygons face out

    // Lighting stuff
    glEnable(GL_LIGHTING);    // Enable lighting

    // Set light model to use ambient light specified by ambientLight[]
    glLightModelfv(GL_LIGHT_MODEL_AMBIENT,ambientLight);


    glEnable(GL_COLOR_MATERIAL);     // Enable material color tracking

    // Front material ambient and diffuse colors track glColor
    glColorMaterial(GL_FRONT,GL_AMBIENT_AND_DIFFUSE);

    // Nice light blue background
    glClearColor(0.0f, 0.0f, 05.f,1.0f);
    }
```

Using a Light Source

Manipulating the ambient light has its uses, but for most applications attempting to model the real world, you must specify one or more specific sources of light. In addition to their intensities and colors, these sources have a location and/or a direction. The placement of these lights can dramatically affect the appearance of your scene.

OpenGL supports at least eight independent light sources located anywhere in your scene or out of the viewing volume. You can locate a light source an infinite distance away and make its light rays parallel or make it a nearby light source radiating outward. You can also specify a spotlight with a specific cone of light radiating from it, as well as manipulate its characteristics.

Which Way Is Up?

When you specify a light source, you tell OpenGL where it is and in which direction it's shining. Often, the light source shines in all directions, but it can be directional. Either way, for any object you draw, the rays of light from any source (other than a pure ambient source) strike the surface of the polygons that make up the object at an angle. Of course, in the case of a directional light, the surfaces of all polygons might not necessarily be illuminated. To calculate the shading effects across the surface of the polygons, OpenGL must be able to calculate the angle.

In Figure 5.20, a polygon (a square) is being struck by a ray of light from some source. The ray makes an angle (A) with the plane as it strikes the surface. The light is then reflected at an angle (B) toward the viewer (or you wouldn't see it). These angles are used in conjunction with the lighting and material properties we have discussed thus far to calculate the apparent color of that location. It happens by design that the locations used by OpenGL are the vertices of the polygon. Because OpenGL calculates the apparent colors for each vertex and then does smooth shading between them, the illusion of lighting is created. Magic!

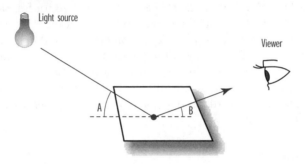

FIGURE 5.20   Light is reflected off objects at specific angles.

From a programming standpoint, these lighting calculations present a slight conceptual difficulty. Each polygon is created as a set of vertices, which are nothing more than points. Each vertex is then struck by a ray of light at some angle. How then do you (or OpenGL) calculate the angle between a point and a line (the ray of light)? Of course, you can't geometrically find the angle between a single point and a line in 3D space because there are an infinite number of possibilities. Therefore, you must associate with each vertex some piece of information that denotes a direction upward from the vertex and away from the surface of the primitive.

Surface Normals

A line from the vertex in the upward direction starts in some imaginary plane (or your polygon) at a right angle. This line is called a normal vector. The term *normal vector* might sound like something the Star Trek crew members toss around, but it just means a line perpendicular to a real or imaginary surface. A vector is a line pointed in some direction, and the word *normal* is just another way for eggheads to say perpendicular (intersecting at a 90° angle). As if the word *perpendicular* weren't bad enough! Therefore, a normal vector is a line pointed in a direction that is at a 90° angle to the surface of your polygon. Figure 5.21 presents examples of 2D and 3D normal vectors.

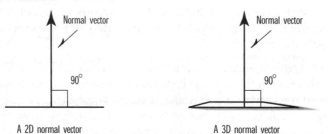

FIGURE 5.21 A 2D and a 3D normal vector.

You might already be asking why we must specify a normal vector for each vertex. Why can't we just specify a single normal for a polygon and use it for each vertex? We can—and for our first few examples, we do. However, sometimes you don't want each normal to be exactly perpendicular to the surface of the polygon. You may have noticed that many surfaces are not flat! You can approximate these surfaces with flat, polygonal sections, but you end up with a jagged or multifaceted surface. Later, we discuss a technique to produce the illusion of smooth curves with flat polygons by "tweaking" surface normals (more magic!). But first things first...

Specifying a Normal

To see how we specify a normal for a vertex, let's look at Figure 5.22—a plane floating above the xz plane in 3D space. We've made this illustration simple to demonstrate the concept. Notice the line through the vertex (1,1,0) that is perpendicular to the plane. If we select any point on this line, say (1,10,0), the line from the first point (1,1,0) to the second point (1,10,0) is our normal vector. The second point specified actually indicates that the direction from the vertex is up in the y direction. This convention is also used to indicate the front and back sides of polygons, as the vector travels up and away from the front surface.

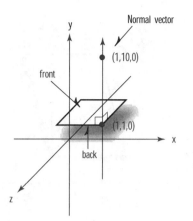

FIGURE 5.22   A normal vector traveling perpendicular from the surface.

You can see that this second point is the number of units in the x, y, and z directions for some point on the normal vector away from the vertex. Rather than specify two points for each normal vector, we can subtract the vertex from the second point on the normal, yielding a single coordinate triplet that indicates the x, y, and z steps away from the vertex. For our example, this is

$$(1,10,0) - (1,1,0) = (1 - 1, 10 - 1, 0) = (0,9,0)$$

Here's another way of looking at this example: If the vertex were translated to the origin, the point specified by subtracting the two original points would still specify the direction pointing away and at a 90° angle from the surface. Figure 5.23 shows the newly translated normal vector.

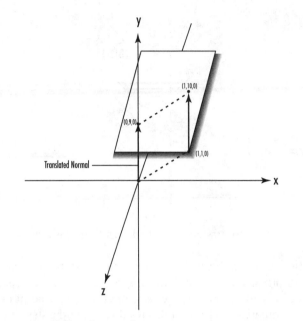

FIGURE 5.23   The newly translated normal vector.

The vector is a directional quantity that tells OpenGL which direction the vertices (or polygon) face. This next code segment shows a normal vector being specified for one of the triangles in the JET sample program:

```
glBegin(GL_TRIANGLES);
    glNormal3f(0.0f, -1.0f, 0.0f);
    glVertex3f(0.0f, 0.0f, 60.0f);
    glVertex3f(-15.0f, 0.0f, 30.0f);
    glVertex3f(15.0f,0.0f,30.0f);
glEnd();
```

The function glNormal3f takes the coordinate triplet that specifies a normal vector pointing in the direction perpendicular to the surface of this triangle. In this example, the normals for all three vertices have the same direction, which is down the negative y-axis. This is a simple example because the triangle is lying flat in the xz plane, and it actually represents a bottom section of the jet. You'll see later that often we want to specify a different normal for each vertex.

The prospect of specifying a normal for every vertex or polygon in your drawing might seem daunting, especially because few surfaces lie cleanly in one of the major planes. Never fear! Shortly we'll present a reusable function that you can call again and again to calculate your normals for you.

POLYGON WINDING

Take special note of the order of the vertices in the jet's triangle. If you view this triangle being drawn from the direction in which the normal vector points, the corners appear counterclockwise around the triangle. This is called *polygon winding*. By default, the front of a polygon is defined as the side from which the vertices appear to be wound in a counterclockwise fashion.

Unit Normals

As OpenGL does its magic, all surface normals must eventually be converted to unit normals. A unit normal is just a normal vector that has a length of 1. The normal in Figure 5.23 has a length of 9. You can find the length of any normal by squaring each component, adding them together, and taking the square root. Divide each component of the normal by the length, and you get a vector pointed in exactly the same direction, but only 1 unit long. In this case, our new normal vector is specified as (0,1,0). This is called *normalization*. Thus, for lighting calculations, all normal vectors must be normalized. Talk about jargon!

You can tell OpenGL to convert your normals to unit normals automatically, by enabling normalization with glEnable and a parameter of GL_NORMALIZE:

```
glEnable(GL_NORMALIZE);
```

This approach does, however, have performance penalties on some implementations. It's far better to calculate your normals ahead of time as unit normals instead of relying on OpenGL to perform this task for you.

You should note that calls to the glScale transformation function also scale the length of your normals. If you use glScale and lighting, you can obtain undesired results from your OpenGL lighting. If you have specified unit normals for all your geometry and used a constant scaling factor with glScale (all geometry is scaled by the same amount), an alternative to GL_NORMALIZE (available in OpenGL 1.2 and later) is GL_RESCALE_NORMALS. You enable this parameter with a call such as

```
glEnable(GL_RESCALE_NORMALS);
```

This call tells OpenGL that your normals are not unit length, but they can all be scaled by the same amount to make them unit length. OpenGL figures this out by examining the modelview matrix. The result is fewer mathematical operations per vertex than are otherwise required.

Because it is better to give OpenGL unit normals to begin with, the math3d library comes with a function that will take any normal vector and "normalize" it for you:

```
void m3dNormalizeVector(M3DVector3f vNormal);
```

Finding a Normal

Figure 5.24 presents another polygon that is not simply lying in one of the axis planes. The normal vector pointing away from this surface is more difficult to guess, so we need an easy way to calculate the normal for any arbitrary polygon in 3D coordinates.

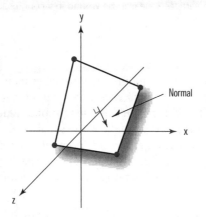

FIGURE 5.24 A nontrivial normal problem.

You can easily calculate the normal vector for any polygon by taking three points that lie in the plane of that polygon. Figure 5.25 shows three points—P1, P2, and P3—that you can use to define two vectors: vector V1 from P1 to P2, and vector V2 from P1 to P3. Mathematically, two vectors in three-dimensional space define a plane. (Your original polygon lies in this plane.) If you take the cross product of those two vectors (written mathematically as V1 X V2), the resulting vector is perpendicular to that plane. Figure 5.26 shows the vector V3 derived by taking the cross product of V1 and V2. Be careful to get the order correct. Cross products are not like multiplication of scalar values. The vector produced by V1 X V2 points in the opposite direction of a vector produced by V2 X V1.

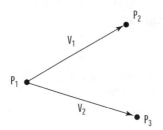

FIGURE 5.25 Two vectors defined by three points on a plane.

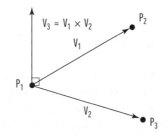

FIGURE 5.26 A normal vector as the cross product of two vectors.

Again, because this is such a useful and often-used method, the math3d library contains a function that calculates a normal vector based on three points on a polygon:

```
void m3dFindNormal(M3DVector3f vNormal, const M3DVector3f vP1,
                   const M3DVector3f vP2, const M3DVector3f vP3);
```

To use this function, pass it a vector to store the normal, and three vectors (each just an array of three floats) from your polygon or triangle (specified in counterclockwise winding order). Note that this returned normal vector is not necessarily unit length (normalized).

Setting Up a Source

Now that you understand the requirements of setting up your polygons to receive and interact with a light source, it's time to turn on the lights! Listing 5.3 shows the SetupRC function from the sample program LITJET. Part of the setup process for this sample program creates a light source and places it to the upper left, slightly behind the viewer. The light source GL_LIGHT0 has its ambient and diffuse components set to the intensities specified by the arrays ambientLight[] and diffuseLight[]. This results in a moderate white light source:

```
GLfloat  ambientLight[] = { 0.3f, 0.3f, 0.3f, 1.0f };
GLfloat  diffuseLight[] = { 0.7f, 0.7f, 0.7f, 1.0f };
...
...
// Set up and enable light 0
glLightfv(GL_LIGHT0,GL_AMBIENT,ambientLight);
glLightfv(GL_LIGHT0,GL_DIFFUSE,diffuseLight);
```

Finally, the light source GL_LIGHT0 is enabled:

```
glEnable(GL_LIGHT0);
```

The light is positioned by this code, located in the ChangeSize function:

```
GLfloat lightPos[] = { -50.f, 50.0f, 100.0f, 1.0f };
```

...

...

```
glLightfv(GL_LIGHT0,GL_POSITION,lightPos);
```

Here, lightPos[] contains the position of the light. The last value in this array is 1.0, which specifies that the designated coordinates are the position of the light source. If the last value in the array is 0.0, it indicates that the light is an infinite distance away along the vector specified by this array. We'll touch more on this issue later. Lights are like geometric objects in that they can be moved around by the modelview matrix. By placing the light's position when the viewing transformation is performed, we ensure that the light is in the proper location regardless of how we transform the geometry.

LISTING 5.3   Light and Rendering Context Setup for LITJET

```
// This function does any needed initialization on the rendering
// context.  Here it sets up and initializes the lighting for
// the scene.
void SetupRC()
    {
    // Light values and coordinates
    GLfloat   ambientLight[] = { 0.3f, 0.3f, 0.3f, 1.0f };
    GLfloat   diffuseLight[] = { 0.7f, 0.7f, 0.7f, 1.0f };

    glEnable(GL_DEPTH_TEST);     // Hidden surface removal
    glFrontFace(GL_CCW);         // Counterclockwise polygons face out
    glEnable(GL_CULL_FACE);      // Do not calculate inside of jet

    // Enable lighting
    glEnable(GL_LIGHTING);

    // Set up and enable light 0
    glLightfv(GL_LIGHT0,GL_AMBIENT,ambientLight);
    glLightfv(GL_LIGHT0,GL_DIFFUSE,diffuseLight);
    glEnable(GL_LIGHT0);

    // Enable color tracking
    glEnable(GL_COLOR_MATERIAL);

    // Set material properties to follow glColor values
    glColorMaterial(GL_FRONT, GL_AMBIENT_AND_DIFFUSE);

    // Light blue background
    glClearColor(0.0f, 0.0f, 1.0f, 1.0f );
```

LISTING 5.3   Continued

```
// Rescale normals to unit length
glEnable(GL_NORMALIZE);
    }
```

Setting the Material Properties

Notice in Listing 5.3 that color tracking is enabled, and the properties to be tracked are the ambient and diffuse reflective properties for the front surface of the polygons. This is just as it was defined in the AMBIENT sample program:

```
// Enable color tracking
glEnable(GL_COLOR_MATERIAL);

// Set material properties to follow glColor values
glColorMaterial(GL_FRONT, GL_AMBIENT_AND_DIFFUSE);
```

Specifying the Polygons

The rendering code from the first two JET samples changes considerably now to support the new lighting model. Listing 5.4 is an excerpt taken from the RenderScene function from LITJET.

LISTING 5.4   Code Sample That Sets Color and Calculates and Specifies Normals and Polygons

```
M3DVector3f vNormal;    // Storage for calculated surface normal

...
...
// Set material color
glColor3ub(128, 128, 128);
glBegin(GL_TRIANGLES);
        glNormal3f(0.0f, -1.0f, 0.0f);
        glVertex3f(0.0f, 0.0f, 60.0f);
        glVertex3f(-15.0f, 0.0f, 30.0f);
        glVertex3f(15.0f,0.0f,30.0f);


        // Vertices for this panel
        {
        M3DVector3f vPoints[3] = {{ 15.0f, 0.0f,  30.0f},
                                  { 0.0f, 15.0f, 30.0f},
                                  { 0.0f,  0.0f,  60.0f}};
```

LISTING 5.4   Continued

```
    // Calculate the normal for the plane
    m3dFindNormal(vNormal, vPoints[0], vPoints[1], vPoints[2]);
    glNormal3fv(vNormal);
    glVertex3fv(vPoints[0]);
    glVertex3fv(vPoints[1]);
    glVertex3fv(vPoints[2]);
    }


    {
    M3DVector3f vPoints[3] = {{ 0.0f, 0.0f, 60.0f },
                              { 0.0f, 15.0f, 30.0f },
                              { -15.0f, 0.0f, 30.0f }};

    m3dFindNormal(vNormal, vPoints[0], vPoints[1], vPoints[2]);
    glNormal3fv(vNormal);
    glVertex3fv(vPoints[0]);
    glVertex3fv(vPoints[1]);
    glVertex3fv(vPoints[2]);
    }
 . . .
glEnd();
```

Notice that we are calculating the normal vector using the m3dFindNormal function from math3d. Also, the material properties are now following the colors set by glColor. One other thing you notice is that not every triangle is blocked by glBegin/glEnd functions. You can specify once that you are drawing triangles, and every three vertices are used for a new triangle until you specify otherwise with glEnd. For very large numbers of polygons, this technique can considerably boost performance by eliminating many unnecessary function calls and primitive batch setup.

Figure 5.27 shows the output from the completed LITJET sample program. The jet is now a single shade of gray instead of multiple colors. We changed the color to make it easier to see the lighting effects on the surface. Even though the plane is one solid "color," you can still see the shape due to the lighting. By rotating the jet around with the arrow keys, you can see the dramatic shading effects as the surface of the jet moves and interacts with the light.

FIGURE 5.27   The output from the LITJET program.

TIP

The most obvious way to improve the performance of this code is to calculate all the normal vectors ahead of time and store them for use in the RenderScene function. Before you pursue this, read Chapter 11, "It's All About the Pipeline: Faster Geometry Throughput," for the material on display lists and vertex arrays. Display lists and vertex arrays provide a means of storing calculated values not only for the normal vectors, but for the polygon data as well. Remember, these examples are meant to demonstrate the concepts. They are not necessarily the most efficient code possible.

Lighting Effects

The ambient and diffuse lights from the LITJET example are sufficient to provide the illusion of lighting. The surface of the jet appears shaded according to the angle of the incident light. As the jet rotates, these angles change and you can see the lighting effects changing in such a way that you can easily guess where the light is coming from.

We ignored the specular component of the light source, however, as well as the specular reflectivity of the material properties on the jet. Although the lighting effects are pronounced, the surface of the jet is rather flatly colored. Ambient and diffuse lighting and material properties are all you need if you are modeling clay, wood, cardboard, cloth, or some other flatly colored object. But for metallic surfaces such as the skin of an airplane, some shine is often desirable.

Specular Highlights

Specular lighting and material properties add needed gloss to the surface of your objects. This shininess has a brightening effect on an object's color and can produce specular highlights when the angle of incident light is sharp in relation to the viewer. A specular highlight is what occurs when nearly all the light striking the surface of an object is reflected away. The white sparkle on a shiny red ball in the sunlight is a good example of a specular highlight.

Specular Light

You can easily add a specular component to a light source. The following code shows the light source setup for the LITJET program, modified to add a specular component to the light:

```
// Light values and coordinates
GLfloat  ambientLight[] = { 0.3f, 0.3f, 0.3f, 1.0f };
GLfloat  diffuseLight[] = { 0.7f, 0.7f, 0.7f, 1.0f };
GLfloat  specular[] = { 1.0f, 1.0f, 1.0f, 1.0f};

...
...

// Enable lighting
glEnable(GL_LIGHTING);

// Set up and enable light 0
glLightfv(GL_LIGHT0,GL_AMBIENT,ambientLight);
glLightfv(GL_LIGHT0,GL_DIFFUSE,diffuseLight);
glLightfv(GL_LIGHT0,GL SPECULAR,specular);
glEnable(GL_LIGHT0);
```

The specular[] array specifies a very bright white light source for the specular component of the light. Our purpose here is to model bright sunlight. The following line simply adds this specular component to the light source GL_LIGHT0:

```
glLightfv(GL_LIGHT0,GL_SPECULAR,specular);
```

If this were the only change you made to LITJET, you wouldn't see any difference in the jet's appearance. We haven't yet defined any specular reflectance properties for the material properties.

Specular Reflectance

Adding specular reflectance to material properties is just as easy as adding the specular component to the light source. This next code segment shows the code from LITJET, again modified to add specular reflectance to the material properties:

```
// Light values and coordinates
GLfloat  specref[] = { 1.0f, 1.0f, 1.0f, 1.0f };
```

```
...
...
```

```
// Enable color tracking
glEnable(GL_COLOR_MATERIAL);

// Set material properties to follow glColor values
glColorMaterial(GL_FRONT, GL_AMBIENT_AND_DIFFUSE);

// All materials hereafter have full specular reflectivity
// with a high shine
glMaterialfv(GL_FRONT, GL_SPECULAR,specref);
glMateriali(GL_FRONT,GL_SHININESS,128);
```

As before, we enable color tracking so that the ambient and diffuse reflectance of the materials follows the current color set by the glColor functions. (Of course, we don't want the specular reflectance to track glColor because we are specifying it separately and it doesn't change.)

Now, we've added the array specref[], which contains the RGBA values for our specular reflectance. This array of all 1s produces a surface that reflects nearly all incident specular light. The following line sets the material properties for all subsequent polygons to have this reflectance:

```
glMaterialfv(GL_FRONT, GL_SPECULAR,specref);
```

Because we do not call glMaterial again with the GL_SPECULAR property, all materials have this property. We set up the example this way on purpose because we want the entire jet to appear made of metal or very shiny composites.

What we have done here in our setup routine is important: We have specified that the ambient and diffuse reflective material properties of all future polygons (until we say otherwise with another call to glMaterial or glColorMaterial) change as the current color changes, but that the specular reflective properties remain the same.

Specular Exponent

As stated earlier, high specular light and reflectivity brighten the colors of the object. For this example, the present extremely high specular light (full intensity) and specular reflectivity (full reflectivity) result in a jet that appears almost totally white or gray except where the surface points away from the light source (in which case, it is black and unlit). To temper this effect, we use the next line of code after the specular component is specified:

```
glMateriali(GL_FRONT,GL_SHININESS,128);
```

The GL_SHININESS property sets the specular exponent of the material, which specifies how small and focused the specular highlight is. A value of 0 specifies an unfocused specular highlight, which is actually what is producing the brightening of the colors evenly across the entire polygon. If you set this value, you reduce the size and increase the focus of the specular highlight, causing a shiny spot to appear. The larger the value, the more shiny and pronounced the surface. The range of this parameter is 1–128 for all conformant implementations of OpenGL.

Listing 5.5 shows the new SetupRC code in the sample program SHINYJET. This is the only code that has changed from LITJET (other than the title of the window) to produce a very shiny and glistening jet. Figure 5.28 shows the output from this program, but to fully appreciate the effect, you should run the program and hold down one of the arrow keys to spin the jet about in the sunlight.

FIGURE 5.28   The output from the SHINYJET program.

LISTING 5.5   Setup from SHINYJET to Produce Specular Highlights on the Jet

```
// This function does any needed initialization on the rendering
// context.  Here it sets up and initializes the lighting for
// the scene.
void SetupRC()
    {
    // Light values and coordinates
    GLfloat   ambientLight[] = { 0.3f, 0.3f, 0.3f, 1.0f };
    GLfloat   diffuseLight[] = { 0.7f, 0.7f, 0.7f, 1.0f };
    GLfloat   specular[] = { 1.0f, 1.0f, 1.0f, 1.0f};
    GLfloat   specref[] =  { 1.0f, 1.0f, 1.0f, 1.0f };
```

LISTING 5.5   Continued

```
glEnable(GL_DEPTH_TEST);      // Hidden surface removal
glFrontFace(GL_CCW);          // Counterclockwise polygons face out
glEnable(GL_CULL_FACE);       // Do not calculate inside of jet

// Enable lighting
glEnable(GL_LIGHTING);

// Set up and enable light 0
glLightfv(GL_LIGHT0,GL_AMBIENT,ambientLight);
glLightfv(GL_LIGHT0,GL_DIFFUSE,diffuseLight);
glLightfv(GL_LIGHT0,GL_SPECULAR,specular);
glEnable(GL_LIGHT0);

// Enable color tracking
glEnable(GL_COLOR_MATERIAL);

// Set material properties to follow glColor values
glColorMaterial(GL_FRONT, GL_AMBIENT_AND_DIFFUSE);

// All materials hereafter have full specular reflectivity
// with a high shine
glMaterialfv(GL_FRONT, GL_SPECULAR,specref);
glMateriali(GL_FRONT,GL_SHININESS,128);


// Light blue background
glClearColor(0.0f, 0.0f, 1.0f, 1.0f );

glEnable(GL_NORMALIZE);
}
```

Normal Averaging

Earlier, we mentioned that by "tweaking" your normals, you can produce apparently
smooth surfaces with flat polygons. This technique, known as *normal averaging,* produces
some interesting optical illusions. Say you have a sphere made up of quads and triangles
like the one shown in Figure 5.29.

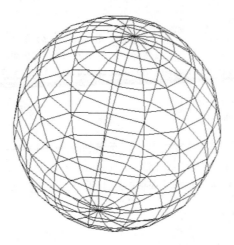

FIGURE 5.29   A typical sphere made up of quads and triangles.

If each face of the sphere had a single normal specified, the sphere would look like a large faceted jewel. If you specify the "true" normal for each vertex, however, the lighting calculations at each vertex produce values that OpenGL smoothly interpolates across the face of the polygon. Thus, the flat polygons are shaded as if they were a smooth surface.

What do we mean by "true" normal? The polygonal representation is only an approximation of the true surface. Theoretically, if we used enough polygons, the surface would appear smooth. This is similar to the idea we used in Chapter 3, "Drawing in Space: Geometric Primitives and Buffers," to draw a smooth curve with a series of short line segments. If we consider each vertex to be a point on the true surface, the actual normal value for that surface is the true normal for the surface.

For our case of the sphere, the normal would point directly out from the center of the sphere through each vertex. We show this graphically for a simple 2D case in Figures 5.30 and 5.31. In Figure 5.30, each flat segment has a normal pointing perpendicular to its surface. We did this just like we did for our LITJET example previously. Figure 5.31, however, shows how each normal is not perpendicular to the line segment but is perpendicular to the surface of the sphere, or the *tangent line* to the surface.

The tangent line touches the curve in one place and does not penetrate it. The 3D equivalent is a tangent plane. In Figure 5.31, you can see the outline of the actual surface and that the normal is actually perpendicular to the line tangent to the surface.

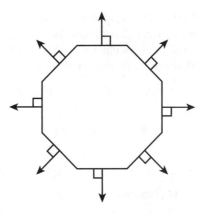

FIGURE 5.30   An approximation with normals perpendicular to each face.

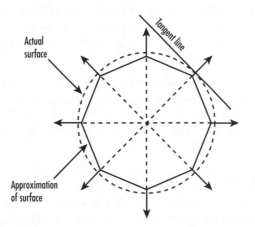

FIGURE 5.31   Each normal is perpendicular to the surface itself.

For a sphere, calculation of the normal is reasonably simple. (The normal actually has the same values as the vertex relative to the center!) For other nontrivial surfaces, the calculation might not be so easy. In such cases, you calculate the normals for each polygon that shares a vertex. The actual normal you assign to that vertex is the average of these normals. The visual effect is a nice, smooth, regular surface, even though it is actually composed of numerous small, flat segments.

Putting It All Together

Now it's time for a more complex sample program. We demonstrate how to use normals to create a smooth surface appearance, move a light around in a scene, create a spotlight, and, finally, identify one of the drawbacks of OpenGL vertex-based lighting.

Our next sample program, SPOT, performs all these tasks. Here, we create a solid sphere in the center of our viewing volume with `glutSolidSphere`. We shine a spotlight on this sphere that we can move around, and we change the "smoothness" of the normals and demonstrate some of the limitations of OpenGL lighting.

So far, we have been specifying a light's position with `glLight` as follows:

```
// Array to specify position
GLfloat  lightPos[] = { 0.0f, 150.0f, 150.0f, 1.0f };
...
...
// Set the light position
glLightfv(GL_LIGHT0,GL_POSITION,lightPos);
```

The array `lightPos[]` contains the x, y, and z values that specify either the light's actual position in the scene or the direction from which the light is coming. The last value, `1.0` in this case, indicates that the light is actually present at this location. By default, the light radiates equally in all directions from this location, but you can change this default to make a spotlight effect.

To make a light source an infinite distance away and coming from the direction specified by this vector, you place `0.0` in this last `lightPos[]` array element. A directional light source, as this is called, strikes the surface of your objects evenly. That is, all the light rays are parallel. In a positional light source, on the other hand, the light rays diverge from the light source.

Creating a Spotlight

Creating a spotlight is no different from creating any other positional light source. The code in Listing 5.6 shows the `SetupRC` function from the SPOT sample program. This program places a blue sphere in the center of the window. It also creates a spotlight that you can move vertically with the up- and down-arrow keys and horizontally with the left- and right-arrow keys. As the spotlight moves over the surface of the sphere, a specular highlight follows it on the surface.

LISTING 5.6   Lighting Setup for the SPOT Sample Program

```
// Light values and coordinates
GLfloat  lightPos[] = { 0.0f, 0.0f, 75.0f, 1.0f };
GLfloat  specular[] = { 1.0f, 1.0f, 1.0f, 1.0f};
GLfloat  specref[] =  { 1.0f, 1.0f, 1.0f, 1.0f };
GLfloat  ambientLight[] = { 0.5f, 0.5f, 0.5f, 1.0f};
GLfloat  spotDir[] = { 0.0f, 0.0f, -1.0f };


// This function does any needed initialization on the rendering
```

LISTING 5.6   Continued

```
// context.  Here it sets up and initializes the lighting for
// the scene.
void SetupRC()
    {
    glEnable(GL_DEPTH_TEST);      // Hidden surface removal
    glFrontFace(GL_CCW);          // Counterclockwise polygons face out
    glEnable(GL_CULL_FACE);          // Do not try to display the back sides

    // Enable lighting
    glEnable(GL_LIGHTING);

    // Set up and enable light 0
    // Supply a slight ambient light so the objects can be seen
    glLightModelfv(GL_LIGHT_MODEL_AMBIENT, ambientLight);

    // The light is composed of just diffuse and specular components
    glLightfv(GL_LIGHT0,GL_DIFFUSE,ambientLight);
    glLightfv(GL_LIGHT0,GL_SPECULAR,specular);
    glLightfv(GL_LIGHT0,GL_POSITION,lightPos);

    // Specific spot effects
    // Cut-off angle is 60 degrees
    glLightf(GL_LIGHT0,GL_SPOT_CUTOFF,60.0f);

    // Enable this light in particular
    glEnable(GL_LIGHT0);

    // Enable color tracking
    glEnable(GL_COLOR_MATERIAL);

    // Set material properties to follow glColor values
    glColorMaterial(GL_FRONT, GL_AMBIENT_AND_DIFFUSE);

    // All materials hereafter have full specular reflectivity
    // with a high shine
    glMaterialfv(GL_FRONT, GL_SPECULAR,specref);
    glMateriali(GL_FRONT, GL_SHININESS,128);


    // Black background
    glClearColor(0.0f, 0.0f, 0.0f, 1.0f );
    }
```

The following line from the listing is actually what makes a positional light source into a spotlight:

```
// Specific spot effects
// Cut-off angle is 60 degrees
glLightf(GL_LIGHT0,GL_SPOT_CUTOFF,60.0f);
```

The GL_SPOT_CUTOFF value specifies the radial angle of the cone of light emanating from the spotlight, from the center line to the edge of the cone. For a normal positional light, this value is 180° so that the light is not confined to a cone. In fact, for spotlights, only values from 0° to 90° are valid. Spotlights emit a cone of light, and objects outside this cone are not illuminated. Figure 5.32 shows how this angle translates to the cone width.

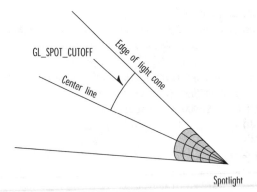

FIGURE 5.32   The angle of the spotlight cone.

Drawing a Spotlight

When you place a spotlight in a scene, the light must come from somewhere. Just because you have a source of light at some location doesn't mean that you see a bright spot there. For our SPOT sample program, we placed a red cone at the spotlight source to show where the light was coming from. Inside the end of this cone, we placed a bright yellow sphere to simulate a light bulb.

CAN YOU SEE THE LIGHT?

In a word, no. Lights in OpenGL cannot be seen by themselves. Spotlights do not create cones of light, and beams of sunlight streaming in a window do not create beams or shafts of light. To create these effects in OpenGL, you will actually have to draw geometry, such as real cones or shafts, often using the blending operations covered later in this book. Lights also go through objects and do not cast shadows. One technique for drawing shadows will be presented soon.

This sample has a pop-up menu that we use to demonstrate several things. The pop-up menu contains items to set flat and smooth shading and to produce a sphere for low, medium, and high *approximation*. Surface approximation means to break the mesh of a curved surface into a finer mesh of polygons (more vertices). Figure 5.33 shows a wireframe representation of a highly approximated sphere next to one that has few polygons.

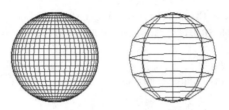

FIGURE 5.33   On the left is a highly approximated sphere; on the right, a sphere made up of fewer polygons.

Figure 5.34 shows our sample in its initial state with the spotlight moved off slightly to one side. (You can use the arrow keys to move the spotlight.) The sphere consists of a few polygons, which are flat shaded. In Windows, use the right mouse button to open a pop-up menu (Ctrl-click on the Mac) where you can switch between smooth and flat shading and between very low, medium, and very high approximation for the sphere. Listing 5.7 shows the complete code for rendering the scene.

FIGURE 5.34   The SPOT sample—low approximation, flat shading.

LISTING 5.7   The Rendering Function for SPOT, Showing How the Spotlight Is Moved

```
// Called to draw scene
void RenderScene(void)
    {
```

LISTING 5.7   Continued

```c
if(iShade == MODE_FLAT)
    glShadeModel(GL_FLAT);
else //      iShade = MODE_SMOOTH;
    glShadeModel(GL_SMOOTH);

// Clear the window with current clearing color
glClear(GL_COLOR_BUFFER_BIT | GL_DEPTH_BUFFER_BIT);

// First place the light
// Save the coordinate transformation
glPushMatrix();
    // Rotate coordinate system
    glRotatef(yRot, 0.0f, 1.0f, 0.0f);
    glRotatef(xRot, 1.0f, 0.0f, 0.0f);

    // Specify new position and direction in rotated coords
    glLightfv(GL_LIGHT0,GL_POSITION,lightPos);
    glLightfv(GL_LIGHT0,GL_SPOT_DIRECTION,spotDir);

    // Draw a red cone to enclose the light source
    glColor3ub(255,0,0);

    // Translate origin to move the cone out to where the light
    // is positioned.
    glTranslatef(lightPos[0],lightPos[1],lightPos[2]);
    glutSolidCone(4.0f,6.0f,15,15);

    // Draw a smaller displaced sphere to denote the light bulb
    // Save the lighting state variables
    glPushAttrib(GL_LIGHTING_BIT);

        // Turn off lighting and specify a bright yellow sphere
        glDisable(GL_LIGHTING);
            glColor3ub(255,255,0);
        glutSolidSphere(3.0f, 15, 15);

    // Restore lighting state variables
    glPopAttrib();

// Restore coordinate transformations
glPopMatrix();
```

LISTING 5.7   Continued

```
// Set material color and draw a sphere in the middle
glColor3ub(0, 0, 255);

if(iTess == MODE_VERYLOW)
    glutSolidSphere(30.0f, 7, 7);
else
    if(iTess == MODE_MEDIUM)
        glutSolidSphere(30.0f, 15, 15);
    else //  iTess = MODE_MEDIUM;
        glutSolidSphere(30.0f, 50, 50);

// Display the results
glutSwapBuffers();
}
```

The variables iTess and iMode are set by the GLUT menu handler and control how many sections the sphere is broken into and whether flat or smooth shading is employed. Note that the light is positioned before any geometry is rendered. As pointed out in Chapter 2, OpenGL is an immediate-mode API: If you want an object to be illuminated, you have to put the light where you want it before drawing the object.

You can see in Figure 5.34 that the sphere is coarsely lit and each flat face is clearly evident. Switching to smooth shading helps a little, as shown in Figure 5.35.

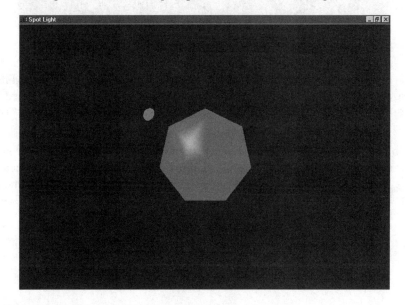

FIGURE 5.35   Smoothly shaded but inadequate approximation.

Increasing the approximation helps, as shown in Figure 5.36, but you still see disturbing artifacts as you move the spotlight around the sphere. These lighting artifacts are one of the drawbacks of OpenGL lighting. A better way to characterize this situation is to say that these artifacts are a drawback of vertex lighting (not necessarily OpenGL!). By lighting the vertices and then interpolating between them, we get a crude approximation of lighting. This approach is sufficient for many cases, but as you can see in our spot example, it is not sufficient in others. If you switch to very high approximation and move the spotlight, you see the lighting blemishes all but vanish.

FIGURE 5.36   Choosing a finer mesh of polygons yields better vertex lighting.

With most OpenGL hardware implementations accelerating transformations and lighting effects, we are able to more finely approximate geometry for better OpenGL-based lighting effects. For the very best quality light effects, we will turn to *shaders*, in Part III, "The Apocrypha."

The final observation you need to make about the SPOT sample appears when you set the sphere for medium approximation and flat shading. As shown in Figure 5.37, each face of the sphere is flatly lit. Each vertex is the same color but is modulated by the value of the normal and the light. With flat shading, each polygon is made the color of the last vertex color specified and not smoothly interpolated between each one.

FIGURE 5.37 A multifaceted sphere.

Shadows

A chapter on color and lighting naturally calls for a discussion of shadows. Adding shadows to your scenes can greatly improve their realism and visual effectiveness. In Figures 5.38 and 5.39, you see two views of a lighted cube. Although both are lit, the one with a shadow is more convincing than the one without the shadow.

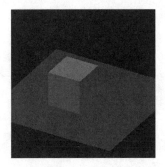

FIGURE 5.38 A lighted cube without a shadow.

FIGURE 5.39   A lighted cube with a shadow.

What Is a Shadow?

Conceptually, drawing a shadow is quite simple. A shadow is produced when an object keeps light from a light source from striking some object or surface behind the object casting the shadow. The area on the shadowed object's surface, outlined by the object casting the shadow, appears dark. We can produce a shadow programmatically by flattening the original object into the plane of the surface in which the object lies. The object is then drawn in black or some dark color, perhaps with some translucence. There are many methods and algorithms for drawing shadows, some quite complex. This book's primary focus is on the OpenGL API. It is our hope that, after you've mastered the tool, some of the additional reading suggested in Appendix A will provide you with a lifetime of learning new applications for this tool. Chapter 14, "Depth Textures and Shadows," covers some new direct support in OpenGL for making shadows; for our purposes in this chapter, we demonstrate one of the simpler methods that works quite well when casting shadows on a flat surface (such as the ground). Figure 5.40 illustrates this flattening.

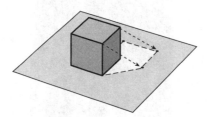

FIGURE 5.40   Flattening an object to create a shadow.

We squish an object against another surface by using some of the advanced matrix manipulations we touched on in the preceding chapter. Here, we boil down this process to make it as simple as possible.

Squish Code

We need to flatten the modelview projection matrix so that any and all objects drawn into it are now in this flattened two-dimensional world. No matter how the object is oriented, it is projected (squished) into the plane in which the shadow lies. The next two considerations are the distance and direction of the light source. The direction of the light source determines the shape of the shadow and influences the size. If you've ever seen your shadow in the early or late hours, you know how long and warped your shadow can appear, depending on the position of the sun.

The function `m3dMakePlanarShadowMatrix` from the math3d library, shown in Listing 5.8, takes the plane equation of the plane in which you want the shadow to appear (three points that cannot be along the same straight line can be fed to `m3dGetPlaneEquation` to get the equation of the plane), and the position of the light source, and returns a transformation matrix that this function constructs. Without delving into the linear algebra, what this function does is build a transformation matrix. If you multiply this matrix by the current modelview matrix, all further drawing is flattened into this plane.

A Shadow Example

To demonstrate the use of this shadow matrix, we suspend our jet in air high above the ground. We place the light source directly above and a bit to the left of the jet. As you use the arrow keys to spin the jet around, the shadow cast by the jet appears flattened on the ground below. The output from this SHADOW sample program is shown in Figure 5.41.

FIGURE 5.41 The output from the SHADOW sample program.

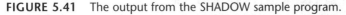

The code in Listing 5.8 shows how the shadow projection matrix was created for this example. Note that we create the matrix once in `SetupRC` and save it in a global variable.

LISTING 5.8   Setting Up the Shadow Projection Matrix

```
GLfloat lightPos[] = { -75.0f, 150.0f, -50.0f, 0.0f };
...
...

// Transformation matrix to project shadow
M3DMatrix44f shadowMat;
...
...

// This function does any needed initialization on the rendering
// context.  Here it sets up and initializes the lighting for
// the scene.
void SetupRC()
    {
    // Any three points on the ground (counterclockwise order)
    M3DVector3f points[3] = {{ -30.0f, -149.0f, -20.0f },
                             { -30.0f, -149.0f, 20.0f },
                             { 40.0f, -149.0f, 20.0f }};

    glEnable(GL_DEPTH_TEST);    // Hidden surface removal
    glFrontFace(GL_CCW);        // Counterclockwise polygons face out
    glEnable(GL_CULL_FACE);     // Do not calculate inside of jet

    // Enable lighting
    glEnable(GL_LIGHTING);

    ...
// Code to set up lighting, etc.
    ...


    // Get the plane equation from three points on the ground
    M3DVector4f vPlaneEquation;
    m3dGetPlaneEquation(vPlaneEquation, points[0], points[1], points[2]);

    // Calculate projection matrix to draw shadow on the ground
    m3dMakePlanarShadowMatrix(shadowMat, vPlaneEquation, lightPos);
    . ..
    }
```

Listing 5.9 shows the rendering code for the shadow example. We first draw the ground. Then we draw the jet as we normally do, restore the modelview matrix, and multiply it by the shadow matrix. This procedure creates our squish matrix. Then we draw the jet again. (We've modified our code to accept a flag telling the DrawJet function to render in color or black.) After restoring the modelview matrix once again, we draw a small yellow sphere to approximate the position of the light. Note that we disable depth testing before we draw a plane below the jet to indicate the ground.

This rectangle lies in the same plane in which our shadow is drawn, and we want to make sure the shadow is drawn. We have never before discussed what happens if we draw two objects or planes in the same location. We have discussed depth testing as a means to determine what is drawn in front of what, however. If two objects occupy the same location, usually the last one drawn is shown. Sometimes, however, an effect called *z-fighting* causes fragments from both objects to be intermingled, resulting in a mess!

LISTING 5.9   Rendering the Jet and Its Shadow

```
// Called to draw scene
void RenderScene(void)
    {
    // Clear the window with current clearing color
    glClear(GL_COLOR_BUFFER_BIT | GL_DEPTH_BUFFER_BIT);

    // Draw the ground; we do manual shading to a darker green
    // in the background to give the illusion of depth
    glBegin(GL_QUADS);
        glColor3ub(0,32,0);
        glVertex3f(400.0f, -150.0f, -200.0f);
        glVertex3f(-400.0f, -150.0f, -200.0f);
        glColor3ub(0,255,0);
        glVertex3f(-400.0f, -150.0f, 200.0f);
        glVertex3f(400.0f, -150.0f, 200.0f);
    glEnd();

    // Save the matrix state and do the rotations
    glPushMatrix();

    // Draw jet at new orientation; put light in correct position
    // before rotating the jet
    glEnable(GL_LIGHTING);
    glLightfv(GL_LIGHT0,GL_POSITION,lightPos);
    glRotatef(xRot, 1.0f, 0.0f, 0.0f);
    glRotatef(yRot, 0.0f, 1.0f, 0.0f);
```

LISTING 5.9   Continued

```
    DrawJet(FALSE);

    // Restore original matrix state
    glPopMatrix();


    // Get ready to draw the shadow and the ground
    // First disable lighting and save the projection state
    glDisable(GL_DEPTH_TEST);
    glDisable(GL_LIGHTING);
    glPushMatrix();

    // Multiply by shadow projection matrix
    glMultMatrixf((GLfloat *)shadowMat);

    // Now rotate the jet around in the new flattened space
    glRotatef(xRot, 1.0f, 0.0f, 0.0f);
    glRotatef(yRot, 0.0f, 1.0f, 0.0f);

    // Pass true to indicate drawing shadow
    DrawJet(TRUE);

    // Restore the projection to normal
    glPopMatrix();

    // Draw the light source
    glPushMatrix();
    glTranslatef(lightPos[0],lightPos[1], lightPos[2]);
    glColor3ub(255,255,0);
    glutSolidSphere(5.0f,10,10);
    glPopMatrix();

    // Restore lighting state variables
    glEnable(GL_DEPTH_TEST);

    // Display the results
    glutSwapBuffers();
    }
```

Sphere World Revisited

Our last example for this chapter is too long to list the source code in its entirety. In the preceding chapter's SPHEREWORLD sample program, we created an immersive 3D world with animation and camera movement. In this chapter, we've revisited Sphere World and have added lights and material properties to the torus and sphere inhabitants. Finally, we have also used our planar shadow technique to add a shadow to the ground! We will keep coming back to this example from time to time as we add more and more of our OpenGL functionality to the code. The output of this chapter's version of SPHEREWORLD is shown in Figure 5.42.

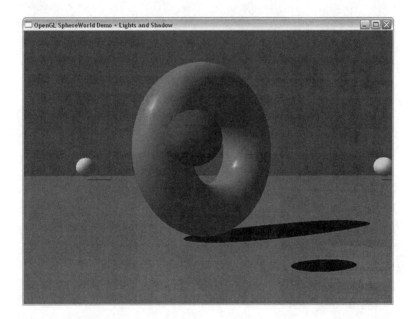

FIGURE 5.42   Fully lit and shadowed Sphere World.

Summary

This chapter introduced some of the more magical and powerful capabilities of OpenGL. We started by adding color to 3D scenes, as well as smooth shading. We then saw how to specify one or more light sources and define their lighting characteristics in terms of ambient, diffuse, and specular components. We explained how the corresponding material properties interact with these light sources and demonstrated some special effects, such as adding specular highlights and softening sharp edges between adjoining triangles.

Also covered were lighting positions and the creation and manipulation of spotlights. The high-level matrix munching function presented here makes shadow generation as easy as it gets for planar shadows.

CHAPTER 6

More on Colors and Materials

by Richard S. Wright Jr.

WHAT YOU'LL LEARN IN THIS CHAPTER:

How To	Functions You'll Use
Blend colors and objects together	glBlendFunc/glBlendFuncSeparate/ glBlendEquation/ glBlendColor
Use alpha testing to eliminate fragments	glAlphaFunc
Add depth cues with fog	glFog, glFogCoord
Render motion-blurred animation	glAccum

In the preceding chapter, you learned that there is more to making a ball appear red than just setting the drawing color to red. Material properties and lighting parameters can go a long way toward adding realism to your graphics, but modeling the real world has a few other challenges that we will address in this chapter. For starters, many effects are accomplished by means of blending colors together. Transparent objects such as stained-glass windows or plastic bottles allow you to see through them, but the light from the objects behind them is blended with the color of the transparent object you are seeing through. This type of transparency is achieved in OpenGL by drawing the background objects first and then blending the foreground object in front with the colors that are already present in the color buffer. A good part of making this technique work requires that we now consider the fourth color component that until now we have been ignoring, *alpha*.

Blending

You have already learned that OpenGL rendering places color values in the color buffer under normal circumstances. You have also learned that depth values for each fragment are also placed in the depth buffer. When depth testing is turned off (disabled), new color values simply overwrite any other values already present in the color buffer. When depth testing is turned on (enabled), new color fragments replace an existing fragment only if they are deemed closer to the near clipping plane than the values already there. Under normal circumstances then, any drawing operation is either discarded entirely, or just completely overwrites any old color values, depending on the result of the depth test. This obliteration of the underlying color values no longer happens the moment you turn on OpenGL blending:

```
glEnable(GL_BLEND);
```

When blending is enabled, the incoming color is combined with the color value already present in the color buffer. How these colors are combined leads to a great many and varied special effects.

Combining Colors

First, we must introduce a more official terminology for the color values coming in and already in the color buffer. The color value already stored in the color buffer is called the *destination* color, and this color value contains the three individual red, green, and blue components, and optionally a stored alpha value as well. A color value that is coming in as a result of more rendering commands that may or may not interact with the destination color is called the *source* color. The source color also contains either three or four color components (red, green, blue, and optionally alpha).

How the source and destination colors are combined when blending is enabled is controlled by the blending equation. By default, the blending equation looks like this:

$$C_f = (C_s * S) + (C_d * D)$$

Here, C_f is the final computed color, C_s is the source color, C_d is the destination color, and S and D are the source and destination blending factors. These blending factors are set with the following function:

```
glBlendFunc(GLenum S, GLenum D);
```

As you can see, S and D are enumerants and not physical values that you specify directly. Table 6.1 lists the possible values for the blending function. The subscripts stand for source, destination, and color (for blend color, to be discussed shortly). R, G, B, and A stand for Red, Green, Blue, and Alpha, respectively.

TABLE 6.1   OpenGL Blending Factors

Function	RGB Blend Factors	Alpha Blend Factor
GL_ZERO	(0,0,0)	0
GL_ONE	(1,1,1)	1
GL_SRC_COLOR	(R_s, G_s, B_s)	A_s
GL_ONE_MINUS_SRC_COLOR	$(1,1,1) - (R_s, G_s, B_s)$	$1 - A_s$

Function	RGB Blend Factors	Alpha Blend Factor
GL_DST_COLOR	(R_d, G_d, B_d)	A_d
GL_ONE_MINUS_DST_COLOR	$(1,1,1) - (R_d, G_d, B_d)$	$1 - A_d$
GL_SRC_ALPHA	(A_s, A_s, A_s)	A_s
GL_ONE_MINUS_SRC_ALPHA	$(1,1,1) - (A_s, A_s, A_s)$	$1 - A_s$
GL_DST_ALPHA	(A_d, A_d, A_d)	A_d
GL_ONE_MINUS_DST_ALPHA	$(1,1,1) - (A_d, A_d, A_d)$	$1 - A_d$
GL_CONSTANT_COLOR	(R_c, G_c, B_c)	A_c
GL_ONE_MINUS_CONSTANT_COLOR	$(1,1,1) - (R_c, G_c, B_c)$	$1 - A_c$
GL_CONSTANT_ALPHA	(A_c, A_c, A_c)	A_c
GL_ONE_MINUS_CONSTANT_ALPHA	$(1,1,1) - (A_c, A_c, A_c)$	$1 - A_c$
GL_SRC_ALPHA_SATURATE	$(f,f,f)*$	1

*Where $f = min(A_s, 1 - A_d)$.

Remember that colors are represented by floating-point numbers, so adding them, subtracting them, and even multiplying them are all perfectly valid operations. Table 6.1 may seem a bit bewildering, so let's look at a common blending function combination:

```
glBlendFunc(GL_SRC_ALPHA, GL_ONE_MINUS_SRC_ALPHA);
```

This function tells OpenGL to take the source (incoming) color and multiply the color (the RGB values) by the alpha value. Add this to the result of multiplying the destination color by one minus the alpha value from the source. Say, for example, that you have the color Red (1.0f, 0.0f, 0.0f, 0.0f) already in the color buffer. This is the destination color, or C_d. If something is drawn over this with the color blue and an alpha of 0.6 (0.0f, 0.0f, 1.0f, 0.6f), you would compute the final color as shown here:

C_d = destination color = (1.0f, 0.0f, 0.0f, 0.0f)

C_s = source color = (0.0f, 0.0f, 1.0f, 0.6f)

S = source alpha = 0.6

D = one minus source alpha = 1.0 – 0.6 = 0.4

Now, the equation

$C_f = (C_s * S) + (C_d * D)$

evaluates to

$C_f = (Blue * 0.6) + (Red * 0.4)$

The final color is a scaled combination of the original red value and the incoming blue value. The higher the incoming alpha value, the more of the incoming color is added and the less of the original color is retained.

This blending function is often used to achieve the effect of drawing a transparent object in front of some other opaque object. This technique does require, however, that you draw the background object or objects first and then draw the transparent object blended over the top. The effect can be quite dramatic. For example, in the REFLECTION sample program, we will use transparency to achieve the illusion of a reflection in a mirrored surface. We begin with a rotating torus with a sphere revolving around it, similar to the view in the Sphere World example from Chapter 5, "Color, Materials, and Lighting: The Basics." Beneath the torus and sphere, we will place a reflective tiled floor. The output from this program is shown in Figure 6.1, and the drawing code is shown in Listing 6.1.

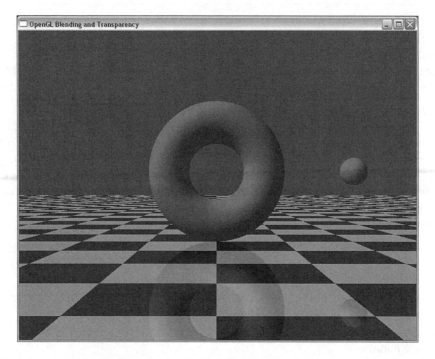

FIGURE 6.1   Using blending to create a fake reflection effect.

LISTING 6.1   Rendering Function for the REFLECTION Program

```
//////////////////////////////////////////////////////////////////////
// Called to draw scene
void RenderScene(void)
    {
    // Clear the window with current clearing color
    glClear(GL_COLOR_BUFFER_BIT | GL_DEPTH_BUFFER_BIT);

    glPushMatrix();
        // Move light under floor to light the "reflected" world
        glLightfv(GL_LIGHT0, GL_POSITION, fLightPosMirror);
        glPushMatrix();
            glFrontFace(GL_CW);                 // geometry is mirrored,
                                                // swap orientation

            glScalef(1.0f, -1.0f, 1.0f);
            DrawWorld();
            glFrontFace(GL_CCW);
        glPopMatrix();

        // Draw the ground transparently over the reflection
        glDisable(GL_LIGHTING);
        glEnable(GL_BLEND);
        glBlendFunc(GL_SRC_ALPHA, GL_ONE_MINUS_SRC_ALPHA);
        DrawGround();
        glDisable(GL_BLEND);
        glEnable(GL_LIGHTING);

        // Restore correct lighting and draw the world correctly
        glLightfv(GL_LIGHT0, GL_POSITION, fLightPos);
        DrawWorld();
    glPopMatrix();

    // Do the buffer Swap
    glutSwapBuffers();
    }
```

The basic algorithm for this effect is to draw the scene upside down first. We use one function to draw the scene, DrawWorld, but to draw it upside down, we scale by –1 to invert the y-axis, reverse our polygon winding, and place the light down beneath us. After drawing the upside-down world, we draw the ground, but we use blending to create a transparent floor over the top of the inverted world. Finally, we turn off blending, put the light back overhead, and draw the world right side up.

Changing the Blending Equation

The blending equation we showed you earlier,

$$C_f = (C_s * S) + (C_d * D)$$

is the *default* blending equation. You can actually choose from five different blending equations, each given in Table 6.2 and selected with the following function:

```
void glBlendEquation(GLenum mode);
```

TABLE 6.2   Available Blend Equation Modes

Mode	Function
GL_FUNC_ADD (default)	$C_f = (C_s * S) + (C_d * D)$
GL_FUNC_SUBTRACT	$C_f = (C_s * S) - (C_d * D)$
GL_FUNC_REVERSE_SUBTRACT	$C_f = (C_d * D) - (C_s * S)$
GL_MIN	$C_f = \min(C_s, C_d)$
GL_MAX	$C_f = \max(C_s, C_d)$

In addition to glBlendFunc, you have even more flexibility with this function:

```
void glBlendFuncSeparate(GLenum srcRGB, GLenum dstRGB, GLenum srcAlpha,
                         GLenum dstAlpha);
```

Whereas glBlendFunc specifies the blend functions for source and destination RGBA values, glBlendFuncSeparate allows you to specify blending functions for the RGB and alpha components separately.

Finally, as shown in Table 6.1, the GL_CONSTANT_COLOR, GL_ONE_MINUS_CONSTANT_COLOR, GL_CONSTANT_ALPHA, and GL_ONE_MINUS_CONSTANT_ALPHA values all allow a constant blending color to be introduced to the blending equation. This constant blending color is initially black (0.0f, 0.0f, 0.0f, 0.0f), but it can be changed with this function:

```
void glBlendColor(GLclampf red, GLclampf green, Glclampf blue, GLclampf alpha);
```

Antialiasing

Another use for OpenGL's blending capabilities is antialiasing. Under most circumstances, individual rendered fragments are mapped to individual pixels on a computer screen. These pixels are square (or squarish), and usually you can spot the division between two colors quite clearly. These *jaggies,* as they are often called, catch the eye's attention and can destroy the illusion that the image is natural. These jaggies are a dead giveaway that the image is computer generated! For many rendering tasks, it is desirable to achieve as much realism as possible, particularly in games, simulations, or artistic endeavors. Figure 6.2 shows the output for the sample program SMOOTHER. In Figure 6.3, we have zoomed in on a line segment and some points to show the jagged edges.

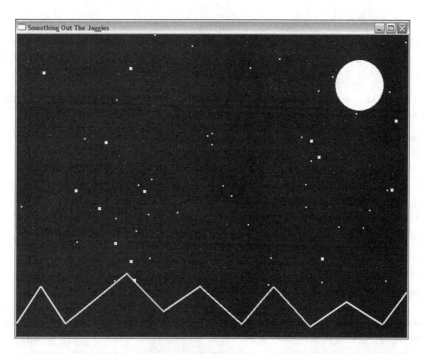

FIGURE 6.2   Output from the program SMOOTHER.

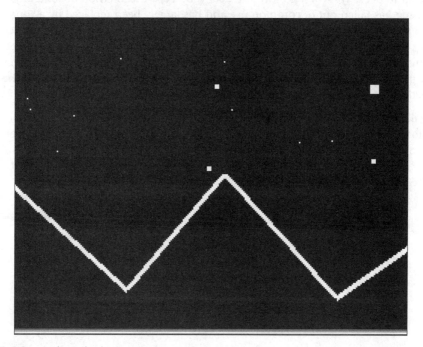

FIGURE 6.3   A closer look at some jaggies.

To get rid of the jagged edges between primitives, OpenGL uses blending to blend the color of the fragment with the destination color of the pixel and its surrounding pixels. In essence, pixel colors are smeared slightly to neighboring pixels along the edges of any primitives.

Turning on antialiasing is simple. First, you must enable blending and set the blending function to be the same as you used in the preceding section for transparency:

```
glEnable(GL_BLEND);
glBlendFunc(GL_SRC_ALPHA, GL_ONE_MINUS_SRC_ALPHA);
```

You also need to make sure the blend equation is set to GL_ADD, but because this is the default and most common blending equation, we don't show it here. After blending is enabled and the proper blending function and equation are selected, you can choose to antialias points, lines, and/or polygons (any solid primitive) by calling glEnable:

```
glEnable(GL_POINT_SMOOTH);    // Smooth out points
glEnable(GL_LINE_SMOOTH);     // Smooth out lines
glEnable(GL_POLYGON_SMOOTH);  // Smooth out polygon edges
```

You should use GL_POLYGON_SMOOTH with care. You might expect to smooth out edges on solid geometry, but there are other tedious rules to making this work. For example, geometry that overlaps requires a different blending mode, and you may need to sort your scene from front to back. We won't go into the details because this method of solid object antialiasing has fallen out of common use and has largely been replaced by a superior route to smoothing edges on 3D geometry called *multisampling*. This feature is discussed in the next section. Without multisampling, you can still get this overlapping geometry problem with antialiased lines that overlap. For wireframe rendering, for example, you can usually get away with just disabling depth testing to avoid the depth artifacts at the line intersections.

Listing 6.2 shows the code from the SMOOTHER program that responds to a pop-up menu that allows the user to switch between antialiased and non-antialiased rendering modes. When this program is run with antialiasing enabled, the points and lines appear smoother (fuzzier). In Figure 6.4, a zoomed-in section shows the same area as Figure 6.3, but now with the jagged edges smoothed out.

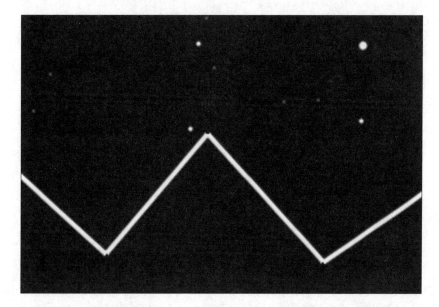

FIGURE 6.4   No more jaggies!

LISTING 6.2   Switching Between Antialiased and Normal Rendering

```
////////////////////////////////////////////////////////////////////////
// Reset flags as appropriate in response to menu selections
void ProcessMenu(int value)
    {
    switch(value)
        {
        case 1:
            // Turn on antialiasing, and give hint to do the best
            // job possible.
            glBlendFunc(GL_SRC_ALPHA, GL_ONE_MINUS_SRC_ALPHA);
            glEnable(GL_BLEND);
            glEnable(GL_POINT_SMOOTH);
            glHint(GL_POINT_SMOOTH_HINT, GL_NICEST);
            glEnable(GL_LINE_SMOOTH);
            glHint(GL_LINE_SMOOTH_HINT, GL_NICEST);
            glEnable(GL_POLYGON_SMOOTH);
            glHint(GL_POLYGON_SMOOTH_HINT, GL_NICEST);
            break;

        case 2:
            // Turn off blending and all smoothing
```

LISTING 6.2   Continued

```
        glDisable(GL_BLEND);
        glDisable(GL_LINE_SMOOTH);
        glDisable(GL_POINT_SMOOTH);
        glDisable(GL_POLYGON_SMOOTH);
        break;

    default:
        break;
    }

// Trigger a redraw
glutPostRedisplay();
}
```

Note especially here the calls to the glHint function discussed in Chapter 2, "Using OpenGL." There are many algorithms and approaches to achieve antialiased primitives. Any specific OpenGL implementation may choose any one of those approaches, and perhaps even support two! You can ask OpenGL, if it does support multiple antialiasing algorithms, to choose one that is very fast (GL_FASTEST) or the one with the most accuracy in appearance (GL_NICEST).

Multisample

One of the biggest advantages to antialiasing is that it smoothes out the edges of primitives and can lend a more natural and realistic appearance to renderings. Point and line smoothing is widely supported, but unfortunately polygon smoothing is not available on all platforms. Even when GL_POLYGON_SMOOTH is available, it is not as convenient a means of having your whole scene antialiased as you might think. Because it is based on the blending operation, you would need to sort all your primitives from *front to back*! Yuck.

A more recent addition to OpenGL to address this shortcoming is *multisampling*. When this feature is supported (it is an OpenGL 1.3 feature), an additional buffer is added to the framebuffer that includes the color, depth, and stencil values. All primitives are sampled multiple times per pixel, and the results are stored in this buffer. These samples are resolved to a single value each time the pixel is updated, so from the programmer's standpoint, it appears automatic and happens "behind the scenes." Naturally, this extra memory and processing that must take place are not without their performance penalties, and some implementations may not support multisampling for multiple rendering contexts.

To get multisampling, you must first obtain a rendering context that has support for a multisampled framebuffer. This varies from platform to platform, but GLUT exposes a bit field (GLUT_MULTISAMPLE) that allows you to request this until you reach the operating system–specific chapters in Part III. For example, to request a multisampled, full-color, double-buffered frame buffer with depth, you would call

```
glutInitDisplayMode(GLUT_DOUBLE | GLUT_RGB | GLUT_DEPTH | GLUT_MULTISAMPLE);
```

You can turn multisampling on and off using the `glEnable`/`glDisable` combination and the `GL_MULTISAMPLE` token:

```
glEnable(GL_MULTISAMPLE);
```

or

```
glDisable(GL_MULTISAMPLE);
```

The sample program MULTISAMPLE is simply the Sphere World sample from the preceding chapter with multisampling selected and enabled. Figure 6.5 shows the difference between two zoomed-in sections from each program. You can see that multisampling really helps smooth out the geometry's edges on the image to the right, lending to a much more pleasing appearance to the rendered output.

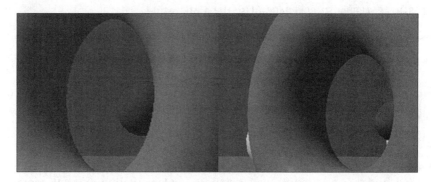

FIGURE 6.5   Zoomed-in view contrasting normal and multisampled rendering.

Another important note about multisampling is that when it is enabled, the point, line, and polygon smoothing features are ignored if enabled. This means you cannot use point and line smoothing at the same time as multisampling. On a given OpenGL implementation, points and lines may look better with smoothing turned on instead of multisampling. To accommodate this, you might turn off multisampling before drawing points and lines and then turn on multisampling for other solid geometry. The following pseudocode shows a rough outline of how to do this:

```
glDisable(GL_MULTISAMPLE);
glEnable(GL_POINT_SMOOTH);

// Draw some smooth points
```

```
// ...
glDisable(GL_POINT_SMOOTH);
glEnable(GL_MULTISAMPLE);
```

Of course if you do not have a multisampled buffer to begin with, OpenGL behaves as if GL_MULTISAMPLE were disabled.

> **STATE SORTING**
>
> Turning different OpenGL features on and off changes the internal state of the driver. These state changes can be costly in terms of rendering performance. Frequently, performance-sensitive programmers will go to great lengths to sort all the drawing commands so that geometry needing the same state will be drawn together. This state sorting is one of the more common techniques to improve rendering speed in games.

The multisample buffers use the RGB values of fragments by default and do not include the alpha component of the colors. You can change this by calling glEnable with one of the following three values:

- GL_SAMPLE_ALPHA_TO_COVERAGE—Use the alpha value.

- GL_SAMPLE_ALPHA_TO_ONE—Set alpha to 1 and use it.

- GL_SAMPLE_COVERAGE—Use the value set with glSampleCoverage.

When GL_SAMPLE_COVERAGE is enabled, the glSampleCoverage function allows you to specify a specific value that is ANDed (bitwise) with the fragment coverage value:

```
void glSampleCoverage(GLclampf value, GLboolean invert);
```

This fine-tuning of how the multisample operation works is not strictly specified by the specification, and the exact results may vary from implementation to implementation.

Applying Fog

Another easy-to-use special effect that OpenGL supports is fog. With fog, OpenGL blends a fog color that you specify with geometry after all other color computations have been completed. The amount of the fog color mixed with the geometry varies with the distance of the geometry from the camera origin. The result is a 3D scene that appears to contain fog. Fog can be useful for slowly obscuring objects as they "disappear" into the background fog; or a slight amount of fog will produce a hazy effect on distant objects, providing a powerful and realistic depth cue. Figure 6.6 shows output from the sample program FOGGED. As you can see, this is nothing more than the ubiquitous Sphere World example with fog turned on.

FIGURE 6.6   Sphere World with fog.

Listing 6.3 shows the few lines of code added to the SetupRC function to produce this effect.

LISTING 6.3   Setting Up Fog for Sphere World

```
// Grayish background
glClearColor(fLowLight[0], fLowLight[1], fLowLight[2], fLowLight[3]);

// Set up Fog parameters
glEnable(GL_FOG);                  // Turn Fog on
glFogfv(GL_FOG_COLOR, fLowLight);  // Set fog color to match background
glFogf(GL_FOG_START, 5.0f);        // How far away does the fog start
glFogf(GL_FOG_END, 30.0f);         // How far away does the fog stop
glFogi(GL_FOG_MODE, GL_LINEAR);    // Which fog equation to use
```

Turning fog on and off is as easy as using the following functions:

```
glEnable/glDisable(GL_FOG);
```

The means of changing fog parameters (how the fog behaves) is to use the `glFog` function. There are several variations on `glFog`:

```
void glFogi(GLenum pname, GLint param);
void glFogf(GLenum pname, GLfloat param);
void glFogiv(GLenum pname, GLint* params);
void glFogfv(GLenum pname, GLfloat* params);
```

The first use of `glFog` shown here is

```
glFogfv(GL_FOG_COLOR, fLowLight); // Set fog color to match background
```

When used with the `GL_FOG_COLOR` parameter, this function expects a pointer to an array of floating-point values that specifies what color the fog should be. Here, we used the same color for the fog as the background clear color. If the fog color does not match the background (there is no strict requirement for this), as objects become fogged, they will become a fog-colored silhouette against the background.

The next two lines allow us to specify how far away an object must be before fog is applied and how far away the object must be for the fog to be fully applied (where the object is completely the fog color):

```
glFogf(GL_FOG_START, 5.0f);     // How far away does the fog start
glFogf(GL_FOG_END, 30.0f);      // How far away does the fog stop
```

The parameter `GL_FOG_START` specifies how far away from the eye fogging begins to take effect, and `GL_FOG_END` is the distance from the eye where the fog color completely overpowers the color of the object. The transition from start to end is controlled by the fog equation, which we set to `GL_LINEAR` here:

```
glFogi(GL_FOG_MODE, GL_LINEAR);       // Which fog equation to use
```

Fog Equations

The fog equation calculates a fog factor that varies from 0 to 1 as the distance of the fragment moves between the start and end distances. OpenGL supports three fog equations: `GL_LINEAR`, `GL_EXP`, and `GL_EXP2`. These equations are shown in Table 6.3.

TABLE 6.3   Three OpenGL Supported Fog Equations

Fog Mode	Fog Equation
GL_LINEAR	$f = (end - c) / (end - start)$
GL_EXP	$f = \exp(-d * c)$
GL_EXP2	$f = \exp(-(d * c)^2)$

In these equations, c is the distance of the fragment from the eye plane, end is the `GL_FOG_END` distance, and start is the `GL_FOG_START` distance. The value d is the fog density. Fog density is typically set with `glFogf`:

```
glFogf(GL_FOG_DENSITY, 0.5f);
```

Note that `GL_FOG_START` and `GL_FOG_END` only have an effect on `GL_LINEAR` fog. Figure 6.7 shows graphically how the fog equation and fog density parameters affect the transition from the original fragment color to the fog color. `GL_LINEAR` is a straight linear progression, whereas the `GL_EXP` and `GL_EXP2` equations show two characteristic curves for their transitions. The fog density value has no effect with linear fog (`GL_LINEAR`), but the other two curves you see here are generally pulled downward with increasing density values. These graphs, for example, show approximately a density value of 0.5.

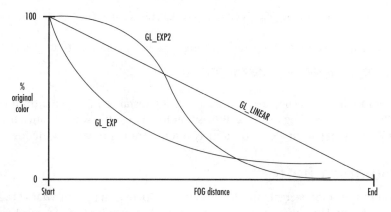

FIGURE 6.7   Fog density equations.

The distance to a fragment from the eye plane can be calculated in one of two ways. Some implementations (notably NVIDIA hardware) will use the actual fragment depth. Other implementations (notably many ATI chipsets) use the vertex distance and interpolate between vertices. The former method is sometimes referred to as fragment fog; and the later, vertex fog. Fragment fog requires more work than vertex fog, but often has a higher quality appearance. Both of the previously mentioned implementations honor the `glHint` parameter `GL_FOG_HINT`. To explicitly request fragment fog (better looking, but more work), call

```
glHint(GL_FOG_HINT, GL_NICEST);
```

For faster, less precise fog, you'd call

```
glHint(GL_FOG_HINT, GL_FASTEST);
```

Remember that hints are implementation dependent, may change over time, and are not required to be acknowledged or used by the driver at all. Indeed, you can't even rely on which fog method will be the default!

Fog Coordinates

Rather than letting OpenGL calculate fog distance for you, you can actually do this yourself. This value is called the fog coordinate and can be set manually with the function `glFogCoordf`:

```
void glFogCoordf(Glfloat fFogDistance);
```

Fog coordinates are ignored unless you change the fog coordinate source with this function call:

```
glFogi(GL_FOG_COORD_SRC, GL_FOG_COORD); // use glFogCoord1f
```

To return to OpenGL-derived fog values, change the last parameter to `GL_FRAGMENT_DEPTH`:

```
glFogi(GL_FOG_COORD_SRC, GL_FRAGMENT_DEPTH);
```

This fog coordinate when specified is used as the fog distance in the equations of Table 6.3. Specifying your own fog distance allows you to change the way distance is calculated. For example, you may want elevation to play a role, lending to volumetric fog effects.

Accumulation Buffer

In addition to the color, stencil, and depth buffers, OpenGL supports what is called the *accumulation buffer*. This buffer allows you to render to the color buffer, and then instead of displaying the results in the window, copy the contents of the color buffer to the accumulation buffer. Several supported copy operations allow you to repeatedly blend, in different ways, the color buffer contents with the accumulated contents in the accumulation buffer (thus its name). When you have finished accumulating an image, you can then copy the accumulation buffer back to the color buffer and display the results with a buffer swap.

The behavior of the accumulation buffer is controlled by one function:

```
void glAccum(GLenumm op, GLfloat value);
```

The first parameter specifies which accumulation operation you want to use, and the second is a floating-point value used to scale the operation. Table 6.4 lists the accumulation operations supported.

TABLE 6.4 OpenGL Accumulation Operations

Operation	Description
GL_ACCUM	Scales the color buffer values by value and adds them to the current contents of the accumulation buffer.
GL_LOAD	Scales the color buffer values by value and replaces the current contents of the accumulation buffer.
GL_RETURN	Scales the color values from the accumulation buffer by value and then copies the values to the color buffer.
GL_MULT	Scales the color values in the accumulation buffer by value and stores the result in the accumulation buffer.
GL_ADD	Scales the color values in the accumulation buffer by value and adds the result to the current accumulation buffer contents.

Because of the large amount of memory that must be copied and processed for accumulation buffer operations, few real-time applications make use of this capability. For non-real-time rendering, OpenGL can produce some astonishing effects that you might not expect from a real-time API. For example, you can render a scene multiple times and move the point of view around by a fraction of a pixel each time. Accumulating these multiple rendering passes blurs the sharp edges and can produce an entire scene fully antialiased with a quality that surpasses anything that can be done with multisampling. You can also use this blurring effect to blur the background or foreground of an image and then render the object of focus clearly afterward, simulating some depth-of-field camera effects.

In our sample program MOTIONBLUR, we will demonstrate yet another use of the accumulation buffer to create what appears to be a motion blur effect. A moving sphere is drawn repeatedly in different positions. Each time it is drawn, it is accumulated to the accumulation buffer, with a smaller weight on subsequent passes. The result is a brighter red sphere with a ghostlike image of itself following along behind. The output from this program is shown in Figure 6.8.

FIGURE 6.8   A motion-blurred flying sphere.

Listing 6.4 shows the DrawGeometry function, which draws all the geometry of the scene. The RenderScene function then repeatedly calls this function and accumulates the results into the accumulation buffer. When that process is finished, the lines

```
glAccum(GL_RETURN, 1.0f);
glutSwapBuffers();
```

copy the accumulation buffer back to the color buffer and perform the buffer swap.

LISTING 6.4   Using the Accumulation Buffer for Motion Blur

```
/////////////////////////////////////////////////////////////
// Draw the ground and the revolving sphere
void DrawGeometry(void)
    {
    // Clear the window with current clearing color
    glClear(GL_COLOR_BUFFER_BIT | GL_DEPTH_BUFFER_BIT);

    glPushMatrix();
        DrawGround();

        // Place the moving sphere
```

LISTING 6.4   Continued

```
            glColor3f(1.0f, 0.0f, 0.0f);
            glTranslatef(0.0f, 0.5f, -3.5f);
            glRotatef(-(yRot * 2.0f), 0.0f, 1.0f, 0.0f);
            glTranslatef(1.0f, 0.0f, 0.0f);
            glutSolidSphere(0.1f, 17, 9);
        glPopMatrix();
        }


//////////////////////////////////////////////////////////////////////
// Called to draw scene. The world is drawn multiple times with each
// frame blended with the last. The current rotation is advanced each
// time to create the illusion of motion blur.
void RenderScene(void)
    {
    GLfloat fPass;
    GLfloat fPasses = 10.0f;

    // Set the current rotation back a few degrees
    yRot = 35.0f;

    for(fPass = 0.0f; fPass < fPasses; fPass += 1.0f)
        {
        yRot += .75f; //1.0f / (fPass+1.0f);

        // Draw sphere
        DrawGeometry();

        // Accumulate to back buffer
        if(fPass == 0.0f)
            glAccum(GL_LOAD, 0.5f);
        else
            glAccum(GL_ACCUM, 0.5f * (1.0f / fPasses));
        }

    // copy accumulation buffer to color buffer and
    // do the buffer Swap
    glAccum(GL_RETURN, 1.0f);
    glutSwapBuffers();
    }
```

Finally, you must remember to ask for an accumulation buffer when you set up your OpenGL rendering context (see the OS-specific chapters in Part III for how to perform this task on your platform). GLUT also provides support for the accumulation buffer by passing the token `GLUT_ACCUM` to the `glutInitDisplayMode` function, as shown here:

```
glutInitDisplayMode(GLUT_DOUBLE ¦ GLUT_RGB ¦ GLUT_DEPTH ¦ GLUT_ACCUM);
```

Other Color Operations

Blending is a powerful OpenGL feature that enables a myriad of special effects algorithms. Aside from direct support for blending, fog, and an accumulation buffer, OpenGL also supports some other means of tweaking color values and fragments as they are written to the color buffer.

Color Masking

After a final color is computed, when it is about to be written to the color buffer, OpenGL allows you to mask out one or more of the color channels with the `glColorMask` function:

```
void glColorMask(GLboolean red, GLboolean green, GLboolean blue,
                                            GLboolean alpha);
```

The parameters are for the red, green, blue, and alpha channels, respectively. Passing `GL_TRUE` allows writing of this channel, and `GL_FALSE` prevents writing to this channel.

Color Logical Operations

Many 2D graphics APIs allow binary logical operations to be performed between the source and the destination colors. OpenGL also supports these types of 2D operations with the `glLogicOp` function:

```
void glLogicOp(GLenum op);
```

The logical operation modes are listed in Table 6.5. The logical operation is not enabled by default and is controlled, as most states are, with `glEnable`/`glDisable` using the value `GL_COLOR_LOGIC_OP`. For example, to turn on the logical operations, you use the following:

```
glEnable(GL_COLOR_LOGIC_OP);
```

TABLE 6.5   Bitwise Color Logical Operations

Argument Value	Operation
GL_CLEAR	0
GL_AND	s & d
GL_AND_REVERSE	s & ~d
GL_COPY	s

Argument Value	Operation
GL_AND_INVERTED	~s & d
NOOP	d
XOR	s xor d
OR	s ¦ d
NOR	~(s ¦ d)
GL_EQUIV	~(s xor d)
GL_INVERT	~d
GL_OR_REVERSE	s ¦ ~d
GL_COPY_INVERTED	~s
GL_OR_INVERTED	~s ¦ d
GL_NAND	~(s & d)
SET	all 1s

Alpha Testing

Alpha testing allows you to tell OpenGL to discard incoming fragments whose alpha value fails the alpha comparison test. Discarded fragments are not written to the color, depth, stencil, or accumulation buffers. This feature allows you to improve performance by dropping values that otherwise might be written to the buffers and to eliminate geometry from the depth buffer that may not be visible in the color buffer (because of very low alpha values). The alpha test value and comparison function are specified with the glAlphaFunc function:

```
void glAlphaFunc(GLenum func, GLclampf ref);
```

The reference value is clamped to the range 0.0 to 1.0, and the comparison function may be specified by any of the constants in Table 6.6. You can turn alpha testing on and off with glEnable/glDisable using the constant GL_ALPHA_TEST. The behavior of this function is similar to the glDepthFunc function (see Appendix C, "API Reference").

TABLE 6.6   Alpha Test Comparison Functions

Constant	Comparison Function
GL_NEVER	Never passes
GL_ALWAYS	Always passes
GL_LESS	Passes if the fragment is less than the reference value
GL_LEQUAL	Passes if the fragment is less than or equal to the reference value
GL_EQUAL	Passes if the fragment is equal to the reference value
GL_GEQUAL	Passes if the fragment is greater than or equal to the reference value
GL_GREATER	Passes if the fragment is greater than the reference value
GL_NOTEQUAL	Passes if the fragment is not equal to the reference value

Dithering

Dithering is a simple operation (in principle) that allows a display system with a small number of discrete colors to simulate displaying a much wider range of colors. For example, the color gray can be simulated by displaying a mix of white and black dots on the screen. More white than black dots make for a lighter gray, whereas more black dots make a darker gray. When your eye is far enough from the display, you cannot see the individual dots, and the blending effect creates the illusion of the color mix. This technique is useful for display systems that support only 8 or 16 bits of color information. Each OpenGL implementation is free to implement its own dithering algorithm, but the effect can be dramatically improved image quality on lower-end color systems. By default, dithering is turned on, and it can be controlled with `glEnable`/`glDisable` and the constant `GL_DITHER`:

```
glEnable(GL_DITHER);    // Initially enabled
```

On higher-end display systems with greater color resolution, the implementation may not need dithering, and dithering may not be employed at a potentially considerable performance savings.

Summary

In this chapter, we took color beyond simple shading and lighting effects. You saw how to use blending to create transparent and reflective surfaces and create antialiased points, lines, and polygons with the blending and multisampling features of OpenGL. You also were introduced to the accumulation buffer and saw at least one common special effect that it is normally used for. Finally, you saw how OpenGL supports other color manipulation features such as color masks, bitwise color operations, and dithering, and how to use the alpha test to discard fragments altogether. Now we progress further in the next chapter from colors, shading, and blending to operations that incorporate real image data.

Included in the source distribution for this chapter, you'll find an update of the Sphere World example from Chapter 5. You can study the source code to see how we have incorporated many of the techniques from this chapter to add some additional depth queuing to the world with fog, partially transparent shadows on the ground, and fully antialiased rendering of all geometry.

CHAPTER 7

Imaging with OpenGL

by Richard S. Wright Jr.

WHAT YOU'LL LEARN IN THIS CHAPTER:

How To	Functions You'll Use
Set the raster position	glRasterPos/glWindowPos
Draw bitmaps	glBitmap
Read and write color images	glReadPixels/glDrawPixels
Magnify, shrink, and flip images	glPixelZoom
Set up operations on colors	glPixelTransfer/glPixelMap
Perform color substitutions	glColorTable
Perform advanced image filtering	glConvolutionFilter2D
Collect statistics on images	glHistogram/glGetHistogram

In the preceding chapters, you learned the basics of OpenGL's acclaimed 3D graphics capabilities. Until now, all output has been the result of three-dimensional primitives being transformed and projected to 2D space and finally rasterized into the color buffer. However, OpenGL also supports reading and writing directly from and to the color buffer. This means image data can be read directly from the color buffer into your own memory buffer, where it can be manipulated or written to a file. This also means you can derive or read image data from a file and place it directly into the color buffer yourself. OpenGL goes beyond merely reading and writing 2D images and has support for a number of imaging operations that can be applied automatically during reading and writing operations. This chapter is all about OpenGL's rich but sometimes overlooked 2D capabilities.

Bitmaps

In the beginning, there were bitmaps. And they were…good enough. The original electronic computer displays were monochrome (one color), typically green or amber, and every pixel on the screen had one of two states: on or off. Computer graphics were simple in the early days, and image data was represented by *bitmaps*—a series of ones and zeros representing on and off pixel values. In a bitmap, each bit in a block of memory corresponds to exactly one pixel's state on the screen. We introduced this idea in the "Filling Polygons, or Stippling Revisited" section in Chapter 3, "Drawing in Space: Geometric Primitives and Buffers." Bitmaps can be used for masks (polygon stippling), fonts and character shapes, and even two-color dithered images. Figure 7.1 shows an image of a horse represented as a bitmap. Even though only two colors are used (black and white dots), the representation of a horse is still apparent. Compare this image with the one in Figure 7.2, which shows a grayscale image of the same horse. In this *pixelmap*, each pixel has one of 256 different intensities of gray. We discuss pixelmaps further in the next section. The term *bitmap* is often applied to images that contain grayscale or full-color data. This description is especially common on the Windows platform in relation to the poorly named .BMP (bitmap) file extension. Many would argue that, strictly speaking, this is a gross misapplication of the term. In this book, we use the term *bitmap* (correctly!) to mean a true binary map of on and off values, and we use the term *pixelmap* (or frequently *pixmap* for short) for image data that contains color or intensity values for each pixel.

FIGURE 7.1   A bitmapped image of a horse.

FIGURE 7.2   A pixmap image of a horse.

Bitmapped Data

The rendering components of the sample program BITMAPS are shown in Listing 7.1. This program uses the same bitmap data used in Chapter 3 for the polygon stippling sample that represents the shape of a small campfire arranged as a pattern of bits measuring 32×32. Remember that bitmaps are built from the bottom up, which means the first row of data actually represents the bottom row of the bitmapped image. This program creates a 512×512 window and fills the window with 16 rows and columns of the campfire bitmap. The output is shown in Figure 7.3. Note that the ChangeSize function sets an orthographic projection matching the window's width and height in pixels.

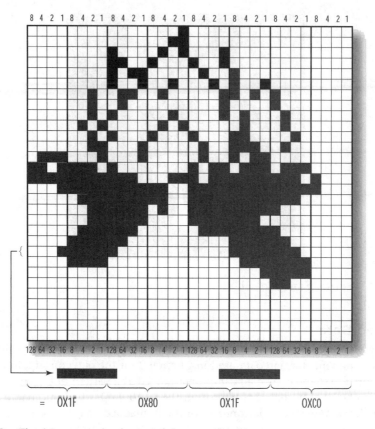

FIGURE 7.3   The 16 rows and columns of the campfire bitmap.

LISTING 7.1   The BITMAPS Sample Program

```
#include "../../shared/gltools.h"     // OpenGL toolkit

// Bitmap of campfire
GLubyte fire[128] = {
                0x00, 0x00, 0x00, 0x00, 0x00, 0x00, 0x00, 0x00,
                0x00, 0x00, 0x00, 0x00, 0x00, 0x00, 0x00, 0x00,
                0x00, 0x00, 0x00, 0x00, 0x00, 0x00, 0x00, 0x00,
                0x00, 0x00, 0x00, 0xc0, 0x00, 0x00, 0x01, 0xf0,
                0x00, 0x00, 0x07, 0xf0, 0x0f, 0x00, 0x1f, 0xe0,
                0x1f, 0x80, 0x1f, 0xc0, 0x0f, 0xc0, 0x3f, 0x80,
                0x07, 0xe0, 0x7e, 0x00, 0x03, 0xf0, 0xff, 0x80,
                0x03, 0xf5, 0xff, 0xe0, 0x07, 0xfd, 0xff, 0xf8,
                0x1f, 0xfc, 0xff, 0xe8, 0xff, 0xe3, 0xbf, 0x70,
```

LISTING 7.1   Continued

```
                      0xde, 0x80, 0xb7, 0x00, 0x71, 0x10, 0x4a, 0x80,
                      0x03, 0x10, 0x4e, 0x40, 0x02, 0x88, 0x8c, 0x20,
                      0x05, 0x05, 0x04, 0x40, 0x02, 0x82, 0x14, 0x40,
                      0x02, 0x40, 0x10, 0x80, 0x02, 0x64, 0x1a, 0x80,
                      0x00, 0x92, 0x29, 0x00, 0x00, 0xb0, 0x48, 0x00,
                      0x00, 0xc8, 0x90, 0x00, 0x00, 0x85, 0x10, 0x00,
                      0x00, 0x03, 0x00, 0x00, 0x00, 0x00, 0x10, 0x00 };

. . .
. . .


///////////////////////////////////////////////////////////////
// Called to draw scene
void RenderScene(void)
    {
    int x, y;

    // Clear the window with current clearing color
    glClear(GL_COLOR_BUFFER_BIT);

    // Set color to white
    glColor3f(1.0f, 1.0f, 1.0f);

    // Loop through 16 rows and columns
    for(y = 0; y < 16; y++)
        {
    // Set raster position for this "square"
    glRasterPos2i(0, y * 32);
        for(x = 0; x < 16; x++)
            // Draw the "fire" bitmap, advance raster position
            glBitmap(32, 32, 0.0, 0.0, 32.0, 0.0, fire);
        }

    // Do the buffer Swap
    glutSwapBuffers();
    }
```

The Raster Position

The real meat of the BITMAPS sample program occurs in the RenderScene function where a set of nested loops draws 16 rows of 16 columns of the campfire bitmap:

```
// Loop through 16 rows and columns
for(y = 0; y < 16; y++)
    {
    // Set raster position for this "square"
    glRasterPos2i(0, y * 32);
    for(x = 0; x < 16; x++)
        // Draw the "fire" bitmap, advance raster position
        glBitmap(32, 32, 0.0, 0.0, 32.0, 0.0, fire);
    }
```

The first loop (y variable) steps the row from 0 to 16. The following function call sets the raster position to the place where you want the bitmap drawn:

```
glRasterPos2i(0, y * 32);
```

The raster position is interpreted much like a call to glVertex in that the coordinates are transformed by the current modelview and projection matrices. The resulting window position becomes the current raster position. All rasterizing operations (bitmaps and pixmaps) occur with the current raster position specifying the image's lower-left corner. If the current raster position falls outside the window's viewport, it is invalid, and any OpenGL operations that require the raster position will fail.

In this example, we deliberately set the OpenGL projection to match the window dimensions so that we could use window coordinates to place the bitmaps. However, this technique may not always be convenient, so OpenGL provides an alternative function that allows you to set the raster position in window coordinates without regard to the current transformation matrix or projection (basically, they are ignored):

```
void glWindowPos2i(GLint x, GLint y);
```

The glWindowPos function comes in two- and three-argument flavors and accepts integers, floats, doubles, and short arguments much like glVertex. See the reference section in Appendix C, "API Reference," for a complete breakdown.

One important note about the raster position is that the color of the bitmap is set when either glRasterPos or glWindowPos is called. This means that the current color *previously* set with glColor is bound to subsequent bitmap operations. Calls to glColor made after the raster position is set will have no effect on the bitmap color.

Drawing the Bitmap

Finally, we get to the command that actually draws the bitmap into the color buffer:

```
glBitmap(32, 32, 0.0, 0.0, 32.0, 0.0, fire);
```

The glBitmap function copies the supplied bitmap to the color buffer at the current raster position and optionally advances the raster position all in one operation. This function has the following syntax:

```
void glBitmap(GLsize width, GLsize height, GLfloat xorig, GLfloat yorig,
              GLfloat xmove, GLfloat ymove, GLubyte *bitmap);
```

The first two parameters, *width* and *height*, specify the width and height of the bitmap (in bits). The next two parameters, *xorig* and *yorig*, specify the floating-point origin of the bitmap. To begin at the lower-left corner of the bitmap, specify 0.0 for both of these arguments. Then *xmove* and *ymove* specify an offset in pixels to move the raster position in the x and y directions after the bitmap is rendered. This is important because it means that the raster operation automatically updates the raster position for the next raster operation. Think about how this would make a bitmapped text system in OpenGL easier to implement! Note that these four parameters are all in floating-point units. The final argument, *bitmap*, is simply a pointer to the bitmap data. Note that when a bitmap is drawn, only the 1s in the image create fragments in the color buffer; 0s have no effect on anything already present.

Pixel Packing

Bitmaps and pixmaps are rarely packed tightly into memory. On many hardware platforms, each row of a bitmap or pixmap should begin on some particular byte-aligned address for performance reasons. Most compilers automatically put variables and buffers at an address alignment optimal for that architecture. OpenGL, by default, assumes a 4-byte alignment, which is appropriate for many systems in use today. The campfire bitmap used in the preceding example was tightly packed, but it didn't cause problems because the bitmap *just happened* to also be 4-byte aligned. Recall that the bitmap was 32 bits wide, exactly 4 bytes. If we had used a 34-bit-wide bitmap (only 2 more bits), we would have had to pad each row with an extra 30 bits of unused storage, for a total of 64 bits (8 bytes is evenly divisible by 4). Although this may seem like a waste of memory, this arrangement allows most CPUs to more efficiently grab blocks of data (such as a row of bits for a bitmap).

You can change how pixels for bitmaps or pixmaps are stored and retrieved by using the following functions:

```
void glPixelStorei(GLenum pname, GLint param);
void glPixelStoref(GLenum pname, GLfloat param);
```

If you want to change to tightly packed pixel data, for example, you make the following function call:

```
glPixelStorei(GL_UNPACK_ALIGNMENT, 1);
```

GL_UNPACK_ALIGNMENT specifies how OpenGL will unpack image data from the data buffer. Likewise, you can use GL_PACK_ALIGNMENT to tell OpenGL how to pack data being read from the color buffer and placed in a user-specified memory buffer. The complete list of pixel storage modes available through this function is given in Table 7.1 and explained in more detail in Appendix C.

TABLE 7.1   glPixelStore Parameters

Parameter Name	Type	Initial Value
GL_PACK_SWAP_BYTES	GLboolean	GL_FALSE
GL_UNPACK_SWAP_BYTES	GLboolean	GL_FALSE
GL_PACK_LSB_FIRST	GLboolean	GL_FALSE
GL_UNPACK_LSB_FIRST	GLboolean	GL_FALSE
GL_PACK_ROW_LENGTH	GLint	0
GL_UNPACK_ROW_LENGTH	GLint	0
GL_PACK_SKIP_ROWS	GLint	0
GL_UNPACK_SKIP_ROWS	GLint	0
GL_PACK_SKIP_PIXELS	GLint	0
GL_UNPACK_SKIP_PIXELS	GLint	0
GL_PACK_ALIGNMENT	GLint	4
GL_UNPACK_ALIGNMENT	GLint	4
GL_PACK_IMAGE_HEIGHT	GLint	0
GL_UNPACK_IMAGE_HEIGHT	GLint	0
GL_PACK_SKIP_IMAGES	GLint	0
GL_UNPACK_SKIP_IMAGES	GLint	0

Pixmaps

Of more interest and somewhat greater utility on today's full-color computer systems are pixmaps. A pixmap is similar in memory layout to a bitmap; however, each pixel may be represented by more than one bit of storage. Extra bits of storage for each pixel allow either intensity (sometimes referred to as *luminance* values) or color component values to be stored. You draw pixmaps at the current raster position just like bitmaps, but you draw them using a new function:

```
void glDrawPixels(GLsizei width, GLsizei height, GLenum format,
                  GLenum type, const void *pixels);
```

The first two arguments specify the width and height of the image in pixels. The third argument specifies the format of the image data, followed by the data type of the data and finally a pointer to the data itself. Unlike glBitmap, this function does not update the raster position and is considerably more flexible in the way you can specify image data.

Each pixel is represented by one or more data elements contained at the *pixels pointer. The color layout of these data elements is specified by the format parameter using one of the constants listed in Table 7.2.

TABLE 7.2 OpenGL Pixel Formats

Constant	Description
GL_RGB	Colors are in red, green, blue order.
GL_RGBA	Colors are in red, green, blue, alpha order.
GL_BGR	Colors are in blue, green, red order.
GL_BGRA	Colors are in blue, green, red, alpha order.
GL_RED	Each pixel contains a single red component.
GL_GREEN	Each pixel contains a single green component.
GL_BLUE	Each pixel contains a single blue component.
GL_ALPHA	Each pixel contains a single alpha component.
GL_LUMINANCE	Each pixel contains a single luminance (intensity) component.
GL_LUMINANCE_ALPHA	Each pixel contains a luminance followed by an alpha component.
GL_STENCIL_INDEX	Each pixel contains a single stencil value.
GL_DEPTH_COMPONENT	Each pixel contains a single depth value.

Two of the formats, GL_STENCIL_INDEX and GL_DEPTH_COMPONENT, are used for reading and writing directly to the stencil and depth buffers. The type parameter interprets the data pointed to by the *pixels parameter. It tells OpenGL what data type within the buffer is used to store the color components. The recognized values are specified in Table 7.3.

TABLE 7.3 Data Types for Pixel Data

Constant	Description
GL_UNSIGNED_BYTE	Each color component is an 8-bit unsigned integer
GL_BYTE	Signed 8-bit integer
GL_BITMAP	Single bits, no color data; same as glBitmap
GL_UNSIGNED_SHORT	Unsigned 16-bit integer
GL_SHORT	Signed 16-bit integer
GL_UNSIGNED_INT	Unsigned 32-bit integer
GL_INT	Signed 32-bit integer
GL_FLOAT	Single-precision float
GL_UNSIGNED_BYTE_3_2_2	Packed RGB values
GL_UNSIGNED_BYTE_2_3_3_REV	Packed RGB values

TABLE 7.3   Continued

Constant	Description
GL_UNSIGNED_SHORT_5_6_5	Packed RGB values
GL_UNSIGNED_SHORT_5_6_5_REV	Packed RGB values
GL_UNSIGNED_SHORT_4_4_4_4	Packed RGBA values
GL_UNSIGNED_SHORT_4_4_4_4_REV	Packed RGBA values
GL_UNSIGNED_SHORT_5_5_5_1	Packed RGBA values
GL_UNSIGNED_SHORT_1_5_5_5_REV	Packed RGBA values
GL_UNSIGNED_INT_8_8_8_8	Packed RGBA values
GL_UNSIGNED_INT_8_8_8_8_REV	Packed RGBA values
GL_UNSIGNED_INT_10_10_10_2	Packed RGBA values
GL_UNSIGNED_INT_2_10_10_10_REV	Packed RGBA values

Packed Pixel Formats

The packed formats listed in Table 7.3 were introduced in OpenGL 1.2 as a means of allowing image data to be stored in a more compressed form that matched a range of color graphics hardware. Display hardware designs could save memory or operate faster on a smaller set of packed pixel data. These packed pixel formats are still found on some PC hardware and may continue to be useful for future hardware platforms.

The packed pixel formats compress color data into as few bits as possible, with the number of bits per color channel shown in the constant. For example, the GL_UNSIGNED_BYTE_3_3_2 format stores 3 bits of the first component, 3 bits of the second component, and 2 bits of the third component. Remember, the specific components (red, green, blue, and alpha) are still ordered according to the *format* parameter of glDrawPixels. The components are ordered from the highest bits (most significant bit, or MSB) to the lowest (least significant bit, or LSB). GL_UNSIGNED_BYTE_2_3_3_REV reverses this order and places the last component in the top 2 bits, and so on. Figure 7.4 shows graphically the bitwise layout for these two arrangements. All the other packed formats are interpreted in the same manner.

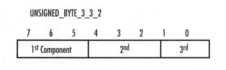

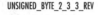

FIGURE 7.4   Sample layout for two packed pixel formats.

A More Colorful Example

Now it's time to put your new pixel knowledge to work with a more colorful and realistic rendition of a campfire. Figure 7.5 shows the output of the next sample program, IMAGE-LOAD. This program loads an image, `fire.tga`, and uses `glDrawPixels` to place the image directly into the color buffer. This program is almost identical to the BITMAPS sample program with the exception that the color image data is read from a targa image file (note the `.tga` file extension) using the glTools function `gltLoadTGA` and then drawn with a call to `glDrawPixels` instead of `glBitmap`. The function that loads the file and displays it is shown in Listing 7.2.

FIGURE 7.5   A campfire image loaded from a file.

LISTING 7.2   The `RenderScene` Function to Load and Display the Image File

```
// Called to draw scene
void RenderScene(void)
    {
    GLbyte *pImage = NULL;
    GLint iWidth, iHeight, iComponents;
    GLenum eFormat;

    // Clear the window with current clearing color
    glClear(GL_COLOR_BUFFER_BIT);

    // Targas are 1 byte aligned
```

LISTING 7.2 Continued

```
glPixelStorei(GL_UNPACK_ALIGNMENT, 1);

// Load the TGA file, get width, height, and component/format information
pImage = gltLoadTGA("fire.tga", &iWidth, &iHeight, &iComponents, &eFormat);

// Use Window coordinates to set raster position
glRasterPos2i(0, 0);

// Draw the pixmap
if(pImage != NULL)
    glDrawPixels(iWidth, iHeight, eFormat, GL_UNSIGNED_BYTE, pImage);

// Don't need the image data anymore
free(pImage);

// Do the buffer Swap
glutSwapBuffers();
}
```

Note the call that reads the targa file:

```
// Load the TGA file, get width, height, and component/format information
pImage = gltLoadTGA("fire.tga", &iWidth, &iHeight, &iComponents, &eFormat);
```

We use this function frequently in other sample programs when the need arises to load image data from a file. The first argument is the filename (with the path if necessary) of the targa file to load. The targa image format is a well-supported and common image file format. Unlike JPEG files, targa files (usually) store an image in its uncompressed form. The gltLoadTGA function opens the file and then reads in and parses the header to determine the width, height, and data format of the file. The number of components can be one, three, or four for luminance, RGB, or RGBA images, respectively. The final parameter is a pointer to a GLenum that receives the corresponding OpenGL image format for the file. If the function call is successful, it returns a newly allocated pointer (using malloc) to the image data read directly from the file. If the file is not found, or some other error occurs, the function returns NULL. The complete listing for the gltLoadTGA function is given in Listing 7.3.

LISTING 7.3 The gltLoadTGA Function to Load Targa Files for Use in OpenGL

```
///////////////////////////////////////////////////////////////////////
// Allocate memory and load targa bits. Returns pointer to new buffer,
// height, and width of texture, and the OpenGL format of data.
```

LISTING 7.3   Continued

```
// Call free() on buffer when finished!
// This only works on pretty vanilla targas... 8, 24, or 32 bit color
// only, no palettes, no RLE encoding.
GLbyte *gltLoadTGA(const char *szFileName,
                   GLint *iWidth, GLint *iHeight,
                   GLint *iComponents, GLenum *eFormat)
    {
    FILE *pFile;                    // File pointer
    TGAHEADER tgaHeader;            // TGA file header
    unsigned long lImageSize;       // Size in bytes of image
    short sDepth;                   // Pixel depth;
    GLbyte    *pBits = NULL;        // Pointer to bits

    // Default/Failed values
    *iWidth = 0;
    *iHeight = 0;
    *eFormat = GL_BGR_EXT;
    *iComponents = GL_RGB8;

    // Attempt to open the file
    pFile = fopen(szFileName, "rb");
    if(pFile == NULL)
        return NULL;

    // Read in header (binary)
    fread(&tgaHeader, 18/* sizeof(TGAHEADER)*/, 1, pFile);

    // Do byte swap for big vs little endian
#ifdef __APPLE__
    BYTE_SWAP(tgaHeader.colorMapStart);
    BYTE_SWAP(tgaHeader.colorMapLength);
    BYTE_SWAP(tgaHeader.xstart);
    BYTE_SWAP(tgaHeader.ystart);
    BYTE_SWAP(tgaHeader.width);
    BYTE_SWAP(tgaHeader.height);
#endif

    // Get width, height, and depth of texture
    *iWidth = tgaHeader.width;
    *iHeight = tgaHeader.height;
    sDepth = tgaHeader.bits / 8;
```

LISTING 7.3   Continued

```
// Put some validity checks here. Very simply, I only understand
// or care about 8, 24, or 32 bit targas.
if(tgaHeader.bits != 8 && tgaHeader.bits != 24 && tgaHeader.bits != 32)
    return NULL;

// Calculate size of image buffer
lImageSize = tgaHeader.width * tgaHeader.height * sDepth;

// Allocate memory and check for success
pBits = malloc(lImageSize * sizeof(GLbyte));
if(pBits == NULL)
    return NULL;

// Read in the bits
// Check for read error. This should catch RLE or other
// weird formats that I don't want to recognize
if(fread(pBits, lImageSize, 1, pFile) != 1)
    {
    free(pBits);
    return NULL;
    }

// Set OpenGL format expected
switch(sDepth)
    {
    case 3:     // Most likely case
        *eFormat = GL_BGR_EXT;
        *iComponents = GL_RGB8;
        break;
    case 4:
        *eFormat = GL_BGRA_EXT;
        *iComponents = GL_RGBA8;
        break;
    case 1:
        *eFormat = GL_LUMINANCE;
        *iComponents = GL_LUMINANCE8;
        break;
    };

// Done with File
fclose(pFile);
```

LISTING 7.3   Continued

```
// Return pointer to image data
return pBits;
}
```

You may notice that the number of components is not set to the integers 1, 3, or 4, but GL_LUMINANCE8, GL_RGB8, and GL_RGBA8. OpenGL recognizes these special constants as a request to maintain full image precision internally when it manipulates the image data. For example, for performance reasons, some OpenGL implementations may down-sample a 24-bit color image to 16 bits internally. This is especially common for texture loads (see Chapter 8, "Texture Mapping: The Basics") on many implementations in which the display output color resolution is only 16 bits, but a higher bit depth image is loaded. These constants are requests to the implementation to store and use the image data as supplied at their full 8-bit-per-channel color depth.

Moving Pixels Around

Writing pixel data to the color buffer can be very useful in and of itself, but you can also read pixel data from the color buffer and even copy data from one part of the color buffer to another. The function to read pixel data works just like glDrawPixels, but in reverse:

```
void glReadPixels(GLint x, GLint y, GLsizei width, GLsizei height,
                  GLenum format, GLenum type, const void *pixels);
```

You specify the *x* and *y* in window coordinates of the lower-left corner of the rectangle to read followed by the *width* and *height* of the rectangle in pixels. The *format* and *type* parameters are the format and type you want the data to have. If the color buffer stores data differently than what you have requested, OpenGL will take care of the necessary conversions. This capability can be very useful, especially after you learn a couple of magic tricks that you can do during this process using the glPixelTransfer function (coming up in the "Pixel Transfer" section). The pointer to the image data, *pixels*, must be valid and must contain enough storage to contain the image data after conversion, or you will likely get a nasty memory exception at runtime. Also be aware that if you specify window coordinates that are out of bounds, you will get data only for the pixels within the actual OpenGL frame buffer.

Copying pixels from one part of the color buffer to another is also easy, and you don't have to allocate any temporary storage during the operation. First, set the raster position using glRasterPos or glWindowPos to the destination corner (remember, the lower-left corner) where you want the image data copied. Then use the following function to perform the copy operation:

```
void glCopyPixels(GLint x, GLint y, GLsizei width,
                  GLsizei height, GLenum type);
```

The *x* and *y* parameters specify the lower-left corner of the rectangle to copy, followed by the *width* and *height* in pixels. The *type* parameter should be GL_COLOR to copy color data. You can also use GL_DEPTH and GL_STENCIL here, and the copy will be performed in the depth or stencil buffer instead. Moving depth and stencil values around can also be useful for some rendering algorithms and special effects.

By default, all these pixel operations operate on the back buffer for double-buffered rendering contexts, and the front buffer for single-buffered rendering contexts. You can change the source or destination of these pixel operations by using these two functions:

```
void glDrawBuffer(GLenum mode);
void glReadBuffer(GLenum mode);
```

The glDrawBuffer function affects where pixels are drawn by either glDrawPixels or glCopyPixels operations. You can use any of the valid buffer constants discussed in Chapter 3: GL_NONE, GL_FRONT, GL_BACK, GL_FRONT_AND_BACK, GL_FRONT_LEFT, GL_FRONT_RIGHT, and so on.

The glReadBuffer function accepts the same constants and sets the target color buffer for read operations performed by glReadPixels or glCopyPixels.

Saving Pixels

You now know enough about how to move pixels around to write another useful function for the glTools library. A counterpart to the targa loading function, gltLoadTGA, is gltWriteTGA. This function reads the color data from the front color buffer and saves it to an image file in the targa file format. You use this function in the next section when you start playing with some interesting OpenGL pixel operations. The complete listing for the gltWriteTGA function is shown in Listing 7.4.

LISTING 7.4   The gltWriteTGA Function to Save the Screen as a Targa File

```
///////////////////////////////////////////////////////////////////
// Capture the current viewport and save it as a targa file.
// Be sure to call SwapBuffers for double buffered contexts or
// glFinish for single buffered contexts before calling this function.
// Returns 0 if an error occurs, or 1 on success.
GLint gltWriteTGA(const char *szFileName)
    {
    FILE *pFile;                    // File pointer
    TGAHEADER tgaHeader;            // TGA file header
    unsigned long lImageSize;       // Size in bytes of image
    GLbyte    *pBits = NULL;        // Pointer to bits
    GLint iViewport[4];             // Viewport in pixels
    GLenum lastBuffer;              // Storage for the current read buffer setting
```

LISTING 7.4   Continued

```
    // Get the viewport dimensions
    glGetIntegerv(GL_VIEWPORT, iViewport);

    // How big is the image going to be (targas are tightly packed)
    lImageSize = iViewport[2] * 3 * iViewport[3];

    // Allocate block. If this doesn't work, go home
    pBits = (GLbyte *)malloc(lImageSize);
    if(pBits == NULL)
        return 0;

    // Read bits from color buffer
    glPixelStorei(GL_PACK_ALIGNMENT, 1);
    glPixelStorei(GL_PACK_ROW_LENGTH, 0);
    glPixelStorei(GL_PACK_SKIP_ROWS, 0);
    glPixelStorei(GL_PACK_SKIP_PIXELS, 0);

    // Get the current read buffer setting and save it. Switch to
    // the front buffer and do the read operation. Finally, restore
    // the read buffer state
    glGetIntegerv(GL_READ_BUFFER, &lastBuffer);
    glReadBuffer(GL_FRONT);
    glReadPixels(0, 0, iViewport[2], iViewport[3], GL_BGR,
                GL_UNSIGNED_BYTE, pBits);
    glReadBuffer(lastBuffer);

    // Initialize the Targa header
    tgaHeader.identsize = 0;
    tgaHeader.colorMapType = 0;
    tgaHeader.imageType = 2;
    tgaHeader.colorMapStart = 0;
    tgaHeader.colorMapLength = 0;
    tgaHeader.colorMapBits = 0;
    tgaHeader.xstart = 0;
    tgaHeader.ystart = 0;
    tgaHeader.width = iViewport[2];
    tgaHeader.height = iViewport[3];
    tgaHeader.bits = 24;
    tgaHeader.descriptor = 0;

    // Do byte swap for big vs little endian
#ifdef __APPLE__
```

LISTING 7.4   Continued

```
    BYTE_SWAP(tgaHeader.colorMapStart);
    BYTE_SWAP(tgaHeader.colorMapLength);
    BYTE_SWAP(tgaHeader.xstart);
    BYTE_SWAP(tgaHeader.ystart);
    BYTE_SWAP(tgaHeader.width);
    BYTE_SWAP(tgaHeader.height);
#endif

    // Attempt to open the file
    pFile = fopen(szFileName, "wb");
    if(pFile == NULL)
        {
        free(pBits);    // Free buffer and return error
        return 0;
        }

    // Write the header
    fwrite(&tgaHeader, sizeof(TGAHEADER), 1, pFile);

    // Write the image data
    fwrite(pBits, lImageSize, 1, pFile);

    // Free temporary buffer and close the file
    free(pBits);
    fclose(pFile);

    // Success!
    return 1;
    }
```

More Fun with Pixels

In this section, we discuss OpenGL's support for magnifying and reducing images, flipping images, and performing some special operations during the transfer of pixel data to and from the color buffer. Rather than having a different sample program for every special effect discussed, we have provided one sample program named OPERATIONS. This sample program ordinarily displays a simple color image loaded from a targa file. A right mouse click is attached to the GLUT menu system, allowing you to select from one of eight drawing modes or to save the modified image to a disk file named screenshot.tga. Listing 7.5 provides the essential elements of the program in its entirety. We dissect this program and explain it piece by piece in the coming sections.

LISTING 7.5   Source Code for the OPERATIONS Sample Program

```cpp
// Operations.cpp
// OpenGL SuperBible
// Demonstrates Imaging Operations
// Program by Richard S. Wright Jr.

#include "../../shared/gltools.h"     // OpenGL toolkit
#include <math.h>


///////////////////////////////////////////////////////////////
// Module globals to save source image data
static GLbyte *pImage = NULL;
static GLint iWidth, iHeight, iComponents;
static GLenum eFormat;

// Global variable to store desired drawing mode
static GLint    iRenderMode = 1;

///////////////////////////////////////////////////////////////
// This function does any needed initialization on the rendering
// context.
void SetupRC(void)
    {
    // Black background
    glClearColor(0.0f, 0.0f, 0.0f, 0.0f);

    // Load the horse image
    glPixelStorei(GL_UNPACK_ALIGNMENT, 1);
    pImage = gltLoadTGA("horse.tga", &iWidth, &iHeight,
                                        &iComponents, &eFormat);

    }

void ShutdownRC(void)
    {
    // Free the original image data
    free(pImage);
    }


///////////////////////////////////////////////////////////////
// Reset flags as appropriate in response to menu selections
void ProcessMenu(int value)
    {
```

LISTING 7.5   Continued

```
if(value == 0)
    // Save image
    gltWriteTGA("ScreenShot.tga");
else
    // Change render mode index to match menu entry index
    iRenderMode = value;

// Trigger Redraw
glutPostRedisplay();
}


///////////////////////////////////////////////////////////////
// Called to draw scene
void RenderScene(void)
    {
    GLint iViewport[4];
    GLbyte *pModifiedBytes = NULL;
    GLfloat invertMap[256];
    GLint i;

    // Clear the window with current clearing color
    glClear(GL_OOLOR_DUFFER_BIT);

    // Current Raster Position always at bottom-left-hand corner
    glRasterPos2i(0, 0);

    // Do image operation, depending on rendermode index
    switch(iRenderMode)
        {
        case 2:     // Flip the pixels
            glPixelZoom(-1.0f, -1.0f);
            glRasterPos2i(iWidth, iHeight);
            break;

        case 3:     // Zoom pixels to fill window
            glGetIntegerv(GL_VIEWPORT, iViewport);
            glPixelZoom((GLfloat) iViewport[2] / (GLfloat)iWidth,
                (GLfloat) iViewport[3] / (GLfloat)iHeight);
            break;

        case 4:     // Just Red
```

LISTING 7.5   Continued

```
            glPixelTransferf(GL_RED_SCALE, 1.0f);
            glPixelTransferf(GL_GREEN_SCALE, 0.0f);
            glPixelTransferf(GL_BLUE_SCALE, 0.0f);
            break;

    case 5:     // Just Green
            glPixelTransferf(GL_RED_SCALE, 0.0f);
            glPixelTransferf(GL_GREEN_SCALE, 1.0f);
            glPixelTransferf(GL_BLUE_SCALE, 0.0f);
            break;

    case 6:     // Just Blue
            glPixelTransferf(GL_RED_SCALE, 0.0f);
            glPixelTransferf(GL_GREEN_SCALE, 0.0f);
            glPixelTransferf(GL_BLUE_SCALE, 1.0f);
            break;

    case 7:     // Black & White, more tricky
            // First draw image into color buffer
            glDrawPixels(iWidth, iHeight, eFormat,
                                GL_UNSIGNED_BYTE, pImage);

            // Allocate space for the luminance map
            pModifiedBytes = (GLbyte *)malloc(iWidth * iHeight);

            // Scale colors according to NSTC standard
            glPixelTransferf(GL_RED_SCALE, 0.3f);
            glPixelTransferf(GL_GREEN_SCALE, 0.59f);
            glPixelTransferf(GL_BLUE_SCALE, 0.11f);

            // Read pixels into buffer (scale above will be applied)
            glReadPixels(0,0,iWidth, iHeight, GL_LUMINANCE,
                            GL_UNSIGNED_BYTE, pModifiedBytes);

            // Return color scaling to normal
            glPixelTransferf(GL_RED_SCALE, 1.0f);
            glPixelTransferf(GL_GREEN_SCALE, 1.0f);
            glPixelTransferf(GL_BLUE_SCALE, 1.0f);
            break;

    case 8:     // Invert colors
            invertMap[0] = 1.0f;
```

LISTING 7.5   Continued

```
            for(i = 1; i < 256; i++)
                invertMap[i] = 1.0f - (1.0f / 255.0f * (GLfloat)i);

            glPixelMapfv(GL_PIXEL_MAP_R_TO_R, 255, invertMap);
            glPixelMapfv(GL_PIXEL_MAP_G_TO_G, 255, invertMap);
            glPixelMapfv(GL_PIXEL_MAP_B_TO_B, 255, invertMap);
            glPixelTransferi(GL_MAP_COLOR, GL_TRUE);
            break;

        case 1:     // Just do a plain old image copy
        default:
                    // This line intentionally left blank
            break;
        }

    // Do the pixel draw
    if(pModifiedBytes == NULL)
        glDrawPixels(iWidth, iHeight, eFormat, GL_UNSIGNED_BYTE,
                                                    pImage);
    else
        {
        glDrawPixels(iWidth, iHeight, GL_LUMINANCE, GL_UNSIGNED_BYTE,
                                                pModifiedBytes);
        free(pModifiedBytes);
        }

    // Reset everything to default
    glPixelTransferi(GL_MAP_COLOR, GL_FALSE);
    glPixelTransferf(GL_RED_SCALE, 1.0f);
    glPixelTransferf(GL_GREEN_SCALE, 1.0f);
    glPixelTransferf(GL_BLUE_SCALE, 1.0f);
    glPixelZoom(1.0f, 1.0f);                     // No Pixel Zooming

    // Do the buffer Swap
    glutSwapBuffers();
    }

. . .
. . .


/////////////////////////////////////////////////////////
// Main program entrypoint
```

LISTING 7.5   Continued

```
int main(int argc, char* argv[])
    {
    glutInit(&argc, argv);
    glutInitDisplayMode(GLUT_RGB | GL_DOUBLE);
    glutInitWindowSize(800 ,600);
    glutCreateWindow("OpenGL Image Operations");
    glutReshapeFunc(ChangeSize);
    glutDisplayFunc(RenderScene);

    // Create the Menu and add choices
    glutCreateMenu(ProcessMenu);
    glutAddMenuEntry("Save Image",0);
    glutAddMenuEntry("DrawPixels",1);
    glutAddMenuEntry("FlipPixels",2);
    glutAddMenuEntry("ZoomPixels",3);
    glutAddMenuEntry("Just Red Channel",4);
    glutAddMenuEntry("Just Green Channel",5);
    glutAddMenuEntry("Just Blue Channel",6);
    glutAddMenuEntry("Black and White", 7);
    glutAddMenuEntry("Invert Colors", 8);
    glutAttachMenu(GLUT_RIGHT_BUTTON);

    SetupRC();          // Do setup

    glutMainLoop();     // Main program loop

    ShutdownRC();       // Do shutdown

    return 0;
    }
```

The basic framework of this program is simple. Unlike with the previous example, IMAGE-LOAD, here the image is loaded and kept in memory for the duration of the program so that reloading the image is not necessary every time the screen must be redrawn. The information about the image and a pointer to the bytes are kept as module global variables, as shown here:

```
static GLbyte *pImage = NULL;
static GLint iWidth, iHeight, iComponents;
static GLenum eFormat;
```

The SetupRC function then does little other than load the image and initialize the global variables containing the image format, width, and height:

```
// Load the horse image
glPixelStorei(GL_UNPACK_ALIGNMENT, 1);
pImage = gltLoadTGA("horse.tga", &iWidth, &iHeight,
                                 &iComponents, &eFormat);
```

When the program terminates, be sure to free the memory allocated by the gltLoadTGA function in ShutdownRC:

```
free(pImage);
```

In the main function, we create a menu and add entries and values for the different operations you want to accomplish:

```
// Create the Menu and add choices
glutCreateMenu(ProcessMenu);
glutAddMenuEntry("Save Image",0);
glutAddMenuEntry("Draw Pixels",1);
glutAddMenuEntry("Flip Pixels",2);
glutAddMenuEntry("Zoom Pixels",3);
glutAddMenuEntry("Just Red Channel",4);
glutAddMenuEntry("Just Green Channel",5);
glutAddMenuEntry("Just Blue Channel",6);
glutAddMenuEntry("Black and White", 7);
glutAddMenuEntry("Invert Colors", 8);
glutAttachMenu(GLUT_RIGHT_BUTTON);
```

These menu selections then set the variable iRenderMode to the desired value or, if the value is 0, save the image as it is currently displayed:

```
void ProcessMenu(int value)
    {
    if(value == 0)
      // Save image
      gltWriteTGA("ScreenShot.tga");
    else
      // Change render mode index to match menu entry index
      iRenderMode = value;

    // Trigger Redraw
    glutPostRedisplay();
    }
```

Finally, the image is actually drawn into the color buffer in the RenderScene function. This function contains a switch statement that uses the iRenderMode variable to select from one of eight different drawing modes. The default case is simply to perform an unaltered glDrawPixels function, placing the image in the lower-left corner of the window, as shown in Figure 7.6. The other cases, however, are now the subject of our discussion.

FIGURE 7.6   The default output of the OPERATIONS sample program.

Pixel Zoom

Another simple yet common operation that you may want to perform on pixel data is stretching or shrinking the image. OpenGL calls this *pixel zoom* and provides a function that performs this operation:

```
void glPixelZoom(GLfloat xfactor, GLfloat yfactor);
```

The two arguments, *xfactor* and *yfactor*, specify the amount of zoom to occur in the x and y directions. Zoom can shrink, expand, or even reverse an image. For example, a zoom factor of 2 causes the image to be written at twice its size along the axis specified, whereas a factor of 0.5 shrinks it by half. As an example, the menu selection Zoom Pixels in the OPERATIONS sample program sets the render mode to 3. The following code lines are then executed before the call to glDrawPixels, causing the x and y zoom factors to stretch the image to fill the entire window:

```
case 3:      // Zoom pixels to fill window
             glGetIntegerv(GL_VIEWPORT, iViewport);
             glPixelZoom((GLfloat) iViewport[2] / (GLfloat)iWidth,
                 (GLfloat) iViewport[3] / (GLfloat)iHeight);
             break;
```

The output is shown in Figure 7.7.

FIGURE 7.7   Using pixel zoom to stretch an image to match the window size.

A negative zoom factor, on the other hand, has the effect of flipping the image along the direction of the zoom. Using such a zoom factor not only reverses the order of the pixels in the image, but also reverses the direction onscreen that the pixels are drawn with respect to the raster position. For example, normally an image is drawn with the lower-left corner being placed at the current raster position. If both zoom factors are negative, the raster position becomes the upper-right corner of the resulting image.

In the OPERATIONS sample program, selecting Flip Pixels inverts the image both horizontally and vertically. As shown in the following code snippet, the pixel zoom factors are both set to -1.0, and the raster position is changed from the lower-left corner of the window to a position that represents the upper-right corner of the image to be drawn (the image's width and height):

```
case 2:      // Flip the pixels
             glPixelZoom(-1.0f, -1.0f);
             glRasterPos2i(iWidth, iHeight);
             break;
```

Figure 7.8 shows the inverted image when this option is selected.

FIGURE 7.8   Image displayed with x and y dimensions inverted.

Pixel Transfer

In addition to zooming pixels, OpenGL supports a set of simple mathematical operations that can be performed on image data as it is transferred either to or from the color buffer. These pixel transfer modes are set with one of the following functions and the pixel transfer parameters listed in Table 7.4:

```
void glPixelTransferi(GLenum pname, GLint param);
void glPixelTransferf(GLenum pname, GLfloat param);
```

TABLE 7.4   Pixel Transfer Parameters

Constant	Type	Default Value
GL_MAP_COLOR	GLboolean	GL_FALSE
GL_MAP_STENCIL	GLboolean	GL_FALSE
GL_RED_SCALE	GLfloat	1.0
GL_GREEN_SCALE	GLfloat	1.0
GL_BLUE_SCALE	GLfloat	1.0
GL_ALPHA_SCALE	GLfloat	1.0
GL_DEPTH_SCALE	GLfloat	1.0
GL_RED_BIAS	GLfloat	0.0
GL_GREEN_BIAS	GLfloat	0.0
GL_BLUE_BIAS	GLfloat	0.0
GL_ALPHA_BIAS	GLfloat	0.0
GL_DEPTH_BIAS	GLfloat	0.0
GL_POST_CONVOLUTION_RED_SCALE	GLfloat	1.0
GL_POST_CONVOLUTION_GREEN_SCALE	GLfloat	1.0
GL_POST_CONVOLUTION_BLUE_SCALE	GLfloat	1.0
GL_POST_CONVOLUTION_ALPHA_SCALE	GLfloat	1.0
GL_POST_CONVOLUTION_RED_BIAS	GLfloat	0.0
GL_POST_CONVOLUTION_GREEN_BIAS	GLfloat	0.0
GL_POST_CONVOLUTION_BLUE_BIAS	GLfloat	0.0
GL_POST_CONVOLUTION_ALPHA_BIAS	GLfloat	0.0
GL_POST_COLOR_MATRIX_RED_SCALE	GLfloat	1.0
GL_POST_COLOR_MATRIX_GREEN_SCALE	GLfloat	1.0
GL_POST_COLOR_MATRIX_BLUE_SCALE	GLfloat	1.0
GL_POST_COLOR_MATRIX_ALPHA_SCALE	GLfloat	1.0
GL_POST_COLOR_MATRIX_RED_BIAS	GLfloat	0.0
GL_POST_COLOR_MATRIX_GREEN_BIAS	GLfloat	0.0
GL_POST_COLOR_MATRIX_BLUE_BIAS	GLfloat	0.0
GL_POST_COLOR_MATRIX_ALPHA_BIAS	GLfloat	0.0

The scale and bias parameters allow you to scale and bias individual color channels. A scaling factor is multiplied by the component value, and a bias value is added to that component value. A scale and bias operation is common in computer graphics for adjusting color channel values. The equation is simple:

New Value = (Old Value * Scale Value) + Bias Value

By default, the scale values are 1.0, and the bias values are 0.0. They essentially have no effect on the component values. Say you want to display a color image's red component values only. To do this, you set the blue and green scale factors to 0.0 before drawing and back to 1.0 afterward:

```
glPixelTransferf(GL_GREEN_SCALE, 0.0f);
glPixelTransfer(GL_BLUE_SCALE, 0.0f);
```

The OPERATIONS sample program includes the menu selections Just Red, Just Green, and Just Blue, which demonstrate this particular example. Each selection turns off all but one color channel to show the image's red, green, or blue color values only:

```
case 4:  // Just Red
        glPixelTransferf(GL_RED_SCALE, 1.0f);
        glPixelTransferf(GL_GREEN_SCALE, 0.0f);
        glPixelTransferf(GL_BLUE_SCALE, 0.0f);
        break;

    case 5:    // Just Green
        glPixelTransferf(GL_RED_SCALE, 0.0f);
        glPixelTransferf(GL_GREEN_SCALE, 1.0f);
        glPixelTransferf(GL_BLUE_SCALE, 0.0f);
        break;

    case 6:    // Just Blue
        glPixelTransferf(GL_RED_SCALE, 0.0f);
        glPixelTransferf(GL_GREEN_SCALE, 0.0f);
        glPixelTransferf(GL_BLUE_SCALE, 1.0f);
        break;
```

After drawing, the pixel transfer for the color channels resets the scale values to 1.0:

```
glPixelTransferf(GL_RED_SCALE, 1.0f);
glPixelTransferf(GL_GREEN_SCALE, 1.0f);
glPixelTransferf(GL_BLUE_SCALE, 1.0f);
```

The post-convolution and post-color matrix scale and bias parameters perform the same operation but wait until after the convolution or color matrix operations have been performed. These operations are available in the imaging subset, which will be discussed shortly.

A more interesting example of the pixel transfer operations is to display a color image in black and white. The OPERATIONS sample does this when you choose the Black and White menu selection. First, the full-color image is drawn to the color buffer:

```
glDrawPixels(iWidth, iHeight, eFormat, GL_UNSIGNED_BYTE, pImage);
```

Next, a buffer large enough to hold just the luminance values for each pixel is allocated:

```
pModifiedBytes = (GLbyte *)malloc(iWidth * iHeight);
```

Remember, a luminance image has only one color channel, and here you allocate 1 byte (8 bits) per pixel. OpenGL automatically converts the image in the color buffer to luminance for use when you call `glReadPixels` but request the data be in the `GL_LUMINANCE` format:

```
glReadPixels(0,0,iWidth, iHeight, GL_LUMINANCE,
                            GL_UNSIGNED_BYTE, pModifiedBytes);
```

The luminance image can then be written back into the color buffer, and you would see the converted black-and-white image:

```
glDrawPixels(iWidth, iHeight, GL_LUMINANCE, GL_UNSIGNED_BYTE,
                                    pModifiedBytes);
```

Using this approach sounds like a good plan, and it almost works. The problem is that when OpenGL converts a color image to luminance, it simply adds the color channels together. If the three color channels add up to a value greater than 1.0, it is simply clamped to 1.0. This has the effect of oversaturating many areas of the image. This effect is shown in Figure 7.9.

FIGURE 7.9 Oversaturation due to OpenGL's default color-to-luminance operation.

To solve this problem, you must set the pixel transfer mode to scale the color value appropriately when OpenGL does the transfer from color to luminance colorspaces. According to the National Television Standards Committee (NTSC) standard, the conversion from RGB colorspace to black and white (grayscale) is

Luminance = (0.3 * Red) + (0.59 * Green) + (0.11 * Blue)

You can easily set up this conversion in OpenGL by calling these functions just before `glReadPixels`:

```
// Scale colors according to NTSC standard
glPixelTransferf(GL_RED_SCALE, 0.3f);
glPixelTransferf(GL_GREEN_SCALE, 0.59f);
glPixelTransferf(GL_BLUE_SCALE, 0.11f);
```

After reading pixels, you return the pixel transfer mode to normal:

```
// Return color scaling to normal
glPixelTransferf(GL_RED_SCALE, 1.0f);
glPixelTransferf(GL_GREEN_SCALE, 1.0f);
glPixelTransferf(GL_BLUE_SCALE, 1.0f);
```

The output is now a nice grayscale representation of the image. Because the figures in this book are not in color, but grayscale, the output onscreen looks exactly like the image in Figure 7.6. Color Plate 3 does, however, show the image (upper left) in full color, and the lower right in grayscale.

Pixel Mapping

In addition to scaling and bias operations, the pixel transfer operation also supports color mapping. A color map is a table used as a lookup to convert one color value (used as an index into the table) to another color value (the color value stored at that index). Color mapping has many applications, such as performing color corrections, making gamma adjustments, or converting to and from different color representations.

You'll notice an interesting example in the OPERATIONS sample program when you select Invert Colors. In this case, a color map is set up to flip all the color values during a pixel transfer. This means all three channels are mapped from the range 0.0 to 1.0 to the range 1.0 to 0.0. The result is an image that looks like a photographic negative.

You enable pixel mapping by calling `glPixelTransfer` with the `GL_MAP_COLOR` parameter set to `GL_TRUE`:

```
glPixelTransferi(GL_MAP_COLOR, GL_TRUE);
```

To set up a pixel map, you must call another function, `glPixelMap`, and supply the map in one of three formats:

```
glPixelMapuiv(GLenum map, GLint mapsize, GLuint *values);
glPixelMapusv(GLenum map, GLint mapsize, GLushort *values);
glPixelMapfv(GLenum map, GLint mapsize, GLfloat *values);
```

The valid map values are listed in Table 7.5.

TABLE 7.5   Pixelmap Parameters

Map Name	Description
GL_PIXEL_MAP_R_TO_R	Remapping of red components
GL_PIXEL_MAP_G_TO_G	Remapping of green components
GL_PIXEL_MAP_B_TO_B	Remapping of blue components
GL_PIXEL_MAP_A_TO_A	Remapping of alpha components

For the example, you set up a map of 256 floating-point values and fill the map with intermediate values from 1.0 to 0.0:

```
GLfloat invertMap[256];
...
...
invertMap[0] = 1.0f;
        for(i = 1; i < 256; i++)
            invertMap[i] = 1.0f - (1.0f / 255.0f * (GLfloat)i);
```

Then you set the red, green, and blue maps to this inversion map and turn on color mapping:

```
glPixelMapfv(GL_PIXEL_MAP_R_TO_R, 255, invertMap);
glPixelMapfv(GL_PIXEL_MAP_G_TO_G, 255, invertMap);
glPixelMapfv(GL_PIXEL_MAP_B_TO_B, 255, invertMap);
glPixelTransferi(GL_MAP_COLOR, GL_TRUE);
```

When `glDrawPixels` is called, the color components are remapped using the inversion table, essentially creating a color negative image. Figure 7.10 shows the output in black and white. Color Plate 3 in the Color insert shows a full-color image of this effect in the upper-right corner.

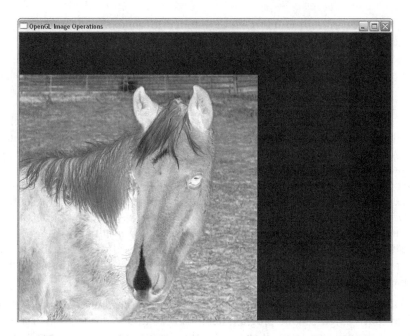

FIGURE 7.10   Using a color map to create a color negative image. (This figure also appears in the Color insert.)

The Imaging "Subset" and Pipeline

All the OpenGL functions covered so far in this chapter for image manipulation have been a part of the core OpenGL API since version 1.0. The only exception is the `glWindowPos` function, which was added in OpenGL 1.4 to make it easier to set the raster position. These features provide OpenGL with adequate support for most image manipulation needs. For more advanced imaging operations, OpenGL may also include, as of version 1.2, an *imaging subset*. The imaging subset is optional, which means vendors may choose not to include this functionality in their implementation. However, if the imaging subset is supported, it is an all-or-nothing commitment to support the entire functionality of these features.

Your application can determine at runtime whether the imaging subset is supported by searching the extension string for the token `"GL_ARB_imaging"`. For example, when you use the glTools library, your code might look something like this:

```
if(gltIsExtSupported("GL_ARB_imaging") == 0)
    {
    // Error, imaging not supported
    ...
    }
else
```

```
    {
    // Do some imaging stuff
    ...
    ...
}
```

You access the imaging subset through the OpenGL extension mechanism, which means you will likely need to use the `glext.h` header file and obtain function pointers for the functions you need to use. Some OpenGL implementations, depending on your platform's development tools, may already have these functions and constants included in the `gl.h` OpenGL header file (for example, in the Apple XCode headers, they are already defined). For compiles on the Macintosh, we use the built-in support for the imaging subset; for other platforms, we use the extension mechanism to obtain function pointers to the imaging functions. This is all done transparently by adding `glee.h` and `glee.c` to your project. These files are located in the `examples/src//shared` directory in the source distribution for this book. It is safe to assume that you'll need these files for most of the rest of the sample programs in this book.

The IMAGING sample program is modeled much like the previous OPERATIONS sample program in that a single sample program demonstrates different operations via the context menu. When the program starts, it checks for the availability of the imaging subset and aborts if it is not found:

```
// Check for imaging subset, must be done after window
// is created or there won't be an OpenGL context to query
if(gltIsExtSupported("GL_ARB_imaging") == 0)
    {
    printf("Imaging subset not supported\r\n");
    return 0;
    }
```

The `RenderScene` function is presented in Listing 7.6. We discuss the various pieces of this function throughout this section.

LISTING 7.6   The `RenderScene` Function from the Sample Program IMAGING

```
/////////////////////////////////////////////////////////////////////
// Called to draw scene
void RenderScene(void)
    {
    GLint i;                    // Looping variable
    GLint iViewport[4];         // Viewport
    GLint iLargest;             // Largest histogram value
    static GLubyte invertTable[256][3]; // Inverted color table
```

LISTING 7.6   Continued

```
// Do a black and white scaling
static GLfloat lumMat[16] = { 0.30f, 0.30f, 0.30f, 0.0f,
                              0.59f, 0.59f, 0.59f, 0.0f,
                              0.11f, 0.11f, 0.11f, 0.0f,
                              0.0f,  0.0f,  0.0f,  1.0f };

static GLfloat mSharpen[3][3] = {  // Sharpen convolution kernel
    {0.0f, -1.0f, 0.0f},
    {-1.0f, 5.0f, -1.0f },
    {0.0f, -1.0f, 0.0f }};

static GLfloat mEmboss[3][3] = {   // Emboss convolution kernel
    { 2.0f, 0.0f, 0.0f },
    { 0.0f, -1.0f, 0.0f },
    { 0.0f, 0.0f, -1.0f }};

static GLint histoGram[256];     // Storage for histogram statistics

// Clear the window with current clearing color
glClear(GL_COLOR_BUFFER_BIT);

// Current Raster Position always at bottom-left-hand corner of window
glRasterPos2i(0, 0);
glGetIntegerv(GL_VIEWPORT, iViewport);
glPixelZoom((GLfloat) iViewport[2] / (GLfloat)iWidth,
                    (GLfloat) iViewport[3] / (GLfloat)iHeight);

if(bHistogram == GL_TRUE)    // Collect Histogram data
    {
    // We are collecting luminance data, use our conversion formula
    // instead of OpenGL's (which just adds color components together)
    glMatrixMode(GL_COLOR);
    glLoadMatrixf(lumMat);
    glMatrixMode(GL_MODELVIEW);

    // Start collecting histogram data, 256 luminance values
    glHistogram(GL_HISTOGRAM, 256, GL_LUMINANCE, GL_FALSE);
    glEnable(GL_HISTOGRAM);
    }

// Do image operation, depending on rendermode index
switch(iRenderMode)
```

LISTING 7.6   Continued

```
        {
    case 5:     // Sharpen image
        glConvolutionFilter2D(GL_CONVOLUTION_2D, GL_RGB, 3, 3,
                                    GL_LUMINANCE, GL_FLOAT, mSharpen);
        glEnable(GL_CONVOLUTION_2D);
        break;

    case 4:     // Emboss image
        glConvolutionFilter2D(GL_CONVOLUTION_2D, GL_RGB, 3, 3,
                                    GL_LUMINANCE, GL_FLOAT, mEmboss);
        glEnable(GL_CONVOLUTION_2D);
        glMatrixMode(GL_COLOR);
        glLoadMatrixf(lumMat);
        glMatrixMode(GL_MODELVIEW);
        break;

    case 3:     // Invert Image
        for(i = 0; i < 255; i++)
            {
            invertTable[i][0] = (GLubyte)(255 - i);
            invertTable[i][1] = (GLubyte)(255 - i);
            invertTable[i][2] = (GLubyte)(255 - i);
            }

        glColorTable(GL_COLOR_TABLE, GL_RGB, 256, GL_RGB,
                                    GL_UNSIGNED_BYTE, invertTable);
        glEnable(GL_COLOR_TABLE);
        break;

    case 2:     // Brighten Image
        glMatrixMode(GL_COLOR);
        glScalef(1.25f, 1.25f, 1.25f);
        glMatrixMode(GL_MODELVIEW);
        break;

    case 1:     // Just do a plain old image copy
    default:
                // This line intentionally left blank
        break;
        }

    // Do the pixel draw
```

LISTING 7.6   Continued

```
glDrawPixels(iWidth, iHeight, eFormat, GL_UNSIGNED_BYTE, pImage);

// Fetch and draw histogram?
if(bHistogram == GL_TRUE)
    {
    // Read histogram data into buffer
    glGetHistogram(GL_HISTOGRAM, GL_TRUE, GL_LUMINANCE, GL_INT, histoGram);

    // Find largest value for scaling graph down
    iLargest = 0;
    for(i = 0; i < 255; i++)
        if(iLargest < histoGram[i])
            iLargest = histoGram[i];

    // White lines
    glColor3f(1.0f, 1.0f, 1.0f);
    glBegin(GL_LINE_STRIP);
        for(i = 0; i < 255; i++)
            glVertex2f((GLfloat)i,
                    (GLfloat)histoGram[i] / (GLfloat) iLargest * 128.0f);
    glEnd();

    bHistogram = GL_FALSE;
    glDisable(GL_HISTOGRAM);
    }


// Reset everything to default
glMatrixMode(GL_COLOR);
glLoadIdentity();
glMatrixMode(GL_MODELVIEW);
glDisable(GL_CONVOLUTION_2D);
glDisable(GL_COLOR_TABLE);

// Show our hard work...
glutSwapBuffers();
}
```

The image-processing subset can be broken down into three major areas of new function-ality: the color matrix and color table, convolutions, and histograms. Bear in mind that image processing is a broad and complex topic all by itself and could easily warrant an entire book on this subject alone. What follows is an overview of this functionality with some simple examples of their use. For a more in-depth discussion on image processing, see the list of suggested references in Appendix A, "Further Reading/References."

OpenGL imaging operations are processed in a specific order along what is called the *imaging pipeline.* In the same way that geometry is processed by the transformation pipeline, image data goes through the imaging operations in a fixed manner. Figure 7.11 breaks down the imaging pipeline operation by operation. The sections that follow describe these operations in more detail.

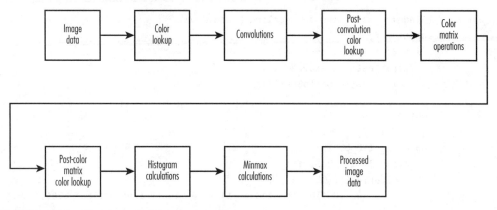

FIGURE 7.11   The OpenGL imaging pipeline.

Color Matrix

The simplest piece of new functionality added with the imaging subset is the color matrix. You can think of color values as coordinates in colorspace—RGB being akin to XYZ on the color axis of the color cube (described in Chapter 5, "Color, Materials, and Lighting: The Basics"). You could think of the alpha color component as the W component of a vector, and it would be transformed appropriately by a 4×4 color matrix. The color matrix is a matrix stack that works just like the other OpenGL matrix stacks (GL_MODELVIEW, GL_PROJECTION, GL_TEXTURE). You can make the color matrix stack the current stack by calling glMatrixMode with the argument GL_COLOR:

```
glMatrixMode(GL_COLOR);
```

All the matrix manipulation routines (glLoadIdentity, glLoadMatrix, and so on) are available for the color matrix. The color matrix stack can be pushed and popped as well, but implementations are required to support only a color stack two elements deep.

A menu item named Increase Contrast in the IMAGING sample program sets the render mode to 2, which causes the RenderScene function to use the color matrix to set a positive scaling factor to the color values, increasing the contrast of the image:

```
case 2:     // Brighten Image
            glMatrixMode(GL_COLOR);
            glScalef(1.25f, 1.25f, 1.25f);
            glMatrixMode(GL_MODELVIEW);
            break;
```

The effect is subtle yet clearly visible when the change occurs onscreen. After rendering, the color matrix is restored to identity:

```
// Reset everything to default
glMatrixMode(GL_COLOR);
glLoadIdentity();
glMatrixMode(GL_MODELVIEW);
```

Color Lookup

With color tables, you can specify a table of color values used to replace a pixel's current color. This functionality is similar to pixel mapping but has some added flexibility in the way the color table is composed and applied. The following function is used to set up a color table:

```
void glColorTable(GLenum target, GLenum internalFormat, GLsizei width,
                  GLenum format, GLenum type,
                  const GLvoid *table);
```

The *target* parameter specifies where in the imaging pipeline the color table is to be applied. This parameter may be one of the size values listed in Table 7.6.

TABLE 7.6 The Place to Apply the Color Lookup Table

Target	Location
GL_COLOR_TABLE	Applied at the beginning of the imaging pipeline
GL_POST_CONVOLUTION_COLOR_TABLE	Applied after the convolution operation
GL_POST_COLOR_MATRIX_COLOR_TABLE	Applied after the color matrix operation
GL_PROXY_COLOR_TABLE	Verify this color table will fit
GL_PROXY_POST_CONVOLUTION_COLOR_TABLE	Verify this color table will fit
GL_PROXY_POST_COLOR_MATRIX_COLOR_TABLE	Verify this color table will fit

You use the GL_PROXY prefixed targets to verify that the supplied color table can be loaded (will fit into memory).

The *internalFormat* parameter specifies the internal OpenGL representation of the color table pointed to by *table*. It can be any of the following symbolic constants: GL_ALPHA, GL_ALPHA4, GL_ALPHA8, GL_ALPHA12, GL_ALPHA16, GL_LUMINANCE, GL_LUMINANCE4, GL_LUMINANCE8, GL_LUMINANCE12, GL_LUMINANCE16, GL_LUMINANCE_ALPHA, GL_LUMINANCE4_ALPHA4,

GL_LUMINANCE6_ALPHA2, GL_LUMINANCE8_ALPHA8, GL_LUMINANCE12_ALPHA4, GL_
LUMINANCE12_ALPHA12, GL_LUMINANCE16_ALPHA16, GL_INTENSITY, GL_INTENSITY4, GL_
INTENSITY8, GL_INTENSTIY12, GL_INTENSITY16, GL_RGB, GL_R3_G3_B2, GL_RGB4, GL_RGB5,
GL_RGB8, GL_RGB10, GL_RGB12, GL_RGB16, GL_RGBA, GL_RGBA2, GL_RGBA4, GL_RGB5_A1,
GL_RGBA8, GL_RGB10_A2, GL_RGBA12, GL_RGBA16. The color component name in this list
should be fairly obvious to you by now, and the numerical suffix simply represents the bit
count of that component's representation.

The *format* and *type* parameters describe the format of the color table being supplied in
the *table* pointer. The values for these parameters all correspond to the same arguments
used in glDrawPixels, and are listed in Tables 7.2 and 7.3.

The following example demonstrates a color table in action. It duplicates the color inversion effect from the OPERATIONS sample program but uses a color table instead of pixel
mapping. When you choose the Invert Color menu selection, the render mode is set to 3,
and the following segment of the RenderScene function is executed:

```
case 3: // Invert Image
    for(i = 0; i < 255; i++)
        {
        invertTable[i][0] = 255 - i;
        invertTable[i][1] = 255 - i;
        invertTable[i][2] = 255 - i;
        }

    glColorTable(GL_COLOR_TABLE, GL_RGB, 256, GL_RGB,
                                GL_UNSIGNED_BYTE, invertTable);
    glEnable(GL_COLOR_TABLE);
```

For a loaded color table to be used, you must also enable the color table with a call to
glEnable with the GL_COLOR_TABLE parameter. After the pixels are drawn, the color table is
disabled:

```
glDisable(GL_COLOR_TABLE);
```

The output from this example matches exactly the image from Figure 7.10.

Proxies

An OpenGL implementation's support for color tables may be limited by system resources.
Large color tables, for example, may not be loaded if they require too much memory. You
can use the proxy color table targets listed in Table 7.6 to determine whether a given color
table fits into memory and can be used. These targets are used in conjunction with
glGetColorTableParameter to see whether a color table will fit. The
glGetColorTableParameter function enables you to query OpenGL about the various

settings of the color tables; it is discussed in greater detail in Appendix C. Here, you can use this function to see whether the width of the color table matches the width requested with the proxy color table call:

```
GLint width;
...
...
glColorTable(GL_PROXY_COLOR_TABLE, GL_RGB, 256, GL_RGB,
                                    GL_UNSIGNED_BYTE, NULL);
glGetColorTableParameteriv(GL_PROXY_COLOR_TABLE, GL_COLOR_TABLE_WIDTH, &width);
if(width == 0) {
    // Error...
...
```

Note that you do not need to specify the pointer to the actual color table for a proxy.

Other Operations

Also in common with pixel mapping, the color table can be used to apply a scaling factor and a bias to color component values. You do this with the following function:

```
void glColorTableParameteriv(GLenum target, GLenum pname, GLint *param);
void glColorTableParameterfv(GLenum target, GLenum pname, GLfloat *param);
```

The glColorTableParameter function's *target* parameter can be GL_COLOR_TABLE, GL_POST_CONVOLUTION_COLOR_TABLE, or GL_POST_COLOR_MATRIX_COLOR_TABLE. The *pname* parameter sets the scale or bias by using the value GL_COLOR_TABLE_SCALE or GL_COLOR_TABLE_BIAS, respectively. The final parameter is a pointer to an array of four elements storing the red, green, blue, and alpha scale or bias values to be used.

You can also actually render a color table by using the contents of the color buffer (after some rendering or drawing operation) as the source data for the color table. The function glCopyColorTable takes data from the current read buffer (the current GL_READ_BUFFER) as its source:

```
void glCopyColorTable(GLenum target, GLenum internalFormat,
                      GLint x, GLint y, GLsizei width);
```

The *target* and *internalFormat* parameters are identical to those used in glColorTable. The color table array is then taken from the color buffer starting at the *x,y* location and taking *width* pixels.

You can replace all or part of a color table by using the glColorSubTable function:

```
void glColorSubTable(GLenum target, GLsizei start, GLsizei count,
                     GLenum format, GLenum type, const void *data);
```

Here, most parameters correspond directly to the glColorTable function, except for *start* and *count*. The *start* parameter is the offset into the color table to begin the replacement, and *count* is the number of color values to replace.

Finally, you can also replace all or part of a color table from the color buffer in a manner similar to glCopyColorTable by using the glCopyColorSubTable function:

```
void glCopyColorSubTable(GLenum target, GLsizei start,
                         GLint x, GLint y, GLsizei width);
```

Again, the source of the color table is the color buffer, with *x* and *y* placing the position to begin reading color values, *start* being the location within the color table to begin the replacement, and *width* being the number of color values to replace.

Convolutions

Convolutions are a powerful image-processing technique, with many applications such as blurring, sharpening, and other special effects. A convolution is a filter that processes pixels in an image according to some pattern of weights called a *kernel*. The convolution replaces each pixel with the weighted average value of that pixel and its neighboring pixels, with each pixel's color values being scaled by the weights in the kernel.

Typically, convolution kernels are rectangular arrays of floating-point values that represent the weights of a corresponding arrangement of pixels in the image. For example, the following kernel from the IMAGING sample program performs a sharpening operation:

```
static GLfloat mSharpen[3][3] = {   // Sharpen convolution kernel
        {0.0f, -1.0f, 0.0f},
        {-1.0f, 5.0f, -1.0f },
        {0.0f, -1.0f, 0.0f }};
```

The center pixel value is 5.0, which places a higher emphasis on that pixel value. The pixels immediately above, below, and to the right and left have a decreased weight, and the corner pixels are not accounted for at all. Figure 7.12 shows a sample block of image data with the convolution kernel superimposed. The 5 in the kernel's center is the pixel being replaced, and you can see the kernel's values as they are applied to the surrounding pixels to derive the new center pixel value (represented by the circle). The convolution kernel is applied to every pixel in the image, resulting in a sharpened image. You can see this process in action by selecting Sharpen Image in the IMAGING sample program.

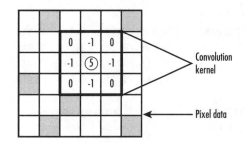

FIGURE 7.12   The sharpening kernel in action.

To apply the convolution filter, the IMAGING program simply calls these two functions before the glDrawPixels operation:

```
glConvolutionFilter2D(GL_CONVOLUTION_2D, GL_RGB, 3, 3,
                               GL_LUMINANCE, GL_FLOAT, mSharpen);
glEnable(GL_CONVOLUTION_2D);
```

The glConvolutionFilter2D function has the following syntax:

```
void glConvolutionFilter2D(GLenum target, GLenum internalFormat,
                    GLsizei width, GLsizei height, GLenum format,
                    GLenum type, const GLvoid *image);
```

The first parameter, *target*, must be GL_CONVOLUTION_2D. The second parameter, *internalFormat*, takes the same values as glColorTable and specifies to which pixel components the convolution is applied. The *width* and *height* parameters are the width and height of the convolution kernel. Finally, *format* and *type* specify the format and type of pixels stored in *image*. In the case of the sharpening filter, the pixel data is in GL_RGB format, and the kernel is GL_LUMINANCE because it contains simply a single weight per pixel (as opposed to having a separate weight for each color channel). Convolution kernels are turned on and off simply with glEnable or glDisable and the parameter GL_CONVOLUTION_2D.

Convolutions are a part of the imaging pipeline and can be combined with other imaging operations. For example, the sharpening filter already demonstrated was used in conjunction with pixel zoom to fill the entire window with the image. For a more interesting example, let's combine pixel zoom with the color matrix and a convolution filter. The following code excerpt defines a color matrix that will transform the image into a black-and-white (grayscale) image and a convolution filter that does embossing:

```
// Do a black and white scaling
    static GLfloat lumMat[16] = { 0.30f, 0.30f, 0.30f, 0.0f,
                                  0.59f, 0.59f, 0.59f, 0.0f,
                                  0.11f, 0.11f, 0.11f, 0.0f,
                                  0.0f,  0.0f,  0.0f,  1.0f };

    static GLfloat mSharpen[3][3] = {  // Sharpen convolution kernel
        {0.0f, -1.0f, 0.0f},
        {-1.0f, 5.0f, -1.0f },
        {0.0f, -1.0f, 0.0f }};

    static GLfloat mEmboss[3][3] = {   // Emboss convolution kernel
        { 2.0f, 0.0f, 0.0f },
        { 0.0f, -1.0f, 0.0f },
        { 0.0f, 0.0f, -1.0f }};
```

When you select Emboss Image from the pop-up menu, the render state is changed to 4, and the following case from the RenderScene function is executed before glDrawPixels:

```
case 4: // Emboss image
        glConvolutionFilter2D(GL_CONVOLUTION_2D, GL_RGB, 3, 3,
                              GL_LUMINANCE, GL_FLOAT, mEmboss);
        glEnable(GL_CONVOLUTION_2D);
        glMatrixMode(GL_COLOR);
        glLoadMatrixf(lumMat);
        glMatrixMode(GL_MODELVIEW);
        break;
```

The embossed image is displayed in Figure 7.13, and is shown in Color Plate 3 in the lower-left corner.

FIGURE 7.13   Using convolutions and the color matrix for an embossed effect.

From the Color Buffer

Convolution kernels can also be loaded from the color buffer. The following function behaves similarly to loading a color table from the color buffer:

```
void glCopyConvolutionFilter2D(GLenum target, GLenum internalFormat,
                               GLint x, GLint y, GLsizei width, GLsizei height);
```

The *target* value must always be GL_CONVOLUTION_2D, and *internalFormat* refers to the format of the color data, as in glConvolutionFilter2D. The kernel is loaded from pixel data from the color buffer located at (*x,y*) and the given *width* and *height*.

Separable Filters

A separable convolution filter is one whose kernel can be represented by the matrix outer product of two one-dimensional filters. For example, in Figure 7.14, one-dimensional row and column matrices are multiplied to yield a final 3×3 matrix (the new kernel filter).

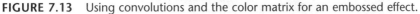

$$\begin{bmatrix} -1 \\ 2 \\ -1 \end{bmatrix} \begin{bmatrix} -1 & 2 & -1 \end{bmatrix} = \begin{bmatrix} 1 & -2 & 1 \\ -2 & 4 & -2 \\ 1 & -2 & 1 \end{bmatrix}$$

FIGURE 7.14   The outer product to two one-dimensional filters.

The following function is used to specify these two one-dimensional filters:

```
void glSeparableFilter2D(GLenum target, GLenum internalFormat,
                         GLsizei width, GLsizei height,
                         GLenum format, GLenum type,
                         void *row, const GLvoid *column);
```

The parameters all have the same meaning as in `glConvolutionFilter2D`, with the exception that now you have two parameters for passing in the address of the filters: *row* and *column*. The *target* parameter, however, must be GL_SEPARABLE_2D in this case.

One-Dimensional Kernels

OpenGL also supports one-dimensional convolution filters, but they are applied only to one-dimensional texture data. They behave in the same manner as two-dimensional convolutions, with the exception that they are applied only to rows of pixels (or actually *texels* in the case of one-dimensional texture maps). These one-dimensional convolutions have one-dimensional kernels, and you can use the corresponding functions for loading and copying the filters:

```
glConvolutionFilter1D(GLenum target, GLenum internalFormat,
                      GLsizei width, GLenum format, GLenum type,
                      const GLvoid *image);


glCopyConvolutionFilter1D(GLenum target, GLenum internalFormat,
                          GLint x, GLint y, GLsizei width);
```

Of course, with these functions the target must be set to GL_CONVOLUTION_1D.

Other Convolution Tweaks

When a convolution filter kernel is applied to an image, along the edges of the image the kernel will overlap and fall outside the image's borders. How OpenGL handles this situation is controlled via the convolution border mode. You set the convolution border mode by using the `glConvolutionParameter` function, which has four variations:

```
glConvolutionParameteri(GLenum target, GLenum pname, GLint param);
glConvolutionParameterf(GLenum target, GLenum pname, GLfloat param);
glConvolutionParameteriv(GLenum target, GLenum pname, GLint *params);
glConvolutionParameterfv(GLenum target, GLenum pname, GLfloat *params);
```

The *target* parameter for these functions can be GL_CONVOLUTION_1D, GL_CONVOLUTION_2D, or GL_SEPARABLE_2D. To set the border mode, you use GL_CONVOLUTION_BORDER_MODE as the *pname* parameter and one of the border mode constants as *param*.

If you set *param* to GL_CONSTANT_BORDER, the pixels outside the image border are computed from a constant pixel value. To set this pixel value, call `glConvolutionParameterfv` with

GL_CONSTANT_BORDER and a floating-point array containing the RGBA values to be used as the constant pixel color.

If you set the border mode to GL_REDUCE, the convolution kernel is not applied to the edge pixels. Thus, the kernel never overlaps the edge of the image. In this case, however, you should note that you are essentially shrinking the image by the width and height of the convolution filter.

The final border mode is GL_REPLICATE_BORDER. In this case, the convolution is applied as if the horizontal and vertical edges of an image are replicated as many times as necessary to prevent overlap.

You can also apply a scale and bias value to kernel values by using GL_CONVOLUTION_FILTER_BIAS and/or GL_CONVOLUTION_FILTER_SCALE for the parameter name (*pname*) and supplying the bias and scale values in *param* or *params*.

Histogram

A histogram is a graphical representation of an image's frequency distribution. In English, it is simply a count of how many times each color value is used in an image, displayed as a sort of bar graph. Histograms may be collected for an image's intensity values or separately for each color channel. Histograms are frequently employed in image processing, and many digital cameras can display histogram data of captured images. Photographers use this information to determine whether the camera captured the full dynamic range of the subject or if perhaps the image is too over- or underexposed. Popular image-processing packages such as Adobe Photoshop also calculate and display histograms, as shown in Figure 7.15.

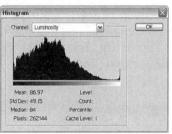

FIGURE 7.15   A histogram display in Photoshop.

When histogram collection is enabled, OpenGL collects statistics about any images as they are written to the color buffer. To prepare to collect histogram data, you must tell OpenGL how much data to collect and in what format you want the data. You do this with the glHistogram function:

```
void glHistogram(GLenum target, GLsizei width,
                 GLenum internalFormat, GLboolean sink);
```

The *target* parameter must be either GL_HISTOGRAM or GL_PROXY_HISTOGRAM (used to determine whether sufficient resources are available to store the histogram). The *width* parameter tells OpenGL how many entries to make in the histogram table. This value must be a power of 2 (1, 2, 4, 8, 16, and so on). The *internalFormat* parameter specifies the data format you expect the histogram to be stored in, corresponding to the valid format parameters for color tables and convolution filters, with the exception that GL_INTENSITY is not included. Finally, you can discard the pixels and not draw anything by specifying GL_TRUE for the *sink* parameter. You can turn histogram data collection on and off with glEnable or glDisable by passing in GL_HISTOGRAM, as in this example:

```
glEnable(GL_HISTOGRAM);
```

After image data has been transferred, you collect the histogram data with the following function:

```
void glGetHistogram(GLenum target, GLboolean reset, GLenum format,
                    GLenum type, GLvoid *values);
```

The only valid value for *target* is GL_HISTOGRAM. Setting *reset* to GL_TRUE clears the histogram data. Otherwise, the histogram becomes cumulative, and each pixel transfer continues to accumulate statistical data in the histogram. The *format* parameter specifies the data format of the collected histogram information, and *type* and *values* are the data type to be used and the address where the histogram is to be placed.

Now, let's look at an example using a histogram. In the IMAGING sample program, selecting Histogram from the menu displays a grayscale version of the image and a graph in the lower-left corner that represents the statistical frequency of each color luminance value. The output is shown in Figure 7.16.

FIGURE 7.16   A histogram of the luminance values of the image.

The first order of business in the `RenderScene` function is to allocate storage for the histogram. The following line creates an array of integers 256 elements long. Each element in the array contains a count of the number of times that corresponding luminance value was used when the image was drawn onscreen:

```
static GLint histoGram[256];    // Storage for histogram statistics
```

Next, if the histogram flag is set (through the menu selection), you tell OpenGL to begin collecting histogram data. The function call to `glHistogram` instructs OpenGL to collect statistics about the 256 individual luminance values that may be used in the image. The sink is set to `false` so that the image is also drawn onscreen:

```
if(bHistogram == GL_TRUE)    // Collect Histogram data
    {
    // We are collecting luminance data, use our conversion formula
    // instead of OpenGL's (which just adds color components together)
    glMatrixMode(GL_COLOR);
    glLoadMatrixf(lumMat);
    glMatrixMode(GL_MODELVIEW);

    // Start collecting histogram data, 256 luminance values
    glHistogram(GL_HISTOGRAM, 256, GL_LUMINANCE, GL_FALSE);
```

```
        glEnable(GL_HISTOGRAM);
        }
```

Note that in this case you also need to set up the color matrix to provide the grayscale color conversion. OpenGL's default conversion to GL_LUMINANCE is simply a summing of the red, green, and blue color components. When you use this conversion formula, the histogram graph will have the same shape as the one from Photoshop for the same image displayed in Figure 7.15.

After the pixels are drawn, you collect the histogram data with the code shown here:

```
// Fetch and draw histogram?
if(bHistogram == GL_TRUE)
    {
    // Read histogram data into buffer
    glGetHistogram(GL_HISTOGRAM, GL_TRUE, GL_LUMINANCE, GL_INT, histoGram);
```

Now you traverse the histogram data and search for the largest collected value. You do this because you will use this value as a scaling factor to fit the graph in the lower-left corner of the display:

```
// Find largest value for scaling graph down
GLint iLargest = 0;
for(i = 0; i < 255; i++)
    if(iLargest < histoGram[i])
        iLargest = histoGram[i];
```

Finally, it's time to draw the graph of statistics. The following code segment simply sets the drawing color to white and then loops through the histogram data creating a single line strip. The data is scaled by the largest value so that the graph is 256 pixels wide and 128 pixels high. When all is done, the histogram flag is reset to false and the histogram data collection is disabled with a call to glDisable:

```
// White lines
glColor3f(1.0f, 1.0f, 1.0f);
glBegin(GL_LINE_STRIP);
    for(i = 0; i < 255; i++)
        glVertex2f((GLfloat)i, (GLfloat)histoGram[i] /
(GLfloat) iLargest * 128.0f);
glEnd();

bHistogram = GL_FALSE;
glDisable(GL_HISTOGRAM);
}
```

Minmax Operations

In the preceding sample, you traversed the histogram data to find the largest luminance component for the rendered image. If you need only the largest or smallest components collected, you can choose not to collect the entire histogram for a rendered image, but instead collect the largest and smallest values. This minmax data collection operates in a similar manner to histograms. First, you specify the format of the data on which you want statistics gathered by using the following function:

```
void glMinmax(GLenum target, GLenum internalFormat, GLboolean sink);
```

Here, *target* is GL_MINMAX, and *internalFormat* and *sink* behave precisely as in glHistogram. You must also enable minmax data collection:

```
glEnable(GL_MINMAX);
```

The minmax data is collected with the glGetMinmax function, which is analogous to glGetHistogram:

```
void glGetMinmax(GLenum target, GLboolean reset, GLenum format,
                                 GLenum type, GLvoid *values);
```

Again, the *target* parameter is GL_MINMAX, and the other parameters map to their counterparts in glGetHistogram.

Summary

In this chapter, we have shown that OpenGL provides first-class support for color image manipulation—from reading and writing bitmaps and color images directly to the color buffer, to color processing operations and color lookup maps. Optionally, many OpenGL implementations go even further by supporting the OpenGL imaging subset. The imaging subset makes it easy to add sophisticated image-processing filters and analysis to your graphics-intensive programs.

We have also laid the groundwork in this chapter for our return to 3D geometry in the next chapter, where we begin coverage of OpenGL's texture mapping capabilities. You'll find that the functions covered in this chapter that load and process image data are used directly when we extend the manipulation of image data by mapping it to 3D primitives.

CHAPTER 8

Texture Mapping: The Basics

by Richard S. Wright Jr.

WHAT YOU'LL LEARN IN THIS CHAPTER:

How To	Functions You'll Use
Load texture images	glTexImage/glTexSubImage
Map textures to geometry	glTexCoord
Change the texture environment	glTexEnv
Set texture mapping parameters	glTexParameter
Generate mipmaps	gluBuildMipmaps
Manage multiple textures	glBindTexture

In the preceding chapter, we covered in detail the groundwork for loading image data into OpenGL. Image data, unless modified by pixel zoom, generally has a one-to-one correspondence between a pixel in an image and a pixel on the screen. In fact, this is where we get the term *pixel* (picture element). In this chapter, we extend this knowledge further by applying images to three-dimensional primitives. When we apply image data to a geometric primitive, we call this a *texture* or *texture map*. Figure 8.1 shows the dramatic difference that can be achieved by texture mapping geometry. The cube on the left is a lit and shaded featureless surface, whereas the cube on the right shows a richness in detail that can be reasonably achieved only with texture mapping.

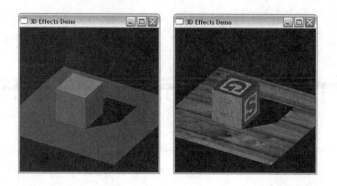

FIGURE 8.1   The stark contrast between textured and untextured geometry.

A texture image when loaded has the same makeup and arrangement as pixmaps, but now a one-to-one correspondence seldom exists between *texels* (the individual picture elements in a texture) and pixels on the screen. This chapter covers the basics of loading a texture map into memory and all the ways in which it may be mapped to and applied to geometric primitives.

Loading Textures

The first necessary step in applying a texture map to geometry is to load the texture into memory. Once loaded, the texture becomes part of the current *texture state* (more on this later). Three OpenGL functions are most often used to load texture data from a memory  buffer (which is, for example, read from a disk file):

```
void glTexImage1D(GLenum target, GLint level, GLint internalformat,
            GLsizei width, GLint border,
            GLenum format, GLenum type, void *data);


void glTexImage2D(GLenum target, GLint level, GLint internalformat,
            GLsizei width, GLsizei height, GLint border,
            GLenum format, GLenum type, void *data);


void glTexImage3D(GLenum target, GLint level, GLint internalformat,
            GLsizei width, GLsizei height, GLsizei depth, GLint border,
            GLenum format, GLenum type, void *data);
```

These three rather lengthy functions tell OpenGL everything it needs to know about how to interpret the texture data pointed to by the *data* parameter.

The first thing you should notice about these functions is that they are essentially three flavors of the same root function, glTexImage. OpenGL supports one-, two-, and three-dimensional texture maps and uses the corresponding function to load that texture and make it current. You should also be aware that OpenGL copies the texture information from *data* when you call one of these functions. This data copy can be quite expensive, and in the section "Texture Objects," later in this chapter, we discuss some ways to help mitigate this problem.

The `target` argument for these functions should be GL_TEXTURE_1D, GL_TEXTURE_2D, or GL_TEXTURE_3D, respectively. You may also specify proxy textures in the same manner in which you used proxies in the preceding chapter, by specifying GL_PROXY_TEXTURE_1D, GL_PROXY_TEXTURE_2D, or GL_PROXY_TEXTURE_3D and using the function glGetTexParameter to retrieve the results of the proxy query.

The *level* parameter specifies the mipmap level being loaded. Mipmaps are covered in an upcoming section called "Mipmapping," so for nonmipmapped textures (just your plain old ordinary texture mapping), always set this to 0 (zero) for the moment.

Next, you have to specify the *internalformat* parameter of the texture data. This information tells OpenGL how many color components you want stored per texel and possibly the storage size of the components and/or whether you want the texture compressed (see the next chapter for information about texture compression). Table 8.1 lists the most common values for this function. A complete listing is given in Appendix C, "API Reference."

TABLE 8.1   Most Common Texture Internal Formats

Constant	Meaning
GL_ALPHA	Store the texels as alpha values
GL_LUMINANCE	Store the texels as luminance values
GL_LUMINANCE_ALPHA	Store the texels with both luminance and alpha values
GL_RGB	Store the texels as red, green, and blue components
GL_RGBA	Store the texels as red, green, blue, and alpha components

The *width*, *height*, and *depth* parameters (where appropriate) specify the dimensions of the texture being loaded. It is important to note that prior to OpenGL 2.0, these dimensions must be integer powers of 2 (1, 2, 4, 8, 16, 32, 64, and so on). There is no requirement that texture maps be square (all dimensions equal), but a texture loaded with non–power of 2 dimensions on older OpenGL implementations will cause texturing to be implicitly disabled. Even though OpenGL 2.0 (and later) allows non–power of two textures, this is no guarantee that they will necessarily be fast on the underlying hardware. Many performance-minded developers still avoid non–power of two textures for this reason.

The *border* parameter allows you to specify a border width for texture maps. Texture borders allow you to extend the width, height, or depth of a texture map by an extra set of texels along the borders. Texture borders play an important role in the discussion of texture filtering to come. For the time being, always set this value to 0 (zero).

The last three parameters—*format*, *type*, and *data*—are identical to the corresponding arguments when you used `glDrawPixels` to place image data into the color buffer. For the sake of convenience, we list the valid constants for *format* and *type* in Tables 8.2 and 8.3.

TABLE 8.2   Texel Formats for `glTexImage`

Constant	Description
GL_RGB	Colors are in red, green, blue order.
GL_RGBA	Colors are in red, green, blue, alpha order.
GL_BGR/GL_BGR_EXT	Colors are in blue, green, red order.
GL_BGRA/GL_BGRA_EXT	Colors are in blue, green, red, alpha order.
GL_RED	Each pixel contains a single red component.
GL_GREEN	Each pixel contains a single green component.
GL_BLUE	Each pixel contains a single blue component.
GL_ALPHA	Each pixel contains a single alpha component.
GL_LUMINANCE	Each pixel contains a single luminance (intensity) component.
GL_LUMINANCE_ALPHA	Each pixel contains a luminance followed by an alpha component.
GL_STENCIL_INDEX	Each pixel contains a single stencil index.
GL_DEPTH_COMPONENT	Each pixel contains a single depth component.

TABLE 8.3   Data Types for Pixel Data

Constant	Description
GL_UNSIGNED_BYTE	Each color component is an 8-bit unsigned integer
GL_BYTE	Signed 8-bit integer
GL_BITMAP	Single bits, no color data; same as `glBitmap`
GL_UNSIGNED_SHORT	Unsigned 16-bit integer
GL_SHORT	Signed 16-bit integer
GL_UNSIGNED_INT	Unsigned 32-bit integer
GL_INT	Signed 32-bit integer
GL_FLOAT	Single-precision float
GL_UNSIGNED_BYTE_3_2_2	Packed RGB values
GL_UNSIGNED_BYTE_2_3_3_REV	Packed RGB values
GL_UNSIGNED_SHORT_5_6_5	Packed RGB values
GL_UNSIGNED_SHORT_5_6_5_REV	Packed RGB values
GL_UNSIGNED_SHORT_4_4_4_4	Packed RGBA values
GL_UNSIGNED_SHORT_4_4_4_4_REV	Packed RGBA values
GL_UNSIGNED_SHORT_5_5_5_1	Packed RGBA values
GL_UNSIGNED_SHORT_1_5_5_5_REV	Packed RGBA values
GL_UNSIGNED_INT_8_8_8_8	Packed RGBA values
GL_UNSIGNED_INT_8_8_8_8_REV	Packed RGBA values
GL_UNSIGNED_INT_10_10_10_2	Packed RGBA values
GL_UNSIGNED_INT_2_10_10_10_REV	Packed RGBA values

Loaded textures are not applied to geometry unless the appropriate texture state is enabled. You can call glEnable or glDisable with GL_TEXTURE_1D, GL_TEXTURE_2D, or GL_TEXTURE_3D to turn texturing on or off for a given texture state. Only one of these texture states may be on at a time for a given texture unit (see the next chapter for a discussion of multitexturing).

A final word about texture loading: Texture data loaded by the glTexImage functions goes through the same pixel and imaging pipeline covered in the preceding chapter. This means pixel packing, pixel zoom, color tables, convolutions, and so on are applied to the texture data when it is loaded.

Using the Color Buffer

One- and two-dimensional textures may also be loaded using data from the color buffer. You can read an image from the color buffer and use it as a new texture by using the following two functions:

```
void glCopyTexImage1D(GLenum target, GLint level, GLenum internalformat,
                      GLint x, GLint y,
                      GLsizei width, GLint border);


void glCopyTexImage2D(GLenum target, GLint level, GLenum internalformat,
                      GLint x, GLint y,
                      GLsizei width, GLsizei height, GLint border);
```

These functions operate similarly to glTexImage, but in this case, x and y specify the location in the color buffer to begin reading the texture data. The source buffer is set using glReadBuffer and behaves just like glReadPixels. Note that there is no glCopyTexImage3D, because you can't get volumetric data from a 2D color buffer!

Updating Textures

Repeatedly loading new textures can become a performance bottleneck in time-sensitive applications such as games or simulation applications. If a loaded texture map is no longer needed, it may be replaced entirely or in part. Replacing a texture map can often be done much more quickly than reloading a new texture directly with glTexImage. The function you use to accomplish this is glTexSubImage, again in three variations:

```
void glTexSubImage1D(GLenum target, GLint level,
                     GLint xOffset,
                     GLsizei width,
                     GLenum format, GLenum type, const GLvoid *data);


void glTexSubImage2D(GLenum target, GLint level,
                     GLint xOffset, GLint yOffset,
```

8

```
                         GLsizei width, GLsizei height,
                         GLenum format, GLenum type, const GLvoid *data);

void glTexSubImage3D(GLenum target, GLint level,
                         GLint xOffset, GLint yOffset, GLint zOffset,
                         GLsizei width, GLsizei height, GLsizei depth,
                         GLenum format, GLenum type, const GLvoid *data);
```

Most of the arguments correspond exactly to the parameters used in glTexImage. The *xOffset, yOffset*, and *zOffset* parameters specify the offsets into the existing texture map to begin replacing texture data. The *width, height*, and *depth* values specify the dimensions of the texture being "inserted" into the existing texture.

A final set of functions allows you to combine reading from the color buffer and inserting or replacing part of a texture. These glCopyTexSubImage variations do just that:

```
void glCopyTexSubImage1D(GLenum target, GLint level,
                         GLint xoffset,
                         GLint x, GLint y,
                         GLsizei width);

void glCopyTexSubImage2D(GLenum target, GLint level,
                         GLint xoffset, GLint yoffset,
                         GLint x, GLint y,
                         GLsizei width, GLsizei height);

void glCopyTexSubImage3D(GLenum target, GLint level,
                         GLint xoffset, GLint yoffset, Glint zoffset,
                         GLint x, GLint y,
                         GLsizei width, GLsizei height);
```

You may have noticed that no glCopyTexImage3D function is listed here. The reason is that the color buffer is 2D, and there simply is no corresponding way to use a 2D color image as a source for a 3D texture. However, you can use glCopyTexSubImage3D to use the color buffer data to set a plane of texels in a three-dimensional texture.

Mapping Textures to Geometry

Loading a texture and enabling texturing cause OpenGL to apply the texture to any of the OpenGL primitives. You must, however, provide OpenGL with information about how to map the texture to the geometry. You do this by specifying a *texture coordinate* for each vertex. Texels in a texture map are addressed not as a memory location (as you would for pixmaps), but as a more abstract (usually floating-point values) texture coordinate.

Typically, texture coordinates are specified as floating-point values that are in the range 0.0 to 1.0. Texture coordinates are named s, t, r, and q (similar to vertex coordinates x, y, z, and w), supporting from one- to three-dimensional texture coordinates, and optionally a way to scale the coordinates.

Figure 8.2 shows one-, two-, and three-dimensional textures and the way the texture coordinates are laid out with respect to their texels.

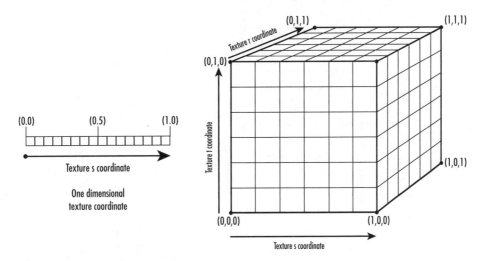

FIGURE 8.2   How texture coordinates address texels.

Because there are no four-dimensional textures, you might ask what the q coordinate is for. The q coordinate corresponds to the w geometric coordinate. This is a scaling factor applied to the other texture coordinates; that is, the actual values used for the texture coordinates are s/q, t/q, and r/q. By default, q is set to 1.0.

You specify a texture coordinate using the glTexCoord function. Much like vertex coordinates, surface normals, and color values, this function comes in a variety of familiar flavors that are all listed in the reference section. The following are three simple variations used in the sample programs:

```
void glTexCoord1f(GLfloat s);
void glTexCoord2f(Glfloat s, GLfloat t);
void glTexCoord3f(GLfloat s, GLfloat t, GLfloat r);
```

One texture coordinate is applied using these functions for each vertex. OpenGL then stretches or shrinks the texture as necessary to apply the texture to the geometry as mapped. (This stretching or shrinking is applied using the current texture *filter;* we'll discuss this issue shortly as well.) Figure 8.3 shows an example of a two-dimensional texture being mapped to a GL_QUAD. Note that the corners of the texture correspond to the corners of the quad. As you do with other vertex properties (materials, normals, and so on), you must specify the texture coordinate before the vertex!

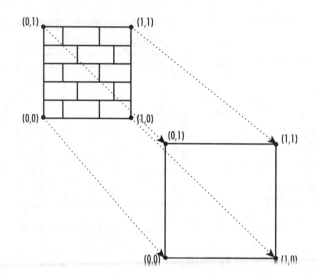

FIGURE 8.3   Applying a two-dimensional texture to a quad.

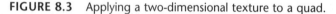

Rarely, however, do you have such a nice fit of a square texture mapped to a square piece of geometry. To help you better understand texture coordinates, we provide another example in Figure 8.4. This figure also shows a square texture map, but the geometry is a triangle. Superimposed on the texture map are the texture coordinates of the locations in the map being extended to the vertices of the triangle.

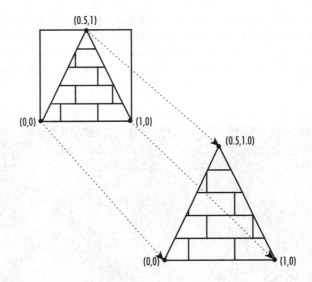

FIGURE 8.4 Applying a portion of a texture map to a triangle.

Texture Matrix

Texture coordinates are also transformed via the texture matrix. The texture matrix stack works just like the other matrices previously discussed (modelview, projection, and color). You make the texture matrix the target of matrix function calls by calling `glMatrixMode` with the argument `GL_TEXTURE`:

```
glMatrixMode(GL_TEXTURE);
```

The texture matrix stack is required to be only two elements deep for the purposes of `glPushMatrix` and `glPopMatrix`. Texture coordinates can be translated, scaled, and even rotated. If you decide to scale your texture coordinates with a q texture coordinate value, this is done after the texture matrix is applied.

A Simple 2D Example

Loading a texture and providing texture coordinates are the fundamental requirements for texture mapping. There are a number of issues we have yet to address, such as coordinate wrapping, texture filters, and the texture environment. What do they mean, and how do we make use of them? Let's pause here first and examine a simple example that uses a 2D texture. In Listing 8.1, we use the functions covered so far and add several new ones. We use this example, then, as a framework to describe these additional texture mapping issues.

Listing 8.1 shows all the pertinent code for the sample program PYRAMID. This program draws a simple lit four-sided pyramid made up of triangles. A stone texture is applied to each face and the bottom of the pyramid. You can spin the pyramid around with the arrow keys much like the samples in earlier chapters. Figure 8.5 shows the output of the PYRAMID program.

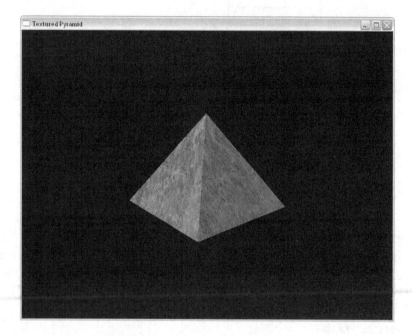

FIGURE 8.5   Output from the PYRAMID sample program.

LISTING 8.1   The PYRAMID Sample Program Source Code

```
// Pyramid.cpp
// Demonstrates Simple Texture Mapping
// OpenGL SuperBible
// Richard S. Wright Jr.
#include "../../Common/GLTools.h"    // GLTools
#include "../../math3d.h"            // 3D Math Library

// Rotation amounts
static GLfloat xRot = 0.0f;
static GLfloat yRot = 0.0f;



// This function does any needed initialization on the rendering
```

LISTING 8.1 Continued

```
// context.  Here it sets up and initializes the lighting for
// the scene.
void SetupRC()
    {
    GLubyte *pBytes;
    GLint iWidth, iHeight, iComponents;
    GLenum eFormat;

    // Light values and coordinates
    . . .
    . . .

    // Load texture
    glPixelStorei(GL_UNPACK_ALIGNMENT, 1);
    pBytes = gltLoadTGA("Stone.tga", &iWidth, &iHeight,
                                        &iComponents, &eFormat);
    glTexImage2D(GL_TEXTURE_2D, 0, iComponents, iWidth, iHeight,
                        0, eFormat, GL_UNSIGNED_BYTE, pBytes);
    free(pBytes);

    glTexParameteri(GL_TEXTURE_2D, GL_TEXTURE_MIN_FILTER, GL_LINEAR);
    glTexParameteri(GL_TEXTURE_2D, GL_TEXTURE_MAG_FILTER, GL_LINEAR);
    glTexParameteri(GL_TEXTURE_2D, GL_TEXTURE_WRAP_S, GL_CLAMP_TO_EDGE);
    glTexParameteri(GL_TEXTURE_2D, GL_TEXTURE_WRAP_T, GL_CLAMP_TO_EDGE);

    glTexEnvi(GL_TEXTURE_ENV, GL_TEXTURE_ENV_MODE, GL_MODULATE);
    glEnable(GL_TEXTURE_2D);
    }


// Called to draw scene
void RenderScene(void)
    {
    M3DVector3f vNormal;
    M3DVector3f vCorners[5] = { { 0.0f, .80f, 0.0f },    // Top            0
                                { -0.5f, 0.0f, -.50f },   // Back left      1
                                { 0.5f, 0.0f, -0.50f },   // Back right     2
                                { 0.5f, 0.0f, 0.5f },     // Front right    3
                                { -0.5f, 0.0f, 0.5f }};   // Front left     4

    // Clear the window with current clearing color
```

LISTING 8.1   Continued

```
    glClear(GL_COLOR_BUFFER_BIT | GL_DEPTH_BUFFER_BIT);

// Save the matrix state and do the rotations
    glPushMatrix();
        // Move object back and do in-place rotation
        glTranslatef(0.0f, -0.25f, -4.0f);
        glRotatef(xRot, 1.0f, 0.0f, 0.0f);
        glRotatef(yRot, 0.0f, 1.0f, 0.0f);

        // Draw the Pyramid
        glColor3f(1.0f, 1.0f, 1.0f);
        glBegin(GL_TRIANGLES);
            // Bottom section - two triangles
            glNormal3f(0.0f, -1.0f, 0.0f);
            glTexCoord2f(1.0f, 1.0f);
            glVertex3fv(vCorners[2]);

            glTexCoord2f(0.0f, 0.0f);
            glVertex3fv(vCorners[4]);

            glTexCoord2f(0.0f, 1.0f);
            glVertex3fv(vCorners[1]);


            glTexCoord2f(1.0f, 1.0f);
            glVertex3fv(vCorners[2]);

            glTexCoord2f(1.0f, 0.0f);
            glVertex3fv(vCorners[3]);

            glTexCoord2f(0.0f, 0.0f);
            glVertex3fv(vCorners[4]);

            // Front Face
            m3dFindNormal(vNormal, vCorners[0], vCorners[4], vCorners[3]);
            glNormal3fv(vNormal);
            glTexCoord2f(0.5f, 1.0f);
            glVertex3fv(vCorners[0]);
            glTexCoord2f(0.0f, 0.0f);
            glVertex3fv(vCorners[4]);
            glTexCoord2f(1.0f, 0.0f);
            glVertex3fv(vCorners[3]);
```

LISTING 8.1   Continued

```
        // Left Face
        m3dFindNormal(vNormal, vCorners[0], vCorners[1], vCorners[4]);
        glNormal3fv(vNormal);
        glTexCoord2f(0.5f, 1.0f);
        glVertex3fv(vCorners[0]);
        glTexCoord2f(0.0f, 0.0f);
        glVertex3fv(vCorners[1]);
        glTexCoord2f(1.0f, 0.0f);
        glVertex3fv(vCorners[4]);

        // Back Face
        m3dFindNormal(vNormal, vCorners[0], vCorners[2], vCorners[1]);
        glNormal3fv(vNormal);
        glTexCoord2f(0.5f, 1.0f);
        glVertex3fv(vCorners[0]);

        glTexCoord2f(0.0f, 0.0f);
        glVertex3fv(vCorners[2]);

        glTexCoord2f(1.0f, 0.0f);
        glVertex3fv(vCorners[1]);

        // Right Face
        m3dFindNormal(vNormal, vCorners[0], vCorners[3], vCorners[2]);
        glNormal3fv(vNormal);
        glTexCoord2f(0.5f, 1.0f);
        glVertex3fv(vCorners[0]);
        glTexCoord2f(0.0f, 0.0f);
        glVertex3fv(vCorners[3]);
        glTexCoord2f(1.0f, 0.0f);
        glVertex3fv(vCorners[2]);
    glEnd();


// Restore the matrix state
glPopMatrix();

// Buffer swap
glutSwapBuffers();

}
```

8

The SetupRC function does all the necessary initialization for this program, including loading the texture using the gltLoadTGA function presented in the preceding chapter and supplying the bits to the glTexImage2D function:

```
// Load texture
pBytes = gltLoadTGA("Stone.tga", &iWidth, &iHeight,
                                        &iComponents, &eFormat);
glTexImage2D(GL_TEXTURE_2D, 0, iComponents, iWidth, iHeight,
                        0, eFormat, GL_UNSIGNED_BYTE, pBytes);
free(pBytes);
```

Of course, texture mapping must also be turned on:

```
glEnable(GL_TEXTURE_2D);
```

The RenderScene function draws the pyramid as a series of texture-mapped triangles. The following excerpt shows one face being constructed as a normal (calculated using the corner vertices) is specified for the face, followed by three texture and vertex coordinates:

```
// Front Face
gltGetNormalVector(vCorners[0], vCorners[4], vCorners[3], vNormal);
glNormal3fv(vNormal);
glTexCoord2f(0.5f, 1.0f);
glVertex3fv(vCorners[0]);
glTexCoord2f(0.0f, 0.0f);
glVertex3fv(vCorners[4]);
glTexCoord2f(1.0f, 0.0f);
glVertex3fv(vCorners[3]);
```

Texture Environment

In the PYRAMID sample program, the pyramid is drawn with white material properties, and the texture is applied in such a way that its colors are scaled by the coloring of the lit geometry. Figure 8.6 shows the untextured pyramid alongside the source texture and the textured but shaded pyramid.

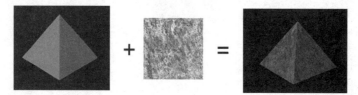

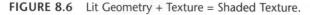

FIGURE 8.6 Lit Geometry + Texture = Shaded Texture.

How OpenGL combines the colors from texels with the color of the underlying geometry is controlled by the *texture environment mode*. You set this mode by calling the `glTexEnv` function:

```
void glTexEnvi(GLenum target, GLenum pname, GLint param);
void glTexEnvf(GLenum target, GLenum pname, GLfloat param);
void glTexEnviv(GLenum target, GLenum pname, GLint *param);
void glTexEnvfv(GLenum target, GLenum pname, GLfloat *param);
```

This function comes in a variety of flavors, as shown here, and controls a number of more advanced texturing options covered in the next chapter. In the PYRAMID sample program, this function set the environment mode to GL_MODULATE before any texture application was performed:

```
glTexEnvi(GL_TEXTURE_ENV, GL_TEXTURE_ENV_MODE, GL_MODULATE);
```

The modulate environment mode multiplies the texel color by the geometry color (after lighting calculations). This is why the shaded color of the pyramid comes through and makes the texture appear to be shaded. Using this mode, you can change the color tone of textures by using colored geometry. For example, a black-and-white brick texture applied to red, yellow, and brown geometry would yield red, yellow, and brown bricks with only a single texture.

If you want to simply replace the color of the underlying geometry, you can specify GL_REPLACE for the environment mode. Doing so replaces fragment colors from the geometry directly with the texel colors. Making this change eliminates any effect on the texture from the underlying geometry. If the texture has an alpha channel, you can enable blending (or use the alpha test), and you can use this mode to create transparent geometry patterned after the alpha channel in the texture map.

If the texture doesn't have an alpha component, GL_DECAL behaves the same way as GL_REPLACE. It simply "decals" the texture over the top of the geometry and any color values that have been calculated for the fragments. However, if the texture has an alpha component, the decal can be applied in such a way that the geometry shows through where the alpha is blended with the underlying fragments.

Textures can also be blended with a constant blending color using the GL_BLEND texture environment. If you set this environment mode, you must also set the texture environment color:

```
GLfloat fColor[4] = { 1.0f, 0.0f, 0.0f, 0.0f };
glTexEnvi(GL_TEXTURE_ENV, GL_TEXTURE_ENV_MODE, GL_BLEND);
glTexEnvfv(GL_TEXTURE_ENV, GL_TEXTURE_ENV_COLOR, fColor);
```

Finally, you can simply add texel color values to the underlying fragment values by setting the environment mode to GL_ADD. Any color component values that exceed 1.0 are clamped, and you may get saturated color values (basically, white or closer to white than you might intend).

We have not presented an exhaustive list of the texture environment constants here. See Appendix C and the next chapter for more modes and texturing effects that are enabled and controlled through this function. We also revisit some additional uses in coming sections and sample programs.

Texture Parameters

More effort is involved in texture mapping than slapping an image on the side of a triangle. Many parameters affect the rendering rules and behaviors of texture maps as they are applied. These texture parameters are all set via variations on the function glTexParameter:

```
void glTexParameterf(GLenum target, GLenum pname, GLfloat param);
void glTexParameteri(GLenum target, GLenum pname, GLint param);
void glTexParameterfv(GLenum target, GLenum pname, GLfloat *params);
void glTexParameteriv(GLenum target, GLenum pname, GLint *params);
```

The first argument, *target*, specifies which texture mode the parameter is to be applied to and may be GL_TEXTURE_1D, GL_TEXTURE_2D, or GL_TEXTURE_3D. The second argument, *pname*, specifies which texture parameter is being set, and finally, the *param* or *params* argument sets the value of the particular texture parameter.

Basic Filtering

Unlike pixmaps being drawn to the color buffer, when a texture is applied to geometry, there is almost never a one-to-one correspondence between texels in the texture map and pixels on the screen. A careful programmer could achieve this result, but only by texturing geometry that was carefully planned to appear onscreen such that the texels and pixels lined up. Consequently, texture images are always either stretched or shrunk as they are applied to geometric surfaces. Because of the orientation of the geometry, a given texture could even be stretched and shrunk at the same time across the surface of some object.

The process of calculating color fragments from a stretched or shrunken texture map is called texture *filtering*. Using the texture parameter function, OpenGL allows you to set both *magnification* and *minification* filters. The parameter names for these two filters are GL_TEXTURE_MAG_FILTER and GL_TEXTURE_MIN_FILTER. For now, you can select from two basic texture filters for them, GL_NEAREST and GL_LINEAR, which correspond to nearest neighbor and linear filtering. Make sure you always choose one of these two filters for the GL_TEXTURE_MIN_FILTER—the default filter setting will not work without mipmaps (see the later section, "Mipmapping").

Nearest neighbor filtering is the simplest and fastest filtering method you can choose. Texture coordinates are evaluated and plotted against a texture's texels, and whichever texel the coordinate falls in, that color is used for the fragment texture color. Nearest neighbor filtering is characterized by large blocky pixels when the texture is stretched especially large. An example is shown in Figure 8.7. You can set the texture filter (for GL_TEXTURE_2D) for both the minification and the magnification filter by using these two function calls:

```
glTexParameteri(GL_TEXTURE_2D, GL_TEXTURE_MAG_FILTER, GL_NEAREST);
glTexParameteri(GL_TEXTURE_2D, GL_TEXTURE_MIN_FILTER, GL_NEAREST);
```

FIGURE 8.7   Nearest neighbor filtering up close.

Linear filtering requires more work than nearest neighbor, but often is worth the extra overhead. On today's commodity hardware, the extra cost of linear filtering is negligible. Linear filtering works by not taking the nearest texel to the texture coordinate, but by applying the weighted average of the texels surrounding the texture coordinate (a linear interpolation). For this interpolated fragment to match the texel color exactly, the texture coordinate needs to fall directly in the center of the texel. Linear filtering is characterized by "fuzzy" graphics when a texture is stretched. This fuzziness, however, often lends to a more realistic and less artificial look than the jagged blocks of the nearest neighbor filtering mode. A contrasting example to Figure 8.7 is shown in Figure 8.8. You can set linear filtering (for GL_TEXTURE_2D) simply enough by using the following lines, which are also included in the SetupRC function in the PYRAMID example:

```
glTexParameteri(GL_TEXTURE_2D, GL_TEXTURE_MAG_FILTER, GL_LINEAR);
glTexParameteri(GL_TEXTURE_2D, GL_TEXTURE_MIN_FILTER, GL_LINEAR);
```

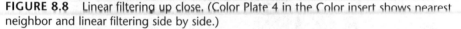

FIGURE 8.8   Linear filtering up close. (Color Plate 4 in the Color insert shows nearest neighbor and linear filtering side by side.)

Texture Wrap

Normally, you specify texture coordinates between 0.0 and 1.0 to map out the texels in a texture map. If texture coordinates fall outside this range, OpenGL handles them according to the current texture wrapping mode. You can set the wrap mode for each coordinate individually by calling glTexParameteri with GL_TEXTURE_WRAP_S, GL_TEXTURE_WRAP_T, or GL_TEXTURE_WRAP_R as the parameter name. The wrap mode can then be set to one of the following values: GL_REPEAT, GL_CLAMP, GL_CLAMP_TO_EDGE, or GL_CLAMP_TO_BORDER.

The GL_REPEAT wrap mode simply causes the texture to repeat in the direction in which the texture coordinate has exceeded 1.0. The texture repeats again for every integer texture coordinate. This mode is very useful for applying a small tiled texture to large geometric surfaces. Well-done seamless textures can lend the appearance of a seemingly much larger texture, but at the cost of a much smaller texture image. The other modes do not repeat, but are "clamped"—thus their name.

If the only implication of the wrap mode is whether the texture repeats, you would need only two wrap modes: repeat and clamp. However, the texture wrap mode also has a great deal of influence on how texture filtering is done at the edges of the texture maps. For GL_NEAREST filtering, there are no consequences to the wrap mode because the texture coordinates are always snapped to some particular texel within the texture map. However, the GL_LINEAR filter takes an average of the pixels surrounding the evaluated texture coordinate, and this creates a problem for texels that lie along the edges of the texture map.

This problem is resolved quite neatly when the wrap mode is GL_REPEAT. The texel samples are simply taken from the next row or column, which in repeat mode wraps back around to the other side of the texture. This mode works perfectly for textures that wrap around an object and meet on the other side (such as spheres).

The clamped texture wrap modes offer a number of options for the way texture edges are handled. For GL_CLAMP, the needed texels are taken from the texture border or the TEXTURE_BORDER_COLOR (set with glTexParameterfv). The GL_CLAMP_TO_EDGE wrap mode forces texture coordinates out of range to be sampled along the last row or column of valid texels. Finally, GL_CLAMP_TO_BORDER uses only border texels whenever the texture coordinates fall outside the range 0.0 to 1.0. Border texels are loaded as an extra row and column surrounding the base image, loaded along with the base texture map.

A typical application of the clamped modes occurs when you must texture a large area that would require a single texture too large to fit into memory, or that may be loaded into a single texture map. In this case, the area is chopped up into smaller "tiles" that are then placed side by side. In such a case, not using a wrap mode such as GL_CLAMP_TO_EDGE can sometimes cause visible filtering artifacts along the seams between tiles. Rarely, even this is not sufficient, and you will have to resort to texture border texels.

Cartoons with Texture

The first example for this chapter used 2D textures because they are usually the simplest and easiest to understand. Most people can quickly get an intuitive feel for putting a 2D picture on the side of a piece of 2D geometry (such as a triangle). We will step back now and present a one-dimensional texture mapping example that is commonly used in computer games to render geometry that appears onscreen shaded like a cartoon. *Toon-shading,* which is often referred to as *cell-shading,* uses a one-dimensional texture map as a lookup table to fill in geometry with a solid color (using GL_NEAREST) from the texture map.

The basic idea is to use a surface normal from the geometry and a vector to the light source to find the intensity of the light striking the surface of the model. The dot product of these two vectors gives a value between 0.0 and 1.0 and is used as a one-dimensional texture coordinate (this is your basic diffuse lighting technique). The sample program TOON presented in Listing 8.2 draws a green torus using this technique. The output from TOON is shown in Figure 8.9.

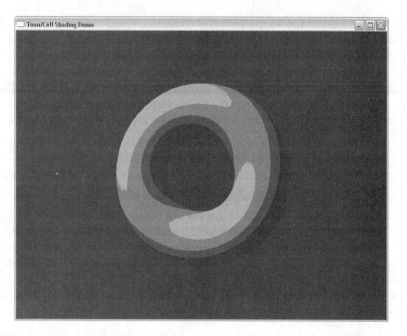

FIGURE 8.9   A cell-shaded torus.

LISTING 8.2   Source Code for the TOON Sample Program

```cpp
// Toon.cpp
// OpenGL SuperBible
// Demonstrates Cell/Toon shading with a 1D texture
// Program by Richard S. Wright Jr.

#include "../../shared/gltools.h"      // OpenGL toolkit
#include "../../shared/math3d.h"
#include <math.h>

// Vector pointing towards the light
M3DVector3f vLightDir = { -1.0f, 1.0f, 1.0f };

// Draw a torus (doughnut), using the current 1D texture for light shading
void toonDrawTorus(GLfloat majorRadius, GLfloat minorRadius,
                          int numMajor, int numMinor, GLTVector3 vLightDir)
    {
    M3DMatrix44f mModelViewMatrix;
    M3DMatrix44f mInvertedLight;
    M3DVector3f vNewLight;
```

LISTING 8.2   Continued

```
M3DVector3f vNormal;
double majorStep = 2.0f*M3D_PI / numMajor;
double minorStep = 2.0f*M3D_PI / numMinor;
int i, j;

// Get the modelview matrix
glGetFloatv(GL_MODELVIEW_MATRIX, mModelViewMatrix);

// Instead of transforming every normal and then dotting it with
// the light vector, we will transform the light into object
// space by multiplying it by the inverse of the modelview matrix
m3dInvertMatrix44(mInvertedLight, mModelViewMatrix);
m3dTransformVector3(vNewLight, vLightDir, mInvertedLight);
vNewLight[0] -= mInvertedLight[12];
vNewLight[1] -= mInvertedLight[13];
vNewLight[2] -= mInvertedLight[14];
m3dNormalizeVector(vNewLight);

// Draw torus as a series of triangle strips
for (i=0; i<numMajor; ++i)
    {
    double a0 = i * majorStep;
    double a1 = a0 + majorStep;
    GLfloat x0 = (GLfloat) cos(a0);
    GLfloat y0 = (GLfloat) sin(a0);
    GLfloat x1 = (GLfloat) cos(a1);
    GLfloat y1 = (GLfloat) sin(a1);

    glBegin(GL_TRIANGLE_STRIP);
    for (j=0; j<=numMinor; ++j)
        {
        double b = j * minorStep;
        GLfloat c = (GLfloat) cos(b);
        GLfloat r = minorRadius * c + majorRadius;
        GLfloat z = minorRadius * (GLfloat) sin(b);

        // First point
        vNormal[0] = x0*c;
        vNormal[1] = y0*c;
        vNormal[2] = z/minorRadius;
        m3dNormalizeVector(vNormal);
```

LISTING 8.2   Continued

```
                    // Texture coordinate is set by intensity of light
                    glTexCoord1f(m3dDotProduct(vNewLight, vNormal));
                    glVertex3f(x0*r, y0*r, z);

                    // Second point
                    vNormal[0] = x1*c;
                    vNormal[1] = y1*c;
                    vNormal[2] = z/minorRadius;
                    m3dNormalizeVector(vNormal);

                    // Texture coordinate is set by intensity of light
                    glTexCoord1f(m3dDotProduct(vNewLight, vNormal));
                    glVertex3f(x1*r, y1*r, z);
                    }
            glEnd();
            }
    }


// Called to draw scene
void RenderScene(void)
    {
    // Rotation angle
    static GLfloat yRot = 0.0f;

    // Clear the window with current clearing color
    glClear(GL_COLOR_BUFFER_BIT | GL_DEPTH_BUFFER_BIT);
        glPushMatrix();
        glTranslatef(0.0f, 0.0f, -2.5f);
        glRotatef(yRot, 0.0f, 1.0f, 0.0f);
        toonDrawTorus(0.35f, 0.15f, 50, 25, vLightDir);
    glPopMatrix();

    // Do the buffer Swap
    glutSwapBuffers();

    // Rotate 1/2 degree more each frame
    yRot += 0.5f;
    }

// This function does any needed initialization on the rendering
// context.
```

LISTING 8.2   Continued

```
void SetupRC()
    {
    // Load a 1D texture with toon shaded values
    // Green, greener...
    GLbyte toonTable[4][3] = { { 0, 32, 0 },
                               { 0, 64, 0 },
                               { 0, 128, 0 },
                               { 0, 192, 0 }};

    // Bluish background
    glClearColor(0.0f, 0.0f, .50f, 1.0f );
    glEnable(GL_DEPTH_TEST);
    glEnable(GL_CULL_FACE);

    glTexEnvi(GL_TEXTURE_ENV, GL_TEXTURE_ENV_MODE, GL_DECAL);
    glTexParameteri(GL_TEXTURE_1D, GL_TEXTURE_MAG_FILTER, GL_NEAREST);
    glTexParameteri(GL_TEXTURE_1D, GL_TEXTURE_MIN_FILTER, GL_NEAREST);
    glTexParameteri(GL_TEXTURE_1D, GL_TEXTURE_WRAP_S, GL_CLAMP);
    glPixelStorei(GL_UNPACK_ALIGNMENT, 1);
    glTexImage1D(GL_TEXTURE_1D, 0, GL_RGB, 4, 0, GL_RGB,
                    GL_UNSIGNED_BYTE, toonTable);

    glEnable(GL_TEXTURE_1D);
    }
```

Mipmapping

Mipmapping is a powerful texturing technique that can improve both the rendering performance and the visual quality of a scene. It does this by addressing two common problems with standard texture mapping. The first is an effect called *scintillation* (aliasing artifacts) that appears on the surface of objects rendered very small onscreen compared to the relative size of the texture applied. Scintillation can be seen as a sort of sparkling that occurs as the sampling area on a texture map moves disproportionately to its size on the screen. The negative effects of scintillation are most noticeable when the camera or the objects are in motion.

The second issue is more performance related, but is due to the same scenario that leads to scintillation. That is, a large amount of texture memory must be loaded and processed through filtering to display a small number of fragments onscreen. This causes texturing performance to suffer greatly as the size of the texture increases.

The solution to both of these problems is to simply use a smaller texture map. However, this solution then creates a new problem: When near the same object, it must be rendered larger, and a small texture map will then be stretched to the point of creating a hopelessly blurry or blocky textured object.

The solution to both of these issues is mipmapping. Mipmapping gets its name from the Latin phrase *multum in parvo,* which means "many things in a small place." In essence, you load not a single image into the texture state, but a whole series of images from largest to smallest into a single "mipmapped" texture state. OpenGL then uses a new set of filter modes to choose the best-fitting texture or textures for the given geometry. At the cost of some extra memory (and possibly considerably more processing work), you can eliminate scintillation and the texture memory processing overhead for distant objects simultaneously, while maintaining higher resolution versions of the texture available when needed.

A mipmapped texture consists of a series of texture images, each one half the size of the previous image. This scenario is shown in Figure 8.10. Mipmap levels do not have to be square, but the halving of the dimensions continues until the last image is 1×1 texel. When one of the dimensions reaches 1, further divisions occur on the other dimension only. Using a square set of mipmaps requires about one-third more memory than not using mipmaps.

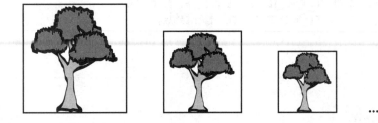

FIGURE 8.10   A series of mipmapped images.

Mipmap levels are loaded with glTexImage. Now the *level* parameter comes into play because it specifies which mip level the image data is for. The first level is 0, then 1, 2, and so on. If mipmapping is not being used, only level 0 is ever loaded. By default, to use mipmaps, all mip levels must be populated. You can, however, specifically set the base and maximum levels to be used with the GL_TEXTURE_BASE_LEVEL and GL_TEXTURE_MAX_LEVEL texture parameters. For example, if you want to specify that only mip levels 0 through 4 need to be loaded, you call glTexParameteri twice as shown here:

```
glTexParameteri(GL_TEXTURE_2D, GL_TEXTURE_BASE_LEVEL, 0);
glTexParameteri(GL_TEXTURE_2D, GL_TEXTURE_MAX_LEVEL, 4);
```

Although GL_TEXTURE_BASE_LEVEL and GL_TEXTURE_MAX_LEVEL control which mip levels are loaded, you can also specifically limit the range of loaded mip levels to be used by using the parameters GL_TEXTURE_MIN_LOD and GL_TEXTURE_MAX_LOD instead.

Mipmap Filtering

Mipmapping adds a new twist to the two basic texture filtering modes GL_NEAREST and GL_LINEAR by giving four permutations for mipmapped filtering modes. They are listed in Table 8.4.

TABLE 8.4 Mipmapped Texture Filters

Constant	Description
GL_NEAREST	Perform nearest neighbor filtering on the base mip level
GL_LINEAR	Perform linear filtering on the base mip level
GL_NEAREST_MIPMAP_NEAREST	Select the nearest mip level and perform nearest neighbor filtering
GL_NEAREST_MIPMAP_LINEAR	Perform a linear interpolation between mip levels and perform nearest neighbor filtering
GL_LINEAR_MIPMAP_NEAREST	Select the nearest mip level and perform linear filtering
GL_LINEAR_MIPMAP_LINEAR	Perform a linear interpolation between mip levels and perform linear filtering; also called *trilinear* mipmapping

Just loading the mip levels with glTexImage does not by itself enable mipmapping. If the texture filter is set to GL_LINEAR or GL_NEAREST, only the base texture level is used, and any mip levels loaded are ignored. You must specify one of the mipmapped filters listed for the loaded mip levels to be used. The constants have the form GL_*FILTER*_MIPMAP_*SELECTOR*, where *FILTER* specifies the texture filter to be used on the mip level selected. The *SELECTOR* specifies how the mip level is selected; for example, GL_NEAREST selects the nearest matching mip level. Using GL_LINEAR for the selector creates a linear interpolation between the two nearest mip levels, which is again filtered by the chosen texture filter. Selecting one of the mipmapped filtering modes without loading the mip levels has the effect of disabling texture mapping.

Which filter you select varies depending on the application and the performance requirements at hand. GL_NEAREST_MIPMAP_NEAREST, for example, gives very good performance and low aliasing (scintillation) artifacts, but nearest neighbor filtering is often not visually pleasing. GL_LINEAR_MIPMAP_NEAREST is often used to speed up games because a higher quality linear filter is used, but a fast selection (nearest) is made between the different-sized mip levels available.

Using nearest as the mipmap selector (as in both examples in the preceding paragraph), however, can also leave an undesirable visual artifact. For oblique views, you can often see the transition from one mip level to another across a surface. It can be seen as a distortion line or a sharp transition from one level of detail to another. The GL_LINEAR_MIPMAP_LINEAR and GL_NEAREST_MIPMAP_LINEAR filters perform an additional interpolation between mip levels to eliminate this transition zone, but at the extra cost of substantially more processing overhead. The GL_LINEAR_MIPMAP_LINEAR filter is often referred to as *trilinear* mipmapping and until recently was the gold standard (highest fidelity) of texture filtering. More recently, *anisotropic* texture filtering (covered in the next chapter) has become widely available on OpenGL hardware but even further increases the cost (performance-wise) of texture mapping.

Generating Mip Levels

As mentioned previously, mipmapping requires approximately one-third more texture memory than just loading the base texture image. It also requires that all the smaller versions of the base texture image be available for loading. Sometimes this can be inconvenient because the lower resolution images may not necessarily be available to either the programmer or the end user of your software. The GLU library does include a function named gluScaleImage that you could use to repeatedly scale and load an image until all the needed mip levels are loaded. More frequently, however, an even more convenient function is available; it automatically creates the scaled images for you and loads them appropriately with glTexImage. This function, gluBuildMipmaps, comes in three flavors and supports one-, two-, and three-dimensional texture maps:

```
int gluBuild1DMipmaps(GLenum target, GLint internalFormat,
                      GLint width,
                      GLenum format, GLenum type, const void *data);

int gluBuild2DMipmaps(GLenum target, GLint internalFormat,
                      GLint width, GLint height,
                      GLenum format, GLenum type, const void *data);

int gluBuild3DMipmaps(GLenum target, GLint internalFormat,
                      GLint width, GLint height, GLint depth,
                      GLenum format, GLenum type, const void *data);
```

The use of these functions closely parallels the use of glTexImage, but they do not have a *level* parameter for specifying the mip level, nor do they provide any support for a texture border. You should also be aware that using these functions may not produce mip level images with the same quality you can obtain with other tools such as Photoshop. The GLU library uses a *box filter* to reduce images, which can lead to an undesirable loss of fine detail as the image shrinks.

With newer versions of the GLU library, you can also obtain a finer-grained control over which mip levels are loaded with these functions:

```
int gluBuild1DMipmapLevels(GLenum target, GLint internalFormat,
                           GLint width,
```

```
                              GLenum format, GLenum type, GLint level,
                              GLint base, GLint max, const void *data);


int gluBuild2DMipmapLevels(GLenum target, GLint internalFormat,
                           GLint width, GLint height,
                           GLenum format, GLenum type, GLint level,
                           GLint base, GLint max, const void *data);


int gluBuild3DMipmapLevels(GLenum target, Glint internalFormat,
                           GLint width, GLint height, GLint depth,
                           GLenum format, GLenum type, GLint level,
                           GLint base, GLint max, const void *data);
```

With these functions, *level* is the mip level specified by the *data* parameter. This texture data is used to build mip levels *base* through *max*.

Hardware Generation of Mipmaps

If you know beforehand that you want all mip levels loaded, you can also use OpenGL hardware acceleration to quickly generate all the necessary mip levels. You do so by setting the texture parameter GL_GENERATE_MIPMAP to GL_TRUE:

```
glTexParameteri(GL_TEXTURE_2D, GL_GENERATE_MIPMAP, GL_TRUE);
```

When this parameter is set, all calls to glTexImage or glTexSubImage that update the base texture map (mip level 0) automatically update all the lower mip levels. By making use of the graphics hardware, this feature is substantially faster than using gluBuildMipmaps. However, you should be aware that this feature was originally an extension and was promoted to the OpenGL core API only as of version 1.4. This is definitely the fastest and easiest way to build mipmaps on-the-fly.

LOD BIAS

When mipmapping is enabled, OpenGL uses a formula to determine which mip level should be selected based on the size of the mipmap levels and the onscreen area the geometry occupies. OpenGL does its best to make a close match between the mipmap level chosen and the texture's representation onscreen. You can tell OpenGL to move its selection criteria back (lean toward larger mip levels) or forward (lean toward smaller mip levels). This can have the effect of increasing performance (using smaller mip levels) or increasing the sharpness of texture-mapped objects (using larger mip levels). This bias one way or the other is selected with the texture environment parameter GL_TEXTURE_LOD_BIAS, as shown here:

```
glTexEnvf(GL_TEXTURE_FILTER_CONTROL, GL_TEXTURE_LOD_BIAS, -1.5);
```

In this example, the texture level of detail is shifted slightly toward using higher levels of detail (smaller level parameters), resulting in sharper looking textures, at the expense of slightly more texture processing overhead.

Texture Objects

So far, you have seen how to load a texture and set texture parameters to affect how texture maps are applied to geometry. The texture image and parameters set with glTexParameter compose the *texture state*. Loading and maintaining the texture state occupies a considerable portion of many texture-heavy OpenGL applications (games in particular).

Especially time-consuming are function calls such as glTexImage, glTexSubImage, and gluBuildMipmaps. These functions move a large amount of memory around and possibly need to reformat the data to match some internal representation. Switching between textures or reloading a different texture image would ordinarily be a costly operation.

Texture objects allow you to load up more than one texture state at a time, including texture images, and switch between them very quickly. The texture state is maintained by the currently bound texture object, which is identified by an unsigned integer. You allocate a number of texture objects with the following function:

```
void glGenTextures(GLsizei n, GLuint *textures);
```

With this function, you specify the number of texture objects and a pointer to an array of unsigned integers that will be populated with the texture object identifiers. You can think of them as handles to different available texture states. To "bind" to one of these states, you call the following function:

```
void glBindTexture(GLenum target, GLuint texture);
```

The target parameter needs to specify GL_TEXTURE_1D, GL_TEXTURE_2D, or GL_TEXTURE_3D, and texture is the specific texture object to bind to. Hereafter, all texture loads and texture parameter settings affect only the currently bound texture object. To delete texture objects, you call the following function:

```
void glDeleteTextures(GLsizei n, GLuint *textures);
```

The arguments here have the same meaning as for glGenTextures. You do not need to generate and delete all your texture objects at the same time. Multiple calls to glGenTextures have very little overhead. Calling glDeleteTextures multiple times may incur some delay, but only because you are deallocating possibly large amounts of texture memory.

You can test texture object names (or handles) to see whether they are valid by using the following function:

```
GLboolean glIsTexture(GLuint texture);
```

This function returns GL_TRUE if the integer is a previously allocated texture object name or GL_FALSE if not.

Managing Multiple Textures

Generally, texture objects are used to load up several textures at program initialization and switch between them quickly during rendering. These texture objects are then deleted when the program shuts down. The TUNNEL sample program loads three textures at startup and then switches between them to render a tunnel. The tunnel has a brick wall pattern with different materials on the floor and ceiling. The output from TUNNEL is shown in Figure 8.11.

FIGURE 8.11   A tunnel rendered with three different textures.

The TUNNEL sample program also shows off mipmapping and the different mipmapped texture filtering modes. Pressing the up- and down-arrow keys moves the point of view back and forth in the tunnel, and the context menu (right-click menu) allows you to switch among six different filtering modes to see how they affect the rendered image. The abbreviated source code is provided in Listing 8.3.

LISTING 8.3   Source Code for the TUNNEL Sample Program

```cpp
// Tunnel.cpp
// Demonstrates mipmapping and using texture objects
// OpenGL SuperBible
// Richard S. Wright Jr.
#include "../../shared/gltools.h"    // GLTools

// Rotation amounts
static GLfloat zPos = -60.0f;

// Texture objects
#define TEXTURE_BRICK    0
#define TEXTURE_FLOOR    1
#define TEXTURE_CEILING 2
#define TEXTURE_COUNT    3
GLuint  textures[TEXTURE_COUNT];
const char *szTextureFiles[TEXTURE_COUNT] =
                                { "brick.tga", "floor.tga", "ceiling.tga" };

///////////////////////////////////////////////////////////////////////////
// Change texture filter for each texture object
void ProcessMenu(int value)
    {
    GLint iLoop;

    for(iLoop = 0; iLoop < TEXTURE_COUNT; iLoop++)
        {
        glBindTexture(GL_TEXTURE_2D, textures[iLoop]);

        switch(value)
            {
            case 0:
                glTexParameteri(GL_TEXTURE_2D, GL_TEXTURE_MIN_FILTER,
                                                        GL_NEAREST);
                break;

            case 1:
                glTexParameteri(GL_TEXTURE_2D, GL_TEXTURE_MIN_FILTER,
                                                        GL_LINEAR);
                break;

            case 2:
                glTexParameteri(GL_TEXTURE_2D, GL_TEXTURE_MIN_FILTER,
```

LISTING 8.3   Continued

```
                                             GL_NEAREST_MIPMAP_NEAREST);
            break;

        case 3:
            glTexParameteri(GL_TEXTURE_2D, GL_TEXTURE_MIN_FILTER,
                                        GL_NEAREST_MIPMAP_LINEAR);
            break;

        case 4:
            glTexParameteri(GL_TEXTURE_2D, GL_TEXTURE_MIN_FILTER,
                                          GL_LINEAR_MIPMAP_NEAREST);
            break;

        case 5:
        default:
            glTexParameteri(GL_TEXTURE_2D, GL_TEXTURE_MIN_FILTER,
                                          GL_LINEAR_MIPMAP_LINEAR);
            break;
        }
    }

    // Trigger Redraw
    glutPostRedisplay();
    }


///////////////////////////////////////////////////////////////////
// This function does any needed initialization on the rendering
// context.  Here it sets up and initializes the texture objects.
void SetupRC()
    {
    GLubyte *pBytes;
    GLint iWidth, iHeight, iComponents;
    GLenum eFormat;
    GLint iLoop;

    // Black background
    glClearColor(0.0f, 0.0f, 0.0f,1.0f);

    // Textures applied as decals, no lighting or coloring effects
    glEnable(GL_TEXTURE_2D);
    glTexEnvi(GL_TEXTURE_ENV, GL_TEXTURE_ENV_MODE, GL_DECAL);
```

LISTING 8.3   Continued

```
    // Load textures
    glGenTextures(TEXTURE_COUNT, textures);
    for(iLoop = 0; iLoop < TEXTURE_COUNT; iLoop++)
        {
        // Bind to next texture object
        glBindTexture(GL_TEXTURE_2D, textures[iLoop]);

        // Load texture, set filter and wrap modes
        pBytes = gltLoadTGA(szTextureFiles[iLoop],&iWidth, &iHeight,
                            &iComponents, &eFormat);
        gluBuild2DMipmaps(GL_TEXTURE_2D, iComponents, iWidth, iHeight, eFormat,
                            GL_UNSIGNED_BYTE, pBytes);
        glTexParameteri(GL_TEXTURE_2D, GL_TEXTURE_MAG_FILTER, GL_LINEAR);
        glTexParameteri(GL_TEXTURE_2D, GL_TEXTURE_MIN_FILTER,
                            GL_LINEAR_MIPMAP_LINEAR);
        glTexParameteri(GL_TEXTURE_2D, GL_TEXTURE_WRAP_S, GL_CLAMP_TO_EDGE);
        glTexParameteri(GL_TEXTURE_2D, GL_TEXTURE_WRAP_T, GL_CLAMP_TO_EDGE);

        // Don't need original texture data any more
        free(pBytes);
        }
    }


//////////////////////////////////////////////////////
// Shut down the rendering context. Just deletes the
// texture objects
void ShutdownRC(void)
    {
    glDeleteTextures(TEXTURE_COUNT, textures);
    }


//////////////////////////////////////////////////////
// Called to draw scene
void RenderScene(void)
    {
    GLfloat z;

    // Clear the window with current clearing color
    glClear(GL_COLOR_BUFFER_BIT);

    // Save the matrix state and do the rotations
```

LISTING 8.3 Continued

```
glPushMatrix();
    // Move object back and do in-place rotation
    glTranslatef(0.0f, 0.0f, zPos);

    // Floor
    for(z = 60.0f; z >= 0.0f; z -= 10)
    {
    glBindTexture(GL_TEXTURE_2D, textures[TEXTURE_FLOOR]);
    glBegin(GL_QUADS);
        glTexCoord2f(0.0f, 0.0f);
        glVertex3f(-10.0f, -10.0f, z);

        glTexCoord2f(1.0f, 0.0f);
        glVertex3f(10.0f, -10.0f, z);

        glTexCoord2f(1.0f, 1.0f);
        glVertex3f(10.0f, -10.0f, z - 10.0f);

        glTexCoord2f(0.0f, 1.0f);
        glVertex3f(-10.0f, -10.0f, z - 10.0f);
    glEnd();

    // Ceiling
    glBindTexture(GL_TEXTURE_2D, textures[TEXTURE_CEILING]);
    glBegin(GL_QUADS);

    . . .
    . . .
    glEnd();
    }

// Restore the matrix state
glPopMatrix();

// Buffer swap
glutSwapBuffers();
}


/////////////////////////////////////////////////////
// Program entry point
int main(int argc, char *argv[])
```

LISTING 8.3   Continued

```
{
// Standard initialization stuff
glutInit(&argc, argv);
glutInitDisplayMode(GLUT_DOUBLE | GLUT_RGB);
glutInitWindowSize(800, 600);
glutCreateWindow("Tunnel");
glutReshapeFunc(ChangeSize);
glutSpecialFunc(SpecialKeys);
glutDisplayFunc(RenderScene);

// Add menu entries to change filter
glutCreateMenu(ProcessMenu);
glutAddMenuEntry("GL_NEAREST",0);
glutAddMenuEntry("GL_LINEAR",1);
glutAddMenuEntry("GL_NEAREST_MIPMAP_NEAREST",2);
glutAddMenuEntry("GL_NEAREST_MIPMAP_LINEAR", 3);
glutAddMenuEntry("GL_LINEAR_MIPMAP_NEAREST", 4);
glutAddMenuEntry("GL_LINEAR_MIPMAP_LINEAR", 5);
glutAttachMenu(GLUT_RIGHT_BUTTON);

// Start up, loop, shut down
SetupRC();
glutMainLoop();
ShutdownRC();

return 0;
}
```

In this example, you first create identifiers for the three texture objects. The array textures will contain three integers, which will be addressed by using the macros TEXTURE_BRICK, TEXTURE_FLOOR, and TEXTURE_CEILING. For added flexibility, you also create a macro that defines the maximum number of textures that will be loaded and an array of character strings containing the names of the texture map files:

```
// Texture objects
#define TEXTURE_BRICK   0
#define TEXTURE_FLOOR  1
#define TEXTURE_CEILING 2
#define TEXTURE_COUNT   3
GLuint  textures[TEXTURE_COUNT];
const char *szTextureFiles[TEXTURE_COUNT] =
                              { "brick.tga", "floor.tga", "ceiling.tga" };
```

The texture objects are allocated in the SetupRC function:

```
glGenTextures(TEXTURE_COUNT, textures);
```

Then a simple loop binds to each texture object in turn and loads its texture state with the texture image and texturing parameters:

```
for(iLoop = 0; iLoop < TEXTURE_COUNT; iLoop++)
    {
    // Bind to next texture object
    glBindTexture(GL_TEXTURE_2D, textures[iLoop]);

    // Load texture, set filter and wrap modes
    pBytes = gltLoadTGA(szTextureFiles[iLoop],&iWidth, &iHeight,
                        &iComponents, &eFormat);
    gluBuild2DMipmaps(GL_TEXTURE_2D, iComponents, iWidth, iHeight, eFormat,
                        GL_UNSIGNED_BYTE, pBytes);
    glTexParameteri(GL_TEXTURE_2D, GL_TEXTURE_MAG_FILTER, GL_LINEAR);
    glTexParameteri(GL_TEXTURE_2D, GL_TEXTURE_MIN_FILTER,
                        GL_LINEAR_MIPMAP_LINEAR);
    glTexParameteri(GL_TEXTURE_2D, GL_TEXTURE_WRAP_S, GL_CLAMP_TO_EDGE);
    glTexParameteri(GL_TEXTURE_2D, GL_TEXTURE_WRAP_T, GL_CLAMP_TO_EDGE);

    // Don't need original texture data any more
    free(pBytes);
    }
```

With each of the three texture objects initialized, you can easily switch between them during rendering to change textures:

```
glBindTexture(GL_TEXTURE_2D, textures[TEXTURE_FLOOR]);
    glBegin(GL_QUADS);
        glTexCoord2f(0.0f, 0.0f);
        glVertex3f(-10.0f, -10.0f, z);

        glTexCoord2f(1.0f, 0.0f);
        glVertex3f(10.0f, -10.0f, z);

        ...
        ...
```

Finally, when the program is terminated, you only need to delete the texture objects for the final cleanup:

```
//////////////////////////////////////////////////
// Shut down the rendering context. Just deletes the
// texture objects
void ShutdownRC(void)
    {
    glDeleteTextures(TEXTURE_COUNT, textures);
    }
```

Also, note that when the mipmapped texture filter is set in the TUNNEL sample program, it is selected only for the minification filter:

```
glTexParameteri(GL_TEXTURE_2D, GL_TEXTURE_MAG_FILTER, GL_LINEAR);
glTexParameteri(GL_TEXTURE_2D, GL_TEXTURE_MIN_FILTER, GL_LINEAR_MIPMAP_LINEAR);
```

This is typically the case because after OpenGL selects the largest available mip level, no larger levels are available to select from. Essentially, this is to say that after a certain threshold is passed, the largest available texture image is used and there are no additional mipmap levels to choose from.

Resident Textures

Most OpenGL implementations support a limited amount of high-performance texture memory. Textures located in this memory are accessed very quickly, and performance is high. Initially, any loaded texture is stored in this memory; however, only a limited amount of memory is typically available, and at some point textures may need to be stored in slower memory. As is often the case, this slower memory may even be located outside the OpenGL hardware (such as in a PC's system memory as opposed to being stored on the graphics card or in AGP memory).

To optimize rendering performance, OpenGL automatically moves frequently accessed textures into this high-performance memory. Textures in this high-performance memory are called *resident* textures. To determine whether a bound texture is resident, you can call glGetTexParameter and find the value associated with GL_TEXTURE_RESIDENT. Testing a group of textures to see whether they are resident may be more useful, and you can perform this test using the following function:

```
GLboolean glAreTexturesResident(GLsizei n, const GLuint *textures,
                                              GLboolean *residences);
```

This function takes the number of texture objects to check, an array of the texture object names, and finally an array of Boolean flags set to GL_TRUE or GL_FALSE to indicate the status of each texture object. If all the textures are resident, the array is left unchanged, and the function returns GL_TRUE. This feature is meant to save the time of having to check through an entire array to see whether all the textures are resident.

Texture Priorities

By default, most OpenGL implementations use a Most Frequently Used (MFU) algorithm to decide which textures can stay resident. However, if several smaller textures are used only slightly more frequently than, say, a much larger texture, texturing performance can suffer considerably. You can provide hints to whatever mechanism an implementation uses to decide texture residency by setting each texture's priority with this function:

```
void glPrioritizeTextures(GLsizei n, const GLuint *textures,
                                     const GLclampf *priorities);
```

This function takes an array of texture object names and a corresponding array of texture object priorities that are clamped between 0 and 1.0. A low priority tells the implementation that this texture object should be left out of resident memory whenever space becomes tight. A higher priority (such as 1.0) tells the implementation that you want that texture object to remain resident if possible, even if the texture seems to be used infrequently.

Bear in mind that texture priorities are only a hint to the implementation. Some OpenGL implementations are known to ignore them completely.

Summary

In this chapter, we extended the simple image loading and display methods from the preceding chapter to applying images as texture maps to real three-dimensional geometry. You learned how to load a texture map and use texture coordinates to map the image to the vertices of geometry. You also learned the different ways in which texture images can be filtered and blended with the geometry color values and how to use mipmaps to improve both performance and visual fidelity. Finally, we discussed how to manage multiple textures and switch between them quickly and easily, and how to tell OpenGL which textures should have priority if any high-performance (or local) texture memory is available.

8

CHAPTER 9

Texture Mapping: Beyond the Basics

by Richard S. Wright Jr.

WHAT YOU'LL LEARN IN THIS CHAPTER:

How To	Functions You'll Use
Add specular highlights to textured objects	`glLightModel`/`glSecondaryColor`
Use anisotropic texture filtering	`glTexParameterf`
Load and use compressed textures	`glCompressedTexImage`/`glCompressedTexSubImage`
Use points as textured quads	`glPointParameter`

Texture mapping is perhaps one of the most exciting features of OpenGL (well, close behind shaders anyway!) and is heavily relied on in the games and simulation industry. In Chapter 8, "Texture Mapping: The Basics," you learned the basics of loading and applying texture maps to geometry. In this chapter, we'll expand on this knowledge and cover some of the finer points of texture mapping in OpenGL.

Secondary Color

Applying texture to geometry, in regard to how lighting works, causes a hidden and often undesirable side effect. In general, you set the texture environment to GL_MODULATE, causing lit geometry to be combined with the texture map in such a way that the textured geometry also appears lit. Normally, OpenGL performs lighting calculations and calculates the color of individual fragments according to the standard light model. These fragment colors are then multiplied by the filtered texel colors being applied to the geometry. However, this process has the side effect of suppressing the visibility of specular highlights on the geometry. Basically, any texture color multiplied by ones (the white spot) is the same texture color. You cannot, by multiplication of any number less than or equal to one, make a color brighter than it already is!

For example, Figure 9.1 shows the original lit SPHEREWORLD sample from Chapter 5, "Color, Materials, and Lighting: The Basics." In this figure, you can see clearly the specular highlights reflecting off the surface of the torus. In contrast, Figure 9.2 shows the SPHERE-WORLD sample from Chapter 8. In this figure, you can see the effects of having the texture applied after the lighting has been added.

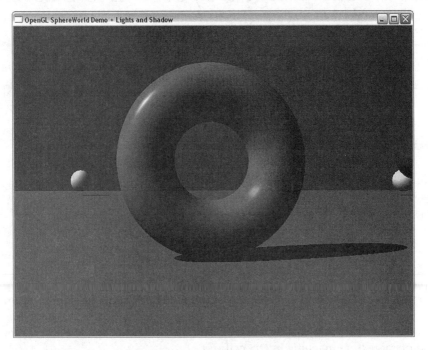

FIGURE 9.1   The original SPHEREWORLD torus with specular highlights.

FIGURE 9.2 The textured torus with muted highlights.

The solution to this problem is to apply (by adding instead of multiplication) the specular highlights after texturing. This technique, called the *secondary specular color,* can be manually applied or automatically calculated by the lighting model. Usually, you do this using the normal OpenGL lighting model and simply turn it on using glLightModeli, as shown here:

```
glLightModeli(GL_LIGHT_MODEL_COLOR_CONTROL, GL_SEPARATE_SPECULAR_COLOR);
```

You can switch back to the normal lighting model by specifying GL_SINGLE_COLOR for the light model parameter:

```
glLightModeli(GL_LIGHT_MODEL_COLOR_CONTROL, GL_COLOR_SINGLE);
```

Figure 9.3 shows the output from this chapter's version of SPHEREWORLD with the restored specular highlights on the torus. We do not provide a listing for this sample because it simply contains the addition of the preceding single line of code.

FIGURE 9.3   Highlights restored to the textured torus.

You can also directly specify a secondary color after texturing when you are not using lighting (lighting is disabled) using the glSecondaryColor function. This function comes in many variations just as glColor does and is fully documented in the reference section. You should also note that if you specify a secondary color, you must also explicitly enable the use of the secondary color by enabling the GL_COLOR_SUM flag:

```
glEnable(GL_COLOR_SUM);
```

Manually setting the secondary color only works when lighting is disabled.

Anisotropic Filtering

Anisotropic texture filtering is not a part of the core OpenGL specification, but it is a widely supported extension that can dramatically improve the quality of texture filtering operations. Texture filtering is covered in the preceding chapter, where you learned about the two basic texture filters: nearest neighbor (GL_NEAREST) and linear (GL_LINEAR). When a texture map is filtered, OpenGL uses the texture coordinates to figure out where in the texture map a particular fragment of geometry falls. The texels immediately around that position are then sampled using either the GL_NEAREST or the GL_LINEAR filtering operations.

This process works perfectly when the geometry being textured is viewed directly perpendicular to the viewpoint, as shown on the left in Figure 9.4. However, when the geometry is viewed from an angle more oblique to the point of view, a regular sampling of the surrounding texels results in the loss of some information in the texture (it looks blurry!). A more realistic and accurate sample would be elongated along the direction of the plane containing the texture. This result is shown on the right in Figure 9.4. Taking this viewing angle into account for texture filtering is called *anisotropic filtering*.

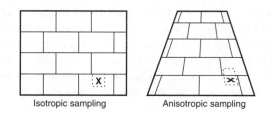

Isotropic sampling   Anisotropic sampling

FIGURE 9.4   Normal texture sampling versus anisotropic sampling.

You can apply anisotropic filtering to any of the basic or mipmapped texture filtering modes; applying it requires three steps. First, you must determine whether the extension is supported. You can do this by querying for the extension string `GL_EXT_texture_filter_anisotropic`. You can use the `glTools` function named `gltIsExtSupported` for this task:

```
if(gltIsExtSupported("GL_EXT_texture_filter_anisotropic"))
    // Set Flag that extension is supported
```

After you determine that this extension is supported, you can find the maximum amount of *anisotropy* supported. You can query for it using `glGetFloatv` and the parameter `GL_MAX_TEXTURE_MAX_ANISOTROPY_EXT`:

```
GLfloat fLargest;
. . .
. . .
glGetFloatv(GL_MAX_TEXTURE_MAX_ANISOTROPY_EXT, &fLargest);
```

The larger the amount of anisotropy applied, the more texels are sampled along the direction of greatest change (along the strongest point of view). A value of `1.0` represents normal texture filtering (called *isotropic* filtering). Bear in mind that anisotropic filtering is not free. The extra amount of work, including other texels, can sometimes result in substantial performance penalties. On modern hardware, this feature is getting quite fast and is becoming a standard feature of popular games, animation, and simulation programs.

Finally, you set the amount of anisotropy you want applied using glTexParameter and the constant GL_TEXTURE_MAX_ANISOTROPY_EXT. For example, using the preceding code, if you want the maximum amount of anisotropy applied, you would call glTexParameterf as shown here:

```
glTexParameterf(GL_TEXTURE_2D, GL_TEXTURE_MAX_ANISOTROPY_EXT, fLargest);
```

This modifier is applied per texture object just like the standard filtering parameters.

The sample program ANISOTROPIC provides a striking example of anisotropic texture filtering in action. This program displays a tunnel with walls, a floor, and ceiling geometry. The arrow keys move your point of view (or the tunnel) back and forth along the tunnel interior. A right mouse click brings up a menu that allows you to select from the various texture filters, and turn on and off anisotropic filtering. Figure 9.5 shows the tunnel using trilinear filtered mipmapping. Notice how blurred the patterns become in the distance, particularly with the bricks.

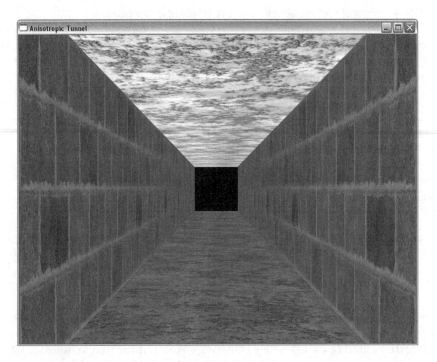

FIGURE 9.5   ANISOTROPIC tunnel sample with trilinear filtering.

Now compare Figure 9.5 with Figure 9.6, in which anisotropic filtering has been enabled. The mortar between the bricks is now clearly visible all the way to the end of the tunnel. In fact, anisotropic filtering can also greatly reduce the visible mipmap transition patterns for the GL_LINEAR_MIPMAP_NEAREST and GL_NEAREST_MIPMAP_NEAREST mipmapped filters.

FIGURE 9.6   ANISOTROPIC tunnel sample with anisotropic filtering.

Texture Compression

Texture mapping can add incredible realism to any 3D rendered scene, with a minimal cost in vertex processing. One drawback to using textures, however, is that they require a lot of memory to store and process. Early attempts at texture compression were crudely storing textures as JPG files and decompressing the textures when loaded before calling glTexImage. These attempts saved disk space or reduced the amount of time required to transmit the image over the network (such as the Internet), but did nothing to alleviate the storage requirements of texture images loaded into graphics hardware memory.

Native support for texture compression was added to OpenGL with version 1.3. Earlier versions of OpenGL may also support texture compression via extension functions of the same name. You can test for this extension by using the GL_ARB_texture_compression string.

Texture compression support in OpenGL hardware can go beyond simply allowing you to load a compressed texture; in most implementations, the texture data stays compressed even in the graphics hardware memory. This allows you to load more texture into less memory and can significantly improve texturing performance due to fewer texture swaps (moving textures around) and fewer memory accesses during texture filtering.

Compressing Textures

Texture data does not have to be initially compressed to take advantage of OpenGL support for compressed textures. You can request that OpenGL compress a texture image when loaded by using one of the values in Table 9.1 for the *internalFormat* parameter of any of the glTexImage functions.

TABLE 9.1   Compressed Texture Formats

Compressed Format	Base Internal Format
GL_COMPRESSED_ALPHA	GL_ALPHA
GL_COMPRESSED_LUMINANCE	GL_LUMINANCE
GL_COMPRESSED_LUMINANCE_ALPHA	GL_LUMINANCE_ALPHA
GL_COMPRESSED_INTENSITY	GL_INTENSITY
GL_COMPRESSED_RGB	GL_RGB
GL_COMPRESSED_RGBA	GL_RGBA

Compressing images this way adds a bit of overhead to texture loads but can increase texture performance due to the more efficient usage of texture memory. If, for some reason, the texture cannot be compressed, OpenGL uses the base internal format listed instead and loads the texture uncompressed.

When you attempt to load and compress a texture in this way, you can find out whether the texture was successfully compressed by using glGetTexLevelParameteriv with GL_TEXTURE_COMPRESSED as the parameter name:

```
GLint compFlag;
. . .
glGetTexLevelParameteriv(GL_TEXTURE_2D, 0, GL_TEXTURE_COMPRESSED, &compFlag);
```

The glGetTexLevelParameteriv function accepts a number of new parameter names pertaining to compressed textures. These parameters are listed in Table 9.2.

TABLE 9.2   Compressed Texture Parameters Retrieved with glGetTexLevelParameter

Parameter	Returns
GL_TEXTURE_COMPRESSED	The value 1 if the texture is compressed, 0 if not
GL_TEXTURE_COMPRESSED_IMAGE_SIZE	The size in bytes of the compressed texture
GL_TEXTURE_INTERNAL_FORMAT	The compression format used
GL_NUM_COMPRESSED_TEXTURE_FORMATS	The number of supported compressed texture formats
GL_COMPRESSED_TEXTURE_FORMATS	An array of constant values corresponding to each supported compressed texture format
GL_TEXTURE_COMPRESSION_HINT	The value of the texture compression hint (GL_NICEST/GL_FASTEST)

When textures are compressed using the values listed in Table 9.1, OpenGL chooses the most appropriate texture compression format. You can use glHint to specify whether you want OpenGL to choose based on the fastest or highest quality algorithm:

```
glHint(GL_TEXTURE_COMPRESSION_HINT, GL_FASTEST);
glHint(GL_TEXTURE_COMPRESSION_HINT, GL_NICEST);
glHint(GL_TEXTURE_COMPRESSION_HINT, GL_DONT_CARE);
```

The exact compression format varies from implementation to implementation. You can obtain a count of compression formats and a list of the values by using GL_NUM_COMPRESSED_TEXTURE_FORMATS and GL_COMPRESSED_TEXTURE_FORMATS. To check for support for a specific set of compressed texture formats, you need to check for a specific extension for those formats. For example, nearly all implementations support the GL_EXT_texture_compression_s3tc texture compression format. If this extension is supported, the compressed texture formats listed in Table 9.3 are all supported, but only for two-dimensional textures.

TABLE 9.3   Compression Formats for GL_EXT_texture_compression_s3tc

Format	Description
GL_COMPRESSED_RGB_S3TC_DXT1	RGB data is compressed; alpha is always 1.0.
GL_COMPRESSED_RGBA_S3TC_DXT1	RGB data is compressed; alpha is either 1.0 or 0.0.
GL_COMPRESSED_RGBA_S3TC_DXT3	RGB data is compressed; alpha is stored as 4 bits.
GL_COMPRESSED_RGBA_S3TC_DXT5	RGB data is compressed; alpha is a weighted average of 8-bit values.

Loading Compressed Textures

Using the functions in the preceding section, you can have OpenGL compress textures in a natively supported format, retrieve the compressed data with the glGetCompressedTexImage function (identical to the glGetTexImage function for uncompressed textures), and save it to disk. On subsequent loads, the raw compressed data can be used, resulting in substantially faster texture loads. Be advised, however, that some vendors may cheat a little when it comes to texture loading in order to optimize texture storage or filtering operations. This technique will work only on fully conformant hardware implementations.

To load precompressed texture data, use one of the following functions:

```
void glCompressedTexImage1D(GLenum target, GLint level, GLenum internalFormat,
                 GLsizei width,
                 GLint border, GLsizei imageSize, void *data);
void glCompressedTexImage2D(GLenum target, GLint level, GLenum internalFormat,
                 GLsizei width, GLsizei height,
                 GLint border, GLsizei imageSize, void *data);
```

```
void glCompressedTexImage3D(GLenum target, GLint level, GLenum internalFormat,
                            GLsizei width, GLsizei height, GLsizei depth,
                            GLint border, Glsizei imageSize, GLvoid *data);
```

These functions are virtually identical to the glTexImage functions from the preceding chapter. The only difference is that the *internalFormat* parameter must specify a supported compressed texture image. If the implementation supports the GL_EXT_texture_compression_s3tc extension, this would be one of the values from Table 9.3. There is also a corresponding set of glCompressedTexSubImage functions for updating a portion or all of an already-loaded texture that mirrors the glTexSubImage functionality from the preceding chapter.

Texture compression is a very popular texture feature. Smaller textures take up less storage, transmit faster over networks, load faster off disk, copy faster to graphics memory, allow for substantially more texture to be loaded onto hardware, and generally texture slightly faster to boot! Don't forget, though, as with so many things in life, there is no such thing as a free lunch. Something may be lost in the compression. The GL_EXT_texture_compression_s3tc method, for example, works by stripping color data out of each texel. For some textures, this results in substantial image quality loss (particularly for textures that contain smooth color gradients). Other times, textures with a great deal of detail are visually nearly identical to the original uncompressed version. The choice of texture compression method (or indeed no compression) can vary greatly depending on the nature of the underlying image.

Texture Coordinate Generation

In Chapter 8, you learned that textures are mapped to geometry using texture coordinates. Often, when you are loading models (see Chapter 11, "It's All About the Pipeline: Faster Geometry Throughput"), texture coordinates are provided for you. If necessary, you can easily map texture coordinates manually to some surfaces such as spheres or flat planes. Sometimes, however, you may have a complex surface for which it is not so easy to manually derive the coordinates. OpenGL can automatically generate texture coordinates for you within certain limitations.

Texture coordinate generation is enabled on the S, T, R, and Q texture coordinates using glEnable:

```
glEnable(GL_TEXTURE_GEN_S);
glEnable(GL_TEXTURE_GEN_T);
glEnable(GL_TEXTURE_GEN_R);
glEnable(GL_TEXTURE_GEN_Q);
```

When texture coordinate generation is enabled, any calls to glTexCoord are ignored, and OpenGL calculates the texture coordinates for each vertex for you. In the same manner that texture coordinate generation is turned on, you turn it off by using glDisable:

```
glDisable(GL_TEXTURE_GEN_S);
glDisable(GL_TEXTURE_GEN_T);
glDisable(GL_TEXTURE_GEN_R);
glDisable(GL_TEXTURE_GEN_Q);
```

You set the function or method used to generate texture coordinates with the following functions:

```
void glTexGenf(GLenum coord, GLenum pname, GLfloat param);
void glTexGenfv(GLenum coord, GLenum pname, GLfloat *param);
```

The first parameter, *coord*, specifies which texture coordinate this function sets. It must be GL_S, GL_T, GL_R, or GL_Q. The second parameter, *pname*, must be GL_TEXTURE_GEN_MODE, GL_OBJECT_PLANE, or GL_EYE_PLANE. The last parameter sets the values of the texture generation function or mode. Note that integer (GLint) and double (GLdouble) versions of these functions are also used.

The pertinent portions of the sample program TEXGEN are presented in Listing 9.1. This program displays a torus that can be manipulated (rotated around) using the arrow keys. A right-click brings up a context menu that allows you to select from the first three texture generation modes we will discuss: Object Linear, Eye Linear, and Sphere Mapping.

LISTING 9.1   Source Code for the TEXGEN Sample Program

```
#include "../../shared/gltools.h"    // gltools library

// Rotation amounts
static GLfloat xRot = 0.0f;
static GLfloat yRot = 0.0f;

GLuint toTextures[2];       // Two texture objects
int iRenderMode = 3;        // Sphere Mapped is default


///////////////////////////////////////////////////////////////////////////////
// Reset flags as appropriate in response to menu selections
void ProcessMenu(int value)
    {
    // Projection plane
    GLfloat zPlane[] = { 0.0f, 0.0f, 1.0f, 0.0f };

    // Store render mode
    iRenderMode = value;

    // Set up textgen based on menu selection
```

LISTING 9.1   Continued

```
    switch(value)
        {
        case 1:
            // Object Linear
            glTexGeni(GL_S, GL_TEXTURE_GEN_MODE, GL_OBJECT_LINEAR);
            glTexGeni(GL_T, GL_TEXTURE_GEN_MODE, GL_OBJECT_LINEAR);
            glTexGenfv(GL_S, GL_OBJECT_PLANE, zPlane);
            glTexGenfv(GL_T, GL_OBJECT_PLANE, zPlane);
            break;

        case 2:
            // Eye Linear
            glTexGeni(GL_S, GL_TEXTURE_GEN_MODE, GL_EYE_LINEAR);
            glTexGeni(GL_T, GL_TEXTURE_GEN_MODE, GL_EYE_LINEAR);
            glTexGenfv(GL_S, GL_EYE_PLANE, zPlane);
            glTexGenfv(GL_T, GL_EYE_PLANE, zPlane);
            break;

        case 3:
        default:
            // Sphere Map
            glTexGeni(GL_S, GL_TEXTURE_GEN_MODE, GL_SPHERE_MAP);
            glTexGeni(GL_T, GL_TEXTURE_GEN_MODE, GL_SPHERE_MAP);
            break;
        }

    glutPostRedisplay();    // Redisplay
    }


///////////////////////////////////////////////////////////////////////
// Called to draw scene
void RenderScene(void)
    {
    // Clear the window with current clearing color
    glClear(GL_COLOR_BUFFER_BIT | GL_DEPTH_BUFFER_BIT);

    // Switch to orthographic view for background drawing
    glMatrixMode(GL_PROJECTION);
    glPushMatrix();
    glLoadIdentity();
    gluOrtho2D(0.0f, 1.0f, 0.0f, 1.0f);
```

LISTING 9.1 Continued

```
glMatrixMode(GL_MODELVIEW);
glBindTexture(GL_TEXTURE_2D, toTextures[1]);    // Background texture

// We will specify texture coordinates
glDisable(GL_TEXTURE_GEN_S);
glDisable(GL_TEXTURE_GEN_T);

// No depth buffer writes for background
glDepthMask(GL_FALSE);

// Background image
glBegin(GL_QUADS);
    glTexCoord2f(0.0f, 0.0f);
    glVertex2f(0.0f, 0.0f);

    glTexCoord2f(1.0f, 0.0f);
    glVertex2f(1.0f, 0.0f);

    glTexCoord2f(1.0f, 1.0f);
    glVertex2f(1.0f, 1.0f);

    glTexCoord2f(0.0f, 1.0f);
    glVertex2f(0.0f, 1.0f);
glEnd();

// Back to 3D land
glMatrixMode(GL_PROJECTION);
glPopMatrix();
glMatrixMode(GL_MODELVIEW);

// Turn texgen and depth writing back on
glEnable(GL_TEXTURE_GEN_S);
glEnable(GL_TEXTURE_GEN_T);
glDepthMask(GL_TRUE);

// May need to switch to stripe texture
if(iRenderMode != 3)
    glBindTexture(GL_TEXTURE_2D, toTextures[0]);

// Save the matrix state and do the rotations
glPushMatrix();
glTranslatef(0.0f, 0.0f, -2.0f);
```

LISTING 9.1   Continued

```
    glRotatef(xRot, 1.0f, 0.0f, 0.0f);
    glRotatef(yRot, 0.0f, 1.0f, 0.0f);

    // Draw the torus
    gltDrawTorus(0.35, 0.15, 61, 37);

    // Restore the matrix state
    glPopMatrix();

    // Display the results
    glutSwapBuffers();
    }
```

Object Linear Mapping

When the texture generation mode is set to GL_OBJECT_LINEAR, texture coordinates are generated using the following function:

```
coord = P1*X + P2*Y + P3*Z + P4*W
```

The X, Y, Z, and W values are the vertex coordinates from the object being textured, and the P1–P4 values are the coefficients for a plane equation. The texture coordinates are then projected onto the geometry from the perspective of this plane. For example, to project texture coordinates for S and T from the plane Z = 0, we would use the following code from the TEXGEN sample program:

```
// Projection plane
GLfloat zPlane[] = { 0.0f, 0.0f, 1.0f, 0.0f };
. . .
. . .
// Object Linear
glTexGeni(GL_S, GL_TEXTURE_GEN_MODE, GL_OBJECT_LINEAR);
glTexGeni(GL_T, GL_TEXTURE_GEN_MODE, GL_OBJECT_LINEAR);
glTexGenfv(GL_S, GL_OBJECT_PLANE, zPlane);
glTexGenfv(GL_T, GL_OBJECT_PLANE, zPlane);
```

Note that the texture coordinate generation function can be based on a different plane equation for each coordinate. Here, we simply use the same one for both the S and the T coordinates.

This technique maps the texture to the object in object coordinates, regardless of any modelview transformation in effect. Figure 9.7 shows the output for TEXGEN when the Object Linear mode is selected. No matter how you reorient the torus, the mapping remains fixed to the geometry.

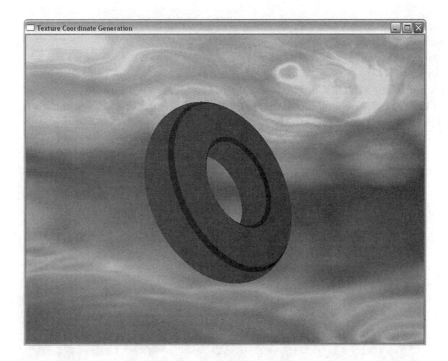

FIGURE 9.7   Torus mapped with object linear coordinates.

Eye Linear Mapping

When the texture generation mode is set to GL_EYE_LINEAR, texture coordinates are generated in a similar manner to GL_OBJECT_LINEAR. The coordinate generation looks the same, except that now the X, Y, Z, and W coordinates indicate the location of the point of view (where the camera or eye is located). The plane equation coefficients are also inverted before being applied to the equation to account for the fact that now everything is in eye coordinates.

The texture, therefore, is basically projected from the plane onto the geometry. As the geometry is transformed by the modelview matrix, the texture will appear to slide across the surface. We set up this capability with the following code from the TEXGEN sample program:

```
// Projection plane
GLfloat zPlane[] = { 0.0f, 0.0f, 1.0f, 0.0f };
. . .
. . .
// Eye Linear
glTexGeni(GL_S, GL_TEXTURE_GEN_MODE, GL_EYE_LINEAR);
```

6

```
glTexGeni(GL_T, GL_TEXTURE_GEN_MODE, GL_EYE_LINEAR);
glTexGenfv(GL_S, GL_EYE_PLANE, zPlane);
glTexGenfv(GL_T, GL_EYE_PLANE, zPlane);
```

The output of the TEXGEN program when the Eye Linear menu option is selected is shown in Figure 9.8. As you move the torus around with the arrow keys, note how the projected texture slides about on the geometry.

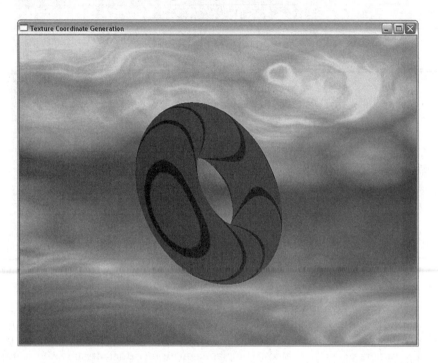

FIGURE 9.8   An example of eye linear texture mapping.

Sphere Mapping

When the texture generation mode is set to GL_SPHERE_MAP, OpenGL calculates texture coordinates in such a way that the object appears to be reflecting the current texture map. This is the easiest mode to set up, with just these two lines from the TEXGEN sample program:

```
glTexGeni(GL_S, GL_TEXTURE_GEN_MODE, GL_SPHERE_MAP);
glTexGeni(GL_T, GL_TEXTURE_GEN_MODE, GL_SPHERE_MAP);
```

You usually can make a well-constructed texture by taking a photograph through a fish-eye lens. This texture then lends a convincing reflective quality to the geometry. For more realistic results, sphere mapping has largely been replaced by cube mapping (discussed next). However, sphere mapping still has some uses because it has significantly less overhead.

In particular, sphere mapping requires only a single texture instead of six, and if true reflectivity is not required, you can obtain adequate results from sphere mapping. Even without a well-formed texture taken through a fish-eye lens, you can also use sphere mapping for an approximate environment map. Many surfaces are shiny and reflect the light from their surroundings, but are not mirror-like in their reflective qualities. In the TEXGEN sample program, we use a suitable environment map for the background (all modes show this background), as well as the source for the sphere map. Figure 9.9 shows the environment-mapped torus against a similarly colored background. Moving the torus around with the arrow keys produces a reasonable approximation of a reflective surface.

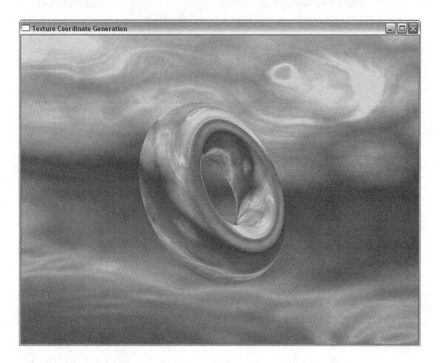

FIGURE 9.9   An environment map using a sphere map.

Cube Mapping

The last two texture generation modes, GL_REFLECTION_MAP and GL_NORMAL_MAP, require the use of a new type of texture target: the cube map. A cube map is treated as a single texture, but is made up of six square (yes, they must be square!) 2D images that make up the six sides of a cube. Figure 9.10 shows the layout of six square textures composing a cube map for the CUBEMAP sample program.

FIGURE 9.10   The layout of six cube faces in the CUBEMAP sample program.

These six 2D tiles represent the view of the world from six different directions (negative and positive X, Y, and Z). Using the texture generation mode `GL_REFLECTION_MAP`, you can then create a realistically reflective surface.

Loading Cube Maps

Cube maps add six new values that can be passed into `glTexImage2D`: `GL_TEXTURE_CUBE_MAP_POSITIVE_X`, `GL_TEXTURE_CUBE_MAP_NEGATIVE_X`, `GL_TEXTURE_CUBE_MAP_POSITIVE_Y`, `GL_TEXTURE_CUBE_MAP_NEGATIVE_Y`, `GL_TEXTURE_CUBE_MAP_POSITIVE_Z`, and `GL_TEXTURE_CUBE_MAP_NEGATIVE_Z`. These constants represent the direction in world coordinates of the cube face surrounding the object being mapped. For example, to load the map for the positive X direction, you might use a function that looks like this:

```
glTexImage2D(GL_TEXTURE_CUBE_MAP_POSITIVE_X, 0, GL_RGBA, iWidth, iHeight,
                              0, GL_RGBA, GL_UNSIGNED_BYTE, pImage);
```

To take this example further, look at the following code segment from the CUBEMAP sample program. Here, we store the name and identifiers of the six cube maps in arrays and then use a loop to load all six images into a single texture object:

```
const char *szCubeFaces[6] = { "pos_x.tga", "neg_x.tga", "pos_y.tga",
                    "neg_y.tga","pos_z.tga", "neg_z.tga" };
```

```
GLenum  cube[6] = {  GL_TEXTURE_CUBE_MAP_POSITIVE_X,
                     GL_TEXTURE_CUBE_MAP_NEGATIVE_X,
                     GL_TEXTURE_CUBE_MAP_POSITIVE_Y,
                     GL_TEXTURE_CUBE_MAP_NEGATIVE_Y,
                     GL_TEXTURE_CUBE_MAP_POSITIVE_Z,
                     GL_TEXTURE_CUBE_MAP_NEGATIVE_Z };

. . .

. . .

    glTexParameteri(GL_TEXTURE_CUBE_MAP, GL_TEXTURE_MAG_FILTER, GL_LINEAR);
    glTexParameteri(GL_TEXTURE_CUBE_MAP, GL_TEXTURE_MIN_FILTER,
                                            GL_LINEAR_MIPMAP_LINEAR);
    glTexParameteri(GL_TEXTURE_CUBE_MAP, GL_TEXTURE_WRAP_S, GL_CLAMP_TO_EDGE);
    glTexParameteri(GL_TEXTURE_CUBE_MAP, GL_TEXTURE_WRAP_T, GL_CLAMP_TO_EDGE);
    glTexParameteri(GL_TEXTURE_CUBE_MAP, GL_TEXTURE_WRAP_R, GL_CLAMP_TO_EDGE);

    GLbyte *pBytes;
    GLint iWidth, iHeight, iComponents;
    GLenum eFormat;

    // Load Cube Map images
    for(i = 0; i < 6; i++)
        {
        // Load this texture map
        glTexParameteri(GL_TEXTURE_CUBE_MAP, GL_GENERATE_MIPMAP, GL_TRUE);
        pBytes = gltLoadTGA(szCubeFaces[i], &iWidth, &iHeight,
                                            &iComponents, &eFormat);
        glTexImage2D(cube[i], 0, iComponents, iWidth, iHeight, 0, eFormat,
                                            GL_UNSIGNED_BYTE, pBytes);
        free(pBytes);
        }
```

To enable the application of the cube map, we now call glEnable with
GL_TEXTURE_CUBE_MAP instead of GL_TEXTURE_2D (we also use the same value in
glBindTexture when using texture objects):

```
glEnable(GL_TEXTURE_CUBE_MAP);
```

If both GL_TEXTURE_CUBE_MAP and GL_TEXTURE_2D are enabled, GL_TEXTURE_CUBE_MAP has
precedence. Also, notice that the texture parameter values (set with glTexParameter) affect
all six images in a single cube texture.

Texture coordinates for cube maps seem a little odd at first glance. Unlike a true 3D texture, the S, T, and R texture coordinates represent a signed vector from the center of the texture map. This vector intersects one of the six sides of the cube map. The texels around this intersection point are then sampled to create the filtered color value from the texture.

Using Cube Maps

The most common use of cube maps is to create an object that reflects its surroundings. The six images used for the CUBEMAP sample program were provided courtesy of The Game Creators, Ltd. (www.thegamecreators.com). This cube map is applied to a sphere, creating the appearance of a mirrored surface. This same cube map is also applied to the skybox, which creates the background being reflected.

A skybox is nothing more than a big box with a picture of the sky on it. Another way of looking at it is as a picture of the sky on a big box! Simple enough. An effective skybox contains six images that contain views from the center of your scene along the six directional axes. If this sounds just like a cube map, congratulations, you're paying attention! For our CUBEMAP sample program a large box is drawn around the scene, and the CUBEMAP texture is applied to the six faces of the cube. The skybox is drawn as a single batch of six GL_QUADS. Each face is then manually textured using glTexCoord3f. For each vertex, a vector is specified that points to that corner of the sky box. The first side (in the negative X direction) is shown here:

```
glBegin(GL_QUADS);
        /////////////////////////////////////////////
        // Negative X
        glTexCoord3f(-1.0f, -1.0f, 1.0f);
        glVertex3f(-fExtent, -fExtent, fExtent);

        glTexCoord3f(-1.0f, -1.0f, -1.0f);
        glVertex3f(-fExtent, -fExtent, -fExtent);

        glTexCoord3f(-1.0f, 1.0f, -1.0f);
        glVertex3f(-fExtent, fExtent, -fExtent);

        glTexCoord3f(-1.0f, 1.0f, 1.0f);
        glVertex3f(-fExtent, fExtent, fExtent);

    . . .
    . . .
```

It is important to remember that in order for the manual selection of texture coordinates via glTexCoord3f to work, you must disable the texture coordinate generation:

```
// Sky Box is manually textured
glDisable(GL_TEXTURE_GEN_S);
```

```
glDisable(GL_TEXTURE_GEN_T);
glDisable(GL_TEXTURE_GEN_R);
DrawSkyBox();
```

To draw the reflective sphere, the CUBEMAP sample sets the texture generation mode to GL_REFLECTION_MAP for all three texture coordinates:

```
glTexGeni(GL_S, GL_TEXTURE_GEN_MODE, GL_REFLECTION_MAP);
glTexGeni(GL_T, GL_TEXTURE_GEN_MODE, GL_REFLECTION_MAP);
glTexGeni(GL_R, GL_TEXTURE_GEN_MODE, GL_REFLECTION_MAP);
```

We must also make sure that texture coordinate generation is enabled:

```
// Use texgen to apply cube map
glEnable(GL_TEXTURE_GEN_S);
glEnable(GL_TEXTURE_GEN_T);
glEnable(GL_TEXTURE_GEN_R);
```

To provide a true reflection, we also take the orientation of the camera into account. The camera's rotation matrix is extracted from the camera class, and inverted. This is then applied to the texture matrix before the cube map is applied. Without this rotation of the texture coordinates, the cube map will not correctly reflect the surrounding skybox. Since the gltDrawSphere function makes no modelview matrix mode changes, we can also leave the matrix mode as GL_TEXTURE until we are through drawing and have restored the texture matrix to its original state (usually this will be the identity matrix):

```
glMatrixMode(GL_TEXTURE);
    glPushMatrix();

    // Invert camera matrix (rotation only) and apply to
    // texture coordinates
    M3DMatrix44f m, invert;
    frameCamera.GetCameraOrientation(m);
    m3dInvertMatrix44(invert, m);
    glMultMatrixf(invert);

      gltDrawSphere(0.75f, 41, 41);

    glPopMatrix();
glMatrixMode(GL_MODELVIEW);
```

Figure 9.11 shows the output of the CUBEMAP sample program. Notice how the sky and surrounding terrain are reflected correctly off the surface of the sphere. Moving the camera around the sphere (by using the arrow keys) reveals the correct background and sky view reflected accurately off the sphere as well.

FIGURE 9.11   Output from the CUBEMAP sample program. (This figure also appears in the Color insert.)

Multitexture

Modern OpenGL hardware implementations support the capability to apply two or more textures to geometry simultaneously. If an implementation supports more than one texture unit, you can query with GL_MAX_TEXTURE_UNITS to see how many texture units are available:

```
GLint iUnits;
glGetIntegerv(GL_MAX_TEXTURE_UNITS, &iUnits);
```

Textures are applied from the base texture unit (GL_TEXTURE0), up to the maximum number of texture units in use (GL_TEXTURE*n*, where *n* is the number of texture units in use). Each texture unit has its own texture environment that determines how fragments are combined with the previous texture unit. Figure 9.12 shows three textures being applied to geometry, each with its own texture environment.

In addition to its own texture environment, each texture unit has its own texture matrix and set of texture coordinates. Each texture unit has its own texture bound to it with different filter modes and edge clamping parameters. You can even use different texture coordinate generation modes for each texture.

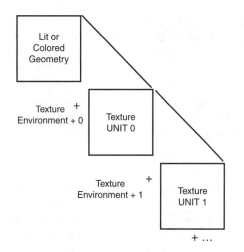

FIGURE 9.12   Multitexture order of operations.

By default, the first texture unit is the active texture unit. All texture commands, with the exception of glTexCoord, affect the currently active texture unit. You can change the current texture unit by calling glActiveTexture with the texture unit identifier as the argument. For example, to switch to the second texture unit and enable 2D texturing on that unit, you would call the following:

```
glActiveTexture(GL_TEXTURE1);
glEnable(GL_TEXTURE_2D);
```

To disable texturing on the second texture unit and switch back to the first (base) texture unit, you would make these calls:

```
glDisable(GL_TEXTURE_2D);
glActiveTexture(GL_TEXTURE0);
```

All calls to texture functions such as glTexParameter, glTexEnv, glTexGen, glTexImage, and glBindTexture are bound only to the current texture unit. When geometry is rendered, texture is applied from all enabled texture units using the texture environment and parameters previously specified.

Multiple Texture Coordinates

Occasionally, you might apply all active textures using the same texture coordinates for each texture, but this is rarely the case. When using multiple textures, you can still specify texture coordinates with glTexCoord; however, these texture coordinates are used only for the first texture unit (GL_TEXTURE0). To specify texture coordinates separately for each texture unit, you need one of the new texture coordinate functions:

```
GlMultiTexCoord1f(GLenum texUnit, GLfloat s);
glMultiTexCoord2f(GLenum texUnit, GLfloat s, GLfloat t);
glMultiTexCoord3f(GLenum texUnit, GLfloat s, GLfloat t, Glfloat r);
```

The *texUnit* parameter is GL_TEXTURE0, GL_TEXTURE1, and so on up to the maximum number of supported texturing units. In these functions, you specify the *s*, *t*, and *r* coordinates of a one-, two-, or three-dimensional texture (including cube maps). You can also use texture coordinate generation on one or more texture units.

A Multitextured Example

Listing 9.2 presents some of the code for the sample program MULTITEXTURE. This program is similar to the CUBEMAP program, and only the important changes are listed here. In this example, we place the CUBEMAP texture on the second texture unit, and on the first texture unit we use a "tarnish" looking texture. When the tarnish texture is multiplied by the cube map texture, we get the same reflective surface as before, but now there are fixed darker spots that appear as blemishes on the mirrored surface. Make note of the fact that each texture unit has its own texture matrix. Therefore, we must take care to apply the inverse of the camera matrix, only to the texture unit containing the reflected cube map. Figure 9.13 shows the output from the MULTITEXTURE program.

FIGURE 9.13   Output from the MULTITEXTURE sample program.

LISTING 9.2   Source Code for the MULTITEXTURE Sample Program

```
#include "../../shared/gltools.h"   // OpenGL toolkit
#include "../../shared/glframe.h"   // Camera class
#include <math.h>


. . .
. . .


// Storage for two texture objects
GLuint      textureObjects[2];
#define CUBE_MAP    0
#define COLOR_MAP   1


. . .
. . .


//////////////////////////////////////////////////////////////////
// This function does any needed initialization on the rendering
// context.
void SetupRC()
    {
    GLbyte *pBytes;
    GLint iWidth, iHeight, iComponents;
    GLenum eFormat;
    int i;

    // Cull backs of polygons
    glCullFace(GL_BACK);
    glFrontFace(GL_CCW);
    glEnable(GL_CULL_FACE);
    glEnable(GL_DEPTH_TEST);

    glGenTextures(2, textureObjects);

    // Set up texture maps

    // Cube Map
    glBindTexture(GL_TEXTURE_CUBE_MAP, textureObjects[CUBE_MAP]);
    glTexParameteri(GL_TEXTURE_CUBE_MAP, GL_TEXTURE_MAG_FILTER, GL_LINEAR);
    glTexParameteri(GL_TEXTURE_CUBE_MAP, GL_TEXTURE_MIN_FILTER,
                                        GL_LINEAR_MIPMAP_LINEAR);
    glTexParameteri(GL_TEXTURE_CUBE_MAP, GL_TEXTURE_WRAP_S, GL_CLAMP_TO_EDGE);
```

LISTING 9.2   Continued

```
glTexParameteri(GL_TEXTURE_CUBE_MAP, GL_TEXTURE_WRAP_T, GL_CLAMP_TO_EDGE);
glTexParameteri(GL_TEXTURE_CUBE_MAP, GL_TEXTURE_WRAP_R, GL_CLAMP_TO_EDGE);

// Load Cube Map images
for(i = 0; i < 6; i++)
    {
    // Load this texture map
    glTexParameteri(GL_TEXTURE_CUBE_MAP, GL_GENERATE_MIPMAP, GL_TRUE);
    pBytes = gltLoadTGA(szCubeFaces[i], &iWidth, &iHeight,
                                            &iComponents, &eFormat);
    glTexImage2D(cube[i], 0, iComponents, iWidth, iHeight,
                            0, eFormat, GL_UNSIGNED_BYTE, pBytes);
    free(pBytes);
    }

// Color map
glBindTexture(GL_TEXTURE_2D, textureObjects[COLOR_MAP]);
glTexParameteri(GL_TEXTURE_2D, GL_TEXTURE_MAG_FILTER, GL_LINEAR);
glTexParameteri(GL_TEXTURE_2D, GL_TEXTURE_MIN_FILTER,
                                    GL_LINEAR_MIPMAP_LINEAR);
glTexParameteri(GL_TEXTURE_2D, GL_TEXTURE_WRAP_S, GL_CLAMP_TO_EDGE);
glTexParameteri(GL_TEXTURE_2D, GL_TEXTURE_WRAP_T, GL_CLAMP_TO_EDGE);

glTexParameteri(GL_TEXTURE_2D, GL_GENERATE_MIPMAP, GL_TRUE);
pBytes = gltLoadTGA("tarnish.tga", &iWidth, &iHeight,
                                        &iComponents, &eFormat);
glTexImage2D(GL_TEXTURE_2D, 0, iComponents, iWidth, iHeight,
                            0, eFormat, GL_UNSIGNED_BYTE, pBytes);
free(pBytes);

/////////////////////////////////////////////////////////////////////
// Set up the texture units

// First texture unit contains the color map
glActiveTexture(GL_TEXTURE0);
glEnable(GL_TEXTURE_2D);
glBindTexture(GL_TEXTURE_2D, textureObjects[COLOR_MAP]);
glTexEnvi(GL_TEXTURE_ENV, GL_TEXTURE_ENV_MODE, GL_DECAL);    // Decal tarnish

// Second texture unit contains the cube map
glActiveTexture(GL_TEXTURE1);
glBindTexture(GL_TEXTURE_CUBE_MAP, textureObjects[CUBE_MAP]);
```

LISTING 9.2 Continued

```
    glTexGeni(GL_S, GL_TEXTURE_GEN_MODE, GL_REFLECTION_MAP);
    glTexGeni(GL_T, GL_TEXTURE_GEN_MODE, GL_REFLECTION_MAP);
    glTexGeni(GL_R, GL_TEXTURE_GEN_MODE, GL_REFLECTION_MAP);
    glEnable(GL_TEXTURE_CUBE_MAP);

    // Multiply this texture by the one underneath
    glTexEnvi(GL_TEXTURE_ENV, GL_TEXTURE_ENV_MODE, GL_MODULATE);
    }


///////////////////////////////////////////////////////////
// Draw the skybox. This is just six quads, with texture
// coordinates set to the corners of the cube map
void DrawSkyBox(void)
    {
    GLfloat fExtent = 15.0f;

    glBegin(GL_QUADS);
        /////////////////////////////////////////////////
        // Negative X
        // Note, we must now use the multitexture version of glTexCoord
        glMultiTexCoord3f(GL_TEXTURE1, -1.0f, -1.0f, 1.0f);
        glVertex3f(-fExtent, -fExtent, fExtent);

        glMultiTexCoord3f(GL_TEXTURE1, -1.0f, -1.0f, -1.0f);
        glVertex3f(-fExtent, -fExtent, -fExtent);

        glMultiTexCoord3f(GL_TEXTURE1, -1.0f, 1.0f, -1.0f);
        glVertex3f(-fExtent, fExtent, -fExtent);

        glMultiTexCoord3f(GL_TEXTURE1, -1.0f, 1.0f, 1.0f);
        glVertex3f(-fExtent, fExtent, fExtent);

    . . .
    . . .

    glEnd();
    }


// Called to draw scene
void RenderScene(void)
```

LISTING 9.2   Continued

```
{
// Clear the window
glClear(GL_COLOR_BUFFER_BIT | GL_DEPTH_BUFFER_BIT);

glPushMatrix();
    frameCamera.ApplyCameraTransform(); // Move the camera about

    // Sky Box is manually textured
    glActiveTexture(GL_TEXTURE0);
    glDisable(GL_TEXTURE_2D);
    glActiveTexture(GL_TEXTURE1);

    glEnable(GL_TEXTURE_CUBE_MAP);
    glDisable(GL_TEXTURE_GEN_S);
    glDisable(GL_TEXTURE_GEN_T);
    glDisable(GL_TEXTURE_GEN_R);
    glTexEnvi(GL_TEXTURE_ENV, GL_TEXTURE_ENV_MODE, GL_DECAL);
    DrawSkyBox();


    // Use texgen to apply cube map
    glEnable(GL_TEXTURE_GEN_S);
    glEnable(GL_TEXTURE_GEN_T);
    glEnable(GL_TEXTURE_GEN_R);
    glTexEnvi(GL_TEXTURE_ENV, GL_TEXTURE_ENV_MODE, GL_MODULATE);

    glActiveTexture(GL_TEXTURE0);
    glEnable(GL_TEXTURE_2D);

    glPushMatrix();
        glTranslatef(0.0f, 0.0f, -3.0f);

        glActiveTexture(GL_TEXTURE1);
        glMatrixMode(GL_TEXTURE);
        glPushMatrix();

        // Invert camera matrix (rotation only) and apply to
        // texture coordinates
        M3DMatrix44f m, invert;
        frameCamera.GetCameraOrientation(m);
        m3dInvertMatrix44(invert, m);
        glMultMatrixf(invert);
```

LISTING 9.2   Continued

```
        glColor3f(1.0f, 1.0f, 1.0f);
        gltDrawSphere(0.75f, 41, 41);

        glPopMatrix();
        glMatrixMode(GL_MODELVIEW);
    glPopMatrix();

glPopMatrix();

// Do the buffer Swap
glutSwapBuffers();
}
```

Texture Combiners

In Chapter 6, "More on Colors and Materials," you learned how to use the blending equation to control the way color fragments were blended together when multiple layers of geometry were drawn in the color buffer (typically back to front). OpenGL's texture combiners allow the same sort of control (only better) for the way multiple texture fragments are combined. By default, you can simply choose one of the texture environment modes (GL_DECAL, GL_REPLACE, GL_MODULATE, or GL_ADD) for each texture unit, and the results of each texture application are then added to the next texture unit. These texture environments were covered in Chapter 8.

Texture combiners add a new texture environment, GL_COMBINE, that allows you to explicitly set the way texture fragments from each texture unit are combined. To use texture combiners, you call glTexEnv in the following manner:

```
glTexEnvi(GL_TEXTURE_ENV, GL_TEXTURE_ENV_MODE, GL_COMBINE);
```

Texture combiners are controlled entirely through the glTexEnv function. Next, you need to select which texture combiner function you want to use. The combiner function selector, which can be either GL_COMBINE_RGB or GL_COMBINE_ALPHA, becomes the second argument to the glTexEnv function. The third argument becomes the texture environment function that you want to employ (for either RGB or alpha values). These functions are listed in Table 9.4. For example, to select the GL_REPLACE combiner for RGB values, you would call the following function:

```
glTexEnvi(GL_TEXTURE_ENV, GL_COMBINE_RGB, GL_REPLACE);
```

This combiner does little more than duplicate the normal GL_REPLACE texture environment.

TABLE 9.4   Texture Combiner Functions

Constant	Function
GL_REPLACE	Arg0
GL_MODULATE	Arg0 * Arg1
GL_ADD	Arg0 + Arg1
GL_ADD_SIGNED	Arg0 + Arg1 − 0.5
GL_INTERPOLATE	(Arg0 * Arg2) + (Arg1 * (1 − Arg2))
GL_SUBTRACT	Arg0 − Arg1
GL_DOT3_RGB/GL_DOT3_RGBA	4*((Arg0r − 0.5) * (Arg1r − 0.5) + (Arg0g − 0.5) * (Arg1g − 0.5) + (Arg0b − 0.5) * (Arg1b − 0.5))

The values of Arg0 – Arg2 are from source and operand values set with more calls to glTexEnv. The values GL_SOURCE*x*_RGB and GL_SOURCE*x*_ALPHA are used to specify the RGB or alpha combiner function arguments, where *x* is 0, 1, or 2. The values for these sources are given in Table 9.5.

TABLE 9.5   Texture Combiner Sources

Constant	Description
GL_TEXTURE	The texture bound to the current active texture unit
GL_TEXTURE*x*	The texture bound to texture unit *x*
GL_CONSTANT	The color (or alpha) value set by the texture environment variable GL_TEXTURE_ENV_COLOR
GL_PRIMARY_COLOR	The color (or alpha) value coming from the original geometry fragment
GL_PREVIOUS	The color (or alpha) value resulting from the previous texture unit's texture environment

For example, to select the texture from texture unit 0 for Arg0, you would make the following function call:

```
glTexEnvi(GL_TEXTURE_ENV, GL_SOURCE0_RGB, GL_TEXTURE0);
```

You also have some additional control over what values are used from a given source for each argument. To set these operands, you use the constant GL_OPERAND*x*_RGB or GL_OPERAND*x*_ALPHA, where *x* is 0, 1, or 2. The valid operands and their meanings are given in Table 9.6.

TABLE 9.6   Texture Combiner Operands

Constant	Meaning
GL_SRC_COLOR	The color values from the source. This may not be used with GL_OPERAND*x*_ALPHA.
GL_ONE_MINUS_SRC_COLOR	One's complement (1-value) of the color values from the source. This may not be used with GL_OPERAND*x*_ALPHA.
GL_SRC_ALPHA	The alpha values of the source.
GL_ONE_MINUS_SRC_ALPHA	One's complement (1-value) of the alpha values from the source.

For example, if you have two textures loaded on the first two texture units, and you want to multiply the color values from both textures during the texture application, you would set it up as shown here:

```
// Tell OpenGL you want to use texture combiners
glTexEnvi(GL_TEXTURE_ENV, GL_TEXTURE_ENV_MODE, GL_COMBINE);

// Tell OpenGL which combiner you want to use (GL_MODULATE for RGB values)
glTexEnvi(GL_TEXTURE_ENV, GL_COMBINE_RGB, GL_MODULATE);

// Tell OpenGL to use texture unit 0's color values for Arg0
glTexEnvi(GL_TEXTURE_ENV, GL_SOURCE0_RGB, GL_TEXTURE0);
glTexEnvi(GL_TEXTURE_ENV, GL_OPERAND0_RGB, GL_SRC_COLOR);

// Tell OpenGL to use texture unit 1's color values for Arg1
glTexEnvi(GL_TEXTURE_ENV, GL_SOURCE0_RGB, GL_TEXTURE1);
glTexenvi(GL_TEXTURE_ENV, GL_OPERAND0_RGB, GL_SRC_COLOR);
```

Finally, with texture combiners, you can also specify a constant RGB or alpha scaling factor. The default parameters for these are as shown here:

```
glTexEnvf(GL_TEXTURE_ENV, GL_RGB_SCALE, 1.0f);
glTexEnvf(GL_TEXTURE_ENV, GL_ALPHA_SCALE, 1.0f);
```

Texture combiners add a lot of flexibility to legacy OpenGL implementations. For ultimate control over how texture layers can be combined, we will later turn to shaders.

Point Sprites

Point sprites are an exciting feature supported by OpenGL version 1.5 and later. Although OpenGL has always supported texture mapped points, prior to version 1.5 this meant a single texture coordinate applied to an entire point. Large textured points were simply large versions of a single filtered texel. With point sprites you can place a 2D textured image anywhere onscreen by drawing a single 3D point.

Probably the most common application of point sprites is for particle systems. A large number of particles moving onscreen can be represented as points to produce a number of visual effects. However, representing these points as small overlapped 2D images can produce dramatic streaming animated filaments. For example, Figure 9.14 shows a well-known screensaver on the Macintosh powered by just such a particle effect.

FIGURE 9.14   A particle effect in the flurry screen saver.

Before point sprites, achieving this type of effect was a matter of drawing a large number of textured quads onscreen. This could be accomplished either by performing a costly rotation to each individual quad to make sure that it faced the camera, or by drawing all particles in a 2D orthographic projection. Point sprites allow you to render a perfectly aligned textured 2D square by sending down a single 3D vertex. At one-quarter the bandwidth of sending down four vertices for a quad, and no client-side matrix monkey business to keep the 3D quad aligned with the camera, point sprites are a potent and efficient feature of OpenGL.

Using Points

Point sprites are very easy to use. Simply bind to a 2D texture, enable GL_POINT_SPRITE, set the texture environment target GL_POINT_SPRITE's GL_COORD_REPLACE parameter to true, and send down 3D points:

```
glBindTexture(GL_TEXTURE_2D, objectID);
glEnable(GL_POINT_SPRITE);
```

```
glTexEnvi(GL_POINT_SPRITE, GL_COORD_REPLACE, GL_TRUE);

glBegin(GL_POINTS);
    . . .
    . . .
glEnd();
```

Figure 9.15 shows the output of the sample program POINTSPRITES. This is an updated version of the SMOOTHER sample program from Chapter 6 that created the star field out of points. In POINTSPRITES, each point now contains a small star image, and the largest point contains a picture of the full moon.

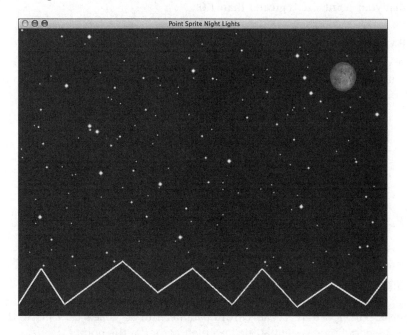

FIGURE 9.15   A star field drawn with point sprites.

One serious limitation to the use of point sprites is that their size is limited by the range of aliased point sizes (this was discussed in Chapter 3, "Drawing in Space: Geometric Primitives and Buffers"). You can quickly determine this implementation-dependent range with the following two lines of code:

```
GLfloat fSizes[2];
GLGetFloatfv(GL_ALIASED_POINT_SIZE_RANGE, fSizes);
```

Following this, the array `fSizes` will contain the minimum and maximum sizes supported for point sprites, and regular aliased points.

Texture Application

Point sprites obey all other 2D texturing rules. The texture environment can be set to GL_DECAL, GL_REPLACE, GL_MODULATE, and so on. They can also be mipmapped and multi-textured. There are a number of ways, however, to get texture coordinates applied to the corners of the points. If GL_COORD_REPLACE is set to false, as shown here

```
glTexEnvi(GL_POINT_SPRITE, GL_COORD_REPLACE, GL_FALSE);
```

then a single texture coordinate is specified with the vertex and applied to the entire point, resulting in one big texel! Setting this value to GL_TRUE, however, causes OpenGL to interpolate the texture coordinates across the face of the point. All of this assumes, of course, that your point size is greater than 1.0!

Point Parameters

A number of features of point sprites (and points in general actually) can be fine-tuned with the function glPointParameter. Figure 9.16 shows the two possible locations of the origin (0,0) of the texture applied to a point sprite.

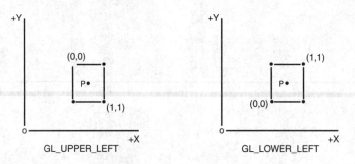

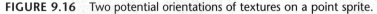

FIGURE 9.16   Two potential orientations of textures on a point sprite.

Setting the GL_POINT_SPRITE_COORD_ORIGIN parameter to GL_LOWER_LEFT places the origin of the texture coordinate system at the lower-left corner of the point:

```
glPointParameteri(GL_POINT_SPRITE_COORD_ORIGIN, GL_LOWER_LEFT);
```

The default orientation for point sprites is GL_UPPER_LEFT.

Other non-texture-related point parameters can also be used to set the minimum and maximum allowable size for points, and to cause point size to be attenuated with distance from the eye point. See the glPointParameter function entry in Appendix C, "API Reference," for details of these other parameters.

Summary

In this chapter, we took texture mapping beyond the simple basics of applying a texture to geometry. You saw how to get improved filtering, obtain better performance and memory efficiency through texture compression, and generate automatic texture coordinates for geometry. You also saw how to add plausible environment maps with sphere mapping and more realistic and correct reflections using cube maps.

In addition, we discussed multitexture and texture combiners. The capability to apply more than one texture at a time is the foundation for many special effects, including hardware support for bump mapping. Using texture combiners, you have a great deal of flexibility in specifying how up to three textures are combined. While fragment programs exposed through the new OpenGL shading language do give you ultimate control over texture application, you can quickly and easily take advantage of these capabilities even on legacy hardware.

Finally, we covered point sprites, a highly efficient means of placing 2D textures onscreen for particle systems, and 2D effects.

6

CHAPTER 10

Curves and Surfaces

by Richard S. Wright Jr.

WHAT YOU'LL LEARN IN THIS CHAPTER:

How To	Functions You'll Use
Draw spheres, cylinders, and disks	gluSphere/gluCylinder/gluDisk
Use maps to render Bézier curves and surfaces	glMap/glEvalCoord
Use evaluators to simplify surface mapping	glMapGrid/glEvalMesh
Create NURBS surfaces	gluNewNurbsRenderer/gluBeginSurface/gluNurbsSurface/ gluEndSurface/gluDeleteNurbsRendererf10
Create trimming curves	gluBeginTrim/gluPwlCurve/gluEndTrim
Tessellate concave and convex polygons	gluTessBeginPolygon/gluTessEndPolygon

The practice of 3D graphics is little more than a computerized version of connect-the-dots. Vertices are laid out in 3D space and connected by flat primitives. Smooth curves and surfaces are approximated using flat polygons and shading tricks. The more polygons used, usually the more smooth and curved a surface may appear. OpenGL, of course, supports smooth curves and surfaces implicitly because you can specify as many vertices as you want and set any desired or calculated values for normals and color values.

OpenGL does provide some additional support, however, that makes the task of constructing more complex surfaces a bit easier. The easiest to use are some GLU functions that render spheres, cylinders, cones (special types of cylinders, as you will see), and flat, round disks, optionally with holes in them. OpenGL also provides top-notch support for complex surfaces that may be difficult to model with a simple mathematical equation: Bézier and NURB curves and surfaces. Finally, OpenGL can take large, irregular, and concave polygons and break them up into smaller, more manageable pieces.

Built-in Surfaces

The OpenGL Utility Library (GLU) that accompanies OpenGL contains a number of functions that render three quadratic surfaces. These quadric functions render spheres, cylinders, and disks. You can specify the radius of both ends of a cylinder. Setting one end's radius to 0 produces a cone. Disks, likewise, provide enough flexibility for you to specify a hole in the center (producing a washer-like surface). You can see these basic shapes illustrated graphically in Figure 10.1.

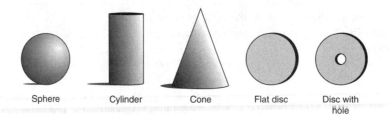

Sphere   Cylinder   Cone   Flat disc   Disc with hole

FIGURE 10.1   Possible quadric shapes.

These quadric objects can be arranged to create more complex models. For example, you could create a 3D molecular modeling program using just spheres and cylinders. Figure 10.2 shows the 3D unit axes drawn with a sphere, three cylinders, three cones, and three disks. This model can be included in any of your own programs via the following `glTools` function:

```
void gltDrawUnitAxes(void)
```

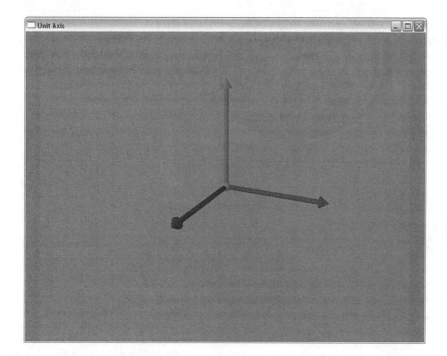

FIGURE 10.2   The x,y,z-axes drawn with quadrics.

Setting Quadric States

The quadric surfaces can be drawn with some flexibility as to whether normals, texture coordinates, and so on are specified. Putting all these options into parameters to a sphere drawing function, for example, would create a function with an exceedingly long list of parameters that must be specified each time. Instead, the quadric functions use an object-oriented model. Essentially, you create a quadric object and set its rendering state with one or more state setting functions. Then you specify this object when drawing one of the surfaces, and its state determines how the surface is rendered. The following code segment shows how to create an empty quadric object and later delete it:

```
GLUquadricObj *pObj;
// . . .
pObj = gluNewQuadric();   // Create and initialize Quadric
// Set Quadric rendering Parameters
// Draw Quadric surfaces
// . . .
gluDeleteQuadric(pObj);   // Free Quadric object
```

10

Note that you create a pointer to the GLUQuadricObj data type, not an instance of the data structure itself. The reason is that the gluNewQuadric function not only allocates space for it, but also initializes the structure members to reasonable default values. Do not confuse these quadric objects with C++ classes; they are really just C data structures.

There are four functions you can use to modify the drawing state of the GLUQuadricObj object and, correspondingly, to any surfaces drawn with it. The first function sets the quadric draw style:

```
void gluQuadricDrawStyle(GLUquadricObj *obj, GLenum drawStyle);
```

The first parameter is the pointer to the quadric object to be set, and the *drawStyle* parameter is one of the values in Table 10.1.

TABLE 10.1   Quadric Draw Styles

Constant	Description
GLU_FILL	Quadric objects are drawn as solid objects.
GLU_LINE	Quadric objects are drawn as wireframe objects.
GLU_POINT	Quadric objects are drawn as a set of vertex points.
GLU_SILHOUETTE	This is similar to a wireframe, except adjoining edges of polygons are not drawn.

The next function specifies whether the quadric surface geometry would be generated with surface normals:

```
void gluQuadricNormals(GLUquadricObj *obj, GLenum normals);
```

Quadrics may be drawn without normals (GLU_NONE), with smooth normals (GLU_SMOOTH), or flat normals (GLU_FLAT). The primary difference between smooth and flat normals is that for smooth normals, one normal is specified for each vertex perpendicular to the surface being approximated, giving a smoothed-out appearance. For flat normals, all normals are face normals, perpendicular to the actual triangle (or quad) face.

You can also specify whether the normals point out of the surface or inward. For example, looking at a lit sphere, you would want normals pointing outward from the surface of the sphere. However, if you were drawing the inside of a sphere—say, as part of a vaulted ceiling—you would want the normals and lighting to be applied to the inside of the sphere. The following function sets this parameter:

```
void gluQuadricOrientation(GLUquadricObj *obj, GLenum orientation);
```

Here, *orientation* can be either GLU_OUTSIDE or GLU_INSIDE. By default, quadric surfaces are wound counterclockwise, with the front faces facing the outsides of the surfaces. The outside of the surface is intuitive for spheres and cylinders; for disks, it is simply the side facing the positive z-axis.

Finally, you can request that texture coordinates be generated for quadric surfaces with the following function:

```
void gluQuadricTexture(GLUquadricObj *obj, GLenum textureCoords);
```

Here, the *textureCoords* parameter can be either GL_TRUE or GL_FALSE. When texture coordinates are generated for quadric surfaces, they are wrapped around spheres and cylinders evenly; they are applied to disks using the center of the texture for the center of the disk, with the edges of the texture lining up with the edges of the disk.

Drawing Quadrics

After the quadric object state has been set satisfactorily, each surface is drawn with a single function call. For example, to draw a sphere, you simply call the following function:

```
void gluSphere(GLUQuadricObj *obj, GLdouble radius, GLint slices, GLint stacks);
```

The first parameter, *obj*, is just the pointer to the quadric object that was previously set up for the desired rendering state. The *radius* parameter is then the radius of the sphere, followed by the number of *slices* and *stacks*. Spheres are drawn with rings of triangle strips (or quad strips, depending on whose GLU library you're using) stacked from the bottom to the top, as shown in Figure 10.3. The number of slices specifies how many triangle sets (or quads) are used to go all the way around the sphere. You could also think of this as the number of lines of latitude and longitude around a globe.

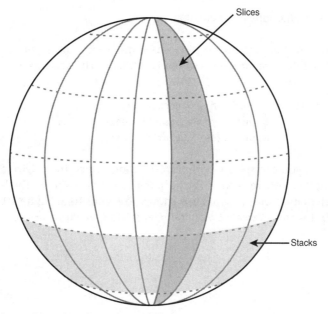

FIGURE 10.3   A quadric sphere's stacks and slices.

10

The quadric spheres are drawn on their sides with the positive z-axis pointing out the top of the spheres. Figure 10.4 shows a wireframe quadric sphere drawn around the unit axes.

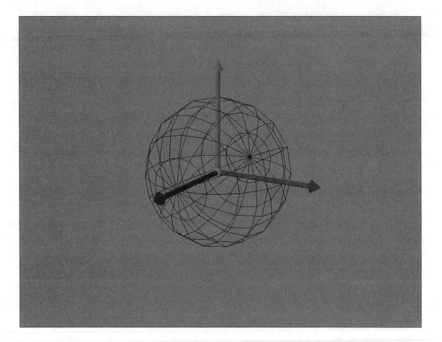

FIGURE 10.4   A quadric sphere's orientation.

Cylinders are also drawn along the positive z-axis and are composed of a number of stacked strips. The following function, which is similar to the gluSphere function, draws a cylinder:

```
void gluCylinder(GLUquadricObj *obj, GLdouble baseRadius,
                 GLdouble topRadius, GLdouble height,
                 GLint slices, GLint stacks);
```

With this function, you can specify both the base radius (near the origin) and the top radius (out along the positive z-axis). The *height* parameter is simply the length of the cylinder. The orientation of the cylinder is shown in Figure 10.5. Figure 10.6 shows the same cylinder, but with the *topRadius* parameter set to 0, making a cone.

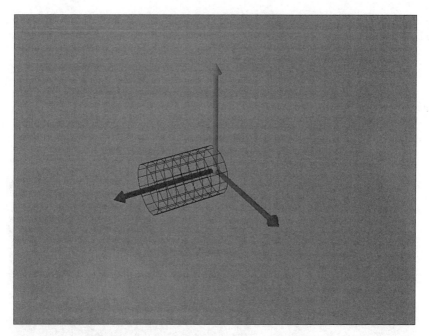

FIGURE 10.5   A quadric cylinder's orientation.

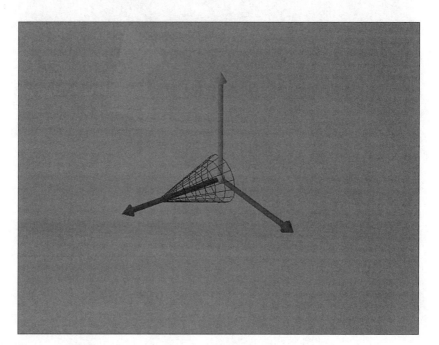

FIGURE 10.6   A quadric cone made from a cylinder.

The final quadric surface is the disk. Disks are drawn with loops of quads or triangle strips, divided into some number of slices. You use the following function to render a disk:

```
void gluDisk(GLUquadricObj *obj, GLdouble innerRadius,
                    GLdouble outerRadius, GLint slices, GLint loops);
```

To draw a disk, you specify both an inner radius and an outer radius. If the inner radius is 0, you get a solid disk like the one shown in Figure 10.7. A nonzero radius gives you a disk with a hole in it, as shown in Figure 10.8. The disk is drawn in the xy plane.

FIGURE 10.7   A quadric disk showing loops and slices.

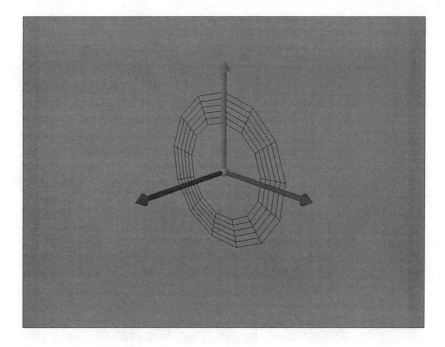

FIGURE 10.8   A quadric disk with a hole in the center.

Modeling with Quadrics

In the sample program SNOWMAN, all the quadric objects are used to piece together a crude model of a snowman. White spheres make up the three sections of the body. Two small black spheres make up the eyes, and an orange cone is drawn for the carrot nose. A cylinder is used for the body of a black top hat, and two disks, one closed and one open, provide the top and the rim of the hat. The output from SNOWMAN is shown in Figure 10.9. Listing 10.1 shows the rendering code that draws the snowman by simply transforming the various quadric surfaces into their respective positions.

FIGURE 10.9   A snowman rendered from quadric objects.

LISTING 10.1   Rendering Code for the SNOWMAN Example

```
void RenderScene(void)
    {
    GLUquadricObj *pObj;    // Quadric Object

    // Clear the window with current clearing color
    glClear(GL_COLOR_BUFFER_BIT | GL_DEPTH_BUFFER_BIT);

    // Save the matrix state and do the rotations
    glPushMatrix();
        // Move object back and do in place rotation
        glTranslatef(0.0f, -1.0f, -5.0f);
        glRotatef(xRot, 1.0f, 0.0f, 0.0f);
        glRotatef(yRot, 0.0f, 1.0f, 0.0f);

        // Draw something
        pObj = gluNewQuadric();
        gluQuadricNormals(pObj, GLU_SMOOTH);
```

LISTING 10.1   Continued

```
        // Main Body
    glPushMatrix();
        glColor3f(1.0f, 1.0f, 1.0f);
        gluSphere(pObj, .40f, 26, 13);   // Bottom

        glTranslatef(0.0f, .550f, 0.0f); // Mid section
        gluSphere(pObj, .3f, 26, 13);

        glTranslatef(0.0f, 0.45f, 0.0f); // Head
        gluSphere(pObj, 0.24f, 26, 13);

        // Eyes
        glColor3f(0.0f, 0.0f, 0.0f);
        glTranslatef(0.1f, 0.1f, 0.21f);
        gluSphere(pObj, 0.02f, 26, 13);

        glTranslatef(-0.2f, 0.0f, 0.0f);
        gluSphere(pObj, 0.02f, 26, 13);

        // Nose
        glColor3f(1.0f, 0.3f, 0.3f);
        glTranslatef(0.1f, -0.12f, 0.0f);
        gluCylinder(pObj, 0.04f, 0.0f, 0.3f, 26, 13);
    glPopMatrix();

    // Hat
    glPushMatrix();
        glColor3f(0.0f, 0.0f, 0.0f);
        glTranslatef(0.0f, 1.17f, 0.0f);
        glRotatef(-90.0f, 1.0f, 0.0f, 0.0f);
        gluCylinder(pObj, 0.17f, 0.17f, 0.4f, 26, 13);

        // Hat brim
        glDisable(GL_CULL_FACE);
        gluDisk(pObj, 0.17f, 0.28f, 26, 13);
        glEnable(GL_CULL_FACE);

        glTranslatef(0.0f, 0.0f, 0.40f);
        gluDisk(pObj, 0.0f, 0.17f, 26, 13);
    glPopMatrix();

    // Restore the matrix state
```

LISTING 10.1   Continued

```
glPopMatrix();

// Buffer swap
glutSwapBuffers();
}
```

Bézier Curves and Surfaces

Quadrics provide built-in support for some very simple surfaces easily modeled with algebraic equations. Suppose, however, you want to create a curve or surface, and you don't have an algebraic equation to start with. It's far from a trivial task to figure out your surface in reverse, starting from what you visualize as the result and working down to a second- or third-order polynomial. Taking a rigorous mathematical approach is time consuming and error-prone, even with the aid of a computer. You can also forget about trying to do it in your head.

Recognizing this fundamental need in the art of computer-generated graphics, Pierre Bézier, an automobile designer for Renault in the 1970s, created a set of mathematical models that could represent curves and surfaces by specifying only a small set of control points. In addition to simplifying the representation of curved surfaces, the models facilitated interactive adjustments to the shape of the curve or surface.

Other types of curves and surfaces and indeed a whole new vocabulary for computer-generated surfaces soon evolved. The mathematics behind this magic show are no more complex than the matrix manipulations in Chapter 4, "Geometric Transformations: The Pipeline," and an intuitive understanding of these curves is easy to grasp. As we did in Chapter 4, we take the approach that you can do a lot with these functions without a deep understanding of their mathematics.

Parametric Representation

A curve has a single starting point, a length, and an endpoint. It's really just a line that squiggles about in 3D space. A surface, on the other hand, has width and length and thus a surface area. We begin by showing you how to draw some smooth curves in 3D space and then extend this concept to surfaces. First, let's establish some common vocabulary and math fundamentals.

When you think of straight lines, you might think of this famous equation:

$$y = mx + b$$

Here, m equals the slope of the line, and b is the y intercept of the line (the place where the line crosses the y-axis). This discussion might take you back to your eighth-grade algebra class, where you also learned about the equations for parabolas, hyperbolas, exponential curves, and so on. All these equations expressed y (or x) in terms of some function of x (or y).

Another way of expressing the equation for a curve or line is as a parametric equation. A parametric equation expresses both x and y in terms of another variable that varies across some predefined range of values that is not explicitly a part of the geometry of the curve. Sometimes in physics, for example, the x, y, and z coordinates of a particle might be in terms of some functions of time, where time is expressed in seconds. In the following, $f()$, $g()$, and $h()$ are unique functions that vary with time (t):

$$x = f(t)$$

$$y = g(t)$$

$$z = h(t)$$

When we define a curve in OpenGL, we also define it as a parametric equation. The parametric parameter of the curve, which we call u, and its range of values is the domain of that curve. Surfaces are described using two parametric parameters: u and v. Figure 10.10 shows both a curve and a surface defined in terms of u and v domains. The important point to realize here is that the parametric parameters (u and v) represent the extents of the equations that describe the curve; they do not reflect actual coordinate values.

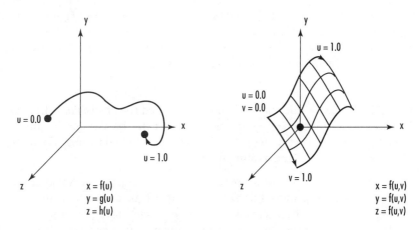

FIGURE 10.10 Parametric representation of curves and surfaces.

Control Points

A curve is represented by a number of control points that influence the shape of the curve. For a Bézier curve, the first and last control points are actually part of the curve. The other control points act as magnets, pulling the curve toward them. Figure 10.11 shows some examples of this concept, with varying numbers of control points.

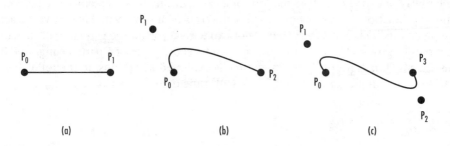

(a)   (b)   (c)

FIGURE 10.11   How control points affect curve shape.

The *order* of the curve is represented by the number of control points used to describe its shape. The *degree* is one less than the order of the curve. The mathematical meaning of these terms pertains to the parametric equations that exactly describe the curve, with the order being the number of coefficients and the degree being the highest exponent of the parametric parameter. If you want to read more about the mathematical basis of Bézier curves, see Appendix A, "Further Reading/References,"

The curve in Figure 10.11(b) is called a *quadratic* curve (degree 2), and Figure 10.11(c) is called a *cubic* (degree 3). Cubic curves are the most typical. Theoretically, you could define a curve of any order, but higher order curves start to oscillate uncontrollably and can vary wildly with the slightest change to the control points.

Continuity

If two curves placed side by side share an endpoint (called the *breakpoint*), they together form a *piecewise* curve. The continuity of these curves at this breakpoint describes how smooth the transition is between them. The four categories of continuity are none, positional (C0), tangential (C1), and curvature (C2).

As you can see in Figure 10.12, no continuity occurs when the two curves don't meet at all. Positional continuity is achieved when the curves at least meet and share a common endpoint. Tangential continuity occurs when the two curves have the same tangent at the breakpoint. Finally, curvature continuity means the two curves' tangents also have the same rate of change at the breakpoint (thus an even smoother transition).

When assembling complex surfaces or curves from many pieces, you usually strive for tangential or curvature continuity. You'll see later that some parameters for curve and surface generation can be chosen to produce the desired continuity.

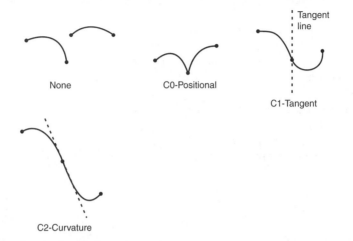

FIGURE 10.12   Continuity of piecewise curves.

Evaluators

OpenGL contains several functions that make it easy to draw Bézier curves and surfaces. To draw them, you specify the control points and the range for the parametric u and v parameters. Then, by calling the appropriate evaluation function (the evaluator), OpenGL generates the points that make up the curve or surface. We start with a 2D example of a Bézier curve and then extend it to three dimensions to create a Bézier surface.

A 2D Curve

The best way to start is to go through an example, explaining it line by line. Listing 10.2 shows some code from the sample program BEZIER in this chapter's subdirectory of the source code distribution on our Web site. This program specifies four control points for a Bézier curve and then renders the curve using an evaluator. The output from Listing 10.2 is shown in Figure 10.13.

LISTING 10.2   Code from BEZIER That Draws a Bézier Curve with Four Control Points

```
// The number of control points for this curve
GLint nNumPoints = 4;

GLfloat ctrlPoints[4][3]= {{  -4.0f, 0.0f, 0.0f},    // End Point
                           { -6.0f, 4.0f, 0.0f},    // Control Point
                           {  6.0f, -4.0f, 0.0f},   // Control Point
                           {  4.0f, 0.0f, 0.0f }};  // End Point
```

10

LISTING 10.2   Continued

```
// This function is used to superimpose the control points over the curve
void DrawPoints(void)
    {
    int i;      // Counting variable

    // Set point size larger to make more visible
    glPointSize(5.0f);

    // Loop through all control points for this example
    glBegin(GL_POINTS);
        for(i = 0; i < nNumPoints; i++)
            glVertex2fv(ctrlPoints[i]);
    glEnd();
    }


// Called to draw scene
void RenderScene(void)
    {
    int i;

    // Clear the window with current clearing color
    glClear(GL_COLOR_BUFFER_BIT);

    // Sets up the bezier
    // This actually only needs to be called once and could go in
    // the setup function
    glMap1f(GL_MAP1_VERTEX_3, // Type of data generated
    0.0f,                     // Lower u range
    100.0f,                   // Upper u range
    3,                        // Distance between points in the data
    nNumPoints,               // number of control points
    &ctrlPoints[0][0]);       // array of control points

    // Enable the evaluator
    glEnable(GL_MAP1_VERTEX_3);

    // Use a line strip to "connect the dots"
    glBegin(GL_LINE_STRIP);
        for(i = 0; i <= 100; i++)
        {
```

LISTING 10.2 Continued

```
        // Evaluate the curve at this point
        glEvalCoord1f((GLfloat) i);
        }
    glEnd();


// Draw the Control Points
    DrawPoints();

    // Flush drawing commands
    glutSwapBuffers();
    }


/////////////////////////////////////////
// Set 2D Projection - negative 10 to positive 10 in X and Y
void ChangeSize(int w, int h)
    {
    // Prevent a divide by zero
    if(h == 0)
        h = 1;

    // Set Viewport to window dimensions
    glViewport(0, 0, w, h);
    glMatrixMode(GL_PROJECTION);
    glLoadIdentity();

    gluOrtho2D(-10.0f, 10.0f, -10.0f, 10.0f);

    // Modelview matrix reset
    glMatrixMode(GL_MODELVIEW);
    glLoadIdentity();
    }
```

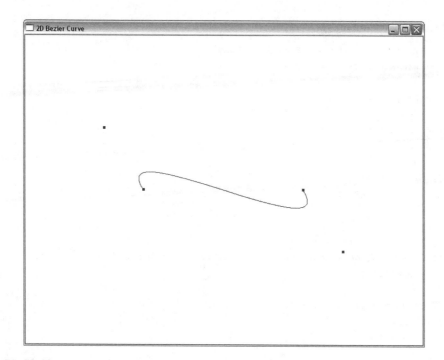

FIGURE 10.13   Output from the BEZIER sample program.

The first thing we do in Listing 10.2 is define the control points for our curve:

```
// The number of control points for this curve
GLint nNumPoints = 4;

GLfloat ctrlPoints[4][3]= {{  -4.0f, 0.0f, 0.0f},    // Endpoint
                           { -6.0f, 4.0f, 0.0f},    // Control point
                           {  6.0f, -4.0f, 0.0f},    // Control point
                           {  4.0f, 0.0f, 0.0f }};   // Endpoint
```

We defined global variables for the number of control points and the array of control points. To experiment, you can change them by adding more control points or just modifying the position of these points.

The DrawPoints function is reasonably straightforward. We call this function from our rendering code to display the control points along with the curve. This capability also is useful when you're experimenting with control-point placement. Our standard ChangeSize function establishes a 2D orthographic projection that spans from –10 to +10 in the x and y directions.

Finally, we get to the rendering code. The `RenderScene` function first calls `glMap1f` (after clearing the screen) to create a mapping for our curve:

```
// Called to draw scene
void RenderScene(void)
    {
    int i;

    // Clear the window with current clearing color
    glClear(GL_COLOR_BUFFER_BIT);

    // Sets up the Bezier
    // This actually only needs to be called once and could go in
    // the setup function
    glMap1f(GL_MAP1_VERTEX_3,    // Type of data generated
    0.0f,                        // Lower u range
    100.0f,                      // Upper u range
    3,                           // Distance between points in the data
    nNumPoints,                  // Number of control points
    &ctrlPoints[0][0]);          // Array of control points
    ...
    ...
```

The first parameter to `glMap1f`, `GL_MAP1_VERTEX_3`, sets up the evaluator to generate vertex coordinate triplets (x, y, and z). You can also have the evaluator generate other values, such as texture coordinates and color information. See Appendix C, "API Reference," for details.

The next two parameters specify the lower and upper bounds of the parametric u value for this curve. The lower value specifies the first point on the curve, and the upper value specifies the last point on the curve. All the values in between correspond to the other points along the curve. Here, we set the range to 0–100.

The fourth parameter to `glMap1f` specifies the number of floating-point values between the vertices in the array of control points. Each vertex consists of three floating-point values (for x, y, and z), so we set this value to 3. This flexibility allows the control points to be placed in an arbitrary data structure, as long as they occur at regular intervals.

The last parameter is a pointer to a buffer containing the control points used to define the curve. Here, we pass a pointer to the first element of the array. After creating the mapping for the curve, we enable the evaluator to make use of this mapping. This capability is maintained through a state variable, and the following function call is all that is needed to enable the evaluator to produce points along the curve:

```
// Enable the evaluator
glEnable(GL_MAP1_VERTEX_3);
```

10

The glEvalCoord1f function takes a single argument: a parametric value along the curve. This function then evaluates the curve at this value and calls glVertex internally for that point. By looping through the domain of the curve and calling glEvalCoord to produce vertices, we can draw the curve with a simple line strip:

```
// Use a line strip to "connect the dots"
glBegin(GL_LINE_STRIP);
    for(i = 0; i <= 100; i++)
        {
        // Evaluate the curve at this point
        glEvalCoord1f((GLfloat) i);
        }
glEnd();
```

Finally, we want to display the control points themselves:

```
// Draw the control points
DrawPoints();
```

Evaluating a Curve

OpenGL can make things even easier than what we've done so far. We set up a grid with the glMapGrid function, which tells OpenGL to create an evenly spaced grid of points over the u domain (the parametric argument of the curve). Then we call glEvalMesh to "connect the dots" using the primitive specified (GL_LINE or GL_POINTS). The two function calls

```
// Use higher level functions to map to a grid, then evaluate the
// entire thing.

// Map a grid of 100 points from 0 to 100
glMapGrid1d(100,0.0,100.0);

// Evaluate the grid, using lines
glEvalMesh1(GL_LINE,0,100);
```

completely replace this code:

```
// Use a line strip to "connect the dots"
glBegin(GL_LINE_STRIP);
    for(i = 0; i <= 100; i++)
        {
        // Evaluate the curve at this point
        glEvalCoord1f((GLfloat) i);
        }
glEnd();
```

As you can see, this approach is more compact and efficient, but its real benefit comes when evaluating surfaces rather than curves.

A 3D Surface

Creating a 3D Bézier surface is much like creating the 2D version. In addition to defining points along the u domain, we must define them along the v domain. Listing 10.3 contains code from our next sample program, BEZ3D, and displays a wire mesh of a 3D Bézier surface. The first change from the preceding example is that we have defined three more sets of control points for the surface along the v domain. To keep this surface simple, we've kept the same control points except for the z value. This way, we create a uniform surface, as if we simply extruded a 2D Bézier along the z-axis.

LISTING 10.3   BEZ3D Code to Create a Bézier Surface

```
// The number of control points for this curve
GLint nNumPoints = 3;

GLfloat ctrlPoints[3][3][3]= {{{  -4.0f, 0.0f, 4.0f},
                              { -2.0f, 4.0f, 4.0f},
                              { 4.0f, 0.0f, 4.0f }},

                             {{  -4.0f, 0.0f, 0.0f},
                              { -2.0f, 4.0f, 0.0f},
                              { 4.0f, 0.0f, 0.0f }},

                             {{  -4.0f, 0.0f, -4.0f},
                              { -2.0f, 4.0f, -4.0f},
                              { 4.0f, 0.0f, -4.0f }}};


// This function is used to superimpose the control points over the curve
void DrawPoints(void)
    {
    int i,j;    // Counting variables

    // Set point size larger to make more visible
    glPointSize(5.0f);

    // Loop through all control points for this example
    glBegin(GL_POINTS);
    for(i = 0; i < nNumPoints; i++)
        for(j = 0; j < 3; j++)
            glVertex3fv(ctrlPoints[i][j]);
```

LISTING 10.3   Continued

```
    glEnd();
    }

// Called to draw scene
void RenderScene(void)
    {
    // Clear the window with current clearing color
    glClear(GL_COLOR_BUFFER_BIT);

    // Save the modelview matrix stack
    glMatrixMode(GL_MODELVIEW);
    glPushMatrix();

    // Rotate the mesh around to make it easier to see
    glRotatef(45.0f, 0.0f, 1.0f, 0.0f);
    glRotatef(60.0f, 1.0f, 0.0f, 0.0f);

    // Sets up the Bezier
    // This actually only needs to be called once and could go in
    // the setup function
    glMap2f(GL_MAP2_VERTEX_3,      // Type of data generated
    0.0f,                          // Lower u range
    10.0f,                         // Upper u range
    3,                             // Distance between points in the data
    3,                             // Dimension in u direction (order)
    0.0f,                          // Lower v range
    10.0f,                         // Upper v range
    9,                             // Distance between points in the data
    3,                             // Dimension in v direction (order)
    &ctrlPoints[0][0][0]);         // array of control points

    // Enable the evaluator
    glEnable(GL_MAP2_VERTEX_3);

    // Use higher level functions to map to a grid, then evaluate the
    // entire thing.

    // Map a grid of 10 points from 0 to 10
    glMapGrid2f(10,0.0f,10.0f,10,0.0f,10.0f);

    // Evaluate the grid, using lines
    glEvalMesh2(GL_LINE,0,10,0,10);
```

LISTING 10.3 Continued

```
// Draw the Control Points
DrawPoints();

// Restore the modelview matrix
glPopMatrix();

// Display the image
glutSwapBuffers();
   }
```

Our rendering code is different now, too. In addition to rotating the figure for a better visual effect, we call `glMap2f` instead of `glMap1f`. This call specifies control points along two domains (u and v) instead of just one (u):

```
// Sets up the Bezier
// This actually only needs to be called once and could go in
// the setup function
glMap2f(GL_MAP2_VERTEX_3,  // Type of data generated
0.0f,                      // Lower u range
10.0f,                     // Upper u range
3,                         // Distance between points in the data
3,                         // Dimension in u direction (order)
0.0f,                      // Lower v range
10.0f,                     // Upper v range
9,                         // Distance between points in the data
3,                         // Dimension in v direction (order)
&ctrlPoints[0][0][0]);     // Array of control points
```

We must still specify the lower and upper range for u, and the distance between points in the u domain is still three. Now, however, we must also specify the lower and upper range in the v domain. The distance between points in the v domain is now nine values because we have a three-dimensional array of control points, with each span in the u domain being three points of three values each ($3 \times 3 = 9$). Then we tell `glMap2f` how many points in the v direction are specified for each u division, followed by a pointer to the control points themselves.

The two-dimensional evaluator is enabled just like the one-dimensional version, and we call `glMapGrid2f` with the number of divisions in the u and v direction:

```
// Enable the evaluator
glEnable(GL_MAP2_VERTEX_3);

// Use higher level functions to map to a grid, then evaluate the
```

10

```
// entire thing.

// Map a grid of 10 points from 0 to 10
glMapGrid2f(10,0.0f,10.0f,10,0.0f,10.0f);
```

After the evaluator is set up, we can call the two-dimensional (meaning u and v) version of glEvalMesh to evaluate our surface grid. Here, we evaluate using lines and specify the u and v domains' values to range from 0 to 10:

```
// Evaluate the grid, using lines
glEvalMesh2(GL_LINE,0,10,0,10);
```

The result is shown in Figure 10.14.

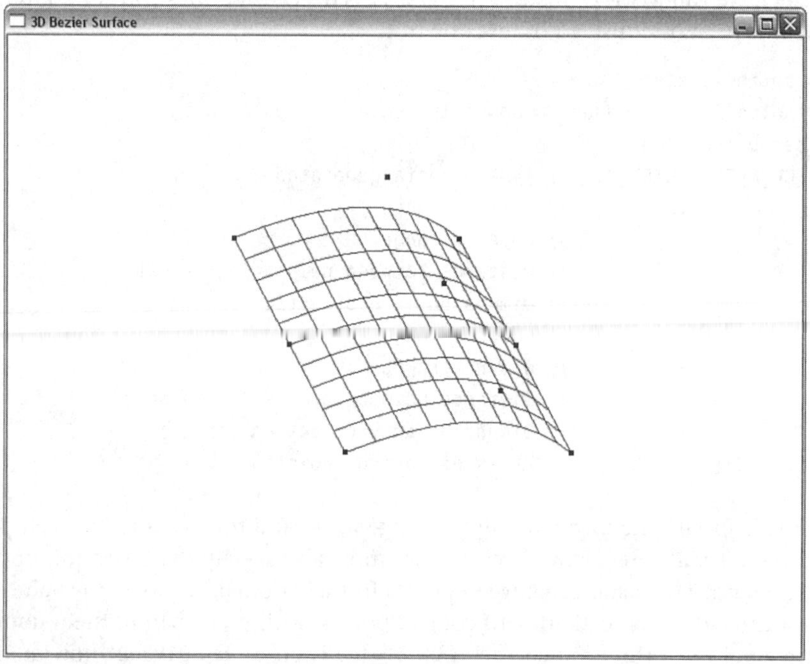

FIGURE 10.14   Output from the BEZ3D program.

Lighting and Normal Vectors
Another valuable feature of evaluators is the automatic generation of surface normals. By simply changing this code

```
// Evaluate the grid, using lines
glEvalMesh2(GL_LINE,0,10,0,10);
```

to this

```
// Evaluate the grid, using polygons
glEvalMesh2(GL_FILL,0,10,0,10);
```

and then calling

```
glEnable(GL_AUTO_NORMAL);
```

in our initialization code, we enable easy lighting of surfaces generated by evaluators. Figure 10.15 shows the same surface as Figure 10.14, but with lighting enabled and automatic normalization turned on. The code for this program appears in the BEZLIT sample in the subdirectory for this chapter in the source code distribution on our Web site. The program is only slightly modified from BEZ3D.

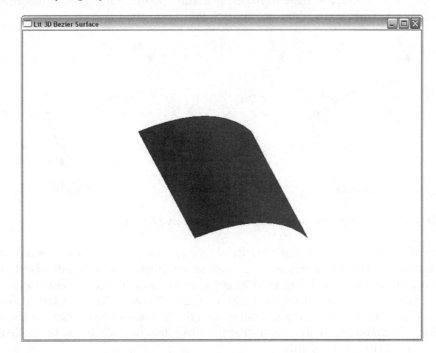

FIGURE 10.15   Output from the BEZLIT program.

NURBS

You can use evaluators to your heart's content to evaluate Bézier surfaces of any degree, but for more complex curves, you have to assemble your Béziers piecewise. As you add more control points, creating a curve that has good continuity becomes difficult. A higher level of control is available through the GLU library's NURBS functions. NURBS stands for *non-uniform rational B-spline.* Mathematicians out there might know immediately that this is just a more generalized form of curves and surfaces that can produce Bézier curves and surfaces, as well as some other kinds (mathematically speaking). These functions allow you to tweak the influence of the control points you specified for the evaluators to produce smoother curves and surfaces with larger numbers of control points.

From Bézier to B-Splines

A Bézier curve is defined by two points that act as endpoints and any number of other control points that influence the shape of the curve. The three Bézier curves in Figure 10.16 have three, four, and five control points specified. The curve is tangent to a line that connects the endpoints with their adjacent control points. For quadratic (three points) and cubic (four points) curves, the resulting Béziers are quite smooth, usually with a continuity of C2 (curvature). For higher numbers of control points, however, the smoothness begins to break down as the additional control points pull and tug on the curve.

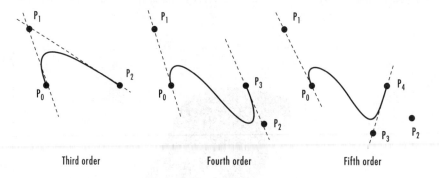

Third order   Fourth order   Fifth order

FIGURE 10.16   Bézier continuity as the order of the curve increases.

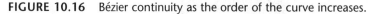

B-splines (bi-cubic splines), on the other hand, work much as the Bézier curves do, but the curve is broken down into segments. The shape of any given segment is influenced only by the nearest four control points, producing a piecewise assemblage of a curve with each segment exhibiting characteristics much like a fourth-order Bézier curve. A long curve with many control points is inherently smoother, with the junction between each segment exhibiting C2 continuity. It also means that the curve does not necessarily have to pass through any of the control points.

Knots

The real power of NURBS is that you can tweak the influence of the four control points for any given segment of a curve to produce the smoothness needed. This control is handled via a sequence of values called *knots*. Two knot values are defined for every control point. The range of values for the knots matches the u or v parametric domain and must be nondescending. The knot values determine the influence of the control points that fall within that range in u/v space. Figure 10.17 shows a curve demonstrating the influence of control points over a curve having four units in the u parametric domain. Points in the middle of the u domain have a greater pull on the curve, and only points between 0 and 3 have any effect on the shape of the curve.

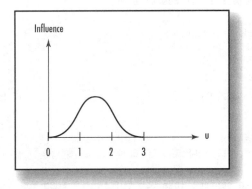

FIGURE 10.17   Control-point influence along the u parameter.

The key here is that one of these influence curves exists at each control point along the u/v parametric domain. The knot sequence then defines the strength of the influence of points within this domain. If a knot value is repeated, points near this parametric value have even greater influence. The repeating of knot values is called *knot multiplicity*. Higher knot multiplicity decreases the curvature of the curve or surface within that region.

Creating a NURBS Surface

The GLU NURBS functions provide a useful high-level facility for rendering surfaces. You don't have to explicitly call the evaluators or establish the mappings or grids. To render a NURBS, you first create a NURBS object that you reference whenever you call the NURBS-related functions to modify the appearance of the surface or curve.

The gluNewNurbsRenderer function creates a renderer for the NURB, and gluDeleteNurbsRenderer destroys it. The following code fragments demonstrate these functions in use:

```
// NURBS object pointer
GLUnurbsObj *pNurb = NULL;
...
...

// Set up the NURBS object
    pNurb = gluNewNurbsRenderer();

...
```

```
// Do your NURBS things...
...
...

// Delete the NURBS object if it was created
if(pNurb)
    gluDeleteNurbsRenderer(pNurb);
```

NURBS Properties

After you have created a NURBS renderer, you can set various high-level NURBS properties for the NURB:

```
// Set sampling tolerance
gluNurbsProperty(pNurb, GLU_SAMPLING_TOLERANCE, 25.0f);

// Fill to make a solid surface (use GLU_OUTLINE_POLYGON to create a
// polygon mesh)
gluNurbsProperty(pNurb, GLU_DISPLAY_MODE, (GLfloat)GLU_FILL);
```

You typically call these functions in your setup routine rather than repeatedly in your rendering code. In this example, GLU_SAMPLING_TOLERANCE defines the fineness of the mesh that defines the surface, and GLU_FILL tells OpenGL to fill in the mesh instead of generating a wireframe.

Defining the Surface

The surface definition is passed as arrays of control points and knot sequences to the gluNurbsSurface function. As shown here, this function is also bracketed by calls to gluBeginSurface and gluEndSurface:

```
// Render the NURB
// Begin the NURB definition
gluBeginSurface(pNurb);

// Evaluate the surface
gluNurbsSurface(pNurb,    // Pointer to NURBS renderer
    8, Knots,             // No. of knots and knot array u direction
    8, Knots,             // No. of knots and knot array v direction
    4 * 3,                // Distance between control points in u dir.
    3,                    // Distance between control points in v dir.
```

```
    &ctrlPoints[0][0][0],// Control points
    4, 4,                // u and v order of surface
    GL_MAP2_VERTEX_3);   // Type of surface

// Done with surface
gluEndSurface(pNurb);
```

You can make more calls to gluNurbsSurface to create any number of NURBS surfaces, but the properties you set for the NURBS renderer are still in effect. Often, this is desired; you rarely want two surfaces (perhaps joined) to have different fill styles (one filled and one a wire mesh).

Using the control points and knot values shown in the next code segment, we produced the NURBS surface shown in Figure 10.18. You can find this NURBS program in this chapter's subdirectory in the source code distribution on our Web site:

```
// Mesh extends four units -6 to +6 along x and y axis
// Lies in Z plane
//                 u   v  (x,y,z)
GLfloat ctrlPoints[4][4][3]= {{{  -6.0f, -6.0f, 0.0f},    // u = 0,   v = 0
                              {  -6.0f, -2.0f, 0.0f},    //          v = 1
                              {  -6.0f,  2.0f, 0.0f},    //          v = 2
                              {  -6.0f,  6.0f, 0.0f}},   //          v = 3

                             {{ -2.0f, -6.0f, 0.0f},    // u = 1    v = 0
                              {  -2.0f, -2.0f, 8.0f},    //          v = 1
                              {  -2.0f,  2.0f, 8.0f},    //          v = 2
                              {  -2.0f,  6.0f, 0.0f}},   //          v = 3

                             {{  2.0f, -6.0f, 0.0f },   // u =2     v = 0
                              {   2.0f, -2.0f, 8.0f },   //          v = 1
                              {   2.0f,  2.0f, 8.0f },   //          v = 2
                              {   2.0f,  6.0f, 0.0f }},  //          v = 3

                             {{  6.0f, -6.0f, 0.0f},    // u = 3    v = 0
                              {   6.0f, -2.0f, 0.0f},    //          v = 1
                              {   6.0f,  2.0f, 0.0f},    //          v = 2
                              {   6.0f,  6.0f, 0.0f}}}; //          v = 3
// Knot sequence for the NURB
GLfloat Knots[8] = {0.0f, 0.0f, 0.0f, 0.0f, 1.0f, 1.0f, 1.0f, 1.0f};
```

10

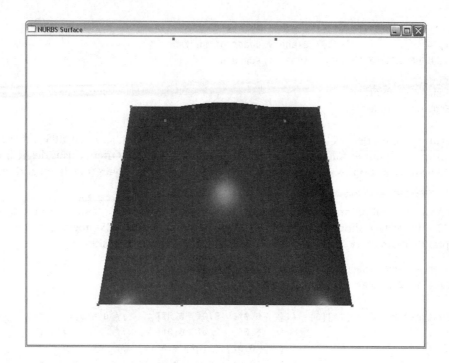

FIGURE 10.18   Output from the NURBS program.

Trimming

Trimming means creating cutout sections from NURBS surfaces. This capability is often used for literally trimming sharp edges of a NURBS surface. You can also create holes in your surface just as easily. The output from the NURBT program is shown in Figure 10.19. This is the same NURBS surface used in the preceding sample (without the control points shown), with a triangular region removed. This program, too, is in the subdirectory for this chapter in the source code distribution on our Web site.

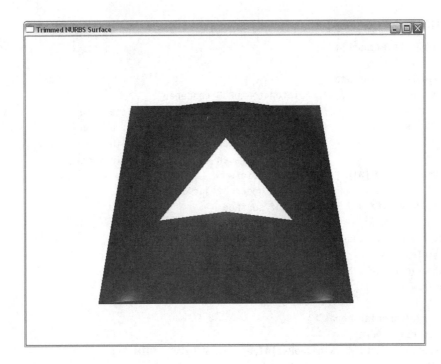

FIGURE 10.19   Output from the NURBT program.

Listing 10.4 shows the code added to the NURBS sample program to produce this trimming effect. Within the gluBeginSurface/gluEndSurface delimiters, we call gluBeginTrim, specify a trimming curve with gluPwlCurve, and finish the trimming curve with gluEndTrim.

LISTING 10.4   Modifications to NURBS to Produce Trimming

```
// Outside trimming points to include entire surface
GLfloat outsidePts[5][2] = /* counterclockwise */
    {{0.0f, 0.0f}, {1.0f, 0.0f}, {1.0f, 1.0f}, {0.0f, 1.0f}, {0.0f, 0.0f}};

// Inside trimming points to create triangle shaped hole in surface
GLfloat insidePts[4][2] = /* clockwise */
    {{0.25f, 0.25f}, {0.5f, 0.5f}, {0.75f, 0.25f}, { 0.25f, 0.25f}};
...
...
...

// Render the NURB
// Begin the NURB definition
```

10

LISTING 10.4   Continued

```
gluBeginSurface(pNurb);

// Evaluate the surface
gluNurbsSurface(pNurb,      // Pointer to NURBS renderer
    8, Knots,               // No. of knots and knot array u direction
    8, Knots,               // No. of knots and knot array v direction
    4 * 3,                  // Distance between control points in u dir.
    3,                      // Distance between control points in v dir.
    &ctrlPoints[0][0][0],// Control points
    4, 4,                   // u and v order of surface
    GL_MAP2_VERTEX_3);     // Type of surface

// Outer area, include entire curve
gluBeginTrim (pNurb);
gluPwlCurve (pNurb, 5, &outsidePts[0][0], 2, GLU_MAP1_TRIM_2);
gluEndTrim (pNurb);

// Inner triangular area
gluBeginTrim (pNurb);
gluPwlCurve (pNurb, 4, &insidePts[0][0], 2, GLU_MAP1_TRIM_2);
gluEndTrim (pNurb);

// Done with surface
gluEndSurface(pNurb);
```

Within the `gluBeginTrim`/`gluEndTrim` delimiters, you can specify any number of curves as long as they form a closed loop in a piecewise fashion. You can also use `gluNurbsCurve` to define a trimming region or part of a trimming region. These trimming curves must, however, be in terms of the unit parametric u and v space. This means the entire u/v domain is scaled from 0.0 to 1.0.

`gluPwlCurve` defines a piecewise linear curve—nothing more than a list of points connected end to end. In this scenario, the inner trimming curve forms a triangle, but with many points, you could create an approximation of any curve needed.

Trimming a curve trims away surface area that is to the right of the curve's winding. Thus, a clockwise-wound trimming curve discards its interior. Typically, an outer trimming curve is specified, which encloses the entire NURBS parameter space. Then smaller trimming regions are specified within this region with clockwise winding. Figure 10.20 illustrates this relationship.

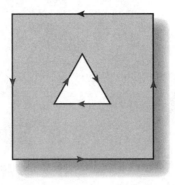

FIGURE 10.20   An area inside clockwise-wound curves is trimmed away.

NURBS Curves

Just as you can have Bézier surfaces and curves, you can also have NURBS surfaces and curves. You can even use `gluNurbsCurve` to do NURBS surface trimming. By this point, we hope you have the basics down well enough to try trimming surfaces on your own. However, another sample, NURBC, is included in the sample source code if you want a starting point to play with.

Tessellation

To keep OpenGL as fast as possible, all geometric primitives must be convex. We made this point in Chapter 3, "Drawing in Space: Geometric Primitives and Buffers." However, many times we have vertex data for a concave or more complex shape that we want to render with OpenGL. These shapes fall into two basic categories, as shown in Figure 10.21. A simple concave polygon is shown on the left, and a more complex polygon with a hole in it is shown on the right. For the shape on the left, you might be tempted to try using `GL_POLYGON` as the primitive type, but the rendering would fail because OpenGL algorithms are optimized for convex polygons. As for the figure on the right...well, there is little hope for that shape at all!

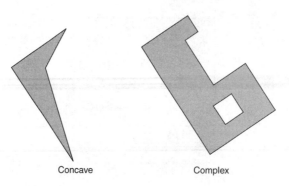

Concave   Complex

FIGURE 10.21   Some nonconvex polygons.

The intuitive solution to both of these problems is to break down the shape into smaller convex polygons or triangles that can be fit together to create the final overall shape. Figure 10.22 shows one possible solution to breaking the shapes in Figure 10.21 into more manageable triangles.

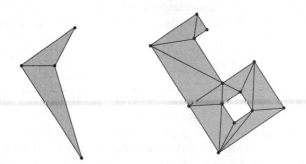

FIGURE 10.22   Complex shapes broken down into triangles.

Breaking down the shapes by hand is tedious at best and possibly error-prone. Fortunately, the OpenGL Utility Library contains functions to help you break concave and complex polygons into smaller, valid OpenGL primitives. The process of breaking down these polygons is called *tessellation*.

The Tessellator

Tessellation works through a tessellator object that must be created and destroyed much in the same way that we did for quadric state objects:

```
GLUtesselator *pTess;
pTess = gluNewTes();
. . .
// Do some tessellation
. . .
gluDeleteDess(pTess);
```

All the tessellation functions use the tessellator object as the first parameter. This allows you to have more than one tessellation object active at a time or interact with libraries or other code that also uses tessellation. The tessellation functions change the tessellator's state and behavior, and this allows you to make sure your changes affect only the object you are currently working with. Alas, yes, GLUtesselator has only one *l* and is thus misspelled!

The tessellator breaks up a polygon and renders it appropriately when you perform the following steps:

1. Create the tessellator object.

2. Set tessellator state and callbacks.

3. Start a polygon.

4. Start a contour.

5. Feed the tessellator the vertices that specify the contour.

6. End the contour.

7. Go back to step 4 if there are more contours.

8. End the polygon.

Each polygon consists of one or more contours. The polygon to the left in Figure 10.21 contains one contour, simply the path around the outside of the polygon. The polygon on the right, however, has two contours: the outside edge and the edge around the inner hole. Polygons may contain any number of contours (several holes) or even nested contours (holes within holes). The actual work of tessellating the polygon does not occur until step 8. This task can sometimes be very time consuming, and if the geometry is static, it may be best to store these function calls in a display list (the next chapter discusses display lists).

10

Tessellator Callbacks

During tessellation, the tessellator calls a number of callback functions that you must provide. You use these callbacks to actually specify the vertex information and begin and end the primitives. The following function registers the callback functions:

```
void gluTessCallback(GLUTesselator *tobj, GLenum which, void (*fn)());
```

The first parameter is the tessellation object. The second specifies the type of callback being registered, and the last is the pointer to the callback function itself. You can specify various callbacks, under the function gluTessCallback. As an example, examine the following lines of code:

```
// Just call glBegin at beginning of triangle batch
gluTessCallback(pTess, GLU_TESS_BEGIN, (CallBack)glBegin);

// Just call glEnd at end of triangle batch
gluTessCallback(pTess, GLU_TESS_END, (CallBack)glEnd);

// Just call glVertex3dv for each  vertex
gluTessCallback(pTess, GLU_TESS_VERTEX, (CallBack)glVertex3dv);
```

The GLU_TESS_BEGIN callback specifies the function to call at the beginning of each new primitive. Specifying glBegin simply tells the tessellator to call glBegin to begin a primitive batch. This may seem pointless, but you can also specify your own function here to do additional processing whenever a new primitive begins. For example, suppose you want to find out how many triangles are used in the final tessellated polygon.

The GLU_TESS_END callback, again, simply tells the tessellator to call glEnd and that you have no other specific code you want to inject into the process. Finally, the GLU_TESS_VERTEX call drops in a call to glVertex3dv to specify the tessellated vertex data. Tessellation requires that vertex data be specified as double precision, and always uses three component vertices. Again, you could substitute your own function here to do some additional processing (such as adding color, normal, or texture coordinate information).

If you're wondering, CallBack is just a typedef defined in gltools.h to represent a generic function pointer for these functions.

For an example of specifying your own callback (instead of cheating and just using existing OpenGL functions), the following code shows the registration of a function to report any errors that may occur during tessellation:

```
///////////////////////////////////////////////////////////////////
// Tessellation error callback
void tessError(GLenum error)
    {
    // Get error message string
```

```
    const char *szError = (const char *)gluErrorString(error);

    // Set error message as window caption
    glutSetWindowTitle(szError);
    }

. . .
. . .


// Register error callback
gluTessCallback(pTess, GLU_TESS_ERROR, (CallBack)tessError);
```

Specifying Vertex Data

To begin a polygon (this corresponds to step 3 shown earlier), you call the following function:

```
void gluTessBeginPolygon(GLUTesselator *tobj, void *data);
```

You first pass in the tessellator object and then a pointer to any user-defined data that you want associated with this tessellation. This data can be sent back to you during tessellation using the callback functions listed for gluTessCallback. Often, this is just NULL. To finish the polygon (step 8) and begin tessellation, call this function:

```
void gluTessEndPolygon(GLUTesselator *tobj);
```

Nested within the beginning and ending of the polygon, you specify one or more contours using the following pair of functions (steps 4 and 6):

```
void gluTessBeginContour(GLUTesselator *tobj);
void gluTessEndContour(GLUTesselator *tobj);
```

Finally, within the contour, you must add the vertices that make up that contour (step 5). The following function feeds the vertices, one at a time, to the tessellator:

```
void gluTessVertex(GLUTesselator *tobj, GLdouble v[3], void *data);
```

The *v* parameter contains the actual vertex data used for tessellator calculations. The *data* parameter is a pointer to the vertex data passed to the callback function specified by GLU_VERTEX. Why two different arguments to specify the same thing? Because the pointer to the vertex data may also point to additional information about the vertex (color, normals, and so on). If you specify your own function for GLU_VERTEX (instead of our cheat), you can access this additional vertex data in the callback routine.

10

Putting It All Together

Now let's look at an example that takes a complex polygon and performs tessellation to render a solid shape. The sample program FLORIDA contains the vertex information to draw the crude, but recognizable, shape of the state of Florida. The program has three modes of rendering, accessible via the context menu: Line Loops, Concave Polygon, and Complex Polygon. The basic shape with Line Loops is shown in Figure 10.23.

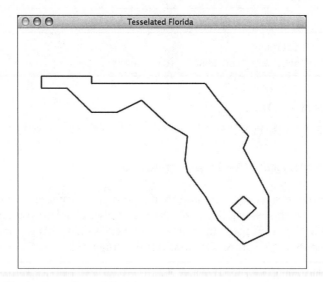

FIGURE 10.23   The basic outline of Florida.

Listing 10.5 shows the vertex data and the rendering code that draws the outlines for the state and Lake Okeechobee.

LISTING 10.5   Vertex Data and Drawing Code for State Outline

```
// Coast Line Data
#define COAST_POINTS 24
GLdouble vCoast[COAST_POINTS][3] = {{-70.0, 30.0, 0.0 },
                                    {-50.0, 30.0, 0.0 },
// ... data removed to save space in text
                                    {-70.0, 25.0, 0.0 }};


// Lake Okeechobee
#define LAKE_POINTS 4
GLdouble vLake[LAKE_POINTS][3] = {{ 10.0, -20.0, 0.0 },
                                  { 15.0, -25.0, 0.0 },
                                  { 10.0, -30.0, 0.0 },
                                  {  5.0, -25.0, 0.0 }};
```

LISTING 10.5   Continued

```
.  .  .
.  .  .

case DRAW_LOOPS:                       // Draw line loops
    {
    glColor3f(0.0f, 0.0f, 0.0f);       // Just black outline

    // Line loop with coastline shape
    glBegin(GL_LINE_LOOP);
    for(i = 0; i < COAST_POINTS; i++)
        glVertex3dv(vCoast[i]);
    glEnd();

    // Line loop with shape of interior lake
    glBegin(GL_LINE_LOOP);
    for(i = 0; i < LAKE_POINTS; i++)
        glVertex3dv(vLake[i]);
    glEnd();
    }
    break;
```

For the Concave Polygon rendering mode, only the outside contour is drawn. This results in a solid filled shape, despite the fact that the polygon is clearly concave. This result is shown in Figure 10.24, and the tessellation code is shown in Listing 10.6.

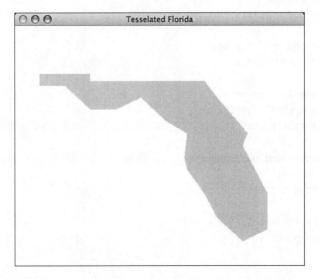

FIGURE 10.24   A solid convex polygon.

10

LISTING 10.6 Drawing a Convex Polygon

```
case DRAW_CONCAVE:                 // Tessellate concave polygon
    {
    // Tessellator object
    GLUtesselator *pTess;

    // Green polygon
    glColor3f(0.0f, 1.0f, 0.0f);

    // Create the tessellator object
    pTess = gluNewTess();

    // Set callback functions
    // Just call glBegin at beginning of triangle batch
    gluTessCallback(pTess, GLU_TESS_BEGIN, (CallBack)glBegin);

    // Just call glEnd at end of triangle batch
    gluTessCallback(pTess, GLU_TESS_END, (CallBack)glEnd);

    // Just call glVertex3dv for each  vertex
    gluTessCallback(pTess, GLU_TESS_VERTEX, (CallBack)glVertex3dv);

    // Register error callback
    gluTessCallback(pTess, GLU_TESS_ERROR, (CallBack)tessError);

    // Begin the polygon
    gluTessBeginPolygon(pTess, NULL);

    // Begin the one and only contour
    gluTessBeginContour(pTess);

    // Feed in the list of vertices
    for(i = 0; i < COAST_POINTS; i++)
        gluTessVertex(pTess, vCoast[i], vCoast[i]); // Can't be NULL

    // Close contour and polygon
    gluTessEndContour(pTess);
    gluTessEndPolygon(pTess);

    // All done with tessellator object
    gluDeleteTess(pTess);
    }
    break;
```

Finally, we present a more complex polygon, one with a hole in it. The Complex Polygon drawing mode draws the solid state, but with a hole representing Lake Okeechobee (a large lake in south Florida, typically shown on maps). The output is shown in Figure 10.25, and the relevant code is presented in Listing 10.7.

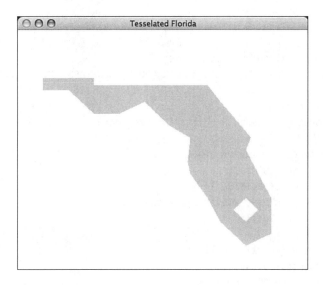

FIGURE 10.25   The solid polygon, but with a hole.

LISTING 10.7   Tessellating a Complex Polygon with Multiple Contours

```
case DRAW_COMPLEX:              // Tessellate, but with hole cut out
    {
    // Tessellator object
    GLUtesselator *pTess;

    // Green polygon
    glColor3f(0.0f, 1.0f, 0.0f);

    // Create the tessellator object
    pTess = gluNewTess();

    // Set callback functions
    // Just call glBegin at beginning of triangle batch
    gluTessCallback(pTess, GLU_TESS_BEGIN, (CallBack)glBegin);

    // Just call glEnd at end of triangle batch
    gluTessCallback(pTess, GLU_TESS_END, (CallBack)glEnd);
```

LISTING 10.7   Continued

```
    // Just call glVertex3dv for each vertex
    gluTessCallback(pTess, GLU_TESS_VERTEX, (CallBack)glVertex3dv);

    // Register error callback
    gluTessCallback(pTess, GLU_TESS_ERROR, (CallBack)tessError);

    // How to count filled and open areas
    gluTessProperty(pTess, GLU_TESS_WINDING_RULE, GLU_TESS_WINDING_ODD);

    // Begin the polygon
    gluTessBeginPolygon(pTess, NULL); // No user data

    // First contour, outline of state
    gluTessBeginContour(pTess);
    for(i = 0; i < COAST_POINTS; i++)
        gluTessVertex(pTess, vCoast[i], vCoast[i]);
    gluTessEndContour(pTess);

    // Second contour, outline of lake
    gluTessBeginContour(pTess);
    for(i = 0; i < LAKE_POINTS; i++)
        gluTessVertex(pTess, vLake[i], vLake[i]);
    gluTessEndContour(pTess);

    // All done with polygon
    gluTessEndPolygon(pTess);

    // No longer need tessellator object
    gluDeleteTess(pTess);
    }
    break;
```

This code contained a new function call:

```
// How to count filled and open areas
gluTessProperty(pTess, GLU_TESS_WINDING_RULE, GLU_TESS_WINDING_ODD);
```

This call tells the tessellator how to decide what areas to fill in and which areas to leave empty when there are multiple contours. The value `GLU_TESS_WINDING_ODD` is actually the default, and we could have skipped this function. However, you should understand how the tessellator handles nested contours. By specifying `ODD`, we are saying that any given point inside the polygon is filled in if it is enclosed in an odd number of contours. The area inside the lake (inner contour) is surrounded by two (an even number) contours and is left unfilled. Points outside the lake but inside the state boundary are enclosed by only one contour (an odd number) and are drawn filled.

Summary

The quadrics library makes creating a few simple surfaces (spheres, cylinders, disks, and cones) child's play. Expanding on this concept into more advanced curves and surfaces could have made this chapter the most intimidating in the entire book. As you have seen, however, the concepts behind these curves and surfaces are not very difficult to understand. Appendix A suggests further reading if you want in-depth mathematical information or tips on creating NURBS-based models.

Other examples from this chapter give you a good starting point for experimenting with NURBS. Adjust the control points and knot sequences to create warped or rumpled surfaces. Also, try some quadratic surfaces and some with higher order than the cubic surfaces. Watch out: One pitfall to avoid as you play with these curves is trying too hard to create one complex surface out of a single NURB. You can find greater power and flexibility if you compose complex surfaces out of several smaller and easy-to-handle NURBS or Bézier surfaces.

Finally, in this chapter, we saw OpenGL's powerful support for automatic polygon tessellation. You learned that you can draw complex surfaces, shapes, and patterns with only a few points that specify the boundaries. You also learned that concave regions and even regions with holes can be broken down into simpler convex primitives using the GLU library's tessellator object.

In the next chapter, you will learn about display lists. As you read that chapter, think about all the work that is being done under the covers to facilitate the power of these functions. Also think about the fact that most of the time, these functions are going to be used to draw static (unchanging) geometry. The techniques of the next chapter will allow you to dramatically increase the performance of what you have just learned here.

10

It's All About the Pipeline: Faster Geometry Throughput

by Richard S. Wright Jr.

WHAT YOU'LL LEARN IN THIS CHAPTER:

How To	Functions You'll Use
Optimize object display with display lists	glNewList/glEndList/glCallList
Store and transfer geometry more efficiently	glEnableClientState/
	glDisableClientState/
	glVertexPointer/glNormalPointer/
	glTexCoordPointer/glColorPointer/
	glEdgeFlagPointer/
	glFogCoordPointer/
	glSecondaryColorPointer/
	glArrayElement/glDrawArrays/
	glInterleavedArrays
Reduce geometric bandwidth	glDrawElements/
	glDrawRangeElements/
	glMultiDrawElements/glBufferData/glBindBuffer

In the preceding chapters, we have covered most of the basic OpenGL rendering techniques and technologies. With this knowledge, there are few 3D scenes you can envision that cannot be realized using only the first half of this book. Getting a detailed image onscreen, however, must often be balanced with the competing goal of performance. For some applications it may be perfectly acceptable to wait for several seconds or even minutes for a completed image to be rendered. For most real-time applications, however, the goal is usually to render a completed and usually dynamic scene many dozens of times per second!

A common hindrance to high performance in real-time applications is geometry through-put. Modern scenes and models are composed of many thousands of vertices, often accompanied by normals, texture coordinates, and other attributes. This is a lot of data that must be operated on by both the CPU and the GPU. In addition, just moving the data from the application to the graphics hardware can be a substantial performance bottleneck.

This chapter focuses exclusively on these issues. OpenGL contains a number of features that allow the programmer a great deal of flexibility and convenience when dealing with the goal of fast geometry throughput, each with its own advantages and disadvantages in terms of speed, flexibility, and ease of use.

Display Lists

So far, all of our primitive batches have been assembled using glBegin/glEnd pairs with individual glVertex calls between them. This is a very flexible means of assembling a batch of primitives, and is incredibly easy to use and understand. Unfortunately, when performance is taken into account, it is also the worst possible way to submit geometry to graphics hardware. Consider the following pseudocode to draw a single lit textured triangle:

```
glBegin(GL_TRIANGLES);
    glNormal3f(x, y, z);
    glTexCoord2f(s, t);
    glVertex3f(x, y, z);

    glNormal3f(x, y, z);
    glTexCoord2f(s, t);
    glVertex3f(x, y, z);

    glNormal3f(x, y, z);
    glTexCoord2f(s, t);
    glVertex3f(x, y, z);
glEnd();
```

For a single triangle, that's 11 function calls. Each of these functions contains potentially expensive validation code in the OpenGL driver. In addition, we must pass 24 different four byte parameters (one at a time!) pushed on the stack, and of course return to the calling function. That's a good bit of work for the CPU to perform to draw a single trian-gle. Now, multiply this by a 3D scene containing 10,000 or more triangles, and it is easy to imagine the graphics hardware sitting idle waiting on the CPU to assemble and submit geometry batches. There are some strategies that will soften the blow, of course. You can use vector-based functions such as glVertex3fv, you can consolidate batches, and you can use strips and fans to reduce redundant transformations and copies. However, the basic

11

approach is flawed from a performance standpoint because it requires many thousands of very small, potentially expensive operations to submit a batch of geometry. This method of submitting geometry batches is often called *immediate mode rendering.* Let's look at how OpenGL processes this data and see how there is an opportunity to dramatically improve this situation.

Batch Processing

OpenGL has been described as a software interface to graphics hardware. As such, you might imagine that OpenGL commands are somehow converted into some specific hardware commands or operators by the driver and then sent on to the graphics card for immediate execution. If so, you would be *mostly* correct. Most OpenGL rendering commands are, in fact, converted into some hardware-specific commands, but these commands are not dispatched immediately to the hardware. Instead, they are accumulated in a local buffer until some threshold is reached, at which point they are *flushed* to the hardware.

The primary reason for this type of arrangement is that trips to the graphics hardware take a long time, at least in terms of computer time. To a human being, this process might take place very quickly, but to a CPU running at many billions of cycles per second, this is like waiting for a cruise ship to sail from North America to Europe and back. You certainly would not put a single person on a ship and wait for the ship to return before loading up the next person. If you have many people to send to Europe, you are going to cram as many people on the ship as you can! This analogy is very accurate: It is faster to send a large amount of data (within some limits) over the system bus to hardware all at once than to break it down into many bursts of smaller packages.

Keeping to the analogy, you also do not have to wait for the first cruise ship to return before you can begin filling the next ship with passengers. Sending the buffer to the graphics hardware (a process called *flushing*) is an *asynchronous* operation. This means that the CPU can move on to other tasks and does not have to wait for the batch of rendering commands just sent to be completed. You can literally have the hardware rendering a given set of commands while the CPU is busy calling a new set of commands for the next graphics image (typically called a *frame* when you're creating an animation). This type of *parallelization* between the graphics hardware and the host CPU is highly efficient and often sought after by performance-conscious programmers.

Three events trigger a flush of the current batch of rendering commands. The first occurs when the driver's command buffer is full. You do not have access to this buffer, nor do you have any control over the size of the buffer. The hardware vendors work hard to tune the size and other characteristics of this buffer to work well with their devices. A flush also occurs when you execute a buffer swap. The buffer swap cannot occur until all pending commands have been executed (you want to see what you have drawn!), so the flush is initiated, followed by the command to perform the buffer swap. A buffer swap is an obvious indicator to the driver that you are done with a given scene and that all commands should be rendered. However, if you are doing single-buffered rendering, OpenGL has no real way of knowing when you're done sending commands and thus when to send the batch of commands to the hardware for execution. To facilitate this process, you can call the following function to manually trigger a flush:

```
void glFlush(void);
```

Some OpenGL commands, however, are not buffered for later execution—for example, `glReadPixels` and `glDrawPixels`. These functions directly access the framebuffer and read or write data directly. These functions actually introduce a pipeline stall, because the currently queued commands must be flushed and executed before you make direct changes to the color buffer. You can forcibly flush the command buffer, and wait for the graphics hardware to complete all its rendering tasks by calling the following function:

```
void glFinish(void);
```

This function is rarely used in practice. Typically this is for platform-specific requirements such as multithreading or multicontext rendering.

Preprocessed Batches

The work done every time you call an OpenGL command is not inconsequential. Commands are *compiled,* or converted, from OpenGL's high-level command language into low-level hardware commands understood by the hardware. For complex geometry, or just large amounts of vertex data, this process is performed many thousands of times, just to draw a single image onscreen. This is, of course, the aforementioned problem with immediate mode rendering. How does our new knowledge of the command buffer help with this situation?

Often, the geometry or other OpenGL data remains the same from frame to frame. For example, a spinning torus is always composed of the same set of triangle strips, with the same vertex data, recalculated with expensive trigonometric functions every frame. The only thing changing frame to frame is the modelview matrix.

A solution to this needlessly repeated overhead is to save a chunk of precomputed data from the command buffer that performs some repetitive rendering task, such as drawing the torus. This chunk of data can later be copied back to the command buffer all at once, saving the many function calls and compilation work done to create the data.

OpenGL provides a facility to create a preprocessed set of OpenGL commands (the chunk of data) that can then be quickly copied to the command buffer for more rapid execution. This precompiled list of commands is called a display list, and creating one or more of them is an easy and straightforward process. Just as you delimit an OpenGL primitive with `glBegin`/`glEnd`, you delimit a display list with `glNewList`/`glEndList`. A display list, however, is named with an integer value that you supply. The following code fragment represents a typical example of display list creation:

```
glNewList(<unsigned integer name>,GL_COMPILE);
...
...
// Some OpenGL Code
...
...
glEndList();
```

The named display list now contains all OpenGL rendering commands that occur between the glNewList and glEndList function calls. The GL_COMPILE parameter tells OpenGL to compile the list but not to execute it yet. You can also specify GL_COMPILE_AND_EXECUTE to simultaneously build the display list and execute the rendering instructions. Typically, however, display lists are built (GL_COMPILE only) during program initialization and then executed later during rendering.

The display list name can be any unsigned integer. However, if you use the same value twice, the second display list overwrites the previous one. For this reason, it is convenient to have some sort of mechanism to keep you from reusing the same display list more than once. This is especially helpful when you are incorporating libraries of code written by someone else who may have incorporated display lists and may have chosen the same display list names.

OpenGL provides built-in support for allocating unique display list names. The following function returns the first of a series of display list integers that are unique:

```
GLuint glGenLists(GLsizei range);
```

The display list names are reserved sequentially, with the first name being returned by the function. You can call this function as often as you want and for as many display list names at a time as you may need. A corresponding function frees display list names and releases any memory allocated for those display lists:

```
void glDeleteLists(GLuint list, GLsizei range);
```

A display list, containing any number of precompiled OpenGL commands, is then executed with a single command:

```
void glCallList(GLuint list);
```

You can also execute a whole array of display lists with this command:

```
void glCallLists(GLsizei n, GLenum type, const GLvoid *lists);
```

The first parameter specifies the number of display lists contained by the array *lists*. The second parameter contains the data type of the array; typically, it is GL_UNSIGNED_BYTE. Conveniently, it is used very often as an offset to address font display lists.

Display List Caveats

A few important points about display lists are worth mentioning here. Although on most implementations, a display list should improve performance, your mileage may vary depending on the amount of effort the vendor puts into optimizing display list creation and execution. It is rare, however, for display lists not to offer a noticeable boost in performance, and they are widely relied on in applications that use OpenGL.

Display lists are typically good at creating precompiled lists of OpenGL commands, especially if the list contains state changes (turning lighting on and off, for example). If you do not create a display list name with glGenLists first, you might get a working display list on some implementations, but not on others. Some commands simply do not make sense in a display list. For example, reading the framebuffer into a pointer with glReadPixels makes no sense in a display list. Likewise, calls to glTexImage2D would store the original image data in the display list, followed by the command to load the image data as a texture. Basically, your textures stored this way would take up twice as much memory! Display lists excel, however, at precompiled lists of static geometry, with texture objects bound either inside or outside the display lists. Finally, display lists cannot contain calls that create display lists. You can have one display list call another, but you cannot put calls to glNewLists/glEndList inside a display list.

Converting to Display Lists

To demonstrate how easy it is to use display lists, and the potential for performance improvement, we have converted the Sphere World sample program to optionally use display lists (see the Sphere World sample program for this chapter). You can select with/without display lists via a context menu available via the right mouse button. We have also added a display to the window caption that displays the frame rate achieved using these two methods.

Converting the Sphere World sample to use display lists requires only a few additional lines of code. First, we add three variables that contain the display list identifiers for the three pieces of static geometry: a sphere, the ground, and the torus.

```
// Display list identifiers
GLuint  sphereList, groundList, torusList;
```

Then, in the SetupRC function, we request three display list names and assign them to our display list variables:

```
// Get Display list names
groundList = glGenLists(3);
sphereList = groundList + 1;
torusList = groundList + 2;
```

Next, we add the code to generate the three display lists. Each display list simply calls the function that draws that piece of geometry:

```
// Prebuild the display lists
glNewList(sphereList, GL_COMPILE);
    gltDrawSphere(0.1f, 40, 20);
glEndList();

// Create torus display list
glNewList(torusList, GL_COMPILE);
    gltDrawTorus(0.35, 0.15, 61, 37);
glEndList();

// Create the ground display list
glNewList(groundList, GL_COMPILE);
    DrawGround();
glEndList();
```

Finally, when drawing the objects, we select either the display list or the direct rendering method based on a flag set by the menu handler. For example, rendering a single sphere becomes this:

```
if(iMethod == 0)
    gltDrawSphere(0.1f, 40, 20);
else
    glCallList(sphereList);
```

Switching to display lists can have an amazing impact on performance. Some OpenGL implementations even try to store display lists in memory on the graphics hardware directly if possible, further reducing the work required to get the data to the graphics processor. Figure 11.1 shows the new improved SPHEREWORLD sample running with display lists activated. Without display lists on the Macintosh this was written on, the frame rate was about 50 fps. With display lists, the frame rate shoots up to over 300!

FIGURE 11.1　SPHEREWORLD with display lists.

Why should you care about rendering performance? The faster and more efficient your rendering code, the more visual complexity you can add to your scene without dragging down the frame rate too much. Higher frame rates yield smoother and better-looking animations. You can also use the extra CPU time to perform other tasks such as physics calculations or lengthy I/O operations on a separate thread.

Vertex Arrays

Display lists are a frequently used and convenient means of precompiling sets of OpenGL commands. In our previous example, the many spheres required a great deal of trigonometric calculations that were saved when we placed the geometry in display lists. You might consider that we could just as easily have created some arrays to store the vertex data for the models and thus saved all the computation time just as easily as with the display lists.

You might be right about this way of thinking—to a point. Some implementations store display lists more efficiently than others, and if all you're really compiling is the vertex data, you can simply place the model's data in one or more arrays and render from the array of precalculated geometry. The only drawback to this approach is that you must still loop through the entire array moving data to OpenGL one vertex at a time. Depending on the amount of geometry involved, taking this approach could incur a substantial performance penalty. The advantage, however, is that, unlike with display lists, the geometry does not have to be static. Each time you prepare to render the geometry, some function could be applied to all the geometry data and perhaps displace or modify it in some way. For example, say a mesh used to render the surface of an ocean could have rippling waves moving across the surface. A swimming whale or jellyfish could also be cleverly modeled with deformable meshes in this way.

With OpenGL, you can, in fact, have the best of both scenarios by using vertex arrays. With vertex arrays, you can precalculate or modify your geometry on the fly but do a bulk transfer of all the geometry data at one time. Basic vertex arrays can be almost as fast as display lists, but without the requirement that the geometry be static. It might also simply be more convenient to store your data in arrays for other reasons and thus also render directly from the same arrays (this approach could also potentially be more memory efficient).

Using vertex arrays in OpenGL involves four basic steps. First, you must assemble your geometry data in one or more arrays. You can do this algorithmically or perhaps by loading the data from a disk file. Second, you must tell OpenGL where the data is. When rendering is performed, OpenGL pulls the vertex data directly from the arrays you have specified. Third, you must explicitly tell OpenGL which arrays you are using. You can have separate arrays for vertices, normals, colors, and so on, and you must let OpenGL know which of these data sets you want to use. Finally, you execute the OpenGL commands to actually perform the rendering using your vertex data.

To demonstrate these four steps, we revisit an old sample from another chapter. We've rewritten the POINTSPRITE sample from Chapter 9, "Texture Mapping: Beyond the Basics," for the STARRYNIGHT sample in this chapter. The STARRYNIGHT sample creates three arrays (for three different-sized stars) that contain randomly initialized positions for stars in a starry sky. We then use vertex arrays to render directly from these arrays, bypassing the glBegin/glEnd mechanism entirely. Figure 11.2 shows the output of the STARRYNIGHT sample program, and Listing 11.1 shows the important portions of the source code.

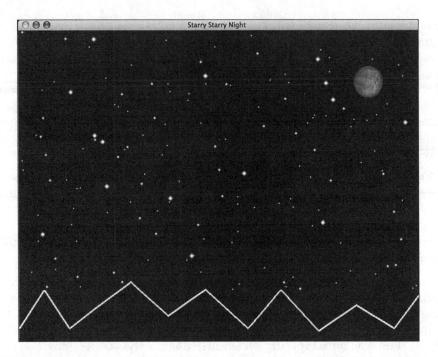

FIGURE 11.2   Output from the STARRYNIGHT program.

LISTING 11.1   Setup and Rendering Code for the STARRYNIGHT Sample

```
// Array of small stars
#define SMALL_STARS 100
M3DVector2f   vSmallStars[SMALL_STARS];

#define MEDIUM_STARS    40
M3DVector2f vMediumStars[MEDIUM_STARS];

#define LARGE_STARS 15
M3DVector2f vLargeStars[LARGE_STARS];


. . .
. . .


/////////////////////////////////////////////////
// Called to draw scene
void RenderScene(void)
    {
    . . .
```

LISTING 11.1 Continued

```
    . . .
// Draw small stars
    glPointSize(7.0f);              // 1.0
    /*
    glBegin(GL_POINTS);
        for(i = 0; i < SMALL_STARS; i++)
            glVertex2fv(vSmallStars[i]);
    glEnd();
    */
    glVertexPointer(2, GL_FLOAT, 0, vSmallStars);
    glDrawArrays(GL_POINTS, 0, SMALL_STARS);


    // Draw medium-sized stars
    glPointSize(12.0f);             // 3.0
    /*glBegin(GL_POINTS);
        for(i = 0; i< MEDIUM_STARS; i++)
            glVertex2fv(vMediumStars[i]);
    glEnd();
    */
    glVertexPointer(2, GL_FLOAT, 0, vMediumStars);
    glDrawArrays(GL_POINTS, 0, MEDIUM_STARS);

    // Draw largest stars
    glPointSize(20.0f);         // 5.5
    /*glBegin(GL_POINTS);
        for(i = 0; i < LARGE_STARS; i++)
            glVertex2fv(vLargeStars[i]);
    glEnd();
    */
    glVertexPointer(2, GL_FLOAT, 0, vLargeStars);
    glDrawArrays(GL_POINTS, 0, LARGE_STARS);

    glDisableClientState(GL_VERTEX_ARRAY);

    . . .
    . . .

    // Swap buffers
    glutSwapBuffers();
    }
```

Loading the Geometry

The first prerequisite to using vertex arrays is that your geometry must be stored in arrays. In Listing 11.1, you see three globally accessible arrays of two-dimensional vectors. They contain x and y coordinate locations for the three groups of stars:

```
// Array of small stars
#define SMALL_STARS 100
M3DVector2f  vSmallStars[SMALL_STARS];

#define MEDIUM_STARS   40
M3DVector2f vMediumStars[MEDIUM_STARS];

#define LARGE_STARS 15
M3DVector2f vLargeStars[LARGE_STARS];
```

Recall that this sample program uses an orthographic projection and draws the stars as points at random screen locations. Each array is populated in the SetupRC function with a simple loop that picks random x and y values that fall within the portion of the window we want the stars to occupy. The following few lines from the listing show how just the small star list is populated:

```
// Populate star list
    for(i = 0; i < SMALL_STARS; i++)
        {
        vSmallStars[i][0] = (GLfloat)(rand() % SCREEN_X);
        vSmallStars[i][1] = (GLfloat)(rand() % (SCREEN_Y - 100))+100.0f;
        }
```

Enabling Arrays

In the RenderScene function, we enable the use of an array of vertices with the following code:

```
// Using vertex arrays
glEnableClientState(GL_VERTEX_ARRAY);
```

This is the first new function for using vertex arrays, and it has a corresponding disabling function:

```
void glEnableClientState(GLenum array);
void glDisableClientState(GLenum array);
```

These functions accept the following constants, turning on and off the corresponding array usage: GL_VERTEX_ARRAY, GL_COLOR_ARRAY, GL_SECONDARY_COLOR_ARRAY, GL_NORMAL_ARRAY, GL_FOG_COORDINATE_ARRAY, GL_TEXURE_COORD_ARRAY, and

GL_EDGE_FLAG_ARRAY. For our STARRYNIGHT example, we are sending down only a list of vertices. As you can see, you can also send down a corresponding array of normals, texture coordinates, colors, and so on.

Here's one question that commonly arises with the introduction of this function: Why did the OpenGL designers add a new glEnableClientState function instead of just sticking with glEnable? A good question. The reason has to do with how OpenGL is designed to operate. OpenGL was designed using a client/server model. The server is the graphics hardware, and the client is the host CPU and memory. On the PC, for example, the server would be the graphics card, and the client would be the PC's CPU and main memory. Because this state of enabled/disabled capability specifically applies to the client side of the picture, a new set of functions was derived.

Where's the Data?

Before we can actually use the vertex data, we must still tell OpenGL where the data is stored. The following single line in the STARRYNIGHT example does this:

```
glVertexPointer(2, GL_FLOAT, 0, vSmallStars);
```

Here, we find our next new function. The glVertexPointer function tells OpenGL where the vertex data is stored. There are also corresponding functions for the other types of vertex array data:

```
void glVertexPointer(GLint size, GLenum type, GLsizei stride,
                                            const void *pointer);
void glColorPointer(GLint size, GLenum type, GLsizei stride,
                                            const void *pointer);
void glTexCoordPointer(GLint size, GLenum type, GLsizei stride,
                                            const void *pointer);
void glSecondaryColorPointer(GLint size, GLenum type, GLsizei stride,
                                            const void *pointer);
void glNormalPointer(GLenum type, GLsizei stride, const void *pData);

void glFogCoordPointer(GLenum type, GLsizei stride, const void *pointer);
void glEdgeFlagPointer(GLenum type, GLsizei stride, const void *pointer);
```

These functions are all closely related and take nearly identical arguments. All but the normal, fog coordinate, and edge flag functions take a *size* argument first. This argument tells OpenGL the number of elements that make up the coordinate type. For example, vertices can consist of two (x,y), three (x,y,z), or four (x,y,z,w) components. Normals, however, are always three components, and fog coordinates and edge flags are always one component; thus, it would be redundant to specify the argument for these functions.

The *type* parameter specifies the OpenGL data type for the array. Not all data types are valid for all vertex array specifications. Table 11.1 lists the seven vertex array functions (index pointers are used for color index mode and are thus excluded here) and the valid data types that can be specified for the data elements.

TABLE 11.1   Valid Vertex Array Sizes and Data Types

Command	Elements	Valid Data Types
glColorPointer	3, 4	GL_BYTE, GL_UNSIGNED_BYTE, GL_SHORT, GL_UNSIGNED_SHORT, GL_INT, GL_UNSIGNED_INT, GL_FLOAT, GL_DOUBLE
glEdgeFlagPointer	1	None specified (always GLboolean)
glFogCoordPointer	1	GL_FLOAT, GL_DOUBLE
glNormalPointer	3	GL_BYTE, GL_SHORT, GL_INT, GL_FLOAT, GL_DOUBLE
glSecondaryColorPointer	3	GL_BYTE, GL_UNSIGNED_BYTE, GL_SHORT, GL_INT, GL_UNSIGNED_INT, GL_FLOAT, GL_DOUBLE
glTexCoordPointer	1, 2, 3, 4	GL_SHORT, GL_INT, GL_FLOAT, GL_DOUBLE
glVertexPointer	2, 3, 4	GL_SHORT, GL_INT, GL_FLOAT, GL_DOUBLE

The *stride* parameter specifies the space in bytes between each array element. Typically, this value is just 0, and array elements have no data gaps between values. Finally, the last parameter is a pointer to the array of data. For arrays, this is simply the name of the array.

This leaves us a little in the dark concerning multitexture. When using the glBegin/glEnd paradigm, we learned a new function for sending texture coordinates for each texture unit, called glMultiTexCoord. When using vertex arrays, you can change the target texture unit for glTexCoordPointer with this function:

glClientActiveTexture(GLenum *texture*);

Here the *target* parameter is GL_TEXTURE0, GL_TEXTURE1, and so forth.

Pull the Data and Draw

Finally, we're ready to render using our vertex arrays. We can actually use the vertex arrays in two different ways. For illustration, first look at the nonvertex array method that simply loops through the array and passes a pointer to each array element to glVertex:

```
glBegin(GL_POINTS);
    for(i = 0; i < SMALL_STARS; i++)
        glVertex2fv(vSmallStars[i]);
glEnd();
```

Because OpenGL now knows about our vertex data, we can have OpenGL look up the vertex values for us with the following code:

```
glBegin(GL_POINTS);
   for(i = 0; i < SMALL_STARS; i++)
      glArrayElement(i);
glEnd();
```

The glArrayElement function looks up the corresponding array data from any arrays that have been enabled with glEnableClientState. If an array has been enabled, and a corresponding array has not been specified (glVertexPointer, glColorPointer, and so on), an illegal memory access will likely cause the program to crash. The advantage to using glArrayElement is that a single function call can now replace several function calls (glNormal, glColor, glVertex, and so forth) needed to specify all the data for a specific vertex. Sometimes you might want to jump around in the array in nonsequential order as well.

Most of the time, however, you will find that you are simply transferring a block of vertex data that needs to be traversed from beginning to end. In these cases (as is the case with the STARRYNIGHT sample), OpenGL can transfer a single block of any enabled arrays with a single function call:

```
void glDrawArrays(GLenum mode, GLint first, GLint count);
```

In this function, mode specifies the primitive to be rendered (one primitive batch per function call). The first parameter specifies where in the enabled arrays to begin retrieving data, and the count parameter tells how many array elements to retrieve. In the case of the STARRYNIGHT example, we rendered the array of small stars as follows:

```
glDrawArrays(GL_POINTS, 0, SMALL_STARS);
```

OpenGL implementations can optimize these block transfers, resulting in significant performance gains over multiple calls to the individual vertex functions such as glVertex and glNormal.

Indexed Vertex Arrays

Indexed vertex arrays are vertex arrays that are not traversed in order from beginning to end, but are traversed in an order that is specified by a separate array of index values. This may seem a bit convoluted, but actually indexed vertex arrays can save memory and reduce transformation overhead. Under ideal conditions, they can actually be faster than display lists!

The reason for this extra efficiency is that the array of vertices can be smaller than the array of indices. Adjoining primitives such as triangles can share vertices in ways not possible by just using triangle strips or fans. For example, using ordinary rendering methods or vertex arrays, there is no other mechanism to share a set of vertices between two adjacent triangle strips. Figure 11.3 shows two triangle strips that share one edge.

Although triangle strips make good use of shared vertices between triangles in the strip, there is no way to avoid the overhead of transforming the vertices shared between the two strips because each strip must be specified individually.

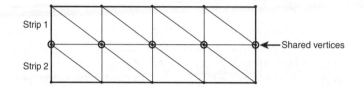

FIGURE 11.3   Two triangle strips in which the vertices share an edge.

Now let's look at a simple example; then we'll look at a more complex model and examine the potential savings of using indexed arrays.

A Simple Cube

We can save a considerable amount of memory if we can reuse a normal or vertex in a vertex array without having to store it more than once. Not only is memory saved, but also a good OpenGL implementation is optimized to transform these vertices only once, saving valuable transformation time.

Instead of creating a vertex array containing all the vertices for a given geometric object, you can create an array containing only the unique vertices for the object. Then you can use another array of index values to specify the geometry. These indices reference the vertex values in the first array. Figure 11.4 shows this relationship.

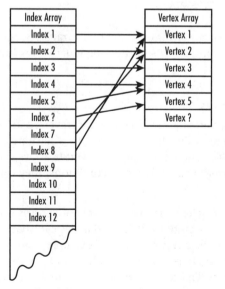

FIGURE 11.4   An index array referencing an array of unique vertices.

Each vertex consists of three floating-point values, but each index is only an integer value. A float and an integer are 4 bytes on most machines, which means you save 8 bytes for each reused vertex for the cost of 4 extra bytes for every vertex. For a small number of vertices, the savings might not be great; in fact, you might even use more memory using an indexed array than you would have by just repeating vertex information. For larger models, however, the savings can be substantial.

Figure 11.5 shows a cube with each vertex numbered. For our next sample program, CUBEDX, we create a cube using indexed vertex arrays.

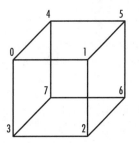

FIGURE 11.5   A cube containing eight unique numbered vertices.

Listing 11.2 shows the code from the CUBEDX program to render the cube using indexed vertex arrays. The eight unique vertices are in the `corners` array, and the indices are in the `indexes` array. In `RenderScene`, we set the polygon mode to `GL_LINE` so that the cube is wireframed.

LISTING 11.2   Code from the CUBEDX Program to Use Indexed Vertex Arrays

```
// Array containing the six vertices of the cube
static GLfloat corners[] = { -25.0f, 25.0f, 25.0f, // 0 // Front of cube
                    25.0f, 25.0f, 25.0f, // 1
                    25.0f, -25.0f, 25.0f,// 2
                    -25.0f, -25.0f, 25.0f,// 3
                    -25.0f, 25.0f, -25.0f,// 4  // Back of cube
                    25.0f, 25.0f, -25.0f,// 5
                    25.0f, -25.0f, -25.0f,// 6
                    -25.0f, -25.0f, -25.0f };// 7


// Array of indexes to create the cube
static GLubyte indexes[] = { 0, 1, 2, 3,      // Front Face
                    4, 5, 1, 0,      // Top Face
                    3, 2, 6, 7,      // Bottom Face
                    5, 4, 7, 6,      // Back Face
                    1, 5, 6, 2,      // Right Face
```

LISTING 11.2   Continued

```
                          4, 0, 3, 7 };    // Left Face

// Rotation amounts
static GLfloat xRot = 0.0f;
static GLfloat yRot = 0.0f;


// Called to draw scene
void RenderScene(void)
    {
    // Clear the window with current clearing color
    glClear(GL_COLOR_BUFFER_BIT | GL_DEPTH_BUFFER_BIT);

    // Make the cube wireframe
    glPolygonMode(GL_FRONT_AND_BACK, GL_LINE);

    // Save the matrix state
    glMatrixMode(GL_MODELVIEW);
    glPushMatrix();
    glTranslatef(0.0f, 0.0f, -200.0f);

    // Rotate about x and y axes
    glRotatef(xRot, 1.0f, 0.0f, 0.0f);
    glRotatef(yRot, 0.0f, 0.0f, 1.0f);

    // Enable and specify the vertex array
    glEnableClientState(GL_VERTEX_ARRAY);
    glVertexPointer(3, GL_FLOAT, 0, corners);

    // Using Drawelements
    glDrawElements(GL_QUADS, 24, GL_UNSIGNED_BYTE, indexes);

    glPopMatrix();

    // Swap buffers
    glutSwapBuffers();
    }
```

OpenGL has native support for indexed vertex arrays, as shown in the glDrawElements function. The key line in Listing 11.2 is

```
glDrawElements(GL_QUADS, 24, GL_UNSIGNED_BYTE, indexes);
```

This line is much like the `glDrawArrays` function mentioned earlier, but now we are specifying an index array that determines the order in which the enabled vertex arrays are traversed. Figure 11.6 shows the output from the program CUBEDX.

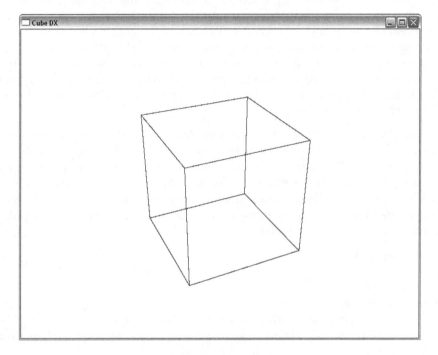

FIGURE 11.6 A wireframe cube drawn with an indexed vertex array.

A variation on `glDrawElement` is the `glDrawRangeElements` function. This function is documented in Appendix C, "API Reference," and simply adds two parameters to specify the range of indices that will be valid. This hint can enable some OpenGL implementations to prefetch the vertex data, a potentially worthwhile performance optimization. A further enhancement is `glMultiDrawArrays`, which allows you to send multiple arrays of indices with a single function call.

One last vertex array function you'll find in the reference section is `glInterleavedArrays`. It allows you to combine several arrays into one aggregate array. There is no change to your access or traversal of the arrays, but the organization in memory can possibly enhance performance on some hardware implementations.

Getting Serious

With a few simple examples behind us, it's time to tackle a more sophisticated model with more vertex data. For this example, we use a model of an F-16 Thunderbird created by Ed Womack at digitalmagician.net. We've used a commercial product called Deep Exploration (version 3.4) from Right Hemisphere that has a handy feature of exporting models as OpenGL code!

We had to modify the code output by Deep Exploration so that it would work with our GLUT framework and run on both the Macintosh and the PC platforms. You can find the code that renders the model in the THUNDERBIRD sample program. Note that the aircraft is broken up into two pieces: the main body and a much smaller glass canopy. For illustrational purposes, the following discussion will refer only to the larger body. We do not include the entire program listing here because it is quite lengthy and mostly meaningless to human beings. It consists of a number of arrays representing 3,704 individual triangles (that's a lot of numbers to stare at!).

The approach taken with this tool is to try to produce the smallest possible amount of code to represent the given model. Deep Exploration has done a reasonable job of compacting the data. There are 3,704 individual triangles, but using a clever indexing scheme, Deep Exploration has encoded this as only 1,898 individual vertices, 2,716 normals, and 2,925 texture coordinates. The following code shows the `DrawBody` function, which loops through the index set and sends OpenGL the texture, normal, and vertex coordinates for each individual triangle:

```
void DrawBody(void)
    {
    int iFace, iPoint;
    glBegin(GL_TRIANGLES);
        for(iFace = 0; iFace < 3704; iFace++)  // Each new triangle starts here
            for(iPoint = 0; iPoint < 3; iPoint++) // Each vertex specified here
                {
                // Lookup the texture value
                glTexCoord2fv(textures[face_indices[iFace][iPoint+6]]);

                // Lookup the normal value
                glNormal3fv(normals[face_indices[iFace][iPoint+3]]);

                // Look up the vertex value
                glVertex3fv(vertices[face_indices[iFace][iPoint]]);
                }
    glEnd();
    }
```

This approach is okay when you must optimize the storage size of the model data—for example, to save memory in an embedded application, reduce storage space, or reduce bandwidth if the model must be transmitted over a network. However, for real-time applications in which performance considerations can sometimes outweigh memory constraints, this code would perform quite poorly because once again you are back to square one, sending vertex data to OpenGL one vertex at a time.

The simplest and perhaps most obvious approach to speeding up this code is simply to place the DrawModel function in a display list. Indeed, this is the approach we used in the THUNDERBIRD program that renders this model. You can see the output of the model in Figure 11.7.

FIGURE 11.7   An F-16 Thunderbird model.

Let's look at the cost of this approach and compare it to rendering the same model with indexed vertex arrays. The Thunderbird model actually comes in two pieces: the main body and a transparent glass canopy. To keep things simple, we are neglecting the cost in these calculations of the separate and much smaller glass canopy.

Measuring the Cost   First, we calculate the amount of memory required to store the original compacted vertex data. We can do this simply by looking at the declarations of the data arrays and knowing how large the base data type is:

```
short face_indices[3704][9] = { ...
```

```
GLfloat vertices [1898][3] = { ...
```

```
GLfloat normals [2716][3] = { ...
```

```
GLfloat textures [2925][2] = { ...
```

The memory for face_indices would be sizeof(short) × 3,704 × 9, which works out to 66,672 bytes. Similarly, we calculate the size of vertices, normals, and textures as 22,776, 32,592, and 23,400 bytes, respectively. This gives us a total memory footprint of 145,440 bytes or about 142KB.

But wait! When we draw the model into the display list, we copy all this data again into the display list, except that now we decompress our packed data so that many vertices are duplicated for adjacent triangles. We, in essence, undo all the work to optimize the storage of the geometry to draw it. We can't calculate exactly how much space the display list takes, but we can get a good estimate by calculating just the size of the geometry. There are 3,704 triangles. Each triangle has three vertices, each of which has a floating-point vertex (three floats), normal (three floats), and texture coordinate (two floats). Assuming 4 bytes for a float (sizeof(float)), we calculate this as shown here:

3,704 (triangle) × 3 (vertices) = 11,112 vertices

Each vertex has three components (x, y, z):

11,112 × 3 = 33,336 floating-point values for geometry

Each vertex has a normal, meaning three more components:

11,112 × 3 = 33,336 floating-point values for normals

Each vertex has a texture, meaning two more components:

11,112 × 2 = 22,224 floating-point values for texture coordinates

This gives a total of 88,896 floats, at 4 bytes each = 355,584 bytes.

Total memory for the display list data and the original data is then 501,024 bytes, just a tad shy of half a megabyte! But don't forget the transformation cost—11,112 (3,704 × 3) vertices must be transformed by the OpenGL geometry pipeline. That's a lot of matrix multiplies!

Creating a Suitable Indexed Array   Just because the data in the THUNDERBIRD sample is stored in arrays does not mean the data is ready to be used as any kind of OpenGL vertex array. In OpenGL, the vertex array, normal array, texture array, and any other arrays that you want to use must all be the same size. The reason is that all the array elements across arrays must be shared. For ordinary vertex arrays, as you march through the set of arrays, array element 0 from the vertex array must go with array element 0 from the normal array, and so on. For indexed arrays, we have the same requirement. Each index must address all the enabled arrays at the same corresponding array element.

For the sample program THUNDERGL, we have created a C++ utility class that processes the existing array data and reindexes the triangles so that all three arrays are the same size and all array elements correspond exactly one to another. Many 3D applications can benefit from reprocessing an unstructured list of triangles and creating a ready-to-go indexed vertex array. This class is easily reusable and extensible, and is placed in the \shared source directory. Listing 11.3 shows the processing of the body and glass canopy elements to get the indexed array ready.

LISTING 11.3   Code to Create the Indexed Vertex Arrays

```
CTriangleMesh    thunderBirdBody;
CTriangleMesh    thunderBirdGlass;


. . .
. . .


// Load Thunderbird body and canopy
// Temporary workspace
M3DVector3f vVerts[3];
M3DVector3f vNorms[3];
M3DVector2f vTex[3];

// Start assembling the body mesh, set maximum size
thunderBirdBody.BeginMesh(3704*3);

// Loop through all the faces
for(int iFace = 0; iFace < 3704; iFace++)
    {
    // Assemble the triangle
    for(int iPoint = 0; iPoint < 3; iPoint++)
        {
        memcpy(&vVerts[iPoint][0],
            &vertices[face_indicies[iFace][iPoint]][0], sizeof(M3DVector3f));
        memcpy(&vNorms[iPoint][0],
            &normals[face_indicies[iFace][iPoint+3]][0], sizeof(M3DVector3f));
        memcpy(&vTex[iPoint][0],
            &textures[face_indicies[iFace][iPoint+6]][0], sizeof(M3DVector2f));
        }

    thunderBirdBody.AddTriangle(vVerts, vNorms, vTex);
    }

// Close the mesh and scale it (it's a little BIG in its original format)
```

LISTING 11.3   Continued

```
thunderBirdBody.EndMesh();
thunderBirdBody.Scale(fScale);

// Now do the same for the canopy
thunderBirdGlass.BeginMesh(352*3);

for(int iFace = 0; iFace < 352; iFace++)
    {
    // Assemble the triangle
    for(int iPoint = 0; iPoint < 3; iPoint++)
        {
        memcpy(&vVerts[iPoint][0],
            &verticesGlass[face_indiciesGlass[iFace][iPoint]][0],
sizeof(M3DVector3f));
        memcpy(&vNorms[iPoint][0],
            &normalsGlass[face_indiciesGlass[iFace][iPoint+3]][0],
sizeof(M3DVector3f));
        memcpy(&vTex[iPoint][0],
            &texturesGlass[face_indiciesGlass[iFace][iPoint+6]][0],
sizeof(M3DVector2f));
        }

    thunderBirdGlass.AddTriangle(vVerts, vNorms, vTex);
    }

thunderBirdGlass.EndMesh();
thunderBirdGlass.Scale(fScale);
```

First, we need to declare storage for our two new triangle meshes:

```
CTriangleMesh    thunderBirdBody;
CTriangleMesh    thunderBirdGlass;
```

Then in the SetupRC function, we populate these triangle meshes with triangles. Because we don't know ahead of time what our savings will be, when we start the mesh, we must tell the class the maximum amount of storage to allocate for workspace. We know that the face array (each containing three vertices) is 3,704 elements long, so the worst possible scenario is 3,704 × 3 unique vertices. As we will see, we will actually do much better than this.

```
thunderBirdBody.BeginMesh(3704*3);
```

Finally, we loop through all the faces, assemble each triangle individually, and send it the AddTriangle method. When all the triangles are added, we scale them using the member function Scale. We did this only because the original model data was bigger than we'd prefer.

```
// Loop through all the faces
for(int iFace = 0; iFace < 3704; iFace++)
    {
    // Assemble the triangle
    for(int iPoint = 0; iPoint < 3; iPoint++)
        {
        memcpy(&vVerts[iPoint][0],
            &vertices[face_indicies[iFace][iPoint]][0], sizeof(M3DVector3f));
        memcpy(&vNorms[iPoint][0],
            &normals[face_indicies[iFace][iPoint+3]][0], sizeof(M3DVector3f));
        memcpy(&vTex[iPoint][0],
            &textures[face_indicies[iFace][iPoint+6]][0], sizeof(M3DVector2f));
        }

    thunderBirdBody.AddTriangle(vVerts, vNorms, vTex);
    }


// Close the mesh and scale it (it's a little BIG in its original format)
thunderBirdBody.EndMesh();
thunderBirdBody.Scale(fScale);
```

We must do this for both the Thunderbird body and the glass canopy.

Comparing the Cost   Now let's compare the cost of our three methods of rendering this model. The CTriangleMesh class reports that the processed body of the Thunderbird consists of 3,265 unique vertices (including matching normals and texture coordinates), and 11,112 indexes (which is the total number of vertices when rendered as triangles). Each vertex and normal has three components (x,y,z), and each texture coordinate has two components. The total number of floating-point values in the mesh data is then calculated this way:

3,265 vertices $\times$ 8 = 26,120 floats

Multiplying each float by 4 bytes yields a memory overhead of 104,480 bytes. We still need to add in the index array of unsigned shorts. That's another 11,112 elements times 2 bytes each = 22,224. This gives a grand total storage overhead of 126,704 bytes. Table 11.2 shows these values side by side. Remember, a kilobyte is 1,024 bytes.

TABLE 11.2   Memory and Transformation Overhead for Three Rendering Methods

Rendering Mode	Memory	Vertices Transformed
Immediate Mode	142KB	11,112
Display List	489KB	11,112
Indexed Vertex Array	123KB	3,265

As it turns out in this case, the Indexed Vertex Array approach wins hands down in terms of memory footprint, and requires less than one-third of the transformation work on the vertices!

In a production program, you might have tools that take this calculated indexed array and write it out to disk with a header that describes the required array dimensions. Reading this mesh or a collection of meshes back into the program then is a simple implementation of a basic model loader. The loaded model's meshes are then exactly in the format required by OpenGL.

Models with sharp edges and corners often have fewer vertices that are candidates for sharing. However, models with large smooth surface areas can stand to gain even more in terms of memory and transformation savings. With the added savings of less geometry to move through memory, and the corresponding savings in matrix operations, indexed vertex arrays can sometimes outperform display lists. For many real-time applications, indexed vertex arrays are often the method of choice for geometric rendering. As you'll soon see, we can take still one more step forward with our vertex arrays and achieve the fastest possible performance, leaving even display lists in the dust!

Back to the point

With all this multiplication and addition going on, we almost forgot that we were trying to render something! The THUNDERGL sample program is a good opportunity to showcase all we have learned so far in this book. Rather than simply render the model against a blank background, we are going to adapt this model to Chapter 9's CUBEMAP sample program. In addition to a nice skybox for the background, we will make use of cube mapping and multitexture to make the glass canopy really look like a glass canopy.

As in the CUBEMAP sample program, we begin by rendering the skybox using the cube map texture. To render the Thunderbird body, we call the function shown in Listing 11.4.

LISTING 11.4   Code to the Entire Thunderbird Model

```
///////////////////////////////////////////////////////////////////////
// Draw the ThunderBird
void DrawThunderBird(void)
    {
    glEnableClientState(GL_VERTEX_ARRAY);
    glEnableClientState(GL_NORMAL_ARRAY);
    glEnableClientState(GL_TEXTURE_COORD_ARRAY);
```

LISTING 11.4   Continued

```
glActiveTexture(GL_TEXTURE1);
glDisable(GL_TEXTURE_CUBE_MAP);
glActiveTexture(GL_TEXTURE0);

glPushMatrix();
    glRotatef(-90.0f, 1.0f, 0.0f, 0.0f);
    glTexEnvi(GL_TEXTURE_2D, GL_TEXTURE_ENV_MODE, GL_MODULATE);
    glBindTexture(GL_TEXTURE_2D, textureObjects[BODY_TEXTURE]);
    thunderBirdBody.Draw();
glPopMatrix();

glActiveTexture(GL_TEXTURE1);
glEnable(GL_TEXTURE_CUBE_MAP);
glActiveTexture(GL_TEXTURE0);

glEnable(GL_BLEND);
glBlendFunc(GL_SRC_ALPHA, GL_ONE_MINUS_SRC_ALPHA);
glTexEnvi(GL_TEXTURE_ENV, GL_TEXTURE_ENV_MODE, GL_MODULATE);
glBindTexture(GL_TEXTURE_2D, textureObjects[GLASS_TEXTURE]);
glTranslatef(0.0f, 0.132f, 0.555f);
glColor4f(1.0f, 1.0f, 1.0f, 0.25f);

glFrontFace(GL_CW);
thunderBirdGlass.Draw();
glFrontFace(GL_CCW);
thunderBirdGlass.Draw();
glDisable(GL_BLEND);

glDisableClientState(GL_VERTEX_ARRAY);
glDisableClientState(GL_NORMAL_ARRAY);
glDisableClientState(GL_TEXTURE_COORD_ARRAY);
    }
```

The model this time is rendered as an indexed vertex array. Just like non-indexed arrays, we must enable the vertex arrays we want to use:

```
glEnableClientState(GL_VERTEX_ARRAY);
glEnableClientState(GL_NORMAL_ARRAY);
glEnableClientState(GL_TEXTURE_COORD_ARRAY);
```

To render the body, we turn off the cube map that is bound to the second texture unit, and just draw the body, using a modulated texture environment so that the shading of the geometry shows through the texture. We will need to do a small rotation to orient the model the way we want it presented:

```
glActiveTexture(GL_TEXTURE1);
glDisable(GL_TEXTURE_CUBE_MAP);
glActiveTexture(GL_TEXTURE0);

glPushMatrix();
glRotatef(-90.0f, 1.0f, 0.0f, 0.0f);
    glTexEnvi(GL_TEXTURE_2D, GL_TEXTURE_ENV_MODE, GL_MODULATE);
    glBindTexture(GL_TEXTURE_2D, textureObjects[BODY_TEXTURE]);
    thunderBirdBody.Draw();
glPopMatrix();
```

The Draw method of the CTriangleMesh class instance thunderBirdBody simply sets the vertex pointers, and calls glDrawElements.

```
// Draw - make sure you call glEnableClientState for these arrays
void CTriangleMesh::Draw(void) {
    // Here's where the data is now
    glVertexPointer(3, GL_FLOAT,0, pVerts);
    glNormalPointer(GL_FLOAT, 0, pNorms);
    glTexCoordPointer(2, GL_FLOAT, 0, pTexCoords);

    // Draw them
    glDrawElements(GL_TRIANGLES, nNumIndexes, GL_UNSIGNED_INT, pIndexes);
    }
```

The glass canopy is a real showcase item here. First we turn cube mapping back on, but on the second texture unit. We have also previously (not shown here) enabled a reflective texture coordinate generation mode for the cube map on this texture unit.

```
glActiveTexture(GL_TEXTURE1);
glEnable(GL_TEXTURE_CUBE_MAP);
glActiveTexture(GL_TEXTURE0);
```

To draw the canopy transparently, we turn on blending and use the standard transparency blending mode. The alpha value for the material is turned way down to make the glass mostly clear:

```
glEnable(GL_BLEND);
glBlendFunc(GL_SRC_ALPHA, GL_ONE_MINUS_SRC_ALPHA);
glColor4f(1.0f, 1.0f, 1.0f, 0.25f);
glBindTexture(GL_TEXTURE_2D, textureObjects[GLASS_TEXTURE]);
```

Then we make a minor position tweak to the canopy and draw it twice:

```
glTranslatef(0.0f, 0.132f, 0.555f);
```

```
glFrontFace(GL_CW);
thunderBirdGlass.Draw();
glFrontFace(GL_CCW);
thunderBirdGlass.Draw();
glDisable(GL_BLEND);
```

Why did we draw the canopy twice? If you recall from Chapter 6, "More on Colors and Materials," the trick to transparency is to draw the background object first. This is the reason we rendered the plane body first, and the canopy second. Regardless of orientation, the canopy either will be hidden via the depth test behind the plane body, or will be drawn second but in front of the body. But the canopy itself has an inside and an outside visible when you look through it from the outside. The simple trick here is to flip front-facing polygons to GL_CW temporarily and draw the object. This draws the back side of the object first, which is also the part of the object farthest away. Restoring front-facing polygons to GL_CCW and drawing the object again draws just the front side of the object, neatly on top of the just-rendered back side. With blending on during this entire operation, you get a nice transparent piece of glass. With the cube map added in as well, you get a very believable glassy reflective surface. The result is shown in Figure 11.8, and in Color Plate 6. Neither image, however, matches the effect of seeing the animation onscreen.

FIGURE 11.8   The final Thunderbird model. (This figure also appears in the Color insert.)

Vertex Buffer Objects

Display lists are a quick and easy way to optimize immediate mode code (code using glBegin/glEnd). At the very worst, a display list will contain a precompiled set of OpenGL data, ready to be copied quickly to the command buffer, and destined for the graphics hardware. At best, an implementation may copy a display list to the graphics hardware, reducing bandwidth to the hardware to essentially nil. This last scenario is highly desirable, but is a bit of a luck-of-the-draw performance optimization. Display lists are also not terribly flexible after they are created!

Vertex arrays, on the other hand, give us all the flexibility we want, and at worst result in block copies (still much faster than immediate mode) to the hardware. Indexed vertex arrays further up the ante by providing a means of reducing the amount of vertex data that must be transferred to the hardware, and reducing the transformation overhead. For dynamic geometry such as cloth, water, or just trees swaying in the wind, vertex arrays are an obvious choice.

There is one more feature of OpenGL that provides the ultimate control over geometric throughput. When you're using vertex arrays, it is possible to transfer individual arrays from your client (CPU-accessible) memory to the graphics hardware. This feature, *vertex buffer objects*, allow you to use and manage vertex array data in a similar manner to how we load and manage textures. Vertex buffer objects, however, are far more flexible than texture objects.

Managing and Using Buffer Objects

The first step to using vertex buffer objects is to use vertex arrays. We have that well covered at this point. The second step is to create the buffer objects in a manner similar to creating texture objects. To do this, we use the function glGenBuffers:

```
void glGenBuffers(GLsizei n, GLuint *buffers);
```

This function works just like the glGenTextures function covered in Chapter 8, "Texture Mapping: The Basics." The first parameter is the number of buffer objects desired, and the second is an array that is filled with new vertex buffer object names. In an identical way, buffers are released with glDeleteBuffers.

Vertex buffer objects are "bound," again reminding us of the use of texture objects. The function glBindBuffer binds the current state to a particular buffer object:

```
void glBindBuffer(GLenum target, GLuint buffer);
```

Here, target refers to the kind of array being bound (again, similar to texture targets). This may be either GL_ARRAY_BUFFER for vertex data (including normals, texture coordinates, etc.) or GL_ELEMENT_ARRAY_BUFFER for array indexes to be used with glDrawElements and the other index-based rendering functions.

Loading the Buffer Objects

To copy your vertex data to the graphics hardware, you first bind to the buffer object in question, then call glBufferData:

```
void glBufferData(GLenum target, GLsizeiptr size, GLvoid *data, GLenum usage);
```

Again target refers to either GL_ARRAY_BUFFER or GL_ELEMENT_ARRAY_BUFFER, and size refers to the size in bytes of the vertex array. The final parameter is a performance usage hint. This can be any one of the values listed in Table 11.3.

TABLE 11.3   Buffer Object Usage Hints

Usage Hint	Description
GL_DYNAMIC_DRAW	The data stored in the buffer object is likely to change frequently but is likely to be used as a source for drawing several times in between changes. This hint tells the implementation to put the data somewhere it won't be too painful to update once in a while.
GL_STATIC_DRAW	The data stored in the buffer object is unlikely to change and will be used possibly many times as a source for drawing. This hint tells the implementation to put the data somewhere it's quick to draw from, but probably not quick to update.
GL_STREAM_DRAW	The data store in the buffer object is likely to change frequently and will be used only once (or at least very few times) in between changes. This hint tells the implementation that you have time-sensitive data such as animated geometry that will be used once and then replaced. It is crucial that the data be placed somewhere quick to update, even at the expense of faster rendering.

Rendering from VBOs

Two things change when rendering from vertex array objects. First, you must bind to the specific vertex array before calling one of the vertex pointer functions. Second, the actual pointer to the array now becomes an offset into the vertex buffer object. For example,

```
glVertexPointer(3, GL_FLOAT,0, pVerts);
```

now becomes this:

```
glBindBuffer(GL_ARRAY_BUFFER, bufferObjects[0]);
glVertexPointer(3, GL_FLOAT,0,  0);
```

This goes for the rendering call as well; for example:

```
glBindBuffer(GL_ELEMENT_ARRAY_BUFFER, bufferObjects[3]);
glDrawElements(GL_TRIANGLES, nNumIndexes, GL_UNSIGNED_SHORT, 0);
```

This offset into the buffer object is technically an offset based on the native architecture's NULL pointer. On most systems, this is just zero.

Back to the Thunderbird!

Let's apply what we have learned to our Thunderbird model so that we can see all of this in a real context. The sample program VBO from this chapter's sample source code is adapted from the THUNDERGL sample program, but it has been retrofitted to use vertex buffer objects. The only change to the main program's source code is that the CTriangleMesh objects have been replaced with CVBOMesh objects. The CVBOMesh class is nothing more than the CTriangleMesh class revved up to use VBOs. Two small changes were made to the header. We defined four values to represent each of our four arrays:

```
#define VERTEX_DATA     0
#define NORMAL_DATA     1
#define TEXTURE_DATA    2
#define INDEX_DATA      3
```

And we need storage for the four buffer objects:

```
GLuint bufferObjects[4];
```

Initializing the Arrays

The biggest change to the original code is in the EndMesh method, shown in Listing 11.5.

LISTING 11.5   The New End Mesh Method

```
void CVBOMesh::EndMesh(void)
    {
    // Create the buffer objects
    glGenBuffers(4, bufferObjects);

    // Copy data to video memory
    // Vertex data
    glBindBuffer(GL_ARRAY_BUFFER, bufferObjects[VERTEX_DATA]);
    glBufferData(GL_ARRAY_BUFFER, sizeof(GLfloat)*nNumVerts*3,
                                        pVerts, GL_STATIC_DRAW);

    // Normal data
    glBindBuffer(GL_ARRAY_BUFFER, bufferObjects[NORMAL_DATA]);
    glBufferData(GL_ARRAY_BUFFER, sizeof(GLfloat)*nNumVerts*3,
                                        pNorms, GL_STATIC_DRAW);

    // Texture coordinates
    glBindBuffer(GL_ARRAY_BUFFER, bufferObjects[TEXTURE_DATA]);
```

LISTING 11.5   Continued

```
glBufferData(GL_ARRAY_BUFFER, sizeof(GLfloat)*nNumVerts*2,
                                  pTexCoords, GL_STATIC_DRAW);

// Indexes
glBindBuffer(GL_ELEMENT_ARRAY_BUFFER, bufferObjects[INDEX_DATA]);
glBufferData(GL_ELEMENT_ARRAY_BUFFER, sizeof(GLushort)*nNumIndexes,
                                  pIndexes, GL_STATIC_DRAW);

// Free older, larger arrays
delete [] pIndexes;
delete [] pVerts;
delete [] pNorms;
delete [] pTexCoords;

// Reassign pointers so they are marked as unused

pIndexes = NULL;
pVerts = NULL;
pNorms = NULL;
pTexCoords = NULL;
}
```

As outlined in the previous section, each array is loaded individually into its own buffer object. Notice that after the data is copied to the buffer object, the original pointer is no longer needed, and all the working space buffers are deleted. This has three implications. First, it frees up client memory, which you can never have enough of. Second, it consumes memory on the graphics hardware, which you never seem to have enough of! Third, you can no longer make changes to the data, because you no longer have access to it. What about dynamic geometry?

Mixing static and dynamic data

There are two methods of handling dynamic or regularly changing geometry. The first is to simply not use VBOs for the arrays that are being regularly updated. For example, if you have a cloth animation, the texture coordinates on your mesh are unlikely to change frame to frame, whereas the vertices are constantly being updated. You can put the texture coordinates in a VBO, and keep the vertex data in a regular vertex array. After you call glBindBuffer, though, you are bound to a particular VBO. Calling glBindBuffer again switches to another VBO. How then do we "unbind" and go back to regular vertex arrays? Simple, just bind to a NULL buffer:

```
glBindBuffer(GL_ARRAY_BUFFER, 0);
```

If the data doesn't need to be updated all that often, another alternative is to map the buffer back into client memory. This actually comes up in the CVBOMesh class Scale function as shown here:

```
glBindBuffer(GL_ARRAY_BUFFER, bufferObjects[VERTEX_DATA]);
M3DVector3f *pVertexData = (M3DVector3f *)glMapBuffer(GL_ARRAY_BUFFER,
                                                      GL_READ_WRITE);


if(pVertexData != NULL)
    {
    for(int i = 0; i < nNumVerts; i++)
        m3dScaleVector3(pVertexData[i], fScaleValue);

    glUnmapBuffer(GL_ARRAY_BUFFER);
    }
```

The glMapBuffer function returns a pointer that you can use to access the vertex data directly. The second parameter to this function is the access permissions and may be GL_READ_WRITE, GL_WRITE_ONLY, or GL_READ_ONLY. When you do this, you must unmap the buffer with glUnmapBuffer before you can use the buffer object again.

Render!

Finally, we are ready to render our model using vertex buffer objects. Listing 11.6 shows the new and improved Draw method. Now, when you run the sample program VBO (which looks just like THUNDERGL!), both the textures and all the geometry are being rendered on the graphics card from local memory. This is the best possible scenario, because the bandwidth to the hardware is virtually nonexistent compared to using vertex arrays, or using worst-case optimized display lists.

LISTING 11.6   The New and Improved Draw Method

```
void CVBOMesh::Draw(void) {
    // Here's where the data is now
    glBindBuffer(GL_ARRAY_BUFFER, bufferObjects[VERTEX_DATA]);
    glVertexPointer(3, GL_FLOAT,0, 0);

    // Normal data
    glBindBuffer(GL_ARRAY_BUFFER, bufferObjects[NORMAL_DATA]);
    glNormalPointer(GL_FLOAT, 0, 0);

    // Texture coordinates
    glBindBuffer(GL_ARRAY_BUFFER, bufferObjects[TEXTURE_DATA]);
    glTexCoordPointer(2, GL_FLOAT, 0, 0);
```

LISTING 11.6   Continued

```
// Indexes
glBindBuffer(GL_ELEMENT_ARRAY_BUFFER, bufferObjects[INDEX_DATA]);
glDrawElements(GL_TRIANGLES, nNumIndexes, GL_UNSIGNED_SHORT, 0);
}
```

Summary

In this chapter, we focused on different methods of improving geometric throughput. We began with display lists, which are an excellent way to quickly optimize legacy immediate mode rendering code. Display lists, however, can also be used conveniently to store many other OpenGL commands such as state changes, lighting setup, and any other frequently repeated tasks.

By packing all the vertex data together in a single data structure (an array), you enable the OpenGL implementation to make potentially valuable performance optimizations. In addition, you can stream the data to disk and back, thus storing the geometry in a format that is ready for use in OpenGL. Although OpenGL does not have a "model format" as some higher level APIs do, the vertex array construct is certainly a good place to start if you want to build your own.

Generally, you can significantly speed up static geometry by using display lists, and you can use vertex arrays whenever you want dynamic geometry. Index vertex arrays, on the other hand, can potentially (but not always) give you the best of both worlds—flexible geometry data and highly efficient memory transfer and geometric processing. For many applications, vertex arrays are used almost exclusively. However, the old glBegin/glEnd construct still has many uses, besides allowing you to create display lists—anytime the amount of geometry fluctuates dynamically from frame to frame, for example. There is little benefit to continually rebuilding a small vertex array from scratch rather than letting the driver do the work with glBegin/glEnd.

Finally, we learned to use vertex buffer objects to get the best possible optimization we can hope for with display lists (storing the geometry on the hardware) yet have the great flexibility of using vertex arrays. We've seen that the best possible way to render static geometry is to represent it as an indexed vertex array, and store it on your graphics card via VBOs. Still, we have only scratched the surface of OpenGL's rich buffer object feature set. In Chapter 18, "Advanced Buffers," you'll learn some more powerful optimizations and whole new capabilities made possible by the ideas introduced in this chapter.

CHAPTER 12

Interactive Graphics

by Richard S. Wright Jr.

WHAT YOU'LL LEARN IN THIS CHAPTER:

How To	Functions You'll Use
Assign OpenGL selection names to primitives or groups of primitives	glInitNames/glPushName/glPopName
Use selection to determine which objects are under the mouse	glSelectBuffer/glRenderMode
Use feedback to get information about where objects are drawn	glFeedbackBuffer/gluPickMatrix

Thus far, you have learned to create some sophisticated 3D graphics using OpenGL, and many applications do no more than generate these scenes. But many graphics applications (notably, games, CAD, 3D modeling, and so on) require more interaction with the scene itself. In addition to menus and dialog boxes, often you need to provide a way for the user to interact with a graphical scene. Typically, this interaction usually happens with a mouse.

Selection, a powerful feature of OpenGL, allows you to take a mouse click at some position over a window and determine which of your objects are beneath it. The act of selecting a specific object on the screen is called *picking*. With OpenGL's selection feature, you can specify a viewing volume and determine which objects fall within that viewing volume. A powerful utility function, gluPickMatrix, produces a matrix for you, based purely on screen coordinates and the pixel dimensions you specify; you use this matrix to create a smaller viewing volume placed beneath the mouse cursor. Then you use selection to test this viewing volume to see which objects are contained by it.

Feedback allows you to get information from OpenGL about how your vertices are transformed and illuminated when they are drawn to the frame buffer. You can use this information to transmit rendering results over a network, send them to a plotter, or add other graphics (say, with GDI, for Windows programmers) to your OpenGL scene that appear to interact with the OpenGL objects. Feedback does not serve the same purpose as selection, but the mode of operation is similar and they can work productively together. You'll see this teamwork later in the SELECT sample program.

Selection

Selection is actually a rendering mode, but in selection mode, no pixels are actually copied to the frame buffer. Instead, primitives that are drawn within the viewing volume (and thus would normally appear in the frame buffer) produce hit records in a selection buffer. This buffer, unlike other OpenGL buffers, is just an array of integer values.

You must set up this selection buffer in advance and name your primitives or groups of primitives (your objects or models) so they can be identified in the selection buffer. You then parse the selection buffer to determine which objects intersected the viewing volume. Named objects that do not appear in the selection buffer fell outside the viewing volume and would not have been drawn in render mode. Although selection mode is fast enough for object picking, using it for general-purpose frustum-culling performs significantly slower than any of the techniques we discussed in Chapter 11, "It's All About the Pipeline: Faster Geometry Throughput." For picking, you specify a viewing volume that corresponds to a small space beneath the mouse pointer and then check which named objects are rendered within that space.

Naming Your Primitives

You can name every single primitive used to render your scene of objects, but doing so is rarely useful. More often, you name groups of primitives, thus creating names for the specific objects or pieces of objects in your scene. Object names, like display list names, are nothing more than unsigned integers.

The names list is maintained on the name stack. After you initialize the name stack, you can push names on the stack or simply replace the name currently on top of the stack. When a hit occurs during selection, all the names currently on the name stack are appended to the end of the selection buffer. Thus, a single hit can return more than one name if needed.

For our first example, we keep things simple. We create a simplified (and not-to-scale) model of the inner planets of the solar system. When the left mouse button is down, we display a message in the window caption naming which planet was clicked. Listing 12.1 shows some of the rendering code for our sample program PLANETS. We have created macro definitions for the sun, Mercury, Venus, Earth, and Mars.

LISTING 12.1   Naming the Sun and Planets in the PLANETS Program

```
/////////////////////////////
// Define object names
#define SUN        1
#define MERCURY    2
#define VENUS      3
#define EARTH      4
#define MARS       5


///////////////////////////////////////////////////////////
// Called to draw scene
void RenderScene(void)
    {
    // Clear the window with current clearing color
    glClear(GL_COLOR_BUFFER_BIT | GL_DEPTH_BUFFER_BIT);

    // Save the matrix state and do the rotations
    glMatrixMode(GL_MODELVIEW);
    glPushMatrix();

        // Translate the whole scene out and into view
        glTranslatef(0.0f, 0.0f, -300.0f);

        // Initialize the names stack
        glInitNames();
        glPushName(0);


        // Name and draw the sun
        glColor3f(1.0f, 1.0f, 0.0f);
        glLoadName(SUN);
        DrawSphere(15.0f);

        // Draw Mercury
        glColor3f(0.5f, 0.0f, 0.0f);
        glPushMatrix();
            glTranslatef(24.0f, 0.0f, 0.0f);
            glLoadName(MERCURY);
            DrawSphere(2.0f);
        glPopMatrix();

        // Draw Venus
        glColor3f(0.5f, 0.5f, 1.0f);
```

LISTING 12.1   Continued

```
    glPushMatrix();
        glTranslatef(60.0f, 0.0f, 0.0f);
        glLoadName(VENUS);
        DrawSphere(4.0f);
    glPopMatrix();

    // Draw the earth
    glColor3f(0.0f, 0.0f, 1.0f);
    glPushMatrix();
        glTranslatef(100.0f,0.0f,0.0f);
        glLoadName(EARTH);
        DrawSphere(8.0f);
    glPopMatrix();

    // Draw Mars
    glColor3f(1.0f, 0.0f, 0.0f);
    glPushMatrix();
        glTranslatef(150.0f, 0.0f, 0.0f);
        glLoadName(MARS);
        DrawSphere(4.0f);
    glPopMatrix();

// Restore the matrix state
glPopMatrix();    // Modelview matrix

glutSwapBuffers();
}
```

In PLANETS, the `glInitNames` function initializes and clears the name stack, and `glPushName` pushes 0 on the stack to put at least one entry on the stack. For the sun and each planet, we call `glLoadName` to name the object or objects about to be drawn. This name, in the form of an unsigned integer, is not pushed on the name stack but rather replaces the current name on top of the stack. Later, we discuss keeping an actual stack of names. For now, we just replace the top name of the name stack each time we draw an object (the sun or a particular planet).

Working with Selection Mode

As mentioned previously, OpenGL can operate in three different rendering modes. The default mode is `GL_RENDER`, in which all the drawing actually occurs onscreen. To use selection, we must change the rendering mode to selection by calling the OpenGL function:

```
glRenderMode(GL_SELECTION);
```

When we actually want to draw again, we use the following call to place OpenGL back in rendering mode:

```
glRenderMode(GL_RENDER);
```

The third rendering mode is GL_FEEDBACK, discussed later in this chapter.

The naming code in Listing 12.1 has no effect unless we first switch the rendering mode to selection mode. Conveniently, you call the same function to render the scene in both GL_RENDER mode and GL_SELECTION mode, as we have done here.

Listing 12.2 provides the GLUT callback code triggered by the clicking of the left mouse button. This code checks for a left button click and then forwards the mouse coordinates to ProcessSelection, which processes the mouse click for this example.

LISTING 12.2   Code That Responds to the Left Mouse Button Click

```
/////////////////////////////////////////////////////////
// Process the mouse click
void MouseCallback(int button, int state, int x, int y)
    {
    if(button == GLUT_LEFT_BUTTON && state == GLUT_DOWN)
        ProcessSelection(x, y);
    }
```

The Selection Buffer

The selection buffer is filled with hit records during the rendering process. A hit record is generated whenever a primitive or collection of primitives is rendered that would have been contained in the viewing volume. Under normal conditions, this is simply anything that would have appeared onscreen.

The selection buffer is an array of unsigned integers, and each hit record occupies at least four elements of the array. The first array index contains the number of names that are on the name stack when the hit occurs. For the PLANETS example (Listing 12.1), this is always 1, because we never really push anything else on top of the name stack. The next two entries contain the minimum and maximum window z coordinates of all the vertices contained by the viewing volume since the last hit record. This value, which ranges [0,1], is scaled to the maximum size of an unsigned integer for storage in the selection buffer. The fourth entry is the bottom of the name stack. If more than one name appears on the name stack (indicated by the first index element), they follow the fourth element. This pattern, illustrated in Figure 12.1, is then repeated for all the hit records contained in the selection buffer. We explain why this pattern can be useful when we discuss picking.

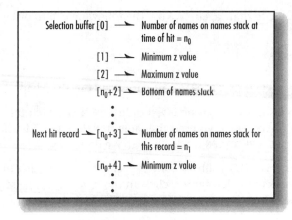

Selection buffer [0] → Number of names on names stack at time of hit = n_0

[1] → Minimum z value

[2] → Maximum z value

$[n_0+2]$ → Bottom of names stack

Next hit record → $[n_0+3]$ → Number of names on names stack for this record = n_1

$[n_0+4]$ → Minimum z value

FIGURE 12.1   Hit record for the selection buffer.

The format of the selection buffer gives you no way of knowing how many hit records you need to parse. The selection buffer is not actually filled until you switch the rendering mode back to GL_RENDER. When you do this with the glRenderMode function, the return value is the number of hit records copied.

Listing 12.3 shows the processing function called when a mouse click occurs for the PLANETS sample program. It shows the selection buffer being allocated and specified with glSelectBuffer. This function takes two arguments: the length of the buffer and a pointer to the buffer itself. You must make sure that you allocate enough elements ahead of time to contain all your hit records. If you do not, the call to glRenderMode will return −1 and the buffer contents will be invalid.

LISTING 12.3   Function to Process the Mouse Click

```
//////////////////////////////////////////////////////////
// Process the selection, which is triggered by a right mouse
// click at (xPos, yPos).
#define BUFFER_LENGTH 64
void ProcessSelection(int xPos, int yPos)
    {
    GLfloat fAspect;

    // Space for selection buffer
    static GLuint selectBuff[BUFFER_LENGTH];

    // Hit counter and viewport storage
    GLint hits, viewport[4];
```

LISTING 12.3 Continued

```
// Set up selection buffer
glSelectBuffer(BUFFER_LENGTH, selectBuff);

// Get the viewport
glGetIntegerv(GL_VIEWPORT, viewport);

// Switch to projection and save the matrix
glMatrixMode(GL_PROJECTION);
glPushMatrix();

// Change render mode
glRenderMode(GL_SELECT);

// Establish new clipping volume to be unit cube around
// mouse cursor point (xPos, yPos) and extending two pixels
// in the vertical and horizontal direction
glLoadIdentity();
gluPickMatrix(xPos, viewport[3] - yPos + viewport[1], 2,2, viewport);

// Apply perspective matrix
fAspect = (float)viewport[2] / (float)viewport[3];
gluPerspective(45.0f, fAspect, 1.0, 425.0);

// Draw the scene
RenderScene();

// Collect the hits
hits = glRenderMode(GL_RENDER);

// If a single hit occurred, display the info.
if(hits == 1)
    ProcessPlanet(selectBuff[3]);

// Restore the projection matrix
glMatrixMode(GL_PROJECTION);
glPopMatrix();

// Go back to modelview for normal rendering
glMatrixMode(GL_MODELVIEW);
    }
```

12

Picking

Picking occurs when you use the mouse position to create and use a modified viewing volume during selection. When you create a smaller viewing volume positioned in your scene under the mouse position, only objects that would be drawn within that viewing volume generate hit records. By examining the selection buffer, you can then see which objects, if any, were clicked on by the mouse.

The `gluPickMatrix` function is a handy utility that creates a matrix describing the new viewing volume:

```
void gluPickMatrix(GLdouble x, GLdouble y, GLdouble width,
                              GLdouble height, GLint viewport[4]);
```

The *x* and *y* parameters are the center of the desired viewing volume in OpenGL window coordinates. You can plug in the mouse position here, and the viewing volume will be centered directly underneath the mouse. The *width* and *height* parameters then specify the dimensions of the viewing volume in window pixels. For clicks near an object, use a large value; for clicks next to the object or directly on the object, use a smaller value. The *viewport* array contains the window coordinates of the currently defined viewport. You can easily obtain this information by calling

```
glGetIntegerv(GL_VIEWPORT, viewport);
```

Remember, as discussed in Chapter 2, "Using OpenGL," that OpenGL window coordinates are the opposite of most systems' window coordinates with respect to the way pixels are counted vertically. Note in Listing 12.3, we subtract the mouse y coordinate from the viewport's height. This yields the proper vertical window coordinate for OpenGL:

```
gluPickMatrix(xPos, viewport[3] - yPos + viewport[1], 2,2, viewport);
```

To use `gluPickMatrix`, you should first save the current projection matrix state (thus saving the current viewing volume). Then call `glLoadIdentity` to create a unit-viewing volume. Calling `gluPickMatrix` then translates this viewing volume to the correct location. Finally, you must apply any further perspective projections you may have applied to your original scene; otherwise, you won't get a true mapping. Here's how it's done for the PLANETS example (from Listing 12.3):

```
// Switch to projection and save the matrix
glMatrixMode(GL_PROJECTION);
glPushMatrix();

// Change render mode
glRenderMode(GL_SELECT);

// Establish new clipping volume to be unit cube around
// mouse cursor point (xPos, yPos) and extending two pixels
```

```
// in the vertical and horizontal direction
glLoadIdentity();
gluPickMatrix(xPos, viewport[3] - yPos + viewport[1], 2,2, viewport);

// Apply perspective matrix (this must MATCH the same call when used
// to set up the scene).
fAspect = (float)viewport[2] / (float)viewport[3];
gluPerspective(45.0f, fAspect, 1.0, 425.0);

// Draw the scene
RenderScene();

// Collect the hits
hits = glRenderMode(GL_RENDER);
```

In this segment, the viewing volume is saved first. Then the selection mode is entered, the viewing volume is modified to include only the area beneath the mouse cursor, and the scene is redrawn via a call to RenderScene. After the scene is rendered, we call glRenderMode again to place OpenGL back into normal rendering mode and get a count of generated hit records.

In the next segment, if a hit occurred (for this example, there is either one hit or none), we pass the entry in the selection buffer that contains the name of the object selected or our ProcessPlanet function. Finally, we restore the projection matrix (thus, the old viewing volume is restored) and switch the active matrix stack back to the modelview matrix, which is usually the default:

```
// If a single hit occurred, display the info.
if(hits == 1)
    ProcessPlanet(selectBuff[3]);

// Restore the projection matrix
glMatrixMode(GL_PROJECTION);
glPopMatrix();

// Go back to modelview for normal rendering
glMatrixMode(GL_MODELVIEW);
```

The ProcessPlanet function simply displays a message in the window's caption telling which planet was clicked. This code is not shown because it is fairly trivial, consisting of no more than a switch statement and some glutSetWindowTitle function calls.

The output from PLANETS is shown in Figure 12.2, where you can see the result of clicking the second planet from the sun.

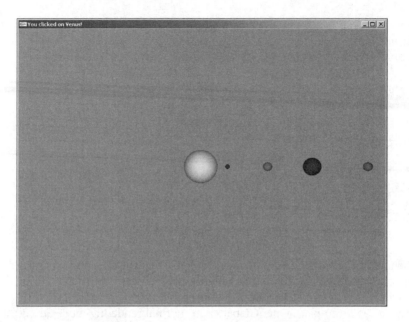

FIGURE 12.2   Output from PLANETS after a planet is clicked.

Although we don't go into any great detail here, it is worth discussing briefly the z values from the selection buffer. In the PLANETS example, each object or model was distinct and off alone in its own space. What if you apply this same method to several objects or models that perhaps overlap? You get multiple hit records! How do you know which one the user clicked? This situation can be tricky and requires some forethought. You can use the z values to determine which object was closest to the user in viewspace, which is the most likely object that was clicked. Still, for some shapes and geometry, if you aren't careful, it can be difficult to sort out precisely what the user intended to pick.

Hierarchical Picking

For the PLANETS example, we didn't push any names on the stack, but rather just replaced the existing one whenever a new object was to be rendered. This single name residing on the name stack was the only name returned in the selection buffer. We can also get multiple names when a selection hit occurs, by placing more than one name on the name stack. This capability is useful, for instance, in drill-down situations when you need to know not only that a particular bolt was selected, but also that it belonged to a particular wheel, on a particular car, and so forth.

To demonstrate multiple names being returned on the name stack, we stick with the astronomy theme of our previous example. Figure 12.3 shows two planets (okay, so use a little imagination)—a large blue planet with a single moon and a smaller red planet with two moons.

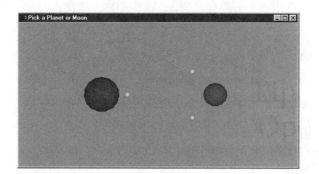

FIGURE 12.3   Two planets with their respective moons.

Rather than just identify the planet or moon that is clicked, we want to also identify the planet that is associated with the particular moon. The code in Listing 12.4 shows our new rendering code for this scene. We push the names of the moons onto the name stack so that it contains the name of the planet as well as the name of the moon when selected.

LISTING 12.4   Rendering Code for the MOONS Sample Program

```
/////////////////////////////
// Define object names
#define EARTH    1
#define MARS     2
#define MOON1    3
#define MOON2    4


/////////////////////////////////////////////////////////////
// Called to draw scene
void RenderScene(void)
    {
    // Clear the window with current clearing color
    glClear(GL_COLOR_BUFFER_BIT | GL_DEPTH_BUFFER_BIT);

    // Save the matrix state and do the rotations
    glMatrixMode(GL_MODELVIEW);
    glPushMatrix();

    // Translate the whole scene out and into view
    glTranslatef(0.0f, 0.0f, -300.0f);

    // Initialize the names stack
```

LISTING 12.4   Continued

```
glInitNames();
glPushName(0);


// Draw the earth
glPushMatrix();
glColor3f(0.0f, 0.0f, 1.0f);
glTranslatef(-100.0f,0.0f,0.0f);
glLoadName(EARTH);
DrawSphere(30.0f);

// Draw the moon
glTranslatef(45.0f, 0.0f, 0.0f);
glColor3f(0.85f, 0.85f, 0.85f);
glPushName(MOON1);
DrawSphere(5.0f);
glPopName();
glPopMatrix();

// Draw Mars
glPushMatrix();
glColor3f(1.0f, 0.0f, 0.0f);
glTranslatef(100.0f, 0.0f, 0.0f);
glLoadName(MARS);
DrawSphere(20.0f);

// Draw Moon1
glTranslatef(-40.0f, 40.0f, 0.0f);
glColor3f(0.85f, 0.85f, 0.85f);
glPushName(MOON1);
DrawSphere(5.0f);
glPopName();

// Draw Moon2
glTranslatef(0.0f, -80.0f, 0.0f);
glPushName(MOON2);
DrawSphere(5.0f);
glPopName();
glPopMatrix();
```

LISTING 12.4   Continued

```
   // Restore the matrix state
   glPopMatrix();    // Modelview matrix

glutSwapBuffers();
   }
```

Now in our `ProcessSelection` function, we still call the `ProcessPlanet` function that we wrote, but this time, we pass the entire selection buffer:

```
// If a single hit occurred, display the info.
if(hits == 1)
    ProcessPlanet(selectBuff);
```

Listing 12.5 shows the more substantial `ProcessPlanet` function for this example. In this instance, the bottom name on the name stack is always the name of the planet because it was pushed on first. If a moon is clicked, it is also on the name stack. This function displays the name of the planet selected, and if it was a moon, that information is also displayed. Sample output is shown in Figure 12.4.

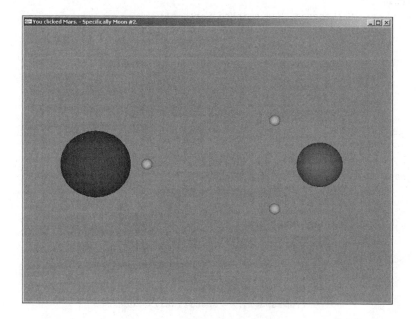

FIGURE 12.4   Sample output from the MOONS sample program.

LISTING 12.5   Code That Parses the Selection Buffer for the MOONS Sample Program

```
/////////////////////////////////////////////////////////
// Parse the selection buffer to see which
// planet/moon was selected
void ProcessPlanet(GLuint *pSelectBuff)
    {
    int id,count;
    char cMessage[64];
    strcpy(cMessage,"Error, no selection detected");

    // How many names on the name stack
    count = pSelectBuff[0];

    // Bottom of the name stack
    id = pSelectBuff[3];

    // Select on Earth or Mars, whichever was picked
    switch(id)
        {
        case EARTH:
            strcpy(cMessage,"You clicked Earth.");

            // If there is another name on the name stack,
            // then it must be the moon that was selected
            // This is what was actually clicked on
            if(count == 2)
                strcat(cMessage," - Specifically the moon.");

            break;

        case MARS:
            strcpy(cMessage,"You clicked Mars.");

            // We know the name stack is only two deep. The precise
            // moon that was selected will be here.
            if(count == 2)
                {
                if(pSelectBuff[4] == MOON1)
                    strcat(cMessage," - Specifically Moon #1.");
                else
                    strcat(cMessage," - Specifically Moon #2.");
                }
            break;
```

LISTING 12.5   Continued

```
    }

// Display the message about planet and moon selection
glutSetWindowTitle(cMessage);
    }
```

Feedback

Feedback, like selection, is a rendering mode that does not produce output in the form of pixels on the screen. Instead, information is written to a feedback buffer indicating how the scene would have been rendered. This information includes transformed vertex data in window coordinates, color data resulting from lighting calculations, and texture data—essentially everything needed to rasterize the primitives.

You enter feedback mode the same way you enter selection mode, by calling `glRenderMode` with a `GL_FEEDBACK` argument. You must reset the rendering mode to `GL_RENDER` to fill the feedback buffer and return to normal rendering mode.

The Feedback Buffer

The feedback buffer is an array of floating-point values specified with the `glFeedbackBuffer` function:

```
void glFeedbackBuffer(GLsizei size, GLenum type, GLfloat *buffer);
```

This function takes the size of the feedback buffer, the type and amount of drawing information wanted, and a pointer to the buffer itself.

Valid values for *type* appear in Table 12.1. The type of data specifies how much data is placed in the feedback buffer for each vertex. Color data is represented by a single value in color index mode or four values for RGBA color mode.

TABLE 12.1   Feedback Buffer Types

Color Data	Vertex Texture Data	Total Values	Type	Coordinates
GL_2D	x, y	N/A	N/A	2
GL_3D	x, y, z	N/A	N/A	3
GL_3D_COLOR	x, y, z	C	N/A	3 + C
GL_3D_COLOR_TEXTURE	x, y, z	C	4	7 + C
GL_4D_COLOR_TEXTURE	x, y, z, w	C	4	8 + C

Feedback Data

The feedback buffer contains a list of tokens followed by vertex data and possibly color and texture data. You can parse for these tokens (see Table 12.2) to determine the types of primitives that would have been rendered. One limitation of feedback occurs when using multiple texture units. In this case, only texture coordinates from the first texture unit are returned.

TABLE 12.2   Feedback Buffer Tokens

Token	Primitive
GL_POINT_TOKEN	Points
GL_LINE_TOKEN	Line
GL_LINE_RESET_TOKEN	Line segment when line stipple is reset
GL_POLYGON_TOKEN	Polygon
GL_BITMAP_TOKEN	Bitmap
GL_DRAW_PIXEL_TOKEN	Pixel rectangle drawn
GL_COPY_PIXEL_TOKEN	Pixel rectangle copied
GL_PASS_THROUGH_TOKEN	User-defined marker

The point, bitmap, and pixel tokens are followed by data for a single vertex and possibly color and texture data. This depends on the data type from Table 12.1 specified in the call to glFeedbackBuffer. The line tokens return two sets of vertex data, and the polygon token is immediately followed by the number of vertices that follow. The user-defined marker (GL_PASS_THROUGH_TOKEN) is followed by a single floating-point value that is user defined. Figure 12.5 shows an example of a feedback buffer's memory layout if a GL_3D type were specified. Here, we see the data for a point, token, and polygon rendered in that order.

```
Feedback buffer  [0]  – GL_POINT_TOKEN
                 [1]  – x coordinate
                 [2]  – y coordinate
                 [3]  – x coordinate
                 [4]  – GL_PASS_THROUGH_TOKEN
                 [5]  – User-defined value
                 [6]  – GL_POLYGON_TOKEN
                 [7]  – Number of vertices
                 [8]  – x coordinate of first vertex
                 [9]  – y coordinate of first vertex
                 [10] – z coordinate of first vertex
                 [11] – x coordinate of second vertex
                  ...
                  ...
                 [n]  z coordinate of last vertex
```

FIGURE 12.5   A sample memory layout for a feedback buffer.

Passthrough Markers

When your rendering code is executing, the feedback buffer is filled with tokens and vertex data as each primitive is specified. Just as you can in selection mode, you can flag certain primitives by naming them. In feedback mode, you can set markers between your primitives, as well. You do so by calling glPassThrough:

```
void glPassThrough(GLfloat token);
```

This function places a GL_PASS_THROUGH_TOKEN in the feedback buffer, followed by the value you specify when calling the function. This process is somewhat similar to naming primitives in selection mode. It's the only way of labeling objects in the feedback buffer.

A Feedback Example

An excellent use of feedback is to obtain window coordinate information regarding any objects you render. You can then use this information to place controls or labels near the objects in the window or other windows around them.

To demonstrate feedback, we use selection to determine which of two objects on the screen has been clicked by the user. Then we enter feedback mode and render the scene again to obtain the vertex information in window coordinates. Using this data, we determine the minimum and maximum x and y values for the object and use those values to draw a focus rectangle around the object. The result is graphical selection and deselection of one or both objects.

Label the Objects for Feedback

Listing 12.6 shows the rendering code for our sample program SELECT. Don't confuse this example with a demonstration of selection mode! Even though selection mode is employed in our example to select an object on the screen, we are demonstrating the process of getting enough information about that object—using feedback—to draw a rectangle around it using OpenGL lines in a 2D orthographic projection. Notice the use of glPassThrough to label the objects in the feedback buffer, right after the calls to glLoadName to label the objects in the selection buffer. Because these functions are ignored when the render mode is GL_RENDER, they have an effect only when rendering for selection or feedback.

LISTING 12.6   Rendering Code for the SELECT Sample Program

```
/////////////////////////
// Object Names
#define TORUS    1
#define SPHERE    2


/////////////////////////////////////////////////////////////
```

LISTING 12.6   Continued

```
// Render the torus and sphere
void DrawObjects(void)
    {
    // Save the matrix state and do the rotations
    glMatrixMode(GL_MODELVIEW);
    glPushMatrix();

    // Translate the whole scene out and into view
    glTranslatef(-0.75f, 0.0f, -2.5f);

    // Initialize the names stack
    glInitNames();
    glPushName(0);

    // Set material color, Yellow
    // torus
    glColor3f(1.0f, 1.0f, 0.0f);
    glLoadName(TORUS);
    glPassThrough((GLfloat)TORUS);
    DrawTorus(40, 20);


    // Draw Sphere
    glColor3f(0.5f, 0.0f, 0.0f);
    glTranslatef(1.5f, 0.0f, 0.0f);
    glLoadName(SPHERE);
    glPassThrough((GLfloat)SPHERE);
    DrawSphere(0.5f);

    // Restore the matrix state
    glPopMatrix();    // Modelview matrix
}


//////////////////////////////////////////////////////////
// Called to draw scene
void RenderScene(void)
    {
    // Clear the window with current clearing color
    glClear(GL_COLOR_BUFFER_BIT | GL_DEPTH_BUFFER_BIT);

    // Draw the objects in the scene
    DrawObjects();
```

LISTING 12.6   Continued

```
    // If something is selected, draw a bounding box around it
    if(selectedObject != 0)
        {
        int viewport[4];

        // Get the viewport
        glGetIntegerv(GL_VIEWPORT, viewport);

        // Remap the viewing volume to match window coordinates (approximately)
        glMatrixMode(GL_PROJECTION);
        glPushMatrix();
        glLoadIdentity();

        // Establish clipping volume (left, right, bottom, top, near, far)
        glOrtho(viewport[0], viewport[2], viewport[3], viewport[1], -1, 1);
        glMatrixMode(GL_MODELVIEW);

        glDisable(GL_LIGHTING);
        glColor3f(1.0f, 0.0f, 0.0f);
        glBegin(GL_LINE_LOOP);
            glVertex2i(boundingRect.left, boundingRect.top);
            glVertex2i(boundingRect.left, boundingRect.bottom);
            glVertex2i(boundingRect.right, boundingRect.bottom);
            glVertex2i(boundingRect.right, boundingRect.top);
        glEnd();
        glEnable(GL_LIGHTING);
        }

    glMatrixMode(GL_PROJECTION);
    glPopMatrix();
    glMatrixMode(GL_MODELVIEW);

    glutSwapBuffers();
    }
```

For this example, the rendering code is broken into two functions: RenderScene and
DrawObjects. RenderScene is our normal top-level rendering function, but we have moved
the actual drawing of the objects that we may select to outside this function. The
RenderScene function draws the objects, but it also draws the bounding rectangle around
an object if it is selected. selectedObject is a variable we will use in a moment to indicate
which object is currently selected.

Step 1: Select the Object

Figure 12.6 shows the output from this rendering code, displaying a torus and sphere. When the user clicks one of the objects, the function ProcessSelection is called (see Listing 12.7). This is similar to the selection code in the previous two examples (in Listings 12.3 and 12.5).

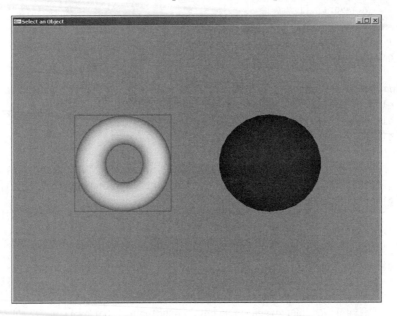

FIGURE 12.6   Output from the SELECT program after the sphere has been clicked.

LISTING 12.7   Selection Processing for the SELECT Sample Program

```
/////////////////////////////////////////////////////////
// Process the selection, which is triggered by a right mouse
// click at (xPos, yPos).
#define BUFFER_LENGTH 64
void ProcessSelection(int xPos, int yPos)
    {
    // Space for selection buffer
    static GLuint selectBuff[BUFFER_LENGTH];

    // Hit counter and viewport storage
    GLint hits, viewport[4];

    // Set up selection buffer
    glSelectBuffer(BUFFER_LENGTH, selectBuff);

    // Get the viewport
```

LISTING 12.7   Continued

```
glGetIntegerv(GL_VIEWPORT, viewport);

// Switch to projection and save the matrix
glMatrixMode(GL_PROJECTION);
glPushMatrix();

// Change render mode
glRenderMode(GL_SELECT);

// Establish new clipping volume to be unit cube around
// mouse cursor point (xPos, yPos) and extending two pixels
// in the vertical and horizontal direction
glLoadIdentity();
gluPickMatrix(xPos, viewport[3] - yPos + viewport[1], 2,2, viewport);

// Apply perspective matrix
gluPerspective(60.0f, fAspect, 1.0, 425.0);

// Draw the scene
DrawObjects();

// Collect the hits
hits = glRenderMode(GL_RENDER);

// Restore the projection matrix
glMatrixMode(GL_PROJECTION);
glPopMatrix();

// Go back to modelview for normal rendering
glMatrixMode(GL_MODELVIEW);

// If a single hit occurred, display the info.
if(hits == 1)
    {
    MakeSelection(selectBuff[3]);
    if(selectedObject == selectBuff[3])
        selectedObject = 0;
    else
        selectedObject = selectBuff[3];
    }

glutPostRedisplay();
    }
```

Step 2: Get Feedback on the Object

Now that we have determined which object was clicked (we saved this in the selectedObject variable), we set up the feedback buffer and render again in feedback mode. Listing 12.8 shows the code that sets up feedback mode for this example and calls DrawObjects to redraw just the torus and sphere scene. This time, however, the glPassThrough functions put markers for the objects in the feedback buffer. Similar to the case of the selection buffer, if you do not allocate enough space for all the data when you call glFeedbackBuffer, glRenderMode will return –1 indicating an error.

LISTING 12.8   Load and Parse the Feedback Buffer

```
/////////////////////////////////////////////////////////
// Go into feedback mode and draw a rectangle around the object
// We need a large buffer to hold all the vertex data!
#define FEED_BUFF_SIZE      32768
void MakeSelection(int nChoice)
    {
    // Space for the feedback buffer
    static GLfloat feedBackBuff[FEED_BUFF_SIZE];

    // Storage for counters, etc.
    int size,i,j,count;

    // Initial minimum and maximum values
    boundingRect.right = boundingRect.bottom = -999999.0f;
    boundingRect.left = boundingRect.top =  999999.0f;

    // Set the feedback buffer
    glFeedbackBuffer(FEED_BUFF_SIZE,GL_2D, feedBackBuff);

    // Enter feedback mode
    glRenderMode(GL_FEEDBACK);

    // Redraw the scene
    DrawObjects();

    // Leave feedback mode
    size = glRenderMode(GL_RENDER);

    // Parse the feedback buffer and get the
    // min and max X and Y window coordinates
    i = 0;
    while(i < size)
        {
```

LISTING 12.8   Continued

```
        // Search for appropriate token
    if(feedBackBuff[i] == GL_PASS_THROUGH_TOKEN)
        if(feedBackBuff[i+1] == (GLfloat)nChoice)
        {
        i+= 2;
        // Loop until next token is reached
        while(i < size && feedBackBuff[i] != GL_PASS_THROUGH_TOKEN)
            {
            // Just get the polygons
            if(feedBackBuff[i] == GL_POLYGON_TOKEN)
                {
                // Get all the values for this polygon
                count = (int)feedBackBuff[++i]; // How many vertices
                i++;

                for(j = 0; j < count; j++)    // Loop for each vertex
                    {
                    // Min and Max X
                    if(feedBackBuff[i] > boundingRect.right)
                        boundingRect.right = feedBackBuff[i];

                    if(feedBackBuff[i] < boundingRect.left)
                        boundingRect.left = feedBackBuff[i];
                    i++;

                    // Min and Max Y
                    if(feedBackBuff[i] > boundingRect.bottom)
                        boundingRect.bottom = feedBackBuff[i];

                    if(feedBackBuff[i] < boundingRect.top)
                        boundingRect.top = feedBackBuff[i];
                    i++;
                    }
                }
            else
                i++;     // Get next index and keep looking
            }
        break;
        }
    i++;
    }
}
```

When the feedback buffer is filled, we search it for GL_PASS_THROUGH_TOKEN. When we find one, we get the next value and determine whether it is the one we are looking for. If so, the only task that remains is to loop through all the polygons for this object and get the minimum and maximum window x and y values. These values are stored in the boundingRect structure and then used by the RenderScene function to draw a focus rectangle around the selected object.

Summary

Selection and feedback are two powerful features of OpenGL that enable you to facilitate the user's active interaction with a scene. Selection and picking are used to identify an object or region of a scene in OpenGL coordinates rather than just window coordinates. Feedback returns valuable information about how an object or a primitive is actually drawn in the window. You can use this information to implement features such as annotations or bounding boxes in your scene.

The reader should note that the features in this chapter are typically implemented in software (the driver), even for hardware accelerated OpenGL implementations. This means that rendering in selection mode, for example, will be very slow compared to hardware rendering. A common means of accounting for this is to render lower resolution "proxies," and render only objects that can be clicked on when performing selection. There are more advanced means of determining object selection that may be preferable for real-time picking. Some of the 3D math books in Appendix A would be a good place to start. Using the techniques in this chapter makes adding this kind of functionality to your application fairly straightforward. You may also find that even with software rendering, the response time from mouse click may be more than fast enough for most purposes.

CHAPTER 13

Occlusion Queries: Why Do More Work Than You Need To?

by Benjamin Lipchak

WHAT YOU'LL LEARN IN THIS CHAPTER:

How To	Functions You'll Use
Create and delete query objects	glGenQueries/glDeleteQueries
Define bounding box occlusion queries	glBeginQuery/glEndQuery
Retrieve the results from an occlusion query	glGetQueryObjectiv

Complex scenes contain hundreds of objects and thousands upon thousands of polygons. Consider the room you're in now, reading this book. Look at all the furniture, objects, and other people or pets, and think of the rendering power needed to accurately represent their complexity. Several readers will find themselves happily sitting on a crate near a computer in an empty studio apartment, but the rest will envision a significant rendering workload around them.

Now think of all the things you can't see: objects hidden behind other objects, in drawers, or even in the next room. From most viewpoints, these objects are invisible to the viewer. If you rendered the scene, the objects would be drawn, but eventually something would draw over the top of them. Why bother doing all that work for nothing?

Enter occlusion queries. In this chapter, we describe a powerful new feature included in OpenGL 1.5 that can save a tremendous amount of vertex and pixel processing at the expense of a bit of extra nontextured fill rate. Often this trade-off is a very favorable one. We explore the use of occlusion detection and witness the dramatic increase in frame rates this technique affords.

The World Before Occlusion Queries

To show off the improved performance possible through the use of occlusion queries, we need an experimental control group. We'll draw a scene without any fancy occlusion detection. The scene is contrived so that there are plenty of objects both visible and hidden at any given time.

First, we'll draw the "main occluder." An *occluder* is a large object in a scene that tends to occlude, or hide, other objects in the scene. An occluder is often low in detail, whereas the objects it occludes may be much higher in detail. Good examples are walls, floors, and ceilings. The main occluder in this scene is a grid made out of six walls, as illustrated in Figure 13.1. Listing 13.1 shows how the walls are actually just scaled cubes.

FIGURE 13.1   Our main occluder is a grid constructed out of six walls.

LISTING 13.1   Main Occluder with Six Scaled and Translated Solid Cubes

```
// Called to draw the occluding grid
void DrawOccluder(void)
{
    glColor3f(0.5f, 0.25f, 0.0f);
```

LISTING 13.1 Continued

```
    glPushMatrix();
    glScalef(30.0f, 30.0f, 1.0f);
    glTranslatef(0.0f, 0.0f, 50.0f);
    glutSolidCube(10.0f);
    glTranslatef(0.0f, 0.0f, -100.0f);
    glutSolidCube(10.0f);
    glPopMatrix();

    glPushMatrix();
    glScalef(1.0f, 30.0f, 30.0f);
    glTranslatef(50.0f, 0.0f, 0.0f);
    glutSolidCube(10.0f);
    glTranslatef(-100.0f, 0.0f, 0.0f);
    glutSolidCube(10.0f);
    glPopMatrix();

    glPushMatrix();
    glScalef(30.0f, 1.0f, 30.0f);
    glTranslatef(0.0f, 50.0f, 0.0f);
    glutSolidCube(10.0f);
    glTranslatef(0.0f, -100.0f, 0.0f);
    glutSolidCube(10.0f);
    glPopMatrix();
}
```

In each grid compartment, we're going to put a highly tessellated textured sphere. These spheres are our "occludees," objects possibly hidden by the occluder. We need the high vertex count and texturing to accentuate the rendering burden so that we can subsequently relieve that burden courtesy of occlusion queries.

Figure 13.2 shows the picture resulting from Listing 13.2. If you find this workload too heavy, feel free to reduce the tessellation in glutSolidSphere from the 100s to smaller numbers. Or if your OpenGL implementation is still hungry for more, go ahead and increase the tessellation, introduce more detailed textures, or consider using shaders as described in subsequent chapters.

FIGURE 13.2   Twenty-seven high-detail spheres will act as our occludees.

LISTING 13.2   Drawing 27 Highly Tessellated Spheres in a Color Cube

```
// Called to draw sphere
void DrawSphere(GLint sphereNum)
{
    ...
    glutSolidSphere(50.0f, 100, 100);
    ...
}

void DrawModels(void)
{
    ...

    // Turn on texturing just for spheres
    glEnable(GL_TEXTURE_2D);
    glEnable(GL_TEXTURE_GEN_S);
    glEnable(GL_TEXTURE_GEN_T);

    // Draw 27 spheres in a color cube
    for (r = 0; r < 3; r++)
    {
```

LISTING 13.2   Continued

```
        for (g = 0; g < 3; g++)
        {
            for (b = 0; b < 3; b++)
            {
                glColor3f(r * 0.5f, g * 0.5f, b * 0.5f);

                glPushMatrix();
                glTranslatef(100.0f * r - 100.0f,
                             100.0f * g - 100.0f,
                             100.0f * b - 100.0f);
                DrawSphere((r*9)+(g*3)+b);
                glPopMatrix();
            }
        }
    }

    glDisable(GL_TEXTURE_2D);
    glDisable(GL_TEXTURE_GEN_S);
    glDisable(GL_TEXTURE_GEN_T);
}
```

Listing 13.2 marks the completion of our picture. If we were happy with the rendering performance, we could end the chapter right here. But if the sphere tessellation or texture detail is cranked up high enough, frame rates should be unacceptable. So read on!

Bounding Boxes

The theory behind occlusion detection is that if an object's *bounding volume* is not visible, neither is the object. A bounding volume is any volume that completely contains the object. The whole point of occlusion detection is to cheaply draw a simple bounding volume to find out whether you can avoid drawing the actual complex object. So the more complex our bounding volume is, the more it negates the purpose of the optimization we're trying to create.

The simplest bounding volume is a cube, also called a *bounding box*. Eight vertices, six faces. You can easily create a bounding box for any object just by scanning for its minimum and maximum coordinates on each of the x-, y-, and z-axes. For our spheres with a 50-unit radius, a bounding box with sides of length 100 units will fit perfectly.

Be aware of the trade-off when using such a simple and arbitrary bounding volume. The bounding volume may have very few vertices, but it will touch many more pixels than the original object would have touched. With a few additional strategically placed vertices, you can turn your bounding box into a more useful shape and significantly reduce the fill-rate overhead. Fortunately, the bounding box is drawn without any fancy texturing or shading, so its overall fill-rate cost will most often be less than the original object anyway. Figure 13.3 shows an example of how different bounding volume shapes affect pixel count and vertex count using a sphere as the occludee. The choice of bounding volume depends entirely on your object shape, since you are no doubt drawing objects more interesting than spheres.

Bounding volume					
Name	tetrahedron	box	octahedron	dodecahedron	icosahedron
# faces	4	6	8	12	20
# vertices	4	8	6	20	12
% of pixels overkill	136%	120%	81%	58%	34%

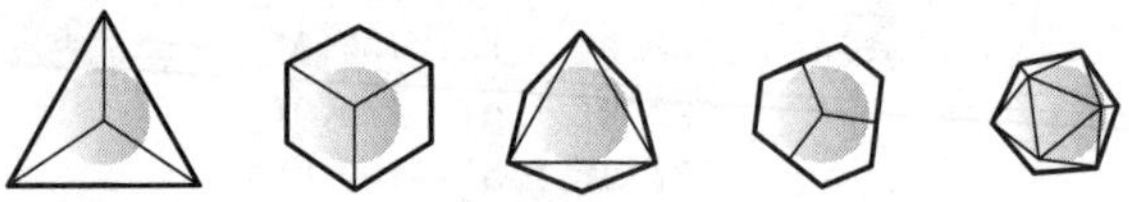

FIGURE 13.3   Various bounding volumes around a sphere with their pros and cons.

When we draw our bounding volumes, we're going to enable an occlusion query that will count the number of fragments that pass the depth test. Therefore, we don't care how the bounding volumes look. In fact, we don't even need to draw them to the screen at all. So we'll shut off all the bells and whistles before rendering the bounding volume, including writes to the depth and color buffers:

```
glShadeModel(GL_FLAT);
// Texturing is already disabled
...
glDisable(GL_LIGHTING);
glDisable(GL_COLOR_MATERIAL);
glDisable(GL_NORMALIZE);
glDepthMask(GL_FALSE);
glColorMask(0, 0, 0, 0);
```

After all this talk about occlusion queries, we're finally going to create some. But first, we need to come up with names for them. Here, we request 27 names, one for each sphere's query, and we provide a pointer to the array of GLuint data where the new names should be stored:

```
// Generate occlusion query names
glGenQueries(27, queryIDs);
```

When we're done with them, we delete the query objects, indicating that there are 27 names to be deleted in the provided GLuint array:

```
glDeleteQueries(27, queryIDs);
```

Occlusion query objects are not bound like other OpenGL objects, such as texture objects and buffer objects. Instead, they're created by a call to glBeginQuery. This marks the beginning of our query. The query object has an internal counter that keeps track of the number of fragments that would make it to the framebuffer—if we hadn't shut off the color buffer's write mask. Beginning the query resets this counter to zero to start a fresh query.

Then we draw our bounding volume. The query object's internal counter is incremented every time a fragment passes the depth test, and thus is not hidden by our main occluder, the grid which we've already drawn. For some algorithms, it's useful to know exactly how many fragments were drawn, but for our purposes here, all we care about is whether the counter is zero or nonzero. This value corresponds to whether any part of the bounding volume is visible or whether all fragments were discarded by the depth test.

When we're finished drawing the bounding volume, we mark the end of the query by calling glEndQuery. This tells OpenGL we're done with this query and lets us continue with another query or ask for the result back. Because we're drawing 27 spheres, we can improve the performance by using 27 different query objects. This way, we can queue up the drawing of all 27 bounding volumes without disrupting the pipeline by waiting to read back the query results in between.

Listing 13.3 illustrates the rendering of the bounding volumes, bracketed by the beginning and ending of the query. Then we proceed to possibly draw the actual spheres. Notice the code for visualizing the bounding volume whereby we leave the color buffer's write mask enabled. This way, we can see and compare the different bounding volume shapes.

LISTING 13.3   Beginning the Query, Drawing the Bounding Volume, Ending the Query, Then Moving on to Redraw the Actual Scene

```
// Called to draw scene objects
void DrawModels(void)
{
    GLint r, g, b;

    // Draw main occluder first
    DrawOccluder();

    if (occlusionDetection || showBoundingVolume)
    {
        // All we care about for bounding box is resulting depth values
        glShadeModel(GL_FLAT);
```

LISTING 13.3   Continued

```
// Texturing is already disabled
if (showBoundingVolume)
{
    glEnable(GL_POLYGON_STIPPLE);
}
else
{
    glDisable(GL_LIGHTING);
    glDisable(GL_COLOR_MATERIAL);
    glDisable(GL_NORMALIZE);
    glDepthMask(GL_FALSE);
    glColorMask(0, 0, 0, 0);
}

// Draw 27 spheres in a color cube
for (r = 0; r < 3; r++)
{
    for (g = 0; g < 3; g++)
    {
        for (b = 0; b < 3; b++)
        {
            if (showBoundingVolume)
                glColor3f(r * 0.5f, g * 0.5f, b * 0.5f);

            glPushMatrix();
            glTranslatef(100.0f * r - 100.0f,
                         100.0f * g - 100.0f,
                         100.0f * b - 100.0f);
            glBeginQuery(GL_SAMPLES_PASSED, queryIDs[(r*9)+(g*3)+b]);
            switch (boundingVolume)
            {
            case 0:
                glutSolidCube(100.0f);
                break;
            case 1:
                glScalef(150.0f, 150.0f, 150.0f);
                glutSolidTetrahedron();
                break;
            case 2:
                glScalef(90.0f, 90.0f, 90.0f);
                glutSolidOctahedron();
                break;
```

LISTING 13.3   Continued

```
                    case 3:
                        glScalef(40.0f, 40.0f, 40.0f);
                        glutSolidDodecahedron();
                        break;
                    case 4:
                        glScalef(65.0f, 65.0f, 65.0f);
                        glutSolidIcosahedron();
                        break;
                    }
                    glEndQuery(GL_SAMPLES_PASSED);
                    glPopMatrix();
                }
            }
        }


    // Restore normal drawing state
    glDisable(GL_POLYGON_STIPPLE);
    glShadeModel(GL_SMOOTH);
    glEnable(GL_LIGHTING);
    glEnable(GL_COLOR_MATERIAL);
    glEnable(GL_NORMALIZE);
    glColorMask(1, 1, 1, 1);
    glDepthMask(GL_TRUE);
    }

// Turn on texturing just for spheres
glEnable(GL_TEXTURE_2D);
glEnable(GL_TEXTURE_GEN_S);
glEnable(GL_TEXTURE_GEN_T);

// Draw 27 spheres in a color cube
for (r = 0; r < 3; r++)
{
    for (g = 0; g < 3; g++)
    {
        for (b = 0; b < 3; b++)
        {
            glColor3f(r * 0.5f, g * 0.5f, b * 0.5f);

            glPushMatrix();
            glTranslatef(100.0f * r - 100.0f,
                         100.0f * g - 100.0f,
```

LISTING 13.3   Continued

```
                         100.0f * b - 100.0f);
                DrawSphere((r*9)+(g*3)+b);
                glPopMatrix();
            }
        }
    }

    glDisable(GL_TEXTURE_2D);
    glDisable(GL_TEXTURE_GEN_S);
    glDisable(GL_TEXTURE_GEN_T);
}
```

DrawSphere contains the magic where we decide whether to actually draw the sphere. Our query results are waiting for us inside the 27 query objects. Let's find out which are hidden and which we have to draw.

Querying the Query Object

The moment of truth is here. The jury is back with its verdict. We want to draw as little as possible, so we're hoping each and every one of our queries resulted in no fragments being touched. But if you think about this grid of spheres, you know that's not going to happen.

No matter from what angle we're looking at our grid, unless we zoom way in, there will always be at least 9 spheres in view. Worst case is you'll see all the spheres on three faces of our grid: 19 spheres. Still, in that worst case, we save ourselves from drawing 8 spheres. That's almost a 30% savings in rendering costs. Best case, we save 66%, skipping 18 spheres. If we zoom in on a single sphere, we could conceivably avoid drawing 26 spheres!

So how do you determine your luck? You simply query the query object. That sounds confusing, but this is a regular old query for OpenGL state. It just happens to be from something called a *query object*. In Listing 13.4, we call glGetQueryObjectiv to see whether the pass counter is zero, in which case we won't draw the sphere.

LISTING 13.4   Checking the Query Results and Drawing the Sphere Only If We Have To

```
// Called to draw sphere
void DrawSphere(GLint sphereNum)
{
    GLboolean occluded = GL_FALSE;

    if (occlusionDetection)
    {
        GLint passingSamples;
```

LISTING 13.4   Continued

```
        // Check if this sphere would be occluded
        glGetQueryObjectiv(queryIDs[sphereNum], GL_QUERY_RESULT,
                            &passingSamples);
        if (passingSamples == 0)
            occluded = GL_TRUE;
    }

    if (!occluded)
    {
        glutSolidSphere(50.0f, 100, 100);
    }
}
```

That's all there is to it. Each sphere's query is checked in turn, and we decide whether to draw the sphere. We've included a mode in which we can disable the occlusion detection to see how badly our performance suffers. Depending on how many spheres are visible, you may see a boost of two times or more thanks to occlusion detection.

In addition to the query result, you can also query to find out whether the result is immediately available. If we didn't render the 27 bounding volumes back to back, and instead asked for each result immediately, the bounding box rendering might still have been in the pipeline and the result may not have been ready yet. You can query GL_QUERY_RESULT_AVAILABLE to find out whether the result is ready. If it's not, querying GL_QUERY_RESULT will stall until the result is available. So instead of stalling, you could find something useful for your application to do while you wait for the results to be ready. In our case, we planned ahead to do a bunch of work in between to be certain our first query result would be ready by the time we finished our 27th bounding volume query.

Other state queries include the currently active query name (which query is in the middle of a glBeginQuery/glEndQuery, if any) and the number of bits in the implementation's pass counter. An implementation is allowed to advertise a 0-bit counter, in which case occlusion queries are useless and shouldn't be used. In Listing 13.5, we check for that case during an application's initialization right after checking for extension availability courtesy of GLee.

LISTING 13.5   Ensuring That Occlusion Queries Are Truly Supported

```
GLint queryCounterBits;

// Make sure required functionality is available!
if (!GLEE_VERSION_1_5 && !GLEE_ARB_occlusion_query)
{
    fprintf(stderr, "Neither OpenGL 1.5 nor GL_ARB_occlusion_query"
                    " extension is available!\n");
```

LISTING 13.5   Continued

```
    Sleep(2000);
    exit(0);
}


// Make sure query counter bits are nonzero
glGetQueryiv(GL_SAMPLES_PASSED, GL_QUERY_COUNTER_BITS, &queryCounterBits);
if (queryCounterBits == 0)
{
    fprintf(stderr, "Occlusion queries not really supported!\n");
    fprintf(stderr, "Available query counter bits: 0\n");
    Sleep(2000);
    exit(0);
}
```

The only other query to be aware of is glIsQuery. This command just checks whether the specified name is the name of an existing query object, in which case it returns GL_TRUE. Otherwise, it returns GL_FALSE.

Best Practices

To maximize this optimization and avoid the most rendering, you should draw the occluders first. This includes any objects inexpensive enough to render that you will always draw them unconditionally. Then conditionally draw the remaining objects in the scene, the occludees, sorted from front to back if your application is designed in a way that permits it. This will increase the chance that objects further from the eye will be occluded, if not by an occluder, then perhaps by a previously drawn fellow occludee.

Requesting the result of a query will stall the pipeline if the corresponding bounding volume hasn't finished rendering yet. We avoided this situation in our example by filling the pipeline with 27 of these bounding volumes, virtually guaranteeing that the result from the first one would be ready by the time we finished issuing the last one. On some implementations, however, the very act of reading back the result may cause the rendering pipeline to drain. This could effectively negate the performance boost you were hoping to achieve. For this reason, applications often wait until a frame of rendering is complete before querying the occlusion results. The cost of reading the result can be hidden in the time spent waiting for a vertical retrace in order to swap buffers, for example. But isn't it too late at that point to make any rendering decisions? This is where you can start making trade-offs between image fidelity and performance: You can use the last frame's occlusion results to educate the next frame's rendering decisions. In the worst case scenario, you fail to render an object that should have just barely become visible in this frame. But that will probably go unnoticed at 60fps, and the very next frame will remedy the situation.

In the same spirit of aggressive optimization, you may choose to skip rendering an object not only when the query result comes back with a zero, but when it is arbitrarily close to zero. You decide how close. Again, you may miss out on a sliver of an object that really should have been rendered, peeking out from behind an occluder. But will anyone notice, or will they just be appreciative of the higher framerates? It depends on how aggressive your threshold is. Beware. If you go too high, then the occludee will visibly pop in and out of the scene as you cross that threshold.

Summary

When rendering complex scenes, sometimes we waste hardware resources by rendering objects that will never be seen. We can try to avoid the extra work by testing whether an object will show up in the final image. By drawing a bounding box, or some other simple bounding volume, around the object, we can cheaply approximate the object in the scene. If occluders in the scene hide the bounding box, they would also hide the actual object. By wrapping the bounding box rendering with a query, we can count the number of pixels that would be hit. If the bounding box hits no pixels, we can guarantee that the original object would also not be drawn, so we can skip rendering it. Performance improvements can be dramatic, depending on the complexity of the objects in the scene and how often they are occluded.

13

CHAPTER 14

Depth Textures and Shadows

by Benjamin Lipchak

WHAT YOU'LL LEARN IN THIS CHAPTER:

How To	Functions You'll Use
Draw your scene from the light's perspective	gluLookAt/gluPerspective
Copy texels from the depth buffer into a depth texture	glCopyTexSubImage2D
Use eye linear texture coordinate generation	glTexGen
Set up shadow comparison	glTexParameter

Shadows are an important visual cue, both in reality and in rendered scenes. At a very basic level, shadows give us information about the location of objects in relation to each other and to light sources, even if the light sources are not visible in the scene. When it comes to games, shadows can make an already immersive environment downright spooky. Imagine turning the corner in a torch-lit dungeon and stepping into the shadow of your worst nightmare. Peter Pan had it easy.

In Chapter 5, "Color, Materials, and Lighting: The Basics," we described a low-tech way of projecting an object onto a flat plane, in effect "squishing" it to appear as a shadow. Another technique utilizing the stencil buffer, known as shadow volumes, has been widely used, but it tends to require significant preprocessing of geometry and high fill rates to the stencil buffer. OpenGL 1.4 introduced a more elegant approach to shadow generation: shadow mapping.

The theory behind shadow mapping is simple. What parts of your scene would fall in shadow? Answer: The parts that light doesn't directly hit. Think of yourself in the light's position in your virtual scene. What would the light see if it were the camera? Everything the light sees would be lit. Everything else falls in shadow. Figure 14.1 will help you visualize the difference between the camera's viewpoint and the light's viewpoint.

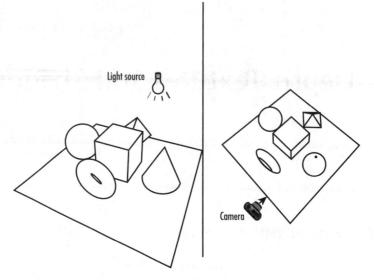

FIGURE 14.1 The camera and the light have different perspectives on the scene.

When the scene is rendered from the light's perspective, the side effect is a depth buffer full of useful information. At every pixel in the resulting depth buffer, we know the relative distance from the light to the nearest surface. These surfaces are lit by the light source. Every other surface farther away from the light source remains in shadow.

What we'll do is take that depth buffer, copy it into a texture, and project it back on the scene, now rendered again from the normal camera angle. We'll use that projected texture to automatically determine which parts of what objects are in light, and which remain in shadow. Sounds easy, but each step of this technique requires careful attention.

Be That Light

Our first step is to draw the scene from the light's perspective. We'll use several built-in GLUT objects to show off how well this technique works, even when casting shadows on nonplanar surfaces, such as other objects in the scene. You can change the viewpoint by manually setting the modelview matrix, but for this example, we use the gluLookAt helper function to facilitate the change:

```
gluLookAt(lightPos[0], lightPos[1], lightPos[2],
          0.0f, 0.0f, 0.0f, 0.0f, 1.0f, 0.0f);
```

Fit the Scene to the Window

In addition to this modelview matrix, we also need to set up the projection matrix to maximize the scene's size in the window. Even if the light is far away from the objects in the scene, to achieve the best utilization of the space in our shadow map, we would still like the scene to fill the available space. We'll set up the near and far clipping planes based on the distance from the light to the nearest and farthest objects in the scene. Also, we'll estimate the field of view to contain the entire scene as closely as possible:

```
GLfloat sceneBoundingRadius = 95.0f; // based on objects in scene

// Save the depth precision for where it's useful
lightToSceneDistance = sqrt(lightPos[0] * lightPos[0] +
                            lightPos[1] * lightPos[1] +
                            lightPos[2] * lightPos[2]);
nearPlane = lightToSceneDistance - sceneBoundingRadius;
// Keep the scene filling the depth texture
fieldOfView = (GLfloat)m3dRadToDeg(2.0f * atan(sceneBoundingRadius /
lightToSceneDistance));

glMatrixMode(GL_PROJECTION);
glLoadIdentity();
gluPerspective(fieldOfView, 1.0f, nearPlane, nearPlane + (2.0f *
sceneBoundingRadius));
```

Given our knowledge of the scene, we can determine a rough bounding radius for all objects. Our scene is centered around the origin at (0,0,0) with objects no more than 95 units away in any direction. Note that since the base plane won't cast shadows on any of our other objects, we don't need to render it into our shadow map. It was therefore not considered when choosing our bounding radius, either. Knowing the position of the light, which will be our eye position when rendering the light's view of the scene, we choose near and far planes to be the distance in eye space from the light to the front and back of the scene's bounding radius, respectively. Finally, the field of view can be estimated by taking twice the inverse tangent of the ratio between the scene's bounding radius and the light-to-scene distance. For a thorough treatment of how to position and orient your shadow frustum to get best shadow map utilization, check out *Robust Shadow Mapping with Light Space Perspective Shadow Maps* by Michael Wimmer and Daniel Scherzer, which can be found in Section 4 of Shader X4, edited by Wolfgang Engel.

No Bells or Whistles, Please

When we draw the first pass of the scene, the light's viewpoint, we don't actually want to see it. We just want to tap into the resulting depth buffer. So we'll draw to the back buffer and never bother swapping. We can further accelerate this pass by masking writes to the color buffer. And because all we care about is the depth values, we obviously don't care about lighting, smooth shading, or anything else that isn't going to affect the result. Shut it all off. In this sample, we don't have any fixed functionality texture mapping or fragment shading in use. If we did, we would disable those as well for this depth pass. All we need to render is the raw geometry:

```
glShadeModel(GL_FLAT);
glDisable(GL_LIGHTING);
glDisable(GL_COLOR_MATERIAL);
glDisable(GL_NORMALIZE);
glColorMask(0, 0, 0, 0);
```

The output from drawing the scene from the light's perspective is invisible, but Figure 14.2 illustrates via grayscale what the depth buffer contains.

FIGURE 14.2   If we could see the depth buffer, this is what it would look like.

A New Kind of Texture

We want to copy the depth values from the depth buffer into a texture for use as the shadow map. OpenGL allows you to copy color values directly into textures via glCopyTexImage2D. Until OpenGL 1.4, this capability was possible only for color values. But now *depth textures* are available.

Depth textures simply add a new type of texture data. We've had base formats with red, green, and blue color data and/or alpha, luminosity, or intensity. To this list, we now add a depth base format. The internal formats that can be requested include GL_DEPTH_COMPO-NENT16, GL_DEPTH_COMPONENT24, and GL_DEPTH_COMPONENT32, each reflecting the number of bits per texel. Typically, you'll want a format that matches the precision of your depth buffer. OpenGL makes it easy by letting you use the generic GL_DEPTH_COMPONENT internal format that usually adopts whichever specific format matches your depth buffer.

After drawing the light's view into the depth buffer, we want to copy that data directly into a depth texture. This saves us the trouble, and potential performance reduction, of using both glReadPixels and glTexImage2D:

```
glCopyTexImage2D(GL_TEXTURE_2D, 0, GL_DEPTH_COMPONENT,
                 0, 0, shadowWidth, shadowHeight, 0);
```

Note that drawing the light's view and regenerating the shadow map needs to be done only when objects in the scene move or the light source moves. If the only thing moving is the camera angle, you can keep using the same depth texture. Remember, when only the camera moves, the light's view of the scene isn't affected. (The camera is invisible.) We can reuse the existing shadow map in this case. The only other time we regenerate the depth texture is when the window size changes, affording us the opportunity to generate a larger depth texture.

Size Matters

When it comes to depth textures, size matters. Earlier we discussed the importance of choosing a projection matrix that maximizes the scene's size in the depth texture. A higher resolution depth texture will also yield more precise shadow results. Because we're rendering the light's viewpoint to our window's back buffer as the basis for our depth texture, that limits its size. With a 1024×768 window, the biggest power-of-two size texture we can create is 1024×512:

```
void ChangeSize(int w, int h)
{
    GLint i;

    windowWidth = shadowWidth = w;
    windowHeight = shadowHeight = h;

    if (!npotTexturesAvailable)
    {
        // Find the largest power of two that will fit in window.

        // Try each width until we get one that's too big
        i = 0;
        while ((1 << i) <= shadowWidth)
            i++;
        shadowWidth = (1 << (i-1));
```

```
        // Now for height
        i = 0;
        while ((1 << i) <= shadowHeight)
            i++;
        shadowHeight = (1 << (i-1));
    }


    RegenerateShadowMap();
}
```

However, if GL_ARB_texture_non_power_of_two is supported (or OpenGL 2.0 is supported, which includes this extension), then we can create a texture that is the same size as the window. To generate a depth texture larger than the window size, an offscreen drawable, such as a Frame Buffer Object (FBO), is required. See Chapter 18, "Advanced Buffers," where we add FBO support to our shadow mapping sample code. Adding FBO support to our sample code is left as an exercise for the reader!

Draw the Shadows First?!

Yes, we will draw the shadows first. But, you ask, if a shadow is defined as the lack of light, why do we need to draw shadows at all? Strictly speaking, you don't need to draw them if you have a single spotlight. If you leave the shadows black, you'll achieve a stark effect that may suit your purposes well. But if you don't want pitch-black shadows and still want to make out details inside the shadowed regions, you'll need to simulate some ambient lighting in your scene:

```
GLfloat lowAmbient[4] = {0.1f, 0.1f, 0.1f, 1.0f};
GLfloat lowDiffuse[4] = {0.35f, 0.35f, 0.35f, 1.0f};

glLightfv(GL_LIGHT0, GL_AMBIENT, lowAmbient);
glLightfv(GL_LIGHT0, GL_DIFFUSE, lowDiffuse);

// Draw objects in the scene, including base plane
DrawModels(GL_TRUE);
```

We've added a bit of diffuse lighting as well to help convey shape information. If you use only ambient lighting, you end up with ambiguously shaped solid-colored regions. Figure 14.3 shows the scene so far, entirely in shadow. Note that you won't see this intermediate stage because we won't swap buffers yet.

FIGURE 14.3   The entire scene is in shadow before the lit areas are drawn.

Some OpenGL implementations support an extension, `GL_ARB_shadow_ambient`, which makes this first shadow drawing pass unnecessary. In this case, both the shadowed regions and the lit regions are drawn simultaneously. More on that optimization later.

And Then There Was Light

Right now, we just have a very dimly lit scene. To make shadows, we need some brightly lit areas to contrast the existing dimly lit areas, turning them into shadows. But how do we determine which areas to light? This is key to the shadow mapping technique. After we've decided where to draw, we'll draw brighter simply by using greater lighting coefficients, twice as bright as the shadowed areas:

```
GLfloat ambientLight[] = { 0.2f, 0.2f, 0.2f, 1.0f};
GLfloat diffuseLight[] = { 0.7f, 0.7f, 0.7f, 1.0f};
  ...
glLightfv(GL_LIGHT0, GL_AMBIENT, ambientLight);
glLightfv(GL_LIGHT0, GL_DIFFUSE, diffuseLight);
```

Projecting Your Shadow Map: The "Why"

The goal here is to project the shadow map (the light's viewpoint) of the scene back onto the scene as if emitted from the light, but viewed from the camera's position. We're projecting those depth values, which represent the distance from the light to the first object hit by the light's rays. Reorienting the texture coordinates into the right coordinate space is going to take a bit of math. If you care only about the "how" and not the "why," you can safely skip over this section. We don't blame you. Math is hard.

In Chapter 4, "Geometric Transformations: The Pipeline," we explained the process of transforming vertices from object space to eye space, then to clip space, on to normalized device coordinates, and finally to window space. We have two different sets of matrices in play performing these transformations: one for the light view and the other for the regular camera view. Figure 14.4 shows the two sets of transformations in use.

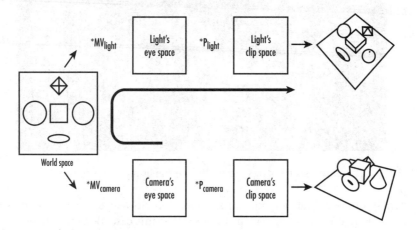

FIGURE 14.4 The large arrow in the center shows the transformations we need to apply to our eye linear texture coordinates.

Any texture projection usually begins with eye linear texture coordinate generation. This process will automatically generate the texture coordinates. Unlike object linear texture coordinate generation, the eye linear coordinates aren't tied to the geometry. Instead, it's as if there is a film projector casting the texture onto the scene. But it doesn't just project onto flat surfaces like a movie screen. Think about what happens when you walk in front of a projector. The movie is projected onto your irregularly shaped body. The same thing happens here.

We need to end up with texture coordinates that will index into our shadow map in the light's clip space. We start off with our projected eye linear texture coordinates in the camera's eye space. So we need to first backtrack to world space and then transform to the light's eye space and finally to the light's clip space. This transformation can be summarized by the following series of matrix multiplications:

$$M = P_{light} * MV_{light} * MV_{camera}^{-1}$$

But wait, there's more. The light's clip space doesn't quite bring us home free. Remember that clip space is in the range [–1,1] for each of the x, y, and z coordinates. The shadow map depth texture, like all standard 2D textures, needs to be indexed in the range [0,1]. Also, the depth texture values against which we're going to be comparing are in the range [0,1], so we'll also need our z texture coordinate in that range. A simple scale by one-half (S) and bias by one-half (B) will do the trick:

$$M = B * S * P_{light} * MV_{light} * MV_{camera}^{-1}$$

If you're unfamiliar with OpenGL matrix notation, you're probably asking why these matrices are in reverse order. After all, we need to apply the inverse of the camera's modelview first, and the bias by one-half translation is the last transformation we need. What's the deal? It's really simple, actually. OpenGL applies a matrix (M) to a coordinate (T) in a seemingly backward way, too. So you want to read everything right to left when thinking about the order of transformations being applied to your coordinate:

$$T' = M * T$$
$$= B * S * P_{light} * MV_{light} * MV_{camera}^{-1} * T$$

This is standard representation. Nothing to see here. Move along.

Projecting Your Shadow Map: The "How"

We understand what matrix transformations need to be applied to our eye linear-generated texture coordinate to have something useful to index into our shadow map texture. But how do we apply these transformations?

We'll set up a texture matrix responsible for achieving the necessary texture coordinate manipulation. Then we'll use the plane equations associated with eye linear texture coordinate generation to put that texture matrix to work. An alternative would be to establish a true texture matrix by calling `glMatrixMode(GL_TEXTURE)` followed by `glLoadIdentity`, `glTranslatef`, `glScalef`, `glMultMatrixf`, and so on; but that would incur an extra matrix multiply, whereas the eye linear plane equations will get applied regardless, so we may as well make full use of them!

To set up the texture matrix, we'll start with an identity matrix and multiply in each of our required transformations discussed in the preceding section:

```
glGetFloatv(GL_PROJECTION_MATRIX, lightProjection);
...
glGetFloatv(GL_MODELVIEW_MATRIX, lightModelview);
...
// Set up texture matrix for shadow map projection,
// which will be rolled into the eye linear
// texture coordinate generation plane equations
```

```
M3DMatrix44f tempMatrix;
m3dLoadIdentity44(tempMatrix);
m3dTranslateMatrix44(tempMatrix, 0.5f, 0.5f, 0.5f);
m3dScaleMatrix44(tempMatrix, 0.5f, 0.5f, 0.5f);
m3dMatrixMultiply44(textureMatrix, tempMatrix, lightProjection);
m3dMatrixMultiply44(tempMatrix, textureMatrix, lightModelview);
// transpose to get the s, t, r, and q rows for plane equations
m3dTransposeMatrix44(textureMatrix, tempMatrix);
```

When setting our light's projection and modelview matrices before drawing the light's view, we conveniently queried and saved off these matrices so we could apply them later to the texture matrix. Our scale and bias operations to map [–1,1] to [0,1] are easily expressed as scales and translations.

But where's the multiplication by the inverse of the camera's modelview matrix? Glad you asked. OpenGL anticipated the need for this transformation when using eye linear texture coordinate generation. A post-multiply by the inverse of the current modelview matrix is applied automatically to the eye plane equations we provided. All you have to do is make sure your camera's modelview is installed at the time you call glTexGenfv:

```
glMatrixMode(GL_MODELVIEW);
glLoadIdentity();
gluLookAt(cameraPos[0], cameraPos[1], cameraPos[2],
          0.0f, 0.0f, 0.0f, 0.0f, 1.0f, 0.0f);

// Set up the eye plane for projecting the shadow map on the scene
glEnable(GL_TEXTURE_GEN_S);
glEnable(GL_TEXTURE_GEN_T);
glEnable(GL_TEXTURE_GEN_R);
glEnable(GL_TEXTURE_GEN_Q);
glTexGenfv(GL_S, GL_EYE_PLANE, &textureMatrix[0]);
glTexGenfv(GL_T, GL_EYE_PLANE, &textureMatrix[4]);
glTexGenfv(GL_R, GL_EYE_PLANE, &textureMatrix[8]);
glTexGenfv(GL_Q, GL_EYE_PLANE, &textureMatrix[12]);
...
glTexGeni(GL_S, GL_TEXTURE_GEN_MODE, GL_EYE_LINEAR);
glTexGeni(GL_T, GL_TEXTURE_GEN_MODE, GL_EYE_LINEAR);
glTexGeni(GL_R, GL_TEXTURE_GEN_MODE, GL_EYE_LINEAR);
glTexGeni(GL_Q, GL_TEXTURE_GEN_MODE, GL_EYE_LINEAR);
```

The Shadow Comparison

We have rendered our light view and copied it into a shadow map. We have our texture coordinates for indexing into the projected shadow map. The scene is dimly lit, ready for the real lights. The moment is near for completing our scene. We just need to combine the ingredients. First, there's some important state we can "set and forget" during initialization.

```
// Hidden surface removal
glEnable(GL_DEPTH_TEST);
glDepthFunc(GL_LEQUAL);
```

We set the depth test to less than or equal so that we can draw the lit pass on top of the dim pass. Otherwise, because the geometry is identical, the lit pass would always fail the depth test, and nothing would show up after the dimly lit shadow pass.

```
// Set up some texture state that never changes
glGenTextures(1, &shadowTextureID);
glBindTexture(GL_TEXTURE_2D, shadowTextureID);
glTexParameteri(GL_TEXTURE_2D, GL_TEXTURE_WRAP_S, GL_CLAMP_TO_EDGE);
glTexParameteri(GL_TEXTURE_2D, GL_TEXTURE_WRAP_T, GL_CLAMP_TO_EDGE);
```

Then we generate and bind to our shadow map, which is the only texture used in this demo. We set our texture coordinate wrap modes to clamp to edge texels. It makes no sense to repeat the projection. For example, if the light affects only a portion of the scene, but the camera is zoomed out to reveal other unlit parts of the scene, you don't want your shadow map to be repeated infinitely across the scene. You want your texture coordinates clamped so that only the lit portion of the scene has the shadow map projected onto it.

Depth textures contain only a single source component representing the depth value. But texture environments expect four components to be returned from a texture lookup: red, green, blue, and alpha. OpenGL gives you flexibility in how you want the single depth component mapped. Choices for the depth texture mode include GL_ALPHA (0,0,0,D), GL_LUMINANCE (D,D,D,1), and GL_INTENSITY (D,D,D,D). We're going to need the depth broadcast to all four channels, so we choose the intensity mode:

```
glTexParameteri(GL_TEXTURE_2D, GL_DEPTH_TEXTURE_MODE, GL_INTENSITY);
```

Obviously, we need to enable texturing to put the shadow map into effect. We set the compare mode to GL_COMPARE_R_TO_TEXTURE. If we don't set this, all we'll get is the depth value in the texture. But we want more than that. We want the depth value compared to our texture coordinate's R component:

```
// Set up shadow comparison
glEnable(GL_TEXTURE_2D);
glTexParameteri(GL_TEXTURE_2D, GL_TEXTURE_COMPARE_MODE,
                GL_COMPARE_R_TO_TEXTURE);
```

The R component of the texture coordinate represents the distance from the light source to the surface of the object being rendered. The shadow map's depth value represents the previously determined distance from the light to the first surface it hits. By comparing one to the other, we can tell whether the surface we are rendering is the first to be hit by a ray of light, or whether that surface is farther away from the light, and hence is in the shadow cast by the first, lit, surface:

D' = (R <= D) ? 1 : 0

Other comparison functions are also available. In fact, OpenGL 1.5 enables you to use all the same relational operators that you can use for depth test comparisons. GL_LEQUAL is the default, so we don't need to change it.

Another two settings we need to consider are the minification and magnification filters. Some implementations may be able to smooth the edges of your shadows if you enable bilinear filtering. On such an implementation, multiple comparisons are performed and the results are averaged. This is called *percentage-closer filtering*.

```
glTexParameteri(GL_TEXTURE_2D, GL_TEXTURE_MIN_FILTER, GL_LINEAR);
glTexParameteri(GL_TEXTURE_2D, GL_TEXTURE_MAG_FILTER, GL_LINEAR);
```

Great. We have a bunch of 0s and 1s. But we don't want to draw black and white. Now what? Easy. We just need to set up a texture environment mode, GL_MODULATE, that multiplies the 0s and 1s by the incoming color resulting from lighting:

```
glTexEnvi(GL_TEXTURE_ENV, GL_TEXTURE_ENV_MODE, GL_MODULATE);
```

Finally, we're done, right? We have drawn our lit areas now. But wait. Where shadows appear, we just drew black over our previous ambient lighting pass. How do we preserve the ambient lighting for shadowed regions? Alpha testing will do the trick. We asked for intensity depth texture mode. Therefore, our 0s and 1s are present in the alpha component as well as the color components. Using an alpha test, we can tell OpenGL to discard any fragments in which we didn't get a 1:

```
// Enable alpha test so that shadowed fragments are discarded
glAlphaFunc(GL_GREATER, 0.9f);
glEnable(GL_ALPHA_TEST);
```

Okay. *Now* we're done. Figure 14.5 shows the output from Listing 14.1, shadows and all.

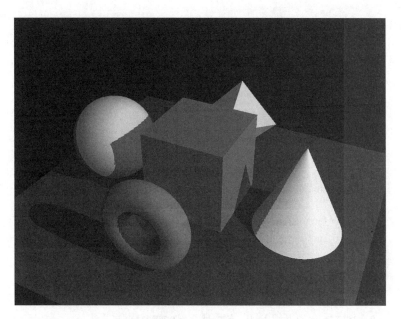

FIGURE 14.5 A brightly lit pass is added to the previous ambient shadow pass.

LISTING 14.1 Drawing the Ambient Shadow and Lit Passes of the Scene

```
// Called to draw scene
void RenderScene(void)
{
    ...

    // Track light position
    glLightfv(GL_LIGHT0, GL_POSITION, lightPos);

    // Clear the window with current clearing color
    glClear(GL_COLOR_BUFFER_BIT | GL_DEPTH_BUFFER_BIT);

    if (showShadowMap)
    {
        // Display shadow map for educational purposes
        ...
    }
    else if (noShadows)
    {
        // Set up some simple lighting
```

LISTING 14.1   Continued

```
        glLightfv(GL_LIGHT0, GL_AMBIENT, ambientLight);
        glLightfv(GL_LIGHT0, GL_DIFFUSE, diffuseLight);

        // Draw objects in the scene, including base plane
        DrawModels(GL_TRUE);
    }
    else
    {

        if (!ambientShadowAvailable)
        {
            GLfloat lowAmbient[4] = {0.1f, 0.1f, 0.1f, 1.0f};
            GLfloat lowDiffuse[4] = {0.35f, 0.35f, 0.35f, 1.0f};

            // Because there is no support for an "ambient"
            // shadow compare fail value, we'll have to
            // draw an ambient pass first...
            glLightfv(GL_LIGHT0, GL_AMBIENT, lowAmbient);
            glLightfv(GL_LIGHT0, GL_DIFFUSE, lowDiffuse);

            // Draw objects in the scene, including base plane
            DrawModels(GL_TRUE);

            // Enable alpha test so that shadowed fragments are discarded
            glAlphaFunc(GL_GREATER, 0.9f);
            glEnable(GL_ALPHA_TEST);
        }

        glLightfv(GL_LIGHT0, GL_AMBIENT, ambientLight);
        glLightfv(GL_LIGHT0, GL_DIFFUSE, diffuseLight);

        // Set up shadow comparison
        glEnable(GL_TEXTURE_2D);
        glTexEnvi(GL_TEXTURE_ENV, GL_TEXTURE_ENV_MODE, GL_MODULATE);
        glTexParameteri(GL_TEXTURE_2D, GL_TEXTURE_COMPARE_MODE,
                        GL_COMPARE_R_TO_TEXTURE);

        // Set up the eye plane for projecting the shadow map on the scene
        glEnable(GL_TEXTURE_GEN_S);
        glEnable(GL_TEXTURE_GEN_T);
        glEnable(GL_TEXTURE_GEN_R);
        glEnable(GL_TEXTURE_GEN_Q);
```

LISTING 14.1   Continued

```
        glTexGenfv(GL_S, GL_EYE_PLANE, &textureMatrix[0]);
        glTexGenfv(GL_T, GL_EYE_PLANE, &textureMatrix[4]);
        glTexGenfv(GL_R, GL_EYE_PLANE, &textureMatrix[8]);
        glTexGenfv(GL_Q, GL_EYE_PLANE, &textureMatrix[12]);

        // Draw objects in the scene, including base plane
        DrawModels(GL_TRUE);

        glDisable(GL_ALPHA_TEST);
        glDisable(GL_TEXTURE_2D);
        glDisable(GL_TEXTURE_GEN_S);
        glDisable(GL_TEXTURE_GEN_T);
        glDisable(GL_TEXTURE_GEN_R);
        glDisable(GL_TEXTURE_GEN_Q);
    }

...
}
```

Two Out of Three Ain't Bad

In Listing 14.1, you'll notice code hinging on the `ambientShadowAvailable` variable. The minimum requirement for the rest of this example is OpenGL 1.4 support, or at least support for the `GL_ARB_shadow` extension. If, however, your implementation supports the `GL_ARB_shadow_ambient` extension, you can cut down on the amount of work significantly.

Currently, we've described three rendering passes: one to draw the light's perspective into the shadow map, one to draw the dimly lit ambient pass, and one to draw the shadow-compared lighting. Remember, the shadow map needs to be regenerated only when the light position or objects in the scene change. So sometimes there are three passes, and other times just two. With `GL_ARB_shadow_ambient`, we can eliminate the ambient pass entirely.

Instead of 0s and 1s resulting from the shadow comparison, this extension allows us to replace another value for the 0s when the comparison fails. So if we set the fail value to one-half, the shadowed regions are still halfway lit, the same amount of lighting we were previously achieving in our ambient pass:

```
if (ambientShadowAvailable)
    glTexParameterf(GL_TEXTURE_2D, GL_TEXTURE_COMPARE_FAIL_VALUE_ARB,
                    0.5f);
```

This way, we also don't need to enable the alpha test.

A Few Words About Polygon Offset

Even on a surface closest to the light source, you will always discover minor differences in the values associated with the R texture coordinate, representing the surface to light distance, and the shadow map's depth value. This can result in "surface acne," whereby the projection of a discretely sampled shadow map onto a continuous surface leads to the surface shadowing itself. You can mitigate this problem by applying a depth offset (a.k.a. polygon offset) when rendering into the shadow map:

```
// Overcome imprecision
glEnable(GL_POLYGON_OFFSET_FILL);
...
glPolygonOffset(factor, 0.0f);
```

Although the polygon offset will help guarantee that surfaces that shouldn't be shadowed won't be, it also artificially shifts the position of shadows. A balance needs to be struck when it comes to polygon offset usage. Figure 14.6 illustrates what you'll see if you don't use enough polygon offset.

FIGURE 14.6   "Shadow acne" can be cleared up with liberal application of polygon offset.

For an in depth discussion of shadow acne, refer to *Eliminate Surface Acne with Gradient Shadow Mapping* by Christian Schüler, published in `Shader X4`, edited by Wolfgang Engel.

Summary

Shadow mapping is a useful technique for achieving realistic lighting without a lot of additional processing. The light's viewpoint can be used to determine which objects are lit and which remain in shadow. Depth textures are special textures designed to store the contents of your depth buffer for use as a shadow map. Eye linear texture coordinate generation is the basis for projected textures. A texture matrix encoded into the eye linear plane equations can be used to reorient the texture coordinates back into the light's clip space. Shadow comparison can be used to make the distinction between shadowed and lit regions. The `GL_ARB_shadow_ambient` extension can be used to reduce the number of passes that must be rendered.

14

PART II

The New Testament

For many years the fixed pipeline reigned supreme as the model for hardware-accelerated 3D graphics. In comparison, the transition to programmable hardware was virtually overnight. In a single generation of consumer graphics hardware, we went from barely configurable texture units and some meager vertex programmability to fully programmable graphics pipelines.

Now, it is possible to dramatically increase realism by writing code that gets executed on the GPU (graphics processing unit). This code can add tremendous flexibility to how vertices and individual fragments onscreen are processed. In addition, these tasks are almost embarrassingly parallel in nature. Multiple execution units designed solely for graphics processing type tasks are getting faster every generation at a rate that far outpaces the increases in regular CPU performance.

Programmable hardware is not the future of graphics hardware, it is the current *state of the art*. Building on the foundation and concepts of the fixed pipeline, shaders usher in a new era of graphics programming and real-time visual effects. Much of the last part of the book is still vital to using OpenGL. For example, we must still load and bind textures, we must still modify and maintain our matrix stacks, and we must still submit batches of vertex data. As you'll soon discover in the following chapters, however, there is a whole lot that can be done after your application turns loose of those vertices!

CHAPTER 15

Programmable Pipeline: This Isn't Your Father's OpenGL

by Benjamin Lipchak

WHAT YOU'LL LEARN IN THIS CHAPTER:

How To	Functions You'll Use
Create shader/program objects	glCreateShader/glCreateProgram
Specify shaders and compile	glShaderSource/glCompileShader
Attach/detach shaders and link	glAttachShader/glDetachShader/glLinkProgram
Switch between programs	glUseProgram
Specify a uniform	glUniform*
Get error and warning information	glGetShaderInfoLog/glGetProgramInfoLog

Graphics hardware has traditionally been designed to quickly perform the same rigid set of hard-coded computations. Different steps of the computation can be skipped, and parameters can be adjusted; but the computations themselves remain fixed. That's why this old paradigm of GPU design is called *fixed functionality*.

There has been a trend toward designing general-purpose graphics processors. Just like CPUs, these GPUs can be programmed with arbitrary sequences of instructions to perform virtually any imaginable computation. The biggest difference is that GPUs are tuned for the floating-point operations most common in the world of graphics.

Think of it this way: Fixed functionality is like a cookie recipe. Prior to OpenGL 2.0 you could change the recipe a bit here and there. Change the amount of each ingredient, change the temperature of the oven. You don't want chocolate chips? Fine. Disable them. But one way or another, you end up with cookies.

Enter programmability with OpenGL 2.0. Want to pick your own ingredients? No problem. Want to cook in a microwave or in a frying pan or on the grill? Have it your way. Instead of cookies, you can bake a cake or grill sirloin or heat up leftovers. The possibilities are endless. The entire kitchen and all its ingredients, appliances, pots, and pans are at your disposal. These are the inputs and outputs, instruction set, and temporary register storage of a programmable pipeline stage.

In this chapter, we cover the conventional OpenGL pipeline and then describe how to replace the programmable portions of it with OpenGL Shading Language shaders.

Out with the Old

Before we talk about replacing it, let's consider the conventional OpenGL rendering pipeline. The first several stages operate per-vertex. Then the primitive is rasterized to produce fragments. Finally, fragments are textured and fogged, and other per-fragment operations are applied before each fragment is written to the framebuffer. Figure 15.1 diagrams the fixed functionality pipeline.

The per-vertex and per-fragment stages of the pipeline are discussed separately in the following sections.

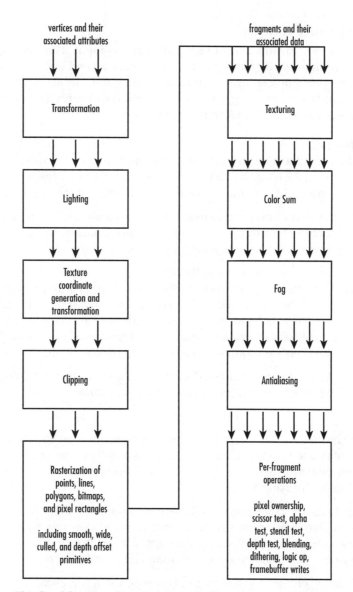

FIGURE 15.1   This fixed functionality rendering pipeline represents the old way of doing things.

15

Fixed Vertex Processing

The per-vertex stages start with a set of vertex attributes as input. These attributes include object-space position, normal, primary and secondary colors, and texture coordinates. The final result of per-vertex processing is clip-space position, front-facing and back-facing primary and secondary colors, a fog coordinate, texture coordinates, and point size. What happens in between is broken into four stages, discussed next.

Vertex Transformation

In fixed functionality, the vertex position is transformed from object space to clip space. This is achieved by multiplying the object-space coordinate first by the modelview matrix to put it into eye space. Then it's multiplied by the projection matrix to reach clip space.

The application has control over the contents of the two matrices, but these matrix multiplications always occur. The only way to "skip" this stage would be to load identity matrices so that you end up with the same position you started with.

Each vertex's normal is also transformed, this time from object space to eye space for use during lighting. The normal is multiplied by the inverse transpose of the modelview matrix, after which it is optionally rescaled or normalized. Lighting wants the normal to be a unit vector, so unless you're passing in unit-length normal vectors and have a modelview matrix that leaves them unit length, you'll need to either rescale them (if your modelview introduced only uniform scaling) or fully normalize them.

Chapter 4, "Geometric Transformations: The Pipeline," and Chapter 5, "Color, Materials, and Lighting: The Basics," covered transformations and normals.

Lighting

Lighting takes the vertex color, normal, and position as its raw data inputs. Its output is two colors, primary and secondary, and in some cases a different set of colors for front and back faces. Controlling this stage are the color material properties, light properties, and a variety of glEnable/glDisable toggles.

Lighting is highly configurable; you can enable some number of lights (up to eight or more), each with myriad parameters such as position, color, and type. You can specify material properties to simulate different surface appearances. You also can enable two-sided lighting to generate different colors for front- and back-facing polygons.

You can skip lighting entirely by disabling it. However, when it is enabled, the same hard-coded equations are always used. See Chapter 5, "Color, Materials, and Lighting: The Basics," and Chapter 6, "More on Color and Materials," for a refresher on fixed functionality lighting details.

Texture Coordinate Generation and Transformation

The final per-vertex stage of the fixed functionality pipeline involves processing the texture coordinates. Each texture coordinate can optionally be generated automatically by OpenGL. There are several choices of generation equations to use. In fact, a different mode can be chosen for each component of each texture coordinate. Or, if generation is disabled, the current texture coordinate associated with the vertex is used instead.

Whether or not texture generation is enabled, each texture coordinate is always transformed by its texture matrix. If it's an identity matrix, the texture coordinate is not affected.

This texture coordinate processing stage is covered in Chapter 8, "Texture Mapping: The Basics," and Chapter 9, "Texture Mapping: Beyond the Basics."

Clipping

If any of the vertices transformed in the preceding sections happens to fall outside the view volume, clipping must occur. Clipped vertices are discarded, and depending on the type of primitive being drawn, new vertices may be generated at the intersection of the primitive and the view volume. Colors, texture coordinates, and other vertex attributes are assigned to the newly generated vertices by interpolating their values along the clipped edge. Figure 15.2 illustrates a clipped primitive.

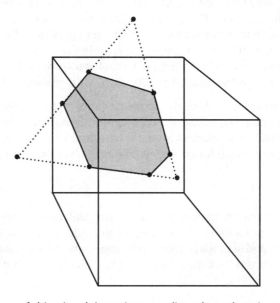

FIGURE 15.2   All three of this triangle's vertices are clipped out, but six new vertices are introduced.

The application may also enable user clip planes. These clip planes further restrict the clip volume so that even primitives within the view volume can be clipped. This technique is often used in medical imaging to "cut" into a volume of, for example, MRI data to inspect tissues deep within the body.

Fixed Fragment Processing

The per-fragment stages start out with a fragment and its associated data as input. This associated data is comprised of various values interpolated across the line or triangle, including one or more texture coordinates, primary and secondary colors, and a fog coordinate. The result of per-fragment processing is a single color that will be passed along to subsequent per-fragment operations, including depth test and blending. Again, four stages of processing are applied, as covered next.

Texture Application and Environment

Texture application is the most important per-fragment stage. Here, you take all the fragment's texture coordinates and its primary color as input. The output will be a new primary color. How this happens is influenced by which texture units are enabled for texturing, which texture images are bound to those units, and what texture function is set up by the texture environment.

For each enabled texture unit, the 1D, 2D, 3D, or cube map texture bound to that unit is used as the source for a lookup. Depending on the format of the texture and the texture function specified on that unit, the result of the texture lookup will either replace or be blended with the fragment's primary color. The resulting color from each enabled texture unit is then fed in as a color input to the next enabled texture unit. The result from the last enabled texture unit is the final output for the texturing stage.

Many configurable parameters affect the texture lookup, including texture coordinate wrap modes, border colors, minification and magnification filters, level-of-detail clamps and biases, depth texture and shadow compare state, and whether mipmap chains are automatically generated. Fixed functionality texturing was covered in detail in Chapters 8 and 9.

Color Sum

The color sum stage starts with two inputs: a primary and a secondary color. The output is a single color. There's not a lot of magic here. If color sum is enabled, or if lighting is enabled, the primary and secondary colors' red, green, and blue channels are added together and then clamped back into the range [0,1]. If color sum is not enabled, the primary color is passed through as the result. The alpha channel of the result always comes from the primary color's alpha. The secondary color's alpha is never used by the fixed functionality pipeline.

Fog Application

If fog is enabled, the fragment's color is blended with a constant fog color based on a computed fog factor. That factor is computed according to one of three hard-coded equations: linear, exponential, or second-order exponential. These equations base the fog factor on the current fog coordinate, which may be the approximate distance from the vertex to the eye, or an arbitrary value set per-vertex by the application.

For more details on fixed functionality fog, see Chapter 6.

Antialiasing Application

Finally, if the fragment belongs to a primitive that has smoothing enabled, one piece of associated data is a coverage value. That value is 1.0 in most cases; but for fragments on the edge of a smooth point, line, or polygon, the coverage is somewhere between 0.0 and 1.0. The fragment's alpha value is multiplied by this coverage value, which, with subsequent blending will produce smooth edges for these primitives. Chapter 6 discusses this behavior.

In with the New

That trip down memory lane was intended to both refresh your memory on the various stages of the current pipeline and give you an appreciation of the configurable but hardcoded computations that happen each step of the way. Now forget everything you just read. We're going to replace the majority of it and roll in the new world order: shaders.

Shaders are also sometimes called *programs,* and the terms are usually interchangeable. And that's what shaders are—application-defined customized programs that take over the responsibilities of fixed functionality pipeline stages. I prefer the term *shader* because it avoids confusion with the typical definition of *program,* which can mean any old application.

Figure 15.3 illustrates the simplified pipeline where previously hard-coded stages are subsumed by custom programmable shaders.

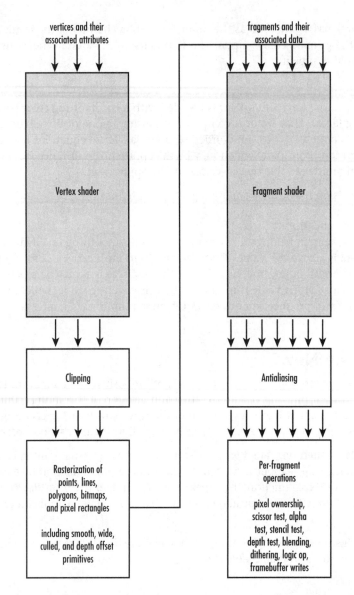

FIGURE 15.3   The block diagram looks simpler, but in reality these shaders can do everything the original fixed stages could do, plus more.

Programmable Vertex Shaders

As suggested by Figure 15.3, the inputs and outputs of a vertex shader remain the same as those of the fixed functionality stages being replaced. The raw vertices and all their attributes are fed into the vertex shader, rather than the fixed transformation stage. Out the other side, the vertex shader spits texture coordinates, colors, point size, and a fog coordinate, which are passed along to the clipper. A vertex shader is a drop-in replacement for the fixed transformation, lighting, and texture coordinate processing per-vertex stages.

Replacing Vertex Transformation

What you do in your vertex shader is entirely up to you. The absolute minimum (if you want anything to draw) would be to output a clip-space vertex position. Every other output is optional and at your sole discretion. How you generate your clip-space vertex position is your call. Traditionally, and to emulate fixed functionality transformation, you would want to multiply your input position by the modelview and projection matrices to get your clip-space output.

But say you have a fixed projection and you're sending in your vertices already in clip space. In that case, you don't need to do any transformation. Just copy the input position to the output position. Or, on the other hand, maybe you want to turn your Cartesian coordinates into polar coordinates. You could add extra instructions to your vertex shader to perform those computations.

Replacing Lighting

If you don't care what the vertex's colors are, you don't have to perform any lighting computations. You can just copy the color inputs to the color outputs; or if you know the colors will never be used later, you don't have to output them at all, and they will become undefined. Beware, if you do try to use them later after not outputting them from the vertex shader, undefined usually means garbage!

If you do want to generate more interesting colors, you have limitless ways of going about it. You could emulate fixed functionality lighting by adding instructions that perform these conventional computations, maybe customizing them here or there. You could also color your vertices based on their positions, their surface normals, or any other input parameter.

Replacing Texture Coordinate Processing

If you don't need texture coordinate generation, you don't need to code it into your vertex shader. The same goes for texture coordinate transformation. If you don't need it, don't waste precious shader cycles implementing it. You can just copy your input texture coordinates to their output counterparts. Or, as with colors, if you won't use the texture coordinate later, don't waste your time outputting it at all. For example, if your GPU supports eight texture coordinates, but you're going to use only three of them for texturing later in the pipeline, there's no point in outputting the other five. Doing so would just consume resources unnecessarily.

After reading the preceding sections, you should have a sufficient understanding of the input and output interfaces of vertex shaders; they are largely the same as their fixed functionality counterparts. But there's been a lot of hand waving about adding code to perform the desired computations within the shader. This would be a great place for an example of a vertex shader, wouldn't it? Alas, this section covers only the what, where, and why of shaders. The second half of this chapter, and the following two chapters for that matter, are devoted to the how, so you'll have to be patient and use your imagination. Consider this the calm before the storm. In a few pages, you'll be staring at more shaders than you ever hoped to see.

Fixed Functionality Glue

In between the vertex shader and the fragment shader, there remain a couple of fixed functionality stages that act as glue between the two shaders. One of them is the clipping stage described previously, which clips the current primitive against the view volume and in so doing possibly adds or removes vertices. After clipping, the perspective divide by W occurs, yielding normalized device coordinates. These coordinates are subjected to viewport transformation and depth range transformation, which yield the final window-space coordinates. Then it's on to rasterization.

Rasterization is the fixed functionality stage responsible for taking the processed vertices of a primitive and turning them into fragments. Whether a point, line, or polygon primitive, this stage produces the fragments to "fill in" the primitive and interpolates all the colors and texture coordinates so that the appropriate value is assigned to each fragment. Figure 15.4 illustrates this process.

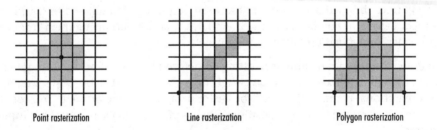

Point rasterization   Line rasterization   Polygon rasterization

FIGURE 15.4   Rasterization turns vertices into fragments.

Depending on how far apart the vertices of a primitive are, the ratio of fragments to vertices tends to be relatively high. For a highly tessellated or distant object, though, you might find all three vertices of a triangle mapping to the same single fragment. As a general rule, significantly more fragments than vertices are processed, but as with all rules, there are exceptions.

Rasterization is also responsible for making lines the desired width and points the desired size. It may apply stipple patterns to lines and polygons. It generates partial coverage values at the edges of smooth points, lines, and polygons, which later are multiplied into the fragment's alpha value during antialiasing application. If requested, rasterization culls out front- or back-facing polygons and applies depth offsets.

In addition to points, lines, and polygons, rasterization also generates the fragments for bitmaps and pixel rectangles (drawn with glDrawPixels). But these primitives don't originate from normal vertices. Instead, where interpolated data is usually assigned to fragments, those values are adopted from the current raster position. See Chapter 7, "Imaging with OpenGL," for more details on this subject.

Programmable Fragment Shaders

The same texture coordinates and colors are available to the fragment shader as were previously available to the fixed functionality texturing stage. The same single-color output is expected out of the fragment shader that was previously expected from the fixed functionality fog stage. Just as with vertex shaders, you may choose your own adventure in between the input interface and the output interface.

Replacing Texturing

The single most important capability of a fragment shader is performing texture lookups. For the most part, these texture lookups are unchanged from fixed functionality in that most of the texture state is set up outside the fragment shader. The texture image is specified and all its parameters are set the same as though you weren't using a fragment shader. The main difference is that you decide within the shader when and whether to perform a lookup and what to use as the texture coordinate.

You're not limited to using texture coordinate 0 to index into texture image 0. You can mix and match coordinates with different textures, using the same texture with different coordinates or the same coordinate with different textures. Or you can even compute a texture coordinate on the fly within the shader. This flexibility was impossible with fixed functionality.

The texture environment previously included a texture function that determined how the incoming fragment color was mixed with the texture lookup results. That function is now ignored, and it's up to the shader to combine colors with texture results. In fact, you might choose to perform no texture lookups at all and rely only on other computations to generate the final color result. A fragment shader could simply copy its primary color input to its color output and call it a day. Not very interesting, but such a "passthrough" shader might be all you need when combined with a fancy vertex shader.

Replacing Color Sum

Replacing the color sum is simple. This stage just adds together the primary and secondary colors. If that's what you want to happen, you just add an instruction to do that. If you're not using the secondary color for anything, ignore it.

15

Replacing Fog

Fog application is not as easy to emulate as color sum, but it's still reasonably easy. First, you need to calculate the fog factor with an equation based on the fragment's fog coordinate and some constant value such as density. Fixed functionality dictated the use of linear, exponential, or second-order exponential equations, but with shaders you can make up your own equation. Then you blend in a constant fog color with the fragment's unfogged color, using the fog factor to determine how much of each goes into the blend. You can achieve all this in just a handful of instructions. Or you can *not* add any instructions and forget about fog. The choice is yours.

OpenGL Shading Language: A First Glimpse

Enough with the hypotheticals. If you've made it this far, you must have worked up an appetite for some real shaders by now. Programming GPUs in a high-level language instead of an assembly language means compact and readable code, and thus higher productivity. The OpenGL Shading Language (GLSL) is the name of this language. It looks a lot like C, but with built-in data types and functions that are useful to vertex and fragment shaders.

Listings 15.1 and 15.2 are your first exposure to GLSL shaders. Consider them to be "Hello World" shaders, even though technically they don't say hello at all.

LISTING 15.1   A Simple GLSL Vertex Shader

```
void main(void)
{
    // This is our Hello World vertex shader
    // notice how comments are preceded by '//'

    // normal MVP transform
    vec4 clipCoord = gl_ModelViewProjectionMatrix * gl_Vertex;
    gl_Position = clipCoord;

    // Copy the primary color
    gl_FrontColor = gl_Color;

    // Calculate NDC
    vec3 ndc = clipCoord.xyz / clipCoord.w;

    // Map from [-1,1] to [0,1] before outputting
    gl_SecondaryColor = (ndc * 0.5) + 0.5;
}
```

LISTING 15.2 A Simple GLSL Fragment Shader

```
// This is our Hello World fragment shader
void main(void)
{
    // Mix primary and secondary colors, 50/50
    gl_FragColor = mix(gl_Color, vec4(vec3(gl_SecondaryColor), 1.0), 0.5);
}
```

If these shaders are not self-explanatory, don't despair! The rest of this chapter will make sense of it all. Basically, the vertex shader emulates fixed functionality vertex transformation by multiplying the object-space vertex position by the modelview/projection matrix. Then it copies its primary color unchanged. Finally, it generates a secondary color based on the post-perspective divide normalized device coordinates. Because they will be in the range [–1,1], you also have to divide by 2 and add 0.5 to map colors to the range [0,1]. The fragment shader is left with the simple task of mixing the primary and secondary colors together. Figure 15.5 shows a sample scene rendered with these shaders.

FIGURE 15.5 Notice how the colors are pastel tinted by the objects' positions in the scene.

15

Managing GLSL Shaders

The new GLSL commands are quite a departure from prior core OpenGL API. There's no more of the Gen/Bind/Delete that you're used to; GLSL gets all newly styled entry points.

Shader Objects

GLSL uses two types of objects: shader objects and program objects. The first objects we will look at, shader objects, are loaded with shader text and compiled.

Creating and Deleting

You create shader objects by calling glCreateShader and passing it the type of shader you want, either vertex or fragment. This function returns a handle to the shader object used to reference it in subsequent calls:

```
GLuint myVertexShader   = glCreateShader(GL_VERTEX_SHADER);
GLuint myFragmentShader = glCreateShader(GL_FRAGMENT_SHADER);
```

Beware that object creation may fail, in which case 0 (zero) will be returned. (If this happens, it's probably due to a simple error in how you called it.) When you're done with your shader objects, you should clean up after yourself:

```
glDeleteShader(myVertexShader);
glDeleteShader(myFragmentShader);
```

Some other OpenGL objects, including texture objects, unbind an object during deletion if it's currently in use. GLSL objects are different. glDeleteShader simply marks the object for future deletion, which will occur as soon as the object is no longer being used.

Specifying Shader Text

Unlike some other shading language APIs out there, GLSL is designed to accept shader text rather than precompiled binaries. This makes it possible for the application to provide a single universal shader regardless of the underlying OpenGL implementation. The OpenGL device driver can then proceed to compile and optimize for the underlying hardware. Another benefit is that the driver can be updated with improved optimization methods, making shaders run faster over time, without any burden on application vendors to patch their applications.

A shader object's goal is simply to accept shader text and compile it. Your shader text can be hard-coded as a string-literal, read from a file on disk, or generated on the fly. One way or another, it needs to be in a string so you can load it into your shader object:

```
GLchar *myStringPtrs[1];
myStringPtrs[0] = vertexShaderText;
glShaderSource(myVertexShader, 1, myStringPtrs, NULL);
myStringPtrs[0] = fragmentShaderText;
glShaderSource(myFragmentShader, 1, myStringPtrs, NULL);
```

`glShaderSource` is set up to accept multiple individual strings. The second argument is a count that indicates how many string pointers to look for. The strings are strung together into a single long string before being compiled. This capability can be useful if you're loading reusable subroutines from a library of functions:

```
GLchar *myStringPtrs[3];
myStringPtrs[0] = vsMainText;
myStringPtrs[1] = myNoiseFuncText;
myStringPtrs[2] = myBlendFuncText;
glShaderSource(myVertexShader, 3, myStringPtrs, NULL);
```

If all your strings are null-terminated, you don't need to specify string lengths in the fourth argument and can pass in NULL instead. But for shader text that is not null-terminated, you need to provide the length; lengths do not include the null terminator if present. You can use –1 for strings that are null-terminated. The following code passes in a pointer to an array of lengths along with the array of string pointers:

```
GLint fsLength = strlen(fragmentShaderText);
myStringPtrs[0] = fragmentShaderText;
glShaderSource(myFragmentShader, 1, myStringPtrs, &fsLength);
```

Compiling Shaders

After your shader text is loaded into a shader object, you need to compile it. Compiling parses your shader and makes sure there are no errors:

```
glCompileShader(myVertexShader);
glCompileShader(myFragmentShader);
```

You can query a flag in each shader object to see whether the compile was successful. Each shader object also has an information log that contains error messages if the compilation failed. It might also contain warnings or other useful information even if your compilation was successful. These logs are primarily intended for use as a tool while you are developing your GLSL application:

```
glCompileShader(myVertexShader);
glGetShaderiv(myVertexShader, GL_COMPILE_STATUS, &success);
if (!success)
{
    GLchar infoLog[MAX_INFO_LOG_SIZE];
    glGetShaderInfoLog(myVertexShader, MAX_INFO_LOG_SIZE, NULL, infoLog);
    fprintf(stderr, "Error in vertex shader compilation!\n");
    fprintf(stderr, "Info log: %s\n", infoLog);
}
```

The returned info log string is always null-terminated. If you don't want to allocate a large static array to store the info log, you can find out the exact size of the info log before querying it:

```
glGetShaderiv(myVertexShader, GL_INFO_LOG_LENGTH, &infoLogSize);
```

Program Objects

The second type of object GLSL uses is a program object. This object acts as a container for shader objects, linking them together into a single executable. You can specify a GLSL shader for each replaceable section of the conventional OpenGL pipeline. Currently, only vertex and fragment stages are replaceable, but that list could be extended in the future to include additional stages.

Creating and Deleting

Program objects are created and deleted the same way as shader objects. The difference is that there's only one kind of program object, so its creation command doesn't take an argument:

```
GLuint myProgram = glCreateProgram();
...
glDeleteProgram(myProgram);
```

Attaching and Detaching

A program object is a container. You need to attach your shader objects to it if you want GLSL instead of fixed functionality:

```
glAttachShader(myProgram, myVertexShader);
glAttachShader(myProgram, myFragmentShader);
```

You can even attach multiple shader objects of the same type to your program object. Similar to loading multiple shader source strings into a single shader object, this makes it possible to include function libraries shared by more than one of your program objects.

You can choose to replace only part of the pipeline with GLSL and leave the rest to fixed functionality. Just don't attach shaders for the parts you want to leave alone. Or if you're switching between GLSL and fixed functionality for part of the pipeline, you can detach a previously attached shader object. You can even detach both shaders, in which case you're back to full fixed functionality:

```
glDetachShader(myProgram, myVertexShader);
glDetachShader(myProgram, myFragmentShader);
```

Linking Programs

Before you can use GLSL for rendering, you have to link your program object. This process takes each of the previously compiled shader objects and links them into a single executable:

```
glLinkProgram(myProgram);
```

You can query a flag in the program object to see whether the link was successful. The object also has an information log that contains error messages if the link failed. The log might also contain warnings or other useful information even if your link was successful:

```
glLinkProgram(myProgram);
glGetProgramiv(myProgram, GL_LINK_STATUS, &success);
if (!success)
{
    GLchar infoLog[MAX_INFO_LOG_SIZE];
    glGetProgramInfoLog(myProgram, MAX_INFO_LOG_SIZE, NULL, infoLog);
    fprintf(stderr, "Error in program linkage!\n");
    fprintf(stderr, "Info log: %s\n", infoLog);
}
```

Validating Programs

If your link was successful, odds are good that your shaders will be executable when it comes time to render. But some things aren't known at link time, such as the values assigned to texture samplers, described in subsequent sections. A sampler may be set to an invalid value, or multiple samplers of different types may be illegally set to the same value. At link time, you don't know what the state is going to be when you render, so errors cannot be thrown at that time. When you validate, however, it looks at the current state so you can find out once and for all whether your GLSL shaders are going to execute when you draw that first triangle:

```
glValidateProgram(myProgram);
glGetProgramiv(myProgram, GL_VALIDATE_STATUS, &success);
if (!success)
{
    GLchar infoLog[MAX_INFO_LOG_SIZE];
    glGetProgramInfoLog(myProgram, MAX_INFO_LOG_SIZE, NULL, infoLog);
    fprintf(stderr, "Error in program validation!\n");
    fprintf(stderr, "Info log: %s\n", infoLog);
}
```

Again, if the validation fails, an explanation and possibly tips for avoiding the failure are included in the program object's info log. Note that validating your program object before rendering with it is not a requirement, but if you do try to use a program object that would have failed validation, your rendering commands will fail and throw OpenGL errors.

Using Programs

Finally, you're ready to turn on your program. Unlike other OpenGL features, GLSL mode is not toggled with glEnable/glDisable. Instead, use this:

```
glUseProgram(myProgram);
```

You can use this function to enable GLSL with a particular program object and also to switch between different program objects. To disable GLSL and switch back to fixed functionality, you also use this function, passing in 0:

```
glUseProgram(0);
```

You can query for the current program object handle at any time:

```
currentProgObj = glGetIntegerv(GL_CURRENT_PROGRAM);
```

Now that you know how to manage your shaders, you can focus on their contents. The syntax of GLSL is largely the same as that of C/C++, so you should be able to dive right in. It should be noted that the latest version of the GLSL specification at the time of publishing is v1.20.

Variables

Variables and functions must be declared in advance. Your variable name can use any letters (case-sensitive), numbers, or an underscore, but it can't begin with a number. Also, your variable cannot begin with the prefix gl_, which is reserved for built-in variables and functions. A list of reserved keywords available in the OpenGL Shading Language specification contains a list of reserved keywords, which are also off-limits.

Basic Types

In addition to the Boolean, integer, and floating-point types found in C, GLSL introduces some data types commonly used in shaders. Table 15.1 lists these basic data types.

TABLE 15.1   Basic Data Types

Type	Description
void	A data type required for functions that don't return a value. Functions that take no arguments can optionally use void as well.
bool	A Boolean variable used primarily for conditionals and loops. It can be assigned to keywords true and false, or any expression that evaluates to a Boolean.
int	A variable represented by a signed integer with at least 16 bits. It can be expressed in decimal, octal, or hexadecimal. It is primarily used for loop counters and array indexing.
float	A floating-point variable approximating IEEE single-precision. It can be expressed in scientific notation (for example, 0.0001 = 1e–4).
bvec2	A two-component Boolean vector.
bvec3	A three-component Boolean vector.
bvec4	A four-component Boolean vector.
ivec2	A two-component integer vector.
ivec3	A three-component integer vector.
ivec4	A four-component integer vector.
vec2	A two-component floating-point vector.
vec3	A three-component floating-point vector.
vec4	A four-component floating-point vector.
mat2 or mat2x2	A 2×2 floating-point matrix. Matrices are accessed in column-major order.
mat3 or mat3x3	A 3×3 floating-point matrix.
mat4 or mat4x4	A 4×4 floating-point matrix.
mat2x3	A 2-column × 3-row floating-point matrix.
mat2x4	A 2-column × 4-row floating-point matrix.
mat3x2	A 3-column × 2-row floating-point matrix.
mat3x4	A 3-column × 4-row floating-point matrix.
mat4x2	A 4-column × 2-row floating-point matrix.
mat4x3	A 4-column × 3-row floating-point matrix.
sampler1D	A special-purpose constant used by built-in texture functions to reference a specific 1D texture. It can be declared only as a uniform or function argument.
sampler2D	A constant used for referencing a 2D texture.
sampler3D	A constant used for referencing a 3D texture.
samplerCube	A constant used for referencing a cube map texture.
sampler1DShadow	A constant used for referencing a 1D depth texture with shadow comparison.
sampler2DShadow	A constant used for referencing a 2D depth texture with shadow comparison.

15

Structures

Structures can be used to group basic data types into a user-defined data type. When defining the structure, you can declare instances of the structure at the same time, or you can declare them later:

```
struct surface {
    float indexOfRefraction;
    float reflectivity;
    vec3 color;
    float turbulence;
} myFirstSurf;

surface mySecondSurf;
```

You can assign one structure to another (=) or compare two structures (==, !=). For both of these operations, the structures must be of the same declared type. Two structures are considered equal if each of their member fields is component-wise equal. To access a single field of a structure, you use the selector (.):

```
vec3 totalColor = myFirstSurf.color + mySecondSurf.color;
```

Structure definitions must contain at least one member. Arrays, discussed next, may be included in structures, but only when a specific array size is provided. Unlike C language structures, GLSL does not allow bit fields. Structures within structures are also not allowed.

```
struct superSurface {
    vec3 points[30];      // Sized arrays are okay
    surface surf;         // Okay, as surface was defined earlier
    struct velocity {     // ILLEGAL!!  Embedded struct
        float speed;
        vec3 direction;
    } velo;
    subSurface sub;       // ILLEGAL!!  Forward declaration
};

struct subSurface {
    int id;
};
```

Arrays

One-dimensional arrays of any type (including structures) can be declared. You don't need to declare the size of the array as long as it is always indexed with a constant integer expression. Otherwise, you must declare its size up front. All the following are acceptable:

```
surface mySurfaces[];
vec4 lightPositions[8];
vec4 moreLightPositions[] = lightPositions;
const int numSurfaces = 5;
surface myFiveSurfaces[numSurfaces];
float[5] values; // another way to size the array
```

You also must declare an explicit size for your array when the array is declared as a parameter or return type in a function declaration or as a member of a structure.

The `length()` method can be used to return the length of an array:

```
lightPositions.length(); // returns array size, in this case 8
```

One last thing: You cannot declare an array of arrays!

Qualifiers

Variables can be declared with an optional type qualifier. Table 15.2 lists the available qualifiers.

TABLE 15.2   Type Qualifiers

Qualifier	Description
const	Constant value initialized during declaration. It is read-only during shader execution. It is also used with a function call argument to indicate that it's a constant that can't be written within the function.
attribute	Read-only per-vertex data, available only within vertex shaders. This data comes from current vertex state or from vertex arrays. It must be declared globally (outside all functions). An attribute must be a floating-point scalar, vector, or matrix, and may not be an array or a structure.
uniform	Another value that remains constant during each shader execution; but unlike a const, a uniform's value is not known at compile time and is initialized outside the shader. A uniform is shared by the currently active vertex and fragment shaders and must be declared globally.
varying	Output of the vertex shader, such as colors or texture coordinates, that corresponds to read-only interpolated input of the fragment shader. A varying must be declared globally; must be a floating-point scalar, vector, or matrix; and may be an array but not a structure.
centroid varying	Identical to a varying when not multisampling, in which case the interpolated value is evaluated at the fragment center. When multisampling, a centroid varying is evaluated at a location that falls within the interior of the primitive being rasterized instead of a fixed location such as the fragment center.

15

TABLE 15.2   Continued

Qualifier	Description
invariant	Used with vertex shader outputs (i.e., varyings and built-ins) and any matching fragment shader varying inputs to indicate that computed values must be consistent across different shaders. If all data flow and control flow are identical leading up to writing an invariant variable, the compiler will guarantee the results to be identical across shaders. This often requires the compiler to sacrifice potential optimizations that might yield slightly different results, so it should not be used unless necessary, such as to avoid Z-fighting artifacts in multipass rendering.
in	A qualifier used with a function call argument to indicate that it's only an input, and any changes to the variable within the called function shouldn't affect the value in the calling function. This is the default behavior for function arguments if no qualifier is present.
out	A qualifier used with a function call argument to indicate that it's only an output, so no value needs to be actually passed into the function.
inout	A qualifier used with a function call argument to indicate that it's both an input and an output. A value is passed in from the calling function, and that value is replaced by the called function.

Built-In Variables

Built-in variables allow interaction with fixed functionality. They don't need to be declared before use. Tables 15.3 and 15.4 list most of the built-in variables. Refer to the GLSL specification for built-in uniforms and constants

TABLE 15.3   Built-in Vertex Shader Variables

Name	Type	Description
gl_Color	vec4	Input attribute corresponding to per-vertex primary color.
gl_SecondaryColor	vec4	Input attribute corresponding to per-vertex secondary color.
gl_Normal	vec3	Input attribute corresponding to per-vertex normal.
gl_Vertex	vec4	Input attribute corresponding to object-space vertex position.
gl_MultiTexCoord*n*	vec4	Input attribute corresponding to per-vertex texture coordinate *n*.
gl_FogCoord	float	Input attribute corresponding to per-vertex fog coordinate.
gl_Position	vec4	Output for transformed vertex position that will be used by fixed functionality primitive assembly, clipping, and culling; all vertex shaders must write to this variable.
gl_ClipVertex	vec4	Output for the coordinate to use for user clip plane clipping.
gl_PointSize	float	Output for the size of the point to be rasterized, measured in pixels.
gl_FrontColor	vec4	Varying output for front primary color.

TABLE 15.3   Continued

Name	Type	Description
gl_BackColor	vec4	Varying output for back primary color.
gl_FrontSecondaryColor	vec4	Varying output for front secondary color.
gl_BackSecondaryColor	vec4	Varying output for back secondary color.
gl_TexCoord[]	vec4	Array of varying outputs for texture coordinates.
gl_FogFragCoord	float	Varying output for the fog coordinate.

TABLE 15.4   Built-in Fragment Shader Variables

Name	Type	Description
gl_Color	vec4	Interpolated read-only input containing the primary color.
gl_SecondaryColor	vec4	Interpolated read-only input containing the secondary color.
gl_TexCoord[]	vec4	Array of interpolated read-only inputs containing texture coordinates.
gl_FogFragCoord	float	Interpolated read-only input containing the fog coordinate.
gl_FragCoord	vec4	Read-only input containing the window-space x, y, z, and 1/w.
gl_FrontFacing	bool	Read-only input whose value is true if part of a front-facing primitive.
gl_PointCoord	vec2	Two-dimensional coordinates ranging from (0.0, 0.0) to (1.0, 1.0) across a point sprite, defined only for point primitives and when GL_POINT_SPRITE is enabled.
gl_FragColor	vec4	Output for the color to use for subsequent per-pixel operations.
gl_FragData[]	vec4	Array of arbitrary data output to be used with glDrawBuffers (see Chapter 18); cannot to be used in combination with gl_FragColor.
gl_FragDepth	float	Output for the depth to use for subsequent per-pixel operations; if unwritten, the fixed functionality depth is used instead.

Expressions

The following sections describe various operators and expressions found in GLSL.

Operators

All the familiar C operators are available in GLSL with few exceptions. See Table 15.5 for a complete list.

TABLE 15.5   Operators in Order of Precedence (From Highest to Lowest)

Operator	Description
( )	Parenthetical grouping, function call, or constructor
[ ]	Array subscript, vector, or matrix selector
.	Structure field selector, vector component selector
++ —	Prefix or postfix increment and decrement
+ - !	Unary addition, subtraction, logical NOT
* /	Multiplication and division
+ -	Binary addition and subtraction
< > <= >= == !=	Less than, greater than, less than or equal to, greater than or equal to, equal to, not equal to
&& ¦¦ ^^	Logical AND, OR, XOR
? :	Conditional
= += -= *= /=	Assignment, arithmetic assignments
,	Sequence

A few operators are missing from GLSL. Because there are no pointers to worry about, you don't need an address-of operator (&) or a dereference operator (*). A typecast operator is not needed because typecasting is not allowed. Bitwise operators (&, ¦, ^, ~, <<, >>, &=, ¦=, ^=, <<=, >>=) are reserved for future use, as are modulus operators (%, %=).

Array Access

Arrays are indexed using integer expressions, with the first array element at index 0:

```
vec4 myFifthColor, ambient, diffuse[6], specular[6];
...
myFifthColor = ambient + diffuse[5] + specular[5];
```

Shader execution is undefined if an attempt is made to access an array with an index less than zero or greater than or equal to the size of the array. If the compiler can determine this at compile time (e.g., the array is indexed by an out-of-range constant expression), the shader will fail to compile entirely.

Constructors

Constructors are special functions primarily used to initialize variables, especially of multi-component data types, including structures and arrays. They take the form of a function call with the name of the function being the same as the name of the type:

```
vec3 myNormal = vec3(0.0, 1.0, 0.0);
```

Constructors are not limited to declaration initializers; they can be used as expressions anywhere in your shader:

```
greenTint = myColor + vec3(0.0, 1.0, 0.0);
```

A single scalar value is assigned to all elements of a vector:

```
ivec4 myColor = ivec4(255);  // all 4 components get 255
```

You can mix and match scalars, vectors, and matrices in your constructor, as long as you end up with enough components to initialize the entire data type. Any extra components are dropped:

```
vec4 myVector1 = vec4(x, vec2(y, z), w);
vec2 myVector2 = vec2(myVector1);        // z, w are dropped
float myFloat = float(myVector2);        // y dropped
```

Matrices are constructed in column-major order. If you provide a single scalar value, that value is used for the diagonal matrix elements, and all other elements are set to 0:

```
// all of these are same 2x2 identity matrix
mat2 myMatrix1 = mat2(1.0, 0.0, 0.0, 1.0);
mat2 myMatrix2 = mat2(vec2(1.0, 0.0), vec2(0.0, 1.0));
mat2 myMatrix3 = mat2(1.0);
mat2 myMatrix4 = mat2(mat4(1.0)); // takes upper 2x2 of the 4x4
```

You can also use constructors to convert between the different scalar types. This is the only way to perform type conversions. No implicit or explicit typecasts or promotions are possible.

The conversion from int to float is obvious. When you are converting from float to int, the fractional part is dropped. When you are converting from int or float to bool, values of 0 or 0.0 are converted to false, and anything else is converted to true. When you are converting from bool to int or float, true is converted to 1 or 1.0, and false is converted to 0 or 0.0:

```
float myFloat = 4.7;
int myInt = int(myFloat);  // myInt = 4
```

Arrays can be initialized by providing in the constructor a value for every element of the array. Either of the following is acceptable:

```
ivec2 cursorPositions[3] = ivec2[3]((0, 0), (10, 20), (15, 40));
ivec2 morePositions[3] = ivec2[]((0, 0), (10, 20), (15, 40));
```

15

Finally, you can initialize structures by providing arguments in the same order and of the same type as the structure definition:

```
struct surface {
    float indexOfRefraction;
    float reflectivity;
    vec3 color;
    float turbulence;
};

surface mySurf = surface(ior, refl, vec3(red, green, blue), turb);
```

Component Selectors

Individual components of a vector can be accessed by using dot notation along with {x,y,z,w}, {r,g,b,a}, or {s,t,p,q}. These different notations are useful for positions and normals, colors, and texture coordinates, respectively. You cannot mix and match selectors from the different notations. Notice the p in place of the usual r texture coordinate. This component has been renamed to avoid ambiguity with the r color component. Here are some examples of component selectors:

```
vec3 myVector = {0.25, 0.5, 0.75};
float myR = myVector.r;   // 0.25
vec2 myYZ = myVector.yz;  // 0.5, 0.75
float myQ = myVector.q;   // ILLEGAL!! accesses component beyond vec3
float myRY = myVector.ry; // ILLEGAL!! mixes two notations
```

You can use the component selectors to rearrange the order of components or replicate them:

```
vec3 myZYX = myVector.zyx;   // reverse order
vec4 mySSTT = myVector.sstt; // replicate s and t twice each
```

You can also use them as write masks on the left side of an assignment to select which components are modified. In this case, you cannot use component selectors more than once:

```
vec4 myColor = vec4(0.0, 1.0, 2.0, 3.0);
myColor.x = -1.0;               // -1.0, 1.0, 2.0, 3.0
myColor.yz = vec2(-2.0, -3.0);  // -1.0, -2.0, -3.0, 3.0
myColor.wx = vec2(0.0, 1.0);    // 1.0, -2.0, -3.0, 0.0
myColor.zz = vec2(2.0, 3.0);    // ILLEGAL!!
```

Another way to get at individual vector components or matrix components is to use array subscript notation. This way, you can use an arbitrarily computed integer index to access your vector or matrix as if it were an array. Shader execution is undefined if an attempt is made to access a component outside the bounds of the vector or matrix.

```
float myY = myVector[1];
```

For matrices, providing a single array index accesses the corresponding matrix column as a vector. Providing a second array index accesses the corresponding vector component:

```
mat3 myMatrix = mat3(1.0);
vec3 myFirstColumn = myMatrix[0]; // first column: 1.0, 0.0, 0.0
float element21 = myMatrix[2][1]; // last column, middle row: 0.0
```

Control Flow

GLSL offers a variety of familiar nonlinear flow mechanisms that reduce code size, make more complex algorithms possible, and make shaders more readable.

Loops

for, while, and do/while loops are all supported with the same syntax as in C/C++. Loops can be nested. You can use continue and break to prematurely move on to the next iteration or break out of the loop:

```
for (l = 0; l < numLights; l++)
{
    if (!lightExists[l])
        continue;
    color += light[l];
}

while (lightNum >= 0)
{
    color += light[lightNum];
    lightNum—;
}

do
{
    color += light[lightNum];
    lightNum—;
} while (lightNum > 0);
```

if/else

You can use `if` and `if/else` clauses to select between multiple blocks of code. These conditionals can also be nested:

```
color = unlitColor;
if (numLights > 0)
{
    color = litColor;
}

if (numLights > 0)
{
    color = litColor;
}
else
{
    color = unlitColor;
}
```

discard

Fragment shaders have a special control flow mechanism called `discard`. It terminates execution of the current fragment's shader. All subsequent per-fragment pipeline stages are skipped, and the fragment is not written to the framebuffer:

```
// e.g., perform an alpha test within your fragment shader
if (color.a < 0.9)
    discard;
```

Functions

Functions are used to modularize shader code. All shaders must define a `main` function, which is the place where execution begins. The `void` parameter list here is optional, but not the void return:

```
void main(void)
{
    ...
}
```

Functions must be either defined or declared with a prototype before use. These definitions or declarations should occur globally, outside any function. Return types are required, as are types for each function argument. Also, arguments can have an optional qualifier in, out, inout, or const (see Table 15.2):

```
// function declaration
bool isAnyComponentNegative(const vec4 v);

// function use
void main()
{
    bool someNeg = isAnyComponentNegative(gl_MultiTexCoord0);
    ...
}

// function definition
bool isAnyComponentNegative(const vec4 v)
{
    if ((v.x < 0.0) || (v.y < 0.0) ||
        (v.z < 0.0) || (v.w < 0.0))
        return true;
    else
        return false;
}
```

Structures are allowed as arguments and return types. Arrays are also allowed as arguments and return types, in which case the declaration and definition would include the array name with size, whereas the function call would just use the array name without brackets or size:

```
vec4 sumMyVectors(int howManyToSum, vec4 v[10]);

void main()
{
    vec4 myColors[10];
    ...
    gl_FragColor = sumMyVectors(6, myColors);
}
```

You can give more than one function the same name, as long as the return type or argument types are different. This is called *function name overloading* and is useful if you want to perform the same type of operation on, for example, different-sized vectors:

```
float multiplyAccumulate(float a, float b, float c)
{
    return (a * b) + c;  // scalar definition
}

vec4 multiplyAccumulate(vec4 a, vec4 b, vec4 c)
```

```
{
    return (a * b) + c;   // 4-vector definition
}
```

Recursive functions are not allowed. In other words, the same function cannot be present more than once in the current call stack. Some compilers may be able to catch this and throw an error, but in any case, shader execution will be undefined.

Approximately 50 built-in functions provide all sorts of useful calculations, ranging from simple arithmetic to trigonometry. You can consult the GLSL specification for the complete list and descriptions.

Texture Lookup Functions

Texture lookup built-in functions deserve special mention. Whereas some of the other built-in functions are provided as a convenience because you could code your own versions relatively easily, texture lookup built-in functions (shown in the following list) are crucial to perform even the most basic texturing.

Texture Lookup Built-in Functions

```
vec4 texture1D(sampler1D sampler, float coord [, float bias] )

vec4 texture1DProj(sampler1D sampler, vec2 coord [, float bias] )

vec4 texture1DProj(sampler1D sampler, vec4 coord [, float bias] )

vec4 texture1DLod(sampler1D sampler, float coord, float lod)

vec4 texture1DProjLod(sampler1D sampler, vec2 coord, float lod)

vec4 texture1DProjLod(sampler1D sampler, vec4 coord, float lod)

vec4 texture2D(sampler2D sampler, vec2 coord [, float bias] )

vec4 texture2DProj(sampler2D sampler, vec3 coord [, float bias] )

vec4 texture2DProj(sampler2D sampler, vec4 coord [, float bias] )

vec4 texture2DLod(sampler2D sampler, vec2 coord, float lod)

vec4 texture2DProjLod(sampler2D sampler, vec3 coord, float lod)

vec4 texture2DProjLod(sampler2D sampler, vec4 coord, float lod)

vec4 texture3D(sampler3D sampler, vec3 coord [, float bias] )

vec4 texture3DProj(sampler3D sampler, vec4 coord [, float bias] )

vec4 texture3DLod(sampler3D sampler, vec3 coord, float lod)

vec4 texture3DProjLod(sampler3D sampler, vec4 coord, float lod)

vec4 textureCube(samplerCube sampler, vec3 coord [, float bias] )

vec4 textureCubeLod(samplerCube sampler, vec3 coord, float lod)

vec4 shadow1D(sampler1DShadow sampler, vec3 coord [, float bias] )
```

```
vec4 shadow2D(sampler2DShadow sampler, vec3 coord [, float bias] )

vec4 shadow1DProj(sampler1DShadow sampler, vec4 coord, [, float bias] )

vec4 shadow2DProj(sampler2DShadow sampler, vec4 coord, [, float bias] )

vec4 shadow1DLod(sampler1DShadow sampler, vec3 coord, float lod)

vec4 shadow2DLod(sampler2DShadow sampler, vec3 coord, float lod)

vec4 shadow1DProjLod(sampler1DShadow sampler, vec4 coord, float lod)

vec4 shadow2DProjLod(sampler2DShadow sampler, vec4 coord, float lod)
```

The lookup is performed on the texture of the type encoded in the function name (1D, 2D, 3D, Cube) currently bound to the sampler represented by the sampler parameter. The "Proj" versions perform a perspective divide on the texture coordinate before lookup. The divisor is the last component of the coordinate vector.

The "Lod" versions, available only in a vertex shader, specify the mipmap level-of-detail (LOD) from which to sample. The non-"Lod" versions sample from the base LOD when used by a vertex shader. Fragment shaders can use only the non-"Lod" versions, where the mipmap LOD is computed as usual based on texture coordinate derivatives. However, fragment shaders can supply an optional bias that will be added to the computed LOD. This bias parameter is not allowed in a vertex shader.

The "shadow" versions perform a depth texture comparison as part of the lookup (see Chapter 14, "Depth Textures and Shadows").

Summary

In this chapter, we outlined the conventional per-vertex and per-fragment pipeline stages, setting the stage for their wholesale replacement by programmable stages. You learned all the nuts and bolts of the OpenGL Shading Language (GLSL). We discussed all the variable types, operators, and flow control mechanisms. We also described how to use the commands for loading and compiling shader objects and linking and using program objects. There was a lot of ground to cover here, but we made it through at a record pace.

This concludes the boring lecture portion of our shader coverage. You now have a solid conceptual foundation for the next two chapters, which will provide practical examples of vertex and fragment shader applications using GLSL. The following chapters will prove much more enjoyable with all the textbook learning behind you.

CHAPTER 16

Vertex Shading: Do-It-Yourself Transform, Lighting, and Texgen

by Benjamin Lipchak

WHAT YOU'LL LEARN IN THIS CHAPTER:

- How to perform per-vertex lighting

- How to generate texture coordinates

- How to calculate per-vertex fog

- How to calculate per-vertex point size

- How to squash and stretch objects

- How to make realistic skin with vertex blending

This chapter is devoted to the application of vertex shaders. We covered the basic mechanics of OpenGL Shading Language (GLSL) shaders in the preceding chapter, but at some point you have to put the textbook down and start learning by doing. Here, we introduce a handful of shaders that perform various real-world tasks. You are encouraged to use these shaders as a starting point for your own experimentation.

Getting Your Feet Wet

Every shader should at the very least output a clip-space vertex coordinate. Lighting and texture coordinate generation (texgen), the other operations typically performed in vertex shaders, may not be necessary. For example, if you're creating a depth texture and all you care about are the final depth values, you wouldn't waste instructions in your shader to output a color or texture coordinates. But one way or another, you always need to output a clip-space position for subsequent primitive assembly and rasterization to occur.

For your first sample shader, you'll perform the bare-bones vertex transformation that would occur automatically by fixed functionality if you weren't using a vertex shader. As an added bonus, you'll copy the incoming color into the outgoing color. Remember, anything that isn't output remains undefined. If you want that color to be available later in the pipeline, you have to copy it from input to output, even if the vertex shader doesn't need to change it in any way.

Figure 16.1 shows the result of the simple shader in Listing 16.1.

FIGURE 16.1   This vertex shader transforms the position to clip space and copies the vertex's color from input to output.

LISTING 16.1   Simple Vertex Shader

```
// simple.vs
//
// Generic vertex transformation,
```

LISTING 16.1   Continued

```
// copy primary color

void main(void)
{
    // multiply object-space position by MVP matrix
    gl_Position = gl_ModelViewProjectionMatrix * gl_Vertex;

    // Copy the primary color
    gl_FrontColor = gl_Color;
}
```

The modelview and projection matrices are traditionally two separate matrices against which the incoming object-space vertex position is multiplied. GLSL conveniently provides a shortcut called gl_ModelViewProjectionMatrix, a concatenation of the two matrices, which we refer to as the MVP matrix. This way we need only perform one matrix multiply in order to transform the vertex position.

An alternative to performing the transform yourself is using the ftransform built-in function, which emulates fixed functionality vertex transformation on the incoming vertex position. Not only is it convenient, but it also guarantees that the result is identical to that achieved by fixed functionality, which is especially useful when rendering in multiple passes. Otherwise, if you mix fixed functionality and your own vertex shader (without ftransform) and draw the same geometry, the subtle floating-point differences in the resulting Z values may result in "Z-fighting" artifacts. The invariant qualifier, described in Chapter 15, "Programmable Pipeline: This Isn't Your Father's OpenGL," can be used when declaring vertex shader outputs to achieve a similar effect. Unlike ftransform, however, invariant is not limited to clip-space position.

Diffuse Lighting

Diffuse lighting takes into account the orientation of a surface relative to the direction of incoming light. The following is the equation for diffuse lighting:

$$C_{diff} = \max\{N \bullet L, 0\} * C_{mat} * C_{li}$$

N is the vertex's unit normal, and L is the unit vector representing the direction from the vertex to the light source. C_{mat} is the color of the surface material, and C_{li} is the color of the light. C_{diff} is the resulting diffuse color. Because the light in the example is white, you can omit that term, as it would be the same as multiplying by {1,1,1,1}. Figure 16.2 shows the result from Listing 16.2, which implements the diffuse lighting equation.

16

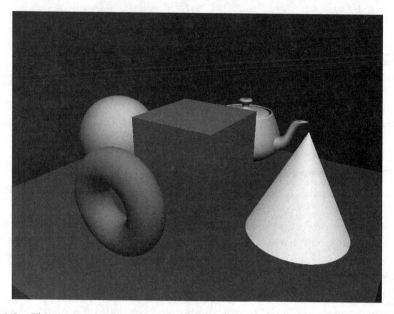

FIGURE 16.2   This vertex shader computes diffuse lighting. (This figure also appears in the Color insert.)

LISTING 16.2   Diffuse Lighting Vertex Shader

```
// diffuse.vp
//
// Generic vertex transformation,
// diffuse lighting based on one
// white light

uniform vec3 lightPos[1];

void main(void)
{
    // normal MVP transform
    gl_Position = gl_ModelViewProjectionMatrix * gl_Vertex;

    vec3 N = normalize(gl_NormalMatrix * gl_Normal);
    vec4 V = gl_ModelViewMatrix * gl_Vertex;
    vec3 L = normalize(lightPos[0] - V.xyz);

    // output the diffuse color
    float NdotL = dot(N, L);
    gl_FrontColor = gl_Color * vec4(max(0.0, NdotL));
}
```

The light position is a uniform vector passed into the shader from the application. This allows you to easily change the light position interactively without having to alter the shader. You can do this using the left- and right-arrow keys while running the VertexShaders sample program. It could have been referenced instead using the built-in uniform variable gl_LightSource[*n*].position to achieve the same effect, in which case the sample program would call glLight* instead of glUniform* to update the position.

After computing the clip-space position as you did in the "simple" shader, the "diffuse" shader proceeds to transform the vertex position to eye space, too. All the lighting calculations are performed in eye space, so you need to transform the normal vector from object space to eye space as well. GLSL provides the gl_NormalMatrix built-in uniform matrix as a convenience for this purpose. It is simply the inverse transpose of the modelview matrix's upper-left 3×3 elements. The last vector you need to compute is the light vector, which is the direction from the vertex position to the light position, so you just subtract one from the other. Note that we're modeling a point light here rather than a directional light.

Both the normal and the light vectors must be unit vectors, so you normalize them before continuing. GLSL supplies a built-in function, normalize, to perform this common task.

The dot product of the two unit vectors, N and L, will be in the range [–1,1]. But because you're interested in the amount of diffuse lighting bouncing off the surface, having a negative contribution doesn't make sense. This is why you clamp the result of the dot product to the range [0,1] by using the max function. The diffuse lighting contribution can then be multiplied by the vertex's diffuse material color to obtain the final lit color.

Specular Lighting

Specular lighting takes into account the orientation of a surface relative to both the direction of incoming light and the view vector. The following is the equation for specular lighting:

$$C_{spec} = \max\{N \bullet H, 0\}^{Sexp} * C_{mat} * C_{li}$$

H is the unit vector representing the direction halfway between the light vector and the view vector, known as the half-angle vector. S_{exp} is the specular exponent, controlling the tightness of the specular highlight. C_{spec} is the resulting specular color. N, L, C_{mat}, and C_{li} represent the same values as in diffuse lighting, although you're free to use different specular and diffuse colors. Because the light in the example is white, you can again omit that term. Figure 16.3 illustrates the output of Listing 16.3, which implements both diffuse and specular lighting equations. Note that the specular term is included only when N • L is also greater than zero—a subtlety not captured in the above equation, but one that's part of the fixed functionality lighting definition.

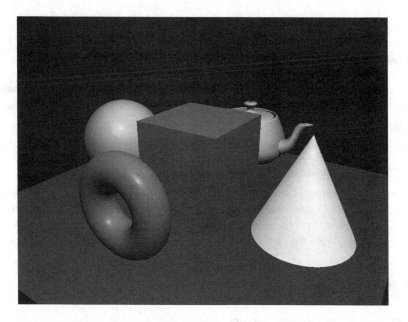

FIGURE 16.3   This vertex shader computes diffuse and specular lighting. (This figure also appears in the Color insert.)

LISTING 16.3   Diffuse and Specular Lighting Vertex Shader

```
// specular.vs
//
// Generic vertex transformation,
// diffuse and specular lighting
// based on one white light

uniform vec3 lightPos[1];

void main(void)
{
    // normal MVP transform
    gl_Position = gl_ModelViewProjectionMatrix * gl_Vertex;

    vec3 N = normalize(gl_NormalMatrix * gl_Normal);
    vec4 V = gl_ModelViewMatrix * gl_Vertex;
    vec3 L = normalize(lightPos[0] - V.xyz);
    vec3 H = normalize(L + vec3(0.0, 0.0, 1.0));
    const float specularExp = 128.0;
```

LISTING 16.3   Continued

```
    // calculate diffuse lighting
    float NdotL = max(0.0, dot(N, L));
    vec4 diffuse = gl_Color * vec4(NdotL);

    // calculate specular lighting
    float NdotH = max(0.0, dot(N, H));
    vec4 specular = vec4(0.0);
    if (NdotL > 0.0)
        specular = vec4(pow(NdotH, specularExp));

    // sum the diffuse and specular components
    gl_FrontColor = diffuse + specular;
}
```

We used a hard-coded constant specular exponent of 128, which provides a nice, tight specular highlight. You can experiment with different values to find one you may prefer. Practice your GLSL skills by turning this scalar value into another uniform that you can control from the application.

Improved Specular Lighting

Specular highlights change rapidly over the surface of an object. Trying to compute them per-vertex and then interpolating the result across a triangle gives relatively poor results. Instead of a nice circular highlight, you end up with a muddy polygonal-shaped highlight.

One way you can improve the situation is to separate the diffuse lighting result from the specular lighting result, outputting one as the vertex's primary color and the other as the secondary color. By adding the diffuse and specular colors together, you effectively saturate the color (that is, exceed a value of 1.0) wherever a specular highlight appears. If you try to interpolate the sum of these colors, the saturation will more broadly affect the entire triangle. However, if you interpolate the two colors separately and then sum them per-fragment, the saturation will occur only where desired, cleaning up some of the muddiness. When using fixed functionality fragment processing, this sum per-fragment is achieved by simply enabling GL_COLOR_SUM. Here is the altered shader code for separating the two lit colors:

```
// put diffuse into primary color
float NdotL = max(0.0, dot(N, L));
gl_FrontColor = gl_Color * vec4(NdotL);

// put specular into secondary color
float NdotH = max(0.0, dot(N, H));
gl_FrontSecondaryColor = (NdotL > 0.0) ?
```

16

```
                         vec4(pow(NdotH, specularExp)) :
                         vec4(0.0);
```

Separating the colors improves things a bit, but the root of the problem is the specular exponent. By raising the specular coefficient to a power, you have a value that wants to change much more rapidly than per-vertex interpolation allows. In fact, if your geometry is not tessellated finely enough, you may lose a specular highlight altogether.

An effective way to avoid this problem is to output just the specular coefficient (N • H), but wait and raise it to a power per-fragment. This way, you can safely interpolate the more slowly changing (N • H). You're not employing fragment shaders until the next chapter, so how do you perform this power computation per-fragment? All you have to do is set up a 1D texture with a table of s^{128} values and send (N • H) out of the vertex shader on a texture coordinate. This is considered custom texgen. Then you will use fixed functionality texture environment to add the specular color from the texture lookup to the interpolated diffuse color from the vertex shader.

The following is the shader code, again altered from the original specular lighting shader:

```
// put diffuse lighting result in primary color
float NdotL = max(0.0, dot(N, L));
gl_FrontColor = gl_Color * vec4(NdotL);

// copy (N.H)*8-7 into texcoord if N.L is positive
float NdotH = 0.0;
if (NdotL > 0.0)
    NdotH = max(0.0, dot(N, H) * 8.0 - 7.0);
gl_TexCoord[0] = vec4(NdotH, 0.0, 0.0, 1.0);
```

Here, the (N • H) has been clamped to the range [0,1]. But if you try raising most of that range to the power of 128, you'll get results so close to zero that they will correspond to texel values of zero. Only the upper 1/8 of (N • H) values will begin mapping to measurable texel values. To make economical use of the 1D texture, you can focus in on this upper 1/8 and fill the entire texture with values from this range, improving the resulting precision. This requires that you scale (N • H) by 8 and bias by –7 so that [0,1] maps to [–7,1]. By using the GL_CLAMP_TO_EDGE wrap mode, values in the range [–7,0] will be clamped to 0. Values in the range of interest, [0,1], will receive texel values between $(7/8)^{128}$ and 1.

The specular contribution resulting from the texture lookup is added to the diffuse color output from the vertex shader using the GL_ADD texture environment function.

Figure 16.4 compares the three specular shaders to show the differences in quality. An even more precise method would be to output only the normal vector from the vertex shader and to encode a cube map texture so that at every N coordinate the resulting texel value is $(N • H)^{128}$. We've left this as another exercise for you.

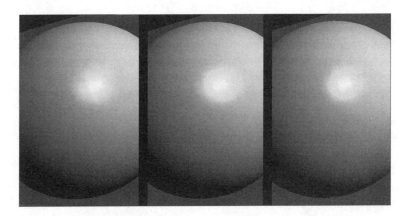

FIGURE 16.4 The per-vertex specular highlight is improved by using separate specular or a specular exponent texture. (This figure also appears in the Color insert.)

Now that you have a decent specular highlight, you can get a little fancier and take the one white light and replicate it into three colored lights. This activity involves performing the same computations, except now you have three different light positions and you have to take the light color into consideration.

As has been the case with all the lighting shaders, you can change the light positions in the sample by using the left- and right-arrow keys. Figure 16.5 shows the three lights in action, produced by Listing 16.4.

FIGURE 16.5 Three lights are better than one. (This figure also appears in the Color insert.)

LISTING 16.4   Three Colored Lights Vertex Shader

```
// 3lights.vs
//
// Generic vertex transformation,
// 3 colored lights

uniform vec3 lightPos[3];
varying vec4 gl_TexCoord[4];

void main(void)
{
    vec3 L[3], H[3];

    // normal MVP transform
    gl_Position = gl_ModelViewProjectionMatrix * gl_Vertex;

    vec3 N = normalize(gl_NormalMatrix * gl_Normal);
    vec4 V = gl_ModelViewMatrix * gl_Vertex;

    // Light colors
    vec4 lightCol[3];
    lightCol[0] = vec4(1.0, 0.25, 0.25, 1.0);
    lightCol[1] = vec4(0.25, 1.0, 0.25, 1.0);
    lightCol[2] = vec4(0.25, 0.25, 1.0, 1.0);

    gl_FrontColor = vec4(0.0);

    for (int i = 0; i < 3; i++)
    {
        // Light vectors
        L[i] = normalize(lightPos[i] - V.xyz);

        // Half-angles
        H[i] = normalize(L[i] + vec3(0.0, 0.0, 1.0));

        float NdotL = max(0.0, dot(N, L[i]));

        // Accumulate the diffuse contributions
        gl_FrontColor += gl_Color * lightCol[i] *
                         vec4(NdotL);
```

LISTING 16.4 Continued

```
        // Put N.H specular coefficients into texcoords
        gl_TexCoord[1+i] = (NdotL > 0.0) ?
            vec4(max(0.0, dot(N, H[i]) * 8.0 - 7.0), 0.0, 0.0, 1.0) :
            vec4(0.0, 0.0, 0.0, 1.0);
    }
}
```

Interesting to note in this sample is the use of a loop construct. Even though GLSL permits them, some older OpenGL implementations may not support loops in hardware. So if your shader is running really slowly, it may be emulating the shader execution in software. "Unrolling" the loop—that is, replicating the code within the loop multiple times into a long linear sequence—could alleviate the problem, but at the expense of making your code less readable.

Per-Vertex Fog

Though fog is specified as a per-fragment rasterization stage that follows texturing, often implementations perform most of the necessary computation per-vertex and then interpolate the results across the primitive. This shortcut is sanctioned by the OpenGL specification because it improves performance with very little loss of image fidelity. The following is the equation for a second-order exponential fog factor, which controls the blending between the fog color and the unfogged fragment color:

$$ff = e^{-(d*fc)^2}$$

In this equation, ff is the computed fog factor. d is the density constant that controls the "thickness" of the fog. fc is the fog coordinate, which is usually the distance from the vertex to the eye, or is approximated by the absolute value of the vertex position's Z component in eye space. In this chapter's sample shaders, you'll compute the actual distance.

In the first sample fog shader, you'll compute only the fog coordinate and leave it to fixed functionality to compute the fog factor and perform the blend. In the second sample, you'll compute the fog factor yourself within the vertex shader and also perform the blending per-vertex. Performing all these operations per-vertex instead of per-fragment is more efficient and provides acceptable results for most uses. Figure 16.6 illustrates the fogged scene, which is nearly identical for the two sample fog shaders, the first of which is shown in Listing 16.5.

16

FIGURE 16.6   Applying per-vertex fog using a vertex shader. (This figure also appears in the Color insert.)

LISTING 16.5   Fog Coordinate Generating Vertex Shader

```
// fogcoord.vs
//
// Generic vertex transformation,
// diffuse and specular lighting,
// per-vertex fogcoord

uniform vec3 lightPos[1];

void main(void)
{
    // normal MVP transform
    gl_Position = gl_ModelViewProjectionMatrix * gl_Vertex;

    vec3 N = normalize(gl_NormalMatrix * gl_Normal);
    vec4 V = gl_ModelViewMatrix * gl_Vertex;
    vec3 L = normalize(lightPos[0] - V.xyz);
    vec3 H = normalize(L + vec3(0.0, 0.0, 1.0));
    const float specularExp = 128.0;
```

LISTING 16.5   Continued

```
    // calculate diffuse lighting
    float NdotL = max(0.0, dot(N, L));
    vec4 diffuse = gl_Color * vec4(NdotL);

    // calculate specular lighting
    float NdotH = max(0.0, dot(N, H));
    vec4 specular = vec4(0.0);
    if (NdotL > 0.0)
        specular = vec4(pow(NdotH, specularExp));

    // calculate fog coordinate: distance from eye
    gl_FogFragCoord = length(V);

    // sum the diffuse and specular components
    gl_FrontColor = diffuse + specular;
}
```

The calculation to find the distance from the eye (0,0,0,1) to the vertex in eye space is trivial. You need only call the built-in length() function, passing in the vertex position vector as an argument.

The following is the altered GLSL code for performing the fog blend within the shader instead of in fixed functionality fragment processing:

```
uniform float density;

...

// calculate 2nd order exponential fog factor
const float e = 2.71828;
float fogFactor = (density * length(V));
fogFactor *= fogFactor;
fogFactor = clamp(pow(e, -fogFactor), 0.0, 1.0);

// sum the diffuse and specular components, then
// blend with the fog color based on fog factor
const vec4 fogColor = vec4(0.5, 0.8, 0.5, 1.0);
gl_FrontColor = mix(fogColor, clamp(diffuse + specular, 0.0, 1.0),
                    fogFactor);
```

16

Per-Vertex Point Size

Applying fog attenuates object colors the farther away they are from the viewpoint. Similarly, you can attenuate point sizes so that points rendered close to the viewpoint are relatively large and points farther away diminish into nothing. Like fog, point attenuation is a useful visual cue for conveying perspective. The computation required is similar as well.

You compute the distance from the vertex to the eye exactly the same as you did for the fog coordinate. Then, to get a point size that falls off exponentially with distance, you square the distance, take its reciprocal, and multiply it by the constant 100,000. This constant is chosen specifically for this scene's geometry so that objects toward the back of the scene, as rendered from the initial camera position, are assigned point sizes of approximately 1, whereas points near the front are assigned point sizes of approximately 10.

In this sample application, you'll set the polygon mode for front- and back-facing polygons to `GL_POINT` so that all the objects in the scene are drawn with points. Also, you must enable `GL_VERTEX_PROGRAM_POINT_SIZE_ARB` so that the point sizes output from the vertex shader are substituted in place of the usual OpenGL point size. Figure 16.7 shows the result of Listing 16.6.

FIGURE 16.7   Per-vertex point size makes distant points smaller. (This figure also appears in the Color insert.)

LISTING 16.6   Point Size Generating Vertex Shader

```
// ptsize.vs
//
// Generic vertex transformation,
// attenuated point size

void main(void)
{
    // normal MVP transform
    gl_Position = gl_ModelViewProjectionMatrix * gl_Vertex;

    vec4 V = gl_ModelViewMatrix * gl_Vertex;

    gl_FrontColor = gl_Color;

    // calculate point size based on distance from eye
    float ptSize = length(V);
    ptSize *= ptSize;
    gl_PointSize = 100000.0 / ptSize;
}
```

Customized Vertex Transformation

You've already customized lighting, texture coordinate generation, and fog coordinate generation. But what about the vertex positions themselves? The next sample shader applies an additional transformation before transforming by the usual modelview/projection matrix.

Figure 16.8 shows the effects of scaling the object-space vertex position by a squash and stretch factor, which can be set independently for each axis as in Listing 16.7.

FIGURE 16.8   Squash and stretch effects customize the vertex transformation.

LISTING 16.7   Squash and Stretch Vertex Shader

```
// stretch.vs
//
// Generic vertex transformation,
// followed by squash/stretch

uniform vec3 lightPos[1];
uniform vec3 squashStretch;

void main(void)
{
    // squash/stretch, followed by normal MVP transform
    vec4 stretchedCoord = gl_Vertex;
    stretchedCoord.xyz *= squashStretch;
    gl_Position = gl_ModelViewProjectionMatrix * stretchedCoord;

    vec3 stretchedNormal = gl_Normal;
    stretchedNormal *= squashStretch;
    vec3 N = normalize(gl_NormalMatrix * stretchedNormal);
    vec4 V = gl_ModelViewMatrix * stretchedCoord;
    vec3 L = normalize(lightPos[0] - V.xyz);
    vec3 H = normalize(L + vec3(0.0, 0.0, 1.0));
```

LISTING 16.7 Continued

```
    // put diffuse lighting result in primary color
    float NdotL = max(0.0, dot(N, L));
    gl_FrontColor = gl_Color * vec4(NdotL);

    // copy (N.H)*8-7 into texcoord if N.L is positive
    float NdotH = 0.0;
    if (NdotL > 0.0)
        NdotH = max(0.0, dot(N, H) * 8.0 - 7.0);
    gl_TexCoord[0] = vec4(NdotH, 0.0, 0.0, 1.0);
}
```

Vertex Blending

Vertex blending is an interesting technique used for skeletal animation. Consider a simple model of an arm with an elbow joint. The forearm and biceps are each represented by a cylinder. When the arm is completely straight, all the "skin" is nicely connected together. But as soon as you bend the arm, as in Figure 16.9, the skin is disconnected and the realism is gone.

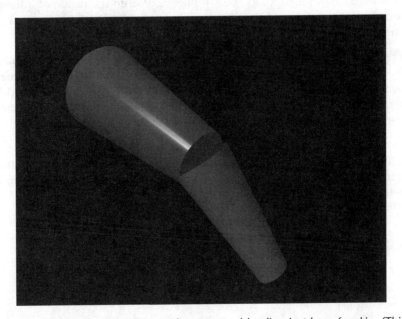

FIGURE 16.9 This simple elbow joint without vertex blending just begs for skin. (This figure also appears in the Color insert.)

16

The way to fix this problem is to employ multiple modelview matrices when transforming each vertex. Both the forearm and the biceps have their own modelview matrix already. The biceps's matrix would orient it relative to the torso if it were attached to a body, or in this case relative to the origin in object-space. The forearm's matrix orients it relative to the biceps. The key to vertex blending is to use a little of each matrix when transforming vertices close to a joint.

You can choose how close to the joint you want the multiple modelview matrices to have influence. We call this the *region of influence*. Vertices outside the region of influence do not require blending. For such a vertex, only the original modelview matrix associated with the object is used. However, vertices that do fall within the region of influence must transform the vertex twice: once with its own modelview matrix and once with the matrix belonging to the object on the other side of the joint. For our example, you blend these two eye-space positions together to achieve the final eye-space position.

The amount of one eye-space position going into the mix versus the other is based on the vertex's blend weight. When drawing the glBegin/glEnd primitives, in addition to the usual normals, colors, and positions, you also specify a weight for each vertex. You use the glVertexAttrib1f function for specifying the weight. Vertices right at the edge of the joint receive weights of 0.5, effectively resulting in a 50% influence by each matrix. On the other extreme, vertices on the edge of the region of influence receive weights of 1.0, whereby the object's own matrix has 100% influence. Within the region of influence, weights vary from 1.0 to 0.5, and they can be assigned linearly with respect to the distance from the joint, or based on some higher-order function.

Any other computations dependent on the modelview matrix must also be blended. In the case of the sample shader, you also perform diffuse and specular lighting. This means the normal vector, which usually is transformed by the inverse transpose of the modelview matrix, now must also be transformed twice just like the vertex position. The two results are blended based on the same weights used for vertex position blending.

By using vertex blending, you can create lifelike flexible skin on a skeleton structure that is easy to animate. Figure 16.10 shows the arm in its new Elastic Man form, thanks to a region of influence covering the entire arm. Listing 16.8 contains the vertex blending shader source.

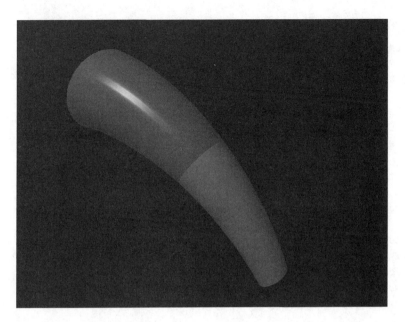

FIGURE 16.10   The stiff two-cylinder arm is now a fun, curvy, flexible object. (This figure also appears in the Color insert.)

LISTING 16.8   Vertex Blending Vertex Shader

```
// skinning.vs
//
// Perform vertex skinning by
// blending between two MV
// matrices

uniform vec3 lightPos;
uniform mat4 mv2;
uniform mat3 mv2IT;
attribute float weight;

void main(void)
{
    // compute each vertex influence
    vec4 V1 = gl_ModelViewMatrix * gl_Vertex;
    vec4 V2 = mv2 * gl_Vertex;
    vec4 V = (V1 * weight) + (V2 * (1.0 - weight));
    gl_Position = gl_ProjectionMatrix * V;
```

16

LISTING 16.8   Continued

```
    // compute each normal influence
    vec3 N1 = gl_NormalMatrix * gl_Normal;
    vec3 N2 = mv2IT * gl_Normal;

    vec3 N = normalize((N1 * weight) + (N2 * (1.0 - weight)));
    vec3 L = normalize(lightPos - V.xyz);
    vec3 H = normalize(L + vec3(0.0, 0.0, 1.0));

    // put diffuse lighting result in primary color
    float NdotL = max(0.0, dot(N, L));
    gl_FrontColor = 0.1 + gl_Color * vec4(NdotL);

    // copy (N.H)*8-7 into texcoord
    float NdotH = 0.0;
    if (NdotL > 0.0)
        NdotH = max(0.0, dot(N, H) * 8.0 - 7.0);
    gl_TexCoord[0] = vec4(NdotH, 0.0, 0.0, 1.0);
}
```

In this example, you use built-in modelview matrix uniforms to access the primary blend matrix. For the secondary matrix, you employ a user-defined uniform matrix.

For normal transformation, you need the inverse transpose of each blend matrix. Shaders do not provide a simple way to access the inverse transpose of a matrix. You continue to use the built-in gl_NormalMatrix for accessing the primary modelview matrix's inverse transpose, but for the secondary matrix's inverse transpose, there is no shortcut. Instead, you must manually compute the inverse of the second modelview matrix within the application and transpose it on the way into OpenGL when calling glUniformMatrix3fv.

Summary

This chapter provided various sample shaders as a jumping-off point for your own exploration of vertex shaders. Specifically, we provided examples of customized lighting, texture coordinate generation, fog, point size, and vertex transformation.

It is refreshing to give vertex shaders their moment in the spotlight. In reality, vertex shaders often play only supporting roles to their fragment shader counterparts, performing menial tasks such as preparing texture coordinates. Fragment shaders end up stealing the show. In the next chapter, we'll start by focusing solely on fragment shaders. Then in the stunning conclusion, we will see our vertex shader friends once again when we combine the two shaders and say goodbye to fixed functionality once and for all.

CHAPTER 17

Fragment Shading: Empower Your Pixel Processing

by Benjamin Lipchak

WHAT YOU'LL LEARN IN THIS CHAPTER:

- How to alter colors

- How to post-process images

- How to light an object per-fragment

- How to perform procedural texture mapping

As you may recall from Chapter 15, "Programmable Pipeline: This Isn't Your Father's OpenGL," fragment shaders replace the texturing, color sum, and fog stages of the fixed functionality pipeline. This is the section of the pipeline where the party is happening. Instead of marching along like a mindless herd of cattle, applying each enabled texture based on its preordained texture coordinate, your fragments are free to choose their own adventure. Mix and match textures and texture coordinates. Or calculate your own texture coordinates. Or don't do any texturing, and just compute your own colors. It's all good.

In their natural habitat, vertex shaders and fragment shaders are most often mated for life. Fragment shaders are the dominant partner, directly producing the eye candy you see displayed on the screen, and thus they receive the most attention. However, vertex shaders play an important supporting role. Because they tend to be executed much less frequently (except for the smallest of triangles), as much of the grunt work as possible is pushed into the vertex shader in the name of performance. The results are then placed into interpolants for use as input by the fragment shader. The vertex shader is a selfless producer, the fragment shader a greedy consumer.

In this chapter, we continue the learning by example we began in the preceding chapter. We present many fragment shaders, both as further exposure to the OpenGL Shading

Language (GLSL) and as a launch pad for your own future dabbling. Because you rarely see fragment shaders alone, after you get the hang of fragment shaders in isolation, we will move on to discuss several examples of vertex shaders and fragment shaders working together in peaceful harmony.

Color Conversion

We almost have to contrive some examples illustrating where fragment shaders are used without vertex shader assistance. But we can easily separate them where we simply want to alter the existing color. For these examples, we use fixed functionality lighting to provide a starting color. Then we go to town on it.

Grayscale

One thing you might want to do in your own work is simulate black-and-white film. Given the incoming red, green, and blue color channel intensities, we would like to calculate a single grayscale intensity to output to all three channels. Red, green, and blue each reflect light differently, which we represent by their different contributions to the final intensity. The weights used in our shader derive from the NTSC standard for converting color television signals for viewing on black and white televisions.

Figure 17.1 shows the vertex shader corresponding to Listing 17.1. This may be the only black-and-white figure in the book that is truly supposed to be black-and-white!

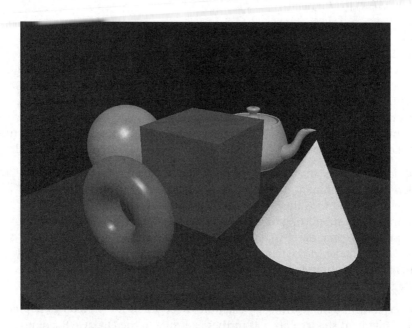

FIGURE 17.1   This fragment shader converts the RGB color into a single grayscale value.

LISTING 17.1   Grayscale Conversion Fragment Shader

```
// grayscale.fs
//
// convert RGB to grayscale

void main(void)
{
    // Convert to grayscale using NTSC conversion weights
    float gray = dot(gl_Color.rgb, vec3(0.299, 0.587, 0.114));

    // replicate grayscale to RGB components
    gl_FragColor = vec4(gray, gray, gray, 1.0);
}
```

The key to all these fragment shaders is that what you write to the color output, gl_FragColor, is what is passed along down the rest of the OpenGL pipeline, eventually to the framebuffer. The primary color input is gl_Color.

Try playing with the contributions of each color channel. Notice how they add up to 1. You can simulate overexposure by making them add up to more than 1, and less than 1 will simulate underexposure.

Sepia Tone

In this next example, we recolorize the grayscale picture with a sepia tone. This tone gives the picture the tint of an Old West photograph. To do this, we first convert to grayscale as before. Then we multiply the gray value by a color vector, which accentuates some color channels and reduces others. Listing 17.2 illustrates this sepia-tone conversion, and the result is as shown in Color Plate 15.

LISTING 17.2   Sepia-Tone Conversion Fragment Shader

```
// sepia.fs
//
// convert RGB to sepia tone

void main(void)
{
    // Convert RGB to grayscale using NTSC conversion weights
    float gray = dot(gl_Color.rgb, vec3(0.299, 0.587, 0.114));

    // convert grayscale to sepia
    gl_FragColor = vec4(gray * vec3(1.2, 1.0, 0.8), 1.0);
}
```

You can choose to colorize with any tint you like. Go ahead and play with the tint factors. Here, we've hard-coded one for sepia. If you're truly ambitious, you could substitute external application-defined uniform constants to make the tint color user-selectable so that you don't have to write a different shader for every tint color.

Inversion

For this next example, we're going for the film negative effect. These shaders are almost too simple to mention. All you have to do is take whatever color you were otherwise going to draw and subtract that color from 1. Black becomes white, and white becomes black. Red becomes cyan. Purple becomes chartreuse. You get the picture.

Figure 17.2 illustrates the color inversion performed in Listing 17.3. Use your imagination or consult the sample code for the grayscale inversion, which is just as straightforward.

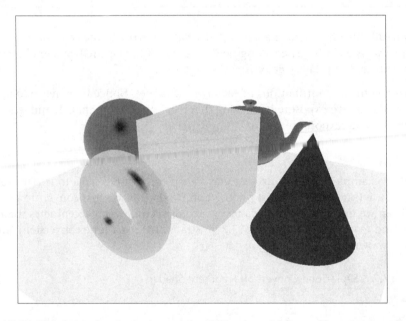

FIGURE 17.2   This fragment shader inverts the RGB color, yielding a film negative effect.

LISTING 17.3   Color Inversion Fragment Shader

```
// colorinvert.fs
//
// invert like a color negative

void main(void)
{
```

LISTING 17.3   Continued

```
// invert color components
gl_FragColor.rgb = 1.0 - gl_Color.rgb;
gl_FragColor.a = 1.0;
}
```

Heat Signature

Now, we attempt our first texture lookup. In this sample shader, we simulate a heat signature effect like the one in the movie *Predator*. Heat is represented by a color spectrum ranging from black to blue to green to yellow to red.

We again use the grayscale conversion, this time as our scalar heat value. This is a cheap trick for demonstration purposes, as the color intensity does not necessarily have any relationship to heat. In reality, the heat value would be passed in as a separate vertex attribute or uniform. We use this value as a texture coordinate to index into a 1D texture populated with the color gradients from black to red. Figure 17.3 shows the results of the heat signature shader in Listing 17.4.

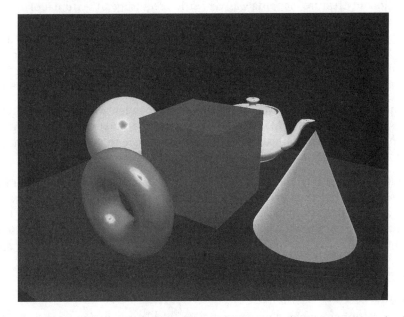

FIGURE 17.3   This fragment shader simulates a heat signature by looking up a color from a 1D texture. (This figure also appears in the Color insert.)

LISTING 17.4   Heat Signature Fragment Shader

```
// heatsig.fs
//
// map grayscale to heat signature

uniform sampler1D sampler0;

void main(void)
{
    // Convert to grayscale using NTSC conversion weights
    float gray = dot(gl_Color.rgb, vec3(0.299, 0.587, 0.114));

    // look up heatsig value
    gl_FragColor = texture1D(sampler0, gray);
}
```

Dependent Texture Lookups

Fixed functionality texture mapping was very strict, requiring all texture lookups to use an interpolated per-vertex texture coordinate. One of the powerful new capabilities made possible by fragment shaders is that you can calculate your own texture coordinates per-fragment. You can even use the result of one texture lookup as the coordinate for another lookup. All these cases are considered dependent texture lookups. They're named that because the lookups are dependent on other preceding operations in the fragment shader.

You may not have noticed, but we just performed a dependent texture lookup in the heat signature shader. First, we had to compute our texture coordinate by doing the grayscale conversion. Then we used that value as a texture coordinate to perform a dependent texture lookup into the 1D heat signature texture.

The dependency chain can continue: You could, for example, take the color from the heat signature shader and use that as a texture coordinate to perform a lookup from a cube map texture, perhaps to gamma-correct your color. Beware, however, that some OpenGL implementations have a hardware limit as to the length of dependency chains, so keep this point in mind if you want to avoid falling into a non-hardware-accelerated driver path!

Per-Fragment Fog

Instead of performing fog blending per-vertex, or calculating the fog factor per-vertex and using fixed functionality fog blending, we compute the fog factor and perform the blend ourselves within the fragment shader in the following example. This example emulates GL_EXP2 fog mode except that it will be more accurate than most fixed functionality implementations, which apply the exponentiation per-vertex instead of per-fragment.

This is most noticeable on low-tessellation geometry that extends from the foreground to the background, such as the floor upon which all the objects in the scene rest. Compare the results of this shader with the fog shaders in the preceding chapter, and you can readily see the difference.

Figure 17.4 illustrates the output of the fog shader in Listing 17.5.

FIGURE 17.4   This fragment shader performs per-fragment fog computation.

LISTING 17.5   Per-Fragment Fog Fragment Shader

```
// fog.fs
//
// per-pixel fog

uniform float density;

void main(void)
{
    const vec4 fogColor = vec4(0.5, 0.8, 0.5, 1.0);

    // calculate 2nd order exponential fog factor
    // based on fragment's Z distance
    const float e = 2.71828;
    float fogFactor = (density * gl_FragCoord.z);
```

LISTING 17.5   Continued

```
    fogFactor *= fogFactor;
    fogFactor = clamp(pow(e, -fogFactor), 0.0, 1.0);

    // Blend fog color with incoming color
    gl_FragColor = mix(fogColor, gl_Color, fogFactor);
}
```

We need to comment on a few things here. One is the built-in function used to blend: `mix`. This function blends two variables of any type, in this case four-component vectors, based on the third argument, which should be in the range [0,1].

Another thing to notice is how we have chosen to make the density an externally set uniform constant rather than a hard-coded inline constant. This way, we can tie the density to keystrokes. When the user hits the left or right arrows, we update the density shader constant with a new value without having to change the shader text at all. As a general rule, constant values that you may want to change at some point should not be hard-coded, but all others should be. By hard-coding a value, you give the OpenGL implementation's optimizing compiler an early opportunity to use this information to possibly make your shader run even faster.

Image Processing

Image processing is another application of fragment shaders that doesn't depend on vertex shader assistance. After drawing the scene without fragment shaders, we can apply convolution kernels to post-process the image in various ways.

To keep the shaders concise and improve the probability of their being hardware-accelerated on a wider range of hardware, we've limited the kernel size to 3×3. Feel free to experiment with larger kernel sizes.

Within the sample application, `glCopyTexImage2D` is called to copy the contents of the framebuffer into a texture. The texture size is chosen to be the largest power-of-two size smaller than the window. (If OpenGL 2.0 or the `ARB_texture_non_power_of_two` extension is supported, the texture can be the same size as the window.) A fragment-shaded quad is then drawn centered within the window with the same dimensions as the texture, with a base texture coordinate ranging from (0,0) in the lower left to (1,1) in the upper right.

The fragment shader takes its base texture coordinate and performs a texture lookup to obtain the center sample of the 3×3 kernel neighborhood. It then proceeds to apply eight different offsets to look up samples for the other eight spots in the neighborhood. Finally, the shader applies some filter to the neighborhood to yield a new color for the center of the neighborhood. Each sample shader provides a different filter commonly used for image-processing tasks.

Blur

Blurring may be the most commonly applied filter in everyday use. It smoothes out high-frequency features, such as the jaggies along object edges. It is also called a low-pass filter because it lets low-frequency features pass through while filtering out high-frequency features.

Because we're using only a 3×3 kernel, the blur is not overly dramatic in a single pass. We could make it more blurry by using a larger kernel or by applying the blur filter multiple times in successive passes. Figure 17.5 shows the results of the blur filter in Listing 17.6 after five passes.

FIGURE 17.5   This fragment shader blurs the scene. (This figure also appears in the Color insert.)

LISTING 17.6   Post-Process Blur Fragment Shader

```
// blur.fs
//
// blur (low-pass) 3x3 kernel

uniform sampler2D sampler0;
uniform vec2 tc_offset[9];

void main(void)
```

LISTING 17.6   Continued

```
{
    vec4 sample[9];

    for (int i = 0; i < 9; i++)
    {
        sample[i] = texture2D(sampler0,
                              gl_TexCoord[0].st + tc_offset[i]);
    }

//   1 2 1
//   2 1 2   / 13
//   1 2 1

    gl_FragColor = (sample[0] + (2.0*sample[1]) + sample[2] +
                    (2.0*sample[3]) + sample[4] + (2.0*sample[5]) +
                    sample[6] + (2.0*sample[7]) + sample[8]) / 13.0;
}
```

The first thing we do in the blur shader is generate our nine texture coordinates. This is accomplished by adding precomputed constant offsets to the interpolated base texture coordinate. The offsets were computed taking into account the size of the texture such that the neighboring texels to the north, south, east, west, northeast, southeast, northwest, and southwest could be obtained by a simple 2D texture lookup.

This neighborhood is obtained the same way in all our image processing shaders. It is the filter applied to the neighborhood that differs in each shader. In the case of the blur filter, the texel neighborhood is multiplied by a 3×3 kernel of coefficients (1s and 2s), which add up to 13. The resulting values are all summed and averaged by dividing by 13, resulting in the new color for the texel. Note that we could have made the kernel coefficient values 1/13 and 2/13 instead of 1 and 2, but that would have required many extra multiplies. It is simpler and cheaper for us to factor out the 1/13 and just apply it at the end.

Try experimenting with the filter coefficients. What if, for example, you put a weight of 1 at each corner and then divide by 4? Notice what happens when you divide by more or less than the sum of the coefficients: The scene grows darker or lighter. That makes sense. If your scene was all white, you would be effectively multiplying the filter coefficients by 1 and adding them up. If you don't divide by the sum of the coefficients, you'll end up with a color other than white.

Sharpen

Sharpening is the opposite of blurring. Some examples of its use include making edges more pronounced and making text more readable. Figure 17.6 illustrates the use of sharpening, applying the filter in two passes.

FIGURE 17.6 This fragment shader sharpens the scene. (This figure also appears in the Color insert.)

Here is the shader code for applying the sharpen filter:

```
// sharpen.fs
//
// 3x3 sharpen kernel

uniform sampler2D sampler0;
uniform vec2 tc_offset[9];

void main(void)
{
    vec4 sample[9];

    for (int i = 0; i < 9; i++)
    {
        sample[i] = texture2D(sampler0,
```

17

```
                              gl_TexCoord[0].st + tc_offset[i]);
   }

//   -1 -1 -1
//   -1  9 -1
//   -1 -1 -1

   gl_FragColor = (sample[4] * 9.0) -
                   (sample[0] + sample[1] + sample[2] +
                    sample[3] + sample[5] +
                    sample[6] + sample[7] + sample[8]);
}
```

Notice how this kernel also sums to 1, as did the blur filter. This operation guarantees that, on average, the filter is not increasing or decreasing the brightness. It's just sharpening the brightness, as desired.

Dilation and Erosion

Dilation and erosion are morphological filters, meaning they alter the shape of objects. Dilation grows the size of bright objects, whereas erosion shrinks the size of bright objects. (They each have the reverse effect on dark objects.) Figures 17.7 and 17.8 show the effects of three passes of dilation and erosion, respectively.

FIGURE 17.7 This fragment shader dilates objects.

Dilation simply finds the maximum value in the neighborhood:

```
// dilation.fs
//
// maximum of 3x3 kernel

uniform sampler2D sampler0;
uniform vec2 tc_offset[9];

void main(void)
{
    vec4 sample[9];
    vec4 maxValue = vec4(0.0);

    for (int i = 0; i < 9; i++)
    {
        sample[i] = texture2D(sampler0,
                              gl_TexCoord[0].st + tc_offset[i]);
        maxValue = max(sample[i], maxValue);
    }

    gl_FragColor = maxValue;
}
```

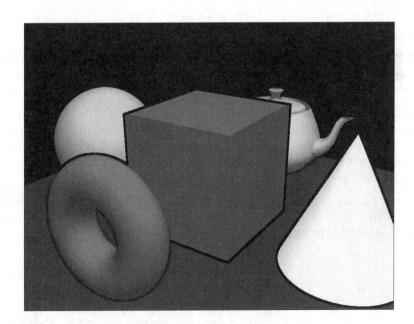

FIGURE 17.8 This fragment shader erodes objects.

Erosion conversely finds the minimum value in the neighborhood:

```
// erosion.fs
//
// minimum of 3x3 kernel

uniform sampler2D sampler0;
uniform vec2 tc_offset[9];

void main(void)
{
    vec4 sample[9];
    vec4 minValue = vec4(1.0);

    for (int i = 0; i < 9; i++)
    {
        sample[i] = texture2D(sampler0,
                        gl_TexCoord[0].st + tc_offset[i]);
        minValue = min(sample[i], minValue);
    }

    gl_FragColor = minValue;
}
```

Edge Detection

One last filter class worthy of mention here is edge detectors. They do just what you would expect—detect edges. Edges are simply places in an image where the color changes rapidly, and edge detection filters pick up on these rapid changes and highlight them.

Three widely used edge detectors are Laplacian, Sobel, and Prewitt. Sobel and Prewitt are gradient filters that detect changes in the first derivative of each color channel's intensity, but only in a single direction. Laplacian, on the other hand, detects zero-crossings of the second derivative, where the intensity gradient suddenly changes from getting darker to getting lighter, or vice versa. It works for edges of any orientation.

Because the differences in their results are subtle, Figure 17.9 shows the results from only one of them, the Laplacian filter. Try out the others and examine their shaders at your leisure in the accompanying sample code.

FIGURE 17.9   This fragment shader implements Laplacian edge detection. (This figure also appears in the Color insert.)

The Laplacian filter code is almost identical to the sharpen code we just looked at:

```
// laplacian.fs
//
// Laplacian edge detection

uniform sampler2D sampler0;
uniform vec2 tc_offset[9];

void main(void)
{
    vec4 sample[9];

    for (int i = 0; i < 9; i++)
    {
        sample[i] = texture2D(sampler0,
                        gl_TexCoord[0].st + tc_offset[i]);
    }

//   -1 -1 -1
//   -1  8 -1
//   -1 -1 -1
```

17

```
    gl_FragColor = (sample[4] * 8.0) -
                   (sample[0] + sample[1] + sample[2] +
                    sample[3] + sample[5] +
                    sample[6] + sample[7] + sample[8]);
}
```

The difference, of course, is that the center kernel value is 8 rather than the 9 present in the sharpen kernel. The coefficients sum up to 0 rather than 1. This explains the blackness of the image. Instead of, on average, retaining its original brightness, the edge detection kernel will produce 0 in areas of the image with no color change.

Lighting

Welcome back to another discussion of lighting shaders. In the preceding chapter, we covered per-vertex lighting. We also described a couple of per-fragment fixed functionality tricks to improve the per-vertex results: separate specular with color sum and power function texture for specular exponent. In this chapter, we perform all our lighting calculations in the fragment shader to obtain the greatest accuracy.

The shaders here will look very familiar. The same lighting equations are implemented, so the code is virtually identical. One new thing is the use of vertex shaders and fragment shaders together. The vertex shader sets up the data that needs to be interpolated across the line or triangle, such as normals and light vectors. The fragment shader then proceeds to do most of the work, resulting in a final color.

Diffuse Lighting

As a refresher, the equation for diffuse lighting follows:

$$C_{diff} = max\{N \bullet L, 0\} * C_{mat} * C_{li}$$

You need a vertex shader that generates both normal and light vectors. Listing 17.7 contains the vertex shader source to generate these necessary interpolants for diffuse lighting.

LISTING 17.7   Diffuse Lighting Interpolant Generating Vertex Shader

```
// diffuse.vs
//
// set up interpolants for diffuse lighting

uniform vec3 lightPos0;
varying vec3 N, L;

void main(void)
```

LISTING 17.7   Continued

```
{
    // vertex MVP transform
    gl_Position = gl_ModelViewProjectionMatrix * gl_Vertex;

    // eye-space normal
    N = gl_NormalMatrix * gl_Normal;

    // eye-space light vector
    vec4 V = gl_ModelViewMatrix * gl_Vertex;
    L = lightPos0 - V.xyz;

    // Copy the primary color
    gl_FrontColor = gl_Color;
}
```

Notice how we are able to give descriptive names N and L to our interpolants, known as *varyings*. They have to match the names used in the fragment shader. All in all, this feature makes the shaders much more readable and less error prone than if we were using generic texture coordinate interpolants. For example, if we weren't careful, we might accidentally output L into texture coordinate 0, whereas the fragment shader is expecting it in texture coordinate 1. No compile error would be thrown. GLSL matches up our custom varyings automatically by name, keeping us out of trouble and at the same time avoiding the need for tedious comments in code explaining the contents of each interpolant.

The diffuse lighting fragment shaders resulting in Figure 17.10 follow in Listing 17.8. Unlike colors produced by specular lighting, diffuse lit colors do not change rapidly across a line or triangle, so you will probably not be able to distinguish between per-vertex and per-fragment diffuse lighting. For this reason, in general, it would be more efficient to perform diffuse lighting in the vertex shader, as we did in the preceding chapter. We perform it here per-fragment simply as a learning exercise.

17

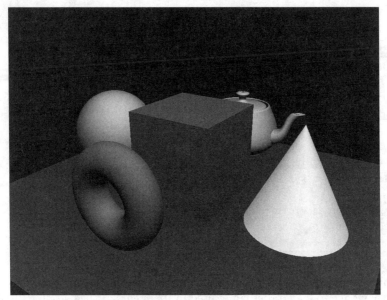

FIGURE 17.10   Per-fragment diffuse lighting.

LISTING 17.8   Diffuse Lighting Fragment Shader

```
// diffuse.fs
//
// per-pixel diffuse lighting

varying vec3 N, L;

void main(void)
{
    // output the diffuse color
    float intensity = max(0.0,
        dot(normalize(N), normalize(L)));

    gl_FragColor = gl_Color;
    gl_FragColor.rgb *= intensity;
}
```

First, we normalize the interpolated normal and light vectors. Then one more dot product, a clamp, and a multiply, and we're finished. Because we want a white light, we can save ourselves the additional multiply by $C_{li} = \{1,1,1,1\}$.

Multiple Specular Lights

Rather than covering specular lighting and multiple light samples independently, we'll cover both at the same time. As a refresher, the specular lighting equation is

$$C_{spec} = \max\{N \bullet H, 0\}^{Sexp} * C_{mat} * C_{li}$$

The vertex shader needs to generate light vector interpolants for all three lights, in addition to the normal vector. We'll calculate the half-angle vector in the fragment shader. Listing 17.9 shows the vertex shader for the three diffuse and specular lights.

LISTING 17.9   Three Lights Vertex Shader

```
// 3lights.vs
//
// set up interpolants for 3 specular lights

uniform vec3 lightPos[3];
varying vec3 N, L[3];

void main(void)
{
    // vertex MVP transform
    gl_Position = gl_ModelViewProjectionMatrix * gl_Vertex;

    vec4 V = gl_ModelViewMatrix * gl_Vertex;

    // eye-space normal
    N = gl_NormalMatrix * gl_Normal;

    // Light vectors
    for (int i = 0; i < 3; i++)
        L[i] = lightPos[i] - V.xyz;

    // Copy the primary color
    gl_FrontColor = gl_Color;
}
```

The fragment shaders will be doing most of the heavy lifting. Figure 17.11 shows the result of Listing 17.10.

17

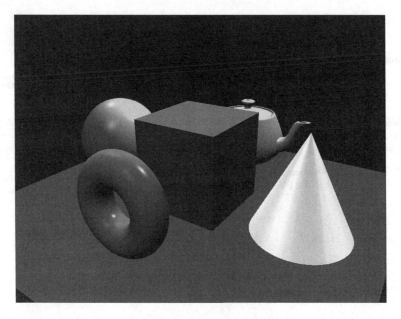

FIGURE 17.11   Per-fragment diffuse and specular lighting with three lights.

LISTING 17.10   Three Diffuse and Specular Lights Fragment Shader

```
// 3lights.fs
//
// 3 specular lights

varying vec3 N, L[3];

void main(void)
{
    const float specularExp = 128.0;

    vec3 NN = normalize(N);

    // Light colors
    vec3 lightCol[3];
    lightCol[0] = vec3(1.0, 0.25, 0.25);
    lightCol[1] = vec3(0.25, 1.0, 0.25);
    lightCol[2] = vec3(0.25, 0.25, 1.0);

    gl_FragColor = vec4(0.0);
```

LISTING 17.10   Continued

```
    for (int i = 0; i < 3; i++)
    {
        vec3 NL = normalize(L[i]);
        vec3 NH = normalize(NL + vec3(0.0, 0.0, 1.0));

        float NdotL = max(0.0, dot(NN, NL));

        // Accumulate the diffuse contributions
        gl_FragColor.rgb += gl_Color.rgb * lightCol[i] *
            NdotL;

        // Accumulate the specular contributions
        if (NdotL > 0.0)
            gl_FragColor.rgb += lightCol[i] *
                pow(max(0.0, dot(NN, NH)), specularExp);
    }

    gl_FragColor.a = gl_Color.a;
}
```

This time, we made each of the three lights a different color instead of white, necessitating an additional multiply by lightCol[n] (C_{li}).

Procedural Texture Mapping

When can you texture map an object without using any textures? When you're using procedural texture maps. This technique enables you to apply colors or other surface properties to an object, just like using conventional texture maps. With conventional texture maps, you load a texture image into OpenGL with glTexImage; then you perform a texture lookup within your fragment shader. However, with procedural texture mapping, you skip the texture loading and texture lookup and instead describe algorithmically what the texture looks like.

Procedural texture mapping has advantages and disadvantages. One advantage is that its storage requirements are measured in terms of a few shader instructions rather than megabytes of texture cache and/or system memory consumed by conventional textures. This frees your storage for other uses, such as vertex buffer objects, discussed in Chapter 11, "It's All About the Pipeline: Faster Geometry Throughput," or some of the advanced buffers discussed in the next chapter.

Another benefit is its virtually limitless resolution. Like vector drawing versus raster drawing, procedural textures scale to any size without loss of quality. Conventional textures require you to increase texture image sizes to improve quality when greatly magnified. Eventually, you'll hit a hardware limit. The only hardware limit affecting procedural texture quality is the floating-point precision of the shader processors, which are required to be at least 24-bit for OpenGL.

A disadvantage of procedural texture maps, and the reason they're not used more frequently, is that the complexity of the texture you want to represent requires an equally complex fragment shader. Everything from simple shapes and colors all the way to complex plasma, fire, smoke, marble, or wood grain can be achieved with procedural textures, given enough shader instructions to work with. But sometimes you just want the company logo or a satellite map or someone's face textured onto your scene. Certainly, conventional textures will always serve a purpose!

Checkerboard Texture

Enough discussion. Let's warm up with our first procedural texture: a 3D checkerboard. Our object will appear to be cut out of a block of alternating white and black cubes. Sounds simple enough, right?

We'll use the object-space position at each fragment to decide what color to make that fragment. So we need a vertex shader that, in addition to transforming the object-space position to clip-space as usual, also copies that object-space position into an interpolant so that it becomes available to the fragment shader. While we're at it, we might as well add diffuse and specular lighting, so our vertex shader needs to output the normal and light vector as well.

Listing 17.11 shows the vertex shader. We'll use it for all three of our procedural texture mapping examples.

LISTING 17.11   Procedural Texture Mapping Vertex Shader

```
// checkerboard.vs
//
// Generic vertex transformation,
// copy object-space position and
// lighting vectors out to interpolants

uniform vec3 lightPos;

varying vec3 N, L, V;

void main(void)
{
    // normal MVP transform
    gl_Position = gl_ModelViewProjectionMatrix * gl_Vertex;
```

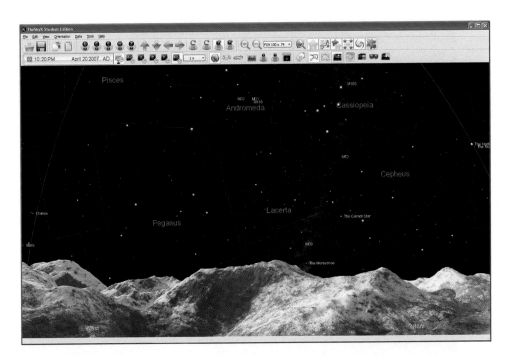

COLOR PLATE 1 (not associated with any chapter)   Software Bisque's next generation sky charting application, *TheSkyX Astronomy Software*, uses only OpenGL fixed pipeline rendering for increased compatibility with older 3D hardware (image courtesy of Software Bisque, Inc.).

COLOR PLATE 2   Shaders allow for unprecedented real-time realism (image courtesy of Software Bisque, Inc.). (For Figure 1.20 in Chapter 1)

COLOR PLATE 3 OpenGL's imaging subset at work: color image, color negative, embossed, and grayscale conversions. (For figures in Chapter 7)

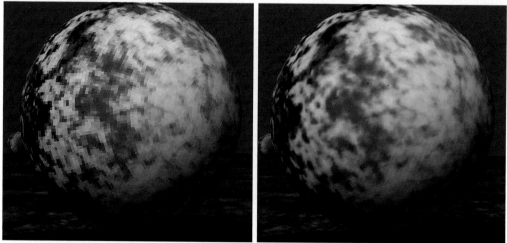

COLOR PLATE 4 Linear filtering up close. (For Figure 8.8 in Chapter 8)

COLOR PLATE 5 Output from the CUBEMAP sample program. (For Figure 9.11 in Chapter 9)

COLOR PLATE 6 The Final Thunderbird model. (For Figure 11.8 in Chapter 11)

COLOR PLATE 7
This vertex shader computes diffuse lighting. (For Figure 16.2 in Chapter 16)

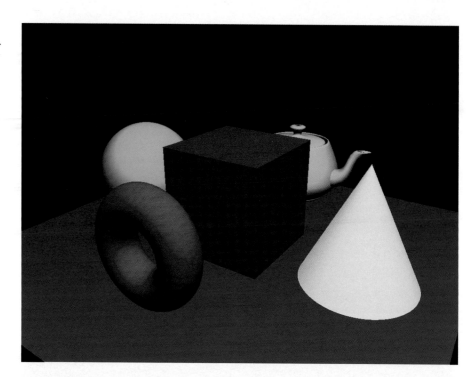

COLOR PLATE 8
This vertex shader computes diffuse and specular lighting. (For Figure 16.3 in Chapter 16)

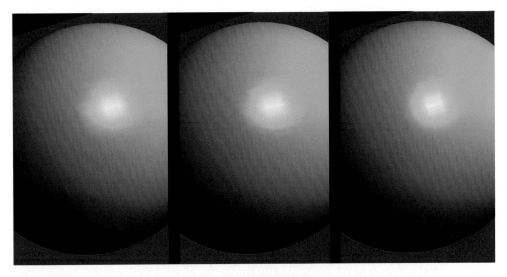

COLOR PLATE 9 The per-vertex specular highlight is improved by using separate specular or a specular exponent texture. (For Figure 16.4 in Chapter 16)

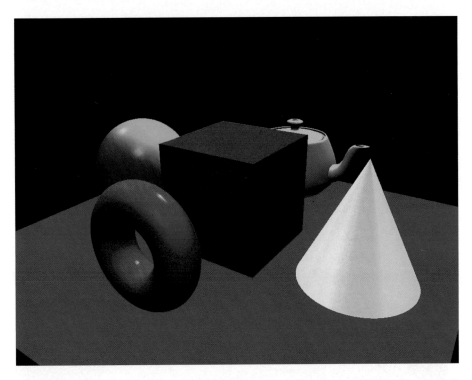

COLOR PLATE 10 Three lights are better than one. (For Figure 16.5 in Chapter 16)

COLOR PLATE 11
Applying per-vertex fog using a vertex shader. (For Figure 16.6 in Chapter 16)

COLOR PLATE 12
Per-vertex point size makes distant points smaller. (For Figure 16.7 in Chapter 16)

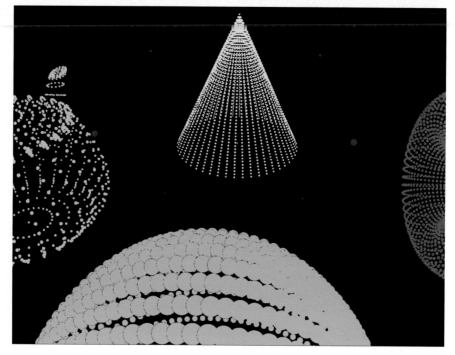

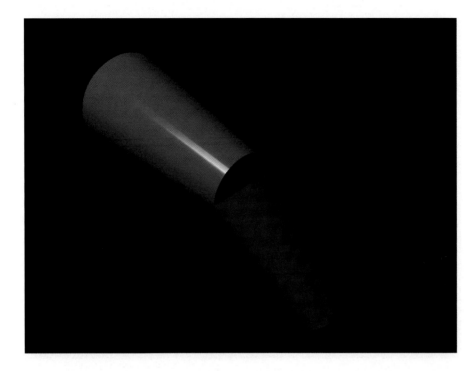

COLOR PLATE 13
This simple elbow joint without vertex blending just begs for skin. (For Figure 16.9 in Chapter 16)

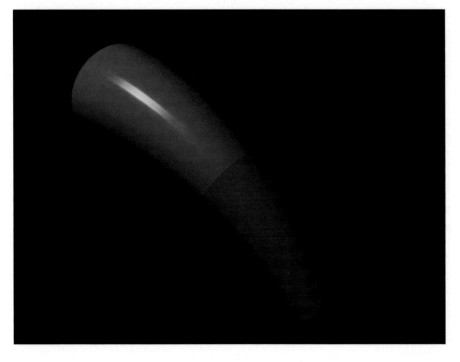

COLOR PLATE 14
The stiff two-cylinder arm is now a fun, curvy, flexible object. (For Figure 16.10 in Chapter 16)

COLOR PLATE 15
This fragment shader performs sepia tone color conversion. (This image shows the result of Listing 17.2 in Chapter 17)

COLOR PLATE 16
This fragment shader simulates a heat signature by looking up a color from a 1D texture. (For Figure 17.3 in Chapter 17)

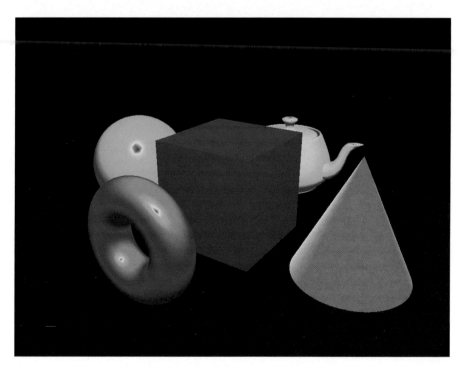

COLOR PLATE 17
This fragment
shader blurs the
scene. (For
Figure 17.5 in
Chapter 17)

COLOR PLATE 18
This fragment
shader sharpens
the scene. (For
Figure 17.6 in
Chapter 17)

COLOR PLATE 19
This fragment shader implements Laplacian edge detection. (For Figure 17.9 in Chapter 17)

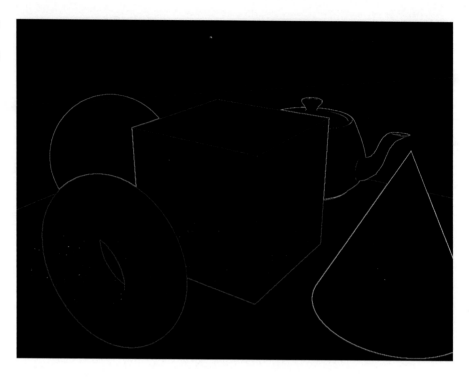

COLOR PLATE 20
An overhead view showing how the beachball colors are assigned. (For Figure 17.14 in Chapter 17)

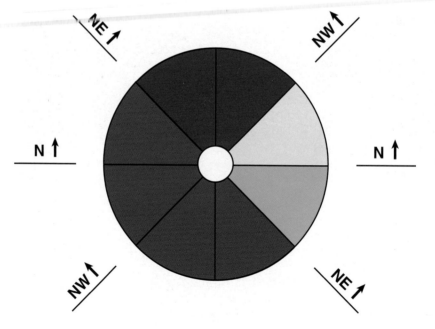

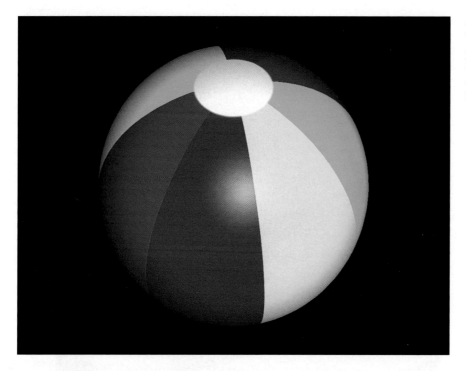

COLOR PLATE 21
You have built your own beach ball from scratch! (For Figure 17.15 in Chapter 17)

COLOR PLATE 22
The toy ball shader describes a relatively complex shape. (For Figure 17.17 in Chapter 17)

COLOR PLATE 23
PBOs improve the performance of our motion blur sample. (For Figure 18.2 in Chapter 18)

COLOR PLATE 24
FBOs improve the image quality of our shadow mapping sample. (For Figure 18.3 in Chapter 18)

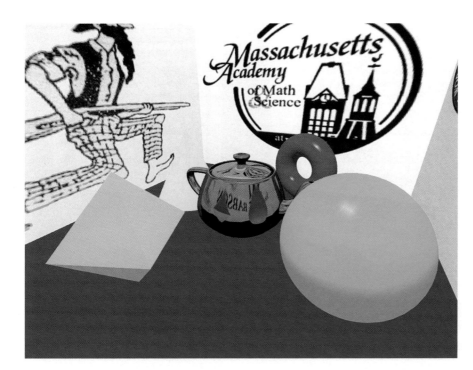

COLOR PLATE 25
Render to texture with FBOs to improve performance of dynamic environment mapping. (For Figure 18.5 in Chapter 18)

COLOR PLATE 26
Fragment shaders can simultaneously output multiple distinct colors to separate color buffers attached to FBOs. (For Figure 18.6 in Chapter 18)

COLOR PLATE 27
Data is thrown away when colors outside [0,1] are clamped (left) rather than mapped to [0,1] (right). (For Chapter 18—not associated with any black and white figure)

COLOR PLATE 28
The HDR image of the silhouetted tree (left) reveals surprising detail when the aperture is adjusted (right). (For Chapter 18—not associated with any black and white figure)

COLOR PLATE 29
The still life sheds its warm candle glow (left) courtesy of a white balance tone mapping shader (right). (For Chapter 18—not associated with any black and white figure)

COLOR PLATE 30
Bloom and afterglow effects help give the impression of extreme brightness even when we can't display colors brighter than 100% white. (For Chapter 18—not associated with any black and white figure)

COLOR PLATE 32 (not associated with any chapter)   This scene from Software Bisque's Seeker solar system simulator is rendered entirely with OpenGL shaders (image courtesy of Software Bisque, Inc.).

LISTING 17.11   Continued

```
    // map object-space position onto unit sphere
    V = gl_Vertex.xyz;

    // eye-space normal
    N = gl_NormalMatrix * gl_Normal;

    // eye-space light vector
    vec4 Veye = gl_ModelViewMatrix * gl_Vertex;
    L = lightPos - Veye.xyz;
}
```

The object we're using for our examples is a sphere. The size of the sphere doesn't matter because we normalize the object-space position at the beginning of the fragment shader. This means that all the positions we deal with in the fragment shader will be in the range [–1,1].

Our strategy for the fragment shader will be to break up the range [–1,1] into eight alternating blocks along each axis. Each block will be assigned an alternating value of 0 or 1 for each axis, as illustrated in Figure 17.12. If the total of the three values is even, we paint it black; otherwise, we paint it white.

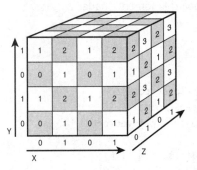

FIGURE 17.12   This diagram illustrates how we assign alternating colors to blocks of fragments.

Figure 17.13 shows the result of Listing 17.12, which implements our checkerboard procedural texture mapping algorithm.

FIGURE 17.13   This 3D checkerboard is generated without using any texture images.

LISTING 17.12   Checkerboard Fragment Shader

```
// checkerboard.fs
//
// 3D solid checker grid

varying vec3 V; // object-space position
varying vec3 N; // eye-space normal
varying vec3 L; // eye-space light vector

const vec3 onColor = vec3(1.0, 1.0, 1.0);
const vec3 offColor = vec3(0.0, 0.0, 0.0);

const float ambientLighting = 0.2;
const float specularExp = 60.0;
const float specularIntensity = 0.75;

const int numSquaresPerSide = 8;


void main (void)
{
```

LISTING 17.12   Continued

```
// Normalize vectors
vec3 NN = normalize(N);
vec3 NL = normalize(L);
vec3 NV = normalize(V);
vec3 NH = normalize(NL + vec3(0.0, 0.0, 1.0));

// Map -1,1 to 0,numSquaresPerSide
vec3 onOrOff = ((NV + 1.0) * float(numSquaresPerSide)) / 2.0;
// mod 2 >= 1
onOrOff = step(1.0, mod(onOrOff, 2.0));
// 3-way xor
onOrOff.x = step(0.5,
    mod(onOrOff.x + onOrOff.y + onOrOff.z, 2.0));

// checkerboard grid
vec3 surfColor = mix(offColor, onColor, onOrOff.x);

// calculate diffuse lighting + 20% ambient
surfColor *= (ambientLighting + vec3(max(0.0, dot(NN, NL))));

// calculate specular lighting w/ 75% intensity
surfColor += (specularIntensity *
    vec3(pow(max(0.0, dot(NN, NH)), specularExp)));

gl_FragColor = vec4(surfColor, 1.0);
}
```

GLSL has a built-in modulo function, mod, which is used to achieve the alternating blocks. Next, we must determine whether the value is within [0,1] or [1,2]. We do this using the step function, which returns 1 if the second argument is greater than or equal to the first, and 0 otherwise.

Now that we have a value of 0 or 1 on each axis, we sum those three values and again perform modulo 2 and a greater-than-or-equal-to comparison. That way, we can assign colors of black or white based on whether the final sum is even or odd. We accomplish this with mix.

You can very easily alter the shaders to change the checkerboard colors or to adjust the number of blocks per row. Give it a try!

17

Beach Ball Texture

In this next sample, we're going to turn our sphere into a beach ball. The ball will have eight longitudinal stripes with alternating primary colors. The north and south poles of the ball will be painted white. Let's get started!

Look at the ball from above. We'll be slicing it up into three half spaces: north-south, northeast-southwest, and northwest-southeast. See Figure 17.14 for a visual depiction. The north slices are assigned full red values, and south slices are assigned no red. The two slices that are both in the southeast half space and the northeast half space are assigned full green, and all other slices receive no green. Notice how the overlapping red and green slice becomes yellow. Finally, all slices in the southwest half space are assigned the color blue.

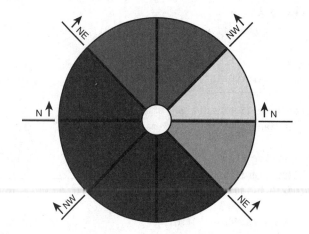

FIGURE 17.14   An overhead view showing how the beach ball colors are assigned. (This figure also appears in the Color insert.)

The east slices nicely alternate from red to yellow to green to blue. But what about the west slices? The easiest way to address them is to effectively copy the east slices and rotate them 180 degrees. We're looking down at the ball from the positive y-axis. If the object-space position's x coordinate is greater than or equal to 0, the position is used as-is. However, if the coordinate is less than 0, we negate both the x-axis and z-axis positions, which maps the original position to its mirror on the opposite side of the beach ball.

The white caps at the poles are simple to add in. After coloring the rest of the ball with stripes, we replace that color with white whenever the absolute value of the y-axis position is close to 1. Figure 17.15 shows the result of the beach ball shaders in Listing 17.13.

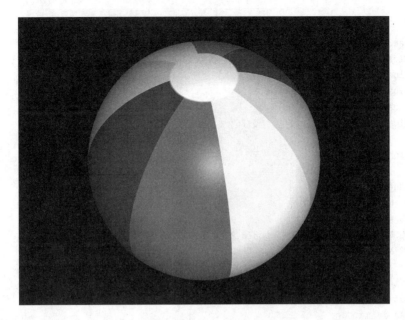

FIGURE 17.15   You have built your own beach ball from scratch! (This figure also appears in the Color insert.)

LISTING 17.13   Beach Ball Fragment Shader

```
// beachball.fs
//
// Longitudinal stripes, end caps

varying vec3 V; // object-space position
varying vec3 N; // eye-space normal
varying vec3 L; // eye-space light vector

const vec3 myRed = vec3(1.0, 0.0, 0.0);
const vec3 myYellow = vec3(1.0, 1.0, 0.0);
const vec3 myGreen = vec3(0.0, 1.0, 0.0);
const vec3 myBlue = vec3(0.0, 0.0, 1.0);
const vec3 myWhite = vec3(1.0, 1.0, 1.0);
const vec3 myBlack = vec3(0.0, 0.0, 0.0);

const vec3 northHalfSpace = vec3(0.0, 0.0, 1.0);
const vec3 northeastHalfSpace = vec3(0.707, 0.0, 0.707);
```

LISTING 17.13   Continued

```
const vec3 northwestHalfSpace = vec3(-0.707, 0.0, 0.707);
const float capSize = 0.03;          // 0 to 1
const float smoothEdgeTol = 0.005;
const float ambientLighting = 0.2;
const float specularExp = 60.0;
const float specularIntensity = 0.75;

void main (void)
{
    // Normalize vectors
    vec3 NN = normalize(N);
    vec3 NL = normalize(L);
    vec3 NH = normalize(NL + vec3(0.0, 0.0, 1.0));
    vec3 NV = normalize(V);

    // Mirror half of ball across X and Z axes
    float mirror = (NV.x >= 0.0) ? 1.0 : -1.0;
    NV.xz *= mirror;

    // Check for north/south, east/west,
    // northeast/southwest, northwest/southeast
    vec4 distance;
    distance.x = dot(NV, northHalfSpace);
    distance.y = dot(NV, northeastHalfSpace);
    distance.z = dot(NV, northwestHalfSpace);

    // set up for white caps on top and bottom
    distance.w = abs(NV.y) - 1.0 + capSize;

    distance = smoothstep(vec4(0.0), vec4(smoothEdgeTol), distance);

    // red, green, red+green=yellow, and blue stripes
    vec3 surfColor = mix(myBlack, myRed, distance.x);
    surfColor += mix(myBlack, myGreen, distance.y*(1.0-distance.z));
    surfColor = mix(surfColor, myBlue, 1.0-distance.y);

    // white caps on top and bottom
    surfColor = mix(surfColor, myWhite, distance.w);
```

LISTING 17.13   Continued

```
    // calculate diffuse lighting + 20% ambient
    surfColor *= (ambientLighting + vec3(max(0.0, dot(NN, NL))));

    // calculate specular lighting w/ 75% intensity
    surfColor += (specularIntensity *
        vec3(pow(max(0.0, dot(NN, NH)), specularExp)));

gl_FragColor = vec4(surfColor, 1.0);
}
```

After remapping all negative x positions as described earlier, we use dot products to determine on which side of each half space the current object-space coordinate falls. The sign of the dot product tells us which side of the half space is in play.

Notice we don't use the built-in step function this time. Instead, we introduce a new and improved version: smoothstep. Instead of transitioning directly from 0 to 1 at the edge of a half space, smoothstep allows for a smooth transition near the edge where values between 0 and 1 are returned. Switch back and forth between step and smoothstep and you'll see how it helps reduce the aliasing jaggies.

Toy Ball Texture

For our final procedural texture mapping feat, we'll transform our sphere into a familiar toy ball, again using no conventional texture images. This ball will have a red star on a yellow background circumscribed by a blue stripe. We will describe all this inside a fragment shader.

The tricky part is obviously the star shape. For each fragment, the shader must determine whether the fragment is within the star, in which case it's painted red, or whether it remains outside the star, in which case it's painted yellow. To make this determination, we first detect whether the fragment is inside or outside five different half spaces, as shown in Figure 17.16.

17

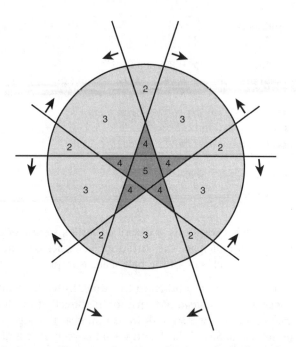

FIGURE 17.16   This diagram illustrates the determination of whether a fragment is inside or outside the star.

Any fragment that is inside at least four of the five half spaces is inside the star. We'll start a counter at –3 and increment it for every half space that the fragment falls within. Then we'll clamp it to the range [0,1]. A 0 indicates that we're outside the star and should paint the fragment yellow. A 1 indicates that we're inside the star and should paint the fragment red.

Adding the blue stripe, like the white caps on the beach ball, is an easy last step. Instead of repainting fragments close to the ends of the ball, we repaint them close to the center, this time along the z-axis. Figure 17.17 illustrates the result of the toy ball shader in Listing 17.14.

FIGURE 17.17   The toy ball shader describes a relatively complex shape. (This figure also appears in the Color insert.)

LISTING 17.14   Toy Ball Fragment Shader

```
// toyball.fs
//
// Based on shader by Bill Licea-Kane

varying vec3 V; // object-space position
varying vec3 N; // eye-space normal
varying vec3 L; // eye-space light vector

const vec3 myRed = vec3(0.6, 0.0, 0.0);
const vec3 myYellow = vec3(0.6, 0.5, 0.0);
const vec3 myBlue = vec3(0.0, 0.3, 0.6);

const vec3 myHalfSpace0 = vec3(0.31, 0.95, 0.0);
const vec3 myHalfSpace1 = vec3(-0.81, 0.59, 0.0);
const vec3 myHalfSpace2 = vec3(-0.81, -0.59, 0.0);
const vec3 myHalfSpace3 = vec3(0.31, -0.95, 0.0);
const vec3 myHalfSpace4 = vec3(1.0, 0.0, 0.0);
```

LISTING 17.14   Continued

```
const float stripeThickness = 0.4;   // 0 to 1
const float starSize = 0.2;          // 0 to ~0.3
const float smoothEdgeTol = 0.005;
const float ambientLighting = 0.2;
const float specularExp = 60.0;
const float specularIntensity = 0.5;

void main (void)
{
    vec4 distVector;
    float distScalar;

    // Normalize vectors
    vec3 NN = normalize(N);
    vec3 NL = normalize(L);
    vec3 NH = normalize(NL + vec3(0.0, 0.0, 1.0));
    vec3 NV = normalize(V);

    // Each flat edge of the star defines a half space.  The interior
    // of the star is any point within at least 4 out of 5 of them.
    // Start with -3 so that it takes adding 4 ins to equal 1.
    float myInOut = -3.0;

    // We need to perform 5 dot products, one for each edge of
    // the star.  Perform first 4 in vector, 5th in scalar.
    distVector.x = dot(NV, myHalfSpace0);
    distVector.y = dot(NV, myHalfSpace1);
    distVector.z = dot(NV, myHalfSpace2);
    distVector.w = dot(NV, myHalfSpace3);
    distScalar = dot(NV, myHalfSpace4);

    // The half-space planes all intersect the origin.  We must
    // offset them in order to give the star some size.
    distVector += starSize;
    distScalar += starSize;

    distVector = smoothstep(0.0, smoothEdgeTol, distVector);
    distScalar = smoothstep(0.0, smoothEdgeTol, distScalar);
    myInOut += dot(distVector, vec4(1.0));
    myInOut += distScalar;
    myInOut = clamp(myInOut, 0.0, 1.0);
```

LISTING 17.14 Continued

```
    // red star on yellow background
    vec3 surfColor = mix(myYellow, myRed, myInOut);

    // blue stripe down middle
    myInOut = smoothstep(0.0, smoothEdgeTol,
                          abs(NV.z) - stripeThickness);
    surfColor = mix(myBlue, surfColor, myInOut);

    // calculate diffuse lighting + 20% ambient
    surfColor *= (ambientLighting + vec3(max(0.0, dot(NN, NL))));

    // calculate specular lighting w/ 50% intensity
    surfColor += (specularIntensity *
        vec3(pow(max(0.0, dot(NN, NH)), specularExp)));

    gl_FragColor = vec4(surfColor, 1.0);
}
```

The half spaces cut through the center of the sphere. This is what we wanted for the beach ball, but for the star we need them offset from the center slightly. This is why we add an extra constant distance to the result of the half-space dot products. The larger you make this constant, the larger your star will be.

Again, we use smoothstep when picking between inside and outside. For efficiency, we put the inside/outside results of the first four half spaces into a four-component vector. This way, we can sum the four components with a single four-component dot product against the vector {1,1,1,1}. The fifth half space's inside/outside value goes into a lonely float and is added to the other four separately because no five-component vector type is available. You could create such a type yourself out of a structure, but you would likely sacrifice performance on most implementations, which natively favor four-component vectors.

If you want to toy with this shader, try this exercise: Convert the star into a six-pointed star by adding another half space and adjusting the existing half-space planes. Prove to yourself how many half spaces your fragments must fall within now to fall within the star, and adjust the myInOut counter's initial value accordingly.

17

Summary

The possible applications of vertex and fragment shaders are limited only by your imagination. We've introduced a few just to spark your creativity and to provide you with some basic building blocks so that you can easily jump right in and start creating your own shaders. Feel free to take these shaders, hack and slash them beyond recognition, and invent and discover better ways of doing things while you're at it. Don't forget the main objective of this book: Make pretty pictures. So get to it!

CHAPTER 18

Advanced Buffers

by Benjamin Lipchak

WHAT YOU'LL LEARN IN THIS CHAPTER:

- How to improve performance with pixel buffer objects (PBOs)

- How to perform offscreen rendering with framebuffer objects (FBOs)

- How to use floating-point textures and color buffers

- How to put it all together and render with high dynamic range

Shaders by now are old hat. Been there, done that. Yawn. The most exciting new advances in OpenGL over the past several years involve buffers. In particular, the flexibility with which you can designate blocks of GPU memory for a variety of purposes enables rendering techniques which were before impossible or too slow to consider using. No longer are vertex arrays, textures, and framebuffers individual and segregated entities. Today you can mix-and-match this data—read it, write it, and render with it from different stages of the OpenGL pipeline. And with new single-precision floating-point data formats, the sky is the limit. Or in deference to IEEE 754, 3.4×10^{38} is the limit.

This chapter covers the OpenGL APIs making this new-found flexibility possible: pixel buffer objects, framebuffer objects, and floating-point internal formats for textures and renderbuffers. Each feature will be explored in isolation with one or two samples. Then they will all join hands on stage for a final curtain call where they team up to provide high dynamic range bloom and afterglow effects.

Pixel Buffer Objects

Pixel buffer objects, commonly referred to as PBOs, are a new class of buffer objects available in OpenGL 2.1. You may remember the original class of buffer objects, vertex buffer objects (VBOs), described in Chapter 11, "It's All About the Pipeline: Faster Geometry Throughput." Although the mechanics are the same, their intended usage is different.

Hint: PBOs are intended to contain pixels instead of vertices.

Like VBOs, PBOs are considered server-side objects. This allows the OpenGL driver to place them in video memory next to the GPU, or wherever else it thinks performance will be optimal. And like VBOs, the same usage hints (what the app plans to do with the data, and how frequently) can influence the decision as to where to place the PBO in memory. If the data will be written once and then used for rendering repeatedly, local video memory may be fastest, whereas if the data is constantly being read back or replaced by the CPU, the PBO may be better situated in host-readable system memory.

By binding a PBO to one of two new buffer object targets, described next, any OpenGL command that traditionally expects a pointer to client memory (that is, memory allocated by your application) to send in or read back blocks of pixel data will now use the PBO as the source or destination for that pixel data. Fear not: When we say pixels, we mean texels too!

How to Use PBOs

The commands are identical to those used for VBOs. In fact, the GL_ARB_pixel_buffer_object extension from which this feature originated introduced no new entrypoints. All it brought to the table were two new tokens for buffer object binding targets, and two new tokens to query back the current bindings. GL_PIXEL_PACK_BUFFER and GL_PIXEL_UNPACK_BUFFER are the new targets. GL_PIXEL_PACK_BUFFER_BINDING and GL_PIXEL_UNPACK_BUFFER_BINDING are used with glGet* to query the current bindings. If no PBO is bound, these return 0.

Here's a refresher on buffer object commands. We generate a name, bind it to create the PBO, initialize its data store, map it to allow direct CPU access and then unmap it, modify a subset of the data store, draw from it, and then delete it:

```
glGenBuffers(1, &pboName);
glBindBuffer(GL_PIXEL_UNPACK_BUFFER, pboName);
glBufferData(GL_PIXEL_UNPACK_BUFFER, width * height,
             myPixelPtr, GL_STATIC_DRAW);
glMapBuffer(GL_PIXEL_UNPACK_BUFFER, GL_WRITE_ONLY);
glUnmapBuffer(GL_PIXEL_UNPACK_BUFFER);
glBufferSubData(GL_PIXEL_UNPACK_BUFFER, width * 5, width, ptrToNewRow5Data);
glDrawPixels(width, height, GL_LUMINANCE, GL_UNSIGNED_BYTE, (GLvoid*)0);
glDeleteBuffers(1, &pboName);
```

Unpacking refers to taking data from the app and unpacking it for use by the OpenGL driver, as in glDrawPixels or glTexImage2D. Packing, on the other hand, is when pixel data is packaged up and returned to the application, such as via glReadPixels or glGetTexImage.

Notice that the call to `glDrawPixels` in the preceding code snippet is passed a pointer value of `0`. Just as for vertex array pointers when a VBO is bound, the pointer is treated as an offset into the currently bound buffer object. The `0` means the driver should start unpacking at the very beginning of the buffer object's data store. A nonzero value would indicate that the unpacking should start some number of bytes past the beginning.

You can use `glBindBuffer` to switch between different PBOs. Binding buffer name `0` to a target will effectively unbind the currently bound PBO, if any, returning to traditional usage of client memory for the associated binding point. Another interesting thing to note is that a buffer object can be simultaneously bound to multiple targets, those for both PBOs and VBOs!

The Benefits of PBOs

There are several specific benefits that summoned PBOs into existence. All of them are performance-related. An application has always been able to send pixels and texels from client memory into the driver, and read them back into client memory, copy them around, and use the data for different purposes. PBOs simply allow the driver to take some shortcuts that can improve performance. These are the specific performance benefits:

- Caching frequently used data close to the GPU

- Avoiding an extra copy from client memory to the driver

- Allowing reads from the framebuffer to be pipelined

- Data repurposing without explicit copies to and from client memory

The first benefit is identical to that achieved with VBOs. Just as frequently used geometry data can be placed into a VBO that the driver might decide to cache in video memory for fast access during rendering, the same can be done for frequently used pixel data. For example, if you redraw the same GUI components, cursor, or other 2D element over and over again, that pixel data has to be unpacked from client memory and sent to the GPU every time. This is because the driver has no way of knowing if the client data has changed in between calls, so it has to assume that the data is different each time. Putting the data into a PBO, where the application can touch it only by calling OpenGL commands like `glBufferData` or `glMapBuffer`, gives the driver an assurance that it can safely relocate your data and reuse it with lower per-draw costs.

The second benefit stems from the typical usage pattern for applications loading textures from disk. Consider your favorite OpenGL game. As you complete one level and move on to the next, don't you hate waiting for that progress bar to advance from one side of the screen to the next? Much of this time is spent loading textures from disk and sending them into the driver. Traditionally, the application allocates client memory, loads the texture data from disk into the client memory, and hands the pointer to the driver with a call like `glTexImage2D`. The driver then needs to copy that data from the client memory

18

into its own memory before returning from the call. Remember, as soon as `glTexImage2D` is complete, the application is allowed to modify that memory and use it again for its next texture if it so chooses! If, instead of allocating its own client memory for the texture, the application calls `glMapBuffer` on a buffer object, the application could load the texture straight from disk into the driver, avoiding an extra explicit copy into client memory along the way. Considering the gigabytes of texture data used by games these days, copying more often than you need to is just a waste!

The third benefit shifts attention away from sending data into the driver, and instead focuses on reading data back out of the driver. In particular, calling `glReadPixels` traditionally reads pixels from the framebuffer and packs them into client memory. Upon return from `glReadPixels`, the data must be ready because the application might start using it immediately. And for that data to be ready, the contents of the framebuffer would first have to be finalized. This means all rendering in the pipeline has to drain out and have its impact on the framebuffer before the pixels can be safely read back. This is why your mother warned you against hanging out with `glReadPixels`. Now you can tell your mother about PBOs. An application can bind a PBO to the `GL_PIXEL_PACK_BUFFER` target before making the call. Because the application has to then use an explicit command, either `glGetBufferSubData` or `glMapBuffer`, to access the results, the driver no longer has to drain the pipeline to ensure that the results are immediately available. If the application can issue the `glReadPixels`, go off and do some other useful work, and then come back later to get the result when it is available, no pipeline stalls are needed!

Finally, we can benefit performance-wise by the flexibility of buffer objects. Looking just at PBOs, we can bind the same buffer object to both the `GL_PIXEL_PACK_BUFFER` and `GL_PIXEL_UNPACK_BUFFER` targets and effectively grab texel data from one place and send it back in as pixel data, or vice versa. (Note that `glCopyTexImage*` already exists to optimize the latter case.) The more interesting combination may be the capability to bind a PBO as a VBO, also known as render to vertex array. Using floating-point formats, you can use the GPU's shader hardware to generate vertex data that can be read back to a PBO, bound as a VBO, and used for subsequent rendering. Though different OpenGL implementations will have different internal gymnastics they need to perform to make this work, from the application's perspective, it can do all this without ever copying data into or out of a client memory buffer.

PBOs in Action

The first sample of the chapter is one that is contrived to demonstrate a couple of the more tricky performance benefits of PBOs, the second and third in the earlier list. For every frame that is drawn, we're going to blend together three textures: (1) an album cover at 50%, incrementally rotated in each new frame, (2) a snapshot of the frame we rendered two frames ago at 25%, and (3) a snapshot of the frame we rendered three frames ago at 25%. The end result is a motion-blurred spinning album cover.

We're going to read back old frames via `glReadPixels` and send them back in as textures via `glTexImage2D` for use as the ghost images for motion blur. To improve performance, we'll bind PBOs so that our reads from the framebuffer are pipelined. Also, we'll map the PBO in order to perform the CPU scaling down to 25% without having to introduce a client memory copy. Clearly there are more optimal ways to achieve this effect, such as using fragment shaders to blend the ghost images at the desired ratios. We're going retro in a number of ways in order to focus on the PBO lessons.

Figure 18.1 shows how three textures are added together per frame to obtain the motion-blurred result. The original album cover at 50% is always contributing, rotated a bit each time. The previous frame does *not* contribute, because we want to give the `glReadPixels` a chance to finish without draining the pipeline. The frame before that, which has finished being read back, is mapped so that the CPU can scale its values by 25%. And finally, the frame before that, already scaled by 25%, makes its final appearance as a ghost image before being recycled as the recipient for the next `glReadPixels`.

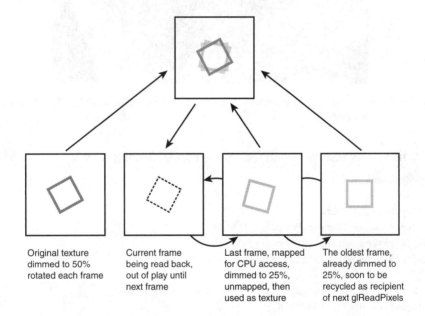

Original texture dimmed to 50% rotated each frame

Current frame being read back, out of play until next frame

Last frame, mapped for CPU access, dimmed to 25%, unmapped, then used as texture

The oldest frame, already dimmed to 25%, soon to be recycled as recipient of next glReadPixels

FIGURE 18.1   Three textures contributing to each final frame.

Figure 18.2 shows the results of the main rendering loop in Listing 18.1. The main rendering loop draws the current frame, starts to read back from it, maps the previous frame for dimming, and sends it back in as a texture.

FIGURE 18.2 PBOs improve the performance of our motion blur sample. (This figure also appears in the Color insert.)

LISTING 18.1 The Main Rendering Loop of the PBO Motion Blur Sample

```
void RenderScene(void)
{
    // Advance old frame
    currentFrame = (currentFrame + 1) % 3;
    int lastFrame = (currentFrame + 2) % 3;
    int frameBeforeThat = (currentFrame + 1) % 3;

    // Rotate the texture matrix for unit 0 (current frame)
    glActiveTexture(GL_TEXTURE0);
    glTranslatef(0.5f, 0.5f, 0.0f);
    glRotatef(angleIncrement, 0.0f, 0.0f, 1.0f);
    glTranslatef(-0.5f, -0.5f, 0.0f);

    // Draw objects in the scene
    int i;
    glBegin(GL_QUADS);
        for (i = 0; i < 3; i++)
            glMultiTexCoord2f(GL_TEXTURE0 + i, 0.0f, 0.0f);
```

LISTING 18.1   Continued

```
            glVertex2f(-1.0f, -1.0f);
        for (i = 0; i < 3; i++)
            glMultiTexCoord2f(GL_TEXTURE0 + i, 0.0f, 1.0f);
        glVertex2f(-1.0f, 1.0f);
        for (i = 0; i < 3; i++)
            glMultiTexCoord2f(GL_TEXTURE0 + i, 1.0f, 1.0f);
        glVertex2f(1.0f, 1.0f);
        for (i = 0; i < 3; i++)
            glMultiTexCoord2f(GL_TEXTURE0 + i, 1.0f, 0.0f);
        glVertex2f(1.0f, -1.0f);
    glEnd();

    // Now read back result
    glBindBuffer(GL_PIXEL_PACK_BUFFER, currentFrame + 1);
    glReadPixels(dataOffsetX, dataOffsetY, dataWidth, dataHeight,
                GL_RGB, GL_UNSIGNED_BYTE, (GLvoid*)0);
    glBindBuffer(GL_PIXEL_PACK_BUFFER, 0);

    frameGood[currentFrame] = GL_TRUE;

    // Prepare the last frame by dividing colors by 4
    glBindBuffer(GL_PIXEL_UNPACK_BUFFER, lastFrame + 1);
    pixels[lastFrame] = (GLubyte*)glMapBuffer(GL_PIXEL_UNPACK_BUFFER,
                                        GL_READ_WRITE);

    for (int y = 0; y < dataHeight; y++)
    {
        for (int x = 0; x < dataWidth; x++)
        {
            GLubyte *ptr = (GLubyte *)pixels[lastFrame] +
                            (y*dataPitch) + (x*3);
            *(ptr + 0) >>= 2;
            *(ptr + 1) >>= 2;
            *(ptr + 2) >>= 2;
        }
    }

    glUnmapBuffer(GL_PIXEL_UNPACK_BUFFER);
    pixels[lastFrame] = NULL;

    glActiveTexture(GL_TEXTURE1);
    glBindTexture(GL_TEXTURE_2D, 2+lastFrame);
```

18

LISTING 18.1   Continued

```
    if (frameGood[lastFrame])
    {
        glTexImage2D(GL_TEXTURE_2D, 0, GL_RGB8, dataWidth, dataHeight,
                     0, GL_RGB, GL_UNSIGNED_BYTE, (GLvoid*)0);
    }
    glBindBuffer(GL_PIXEL_UNPACK_BUFFER, 0);

    glActiveTexture(GL_TEXTURE2);
    glBindTexture(GL_TEXTURE_2D, 2+frameBeforeThat);

    // Flush drawing commands
    glutSwapBuffers();
}
```

Oh, Where Is the Home Where the PBOs Roam?

You have seen PBOs used in conjunction with basic commands like glTexImage2D and glReadPixels. But what is the full list of commands where GL_PIXEL_PACK_BUFFER and GL_PIXEL_UNPACK_BUFFER come into play? I'm glad you asked.

GL_PIXEL_PACK_BUFFER affects glGetCompressedTexImage, glGetConvolutionFilter, glGetHistogram, glGetMinmax, glGetPixelMap, glGetPolygonStipple, glGetSeparableFilter, glGetTexImage, and glReadPixels.

GL_PIXEL_UNPACK_BUFFER affects glBitmap, glColorSubTable, glColorTable, glCompressedTexImage*, glCompressedTexSubImage*, glConvolutionFilter*, glDrawPixels, glPixelMap, glPolygonStipple, glSeparableFilter2D, glTexImage*, and glTexSubImage*.

The OpenGL 2.1 specification requires that any of these commands be usable with PBOs. Many of them are rarely used, so your mileage may vary!

Framebuffer Objects

Framebuffer objects, known as FBOs, allow you to divert your rendering away from your window's framebuffer to one or more offscreen framebuffers that you create. Offscreen simply means that the content of the framebuffers is not visible until it is first copied back to the original window. This is similar to rendering to your back buffer, which isn't visible until swapped.

Why would you want to do this, especially if rendering to an FBO doesn't show up on the screen?! My answer is threefold, with more details following in subsequent sections:

- FBOs aren't limited to the size of your window.

- Textures can be attached to FBOs, allowing direct rendering to textures without an explicit glCopyTexImage.

- FBOs can contain multiple color buffers, which can be written to simultaneously from a fragment shader.

FBOs are new enough that they are not yet part of the core OpenGL API. You need to check for the GL_EXT_framebuffer_object extension before using them.

How to Use FBOs

The first thing to understand is that an FBO is just a container for images. Consider the traditional framebuffer that comes with your window. It is also a container of images. At minimum you always have a front buffer, which holds the colors you see on the screen. Almost always you have a back buffer, which is the staging area for your in-progress rendering. Often you have a depth buffer, and sometimes a stencil buffer too. These individual 2D surfaces compose the framebuffer.

Creating and Destroying

You create and destroy your FBO container using familiar commands:

```
glGenFramebuffersEXT(1, &fboName);
glBindFramebufferEXT(GL_FRAMEBUFFER_EXT, fboName);
glDeleteFramebuffersEXT(1, &fboName);
```

In addition to creating new FBOs, glBindFramebufferEXT is also used for switching between FBOs. Binding to name 0 will effectively unbind the current FBO, if any, and redirect rendering to your window's framebuffer.

Now, with what shall we fill our initially empty container? There are two types of images that can be attached to the FBO. The first you're already familiar with: textures. Since this book is nearing its end, I trust that by now you're an expert at creating textures. The second type of image is called a renderbuffer. Both textures and renderbuffers will serve as the targets for rendering. The main difference is that renderbuffers cannot be used for subsequent texturing. Also, whereas you can create depth textures (see Chapter 14), stencil textures don't exist. So, if you need a stencil buffer attachment, or if you don't intend to turn around and use your FBO attachment as a texture, renderbuffers are for you.

Renderbuffers again use a familiar interface:

```
glGenRenderbuffersEXT(1, &rbName);
glBindRenderbufferEXT(GL_RENDERBUFFER_EXT, rbName);
glRenderbufferStorageEXT(GL_RENDERBUFFER_EXT, GL_RGBA8, width, height);
glDeleteRenderbuffersEXT(1, &rbName);
```

18

glRenderbufferStorageEXT establishes the size and internal format of your renderbuffer. Accepted formats are the same as those accepted by glTexImage*, with the addition of GL_STENCIL_INDEX{1¦4¦8¦16}_EXT formats. You can find the maximum dimensions supported by your OpenGL implementation by calling glGetIntegerv with the parameter GL_MAX_RENDERBUFFER_SIZE_EXT.

Attaching Images

Now to attach our images to our FBO. One requirement is that all attached images have to be the same size. This is a very reasonable requirement. Imagine if the color buffers and depth buffer in your traditional framebuffer were different sizes. What would that even mean? It would be chaos! Another requirement is that all attached color buffers must be the same format. This time I could make arguments for wanting to render simultaneously to different color formats, but alas this is a restriction we're currently stuck with. Here are examples of the four commands for attaching images to our FBO:

```
glFramebufferTexture1DEXT(GL_FRAMEBUFFER_EXT, GL_COLOR_ATTACHMENT0_EXT,
                    GL_TEXTURE_1D, my1DTexName, mipLevel);
glFramebufferTexture2DEXT(GL_FRAMEBUFFER_EXT, GL_COLOR_ATTACHMENT0_EXT,
                    GL_TEXTURE_2D, my2DTexName, mipLevel);
glFramebufferTexture3DEXT(GL_FRAMEBUFFER_EXT, GL_COLOR_ATTACHMENT0_EXT,
                    GL_TEXTURE_3D, my3DTexName, mipLevel, zOffset);
glFramebufferRenderbufferEXT(GL_FRAMEBUFFER_EXT, GL_COLOR_ATTACHMENT0_EXT,
                    GL_RENDERBUFFER_EXT, rbName);
```

The second argument in each command is the name of the attachment point. This can be GL_DEPTH_ATTACHMENT_EXT, GL_STENCIL_ATTACHMENT_EXT, or GL_COLOR_ATTACHMENTn_EXT where n is 0 through 15. However, today's implementations tend to support fewer than 16 simultaneous color attachments. You can find the limit of an OpenGL implementation by calling glGetIntegerv with parameter GL_MAX_COLOR_ATTACHMENTS_EXT.

When attaching textures, you need to specify which mipmap level you're targeting. Remember that a texture is actually an array of images representing the mipmap chain. If your texture isn't mipmapped, or you'll be using mipmap generation (more on this later), specifying level 0 is appropriate to target the texture's base level.

All attached images must be 2D. Renderbuffers and 2D textures naturally fall into this category. Any 1D textures are treated as 2D images with height 1. You can attach one or more individual cube map faces by specifying the face as the texture target. When attaching a 3D texture, you need to indicate which layer of the 3D texture is being attached via the zOffset parameter.

You may at this point have already asked yourself, "What happens if I have a texture attached to the current FBO and also bound to a texture unit that's currently in use? Isn't there a paradox in which I'm currently rendering from the same surface I'm rendering to?" The answer is, "Yes, there's a paradox, and you'll tear apart the very fabric of space and time, causing the universe to cease existence." Or your rendering will be undefined. Either way, don't do it, I implore you.

Draw Buffers

There's been a lot of talk about multiple color attachments, but how do we address them? For starters, let's look at the output from OpenGL Shading Language (GLSL) fragment shaders. Most often the fragment shader will output a single color to the built-in variable gl_FragColor. However, it may choose instead to output multiple colors to the gl_FragData[*n*] array. A fragment shader will fail to compile if it tries to do both!

The single or multiple color outputs still need to be mapped to the FBO's color attachments. The default behavior is for a single color output to be sent down to color attachment 0. However, this can be altered by a call to either glDrawBuffer or glDrawBuffers, the latter new in OpenGL 2.0 to go along with gl_FragData[*n*].

When no FBO is bound, glDrawBuffer will behave as it always has, meaning that a single color is mapped to one or more color buffers associated with the window, most popularly GL_BACK_LEFT. However, when an FBO is bound, glDrawBuffer no longer accepts the traditional values of front/back/left/right color buffers. Instead it will accept GL_COLOR_ATTACHMENT*n*_EXT or GL_NONE, causing a single color output to be sent to the designated color attachment of the FBO or nowhere, respectively.

glDrawBuffers handles the mapping of multiple color outputs from the fragment shader to multiple color attachments of the FBO. In the rare case in which no FBO is bound, you can still direct the multiple colors to individual color buffers of the traditional framebuffer. For example, if you have double-buffering and stereo support in your window, you can target each buffer individually:

```
GLenum bufs[4] = {GL_FRONT_LEFT, GL_FRONT_RIGHT, GL_BACK_LEFT, GL_BACK_RIGHT};
glDrawBuffers(4, bufs);
```

However, the common case is going to entail using these multiple color outputs while an FBO is bound, as such:

```
GLenum bufs[4] = {GL_COLOR_ATTACHMENT0_EXT, GL_COLOR_ATTACHMENT1_EXT,
                  GL_COLOR_ATTACHMENT2_EXT, GL_COLOR_ATTACHMENT3_EXT};
glDrawBuffers(4, bufs);
```

Of course, there's no reason you need to map the color outputs from gl_FragData[0] to GL_COLOR_ATTACHMENT0_EXT. You can mix it up however you like, or set an entry in the draw buffers list to GL_NONE if you don't need one of the outputs from the fragment shader. There is a limit to how long a list of draw buffers you can pass in to glDrawBuffers. You can discover the limit by calling glGetIntegerv with parameter GL_MAX_DRAW_BUFFERS.

Framebuffer Completeness

Framebuffer completeness is similar in concept to texture completeness. If a texture doesn't have all required mipmap levels specified with the right size and consistent format, that texture is incomplete. Here are the rules for framebuffer completeness, each preceded by its associated error condition:

- GL_FRAMEBUFFER_INCOMPLETE_ATTACHMENT_EXT: All attachment points are framebuffer attachment complete. That is, either each attachment point has no image attached, or the image has nonzero width and height, a valid zOffset if a 3D texture, and an appropriate internal format depending on whether it is attached to a color, depth, or stencil attachment point.

- GL_FRAMEBUFFER_INCOMPLETE_MISSING_ATTACHMENT_EXT: There is at least one image attached to the FBO.

- GL_FRAMEBUFFER_INCOMPLETE_DIMENSIONS_EXT: All attached images have the same dimensions.

- GL_FRAMEBUFFER_INCOMPLETE_FORMATS_EXT: All color attachments have the same internal format.

- GL_FRAMEBUFFER_INCOMPLETE_DRAW_BUFFER_EXT: All non-GL_NONE color attachments referenced by the most recent call to glDrawBuffer or glDrawBuffers against the FBO must have corresponding images attached to the FBO.

- GL_FRAMEBUFFER_INCOMPLETE_READ_BUFFER_EXT: The color attachment referenced by the most recent call to glReadBuffer against the FBO, if non-GL_NONE, must have a corresponding image attached to the FBO.

- GL_FRAMEBUFFER_UNSUPPORTED_EXT: The combination of internal formats of the attached images does not violate an implementation-dependent set of restrictions.

The last one in the list is essentially an implementation's ejection seat, allowing it to bail out for any reason. So even if you're vigilantly obeying all the listed rules, you still need to check for framebuffer completeness in case you hit one of the undocumented implementation-dependent limitations.

To make it easier to determine the cause of framebuffer incompleteness, there is a command for this purpose that will return the offending problem from the preceding list, or GL_FRAMEBUFFER_COMPLETE_EXT if all is well with your FBO:

```
GLenum status = glCheckFramebufferStatusEXT(GL_FRAMEBUFFER_EXT);
switch (status)
{
    case GL_FRAMEBUFFER_COMPLETE_EXT:
        break;
```

```
    case GL_FRAMEBUFFER_UNSUPPORTED_EXT:
        /* choose different formats */
        break;
    default:
        /* programming error; will fail on all hardware */
        assert(0);
}
```

If you attempt to perform any command that reads from or writes to the framebuffer while an FBO is bound and the FBO is incomplete, the command will simply return after throwing a new kind of error, `GL_INVALID_FRAMEBUFFER_OPERATION_EXT`, which is retrievable with `glGetError`.

Mipmap Generation

There's one last consideration before moving on to practical applications of FBOs. Automatic mipmap generation can work efficiently only when it is fully aware when the application is making changes to the texture. If the texture is altered as a side effect of being attached to an FBO, automatic mipmap generation does not take place! For this reason, a new command is added to request manual mipmap generation. You just supply the texture target on the currently active texture unit:

```
glGenerateMipmapEXT(GL_TEXTURE_2D);
```

I like to consider it semiautomatic on-demand mipmap generation. It still beats doing it yourself in the application!

Offscreen Rendering

For our first FBO sample we'll revisit shadow mapping from Chapter 14, "Depth Textures and Shadows." Recall how the size of our shadow map was limited to the size of our window because the depth texture was being copied from the window framebuffer's depth buffer. The size of the shadow map is directly related to the resulting image quality. "But my desktop is small and I can't make my window bigger!" you say. Or "I don't *like* big windows." Fear not. Your misery will be short-lived.

We'll create an FBO, attach a nice big renderbuffer to the depth attachment point, and proceed to reap the image quality rewards. Figure 18.3 compares the original shadow map results with those obtained with FBOs, as set up in Listing 18.2. FBO shadow map results are also included in the color insert.

FIGURE 18.3   Notice the jagged edges of the shadows in the original shadow mapping sample from Chapter 14 compared to the updated sample that uses a large depth renderbuffer attached to an FBO.

LISTING 18.2   FBO Setup Code Added to the Shadow Mapping Sample

```
void SetupRC()
{
    ...

    // Set up some renderbuffer state
    glGenFramebuffersEXT(1, &framebufferID);
    glBindFramebufferEXT(GL_FRAMEBUFFER_EXT, framebufferID);
    glGenRenderbuffersEXT(1, &renderbufferID);
    glBindRenderbufferEXT(GL_RENDERBUFFER_EXT, renderbufferID);
    glRenderbufferStorageEXT(GL_RENDERBUFFER_EXT, GL_DEPTH_COMPONENT32,
                             maxTexSize, maxTexSize);
    glFramebufferRenderbufferEXT(GL_FRAMEBUFFER_EXT, GL_DEPTH_ATTACHMENT_EXT,
                                 GL_RENDERBUFFER_EXT, renderbufferID);
    glDrawBuffer(GL_NONE);
    glReadBuffer(GL_NONE);
    GLenum fboStatus = glCheckFramebufferStatusEXT(GL_FRAMEBUFFER_EXT);
    if (fboStatus != GL_FRAMEBUFFER_COMPLETE_EXT)
    {
        fprintf(stderr, "FBO Error!\n");
    }
    glBindFramebufferEXT(GL_FRAMEBUFFER_EXT, 0);

    RegenerateShadowMap();
}
```

Notice how the draw buffer and read buffer are both set to GL_NONE. This is because our FBO doesn't have any color attachments. All we need is a depth attachment.

The only other difference in this version of the sample is that we bind the FBO right before rendering the shadow pass, then unbind it after copying the result into a depth texture.

Rendering to Textures

By attaching textures to an FBO, you can render directly to a texture. Without FBOs, you have to render to the back buffer and copy it to a texture, not to mention that you're limited to the window size as emphasized in the previous sample. If you're generating a static texture once and then using it repeatedly, saving the one extra copy won't gain you anything. But if you're regenerating the texture every frame, as in the next sample, avoiding that extra copy can mean a substantial performance boost—especially because our cube map environment map is actually six 2D textures in one! Figure 18.4 shows the six views of our scene that compose the environment map.

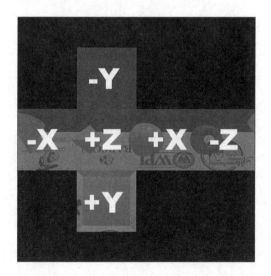

FIGURE 18.4   Six views of the scene. And, yes, they're supposed to appear upside down.

In Listing 18.3, we set up an FBO with a renderbuffer attached for depth. Then one at a time we attach a different cube map face and render each of the six views. Using standard GL_REFLECTION_MAP texture coordinate generation, the teapot's normals are used as a basis for accessing the environment map, causing the teapot to appear to reflect the rest of the scene.

LISTING 18.3   FBO Setup and Use During Environment Map Generation

```
void SetupRC()
{
    ...

    // Set up some renderbuffer state
    glGenFramebuffersEXT(1, &framebufferID);
    glBindFramebufferEXT(GL_FRAMEBUFFER_EXT, framebufferID);
    glGenRenderbuffersEXT(1, &renderbufferID);
    glBindRenderbufferEXT(GL_RENDERBUFFER_EXT, renderbufferID);
    glRenderbufferStorageEXT(GL_RENDERBUFFER_EXT, GL_DEPTH_COMPONENT32,
                             envMapSize, envMapSize);
    glFramebufferRenderbufferEXT(GL_FRAMEBUFFER_EXT, GL_DEPTH_ATTACHMENT_EXT,
                                 GL_RENDERBUFFER_EXT, renderbufferID);
    glBindFramebufferEXT(GL_FRAMEBUFFER_EXT, 0);
}

// Called to regenerate the envmap
void RegenerateEnvMap(void)
{
    // generate 6 views from origin of teapot (0,0,0)

    glMatrixMode(GL_PROJECTION);
    glLoadIdentity();
    gluPerspective(90.0f, 1.0f, 1.0f, 125.0f);
    glViewport(0, 0, envMapSize, envMapSize);

    if (useFBO)
        glBindFramebufferEXT(GL_FRAMEBUFFER_EXT, framebufferID);

    for (GLenum i = GL_TEXTURE_CUBE_MAP_POSITIVE_X;
         i < GL_TEXTURE_CUBE_MAP_POSITIVE_X+6; i++)
    {
        glMatrixMode(GL_MODELVIEW);
        glLoadIdentity();

        switch (i)
        {
        case GL_TEXTURE_CUBE_MAP_POSITIVE_X:
            // +X
            gluLookAt(0.0f, 0.0f, 0.0f,
                      1.0f, 0.0f, 0.0f, 0.0f, -1.0f, 0.0f);
            break;
```

LISTING 18.3   Continued

```
    case GL_TEXTURE_CUBE_MAP_NEGATIVE_X:
        // -X
        gluLookAt(0.0f, 0.0f, 0.0f,
                  -1.0f, 0.0f, 0.0f, 0.0f, -1.0f, 0.0f);
        break;
    case GL_TEXTURE_CUBE_MAP_POSITIVE_Y:
        // +Y
        gluLookAt(0.0f, 0.0f, 0.0f,
                  0.0f, 1.0f, 0.0f, 0.0f, 0.0f, 1.0f);
        break;
    case GL_TEXTURE_CUBE_MAP_NEGATIVE_Y:
        // -Y
        gluLookAt(0.0f, 0.0f, 0.0f,
                  0.0f, -1.0f, 0.0f, 0.0f, 0.0f, -1.0f);
        break;
    case GL_TEXTURE_CUBE_MAP_POSITIVE_Z:
        // +Z
        gluLookAt(0.0f, 0.0f, 0.0f,
                  0.0f, 0.0f, 1.0f, 0.0f, -1.0f, 0.0f);
        break;
    case GL_TEXTURE_CUBE_MAP_NEGATIVE_Z:
        // -Z
        gluLookAt(0.0f, 0.0f, 0.0f,
                  0.0f, 0.0f, -1.0f, 0.0f, -1.0f, 0.0f);
        break;
    default:
        assert(0);
        break;
    }

    if (useFBO)
        glFramebufferTexture2DEXT(GL_FRAMEBUFFER_EXT,
                                  GL_COLOR_ATTACHMENT0_EXT, i,
                                  envMapTextureID, 0);

    // Clear the window with current clearing color
    glClear(GL_COLOR_BUFFER_BIT | GL_DEPTH_BUFFER_BIT);

    // Draw objects in the scene except for the teapot
    DrawModels(GL_FALSE);

    if (!useFBO)
```

18

LISTING 18.3   Continued

```
            glCopyTexImage2D(i, 0, GL_RGBA8, 0, 0, envMapSize, envMapSize, 0);
    }

    if (useFBO)
    {
        glGenerateMipmapEXT(GL_TEXTURE_CUBE_MAP);
        GLenum fboStatus = glCheckFramebufferStatusEXT(GL_FRAMEBUFFER_EXT);
        if (fboStatus != GL_FRAMEBUFFER_COMPLETE_EXT)
        {
            fprintf(stderr, "FBO Error!\n");
        }

        glBindFramebufferEXT(GL_FRAMEBUFFER_EXT, 0);
    }
}
```

Notice the `glCopyTexImage2D` call in the listing, which we can avoid entirely when FBOs
are enabled. That's six copies we're avoiding every time we regenerate the environment
map. And because objects in the scene are moving every frame, our environment map has
to be regenerated with every frame, too. Also notice the call to `glGenerateMipmapEXT`,
which semiautomatically generates the mipmap chain. Using mipmapping significantly
improves image quality by reducing aliasing. See the resulting image in Figure 18.5.

FIGURE 18.5 Dynamic environment mapping benefits from FBOs. (This figure also appears in the Color insert.)

Multiple Render Targets

To demonstrate the capability to render to multiple color buffers simultaneously, we'll render our scene to an FBO-attached texture, then run that texture through a fragment shader that applies four different image transformations simultaneously: edge detection, color inversion, blur, and grayscale. See Listing 18.4.

LISTING 18.4 A GLSL Fragment Shader Outputting Four Different Colors

```
// multirender.fs
//
// 4 different outputs!

uniform sampler2D sampler0;
uniform vec2 tc_offset[9];

void main(void)
{
    vec4 sample[9];

    // enhance the blur by adding an LOD bias
    for (int i = 0; i < 9; i++)
```

LISTING 18.4   Continued

```
{
    sample[i] = texture2D(sampler0,
                          gl_TexCoord[0].st + (tc_offset[i] * 3.0), 3.0);
}

// output 0 is a blur
gl_FragData[0] = (sample[0] + (2.0*sample[1]) + sample[2] +
                 (2.0*sample[3]) + (2.0*sample[5]) +
                 sample[6] + (2.0*sample[7]) + sample[8]) / 12.0;

// now grab the unbiased samples again
for (int i = 0; i < 9; i++)
{
    sample[i] = texture2D(sampler0,
                          gl_TexCoord[0].st + tc_offset[i]);
}

// output 1 is a Laplacian edge-detect
gl_FragData[1] = (sample[4] * 8.0) -
                 (sample[0] + sample[1] + sample[2] +
                  sample[3] + sample[5] +
                  sample[6] + sample[7] + sample[8]);

// output 2 is grayscale
gl_FragData[2] = vec4(vec3(dot(sample[4].rgb, vec3(0.3, 0.59, 0.11))), 1.0);

// output 3 is an inverse
gl_FragData[3] = vec4(vec3(1.0) - sample[4].rgb, 1.0);
}
```

The four color outputs from the fragment shader are mapped to an FBO with four color attachments, again textures. The four textures with four different framebuffer effects are then tiled in a final pass to the window after unbinding the FBO. See Listing 18.5 for the relevant FBO setup code, and Figure 18.6 for the end result.

LISTING 18.5   Set Up Two FBOs with Different Attachments

```
// Set up some renderbuffer state
glGenRenderbuffersEXT(1, &renderbufferID);
glBindRenderbufferEXT(GL_RENDERBUFFER_EXT, renderbufferID);
glRenderbufferStorageEXT(GL_RENDERBUFFER_EXT, GL_DEPTH_COMPONENT32,
                         fboWidth, fboHeight);
```

LISTING 18.5   Continued

```
glGenFramebuffersEXT(2, framebufferID);
glBindFramebufferEXT(GL_FRAMEBUFFER_EXT, framebufferID[0]);
glFramebufferRenderbufferEXT(GL_FRAMEBUFFER_EXT, GL_DEPTH_ATTACHMENT_EXT,
                            GL_RENDERBUFFER_EXT, renderbufferID);
glFramebufferTexture2DEXT(GL_FRAMEBUFFER_EXT, GL_COLOR_ATTACHMENT0_EXT,
                          GL_TEXTURE_2D, renderTextureID[0], 0);

glBindFramebufferEXT(GL_FRAMEBUFFER_EXT, framebufferID[1]);
for (int i = 0; i < maxDrawBuffers; i++)
{
    glFramebufferTexture2DEXT(GL_FRAMEBUFFER_EXT, GL_COLOR_ATTACHMENT0_EXT + i,
                              GL_TEXTURE_2D, renderTextureID[i+1], 0);
}
glBindFramebufferEXT(GL_FRAMEBUFFER_EXT, 0);

...

GLenum buf[4] = {GL_COLOR_ATTACHMENT0_EXT, GL_COLOR_ATTACHMENT1_EXT,
                 GL_COLOR_ATTACHMENT2_EXT, GL_COLOR_ATTACHMENT3_EXT};
glDrawBuffers(maxDrawBuffers, buf);
```

FIGURE 18.6   These four postprocessing effects were generated in parallel, saving three extra passes! (This figure also appears in the Color insert.)

Floating-Point Textures

The GL_ARB_texture_float extension makes available 12 new internal formats for textures, each of the six base color formats in both 16-bit and 32-bit floating-point flavors:

GL_RGBA16F_ARB	GL_RGBA32F_ARB
GL_RGB16F_ARB	GL_RGB32F_ARB
GL_ALPHA16F_ARB	GL_ALPHA32F_ARB
GL_INTENSITY16F_ARB	GL_INTENSITY32F_ARB
GL_LUMINANCE16F_ARB	GL_LUMINANCE32F_ARB
GL_LUMINANCE_ALPHA16F_ARB	GL_LUMINANCE_ALPHA32F_ARB

For nonfloat internal formats, when you call glTexImage* with an integer data type (e.g., GL_UNSIGNED_BYTE), the values are normalized to the range [0,1]. GL_FLOAT type data passed in for use with a nonfloat internal format gets clamped to [0,1]. With the new floating-point internal formats, no normalization or clamping takes place. What you specify is what will be stored, and with the precision and range associated with your choice of 16-bit or 32-bit floats.

Older-generation hardware may not have full support for some functionality when used in conjunction with floating-point textures, such as mipmapping or wrap modes that might sample from the border color (e.g., GL_CLAMP and GL_CLAMP_TO_BORDER). When targeting older hardware, you may witness unexpected rendering or the rendering may be emulated in software with abysmal performance. Beware!

Not only can you render from textures with these new formats, but courtesy of FBO's render-to-texture capabilities, you can also attach floating-point textures to an FBO and render to them. In fact, even renderbuffers can have floating-point internal formats. However, due to implementation-dependent restrictions, always remember to check the completeness of your FBOs with glCheckFramebufferStatusEXT before assuming that anything will work!

Note that there is also an extension, GL_ARB_color_buffer_float, that in coordination with window system-specific extensions (WGL_ARB_pixel_format_float and GLX_ARB_fbconfig_float) allow floating-point rendering directly to the window's framebuffer. However, FBOs cover 99% of interesting cases and are easier to use and more portable. That's probably why the GL_ARB_texture_float extension is the one most widely adopted, and the one we'll be using here.

High Dynamic Range

Now that we have floating-point textures, what are we going to use them for? The short answer is anything you want. No longer limited to capturing 256 shades of colors between 0.0 and 1.0, you can put any arbitrary data into these floating-point buffers.

This high-precision data combined with shader programmability is ushering in a new trend in computing called GPGPU (General-Purpose Graphics Processing Units). Essentially, you can use your GPU as a generic math coprocessor! Considering that some users have a GPU more powerful (and expensive) than their CPU, it would be a shame to tap into it only when drawing pretty pictures on the screen.

Since pretty pictures are our specialty, let's look at an application of floating-point textures that falls into that category: High Dynamic Range (HDR). Take a quick look around. Maybe you have a light bulb in sight. Look out the window, and perhaps you'll see the sun or the moon. (I apologize to those readers outside the Earth's solar system—you'll have to bear with me.) Each light source on its own looks bright. But they're not all equally bright, are they? Staring at a light bulb may leave temporary marks on your retina, but staring at the sun could blind you. Don't try this, just take my word for it.

You might want to model a 60-watt light bulb in your virtual scene. What color do you assign it? Well, it's totally bright white, so that would be (1,1,1,1), right? Now you're in a bit of a pickle when you want to add a 120-watt light bulb, or the sun, which might be approximated by a 1000-watt light bulb. Something can be white, but there's always something brighter white. (To quote the wisdom of Nigel Tufnel in *This Is Spinal Tap,* "These go to eleven.")

In the realm of HDR, we want to remove the artificial limits in which colors are always represented in the range [0,1]. We can work with them as floating-point values with dynamic ranges as high as +/– 3.4×10^{38}. Since there is no common display hardware capable of outputting such a high range (film comes only slightly closer than CRTs or LCDs), this representation will only help us while making intermediate calculations. Eventually we'll have to map back into the [0,1] low dynamic range, but only when we're ready.

OpenEXR File Format

Industrial Light and Magic has made our demonstration of floating-point textures easier by creating an open standard format for storing HDR images. They also make available open-source sample code for working with the format. And to top it off, they provide a number of interesting sample images that we're free to use as we please.

Incorporating the code for loading images was a breeze, as evident in Listing 18.6.

LISTING 18.6   Loading OpenEXR Images into Floating-Point Textures

```
void SetupTextures(int whichEXR)
{
    Array2D<Rgba> pixels;
    char name[256];

    switch (whichEXR)
    {
```

LISTING 18.6   Continued

```
   case 0:
       strcpy(name, "openexr-images/Blobbies.exr");
       break;

...

   default:
       assert(0);
       break;
   }
   RgbaInputFile file(name);
   Box2i dw = file.dataWindow();

   npotTextureWidth = dw.max.x - dw.min.x + 1;
   npotTextureHeight = dw.max.y - dw.min.y + 1;
   pixels.resizeErase(npotTextureHeight, npotTextureWidth);

   file.setFrameBuffer(&pixels[0][0] - dw.min.x - dw.min.y * npotTextureWidth,
                       1, npotTextureWidth);
   file.readPixels(dw.min.y, dw.max.y);

   // Stick the texels into a GL formatted buffer
   potTextureWidth = npotTextureWidth;
   potTextureHeight = npotTextureHeight;

   if (!npotTexturesAvailable)
   {
       while (potTextureWidth & (potTextureWidth-1))
           potTextureWidth++;
       while (potTextureHeight & (potTextureHeight-1))
           potTextureHeight++;
   }

   if ((potTextureWidth > maxTexSize) || (potTextureHeight > maxTexSize))
   {
       fprintf(stderr, "Texture is too big!\n");
       Sleep(2000);
       exit(0);
   }

   if (fTexels)
       free(fTexels);
```

LISTING 18.6   Continued

```
    fTexels = (GLfloat*)malloc(potTextureWidth * potTextureHeight *
                               3 * sizeof(GLfloat));
GLfloat *ptr = fTexels;
for (int v = 0; v < potTextureHeight; v++)
{
    for (int u = 0; u < potTextureWidth; u++)
    {
        if ((v >= npotTextureHeight) || (u >= npotTextureWidth))
        {
            ptr[0] = 0.0f;
            ptr[1] = 0.0f;
            ptr[2] = 0.0f;
        }
        else
        {
            // invert texture vertically
            Rgba texel = pixels[npotTextureHeight - v - 1][u];
            ptr[0] = texel.r;
            ptr[1] = texel.g;
            ptr[2] = texel.b;
        }
        ptr += 3;
    }
}

// pick up new aspect ratio
AlterAspect();

glTexParameteri(GL_TEXTURE_2D, GL_GENERATE_MIPMAP, 1);
glTexImage2D(GL_TEXTURE_2D, 0, GL_RGB16F_ARB, potTextureWidth,
             potTextureHeight, 0, GL_RGB, GL_FLOAT, fTexels);
glTexParameteri(GL_TEXTURE_2D, GL_TEXTURE_MAG_FILTER, GL_LINEAR);
glTexParameteri(GL_TEXTURE_2D, GL_TEXTURE_MIN_FILTER,
                GL_LINEAR_MIPMAP_LINEAR);
glTexParameteri(GL_TEXTURE_2D, GL_TEXTURE_WRAP_S, GL_CLAMP_TO_EDGE);
glTexParameteri(GL_TEXTURE_2D, GL_TEXTURE_WRAP_T, GL_CLAMP_TO_EDGE);
}
```

18

We create an RGBAInputFile instance, passing in a string with the path to the EXR file. We check the image's width and height via RGBAInputFile::dataWindow, and then establish an Array2D<Rgba> of RGBA pixels of the appropriate size via

Array2D::resizeErase. We extract the texels from the file by first pointing at our array via RGBAInputFile::setFrameBuffer and then kicking off the transfer via RGBAInputFile::readPixels. So far this has all been performed using the OpenEXR library.

To dump the data into the OpenGL driver, we first ensure that the texture isn't too big to be supported. Also, we may need to bump up our texture size to the next power-of-two in case the underlying OpenGL implementation doesn't handle NPOT textures. In this case, we'll just frame the texture with black. Then we signal the aspect ratio elsewhere so that the proper viewport and mouse mapping can be established. Finally, we make the OpenGL calls to send in our texels to be stored as 16-bit floats with GL_RGB16F_ARB.

Tone Mapping

We have one final hurdle to cross. We need to map our high dynamic range floating-point data back to the range [0,1], which will then be displayed on a low dynamic range computer display. Doing this range reduction, while attempting to maintain important visual characteristics, is known as tone mapping. One very simple way of tone mapping is to simply clamp any value greater than 1.0. In other circles, this is known as saturating or clipping a color. It's a bit of a cop-out, but for educational purposes it's useful to look at the results of this. See Listing 18.7 and Figure 18.7, where we lose all detail in the bright portions of the image, which become a uniform white.

LISTING 18.7   This Tone Mapping Shader Drops the Ball and Just Clamps

```
// clamped.fs
//
// No tone mapping: clamp [0,oo) -> [0,1]

uniform sampler2D sampler0;

void main(void)
{
    vec4 sample = texture2D(sampler0,
                            gl_TexCoord[0].st);

    // clamp color
    gl_FragColor.rgb = clamp(sample.rgb, 0.0, 1.0);
    gl_FragColor.a = 1.0;
}
```

FIGURE 18.7 Clamping does not make for good tone mapping!

A very simple but often adequate tone mapping technique manages to map the entire range of positive floats down to the range [0,1] using the equation X = Y/(Y+1). Right off the bat, values of 1.0 get cut in half to 0.5. But you can be assured that no matter how bright your scene gets, there will always be a home for every wattage of light bulb, as it were. See Listing 18.8 and Figure 18.8, where suddenly the details in the bright regions pop out.

LISTING 18.8 General-Purpose Tone Mapping Shader

```
// trival.fs
//
// Trivial tone mapping: map [0,oo) -> [0,1)

uniform sampler2D sampler0;

void main(void)
{
    vec4 sample = texture2D(sampler0,
                            gl_TexCoord[0].st);

    // invert color components
```

LISTING 18.8   Continued

```
    gl_FragColor.rgb = sample.rgb / (sample.rgb + 1.0);
    gl_FragColor.a = 1.0;
}
```

FIGURE 18.8   Every brightness level gets mapped now, but those that used to be in the range [0,1] have been further diminished.

If you go into a movie theatre after being in the bright sun, you'll see a whole lot of black. But over time, you'll start to be able to make out details in your surroundings. Believe it or not, pirates wore a patch over one eye not because of disfigurement or fashion trends, but so that one eye would always be sensitive in darkness, for example, when going below deck on a sunny day. To pick out detail in the extra bright areas or extra dark areas of an HDR image, we can use a tone mapping method that works sort of like our eyes do. Using the cursor to choose which part of the image our eyes are accustomed to, we'll take the local maximum brightness from that area and scale it down to 1.0. See Listing 18.9 and Figure 18.9.

LISTING 18.9   Custom Auto-Exposure Tone Mapping

```
// iris.fs
//
// Iris tone mapping: map [0,max] -> [0,1]
// for a local maximum "max" set externally
```

LISTING 18.9 Continued

```
uniform sampler2D sampler0;
uniform vec3 max;

void main(void)
{
    vec4 sample = texture2D(sampler0,
                            gl_TexCoord[0].st);

    // scale all color channels evenly
    float maxMax = (max.r > max.g) ? max.r : max.g;
    maxMax = (maxMax > max.b) ? maxMax : max.b;

    gl_FragColor.rgb = sample.rgb / maxMax;
    gl_FragColor.a = 1.0;
}
```

FIGURE 18.9 Who knew there was this much detail in the foreground trees?

One last variation of the tone mapping implemented for the floating-point textures sample scales each color channel independently, no longer maintaining the original hue. This is not unlike white balancing. In the color insert (Color Plate 29), you can see how it turns an otherwise warm orange candle glow into true white. Cameras often perform this function to compensate for the discoloration caused by artificial lighting.

There are more complex methods of compressing HDR images so that details in both the lightest and the darkest regions are presented simultaneously. I encourage you to pursue HDR compression further if you're interested.

Making Your Whites Whiter and Your Brights Brighter

Sorry, Clorox. I couldn't resist. For our last sample, I'll show how to make good old (1,1,1,1) white look brighter than ever using a bloom effect. This gives the appearance of film overexposure with saturated surfaces bleeding past their edges. If you've played any recent games with the eye candy cranked up, you probably know what I'm talking about.

Even if you don't have support for floating-point textures, you can still take advantage of the bloom effect. It may look a little muted because bright areas will quickly lose their brightness as they're blurred. But you may find second-rate bloom to be better than no bloom at all, so give it a try.

Drawing the Scene

In the first pass, we draw our scene. We'll borrow the toy ball procedural texture shader from Chapter 17, "Fragment Shading: Empower Your Pixel Processing." This time, however, instead of painting the star with a red diffuse material color, we will make the star emit a red glow. The intensity of the glow will be based on how quickly the ball is spinning. See Listing 18.10. Figure 18.10 illustrates the result of this first pass.

LISTING 18.10   Toy Ball Makes a Reappearance Now with a Healthy Glow

```
// hdrball.fs
//
// Based on toy ball shader by Bill Licea-Kane
// with HDR additions from Benj Lipchak

varying vec3 V; // object-space position
varying vec3 N; // eye-space normal
varying vec3 L; // eye-space light vector

uniform float bloomLimit;    // minimum brightness for bloom
uniform float starIntensity; // how bright is the star?

const vec3 myRed = vec3(1.1, 0.2, 0.2);
const vec3 myYellow = vec3(0.6, 0.5, 0.0);
const vec3 myBlue = vec3(0.0, 0.3, 0.6);
```

LISTING 18.10   Continued

```
const vec3 myHalfSpace0 = vec3(0.31, 0.95, 0.0);
const vec3 myHalfSpace1 = vec3(-0.81, 0.59, 0.0);
const vec3 myHalfSpace2 = vec3(-0.81, -0.59, 0.0);
const vec3 myHalfSpace3 = vec3(0.31, -0.95, 0.0);
const vec3 myHalfSpace4 = vec3(1.0, 0.0, 0.0);

const float stripeThickness = 0.4;   // 0 to 1
const float starSize = 0.2;          // 0 to ~0.3
const float smoothEdgeTol = 0.005;
const float ambientLighting = 0.2;
const float specularExp = 60.0;
const float specularIntensity = 0.5;

void main (void)
{
    vec4 distVector;
    float distScalar;

    // Normalize vectors
    vec3 NN = normalize(N);
    vec3 NL = normalize(L);
    vec3 NH = normalize(NL + vec3(0.0, 0.0, 1.0));
    vec3 NV = normalize(V);

    // Each flat edge of the star defines a half-space.  The interior
    // of the star is any point within at least 4 out of 5 of them.
    // Start with -3 so that it takes adding 4 ins to equal 1.
    float myInOut = -3.0;

    // We need to perform 5 dot products, one for each edge of
    // the star.  Perform first 4 in vector, 5th in scalar.
    distVector.x = dot(NV, myHalfSpace0);
    distVector.y = dot(NV, myHalfSpace1);
    distVector.z = dot(NV, myHalfSpace2);
    distVector.w = dot(NV, myHalfSpace3);
    distScalar = dot(NV, myHalfSpace4);

    // The half-space planes all intersect the origin.  We must
    // offset them in order to give the star some size.
    distVector += starSize;
    distScalar += starSize;
```

LISTING 18.10   Continued

```
distVector = smoothstep(0.0, smoothEdgeTol, distVector);
distScalar = smoothstep(0.0, smoothEdgeTol, distScalar);
myInOut += dot(distVector, vec4(1.0));
myInOut += distScalar;
myInOut = clamp(myInOut, 0.0, 1.0);

// calculate diffuse lighting + 20% ambient
vec3 diffuse = (ambientLighting + vec3(max(0.0, dot(NN, NL))));

// colors
vec3 yellow = myYellow * diffuse;
vec3 blue = myBlue * diffuse;
vec3 red = myRed * starIntensity;

// red star on yellow background
vec3 surfColor = mix(yellow, red, myInOut);

// blue stripe down middle
myInOut = smoothstep(0.0, smoothEdgeTol,
                     abs(NV.z) - stripeThickness);
surfColor = mix(blue, surfColor, myInOut);

// calculate specular lighting w/ 50% intensity
surfColor += (specularIntensity *
    vec3(pow(max(0.0, dot(NN, NH)), specularExp)));

gl_FragData[0] = vec4(surfColor, 1.0);

// bright pass: only output colors with some component >= bloomLimit
vec3 brightColor = max(surfColor - vec3(bloomLimit), vec3(0.0));
float bright = dot(brightColor, vec3(1.0));
bright = smoothstep(0.0, 0.5, bright);
gl_FragData[1] = vec4(mix(vec3(0.0), surfColor, bright), 1.0);
}
```

FIGURE 18.10   Our glowing toy ball after the first pass. The red tinted glow appears white due to floating-point clamping because all color channels exceed 1.0.

One important difference between this new version of the toy ball and the old one is the calculation of the red star color, which is no longer dependent on the lighting equation. Instead, it is multiplied by an externally set uniform, starIntensity. The other key difference is that it's outputting two colors to the gl_FragData array. More on that next.

Bright Pass

While rendering the entire toy ball during the first pass, we'll also render a modified version to a second FBO color attachment. This version will contain only the brightest parts of the scene, those brighter than 1.0. (This threshold is adjustable via the bloomLimit uniform in the shader.) All dimmer parts of the scene are drawn black. We use the smooth-step built-in function so there's a gentle transition from bright to black. See Figure 18.11 for a look at the intermediate results from the bright pass.

18

FIGURE 18.11   The bright pass will be the foundation for our bloom generation.

Gaussian Blur with a Little Help

Bloom needs some serious blurring to achieve a decent effect. We'll use a 5×5 kernel, which already pushes the limits of interactivity, especially on older hardware. So how can we get a more bountiful blur than this? The answer lies in some filtering that is always at our fingertips: mipmap generation.

By calling `glGenerateMipmapsEXT` on the FBO-attached texture containing the bright pass results, we get access to an array of images, each of which is more blurred than the last courtesy of downsampling, as shown in Figure 18.12. It isn't a beautiful Gaussian blur, but after we apply our 5×5 kernel in Listing 18.11, the results are quite nice, as shown in Figure 18.13. We apply the blur filter to the first four levels of the texture by setting both `GL_TEXTURE_BASE_LEVEL` and `GL_TEXTURE_MAX_LEVEL` to 0, then 1, then 2, and finally 3.

FIGURE 18.12   The bright pass is progressively downsampled.

LISTING 18.11   5×5 Gaussian Blur Kernel

```
// gaussian.fs
//
// gaussian 5x5 kernel

uniform sampler2D sampler0;
uniform vec2 tc_offset[25];

void main(void)
{
    vec4 sample[25];

    for (int i = 0; i < 25; i++)
    {
        sample[i] = texture2D(sampler0,
                        gl_TexCoord[0].st + tc_offset[i]);
    }

//    1  4  7  4 1
//    4 16 26 16 4
//    7 26 41 26 7 / 273
//    4 16 26 16 4
//    1  4  7  4 1
```

LISTING 18.11   Continued

```
gl_FragColor =
    ((1.0  * (sample[0] + sample[4] + sample[20] + sample[24])) +
     (4.0  * (sample[1] + sample[3] + sample[5] + sample[9] +
              sample[15] + sample[19] + sample[21] + sample[23])) +
     (7.0  * (sample[2] + sample[10] + sample[14] + sample[22])) +
     (16.0 * (sample[6] + sample[8] + sample[16] + sample[18])) +
     (26.0 * (sample[7] + sample[11] + sample[13] + sample[17])) +
     (41.0 * sample[12])
    ) / 273.0;
}
```

FIGURE 18.13   The downsampled levels are now blurred.

Notice the red halo around the bloom most evident with the coarsest blur. This is a pleasant side effect of the blurring. Remember that the original star color is tinted red. Whereas in the middle of the bloom the colors are too bright to escape pure saturated whiteness, at the fringes where they are mixed with dimmer colors, the true redness of the glow has a chance to come through.

The Sum Is Greater Than Its Parts

All that's left is to add everything up in the window's framebuffer. We have the original scene and four levels worth of blur. This is not a difficult step. Figure 18.14 shows the results of Listing 18.12.

FIGURE 18.14   Our toy ball is finally in full bloom.

LISTING 18.12   Math Is Hard, Especially Addition

```
// combine.fs
//
// take incoming textures and
// add them together

uniform bool afterGlow;

uniform sampler2D sampler0;
uniform sampler2D sampler1;
uniform sampler2D sampler2;
uniform sampler2D sampler3;
uniform sampler2D sampler4;
uniform sampler2D sampler5;

void main(void)
{
    vec4 temp;

    temp = texture2D(sampler0, gl_TexCoord[0].st);
    temp += texture2D(sampler1, gl_TexCoord[0].st);
    temp += texture2D(sampler2, gl_TexCoord[0].st);
```

LISTING 18.12   Continued

```
    temp += texture2D(sampler3, gl_TexCoord[0].st);
    temp += texture2D(sampler4, gl_TexCoord[0].st);

    if (afterGlow)
    {
        temp *= 0.6;
        temp += 0.4 * texture2D(sampler5, gl_TexCoord[0].st);
    }

    gl_FragColor = temp;
}
```

PBOs Make a Comeback

What's that last texture we're blending into the final frame? Afterglow is just a ghost image simulating retinal burn-in. This is reminiscent of our first PBO sample, and again we'll use a PBO to read back the window's framebuffer contents and send it back in as a texture, all without touching client memory. See Color Plate 30 in the color insert for the final toy ball image with both bloom and afterglow.

This could also be achieved by rendering the last pass to an FBO, saving the attached texture for use as the next frame's afterglow, and then adding one more pass to get the result into the window. Or you could use a simple call to glCopyTexImage. But then we wouldn't be able to exercise our new friend, the PBO. Where's the fun in that?

Summary

PBOs, FBOs, and floating-point textures, when teamed up with shader programmability, open up a universe of possibilities. Squeezing this much potential into one chapter is certainly overambitious. I hope you at least have a sense for the immense GPU power at your disposal. Please go forth and use this power for good, not evil.

PART III

The Apocrypha

Now we come to some important material that lies outside the true canon of pure OpenGL. Although OpenGL itself remains purely a platform-independent abstraction of graphics hardware, there is always the need to interface OpenGL with native OSs and windowing systems. On each platform, there are families of nonportable binding functions that glue OpenGL to the native window or display system. This part of the book is about those interfaces.

The three most popular platforms for OpenGL today are undoubtedly Windows, Mac OS X, and UNIX. You'll find here specific chapters that will take you through the peculiarities of using OpenGL on these platforms. Finally, we will strip OpenGL down to its bare essentials for use on hand-held and embedded systems. OpenGL is by far the most popular 3D graphics API today, used in nearly every application category, on nearly every platform where 3D hardware can be found.

OpenGL. It's everywhere. Do the math.

CHAPTER 19

Wiggle: OpenGL on Windows

by Richard S. Wright Jr.

WHAT YOU'LL LEARN IN THIS CHAPTER:

How To	Functions You'll Use
Request and select an OpenGL pixel format	`ChoosePixelFormat/` `DescribePixelFormat/` `SetPixelFormat`
Create and use OpenGL rendering contexts	`wglCreateContext/` `wglDeleteContext/` `wglMakeCurrent`
Respond to window messages	`WM_PAINT/WM_CREATE/` `WM_DESTROY/WM_SIZE`
Use double buffering in Windows	`SwapBuffers`

OpenGL is purely a low-level graphics API, with user interaction and the screen or window handled by the host environment. To facilitate this partnership, each environment usually has some extensions that "glue" OpenGL to its own window management and user interface functions. This glue is code that associates OpenGL drawing commands with a particular window. It is also necessary to provide functions for setting buffer modes, color depths, and other drawing characteristics.

For Microsoft Windows, this glue code is embodied in a set of functions added to the Windows API. They are called the *wiggle functions* because they are prefixed with wgl rather than gl. These gluing functions are explained in this chapter, where we dispense with using the GLUT library for our OpenGL framework and build full-fledged Windows applications that can take advantage of all the operating system's features. You will see what characteristics a Windows window must have to support OpenGL graphics. You will learn which messages a well-behaved OpenGL window should handle and how. The concepts of this chapter are introduced gradually, as we build a model OpenGL program that provides a framework for Windows-specific OpenGL support.

So far in this book, you've needed no prior knowledge of 3D graphics and only a rudimentary knowledge of C programming. For this chapter, however, we assume you have at least an entry-level knowledge of Windows programming. Otherwise, we would have wound up writing a book twice the size of this one, and we would have spent more time on the details of Windows programming and less on OpenGL programming.

OpenGL Implementations on Windows

OpenGL became available for the Win32 platform with the release of Windows NT version 3.5. It was later released as an add-on for Windows 95 and then became a shipping part of the Windows 95 operating system (OSR2). OpenGL is now a native API on any Win32 platform (Windows 95/98/ME, Windows NT/2000/XP, and Vista), with its functions exported from `opengl32.dll`. You need to be aware of four flavors of OpenGL on Windows: Generic, ICD, MCD, and the Extended. Each has its pros and cons from both the user and the developer point of view. You should at least have a high-level understanding of how these implementations work and what their drawbacks might be.

Generic OpenGL

A generic implementation of OpenGL is simply a software implementation that does not use specific 3D hardware. The Microsoft implementation bundled with all versions of Windows is a generic implementation. The Silicon Graphics Incorporated (SGI) OpenGL for Windows implementation (no longer widely available) optionally made use of MMX instructions, but because it was not considered dedicated 3D hardware, it was still considered a generic software implementation. Another implementation called *MESA* (www.mesa3d.org) is not strictly a "real" OpenGL implementation—it's a "work-a-like"— but for most purposes, you can consider it to be so. MESA can also be hooked to hardware, but this should be considered a special case of the mini-driver (discussed shortly).

Although the MESA implementation has kept up with OpenGL's advancing feature set over the years, the Microsoft generic implementation has not been updated since OpenGL version 1.1. Not to worry, we will soon show you how to get to all the OpenGL functionality your graphics card supports.

Installable Client Driver

The Installable Client Driver (ICD) was the original hardware driver interface provided for Windows NT. The ICD must implement the entire OpenGL pipeline using a combination of software and the specific hardware for which it was written. Creating an ICD from scratch is a considerable amount of work for a vendor to undertake.

The ICD drops in and works with Microsoft's OpenGL implementation. Applications linked to `opengl32.dll` are automatically dispatched to the ICD driver code for OpenGL calls. This mechanism is ideal because applications do not have to be recompiled to take advantage of OpenGL hardware should it become available. The ICD is actually a part of the display driver and does not affect the existing openGL32.dll system DLL. This driver model provides the vendor with the most opportunities to optimize its driver and hardware combination.

Mini-Client Driver

The Mini-Client Driver (MCD) was a compromise between a software and a hardware implementation. Most early PC 3D hardware provided hardware-accelerated rasterization only. (See "The Pipeline" section in Chapter 2, "Using OpenGL.") The MCD driver model allowed applications to use Microsoft's generic implementation for features that were not available in hardware. For example, transform and lighting could come from Microsoft's OpenGL software, but the actual rasterizing of lit shaded triangles would be handled by the hardware.

The MCD driver implementation made it easy for hardware vendors to create OpenGL drivers for their hardware. Most of the work was done by Microsoft, and whatever features the vendors did not implement in hardware were handed back to the Microsoft generic implementation.

The MCD driver model showed great promise for bringing OpenGL to the PC mass market. Initially available for Windows NT, a software development kit (SDK) was provided to hardware vendors to create MCD drivers for Windows 98, and Microsoft encouraged hardware vendors to use it for their OpenGL support. After many hardware vendors had completed their MCD drivers, Microsoft decided not to license the code for public release. This gave their own proprietary 3D API a temporary advantage in the consumer marketplace.

The MCD driver model today is largely obsolete, but a few implementations are still in use in legacy NT-based systems. One reason for its demise is that the MCD driver model cannot support Intel's Accelerated Graphics Port (AGP) texturing efficiently. Another is that SGI began providing an optimized ICD driver kit to vendors that made writing ICDs almost as easy as writing MCDs. (This move was a response to Microsoft's withdrawal of support for OpenGL MCDs on Windows 98.)

Mini-Driver

A mini-driver is not a real display driver. Instead, it is a drop-in replacement for opengl32.dll that makes calls to a hardware vendor's proprietary 3D hardware driver. Typically, these mini-drivers convert OpenGL calls to roughly equivalent calls in a vendor's proprietary 3D API. The first mini-driver was written by 3dfx for its Voodoo graphics card. This DLL drop-in converted OpenGL calls into the Voodoo's native Glide (the 3dfx 3D API) programming interface.

Although mini-drivers popularized OpenGL for games, they often had missing OpenGL functions or features. Any application that used OpenGL did not necessarily work with a mini-driver. Typically, these drivers provided only the barest functionality needed to run a popular game. Though not widely documented, Microsoft even made an OpenGL to D3D translation layer that was used on Windows XP to accelerate some games when an ICD was not present. Fortunately, the widespread popularity of OpenGL has made the mini-driver obsolete on newer commodity PCs.

OpenGL on Vista

A variation of this mini-driver still exists on Windows Vista, but is not exposed to developers. Microsoft has implemented an OpenGL to D3D emulator that supports OpenGL version 1.4. This implementation looks like an ICD, but shows up only if a real ICD is not installed. As of the initial release of Vista, there is no way to turn on this implementation manually. Only a few games (selected by Microsoft) are "tricked" into seeing this implementation. Vista, like XP, does not ship with ICD drivers on the distribution media. After a user downloads a new display driver from their vendor's Web site, however, they will get a true ICD-based driver, and full OpenGL support in both Windowed and full-screen games.

Extended OpenGL

If you are developing software for any version of Microsoft Windows, you are most likely making use of header files and an import library that works with Microsoft's `opengl32.dll`. This DLL is designed to provide a generic (software-rendered) fallback if 3D hardware is not installed, and has a dispatch mechanism that works with the official ICD OpenGL driver model for hardware-based OpenGL implementations. Using this header and import library alone gives you access only to functions and capabilities present in OpenGL 1.1.

As of this edition, most desktop drivers support OpenGL version 2.1. Take note, however, that OpenGL 1.1 is still a very capable and full-featured graphics API and is suitable for a wide range of graphical applications, including games and business graphics. Even without the additional features of OpenGL 1.2 and beyond, graphics hardware performance has increased exponentially, and most PC graphics cards have the entire OpenGL pipeline implemented in special-purpose hardware. OpenGL 1.1 can still produce screaming-fast and highly complex 3D renderings!

Many applications still will require, or at least be significantly enhanced by, use of the newer OpenGL innovations. To get to the newer OpenGL features (which are widely supported), you need to use the same OpenGL extension mechanism that you use to get to vendor-specific OpenGL enhancements. OpenGL extensions were introduced in Chapter 2, and the specifics of using this extension mechanism on Windows are covered later in this chapter in the section "OpenGL and WGL Extensions."

This may sound like a bewildering environment in which to develop 3D graphics—especially if you plan to port your applications to, say, the Macintosh platform, where OpenGL features are updated more consistently with each OS release. Some strategies, however, can make such development more manageable. First, you can call the following function so that your application can tell at runtime which OpenGL version the hardware driver supports:

```
glGetString(GL_VERSION);
```

This way, you can gracefully decide whether the application is going to be able to run at all on the user's system. Because OpenGL and its extensions are dynamically loaded, there is no reason your programs should not at least start and present the user with a friendly and informative error or diagnostic message.

You also need to think carefully about what OpenGL features your application *must* have. Can the application be written to use only OpenGL 1.1 features? Will the application be usable at all if no hardware is present and the user must use the built-in software renderer? If the answer to either of these questions is yes, you should first write your application's rendering code using only the import library for OpenGL 1.1. This gives you the widest possible audience for your application.

When you have the basic rendering code in place, you can go back and consider performance optimizations or special visual effects available with newer OpenGL features that you want to make available in your program. By checking the OpenGL version early in your program, you can introduce different rendering paths or functions that will optionally perform better or provide additional visual effects to your rendering. For example, static texture maps could be replaced with fragment programs, or standard fog replaced with volumetric fog made possible through vertex programs. Using the latest and greatest features allows you to really show off your program, but if you rely on them exclusively, you may be severely limiting your audience...and sales.

Bear in mind that the preceding advice should be weighed heavily against the type of application you are developing. If you are making an immersive and fast-paced 3D game, worrying about users with OpenGL 1.1 does not make much sense. On the other hand, a program that, say, generates interactive 3D weather maps can certainly afford to be more conservative.

Many, if not most, modern applications really *must* have some newer OpenGL feature; for example, a medical visualization package may require that 3D texturing or the imaging subset be available. In these types of more specialized or vertical markets, your application will simply have to require some minimal OpenGL support to run. The OpenGL version required in these cases will be listed among any other minimum system requirements that you specify are needed for your software. Again, your application can check for these details at startup.

Basic Windows Rendering

The GLUT library provided only one window, and OpenGL function calls always produced output in that window. (Where else would they go?) Your own real-world Windows applications, however, will often have more than one window. In fact, dialog boxes, controls,

19

and even menus are actually windows at a fundamental level; having a useful program that contains only one window is nearly impossible (well, okay, maybe games are an important exception!). How does OpenGL know where to draw when you execute your rendering code? Before we answer this question, let's first review how we normally draw in a window without using OpenGL.

GDI Device Contexts

There are many technology options for drawing into a Windows window. The oldest and most widely supported is the Windows GDI (graphics device interface). GDI is strictly a 2D drawing interface, and was widely hardware accelerated before Windows Vista. Although GDI is still available on Vista, it is no longer hardware accelerated; the preferred high-level drawing technology is based on the .NET framework and is called the Windows Presentation Foundation (WPF). WPF is also available via a download for Windows XP. Over the years some minor 2D API variations have come and gone, as well as several incarnations of Direct3D. On Vista, the new low-level rendering interface is called Windows Graphics Foundation (WGF) and is essentially just Direct 3D version 10.

The one native rendering API common to all versions of Windows (even Windows Mobile) is GDI. This is fortunate because GDI is how we initialize OpenGL and interact with OpenGL on all versions of Windows (except Windows Mobile, where OpenGL is not natively supported by Microsoft). On Vista, GDI is no longer hardware accelerated, but this is irrelevant because we will never (at least when using OpenGL) use GDI for any drawing operations anyway.

When you're using GDI, each window has a device context that actually receives the graphics output, and each GDI function takes a device context as an argument to indicate which window you want the function to affect. You can have multiple device contexts, but only one for each window.

Before you jump to the conclusion that OpenGL should work in a similar way, remember that the GDI is Windows specific. Other environments do not have device contexts, window handles, and the like. Although the ideas may be similar, they are certainly not called the same thing and might work and behave differently. OpenGL, on the other hand, was designed to be completely portable among environments and hardware platforms (and it didn't start on Windows anyway!). Adding a device context parameter to the OpenGL functions would render your OpenGL code useless in any environment other than Windows.

OpenGL does have a context identifier, however, and it is called the *rendering context*. The rendering context is similar in many respects to the GDI device context because it is the rendering context that remembers current colors, state settings, and so on, much like the device context holds onto the current brush or pen color for Windows.

Pixel Formats

The Windows concept of the device context is limited for 3D graphics because it was designed for 2D graphics applications. In Windows, you request a device context identifier for a given window. The nature of the device context depends on the nature of the device. If your desktop is set to 16-bit color, the device context Windows gives you knows about and understands 16-bit color only. You cannot tell Windows, for example, that one window is to be a 16-bit color window and another is to be a 32-bit color window.

Although Windows lets you create a memory device context, you still have to give it an existing window device context to emulate. Even if you pass in NULL for the window parameter, Windows uses the device context of your desktop. You, the programmer, have no control over the intrinsic characteristics of a window's device context.

Any window or device that will be rendering 3D graphics has far more characteristics to it than simply color depth, especially if you are using a hardware rendering device (3D graphics card). Up until now, GLUT has taken care of these details for you. When you initialized GLUT, you told it what buffers you needed (double or single color buffer, depth buffer, stencil, and alpha).

Before OpenGL can render into a window, you must first configure that window according to your rendering needs. Do you want hardware or software rendering? Will the rendering be single or double buffered? Do you need a depth buffer? How about stencil, destination alpha, or an accumulation buffer? After you set these parameters for a window, you cannot change them later. To switch from a window with only a depth and color buffer to a window with only a stencil and color buffer, you have to destroy the first window and re-create a new window with the characteristics you need.

Describing a Pixel Format

The 3D characteristics of the window are set one time, usually just after window creation. The collective name for these settings is the pixel format. Windows provides a structure named PIXELFORMATDESCRIPTOR that describes the pixel format. This structure is defined as follows:

```
typedef struct tagPIXELFORMATDESCRIPTOR {
WORD  nSize;            // Size of this structure
WORD  nVersion;         // Version of structure (should be 1)
DWORD dwFlags;          // Pixel buffer properties
BYTE  iPixelType;       // Type of pixel data (RGBA or Color Index)
BYTE  cColorBits;       // Number of color bit planes in color buffer
BYTE  cRedBits;         // How many bits for red
BYTE  cRedShift;        // Shift count for red bits
BYTE  cGreenBits;       // How many bits for green
BYTE  cGreenShift;      // Shift count for green bits
BYTE  cBlueBits;        // How many bits for blue
BYTE  cBlueShift;       // Shift count for blue bits
```

19

```
BYTE    cAlphaBits;        // How many bits for destination alpha
BYTE    cAlphaShift;       // Shift count for destination alpha
BYTE    cAccumBits;        // How many bits for accumulation buffer
BYTE    cAccumRedBits;     // How many red bits for accumulation buffer
BYTE    cAccumGreenBits;   // How many green bits for accumulation buffer
BYTE    cAccumBlueBits;    // How many blue bits for accumulation buffer
BYTE    cAccumAlphaBits;   // How many alpha bits for accumulation buffer
BYTE    cDepthBits;        // How many bits for depth buffer
BYTE    cStencilBits;      // How many bits for stencil buffer
BYTE    cAuxBuffers;       // How many auxiliary buffers
BYTE    iLayerType;        // Obsolete - ignored
BYTE    bReserved;         // Number of overlay and underlay planes
DWORD dwLayerMask;         // Obsolete - ignored
DWORD dwVisibleMask;       // Transparent color of underlay plane
DWORD dwDamageMask;        // Obsolete - ignored
} PIXELFORMATDESCRIPTOR;
```

For a given OpenGL device (hardware or software), the values of these members are not arbitrary. Only a limited number of pixel formats is available for a given window. Pixel formats are said to be exported by the OpenGL driver or software renderer. Most of these structure members are self-explanatory, but a few require some additional explanation, as listed in Table 19.1.

TABLE 19.1   PIXELFORMATDESCRIPTOR Fields

Field	Description
nSize	The size of the structure; set to sizeof(PIXELFORMATDESCRIPTOR);.
nVersion	Set to 1.
dwFlags	A set of bit flags that specify properties of the pixel buffer. Most of these flags are not mutually exclusive, but a few are used only when requesting or describing the pixel format. Table 19.2 lists the valid flags for this member.
iPixelType	The type of color buffer. Only two values are valid: PFD_TYPE_RGBA and PFD_TYPE_COLORINDEX. PFD_TYPE_COLORINDEX allows you to request or describe the pixel format as color index mode. This rendering mode should be considered obsolete on modern hardware and is mostly ignored throughout this book.
cColorBits	The number of bits of color depth in the color buffer. Typical values are 8, 16, 24, and 32. The 32-bit color buffers may or may not be used to store destination alpha values. Only Microsoft's generic implementation on Windows 2000, Windows XP, and later supports destination alpha.
cRedBits	The number of bits in the color buffer dedicated for the red color component.
cGreenBits	The number of bits in the color buffer dedicated for the green color component.
cBlueBits	The number of bits in the color buffer dedicated for the blue color component.
cAlphaBits	The number of bits used for the alpha buffer. Destination alpha is not supported by Microsoft's generic implementation, but many hardware implementations are beginning to support it.

TABLE 19.1   Continued

Field	Description
cAccumBits	The number of bits used for the accumulation buffer.
cDepthBits	The number of bits used for the depth buffer. Typical values are 0, 16, 24, and 32. The more bits dedicated to the depth buffer, the more accurate depth testing will be.
cStencilBits	The number of bits used for the stencil buffer.
cAuxBuffers	The number of auxiliary buffers. In implementations that support auxiliary buffers, rendering can be redirected to an auxiliary buffer from the color buffer and swapped to the screen later.
iLayerType	Obsolete (ignored).
bReserved	The number of overlay and underlay planes supported by the implementation. Bits 0 through 3 specify the number of overlay planes (up to 15), and bits 4 through 7 specify the number of underlay planes (also up to 15). Windows Vista no longer supports overlays.
dwLayerMask	Obsolete (ignored).
dwVisibleMask	The transparent color of an underlay plane. This is not supported on Windows Vista.
dwDamageMask	Obsolete (ignored).

TABLE 19.2   Valid Flags to Describe the Pixel Rendering Buffer

Bit Flag	Description
PFD_DRAW_TO_WINDOW	The buffer's output is displayed in a window.
PFD_DRAW_TO_BITMAP	The buffer's output is written to a Windows bitmap.
PFD_SUPPORT_GDI	The buffer supports Windows GDI drawing. Most implementations allow this only for single-buffered windows or bitmaps.
PFD_SUPPORT_OPENGL	The buffer supports OpenGL drawing.
PFD_GENERIC_ACCELERATED	The buffer is accelerated by an MCD device driver that accelerates this format.
PFD_GENERIC_FORMAT	The buffer is rendered by a software implementation. This bit is also set with PFD_GENERIC_ACCELERATED for MCD drivers. Only if this bit is clear is the hardware driver an ICD.
PFD_NEED_PALETTE	The buffer is on a palette-managed device. This flag is set on Windows when running in 8-bit (256-color) mode and requires a 3-3-2 color palette.
PFD_NEED_SYSTEM_PALETTE	This flag indicates that OpenGL hardware supports rendering in 256-color mode. A 3-3-2 palette must be realized to enable hardware acceleration. Although documented, this flag can be considered obsolete. No mainstream hardware accelerator that supported accelerated rendering in 256-color mode ever shipped for Windows.
PFD_DOUBLEBUFFER	The color buffer is double buffered.
PFD_STEREO	The color buffer is stereoscopic. This is not supported by Microsoft's generic implementation. Most PC vendors that support stereo do so with custom extensions for their hardware.

19

TABLE 19.2 Continued

Bit Flag	Description
PFD_SWAP_LAYER_BUFFERS	This flag is used if overlay and underlay planes are supported. If set, these planes may be swapped independently of the color buffer. These planes are no longer possible on Windows Vista.
PFD_DEPTH_DONTCARE	This flag is used only when requesting a pixel format. It indicates that you do not need a depth buffer. Some implementations can save memory and enhance performance by not allocating memory for the depth buffer.
PFD_DOUBLE_BUFFER_DONTCARE	This flag is used only when requesting a pixel format. It indicates that you do not plan to use double buffering. Although you can force rendering to the front buffer only, this flag allows an implementation to save memory and potentially enhance performance.
PFD_SWAP_COPY	This is a hint (which means it may be ignored!) that the buffer swap should be accomplished by means of a bulk copy of the back buffer to the front buffer.
PFD_SWAP_EXCHANGE	This is a hint (which means it may be ignored!) that the front and back buffers should be exchanged when the buffer swap occurs.

Enumerating Pixel Formats

The pixel format for a window is identified by a one-based integer index number. An implementation exports a number of pixel formats from which to choose. To set a pixel format for a window, you must select one of the available formats exported by the driver. You can use the DescribePixelFormat function to determine the characteristics of a given pixel format. You can also use this function to find out how many pixel formats are exported by the driver. The following code shows how to enumerate all the pixel formats available for a window:

```
PIXELFORMATDESCRIPTOR pfd;       // Pixel format descriptor
int nFormatCount;                // How many pixel formats exported
. . .

// Get the number of pixel formats
// Will need a device context
pfd.nSize = sizeof(PIXELFORMATDESCRIPTOR);
nFormatCount = DescribePixelFormat(hDC, 1, 0, NULL);

// Retrieve each pixel format
for(int i = 1; i <= nFormatCount; i++)
    {
    // Get description of pixel format
    DescribePixelFormat(hDC, i, pfd.nSize, &pfd);

. . .
. . .
}
```

The `DescribePixelFormat` function returns the maximum pixel format index. You can use an initial call to this function as shown to determine how many are available. An interesting utility program called GLView is included in the source distribution for this chapter. This program enumerates all pixel formats available for your display driver for the given resolution and color depths. Figure 19.1 shows the output from this program when a double-buffered pixel format is selected. (A single-buffered pixel format would contain a flickering block animation.)

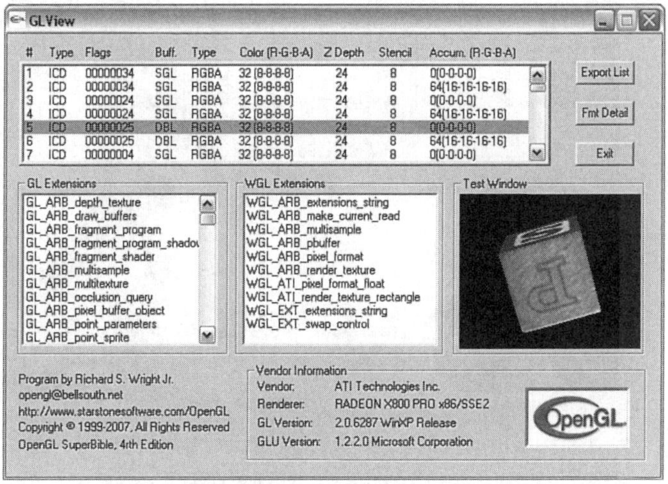

FIGURE 19.1   The GLView program shows all pixel formats for a given device.

The Microsoft Foundation Classes (MFC) source code is included for this program. This is a bit more complex than your typical sample program, and GLView is provided more as a tool for your use than as a programming example. The important code for enumerating pixel formats was presented earlier and is less than a dozen lines long. If you are familiar with MFC already, examination of this source code will show you how to integrate OpenGL rendering into any `CWnd` derived window class.

The list box lists all the available pixel formats and displays their characteristics (driver type, color depth, and so on). A sample window in the lower-right corner displays a rotating cube using a window created with the highlighted pixel format. The `glGetString` function enables you to find out the name of the vendor for the OpenGL driver, as well as other version information. Finally, a list box displays all the OpenGL and WGL extensions exported by the driver (WGL extensions are covered later in this chapter).

19

If you experiment with this program, you'll discover that not all pixel formats can be used to create an OpenGL window, as shown in Figure 19.2. Even though the driver exports these pixel formats, it does not mean that you can create an OpenGL-enabled window with one of them. The most important criterion is that the pixel format color depth must match the color depth of your desktop. That is, you can't create a 16-bit color pixel format for a 32-bit color desktop, or vice versa.

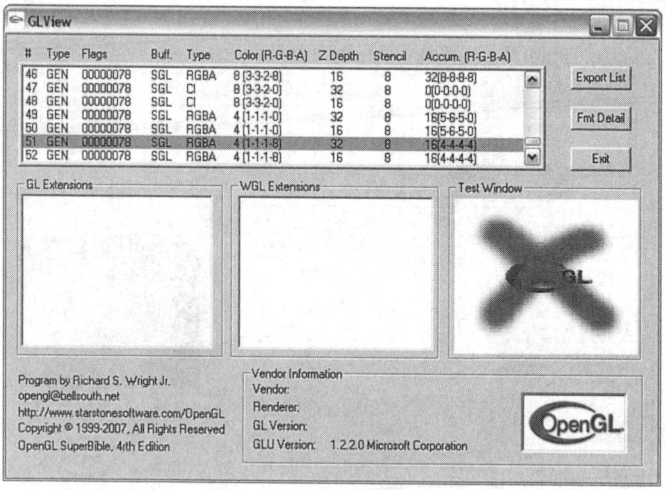

FIGURE 19.2   The GLView program showing an invalid pixel format.

Make special note of the fact that at least 24 pixel formats are always enumerated, sometimes more. If you are running without an OpenGL hardware driver, you will see exactly 24 pixel formats listed (all belonging to the Microsoft Generic Implementation). If you have a hardware accelerator (either an MCD or an ICD), you'll note that the accelerated pixel formats are listed first, followed by the 24 generic pixel formats belonging to Microsoft. This means that when hardware acceleration is present, you actually can choose from two implementations of OpenGL. The first are the hardware-accelerated pixel formats belonging to the hardware accelerator. The second are the pixel formats for Microsoft's software implementation.

Knowing this bit of information can be useful. For one thing, it means that a software implementation is always available for rendering to bitmaps or printer devices. It also means that if you so desire (for debugging purposes, perhaps), you can force software rendering, even when an application might typically select hardware acceleration.

One final thing you may notice is that many pixel formats look the same. In these cases, the pixel formats are supporting *multisampled* buffers. This feature came along after the PIXELFORMATDESCRIPTOR was cast in stone, and we'll have more to say about this later in the chapter.

Selecting and Setting a Pixel Format

Enumerating all the available pixel formats and examining each one to find one that meets your needs could turn out to be quite tedious. Windows provides a shortcut function that makes this process somewhat simpler. The ChoosePixelFormat function allows you to create a pixel format structure containing the desired attributes of your 3D window. The ChoosePixelFormat function then finds the closest match possible (with preference for hardware-accelerated pixel formats) and returns the most appropriate index. The pixel format is then set with a call to another new Windows function, SetPixelFormat. The following code segment shows the use of these two functions:

```
int nPixelFormat;

. . .

static PIXELFORMATDESCRIPTOR pfd = {
    sizeof(PIXELFORMATDESCRIPTOR),  // Size of this structure
    1,                              // Version of this structure
    PFD_DRAW_TO_WINDOW |            // Draw to window (not to bitmap)
    PFD_SUPPORT_OPENGL |            // Support OpenGL calls in window
    PFD_DOUBLEBUFFER,               // Double buffered mode
    PFD_TYPE_RGBA,                  // RGBA color mode
    32,                             // Want 32-bit color
    0,0,0,0,0,0,                    // Not used to select mode
    0,0,                            // Not used to select mode
    0,0,0,0,0,                      // Not used to select mode
    16,                             // Size of depth buffer
    0,                              // No stencil
    0,                              // No auxiliary buffers
    0,                              // Obsolete or reserved
    0,                              // No overlay and underlay planes
    0,                              // Obsolete or reserved layer mask
    0,                              // No transparent color for underlay plane
    0};                             // Obsolete

// Choose a pixel format that best matches that described in pfd
// for the given device context
nPixelFormat = ChoosePixelFormat(hDC, &pfd);

// Set the pixel format for the device context
SetPixelFormat(hDC, nPixelFormat, &pfd);
```

Initially, the PIXELFORMATDESCRIPTOR structure is filled with the desired characteristics of the 3D-enabled window. In this case, you want a double-buffered pixel format that renders into a window, so you request 32-bit color and a 16-bit depth buffer. If the current implementation supports 24-bit color at best, the returned pixel format will be a valid 24-bit color format. Depth buffer resolution is also subject to change. An implementation might support only a 24-bit or 32-bit depth buffer. In any case, `ChoosePixelFormat` always tries to return a valid pixel format, and if at all possible, it returns one that is hardware-accelerated.

Some programmers and programming needs might require more sophisticated selection of a pixel format. In these cases, you need to enumerate and inspect all available pixel formats or use the WGL extension presented later in this chapter. For most uses, however, the preceding code is sufficient to prime your window to receive OpenGL rendering commands.

The OpenGL Rendering Context

A typical Windows application can consist of many windows. You can even set a pixel format for each one (using that windows device context) if you want! But `SetPixelFormat` can be called only once per window. When you call an OpenGL command, how does it know which window to send its output to? In the previous chapters, we used the GLUT framework, which provided a single window to display OpenGL output. Recall that with normal Windows GDI-based drawing, each window has its own device context.

To accomplish the portability of the core OpenGL functions, each environment must implement some means of specifying a current rendering window before executing any OpenGL commands. Just as the Windows GDI functions use the windows device contexts, the OpenGL environment is embodied in what is known as the *rendering context.* Just as a device context remembers settings about drawing modes and commands for the GDI, the rendering context remembers OpenGL settings and commands.

You create an OpenGL rendering context by calling the `wglCreateContext` function. This function takes one parameter: the device context of a window with a valid pixel format. The data type of an OpenGL rendering context is `HGLRC`. The following code shows the creation of an OpenGL rendering context:

```
HGLRC hRC;    // OpenGL rendering context
HDC hDC;    // Windows device context
. . .
// Select and set a pixel format
. . .
hRC = wglCreateContext(hDC);
```

A rendering context is created that is compatible with the window for which it was created. You can have more than one rendering context in your application—for instance, two windows that are using different drawing modes, perspectives, and so on. However, for OpenGL commands to know which window they are operating on, only one rendering context can be active at any one time per thread. When a rendering context is made active, it is said to be *current.*

When made current, a rendering context is also associated with a device context and thus with a particular window. Now, OpenGL knows which window into which to render. You can even move an OpenGL rendering context from window to window, but each window must have the same pixel format. To make a rendering context current and associate it with a particular window, you call the `wglMakeCurrent` function. This function takes two parameters, the device context of the window and the OpenGL rendering context:

```
void wglMakeCurrent(HDC hDC, HGLRC hRC);
```

Putting It All Together

We've covered a lot of ground over the past several pages. We've described each piece of the puzzle individually, but now let's look at all the pieces put together. In addition to seeing all the OpenGL-related code, we should examine some of the minimum requirements for any Windows program to support OpenGL. Our sample program for this section is GLRECT. It should look somewhat familiar because it is also the first GLUT-based sample program from Chapter 2. Now, however, the program is a full-fledged Windows program written with nothing but C++ and the Win32 API. Figure 19.3 shows the output of the new program, complete with a bouncing square.

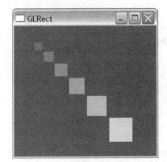

FIGURE 19.3   Output from the GLRECT program with a bouncing square.

Creating the Window

The starting place for any low-level Windows-based GUI program is the `WinMain` function. In this function, you register the window type, create the window, and start the message pump. Listing 19.1 shows the `WinMain` function for the first sample.

LISTING 19.1   The `WinMain` Function of the GLRECT Sample Program

```
// Entry point of all Windows programs
int APIENTRY WinMain(    HINSTANCE    hInstance,
                         HINSTANCE    hPrevInstance,
                         LPSTR        lpCmdLine,
```

LISTING 19.1 Continued

```
                          int           nCmdShow)
{
MSG        msg;        // Windows message structure
WNDCLASS   wc;         // Windows class structure
HWND       hWnd;       // Storage for window handle


// Register window style
wc.style        = CS_HREDRAW | CS_VREDRAW | CS_OWNDC;
wc.lpfnWndProc  = (WNDPROC) WndProc;
wc.cbClsExtra   = 0;
wc.cbWndExtra   = 0;
wc.hInstance    = hInstance;
wc.hIcon        = NULL;
wc.hCursor      = LoadCursor(NULL, IDC_ARROW);

// No need for background brush for OpenGL window
wc.hbrBackground  = NULL;


wc.lpszMenuName   = NULL;
wc.lpszClassName  = lpszAppName;

// Register the window class
if(RegisterClass(&wc) == 0)
    return FALSE;


// Create the main application window
hWnd = CreateWindow(
        lpszAppName,
        lpszAppName,

        // OpenGL requires WS_CLIPCHILDREN and WS_CLIPSIBLINGS
        WS_OVERLAPPEDWINDOW | WS_CLIPCHILDREN | WS_CLIPSIBLINGS,

        // Window position and size
        100, 100,
        250, 250,
        NULL,
        NULL,
        hInstance,
        NULL);
```

LISTING 19.1   Continued

```
// If window was not created, quit
if(hWnd == NULL)
    return FALSE;


// Display the window
ShowWindow(hWnd,SW_SHOW);
UpdateWindow(hWnd);

// Process application messages until the application closes
while( GetMessage(&msg, NULL, 0, 0))
    {
    TranslateMessage(&msg);
    DispatchMessage(&msg);
    }

return msg.wParam;
}
```

This listing pretty much contains your standard Windows GUI startup code. Only two points really bear mentioning here. The first is the choice of window styles set in CreateWindow. You can generally use whatever window styles you like, but you do need to set the WS_CLIPCHILDREN and WS_CLIPSIBLINGS styles. These styles were required in earlier versions of Windows, but later versions have dropped them as a strict requirement. The purpose of these styles is to keep the OpenGL rendering context from rendering into other windows, which can happen in GDI. However, an OpenGL rendering context must be associated with only one window at a time.

The second note you should make about this startup code is the use of CS_OWNDC for the window style. Why you need this innocent-looking flag requires a bit more explanation. You need a device context for both GDI rendering and for OpenGL double-buffered page flipping. To understand what CS_OWNDC has to do with this, you first need to take a step back and review the purpose and use of a windows device context.

First, You Need a Device Context

Before you can draw anything in a window with GDI, you first need the window's device context. You need it whether you're doing OpenGL, GDI, or even Direct3D programming. Any drawing or painting operation in Windows (even if you're drawing on a bitmap in memory) requires a device context that identifies the specific object being drawn on. You retrieve the device context to a window with a simple function call:

```
HDC hDC = GetDC(hWnd);
```

The *hDC* variable is your handle to the device context of the window identified by the window handle *hWnd*. You use the device context for all GDI functions that draw in the window. You also need the device context for creating an OpenGL rendering context, making it current, and performing the buffer swap. You tell Windows that you don't need the device context for the window any longer with another simple function call, using the same two values:

```
ReleaseDC(hWnd, hDC);
```

The standard Windows programming wisdom is that you retrieve a device context, use it for drawing, and then release it again as soon as possible. This advice dates back to the pre-Win32 days; under Windows 3.1 and earlier, you had a small pool of memory allocated for system resources, such as the windows device context. What happened when Windows ran out of system resources? If you were lucky, you got an error message. If you were working on something really important, the operating system could somehow tell, and it would instead crash and take all your work with it. Well, at least it seemed that way!

The best way to spare your users this catastrophe was to make sure that the GetDC function succeeded. If you did get a device context, you did all your work as quickly as possible (typically within one message handler) and then released the device context so that other programs could use it. The same advice applied to other system resources such as pens, fonts, and brushes.

Enter Win32

Windows NT and the subsequent Win32-based operating systems were a tremendous blessing for Windows programmers, in more ways than can be recounted here. Among their many benefits was that you could have all the system resources you needed until you exhausted available memory or your application crashed. (At least it wouldn't crash the OS!) It turns out that the GetDC function is, in computer time, quite an expensive function call to make. If you got the device context when the window was created and hung on to it until the window was destroyed, you could speed up your window painting considerably. You could hang on to brushes, fonts, and other resources that would have to be created or retrieved and potentially reinitialized each time the window was invalidated.

An old popular example of this Win32 benefit was a program that created random rectangles and put them in random locations in the window. (This was a GDI sample.) The difference between code written the old way and code written the new way was astonishingly obvious. Wow—Win32 was great!

Three Steps Forward, Two Steps Back

Windows 95, 98, and ME brought Win32 programming to the mainstream, but still had a few of the old 16-bit limitations deep down in the plumbing. The situation with losing system resources was considerably improved, but it was not eliminated entirely. The operating system could still run out of resources, but (according to Microsoft) it was unlikely. Alas, life is not so simple. Under Windows NT, when an application terminates, all allocated system resources are automatically returned to the operating system. Under Windows 95, 98, or ME, you have a resource leak if the program crashes or the application fails to release the resources it allocated. Eventually, you will start to stress the system, and you can run out of system resources (or device contexts).

What happens when Windows doesn't have enough device contexts to go around? Well, it just takes one from someone who is being a hog with them. This means that if you call GetDC and don't call ReleaseDC, Windows 95, 98, or ME might just appropriate your device context when it becomes stressed. The next time you call wglMakeCurrent or SwapBuffers, your device context handle might not be valid. Your application might crash or mysteriously stop rendering. Ask someone in customer support how well it goes over when you try to explain to a customer that his or her problem with your application is really Microsoft's fault!

All Is Not Lost

You actually have a way to tell Windows to create a device context just for your window's use. This feature is useful because every time you call GetDC, you have to reselect your fonts, the mapping mode, and so on. If you have your own device context, you can do this sort of initialization only once. Plus, you don't have to worry about your device context handle being yanked out from under you. Doing this is simple: You simply specify CS_OWNDC as one of your class styles when you register the window. A common error is to use CS_OWNDC as a window style when you call Create. There are window styles and there are class styles, but you can't mix and match.

Code to register your window style generally looks something like this:

```
WNDCLASS wc; // Windows class structure
...
...
// Register window style
wc.style = CS_HREDRAW | CS_VREDRAW | CS_OWNDC;
wc.lpfnWndProc = (WNDPROC) WndProc;
...
...
wc.lpszClassName = lpszAppName;
// Register the window class
if(RegisterClass(&wc) == 0)
return FALSE;
```

You then specify the class name when you create the window:

```
hWnd = CreateWindow( wc.lpszClassName, szWindowName, ...
```

Graphics programmers should always use CS_OWNDC in the window class registration. This ensures that you have the most robust code possible on any Windows platform. Another consideration is that many older OpenGL hardware drivers have bugs because they expect CS_OWNDC to be specified. They might have been originally written for NT, so the drivers do not account for the possibility that the device context might become invalid. The driver might also trip up if the device context does not retain its configuration (as is the case in the GetDC/ReleaseDC scenario).

Regardless of the specifics, some older drivers are not very stable unless you specify the CS_OWNDC flag. Today's drivers rarely have this issue anymore, but one thing you learn as an application developer is that it's amazing where your code may end up sometimes! Still, the other reasons outlined here provide plenty of incentive to make what is basically a minor code adjustment.

Using the OpenGL Rendering Context

The real meat of the GLRECT sample program is in the window procedure, WndProc. The window procedure receives window messages from the operating system and responds appropriately. This model of programming, called *message* or *event-driven programming,* is the foundation of the modern Windows GUI.

When a window is created, it first receives a WM_CREATE message from the operating system. This is the ideal location to create and set up the OpenGL rendering context. A window also receives a WM_DESTROY message when it is being destroyed. Naturally, this is the ideal place to put cleanup code. Listing 19.2 shows the SetDCPixelFormat format, which is used to select and set the pixel format, along with the window procedure for the application. This function contains the same basic functionality that we have been using with the GLUT framework.

LISTING 19.2   Setting the Pixel Format and Handling the Creation and Deletion of the OpenGL Rendering Context

```
/////////////////////////////////////////
// Select the pixel format for a given device context
void SetDCPixelFormat(HDC hDC)
    {
    int nPixelFormat;

    static PIXELFORMATDESCRIPTOR pfd = {
        sizeof(PIXELFORMATDESCRIPTOR),  // Size of this structure
        1,                              // Version of this structure
        PFD_DRAW_TO_WINDOW |            // Draw to window (not to bitmap)
        PFD_SUPPORT_OPENGL |            // Support OpenGL calls in window
        PFD_DOUBLEBUFFER,               // Double-buffered mode
        PFD_TYPE_RGBA,                  // RGBA color mode
        32,                             // Want 32-bit color
        0,0,0,0,0,0,                    // Not used to select mode
        0,0,                            // Not used to select mode
```

LISTING 19.2   Continued

```
        0,0,0,0,0,                      // Not used to select mode
        16,                             // Size of depth buffer
        0,                              // Not used here
        0,                              // Not used here
        0,                              // Not used here
        0,                              // Not used here
        0,0,0 };                        // Not used here

    // Choose a pixel format that best matches that described in pfd
    nPixelFormat = ChoosePixelFormat(hDC, &pfd);

    // Set the pixel format for the device context
    SetPixelFormat(hDC, nPixelFormat, &pfd);
    }


/////////////////////////////////////////////////////////////////////
// Window procedure, handles all messages for this program
LRESULT CALLBACK WndProc(HWND     hWnd,
            UINT      message,
            WPARAM    wParam,
            LPARAM    lParam)
    {
    static HGLRC hRC = NULL;     // Permanent rendering context
    static HDC hDC = NULL;       // Private GDI device context

    switch (message)
            {
        // Window creation, set up for OpenGL
    case WM_CREATE:
            // Store the device context
            hDC = GetDC(hWnd);

            // Select the pixel format
            SetDCPixelFormat(hDC);

            // Create the rendering context and make it current
            hRC = wglCreateContext(hDC);
            wglMakeCurrent(hDC, hRC);

            // Create a timer that fires 30 times a second
            SetTimer(hWnd,33,1,NULL);
            break;
```

LISTING 19.2   Continued

```
// Window is being destroyed, clean up
case WM_DESTROY:
    // Kill the timer that we created
    KillTimer(hWnd,101);

    // Deselect the current rendering context and delete it
    wglMakeCurrent(hDC,NULL);
    wglDeleteContext(hRC);

    // Tell the application to terminate after the window
    // is gone.
    PostQuitMessage(0);
    break;

// Window is resized.
case WM_SIZE:
    // Call our function which modifies the clipping
    // volume and viewport
    ChangeSize(LOWORD(lParam), HIWORD(lParam));
    break;

// Timer moves and bounces the rectangle, simply calls
// our previous OnIdle function, then invalidates the
// window so it will be redrawn.
case WM_TIMER:
    {
    IdleFunction();

    InvalidateRect(hWnd,NULL,FALSE);
    }
    break;

// The painting function. This message is sent by Windows
// whenever the screen needs updating.
case WM_PAINT:
    {
    // Call OpenGL drawing code
    RenderScene();

    // Call function to swap the buffers
    SwapBuffers(hDC);
```

LISTING 19.2 Continued

```
            // Validate the newly painted client area
            ValidateRect(hWnd,NULL);
            }
            break;


        default:   // Passes it on if unprocessed
            return (DefWindowProc(hWnd, message, wParam, lParam));
        }

    return (0L);
    }
```

Initializing the Rendering Context

The first thing you do when the window is being created is retrieve the device context (remember, you hang on to it) and set the pixel format:

```
// Store the device context
hDC = GetDC(hWnd);

// Select the pixel format
SetDCPixelFormat(hDC);
```

Then you create the OpenGL rendering context and make it current:

```
// Create the rendering context and make it current
hRC = wglCreateContext(hDC);
wglMakeCurrent(hDC, hRC);
```

The last task you handle while processing the WM_CREATE message is creating a Windows timer for the window. You will use this shortly to affect the animation loop:

```
// Create a timer that fires 30 times a second
SetTimer(hWnd,33,1,NULL);
break;
```

Note that WM_TIMER is not the best way to achieve high frame rates. We'll revisit this issue later, but for now, it serves our purposes.

At this point, the OpenGL rendering context has been created and associated with a window with a valid pixel format. From this point forward, all OpenGL rendering commands will be routed to this context and window.

19

Shutting Down the Rendering Context

When the window procedure receives the WM_DESTROY message, the OpenGL rendering context must be deleted. Before you delete the rendering context with the wglDeleteContext function, you must first call wglMakeCurrent again, but this time with NULL as the parameter for the OpenGL rendering context:

```
// Deselect the current rendering context and delete it
wglMakeCurrent(hDC,NULL);
wglDeleteContext(hRC);
```

Before deleting the rendering context, you should delete any display lists, texture objects, or other OpenGL-allocated memory.

Other Windows Messages

All that is required to enable OpenGL to render into a window is creating and destroying the OpenGL rendering context. However, to make your application well behaved, you need to follow some conventions with respect to message handling. For example, you need to set the viewport when the window changes size, by handling the WM_SIZE message:

```
// Window is resized.
case WM_SIZE:
    // Call our function which modifies the clipping
    // volume and viewport
    ChangeSize(LOWORD(lParam), HIWORD(lParam));
    break;
```

The processing that happens in response to the WM_SIZE message is the same as in the function you handed off to glutReshapeFunc in GLUT-based programs. The window procedure also receives two parameters: lParam and wParam. The low word of lParam is the new width of the window, and the high word is the height.

This example uses the WM_TIMER message handler to do the idle processing. The process is not really idle, but the previous call to SetTimer causes the WM_TIMER message to be received on a fairly regular basis (*fairly* because the exact interval is not guaranteed).

Other Windows messages handle things such as keyboard activity (WM_CHAR, WM_KEYDOWN) and mouse movements (WM_MOUSEMOVE).

The WM_PAINT message bears closer examination. This message is sent to a window whenever Windows needs to draw or redraw its contents. To tell Windows to redraw a window anyway, you invalidate the window with one function call in the WM_TIMER message handler:

```
IdleFunction();
InvalidateRect(hWnd,NULL,FALSE);
```

Here, `IdleFunction` updates the position of the square, and `InvalidateRect` tells Windows to redraw the window (now that the square has moved).

Most Windows programming books show you a `WM_PAINT` message handler with the well-known `BeginPaint`/`EndPaint` function pairing. `BeginPaint` retrieves the device context so it can be used for GDI drawing, and `EndPaint` releases the context and validates the window. In our previous discussion of why you need the `CS_OWNDC` class style, we pointed out that using this function pairing is generally a bad idea for high-performance graphics applications. The following code shows roughly the equivalent functionality, without any GDI overhead:

```
// The painting function. This message is sent by Windows
// whenever the screen needs updating.
case WM_PAINT:
    {
    // Call OpenGL drawing code
    RenderScene();

    // Call function to swap the buffers
    SwapBuffers(hDC);

    // Validate the newly painted client area
    ValidateRect(hWnd,NULL);
    }
    break;
```

Because this example has a device context (hDC), you don't need to continually get and release it. We've mentioned the `SwapBuffers` function previously but not fully explained it. This function takes the device context as an argument and performs the buffer swap for double-buffered rendering. This is why you need the device context readily available when rendering.

Notice that you must manually validate the window with the call to `ValidateRect` after rendering. Without the `BeginPaint`/`EndPaint` functionality in place, there is no way to tell Windows that you have finished drawing the window contents. One alternative to using `WM_TIMER` to invalidate the window (thus forcing a redraw) is to simply not validate the window. If the window procedure returns from a `WM_PAINT` message and the window is not validated, the operating system generates another `WM_PAINT` message. This chain reaction causes an endless stream of repaint messages. One problem with this approach to animation is that it can leave little opportunity for other window messages to be processed. Although rendering might occur very quickly, the user might find it difficult or impossible to resize the window or use the menu, for example.

19

OpenGL and Windows Fonts

One nice feature of Windows is its support for TrueType fonts. These fonts have been native to Windows since before Windows became a 32-bit operating system. TrueType fonts enhance text appearance because they are device independent and can be easily scaled while still keeping a smooth shape. TrueType fonts are vector fonts, not bitmap fonts. What this means is that the character definitions consist of a series of point and curve definitions. When a character is scaled, the overall shape and appearance remain smooth.

Textual output is a part of nearly any Windows application, and 3D applications are no exception. Microsoft provided support for TrueType fonts in OpenGL with two new wiggle functions. You can use the first, wglUseFontOutlines, to create 3D font models that can be used to create 3D text effects. The second, wglUseFontBitmaps, creates a series of font character bitmaps that can be used for 2D text output in a double-buffered OpenGL window.

3D Fonts and Text

The wglUseFontOutlines function takes a handle to a device context. It uses the TrueType font currently selected into that device context to create a set of display lists for that font. Each display list renders just one character from the font. Listing 19.3 shows the SetupRC function from the sample program TEXT3D, where you can see the entire process of creating a font, selecting it into the device context, creating the display lists, and, finally, deleting the (Windows) font.

LISTING 19.3   Creating a Set of 3D Characters

```
void SetupRC(HDC hDC)
    {
    // Set up the font characteristics
    HFONT hFont;
    GLYPHMETRICSFLOAT agmf[128]; // Throw away
    LOGFONT logfont;

    logfont.lfHeight = -10;
    logfont.lfWidth = 0;
    logfont.lfEscapement = 0;
    logfont.lfOrientation = 0;
    logfont.lfWeight = FW_BOLD;
    logfont.lfItalic = FALSE;
    logfont.lfUnderline = FALSE;
    logfont.lfStrikeOut = FALSE;
    logfont.lfCharSet = ANSI_CHARSET;
    logfont.lfOutPrecision = OUT_DEFAULT_PRECIS;
    logfont.lfClipPrecision = CLIP_DEFAULT_PRECIS;
    logfont.lfQuality = DEFAULT_QUALITY;
    logfont.lfPitchAndFamily = DEFAULT_PITCH;
```

LISTING 19.3 Continued

```
    strcpy(logfont.lfFaceName,"Arial");

    // Create the font and display list
    hFont = CreateFontIndirect(&logfont);
    SelectObject (hDC, hFont);


    // Create display lists for glyphs 0 through 128 with 0.1 extrusion
    // and default deviation. The display list numbering starts at 1000
    // (it could be any number).
    nFontList = glGenLists(128);
    wglUseFontOutlines(hDC, 0, 128, nFontList, 0.0f, 0.5f,
            WGL_FONT_POLYGONS, agmf);

    DeleteObject(hFont);

    . . .
    . . .
    }
```

The function call to wglUseFontOutlines is the key function call to create your 3D character set:

```
wglUseFontOutlines(hDC, 0, 128, nFontList, 0.0f, 0.5f,
            WGL_FONT_POLYGONS, agmf);
```

The first parameter is the handle to the device context where the desired font has been selected. The next two parameters specify the range of characters (called *glyphs*) in the font to use. In this case, you use the 1st through 127th characters. (The indexes are zero based.) The third parameter, nFontList, is the beginning of the range of display lists created previously. It is important to allocate your display list space before using either of the WGL font functions. The next parameter is the chordal deviation. Think of it as specifying how smooth you want the font to appear, with 0.0 being the most smooth.

The 0.5f is the extrusion of the character set. The 3D characters are defined to lie in the xy plane. The extrusion determines how far along the z-axis the characters extend. WGL_FONT_POLYGONS tells OpenGL to create the characters out of triangles and quads so that they are solid. When this information is specified, normals are also calculated and supplied for each letter. Only one other value is valid for this parameter: WGL_FONT_LINES. It produces a wireframe version of the character set and does not generate normals.

The last argument is an array of type GLYPHMETRICSFLOAT, which is defined in this way:

```
typedef struct _GLYPHMETRICSFLOAT {
  FLOAT         gmfBlackBoxX;        // Extent of character cell in x direction
```

19

```
FLOAT         gmfBlackBoxY;         // Extent of character cell in y direction
POINTFLOAT    gmfptGlyphOrigin;     // Origin of character cell
FLOAT         gmfCellIncX;          // Horizontal distance to origin of next cell
FLOAT         gmfCellIncY;          // Vertical distance to origin of next cell
}; GLYPHMETRICSFLOAT
```

Windows fills in this array according to the selected font's characteristics. These values can be useful when you want to determine the size of a string rendered with 3D characters.

When the display list for each character is called, it renders the character and advances the current position to the right (positive x direction) by the width of the character cell. This is like calling `glTranslate` after each character, with the translation in the positive x direction. You can use the `glCallLists` function in conjunction with `glListBase` to treat a character array (a string) as an array of offsets from the first display list in the font. A simple text output method is shown in Listing 19.4. The output from the TEXT3D program appears in Figure 19.4.

LISTING 19.4   Rendering a 3D Text String

```
void RenderScene(void)
    {
    glClear(GL_COLOR_BUFFER_BIT | GL_DEPTH_BUFFER_BIT);

    // Blue 3D text
    glColor3ub(0, 0, 255);

    glPushMatrix();
    glListBase(nFontList);
    glCallLists (6, GL_UNSIGNED_BYTE, "OpenGL");
    glPopMatrix();
    }
```

FIGURE 19.4   Sample 3D text in OpenGL.

2D Fonts and Text

The `wglUseFontBitmaps` function is similar to its 3D counterpart. This function does not extrude the bitmaps into 3D, however, but instead creates a set of bitmap images of the glyphs in the font. You output images to the screen using the bitmap functions discussed in Chapter 7, "Imaging with OpenGL." Each character rendered advances the raster position to the right in a similar manner to the 3D text.

Listing 19.5 shows the code to set up the coordinate system for the window (`ChangeSize` function), create the bitmap font (`SetupRC` function), and finally render some text (`RenderScene` function). The output from the TEXT2D sample program is shown in Figure 19.5.

LISTING 19.5   Creating and Using a 2D Font

```
/////////////////////////////////////////////////////////////////
// Window has changed size. Reset to match window coordinates
void ChangeSize(GLsizei w, GLsizei h)
    {
    GLfloat nRange = 100.0f;
    GLfloat fAspect;

    // Prevent a divide by zero
    if(h == 0)
        h = 1;

    fAspect = (GLfloat)w/(GLfloat)h;

    // Set Viewport to window dimensions
    glViewport(0, 0, w, h);

    glMatrixMode(GL_PROJECTION);
    glLoadIdentity();

    gluOrtho2D(0,400, 400, 0);

    // Viewing transformation
    glMatrixMode(GL_MODELVIEW);
    glLoadIdentity();
    }


/////////////////////////////////////////////////////////
// Set up. Use a Windows font to create the bitmaps
void SetupRC(HDC hDC)
    {
```

LISTING 19.5   Continued

```
    // Set up the Font characteristics
    HFONT hFont;
    LOGFONT logfont;

    logfont.lfHeight = -20;
    logfont.lfWidth = 0;
    logfont.lfEscapement = 0;
    logfont.lfOrientation = 0;
    logfont.lfWeight = FW_BOLD;
    logfont.lfItalic = FALSE;
    logfont.lfUnderline = FALSE;
    logfont.lfStrikeOut = FALSE;
    logfont.lfCharSet = ANSI_CHARSET;
    logfont.lfOutPrecision = OUT_DEFAULT_PRECIS;
    logfont.lfClipPrecision = CLIP_DEFAULT_PRECIS;
    logfont.lfQuality = DEFAULT_QUALITY;
    logfont.lfPitchAndFamily = DEFAULT_PITCH;
    strcpy(logfont.lfFaceName,"Arial");

    // Create the font and display list
    hFont = CreateFontIndirect(&logfont);
    SelectObject (hDC, hFont);

    // Create display lists for glyphs 0 through 128
    nFontList = glGenLists(128);
    wglUseFontBitmaps(hDC, 0, 128, nFontList);

    DeleteObject(hFont);    // Don't need original font anymore

    // Black Background
    glClearColor(0.0f, 0.0f, 0.0f, 1.0f );
    }

///////////////////////////////////////////////////
// Draw everything (just the text)
void RenderScene(void)
    {
    glClear(GL_COLOR_BUFFER_BIT);

    // Blue 3D Text - Note color is set before the raster position
    glColor3f(1.0f, 1.0f, 1.0f);
    glRasterPos2i(0, 200);
```

LISTING 19.5   Continued

```
glListBase(nFontList);
glCallLists (13, GL_UNSIGNED_BYTE, "OpenGL Rocks!");
    }
```

FIGURE 19.5   Output from the TEXT2D sample program.

Note that `wglUseFontBitmaps` is a much simpler function. It requires only the device context handle, the beginning and last characters, and the first display list name to be used:

```
wglUseFontBitmaps(hDC, 0, 128, nFontList);
```

Because bitmap fonts are created based on the actual font and map directly to pixels on the screen, the `lfHeight` member of the `LOGFONT` structure is used exactly in the same way it is for GDI font rasterization.

Full-Screen Rendering

With OpenGL becoming popular among PC game developers, a common question is "How do I do full-screen rendering with OpenGL?" The truth is, if you've read this chapter, you already know how to do full-screen rendering with OpenGL—it's just like rendering into any other window! The real question is "How do I create a window that takes up the entire screen and has no borders?" After you do this, rendering into this window is no different from rendering into any other window in any other sample in this book.

Even though this issue isn't strictly related to OpenGL, it is of enough interest to a wide number of our readers that we give this topic some coverage here.

Creating a Frameless Window

The first task is to create a window that has no border or caption. This procedure is quite simple. Following is the window creation code from the GLRECT sample program. We've made one small change by making the window style WS_POPUP instead of WS_OVERLAPPED-WINDOW:

```
// Create the main application window
hWnd = CreateWindow(lpszAppName,
                    lpszAppName,

                    // OpenGL requires WS_CLIPCHILDREN and WS_CLIPSIBLINGS
                    WS_POPUP | WS_CLIPCHILDREN | WS_CLIPSIBLINGS,

                    // Window position and size
                    100, 100,
                    250, 250,
                    NULL,
                    NULL,
                    hInstance,
                    NULL);
```

The result of this change is shown in Figure 19.6.

FIGURE 19.6   A window with no caption or border.

As you can see, without the proper style settings, the window has neither a caption nor a border of any kind. Don't forget to take into account that now the window no longer has a close button on it. The user will have to press Alt+F4 to close the window and exit the program. Most user-friendly programs watch for a keystroke such as the Esc key or Q to terminate the program.

Creating a Full-Screen Window

Creating a window the size of the screen is almost as trivial as creating a window with no caption or border. The parameters of the CreateWindow function allow you to specify where onscreen the upper-left corner of the window will be positioned and the width and height of the window. To create a full-screen window, you always use (0,0) as the upper-left corner. The only trick would be determining what size the desktop is so you know how wide and high to make the window. You can easily determine this information by using the Windows function GetDeviceCaps.

Listing 19.6 shows the new WinMain function from GLRECT, which is now the new sample FSCREEN. To use GetDeviceCaps, you need a device context handle. Because you are in the process of creating the main window, you need to use the device context from the desktop window.

LISTING 19.6   Creating a Full-Screen Window

```
// Entry point of all Windows programs
int APIENTRY WinMain(  HINSTANCE      hInstance,
                       HINSTANCE      hPrevInstance,
                       LPSTR          lpCmdLine,
                       int            nCmdShow)
    {
    MSG         msg;          // Windows message structure
    WNDCLASS    wc;           // Windows class structure
    HWND        hWnd;         // Storage for window handle
    HWND        hDesktopWnd;  // Storage for desktop window handle
    HDC         hDesktopDC;   // Storage for desktop window device context
    int         nScreenX, nScreenY; // Screen Dimensions

    // Register Window style
    wc.style              = CS_HREDRAW | CS_VREDRAW | CS_OWNDC;
    wc.lpfnWndProc        = (WNDPROC) WndProc;
    wc.cbClsExtra         = 0;
    wc.cbWndExtra         = 0;
    wc.hInstance          = hInstance;
    wc.hIcon              = NULL;
    wc.hCursor            = LoadCursor(NULL, IDC_ARROW);

    // No need for background brush for OpenGL window
    wc.hbrBackground      = NULL;
    wc.lpszMenuName       = NULL;
    wc.lpszClassName      = lpszAppName;

    // Register the window class
    if(RegisterClass(&wc) == 0)
        return FALSE;
```

19

LISTING 19.6   Continued

```
// Get the Window handle and Device context to the desktop
hDesktopWnd = GetDesktopWindow();
hDesktopDC = GetDC(hDesktopWnd);

// Get the screen size
nScreenX = GetDeviceCaps(hDesktopDC, HORZRES);
nScreenY = GetDeviceCaps(hDesktopDC, VERTRES);

// Release the desktop device context
ReleaseDC(hDesktopWnd, hDesktopDC);

// Create the main application window
hWnd = CreateWindow(lpszAppName,
                    lpszAppName,
        // OpenGL requires WS_CLIPCHILDREN and WS_CLIPSIBLINGS
          WS_POPUP | WS_CLIPCHILDREN | WS_CLIPSIBLINGS,
                    // Window position and size
                    0, 0,
                    nScreenX, nScreenY,
                    NULL,
                    NULL,
                    hInstance,
                    NULL);


// If window was not created, quit
if(hWnd == NULL)
    return FALSE;

// Display the window
ShowWindow(hWnd,SW_SHOW);
UpdateWindow(hWnd);

// Process application messages until the application closes
while( GetMessage(&msg, NULL, 0, 0))
    {
    TranslateMessage(&msg);
    DispatchMessage(&msg);
    }

return msg.wParam;
}
```

The key code here is the lines that get the desktop window handle and device context. The device context can then be used to obtain the screen's horizontal and vertical resolution:

```
hDesktopWnd = GetDesktopWindow();
hDesktopDC = GetDC(hDesktopWnd);

// Get the screen size
nScreenX = GetDeviceCaps(hDesktopDC, HORZRES);
nScreenY = GetDeviceCaps(hDesktopDC, VERTRES);

// Release the desktop device context
ReleaseDC(hDesktopWnd, hDesktopDC);
```

If your system has multiple monitors, you should note that the values returned here would be for the primary display device. You might also be tempted to force the window to be a topmost window (using the WS_EX_TOPMOST window style). However, doing so makes it possible for your window to lose focus but remain on top of other active windows. This may confuse the user when the program stops responding to keyboard strokes.

You may also want to take a look at the Win32 function ChangeDisplaySettings in your Windows SDK documentation. This function allows you to dynamically change the desktop size at runtime and restore it when your application terminates. This capability may be desirable if you want to have a full-screen window but at a lower or higher display resolution than the default. If you do change the desktop settings, you must not create the rendering window or set the pixelformat until after the desktop settings have changed. OpenGL rendering contexts created under one environment (desktop settings) are not likely to be valid in another.

Multithreaded Rendering

A powerful feature of the Win32 API is multithreading. The topic of threading is beyond the scope of a book on computer graphics. Basically, a thread is the unit of execution for an application. Most programs execute instructions sequentially from the start of the program until the program terminates. A thread of execution is the path through the machine code that the CPU traverses as it fetches and executes instructions. By creating multiple threads using the Win32 API, you can create multiple paths through your source code that are followed simultaneously.

Think of multithreading as being able to call two functions at the same time and then have them executed simultaneously. Of course, the CPU cannot actually execute two code paths simultaneously, so it switches between threads during normal program flow much the same way a multitasking operating system switches between tasks. If you have more than one processor, or a multicore CPU, multithreaded programs can experience quite substantial performance gains as the work required is split between two execution units.

Even on a single CPU system, a program carefully designed for multithreaded execution can outperform a single-threaded application in many circumstances. On a single processor machine, one thread can service I/O requests, for example, while another handles the GUI.

Some OpenGL implementations take advantage of a multiprocessor system. If, for example, the transformation and lighting units of the OpenGL pipeline are not hardware accelerated, a driver can create another thread so that these calculations are performed by one CPU while another CPU feeds the transformed data to the rasterizer. Threads within a driver can also be used to offload command assembly and dispatch, decreasing the latency of many OpenGL calls.

You might think that using two threads to do your OpenGL rendering would speed up your rendering as well. You could perhaps have one thread draw the background objects in a scene while another thread draws the more dynamic elements. This approach is almost always a bad idea. Although you can create two OpenGL rendering contexts for two different threads, most drivers fail if you try to render with both of them in the same window. Technically, this multithreading should be possible, and the Microsoft generic implementation will succeed if you try it, as might many hardware implementations. In the real world, the extra work you place on the driver with two contexts trying to share the same framebuffer will most likely outweigh any performance benefit you hope to gain from using multiple threads.

Multithreading can benefit your OpenGL rendering on a multiprocessor system or even on a single processor system in at least two ways. In the first scenario, you have two different windows, each with its own rendering context and thread of execution. This case could still stress some drivers (some of the low-end game boards are stressed just by two applications using OpenGL simultaneously!), but many professional OpenGL implementations can handle it quite well.

The second example is if you are writing a game or a real-time simulation. You can have a worker thread perform physics calculations or artificial intelligence or handle player interaction while another thread does the OpenGL rendering. This scenario requires careful sharing of data between threads but can provide a substantial performance boost on a dual-processor machine, and even a single-processor machine can improve the responsiveness of your program. Although we've made the disclaimer that multithreaded programming is outside the scope of this book, we present for your examination the sample program RTHREAD in the source distribution for this chapter. This program creates and uses a rendering thread. This program also demonstrates the use of the OpenGL WGL extensions.

OpenGL and WGL Extensions

On the Windows platform, you do not have direct access to the OpenGL driver. All OpenGL function calls are routed through the opengl32.dll system file. Because this DLL understands only OpenGL 1.1 entrypoints (function names), you must have a mechanism to get a pointer to an OpenGL function supported directly by the driver. Fortunately, the Windows OpenGL implementation has a function named `wglGetProcAddress` that allows you to retrieve a pointer to an OpenGL function supported by the driver, but not necessarily natively supported by `opengl32.dll`:

```
PROC wglGetProcAddress(LPSTR lpszProc);
```

This function takes the name of an OpenGL function or extension and returns a function pointer that you can use to call that function directly. For this to work, you must know the function prototype for the function so you can create a pointer to it and subsequently call the function.

OpenGL extensions (and post-version 1.1 features) come in two flavors. Some are simply new constants and enumerants recognized by a vendor's hardware driver. Others require that you call new functions added to the API. The number of extensions is extensive, especially when you add in the newer OpenGL core functionality and vendor-specific extensions. Complete coverage of all OpenGL extensions would require an entire book in itself (if not an encyclopedia!). You can find a registry of extensions on the Internet and among the Web sites listed in Appendix A, "Further Reading/References."

Fortunately, the following two header files give you programmatic access to most OpenGL extensions:

```
#include <wglext.h>
#include <glext.h>
```

These files can be found at the OpenGL extension registry Web site. They are also maintained by most graphics card vendors (see their developer support Web sites), and the latest version as of this book's printing is included in the source code distribution on our Web site The `wglext.h` header contains a number of extensions that are Windows specific, and the `glext.h` header contains both standard OpenGL extensions and many vendor-specific OpenGL extensions.

Simple Extensions

Because this book covers known OpenGL features up to version 2.1, you may have already discovered that many of the sample programs in this book use these extensions for Windows builds of the sample code found in previous chapters. For example, in Chapter 9, "Texture Mapping: Beyond the Basics," we showed you how to add specular highlights to textured geometry using OpenGL's separate specular color with the following function call:

```
glLightModeli(GL_LIGHT_MODEL_COLOR_CONTROL, GL_SEPARATE_SPECULAR_COLOR);
```

However, this capability is not present in OpenGL 1.1, and the `GL_LIGHT_MODEL_COLOR_CONTROL` and `GL_SEPARATE_SPECULAR_COLOR` constants are not defined in the Windows version of gl.h. They are, however, found in glext.h, and this file is already included automatically in all the samples in this book via the gltools.h header file. The glLightModeli function, on the other hand, has been around since OpenGL 1.0. These kinds of simple extensions simply pass new tokens to existing entry-points (functions) and require only that you have the constants defined and know that the extension or feature is supported by the hardware.

Even if the OpenGL version is still reported as 1.1, this capability may still be included in the driver. This feature was originally an extension that was later promoted to the OpenGL core functionality. You can check for this and other easy-to-access extensions (no function pointers needed) quickly by using the following GlTools function:

```
bool gltIsExtSupported(const char *szExtension);
```

In the case of separate specular color, you might just code something like this:

```
if(gltIsExtSupported(GL_EXT_separate_specular_color))
    RenderOnce();
else
    UseMultiPassTechnique();
```

Here, you call the RenderOnce function if the extension (or feature) is supported, and the UserMultiPassTechnique function to render an alternate (drawn twice and blended together) and slower way to achieve the same effect.

Using New Entrypoints

A more complex extension example comes from the IMAGING sample program in Chapter 7. In this case, the optional imaging subset not only is missing from the Windows version of gl.h, but is optional in all subsequent versions of OpenGL as well. This is an example of the type of feature that has to be there, or there is no point in continuing. Thus, you first check for the presence of the imaging subset by checking for its extension string:

```
// Check for imaging subset, must be done after window
// is created or there won't be an OpenGL context to query
if(gltIsExtSupported("GL_ARB_imaging") == 0)
  {
  printf("Imaging subset not supported\r\n");
  return 0;
  }
```

The function prototype typedefs for the functions used are found in glext.h, and you use them to create function pointers to each of the functions you want to call. On the Macintosh platform, the standard system headers already contain these functions:

```
#ifndef __APPLE__
// These typdefs are found in glext.h
PFNGLHISTOGRAMPROC                 glHistogram = NULL;
PFNGLGETHISTOGRAMPROC              glGetHistogram = NULL;
PFNGLCOLORTABLEPROC                glColorTable = NULL;
PFNGLCONVOLUTIONFILTER2DPROC       glConvolutionFilter2D = NULL;
#endif
```

Now you use the glTools function gltGetExtensionPointer to retrieve the function pointer to the function in question. This function is simply a portability wrapper for wglGetProcAddress on Windows and an admittedly more complex method on the Apple of getting the function pointers:

```
#ifndef __APPLE__
glHistogram = gltGetExtensionPointer("glHistogram");
glGetHistogram = gltGetExtensionPointer("glGetHistogram");
glColorTable = gltGetExtensionPointer("glColorTable");
glConvolutionFilter2D = gltGetExtensionPointer("glConvolutionFilter2D");
#endif
```

Then you simply use the extension as if it were a normally supported part of the API:

```
// Start collecting histogram data, 256 luminance values
glHistogram(GL_HISTOGRAM, 256, GL_LUMINANCE, GL_FALSE);
glEnable(GL_HISTOGRAM);
```

Auto-Magic Extensions

Most normal developers would fairly quickly grow weary of always having to query for new function pointers at the beginning of the program. There is a faster way, and in fact, we used this shortcut for all the samples in this book. The GLEE library (GL Easy Extension library) is included in the \shared directory with the source distribution for the book on our Web site. Automatically gaining access to all the function pointers supported by the driver is a simple matter of adding glee.c to your project, and glee.h to the top of your header list.

GLEE is quite clever; the new functions initialize themselves the first time they are called. This removes the need to perform any specialized initialization to gain access to all the OpenGL functionality available by a particular driver on Windows. This does not, however, remove the need to check for which version of OpenGL is currently supported by the driver. If an entrypoint does not exist in the driver, the GLEE library will simply return from the function call and do nothing.

WGL Extensions

Several Windows-specific WGL extensions are also available. You access the WGL extensions' entrypoints in the same manner as the other extensions—using the wglGetProcAddress function. There is, however, an important exception. Typically, among the many WGL extensions, only two are advertised by using glGetString(GL_EXTENSIONS). One is the swap interval extension (which allows you to synchronize buffer swaps with the vertical retrace), and the other is the WGL_ARB_extensions_string extension. This extension provides yet another entrypoint that is used exclusively to query for the WGL extensions. The ARB extensions string function is prototyped like this:

```
const char *wglGetExtensionsStringARB(HDC hdc);
```

This function retrieves the list of WGL extensions in the same manner in which you previously would have used glGetString. Using the wglext.h header file, you can retrieve a pointer to this function like this:

```
PFNWGLGETEXTENSIONSSTRINGARBPROC *wglGetExtensionsStringARB;
wglGetExtensionsStringARB = (PFNWGLGETEXTENSIONSSTRINGARBPROC)
                    wglGetProcAddress("wglGetExtensionsStringARB");
```

glGetString returns the WGL_ARB_extensions_string identifier, but often developers skip this check and simply look for the entrypoint, as shown in the preceding code fragment. This approach usually works with most OpenGL extensions, but you should realize that this is, strictly speaking, "coloring outside the lines." Some vendors export extensions on an "experimental" basis, and these extensions may not be officially supported, or the functions may not function properly if you skip the extension string check. Also, more than one extension may use the same function or functions. Testing only for function availability provides no information on the availability or the reliability of the specific extension or extensions that are supported.

Extended Pixel Formats

Perhaps one of the most important WGL extensions available for Windows is the WGL_ARB_pixel_format extension. This extension provides a mechanism that allows you to check for and select pixel format features that did not exist when PIXELFORMATDESCRIPTOR was first created. For example, if your driver supports multisampled rendering (for full-scene antialiasing, for example), there is no way to select a pixel format with this support using the old PIXELFORMATDESCRIPTOR fields. If this extension is supported, the driver exports the following functions:

```
BOOL wglGetPixelFormatAttribivARB(HDC hdc, GLint iPixelFormat,
                        GLint iLayerPlane, GLuint nAttributes,
                        const GLint *piAttributes, GLint *piValues);
```

```
BOOL wglGetPixelFormatAttribfvARB(HDC hdc, GLint iPixelFormat,
                                  GLint iLayerPlane, GLuint nAttributes,
                                  const GLint *piAttributes, GLfloat *pfValues);
```

These two variations of the same function allow you to query a particular pixel format index and retrieve an array containing the attribute data for that pixel format. The first argument, *hdc*, is the device context of the window that the pixel format will be used for, followed by the pixel format index. The *iLayerPlane* argument specifies which layer plane to query (0 on Vista, or if your implementation does not support layer planes). Next, *nAttributes* specifies how many attributes are being queried for this pixel format, and the array *piAttributes* contains the list of attribute names to be queried. The attributes that can be specified are listed in Table 19.3. The final argument is an array that will be filled with the corresponding pixel format attributes.

TABLE 19.3   Pixelformat Attributes

Constant	Description
WGL_NUMBER_PIXEL_FORMATS_ARB	Number of pixel formats for this device.
WGL_DRAW_TO_WINDOW_ARB	Nonzero if the pixel format can be used with a window.
WGL_DRAW_TO_BITMAP_ARB	Nonzero if the pixel format can be used with a memory Device Independent Bitmap (DIB).
WGL_DEPTH_BITS_ARB	Number of bits in the depth buffer.
WGL_STENCIL_BITS_ARB	Number of bits in the stencil buffer.
WGL_ACCELERATION_ARB	One of the values in Table 19.4 that specifies which, if any, hardware driver is used.
WGL_NEED_PALETTE_ARB	Nonzero if a palette is required.
WGL_NEED_SYSTEM_PALETTE_ARB	Nonzero if the hardware supports one palette only in 256-color mode.
WGL_SWAP_LAYER_BUFFERS_ARB	Nonzero if the hardware supports swapping layer planes.
WGL_SWAP_METHOD_ARB	Method by which the buffer swap is accomplished for double-buffered pixel formats. It is one of the values listed in Table 19.5.
WGL_NUMBER_OVERLAYS_ARB	Number of overlay planes.
WGL_NUMBER_UNDERLAYS_ARB	Number of underlay planes.
WGL_TRANSPARENT_ARB	Nonzero if transparency is supported.
WGL_TRANSPARENT_RED_VALUE_ARB	Transparent red color.
WGL_TRANSPARENT_GREEN_VALUE_ARB	Transparent green color.
WGL_TRANSPARENT_BLUE_VALUE_ARB	Transparent blue color.
WGL_TRANSPARENT_ALPHA_VALUE_ARB	Transparent alpha color.
WGL_SHARE_DEPTH_ARB	Nonzero if layer planes share a depth buffer with the main plane.
WGL_SHARE_STENCIL_ARB	Nonzero if layer planes share a stencil buffer with the main plane.
WGL_SHARE_ACCUM_ARB	Nonzero if layer planes share an accumulation buffer with the main plane.

TABLE 19.3   Continued

Constant	Description
WGL_SUPPORT_GDI_ARB	Nonzero if GDI rendering is supported (front buffer only).
WGL_SUPPORT_OPENGL_ARB	Nonzero if OpenGL is supported.
WGL_DOUBLE_BUFFER_ARB	Nonzero if double buffered.
WGL_STEREO_ARB	Nonzero if left and right buffers are supported.
WGL_PIXEL_TYPE_ARB	WGL_TYPE_RGBA_ARB for RGBA color modes; WGL_TYPE_COLORINDEX_ARB for color index mode.
WGL_COLOR_BITS_ARB	Number of bit planes in the color buffer.
WGL_RED_BITS_ARB	Number of red bit planes in the color buffer.
WGL_RED_SHIFT_ARB	Shift count for red bit planes.
WGL_GREEN_BITS_ARB	Number of green bit planes in the color buffer.
WGL_GREEN_SHIFT_ARB	Shift count for green bit planes.
WGL_BLUE_BITS_ARB	Number of blue bit planes in the color buffer.
WGL_BLUE_SHIFT_ARB	Shift count for blue bit planes.
WGL_ALPHA_BITS_ARB	Number of alpha bit planes in the color buffer.
WGL_ALPHA_SHIFT_ARB	Shift count for alpha bit planes.
WGL_ACCUM_BITS_ARB	Number of bit planes in the accumulation buffer.
WGL_ACCUM_RED_BITS_ARB	Number of red bit planes in the accumulation buffer.
WGL_ACCUM_GREEN_BITS_ARB	Number of green bit planes in the accumulation buffer.
WGL_ACCUM_BLUE_BITS_ARB	Number of blue bit planes in the accumulation buffer.
WGL_ACCUM_ALPHA_BITS_ARB	Number of alpha bit planes in the accumulation buffer.
WGL_AUX_BUFFERS_ARB	Number of auxiliary buffers

TABLE 19.4   Acceleration Flags for WGL_ACCELERATION_ARB

Constant	Description
WGL_NO_ACCELERATION_ARB	Software rendering, no acceleration
WGL_GENERIC_ACCELERATION_ARB	Acceleration via an MCD driver
WGL_FULL_ACCELERATION_ARB	Acceleration via an ICD driver

TABLE 19.5   Buffer Swap Values for WGL_SWAP_METHOD_ARB

Constant	Description
WGL_SWAP_EXCHANGE_ARB	Swapping exchanges the front and back buffers.
WGL_SWAP_COPY_ARB	The back buffer is copied to the front buffer.
WGL_SWAP_UNDEFINED_ARB	The back buffer is copied to the front buffer, but the back buffer contents remain undefined after the buffer swap.

There is, however, a Catch-22 to these and all other OpenGL extensions. You must have a valid OpenGL rendering context before you can call either glGetString or wglGetProcAddress. This means that you must first create a temporary window, set a pixel format (we can actually cheat and just specify 1, which will be the first hardware acceler-ated format) and then obtain a pointer to one of the `wglGetPixelFormatAttribARB` func-tions. A convenient place to do this might be the splash screen or perhaps an initial options dialog box that is presented to the user. You should not, however, try to use the Windows desktop because your application does not own it!

The following simple example queries for a single attribute—the number of pixel formats supported—so that you know how many you may need to look at:

```
int attrib[] = { WGL_NUMBER_PIXEL_FORMATS_ARB };
int nResults[0];
wglGetPixelFormatAttributeivARB(hDC, 1, 0, 1, attrib, nResults);
// nResults[0] now contains the number of exported pixel formats
```

For a more detailed example showing how to look for a specific pixel format (including a multisampled pixel format), see the SPHEREWORLD32 sample program coming up next.

Win32 to the Max

SPHEREWORLD32 is a Win32-specific version of the Sphere World example we have returned to again and again throughout this book. SPHEREWORLD32 allows you to select windowed or full-screen mode, changes the display settings if necessary, and detects and allows you to select a multisampled pixel format. Finally, you use the Windows-specific font features to display the frame rate and other information onscreen. When in full-screen mode, you can even Alt+Tab away from the program, and the window will be mini-mized until reselected.

The complete source to this "ultimate" Win32 sample program contains extensive comments to explain every aspect of the program. In the initial dialog box that is displayed (see Figure 19.7), you can select full-screen or windowed mode, multisampled rendering (if available), and whether you want to enable the swap interval extension. A sample screen of the running program is shown in Figure 19.8.

FIGURE 19.7   The initial Options dialog box for SPHEREWORLD32.

Multisampled Frame Buffer
FPS: 435.4
OpenGL Rocks!

FIGURE 19.8   Output from the SPHEREWORLD32 sample program.

Summary

This chapter introduced you to using OpenGL on the Win32 platform. You read about the different driver models and implementations available for Windows and what to watch. You also learned how to enumerate and select a pixel format to get the kind of hardware-accelerated or software rendering support you want. You've now seen the basic framework for a Win32 program that replaces the GLUT framework, so you can write true native Win32 (actually, all this works under Win64 too!) application code. We also showed you how to create a full-screen window for games or simulation-type applications. Additionally, we discussed some of the Windows-specific features of OpenGL on Windows, such as support for TrueType fonts and multiple rendering threads.

Finally, we offer in the source code the ultimate OpenGL on Win32 sample program, SPHEREWORLD32. This program demonstrated how to use a number of Windows-specific features and WGL extensions if they were available. It also demonstrated how to construct a well-behaved program that will run on everything from an old 8-bit color display to the latest 32-bit full-color mega-3D game accelerator.

CHAPTER 20

OpenGL on Mac OS X

by Richard S. Wright Jr.

WHAT YOU'LL LEARN IN THIS CHAPTER:

How To	Functions You'll Use
Choose appropriate pixel formats for OpenGL rendering	`aglChoosePixelFormat`
Manage OpenGL drawing contexts	`aglCreateContext/aglDestroyContext/` `aglSetCurrentContext/aglSetDrawable`
Do double-buffered drawing	`aglSwapBuffers`
Create bitmap text fonts	`aglUseFont`

OpenGL is the native and preferred 3D rendering API on the Mac OS X platform. In fact, OpenGL is used at the lowest levels of the operating system for the desktop, GUI, and Mac OS X's own 2D graphics APIs and compositing engine (Quartz). The importance of OpenGL on the Mac platform cannot be overstated. With its favored status in the eyes of Apple (somewhat analogous to Direct3D's status with Microsoft), it enjoys significant support, and investment by Apple in continual tuning and extension to the API.

There are four programming interfaces to OpenGL on the Mac, each with its own personality. Which one you use will vary greatly depending on how you prefer to create applications on the Mac, and for your specific rendering needs. Table 20.1 lists these four interfaces. We will cover the first three of these in some detail.

TABLE 20.1   OpenGL Interface Technologies in OS X

Name	Description
GLUT	Provides a complete framework for simple rendering-based applications.
AGL	Provides the OpenGL interface to developers using Carbon as their framework.
NSOpenGL	Provides the OpenGL interface for developers using the Cocoa object-oriented framework for their applications.
CGL	Is the lowest-level OpenGL interface, available to all application technologies. Both the AGL and NSOpenGL interfaces are layered on top of CGL.

We use these interfaces to do the setup for OpenGL in a window, or on a display device. After that is out of the way, OpenGL is just OpenGL!

Remember, this chapter is not about OS X programming, but about using OpenGL on OS X. If you are brand new to the Mac, the GLUT section should get you going. The sections following that will assume some prior Mac programming experience. You can probably still get things up and going, but the material will offer less insight into how to develop on OS X than it will on how to use OpenGL.

GLUT

Both the simplest and most portable access to OpenGL on the Mac comes via the GLUT library. Nearly all the samples in this book are written using the GLUT library, because it is available for not only the Mac, but also Windows, and nearly every variant of UNIX as well. GLUT is included in OS X automatically, so there is nothing else to install besides the standard Apple developer tools. When browsing the source distribution for the book, you'll find a /Projects/Apple folder containing Xcode project files for every chapter, except the non–Apple operating system specific chapters in Part III, "The Apocrypha." For your reference, all the screen shots in this chapter were made using Xcode version 2.4.1, running under OS X version 10.4.8.

Setting Up a GLUT Project

Since the majority of examples in this book are GLUT projects, we aren't going to go through the actual programming involved in using GLUT, because this was pretty well covered in Chapter 2, "Using OpenGL," not to mention nearly every chapter since! We will, however, at least walk you through setting up a brand-new Xcode GLUT project. This is undoubtedly the simplest way to get going if you just want to experiment with OpenGL on a Mac. Less experienced programmers seeking to get started right away with OpenGL should definitely start with GLUT. More experienced Mac programmers can probably skip right ahead to one of the next sections, OpenGL with Carbon or OpenGL with Cocoa.

To begin with, start Xcode (Xcode is Apple's free development environment for the Mac, and comes on every OS X installation CD). Select New Project from the main menu, and specify a Cocoa application as shown in Figure 20.1.

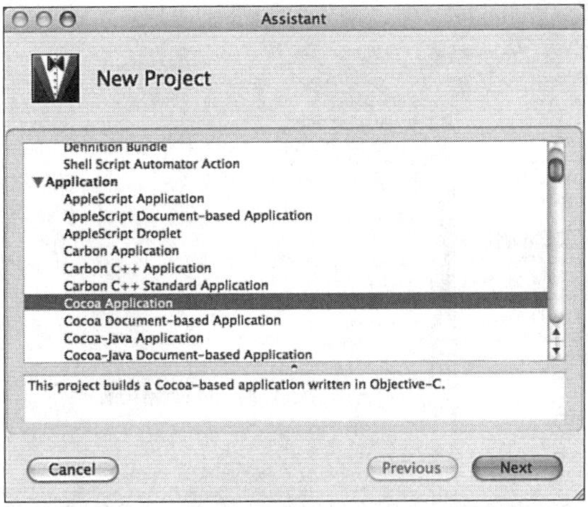

FIGURE 20.1   GLUT-based programs start life as a Cocoa application.

GLUT is actually layered on top of the Cocoa interface, which we'll discuss later. The New Project Assistant will then create a simple Cocoa skeleton application for us. We'll need to make some changes to the defaults, however, before we can get started coding.

Application Frameworks

To begin with, we need to add a couple of application frameworks. An application framework is a dynamically loaded "plug-in" for Mac applications. If you are already familiar with Windows programming, these are analogous to DLLs, except they also contain all the headers and other resources you need to program with them. To add a library of functionality to your application, you add that library's framework. A large number of frameworks ship standard on OS X, including GLUT and OpenGL.

To see the default frameworks included in your project, expand the Frameworks folder in the Groups & Files pane, as shown in Figure 20.2.

To add the GLUT and OpenGL frameworks, right-click (or Ctrl-click) on the Frameworks folder, select Add, and then select Existing Frameworks from the pop-up menu. The frameworks are stored in the /System/Library/Frameworks folder. Frameworks are actually whole folders containing all the data needed to include the library into your application. Select and add both the GLUT and the OpenGL frameworks. You can also perform a multiple selection by holding down the Apple key while clicking the framework name.

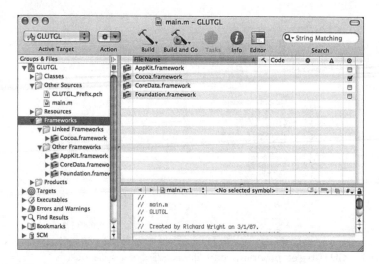

FIGURE 20.2   The initial project screen for a new GLUT-based program.

Ditching Cocoa

Finally, we just need the source code for our GLUT-based program. First we have to get rid of the default Cocoa source module created for us. Click on the main.m file in the Other Sources folder, also shown in Figure 20.2, and press the Delete key. A confirmation dialog will appear; click Delete References & Files. This not only removes the file from the project, but deletes the file itself.

Of course, now we have no source code for our program! You can add a new or existing C or C++ file to the project with a right-click (or Ctrl-click) on the Other Sources folder. You can select one of the sample programs in source distribution or create your own fresh new program.

If you are not using our gltools helper functions and classes, you need to know what standard headers you need to include for GLUT. These headers below bring in OpenGL, the utility library, and GLUT functions:

```
#include <OpenGL/gl.h>    // Apple OpenGL headers
#include <OpenGL/glu.h>   // OpenGL Utilities
#include <Glut/glut.h>    // Apple's Implementation of GLUT
```

Finally, if you are new to the Mac platform, one of the most frustrating things to figure out on your own is where files go. If you perform a standard C runtime fopen, for example, where is the working directory? For GLUT-based programs, the current active directory is located inside the application bundle in the /Resources folder. This folder is not set to the current working directory until after you call glutInit. If you are going to load textures or data files, you place these files here (see most of the previous chapters' sample programs for an example of this).

To open an application's bundle and look inside, right-click (or Ctrl-click) and select Show Package Contents. Application bundles on the Mac are nothing more than a standard application folder hierarchy. You can also directly add files to this folder as part of the Xcode build process. Right-click on the `Resources` folder and select Add Existing Files. Select any data files or textures you want packaged automatically, and you're ready to go!

OpenGL with Carbon

Carbon is the name of an application development technology for OS X. Carbon is essentially just an API, but it is a comprehensive API used for creating C and C++ applications on Mac OS X. Carbon was the primary means by which application developers moved old OS 9 applications to the new more modern and UNIX-based OS X. Carbon-based applications (I don't know why, but I just *love* that term!) usually access OpenGL via the `agl` (Apple GL) framework.

We'll begin our first sample program, CARBONGL, with a simple Carbon-based program that displays an empty window. To make things a little more interesting, we'll port our vertex buffer object–based THUNDERBIRD sample program in Chapter 11 from GLUT to Carbon.

Setting Up for OpenGL

Before we can begin, we must add the OpenGL framework just as we did in the preceding section. However, instead of GLUT, you also need to add the AGL framework. The AGL library is Apple's API glue that brings OpenGL into Carbon managed windows. Adding these frameworks brings in the libraries during the link phase when you build your Xcode projects. To include the functions from these libraries, you also need to include these two headers:

```
#include <OpenGL/gl.h>
#include <Agl/agl.h>
```

In all of our GLUT-based sample programs, the `/Resources` folder inside the application bundle was automatically set as the default working directory for the program. This is extremely convenient, but not the default for OS X programs. GLUT did the heavy lifting for us, but now we must have a little cheat to set this ourselves. These first few lines after our `main` function will do the trick:

```
int main(int argc, char* argv[])
    {
    . . .
    // Little cheat to get working directory back
    // to /Resources like it is in GLUT
    char *parentdir;
    char *c;
```

20

```
    parentdir = strdup(argv[0]);
    c = (char*) parentdir;

    while (*c != '\0')      // go to end
      c++;

    while (*c != '/')       // back up to parent
        c—;

    *c++ = '\0';            // cut off last part (binary name)

    // Change to Resources directory. Any files need to be placed there
    chdir(parentdir);
    chdir("../Resources");
    free(parentdir);
```

There are four main things that every windowed OpenGL program must perform: setup, shutdown, rendering, and handling window size changes. In GLUT we registered callback functions for these tasks that were called at the appropriate time. In every platform-specific program these same tasks are still the foundation of a sound rendering framework. Setup occurs sometime after the window is created (often immediately), with shutdown occurring when the window is being destroyed. OpenGL rendering is wired into the normal event-driven paint or draw messages. Finally, when notified that a window has changed size, it's time to reset the viewport and potentially the projection as well.

With Carbon, we can register for notifications of some of these events. We'll bring OpenGL to life right after we create the window. Then we register for the following carbon events in the window's event handler: kEventWindowClose, kEventWindowDrawContent, and kEventWindowBoundsChanged. Listing 20.1 shows a modified version of the standard Carbon window creation code produced by the New Project Assistant in Xcode. This specific code is used in our CARBONGL sample program for this chapter. We have added tokens for our additional event notifications, and note the call to SetupGL that is called right after we have created the window. We are going to look at that next.

LISTING 20.1   Initializing the Carbon Window

```
static OSStatus HandleNew()
{
    OSStatus                err;
    WindowRef               window;
    static const EventTypeSpec    kWindowEvents[] =
    {
        { kEventClassCommand, kEventCommandProcess },
        { kEventClassWindow, kEventWindowDrawContent }, // when to draw
```

LISTING 20.1   Continued

```
        { kEventClassWindow, kEventWindowClose },         // window being closed
        { kEventClassWindow, kEventWindowBoundsChanged }// window resized
    };

    Rect            windowRect;
    int             windowAttributes;

    // Set window dimensions here
    SetRect(&windowRect, 10, 60, 800, 600);

    // Set Window attributes
    windowAttributes =
                    kWindowStandardHandlerAttribute ¦ kWindowCloseBoxAttribute
                    kWindowCollapseBoxAttribute ¦
                    kWindowResizableAttribute ¦ kWindowStandardDocumentAttributes;

    // Create the Window
    CreateNewWindow(kDocumentWindowClass, windowAttributes,
                                            &windowRect, &window);
    SetWTitle(window, "\pCarbonGL");

    // Install a command handler on the window. We don't use this handler
    // yet, but nearly all Carbon apps will need to handle commands, so this
    // saves everyone a little typing.
    InstallWindowEventHandler(window, GetWindowEventHandlerUPP(),
                        GetEventTypeCount( kWindowEvents ), kWindowEvents,
                        NULL, NULL );


    // Position new windows in a staggered arrangement on the main screen
    RepositionWindow( window, NULL, kWindowCascadeOnMainScreen );

    SetupGL(window);
    ChangeSize(800, 600);

    // The window was created hidden, so show it
    ShowWindow( window );

CantCreateWindow:
    return err;
}
```

20

Setting the Pixel Format

Before OpenGL can be initialized for a window, you must first select an appropriate *pixel format*. A pixel format describes the hardware buffer configuration for 3D rendering, things like the depth of the color buffer, the size of the stencil buffer, and whether the buffer is onscreen (the default) or offscreen. The pixel format is described by the AGL data type AGLPixelFormat.

To select an appropriate pixel format for your needs, you first construct an array of integer attributes. For example, the following array requests a double-buffered pixel format with red, green, blue, and alpha components in the destination buffer, and a 16-bit depth buffer. You may get other attributes as well, but you are essentially saying these are all you really care about:

```
static GLint glAttributes[] = {
                AGL_DOUBLEBUFFER, GL_TRUE,  // Double buffered
                AGL_RGBA,         GL_TRUE,  // Four-component color
                AGL_DEPTH_SIZE,   16,       // 16-bit (at least) depth buffer
                AGL_NONE };                 // Terminator
```

Note that you must terminate the array with AGL_NONE. Next, you pass this array to aglChoosePixelFormat. This function searches for an appropriate specific pixel format that matches your request as closely as possible. This returns either a valid AGLPixelFormat, or NULL if the request could not be fulfilled.

```
AGLPixelFormat openGLFormat = aglChoosePixelFormat(NULL, 0, glAttributes);
if(openGLFormat == NULL)
     // Something has gone wrong...deal with it!
```

Most attributes are followed by either a Boolean flag or an integer value. For example, AGL_DEPTH_SIZE is expected to be followed by an integer value that specifies the number of bits desired for the depth buffer. The available attributes and their meanings are listed in Table 20.2.

TABLE 20.2 AGL Pixel Format Attribute List Constants

Constant	Description
AGL_NONE	This constant terminates the attribute list.
AGL_ALL_RENDERERS	Select the pixelformat from all available renderers, including non-conformat or special-purpose renderers.
AGL_BUFFER_SIZE	The value following it is the sum of all the color bits in the color buffer. Ignored if AGL_RGBA is also in the list.
AGL_LEVEL	The value following it specifies the number of overlay planes desired, or if negative the number of underlay planes.
AGL_RGBA	The value following is GL_TRUE if four-component color values are to be used, GL_FALSE for color index mode.
AGL_DOUBLEBUFFER	The value following is GL_TRUE if double buffering is desired, GL_FALSE if only a single-buffered format is required.

TABLE 20.2   Continued

Constant	Description
AGL_STEREO	If the value following is GL_TRUE, the color buffers exist in left-right pairs.
AGL_AUX_BUFFERS	The value following is the number of auxiliary buffers available.
AGL_RED_SIZE	The value following is the desired size of the number of red component bits in a GL_RGBA pixel format.
AGL_GREEN_SIZE	The value following is the desired size of the number of green component bits in a GL_RGBA pixel format.
AGL_BLUE_SIZE	The value following is the desired size of the number of blue component bits in a GL_RGBA pixel format.
AGL_ALPHA_SIZE	The value following is the desired size of the number of alpha component bits in a GL_RGBA pixel format.
AGL_DEPTH_SIZE	The value following is the desired number of bits in the depth buffer.
AGL_STENCIL_SIZE	The value following is the desired number of bits in the stencil buffer.
AGL_ACCUM_RED_SIZE	The value following is the number of bits of the red component in the accumulation buffer.
AGL_ACCUM_GREEN_SIZE	The value following is the number of bits of the green component in the accumulation buffer.
AGL_ACCUM_BLUE_SIZE	The value following is the number of bits of the blue component in the accumulation buffer.
AGL_ACCUM_ALPHA_SIZE	The value following is the number of bits of the alpha component in the accumulation buffer.
AGL_PIXEL_SIZE	The value following is the total number of bits used to store a single pixel in the frame buffer.
AGL_MINIMUM_POLICY	This flag specifies never to select a pixel format containing buffers smaller than specified (for example, asking for a 16-bit depth buffer with AGL_DEPTH_SIZE).
AGL_MAXIMUM_POLICY	This flag specifies that the largest available buffer should be selected if a nonzero buffer size is requested (for example, you might get a 32-bit depth buffer, even though you only asked for 16 bits).
AGL_OFFSCREEN	Set to GL_TRUE to select only a renderer capable of rendering to an off-screen buffer.
AGL_FULLSCREEN	Set to GL_TRUE to request a pixel format that can be used to render to a full-screen device. This attribute requires a Gdevice pointer be used in aglChoosePixelformat.
AGL_SAMPLE_BUFFERS_ARB	The value following this attribute is the number of multisample buffers.
AGL_SAMPLES_ARB	The value following is the number of samples per multisample buffer.
AGL_AUX_DEPTH_STENCIL	The value following is the independent depth and/or stencil buffers for the auxiliary buffer.
AGL_COLOR_FLOAT	Set the value following this field to GL_TRUE to request a floating-point color buffer.
AGL_MULTISAMPLE	This value hints to the driver that you prefer multisampling.
AGL_SUPERSAMPLE	This value hints to the driver that you prefer supersampling.
AGL_SAMPLE_ALPHA	This attribute requests alpha filtering when multisampling.

20

The Rendering Context

After an appropriate pixel format is selected, it is used to create an OpenGL *rendering context*. The rendering context can be thought of as a handle to a live and running OpenGL state machine and renderer; it is the conduit through which your OpenGL commands reach the hardware. The AGLContext data type represents the AGL OpenGL rendering context:

```
static AGLContext    openGLContext = NULL;    // OpenGL rendering context
```

In our CARBONGL sample program, this is a module global variable in the main.cpp file. The setup after the selection of the pixel format continues:

```
// Create the context
openGLContext  = aglCreateContext(openGLFormat, NULL);
if(openGLContext == NULL)
    return false;      // Handle failure gracefully please!

// No longer needed
aglDestroyPixelFormat(openGLFormat);

// Point to window and make current
aglSetDrawable(openGLContext, GetWindowPort(windowRef));
aglSetCurrentContext(openGLContext);

// OpenGL is up...go load up geometry and stuff
SetupRC();
```

The aglCreateContext takes the pixel format as the first argument, and NULL as the second parameter. This second parameter may optionally be a preexisting rendering context that will share its object state (all display lists, texture objects, vertex buffers, etc.) with the new context. After the rendering context is created, the pixel format is no longer needed, and can be destroyed with aglDestroyPixelFormat.

Finally, we set the rendering context to point to our carbon window, and make it current:

```
// Point to window and make current
aglSetDrawable(openGLContext, GetWindowPort(windowRef));
aglSetCurrentContext(openGLContext);
```

The AGL interface allows for multiple OpenGL rendering contexts, each of which can be set to render to different windows. However, only one context may be current at any one time. All OpenGL commands on the current thread will render to whichever rendering context is currently current.

Now that OpenGL is alive and well, it is ready to accept commands. The `SetupRC` function is in `thundergl.cpp`, which has been borrowed from the THUNDERGL sample program in Chapter 11, "It's All About the Pipeline: Faster Geometry Throughput." If you recall, this function loads all the needed textures, and sets up the vertex buffer objects for the Thunderbird model.

Cleanup

Before we get to rendering, let's talk about cleanup while the startup is still fresh on your mind. When the window is being destroyed, we first want to call the `ShutdownRC` function in `thundergl.cpp` to free the texture objects and other data:

```
ShutdownRC();
```

Then we must set the current context to `NULL`, and set the context's drawable to `NULL`. Finally, we can destroy the context altogether:

```
// Unbind to context
aglSetCurrentContext (NULL);

// Remove drawable
aglSetDrawable (openGLContext, NULL);
aglDestroyContext (openGLContext);
```

The Big Event!

Now it's time for the big event, or perhaps *events* would be more appropriate. In the event handler for the CARBONGL sample program's main window, there are three events that pertain directly to our rendering needs. The first is received whenever the window changes size:

```
// Size of window has changed
case kEventWindowBoundsChanged:
    if(openGLContext)
    {
    aglUpdateContext(openGLContext);

    GetWindowPortBounds(window, &windowRect);
    ChangeSize(windowRect.right - windowRect.left,
                        windowRect.bottom - windowRect.top);
    InvalWindowRect(window, &windowRect);
    }
break;
```

In addition to calling ChangeSize (which, as you recall from THUNDERGL, simply resets the viewport and projection), you must also call aglUpdateContext anytime something about the window or screen changes. This includes size changes, and screen resolution mode changes. The call to the function InvalWindowRect ensures that the window gets redrawn whenever the window size changes. Drawing or redrawing (there is no real difference!) is handled by the following bit of code:

```
// Draw/Render contents
case kEventWindowDrawContent:
    {
    RenderScene();
    aglSwapBuffers(openGLContext);

    GetWindowPortBounds(window, &windowRect);
    InvalWindowRect(window, &windowRect);
    }
break;
```

The RenderScene function is again simply brought over from the GLUT-based THUNDERGL sample program. Since we have previously established a double-buffered context, we must issue a command to perform the buffer swap after rendering:

```
aglSwapBuffers(openGLContext);
```

The only argument to this function is the previously created OpenGL rendering context identifier. In order to facilitate the animated effect, the last thing the drawing handler does is request another draw event!

```
GetWindowPortBounds(window, &windowRect);
InvalWindowRect(window, &windowRect);
```

This provides a fairly high frame rate, rendering about as fast as is possible without hacking outside of the carbon event framework. One of the reasons we do this, really, is so that that we have something to show off in the next section! In the meantime, you can see the fruits of our labor in Figure 20.3.

FIGURE 20.3   The CARBONGL sample showing THUNDERGL ported from GLUT to native Carbon.

Bitmap Fonts

Another useful feature of the AGL framework is support for bitmap fonts in OpenGL. Essentially, the function `aglUseFont` will take an existing font and convert it into a series of display lists, each containing a `glBitmap` call (see Chapter 7, "Imaging with OpenGL") for a single character, followed by an advance of the raster position. Setting up a set of font bitmaps could not be much easier:

```
short fontID;
GetFNum((const unsigned char *)"/pTimes", &fontID);

fontStart = glGenLists(96);
aglUseFont(openGLContext, fontID, bold, 14, ' ', 96, fontStart);
```

Setting Up the Font

On OS X, fonts are identified by a unique short integer. The `GetFNum` takes the font face name, and returns this value. Before generating the font bitmap display lists, we call `glGenLists` to reserve a range of display list IDs (see Chapter 11) large enough to hold the range of characters we are interested in. The `aglUseFont` function is listed here for convenience:

20

```
GLboolean aglUseFont(AGLcontext ctx, GLint fontID, Style face,
                     GLint size, GLint first, GLint count, GLint base);
```

The first two parameters are the AGL OpenGL rendering context pointer, and the font identifier. The face parameter can be one of the typical font face styles: normal, bold, italic, underline, outline, shadow, condense, or extend. These face styles can also be logically or'd together (e.g., italic ¦ underline). These are followed by the point size of the font.

The last three parameters specify the first character to begin with (in our sample, we started with the space ' ', the number of characters to include in our font set (96 which is usually the majority of normally printable characters), and finally the display list ID to use as the starting point for our list of display lists.

Using the Font

In the CARBONGLFONTS sample program, we have reused our previous carbon framework, but have added a frame rate display. The frame rate is simply the average number of frames rendered per second, estimated by averaging the time to render 100 frames. This is done repeatedly, and a static string containing the information is displayed constantly. To begin, we make sure the current color is white, and set the raster position:

```
glColor3f(1.0f, 1.0f, 1.0f); // Just in case it gets changed
glWindowPos2f(10.0f, 10.0f);
```

Font rendering via this mechanism is based on display lists, so we must be careful when mixing these font bitmaps with any other code that uses display lists. First we must set the display list base to the beginning of our display list range, but subtract the first character's ASCII value.

```
glListBase(fontStart - ' ');
```

Then we use the glCallLists function to render an array of display list names. This array just happens to be the ASCII text of the string we want to display. Each character's ASCII numerical value is added to the list base value, and the resulting display list is executed:

```
glCallLists(strlen(cBuffer), GL_BYTE, cBuffer);
```

The result is a sequence of display lists being called, each of which displays a single letter from the string and advances the raster position for the next letter. The final result is seen in Figure 20.4, which shows a single frame of the animation along with the average frame rate of the last 100 frames displayed in the lower-left corner.

FPS: 412.1

FIGURE 20.4 The CARBONGLFONT sample with frame rate display.

OpenGL with Cocoa

There are many programming languages available to developers on Mac OS X. One very popular language on the Mac (but not quite so popular elsewhere) is Objective-C. To the uninitiated, Objective-C may appear as a strange blend of C and C++ with some completely new syntax thrown in. But Objective-C is also the foundation of a very popular application development technology called Cocoa.

Cocoa is best described as both a collection of application framework classes and a visual programming paradigm. Developers do quite a bit of work in Interface Builder, designing user interfaces, assigning properties, and even making connections between events. Objective-C classes are subclassed from controls, or are created from scratch to add application functionality. Fortunately, OpenGL is a first-class citizen in this development environment.

Creating a Cocoa Program

A Cocoa-based program can be created using the New Project Assistant in Xcode. Figure 20.1 shows how we did this when we created our first GLUT-based program. This time, however, we will not replace the generated project with GLUT-based code. Figure 20.5 shows our newly created COCOAGL project.

20

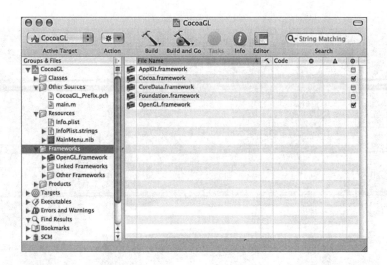

FIGURE 20.5   The initial COCOAGL project.

Adding an OpenGL View

Cocoa applications store resources and GUI layouts in a NIB file (which for historic reasons stands for NEXTSTEP Interface Builder). Double-click the `MainMenu.nib` file under the `Resources` folder. This will start Interface Builder and open the main nib for editing. You should see a screen similar to that shown in Figure 20.6, with the main window already open.

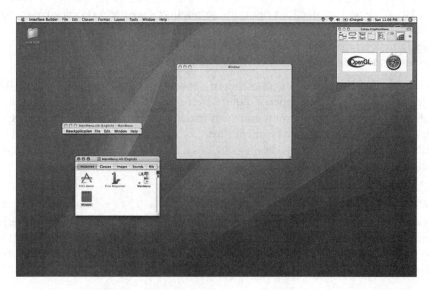

FIGURE 20.6   Interface Builder—ready to go!

If the tool palette does not already have the Cocoa-GraphicsView displayed, advance by clicking the far-right toolbar button. Click and drag an OpenGL view from the palette to the main window and resize it to fill most of the main window. Just to make the OpenGL view stand out, we have also changed the main window background to metallic (or textured, depending on the version of your tools). You can see in Figure 20.7 that we now have an NSOpenGLView ready to go in the center of the window.

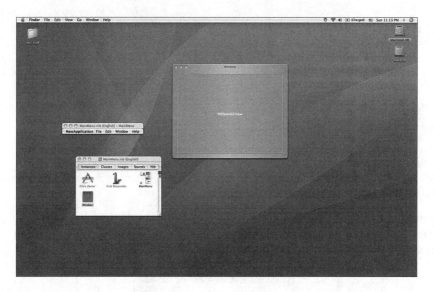

FIGURE 20.7 A very basic interface window.

Creating a Custom OpenGL Class

The next task is to create a custom class derived from NSOpenGLView and associate it with the OpenGL view in the window. Click the MainMenu.nib window and click the Classes button. In the search edit control type NSOpenGLView. Right-click on this class and select Subclass NSOpenGLView, as shown in Figure 20.8. For this sample program, we will again be reusing the Thunderbird demo, so call the new subclass ThunderGLView.

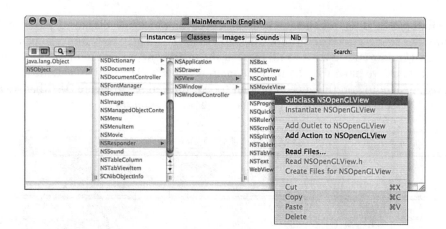

FIGURE 20.8   Subclassing the NSOpenGLView.

Right-click again, and select Create Files for ThunderGLView. Save both the
ThunderGLView.h and the ThunderGLView.m files. Finally, we must associate this new
class with the NSOpenGLView in the main window.

To do this, select the NSOpenGLView window and bring up the Inspector (Tools, Show
Inspector on the main menu). Change the combo box on the inspector to Custom Class
and highlight the ThunderGLView class, as shown in Figure 20.9.

FIGURE 20.9   Assigning the custom class to the NSOpenGLView.

Now save the interface file and close Interface Builder. Time to write some code!

Wiring It All Together

Back in the Xcode project window, you'll see the ThunderGLView header and implementation files. These contain the stubbed definition of the `ThunderGLView` class, derived from NSOpenGLView. Interface builder has already wired this class to our OpenGL view in the main window, and we now only need to add the class framework and OpenGL rendering code.

The edited header file for the new class is trivial and simply contains a member pointer to an `NSTimer` that will be used for animation:

```
#import <Cocoa/Cocoa.h>

@interface ThunderGLView : NSOpenGLView
{
    NSTimer *pTimer;
}
@end
```

In the implementation file, we add an idle function, and again the same four top-level rendering tasks wired into the Cocoa framework that every other sample in this book has needed: initialization, shutdown, render a frame, and handle window size changes. The entire source to `ThunderGLView.m` is given in Listing 20.2.

LISTING 20.2   Implementation of the `ThunderGLView` Class

```
#import "ThunderGLView.h"
#include <OpenGL/gl.h>

// Functions in ThunderGL.cpp
void SetupRC(void);
void ShutdownRC(void);
void RenderScene(void);
void ChangeSize(int w, int h);

@implementation ThunderGLView

- (void)idle:(NSTimer *)pTimer
    {
    [self drawRect:[self bounds]];
    }

// Do setup
 - (void) prepareOpenGL
    {
    SetupRC();
```

20

LISTING 20.2   Continued

```
pTimer = [NSTimer timerWithTimeInterval:(0.0) target:self
        selector:@selector(idle:) userInfo:nil repeats:YES];
[[NSRunLoop currentRunLoop]addTimer:pTimer forMode:NSDefaultRunLoopMode];
}

// Do cleanup
- (void) clearGLContext
    {
    ShutdownRC();
    }

// Changed size
- (void)reshape
    {
    NSRect rect = [self bounds];
    ChangeSize(rect.size.width, rect.size.height);
    }

// Paint
-(void) drawRect: (NSRect) bounds
    {
    RenderScene();

    glFlush(); // All done!
    }
@end
```

Note that we had to declare the following functions, which are in the original
ThunderGL.cpp file:

```
// Functions in ThunderGL.cpp
void SetupRC(void);
void ShutdownRC(void);
void RenderScene(void);
void ChangeSize(int w, int h);
```

Fortunately, it is possible to call C and C++ code from Objective-C. There are a few caveats
to doing this, but the least troublesome to follow through on is to keep your C/C++ source
code separate from your Objective-C source code by placing them in different source files,
and provide a C-only API between code modules. It is possible to share C++ classes
between the two languages as well, but many developers find this more trouble than it's

worth. Consequently, we will need to declare the preceding four functions in thundergl.cpp as having the "C" calling convention.

This is simple to do; we just place the following declarations near the top of thundergl.cpp:

```
extern "C" {
void SetupRC(void);
void ShutdownRC(void);
void RenderScene(void);
void ChangeSize(int w, int h);
}
```

Figure 20.10 shows our completed Cocoa based project.

FIGURE 20.10 OpenGL in a Cocoa view.

Hang on a Second There!

At this point in time, the astute reader may be imagining the sound of screeching tires on pavement. Was that a glFlush you saw after RenderScene in Listing 20.2 instead of some sort of buffer swap call? Indeed it was, and this brings us to an interesting subtlety of OpenGL on Mac OS X (as well as a nice segue into the next section).

20

On Mac OS X, the entire desktop is actually OpenGL accelerated. Anytime you are rendering with OpenGL, you are always rendering to an offscreen buffer. A buffer swap does nothing but signal the OS that your rendering is ready to be composited with the rest of the desktop. You can think of the desktop compositing engine as your front buffer. Thus, in windowed OpenGL applications (this applies to both Cocoa and Carbon), *all* OpenGL windows are *really* single buffered. Depending on how you look at it, it would also be okay to say that *all* OpenGL windows are *really* double buffered, with the desktop composite being the front buffer. Pick whichever one helps you sleep best at night! In fact, if you were to execute a `glDrawBuffer(GL_FRONT)`, the drivers on the Mac actually would fall into a triple-buffered mode! In reality, all OpenGL windows on the Mac should be treated as single buffered. The buffer swap calls are really just doing a glFlush, unless you are working with a full screen context. For this (and many others—the least of which is that you are bypassing the driver's own good sense as to when to flush) you should avoid `glFlush` in Cocoa views until you have completed all of your OpenGL rendering.

Full-Screen Rendering

Many OpenGL applications will need to render to the entire screen, rather than live within the confines of a window. This would include many games, media players, Kiosk hosted applications, and other specialized types of applications. One way to accomplish this is to simply make a large window that is the size of the entire display. This, however, is not the most optimal approach.

In the previous section, we discussed the fact that OpenGL windows are copied and composited into the Mac OS X desktop at either the buffer swap or a call to glFlush or glFinish. This operation can result in a large amount of memory being moved and operated on. All of the OpenGL interface technologies listed in Table 20.1 have support for full-screen rendering. In full-screen mode, the application completely takes over the screen and no other windows can be displayed until the application releases the screen. Rendering occurs in the back buffer, and a buffer swap occurs to display the next frame. Full-screen rendering can be significantly faster than windowed rendering as long as your performance is not already geometry or CPU bound.

Managing the Display

A handful of the Quartz Display Services functions come in handy when we're performing full-screen rendering. We may want to change the display mode, for example; and if not, we still will need a way to determine the screen resolution for our perspective projection computations. We cannot rely on window bounds changes because when we're rendering to a full-screen context, there actually is no window!

For simplicity, we are going to ignore the complex issue of multiple monitors and display devices, and restrict our interests to the main display (the one with the menu bar). We must first get a display ID that uniquely identifies a particular display. To get the main display, this is one simple function call:

```
CGDirectDisplayID gCGDisplayID = CGMainDisplayID();
```

The display ID can now be used to query the display services and determine what resolution the display is currently operating at:

```
int nScreenWidth = CGDisplayPixelsWide(gCGDisplayID);
int nScreenHeight = CGDisplayPixelsHigh(gCGDisplayID);
```

If you are content to run full-screen at the default resolution, you can stop there. Each display mode has again a unique reference. You can search for the best matching display mode with this function:

```
CFDictionaryRef refDisplayMode =
          CGDisplayBestModeForParameters(
          gCGDisplayID, 32, nWidth, nHeight, NULL);
```

Here we set nWidth and nHeight to the desired screen resolution. As long as refDisplayMode doesn't come back as zero, you have a valid identifier for the requested display mode. Note, you may not get exactly what you want with this function. For example, if you request a screen resolution of 725×590, you are likely to just get 800×600 since that is the nearest valid display mode.

With a valid display mode in hand, we can change the display mode with a single function call. However, before you do that, you should *capture* the display:

```
CGDisplayCapture(gCGDisplayID);
```

Capturing the display tells the operating system that your application is in charge of the display. If you do not call this when you change the display mode, all other running applications will receive display change notifications, and will likely resize their windows appropriately. This often leaves a mess on your desktop when your application terminates. To release the display when your program terminates, call this:

```
CGReleaseAllDisplays();
```

Now that you know how to behave yourself when changing display modes, you can do so:

```
CGDisplaySwitchToMode(gCGDisplayID, refDisplayMode);
```

When your application terminates, the display mode will automatically be restored. This is a nice feature, in case your program does happen to crash; it's just not polite to leave behind a mess on the desktop.

20

AGL Full-Screen Support

With the display mode querying and changing out of the way, it's time to get back to creating our OpenGL context. Since our last AGL-based program contained a frame rate display, we will go the AGL route for creating a full-screen rendering context. You will easily be able to see for yourself the difference in frame rate between a maximized window and a real full-screen context.

Retrofitting the previous CARBONGL sample program to the new FULLSCREEN sample program is fairly straightforward. Start by adding a few new variables at the top to hold the screen width and height, and a flag for whether we want the display mode changed:

```
static AGLContext      openGLContext = NULL;    // OpenGL rendering context
static int             nScreenWidth = 800;      // Set these to what you "want"
static int             nScreenHeight = 600;

// Set to false to ignore above and keep current resolution.
static bool            bChangeDisplayMode = false;
```

If the bChangeDisplayMode flag is left false, the values of nScreenWidth and nScreenHeight are reset to the current display's resolution. Aside from removing the kEventWindowBoundsChanged handler, all the changes are in the SetupGL function, shown in Listing 20.3.

LISTING 20.3   The New AGL-Based Setup for Full-Screen Rendering

```
bool SetupGL(void)
    {
    static AGLPixelFormat    openGLFormat = NULL;       // OpenGL pixel format

    static GLint glAttributes[] = {
                    AGL_FULLSCREEN,                  // Full-Screen
                    AGL_NO_RECOVERY,
                    // Uncomment to get FSAA
    //              AGL_SAMPLE_BUFFERS_ARB, 1,  // (only one supported)
    //              AGL_SAMPLES_ARB,  4,        // Number of samples at a point
                    AGL_DOUBLEBUFFER, GL_TRUE,  // Double buffered
                    AGL_RGBA,         GL_TRUE,  // Four-component color
                    AGL_DEPTH_SIZE,   16,       // 16-bit (min) depth buffer
                    AGL_NONE };                 // Terminator

    // Get the main display and capture it.
    CGDirectDisplayID gCGDisplayID = CGMainDisplayID();
    CGDisplayCapture(gCGDisplayID);
```

LISTING 20.3   Continued

```
// Change display mode if necessary
if(bChangeDisplayMode)
    {
    CFDictionaryRef refDisplayMode =
        CGDisplayBestModeForParameters(
        gCGDisplayID, 32, nScreenWidth, nScreenHeight, NULL);

        // Screen will revert when this program ends
        CGDisplaySwitchToMode(gCGDisplayID, refDisplayMode);
    }

// Get the screen resolution (even if we have changed it)
nScreenWidth = CGDisplayPixelsWide(gCGDisplayID);
nScreenHeight = CGDisplayPixelsHigh(gCGDisplayID);

// Initialize OpenGL
// Choose pixelformat based on attribute list, and the main display device
GDHandle gdevice = GetMainDevice();
openGLFormat  = aglChoosePixelFormat(&gdevice, 1, glAttributes);
if(openGLFormat == NULL)
    return false;

// Create the context
openGLContext  = aglCreateContext(openGLFormat, NULL);
if(openGLContext == NULL)
    return false;

// Don't need this anymore
aglDestroyPixelFormat(openGLFormat);

// Tell AGL to go full-screen
aglEnable(openGLContext, AGL_FS_CAPTURE_SINGLE);
aglSetFullScreen(openGLContext, 0, 0, 0, 0);
aglSetCurrentContext(openGLContext);

// OpenGL is up...go load up geometry and stuff
SetupRC();

// Reset projection
ChangeSize(nScreenWidth, nScreenHeight);
```

20

LISTING 20.3   Continued

```
    // Set up the font
    fontStart = glGenLists(96);
    short fontID;
    GetFNum((const unsigned char *)"/pTimes", &fontID);
    aglUseFont(openGLContext, fontID,  bold, 14, ' ', 96, fontStart);

    glListBase(fontStart - ' ');

    HideCursor();   // Hide the cursor (personal preference)

    return true;
    }
```

AGL Changes

The glAttributes list contains a few new tokens. The AGL_FULLSCREEN token requests a full-screen pixel format, and the AGL_NO_RECOVERY says we are uninterested in a software fallback that does not support full-screen.

At lower resolutions, aliasing artifacts are especially noticeable, so this seems a good place to show off multisampling as well. Uncomment the two lines containing AGL_SAMPLE_BUFFERS_ARB and AGL_SAMPLES_ARB to request a multisampling pixel format. You will also notice that frame rates are noticeably smaller when this is enabled.

Also, different in this version is the call to aglChoosePixelFormat. Here you see that the AGLDevice parameter cannot be NULL for full-screen contexts, but must contain an array of devices. For our purposes, we pass in only the main display device ID:

```
GDHandle gdevice = GetMainDevice();
openGLFormat   = aglChoosePixelFormat(&gdevice, 1, glAttributes);
```

Finally, we tell AGL that we want to go full-screen.

```
aglEnable(openGLContext, AGL_FS_CAPTURE_SINGLE);
aglSetFullScreen(openGLContext, 0, 0, 0, 0);
```

The first line tells AGL to "capture" the screen when it goes full-screen, and the second line makes the change to full-screen mode. After this, all OpenGL rendering goes to the full-screen context, and any application windows you or any other application have open will not be visible.

These two lines of code can actually be used to capture the screen and change the display mode (by filling in some of those zeros). However, if you specify an invalid display resolution, the display mode will not change. The previous approach using `CGDisplayBestModeForParameters` is better since it is more likely to "guess" a valid display mode based on your request.

Final Touches

Finally, our last OpenGL-related modification is to call the `ChangeSize` function with the (potentially) new screen width and height:

```
ChangeSize(nScreenWidth, nScreenHeight);
```

Also, for games and many full-screen applications, the mouse cursor is an unnecessary distraction. You can turn that off easily:

```
HideCursor();
```

Turning it back on is equally obvious:

```
ShowCursor();
```

Summary

We have taken a whirlwind tour of the most important OpenGL technologies available on Mac OS X. We started with GLUT, which is the toolkit we used for most of this book's sample programs. You now even know how to start your own GLUT-based masterpiece from scratch with Xcode. We followed that up with coverage for the more experienced Mac programmers using either Carbon or the Cocoa application frameworks. We finished with an example of full-screen rendering, and explained why it was inherently faster than rendering in any window would be.

OpenGL is a core foundational technology for the Macintosh. A basic understanding of OpenGL, and how applications can natively interact with it, is an essential skill for any Mac OS X developer. This chapter only scratched the surface of a potentially deep and complex topic. We have purposely stayed in the shallow end of the pool, as it were, so that you can get going quickly and experiment as much as possible with OpenGL on this wonderful platform. In Appendix A, "Further Reading/References," you'll find some additional great coverage of this exciting topic.

20

CHAPTER 21

OpenGL on Linux

by Nicholas Haemel

WHAT YOU'LL LEARN IN THIS CHAPTER:

How To	Functions You'll Use
Manage visuals	glXChooseVisual/glXChooseFBConfig
Create GLX windows	glXCreateWindow
Manage OpenGL drawing contexts	glXCreateContext/glXDestroyContext/glXMakeCurrent
Create OpenGL windows	glXCreateWindow
Do double-buffered drawing	glXSwapBuffers
Create bitmap text fonts	glXUseXFont

Now that you have had a chance to learn how to use OpenGL on Windows and Mac OS, it's time for Linux to get some attention! Just like other platforms, Linux supports 3D rendering through the OpenGL API.

In this chapter we will take a look at how Linux supports OpenGL, what interfaces are available for developers, and how to set up an application. We will also hit GLUT, context management, and how to allocate, render to, and deal with windows on X Windows.

The Basics

OpenGL has long been supported on various versions of Linux, Unix, and so on. On Unix, native hardware support has often been built into the box. For Linux, Mesa3D comes installed with most X Server configurations. Also, most 3D hardware vendors provide some form of 3D acceleration for Linux, usually with proprietary closed-source drivers.

Before there was OpenGL, there was IRIS GL. This was a standard released by SGI. Next came the public interface for 3D graphics, OpenGL. Brian Paul started a project to implement support for OpenGL, called Mesa. At the time there were very few functional implementations. SGI, the founders of OpenGL, had very few computers available that supported OpenGL. In 1995, the first release of Mesa opened the door to wider support that was not tied to a hardware vendor. Because Mesa was a hardware independent software implementation, it was slower than most native implementations.

More recently hardware vendors have provided OpenGL support through both open- and closed-source drivers. Currently, both ATI and NVIDIA provide OpenGL drivers supporting at least OpenGL 2.0. The most recent version of Mesa supports OpenGL 1.5.

The X Window System is a graphical user interface that provides a more pleasing environment for users than a command prompt. This is similar to the interfaces for Microsoft Windows and Mac OS. X Windows are not limited to running only on the system they reside on. For instance, if you are away from your computer, you can connect to your X Server from a different computer as if you were sitting in your own desk chair.

Many different X Window environments or window desktop managers are available, such as KDE and Gnome. Each has a unique look and feel. These environments run on top of a core server. For Linux this is usually XFree86, an open-source implementation of an X Server. We will be running our OpenGL applications inside X Windows on Linux, taking advantage of XFree86

Setup

Let's take a quick look at making sure OpenGL is supported on your system. Without that, the rest of this chapter is pretty meaningless. Try running the `glxinfo` command as shown here:

```
glxinfo |grep rendering
```

You should get one of two responses:

```
direct rendering: Yes
direct rendering: No
```

If the answer is yes, good news! You have hardware support for 3D rendering. If no, you may not have hardware that supports OpenGL, or you may not have drivers installed for OpenGL. If hardware support is not available, try running the following:

```
glxinfo |grep "OpenGL vendor"
glxinfo |grep "OpenGL version"
```

This will print out the currently installed OpenGL driver information. Remember to be careful about capitalization! If you do not have hardware drivers but do have Mesa installed, the information for the Mesa driver will be displayed. You will also get the current version of OpenGL that your Mesa implementation supports.

If the `glxinfo` command fails, or no vendor/version information is available, your distro is not set up for rendering with OpenGL. You have some options. You can install Mesa, or you can procure a video card that does support OpenGL rendering on Linux.

Setting Up Mesa

The latest version of Mesa can be downloaded from the Mesa 3D Web site; http://www.mesa3d.org. From there you can get the download link for SourceForge. Once it's downloaded, unpack the files (example shown for Mesa 6.5.2):

```
gunzip MesaLib-6.5.2.tar.gz
tar xf MesaLib-6.5.2.tar
```

Next, you will need to compile the source that you have just unpacked. Go to the directory that was just created from the tar package and run the following:

```
make linux-x86
```

This will take a little while, but will build the Mesa package for your system. After it has finished, a bunch of libraries will have been created. Now you will need to install the libraries and headers to allow the OS to find them when necessary. Installs typically touch files that are locked for administrator modification only. Before running the install, you might want to switch to the root account by using the *su* command. To do the install, run the following command:

```
make install
```

These are usually located in the following directories:

```
Libraries: usr/X11R6/lib
Includes: usr/include/
```

You have finished the Mesa install. If you have more questions about the Mesa setup or install, visit the Mesa 3D Web site.

Setting Up Hardware Drivers

Hardware support for OpenGL is a little different to set up than Mesa. Each vendor has its own process. ATI and NVIDIA provide proprietary driver packages that can be downloaded. The install process is usually very simple, just a matter of running the downloaded package.

Some hardware vendors may also provide an open-source version of their display drivers. Although it is nice to have the source for the driver build, these drivers are often slower and have fewer features than their proprietary counterparts. This is usually because of the trade secrets included in proprietary versions. Also the hardware interfaces for proprietary drivers may use a less generic and more optimized path.

More Setup Details

For those who want to dig a little deeper into OpenGL setup, you can look into your X Server configuration. Your config file can be found in /etc/X11. This file is used to set the parameters of the X Server. The "Module" section specifies which modules will be loaded with your X Server. Here, there may be load lines (as shown below) for DRI (Direct Rendering Infrastructure), OpenGL, and GLX.

```
Load "glx"
Load "dri"
Load "GLcore"
```

Be careful in this file. Changes here can result in your X Server no longer loading.

Setting Up GLUT

GLUT may not be already installed on your system. If that's the case, it can be downloaded from the OpenGL SuperBible Web site, http://www.opengl.org/superbible. Copy the glut download to your system. Then go to the GLUT directory and perform the following commands:

```
./mkmkfiles.imake
make
make install
```

The first command makes the makefiles you will use to compile the code. This is done because different resources may be located in different places on individual systems. The second command actually compiles the code. And the third installs the result. One note: Make sure you have the correct permissions for the directory and all subcomponents, or running mkmkfiles will fail. You will also need to assume root privileges.

To use GLUT in your applications, you will need to add the GLUT library to your link command in your makefiles:

```
-lglut
```

Mesa 3D also supplies a version of GLUT that can be downloaded and installed.

Building OpenGL Apps

Now that we've gone through all that setup and our system is prepped for running and compiling OpenGL programs, let's take a look at how to build these programs. If you have spent time working with Linux, you are probably already familiar with creating makefiles. If so, skip ahead.

Makefiles are used on Linux systems to compile and link source code, creating an executable file. They hold the instructions for the compiler and linker, telling them where to find files and what to do with them. A sample makefile is shown below. It can be modified and expanded to accommodate your own projects.

```
LIBDIRS = -L/usr/X11R6/lib -L/usr/X11R6/lib64 -L/usr/local/lib
INCDIRS = -I/usr/include -L/usr/local/include -L/usr/X11R6/include
    COMPILERFLAGS = -Wall

CC = gcc
CFLAGS = $(COMPILERFLAGS) -g $(INCDIRS)
LIBS = -lX11 -lXi -lXmu -lglut -lGL -lGLU -lm

example : example.o
    $(CC) $(CFLAGS) -o example $(LIBDIRS) example.c $(LIBS)
clean:
    rm -f *.o
```

The first line creates a variable that contains the link parameters for libraries to be included. The one used here will look in the standard lib directory for X11 and the location for 64-bit specific libraries.

The second line lists the include paths the compiler should use when trying to find header files. The next line specifies the compile flags to use with this instance. Then LIBS = selects all the libraries that need to be linked into our program.

Finally we compile and link the single source file for the example, called example.c. The last line cleans up intermediate objects that were created during the process. This example can be used while substituting your file in the script. Other files can also be compiled together as well. There are many good resources and tutorials on the Web for more information on makefiles.

GLUT

GLUT has been covered earlier in this book. It is basically a very useful set of functions that help make interfacing with OpenGL and the system much more user friendly, taking care of many of the unsightly details. OpenGL code written with GLUT is also platform agnostic, making the code very portable.

GLUT is available for download and installation on Linux. This helps make any applications that use GLUT very portable since the code can be compiled on Windows, Mac, and Linux. It is also a good way to get applications up and running quickly, since no window management is required. GLUT will be used for the first sample app in this chapter.

On the other hand, GLUT does not allow for very direct interface with the X Server. This means that some things that can be done by directly communicating with the OS or X are more difficult or impossible when using GLUT. That said, GLUT will be used for the first sample program so that we can concentrate on other functionality. You will have to decide what level of control you will need in determining whether GLUT will suffice or if you should directly use GLX.

GLX—Dealing with the X Windows Interface

On X Windows an interface is provided to allow applications to connect OpenGL with X Windows, very similar to WGL on Microsoft Windows and AGL on Mac. There are many different versions of GLX. Version 1.4 is the most recent version but is very similar to GLX version 1.3. GLX 1.2 is currently the most commonly supported version on most Linux distributions. GLX is a much more direct interface that will allow for greater control over your applications system interface. Using GLX will enable you to tweak all the window and surface properties available in X Windows/GLX. Although GLUT can make it easy to get an application running quickly, it does not allow for the options available with a direct interface. In this section we will go through what GLX can do and how to use it. We will focus mainly on version 1.3 and point out what is different between versions 1.2 and 1.3.

To find more information about your installation of GLX, you can use the `glxinfo` command again. Try the following:

```
glxinfo ¦grep "glx vendor"
glxinfo ¦grep "glx version"
```

This will display the GLX information for both server and client components of X Windows. The effective version you can use is the older of the server and client versions. So if your client reports `1.3` and your server reports `1.2`, you are essentially using version `1.2`. This means you can't pick and choose which version of GLX you want to work with. Instead, your code needs to be able to support the versions of GLX it is likely to encounter.

Displays and X

Now that we have covered how to examine your system, getting it ready for OpenGL execution and development, it's time to look at actual code. The next sections examine code constructs used to interface with X Windows and GLX. Before we get too far into GLX, there are a few prerequisites. Remember that X Windows supports client and server components running on separate systems, essentially allowing you to run your desktop from somewhere else. Before we can create a window, we need to find out what display the application will be executing on. The display will help the X Server understand where we are rendering. Use the `XOpenDisplay()` function to get the current display.

```
Display *dpy = XOpenDisplay(getenv("DISPLAY"));
```

This will give us a display pointer for the default display we can use later to tell the X Server where we are. After our application is done, it also needs to close the display using the `XCloseDisplay()` function. This tells the X Server that we are finished and it can close the connection:

```
XCloseDisplay(Display * display);
```

Config Management and Visuals

GLX 1.3+

Configs on Linux are very similar to configs on OpenGL ES or pixel formats on Microsoft Windows. Configs can be a little difficult to handle since there are so many factors all tied together. For starters, you can use the glXGetFBConfigs interface to get information on all the configs supported:

```
GLXFBConfig *glXGetFBConfigs(Display * dpy, int screen, int *nelements);
```

Use the display handle that you got from calling XOpenDisplay. For our purposes we can use the default screen for the screen parameter. When the call returns, nelements will tell you how many configs were returned.

There's more to each config than its index. Each config has a unique set of attributes that represent the functionality of that config. These attributes and a description of what they do are listed in Table 21.1.

TABLE 21.1   GLX Config Attribute List

Attribute	Description
GLX_BUFFER SIZE	Total number of bits of color buffer.
GLX_RED_SIZE	Number of bits in red channel of color buffer.
GLX_GREEN_SIZE	Number of bits in green channel of color buffer.
GLX_BLUE_SIZE	Number of bits in blue channel of color buffer.
GLX_ALPHA_SIZE	Number of bits in alpha channel of color buffer.
GLX_DEPTH_SIZE	Number of bits per pixel in depth buffer.
GLX_STENCIL_SIZE	Number of bits per pixel in stencil buffer.
GLX_CONFIG_CAVEAT	Set to one of the following caveats: GLX_NONE, GLX_SLOW_CONFIG, or GLX_NON_CONFORMANT_CONFIG. These can warn of potential issues for this config. A slow config may be software emulated because it exceeds HW limits. A nonconformant config will not pass the conformance test.
GLX_X_RENDERABLE	Is set to GLX_TRUE if the X Server can render to this surface.
GLX_VISUAL_ID	The XID of the related visual.
GLX_X_VISUAL_TYPE	Type of an X visual if config supports window rendering (associated visual exists).
GLX_DRAWABLE_TYPE	Valid surface targets supported. May be any or all of GLX_WINDOW_BIT, GLX_PIXMAP_BIT, or GLX_PBUFFER_BIT.
GLX_RENDER_TYPE	Bitfield indicating the types of contexts that can be bound. May be GLX_RGBA_BIT or GLX_COLOR_INDEX_BIT.
GLX_FBCONFIG_ID	The XID for the GLXFBConfig.
GLX_LEVEL	The frame buffer level.
GLX_DOUBLEBUFFER	Is GLX_TRUE if color buffers are double buffered.

21

TABLE 21.1   Continued

Attribute	Description
GLX_STEREO	Is GLX_TRUE if color buffers support stereo rendering.
GLX_SAMPLE_BUFFERS	Number of multisample buffers. Must be 0 or 1.
GLX_SAMPLES	Number of samples per pixel for multisample buffers. Will be 0 if GLX_SAMPLE_BUFFERS is 0.
GLX_TRANSPARENT_TYPE	Indicates support of transparency. Value may be GLX_NONE, GLX_TRANSPARENT_RGB, or GLX_TRANSPARENT_INDEX. If transparency is supported, a transparent pixel is drawn when the pixel's components are all equal to the respective transparent RGB values.
GLX_TRANSPARENT_RED_VALUE	Red value a framebuffer pixel must have to be transparent.
GLX_TRANSPARENT_GREEN_VALUE	Green value a framebuffer pixel must have to be transparent.
GLX_TRANSPARENT_BLUE_VALUE	Blue value a framebuffer pixel must have to be transparent.
GLX_TRANSPARENT_ALPHA_VALUE	Alpha value a framebuffer pixel must have to be transparent.
GLX_TRANSPARENT_INDEX_VALUE	Index value a framebuffer pixel must have to be transparent. For color index configs only.
GLX_MAX_PBUFFER_WIDTH	Maximum width that can be used to create a pBuffer.
GLX_MAX_PBUFFER_HEIGHT	Maximum height that can be used to create a pBuffer.
GLX_MIN_PBUFFER_PIXELS	Largest total size of a pBuffer, in pixels.
GLX_AUX_BUFFERS	Number of supported auxiliary buffers.
GLX_ACCUM_RED_SIZE	Number of bits in red channel of the auxiliary buffer.
GLX_ACCUM_GREEN_SIZE	Number of bits in green channel of the auxiliary buffer.
GLX_ACCUM_BLUE_SIZE	Number of bits in blue channel of the auxiliary buffer.
GLX_ACCUM_ALPHA_SIZE	Number of bits in alpha channel of the auxiliary buffer.

Each of these attributes can be queried for a given format by using the glXGetFBConfigAttrib command:

```
Glint glXGetFBConfigAttrib(Display * dpy, GLXFBConfig config,
    int attribute, int *value);
```

Set the config parameter to the config number you are interested in querying and the attribute parameter to the attribute you are interested in. The result will be returned in the value parameter. If the glXGetFBConfigAttrib call fails, it may return the error GLX_BAD_ATTRIBUTE if the attribute you are requesting doesn't exist.

GLX also provides a method for getting a subset of the full config selection that meet a set of criteria. This can help narrow down the total set of configs to just those you care about, making it much easier to find a config that will work for your application. For instance, if you have an application that wants to render in a window, the config you select needs to support rendering to a window:

```
GLXFBConfig *glXChooseFBConfig(Display * dpy, int screen,
    const int *attrib_list, int *nelements);
```

Pass in the screen you are interested in. Also specify the elements that are required for a config match. This is done with a NULL-terminated list of parameter and value pairs. These attributes are the same config attributes that are listed in Table 21.1.

```
attrib_list = {attribute1, attribute_value1,
               attribute2, attribute_value2,
               attribute3, attribute_value3,
               0};
```

Similar to `glXGetFBConfigs`, the number of elements that matched the attribute list is returned in `nelements`. A pointer to a list of matching configs is returned by the function. Remember to use XFree to clean up the memory that was returned by the `glXChooseFBConfig` call. All configs returned will match the minimum criteria you set in the attrib list.

There are a few key attributes you may want to pay attention to when creating a config—for example,`GLX_X_RENDERABLE` should be `GLX_TRUE` so that you can use OpenGL to render; `GLX_DRAWABLE_TYPE` needs to include `GLX_WINDOW_BIT` if you are rendering to a window; `GLX_RENDER_TYPE` should be `GLX_RGBA_BIT`; and `GLX_CONFIG_CAVEAT` should be set to `GLX_NONE` or at the very least should not have the `GLX_SLOW_CONFIG` bit set. After that you may also want to make sure that the color, depth, and stencil channels meet your minimum requirements. The pBuffer, accumulation, and transparency values are less commonly used.

For attributes you don't specify, the `glXChooseFBConfigs` command will use the defaults. These are listed in the GLX specification. The sort mechanism orders the configs using relative attribute priorities. The order for the highest priority attributes is `GLX_CONFIG_CAVEAT`, the color buffer bit depths, `GLX_BUFFER_SIZE`, and then `GLX_DOUBLE-BUFFER`.

If a config has the `GLX_WINDOW_BIT` set for the `GLX_DRAWABLE_TYPE` attribute, the config will have an associated X visual. The visual can be queried using the following command:

```
XVisualInfo *glXGetVisualFromFBConfig(Display * dpy, GLXFBConfig config);
```

NULL will be returned if there isn't an associated X visual. Don't forget to free the returned memory with XFree.

PBuffers will not be discussed since they are being phased out. They are difficult to implement, difficult to use, and often much slower than normal rendering. Pixmaps fall into the same category. Instead, frame buffer objects replace this functionality. Also, color index mode is not covered here. It also is generally deprecated and not supported on most PC-based implementations.

GLX 1.2

With older versions of GLX, none of the preceding config interfaces is available. Instead of finding a config and then getting the corresponding visual, you can just search for a visual directly:

```
XVisualInfo *glXChooseVisual (Display * dpy, GLXFBConfig config);
```

Pass in the screen you will use for your window and a list of visual attributes. The possible attributes are listed in Table 21.2. Some attribute tokens can simply be added to the list, but most must be paired with a corresponding value, just as is done for glXChooseFBConfig in GLX 1.3. These attributes are noted in their descriptions.

TABLE 21.2   Visual Attribute List

Attribute	Description
GLX_USE_GL	Ignored since only GL visuals are searched.
GLX_BUFFER SIZE	Total depth in bits of the color buffer. Follow with integer indicating minimum size.
GLX_RGBA	Requires visual to support TrueColor and DirectColor. This means colors will be stored in separate red, green, blue, and alpha channels.
GLX_RED_SIZE	Number of bits in red channel of color buffer. Follow with integer indicating minimum size.
GLX_GREEN_SIZE	Number of bits in green channel of color buffer. Follow with integer indicating minimum size.
GLX_BLUE_SIZE	Number of bits in blue channel of color buffer. Follow with integer indicating minimum size.
GLX_ALPHA_SIZE	Number of bits in alpha channel of color buffer. Follow with integer indicating minimum size.
GLX_DEPTH_SIZE	Number of bits in depth buffer. Follow with integer indicating minimum size.
GLX_STENCIL_SIZE	Number of bits in stencil buffer. Follow with integer indicating minimum size.
GLX_DOUBLEBUFFER	Requires matching visual to be double buffered.
GLX_STEREO	Requires matching visual to support stereo rendering.
GLX_AUX_BUFFERS	The number of supported auxiliary buffers. Follow with integer indicating minimum number of aux buffers.
GLX_ACCUM_RED_SIZE	Number of bits in red channel of the accumulation buffer. Follow with integer indicating minimum size.
GLX_ACCUM_GREEN_SIZE	Number of bits in green channel of the accumulation buffer. Follow with integer indicating minimum size.
GLX_ACCUM_BLUE_SIZE	Number of bits in blue channel of the accumulation buffer. Follow with integer indicating minimum size.
GLX_ACCUM_ALPHA_SIZE	Number of bits in alpha channel of the accumulation buffer. Follow with integer indicating minimum size.
GLX_LEVEL	The frame buffer level. Followed by an integer indicating the exact level.

The last item in the list of visual attributes must be NULL. If no matching visuals are found, NULL is returned. Returned visuals will need to be freed with XFree.

GLX 1.2 also provides a method for querying attributes of a visual. `glXGetConfig` will take a visual and one of the attributes listed in Table 21.2, providing the result:

```
int glXGetConfig(Display * dpy, XVisualInfo *visual, int attribute, int *value);
```

Windows and Render Surfaces

Alright, now that we got through the messy stuff, let's create a window. X provides an interface to create windows, `XCreateWindow`. This returns a handle for the new X window. The command needs a parent window at creation time; you can also use the main X window for this. You should already be familiar with the display parameter here. Also, you need to tell X how big to make the window and where to put it with the x,y position and width/height parameters.

```
Window XCreateWindow(Display * dpy, Window parent, int x, int y, unsigned int width,
    unsigned int height, unsigned int border_width, int depth, unsigned int class,
    Visual *visual, unsigned_long valuemask, XSetWindowAttributes *attributes);
```

Also tell X what kind of a window you want with the `window` class. This can be one of three values: `InputOnly`, `InputOutput`, or `CopyFromParent`. `CopyFromParent` will use the value that the parent window was created with. The `attributes` and `valuemask` fields let you tell X what types of characteristics the window should have. The `attributes` field holds the values and the `valuemask` tells X which values it should pay attention to. To get more information on attributes, check out X Server documentation.

GLX 1.3+

After the X window has been created and you are on a system supporting GLX 1.3, you can create the GLX window association. The GLX call must be made with a config that is compatible with the visual used when calling `XCreateWindow`. `glXGetVisualFromFBConfig` is helpful for that. Use the `glXCreateWindow` command to create a new onscreen OpenGL rendering area that will be associated with the specified X window:

```
GLXWindow glXCreateWindow(Display * dpy, GLXFBConfig config, Window win,
                const int *attrib_list);
```

You can use the config as returned from the work in the preceding section. The `attrib_list` currently does not support any parameters and is for future expansion. Pass in NULL.

`glXCreateWindow` will throw an error and fail if any of the following conditions is true: if the config is not compatible with the window visual, if the config doesn't support window rendering, if the window parameter is invalid, if a `GLXFBConfig` has already been associated with the window, if the `GLXFBConfig` is invalid, or if there was a general failure creating the GLX window. Also remember that `glXCreateWindow` is supported only in GLX 1.3 or later. It does not work on older versions. Remember we checked the versions earlier by running `glxinfo ¦grep "glx version"` in a terminal.

After you are done rendering, you will also have to clean up the windows you have created. To destroy the GLX window, call `glxDestroyWindow` with the GLX window handle you got when you called `glXCreateWindow`:

```
glXDestroyWindow(Display * dpy, GLXWindow window);
```

To destroy the X window you also created, you can use the similarly named `XDestroyWindow` command, and pass back the X window handle:

```
XDestroyWindow(Display * dpy, Window win);
```

GLX 1.2

To create a window in GLX1.2, you do not need to use any special GLX commands. Instead, simply call `XCreateWindow`. The X window will also need to be destroyed as described previously.

Context Management

A context is a set of OpenGL state that is associated with a handle. Once created, the context can then be used to render with. Multiple contexts can be created, but only one can be bound to a render surface at a time. At least one context is necessary to be able to render. The methods for creating contexts and setting the current context are slightly different for GLX 1.3+ and GLX 1.2.

GLX 1.3+

For GLX 1.3+, you can create a new context with the `glXCreateNewContext` command. When successful, this function returns a context handle you can use when telling GLX which context you want to use when rendering. The config you use to create this context needs to be compatible with the render surface you intend to draw on. For common cases, it is easiest to use the same config that was used to create the GLX window.

```
GLXContext glXCreateNewContext(Display * dpy, GLXFBConfig config,
        int render_type, GLXContext share_list, bool direct);
```

The `render_type` parameter will accept `GLX_RGBA_TYPE` or `GLX_COLOR_INDEX_TYPE`. `GLX_RGBA_TYPE` should be used since we are not using color index mode. Normally you should also pass NULL in the `share_list` parameter. However, if you have multiple contexts for an app and would like to share GL objects such as display lists, VBOs, textures, and so forth, you can pass in the first context's handle when creating the second. This will cause both contexts to use the same namespace. Specifying `TRUE` for the direct parameter requests a direct hardware context for a local X Server connection, and `FALSE` creates a context that renders through the X Server.

If creation fails, the function will return NULL; otherwise, it will initialize the context to default OpenGL state. The function will throw an error if you pass an invalid handle as the `share_list` parameter, if the config is invalid, or if the system is out of resources.

To use a context you have created, you can call `glXMakeContextCurrent`:

```
glXMakeContextCurrent(Display * dpy, GLXDrawable draw, GLXDrawable read,
    GLXContext ctx);
```

It is most common to specify the same drawable for `read` and `draw` targets when making a context current. This means that the same context will be used for both read and draw operations. If a different context was bound before you made this call, it will be flushed and marked as no longer current. If the context you pass is not valid or either drawable is no longer valid, the function will throw an error. It will also throw an error if the context's config is not compatible with the config used to create the drawables. Contexts can be released from a thread by passing `None` in the `read` and `draw` drawable parameters, and NULL as the context. If `None` is not passed for the drawables when trying to free a context, GLX will throw an error.

GLX will allow you to query certain things from a context as well. Use the `glXQueryContext` command to query `GLX_FBCONFIG_ID`, `GLX_RENDER_TYPE`, or `GLX_SCREEN` attributes associated with the context:

```
int glXQueryContext(Display * dpy, GLXContext ctx, int attribute, int *value);
```

There are a few other context-related commands in GLX, but these are mostly self-descriptive. `glXGetCurrentReadDrawable` is supported only in GLX 1.3:

```
GLXDrawable glXGetCurrentReadDrawable(void);
```

In addition, the following functions are supported by both GLX 1.2 and 1.3.

```
GLXContext glXGetCurrentContext(void);
GLXDrawable glXGetCurrentDrawable(void);
Display glXGetCurrentDisplay(void);
```

Once finished with a context, it is important to destroy it so that the implementation can free the related resources. Use the `glXDestroyContext` command for both GLX 1.2 and 1.3:

```
glXDestroyContext(Display * dpy, GLXContext ctx);
```

If the context is currently bound to any thread, the context will not be destroyed until it is no longer current. The function will throw an error if you pass an invalid context handle.

One other handy feature provided by GLX 1.2/1.3 is the capability to copy data from one context to another using `glXCopyContext`. Just pass in the source and destination context handles. A mask is used to specify the pieces of OpenGL state that you would like to copy. These are the same values that may be passed into `glPushAttrib/glPopAttrib`. To copy everything, you can pass `GL_ALL_ATTRIB_BITS`. Client-side state will not be copied.

```
glXCopyContext(Display * dpy, GLXContext source, GLXContext dest, unsigned long
mask);
```

To find out if a context is a direct context, you can call `glXIsDirect` for GLX 1.2/1.3. This will return `true` if the context is a direct rendering context.

```
glXIsDirect(Display * dpy, GLXContext ctx);
```

GLX 1.2

Most of the context interfaces provided previously can be used only in GLX 1.3. However, there are some similar methods that can be used on older GLX versions. To create a context in GLX 1.2, call `glXCreateContext`. This command is very similar to `glXCreateNewContext` except it takes visual info in place of config info and does not accept a render type parameter.

```
GLXContext glXCreateContext(Display * dpy, XVisualInfo* visual,
                           GLXContext share_list, Bool direct);
```

To make a context current, call `glXMakeCurrent` with the context to be rendered with. Here, only one parameter is accepted for the drawable. In GLX 1.2 the same drawable will be used for both draw and read operations.

```
Bool glXMakeCurrent(Display * dpy, GLXDrawable drawable, GLXContext ctx);
```

To unbind the context from the current thread, pass `None` as the drawable and NULL as the context.

Synchronization

GLX has several synchronization commands that are similar to those on other OSs. Making a call to `glXWaitGL` will guarantee that all GL rendering will finish for a window before other native rendering occurring after the call to `glXWaitGL` is allowed to proceed. These might be window decorations drawn by the window manager like scroll bars and buttons, or 2D drawing. This allows an app to ensure that all rendering happens in the correct order and that rendering is not incorrectly overlapped or overwritten.

```
void glXWaitGL(void);
```

Likewise, a call to `glXWaitX` ensures that all native rendering made before the call to `glXWaitX` completes before any OpenGL rendering after the call is allowed to happen.

```
void glXWaitX(void);
```

When using a double-buffered config, a call to `glXSwapBuffers` will present the contents of the back buffer to the window. The call also performs a `glFlush` before the swap occurs. Afterward, the contents of the new back buffer are undefined. GLX will throw an error if the drawable is invalid, the display is invalid, or if the window is no longer valid.

```
void glXSwapBuffers(Display *dpy, GLXDrawable draw);
```

GLX Strings

Several different strings can be queried from GLX. First, you can get a string with all the supported extension strings listed by calling `glXQueryExtensionsString`:

```
const char *glXQueryExtensionsString(Display *dpy, int screen);
```

You can also call `glXGetClientString` or `glXQueryServerString` to find out information about the client library or the server, respectively. Pass it one of the following enums in the name field: `GLX_VENDOR`, `GLX_VERSION`, or `GLX_EXTENSIONS`.

```
const char *glXGetClientString(Display *dpy,  int name);
const char *glXQueryServerString(Display *dpy, int screen, int name);
```

The Rest of GLX

There are a few less-common components of GLX we haven't covered yet. Let's take a quick look at them. The first is a simple method of querying the current GLX version. This function returns integers, which are easier to parse than the version string returned when the string query functions are used. This is helpful for determining what version of GLX you are dealing with from inside your application. The version is broken down into major and minor components:

```
bool glXQueryVersion(Display *dpy, int *major, int *minor);
```

You can query certain state from the current drawable. GLX provides the function `glXQueryDrawable` to allow applications to get information on how the drawable is set up. Pass in the attribute you are interested in: `GLX_WIDTH`, `GLX_HEIGHT`, `GLX_PRESERVED_CONTENTS`, `GLX_LARGEST_PBUFFER`, or `GLX_FBCONFIG_ID`. The result will be returned in the value field. You will also need to specify the drawable you are interested in.

```
void glXQueryDrawable(Display *dpy, GLXDrawable draw, int attribute, unsigned int
*value);
```

There is also a set of functions for creating, dealing with, and deleting pixmaps and pBuffers. These will not be covered since we are not covering and do not recommend you use pixmaps or pBuffers.

X Fonts

The X environment provides for automatic bitmap font generation. This makes it easier for applications to render text in OpenGL, since each character does not need to be stored in the application as a texture. GLX extends this functionality, making it even easier to use. First, call into X and load the font you want to use, and then create display lists to hold the characters, one for each character. Next, call glXUseFont to load the fonts into the display lists:

```
void glXUseXFont(Font font, int first, int count, int list_base);
```

Now you are ready to use the display lists for rendering. Each list will hold a call to glBitmap. You can use glRasterPos to set the screen position and then glCallLists to draw characters. The first sample app demonstrates how to use the display list generation function to simplify writing text to the screen. Figure 21.1 shows the output of this simple demo. Listing 21.1 shows the important steps in this app. First a font is chosen and display list names are generated for the characters. Next glXUseFont is called to populate the display lists. Last, glCallLists is used to render each character.

FIGURE 21.1   The simple font text example.

LISTING 21.1   The font.c Sample Program

```c
char *szString =  "GLX Fonts";

// Load a courier font with size 48pix.
XFontStruct *xFont = XLoadQueryFont(dpy,
    "-*-courier-bold-r-normal—48-*-*-*-*-*-*-*");

// Generate display list names
uiDListStart = glGenLists(96);

// Have GLX generate the display lists for the characters
glXUseXFont(xFont->fid, ' ', 96, uiDListStart);

// Save the display list bit
glPushAttrib(GL_LIST_BIT);

// Set up the display list offset
glListBase(uiDListStart - ' ' );
```

LISTING 21.1   Continued

```
// Now call the appropriate lists for the characters
// in the string
glCallLists(strlen(szString), GL_UNSIGNED_BYTE, (GLubyte*)szString);

// Restore the display list bit
glPopAttrib();
```

Extending GLX

GLX and OpenGL can be extended beyond what is in the core specification. Vendors can write new extensions to that functionality for applications to use. This allows applications to have options that either are vendor-specific or are available before they can become part of the core specification. You can query the list of extensions available for GLX on a system by calling glXQueryExtensionString. An application can also call glGetString(GL_EXTENSIONS) to get the OpenGL extensions available.

After you know which extensions are available, you may have to get new entry points to use them. GLX provides a method to get these. The glXGetProcAddress provides extension function addresses for extensions. This function is available only for GLX versions 1.4 and newer.

```
void (*glXGetProcAddress(const ubyte *procname))();
```

There are a large number of extensions registered for OpenGL. You can take a look at what is available by browsing the extension registry on the OpenGL Web page. For GLX versions before 1.4, you can use the ARB extension version, as shown next, but be sure to check that it exists in the extension string first!

```
void (*glXGetProcAddressARB(const ubyte *procname))();
```

Putting It All Together

Now, for the fun part! Let's put all this GLX stuff together and create an app that uses GLX instead of GLUT for window creation and maintenance. GLUT is great for creating quick, simple apps but does not allow very granular control over the GLX environment.

Because many X Servers packaged with Linux do not yet support GLX 1.3, our example uses the GLX 1.2 interfaces. The first step is to open a connection to the X Server:

```
rcx->dpy = XOpenDisplay(NULL);
```

Then, let's check the supported GLX version to make sure that the functionality we will use later is supported:

```
glXQueryVersion(rcx->dpy, &nMajorVer, &nMinorVer);
printf("Supported GLX version - %d.%d\n", nMajorVer, nMinorVer);

if(nMajorVer == 1 && nMinorVer < 2)
{
    printf("ERROR: GLX 1.2 or greater is necessary\n");
    XCloseDisplay(rcx->dpy);
    exit(0);
}
```

Now that we know we are good to go, look for a visual that meets our requirements. We aren't very picky here since this app doesn't have any complex interactions with the framebuffer.

```
static int attributes[] = { GLX_RGBA,
                            GLX_DOUBLEBUFFER,
                            GLX_DEPTH_SIZE, 16,
                            GLX_RED_SIZE, 8,
                            GLX_BLUE_SIZE, 8,
                            GLX_GREEN_SIZE, 8,
                            0 };

visualInfo = glXChooseVisual(rcx->dpy,
            DefaultScreen(rcx->dpy), attributes);
```

After we have a visual, we can use it to create a new X window. Before calling into XCreateWindow, we have to figure out what things we want the window to do. Pick the events that will be of interest and add them to the event mask. Do the same with the window mask. Set the desired border size and gravity. We also have to create a color map for the window to use. While we are at it, map the window to the display:

```
winAttribs.event_mask = ExposureMask | VisibilityChangeMask |
                        KeyPressMask | PointerMotionMask      |
                        StructureNotifyMask ;

winAttribs.border_pixel = 0;
winAttribs.bit_gravity = StaticGravity;
winAttribs.colormap = XCreateColormap(rcx->dpy,
                    RootWindow(rcx->dpy, visualInfo->screen),
                    visualInfo->visual, AllocNone);
winmask = CWBorderPixel | CWBitGravity | CWEventMask| CWColormap;
```

```
rcx->win = XCreateWindow(rcx->dpy, DefaultRootWindow(rcx->dpy), 20, 20,
                         rcx->nWinWidth, rcx->nWinHeight, 0,
                         visualInfo->depth, InputOutput,
                         visualInfo->visual, winmask, &winAttribs);

XMapWindow(rcx->dpy, rcx->win);
```

Great! We have a window! There are still a few steps that need to be completed before we can render. First let's create a context and make it the current context. Remember, we will need the visual that we used to create the window to create the context.

```
rcx->ctx = glXCreateContext(rcx->dpy, visualInfo, 0, True);
glXMakeCurrent(rcx->dpy, rcx->win, rcx->ctx);
```

After a context is bound, we can make GL calls. So first we need to set the viewport and scissor rectangle:

```
glViewport(0,0,rcx->nWinWidth,rcx->nWinHeight);
glScissor(0,0,rcx->nWinWidth,rcx->nWinHeight);
```

Next, clear the color buffer and the matrices we care about. Also set the viewing frustum:

```
glClearColor(0.0f, 1.0f, 1.0f, 1.0f);
glClear(GL_COLOR_BUFFER_BIT);

glMatrixMode(GL_MODELVIEW);
glLoadIdentity();
glMatrixMode(GL_PROJECTION);
glLoadIdentity();

// Set the frustum
glFrustum(fXLeft, fXRight, fYBottom, fYTop, 0.1f, 100.f);
```

OpenGL setup now is complete, and we can concentrate on rendering something. This little demo application draws two eyeballs that do their best to follow your mouse pointer around the window. Some math is done to figure out where to put the eyeballs, where the mouse pointer is, and where the eyeballs should be looking. You can take a look at the full source available on the download site to see how all this works together. Only the important snippets will be listed here since this chapter is not introducing new OpenGL functionality. Figure 21.2 shows the output of the GLX demo.

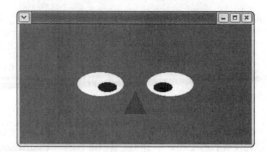

FIGURE 21.2   Here's looking at you!

Several events will cause the contents of the OpenGL window to be redrawn, like uncover events, window moves or resizes. Also any mouse pointer movement will send similar events. These mouse motion events are used to update the eyeball positions. Afterward, glXSwapBuffers is called:

```
glClear(GL_COLOR_BUFFER_BIT);

// Clear matrix stack
glMatrixMode(GL_PROJECTION);
glLoadIdentity();

glMatrixMode(GL_MODELVIEW);
glLoadIdentity();

// Draw left eyeball
glColor3f(1.0, 1.0, 1.0);
glScalef(0.20, 0.20, 1.0);
glTranslatef(-1.5, 0.0, 0.0);
DrawCircle();

// Draw left pupil
glColor3f(0.0, 0.0, 0.0);
glScalef(0.40, 0.40, 1.0);
glTranslatef(fLeftX, fLeftY, 0.0);
DrawCircle();

// Draw right eyeball
glColor3f(1.0, 1.0, 1.0);
glLoadIdentity();
glScalef(0.20, 0.20, 1.0);
glTranslatef(1.5, 0.0, 0.0);
DrawCircle();
```

```
// Draw right pupil
glColor3f(0.0, 0.0, 0.0);
glScalef(0.40, 0.40, 1.0);
glTranslatef(fRightX, fRightY, 0.0);
DrawCircle();

// Clear matrix stack
glMatrixMode(GL_MODELVIEW);
glLoadIdentity();

// Draw nose
glColor3f(0.5, 0.0, 0.7);
glScalef(0.20, 0.20, 1.0);
glTranslatef(0.0, -1.5, 0.0);

glBegin(GL_TRIANGLES);
  glVertex2f(0.0, 1.0);
  glVertex2f(-0.5, -1.0);
  glVertex2f(0.5, -1.0);
glEnd();

// Display rendering
glXSwapBuffers(rcx->dpy, rcx->win);
```

Before the app closes, there is some cleanup that needs to be done. Remember, when we started the application, a connection to the X Server was opened, an X window was created, and a context was created and bound. Now before the app exits these have to be cleaned up. Note that the context will be unbound from the thread before it is destroyed.

```
glXMakeCurrent(rcx->dpy, None, NULL);

glXDestroyContext(rcx->dpy, rcx->ctx);
rcx->ctx = NULL;

XDestroyWindow(rcx->dpy, rcx->win);
rcx->win = (Window)NULL;

XCloseDisplay(rcx->dpy);
rcx->dpy = 0;
```

Summary

OpenGL is an important part of Linux because it is the main hardware accelerated 3D interface. Although we have seen how GLUT can be used with Linux, GLX is also very important for defining buffer resources, window management, and other Linux-specific interfaces with OpenGL. There are also other helpful interfaces available on Linux, like XFonts, that can make rendering easier for applications.

GLX 1.3 provides an interface to Linux and OpenGL that allows intricate control of the rendering environment. It has many similarities to its WGL and AGL counterparts. GLX 1.2 also offers a functional interface to Linux for OpenGL applications and is currently more widely supported.

CHAPTER 22

OpenGL ES: OpenGL on the Small

by Nicholas Haemel

WHAT YOU'LL LEARN IN THIS CHAPTER:

How To	Functions You'll Use
Choose configs	`eglGetConfig/eglChooseConfig/eglGetConfigAttrib`
Create EGL windows	`eglCreateWindowSurface`
Manage EGL contexts	`eglCreateContext/eglDestroyContext/eglMakeCurrent`
Post buffers to the window and synchronize	`eglSwapBuffers/eglSwapInterval/eglWaitGL`

This chapter is a peek into the world of OpenGL ES rendering. This set of APIs is intended for use in embedded environments where traditionally resources are much more limited. OpenGL ES dares to go where other rendering APIs can only dream of.

There is a lot of ground to cover, but we will go over much of the basics. We'll take a look at the different versions of OpenGL ES and what the differences are. We will also go over the windowing interfaces designed for use with OpenGL ES. Also, we will touch on some issues specific to dealing with embedded environments.

OpenGL on a Diet

You will find that OpenGL ES is very similar to regular OpenGL. This isn't accidental; the OpenGL ES specifications were developed from different versions of OpenGL. As you have seen up until now, OpenGL provides a great interface for rendering. It is very flexible and can be used in many applications, from gaming to workstations to medical imaging.

What's the ES For?

Over time, the OpenGL API has been expanded and added to in order to support new features. This has caused the OpenGL application interface to become bloated, providing many different methods of doing the same thing. Take, for instance, drawing a single point. The first available method was drawing in immediate mode, in which you use glBegin/glEnd with the vertex information defined in between. Also, display lists were available, allowing immediate mode commands to be captured into a list that can be replayed again and again. Using the newer glDrawArrays method allows you to put your points in a prespecified array for rendering convenience. And Buffer Objects allow you to do something similar, but from local GPU memory.

The simple action of drawing a point can be done four different ways, each having different advantages. Although it is nice to have many choices when implementing your own application, all of this flexibility has produced a very large API. This in turn requires a very large and complex driver to support it. In addition, special hardware is often required to make each path efficient and fast.

Because of the public nature of OpenGL, it has been a great candidate for use in many different applications outside of the personal computer. But implementers had a hard time conforming to the entire OpenGL spec for these limited hardware applications. For this reason, a new version was necessary; one with Embedded Systems specifically in mind, hence the ES moniker.

A Brief History

As hardware costs have come down and more functionality can be fit into smaller areas on semiconductors, the user interfaces have become more and more complex for embedded devices. A common example is the automobile. In the 1980s the first visual feedback from car computers was provided in the form of single- and multiline text. These interfaces provided warnings about seatbelt usage, current gas mile usage, and so on. After that, two-dimensional displays became prevalent. These often used bitmap-like rendering to present 2D graphics. Most recently, 3D-capable systems have been integrated to help support GPS navigation and other graphic-intensive features. A similar technological history exists for aeronautical instrumentation and cellphones.

The early embedded 3D interfaces were often proprietary and tied closely to the specific hardware features present. This was often the case because the supported feature set was small and varied greatly from device to device. But as 3D engine complexity increased and was used in more and more devices, a standard interface became more important and useful. It was very difficult to port an application from device to device when 3D APIs were so different.

With this in mind, a consortium was formed to help define an interface that would be flexible and portable, yet tailored to embedded environments and conscious of their limitations. This body would be called the Khronos Group.

Khronos

The Khronos Group was originally founded in 2000 by members of the OpenGL ARB, the OpenGL governing body. Many capable media APIs existed for the PC space, but the goal of Khronos was to help define interfaces that were more applicable to devices beyond the personal computer. The first embedded API it developed was OpenGL ES.

Khronos consists of many industry leaders in both hardware and software. Some of the current members are Motorola, Texas Instruments, AMD, Sun Microsystems, Intel, NVIDIA, and Nokia. The complete list is long and distinguished. You can visit the Khronos Web site for more information (www.khronos.org).

Version Development

The first version of OpenGL ES released, cleverly called ES 1.0, was an attempt to drastically reduce the API footprint of a full-featured PC API. This release used the OpenGL 1.3 specification as a basis. Although very capable, OpenGL ES 1.0 removed many less frequently used or very complex portions of the full OpenGL specification. Just like its big brother, OpenGL ES 1.0 defines a fixed functionality pipe for vertex transform and fragment processing.

Being the first release, it was targeted at implementations that supported hardware-accelerated paths for some portions of the pipeline and possibly software implementations for others. In limited devices it is very common to have both software and hardware work together to enable the entire rendering path.

ES 1.1 was completed soon after the first specification had been released. Although very similar to OpenGL ES 1.0, the 1.1 specification is written from the OpenGL 1.5 specification. In addition, a more advanced texture path is supported. A buffer object and draw texture interface has also been added. All in all, the ES 1.1 release was very similar to ES 1.0 but added a few new interesting features.

ES 2.0 was a complete break from the pack. It is not backward compatible with the ES 1.x versions. The biggest difference is that the fixed functionality portions of the pipeline have been removed. Instead, programmable shaders are used to perform the vertex and fragment processing steps. The ES 2.0 specification is based on the OpenGL 2.0 specification.

To fully support programmable shaders, ES 2.0 employs the OpenGL ES Shading Language. This is a high-level shading language that is very similar to the OpenGL Shading Language that is defined for use with OpenGL 2.0+. The reason ES 2.0 is such a large improvement is that all the fixed functionality no longer encumbers the API. This means applications can then implement and use only the features they need in their own shaders. The driver and hardware are relieved from tracking state that may never be used. Of course, the other side of the coin is that applications that want to use portions of the old fixed-function pipeline will need to implement these in app-defined shaders.

There is one more ES version worth mentioning, OpenGL ES SC 1.0. This special version is designed for execution environments with extreme reliability restraints. These applications are considered "Safety Critical," hence the SC designator. Typical applications are in avionics, automobile, and military environments. In these areas 3D applications are often used for instrumentation, mapping, and representing terrain.

The ES SC 1.0 specification uses the OpenGL ES 1.0 specification as a base, which was derived from OpenGL 1.3. Some things are removed from the core ES 1.0 version to reduce implementation costs, and many features from core OpenGL are added back. The most important re-additions are display lists, immediate mode rendering (`glBegin`/`glEnd`), draw pixels, and bitmap rendering. These cumbersome features are included to minimize the complexity of porting older safety critical systems that may already use these features.

So, to recap, the OpenGL ES versions currently defined and the related OpenGL version are listed in Table 22.1.

TABLE 22.1   Base OpenGL versions for ES

OpenGL ES	OpenGL
ES 1.0	GL 1.3
ES 1.1	GL 1.5
ES 2.0	GL 2.0
ES SC 1.0	GL 1.3

Which Version Is Right for You?

Often hardware is created with a specific API in mind. These platforms usually will support only a single accelerated version of ES. It is sometimes helpful to think of the different versions of ES as profiles that represent the functionality of the underlying hardware. For this reason, if you are developing for a specific platform, you may not have a choice as to which version of ES to use.

For traditional GL, typically new hardware will be designed to support the latest version available. ES is a little different. The type of features targeted for new hardware are chosen based on several factors; targeted production cost, typical uses, and system support are a few. For instance, adding hardware functionality for supporting ES 2.0 on an entry-level cellphone may not make sense if it is not intended to be used as a game platform.

The following sections define each specification in much more detail. The Khronos Group has chosen to define the OpenGL ES specifications relative to their OpenGL counterparts. This provides a convenient way to define the entire specification without having to fully describe each interface. Most developers are already familiar with the parent OpenGL specification, making the consumption of the ES version very efficient. For those who are not, cross-referencing the relevant full OpenGL specification is a great way to get the rest of the picture.

Before we get started, it is important to note that the ES 1.x specifications support multiple profiles. The Common profile is designed as the usual interface for heavier-weight implementations. The Common-Lite profile is designed for thinner, leaner applications.

The Common profile is a superset of the Common-Lite profile. The Common-Lite profile does not support floating-point interfaces, whereas the Common profile does. But the Common-Lite profile can use an extension definition of fixed point to use interfaces that whole numbers are not suitable for.

To get the most out of this chapter, you should be very comfortable with most of the OpenGL feature set. This chapter is more about showing you what the major differences are between regular OpenGL and OpenGL ES and less about describing each feature again in detail.

ES 1.0

OpenGL ES 1.0 is written as a difference specification to OpenGL 1.3, which means that the new specification is defined by the differences between it and the reference. We will review OpenGL ES 1.0 relative to the OpenGL 1.3 specification and highlight the important differences.

Vertex Specification

The first major change for ES 1.0 is the removal of the `glBegin`/`glEnd` entrypoints and rendering mechanism. With this, edge flag support is also removed. Although the use of `glBegin`/`glEnd` provides a simple mechanism for rendering, the required driver-side support is usually complex. Vertex arrays can be used for vertex specification just as effectively, although the more complex `glInterleavedArrays` and `glDrawRangeElements` are not supported.

Also, the primitive types `GL_QUAD`, `GL_QUAD_STRIPS`, and `GL_POLYGON` are no longer supported. Other primitive types can be used just as effectively. By the same token, the `glRect` commands have been removed. Color index mode is removed. For vertex specification, only the types `float`, `short`, and `byte` are accepted for vertex data. For color components `ubyte` can also be used.

Even though immediate mode rendering has been removed, ES 1.0 still supports several entrypoints for setting the current render state. This can help reduce the amount of data overhead required per-vertex for state that may not change frequently when drawing with arrays. `glNormal3f`, `glMultiTexCoord4f` and `glColor3f` are all still available.

```
glNormal3f(GLfloat coords);
glMultiTexCoord4f(GLenum texture, GLfloat coords);
glColor4f(GLfloat components);
```

The Common-Lite profile supports these entrypoints as well, but replaces the floating-point parameters with fixed-point.

Transforms

The full transform pipeline still exists, but some changes have been made to simplify complex operations. No texture generation exists, and support for the color matrix has been removed. Because of data type limitations, all double-precision matrix specification is removed. Also, the transpose versions of matrix specification entrypoints have been removed.

OpenGL usually requires an implementation to support a matrix stack depth of at least 32. To ease memory requirements for OpenGL ES 1.0 implementations, a stack depth of only 16 is required. Also, user-specified clip planes are not supported.

Coloring

The full lighting model is supported with a few exceptions. Local viewer has been removed, as has support for different front and back materials. The only supported color material mode is GL_AMBIENT_AND_DIFFUSE. Secondary color is also removed.

Rasterization

There are also a few important changes to the rasterization process. Point and line antialiasing is supported because it is a frequently used feature. However, line stipple and polygon stipple have been removed. These features tend to be very difficult to implement and are not as commonly used except by a few CAD apps. Polygon smooth has also been removed. Polygon offset is still available, but only for filled triangles, not for lines or points.

All support for directly drawing pixel rectangles has been removed. This means glDrawPixels, glPixelTransfer, glPixelZoom, and all related functionality is not supported. Therefore the imaging subset is also not supported. glBitmap rendering is removed as well. glPixelStorei is still supported to allow for glReadPixels pack alignment. These paths tend to be complex in hardware. It is still possible to emulate glDrawPixels by creating a texture with color buffer data that would have been used for a glDrawPixels call and then drawing a screen-aligned textured polygon .

Texturing

Texturing is another complex feature that can be simplified for a limited API. For starters, 1D textures are redundant since they can be emulated with a 2D texture of height 1. Also, 3D and cube map textures are removed because of their added complexity and less frequent use. Borders are not supported. To simplify 2D textures, only a few image formats are supported: GL_RGB, GL_RGBA, GL_LUMINANCE, GL_ALPHA, and GL_LUMINANCE_ALPHA. glCopyTexImage2D and glCopyTexSubImage are supported, as well as compressed textures. However, glGetCompressedTexImage is not supported and compressed formats are illegal as internal formats for glTexImage2D calls, so compressed textures have to be compressed offline using vendor-provided tools.

The texture environment remains intact except for combine mode, which is not supported. Both GL_CLAMP_TO_EDGE and GL_REPEAT wrap modes are supported. GL_CLAMP and `GL_CLAMP_TO_BORDER` are not supported. Controls over mipmap image levels and LOD range are also removed.

Per-Fragment Operations

Most per-fragment operations, such as scissoring, stenciling, and depth test, remain intact since most of them provide unique and commonly used functionality. Blending is included but operations other than `GL_ADD` are not supported. So `glBlendEquation` and `glBlendColor` are no longer necessary.

Framebuffer Operations

Of course, all color index operations are not supported for whole framebuffer operations since color index is not supported. In addition, accumulation buffers are not supported. Also, drawing to multiple color buffers is not supported, so `glDrawBuffer` is not available. Similarly, `glReadPixels` is supported but `glReadBuffer` is not since the only valid rendering target is the front buffer. As has been previously mentioned, `glCopyPixels` is also gone.

Other Functionality

Evaluators are not supported. Selection and feedback are not supported.

State

OpenGL ES 1.0 has decided to limit access to internal state. This helps reduce duplication of state storage for implementations and can provide for more optimal implementation. Generally, all dynamic state is not accessible whereas static state is available. Only the following functions are allowed for accessing state:

```
glGetIntegerv(GLenum pname, Glint *params);
glGetString(GLenum pname);
```

Hints are queryable. Also, independent hardware limits are supported, such as `GL_MODELVIEW_MATRIX_STACK_DEPTH`, `GL_MAX_TEXTURE_SIZE`, and `GL_ALIASED_POINT_RANGE`.

Core Additions

For the most part, OpenGL ES is a subset of OpenGL functionality. But there are also a few additions. These take the form of extensions that are accepted as core additions to the ES specification. That means they are required to be supported by any implementation that is conformant, unless the extension is optional (`OES_query_matrix`).

Byte Coordinates—`OES_byte_coordinates`   This, along with the next extension, are two of the biggest enablers for limited embedded systems. This extension allows byte data usage for vertex and texture coordinates.

Fixed Point—`OES_fixed_point`   This extension introduces a new integer-based fixed-point data type for use in defining vertex data. The new interfaces mirror the floating-point versions with the new data type. The new commands are `glNormal3x`, `glMultiTexCord4x`, glVertexPointer, glColorPointer, glNormalPointer, glTexCordPointer, glDepthRange, glLoadMatrixx, glMultMatrixx, glRotatex, glScalex, glTranslatex, glFrustumx, glOrthox, glMaterialx[v], glLight[v], glLightModelx[v], glPointSizex, glLineWidthx, glPolygonOffsetx, glTexParameterx, glTexEnvx[v], glFogx[v], glSampleCoveragex, glAlphaFuncx, glClearColorx, and glClearDepthx.

Single-Precision Commands—OES_single_precision   This extension adds a few new single-precision entrypoints as alternatives to the original double-precision versions. The supported functions are glDepthRangef, glFrustrumf, glOrthof, and glClearDepthf.

Compressed Paletted Textures—OES_compressed_paletted_texture   This extension provides for specifying compressed texture images in color index formats, along with a color palette. It also adds ten new internal texture formats to allow for texture specification.

Read Format—OES_read_format   Read Format is a required extension. With this extension, the optimal type and format combinations for use with glReadPixels can be queried. The format and type have to be within the set of supported texture image values. These are stored as state variables with the names GL_IMPLEMENTATION_COLOR_READ_FORMAT_OES and GL_IMPLEMENTATION_COLOR_READ_TYPE_OES. This prevents the ES implementation from having to do a software conversion of the pixel buffer.

Query Matrix—OES_query_matrix   This is an optional extension that allows access to certain matrix states. If this extension is supported, the modelview, texture, and projection matrix can be queried. The extension allows for retrieval in a fixed-point format for the profiles that require it. (Common-Lite)

ES 1.1

The ES 1.1x specification is similar to the 1.0 specification. The biggest change is that OpenGL 1.5 is used for the base of this revision, instead of OpenGL 1.3. So most of the new features in OpenGL 1.5 are also available in ES 1.1x. In addition to the OpenGL 1.5 features, there are a few new core extensions. In this section we will cover the major changes to ES 1.1 with reference to ES 1.0 instead of beginning from scratch.

Vertex Processing and Coloring

Most of the vertex specification path is the same as the ES 1.0 path. There are a few additions to commands that can be used to define vertex information. Color information can be defined using unsigned bytes:

glColor4ub[v](GLubyte red, GLubyte green, GLubyte blue, GLubyte alpha);

Also, buffer objects were added to the OpenGL 1.5 specification and are included in the OpenGL ES 1.1 specification. Some aspects of buffer objects allowed for flexible usage. For instance, after a buffer object is specified, OpenGL 1.5 allows for that buffer to be mapped back to system memory so that the application can update it, as well as updating buffers by GL. And to support this access method, different usage indicators are given when glBufferData is called on a buffer.

For the ES version, the multiple usage profiles for buffer objects are removed. Instead, the only supported usage is GL_STATIC_DRAW. This means that the buffer object data is intended to be specified once, and then repeatedly rendered from. When ES can expect this behavior, it can optimize the handling and efficiency of the buffer object. In addition, system limitations in an embedded environment may not allow for the video memory holding the buffer object to be mapped to the application directly. Since all other usage methods are not supported, GL_STREAM_DRAW, GL_STREAM_COPY, GL_STREAM_READ, GL_STATIC_READ, GL_DYNAMIC_COPY, and GL_DYNAMIC_READ tokens are not accepted. Also, the glMapBuffer and glUnmapBuffer commands are not supported.

Clip planes were not supported in ES 1.0, but have been added to ES 1.1 in a limited fashion. The new minimum number of supported clip planes is one instead of six. Also, the commands for setting clip planes take lower precision plane equations. The precision is dependent on the profile.

Query functions are generally not supported in the previous version of ES. For lighting state, several functions were added to permit query. These are glGetMaterialfv and glGetLightfv.

Rasterization
Point parameters are also added. The interface is more limited than the standard OpenGL 1.5 interface. Only the glPointParameterf[v] interface is supported.

Texturing
The level of texturing support in ES 1.1 has been expanded. One of the major changes is the re-addition of mipmapping. This helps relieve applications from having to store all the mipmap data or calculate it at runtime. Also, glIsTexture is added back to the interface to help determine what textures have been instantiated. As part of the generate mipmap support, the GL_GENERATE_MIPMAP hint is supported.

Only GL_TEX_ENV_COLOR and GL_TEX_ENV_MODE were previously supported, and in a limited capacity at that. But OpenGL ES 1.1 adds all of the texture environment back in.

State
One of the fundamental changes in level of support for ES 1.1 is state queries. A premise for the ES 1.0 spec was to limit the amount of interaction between the application and GL. This helps to simplify the interface to allow for a leaner implementation. As part of this effort, all dynamic state queries were removed from the GL interface.

Now, many of the dynamic GL state queries are available again. This is helpful for application development, since querying state can be an important debug tool. For the most part, any state that is accepted in ES 1.1 can be queried. But the same limitations that exist in the state command interface exist in the query interface. For instance, glGetMaterialiv is not supported while glGetMaterialfv is, and state interface supports only the "fv" interface. So the query interfaces parallel the state interfaces. In the same respect, only query interfaces for the supported data types for a given profile are valid.

Texture data queries are still limited. The only valid state queries are the following:
GL_TEXTURE_2D, GL_TEXTURE_BINDING_2D, GL_TEXTURE_MIN_FILTER,
GL_TEXTURE_MAG_FILTER, GL_TEXTURE_WRAP_S, GL_TEXTURE_WRAP_T, and
GL_GENERATE_MIPMAP.

Core Additions

Most of the same extensions are included in the OpenGL ES 1.1 specification as are in 1.0.
However, the optional OES_query_matrix extension has been replaced by a new extension
that also allows matrices to be queried. Several additional extensions are added to the 1.0
set to further extend ES functionality. The OpenGL ES 1.0 extensions that are also part of
the ES 1.1 specification are OES_byte_coordinates, OES_fixed_point, OES_single_preci-
sion, OES_read_format, OES_query_matrix, and OES_compressed_paletted_texture. These
are already described in the preceding section.

Matrix Palette—OES_matrix_palette   Most embedded systems have to keep object
models simple due to limited resources. This can be a problem when we're trying to model
people, animals, or other complex objects. As body parts move, when a bone modeling
method is used, there can be gaps between different parts. Imagine standing one cylinder
on top of another, and then tilting the top one off-axis. The result is a developing gap
between the two cylinders, which in a game might represent an upper arm and a lower
arm of a human character.

This is a hard problem to solve without complex meshes connecting each piece that need
to be recalculated on every frame. That sort of solution is usually well out of the reach of
most embedded systems.

Another solution is to use a new OpenGL ES extension that enables the technique of
vertex skinning. This stitches together the ends of each "bone," eliminating the gap. The
final result is a smooth, texturable surface connecting each bone.

When this extension is enabled, a palette of matrices can be supported. These are not
part of the matrix stack, but can be enabled by setting the GL_MATRIX_MODE to
GL_MATRIX_PALETTE_OES. Each implementation can support a different number of matrices
and vertex units. The application can then define a set of indices, one for each bone.
There is also an associated weight for each index. The final vertex is then the sum of each
index weight times its respective matrix palette times the vertex. The normal is calculated
in a similar way.

To select the current matrix, use the glCurrentPaletteMatrix command, passing in an
index for the specific palette matrix to modify. The matrix can then be set using the
normal load matrix commands. Alternatively, the current palette matrix can be loaded
from the modelview matrix by using the glLoadPaletteFromModelViewMatrixOES
command. You will have to enable two new vertex arrays, GL_MATRIX_INDEX_ARRAY and
GL_WEIGHT_ARRAY. Also, the vertex array pointers will need to be set using the
glWeightPointer and glMatrixIndexPointer commands:

```
glCurrentPaletteMatrixOES(GLuint index);
glLoadPaletteFromModelViewMatrixOES();
glMatrixIndexPointerOES(GLint size, GLenum type, sizei stride, void *pointer);
glWeightPointerOES(Glint size, GLenum type, sizei stride, void *pointer);
```

Point Sprites—OES_point_sprite   Point sprites do not exist as core functionality in OpenGL 1.5. Instead, they are supported as the ARB_point_sprite extension and then later in OpenGL 2.0. The OES_point_sprite core extension is very similar to the ARB version that was written for OpenGL 1.5, but takes into account the embedded system environment. Mainly this means that instead of using token names that end in "ARB," token names end in "OES."

Point Size Array—OES_point_size_array   To support quick and efficient rendering of particle systems, the OES_point_size_array extension was added. This allows a vertex array to be defined that will contain point sizes. This allows the application to render an entire series of points with varying sizes in one glDrawArrays call. Without this extension the GL point size state would have to be changed between rendering each point that had a different size.

Matrix Get—OES_matrix_get   Because some applications would like to read matrix state back, particularly useful after having done a series of matrix transforms or multiplications, the new required OES_matrix_get extension was added to provide a query path suited to ES. The Common profile is permitted to query for float values whereas the Common-Lite profile must use a fixed-point representation. The commands are glGetFloatv and glGetFixedv, respectively; they return matrix data as a single array. This extension is in addition to OES_query_matrix.

Draw Texture—OES_draw_texture   In certain environments, ES may be the only API for rendering, or it may be inconvenient for an application to switch between two APIs. Although 2D-like rendering can be done with OpenGL, it can be cumbersome. This extension is intended to help resolve this problem as well as provide a method for quickly drawing font glyphs and backgrounds.

With this extension, a screen-aligned texture can be drawn to a rectangle region on the screen. This may be done using the glDrawTex commands:

```
glDrawTex{sifx}OES(T Xs, T Ys, T Zs, T Ws, T Hs);
glDrawTex{sifx}vOES(T *coords);
```

In addition, a specific region of a texture for use can be defined. The entire texture does not need to be used for a glDrawTex call. This may be done by calling glTexParameter with the GL_TEXTURE_CROP_RECT_OES token and the four texture coordinates to use as the texture crop rectangle. By default, the crop rectangle is 0,0,0,0. The texture crop rectangle will not affect any other GL commands besides glDrawTex.

ES 2.0

The first two major OpenGL ES specifications were largely complexity reductions from existing OpenGL specifications. ES 2.0 extends this trend by wholesale removal of large parts of core OpenGL 2.0, making even greater strides in rendering path consolidation.

At the same time, ES 2.0 provides more control over the graphics pipeline than was previously available. Instead of supporting a slimmed-down version of the fixed-function pipeline, the fixed-function pipeline has been completely removed. In its place is a programmable shader path that allows applications to decide individually which vertex and fragment processing steps are important.

One prevalent change in ES 2.0 is the support of floating-point data types in commands. Previously, floating-point data needed to be emulated using fixed-point types, which are still available in ES 2.0. Also, the data types byte, unsigned byte, short, and unsigned short are not used for OpenGL commands.

Vertex Processing and Coloring

As with the preceding versions, display list and immediate mode render are not supported. Vertex arrays or vertex buffer objects must be used for vertex specification. The vertex buffer object interface now supports mapping and unmapping buffers just as OpenGL 2.0 does. Predetermined array types are no longer supported (glVertexPointer, glNormalPointer, etc.). The only remaining method for specifying vertex data is the use of generic attributes through the following entrypoints.

```
glVertexAttribPointer(GLuint index, GLuint size, GLenum type,
        GLboolean normalized, sizei stride, const void *ptr);
```

In addition, glInterleavedArrays and glArrayElement are no longer supported. Also, normal rescale, normalization, and texture coordinate generation are not supported. Because the fixed-function pipeline has been removed, these features are no longer relevant. If desirable, similar functionality can be implemented in programmable shaders.

Because the fixed-function pipeline has been removed, all lighting state is also removed. Lighting models can be represented in programmable shaders as well.

Programmable Pipeline

OpenGL ES 2.0 has replaced the fixed-function pipeline with support for programmable shaders. In OpenGL 2.0, which also supports programmable GLSL shaders, the implementation model allows applications to compile source at runtime using shader source strings. OpenGL ES 2.0 uses a shading language similar to the GLSL language specification, called the OpenGL ES Shading Language. This version has changes that are specific to embedded environments and hardware they contain.

Although a built-in compiler is very easy to use, including the compiler in the OpenGL driver can be large (several megabytes) and the compile process can be very CPU intensive. These limitations do not work well with smaller handheld embedded systems, which have much more stringent limitations for both memory and processing power.

For this reason, OpenGL ES has provided two different paths for the compilation of shaders. The first is similar to OpenGL 2.0, allowing applications to compile and link shaders using shader source strings at runtime. The second is a method for compiling shaders offline and then loading the compiled result at runtime. Neither method individually is required, but an OpenGL ES 2.0 implementation must support at least one.

Many of the original OpenGL 2.0 commands are still part of ES. The same semantics of program and shader management are still in play. The first step in using the programmable pipeline is to create the necessary shader and program objects. This is done with the following commands:

```
glCreateShader(void);
glCreateProgram(void);
```

After that, shader objects can be attached to program objects:

```
glAttachShader(GLuint program, GLuint shader);
```

Shaders can be compiled before or after attachment if the compile method is supported. But the shader source needs to be specified first. These methods are covered in the following extension sections: "Shader Source Loading and Compiling" and "Loading Shaders." Also, generic attribute channels can be bound to names during this time:

```
glBindAttribLocation(GLuint program, GLuint index, const char *name);
```

The program can then be linked. If the shader binary interface is supported, the shader binaries for the compiled shaders need to be loaded before the link method is called. A single binary can be loaded for a fragment-vertex pair if they were compiled together offline.

```
glLinkProgram(GLuint program);
```

After the program has been successfully linked, it can be set as the currently executing program by calling glUseProgram. Also, at this point uniforms can be set as needed. All the normal OpenGL 2.0 attribute and uniform interfaces are supported. However, the transpose bit for setting uniform matrices must be GL_FALSE. This feature is not essential to the functioning of the programmable pipeline. Trying to draw without a valid program bound will generate undefined results.

```
glUseProgram(GLuint program);
glUniform{1234}{if}(GLint location, T values);
glUniform{1234}{if}v(GLint location, sizei count, T value);
```

```
glUniformMatrix{234}fv(GLint location, sizei count,
                       GLboolean transpose, T value);
```

Using the programmable pipeline in OpenGL ES 2.0 is pretty straightforward if you are familiar with using GLSL. If you don't have much GLSL experience, it may be helpful to do some work with programmable shaders in OpenGL 2.0 first since programming for a PC is usually more user-friendly than most embedded environments. For more information and the semantics of using shaders and programs, see chapters 15 through 17. To get a better idea of how the two OpenGL ES shader compilation models are used, see the related extensions at the end of this section.

Rasterization

Handling of points has also changed. Only aliased points are supported. Also, point sprites are always enabled for point rendering. Several aspects of point sprite handling have also changed. Vertex shaders are responsible for outputting point size; there is no other way for point size to be specified. GL_COORD_REPLACE can be used to generate point texture coordinates from 0 to 1 for s and t coordinates. Also, the point coordinate origin is set to GL_UPPER_LEFT and cannot be changed.

Antialiased lines are not supported. OpenGL ES 2.0 also has the same limitations as ES 1.1 for polygon support.

Texturing

Texture support has been expanded for ES 2.0. In addition to 2D textures, cubemaps are supported. Depth textures still are not supported and 3D textures remain optional. Non-power-of-two textures support was promoted to OpenGL 2.0 and is included as part of the ES 2.0 specification as well. But for ES, non-power-of-two textures are valid only for 2D textures when mipmapping is not in use and the texture wrap mode is set to clamp to edge.

Fragment Operations

There are also a few changes to the per-fragment operations allowed in ES 2.0. It is required that there be at least one config available that supports both a depth buffer and a stencil buffer. This will guarantee that an application depending on the use of depth information and stencil compares will function on any implementation that supports OpenGL ES 2.0.

A few things have also been removed from the OpenGL 2.0 spec. First, the alpha test stage has been removed since an application can implement this stage in a fragment shader. The glLogicOp interface is no longer supported. And occlusion queries are also not part of OpenGL ES.

Blending works as it does in OpenGL 2.0, but the scope is more limited. glBlendEquation and glBlendEquationSeparate can only support the following modes; GL_FUNC_ADD, GL_FUNC_SUBTRACT, GL_FUNC_REVERSE_SUBTRACT.

State

OpenGL ES 2.0 supports the same state and state queries as OpenGL ES 1.1. But the state that is not part of ES 2.0 cannot be queried, for instance, `GL_CURRENT_COLOR` and `GL_CURRENT_NORMAL`. Vertex array data state is also not queryable since ES 2.0 does not support named arrays. Queries have been added for shader and program state and these are the same as in OpenGL 2.0.

Core Additions

The number of core additions and extensions has dramatically increased to support the more flexible nature of ES 2.0. Some of these are required but most are optional. You may notice there are many layered extensions for things like texturing. With the use of this model, an optional core extension definition is created for compatibility purposes, while still allowing implementations to decide exactly what components should be implemented and to what level.

Two required extensions are promoted along from ES 1.1 and ES 1.0: `OES_read_format` and `OES_compressed_paletted_texture`.

Framebuffer Objects—`OES_framebuffer_object`   The framebuffer object extension was originally written against OpenGL 2.0, and is required to be supported in OpenGL ES 2.0. This extension creates the concept of a "frame-buffer-attachable image." This image is similar to the window render surfaces. The main intention is to allow other surfaces to be bound to the GL framebuffer. This allows direct rendering to arbitrary surfaces that can later be used as texture images, among other things. Because this extension details many intricate interactions, only the broad strokes will be represented here. Refer to the ES 2.0 specification and the `EXT_framebuffer_object` description for more information on usage, and to Chapter 18, "Advanced Buffers," for the OpenGL 2.0 explanation of framebuffer objects.

Framebuffer Texture Mipmap Rendering—`OES_fbo_render_mipmap`   When rendering to a framebuffer object that is used as a mipmapped texture, this optional extension allows for rendering into any of the mipmap levels of the attached framebuffer object. This can be done using the `glFramebufferTexture2DOES` and `glFramebufferTexture3DOES` commands.

Render Buffer Storage Formats   To increase the data type options for render buffer storage formats, the following extensions have been added: `OES_rgb_rgba`, `OES_depth24`, `OES_depth32`, `OES_stencil1`, `OES_stencil_4`, and `OES_stencil8`. Of these, only `OES_stencil8` is required. These new formats are relevant only for use with framebuffer objects and are designed to extend framebuffer object compatibility.

Half-Float Vertex Format—`OES_vertex_half_float`   With this optional extension it is possible to specify vertex data with 16 bit floating-point values. When this is done, the required storage for vertex data can be significantly reduced from the size of larger data types. Also, the smaller data type can have a positive effect on the efficiency of the vertex transform portions of the pipeline. Use of half-floats for data like colors often does not have any adverse effects, especially for limited display color depth.

Floating-Point Textures   Two new optional extensions, `OES_texture_half_float` and `OES_texture_float`, define new texture formats using floating-point components. The `OES_texture_float` uses a 32-bit floating format whereas `OES_texture_half_float` uses a 16-bit format. Both extensions support `GL_NEAREST` magnification as well as `GL_NEAREST`, and `GL_NEAREST_MIPMAP_NEAREST` minification filters. To use the other minification and magnification filters defined in OpenGL ES, the support of `OES_texture_half_float_linear` and `OES_texture_float_linear` extension is required.

Unsigned Integer Element Indices—`OES_element_index_uint`   Element index use in OpenGL ES is inherently limited by the maximum size of the index data types. The use of unsigned bytes and unsigned shorts allows for only 65,536 elements to be used. This optional extension allows for the use of element indexing with unsigned integers, extending the maximum reference index to beyond what current hardware could store.

Mapping Buffers—`OES_mapbuffer`   For vertex buffer object support in previous OpenGL ES versions, the capability to specify and use anything other than a static buffer was removed. When this optional extension is available, use of the tokens `GL_STREAM_DRAW`, `GL_STREAM_COPY`, `GL_STREAM_READ`, `GL_STATIC_READ`, `GL_DYNAMIC_COPY`, and `GL_DYNAMIC_READ` are valid, as well as the `glMapBuffer` and `glUnmapBuffer` entrypoints. This permits applications to map and edit VBOs that already have been defined.

3D Textures—`OES_texture_3D`   Generally, most ES applications do not require support for 3D textures. This extension was kept as optional to allow implementations to decide whether support could be accelerated and would be useful on an individual basis. Also, texture wrap modes and mipmapping are supported for 3D textures that have power-of-two dimensions. Non-power-of-two 3D textures only support `GL_CLAMP_TO_EDGE` for mipmapping and texture wrap.

Non-Power-of-Two Extended Support—`OES_texture_npot`   For non-power-of-two textures, the optional `OES_texture_npot` extension provides two additional wrap modes. `GL_REPEAT` and `GL_MIRRORED_REPEAT` are allowed as texture wrap modes and minification filters when this extension is supported.

High-Precision Floats and Integers in Fragment Shaders—`OES_fragment_precision_high` This optional extension allows for support of the high-precision qualifier for integers and floats defined in fragment shaders.

Ericsson Compressed Texture Format—`OES_compressed_ETC1_RGB8_texture`   The need for compressed texture support in OpenGL ES has long been understood, but format specification and implementation has been left to each individual implementer. This optional extension formalizes one of these formats for use on multiple platforms.

To load a compressed texture using the `ETC_RGB8` format, call `glCompressedTexImage2D` with an internal format of `GL_ETC1_RGB8_OES`. This format defines a scheme by which each 4×4 texel block is grouped. A base color is then derived, and modifiers for each texel are selected from a table. The modifiers are then added to the base color and clamped to 0–255 to determine the final texel color. The full `OES_compressed_ETC1_RGB8_texture` description has more details on this process.

Shader Source Loading and Compiling—OES_shader_source   This extension is one of the two methods for loading shaders. If this extension is not supported, OES_shader_binary must be. This version is the most like OpenGL 2.0. There are several entrypoints that are valid only for this extension and are used for loading uncompiled shader source.

After the creation of a shader, the source must be set for the shader using the glShaderSource function. This can be done before or after the shader is attached to a program, but must be done before glCompileShader is called. After the source has been set, but before glLinkProgram is called if the shader is attached to a program, the shader must be compiled with a call to glCompileShader.

```
glShaderSource(GLuint shader, sizei count, const char **string,
               const int *length);
glCompileShaer(GLuint shader);
```

Because the shader source path has been added back to the programmable pipeline, several shader-specific queries are also available. glGetShaderInfoLog can be used to query information specific to a shader. Compile info is usually the most important information stored in the log. glGetShaderSource can be used to query the shader strings.

```
glGetShaderInfoLog(GLuint shader, sizei bufsize, sizei *length, char *infolog);
glGetShaderSource(GLuint shader, sizei bufsize, sizei *length, char *source);
```

Different implementations of OpenGL ES 2.0 may have different levels of internal precision when executing linked programs. Both the precision and the range can be checked for both shader types, vertex and fragment, with the glGetShaderPrecisionFormatOES. Each precision-specific data type, GL_LOW_FLOAT, GL_MEDIUM_FLOAT, GL_HIGH_FLOAT, GL_LOW_INT, GL_MEDIUM_INT, and GL_HIGH_INT, can be queried individually. The results of the queries are log base 2 numbers.

```
glGetShaderPrecisionFormatOES(GLenum shadertype, sizei bufsize,
                              sizei *length, char *source);
```

The last function added with this extension is glReleaseShaderCompilerOES. The resources that need to be initialized to successfully compile a shader can be extensive. Generally, an application will compile and link all shaders/programs it will use before executing any draw calls. This new command signals to the implementation that the compiler will not be used for a while and any allocated resources can be freed. The call does not mean that shaders are no longer allowed to be compiled, though.

Loading Shaders—OES_shader_binary   This extension is the other method for loading shaders. If this extension is not supported, OES_shader_source must be. This extension is intended to address the resource issues related to including a compiler in the OpenGL ES implementation. A compiler can require large amounts of storage, and the execution of an optimizing compiler on shaders during execution can steal large amounts of CPU time.

Using this method allows applications to compile shaders offline for execution on a specific system. These compiled shaders can then be loaded at execution time. This solves the storage problems related to including a compiler and eliminates any compile-time stalls.

This extension also supports use of the command `glGetShaderPrecisionFormatOES`. See the earlier description under "`OES_shader_source`" to get a detailed explanation.

One new command has been added to load compiled shader source, `glShaderBinaryOES`. This command can be used to load a single binary for multiple shaders that were all compiled offline together. These shaders are all listed together on the `glShaderBinaryOES` call, with "n" being the count of shader handles. For OpenGL ES 2.0, the binary format is always `GL_PLATFORM_BINARY`.

```
glShaderBinaryOES(GLint n, GLuint *shaders, GLenum binaryformat,
                const void *binary, GLint length);
```

Shaders are compiled offline using an implementation-specific interface that is defined by individual vendors. These compiles will return a shader binary that will be used at execution time. It is best to compile both the vertex and the fragment shaders for an intended program at the same time, together. This gives the compiler the most opportunity to optimize the compiled shader code, eliminating any unnecessary steps such as outputting interpolants in vertex shaders that are never read in the fragment shader.

There is an additional link-time caveat. `glLinkProgram` is allowed to fail if optimized vertex and fragment shader source pairs are not linked together. This is because it is possible for the vertex shader to need a recompile based on the needs of the fragment shader.

ES SC

The last version of OpenGL ES we will present is OpenGL ES SC. This is the safety-critical specification. At this time there is only one release of SC, version 1.0. The SC specification is important for execution in places where an application or driver crash can have serious implications, such as for aircraft instrumentation or on an automobile's main computer. Also, many of the removed features for SC were pulled out to make testing easier, since safety-critical components must go through a much more extensive testing and certification process than a normal PC component.

Because the industry in many of these safety-critical areas tends to progress slowly, many embedded applications use older features of OpenGL that are removed from the newer versions of OpenGL ES. You will find that many of these features are still present in OpenGL ES SC. SC has been written against the OpenGL 1.3 specification. Interface versions specific to the `byte`, `short`, and `unsigned short` data types have been removed to help reduce the number of entrypoints.

22

Vertex Processing and Coloring

In SC, immediate mode rendering has been added back in for all primitive types except GL_QUADS, GL_QUAD_STRIP, and GL_POLYGON. These can be simulated using other primitive types. Edge flags are not supported. Also, the vertex data entry routines have been reduced to include only the following:

```
glBegin(GLenum mode);
glEnd();
glVertex{2,3}f[v](T coords);
glNormal3f[v](GLfloat coords);
glMultiTexCoord2f(GLenum texture, GLfloat coords);
glColor4{f,fv,ub}(GLfloat components);
```

Rendering with vertex arrays is also supported in the same capacity as OpenGL ES 1.0, but generally only support GL_FLOAT as the array data type (color arrays can also be GL_UNSIGNED_BYTE). Also, all the float versions of matrix specification and manipulation functions are supported, whereas the double versions are not since doubles are generally not supported in OpenGL ES. But the transpose versions of the commands are also not supported. Texture coordinate generation is not available.

Many SC systems rely on OpenGL ES to do all graphic rendering, including 2D, menus, and such. So, bitmaps are an important part of menus and 2D rendering and are available on SC. Because bitmaps are supported in SC, a method for setting the current raster position is also necessary. The glRasterPos entrypoint has been included to fulfill this need:

```
glRasterPos3f(GLfloat coords);
glBitmap(sizei width, sizei height, GLfloat xorig, GLfloat yorig,
        GLfloat xmove, GLfloat ymove, const GLubyte *bitmap);
```

Most of the lighting model stays intact and at least two lights must be supported. But two-sided lighting has been removed, and with it go differing front and back materials. Also, local viewer is not available and the only color material mode is GL_AMBIENT_AND_DIFFUSE.

Rasterization

The rasterization path is very similar to the OpenGL 1.3 path. Point rendering is fully supported. Also, line and polygon stippling is supported. But as with the other ES versions, point and line polygon modes are not supported. Neither is GL_POLYGON_SMOOTH or multisample. As in OpenGL ES 1.0, only 2D textures are supported.

Fragment Operations

Fragment operations will seem familiar. Depth test is included as well as alpha test, scissoring, and blending. This specification also still allows use of color mask and depth mask.

State

Most states that are available for rendering are also available for querying. Most entry-points are also supported unless they are duplicates or are for a data type that is not supported.

Core Additions

Even the SC version of OpenGL ES has several core additions. These are `OES_single_precision`, `EXT_paletted_texture`, and `EXT_shared_texture_palette`. Single precision has already been covered in previous versions of ES. Paletted texture support is very similar to the compressed paletted texture support offered in other versions of ES and is not described in detail here. Shared paletted textures expand on paletted textures by allowing for a common, shared palette.

The ES Environment

Now that we have seen what the specs actually look like, we are almost ready to take a peek at an example. Figure 22.1 shows an example of OpenGL ES running on a cell phone. To see a color version, flip to the Color Insert section of the book. But before that, there are a few issues unique to embedded systems that you should keep in mind while working with OpenGL ES and targeting embedded environments.

FIGURE 22.1   OpenGL ES rendering on a cellphone.

Application Design Considerations

For first-timers to the embedded world, things are a bit different here than when working on a PC. The ES world spans a wide variety of hardware profiles. The most capable of these might be multicore systems with extensive dedicated graphics resources, such as the Sony PlayStation 3. Alternatively, and probably more often, you may be developing for or porting to an entry-level cellphone with a 50MHz processor and 16MB of storage.

On limited systems, special attention must be paid to instruction count because every cycle counts if you are looking to maintain reasonable performance. Certain operations can be very slow. An example might be finding the sine of an angle. Instead of calling sin() in a math library, it would be much faster to do a lookup in a precalculated table if a close approximation would do the job. In general, the types of calculations and algorithms that might be part of a PC application should be updated for use in an embedded system. One example might be physics calculations, which are often very expensive. These can usually be simplified and approximated for use on embedded systems like cellphones.

On systems that support only ES 1.x, it's also important to be aware of native floating-point support. Many of these systems do not have the capability to perform floating-point operations directly. This means all floating-point operations will be emulated in software. These operations are generally very slow and should be avoided at all costs. This is the reason that ES has provided for an interface that does not require floating-point data usage.

Dealing with a Limited Environment

Not only can the environment be limiting when working on embedded systems, but the graphics processing power itself is unlikely to be on par with the bleeding edge of PC graphics. This limitation also creates specific areas that need special attention when you're looking to optimize the performance of your app, or just to get it to load and run at all!

It may be helpful to create a budget for storage space. In this way you can break up the maximum graphics/system memory available into pieces for each memory-intensive category. This will help to provide a perspective on how much data each unique piece of your app can use and when you are starting to run low.

One of the most obvious areas is texturing. Large detailed textures can help make a PC targeted application provide a rich and detailed environment. This is great for the user experience. But in most embedded systems textures can be a huge resource hog. Many of the older platforms may not have full hardware support for texturing. OpenGL ES 1.x implementations may also be limited in the texture environment that can be hardware accelerated. You'll want to refer to the documentation for your platform for this information. But these issues can cause large performance drops when many fragments are textured, especially if each piece of overlapping geometry is textured and drawn in the wrong order.

In addition to core hardware texturing performance, texture sizes can also be a major limitation. Both 3D and cube map textures can quickly add up to a large memory footprint. This is one reason why only 2D textures are supported in ES 1.x and 3D textures are optional for ES 2.0. Usually when the amount of graphics and system memory is limited, the screen size is also small. This means that a much smaller texture can be used with similar visual results. Also, it may be worth avoiding multitexture because it requires multiple texture passes as well as more texture memory.

Vertex count can also have an adverse effect on performance. Earlier ES platforms often performed vertex transform on the CPU instead of on dedicated graphics resources. This can be especially slow when using lighting on ES 1.x. To reduce vertex counts, difficult decisions have to be made about which parts of object models are important and require higher tessellation, and which are less important or may not suffer if rendered with less tessellation.

Vertex storage can also impact memory, similar to textures. In addition to setting a cap for the total memory used for vertices, it may also be helpful to decide which parts of a scene are important and divide up the vertex allotment along those lines.

One trick to keeping rendering smooth while many objects are on the screen is to change the vertex counts for objects relative to their distance from the viewer. This is a level-of-detail approach to geometry management. For instance, if you would like to generate a forest scene, three different models of trees could be used. One level would have a very small vertex count and would be used to render the farthest of the trees. A medium vertex count could be used for trees of intermediate distance, and a larger count would be used on the closest. This would allow many trees to be rendered much quicker than if they were all at a high detail level. Because the least detailed trees are the farthest away, and may also be partially occluded, it is unlikely the lower detail would be noticed. But there may be significant savings in vertex processing as a result.

Fixed-Point Math

You may ask yourself, "What is fixed-point math and why should I care?" The truth is that you may not care if your hardware supports floating-point numbers and the version of OpenGL ES you are using does as well. But there are many platforms that do not natively support floating point. Floating-point calculations in CPU emulation are very slow and should be avoided. In those instances, a representation of a floating-point number can be used to communicate nonwhole numbers. I definitely am not going to turn this into a math class! But instead a few basic things about fixed-point math will be covered to give you an idea of what's involved. If you need to know more, there are many great resources available that go to great lengths in discussing fixed-point math.

First, let's review how floating-point numbers work. There are basically two components to a floating-point number: The mantissa describes the fractional value, and the exponent is the scale or power. In this way large numbers are represented with the same number of significant digits as small numbers. They are related by $m * 2^e$ where m is the mantissa and e is the exponent.

Fixed-point representation is different. It looks more like a normal integer. The bits are divided into two parts, with one part being the integer portion and the other part being the fractional. The position between the integer and fractional components is the "imaginary point." There also may be a sign bit. Putting these pieces together, a fixed-point format of s15.16 means that there is 1 sign bit, 15 bits represent the integer, and 16 bits represent the fraction. This is the format used natively by OpenGL ES to represent fixed-point numbers.

Addition of two fixed-point numbers is simple. Because a fixed-point number is basically an integer with an arbitrary "point," the two numbers can be added together with a common scalar addition operation. The same is true for subtraction. There is one requirement for performing these operations. The fixed-point numbers must be in the same format. If they are not, one must be converted to the format of the other first. So to add or subtract a number with format s23.8 and one with s15.16, one format has to be picked and both numbers converted to that format.

Multiplication and division are a bit more complex. When two fixed-point numbers are multiplied together, the imaginary point of the result will be the sum of that in the two operands. For instance, if you were multiplying two numbers with formats of s23.8 together, the result would be in the format of s15.16. So it is often helpful to first convert the operands into a format that will allow for a reasonably accurate result format. You probably don't want to multiply two s15.16 formats together if they are greater than 1.0—the result format would have no integer portion! Division is very similar, except the size of the fractional component of the second number is subtracted from the first.

When using fixed-point numbers, you have to be especially careful about overflow issues. With normal floating point, when the fractional component would overflow, the exponent portion is modified to preserve accuracy and prevent the overflow. This is not the case for fixed point. To avoid overflowing fixed-point numbers when performing operations that might cause problems, the format can be altered. The numbers can be converted to a format that has a larger integer component, and then converted back before calling into OpenGL ES. With multiplication similar issues result in precision loss of the fractional component when the result is converted back to one of the operand formats. There are also math packages available to help you convert to and from fixed-point formats, as well as perform math functions. This is probably the easiest way to handle fixed-point math if you need to use it for an entire application.

That's it! Now you have an idea how to do basic math operations using fixed-point formats. This will help get you started if you find yourself stuck having to use fixed-point values when working with embedded systems. There are many great references for learning more about fixed-point math. One is *Essential Mathematics for Games and Interactive Applications* by James Van Verth and Lars Bishop (Elsevier, Inc. 2004).

EGL: A New Windowing Environment

You have already heard about glx, agl, and wgl. These are the OpenGL-related system interfaces for OSs like Linux, Apple's Mac OS, and Microsoft Windows. These interfaces are necessary to do the setup and management for system-side resources that OpenGL will use. The EGL implementation often is also provided by the graphics hardware vendor. Unlike the other windowing interfaces, EGL is not OS specific. It has been designed to run under Windows, Linux, or embedded OSs such as Brew and Symbian. A block diagram of how EGL and OpenGL ES fit into an embedded system is shown in Figure 22.2

EGL has its own native types just like OpenGL does. EGLBoolean has two values that are named similarly to their OpenGL counterparts: `EGL_TRUE` and `EGL_FALSE`. EGL also defines the type `EGLint`. This is an integer that is sized the same as the native platform integer type. The most current version of EGL as of this writing is EGL 1.2

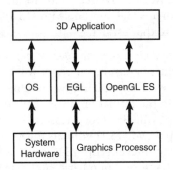

FIGURE 22.2   A typlical embedded system diagram.

EGL Displays

Most EGL entrypoints take a parameter called `EGLDisplay`. This is a reference to the rendering target where drawing can take place. It might be easiest to think of this as corresponding to a physical monitor. The first step in setting up EGL will be to get the default display. This can be done through the following function:

```
EGLDisplay eglGetDisplay(NativeDisplayType display_id);
```

The native display id that is taken as a parameter is dependent on the system. For instance, if you were working with an EGL implementation on Windows, the `display_id` parameter you pass would be the device context. You can also pass `EGL_DEFAULT_DISPLAY` if you don't have the display id and just want to render on the default device. If `EGL_NO_DISPLAY` is returned, an error occurred.

Now that you have a display handle, you can use it to initialize EGL. If you try to use other EGL interfaces without initializing EGL first, you will get an `EGL_NOT_INITIALIZED` error.

```
EGLBoolean eglInitialize(EGLDisplay dpy, EGLint *major, EGLint *minor);
```

The other two parameters returned are the major and minor EGL version numbers. By calling the initialize command, you tell EGL you are getting ready to do rendering, which will allow it to allocate and set up any necessary resources.

The main addition to EGL 1.2 is the `eglBindAPI` interface. This allows an application to select from different rendering APIs, such as OpenGL ES and OpenVG. Only one context can be current for each API per thread. Use this interface to tell EGL which interface it should use for subsequent calls to `eglMakeCurrent in a thread`. Pass in one of two tokens to signify the correct API; EGL_OPENVG_API, EGL_OPENGL_ES_API. The call will fail if an invalid enum is passed in. The default value is EGL_OPENGL_ES_API. So unless you plan to switch between multiple APIs, you don't need to set EGL_OPENGL_ES_API to get OpenGL ES.

```
EGLBoolean eglBindAPI(EGLenum api);
```

EGL also provides a method to query the current API, `eglQueryAPI`. This interface returns one of the two enums previously listed.

```
EGLBoolean eglBindAPI(EGLenum api);
```

On exit of your application, or after you are done rendering, a call must be made to EGL again to clean up all allocated resources. After this call is made, further references to EGL resources with the current display will be invalid until `eglInitialize` is called on it again.

```
EGLBoolean eglTerminate(EGLDisplay dpy);
```

Also on exit and when finished rendering from a thread, call `eglReleaseThread`. This allows EGL to release any resources it has allocated in that thread. If a context is still bound, `eglReleaseThread` will release it as well. It is still valid to make EGL calls after calling `eglReleaseThread`, but that will cause EGL to reallocate any state it just released.

```
EGLBoolean eglReleaseThread(EGLDisplay dpy);
```

Creating a Window

As on most platforms, creating a window to render in can be a complex task. Windows are created in the native operating system. Later we will look at how to tell EGL about native windows. Thankfully the process is similar enough to that for Windows and Linux.

Display Configs

An EGL config is analogous to a pixel format on Windows or visuals on Linux. Each config represents a group of attributes or properties for a set of render surfaces. In this case the render surface will be a window on a display. It is typical for an implementation to support multiple configs. Each config is identified by a unique number. Different constants are defined that correlate to attributes of a config. They are defined in Table 22.2.

TABLE 22.2   EGL Config Attribute List

Attribute	Description
EGL_BUFFER SIZE	Total depth in bits of color buffer.
EGL_RED_SIZE	Number of bits in red channel of color buffer.
EGL_GREEN_SIZE	Number of bits in green channel of color buffer.
EGL_BLUE_SIZE	Number of bits in blue channel of color buffer.
EGL_ALPHA_SIZE	Number of bits in alpha channel of color buffer.
EGL_DEPTH_SIZE	Number of bits in depth buffer.
EGL_LUMINANCE_SIZE	Number of bits of luminance in the color buffer
EGL_STENCIL_SIZE	Number of bits in stencil buffer.
EGL_BIND_TO_TEXTURE_RGB	True if config is bindable to RGB textures.
EGL_BIND_TO_TEXTURE_RGBA	True if config is bindable to RGBA textures.
EGL_CONFIG_CAVEAT	Set to one of the following caveats: EGL_NONE, EGL_SLOW_CONFIG, or EGL_NON_CONFORMANT_CONFIG. These can warn of potential issues for this config. A slow config may be software emulated because it exceeds hardware limits. A nonconformant config will not pass the conformance test.
EGL_CONFIG_ID	Unique identifier for this config.
EGL_LEVEL	Framebuffer level.
EGL_NATIVE_RENDERABLE	Is set to EGL_TRUE if native APIs can render to this surface.
EGL_NATIVE_VISUAL_ID	May represent the id of the native visual if the config supports a window, otherwise is 0.
EGL_NATIVE_VISUAL_TYPE	Type of a native visual if config supports window rendering.
EGL_RENDERABLE_TYPE	Native type of visual. May be EGL_OPENGL_ES_BIT or EGL_OPENVG_BIT
EGL_SURFACE_TYPE	Valid surface targets supported. May be any or all of EGL_WINDOW_BIT, EGL_PIXMAP_BIT, or EGL_PBUFFER_BIT.
EGL_COLOR_BUFFER_TYPE	Type of color buffer. May be EGL_RGB_BUFFER or EGL_LUMINANCE_BUFFER.
EGL_MIN_SWAP_INTERVAL	Smallest value that can be accepted by eglSwapInterval. Smaller values will be clamped to this minimum.
EGL_MAX_SWAP_INTERVAL	Largest value that can be accepted by eglSwapInterval. Larger values will be clamped to this maximum.
EGL_SAMPLE_BUFFERS	Number of multisample buffers supported. Must be 0 or 1.
EGL_SAMPLES	Number of samples per pixel for multisample buffers. Will be 0 if EGL_SAMPLE_BUFFERS is 0.
EGL_ALPHA_MASK_SIZE	Number of bits of alpha mask
EGL_TRANSPARENT_TYPE	Indicates support of transparency. Value may be EGL_NONE or EGL_TRANSPARENT_RGB. If transparency is supported, a transparent pixel is drawn when the pixel's components are all equal to the respective transparent RGB values.
EGL_TRANSPARENT_RED_VALUE	Red value a framebuffer pixel must have to be transparent.

TABLE 22.2   Continued

Attribute	Description
EGL_TRANSPARENT_GREEN_VALUE	Green value a framebuffer pixel must have to be transparent.
EGL_TRANSPARENT_BLUE_VALUE	Blue value a framebuffer pixel must have to be transparent.
EGL_MAX_PBUFFER_WIDTH	Maximum width that can be used to create a pBuffer.
EGL_MAX_PBUFFER_HEIGHT	Maximum height that can be used to create a pBuffer.
EGL_MAX_PBUFFER_PIXELS	Largest total size of a pBuffer, in pixels.

It is necessary to choose a config before creating a render surface. But with all the possible combinations of attributes, the process may seem difficult. EGL has provided several tools to help you decide which config will best support your needs. If you have an idea of the kind of options you need for a window, you can use the eglChooseConfig interface to let EGL choose the best config for your requirements.

```
EGLBoolean eglChooseConfig(EGLDisplay dpy, const EGLint *attrib_list,
                           EGLConfig *configs,EGLint config_size,
                           EGLint *num_configs);
```

First decide how many matches you are willing to look through. Then allocate memory to hold the returned config handles. The matching config handles will be returned through the configs pointer. The number of configs will be returned through the num_config pointer. Next comes the tricky part. You have to decide which parameters are important to you in a functional config. Then, you create a list of each attrib followed by the corresponding value. For simple applications, some important attributes might be the bit depths of the color and depth buffers, and the surface type. The list must be terminated with EGL_NONE. An example of an attribute list is shown here:

```
EGLint attributes[] = {EGL_BUFFER_SIZE,      24,
                       EGL_RED_SIZE,          6,
                       EGL_GREEN_SIZE,        6,
                       EGL_BLUE_SIZE,         6,
                       EGL_DEPTH_SIZE,        12,
                       EGL_SURFACE_TYPE,      EGL_WINDOW_BIT,
                       EGL_NONE};
```

For attributes that are not specified in the array, the default values will be used. During the search for a matching config, some of the attributes you list are required to make an exact match whereas others are not. Table 22.3 lists the default values and the compare method for each attribute.

TABLE 22.3   EGL Config Attribute List

Attribute	Compare Operator	Default
EGL_BUFFER SIZE	Minimum	0
EGL_RED_SIZE	Minimum	0
EGL_GREEN_SIZE	Minimum	0
EGL_BLUE_SIZE	Minimum	0
EGL_ALPHA_SIZE	Minimum	0
EGL_DEPTH_SIZE	Minimum	0
EGL_LUMINANCE_SIZE	Minimum	0
EGL_STENCIL_SIZE	Minimum	0
EGL_BIND_TO_TEXTURE_RGB	Equal	EGL_DONT_CARE
EGL_BIND_TO_TEXTURE_RGBA	Equal	EGL_DONT_CARE
EGL_CONFIG_CAVEAT	Equal	EGL_DONT_CARE
EGL_CONFIG_ID	Equal	EGL_DONT_CARE
EGL_LEVEL	Equal	0
EGL_NATIVE_RENDERABLE	Equal	EGL_DONT_CARE
EGL_NATIVE_VISUAL_TYPE	Equal	EGL_DONT_CARE
EGL_RENDERABLE_TYPE	Mask	EGL_OPENGL_ES_BIT
EGL_SURFACE_TYPE	Equal	EGL_WINDOW_BIT
EGL_COLOR_BUFFER_TYPE	Equal	EGL_RGB_BUFFER
EGL_MIN_SWAP_INTERVAL	Equal	EGL_DONT_CARE
EGL_MAX_SWAP_INTERVAL	Equal	EGL_DONT_CARE
EGL_SAMPLE_BUFFERS	Minimum	0
EGL_SAMPLES	Minimum	0
EGL_ALPHA_MASK_SIZE	Minimum	0
EGL_TRANSPARENT_TYPE	Equal	EGL_NONE
EGL_TRANSPARENT_RED_VALUE	Equal	EGL_DONT_CARE
EGL_TRANSPARENT_GREEN_VALUE	Equal	EGL_DONT_CARE
EGL_TRANSPARENT_BLUE_VALUE	Equal	EGL_DONT_CARE

EGL uses a set of rules to sort the matching results before they are returned to you. Basically, the caveat field is matched first, followed by the color buffer channel depths, then the total buffer size, and next the sample buffer information. So the config that is the best match should be first. After you have received the matching configs, you can peruse the results to find the best option for you. The first one will often be sufficient.

To analyze the attributes for each config, you can use `eglGetConfigAttrib`. This will allow you to query the attributes for a config, one at a time:

```
EGLBoolean eglGetConfigAttrib(EGLDisplay dpy, EGLConfig config,
                        EGLint attribute, EGLint *value);
```

If you prefer a more "hands-on" approach to choosing a config, a more direct method for accessing supported configs is also provided. You can use `eglGetConfigs` to get all the configs supported by EGL:

```
EGLBoolean eglGetConfigs(EGLDisplay dpy, EGLConfig *configs,
                         EGLint config_size, EGLint *num_configs);
```

This function is very similar to `eglChooseConfig` except that it will return a list that is not dependent on some search criteria. The number of configs returned will be either the maximum available or the number passed in by `config_size`, whichever is smaller. Here also a buffer needs to be preallocated based on the expected number of formats. After you have the list, it is up to you to pick the best option, examining each with `eglGetConfigAttrib`. It is unlikely that multiple different platforms will have the same configs or list configs in the same order. So it is important to properly select a config instead of blindly using the config handle.

Creating Rendering Surfaces

Now that we know how to pick a config that will support our needs, it's time to look at creating an actual render surface. The focus will be window surfaces, although it is also possible to create nondisplayable surfaces such as pBuffers and pixmaps. The first step will be to create a native window that has the same attributes as those in the config you chose. Then you can use the window handle to create a window surface. The window handle type will be related to the platform or OS you are using. In this way the same interface will support many different OSs without having to define a new method for each.

```
EGLSurface eglCreateWindowSurface(EGLDisplay dpy, EGLConfig config,
                         NativeWindowType win, EGLint *attrib_list);
```

The handle for the onscreen surface is returned if the call succeeds. The `attrib_list` parameter is intended to specify window attributes, but currently none is defined. After you are done rendering, you'll have to destroy your surface using the `eglDestroySurface` function:

```
EGLBoolean eglDestroySurface(EGLDisplay dpy, EGLSurface surface);
```

After a window render surface has been created and the hardware resources have been configured, you are almost ready to go!

Context Management

The last step is to create a render context to use. The rendering context is a set of state used for rendering. At least one context must be supported.

```
EGLContext eglCreateContext(EGLDisplay dpy, EGLConfig config,
             EGLContext share_context, const EGLint *attrib_list);
```

To create a context, call the `eglCreateContext` function with the display handle you have been using all along. Also pass in the config used to create the render surface. The config used to create the context must be compatible with the config used to create the window. The `share_context` parameter is used to share objects like textures and shaders between contexts. Pass in the context you would like to share with. Normally you will pass `EGL_NO_CONTEXT` here since sharing is not necessary. The context handle is passed back if the context was successfully created; otherwise, `EGL_NO_CONTEXT` is returned.

Now that you have a rendering surface and a context, you're ready to go! The last thing to do is to tell EGL which context you'd like to use, since you can use multiple contexts for rendering. Use `eglMakeCurrent` to set a context as current. You can use the surface you just created as both the read and the draw surfaces.

```
EGLBoolean eglMakeCurrent(EGLDisplay dpy, EGLSurface draw,
                          EGLSurface read, EGLContext ctx);
```

You will get an error if the draw or read surfaces are invalid or if they are not compatible with the context. To release a bound context, you can call `eglMakeCurrent` with `EGL_NO_CONTEXT` as the context. You must use `EGL_NO_SURFACE` as the read and write surfaces when releasing a context. To delete a context you are finished with, call `eglDestroyContext`:

```
EGLBoolean eglDestroyContex(EGLDisplay dpy, EGLContext ctx);
```

Presenting Buffers and Rendering Synchronization

For rendering, there are certain EGL functions you may need in order to help keep things running smoothly. The first is `eglSwapBuffers`. This interface allows you to present a color buffer to a window. Just pass in the window surface you would like to post to:

```
EGLBoolean eglSwapBuffers(EGLDisplay dpy, EGLSurface surface);
```

Just because `eglSwapBuffers` is called doesn't mean it's the best time to actually post the buffer to the monitor. It's possible that the display is in the middle of displaying a frame when `eglSwapBuffers` is called. This case causes an artifact called tearing that looks like the frame is slightly skewed on a horizontal line. EGL provides a way to decide if it should wait until the current drawing is complete before posting the swapped buffer to the monitor:

```
EGLBoolean eglSwapInterval(EGLDisplay dpy, EGLint interval);
```

By setting the swap interval to 0, you are telling EGL to not synchronize swaps and that an `eglSwapBuffers` call should be posted immediately. The default value is 1, which means each swap will be synchronized with the next post to the monitor. The interval is clamped to the values of `EGL_MIN_SWAP_INTERVAL` and `EGL_MAX_SWAP_INTERVAL`.

If you plan to render to your window using other APIs besides OpenGL ES/EGL, there are some things you can do to ensure that rendering is posted in the right order:

```
EGLBoolean eglWaitGL(void);


EGLBoolean eglWaitNative(EGLint engine);
```

Use `eglWaitGL` to prevent other API rendering from operating on a window surface before OpenGL ES rendering completes. Use `eglWaitNative` to prevent OpenGL ES from executing before native API rendering completes. The engine parameter can be defined in EGL extensions specific to an implementation, but `EGL_CORE_NATIVE_ENGINE` can also be used and will refer to the most common native rendering engine besides OpenGL ES. This is implementation/system specific.

More EGL Stuff

We have covered the most important and commonly used EGL interfaces. There are a few more EGL functions left to talk about that are more peripheral to the common execution path.

EGL Errors

EGL provides a method for getting EGL-specific errors that may be thrown during EGL execution. Most functions return `EGL_TRUE` or `EGL_FALSE` to indicate whether they were successful, but in the event of a failure, a Boolean provides very little information on what went wrong. In this case, `eglGetError` may be called to get more information:

```
EGLint eglGetError();
```

The last thrown error is returned. This will be one of the following self-explanatory errors: `EGL_SUCCESS`, `EGL_NOT_INITIALIZED`, `EGL_BAD_ACCESS`, `EGL_BAD_ALLOC`, `EGL_BAD_ATTRIBUTE`, `EGL_BAD_CONTEXT`, `EGL_BAD_CONFIG`, `EGL_BAD_CURRENT_SURFACE`, `EGL_BAD_DISPLAY`, `EGL_BAD_SURFACE`, `EGL_BAD_MATCH`, `EGL_BAD_PARAMETER`, `EGL_BAD_NATIVE_PIXMAP`, `EGL_BAD_NATIVE_WINDOW`, or `EGL_CONTEXT_LOST`.

Getting EGL Strings

There are a few EGL state strings that may be of interest. These include the EGL version string and extension string. To get these, use the `eglQueryString` interface with the `EGL_VERSION` and `EGL_EXTENSIONS` enums:

```
const char *eglQueryString(EGLDisplay dpy, EGLint name);
```

Extending EGL

Like OpenGL, EGL provides support for various extensions. These are often extensions specific to the current platform and can provide for extended functionality beyond that of the core specification. To find out what extensions are available on your system, you can use the `eglQueryString` function previously discussed. To get more information on specific extensions, you can visit the Khronos Web site listed in the reference section. Some of these extensions may require additional entrypoints. To get the entrypoint address for these extensions, pass the name of the new entrypoint into the following function:

```
void (*eglGetProcAddress(const char *procname))();
```

Use of this entrypoint is very similar to `wglGetProcAddress`. A NULL return means the entry point does not exist. But just because a non-NULL address is returned does not mean the function is actually supported. The related extensions must exist in the EGL extension string or the OpenGL ES extension string. It is important to ensure that you have a valid function pointer (non-NULL) returned from calling `eglGetProcAddress`.

Negotiating Embedded Environments

After examining all the different versions of OpenGL ES and EGL, it's time to look closer at the environment of an embedded system and how it will affect an OpenGL ES application. The environment will play an important role in how you approach creating ES applications.

Popular Operating Systems

Because OpenGL ES is not limited to certain platforms as many 3D APIs are, a wide variety of OSs have been used. This decision is often already made for you, because most embedded systems are designed for use with certain OSs, and certain OSs are intended for use on specific hardware.

One of the most apparent platforms is Microsoft Windows CE/Windows Pocket PC/Windows Mobile. The Microsoft OSs are currently most prevalent on PDA type systems. Also, slimmed-down versions of Linux are very popular for their flexibility and extensibility. Brew and Symbian are common in the cellphone arena. Each of these options often has its own SDK for developing, compiling, loading, and debugging applications. For our example, we will target PC-based systems running Windows, although this code can be compiled for any target.

Embedded Hardware

The number of hardware implementations supporting OpenGL ES is rapidly growing. Many hardware vendors create their own proprietary implementations for inclusion in their products. Some of these are Ericsson, Nokia, and Motorola.

Other companies provide standalone support for integration into embedded solutions, like the AMD Imageon processors. And some provide licensing for IP-enabling OpenGL ES support, such as PowerVR (www.imgtec.com/PowerVR/Products/index.asp). There are many ways OpenGL ES hardware support can find its way into an embedded system near you!

Vendor-Specific Extensions

Each OpenGL ES vendor often has a set of extensions that are specific to its hardware and implementation. These often extend the number and types of formats available. Because these extensions are useful only for limited sets of hardware, they are not discussed here.

For the Home Gamer

For those of us not lucky enough to be working on a hardware emulator or hardware itself, there are other options if you would still like to try your hand at OpenGL ES. There are several OpenGL ES implementations available that will execute on a full-scale operating system. These are also great for doing initial development.

At the time of writing, a software implementation of OpenGL ES1.1 is available on Sourceforge called Vincent (http://ogl-es.sourceforge.net/index.htm). The project is open source, so anyone can try it. Unfortunately, at this time the only supported target environments are Microsoft Windows Mobile OSs and the ARM processor. This makes it difficult for the ordinary programmer to try out. But if you have experience with Windows CE, this might be a good place to start. A version of Vincent has been started that targets OpenGL ES 2.x, but currently is not ready for use.

Another option is PowerVR by Imagination Technologies. PowerVR is an IP-based technology that can be integrated into proprietary designs. They also have a free download for the PowerVR SDK. This is a package that includes an OpenGL ES emulator that will run on Microsoft Windows and Linux systems.

Hybrid Graphics Ltd. has also released a development package called Rasteroid that provides OpenGL ES emulator capabilities (http://www.hybrid.fi/main/products/devtools.php). This SDK is also freely downloadable for application development purposes.

Putting OpenGL ES into Action

Time for the meat and potatoes! Now that we have seen what OpenGL ES looks like, how it works, and the type of hardware and environments that are used, let's look at an actual example. We will walk through a simple OpenGL ES application using a PC emulator. The setup will be based on the Hybrid Graphics Rasteroid SDK. This platform will work only on Microsoft Windows–based systems. For those of you with other OSs, take a peek at what the PowerVR emulator has to offer. It also supports both Mac OS and Linux environments.

To successfully compile, link, and execute this program, you will need to download and install the Rasteroid SDK. How this relates to the sample code is described in the Readme.txt document that accompanies the source.

Setting Up the Environment

First things first: To render to the screen we will need a window. But before anything can be done with EGL, we need to create an OS-specific window. Then, the EGL display can be queried. Pass in the display you want; in this case we will ask for the default display:

```
programInfo->display = eglGetDisplay(EGL_DEFAULT_DISPALY);
```

After you have the display handle, you'll use it in many other EGL calls to signify which device you are referring to. Next, initialize EGL. Without initialization, most other calls are invalid and will throw an error.

```
eglInitialize(programInfo->display, &majorVer, &minorVer);
```

EGL will tell you what its major and minor versions are when you initialize it. Now that EGL has been "turned on," we need to choose a config. First, select the attributes you need; then, pass them into `eglChooseConfig`:

```
EGLint attribs[] =
{
    EGL_RED_SIZE,                            6,
    EGL_GREEN_SIZE,                          6,
    EGL_BLUE_SIZE,                           6,
    EGL_RENDERABLE_TYPE,      EGL_OPENGL_ES_BIT,
    EGL_SURFACE_TYPE,            EGL_WINDOW_BIT,
    EGL_NONE
};

    eglChooseConfig(programInfo->display, attribs, returnedConfigs, 1,
                &matchingConfigCnt);
    programInfo->config = returnedConfigs[0];
```

In this case we are only interested in getting one match. We will assume that the returned config will work for us since it matches the attribute criteria. For more robustness, an app can choose to have all matches returned, and then parse through the results to find the one that will work best. This is a simple application and will not require a special config. Store the config away.

Now that EGL is initialized and we know what config we want to use, we can create an EGL window surface to go along with the native window created earlier. Choose which surface attributes are desirable and call `eglCreateWindowSurface` using the config that was the best match and the native window handle that was returned when we created an

OS window:

```
EGLint surfAttribs[] =
{
    EGL_COLORSPACE,              EGL_COLORSPACE_sRGB,
    EGL_NONE
};

programInfo->windowSurface = eglCreateWindowSurface(programInfo->display,
                programInfo->config,
                (NativeWindowType)surfDesc.nativePtr,
                surfAttribs);
```

Again, store away the returned window surface handle for use later. Now that the window setup is all squared away, it's time to focus on more OpenGL-related stuff. We will need a context in order to make any OpenGL calls. Call `eglCreateContext` to get one, and use the display and config values we stored away to tell EGL where and what kind of context we need:

```
programInfo->esContext = eglCreateContext(programInfo->display,
                                          programInfo->config,
                                          NULL,
                                          NULL);
```

Keep the context handle so we know which context will be used. Now that a context has been created, make it the current context so it can actually be used for rendering. To do this, we will use all the handles we have spent all this time allocating:

```
eglMakeCurrent(programInfo->display, programInfo->windowSurface,
                programInfo->windowSurface, programInfo->esContext);
```

After the context is created and made current, OpenGL calls can now be made. But before we get to the OpenGL stuff, there is one last task. EGL still needs to be told what kind of rendering we will do to the surfaces we allocated. Do this with the `eglBindAPI` call. We are interested only in EGL rendering, so no surprise here.

```
eglBindAPI(EGL_OPENGL_ES_API);
```

Setting Up OpenGL ES State

Now that we have a current context, we can initialize the OpenGL state that needs to be set for rendering. First, set the viewport and scissor rectangle to the size of the window that was just created:

```
glViewport(0, 0, x, y);
glScissor(0, 0, x, y);
```

Next, clear the projection matrix:

```
glMatrixMode(GL_PROJECTION);
glLoadIdentity();
```

Then, call `glFrustrumf` to set up a projection matrix that matches our window. The parameters are calculated based on the window size:

```
glFrustumf(fXLeft, fXRight, fYBottom, fYTop, 0.1f, 100.f);
```

One last thing: There is some OpenGL state that can be set up now since it will not change while we are rendering. First set the shade model to flat, and then set the raster color. Also, turn on vertex arrays since that is what we will use to specify our geometry. And we will have to set the vertex pointer to our vertex data that has been predefined.

```
glShadeModel(GL_FLAT);
glColor4x(0x00000, 0x10000, 0x10000, 0x10000);

glEnableClientState(GL_VERTEX_ARRAY);
glVertexPointer(3, GL_BYTE, 0, verts);
```

That's it! EGL is now set up and ready for rendering. OpenGL ES state is also set up and ready to go.

Rendering

Rasteroid works much like GLUT. There is a rendering loop that gets called when the scene needs to be updated. We will use this loop to trigger all of our rendering. In addition to normal window redraw triggers, the draw function will be called periodically, allowing us to animate rendering.

Because this sample code is meant to demonstrate EGL and ES, the actual rendering is not very fancy. We will focus all of our rendering efforts on a single triangle!

The first task will be to update the window specific state. This was covered previously. Next, a clear color will be chosen and the color buffer cleared

```
glClearColor(fClearColor, fClearColor, fClearColor, 1.0f);
glClear(GL_COLOR_BUFFER_BIT);
```

Now, let's set up the model view matrix to prepare for rendering. We'll throw in a little rotation to keep things mildly interesting:

```
glMatrixMode(GL_MODELVIEW);
glLoadIdentity();
glTranslatef(0.f, 0.f, -20.f);
```

```
// rotate based on application execution time
glRotatef((GLfloat)(time*35.0f), -1.0f, -3.0f, 0.0f);
glRotatef((GLfloat)(time*20.0f),  0.5f, 0.0f,  7.0f);
```

At long last, it's time to draw! We'll just make one glDrawArrays call:

```
glDrawArrays(GL_TRIANGLE_STRIP, 0, 3);
```

There is one thing left to do. The drawing we just completed needs to be presented to the window surface. This is done with the eglSwapBuffers command:

```
eglSwapBuffers(programInfo->display, programInfo->windowSurface);
```

Figure 22.3 shows the result of our labor. This app isn't too fancy, but in this chapter our focus is on getting OpenGL ES working and using EGL to interface with the environment.

FIGURE 22.3   A spinning triangle in ES.

Cleaning Up

Before we are done, some cleanup is necessary. When the app exits, all the OpenGL ES and EGL state we set up needs to be released so that the system knows we are done drawing. First, release the context we created by calling eglMakeCurrent with NULL:

```
eglMakeCurrent(programInfo->display, NULL, NULL, NULL);
```

After the context is no longer current, it can be deleted:

```
eglDestroyContext(programInfo->display, programInfo->esContext);
```

Now that the context is cleaned up, we can clean up the surface and tell EGL we are done for now:

```
eglDestroySurface(programInfo->display, programInfo->windowSurface);
eglTerminate(programInfo->display);
eglReleaseThread();
```

Summary

We have covered a lot of ground in this chapter. First, OpenGL ES 1.0 was examined. This was the first OpenGL ES specification and was based on OpenGL 1.3. It uses the same type of fixed functionality pipeline to render. Next, OpenGL ES 1.1 was reviewed. This version, based on OpenGL 1.5, was a step up from OpenGL ES 1.0 and added many new features from its OpenGL counterpart. Then came OpenGL ES 2.0, based on OpenGL 2.0. This version takes a whole new approach by eliminating fixed function rendering altogether and introducing programmable shaders in its place. Last was OpenGL ES SC 1.0. This version provided compatibility features allowing it to work well in environments that require reliable execution.

We also were introduced to EGL and how it can be used to do window management with OpenGL ES. In addition, we have gone over some of the differences in working with an embedded environment. There are many setups in which OpenGL ES can operate. And for development on a PC, emulators have been created that can be used to simulate an OpenGL ES capable system. Finally, we saw an example of how to create an OpenGL ES application on a normal PC.

APPENDIX A
Further Reading/References

Real-time 3D graphics and OpenGL are popular topics, and there's more information and techniques in practice than can ever be published in a single book. You might find the following resources helpful as you further your knowledge and experience.

Other Good OpenGL Books

OpenGL Programming Guide, 5th Edition: The Official Guide to Learning OpenGL, Version 2. OpenGL Architecture Board, Dave Shreiner, Mason Woo, and Jackie Neider. Addison-Wesley, 2005.

OpenGL Shading Language, 2nd Edition. Randi J. Rost. Addison-Wesley, 2006.

OpenGL Distilled. Paul Martz. Addison-Wesley, 2006.

OpenGL Programming on Mac OS X: Architecture, Performance, and Integration. Robert P. Kuehne and J. D. Sullivan. Addison-Wesley, 2007.

OpenGL Programming for the X Window System. Mark J. Kilgard. Addison-Wesley, 1996.

Interactive Computer Graphics: A Top-Down Approach with OpenGL, 4th Edition. Edward Angel. Addison-Wesley, 2005.

The OpenGL Extensions Guide. Eric Lengyel. Charles River Media, 2003.

Advanced Graphics Programming Using OpenGL. Tom McReynolds and David Blythe. The Morgan Kaufmann Series in Computer Graphics, 2005.

More OpenGL Game Programming. Dave Astle, Editor. Thomson Course Technology, 2006.

3D Graphics Books

3D Computer Graphics, 3rd Edition. Alan Watt. Addison-Wesley, 1999.

3D Math Primer for Graphics and Game Development. Fletcher Dunn and Ian Parbery. Wordware Publishing, 2002.

Advanced Animation and Rendering Techniques: Theory and Practice. Alan Watt and Mark Watt (contributor). Addison-Wesley, 1992.

Introduction to Computer Graphics. James D. Foley, Andries van Dam, Steven K. Feiner, John F. Hughes, and Richard L. Phillips. Addison-Wesley, 1993.

Open Geometry: OpenGL + Advanced Geometry. Georg Glaeser and Hellmuth Stachel. Springer-Verlag, 1999.

Mathematics for 3D Game Programming & Computer Graphics, 2nd Edition. Eric Lengyel. Charles River Media, 2003.

Essential Mathematics for Games and Interactive Applications, James Van Verth and Lars Bishop. The Morgan Kaufmann Series in Interactive 3d Technology

Shader X 4: Advanced Rendering Techniques. Wolfgang Engel, Editor. Charles River Media, 2006.

Texturing & Modeling: A Procedural Approach, 3rd Edition. David S. Ebert, F. Kenton Musgrave, Darwyn Peachey, Ken Perlin, Steven Worley. The Morgan Kaufmann Series in Computer Graphics

Web Sites

The OpenGL SuperBible Web site:

`www.opengl.org/superbible`

The official OpenGL Web site:

`www.opengl.org`

The OpenGL SDK (lots of tutorials and tools):

`www.opengl.org/sdk/`

The preceding three Web sites are the gateways to OpenGL information on the Web, and of course, the official source of information for all things OpenGL and SuperBible related. The following sites also pertain to information covered in this book and offer vendor-specific OpenGL support, tutorials, demos, and news.

The Khronos Group OpenGL ES home page:

`www.khronos.org/opengles/`

The OpenGL Extension Registry:

`www.opengl.org/registry/`

AMD/ATI's developer home page:

`www.ati.amd.com/developer/`

NVIDIA's developer home page:

`developer.nvidia.com/`

The Mesa 3D OpenGL "work-a-like":

`www.mesa3d.org`

Open source X Window System

`www.xfree86.org`

A

Glossary

Aliasing   Technically, the loss of signal information in an image reproduced at some finite resolution. It is most often characterized by the appearance of sharp jagged edges along points, lines, or polygons due to the nature of having a limited number of fixed-sized pixels.

Alpha   A fourth color value added to provide a degree of transparency to the color of an object. An alpha value of 0.0 means complete transparency; 1.0 denotes no transparency (opaque).

Ambient light   Light in a scene that doesn't come from any specific point source or direction. Ambient light illuminates all surfaces evenly and on all sides. In the OpenGL lighting model, ambient light approximates how light is collectively scattered off all the surfaces in a scene.

Antialiasing   A rendering method used to smooth lines and curves and polygon edges. This technique averages the color of pixels adjacent to the line. It has the visual effect of softening the transition from the pixels on the line and those adjacent to the line, thus providing a smoother appearance. Full-scene Antialiasing is supported by OpenGL via the multisampling feature.

ARB   The Architecture Review Board. The committee body consisting of 3D graphics hardware vendors, previously charged with maintaining the OpenGL specification. The OpenGL ARB is now the name of the Khronos working group that is responsible for maintenance of the OpenGL specification.

Aspect ratio   The ratio of the width of a window to the height of the window. Specifically, the width of the window in pixels divided by the height of the window in pixels.

AUX library   A window-system-independent utility library. Limited but useful for quick and portable OpenGL demonstration programs. Now largely replaced by the GLUT library.

Bézier curve   A curve whose shape is defined by control points near the curve rather than by the precise set of points that define the curve itself.

Bitplane   An array of bits mapped directly to screen pixels.

Buffer   An area of memory used to store image information. This can be color, depth, or blending information. The red, green, blue, and alpha buffers are often collectively referred to as the color buffer.

Cartesian   A coordinate system based on three directional axes placed at a 90° orientation to one another. These coordinates are labeled x, y, and z.

Clip coordinates   The 4D geometric coordinates that result from the modelview and projection transformation.

Clipping   The elimination of a portion of a single primitive or group of primitives. The points that would be rendered outside the clipping region or volume are not drawn. The clipping volume is generally specified by the projection matrix. Clipped primitives are reconstructed such that the edges of the primitive do not lie outside the clipping region.

Color index mode   A color mode in which colors in a scene are selected from a fixed number of colors available in a palette. These entries are referenced by an index into the palette. This mode is rarely used and even more rarely hardware accelerated.

Convex   A reference to the shape of a polygon. A convex polygon has no indentations, and no straight line can be drawn through the polygon that intersects it more than twice (once entering, once leaving).

Culling   The elimination of graphics primitives that would not be seen if rendered. Backface culling eliminates the front or back face of a primitive so that the face isn't drawn. Frustum culling eliminates whole objects that would fall outside the viewing frustum.

Destination color   The stored color at a particular location in the color buffer. This terminology is usually used when describing blending operations to distinguish between the color already present in the color buffer and the color coming into the color buffer (source color).

Display list   A compiled list of OpenGL functions and commands. When called, a display list executes faster than a manually called list of single commands.

Dithering   A method used to simulate a wider range of color depth by placing different-colored pixels together in patterns that give the illusion of shading between the two colors.

Double buffered   A drawing technique used by OpenGL. The image to be displayed is assembled in memory and then placed on the screen in a single update operation, rather than built primitive by primitive on the screen. Double buffering is a much faster and smoother update operation and can produce animations.

Extruded   The process of taking a 2D image or shape and adding a third dimension uniformly across the surface. This process can transform 2D fonts into 3D lettering.

Eye coordinates   The coordinate system based on the position of the eye. The eye's position is placed at (0, 0, 0) and looks down the negative z-axis.

Frustum   A truncated pyramid-shaped viewing volume that creates a perspective view. (Near objects are large; far objects are small.)

GLSL   Acronym for the OpenGL Shading Language, a high-level C-like shading language.

GLUT library   The OpenGL Utility Toolkit. A window-system-independent utility library useful for creating sample programs and simple 3D rendering programs that are independent of the operating system and windowing system. Typically used to provide portability between Windows, X-Window, Linux, and so on.

Immediate mode   A graphics rendering mode in which commands and functions are sent individually and have an immediate effect on the state of the rendering engine.

Implementation   A software- or hardware-based device that performs OpenGL rendering operations.

Khronos Group   An industry consortium that now manages the maintenance and promotion of the OpenGL specification in addition to several other industry standards

Literal   A value, not a variable name. A specific string or numeric constant embedded directly in source code.

Matrix   A 2D array of numbers. Matrices can be operated on mathematically and are used to perform coordinate transformations.

Mipmapping   A technique that uses multiple levels of detail for a texture. This technique selects from among the different sizes of an image available, or possibly combines the two nearest sized matches to produce the final fragments used for texturing.

Modelview matrix   The OpenGL matrix that transforms primitives to eye coordinates from object coordinates.

Normal   A directional vector that points perpendicularly to a plane or surface. When used, normals are applied to each vertex in a primitive.

Normalize   The reduction of a normal to a unit normal. A unit normal is a vector that has a length of exactly 1.0.

NURBS   An acronym for non-uniform rational B-spline. This is a method of specifying parametric curves and surfaces.

Orthographic   A drawing mode in which no perspective or foreshortening takes place. Also called parallel projection. The lengths and dimensions of all primitives are undistorted regardless of orientation or distance from the viewer.

B

Palette   A set of colors available for drawing operations. For 8-bit Windows color modes, the palette contains 256 color entries, and all pixels in the scene can be colored from only this set.

Parametric curve   A curve whose shape is determined by one (for a curve) or two (for a surface) parameters. These parameters are used in separate equations that yield the individual x, y, and z values of the points along the curve.

Perspective   A drawing mode in which objects farther from the viewer appear smaller than nearby objects.

Pixel   Condensed from the words *picture element.* This is the smallest visual division available on the computer screen. Pixels are arranged in rows and columns and are individually set to the appropriate color to render any given image.

Pixmap   A two-dimensional array of color values that compose a color image. Pixmaps are so called because each picture element corresponds to a pixel on the screen.

Polygon   A 2D shape drawn with three or more sides.

Primitive   A 2D polygonal shape defined by OpenGL. All objects and scenes are composed of various combinations of primitives.

Projection   The transformation of lines, points, and polygons from eye coordinates to clipping coordinates on the screen.

Quadrilateral   A polygon with exactly four sides.

Rasterize   The process of converting projected primitives and bitmaps into pixel fragments in the frame buffer.

Render   The conversion of primitives in object coordinates to an image in the frame buffer. The rendering pipeline is the process by which OpenGL commands and statements become pixels on the screen.

Retained mode   A style of 3D programming in which an object's representation is held in memory by the programming library.

Scintillation   A sparkling or flashing effect produced on objects when a nonmipmapped texture map is applied to a polygon that is significantly smaller than the size of the texture being applied. This term is also applied to aliasing artifacts.

Shader   A small program that is executed by the graphics hardware, often in parallel, to operate on individual vertices or pixels. See also *GLSL.*

Source color   The color of the incoming fragment, as opposed to the color already present in the color buffer (destination color). This terminology is usually used when describing how the source and destination colors are combined during a blending operation.

Specification   The design document that specifies OpenGL operation and fully describes how an implementation must work.

Spline   A general term used to describe any curve created by placing control points near the curve, which have a pulling effect on the curve's shape. This is similar to the reaction of a piece of flexible material when pressure is applied at various points along its length.

Stipple   A binary bit pattern used to mask out pixel generation in the frame buffer. This is similar to a monochrome bitmap, but one-dimensional patterns are used for lines and two-dimensional patterns are used for polygons.

Tessellation   The process of breaking down a complex 2D polygon into a planar mesh of convex polygons.

Texel   Similar to pixel (picture element), a texel is a *texture element*. A texel represents a color from a texture that is applied to a pixel fragment in the frame buffer.

Texture   An image pattern of colors applied to the surface of a primitive.

Texture mapping   The process of applying a texture image to a surface. The surface does not have to be planar (flat). Texture mapping is often used to wrap an image around a curved object or to produce patterned surfaces such as wood or marble.

Transformation   The manipulation of a coordinate system. This can include rotation, translation, scaling (both uniform and nonuniform), and perspective division.

Translucence   A degree of transparency of an object. In OpenGL, this is represented by an alpha value ranging from 1.0 (opaque) to 0.0 (transparent).

Vertex   A single point in space. Except when used for point and line primitives, it also defines the point at which two edges of a polygon meet.

Viewing volume   The area in 3D space that can be viewed in the window. Objects and points outside the viewing volume are clipped (cannot be seen).

Viewport   The area within a window that is used to display an OpenGL image. Usually, this encompasses the entire client area. Stretched viewports can produce enlarged or shrunken output within the physical window.

Wireframe   The representation of a solid object by a mesh of lines rather than solid shaded polygons. Wireframe models are usually rendered faster and can be used to view both the front and the back of an object at the same time.

B

API Reference

Overview of Appendix C

Appendix C is composed of API reference pages, covering OpenGL. These pages come from several different sources.

The following OpenGL reference pages are Copyright © 2003-2005 3Dlabs Inc. Ltd. and may be distributed subject to the terms and conditions set forth in the Open Publication License, v 1.0, 8 June 1999. For details, see http://opencontent.org/openpub/.

glAttachShader, glBindAttribLocation, glCompileShader, glCreateProgram, glCreateShader, glDeleteProgram, glDeleteShader, glDetachShader, glDrawBuffers, glEnableVertexAttribArray/glDisableVertexAttribArray, glGetActiveAttrib, glGetActiveUniform, glGetAttachedShaders, glGetAttribLocation, glGetProgramiv, glGetProgramInfoLog, glGetShaderiv, glGetShaderInfoLog, glGetUniform, glGetUniformLocation, glGetVertexAttrib, glGetVertexAttribPointerv, glIsProgram, glIsShader, glLinkProgram, glShaderSource, glUniform/glUniformMatrix, glUseProgram, glValidateProgram, glVertexAttrib, glVertexAttribPointer

The following OpenGL reference pages are Copyright © 2007 The Khronos Group Inc. and licensed under the Khronos Free Use License. For details, see http://www.khronos.org/help/legal/KFUL/.

glBlendEquationSeparate, glStencilFuncSeparate, glStencilMaskSeparate, glStencilOpSeparate

The following OpenGL reference pages were written for this book and offered back to the community for free use. They are Copyright © 2005 Addison-Wesley and may be distributed subject to the terms and conditions set forth in the Open Publication License, v 1.0, 8 June 1999. For details, see http://opencontent.org/openpub/.

glBeginQuery/glEndQuery, glBindBuffer, glBufferData, glBufferSubData, glDeleteBuffers, glDeleteQueries, glGenBuffers, glGenQueries, glGetBufferParameteriv, glGetBufferPointerv, glGetBufferSubData, glGetQueryiv, glGetQueryObject, glIsBuffer, glIsQuery, glMapBuffer/glUnmapBuffer

glAccum

Operate on the accumulation buffer

C Specification

```
void glAccum(GLenum op, GLfloat value);
```

Parameters

op   Specifies the accumulation buffer operation. Symbolic constants GL_ACCUM, GL_LOAD, GL_ADD, GL_MULT, and GL_RETURN are accepted.

value   Specifies a floating-point value used in the accumulation buffer operation. op determines how value is used.

Description

The accumulation buffer is an extended-range color buffer. Images are not rendered into it. Rather, images rendered into one of the color buffers are added to the contents of the accumulation buffer after rendering. Effects such as antialiasing (of points, lines, and polygons), motion blur, and depth of field can be created by accumulating images generated with different transformation matrices.

Each pixel in the accumulation buffer consists of red, green, blue, and alpha values. The number of bits per component in the accumulation buffer depends on the implementation. You can examine this number by calling glGetIntegerv four times, with arguments GL_ACCUM_RED_BITS, GL_ACCUM_GREEN_BITS, GL_ACCUM_BLUE_BITS, and GL_ACCUM_ALPHA_BITS. Regardless of the number of bits per component, the range of values stored by each component is [-1,1] . The accumulation buffer pixels are mapped one-to-one with frame buffer pixels.

glAccum operates on the accumulation buffer. The first argument, op, is a symbolic constant that selects an accumulation buffer operation. The second argument, value, is a floating-point value to be used in that operation. Five operations are specified: GL_ACCUM, GL_LOAD, GL_ADD, GL_MULT, and GL_RETURN.

All accumulation buffer operations are limited to the area of the current scissor box and applied identically to the red, green, blue, and alpha components of each pixel. If a glAccum operation results in a value outside the range [-1,1] , the contents of an accumulation buffer pixel component are undefined.

The operations are as follows:

GL_ACCUM

Obtains R, G, B, and A values from the buffer currently selected for reading (see glReadBuffer). Each component value is divided by $2^n - 1$, where n is the number of bits allocated to each color component in the currently selected buffer. The result is a floating-point value in the range [0,1] , which is multiplied by value and added to the corresponding pixel component in the accumulation buffer, thereby updating the accumulation buffer.

GL_LOAD

Similar to GL_ACCUM, except that the current value in the accumulation buffer is not used in the calculation of the new value. That is, the R, G, B, and A values from the currently selected buffer are divided by $2^n - 1$, multiplied by value, and then stored in the corresponding accumulation buffer cell, overwriting the current value.

GL_ADD

Adds value to each R, G, B, and A in the accumulation buffer.

GL_MULT

Multiplies each R, G, B, and A in the accumulation buffer by value and returns the scaled component to its corresponding accumulation buffer location.

GL_RETURN

Transfers accumulation buffer values to the color buffer or buffers currently selected for writing. Each R, G, B, and A component is multiplied by value, then multiplied by $2^n - 1$, clamped to the range $[0, 2^n - 1]$, and stored in the corresponding display buffer cell. The only fragment operations that are applied to this transfer are pixel ownership, scissor, dithering, and color writemasks.

To clear the accumulation buffer, call glClearAccum with R, G, B, and A values to set it to, then call glClear with the accumulation buffer enabled.

Notes

Only pixels within the current scissor box are updated by a glAccum operation.

Errors

GL_INVALID_ENUM is generated if *op* is not an accepted value.

GL_INVALID_OPERATION is generated if there is no accumulation buffer.

GL_INVALID_OPERATION is generated if glAccum is executed between the execution of glBegin and the corresponding execution of glEnd.

Associated Gets

glGet with argument GL_ACCUM_RED_BITS
glGet with argument GL_ACCUM_GREEN_BITS
glGet with argument GL_ACCUM_BLUE_BITS
glGet with argument GL_ACCUM_ALPHA_BITS

See Also

glClear, glClearAccum, glCopyPixels, glDrawBuffer, glGet, glReadBuffer, glReadPixels, glScissor, glStencilOp

glActiveTexture

Select active texture unit

C Specification

void **glActiveTexture**(GLenum *texture*);

Parameters

texture   Specifies which texture unit to make active. The number of texture units is implementation dependent, but must be at least two. *texture* must be one of GL_TEXTURE*i*, where *i* ranges from 0 to the larger of (GL_MAX_TEXTURE_COORDS − 1) and (GL_MAX_COMBINED_TEXTURE_IMAGE_UNITS − 1). The initial value is GL_TEXTURE0.

Description

glActiveTexture selects which texture unit subsequent texture state calls will affect. The number of texture units an implementation supports is implementation dependent, but must be at least 2.

Vertex arrays are client-side GL resources, which are selected by the glClientActiveTexture routine.

Notes

glActiveTexture is only supported if the GL version is 1.3 or greater, or if ARB_multitexture is included in the string returned by glGetString when called with the argument GL_EXTENSIONS.

Errors

GL_INVALID_ENUM is generated if *texture* is not one of GL_TEXTURE*i*, where *i* ranges from 0 to the larger of (GL_MAX_TEXTURE_COORDS − 1) and (GL_MAX_COMBINED_TEXTURE_IMAGE_UNITS − 1).

Associated Gets

glGet with argument GL_ACTIVE_TEXTURE, GL_MAX_TEXTURE_COORDS, or GL_MAX_COMBINED_TEXTURE_IMAGE_UNITS

See Also

glClientActiveTexture, glMultiTexCoord, glTexParameter

glAlphaFunc

Specify the alpha test function

C Specification

```
void glAlphaFunc(GLenum func, GLclampf ref);
```

Parameters

func   Specifies the alpha comparison function. Symbolic constants GL_NEVER, GL_LESS, GL_EQUAL, GL_LEQUAL, GL_GREATER, GL_NOTEQUAL, GL_GEQUAL, and GL_ALWAYS are accepted. The initial value is GL_ALWAYS.

ref   Specifies the reference value that incoming alpha values are compared to. This value is clamped to the range [0,1] , where 0 represents the lowest possible alpha value and 1 the highest possible value. The initial reference value is 0.

Description

The alpha test discards fragments depending on the outcome of a comparison between an incoming fragment's alpha value and a constant reference value. glAlphaFunc specifies the reference value and the comparison function. The comparison is performed only if alpha testing is enabled. By default, it is not enabled. (See glEnable and glDisable of GL_ALPHA_TEST.)

func and *ref* specify the conditions under which the pixel is drawn. The incoming alpha value is compared to *ref* using the function specified by *func*. If the value passes the comparison, the incoming fragment is drawn if it also passes subsequent stencil and depth buffer tests. If the value fails the comparison, no change is made to the frame buffer at that pixel location. The comparison functions are as follows:

GL_NEVER
Never passes.

GL_LESS
Passes if the incoming alpha value is less than the reference value.

GL_EQUAL
Passes if the incoming alpha value is equal to the reference value.

GL_LEQUAL
Passes if the incoming alpha value is less than or equal to the reference value.

GL_GREATER
Passes if the incoming alpha value is greater than the reference value.

GL_NOTEQUAL
Passes if the incoming alpha value is not equal to the reference value.

GL_GEQUAL
Passes if the incoming alpha value is greater than or equal to the reference value.

GL_ALWAYS
Always passes (initial value).

glAlphaFunc operates on all pixel write operations, including those resulting from the scan conversion of points, lines, polygons, and bitmaps, and from pixel draw and copy operations. glAlphaFunc does not affect screen clear operations.

Notes

Alpha testing is performed only in RGBA mode.

Errors

GL_INVALID_ENUM is generated if *func* is not an accepted value.

GL_INVALID_OPERATION is generated if glAlphaFunc is executed between the execution of glBegin and the corresponding execution of glEnd.

Associated Gets

glGet with argument GL_ALPHA_TEST_FUNC
glGet with argument GL_ALPHA_TEST_REF
glIsEnabled with argument GL_ALPHA_TEST

See Also

glBlendFunc, glClear, glDepthFunc, glEnable, glStencilFunc

glAreTexturesResident

Determine if textures are loaded in texture memory

C Specification

GLboolean **glAreTexturesResident**(GLsizei   *n*,
                                    const GLuint * *textures*,
                                    GLboolean *   *residences*);

Parameters

n   Specifies the number of textures to be queried.

textures   Specifies an array containing the names of the textures to be queried.

residences   Specifies an array in which the texture residence status is returned. The resi-
                 dence status of a texture named by an element of *textures* is returned in the
                 corresponding element of *residences*.

Description

GL establishes a "working set" of textures that are resident in texture memory. These textures can
be bound to a texture target much more efficiently than textures that are not resident.

glAreTexturesResident queries the texture residence status of the *n* textures named by the
elements of *textures*. If all the named textures are resident, glAreTexturesResident returns
GL_TRUE, and the contents of *residences* are undisturbed. If not all the named textures are resident, glAreTexturesResident returns GL_FALSE, and detailed status is returned in the *n* elements
of *residences*. If an element of *residences* is GL_TRUE, then the texture named by the corresponding element of *textures* is resident.

The residence status of a single bound texture may also be queried by calling
glGetTexParameter with the *target* argument set to the target to which the texture is bound, and
the *pname* argument set to GL_TEXTURE_RESIDENT. This is the only way that the residence status of
a default texture can be queriedglAreTexturesResident.

Notes

glAreTexturesResident is available only if the GL version is 1.1 or greater.

glAreTexturesResident returns the residency status of the textures at the time of invocation.
It does not guarantee that the textures will remain resident at any other time.

If textures reside in virtual memory (there is no texture memory), they are considered always
resident.

Some implementations may not load a texture until the first use of that texture.

Errors

GL_INVALID_VALUE is generated if n is negative.

GL_INVALID_VALUE is generated if any element in **textures** is 0 or does not name a texture. In
that case, the function returns GL_FALSE and the contents of **residences** is indeterminate.

GL_INVALID_OPERATION is generated if glAreTexturesResident is executed between the
execution of glBegin and the corresponding execution of glEnd.

Associated Gets

glGetTexParameter with parameter name GL_TEXTURE_RESIDENT retrieves the residence status
of a currently bound texture.

See Also

glBindTexture, glGetTexParameter, glPrioritizeTextures, glTexImage1D,
glTexImage2D, glTexImage3D, glTexParameter

glArrayElement

Render a vertex using the specified vertex array element

C Specification

void **glArrayElement**(GLint *i*);

Parameters

i   Specifies an index into the enabled vertex data arrays.

Description

glArrayElement commands are used within glBegin/glEnd pairs to specify vertex and attribute data for point, line, and polygon primitives. If GL_VERTEX_ARRAY is enabled when glArrayElement is called, a single vertex is drawn, using vertex and attribute data taken from location i of the enabled arrays. If GL_VERTEX_ARRAY is not enabled, no drawing occurs but the attributes corresponding to the enabled arrays are modified.

Use glArrayElement to construct primitives by indexing vertex data, rather than by streaming through arrays of data in first-to-last order. Because each call specifies only a single vertex, it is possible to explicitly specify per-primitive attributes such as a single normal for each triangle.

Changes made to array data between the execution of glBegin and the corresponding execution of glEnd may affect calls to glArrayElement that are made within the same glBegin/glEnd period in nonsequential ways. That is, a call to glArrayElement that precedes a change to array data may access the changed data, and a call that follows a change to array data may access original data.

Notes

glArrayElement is available only if the GL version is 1.1 or greater.

glArrayElement is included in display lists. If glArrayElement is entered into a display list, the necessary array data (determined by the array pointers and enables) is also entered into the display list. Because the array pointers and enables are client-side state, their values affect display lists when the lists are created, not when the lists are executed.

Errors

GL_INVALID_VALUE may be generated if i is negative.

GL_INVALID_OPERATION is generated if a nonzero buffer object name is bound to an enabled array and the buffer object's data store is currently mapped.

See Also

glClientActiveTexture, glColorPointer, glDrawArrays, glEdgeFlagPointer, glFogCoordPointer, glGetPointerv, glIndexPointer, glInterleavedArrays, glNormalPointer, glSecondaryColorPointer, glTexCoordPointer, glVertexPointer

glAttachShader

Attach a shader object to a program object

C Specification

void **glAttachShader**(GLuint   *program*,
                     GLuint   *shader*);

Parameters

program   Specifies the program object to which a shader object will be attached.
shader   Specifies the shader object that is to be attached.

Description

In order to create an executable, there must be a way to specify the list of things that will be linked together. Program objects provide this mechanism. Shaders that are to be linked together in a program object must first be attached to that program object. glAttachShader attaches the shader object specified by *shader* to the program object specified by *program*. This indicates that *shader* will be included in link operations that will be performed on *program*.

All operations that can be performed on a shader object are valid whether or not the shader object is attached to a program object. It is permissible to attach a shader object to a program object before source code has been loaded into the shader object or before the shader object has been compiled. It is permissible to attach multiple shader objects of the same type because each may contain a portion of the complete shader. It is also permissible to attach a shader object to more than one program object. If a shader object is deleted while it is attached to a program object, it will be flagged for deletion, and deletion will not occur until glDetachShader is called to detach it from all program objects to which it is attached.

Notes
glAttachShader is available only if the GL version is 2.0 or greater.

Errors
GL_INVALID_VALUE is generated if either *program* or *shader* is not a value generated by OpenGL.

GL_INVALID_OPERATION is generated if *program* is not of type GL_PROGRAM_OBJECT.

GL_INVALID_OPERATION is generated if *shader* is not of type GL_SHADER_OBJECT.

GL_INVALID_OPERATION is generated if *shader* is already attached to *program*.

GL_INVALID_OPERATION is generated if glAttachShader is executed between the execution of glBegin and the corresponding execution of glEnd.

Associated Gets
glGetAttachedShaders with the handle of a valid program object
glIsProgram
glIsShader

See Also
glCompileShader, glDetachShader, glLinkProgram, glShaderSource

glBegin

Delimit the vertices of a primitive or a group of like primitives

C Specification
void **glBegin**(GLenum *mode*);

Parameters
mode   Specifies the primitive or primitives that will be created from vertices presented between glBegin and the subsequent glEnd. Ten symbolic constants are accepted: GL_POINTS, GL_LINES, GL_LINE_STRIP, GL_LINE_LOOP, GL_TRIANGLES, GL_TRIANGLE_STRIP, GL_TRIANGLE_FAN, GL_QUADS, GL_QUAD_STRIP, and GL_POLYGON.

C Specification
void **glEnd**(*void*);

Description
glBegin and glEnd delimit the vertices that define a primitive or a group of like primitives. glBegin accepts a single argument that specifies in which of ten ways the vertices are interpreted. Taking *n* as an integer count starting at one, and *N* as the total number of vertices specified, the interpretations are as follows:

GL_POINTS

Treats each vertex as a single point. Vertex *n* defines point *n*. *N* points are drawn.

GL_LINES

Treats each pair of vertices as an independent line segment. Vertices $2n - 1$ and $2n$ define line *n*. $\frac{N}{2}$ lines are drawn.

GL_LINE_STRIP

Draws a connected group of line segments from the first vertex to the last. Vertices n and $n + 1$ define line n. $N - 1$ lines are drawn.

GL_LINE_LOOP

Draws a connected group of line segments from the first vertex to the last, then back to the first. Vertices n and $n + 1$ define line n. The last line, however, is defined by vertices N and 1. N lines are drawn.

GL_TRIANGLES

Treats each triplet of vertices as an independent triangle. Vertices $3n - 2$, $3n - 1$, and $3n$ define triangle n. $\dfrac{N}{3}$ triangles are drawn.

GL_TRIANGLE_STRIP

Draws a connected group of triangles. One triangle is defined for each vertex presented after the first two vertices. For odd n, vertices n, $n + 1$, and $n + 2$ define triangle n. For even n, vertices $n + 1$, n, and $n + 2$ define triangle n. $N - 2$ triangles are drawn.

GL_TRIANGLE_FAN

Draws a connected group of triangles. One triangle is defined for each vertex presented after the first two vertices. Vertices 1, $n + 1$, and $n + 2$ define triangle n. $N - 2$ triangles are drawn.

GL_QUADS

Treats each group of four vertices as an independent quadrilateral. Vertices $4n - 3$, $4n - 2$, $4n - 1$, and $4n$ define quadrilateral n. $\dfrac{N}{4}$ quadrilaterals are drawn.

GL_QUAD_STRIP

Draws a connected group of quadrilaterals. One quadrilateral is defined for each pair of vertices presented after the first pair. Vertices $2n - 1$, $2n$, $2n + 2$, and $2n + 1$ define quadrilateral n. $\dfrac{N}{2}$ quadrilaterals are drawn. Note that the order in which vertices are used to construct a quadrilateral from strip data is different from that used with independent data.

GL_POLYGON

Draws a single, convex polygon. Vertices 1 through N define this polygon.

Only a subset of GL commands can be used between glBegin and glEnd. The commands are glVertex, glColor, glIndex, glNormal, glTexCoord, glEvalCoord, glEvalPoint, glArrayElement, glMaterial, and glEdgeFlag. Also, it is acceptable to use glCallList or glCallLists to execute display lists that include only the preceding commands. If any other GL command is executed between glBegin and glEnd, the error flag is set and the command is ignored.

Regardless of the value chosen for *mode*, there is no limit to the number of vertices that can be defined between glBegin and glEnd. Lines, triangles, quadrilaterals, and polygons that are incompletely specified are not drawn. Incomplete specification results when either too few vertices are provided to specify even a single primitive or when an incorrect multiple of vertices is specified. The incomplete primitive is ignored; the rest are drawn.

The minimum specification of vertices for each primitive is as follows: 1 for a point, 2 for a line, 3 for a triangle, 4 for a quadrilateral, and 3 for a polygon. Modes that require a certain multiple of vertices are GL_LINES (2), GL_TRIANGLES (3), GL_QUADS (4), and GL_QUAD_STRIP (2).

Errors

GL_INVALID_ENUM is generated if *mode* is set to an unaccepted value.

GL_INVALID_OPERATION is generated if glBegin is executed between a glBegin and the corresponding execution of glEnd.

GL_INVALID_OPERATION is generated if glEnd is executed without being preceded by a glBegin.

GL_INVALID_OPERATION is generated if a command other than glVertex, glColor, glSecondaryColor, glIndex, glNormal, glFogCoord, glTexCoord, glMultiTexCoord, glEvalCoord, glEvalPoint, glArrayElement, glMaterial, glEdgeFlag, glCallList, or glCallLists is executed between the execution of glBegin and the corresponding execution glEnd.

Execution of glEnableClientState, glDisableClientState, glEdgeFlagPointer, glFogCoordPointer, glTexCoordPointer, glColorPointer, glSecondaryColorPointer, glIndexPointer, glNormalPointer, glVertexPointer, glInterleavedArrays, or glPixelStore is not allowed after a call to glBegin and before the corresponding call to glEnd, but an error may or may not be generated.

See Also

glArrayElement, glCallList, glCallLists, glColor, glEdgeFlag, glEvalCoord, glEvalPoint, glFogCoord, glIndex, glMaterial, glMultiTexCoord, glNormal, glSecondaryColor, glTexCoord, glVertex

glBeginQuery

Delimit the boundaries of a query object

C Specification

void **glBeginQuery**(GLenum *target*, GLuint *id*);

Parameters

target   Specifies the target type of query object established between glBeginQuery and the subsequent glEndQuery. The symbolic constant must be GL_SAMPLES_PASSED.

id   Specifies the name of a query object.

C Specification

void **glEndQuery**(GLenum *target*);

Parameters

target   Specifies the target type of query object to be concluded. The symbolic constant must be GL_SAMPLES_PASSED.

Description

glBeginQuery and glEndQuery delimit the boundaries of a query object. If a query object with name *id* does not yet exist it is created.

When glBeginQuery is executed, the query object's samples-passed counter is reset to 0. Subsequent rendering will increment the counter once for every sample that passes the depth test. When glEndQuery is executed, the samples-passed counter is assigned to the query object's result value. This value can be queried by calling glGetQueryObject with pnameGL_QUERY_RESULT.

Querying the GL_QUERY_RESULT implicitly flushes the GL pipeline until the rendering delimited by the query object has completed and the result is available. GL_QUERY_RESULT_AVAILABLE can be queried to determine if the result is immediately available or if the rendering is not yet complete.

Notes

If the samples-passed count exceeds the maximum value representable in the number of available bits, as reported by glGetQueryiv with pnameGL_QUERY_COUNTER_BITS, the count becomes undefined.

An implementation may support 0 bits in its samples-passed counter, in which case query results are always undefined and essentially useless.

When SAMPLE_BUFFERS is 0, the samples-passed counter will increment once for each fragment that passes the depth test. When SAMPLE_BUFFERS is 1, an implementation may either increment the samples-passed counter individually for each sample of a fragment that passes the depth test, or it may choose to increment the counter for all samples of a fragment if any one of them passes the depth test.

glBeginQuery and glEndQuery are available only if the GL version is 1.5 or greater.

Errors

GL_INVALID_ENUM is generated if *target* is not GL_SAMPLES_PASSED.

GL_INVALID_OPERATION is generated if glBeginQuery is executed while a query object of the same *target* is already active.

GL_INVALID_OPERATION is generated if glEndQuery is executed when a query object of the same *target* is not active.

GL_INVALID_OPERATION is generated if *id* is 0.

GL_INVALID_OPERATION is generated if *id* is the name of an already active query object.

GL_INVALID_OPERATION is generated if glBeginQuery or glEndQuery is executed between the execution of glBegin and the corresponding execution of glEnd.

See Also

glDeleteQueries, glGenQueries, glGetQueryiv, glGetQueryObject, glIsQuery

glBindAttribLocation

Associate a generic vertex attribute index with a named attribute variable

C Specification

```
void glBindAttribLocation(GLuint          program,
                          GLuint          index,
                          const GLchar *  name);
```

Parameters

program   Specifies the handle of the program object in which the association is to be made.

index   Specifies the index of the generic vertex attribute to be bound.

name   Specifies a null terminated string containing the name of the vertex shader attribute variable to which *index* is to be bound.

Description

glBindAttribLocation is used to associate a user-defined attribute variable in the program object specified by *program* with a generic vertex attribute index. The name of the user-defined attribute variable is passed as a null terminated string in *name*. The generic vertex attribute index to be bound to this variable is specified by *index*. When *program* is made part of current state, values provided via the generic vertex attribute *index* will modify the value of the user-defined attribute variable specified by *name*.

If *name* refers to a matrix attribute variable, *index* refers to the first column of the matrix. Other matrix columns are then automatically bound to locations *index* + 1 for a matrix of type mat2; *index* + 1 and *index* + 2 for a matrix of type mat3; and *index* + 1, *index* + 2, and *index* + 3 for a matrix of type mat4.

This command makes it possible for vertex shaders to use descriptive names for attribute variables rather than generic variables that are numbered from 0 to GL_MAX_VERTEX_ATTRIBS -1. The values sent to each generic attribute index are part of current state, just like standard vertex attributes such as color, normal, and vertex position. If a different program object is made current by calling glUseProgram, the generic vertex attributes are tracked in such a way that the same values will be observed by attributes in the new program object that are also bound to *index*.

Attribute variable name-to-generic attribute index bindings for a program object can be explicitly assigned at any time by calling glBindAttribLocation. Attribute bindings do not go into effect until glLinkProgram is called. After a program object has been linked successfully, the index values for generic attributes remain fixed (and their values can be queried) until the next link command occurs.

Applications are not allowed to bind any of the standard OpenGL vertex attributes using this command, as they are bound automatically when needed. Any attribute binding that occurs after the program object has been linked will not take effect until the next time the program object is linked.

Notes

glBindAttribLocation is available only if the GL version is 2.0 or greater.

glBindAttribLocation can be called before any vertex shader objects are bound to the specified program object. It is also permissible to bind a generic attribute index to an attribute variable name that is never used in a vertex shader.

If *name* was bound previously, that information is lost. Thus you cannot bind one user-defined attribute variable to multiple indices, but you can bind multiple user-defined attribute variables to the same index.

Applications are allowed to bind more than one user-defined attribute variable to the same generic vertex attribute index. This is called *aliasing*, and it is allowed only if just one of the aliased attributes is active in the executable program, or if no path through the shader consumes more than one attribute of a set of attributes aliased to the same location. The compiler and linker are allowed to assume that no aliasing is done and are free to employ optimizations that work only in the absence of aliasing. OpenGL implementations are not required to do error checking to detect aliasing. Because there is no way to bind standard attributes, it is not possible to alias generic attributes with conventional ones (except for generic attribute 0).

Active attributes that are not explicitly bound will be bound by the linker when glLinkProgram is called. The locations assigned can be queried by calling glGetAttribLocation.

OpenGL copies the *name* string when glBindAttribLocation is called, so an application may free its copy of the *name* string immediately after the function returns.

Errors

GL_INVALID_VALUE is generated if *index* is greater than or equal to GL_MAX_VERTEX_ATTRIBS.

GL_INVALID_OPERATION is generated if *name* starts with the reserved prefix "gl_".

GL_INVALID_VALUE is generated if *program* is not a value generated by OpenGL.

GL_INVALID_OPERATION is generated if *program* is not of type GL_PROGRAM_OBJECT.

GL_INVALID_OPERATION is generated if glBindAttribLocation is executed between the execution of glBegin and the corresponding execution of glEnd.

Associated Gets

glGet with argument GL_MAX_VERTEX_ATTRIBS
glGetActiveAttrib with argument *program*
glGetAttribLocation with arguments *program* and *name*
glIsProgram

See Also

glDisableVertexAttribArray, glEnableVertexAttribArray, glUseProgram, glVertexAttrib, glVertexAttribPointer

glBindBuffer

Bind a named buffer object

C Specification

void **glBindBuffer**(GLenum *target*,
                  GLuint *buffer*);

Parameters

target   Specifies the target to which the buffer object is bound. The symbolic constant must be GL_ARRAY_BUFFER, GL_ELEMENT_ARRAY_BUFFER, GL_PIXEL_PACK_BUFFER, or GL_PIXEL_UNPACK_BUFFER.

buffer   Specifies the name of a buffer object.

Description

glBindBuffer lets you create or use a named buffer object. Calling glBindBuffer with *target* set to GL_ARRAY_BUFFER, GL_ELEMENT_ARRAY_BUFFER, GL_PIXEL_PACK_BUFFER or GL_PIXEL_UNPACK_BUFFER and *buffer* set to the name of the new buffer object binds the buffer object name to the target. When a buffer object is bound to a target, the previous binding for that target is automatically broken.

Buffer object names are unsigned integers. The value zero is reserved, but there is no default buffer object for each buffer object target. Instead, *buffer* set to zero effectively unbinds any buffer object previously bound, and restores client memory usage for that buffer object target. Buffer object names and the corresponding buffer object contents are local to the shared display-list space (see glXCreateContext) of the current GL rendering context; two rendering contexts share buffer object names only if they also share display lists.

You may use glGenBuffers to generate a set of new buffer object names.

The state of a buffer object immediately after it is first bound is an unmapped zero-sized memory buffer with READ_WRITE access and STATIC_DRAW usage.

While a nonzero buffer object name is bound, GL operations on the target to which it is bound affect the bound buffer object, and queries of the target to which it is bound return state from the bound buffer object. While buffer object name zero is bound, as in the initial state, attempts to modify or query state on the target to which it is bound generates an INVALID_OPERATION error.

When vertex array pointer state is changed, for example by a call to glNormalPointer, the current buffer object binding (GL_ARRAY_BUFFER_BINDING) is copied into the corresponding client state for the vertex array type being changed, for example GL_NORMAL_ARRAY_BUFFER_BINDING. While a nonzero buffer object is bound to the GL_ARRAY_BUFFER target, the vertex array pointer parameter that is traditionally interpreted as a pointer to client-side memory is instead interpreted as an offset within the buffer object measured in basic machine units.

While a nonzero buffer object is bound to the GL_ARRAY_ELEMENT_BUFFER target, the indices parameter of glDrawElements, glDrawRangeElements, or glMultiDrawElements that is traditionally interpreted as a pointer to client-side memory is instead interpreted as an offset within the buffer object measured in basic machine units.

While a nonzero buffer object is bound to the GL_PIXEL_PACK_BUFFER target, the following commands are affected: glGetCompressedTexImage, glGetConvolutionFilter, glGetHistogram, glGetMinmax, glGetPixelMap, glGetPolygonStipple, glGetSeparableFilter, glGetTexImage, and glReadPixels. The pointer parameter that is traditionally interpreted as a pointer to client-side memory where the pixels are to be packed is instead interpreted as an offset within the buffer object measured in basic machine units.

While a nonzero buffer object is bound to the GL_PIXEL_UNPACK_BUFFER target, the following commands are affected: glBitmap, glColorSubTable, glColorTable, glCompressedTexImage1D, glCompressedTexImage2D, glCompressedTexImage3D, glCompressedTexSubImage1D, glCompressedTexSubImage2D, glCompressedTexSubImage3D, glConvolutionFilter1D, glConvolutionFilter2D, glDrawPixels, glPixelMap, glPolygonStipple, glSeparableFilter2D, glTexImage1D, glTexImage2D, glTexImage3D, glTexSubImage1D, glTexSubImage2D, and glTexSubImage3D. The pointer parameter that is traditionally interpreted as a pointer to client-side memory from which the pixels are to be unpacked is instead interpreted as an offset within the buffer object measured in basic machine units.

A buffer object binding created with glBindBuffer remains active until a different buffer object name is bound to the same target, or until the bound buffer object is deleted with glDeleteBuffers.

Once created, a named buffer object may be re-bound to any target as often as needed. However, the GL implementation may make choices about how to optimize the storage of a buffer object based on its initial binding target.

Notes
glBindBuffer is available only if the GL version is 1.5 or greater.

GL_PIXEL_PACK_BUFFER and GL_PIXEL_UNPACK_BUFFER are available only if the GL version is 2.1 or greater.

Errors
GL_INVALID_ENUM is generated if *target* is not one of the allowable values.

GL_INVALID_OPERATION is generated if glBindBuffer is executed between the execution of glBegin and the corresponding execution of glEnd.

Associated Gets
glGet with argument GL_ARRAY_BUFFER_BINDING

glGet with argument GL_ELEMENT_ARRAY_BUFFER_BINDING

glGet with argument GL_PIXEL_PACK_BUFFER_BINDING

glGet with argument GL_PIXEL_UNPACK_BUFFER_BINDING

See Also
glDeleteBuffers, glGenBuffers, glGet, glIsBuffer

glBindTexture

Bind a named texture to a texturing target

C Specification
void **glBindTexture**(GLenum *target*,
                    GLuint *texture*);

Parameters
target   Specifies the target to which the texture is bound. Must be either GL_TEXTURE_1D, GL_TEXTURE_2D, GL_TEXTURE_3D, or GL_TEXTURE_CUBE_MAP.

texture   Specifies the name of a texture.

Description
glBindTexture lets you create or use a named texture. Calling glBindTexture with *target* set to GL_TEXTURE_1D, GL_TEXTURE_2D, GL_TEXTURE_3D or GL_TEXTURE_CUBE_MAP and *texture* set to the name of the new texture binds the texture name to the target. When a texture is bound to a target, the previous binding for that target is automatically broken.

Texture names are unsigned integers. The value zero is reserved to represent the default texture for each texture target. Texture names and the corresponding texture contents are local to the shared display-list space (see glXCreateContext) of the current GL rendering context; two rendering contexts share texture names only if they also share display lists.

You may use glGenTextures to generate a set of new texture names.

When a texture is first bound, it assumes the specified target: A texture first bound to GL_TEXTURE_1D becomes one-dimensional texture, a texture first bound to GL_TEXTURE_2D becomes two-dimensional texture, a texture first bound to GL_TEXTURE_3D becomes three-dimensional texture, and a texture first bound to GL_TEXTURE_CUBE_MAP becomes a cube-mapped texture. The state of a one-dimensional texture immediately after it is first bound is equivalent to the state of the default GL_TEXTURE_1D at GL initialization, and similarly for two- and three-dimensional textures and cube-mapped textures.

While a texture is bound, GL operations on the target to which it is bound affect the bound texture, and queries of the target to which it is bound return state from the bound texture. If texture mapping is active on the target to which a texture is bound, the bound texture is used. In effect, the texture targets become aliases for the textures currently bound to them, and the texture name zero refers to the default textures that were bound to them at initialization.

A texture binding created with glBindTexture remains active until a different texture is bound to the same target, or until the bound texture is deleted with glDeleteTextures.

Once created, a named texture may be re-bound to its same original target as often as needed. It is usually much faster to use glBindTexture to bind an existing named texture to one of the texture targets than it is to reload the texture image using glTexImage1D, glTexImage2D, or glTexImage3D. For additional control over performance, use glPrioritizeTextures. glBindTexture is included in display lists.

Notes

glBindTexture is available only if the GL version is 1.1 or greater.

GL_TEXTURE_CUBE_MAP is available only if the GL version is 1.3 or greater.

Errors

GL_INVALID_ENUM is generated if *target* is not one of the allowable values.

GL_INVALID_OPERATION is generated if *texture* was previously created with a target that doesn't match that of *target*.

GL_INVALID_OPERATION is generated if glBindTexture is executed between the execution of glBegin and the corresponding execution of glEnd.

Associated Gets

glGet with argument GL_TEXTURE_BINDING_1D

glGet with argument GL_TEXTURE_BINDING_2D

glGet with argument GL_TEXTURE_BINDING_3D

See Also

glAreTexturesResident, glDeleteTextures, glGenTextures, glGet, glGetTexParameter, glIsTexture, glPrioritizeTextures, glTexImage1D, glTexImage2D, glTexParameter

glBitmap

Draw a bitmap

C Specification

```
void glBitmap(GLsizei        width,
              GLsizei        height,
              GLfloat        xorig,
              GLfloat        yorig,
              GLfloat        xmove,
              GLfloat        ymove,
              const GLubyte * bitmap);
```

Parameters

width, *height*   Specify the pixel width and height of the bitmap image.

xorig, *yorig*   Specify the location of the origin in the bitmap image. The origin is measured from the lower-left corner of the bitmap, with right and up being the positive axes.

xmove, *ymove*   Specify the x and y offsets to be added to the current raster position after the bitmap is drawn.

bitmap   Specifies the address of the bitmap image.

Description

A bitmap is a binary image. When drawn, the bitmap is positioned relative to the current raster position, and frame buffer pixels corresponding to 1's in the bitmap are written using the current raster color or index. Frame buffer pixels corresponding to 0's in the bitmap are not modified.

glBitmap takes seven arguments. The first pair specifies the width and height of the bitmap image. The second pair specifies the location of the bitmap origin relative to the lower-left corner of the bitmap image. The third pair of arguments specifies x and *y* offsets to be added to the current raster position after the bitmap has been drawn. The final argument is a pointer to the bitmap image itself.

If a nonzero named buffer object is bound to the GL_PIXEL_UNPACK_BUFFER target (see glBindBuffer) while a bitmap image is specified, bitmap is treated as a byte offset into the buffer object's data store.

The bitmap image is interpreted like image data for the glDrawPixels command, with *width* and *height* corresponding to the width and height arguments of that command, and with *type* set to GL_BITMAP and *format* set to GL_COLOR_INDEX. Modes specified using glPixelStore affect the interpretation of bitmap image data; modes specified using glPixelTransfer do not.

If the current raster position is invalid, glBitmap is ignored. Otherwise, the lower-left corner of the bitmap image is positioned at the window coordinates

$$x_w = |\ x_r - x_o\ |$$
$$y_w = |\ y_r - y_o\ |$$

where (x_r, y_r) is the raster position and (x_o, y_o) is the bitmap origin. Fragments are then generated for each pixel corresponding to a 1 (one) in the bitmap image. These fragments are generated using the current raster z coordinate, color or color index, and current raster texture coordinates. They are then treated just as if they had been generated by a point, line, or polygon, including texture mapping, fogging, and all per-fragment operations such as alpha and depth testing.

After the bitmap has been drawn, the x and y coordinates of the current raster position are offset by *xmove* and *ymove*. No change is made to the z coordinate of the current raster position, or to the current raster color, texture coordinates, or index.

Notes

To set a valid raster position outside the viewport, first set a valid raster position inside the viewport, then call glBitmap with NULL as the *bitmap* parameter and with *xmove* and *ymove* set to the offsets of the new raster position. This technique is useful when panning an image around the viewport.

Errors

GL_INVALID_VALUE is generated if *width* or *height* is negative.

GL_INVALID_OPERATION is generated if a nonzero buffer object name is bound to the GL_PIXEL_UNPACK_BUFFER target and the buffer object's data store is currently mapped.

GL_INVALID_OPERATION is generated if a nonzero buffer object name is bound to the GL_PIXEL_UNPACK_BUFFER target and the data would be unpacked from the buffer object such that the memory reads required would exceed the data store size.

GL_INVALID_OPERATION is generated if glBitmap is executed between the execution of glBegin and the corresponding execution of glEnd.

Associated Gets

glGet with argument GL_CURRENT_RASTER_POSITION
glGet with argument GL_CURRENT_RASTER_COLOR
glGet with argument GL_CURRENT_RASTER_SECONDARY_COLOR
glGet with argument GL_CURRENT_RASTER_DISTANCE
glGet with argument GL_CURRENT_RASTER_INDEX
glGet with argument GL_CURRENT_RASTER_TEXTURE_COORDS
glGet with argument GL_CURRENT_RASTER_POSITION_VALID
glGet with argument GL_PIXEL_UNPACK_BUFFER_BINDING

See Also

glBindBuffer, glDrawPixels, glPixelStore, glPixelTransfer, glRasterPos, glWindowPos

glBlendColor

Set the blend color

C Specification
```
void glBlendColor(GLclampf red,
                  GLclampf green,
                  GLclampf blue,
                  GLclampf alpha);
```

Parameters
red, green, blue, alpha   Specify the components of GL_BLEND_COLOR

Description
The GL_BLEND_COLOR may be used to calculate the source and destination blending factors. The color components are clamped to the range [0,1] before being stored. See glBlendFunc for a complete description of the blending operations. Initially the GL_BLEND_COLOR is set to (0, 0, 0, 0).

Notes
glBlendColor is part of the ARB_imaging subset. glBlendColor is present only if ARB_imaging is returned when glGetString is called with GL_EXTENSIONS as its argument.

Errors
GL_INVALID_OPERATION is generated if glBlendColor is executed between the execution of glBegin and the corresponding execution of glEnd.

Associated Gets
glGet with an argument of GL_BLEND_COLOR

See Also
glBlendEquation, glBlendFunc, glGetString

glBlendEquation

Specify the equation used for both the RGB blend equation and the Alpha blend equation

C Specification
```
void glBlendEquation(GLenum mode);
```

Parameters
mode   Specifies how source and destination colors are combined. It must be GL_FUNC_ADD, GL_FUNC_SUBTRACT, GL_FUNC_REVERSE_SUBTRACT, GL_MIN, GL_MAX.

Description
The blend equations determine how a new pixel (the "source" color) is combined with a pixel already in the framebuffer (the "destination" color). This function sets both the RGB blend equation and the alpha blend equation to a single equation.

These equations use the source and destination blend factors specified by either glBlendFunc or glBlendFuncSeparate. See glBlendFunc or glBlendFuncSeparate for a description of the various blend factors.

In the equations that follow, source and destination color components are referred to as (R_s, G_s, B_s, A_s) and (R_d, G_d, B_d, A_d), respectively. The result color is referred to as (R_r, G_r, B_r, A_r). The source and destination blend factors are denoted (s_R, s_G, s_B, s_A) and (d_R, d_G, d_B, d_A), respectively. For these equations all color components are understood to have values in the range [0,1].

Mode	RGB Components	Alpha Component
GL_FUNC_ADD	$Rr = min\ (1, R_s\ s_R + R_d\ d_R)$	$Ar = min\ (1, A_s\ s_A + A_d\ d_A)$
	$Gr = min\ (1, G_s\ s_G + G_d\ d_G)$	
	$Br = min\ (1, B_s\ s_B + B_d\ d_B)$	
GL_FUNC_SUBTRACT	$Rr = max\ (0, R_s\ s_R - R_d\ d_R)$	$Ar = max\ (0, A_s\ s_A - A_d\ d_A)$
	$Gr = max\ (0, G_s\ s_G - G_d\ d_G)$	
	$Br = max\ (0, B_s\ s_B - B_d\ d_B)$	
GL_FUNC_REVERSE_SUBTRACT	$Rr = max\ (0, R_d\ d_R - R_s\ s_R)$	$Ar = max\ (0, A_d\ d_A - A_s\ s_A)$
	$Gr = max\ (0, G_d\ d_G - G_s\ s_G)$	
	$Br = max\ (0, B_d\ d_B - B_s\ s_B)$	
GL_FUNC_MIN	$Rr = min\ (R_s, R_d)$	$Ar = min\ (A_s, A_d)$
	$Gr = min\ (G_s, G_d)$	
	$Br = min\ (B_s, B_d)$	
GL_FUNC_MAX	$Rr = max\ (R_s, R_d)$	$Ar = max\ (A_s, A_d)$
	$Gr = max\ (G_s, G_d)$	
	$Br = max\ (B_s, B_d)$	

The results of these equations are clamped to the range [0,1] .

The GL_MIN and GL_MAX equations are useful for applications that analyze image data (image thresholding against a constant color, for example). The GL_FUNC_ADD equation is useful for antialiasing and transparency, among other things.

Initially, both the RGB blend equation and the alpha blend equation are set to GL_FUNC_ADD.

Notes

The GL_MIN, and GL_MAX equations do not use the source or destination factors, only the source and destination colors.

Errors

GL_INVALID_ENUM is generated if *mode* is not one of GL_FUNC_ADD, GL_FUNC_SUBTRACT, GL_FUNC_REVERSE_SUBTRACT, GL_MAX, or GL_MIN.

GL_INVALID_OPERATION is generated if glBlendEquation is executed between the execution of glBegin and the corresponding execution of glEnd.

Associated Gets

glGet with an argument of GL_BLEND_EQUATION_RGB
glGet with an argument of GL_BLEND_EQUATION_ALPHA

See Also

glGetString, glBlendColor, glBlendFuncglBlendFuncSeparate

glBlendEquationSeparate

Set the RGB blend equation and the alpha blend equation separately

C Specification

void **glBlendEquationSeparate**(GLenum *modeRGB*,
                                 GLenum *modeAlpha*);

Parameters

modeRGB   Specifies the RGB blend equation, how the red, green, and blue components of the source and destination colors are combined. It must be GL_FUNC_ADD, GL_FUNC_SUBTRACT, GL_FUNC_REVERSE_SUBTRACT, GL_MIN, GL_MAX.

modeAlpha   Specifies the alpha blend equation, how the alpha component of the source and destination colors are combined. It must be GL_FUNC_ADD, GL_FUNC_SUBTRACT, GL_FUNC_REVERSE_SUBTRACT, GL_MIN, GL_MAX.

Description

The blend equations determines how a new pixel (the "source" color) is combined with a pixel already in the framebuffer (the "destination" color). This function specifies one blend equation for the RGB-color components and one blend equation for the alpha component.

The blend equations use the source and destination blend factors specified by either glBlendFunc or glBlendFuncSeparate. See glBlendFunc or glBlendFuncSeparate for a description of the various blend factors.

In the equations that follow, source and destination color components are referred to as (R_s, G_s, B_s, A_s) and (R_d, G_d, B_d, A_d), respectively. The result color is referred to as (R_r, G_r, B_r, A_r). The source and destination blend factors are denoted (s_R, s_G, s_B, s_A) and (d_R, d_G, d_B, d_A), respectively. For these equations all color components are understood to have values in the range [0,1].

Mode	RGB Components	Alpha Component
GL_FUNC_ADD	$Rr = min\,(1, R_s\,s_R + R_d\,d_R)$	$Ar = min\,(1, A_s\,s_A + A_d\,d_A)$
	$Gr = min\,(1, G_s\,s_G + G_d\,d_G)$	
	$Br = min\,(1, B_s\,s_B + B_d\,d_B)$	
GL_FUNC_SUBTRACT	$Rr = max\,(0, R_s\,s_R - R_d\,d_R)$	$Ar = max\,(0, A_s\,s_A - A_d\,d_A)$
	$Gr = max\,(0, G_s\,s_G - G_d\,d_G)$	
	$Br = max\,(0, B_s\,s_B - B_d\,d_B)$	
GL_FUNC_REVERSE_SUBTRACT	$Rr = max\,(0, R_d\,d_R - R_s\,s_R)$	$Ar = max\,(0, A_d\,d_A - A_s\,s_A)$
	$Gr = max\,(0, G_d\,d_G - G_s\,s_G)$	
	$Br = max\,(0, B_d\,d_B - B_s\,s_B)$	
GL_FUNC_MIN	$Rr = min\,(R_s, R_d)$	$Ar = min\,(A_s, A_d)$
	$Gr = min\,(G_s, G_d)$	
	$Br = min\,(B_s, B_d)$	
GL_FUNC_MAX	$Rr = max\,(R_s, R_d)$	$Ar = max\,(A_s, A_d)$
	$Gr = max\,(G_s, G_d)$	
	$Br = max\,(B_s, B_d)$	

The results of these equations are clamped to the range [0,1].

The GL_MIN and GL_MAX equations are useful for applications that analyze image data (image thresholding against a constant color, for example). The GL_FUNC_ADD equation is useful for antialiasing and transparency, among other things.

Initially, both the RGB blend equation and the alpha blend equation are set to GL_FUNC_ADD.

Notes

glBlendEquationSeparate is available only if the GL version is 2.0 or greater.

The GL_MIN, and GL_MAX equations do not use the source or destination factors, only the source and destination colors.

Errors

GL_INVALID_ENUM is generated if either *modeRGB* or *modeAlpha* is not one of GL_FUNC_ADD, GL_FUNC_SUBTRACT, GL_FUNC_REVERSE_SUBTRACT, GL_MAX, or GL_MIN.

GL_INVALID_OPERATION is generated if glBlendEquationSeparate is executed between the execution of glBegin and the corresponding execution of glEnd.

Associated Gets

glGet with an argument of GL_BLEND_EQUATION_RGB
glGet with an argument of GL_BLEND_EQUATION_ALPHA

See Also

glGetString, glBlendColor, glBlendFunc, glBlendFuncSeparate

glBlendFunc

Specify pixel arithmetic

C Specification

void **glBlendFunc**(GLenum *sfactor*,
                     GLenum *dfactor*);

Parameters

sfactor   Specifies how the red, green, blue, and alpha source blending factors are computed. The
            following symbolic constants are accepted: GL_ZERO, GL_ONE, GL_SRC_COLOR,
            GL_ONE_MINUS_SRC_COLOR, GL_DST_COLOR, GL_ONE_MINUS_DST_COLOR,
            GL_SRC_ALPHA, GL_ONE_MINUS_SRC_ALPHA, GL_DST_ALPHA,
            GL_ONE_MINUS_DST_ALPHA, GL_CONSTANT_COLOR, GL_ONE_MINUS_CONSTANT_COLOR,
            GL_CONSTANT_ALPHA, GL_ONE_MINUS_CONSTANT_ALPHA, and
            GL_SRC_ALPHA_SATURATE. The initial value is GL_ONE.

dfactor   Specifies how the red, green, blue, and alpha destination blending factors are
            computed. The following symbolic constants are accepted: GL_ZERO, GL_ONE,
            GL_SRC_COLOR, GL_ONE_MINUS_SRC_COLOR, GL_DST_COLOR,
            GL_ONE_MINUS_DST_COLOR, GL_SRC_ALPHA, GL_ONE_MINUS_SRC_ALPHA,
            GL_DST_ALPHA, GL_ONE_MINUS_DST_ALPHA. GL_CONSTANT_COLOR,
            GL_ONE_MINUS_CONSTANT_COLOR, GL_CONSTANT_ALPHA, and
            GL_ONE_MINUS_CONSTANT_ALPHA. The initial value is GL_ZERO.

Description

In RGBA mode, pixels can be drawn using a function that blends the incoming (source) RGBA values with the RGBA values that are already in the frame buffer (the destination values). Blending is initially disabled. Use glEnable and glDisable with argument GL_BLEND to enable and disable blending.

glBlendFunc defines the operation of blending when it is enabled. *sfactor* specifies which method is used to scale the source color components. *dfactor* specifies which method is used to scale the destination color components. The possible methods are described in the following table. Each method defines four scale factors, one each for red, green, blue, and alpha. In the table and in subsequent equations, source and destination color components are referred to as (R_s,G_s,B_s,A_s) and (R_d,G_d,B_d,A_d). The color specified by glBlendColor is referred to as (R_c,G_c,B_c,A_c). They are understood to have integer values between 0 and (k_R,k_G,k_B,k_A), where

$$k_c = 2^{m_c} - 1$$

and (m_R,m_G,m_B,m_A) is the number of red, green, blue, and alpha bitplanes.

Source and destination scale factors are referred to as (s_R,s_G,s_B,s_A) and (d_R,d_G,d_B,d_A). The scale factors described in the table, denoted (f_R,f_G,f_B,f_A), represent either source or destination factors. All scale factors have range [0,1].

Parameter	(fR, fG, fB, fA)
GL_ZERO	$(0,0,0,0)$
GL_ONE	$(1,1,1,1)$
GL_SRC_COLOR	$(\dfrac{R_s}{k_R}, \dfrac{G_s}{k_G}, \dfrac{B_s}{k_B}, \dfrac{A_s}{k_A})$
GL_ONE_MINUS_SRC_COLOR	$(1,1,1,1) - (\dfrac{R_s}{k_R}, \dfrac{G_s}{k_G}, \dfrac{B_s}{k_B}, \dfrac{A_s}{k_A})$
GL_DST_COLOR	$(\dfrac{R_d}{k_R}, \dfrac{G_d}{k_G}, \dfrac{B_d}{k_B}, \dfrac{A_d}{k_A})$
GL_ONE_MINUS_DST_COLOR	$(1,1,1,1) - (\dfrac{R_d}{k_R}, \dfrac{G_d}{k_G}, \dfrac{B_d}{k_B}, \dfrac{A_d}{k_A})$
GL_SRC_ALPHA	$(\dfrac{A_s}{k_A}, \dfrac{A_s}{k_A}, \dfrac{A_s}{k_A}, \dfrac{A_s}{k_A})$
GL_ONE_MINUS_SRC_ALPHA	$(1,1,1,1) - (\dfrac{A_s}{k_A}, \dfrac{A_s}{k_A}, \dfrac{A_s}{k_A}, \dfrac{A_s}{k_A})$
GL_DST_ALPHA	$(\dfrac{A_d}{k_A}, \dfrac{A_d}{k_A}, \dfrac{A_d}{k_A}, \dfrac{A_d}{k_A})$
GL_ONE_MINUS_DST_ALPHA	$(1,1,1,1) - (\dfrac{A_d}{k_A}, \dfrac{A_d}{k_A}, \dfrac{A_d}{k_A}, \dfrac{A_d}{k_A})$
GL_CONSTANT_COLOR	(R_c, G_c, B_c, A_c)
GL_ONE_MINUS_CONSTANT_COLOR	$(1,1,1,1) - (R_c, G_c, B_c, A_c)$
GL_CONSTANT_ALPHA	(A_c, A_c, A_c, A_c)
GL_ONE_MINUS_CONSTANT_ALPHA	$(1,1,1,1) - (A_c, A_c, A_c, A_c)$
GL_SRC_ALPHA_SATURATE	$(i,i,i,1)$

In the table,

$$i = \frac{min\,(A_s, k_A - A_d)}{k_A}$$

To determine the blended RGBA values of a pixel when drawing in RGBA mode, the system uses the following equations:

$$R_d = min\,(k_R, R_s\,s_R + R_d\,d_R)$$
$$G_d = min\,(k_G, G_s\,s_G + G_d\,d_G)$$
$$B_d = min\,(k_B, B_s\,s_B + B_d\,d_B)$$
$$A_d = min\,(k_A, A_s\,s_A + A_d\,d_A)$$

Despite the apparent precision of the above equations, blending arithmetic is not exactly specified, because blending operates with imprecise integer color values. However, a blend factor that should be equal to 1 is guaranteed not to modify its multiplicand, and a blend factor equal to 0 reduces its multiplicand to 0. For example, when sfactor is GL_SRC_ALPHA, dfactor is GL_ONE_MINUS_SRC_ALPHA, and A_s is equal to k_A, the equations reduce to simple replacement:

$$R_d = R_s G_d = G_s B_d = B_s A_d = A_s$$

Examples

Transparency is best implemented using blend function (GL_SRC_ALPHA, GL_ONE_MINUS_SRC_ALPHA) with primitives sorted from farthest to nearest. Note that this transparency calculation does not require the presence of alpha bitplanes in the frame buffer.

Blend function (GL_SRC_ALPHA, GL_ONE_MINUS_SRC_ALPHA) is also useful for rendering antialiased points and lines in arbitrary order.

Polygon antialiasing is optimized using blend function (GL_SRC_ALPHA_SATURATE, GL_ONE) with polygons sorted from nearest to farthest. (See the glEnable, glDisable reference page and the GL_POLYGON_SMOOTH argument for information on polygon antialiasing.) Destination alpha bitplanes, which must be present for this blend function to operate correctly, store the accumulated coverage.

Notes

Incoming (source) alpha is correctly thought of as a material opacity, ranging from 1.0 (K_A), representing complete opacity, to 0.0 (0), representing complete transparency.

When more than one color buffer is enabled for drawing, the GL performs blending separately for each enabled buffer, using the contents of that buffer for destination color. (See glDrawBuffer.)

Blending affects only RGBA rendering. It is ignored by color index renderers.

GL_CONSTANT_COLOR, GL_ONE_MINUS_CONSTANT_COLOR, GL_CONSTANT_ALPHA, GL_ONE_MINUS_CONSTANT_ALPHA are available only if the GL version is 1.4 or greater or if the ARB_imaging is supported by your implementation.

GL_SRC_COLOR and GL_ONE_MINUS_SRC_COLOR are valid only for sfactor if the GL version is 1.4 or greater.

GL_DST_COLOR and GL_ONE_MINUS_DST_COLOR are valid only for dfactor if the GL version is 1.4 or greater.

Errors

GL_INVALID_ENUM is generated if either sfactor or dfactor is not an accepted value.

GL_INVALID_OPERATION is generated if glBlendFunc is executed between the execution of glBegin and the corresponding execution of glEnd.

Associated Gets

glGet with argument GL_BLEND_SRC
glGet with argument GL_BLEND_DST
glIsEnabled with argument GL_BLEND

See Also

glAlphaFunc, glBlendColor, glBlendEquation, glBlendFuncSeparate, glClear, glDrawBuffer, glEnable, glLogicOp, glStencilFunc

glBlendFuncSeparate

Specify pixel arithmetic for RGB and alpha components separately

C Specification

```
void glBlendFuncSeparate(GLenum srcRGB,
                         GLenum dstRGB,
                         GLenum srcAlpha,
                         GLenum dstAlpha);
```

Parameters

srcRGB	Specifies how the red, green, and blue blending factors are computed. The following symbolic constants are accepted: GL_ZERO, GL_ONE, GL_SRC_COLOR, GL_ONE_MINUS_SRC_COLOR, GL_DST_COLOR, GL_ONE_MINUS_DST_COLOR, GL_SRC_ALPHA, GL_ONE_MINUS_SRC_ALPHA, GL_DST_ALPHA, GL_ONE_MINUS_DST_ALPHA, GL_CONSTANT_COLOR, GL_ONE_MINUS_CONSTANT_COLOR, GL_CONSTANT_ALPHA, GL_ONE_MINUS_CONSTANT_ALPHA, and GL_SRC_ALPHA_SATURATE. The initial value is GL_ONE.
dstRGB	Specifies how the red, green, and blue destination blending factors are computed. The following symbolic constants are accepted: GL_ZERO, GL_ONE, GL_SRC_COLOR, GL_ONE_MINUS_SRC_COLOR, GL_DST_COLOR, GL_ONE_MINUS_DST_COLOR, GL_SRC_ALPHA, GL_ONE_MINUS_SRC_ALPHA, GL_DST_ALPHA, GL_ONE_MINUS_DST_ALPHA. GL_CONSTANT_COLOR, GL_ONE_MINUS_CONSTANT_COLOR, GL_CONSTANT_ALPHA, and GL_ONE_MINUS_CONSTANT_ALPHA. The initial value is GL_ZERO.
srcAlpha	Specifies how the alpha source blending factor is computed. The same symbolic constants are accepted as for *srcRGB*. The initial value is GL_ONE.
dstAlpha	Specifies how the alpha destination blending factor is computed. The same symbolic constants are accepted as for *dstRGB*. The initial value is GL_ZERO.

Description

In RGBA mode, pixels can be drawn using a function that blends the incoming (source) RGBA values with the RGBA values that are already in the frame buffer (the destination values). Blending is initially disabled. Use glEnable and glDisable with argument GL_BLEND to enable and disable blending.

glBlendFuncSeparate defines the operation of blending when it is enabled. *srcRGB* specifies which method is used to scale the source RGB-color components. *dstRGB* specifies which method is used to scale the destination RGB-color components. Likewise, *srcAlpha* specifies which method is used to scale the source alpha color component, and *dstAlpha* specifies which method is used to scale the destination alpha component. The possible methods are described in the following table. Each method defines four scale factors, one each for red, green, blue, and alpha.

In the table and in subsequent equations, source and destination color components are referred to as (R_s, G_s, B_s, A_s) and (R_d, G_d, B_d, A_d). The color specified by glBlendColor is referred to as (R_c, G_c, B_c, A_c). They are understood to have integer values between 0 and (k_R, k_G, k_B, k_A), where

$$k_c = 2^{m_c} - 1$$

and (m_R, m_G, m_B, m_A) is the number of red, green, blue, and alpha bitplanes.

Source and destination scale factors are referred to as (s_R, s_G, s_B, s_A) and (d_R, d_G, d_B, d_A). All scale factors have range [0,1].

Parameter	RGB Factor	Alpha Factor
GL_ZERO	$(0,0,0)$	0
GL_ONE	$(1,1,1)$	1
GL_SRC_COLOR	$(\frac{R_s}{k_R}, \frac{G_s}{k_G}, \frac{B_s}{k_B})$	$\frac{A_s}{k_A}$
GL_ONE_MINUS_SRC_COLOR	$(1,1,1,1) - (\frac{R_s}{k_R}, \frac{G_s}{k_G}, \frac{B_s}{k_B})$	$1 - \frac{A_s}{k_A}$
GL_DST_COLOR	$(\frac{R_d}{k_R}, \frac{G_d}{k_G}, \frac{B_d}{k_B})$	$\frac{A_d}{k_A}$

Parameter	RGB Factor	Alpha Factor
GL_ONE_MINUS_DST_COLOR	$(1,1,1) - (\frac{R_d}{k_R}, \frac{G_d}{k_G}, \frac{B_d}{k_B})$	$1 - \frac{A_d}{k_A}$
GL_SRC_ALPHA	$(\frac{A_s}{k_A}, \frac{A_s}{k_A}, \frac{A_s}{k_A})$	$\frac{A_s}{k_A}$
GL_ONE_MINUS_SRC_ALPHA	$(1,1,1) - (\frac{A_s}{k_A}, \frac{A_s}{k_A}, \frac{A_s}{k_A})$	$1 - \frac{A_s}{k_A}$
GL_DST_ALPHA	$(\frac{A_d}{k_A}, \frac{A_d}{k_A}, \frac{A_d}{k_A})$	$\frac{A_d}{k_A}$
GL_ONE_MINUS_DST_ALPHA	$(1,1,1) - (\frac{A_d}{k_A}, \frac{A_d}{k_A}, \frac{A_d}{k_A})$	$1 - \frac{A_d}{k_A}$
GL_CONSTANT_COLOR	(R_c, G_c, B_c)	A_c
GL_ONE_MINUS_CONSTANT_COLOR	$(1,1,1) - (R_c, G_c, B_c)$	$1 - A_c$
GL_CONSTANT_ALPHA	(A_c, A_c, A_c)	A_c
GL_ONE_MINUS_CONSTANT_ALPHA	$(1,1,1) - (A_c, A_c, A_c)$	$1 - A_c$
GL_SRC_ALPHA_SATURATE	(i,i,i)	1

In the table,
$i = min\ (A_s, 1 - A_d)$

To determine the blended RGBA values of a pixel when drawing in RGBA mode, the system uses the following equations:

$R_d = min\ (k_R, R_s\ s_R + R_d\ d_R)\ G_d = min\ (k_G, G_s\ s_G + G_d\ d_G)\ B_d = min\ (k_B, B_s\ s_B + B_d\ d_B)\ A_d = min\ (k_A, A_s\ s_A + A_d\ d_A)$

Despite the apparent precision of the above equations, blending arithmetic is not exactly specified, because blending operates with imprecise integer color values. However, a blend factor that should be equal to 1 is guaranteed not to modify its multiplicand, and a blend factor equal to 0 reduces its multiplicand to 0. For example, when *srcRGB* is GL_SRC_ALPHA, *dstRGB* is GL_ONE_MINUS_SRC_ALPHA, and A_s is equal to k_A, the equations reduce to simple replacement:

$R_d = R_s G_d = G_s B_d = B_s A_d = A_s$

Notes

glBlendFuncSeparate is available only if the GL version is 1.4 or greater.

Incoming (source) alpha is correctly thought of as a material opacity, ranging from 1.0 (K_A), representing complete opacity, to 0.0 (0), representing complete transparency.

When more than one color buffer is enabled for drawing, the GL performs blending separately for each enabled buffer, using the contents of that buffer for destination color. (See glDrawBuffer.)

Blending affects only RGBA rendering. It is ignored by color index renderers.

GL_CONSTANT_COLOR, GL_ONE_MINUS_CONSTANT_COLOR, GL_CONSTANT_ALPHA, GL_ONE_MINUS_CONSTANT_ALPHA are available only if the GL version is 1.4 or greater or if the ARB_imaging is supported by your implementation.

GL_SRC_COLOR and GL_ONE_MINUS_SRC_COLOR are valid only for *srcRGB* if the GL version is 1.4 or greater.

GL_DST_COLOR and GL_ONE_MINUS_DST_COLOR are valid only for *dstRGB* if the GL version is 1.4 or greater.

Errors

GL_INVALID_ENUM is generated if either *srcRGB* or *dstRGB* is not an accepted value.

GL_INVALID_OPERATION is generated if glBlendFuncSeparate is executed between the execution of glBegin and the corresponding execution of glEnd.

Associated Gets

glGet with argument GL_BLEND_SRC_RGB
glGet with argument GL_BLEND_SRC_ALPHA
glGet with argument GL_BLEND_DST_RGB
glGet with argument GL_BLEND_DST_ALPHA
glIsEnabled with argument GL_BLEND

See Also

glAlphaFunc, glBlendColor, glBlendFunc, glBlendEquation, glClear, glDrawBuffer, glEnable, glLogicOp, glStencilFunc

glBufferData

Create and initialize a buffer object's data store

C Specification

```
void glBufferData(GLenum          target,
                  GLsizeiptr      size,
                  const GLvoid *  data,
                  GLenum          usage);
```

Parameters

target   Specifies the target buffer object. The symbolic constant must be GL_ARRAY_BUFFER, GL_ELEMENT_ARRAY_BUFFER, GL_PIXEL_PACK_BUFFER, or GL_PIXEL_UNPACK_BUFFER.

size   Specifies the size in bytes of the buffer object's new data store.

data   Specifies a pointer to data that will be copied into the data store for initialization, or NULL if no data is to be copied.

usage   Specifies the expected usage pattern of the data store. The symbolic constant must be GL_STREAM_DRAW, GL_STREAM_READ, GL_STREAM_COPY, GL_STATIC_DRAW, GL_STATIC_READ, GL_STATIC_COPY, GL_DYNAMIC_DRAW, GL_DYNAMIC_READ, or GL_DYNAMIC_COPY.

Description

glBufferData creates a new data store for the buffer object currently bound to *target*. Any preexisting data store is deleted. The new data store is created with the specified *size* in bytes and *usage*. If *data* is not NULL, the data store is initialized with data from this pointer. In its initial state, the new data store is not mapped, it has a NULL mapped pointer, and its mapped access is GL_READ_WRITE.

usage is a hint to the GL implementation as to how a buffer object's data store will be accessed. This enables the GL implementation to make more intelligent decisions that may significantly impact buffer object performance. It does not, however, constrain the actual usage of the data store. *usage* can be broken down into two parts: first, the frequency of access (modification and usage), and second, the nature of that access.

The frequency of access may be one of these:

STREAM

The data store contents will be modified once and used at most a few times.

STATIC

The data store contents will be modified once and used many times.

DYNAMIC

The data store contents will be modified repeatedly and used many times.

The nature of access may be one of these:

DRAW

The data store contents are modified by the application, and used as the source for GL drawing and image specification commands.

READ

The data store contents are modified by reading data from the GL, and used to return that data when queried by the application.

COPY

The data store contents are modified by reading data from the GL, and used as the source for GL drawing and image specification commands.

Notes

glBufferData is available only if the GL version is 1.5 or greater.

Targets GL_PIXEL_PACK_BUFFER and GL_PIXEL_UNPACK_BUFFER are available only if the GL version is 2.1 or greater.

If *data* is NULL, a data store of the specified size is still created, but its contents remain uninitialized and thus undefined.

Clients must align data elements consistent with the requirements of the client platform, with an additional base-level requirement that an offset within a buffer to a datum comprising *NN*.

Errors

GL_INVALID_ENUM is generated if *target* is not GL_ARRAY_BUFFER, GL_ELEMENT_ARRAY_BUFFER, GL_PIXEL_PACK_BUFFER, or GL_PIXEL_UNPACK_BUFFER.

GL_INVALID_ENUM is generated if *usage* is not GL_STREAM_DRAW, GL_STREAM_READ, GL_STREAM_COPY, GL_STATIC_DRAW, GL_STATIC_READ, GL_STATIC_COPY, GL_DYNAMIC_DRAW, GL_DYNAMIC_READ, or GL_DYNAMIC_COPY.

GL_INVALID_VALUE is generated if *size* is negative.

GL_INVALID_OPERATION is generated if the reserved buffer object name 0 is bound to *target*.

GL_OUT_OF_MEMORY is generated if the GL is unable to create a data store with the specified *size*.

GL_INVALID_OPERATION is generated if glBufferData is executed between the execution of glBegin and the corresponding execution of glEnd.

Associated Gets

glGetBufferSubData

glGetBufferParameteriv with argument GL_BUFFER_SIZE or GL_BUFFER_USAGE

See Also

glBindBuffer, glBufferSubData, glMapBuffer, glUnmapBuffer

glBufferSubData

Update a subset of a buffer object's data store

C Specification

```
void glBufferSubData(GLenum        target,
                     GLintptr      offset,
                     GLsizeiptr    size,
                     const GLvoid * data);
```

Parameters

target   Specifies the target buffer object. The symbolic constant must be GL_ARRAY_BUFFER, GL_ELEMENT_ARRAY_BUFFER, GL_PIXEL_PACK_BUFFER, or GL_PIXEL_UNPACK_BUFFER.

offset   Specifies the offset into the buffer object's data store where data replacement will begin, measured in bytes.

size   Specifies the size in bytes of the data store region being replaced.

data   Specifies a pointer to the new data that will be copied into the data store.

Description

glBufferSubData redefines some or all of the data store for the buffer object currently bound to *target*. Data starting at byte offset *offset* and extending for *size* bytes is copied to the data store from the memory pointed to by *data*. An error is thrown if *offset* and *size* together define a range beyond the bounds of the buffer object's data store.

Notes

glBufferSubData is available only if the GL version is 1.5 or greater.

Targets GL_PIXEL_PACK_BUFFER and GL_PIXEL_UNPACK_BUFFER are available only if the GL version is 2.1 or greater.

When replacing the entire data store, consider using glBufferSubData rather than completely recreating the data store with glBufferData. This avoids the cost of reallocating the data store.

Consider using multiple buffer objects to avoid stalling the rendering pipeline during data store updates. If any rendering in the pipeline makes reference to data in the buffer object being updated by glBufferSubData, especially from the specific region being updated, that rendering must drain from the pipeline before the data store can be updated.

Clients must align data elements consistent with the requirements of the client platform, with an additional base-level requirement that an offset within a buffer to a datum comprising *NN*.

Errors

GL_INVALID_ENUM is generated if *target* is not GL_ARRAY_BUFFER, GL_ELEMENT_ARRAY_BUFFER, GL_PIXEL_PACK_BUFFER, or GL_PIXEL_UNPACK_BUFFER.

GL_INVALID_VALUE is generated if offset or size is negative, or if together they define a region of memory that extends beyond the buffer object's allocated data store.

GL_INVALID_OPERATION is generated if the reserved buffer object name 0 is bound to *target*.

GL_INVALID_OPERATION is generated if the buffer object being updated is mapped.

GL_INVALID_OPERATION is generated if glBufferSubData is executed between the execution of glBegin and the corresponding execution of glEnd.

Associated Gets

glGetBufferSubData

See Also

glBindBuffer, glBufferData, glMapBuffer, glUnmapBuffer

glCallList

Execute a display list

C Specification

void **glCallList**(GLuint *list*);

Parameters

list   Specifies the integer name of the display list to be executed.

Description

glCallList causes the named display list to be executed. The commands saved in the display list are executed in order, just as if they were called without using a display list. If list has not been defined as a display list, glCallList is ignored.

glCallList can appear inside a display list. To avoid the possibility of infinite recursion resulting from display lists calling one another, a limit is placed on the nesting level of display lists during display-list execution. This limit is at least 64, and it depends on the implementation.

GL state is not saved and restored across a call to glCallList. Thus, changes made to GL state during the execution of a display list remain after execution of the display list is completed. Use glPushAttrib, glPopAttrib, glPushMatrix, and glPopMatrix to preserve GL state across glCallList calls.

Notes

Display lists can be executed between a call to glBegin and the corresponding call to glEnd, as long as the display list includes only commands that are allowed in this interval.

Associated Gets

glGet with argument GL_MAX_LIST_NESTING
glIsList

See Also

glCallLists, glDeleteLists, glGenLists, glNewList, glPushAttrib, glPushMatrix

glCallLists

Execute a list of display lists

C Specification

```
void glCallLists(GLsizei        n,
                 GLenum         type,
                 const GLvoid * lists);
```

Parameters

n   Specifies the number of display lists to be executed.

type   Specifies the type of values in lists. Symbolic constants GL_BYTE, GL_UNSIGNED_BYTE, GL_SHORT, GL_UNSIGNED_SHORT, GL_INT, GL_UNSIGNED_INT, GL_FLOAT, GL_2_BYTES, GL_3_BYTES, and GL_4_BYTES are accepted.

lists   Specifies the address of an array of name offsets in the display list. The pointer type is void because the offsets can be bytes, shorts, ints, or floats, depending on the value of type.

Description

glCallLists causes each display list in the list of names passed as lists to be executed. As a result, the commands saved in each display list are executed in order, just as if they were called without using a display list. Names of display lists that have not been defined are ignored.

glCallLists provides an efficient means for executing more than one display list. type allows lists with various name formats to be accepted. The formats are as follows:

GL_BYTE

lists is treated as an array of signed bytes, each in the range -128 through 127.

GL_UNSIGNED_BYTE

lists is treated as an array of unsigned bytes, each in the range 0 through 255.

GL_SHORT

lists is treated as an array of signed two-byte integers, each in the range -32768 through 32767.

GL_UNSIGNED_SHORT

lists is treated as an array of unsigned two-byte integers, each in the range 0 through 65535.

GL_INT

lists is treated as an array of signed four-byte integers.

GL_UNSIGNED_INT

lists is treated as an array of unsigned four-byte integers.

GL_FLOAT

lists is treated as an array of four-byte floating-point values.

GL_2_BYTES

lists is treated as an array of unsigned bytes. Each pair of bytes specifies a single display-list name. The value of the pair is computed as 256 times the unsigned value of the first byte plus the unsigned value of the second byte.

GL_3_BYTES

lists is treated as an array of unsigned bytes. Each triplet of bytes specifies a single display-list name. The value of the triplet is computed as 65536 times the unsigned value of the first byte, plus 256 times the unsigned value of the second byte, plus the unsigned value of the third byte.

GL_4_BYTES

lists is treated as an array of unsigned bytes. Each quadruplet of bytes specifies a single display-list name. The value of the quadruplet is computed as 16777216 times the unsigned value of the first byte, plus 65536 times the unsigned value of the second byte, plus 256 times the unsigned value of the third byte, plus the unsigned value of the fourth byte.

The list of display-list names is not null-terminated. Rather, *n* specifies how many names are to be taken from `lists`.

An additional level of indirection is made available with the `glListBase` command, which specifies an unsigned offset that is added to each display-list name specified in *lists* before that display list is executed.

`glCallLists` can appear inside a display list. To avoid the possibility of infinite recursion resulting from display lists calling one another, a limit is placed on the nesting level of display lists during display-list execution. This limit must be at least 64, and it depends on the implementation.

GL state is not saved and restored across a call to `glCallLists`. Thus, changes made to GL state during the execution of the display lists remain after execution is completed. Use `glPushAttrib`, `glPopAttrib`, `glPushMatrix`, and `glPopMatrix` to preserve GL state across `glCallLists` calls.

Notes

Display lists can be executed between a call to `glBegin` and the corresponding call to `glEnd`, as long as the display list includes only commands that are allowed in this interval.

Errors

GL_INVALID_VALUE is generated if *n* is negative.

GL_INVALID_ENUM is generated if *type* is not one of GL_BYTE, GL_UNSIGNED_BYTE, GL_SHORT, GL_UNSIGNED_SHORT, GL_INT, GL_UNSIGNED_INT, GL_FLOAT, GL_2_BYTES, GL_3_BYTES, GL_4_BYTES.

Associated Gets

`glGet` with argument GL_LIST_BASE

`glGet` with argument GL_MAX_LIST_NESTING

`glIsList`

See Also

`glCallList`, `glDeleteLists`, `glGenLists`, `glListBase`, `glNewList`, `glPushAttrib`, `glPushMatrix`

glClear

Clear buffers to preset values

C Specification

void **glClear**(GLbitfield *mask*);

Parameters

mask   Bitwise OR of masks that indicate the buffers to be cleared. The four masks are GL_COLOR_BUFFER_BIT, GL_DEPTH_BUFFER_BIT, GL_ACCUM_BUFFER_BIT, and GL_STENCIL_BUFFER_BIT.

Description

glClear sets the bitplane area of the window to values previously selected by glClearColor, glClearIndex, glClearDepth, glClearStencil, and glClearAccum. Multiple color buffers can be cleared simultaneously by selecting more than one buffer at a time using glDrawBuffer.

The pixel ownership test, the scissor test, dithering, and the buffer writemasks affect the operation of glClear. The scissor box bounds the cleared region. Alpha function, blend function, logical operation, stenciling, texture mapping, and depth-buffering are ignored by glClear.

glClear takes a single argument that is the bitwise OR of several values indicating which buffer is to be cleared.

The values are as follows:

GL_COLOR_BUFFER_BIT
Indicates the buffers currently enabled for color writing.
GL_DEPTH_BUFFER_BIT
Indicates the depth buffer.
GL_ACCUM_BUFFER_BIT
Indicates the accumulation buffer.
GL_STENCIL_BUFFER_BIT
Indicates the stencil buffer.
The value to which each buffer is cleared depends on the setting of the clear value for that buffer.

Notes

If a buffer is not present, then a glClear directed at that buffer has no effect.

Errors

GL_INVALID_VALUE is generated if any bit other than the four defined bits is set in *mask*.

GL_INVALID_OPERATION is generated if glClear is executed between the execution of glBegin and the corresponding execution of glEnd.

Associated Gets

glGet with argument GL_ACCUM_CLEAR_VALUE
glGet with argument GL_DEPTH_CLEAR_VALUE
glGet with argument GL_INDEX_CLEAR_VALUE
glGet with argument GL_COLOR_CLEAR_VALUE
glGet with argument GL_STENCIL_CLEAR_VALUE

See Also

glClearAccum, glClearColor, glClearDepth, glClearIndex, glClearStencil, glColorMask, glDepthMask, glDrawBuffer, glScissor, glStencilMask

glClearAccum

Specify clear values for the accumulation buffer

C Specification

```
void glClearAccum(GLfloat red,
                  GLfloat green,
                  GLfloat blue,
                  GLfloat alpha);
```

Parameters

red, *green*, *blue*, *alpha*   Specify the red, green, blue, and alpha values used when the accumulation buffer is cleared. The initial values are all 0.

Description

glClearAccum specifies the red, green, blue, and alpha values used by glClear to clear the accumulation buffer.

Values specified by glClearAccum are clamped to the range [-1,1].

Errors

GL_INVALID_OPERATION is generated if glClearAccum is executed between the execution of glBegin and the corresponding execution of glEnd.

Associated Gets

glGet with argument GL_ACCUM_CLEAR_VALUE

See Also

glAccum, glClear

glClearColor

Specify clear values for the color buffers

C Specification

void **glClearColor**(GLclampf *red*,
                     GLclampf *green*,
                     GLclampf *blue*,
                     GLclampf *alpha*);

Parameters

red, *green*, *blue*, *alpha*   Specify the red, green, blue, and alpha values used when the color buffers are cleared. The initial values are all 0.

Description

glClearColor specifies the red, green, blue, and alpha values used by glClear to clear the color buffers. Values specified by glClearColor are clamped to the range [0,1].

Errors

GL_INVALID_OPERATION is generated if glClearColor is executed between the execution of glBegin and the corresponding execution of glEnd.

Associated Gets

glGet with argument GL_COLOR_CLEAR_VALUE

See Also

glClear

glClearDepth

Specify the clear value for the depth buffer

C Specification

void **glClearDepth**(GLclampd *depth*);

Parameters

depth   Specifies the depth value used when the depth buffer is cleared. The initial value is 1.

Description

glClearDepth specifies the depth value used by glClear to clear the depth buffer. Values specified by glClearDepth are clamped to the range [0,1].

Errors

GL_INVALID_OPERATION is generated if glClearDepth is executed between the execution of glBegin and the corresponding execution of glEnd.

Associated Gets

glGet with argument GL_DEPTH_CLEAR_VALUE

See Also

glClear

glClearIndex

Specify the clear value for the color index buffers

C Specification

void **glClearIndex**(GLfloat c);

Parameters

c   Specifies the index used when the color index buffers are cleared. The initial value is 0.

Description

glClearIndex specifies the index used by glClear to clear the color index buffers. c is not clamped. Rather, c is converted to a fixed-point value with unspecified precision to the right of the binary point. The integer part of this value is then masked with $2^m - 1$, where m is the number of bits in a color index stored in the frame buffer.

Errors

GL_INVALID_OPERATION is generated if glClearIndex is executed between the execution of glBegin and the corresponding execution of glEnd.

Associated Gets

glGet with argument GL_INDEX_CLEAR_VALUE
glGet with argument GL_INDEX_BITS

See Also

glClear

glClearStencil

Specify the clear value for the stencil buffer

C Specification

void **glClearStencil**(GLint s);

Parameters

s   Specifies the index used when the stencil buffer is cleared. The initial value is 0.

Description

glClearStencil specifies the index used by glClear to clear the stencil buffer. s is masked with $2^m - 1$, where m is the number of bits in the stencil buffer.

Errors

GL_INVALID_OPERATION is generated if glClearStencil is executed between the execution of glBegin and the corresponding execution of glEnd.

Associated Gets

glGet with argument GL_STENCIL_CLEAR_VALUE
glGet with argument GL_STENCIL_BITS

See Also

glClear, glStencilFunc, glStencilFuncSeparate, glStencilMask, glStencilMaskSeparate, glStencilOp, glStencilOpSeparate

glClientActiveTexture

Select active texture unit

C Specification

```
void glClientActiveTexture(GLenum texture);
```

Parameters

texture   Specifies which texture unit to make active. The number of texture units is implementation dependent, but must be at least two. *texture* must be one of GL_TEXTURE*i*, where *i* ranges from 0 to the value of GL_MAX_TEXTURE_COORDS - 1, which is an implementation-dependent value. The initial value is GL_TEXTURE0.

Description

glClientActiveTexture selects the vertex array client state parameters to be modified by glTexCoordPointer, and enabled or disabled with glEnableClientState or glDisableClientState, respectively, when called with a parameter of GL_TEXTURE_COORD_ARRAY.

Notes

glClientActiveTexture is supported only if the GL version is 1.3 or greater, or ARB_multitexture is included in the string returned by glGetString when called with the argument GL_EXTENSIONS.

Errors

GL_INVALID_ENUM is generated if *texture* is not one of GL_TEXTURE*i*, where *i* ranges from 0 to the value of GL_MAX_TEXTURE_COORDS - 1.

Associated Gets

glGet with argument GL_CLIENT_ACTIVE_TEXTURE or GL_MAX_TEXTURE_COORDS

See Also

glActiveTexture, glDisableClientState, glEnableClientState, glMultiTexCoord, glTexCoordPointer

glClipPlane

Specify a plane against which all geometry is clipped

C Specification

```
void glClipPlane(GLenum          plane,
                 const GLdouble * equation);
```

Parameters

plane   Specifies which clipping plane is being positioned. Symbolic names of the form GL_CLIP_PLANE*i*, where *i* is an integer between 0 and GL_MAX_CLIP_PLANES-1, are accepted.

equation   Specifies the address of an array of four double-precision floating-point values. These values are interpreted as a plane equation.

Description

Geometry is always clipped against the boundaries of a six-plane frustum in x, y, and z. glClipPlane allows the specification of additional planes, not necessarily perpendicular to the x, y, or z axis, against which all geometry is clipped. To determine the maximum number of additional clipping planes, call glGetIntegerv with argument GL_MAX_CLIP_PLANES. All implementations support at least six such clipping planes. Because the resulting clipping region is the intersection of the defined half-spaces, it is always convex.

glClipPlane specifies a half-space using a four-component plane equation. When glClipPlane is called, *equation* is transformed by the inverse of the modelview matrix and stored in the resulting eye coordinates. Subsequent changes to the modelview matrix have no effect on the stored plane-equation components. If the dot product of the eye coordinates of a vertex with the stored plane equation components is positive or zero, the vertex is *in* with respect to that clipping plane. Otherwise, it is *out*.

To enable and disable clipping planes, call glEnable and glDisable with the argument GL_CLIP_PLANE*i*, where *i* is the plane number.

All clipping planes are initially defined as (0, 0, 0, 0) in eye coordinates and are disabled.

Notes
It is always the case that GL_CLIP_PLANE*i* = GL_CLIP_PLANE0 + *i*.

Errors
GL_INVALID_ENUM is generated if plane is not an accepted value.

GL_INVALID_OPERATION is generated if glClipPlane is executed between the execution of glBegin and the corresponding execution of glEnd.

Associated Gets
glGetClipPlane
glIsEnabled with argument GL_CLIP_PLANE*i*

See Also
glEnable

glColor

Set the current color

C Specification
```
void glColor3b(GLbyte red,
               GLbyte green,
               GLbyte blue);
void glColor3s(GLshort red,
               GLshort green,
               GLshort blue);
void glColor3i(GLint red,
               GLint green,
               GLint blue);
void glColor3f(GLfloat red,
               GLfloat green,
               GLfloat blue);
void glColor3d(GLdouble red,
               GLdouble green,
               GLdouble blue);
void glColor3ub(GLubyte red,
                GLubyte green,
                GLubyte blue);
void glColor3us(GLushort red,
                GLushort green,
                GLushort blue);
void glColor3ui(GLuint red,
                GLuint green,
                GLuint blue);
```

```
void glColor4b(GLbyte red,
               GLbyte green,
               GLbyte blue,
               GLbyte alpha);
void glColor4s(GLshort red,
               GLshort green,
               GLshort blue,
               GLshort alpha);
void glColor4i(GLint red,
               GLint green,
               GLint blue,
               GLint alpha);
void glColor4f(GLfloat red,
               GLfloat green,
               GLfloat blue,
               GLfloat alpha);
void glColor4d(GLdouble red,
               GLdouble green,
               GLdouble blue,
               GLdouble alpha);
void glColor4ub(GLubyte red,
               GLubyte green,
               GLubyte blue,
               GLubyte alpha);
void glColor4us(GLushort red,
               GLushort green,
               GLushort blue,
               GLushort alpha);
void glColor4ui(GLuint red,
               GLuint green,
               GLuint blue,
               GLuint alpha);
```

Parameters

red, *green*, *blue*   Specify new red, green, and blue values for the current color.

alpha   Specifies a new alpha value for the current color. Included only in the four-argument glColor4 commands.

C Specification

```
void glColor3bv(const GLbyte * v);
void glColor3sv(const GLshort * v);
void glColor3iv(const GLint * v);
void glColor3fv(const GLfloat * v);
void glColor3dv(const GLdouble * v);
void glColor3ubv(const GLubyte * v);
void glColor3usv(const GLushort * v);
void glColor3uiv(const GLuint * v);
void glColor4bv(const GLbyte * v);
void glColor4sv(const GLshort * v);
void glColor4iv(const GLint * v);
void glColor4fv(const GLfloat * v);
void glColor4dv(const GLdouble * v);
void glColor4ubv(const GLubyte * v);
```

```
void glColor4usv(const GLushort * v);
void glColor4uiv(const GLuint * v);
```

Parameters

v   Specifies a pointer to an array that contains red, green, blue, and (sometimes) alpha values.

Description

The GL stores both a current single-valued color index and a current four-valued RGBA color. glColor sets a new four-valued RGBA color. glColor has two major variants: glColor3 and glColor4. glColor3 variants specify new red, green, and blue values explicitly and set the current alpha value to 1.0 (full intensity) implicitly. glColor4 variants specify all four color components explicitly.

glColor3b, glColor4b, glColor3s, glColor4s, glColor3i, and glColor4i take three or four signed byte, short, or long integers as arguments. When v is appended to the name, the color commands can take a pointer to an array of such values.

Current color values are stored in floating-point format, with unspecified mantissa and exponent sizes. Unsigned integer color components, when specified, are linearly mapped to floating-point values such that the largest representable value maps to 1.0 (full intensity), and 0 maps to 0.0 (zero intensity). Signed integer color components, when specified, are linearly mapped to floating-point values such that the most positive representable value maps to 1.0, and the most negative representable value maps to -1.0. (Note that this mapping does not convert 0 precisely to 0.0.) Floating-point values are mapped directly.

Neither floating-point nor signed integer values are clamped to the range [0,1] before the current color is updated. However, color components are clamped to this range before they are interpolated or written into a color buffer.

Notes

The initial value for the current color is (1, 1, 1, 1).

The current color can be updated at any time. In particular, glColor can be called between a call to glBegin and the corresponding call to glEnd.

Associated Gets

glGet with argument GL_CURRENT_COLOR
glGet with argument GL_RGBA_MODE

See Also

glColorPointer, glIndex, glSecondaryColor

glColorMask

Enable and disable writing of frame buffer color components

C Specification

```
void glColorMask(GLboolean red,
                 GLboolean green,
                 GLboolean blue,
                 GLboolean alpha);
```

Parameters

red, green, blue, alpha   Specify whether red, green, blue, and alpha can or cannot be written into the frame buffer. The initial values are all GL_TRUE, indicating that the color components can be written.

Description

glColorMask specifies whether the individual color components in the frame buffer can or cannot be written. If red is GL_FALSE, for example, no change is made to the red component of any pixel in any of the color buffers, regardless of the drawing operation attempted.

Changes to individual bits of components cannot be controlled. Rather, changes are either enabled or disabled for entire color components.

Errors

GL_INVALID_OPERATION is generated if glColorMask is executed between the execution of glBegin and the corresponding execution of glEnd.

Associated Gets

glGet with argument GL_COLOR_WRITEMASK

glGet with argument GL_RGBA_MODE

See Also

glClear, glColor, glColorPointer, glDepthMask, glIndex, glIndexPointer, glIndexMask, glStencilMask

glColorMaterial

Cause a material color to track the current color

C Specification

```
void glColorMaterial(GLenum face,
                     GLenum mode);
```

Parameters

face   Specifies whether front, back, or both front and back material parameters should track the current color. Accepted values are GL_FRONT, GL_BACK, and GL_FRONT_AND_BACK. The initial value is GL_FRONT_AND_BACK.

mode   Specifies which of several material parameters track the current color. Accepted values are GL_EMISSION, GL_AMBIENT, GL_DIFFUSE, GL_SPECULAR, and GL_AMBIENT_AND_DIFFUSE. The initial value is GL_AMBIENT_AND_DIFFUSE.

Description

glColorMaterial specifies which material parameters track the current color. When GL_COLOR_MATERIAL is enabled, the material parameter or parameters specified by mode, of the material or materials specified by face, track the current color at all times.

To enable and disable GL_COLOR_MATERIAL, call glEnable and glDisable with argument GL_COLOR_MATERIAL. GL_COLOR_MATERIAL is initially disabled.

Notes

glColorMaterial makes it possible to change a subset of material parameters for each vertex using only the glColor command, without calling glMaterial. If only such a subset of parameters is to be specified for each vertex, calling glColorMaterial is preferable to calling glMaterial.

Call glColorMaterial before enabling GL_COLOR_MATERIAL.

Calling glDrawElements, glDrawArrays, or glDrawRangeElements may leave the current color indeterminate, if the color array is enabled. If glColorMaterial is enabled while the current color is indeterminate, the lighting material state specified by face and mode is also indeterminate.

If the GL version is 1.1 or greater, and GL_COLOR_MATERIAL is enabled, evaluated color values affect the results of the lighting equation as if the current color were being modified, but no change is made to the tracking lighting parameter of the current color.

Errors

GL_INVALID_ENUM is generated if face or mode is not an accepted value.

GL_INVALID_OPERATION is generated if glColorMaterial is executed between the execution of glBegin and the corresponding execution of glEnd.

Associated Gets

glIsEnabled with argument GL_COLOR_MATERIAL

glGet with argument GL_COLOR_MATERIAL_PARAMETER

glGet with argument GL_COLOR_MATERIAL_FACE

See Also

glColor, glColorPointer, glDrawArrays, glDrawElements, glDrawRangeElements, glEnable, glLight, glLightModel, glMaterial

glColorPointer

Define an array of colors

C Specification

```
void glColorPointer(GLint          size,
                    GLenum         type,
                    GLsizei        stride,
                    const GLvoid * pointer);
```

Parameters

size   Specifies the number of components per color. Must be 3 or 4. The initial value is 4.

type   Specifies the data type of each color component in the array. Symbolic constants GL_BYTE, GL_UNSIGNED_BYTE, GL_SHORT, GL_UNSIGNED_SHORT, GL_INT, GL_UNSIGNED_INT, GL_FLOAT, and GL_DOUBLE are accepted. The initial value is GL_FLOAT.

stride   Specifies the byte offset between consecutive colors. If stride is 0, the colors are understood to be tightly packed in the array. The initial value is 0.

pointer   Specifies a pointer to the first component of the first color element in the array. The initial value is 0.

Description

glColorPointer specifies the location and data format of an array of color components to use when rendering. size specifies the number of components per color, and must be 3 or 4. type specifies the data type of each color component, and stride specifies the byte stride from one color to the next, allowing vertices and attributes to be packed into a single array or stored in separate arrays. (Single-array storage may be more efficient on some implementations; see glInterleavedArrays.)

If a nonzero named buffer object is bound to the GL_ARRAY_BUFFER target (see glBindBuffer) while a color array is specified, pointer is treated as a byte offset into the buffer object's data store. Also, the buffer object binding (GL_ARRAY_BUFFER_BINDING) is saved as color vertex array client-side state (GL_COLOR_ARRAY_BUFFER_BINDING).

When a color array is specified, size, type, stride, and pointer are saved as client-side state, in addition to the current vertex array buffer object binding.

To enable and disable the color array, call glEnableClientState and glDisableClientState with the argument GL_COLOR_ARRAY. If enabled, the color array is used when glDrawArrays, glMultiDrawArrays, glDrawElements, glMultiDrawElements, glDrawRangeElements, or glArrayElement is called.

Notes

glColorPointer is available only if the GL version is 1.1 or greater.

The color array is initially disabled and isn't accessed when glArrayElement, glDrawElements, glDrawRangeElements, glDrawArrays, glMultiDrawArrays, or glMultiDrawElements is called.

Execution of glColorPointer is not allowed between the execution of glBegin and the corresponding execution of glEnd, but an error may or may not be generated. If no error is generated, the operation is undefined.

glColorPointer is typically implemented on the client side.

Color array parameters are client-side state and are therefore not saved or restored by glPushAttrib and glPopAttrib. Use glPushClientAttrib and glPopClientAttrib instead.

Errors

GL_INVALID_VALUE is generated if *size* is not 3 or 4.

GL_INVALID_ENUM is generated if *type* is not an accepted value.

GL_INVALID_VALUE is generated if *stride* is negative.

Associated Gets

glIsEnabled with argument GL_COLOR_ARRAY

glGet with argument GL_COLOR_ARRAY_SIZE

glGet with argument GL_COLOR_ARRAY_TYPE

glGet with argument GL_COLOR_ARRAY_STRIDE

glGet with argument GL_COLOR_ARRAY_BUFFER_BINDING

glGet with argument GL_ARRAY_BUFFER_BINDING

glGetPointerv with argument GL_COLOR_ARRAY_POINTER

See Also

glArrayElement, glBindBuffer, glColor, glDisableClientState, glDrawArrays, glDrawElements, glDrawRangeElements, glEdgeFlagPointer, glEnableClientState, glFogCoordPointer, glIndexPointer, glInterleavedArrays, glMultiDrawArrays, glMultiDrawElements, glNormalPointer, glPopClientAttrib, glPushClientAttrib, glSecondaryColorPointer, glTexCoordPointer, glVertexAttribPointer, glVertexPointer

glColorSubTable

Respecify a portion of a color table

C Specification

```
void glColorSubTable(GLenum        target,
                     GLsizei       start,
                     GLsizei       count,
                     GLenum        format,
                     GLenum        type,
                     const GLvoid * data);
```

Parameters

target   Must be one of GL_COLOR_TABLE, GL_POST_CONVOLUTION_COLOR_TABLE, or GL_POST_COLOR_MATRIX_COLOR_TABLE.

start   The starting index of the portion of the color table to be replaced.

count   The number of table entries to replace.

format   The format of the pixel data in *data*. The allowable values are GL_RED, GL_GREEN, GL_BLUE, GL_ALPHA, GL_LUMINANCE, GL_LUMINANCE_ALPHA, GL_RGB, GL_BGR, GL_RGBA, and GL_BGRA.

type   The type of the pixel data in *data*. The allowable values are GL_UNSIGNED_BYTE, GL_BYTE, GL_UNSIGNED_SHORT, GL_SHORT, GL_UNSIGNED_INT, GL_INT, GL_FLOAT, GL_UNSIGNED_BYTE_3_3_2, GL_UNSIGNED_BYTE_2_3_3_REV, GL_UNSIGNED_SHORT_5_6_5, GL_UNSIGNED_SHORT_5_6_5_REV, GL_UNSIGNED_SHORT_4_4_4_4, GL_UNSIGNED_SHORT_4_4_4_4_REV, GL_UNSIGNED_SHORT_5_5_5_1, GL_UNSIGNED_SHORT_1_5_5_5_REV, GL_UNSIGNED_INT_8_8_8_8, GL_UNSIGNED_INT_8_8_8_8_REV, GL_UNSIGNED_INT_10_10_10_2, and GL_UNSIGNED_INT_2_10_10_10_REV.

data   Pointer to a one-dimensional array of pixel data that is processed to replace the specified region of the color table.

Description

glColorSubTable is used to respecify a contiguous portion of a color table previously defined using glColorTable. The pixels referenced by *data* replace the portion of the existing table from indices *start* to *start + count* − 1, inclusive. This region may not include any entries outside the range of the color table as it was originally specified. It is not an error to specify a subtexture with width of 0, but such a specification has no effect.

If a nonzero named buffer object is bound to the GL_PIXEL_UNPACK_BUFFER target (see glBindBuffer) while a portion of a color table is respecified, *data* is treated as a byte offset into the buffer object's data store.

Notes

glColorSubTable is present only if ARB_imaging is returned when glGetString is called with an argument of GL_EXTENSIONS.

Errors

GL_INVALID_ENUM is generated if *target* is not one of the allowable values.

GL_INVALID_ENUM is generated if *format* is not one of the allowable values.

GL_INVALID_ENUM is generated if *type* is not one of the allowable values.

GL_INVALID_VALUE is generated if *start + count* > *width*.

GL_INVALID_OPERATION is generated if a nonzero buffer object name is bound to the GL_PIXEL_UNPACK_BUFFER target and the buffer object's data store is currently mapped.

GL_INVALID_OPERATION is generated if a nonzero buffer object name is bound to the GL_PIXEL_UNPACK_BUFFER target and the data would be unpacked from the buffer object such that the memory reads required would exceed the data store size.

GL_INVALID_OPERATION is generated if a nonzero buffer object name is bound to the GL_PIXEL_UNPACK_BUFFER target and *data* is not evenly divisible into the number of bytes needed to store in memory a datum indicated by *type*.

GL_INVALID_OPERATION is generated if glColorSubTable is executed between the execution of glBegin and the corresponding execution of glEnd.

Associated Gets

glGetColorTable, glGetColorTableParameter

glGet with argument GL_PIXEL_UNPACK_BUFFER_BINDING

See Also

glColorTable, glColorTableParameter, glCopyColorTable, glCopyColorSubTable, glGetColorTable

glColorTable

Define a color lookup table

C Specification

```
void glColorTable(GLenum          target,
                  GLenum          internalformat,
                  GLsizei         width,
                  GLenum          format,
                  GLenum          type,
                  const GLvoid *  data);
```

Parameters

target   Must be one of GL_COLOR_TABLE, GL_POST_CONVOLUTION_COLOR_TABLE, GL_POST_COLOR_MATRIX_COLOR_TABLE, GL_PROXY_COLOR_TABLE, GL_PROXY_POST_CONVOLUTION_COLOR_TABLE, or GL_PROXY_POST_COLOR_MATRIX_COLOR_TABLE.

internalformat	The internal format of the color table. The allowable values are GL_ALPHA, GL_ALPHA4, GL_ALPHA8, GL_ALPHA12, GL_ALPHA16, GL_LUMINANCE, GL_LUMINANCE4, GL_LUMINANCE8, GL_LUMINANCE12, GL_LUMINANCE16, GL_LUMINANCE_ALPHA, GL_LUMINANCE4_ALPHA4, GL_LUMINANCE6_ALPHA2, GL_LUMINANCE8_ALPHA8, GL_LUMINANCE12_ALPHA4, GL_LUMINANCE12_ALPHA12, GL_LUMINANCE16_ALPHA16, GL_INTENSITY, GL_INTENSITY4, GL_INTENSITY8, GL_INTENSITY12, GL_INTENSITY16, GL_R3_G3_B2, GL_RGB, GL_RGB4, GL_RGB5, GL_RGB8, GL_RGB10, GL_RGB12, GL_RGB16, GL_RGBA, GL_RGBA2, GL_RGBA4, GL_RGB5_A1, GL_RGBA8, GL_RGB10_A2, GL_RGBA12, and GL_RGBA16.
width	The number of entries in the color lookup table specified by *data*.
format	The format of the pixel data in *data*. The allowable values are GL_RED, GL_GREEN, GL_BLUE, GL_ALPHA, GL_LUMINANCE, GL_LUMINANCE_ALPHA, GL_RGB, GL_BGR, GL_RGBA, and GL_BGRA.
type	The type of the pixel data in *data*. The allowable values are GL_UNSIGNED_BYTE, GL_BYTE, GL_UNSIGNED_SHORT, GL_SHORT, GL_UNSIGNED_INT, GL_INT, GL_FLOAT, GL_UNSIGNED_BYTE_3_3_2, GL_UNSIGNED_BYTE_2_3_3_REV, GL_UNSIGNED_SHORT_5_6_5, GL_UNSIGNED_SHORT_5_6_5_REV, GL_UNSIGNED_SHORT_4_4_4_4, GL_UNSIGNED_SHORT_4_4_4_4_REV, GL_UNSIGNED_SHORT_5_5_5_1, GL_UNSIGNED_SHORT_1_5_5_5_REV, GL_UNSIGNED_INT_8_8_8_8, GL_UNSIGNED_INT_8_8_8_8_REV, GL_UNSIGNED_INT_10_10_10_2, and GL_UNSIGNED_INT_2_10_10_10_REV.
data	Pointer to a one-dimensional array of pixel data that is processed to build the color table.

Description

glColorTable may be used in two ways: to test the actual size and color resolution of a lookup table given a particular set of parameters, or to load the contents of a color lookup table. Use the targets GL_PROXY_* for the first case and the other targets for the second case.

If a nonzero named buffer object is bound to the GL_PIXEL_UNPACK_BUFFER target (see glBindBuffer) while a color table is specified, *data* is treated as a byte offset into the buffer object's data store.

If *target* is GL_COLOR_TABLE, GL_POST_CONVOLUTION_COLOR_TABLE, or GL_POST_COLOR_MATRIX_COLOR_TABLE, glColorTable builds a color lookup table from an array of pixels. The pixel array specified by *width*, *format*, *type*, and *data* is extracted from memory and processed just as if glDrawPixels were called, but processing stops after the final expansion to RGBA is completed.

The four scale parameters and the four bias parameters that are defined for the table are then used to scale and bias the R, G, B, and A components of each pixel. (Use glColorTableParameter to set these scale and bias parameters.)

Next, the R, G, B, and A values are clamped to the range [0,1]. Each pixel is then converted to the internal format specified by *internalformat*. This conversion simply maps the component values of the pixel (R, G, B, and A) to the values included in the internal format (red, green, blue, alpha, luminance, and intensity). The mapping is as follows:

Internal Format	Red	Green	Blue	Alpha	Luminance	Intensity
GL_ALPHA				A		
GL_LUMINANCE					R	
GL_LUMINANCE_ALPHA				A	R	
GL_INTENSITY						R
GL_RGB	R	G	B			
GL_RGBA	R	G	B	A		

Finally, the red, green, blue, alpha, luminance, and/or intensity components of the resulting pixels are stored in the color table. They form a one-dimensional table with indices in the range [0,*width* – 1].

If *target* is GL_PROXY_*, glColorTable recomputes and stores the values of the proxy color table's state variables GL_COLOR_TABLE_FORMAT, GL_COLOR_TABLE_WIDTH, GL_COLOR_TABLE_RED_SIZE, GL_COLOR_TABLE_GREEN_SIZE, GL_COLOR_TABLE_BLUE_SIZE, GL_COLOR_TABLE_ALPHA_SIZE, GL_COLOR_TABLE_LUMINANCE_SIZE, and GL_COLOR_TABLE_INTEN-SITY_SIZE. There is no effect on the image or state of any actual color table. If the specified color table is too large to be supported, then all the proxy state variables listed above are set to zero. Otherwise, the color table could be supported by glColorTable using the corresponding non-proxy target, and the proxy state variables are set as if that target were being defined.

The proxy state variables can be retrieved by calling glGetColorTableParameter with a target of GL_PROXY_*. This allows the application to decide if a particular glColorTable command would succeed, and to determine what the resulting color table attributes would be.

If a color table is enabled, and its width is nonzero, then its contents are used to replace a subset of the components of each RGBA pixel group, based on the internal format of the table.

Each pixel group has color components (R, G, B, A) that are in the range [0.0,1.0]. The color components are rescaled to the size of the color lookup table to form an index. Then a subset of the components based on the internal format of the table are replaced by the table entry selected by that index. If the color components and contents of the table are represented as follows:

Representation	Meaning
r	Table index computed from R
g	Table index computed from G
b	Table index computed from B
a	Table index computed from A
L[i]	Luminance value at table index i
I[i]	Intensity value at table index i
R[i]	Red value at table index i
G[i]	Green value at table index i
B[i]	Blue value at table index i
A[i]	Alpha value at table index i

then the result of color table lookup is as follows:

Resulting Texture Components

Table Internal Format	R	G	B	A
GL_ALPHA	R	G	B	A[a]
GL_LUMINANCE	L[r]	L[g]	L[b]	At
GL_LUMINANCE_ALPHA	L[r]	L[g]	L[b]	A[a]
GL_INTENSITY	I[r]	I[g]	I[b]	I[a]
GL_RGB	R[r]	G[g]	B[b]	A
GL_RGBA	R[r]	G[g]	B[b]	A[a]

When GL_COLOR_TABLE is enabled, the colors resulting from the pixel map operation (if it is enabled) are mapped by the color lookup table before being passed to the convolution operation. The colors resulting from the convolution operation are modified by the post convolution color lookup table when GL_POST_CONVOLUTION_COLOR_TABLE is enabled. These modified colors are then sent to the color matrix operation. Finally, if GL_POST_COLOR_MATRIX_COLOR_TABLE is enabled, the colors resulting from the color matrix operation are mapped by the post color matrix color lookup table before being used by the histogram operation.

Notes

glColorTable is present only if ARB_imaging is returned when glGetString is called with an argument of GL_EXTENSIONS.

If *target* is set to GL_COLOR_TABLE, GL_POST_CONVOLUTION_COLOR_TABLE, or GL_POST_COLOR_MATRIX_COLOR_TABLE, then *width* must be a power of two or a GL_INVALID_VALUE error is generated.

Errors

GL_INVALID_ENUM is generated if *target* is not one of the allowable values.

GL_INVALID_ENUM is generated if *internalformat* is not one of the allowable values.

GL_INVALID_ENUM is generated if *format* is not one of the allowable values.

GL_INVALID_ENUM is generated if *type* is not one of the allowable values.

GL_INVALID_VALUE is generated if *width* is less than zero.

GL_TABLE_TOO_LARGE is generated if the requested color table is too large to be supported by the implementation, and *target* is not a GL_PROXY_* target.

GL_INVALID_OPERATION is generated if a nonzero buffer object name is bound to the GL_PIXEL_UNPACK_BUFFER target and the buffer object's data store is currently mapped.

GL_INVALID_OPERATION is generated if a nonzero buffer object name is bound to the GL_PIXEL_UNPACK_BUFFER target and the data would be unpacked from the buffer object such that the memory reads required would exceed the data store size.

GL_INVALID_OPERATION is generated if a nonzero buffer object name is bound to the GL_PIXEL_UNPACK_BUFFER target and *data* is not evenly divisible into the number of bytes needed to store in memory a datum indicated by *type*.

GL_INVALID_OPERATION is generated if glColorTable is executed between the execution of glBegin and the corresponding execution of glEnd.

Associated Gets

glGetColorTableParameter

glGet with argument GL_PIXEL_UNPACK_BUFFER_BINDING

See Also

glColorSubTable, glColorTableParameter, glCopyColorTable, glCopyColorSubTable, glGetColorTable

glColorTableParameter

Set color lookup table parameters

C Specification

```
void glColorTableParameterfv(GLenum          target,
                             GLenum          pname,
                             const GLfloat * params);
void glColorTableParameteriv(GLenum          target,
                             GLenum          pname,
                             const GLint *   params);
```

Parameters

target	The target color table. Must be GL_COLOR_TABLE, GL_POST_CONVOLUTION_COLOR_TABLE, or GL_POST_COLOR_MATRIX_COLOR_TABLE.
pname	The symbolic name of a texture color lookup table parameter. Must be one of GL_COLOR_TABLE_SCALE or GL_COLOR_TABLE_BIAS.
params	A pointer to an array where the values of the parameters are stored.

Description

glColorTableParameter is used to specify the scale factors and bias terms applied to color components when they are loaded into a color table. *target* indicates which color table the scale and bias terms apply to; it must be set to GL_COLOR_TABLE, GL_POST_CONVOLUTION_COLOR_TABLE, or GL_POST_COLOR_MATRIX_COLOR_TABLE.

pname must be GL_COLOR_TABLE_SCALE to set the scale factors. In this case, *params* points to an array of four values, which are the scale factors for red, green, blue, and alpha, in that order.

pname must be GL_COLOR_TABLE_BIAS to set the bias terms. In this case, *params* points to an array of four values, which are the bias terms for red, green, blue, and alpha, in that order.

The color tables themselves are specified by calling glColorTable.

Notes

glColorTableParameter is available only if ARB_imaging is returned from calling glGetString with an argument of GL_EXTENSIONS.

Errors

GL_INVALID_ENUM is generated if *target* or *pname* is not an acceptable value.

GL_INVALID_OPERATION is generated if glColorTableParameter is executed between the execution of glBegin and the corresponding execution of glEnd.

Associated Gets

glGetColorTableParameter

See Also

glColorTable, glPixelTransfer

glCompileShader

Compile a shader object

C Specification

void **glCompileShader**(GLuint *shader*);

Parameters

shader   Specifies the shader object to be compiled.

Description

glCompileShader compiles the source code strings that have been stored in the shader object specified by *shader*.

The compilation status will be stored as part of the shader object's state. This value will be set to GL_TRUE if the shader was compiled without errors and is ready for use, and GL_FALSE otherwise. It can be queried by calling glGetShader with arguments *shader* and GL_COMPILE_STATUS.

Compilation of a shader can fail for a number of reasons as specified by the OpenGL Shading Language Specification. Whether or not the compilation was successful, information about the compilation can be obtained from the shader object's information log by calling glGetShaderInfoLog.

Notes

glCompileShader is available only if the GL version is 2.0 or greater.

Errors

GL_INVALID_VALUE is generated if *shader* is not a value generated by OpenGL.

GL_INVALID_OPERATION is generated if *shader* is not of type GL_SHADER_OBJECT.

GL_INVALID_OPERATION is generated if glCompileShader is executed between the execution of glBegin and the corresponding execution of glEnd.

Associated Gets

glGetShaderInfoLog with argument *shader*

glGetShader with arguments *shader* and GL_COMPILE_STATUS

glIsShader

See Also

glCreateShader, glLinkProgram, glShaderSource

glCompressedTexImage1D

Specify a one-dimensional texture image in a compressed format

C Specification

```
void glCompressedTexImage1D(GLenum        target,
                            GLint         level,
                            GLenum        internalformat,
                            GLsizei       width,
                            GLint         border,
                            GLsizei       imageSize,
                            const GLvoid * data);
```

Parameters

target	Specifies the target texture. Must be GL_TEXTURE_1D or GL_PROXY_TEXTURE_1D.
level	Specifies the level-of-detail number. Level 0 is the base image level. Level *n* is the *n*th mipmap reduction image.
internalformat	Specifies the format of the compressed image data stored at address *data*.
width	Specifies the width of the texture image including the border if any. If the GL version does not support non-power-of-two sizes, this value must be $2^n + 2$ (*border*) for some integer *n*. All implementations support texture images that are at least 64 texels wide. The height of the 1D texture image is 1.
border	Specifies the width of the border. Must be either 0 or 1.
imageSize	Specifies the number of unsigned bytes of image data starting at the address specified by *data*.
data	Specifies a pointer to the compressed image data in memory.

Description

Texturing maps a portion of a specified texture image onto each graphical primitive for which texturing is enabled. To enable and disable one-dimensional texturing, call glEnable and glDisable with argument GL_TEXTURE_1D.

glCompressedTexImage1D loads a previously defined, and retrieved, compressed one-dimensional texture image if *target* is GL_TEXTURE_1D (see glTexImage1D).

If *target* is GL_PROXY_TEXTURE_1D, no data is read from *data*, but all of the texture image state is recalculated, checked for consistency, and checked against the implementation's capabilities. If the implementation cannot handle a texture of the requested texture size, it sets all of the image state to 0, but does not generate an error (see glGetError). To query for an entire mipmap array, use an image array level greater than or equal to 1.

internalformat must be extension-specified compressed-texture format. When a texture is loaded with glTexImage1D using a generic compressed texture format (e.g., GL_COMPRESSED_RGB) the GL selects from one of its extensions supporting compressed textures. In order to load the compressed texture image using glCompressedTexImage1D, query the compressed texture image's size and format using glGetTexLevelParameter.

If a nonzero named buffer object is bound to the GL_PIXEL_UNPACK_BUFFER target (see glBindBuffer) while a texture image is specified, *data* is treated as a byte offset into the buffer object's data store.

Notes

glCompressedTexImage1D is available only if the GL version is 1.3 or greater.

Non-power-of-two textures are supported if the GL version is 2.0 or greater, or if the implementation exports the GL_ARB_texture_non_power_of_two extension.

Errors

GL_INVALID_ENUM is generated if *internalformat* is of the generic compressed internal formats: GL_COMPRESSED_ALPHA, GL_COMPRESSED_LUMINANCE, GL_COMPRESSED_LUMINANCE_ALPHA, GL_COMPRESSED_INTENSITY, GL_COMPRESSED_RGB, or GL_COMPRESSED_RGBA.

GL_INVALID_VALUE is generated if *imageSize* is not consistent with the format, dimensions, and contents of the specified compressed image data.

GL_INVALID_OPERATION is generated if parameter combinations are not supported by the specific compressed internal format as specified in the specific texture compression extension.

GL_INVALID_OPERATION is generated if a nonzero buffer object name is bound to the GL_PIXEL_UNPACK_BUFFER target and the buffer object's data store is currently mapped.

GL_INVALID_OPERATION is generated if a nonzero buffer object name is bound to the GL_PIXEL_UNPACK_BUFFER target and the data would be unpacked from the buffer object such that the memory reads required would exceed the data store size.

GL_INVALID_OPERATION is generated if glCompressedTexImage1D is executed between the execution of glBegin and the corresponding execution of glEnd.

Undefined results, including abnormal program termination, are generated if *data* is not encoded in a manner consistent with the extension specification defining the internal compression format.

Associated Gets

glGetCompressedTexImage

glGet with argument GL_TEXTURE_COMPRESSED

glGet with argument GL_PIXEL_UNPACK_BUFFER_BINDING

glGetTexLevelParameter with arguments GL_TEXTURE_INTERNAL_FORMAT and GL_TEXTURE_COMPRESSED_IMAGE_SIZE

glIsEnabled with argument GL_TEXTURE_1D

See Also

glActiveTexture, glColorTable, glCompressedTexImage2D, glCompressedTexImage3D, glCompressedTexSubImage1D, glCompressedTexSubImage2D, glCompressedTexSubImage3D, glConvolutionFilter1D, glCopyPixels, glCopyTexImage1D, glCopyTexImage2D, glCopyTexSubImage1D, glCopyTexSubImage2D, glCopyTexSubImage3D, glDrawPixels, glMatrixMode, glPixelStore, glPixelTransfer, glTexEnv, glTexGen, glTexImage2D, glTexImage3D, glTexSubImage1D, glTexSubImage2D, glTexSubImage3D, glTexParameter

glCompressedTexImage2D

Specify a two-dimensional texture image in a compressed format

C Specification

```
void glCompressedTexImage2D(GLenum        target,
                            GLint         level,
                            GLenum        internalformat,
                            GLsizei       width,
                            GLsizei       height,
                            GLint         border,
                            GLsizei       imageSize,
                            const GLvoid * data);
```

Parameters

target	Specifies the target texture. Must be GL_TEXTURE_2D, GL_PROXY_TEXTURE_2D, GL_TEXTURE_CUBE_MAP_POSITIVE_X, GL_TEXTURE_CUBE_MAP_NEGATIVE_X, GL_TEXTURE_CUBE_MAP_POSITIVE_Y, GL_TEXTURE_CUBE_MAP_NEGATIVE_Y, GL_TEXTURE_CUBE_MAP_POSITIVE_Z, GL_TEXTURE_CUBE_MAP_NEGATIVE_Z, or GL_PROXY_TEXTURE_CUBE_MAP.
level	Specifies the level-of-detail number. Level 0 is the base image level. Level n is the nth mipmap reduction image.
internalformat	Specifies the format of the compressed image data stored at address *data*. Must be one of the following constants: GL_COMPRESSED_ALPHA, GL_COMPRESSED_LUMINANCE, GL_COMPRESSED_LUMINANCE_ALPHA, GL_COMPRESSED_INTENSITY, GL_COMPRESSED_RGB, GL_COMPRESSED_RGBA, GL_COMPRESSED_SLUMINANCE, or GL_COMPRESSED_SLUMINANCE_ALPHA. GL_COMPRESSED_SRGB, GL_COMPRESSED_SRGBA, GL_COMPRESSED_SRGB_ALPHA,
width	Specifies the width of the texture image including the border if any. If the GL version does not support non-power-of-two sizes, this value must be $2^n + 2$ (*border*) for some integer n. All implementations support texture images that are at least 64 texels wide.
height	Specifies the height of the texture image including the border if any. If the GL version does not support non-power-of-two sizes, this value must be Must be $2^n + 2$ (*border*) for some integer n. All implementations support texture images that are at least 64 texels wide.
border	Specifies the width of the border. Must be either 0 or 1.
imageSize	Specifies the number of unsigned bytes of image data starting at the address specified by *data*.
data	Specifies a pointer to the compressed image data in memory.

Description

Texturing maps a portion of a specified texture image onto each graphical primitive for which texturing is enabled. To enable and disable two-dimensional texturing, call glEnable and glDisable with argument GL_TEXTURE_2D. To enable and disable texturing using cube-mapped textures, call glEnable and glDisable with argument GL_TEXTURE_CUBE_MAP.

glCompressedTexImage2D loads a previously defined, and retrieved, compressed two-dimensional texture image if *target* is GL_TEXTURE_2D (see glTexImage2D).

If *target* is GL_PROXY_TEXTURE_2D, no data is read from *data*, but all of the texture image state is recalculated, checked for consistency, and checked against the implementation's capabilities. If the implementation cannot handle a texture of the requested texture size, it sets all of the image state to 0, but does not generate an error (see glGetError). To query for an entire mipmap array, use an image array level greater than or equal to 1.

internalformat must be an extension-specified compressed-texture format. When a texture is loaded with glTexImage2D using a generic compressed texture format (e.g., GL_COMPRESSED_RGB), the GL selects from one of its extensions supporting compressed textures. In order to load the compressed texture image using glCompressedTexImage2D, query the compressed texture image's size and format using glGetTexLevelParameter.

If a nonzero named buffer object is bound to the GL_PIXEL_UNPACK_BUFFER target (see glBindBuffer) while a texture image is specified, *data* is treated as a byte offset into the buffer object's data store.

Notes

glCompressedTexImage2D is available only if the GL version is 1.3 or greater.

Non-power-of-two textures are supported if the GL version is 2.0 or greater, or if the implementation exports the GL_ARB_texture_non_power_of_two extension.

The GL_COMPRESSED_SRGB, GL_COMPRESSED_SRGBA, GL_COMPRESSED_SRGB_ALPHA, GL_COMPRESSED_SLUMINANCE, and GL_COMPRESSED_SLUMINANCE_ALPHA internal formats are only available if the GL version is 2.1 or greater.

Errors

GL_INVALID_ENUM is generated if *internalformat* is not one of these generic compressed internal formats: GL_COMPRESSED_ALPHA, GL_COMPRESSED_LUMINANCE, GL_COMPRESSED_LUMINANCE_ALPHA, GL_COMPRESSED_INTENSITY, GL_COMPRESSED_RGB, GL_COMPRESSED_RGBA, GL_COMPRESSED_SLUMINANCE, GL_COMPRESSED_SLUMINANCE_ALPHA, GL_COMPRESSED_SRGB, GL_COMPRESSED_SRGBA, or GL_COMPRESSED_SRGB_ALPHA.

GL_INVALID_VALUE is generated if *imageSize* is not consistent with the format, dimensions, and contents of the specified compressed image data.

GL_INVALID_OPERATION is generated if parameter combinations are not supported by the specific compressed internal format as specified in the specific texture compression extension.

GL_INVALID_OPERATION is generated if a nonzero buffer object name is bound to the GL_PIXEL_UNPACK_BUFFER target and the buffer object's data store is currently mapped.

GL_INVALID_OPERATION is generated if a nonzero buffer object name is bound to the GL_PIXEL_UNPACK_BUFFER target and the data would be unpacked from the buffer object such that the memory reads required would exceed the data store size.

GL_INVALID_OPERATION is generated if glCompressedTexImage2D is executed between the execution of glBegin and the corresponding execution of glEnd.

Undefined results, including abnormal program termination, are generated if *data* is not encoded in a manner consistent with the extension specification defining the internal compression format.

Associated Gets

glGetCompressedTexImage

glGet with argument GL_TEXTURE_COMPRESSED

glGet with argument GL_PIXEL_UNPACK_BUFFER_BINDING

glGetTexLevelParameter with arguments GL_TEXTURE_INTERNAL_FORMAT and GL_TEXTURE_COMPRESSED_IMAGE_SIZE

glIsEnabled with argument GL_TEXTURE_2D

See Also

glActiveTexture, glColorTable, glCompressedTexImage1D, glCompressedTexImage3D, glCompressedTexSubImage1D, glCompressedTexSubImage2D, glCompressedTexSubImage3D, glConvolutionFilter1D, glCopyPixels, glCopyTexImage1D, glCopyTexSubImage1D, glCopyTexSubImage2D, glCopyTexSubImage3D, glDrawPixels, glMatrixMode, glPixelStore, glPixelTransfer, glTexEnv, glTexGen, glTexImage2D, glTexImage3D, glTexSubImage1D, glTexSubImage2D, glTexSubImage3D, glTexParameter

glCompressedTexImage3D

Specify a three-dimensional texture image in a compressed format

C Specification

```
void glCompressedTexImage3D(GLenum       target,
                            GLint        level,
                            GLenum       internalformat,
                            GLsizei      width,
                            GLsizei      height,
                            GLsizei      depth,
                            GLint        border,
                            GLsizei      imageSize,
                            const GLvoid * data);
```

Parameters

target	Specifies the target texture. Must be GL_TEXTURE_3D or GL_PROXY_TEXTURE_3D.
level	Specifies the level-of-detail number. Level 0 is the base image level. Level n is the nth mipmap reduction image.
internalformat	Specifies the format of the compressed image data stored at address data. Must be one of the following constants: GL_COMPRESSED_ALPHA, GL_COMPRESSED_LUMINANCE, GL_COMPRESSED_LUMINANCE_ALPHA, GL_COMPRESSED_INTENSITY, GL_COMPRESSED_RGB, GL_COMPRESSED_RGBA, GL_COMPRESSED_SRGB, GL_COMPRESSED_SRGBA, GL_COMPRESSED_SRGB_ALPHA, GL_COMPRESSED_SLUMINANCE, or GL_COMPRESSED_SLUMINANCE_ALPHA.
width	Specifies the width of the texture image including the border if any. If the GL version does not support non-power-of-two sizes, this value must be $2^n + 2$ (border) for some integer n. All implementations support texture images that are at least 64 texels wide.
height	Specifies the height of the texture image including the border if any. If the GL version does not support non-power-of-two sizes, this value must be $2^n + 2$ (border) for some integer n. All implementations support texture images that are at least 64 texels wide.
depth	Specifies the depth of the texture image including the border if any. If the GL version does not support non-power-of-two sizes, this value must be $2^n + 2$ (border) for some integer n. All implementations support texture images that are at least 64 texels wide.
border	Specifies the width of the border. Must be either 0 or 1.
imageSize	Specifies the number of unsigned bytes of image data starting at the address specified by data.
data	Specifies a pointer to the compressed image data in memory.

Description

Texturing maps a portion of a specified texture image onto each graphical primitive for which texturing is enabled. To enable and disable three-dimensional texturing, call glEnable and glDisable with argument GL_TEXTURE_3D.

glCompressedTexImage3D loads a previously defined, and retrieved, compressed three-dimensional texture image if target is GL_TEXTURE_3D (see glTexImage3D).

If target is GL_PROXY_TEXTURE_3D, no data is read from data, but all of the texture image state is recalculated, checked for consistency, and checked against the implementation's capabilities. If the implementation cannot handle a texture of the requested texture size, it sets all of the image state to

0, but does not generate an error (see glGetError). To query for an entire mipmap array, use an image array level greater than or equal to 1.

internalformat must be an extension-specified compressed-texture format. When a texture is loaded with glTexImage2D using a generic compressed texture format (e.g., GL_COMPRESSED_RGB), the GL selects from one of its extensions supporting compressed textures. In order to load the compressed texture image using glCompressedTexImage3D, query the compressed texture image's size and format using glGetTexLevelParameter.

If a nonzero named buffer object is bound to the GL_PIXEL_UNPACK_BUFFER target (see glBindBuffer) while a texture image is specified, *data* is treated as a byte offset into the buffer object's data store.

Notes

glCompressedTexImage3D is available only if the GL version is 1.3 or greater.

Non-power-of-two textures are supported if the GL version is 2.0 or greater, or if the implementation exports the GL_ARB_texture_non_power_of_two extension.

The GL_COMPRESSED_SRGB, GL_COMPRESSED_SRGBA, GL_COMPRESSED_SRGB_ALPHA, GL_COMPRESSED_SLUMINANCE, and GL_COMPRESSED_SLUMINANCE_ALPHA internal formats are only available if the GL version is 2.1 or greater.

Errors

GL_INVALID_ENUM is generated if *internalformat* is not one of these generic compressed internal formats: GL_COMPRESSED_ALPHA, GL_COMPRESSED_LUMINANCE, GL_COMPRESSED_LUMINANCE_ALPHA, GL_COMPRESSED_INTENSITY, GL_COMPRESSED_RGB, GL_COMPRESSED_RGBA, GL_COMPRESSED_SLUMINANCE, GL_COMPRESSED_SLUMINANCE_ALPHA, GL_COMPRESSED_SRGB, GL_COMPRESSED_SRGBA, or GL_COMPRESSED_SRGB_ALPHA.

GL_INVALID_VALUE is generated if *imageSize* is not consistent with the format, dimensions, and contents of the specified compressed image data.

GL_INVALID_OPERATION is generated if parameter combinations are not supported by the specific compressed internal format as specified in the specific texture compression extension.

GL_INVALID_OPERATION is generated if a nonzero buffer object name is bound to the GL_PIXEL_UNPACK_BUFFER target and the buffer object's data store is currently mapped.

GL_INVALID_OPERATION is generated if a nonzero buffer object name is bound to the GL_PIXEL_UNPACK_BUFFER target and the data would be unpacked from the buffer object such that the memory reads required would exceed the data store size.

GL_INVALID_OPERATION is generated if glCompressedTexImage3D is executed between the execution of glBegin and the corresponding execution of glEnd.

Undefined results, including abnormal program termination, are generated if *data* is not encoded in a manner consistent with the extension specification defining the internal compression format.

Associated Gets

glGetCompressedTexImage

glGet with argument GL_TEXTURE_COMPRESSED

glGet with argument GL_PIXEL_UNPACK_BUFFER_BINDING

glGetTexLevelParameter with arguments GL_TEXTURE_INTERNAL_FORMAT and GL_TEXTURE_COMPRESSED_IMAGE_SIZE

glIsEnabled with argument GL_TEXTURE_3D

See Also

glActiveTexture, glColorTable, glCompressedTexImage1D, glCompressedTexImage2D, glCompressedTexSubImage1D, glCompressedTexSubImage2D, glCompressedTexSubImage3D, glConvolutionFilter1D, glCopyPixels, glCopyTexImage1D, glCopyTexSubImage1D, glCopyTexSubImage2D, glCopyTexSubImage3D, glDrawPixels, glMatrixMode, glPixelStore, glPixelTransfer, glTexEnv, glTexGen, glTexImage1D, glTexImage2D, glTexSubImage1D, glTexSubImage2D, glTexSubImage3D, glTexParameter

glCompressedTexSubImage1D

Specify a one-dimensional texture subimage in a compressed format

C Specification

```
void glCompressedTexSubImage1D(GLenum          target,
                               GLint           level,
                               GLint           xoffset,
                               GLsizei         width,
                               GLenum          format,
                               GLsizei         imageSize,
                               const GLvoid *  data);
```

Parameters

target	Specifies the target texture. Must be GL_TEXTURE_1D.
level	Specifies the level-of-detail number. Level 0 is the base image level. Level *n* is the *n*th mipmap reduction image.
xoffset	Specifies a texel offset in the x direction within the texture array.
width	Specifies the width of the texture subimage.
format	Specifies the format of the compressed image data stored at address *data*.
imageSize	Specifies the number of unsigned bytes of image data starting at the address specified by *data*.
data	Specifies a pointer to the compressed image data in memory.

Description

Texturing maps a portion of a specified texture image onto each graphical primitive for which texturing is enabled. To enable and disable one-dimensional texturing, call glEnable and glDisable with argument GL_TEXTURE_1D.

glCompressedTexSubImage1D redefines a contiguous subregion of an existing one-dimensional texture image. The texels referenced by *data* replace the portion of the existing texture array with x indices *xoffset* and *xoffset* + *width* – 1, inclusive. This region may not include any texels outside the range of the texture array as it was originally specified. It is not an error to specify a subtexture with width of 0, but such a specification has no effect.

format must be an extension-specified compressed-texture format. The *format* of the compressed texture image is selected by the GL implementation that compressed it (see glTexImage1D), and should be queried at the time the texture was compressed with glGetTexLevelParameter.

If a nonzero named buffer object is bound to the GL_PIXEL_UNPACK_BUFFER target (see glBindBuffer) while a texture image is specified, *data* is treated as a byte offset into the buffer object's data store.

Notes

glCompressedTexSubImage1D is available only if the GL version is 1.3 or greater.

Errors

GL_INVALID_ENUM is generated if *format* is one of these generic compressed internal formats: GL_COMPRESSED_ALPHA, GL_COMPRESSED_LUMINANCE, GL_COMPRESSED_LUMINANCE_ALPHA, GL_COMPRESSED_INTENSITY, GL_COMPRESSED_RGB, GL_COMPRESSED_RGBA, GL_COMPRESSED_SLUMINANCE, GL_COMPRESSED_SLUMINANCE_ALPHA, GL_COMPRESSED_SRGB, GL_COMPRESSED_SRGBA, or GL_COMPRESSED_SRGB_ALPHA.

GL_INVALID_VALUE is generated if *imageSize* is not consistent with the format, dimensions, and contents of the specified compressed image data.

GL_INVALID_OPERATION is generated if parameter combinations are not supported by the specific compressed internal format as specified in the specific texture compression extension.

GL_INVALID_OPERATION is generated if a nonzero buffer object name is bound to the GL_PIXEL_UNPACK_BUFFER target and the buffer object's data store is currently mapped.

GL_INVALID_OPERATION is generated if a nonzero buffer object name is bound to the GL_PIXEL_UNPACK_BUFFER target and the data would be unpacked from the buffer object such that the memory reads required would exceed the data store size.

GL_INVALID_OPERATION is generated if glCompressedTexSubImage1D is executed between the execution of glBegin and the corresponding execution of glEnd.

Undefined results, including abnormal program termination, are generated if *data* is not encoded in a manner consistent with the extension specification defining the internal compression format.

Associated Gets

glGetCompressedTexImage

glGet with argument GL_TEXTURE_COMPRESSED

glGet with argument GL_PIXEL_UNPACK_BUFFER_BINDING

glGetTexLevelParameter with arguments GL_TEXTURE_INTERNAL_FORMAT and GL_TEXTURE_COMPRESSED_IMAGE_SIZE

glIsEnabled with argument GL_TEXTURE_1D

See Also

glActiveTexture, glColorTable, glCompressedTexImage1D, glCompressedTexImage2D, glCompressedTexImage3D, glCompressedTexSubImage2D, glCompressedTexSubImage3D, glConvolutionFilter1D, glCopyPixels, glCopyTexImage1D, glCopyTexImage2D, glCopyTexSubImage1D, glCopyTexSubImage2D, glCopyTexSubImage3D, glDrawPixels, glMatrixMode, glPixelStore, glPixelTransfer, glTexEnv, glTexGen, glTexImage2D, glTexImage3D, glTexSubImage1D, glTexSubImage2D, glTexSubImage3D, glTexParameter

glCompressedTexSubImage2D

Specify a two-dimensional texture subimage in a compressed format

C Specification

```
void glCompressedTexSubImage2D(GLenum        target,
                               GLint         level,
                               GLint         xoffset,
                               GLint         yoffset,
                               GLsizei       width,
                               GLsizei       height,
                               GLenum        format,
                               GLsizei       imageSize,
                               const GLvoid * data);
```

Parameters

target   Specifies the target texture. Must be GL_TEXTURE_2D, GL_TEXTURE_CUBE_MAP_
           POSITIVE_X, GL_TEXTURE_CUBE_MAP_NEGATIVE_X, GL_TEXTURE_CUBE_MAP_
           POSITIVE_Y, GL_TEXTURE_CUBE_MAP_NEGATIVE_Y, GL_TEXTURE_CUBE_MAP_
           POSITIVE_Z, GL_TEXTURE_CUBE_MAP_NEGATIVE_Z, or
           GL_PROXY_TEXTURE_CUBE_MAP.

level   Specifies the level-of-detail number. Level 0 is the base image level. Level *n* is the *n*th
           mipmap reduction image.

xoffset   Specifies a texel offset in the x direction within the texture array.

yoffset   Specifies a texel offset in the y direction within the texture array.

width   Specifies the width of the texture subimage.

height   Specifies the height of the texture subimage.

format   Specifies the format of the compressed image data stored at address *data*.

imageSize Specifies the number of unsigned bytes of image data starting at the address specified
           by *data*.

data   Specifies a pointer to the compressed image data in memory.

Description

Texturing maps a portion of a specified texture image onto each graphical primitive for which texturing is enabled. To enable and disable two-dimensional texturing, call glEnable and glDisable with argument GL_TEXTURE_2D. To enable and disable texturing using cube-mapped texture, call glEnable and glDisable with argument GL_TEXTURE_CUBE_MAP.

glCompressedTexSubImage2D redefines a contiguous subregion of an existing two-dimensional texture image. The texels referenced by *data* replace the portion of the existing texture array with x indices *xoffset* and *xoffset* + *width* – 1, and the y indices *yoffset* and *yoffset* + *height* – 1, inclusive. This region may not include any texels outside the range of the texture array as it was originally specified. It is not an error to specify a subtexture with width of 0, but such a specification has no effect.

format must be an extension-specified compressed-texture format. The *format* of the compressed texture image is selected by the GL implementation that compressed it (see glTexImage2D) and should be queried at the time the texture was compressed with glGetTexLevelParameter.

If a nonzero named buffer object is bound to the GL_PIXEL_UNPACK_BUFFER target (see glBindBuffer) while a texture image is specified, *data* is treated as a byte offset into the buffer object's data store.

Notes

glCompressedTexSubImage2D is available only if the GL version is 1.3 or greater.

GL_TEXTURE_CUBE_MAP_POSITIVE_X, GL_TEXTURE_CUBE_MAP_NEGATIVE_X, GL_TEXTURE_CUBE_MAP_POSITIVE_Y, GL_TEXTURE_CUBE_MAP_NEGATIVE_Y, GL_TEXTURE_CUBE_MAP_POSITIVE_Z, GL_TEXTURE_CUBE_MAP_NEGATIVE_Z, or GL_PROXY_TEXTURE_CUBE_MAP are available only if the GL version is 1.3 or greater.

Errors

GL_INVALID_ENUM is generated if *format* is one of these generic compressed internal formats: GL_COMPRESSED_ALPHA, GL_COMPRESSED_LUMINANCE, GL_COMPRESSED_LUMINANCE_ALPHA, GL_COMPRESSED_INTENSITY, GL_COMPRESSED_RGB, GL_COMPRESSED_RGBA, GL_COMPRESSED_SLUMINANCE, GL_COMPRESSED_SLUMINANCE_ALPHA, GL_COMPRESSED_SRGB, GL_COMPRESSED_SRGBA, or GL_COMPRESSED_SRGB_ALPHA.

GL_INVALID_VALUE is generated if *imageSize* is not consistent with the format, dimensions, and contents of the specified compressed image data.

GL_INVALID_OPERATION is generated if parameter combinations are not supported by the specific compressed internal format as specified in the specific texture compression extension.

GL_INVALID_OPERATION is generated if a nonzero buffer object name is bound to the GL_PIXEL_UNPACK_BUFFER target and the buffer object's data store is currently mapped.

GL_INVALID_OPERATION is generated if a nonzero buffer object name is bound to the GL_PIXEL_UNPACK_BUFFER target and the data would be unpacked from the buffer object such that the memory reads required would exceed the data store size.

GL_INVALID_OPERATION is generated if glCompressedTexSubImage2D is executed between the execution of glBegin and the corresponding execution of glEnd.

Undefined results, including abnormal program termination, are generated if *data* is not encoded in a manner consistent with the extension specification defining the internal compression format.

Associated Gets

glGetCompressedTexImage

glGet with argument GL_TEXTURE_COMPRESSED

glGet with argument GL_PIXEL_UNPACK_BUFFER_BINDING

glGetTexLevelParameter with arguments GL_TEXTURE_INTERNAL_FORMAT and GL_TEXTURE_COMPRESSED_IMAGE_SIZE

glIsEnabled with argument GL_TEXTURE_2D or GL_TEXTURE_CUBE_MAP

See Also

glActiveTexture, glColorTable, glCompressedTexImage1D, glCompressedTexImage2D, glCompressedTexImage3D, glCompressedTexSubImage1D, glCompressedTexSubImage3D, glConvolutionFilter1D, glCopyPixels, glCopyTexImage1D, glCopyTexImage2D, glCopyTexSubImage1D, glCopyTexSubImage2D, glCopyTexSubImage3D, glDrawPixels, glMatrixMode, glPixelStore, glPixelTransfer, glTexEnv, glTexGen, glTexImage2D, glTexImage3D, glTexSubImage1D, glTexSubImage2D, glTexSubImage3D, glTexParameter

glCompressedTexSubImage3D

Specify a three-dimensional texture subimage in a compressed format

C Specification

```
void glCompressedTexSubImage3D(GLenum         target,
                               GLint          level,
                               GLint          xoffset,
                               GLint          yoffset,
                               GLint          zoffset,
                               GLsizei        width,
                               GLsizei        height,
                               GLsizei        depth,
                               GLenum         format,
                               GLsizei        imageSize,
                               const GLvoid * data);
```

Parameters

target	Specifies the target texture. Must be GL_TEXTURE_3D.
level	Specifies the level-of-detail number. Level 0 is the base image level. Level n is the nth mipmap reduction image.
xoffset	Specifies a texel offset in the x direction within the texture array.
yoffset	Specifies a texel offset in the y direction within the texture array.
width	Specifies the width of the texture subimage.
height	Specifies the height of the texture subimage.
depth	Specifies the depth of the texture subimage.
format	Specifies the format of the compressed image data stored at address data.
imageSize	Specifies the number of unsigned bytes of image data starting at the address specified by data.
data	Specifies a pointer to the compressed image data in memory.

Description

Texturing maps a portion of a specified texture image onto each graphical primitive for which texturing is enabled. To enable and disable three-dimensional texturing, call glEnable and glDisable with argument GL_TEXTURE_3D.

glCompressedTexSubImage3D redefines a contiguous subregion of an existing three-dimensional texture image. The texels referenced by data replace the portion of the existing texture array with x indices xoffset and xoffset + width – 1, and the y indices yoffset and yoffset + height – 1, and the z indices zoffset and zoffset + depth – 1, inclusive. This region may not include any texels outside the range of the texture array as it was originally specified. It is not an error to specify a subtexture with width of 0, but such a specification has no effect.

format must be an extension-specified compressed-texture format. The format of the compressed texture image is selected by the GL implementation that compressed it (see glTexImage3D) and should be queried at the time the texture was compressed with glGetTexLevelParameter.

If a nonzero named buffer object is bound to the GL_PIXEL_UNPACK_BUFFER target (see glBindBuffer) while a texture image is specified, *data* is treated as a byte offset into the buffer object's data store.

Notes

glCompressedTexSubImage3D is available only if the GL version is 1.3 or greater.

Errors

GL_INVALID_ENUM is generated if *format* is one of these generic compressed internal formats: GL_COMPRESSED_ALPHA, GL_COMPRESSED_LUMINANCE, GL_COMPRESSED_LUMINANCE_ALPHA, GL_COMPRESSED_INTENSITY, GL_COMPRESSED_RGB, GL_COMPRESSED_RGBA, GL_COMPRESSED_SLUMINANCE, GL_COMPRESSED_SLUMINANCE_ALPHA, GL_COMPRESSED_SRGB, GL_COMPRESSED_SRGBA, or GL_COMPRESSED_SRGB_ALPHA.

GL_INVALID_VALUE is generated if *imageSize* is not consistent with the format, dimensions, and contents of the specified compressed image data.

GL_INVALID_OPERATION is generated if parameter combinations are not supported by the specific compressed internal format as specified in the specific texture compression extension.

GL_INVALID_OPERATION is generated if a nonzero buffer object name is bound to the GL_PIXEL_UNPACK_BUFFER target and the buffer object's data store is currently mapped.

GL_INVALID_OPERATION is generated if a nonzero buffer object name is bound to the GL_PIXEL_UNPACK_BUFFER target and the data would be unpacked from the buffer object such that the memory reads required would exceed the data store size.

GL_INVALID_OPERATION is generated if glCompressedTexSubImage3D is executed between the execution of glBegin and the corresponding execution of glEnd.

Undefined results, including abnormal program termination, are generated if *data* is not encoded in a manner consistent with the extension specification defining the internal compression format.

Associated Gets

glGetCompressedTexImage
glGet with argument GL_TEXTURE_COMPRESSED
glGet with argument GL_PIXEL_UNPACK_BUFFER_BINDING
glGetTexLevelParameter with arguments GL_TEXTURE_INTERNAL_FORMAT and GL_TEXTURE_COMPRESSED_IMAGE_SIZE
glIsEnabled with argument GL_TEXTURE_3D

See Also

glActiveTexture, glColorTable, glCompressedTexImage1D, glCompressedTexImage2D, glCompressedTexImage3D, glCompressedTexSubImage1D, glCompressedTexSubImage2D, glConvolutionFilter1D, glCopyPixels, glCopyTexImage1D, glCopyTexImage2D, glCopyTexSubImage1D, glCopyTexSubImage2D, glCopyTexSubImage3D, glDrawPixels, glMatrixMode, glPixelStore, glPixelTransfer, glTexEnv, glTexGen, glTexImage2D, glTexImage3D, glTexSubImage1D, glTexSubImage2D, glTexSubImage3D, glTexParameter

glConvolutionFilter1D

Define a one-dimensional convolution filter

C Specification

```
void glConvolutionFilter1D(GLenum          target,
                           GLenum          internalformat,
                           GLsizei         width,
                           GLenum          format,
                           GLenum          type,
                           const GLvoid *  data);
```

Parameters

target	Must be GL_CONVOLUTION_1D.
internalformat	The internal format of the convolution filter kernel. The allowable values are GL_ALPHA, GL_ALPHA4, GL_ALPHA8, GL_ALPHA12, GL_ALPHA16, GL_LUMINANCE, GL_LUMINANCE4, GL_LUMINANCE8, GL_LUMINANCE12, GL_LUMINANCE16, GL_LUMINANCE_ALPHA, GL_LUMINANCE4_ALPHA4, GL_LUMINANCE6_ALPHA2, GL_LUMINANCE8_ALPHA8, GL_LUMINANCE12_ALPHA4, GL_LUMINANCE12_ALPHA12, GL_LUMINANCE16_ALPHA16, GL_INTENSITY, GL_INTENSITY4, GL_INTENSITY8, GL_INTENSITY12, GL_INTENSITY16, GL_R3_G3_B2, GL_RGB, GL_RGB4, GL_RGB5, GL_RGB8, GL_RGB10, GL_RGB12, GL_RGB16, GL_RGBA, GL_RGBA2, GL_RGBA4, GL_RGB5_A1, GL_RGBA8, GL_RGB10_A2, GL_RGBA12, or GL_RGBA16.
width	The width of the pixel array referenced by *data*.
format	The format of the pixel data in *data*. The allowable values are GL_ALPHA, GL_LUMINANCE, GL_LUMINANCE_ALPHA, GL_INTENSITY, GL_RGB, and GL_RGBA.
type	The type of the pixel data in *data*. Symbolic constants GL_UNSIGNED_BYTE, GL_BYTE, GL_BITMAP, GL_UNSIGNED_SHORT, GL_SHORT, GL_UNSIGNED_INT, GL_INT, GL_FLOAT, GL_UNSIGNED_BYTE_3_3_2, GL_UNSIGNED_BYTE_2_3_3_REV, GL_UNSIGNED_SHORT_5_6_5, GL_UNSIGNED_SHORT_5_6_5_REV, GL_UNSIGNED_SHORT_4_4_4_4, GL_UNSIGNED_SHORT_4_4_4_4_REV, GL_UNSIGNED_SHORT_5_5_5_1, GL_UNSIGNED_SHORT_1_5_5_5_REV, GL_UNSIGNED_INT_8_8_8_8, GL_UNSIGNED_INT_8_8_8_8_REV, GL_UNSIGNED_INT_10_10_10_2, and GL_UNSIGNED_INT_2_10_10_10_REV are accepted.
data	Pointer to a one-dimensional array of pixel data that is processed to build the convolution filter kernel.

Description

glConvolutionFilter1D builds a one-dimensional convolution filter kernel from an array of pixels.

The pixel array specified by *width*, *format*, *type*, and *data* is extracted from memory and processed just as if glDrawPixels were called, but processing stops after the final expansion to RGBA is completed.

If a nonzero named buffer object is bound to the GL_PIXEL_UNPACK_BUFFER target (see glBindBuffer) while a convolution filter is specified, *data* is treated as a byte offset into the buffer object's data store.

The R, G, B, and A components of each pixel are next scaled by the four 1D GL_CONVOLUTION_FILTER_SCALE parameters and biased by the four 1D GL_CONVOLUTION_FILTER_BIAS parameters. (The scale and bias parameters are set by glConvolutionParameter using the GL_CONVOLUTION_1D target and the names GL_CONVOLUTION_FILTER_SCALE and GL_CONVOLUTION_FILTER_BIAS. The parameters themselves are vectors of four values that are applied to red, green, blue, and alpha, in that order.) The R, G, B, and A values are not clamped to [0,1] at any time during this process.

Each pixel is then converted to the internal format specified by *internalformat*. This conversion simply maps the component values of the pixel (R, G, B, and A) to the values included in the internal format (red, green, blue, alpha, luminance, and intensity). The mapping is as follows:

Internal Format	Red	Green	Blue	Alpha	Luminance	Intensity
GL_ALPHA		A				
GL_LUMINANCE					R	
GL_LUMINANCE_ALPHA				A	R	
GL_INTENSITY						R
GL_RGB	R	G	B			
GL_RGBA	R	G	B	A		

The red, green, blue, alpha, luminance, and/or intensity components of the resulting pixels are stored in floating-point rather than integer format. They form a one-dimensional filter kernel image indexed with coordinate *i* such that *i* starts at 0 and increases from left to right. Kernel location *i* is derived from the *i*th pixel, counting from 0.

Note that after a convolution is performed, the resulting color components are also scaled by their corresponding GL_POST_CONVOLUTION_*c*_SCALE parameters and biased by their corresponding GL_POST_CONVOLUTION_*c*_BIAS parameters (where *c* takes on the values RED, GREEN, BLUE, and ALPHA). These parameters are set by glPixelTransfer.

Notes

glConvolutionFilter1D is present only if ARB_imaging is returned when glGetString is called with an argument of GL_EXTENSIONS.

Errors

GL_INVALID_ENUM is generated if *target* is not GL_CONVOLUTION_1D.

GL_INVALID_ENUM is generated if *internalformat* is not one of the allowable values.

GL_INVALID_ENUM is generated if *format* is not one of the allowable values.

GL_INVALID_ENUM is generated if *type* is not one of the allowable values.

GL_INVALID_VALUE is generated if *width* is less than zero or greater than the maximum supported value. This value may be queried with glGetConvolutionParameter using target GL_CONVOLUTION_1D and name GL_MAX_CONVOLUTION_WIDTH.

GL_INVALID_OPERATION is generated if *format* is one of GL_UNSIGNED_BYTE_3_3_2, GL_UNSIGNED_BYTE_2_3_3_REV, GL_UNSIGNED_SHORT_5_6_5, or GL_UNSIGNED_SHORT_5_6_5_REV and *type* is not GL_RGB.

GL_INVALID_OPERATION is generated if *format* is one of GL_UNSIGNED_SHORT_4_4_4_4, GL_UNSIGNED_SHORT_4_4_4_4_REV, GL_UNSIGNED_SHORT_5_5_5_1, GL_UNSIGNED_SHORT_1_5_5_5_REV, GL_UNSIGNED_INT_8_8_8_8, GL_UNSIGNED_INT_8_8_8_8_REV, GL_UNSIGNED_INT_10_10_10_2, or GL_UNSIGNED_INT_2_10_10_10_REV and *type* is neither GL_RGBA nor GL_BGRA.

GL_INVALID_OPERATION is generated if a nonzero buffer object name is bound to the GL_PIXEL_UNPACK_BUFFER target and the buffer object's data store is currently mapped.

GL_INVALID_OPERATION is generated if a nonzero buffer object name is bound to the GL_PIXEL_UNPACK_BUFFER target and the data would be unpacked from the buffer object such that the memory reads required would exceed the data store size.

GL_INVALID_OPERATION is generated if a nonzero buffer object name is bound to the GL_PIXEL_UNPACK_BUFFER target and *data* is not evenly divisible into the number of bytes needed to store in memory a datum indicated by *type*.

GL_INVALID_OPERATION is generated if glConvolutionFilter1D is executed between the execution of glBegin and the corresponding execution of glEnd.

Associated Gets

glGetConvolutionParameter, glGetConvolutionFilter
glGet with argument GL_PIXEL_UNPACK_BUFFER_BINDING

See Also

glConvolutionFilter2D, glSeparableFilter2D, glConvolutionParameter, glPixelTransfer

glConvolutionFilter2D

Define a two-dimensional convolution filter

C Specification

```
void glConvolutionFilter2D(GLenum          target,
                           GLenum          internalformat,
                           GLsizei         width,
                           GLsizei         height,
                           GLenum          format,
                           GLenum          type,
                           const GLvoid *  data);
```

Parameters

target   Must be GL_CONVOLUTION_2D.

internalformat The internal format of the convolution filter kernel. The allowable values are GL_ALPHA, GL_ALPHA4, GL_ALPHA8, GL_ALPHA12, GL_ALPHA16, GL_LUMINANCE, GL_LUMINANCE4, GL_LUMINANCE8, GL_LUMINANCE12, GL_LUMINANCE16, GL_LUMINANCE_ALPHA, GL_LUMINANCE4_ALPHA4, GL_LUMINANCE6_ALPHA2, GL_LUMINANCE8_ALPHA8, GL_LUMINANCE12_ALPHA4, GL_LUMINANCE12_ALPHA12, GL_LUMINANCE16_ALPHA16, GL_INTENSITY, GL_INTENSITY4, GL_INTENSITY8, GL_INTENSITY12, GL_INTENSITY16, GL_R3_G3_B2, GL_RGB, GL_RGB4, GL_RGB5, GL_RGB8, GL_RGB10, GL_RGB12, GL_RGB16, GL_RGBA, GL_RGBA2, GL_RGBA4, GL_RGB5_A1, GL_RGBA8, GL_RGB10_A2, GL_RGBA12, or GL_RGBA16.

width   The width of the pixel array referenced by *data*.

height   The height of the pixel array referenced by *data*.

format   The format of the pixel data in *data*. The allowable values are GL_RED, GL_GREEN, GL_BLUE, GL_ALPHA, GL_RGB, GL_BGR, GL_RGBA, GL_BGRA, GL_LUMINANCE, and GL_LUMINANCE_ALPHA.

type   The type of the pixel data in *data*. Symbolic constants GL_UNSIGNED_BYTE, GL_BYTE, GL_BITMAP, GL_UNSIGNED_SHORT, GL_SHORT, GL_UNSIGNED_INT, GL_INT, GL_FLOAT, GL_UNSIGNED_BYTE_3_3_2, GL_UNSIGNED_BYTE_2_3_3_REV, GL_UNSIGNED_SHORT_5_6_5, GL_UNSIGNED_SHORT_5_6_5_REV, GL_UNSIGNED_SHORT_4_4_4_4, GL_UNSIGNED_SHORT_4_4_4_4_REV, GL_UNSIGNED_SHORT_5_5_5_1, GL_UNSIGNED_SHORT_1_5_5_5_REV, GL_UNSIGNED_INT_8_8_8_8, GL_UNSIGNED_INT_8_8_8_8_REV, GL_UNSIGNED_INT_10_10_10_2, and GL_UNSIGNED_INT_2_10_10_10_REV are accepted.

data   Pointer to a two-dimensional array of pixel data that is processed to build the convolution filter kernel.

Description

glConvolutionFilter2D builds a two-dimensional convolution filter kernel from an array of pixels.

The pixel array specified by *width*, *height*, *format*, *type*, and *data* is extracted from memory and processed just as if glDrawPixels were called, but processing stops after the final expansion to RGBA is completed.

If a nonzero named buffer object is bound to the GL_PIXEL_UNPACK_BUFFER target (see glBindBuffer) while a convolution filter is specified, *data* is treated as a byte offset into the buffer object's data store.

The R, G, B, and A components of each pixel are next scaled by the four 2D GL_CONVOLUTION_FILTER_SCALE parameters and biased by the four 2D GL_CONVOLUTION_FILTER_BIAS parameters. (The scale and bias parameters are set by glConvolutionParameter using the GL_CONVOLUTION_2D target and the names GL_CONVOLUTION_FILTER_SCALE and GL_CONVOLUTION_FILTER_BIAS. The parameters themselves are vectors of four values that are applied to red, green, blue, and alpha, in that order.) The R, G, B, and A values are not clamped to [0,1] at any time during this process.

Each pixel is then converted to the internal format specified by *internalformat*. This conversion simply maps the component values of the pixel (R, G, B, and A) to the values included in the internal format (red, green, blue, alpha, luminance, and intensity). The mapping is as follows:

Internal Format	Red	Green	Blue	Alpha	Luminance	Intensity
GL_ALPHA				A		
GL_LUMINANCE					R	
GL_LUMINANCE_ALPHA				A	R	
GL_INTENSITY						R
GL_RGB	R	G	B			
GL_RGBA	R	G	B	A		

The red, green, blue, alpha, luminance, and/or intensity components of the resulting pixels are stored in floating-point rather than integer format. They form a two-dimensional filter kernel image indexed with coordinates *i* and *j* such that *i* starts at zero and increases from left to right, and *j* starts at zero and increases from bottom to top. Kernel location *i,j* is derived from the Nth pixel, where N is $i + j*width$.

Note that after a convolution is performed, the resulting color components are also scaled by their corresponding GL_POST_CONVOLUTION_*c*_SCALE parameters and biased by their corresponding GL_POST_CONVOLUTION_*c*_BIAS parameters (where *c* takes on the values RED, GREEN, BLUE, and ALPHA). These parameters are set by glPixelTransfer.

Notes

glConvolutionFilter2D is present only if ARB_imaging is returned when glGetString is called with an argument of GL_EXTENSIONS.

Errors

GL_INVALID_ENUM is generated if *target* is not GL_CONVOLUTION_2D.

GL_INVALID_ENUM is generated if *internalformat* is not one of the allowable values.

GL_INVALID_ENUM is generated if *format* is not one of the allowable values.

GL_INVALID_ENUM is generated if *type* is not one of the allowable values.

GL_INVALID_VALUE is generated if *width* is less than zero or greater than the maximum supported value. This value may be queried with glGetConvolutionParameter using target GL_CONVOLUTION_2D and name GL_MAX_CONVOLUTION_WIDTH.

GL_INVALID_VALUE is generated if *height* is less than zero or greater than the maximum supported value. This value may be queried with glGetConvolutionParameter using target GL_CONVOLUTION_2D and name GL_MAX_CONVOLUTION_HEIGHT.

GL_INVALID_OPERATION is generated if *height* is one of GL_UNSIGNED_BYTE_3_3_2, GL_UNSIGNED_BYTE_2_3_3_REV, GL_UNSIGNED_SHORT_5_6_5, or GL_UNSIGNED_SHORT_5_6_5_REV and *format* is not GL_RGB.

GL_INVALID_OPERATION is generated if *height* is one of GL_UNSIGNED_SHORT_4_4_4_4, GL_UNSIGNED_SHORT_4_4_4_4_REV, GL_UNSIGNED_SHORT_5_5_5_1, GL_UNSIGNED_SHORT_1_5_5_5_REV, GL_UNSIGNED_INT_8_8_8_8, GL_UNSIGNED_INT_8_8_8_8_REV, GL_UNSIGNED_INT_10_10_10_2, or GL_UNSIGNED_INT_2_10_10_10_REV and *format* is neither GL_RGBA nor GL_BGRA.

GL_INVALID_OPERATION is generated if a nonzero buffer object name is bound to the GL_PIXEL_UNPACK_BUFFER target and the buffer object's data store is currently mapped.

GL_INVALID_OPERATION is generated if a nonzero buffer object name is bound to the GL_PIXEL_UNPACK_BUFFER target and the data would be unpacked from the buffer object such that the memory reads required would exceed the data store size.

GL_INVALID_OPERATION is generated if a nonzero buffer object name is bound to the GL_PIXEL_UNPACK_BUFFER target and *data* is not evenly divisible into the number of bytes needed to store in memory a datum indicated by *type*.

GL_INVALID_OPERATION is generated if glConvolutionFilter2D is executed between the execution of glBegin and the corresponding execution of glEnd.

Associated Gets
glGetConvolutionParameter, glGetConvolutionFilter

See Also
glConvolutionFilter1D, glSeparableFilter2D, glConvolutionParameter, glPixelTransfer

glConvolutionParameter

Set convolution parameters

C Specification
void **glConvolutionParameterf**(GLenum *target*,
                                 GLenum *pname*,
                                 GLfloat *params*);
void **glConvolutionParameteri**(GLenum *target*,
                                 GLenum *pname*,
                                 GLint *params*);

Parameters
target   The target for the convolution parameter. Must be one of GL_CONVOLUTION_1D, GL_CONVOLUTION_2D, or GL_SEPARABLE_2D.

pname   The parameter to be set. Must be GL_CONVOLUTION_BORDER_MODE.

params   The parameter value. Must be one of GL_REDUCE, GL_CONSTANT_BORDER, GL_REPLICATE_BORDER.

C Specification
void **glConvolutionParameterfv**(GLenum   *target*,
                                  GLenum   *pname*,
                                  const GLfloat * *params*);
void **glConvolutionParameteriv**(GLenum   *target*,
                                  GLenum   *pname*,
                                  const GLint *   *params*);

Parameters
target   The target for the convolution parameter. Must be one of GL_CONVOLUTION_1D, GL_CONVOLUTION_2D, or GL_SEPARABLE_2D.

pname   The parameter to be set. Must be one of GL_CONVOLUTION_BORDER_MODE, GL_CONVOLUTION_BORDER_COLOR, GL_CONVOLUTION_FILTER_SCALE, or GL_CONVOLUTION_FILTER_BIAS.

params   The parameter value. If *pnamev* is GL_CONVOLUTION_BORDER_MODE, *paramsv* must be one of GL_REDUCE, GL_CONSTANT_BORDER, or GL_REPLICATE_BORDER. Otherwise, must be a vector of four values (for red, green, blue, and alpha, respectively) to be used for scaling (when *pnamev* is GL_CONVOLUTION_FILTER_SCALE), or biasing (when *pnamev* is GL_CONVOLUTION_FILTER_BIAS) a convolution filter kernel or setting the constant border color (when *pnamev* is GL_CONVOLUTION_BORDER_COLOR.

Description

glConvolutionParameter sets the value of a convolution parameter.

target selects the convolution filter to be affected: GL_CONVOLUTION_1D, GL_CONVOLUTION_2D, or GL_SEPARABLE_2D for the 1D, 2D, or separable 2D filter, respectively.

pname selects the parameter to be changed. GL_CONVOLUTION_FILTER_SCALE and GL_CONVOLUTION_FILTER_BIAS affect the definition of the convolution filter kernel; see glConvolutionFilter1D, glConvolutionFilter2D, and glSeparableFilter2D for details. In these cases, *params*v is an array of four values to be applied to red, green, blue, and alpha values, respectively. The initial value for GL_CONVOLUTION_FILTER_SCALE is (1, 1, 1, 1), and the initial value for GL_CONVOLUTION_FILTER_BIAS is (0, 0, 0, 0).

A *pname* value of GL_CONVOLUTION_BORDER_MODE controls the convolution border mode. The accepted modes are:

GL_REDUCE

The image resulting from convolution is smaller than the source image. If the filter width is Wf and height is Hf, and the source image width is Ws and height is Hs, then the convolved image width will be $Ws - Wf + 1$ and height will be $Hs - Hf + 1$. (If this reduction would generate an image with zero or negative width and/or height, the output is simply null, with no error generated.) The coordinates of the image resulting from convolution are zero through $Ws - Wf$ in width and zero through $Hs - Hf$ in height.

GL_CONSTANT_BORDER

The image resulting from convolution is the same size as the source image, and processed as if the source image were surrounded by pixels with their color specified by the GL_CONVOLUTION_BORDER_COLOR.

GL_REPLICATE_BORDER

The image resulting from convolution is the same size as the source image, and processed as if the outermost pixel on the border of the source image were replicated.

Notes

glConvolutionParameter is present only if ARB_imaging is returned when glGetString is called with an argument of GL_EXTENSIONS.

In cases where errors can result from the specification of invalid image dimensions, it is the dimensions after convolution that are tested, not the dimensions of the source image. For example, glTexImage1D requires power-of-two image size. When GL_REDUCE border mode is in effect, the source image must be larger than the final power-of-two size by one less than the size of the 1D filter kernel.

Errors

GL_INVALID_ENUM is generated if *target* is not one of the allowable values.

GL_INVALID_ENUM is generated if *pname* is not one of the allowable values.

GL_INVALID_ENUM is generated if *pname* is GL_CONVOLUTION_BORDER_MODE and *params* is not one of GL_REDUCE, GL_CONSTANT_BORDER, or GL_REPLICATE_BORDER.

GL_INVALID_OPERATION is generated if glConvolutionParameter is executed between the execution of glBegin and the corresponding execution of glEnd.

Associated Gets

glGetConvolutionParameter

See Also

glConvolutionFilter1D, glConvolutionFilter2D, glSeparableFilter2D, glGetConvolutionParameter

glCopyColorSubTable

Respecify a portion of a color table

C Specification

void **glCopyColorSubTable**(GLenum *target*,
                            GLsizei *start*,
                            GLint   *x*,
                            GLint   *y*,
                            GLsizei *width*);

Parameters

target   Must be one of GL_COLOR_TABLE, GL_POST_CONVOLUTION_COLOR_TABLE, or
           GL_POST_COLOR_MATRIX_COLOR_TABLE.
start   The starting index of the portion of the color table to be replaced.
x, y   The window coordinates of the left corner of the row of pixels to be copied.
width   The number of table entries to replace.

Description

glCopyColorSubTable is used to respecify a contiguous portion of a color table previously
defined using glColorTable. The pixels copied from the framebuffer replace the portion of the existing table from indices *start* to *start* + *x* − 1, inclusive. This region may not include any entries
outside the range of the color table, as was originally specified. It is not an error to specify a subtexture with width of 0, but such a specification has no effect.

Notes

glCopyColorSubTable is present only if ARB_imaging is returned when glGetString is called
with an argument of GL_EXTENSIONS.

Errors

GL_INVALID_VALUE is generated if *target* is not a previously defined color table.
GL_INVALID_VALUE is generated if *target* is not one of the allowable values.
GL_INVALID_VALUE is generated if *start* + *x* > *width*.
GL_INVALID_OPERATION is generated if glCopyColorSubTable is executed between the execu-
tion of glBegin and the corresponding execution of glEnd.

Associated Gets

glGetColorTable, glGetColorTableParameter

See Also

glColorSubTable, glColorTableParameter, glCopyColorTable, glCopyColorSubTable,
glGetColorTable

glCopyColorTable

Copy pixels into a color table

C Specification

void **glCopyColorTable**(GLenum *target*,
                         GLenum *internalformat*,
                         GLint   *x*,
                         GLint   *y*,
                         GLsizei *width*);

Parameters

target   The color table target. Must be GL_COLOR_TABLE,
                GL_POST_CONVOLUTION_COLOR_TABLE, or
                GL_POST_COLOR_MATRIX_COLOR_TABLE.

internalformat	The internal storage format of the texture image. Must be one of the following symbolic constants: GL_ALPHA, GL_ALPHA4, GL_ALPHA8, GL_ALPHA12, GL_ALPHA16, GL_LUMINANCE, GL_LUMINANCE4, GL_LUMINANCE8, GL_LUMINANCE12, GL_LUMINANCE16, GL_LUMINANCE_ALPHA, GL_LUMINANCE4_ALPHA4, GL_LUMINANCE6_ALPHA2, GL_LUMINANCE8_ALPHA8, GL_LUMINANCE12_ALPHA4, GL_LUMINANCE12_ALPHA12, GL_LUMINANCE16_ALPHA16, GL_INTENSITY, GL_INTENSITY4, GL_INTENSITY8, GL_INTENSITY12, GL_INTENSITY16, GL_R3_G3_B2, GL_RGB, GL_RGB4, GL_RGB5, GL_RGB8, GL_RGB10, GL_RGB12, GL_RGB16, GL_RGBA, GL_RGBA2, GL_RGBA4, GL_RGB5_A1, GL_RGBA8, GL_RGB10_A2, GL_RGBA12, or GL_RGBA16.
x	The x coordinate of the lower-left corner of the pixel rectangle to be transferred to the color table.
y	The y coordinate of the lower-left corner of the pixel rectangle to be transferred to the color table.
width	The width of the pixel rectangle.

Description

glCopyColorTable loads a color table with pixels from the current GL_READ_BUFFER (rather than from main memory, as is the case for glColorTable).

The screen-aligned pixel rectangle with lower-left corner at (x,\ y) having width *width* and height 1 is loaded into the color table. If any pixels within this region are outside the window that is associated with the GL context, the values obtained for those pixels are undefined.

The pixels in the rectangle are processed just as if glReadPixels were called, with *internalformat* set to RGBA, but processing stops after the final conversion to RGBA.

The four scale parameters and the four bias parameters that are defined for the table are then used to scale and bias the R, G, B, and A components of each pixel. The scale and bias parameters are set by calling glColorTableParameter.

Next, the R, G, B, and A values are clamped to the range [0,1]. Each pixel is then converted to the internal format specified by *internalformat*. This conversion simply maps the component values of the pixel (R, G, B, and A) to the values included in the internal format (red, green, blue, alpha, luminance, and intensity). The mapping is as follows:

Internal Format	Red	Green	Blue	Alpha	Luminance	Intensity
GL_ALPHA				A		
GL_LUMINANCE					R	
GL_LUMINANCE_ALPHA				A	R	
GL_INTENSITY						R
GL_RGB	R	G	B			
GL_RGBA	R	G	B	A		

Finally, the red, green, blue, alpha, luminance, and/or intensity components of the resulting pixels are stored in the color table. They form a one-dimensional table with indices in the range [0,*width* − 1].

Notes

glCopyColorTable is available only if ARB_imaging is returned from calling glGetString with an argument of GL_EXTENSIONS.

Errors

GL_INVALID_ENUM is generated when *target* is not one of the allowable values.

GL_INVALID_VALUE is generated if *width* is less than zero.

GL_INVALID_VALUE is generated if *internalformat* is not one of the allowable values.

GL_TABLE_TOO_LARGE is generated if the requested color table is too large to be supported by the implementation.

GL_INVALID_OPERATION is generated if glCopyColorTable is executed between the execution of glBegin and the corresponding execution of glEnd.

Associated Gets

glGetColorTable, glGetColorTableParameter

See Also

glColorTable, glColorTableParameter, glReadPixels

glCopyConvolutionFilter1D

Copy pixels into a one-dimensional convolution filter

C Specification

```
void glCopyConvolutionFilter1D(GLenum  target,
                               GLenum  internalformat,
                               GLint   x,
                               GLint   y,
                               GLsizei width);
```

Parameters

target   Must be GL_CONVOLUTION_1D.

internalformat The internal format of the convolution filter kernel. The allowable values are
               GL_ALPHA, GL_ALPHA4, GL_ALPHA8, GL_ALPHA12, GL_ALPHA16,
               GL_LUMINANCE, GL_LUMINANCE4, GL_LUMINANCE8, GL_LUMINANCE12,
               GL_LUMINANCE16, GL_LUMINANCE_ALPHA, GL_LUMINANCE4_ALPHA4,
               GL_LUMINANCE6_ALPHA2, GL_LUMINANCE8_ALPHA8,
               GL_LUMINANCE12_ALPHA4, GL_LUMINANCE12_ALPHA12,
               GL_LUMINANCE16_ALPHA16, GL_INTENSITY, GL_INTENSITY4,
               GL_INTENSITY8, GL_INTENSITY12, GL_INTENSITY16, GL_R3_G3_B2, GL_RGB,
               GL_RGB4, GL_RGB5, GL_RGB8, GL_RGB10, GL_RGB12, GL_RGB16, GL_RGBA,
               GL_RGBA2, GL_RGBA4, GL_RGB5_A1, GL_RGBA8, GL_RGB10_A2, GL_RGBA12, or
               GL_RGBA16.

x, y   The window space coordinates of the lower-left coordinate of the pixel array to
               copy.

width   The width of the pixel array to copy.

Description

glCopyConvolutionFilter1D defines a one-dimensional convolution filter kernel with pixels from the current GL_READ_BUFFER (rather than from main memory, as is the case for glConvolutionFilter1D).

The screen-aligned pixel rectangle with lower-left corner at (x,\ y), width *width* and height 1 is used to define the convolution filter. If any pixels within this region are outside the window that is associated with the GL context, the values obtained for those pixels are undefined.

The pixels in the rectangle are processed exactly as if glReadPixels had been called with *format* set to RGBA, but the process stops just before final conversion. The R, G, B, and A components of each pixel are next scaled by the four 1D GL_CONVOLUTION_FILTER_SCALE parameters and biased by the four 1D GL_CONVOLUTION_FILTER_BIAS parameters. (The scale and bias parameters are set by glConvolutionParameter using the GL_CONVOLUTION_1D target and the names GL_CONVOLUTION_FILTER_SCALE and GL_CONVOLUTION_FILTER_BIAS. The parameters themselves are vectors of four values that are applied to red, green, blue, and alpha, in that order.) The R, G, B, and A values are not clamped to [0,1] at any time during this process.

Each pixel is then converted to the internal format specified by *internalformat*. This conversion simply maps the component values of the pixel (R, G, B, and A) to the values included in the internal format (red, green, blue, alpha, luminance, and intensity). The mapping is as follows:

Internal Format	Red	Green	Blue	Alpha	Luminance	Intensity
GL_ALPHA			A			
GL_LUMINANCE					R	
GL_LUMINANCE_ALPHA				A	R	
GL_INTENSITY						R
GL_RGB	R	G	B			
GL_RGBA	R	G	B	A		

The red, green, blue, alpha, luminance, and/or intensity components of the resulting pixels are stored in floating-point rather than integer format.

Pixel ordering is such that lower x screen coordinates correspond to lower *i* filter image coordinates.

Note that after a convolution is performed, the resulting color components are also scaled by their corresponding GL_POST_CONVOLUTION_*c*_SCALE parameters and biased by their corresponding GL_POST_CONVOLUTION_*c*_BIAS parameters (where *c* takes on the values RED, GREEN, BLUE, and ALPHA). These parameters are set by glPixelTransfer.

Notes

glCopyConvolutionFilter1D is present only if ARB_imaging is returned when glGetString is called with an argument of GL_EXTENSIONS.

Errors

GL_INVALID_ENUM is generated if *target* is not GL_CONVOLUTION_1D.

GL_INVALID_ENUM is generated if *internalformat* is not one of the allowable values.

GL_INVALID_VALUE is generated if *width* is less than zero or greater than the maximum supported value. This value may be queried with glGetConvolutionParameter using target GL_CONVOLUTION_1D and name GL_MAX_CONVOLUTION_WIDTH.

GL_INVALID_OPERATION is generated if glCopyConvolutionFilter1D is executed between the execution of glBegin and the corresponding execution of glEnd.

Associated Gets

glGetConvolutionParameter, glGetConvolutionFilter

See Also

glConvolutionFilter1D, glConvolutionParameter, glPixelTransfer

---

glCopyConvolutionFilter2D

Copy pixels into a two-dimensional convolution filter

C Specification

```
void glCopyConvolutionFilter2D(GLenum   target,
                               GLenum   internalformat,
                               GLint    x,
                               GLint    y,
                               GLsizei  width,
                               GLsizei  height);
```

Parameters

target	Must be GL_CONVOLUTION_2D.
internalformat	The internal format of the convolution filter kernel. The allowable values are GL_ALPHA, GL_ALPHA4, GL_ALPHA8, GL_ALPHA12, GL_ALPHA16, GL_LUMINANCE, GL_LUMINANCE4, GL_LUMINANCE8, GL_LUMINANCE12, GL_LUMINANCE16, GL_LUMINANCE_ALPHA, GL_LUMINANCE4_ALPHA4, GL_LUMINANCE6_ALPHA2, GL_LUMINANCE8_ALPHA8, GL_LUMINANCE12_ALPHA4, GL_LUMINANCE12_ALPHA12, GL_LUMINANCE16_ALPHA16, GL_INTENSITY, GL_INTENSITY4, GL_INTENSITY8, GL_INTENSITY12, GL_INTENSITY16, GL_R3_G3_B2, GL_RGB, GL_RGB4, GL_RGB5, GL_RGB8, GL_RGB10, GL_RGB12, GL_RGB16, GL_RGBA, GL_RGBA2, GL_RGBA4, GL_RGB5_A1, GL_RGBA8, GL_RGB10_A2, GL_RGBA12, or GL_RGBA16.
x, y	The window space coordinates of the lower-left coordinate of the pixel array to copy.
width	The width of the pixel array to copy.
height	The height of the pixel array to copy.

Description

glCopyConvolutionFilter2D defines a two-dimensional convolution filter kernel with pixels from the current GL_READ_BUFFER (rather than from main memory, as is the case for glConvolutionFilter2D).

The screen-aligned pixel rectangle with lower-left corner at (x,\ y), width *width* and height *height* is used to define the convolution filter. If any pixels within this region are outside the window that is associated with the GL context, the values obtained for those pixels are undefined.

The pixels in the rectangle are processed exactly as if glReadPixels had been called with *format* set to RGBA, but the process stops just before final conversion. The R, G, B, and A components of each pixel are next scaled by the four 2D GL_CONVOLUTION_FILTER_SCALE parameters and biased by the four 2D GL_CONVOLUTION_FILTER_BIAS parameters. (The scale and bias parameters are set by glConvolutionParameter using the GL_CONVOLUTION_2D target and the names GL_CONVOLUTION_FILTER_SCALE and GL_CONVOLUTION_FILTER_BIAS. The parameters themselves are vectors of four values that are applied to red, green, blue, and alpha, in that order.) The R, G, B, and A values are not clamped to [0,1] at any time during this process.

Each pixel is then converted to the internal format specified by *internalformat*. This conversion simply maps the component values of the pixel (R, G, B, and A) to the values included in the internal format (red, green, blue, alpha, luminance, and intensity). The mapping is as follows:

Internal Format	Red	Green	Blue	Alpha	Luminance	Intensity
GL_ALPHA				A		
GL_LUMINANCE					R	
GL_LUMINANCE_ALPHA				A	R	
GL_INTENSITY						R
GL_RGB	R	G	B			
GL_RGBA	R	G	B	A		

The red, green, blue, alpha, luminance, and/or intensity components of the resulting pixels are stored in floating-point rather than integer format.

Pixel ordering is such that lower x screen coordinates correspond to lower *i* filter image coordinates, and lower y screen coordinates correspond to lower *j* filter image coordinates.

Note that after a convolution is performed, the resulting color components are also scaled by their corresponding GL_POST_CONVOLUTION_*c*_SCALE parameters and biased by their corresponding GL_POST_CONVOLUTION_*c*_BIAS parameters (where *c* takes on the values RED, GREEN, BLUE, and ALPHA). These parameters are set by glPixelTransfer.

Notes

glCopyConvolutionFilter2D is present only if ARB_imaging is returned when glGetString is called with an argument of GL_EXTENSIONS.

Errors

GL_INVALID_ENUM is generated if *target* is not GL_CONVOLUTION_2D.

GL_INVALID_ENUM is generated if *internalformat* is not one of the allowable values.

GL_INVALID_VALUE is generated if *width* is less than zero or greater than the maximum supported value. This value may be queried with glGetConvolutionParameter using target GL_CONVOLUTION_2D and name GL_MAX_CONVOLUTION_WIDTH.

GL_INVALID_VALUE is generated if *height* is less than zero or greater than the maximum supported value. This value may be queried with glGetConvolutionParameter using target GL_CONVOLUTION_2D and name GL_MAX_CONVOLUTION_HEIGHT.

GL_INVALID_OPERATION is generated if glCopyConvolutionFilter2D is executed between the execution of glBegin and the corresponding execution of glEnd.

Associated Gets

glGetConvolutionParameter, glGetConvolutionFilter

See Also

glConvolutionFilter2D, glConvolutionParameter, glPixelTransfer

glCopyPixels

Copy pixels in the frame buffer

C Specification

```
void glCopyPixels(GLint    x,
                  GLint    y,
                  GLsizei  width,
                  GLsizei  height,
                  GLenum   type);
```

Parameters

x, y   Specify the window coordinates of the lower-left corner of the rectangular
                 region of pixels to be copied.

width, height Specify the dimensions of the rectangular region of pixels to be copied. Both
                 must be nonnegative.

type   Specifies whether color values, depth values, or stencil values are to be copied.
                 Symbolic constants GL_COLOR, GL_DEPTH, and GL_STENCIL are accepted.

Description

glCopyPixels copies a screen-aligned rectangle of pixels from the specified frame buffer location to a region relative to the current raster position. Its operation is well defined only if the entire pixel source region is within the exposed portion of the window. Results of copies from outside the window, or from regions of the window that are not exposed, are hardware dependent and undefined.

x and *y* specify the window coordinates of the lower-left corner of the rectangular region to be copied. *width* and *height* specify the dimensions of the rectangular region to be copied. Both *width* and *height* must not be negative.

Several parameters control the processing of the pixel data while it is being copied. These parameters are set with three commands: glPixelTransfer, glPixelMap, and glPixelZoom. This reference page describes the effects on glCopyPixels of most, but not all, of the parameters specified by these three commands.

glCopyPixels copies values from each pixel with the lower-left corner at $(x + i, y + j)$ for $0 <= i < width$ and $0 <= j < height$. This pixel is said to be the ith pixel in the jth row. Pixels are copied in row order from the lowest to the highest row, left to right in each row.

type specifies whether color, depth, or stencil data is to be copied. The details of the transfer for each data type are as follows:

GL_COLOR

Indices or RGBA colors are read from the buffer currently specified as the read source buffer (see glReadBuffer). If the GL is in color index mode, each index that is read from this buffer is converted to a fixed-point format with an unspecified number of bits to the right of the binary point. Each index is then shifted left by GL_INDEX_SHIFT bits, and added to GL_INDEX_OFFSET. If GL_INDEX_SHIFT is negative, the shift is to the right. In either case, zero bits fill otherwise unspecified bit locations in the result. If GL_MAP_COLOR is true, the index is replaced with the value that it references in lookup table GL_PIXEL_MAP_I_TO_I. Whether the lookup replacement of the index is done or not, the integer part of the index is then ANDed with $2^b - 1$, where b is the number of bits in a color index buffer.

If the GL is in RGBA mode, the red, green, blue, and alpha components of each pixel that is read are converted to an internal floating-point format with unspecified precision. The conversion maps the largest representable component value to 1.0, and component value 0 to 0.0. The resulting floating-point color values are then multiplied by GL_c_SCALE and added to GL_c_BIAS, where c is RED, GREEN, BLUE, and ALPHA for the respective color components. The results are clamped to the range [0,1]. If GL_MAP_COLOR is true, each color component is scaled by the size of lookup table GL_PIXEL_MAP_c_TO_c, then replaced by the value that it references in that table. c is R, G, B, or A.

If the ARB_imaging extension is supported, the color values may be additionally processed by color-table lookups, color-matrix transformations, and convolution filters.

The GL then converts the resulting indices or RGBA colors to fragments by attaching the current raster position z coordinate and texture coordinates to each pixel, then assigning window coordinates $(x_r + i, y_r + j)$, where (x_r, y_r) is the current raster position, and the pixel was the ith pixel in the jth row. These pixel fragments are then treated just like the fragments generated by rasterizing points, lines, or polygons. Texture mapping, fog, and all the fragment operations are applied before the fragments are written to the frame buffer.

GL_DEPTH

Depth values are read from the depth buffer and converted directly to an internal floating-point format with unspecified precision. The resulting floating-point depth value is then multiplied by GL_DEPTH_SCALE and added to GL_DEPTH_BIAS. The result is clamped to the range [0,1].

The GL then converts the resulting depth components to fragments by attaching the current raster position color or color index and texture coordinates to each pixel, then assigning window coordinates $(x_r + i, y_r + j)$, where (x_r, y_r) is the current raster position, and the pixel was the ith pixel in the jth row. These pixel fragments are then treated just like the fragments generated by rasterizing points, lines, or polygons. Texture mapping, fog, and all the fragment operations are applied before the fragments are written to the frame buffer.

GL_STENCIL

Stencil indices are read from the stencil buffer and converted to an internal fixed-point format with an unspecified number of bits to the right of the binary point. Each fixed-point index is then shifted left by GL_INDEX_SHIFT bits, and added to GL_INDEX_OFFSET. If GL_INDEX_SHIFT is negative, the shift is to the right. In either case, zero bits fill otherwise unspecified bit locations in the result. If GL_MAP_STENCIL is true, the index is replaced with the value that it references in lookup table GL_PIXEL_MAP_S_TO_S. Whether the lookup replacement of the index is done or not, the integer part of the index is then ANDed with $2^b - 1$, where b is the number of bits in the stencil buffer. The resulting stencil indices are then written to the stencil buffer such that the index read from the ith location of the jth row is written to location $(x_r + i, y_r + j)$, where (x_r, y_r) is the current raster position. Only the pixel ownership test, the scissor test, and the stencil writemask affect these write operations.

The rasterization described thus far assumes pixel zoom factors of 1.0. If glPixelZoom is used to change the x and y pixel zoom factors, pixels are converted to fragments as follows. If (x_r, y_r) is the current raster position, and a given pixel is in the ith location in the jth row of the source pixel rectangle, then fragments are generated for pixels whose centers are in the rectangle with corners at

$$(x_r + zoom_x \; i, y_r + zoom_y \; j)$$

and

$$(x_r + zoom_x \; (i + 1), y_r + zoom_y \; (j + 1))$$

where $zoom_x$ is the value of GL_ZOOM_X and $zoom_y$ is the value of GL_ZOOM_Y.

Examples

To copy the color pixel in the lower-left corner of the window to the current raster position, use glCopyPixels(0, 0, 1, 1, GL_COLOR);

Notes

Modes specified by glPixelStore have no effect on the operation of glCopyPixels.

Errors

GL_INVALID_ENUM is generated if *type* is not an accepted value.

GL_INVALID_VALUE is generated if either *width* or *height* is negative.

GL_INVALID_OPERATION is generated if *type* is GL_DEPTH and there is no depth buffer.

GL_INVALID_OPERATION is generated if *type* is GL_STENCIL and there is no stencil buffer.

GL_INVALID_OPERATION is generated if glCopyPixels is executed between the execution of glBegin and the corresponding execution of glEnd.

Associated Gets

glGet with argument GL_CURRENT_RASTER_POSITION

glGet with argument GL_CURRENT_RASTER_POSITION_VALID

See Also

glColorTable, glConvolutionFilter1D, glConvolutionFilter2D, glDepthFunc, glDrawBuffer, glDrawPixels, glMatrixMode, glPixelMap, glPixelTransfer, glPixelZoom, glRasterPos, glReadBuffer, glReadPixels, glSeparableFilter2D, glStencilFunc, glWindowPos

glCopyTexImage1D

Copy pixels into a 1D texture image

C Specification

```
void glCopyTexImage1D(GLenum   target,
                      GLint    level,
                      GLenum   internalformat,
                      GLint    x,
                      GLint    y,
                      GLsizei  width,
                      GLint    border);
```

Parameters

target   Specifies the target texture. Must be GL_TEXTURE_1D.

level   Specifies the level-of-detail number. Level 0 is the base image level. Level n is the nth mipmap reduction image.

internalformat   Specifies the internal format of the texture. Must be one of the following symbolic constants: GL_ALPHA, GL_ALPHA4, GL_ALPHA8, GL_ALPHA12, GL_ALPHA16, GL_COMPRESSED_ALPHA, GL_COMPRESSED_LUMINANCE, GL_COMPRESSED_LUMINANCE_ALPHA, GL_COMPRESSED_INTENSITY,

GL_COMPRESSED_RGB, GL_COMPRESSED_RGBA, GL_DEPTH_COMPONENT, GL_DEPTH_COMPONENT16, GL_DEPTH_COMPONENT24, GL_DEPTH_COMPONENT32, GL_LUMINANCE, GL_LUMINANCE4, GL_LUMINANCE8, GL_LUMINANCE12, GL_LUMINANCE16, GL_LUMINANCE_ALPHA, GL_LUMINANCE4_ALPHA4, GL_LUMINANCE6_ALPHA2, GL_LUMINANCE8_ALPHA8, GL_LUMINANCE12_ALPHA4, GL_LUMINANCE12_ALPHA12, GL_LUMINANCE16_ALPHA16, GL_INTENSITY, GL_INTENSITY4, GL_INTENSITY8, GL_INTENSITY12, GL_INTENSITY16, GL_RGB, GL_R3_G3_B2, GL_RGB4, GL_RGB5, GL_RGB8, GL_RGB10, GL_RGB12, GL_RGB16, GL_RGBA, GL_RGBA2, GL_RGBA4, GL_RGB5_A1, GL_RGBA8, GL_RGB10_A2, GL_RGBA12, GL_RGBA16, GL_SLUMINANCE, GL_SLUMINANCE8, GL_SLUMINANCE_ALPHA, GL_SLUMINANCE8_ALPHA8, GL_SRGB, GL_SRGB8, GL_SRGB_ALPHA, or GL_SRGB8_ALPHA8.

x, y   Specify the window coordinates of the left corner of the row of pixels to be copied.

width   Specifies the width of the texture image. Must be 0 or $2^n + 2$ (*border*) for some integer *n*. The height of the texture image is 1.

border Specifies the width of the border. Must be either 0 or 1.

Description

glCopyTexImage1D defines a one-dimensional texture image with pixels from the current GL_READ_BUFFER.

The screen-aligned pixel row with left corner at (*x,y*) and with a length of *width* + 2 (*border*) defines the texture array at the mipmap level specified by *level*. *internalformat* specifies the internal format of the texture array.

The pixels in the row are processed exactly as if glCopyPixels had been called, but the process stops just before final conversion. At this point all pixel component values are clamped to the range [0,1] and then converted to the texture's internal format for storage in the texel array.

Pixel ordering is such that lower *x* screen coordinates correspond to lower texture coordinates.

If any of the pixels within the specified row of the current GL_READ_BUFFER are outside the window associated with the current rendering context, then the values obtained for those pixels are undefined.

glCopyTexImage1D defines a one-dimensional texture image with pixels from the current GL_READ_BUFFER.

When *internalformat* is one of the sRGB types, the GL does not automatically convert the source pixels to the sRGB color space. In this case, the glPixelMap function can be used to accomplish the conversion.

Notes

glCopyTexImage1D is available only if the GL version is 1.1 or greater.

Texturing has no effect in color index mode.

1, 2, 3, and 4 are not accepted values for *internalformat*.

An image with 0 width indicates a NULL texture.

When the ARB_imaging extension is supported, the RGBA components copied from the framebuffer may be processed by the imaging pipeline. See glTexImage1D for specific details.

GL_DEPTH_COMPONENT, GL_DEPTH_COMPONENT16, GL_DEPTH_COMPONENT24, and GL_DEPTH_COMPONENT32 are available only if the GL version is 1.4 or greater.

Non-power-of-two textures are supported if the GL version is 2.0 or greater, or if the implementation exports the GL_ARB_texture_non_power_of_two extension.

The GL_SRGB, GL_SRGB8, GL_SRGB_ALPHA, GL_SRGB8_ALPHA8, GL_SLUMINANCE, GL_SLUMINANCE8, GL_SLUMINANCE_ALPHA, and GL_SLUMINANCE8_ALPHA8 internal formats are only available if the GL version is 2.1 or greater. See glTexImage1D for specific details about sRGB conversion.

Errors

GL_INVALID_ENUM is generated if *target* is not one of the allowable values.

GL_INVALID_VALUE is generated if *level* is less than 0.

GL_INVALID_VALUE may be generated if *level* is greater than $log_2\ max$, where *max* is the returned value of GL_MAX_TEXTURE_SIZE.

GL_INVALID_VALUE is generated if *internalformat* is not an allowable value.

GL_INVALID_VALUE is generated if *width* is less than 0 or greater than 2 + GL_MAX_TEXTURE_SIZE.

GL_INVALID_VALUE is generated if non-power-of-two textures are not supported and the *width* cannot be represented as $2^n + 2$ (*border*) for some integer value of *n*.

GL_INVALID_VALUE is generated if *border* is not 0 or 1.

GL_INVALID_OPERATION is generated if glCopyTexImage1D is executed between the execution of glBegin and the corresponding execution of glEnd.

GL_INVALID_OPERATION is generated if *internalformat* is GL_DEPTH_COMPONENT, GL_DEPTH_COMPONENT16, GL_DEPTH_COMPONENT24, or GL_DEPTH_COMPONENT32 and there is no depth buffer.

Associated Gets

glGetTexImage

glIsEnabled with argument GL_TEXTURE_1D

See Also

glCopyPixels, glCopyTexImage2D, glCopyTexSubImage1D, glCopyTexSubImage2D, glPixelStore, glPixelTransfer, glTexEnv, glTexGen, glTexImage1D, glTexImage2D, glTexSubImage1D, glTexSubImage2D, glTexParameter

glCopyTexImage2D

Copy pixels into a 2D texture image

C Specification

```
void glCopyTexImage2D(GLenum  target,
                      GLint   level,
                      GLenum  internalformat,
                      GLint   x,
                      GLint   y,
                      GLsizei width,
                      GLsizei height,
                      GLint   border);
```

Parameters

target   Specifies the target texture. Must be GL_TEXTURE_2D, GL_TEXTURE_CUBE_MAP_POSITIVE_X, GL_TEXTURE_CUBE_MAP_NEGATIVE_X, GL_TEXTURE_CUBE_MAP_POSITIVE_Y, GL_TEXTURE_CUBE_MAP_NEGATIVE_Y, GL_TEXTURE_CUBE_MAP_POSITIVE_Z, GL_TEXTURE_CUBE_MAP_NEGATIVE_Z, or GL_PROXY_TEXTURE_CUBE_MAP.

level   Specifies the level-of-detail number. Level 0 is the base image level. Level *n* is the *n*th mipmap reduction image.

internalformat Specifies the internal format of the texture. Must be one of the following symbolic constants: GL_ALPHA, GL_ALPHA4, GL_ALPHA8, GL_ALPHA12, GL_ALPHA16, GL_COMPRESSED_ALPHA, GL_COMPRESSED_LUMINANCE, GL_COMPRESSED_LUMINANCE_ALPHA, GL_COMPRESSED_INTENSITY, GL_COMPRESSED_RGB, GL_COMPRESSED_RGBA, GL_DEPTH_COMPONENT, GL_DEPTH_COMPONENT16, GL_DEPTH_COMPONENT24, GL_DEPTH_COMPONENT32,

GL_LUMINANCE, GL_LUMINANCE4, GL_LUMINANCE8, GL_LUMINANCE12, GL_LUMINANCE16, GL_LUMINANCE_ALPHA, GL_LUMINANCE4_ALPHA4, GL_LUMINANCE6_ALPHA2, GL_LUMINANCE8_ALPHA8, GL_LUMINANCE12_ALPHA4, GL_LUMINANCE12_ALPHA12, GL_LUMINANCE16_ALPHA16, GL_INTENSITY, GL_INTENSITY4, GL_INTENSITY8, GL_INTENSITY12, GL_INTENSITY16, GL_RGB, GL_R3_G3_B2, GL_RGB4, GL_RGB5, GL_RGB8, GL_RGB10, GL_RGB12, GL_RGB16, GL_RGBA, GL_RGBA2, GL_RGBA4, GL_RGB5_A1, GL_RGBA8, GL_RGB10_A2, GL_RGBA12, GL_RGBA16, GL_SLUMINANCE, GL_SLUMINANCE8, GL_SLUMINANCE_ALPHA, GL_SLUMINANCE8_ALPHA8, GL_SRGB, GL_SRGB8, GL_SRGB_ALPHA, or GL_SRGB8_ALPHA8.

x, y	Specify the window coordinates of the lower-left corner of the rectangular region of pixels to be copied.
width	Specifies the width of the texture image. Must be 0 or $2^n + 2$ (*border*) for some integer n.
height	Specifies the height of the texture image. Must be 0 or $2^m + 2$ (*border*) for some integer m.
border	Specifies the width of the border. Must be either 0 or 1.

Description

glCopyTexImage2D defines a two-dimensional texture image, or cube-map texture image with pixels from the current GL_READ_BUFFER.

The screen-aligned pixel rectangle with lower-left corner at (x, y) and with a width of *width* + 2 (*border*) and a height of *height* + 2 (*border*) defines the texture array at the mipmap level specified by *level*. *internalformat* specifies the internal format of the texture array.

The pixels in the rectangle are processed exactly as if glCopyPixels had been called, but the process stops just before final conversion. At this point all pixel component values are clamped to the range [0,1] and then converted to the texture's internal format for storage in the texel array.

Pixel ordering is such that lower *x* and *y* screen coordinates correspond to lower *s* and *t* texture coordinates.

If any of the pixels within the specified rectangle of the current GL_READ_BUFFER are outside the window associated with the current rendering context, then the values obtained for those pixels are undefined.

When *internalformat* is one of the sRGB types, the GL does not automatically convert the source pixels to the sRGB color space. In this case, the glPixelMap function can be used to accomplish the conversion.

Notes

glCopyTexImage2D is available only if the GL version is 1.1 or greater.

Texturing has no effect in color index mode.

1, 2, 3, and 4 are not accepted values for *internalformat*.

An image with height or width of 0 indicates a NULL texture.

When the ARB_imaging extension is supported, the RGBA components read from the framebuffer may be processed by the imaging pipeline. See glTexImage1D for specific details.

GL_TEXTURE_CUBE_MAP_POSITIVE_X, GL_TEXTURE_CUBE_MAP_NEGATIVE_X, GL_TEXTURE_CUBE_MAP_POSITIVE_Y, GL_TEXTURE_CUBE_MAP_NEGATIVE_Y, GL_TEXTURE_CUBE_MAP_POSITIVE_Z, GL_TEXTURE_CUBE_MAP_NEGATIVE_Z, or GL_PROXY_TEXTURE_CUBE_MAP are available only if the GL version is 1.3 or greater.

GL_DEPTH_COMPONENT, GL_DEPTH_COMPONENT16, GL_DEPTH_COMPONENT24, and GL_DEPTH_COMPONENT32 are available only if the GL version is 1.4 or greater.

The GL_SRGB, GL_SRGB8, GL_SRGB_ALPHA, GL_SRGB8_ALPHA8, GL_SLUMINANCE, GL_SLUMINANCE8, GL_SLUMINANCE_ALPHA, and GL_SLUMINANCE8_ALPHA8 internal formats are only available if the GL version is 2.1 or greater. See glTexImage2D for specific details about sRGB conversion.

Errors

GL_INVALID_ENUM is generated if *target* is not GL_TEXTURE_2D.

GL_INVALID_VALUE is generated if *level* is less than 0.

GL_INVALID_VALUE may be generated if *level* is greater than log_2 *max*, where *max* is the returned value of GL_MAX_TEXTURE_SIZE.

GL_INVALID_VALUE is generated if *width* is less than 0 or greater than 2 + GL_MAX_TEXTURE_SIZE.

GL_INVALID_VALUE is generated if non-power-of-two textures are not supported and the *width* or *depth* cannot be represented as $2^k + 2$ (*border*) for some integer *k*.

GL_INVALID_VALUE is generated if *border* is not 0 or 1.

GL_INVALID_VALUE is generated if *internalformat* is not an accepted format.

GL_INVALID_OPERATION is generated if glCopyTexImage2D is executed between the execution of glBegin and the corresponding execution of glEnd.

GL_INVALID_OPERATION is generated if *internalformat* is GL_DEPTH_COMPONENT, GL_DEPTH_COMPONENT16, GL_DEPTH_COMPONENT24, or GL_DEPTH_COMPONENT32 and there is no depth buffer.

Associated Gets

glGetTexImage

glIsEnabled with argument GL_TEXTURE_2D or GL_TEXTURE_CUBE_MAP

See Also

glCopyPixels, glCopyTexImage1D, glCopyTexSubImage1D, glCopyTexSubImage2D, glPixelStore, glPixelTransfer, glTexEnv, glTexGen, glTexImage1D, glTexImage2D, glTexSubImage1D, glTexSubImage2D, glTexParameter

glCopyTexSubImage1D

Copy a one-dimensional texture subimage

C Specification

```
void glCopyTexSubImage1D(GLenum  target,
                         GLint   level,
                         GLint   xoffset,
                         GLint   x,
                         GLint   y,
                         GLsizei width);
```

Parameters

target	Specifies the target texture. Must be GL_TEXTURE_1D.
level	Specifies the level-of-detail number. Level 0 is the base image level. Level *n* is the *n*th mipmap reduction image.
xoffset	Specifies the texel offset within the texture array.
x, y	Specify the window coordinates of the left corner of the row of pixels to be copied.
width	Specifies the width of the texture subimage.

Description

glCopyTexSubImage1D replaces a portion of a one-dimensional texture image with pixels from the current GL_READ_BUFFER (rather than from main memory, as is the case for glTexSubImage1D).

The screen-aligned pixel row with left corner at (x,\ y), and with length *width* replaces the portion of the texture array with x indices *xoffset* through *xoffset* + *width* – 1, inclusive. The destination in the texture array may not include any texels outside the texture array as it was originally specified.

The pixels in the row are processed exactly as if glCopyPixels had been called, but the process stops just before final conversion. At this point, all pixel component values are clamped to the range [0,1] and then converted to the texture's internal format for storage in the texel array.

It is not an error to specify a subtexture with zero width, but such a specification has no effect. If any of the pixels within the specified row of the current GL_READ_BUFFER are outside the read window associated with the current rendering context, then the values obtained for those pixels are undefined.

No change is made to the *internalformat*, *width*, or *border* parameters of the specified texture array or to texel values outside the specified subregion.

Notes

glCopyTexSubImage1D is available only if the GL version is 1.1 or greater.

Texturing has no effect in color index mode.

glPixelStore and glPixelTransfer modes affect texture images in exactly the way they affect glDrawPixels.

When the ARB_imaging extension is supported, the RGBA components copied from the frame-buffer may be processed by the imaging pipeline. See glTexImage1D for specific details.

Errors

GL_INVALID_ENUM is generated if /*target* is not GL_TEXTURE_1D.

GL_INVALID_OPERATION is generated if the texture array has not been defined by a previous glTexImage1D or glCopyTexImage1D operation.

GL_INVALID_VALUE is generated if *level* is less than 0.

GL_INVALID_VALUE may be generated if $level > log_2 (max)$, where *max* is the returned value of GL_MAX_TEXTURE_SIZE.

GL_INVALID_VALUE is generated if $xoffset < - b$, or $(xoffset + width) > (w - b)$, where *w* is the GL_TEXTURE_WIDTH and *b* is the GL_TEXTURE_BORDER of the texture image being modified. Note that *w* includes twice the border width.

Associated Gets

glGetTexImage

glIsEnabled with argument GL_TEXTURE_1D

See Also

glCopyPixels, glCopyTexImage1D, glCopyTexImage2D, glCopyTexSubImage2D, glCopyTexSubImage3D, glPixelStore, glPixelTransfer, glReadBuffer, glTexEnv, glTexGen, glTexImage1D, glTexImage2D, glTexImage3D, glTexParameter, glTexSubImage1D, glTexSubImage2D, glTexSubImage3D

glCopyTexSubImage2D

Copy a two-dimensional texture subimage

C Specification

```
void glCopyTexSubImage2D(GLenum  target,
                         GLint   level,
                         GLint   xoffset,
                         GLint   yoffset,
                         GLint   x,
                         GLint   y,
                         GLsizei width,
                         GLsizei height);
```

Parameters

/target   Specifies the target texture. Must be GL_TEXTURE_2D, GL_TEXTURE_CUBE_MAP_
                POSITIVE_X, GL_TEXTURE_CUBE_MAP_NEGATIVE_X, GL_TEXTURE_CUBE_MAP_
                POSITIVE_Y, GL_TEXTURE_CUBE_MAP_NEGATIVE_Y, GL_TEXTURE_CUBE_MAP_
                POSITIVE_Z, GL_TEXTURE_CUBE_MAP_NEGATIVE_Z, or
                GL_PROXY_TEXTURE_CUBE_MAP.

level   Specifies the level-of-detail number. Level 0 is the base image level. Level n is the nth
                mipmap reduction image.

xoffset   Specifies a texel offset in the x direction within the texture array.

yoffset   Specifies a texel offset in the y direction within the texture array.

x, y   Specify the window coordinates of the lower-left corner of the rectangular region of
                pixels to be copied.

width   Specifies the width of the texture subimage.

height   Specifies the height of the texture subimage.

Description

glCopyTexSubImage2D replaces a rectangular portion of a two-dimensional texture image or cube-map texture image with pixels from the current GL_READ_BUFFER (rather than from main memory, as is the case for glTexSubImage2D).

The screen-aligned pixel rectangle with lower-left corner at (*x,y*) and with width *width* and height *height* replaces the portion of the texture array with x indices *xoffset* through *xoffset* + *width* – 1, inclusive, and y indices *yoffset* through *yoffset* + *height* – 1, inclusive, at the mipmap level specified by *level*.

The pixels in the rectangle are processed exactly as if glCopyPixels had been called, but the process stops just before final conversion. At this point, all pixel component values are clamped to the range [0,1] and then converted to the texture's internal format for storage in the texel array.

The destination rectangle in the texture array may not include any texels outside the texture array as it was originally specified. It is not an error to specify a subtexture with zero width or height, but such a specification has no effect.

If any of the pixels within the specified rectangle of the current GL_READ_BUFFER are outside the read window associated with the current rendering context, then the values obtained for those pixels are undefined.

No change is made to the *internalformat*, *width*, *height*, or *border* parameters of the specified texture array or to texel values outside the specified subregion.

Notes

glCopyTexSubImage2D is available only if the GL version is 1.1 or greater.

GL_TEXTURE_CUBE_MAP_POSITIVE_X, GL_TEXTURE_CUBE_MAP_NEGATIVE_X, GL_TEXTURE_CUBE_MAP_POSITIVE_Y, GL_TEXTURE_CUBE_MAP_NEGATIVE_Y, GL_TEXTURE_CUBE_MAP_POSITIVE_Z, GL_TEXTURE_CUBE_MAP_NEGATIVE_Z, or GL_PROXY_TEXTURE_CUBE_MAP are available only if the GL version is 1.3 or greater.

Texturing has no effect in color index mode.

glPixelStore and glPixelTransfer modes affect texture images in exactly the way they affect glDrawPixels.

When the ARB_imaging extension is supported, the RGBA components read from the frame-buffer may be processed by the imaging pipeline. See glTexImage1D for specific details.

Errors

GL_INVALID_ENUM is generated if */target* is not GL_TEXTURE_2D.

GL_INVALID_OPERATION is generated if the texture array has not been defined by a previous glTexImage2D or glCopyTexImage2D operation.

GL_INVALID_VALUE is generated if *level* is less than 0.

GL_INVALID_VALUE may be generated if *level* > log_2 (*max*) , where *max* is the returned value of GL_MAX_TEXTURE_SIZE.

GL_INVALID_VALUE is generated if *xoffset* <–*b*, (*xoffset* + *width*) > (*w* – *b*) , *yoffset* <–*b*, or (*yoffset* + *height*) > (*h* – *b*) , where *w* is the GL_TEXTURE_WIDTH, *h* is the GL_TEXTURE_HEIGHT, and *b* is the GL_TEXTURE_BORDER of the texture image being modified. Note that *w* and *h* include twice the border width.

GL_INVALID_OPERATION is generated if glCopyTexSubImage2D is executed between the execution of glBegin and the corresponding execution of glEnd.

Associated Gets
glGetTexImage
glIsEnabled with argument GL_TEXTURE_2D

See Also
glCopyPixels, glCopyTexImage1D, glCopyTexImage2D, glCopyTexSubImage1D, glCopyTexSubImage3D, glPixelStore, glPixelTransfer, glReadBuffer, glTexEnv, glTexGen, glTexImage1D, glTexImage2D, glTexImage3D, glTexParameter, glTexSubImage1D, glTexSubImage2D, glTexSubImage3D

glCopyTexSubImage3D

Copy a three-dimensional texture subimage

C Specification
```
void glCopyTexSubImage3D(GLenum   target,
                         GLint    level,
                         GLint    xoffset,
                         GLint    yoffset,
                         GLint    zoffset,
                         GLint    x,
                         GLint    y,
                         GLsizei width,
                         GLsizei height);
```

Parameters
/target	Specifies the target texture. Must be GL_TEXTURE_3D
level	Specifies the level-of-detail number. Level 0 is the base image level. Level *n* is the *n*th mipmap reduction image.
xoffset	Specifies a texel offset in the x direction within the texture array.
yoffset	Specifies a texel offset in the y direction within the texture array.
zoffset	Specifies a texel offset in the z direction within the texture array.
x, y	Specify the window coordinates of the lower-left corner of the rectangular region of pixels to be copied.
width	Specifies the width of the texture subimage.
height	Specifies the height of the texture subimage.

Description
glCopyTexSubImage3D replaces a rectangular portion of a three-dimensional texture image with pixels from the current GL_READ_BUFFER (rather than from main memory, as is the case for glTexSubImage3D).

The screen-aligned pixel rectangle with lower-left corner at (*x*,\ *y*) and with width *width* and height *height* replaces the portion of the texture array with x indices *xoffset* through *xoffset* + *width* – 1, inclusive, and y indices *yoffset* through *yoffset* + *height* – 1, inclusive, at z index *zoffset* and at the mipmap level specified by *level*.

The pixels in the rectangle are processed exactly as if glCopyPixels had been called, but the process stops just before final conversion. At this point, all pixel component values are clamped to the range [0,1] and then converted to the texture's internal format for storage in the texel array.

The destination rectangle in the texture array may not include any texels outside the texture array as it was originally specified. It is not an error to specify a subtexture with zero width or height, but such a specification has no effect.

If any of the pixels within the specified rectangle of the current GL_READ_BUFFER are outside the read window associated with the current rendering context, then the values obtained for those pixels are undefined.

No change is made to the *internalformat*, *width*, *height*, *depth*, or *border* parameters of the specified texture array or to texel values outside the specified subregion.

Notes

glCopyTexSubImage3D is available only if the GL version is 1.2 or greater.

Texturing has no effect in color index mode.

glPixelStore and glPixelTransfer modes affect texture images in exactly the way they affect glDrawPixels.

When the ARB_imaging extension is supported, the RGBA components copied from the frame-buffer may be processed by the imaging pipeline, as if they were a two-dimensional texture. See glTexImage2D for specific details.

Errors

GL_INVALID_ENUM is generated if /*target* is not GL_TEXTURE_3D.

GL_INVALID_OPERATION is generated if the texture array has not been defined by a previous glTexImage3D operation.

GL_INVALID_VALUE is generated if *level* is less than 0.

GL_INVALID_VALUE may be generated if *level* $> log_2$ (*max*) , where *max* is the returned value of GL_MAX_3D_TEXTURE_SIZE.

GL_INVALID_VALUE is generated if *xoffset* $<- b$, (*xoffset* + *width*) $> (w - b)$, *yoffset* $<- b$, (*yoffset* + *height*) $> (h - b)$, *zoffset* $<-b$, or *zoffset* $> (d - b)$, where *w* is the GL_TEXTURE_WIDTH, *h* is the GL_TEXTURE_HEIGHT, *d* is the GL_TEXTURE_DEPTH, and *b* is the GL_TEXTURE_BORDER of the texture image being modified. Note that *w*, *h*, and *d* include twice the border width.

GL_INVALID_OPERATION is generated if glCopyTexSubImage3D is executed between the execution of glBegin and the corresponding execution of glEnd.

Associated Gets

glGetTexImage

glIsEnabled with argument GL_TEXTURE_3D

See Also

glCopyPixels, glCopyTexImage1D, glCopyTexImage2D, glCopyTexSubImage1D, glCopyTexSubImage2D, glPixelStore, glPixelTransfer, glReadBuffer, glTexEnv, glTexGen, glTexImage1D, glTexImage2D, glTexImage3D, glTexParameter, glTexSubImage1D, glTexSubImage2D, glTexSubImage3D

glCreateProgram

Create a program object

C Specification

GLuint **glCreateProgram**(*void*);

Description

glCreateProgram creates an empty program object and returns a nonzero value by which it can be referenced. A program object is an object to which shader objects can be attached. This provides a mechanism to specify the shader objects that will be linked to create a program. It also provides a means for checking the compatibility of the shaders that will be used to create a program (for instance, checking the compatibility between a vertex shader and a fragment shader). When no longer needed as part of a program object, shader objects can be detached.

One or more executables are created in a program object by successfully attaching shader objects to it with glAttachShader, successfully compiling the shader objects with glCompileShader, and successfully linking the program object with glLinkProgram. These executables are made part of current state when glUseProgram is called. Program objects can be deleted by calling glDeleteProgram. The memory associated with the program object will be deleted when it is no longer part of current rendering state for any context.

Notes

glCreateProgram is available only if the GL version is 2.0 or greater.

Like display lists and texture objects, the name space for program objects may be shared across a set of contexts, as long as the server sides of the contexts share the same address space. If the name space is shared across contexts, any attached objects and the data associated with those attached objects are shared as well.

Applications are responsible for providing the synchronization across API calls when objects are accessed from different execution threads.

Errors

This function returns 0 if an error occurs creating the program object.

GL_INVALID_OPERATION is generated if glCreateProgram is executed between the execution of glBegin and the corresponding execution of glEnd.

Associated Gets

glGet with the argument GL_CURRENT_PROGRAM

glGetActiveAttrib with a valid program object and the index of an active attribute variable

glGetActiveUniform with a valid program object and the index of an active uniform variable

glGetAttachedShaders with a valid program object

glGetAttribLocation with a valid program object and the name of an attribute variable

glGetProgram with a valid program object and the parameter to be queried

glGetProgramInfoLog with a valid program object

glGetUniform with a valid program object and the location of a uniform variable

glGetUniformLocation with a valid program object and the name of a uniform variable

glIsProgram

See Also

glAttachShader, glBindAttribLocation, glCreateShader, glDeleteProgram, glDetachShader, glLinkProgram, glUniform, glUseProgram, glValidateProgram

glCreateShader

Create a shader object

C Specification

GLuint **glCreateShader**(GLenum *shaderType*);

Parameters

shaderType   Specifies the type of shader to be created. Must be either GL_VERTEX_SHADER or GL_FRAGMENT_SHADER.

Description

glCreateShader creates an empty shader object and returns a nonzero value by which it can be referenced. A shader object is used to maintain the source code strings that define a shader.

shaderType indicates the type of shader to be created. Two types of shaders are supported. A shader of type GL_VERTEX_SHADER is a shader that is intended to run on the programmable vertex processor and replace the fixed functionality vertex processing in OpenGL. A shader of type GL_FRAGMENT_SHADER is a shader that is intended to run on the programmable fragment processor and replace the fixed functionality fragment processing in OpenGL.

When created, a shader object's GL_SHADER_TYPE parameter is set to either GL_VERTEX_SHADER or GL_FRAGMENT_SHADER, depending on the value of shaderType.

Notes

glCreateShader is available only if the GL version is 2.0 or greater.

Like display lists and texture objects, the name space for shader objects may be shared across a set of contexts, as long as the server sides of the contexts share the same address space. If the name space is shared across contexts, any attached objects and the data associated with those attached objects are shared as well.

Applications are responsible for providing the synchronization across API calls when objects are accessed from different execution threads.

Errors

This function returns 0 if an error occurs creating the shader object.

GL_INVALID_ENUM is generated if *shaderType* is not an accepted value.

GL_INVALID_OPERATION is generated if glCreateShader is executed between the execution of glBegin and the corresponding execution of glEnd.

Associated Gets

glGetShader with a valid shader object and the parameter to be queried

glGetShaderInfoLog with a valid shader object

glGetShaderSource with a valid shader object

glIsShader

See Also

glAttachShader, glCompileShader, glDeleteShader, glDetachShader, glShaderSource

glCullFace

Specify whether front- or back-facing facets can be culled

C Specification

void **glCullFace**(GLenum *mode*);

Parameters

mode   Specifies whether front- or back-facing facets are candidates for culling. Symbolic constants GL_FRONT, GL_BACK, and GL_FRONT_AND_BACK are accepted. The initial value is GL_BACK.

Description

glCullFace specifies whether front- or back-facing facets are culled (as specified by *mode*) when facet culling is enabled. Facet culling is initially disabled. To enable and disable facet culling, call the glEnable and glDisable commands with the argument GL_CULL_FACE. Facets include triangles, quadrilaterals, polygons, and rectangles.

glFrontFace specifies which of the clockwise and counterclockwise facets are front-facing and back-facing. See glFrontFace.

Notes

If *mode* is GL_FRONT_AND_BACK, no facets are drawn, but other primitives such as points and lines are drawn.

Errors

GL_INVALID_ENUM is generated if *mode* is not an accepted value.

GL_INVALID_OPERATION is generated if glCullFace is executed between the execution of glBegin and the corresponding execution of glEnd.

Associated Gets

glIsEnabled with argument GL_CULL_FACE

glGet with argument GL_CULL_FACE_MODE

See Also

glEnable, glFrontFace

glDeleteBuffers

Delete named buffer objects

C Specification

void **glDeleteBuffers**(GLsizei   n,
                        const GLuint * buffers);

Parameters

n   Specifies the number of buffer objects to be deleted.
buffers   Specifies an array of buffer objects to be deleted.

Description

glDeleteBuffers deletes n buffer objects named by the elements of the array buffers. After a buffer object is deleted, it has no contents, and its name is free for reuse (for example by glGenBuffers). If a buffer object that is currently bound is deleted, the binding reverts to 0 (the absence of any buffer object, which reverts to client memory usage).

glDeleteBuffers silently ignores 0's and names that do not correspond to existing buffer objects.

Notes

glDeleteBuffers is available only if the GL version is 1.5 or greater.

Errors

GL_INVALID_VALUE is generated if n is negative.

GL_INVALID_OPERATION is generated if glDeleteBuffers is executed between the execution of glBegin and the corresponding execution of glEnd.

Associated Gets

glIsBuffer

See Also

glBindBuffer, glGenBuffers, glGet

glDeleteLists

Delete a contiguous group of display lists

C Specification

void **glDeleteLists**(GLuint list,
                      GLsizei range);

Parameters

list   Specifies the integer name of the first display list to delete.
range   Specifies the number of display lists to delete.

Description

glDeleteLists causes a contiguous group of display lists to be deleted. list is the name of the first display list to be deleted, and range is the number of display lists to delete. All display lists d with $list <= d <= list + range - 1$ are deleted.

All storage locations allocated to the specified display lists are freed, and the names are available for reuse at a later time. Names within the range that do not have an associated display list are ignored. If range is 0, nothing happens.

Errors

GL_INVALID_VALUE is generated if range is negative.

GL_INVALID_OPERATION is generated if glDeleteLists is executed between the execution of glBegin and the corresponding execution of glEnd.

See Also

glCallList, glCallLists, glGenLists, glIsList, glNewList

glDeleteProgram

Delete a program object

C Specification

void **glDeleteProgram**(GLuint *program*);

Parameters

program   Specifies the program object to be deleted.

Description

glDeleteProgram frees the memory and invalidates the name associated with the program object specified by *program*. This command effectively undoes the effects of a call to glCreateProgram.

If a program object is in use as part of current rendering state, it will be flagged for deletion, but it will not be deleted until it is no longer part of current state for any rendering context. If a program object to be deleted has shader objects attached to it, those shader objects will be automatically detached but not deleted unless they have already been flagged for deletion by a previous call to glDeleteShader. A value of 0 for *program* will be silently ignored.

To determine whether a program object has been flagged for deletion, call glGetProgram with arguments *program* and GL_DELETE_STATUS.

Notes

glDeleteProgram is available only if the GL version is 2.0 or greater.

Errors

GL_INVALID_VALUE is generated if *program* is not a value generated by OpenGL.

GL_INVALID_OPERATION is generated if glDeleteProgram is executed between the execution of glBegin and the corresponding execution of glEnd.

Associated Gets

glGet with argument GL_CURRENT_PROGRAM

glGetProgram with arguments *program* and GL_DELETE_STATUS

glIsProgram

See Also

glCreateShader, glDetachShader, glUseProgram

glDeleteQueries

Delete named query objects

C Specification

void **glDeleteQueries**(GLsizei   *n*,
                    const GLuint * *ids*);

Parameters

n   Specifies the number of query objects to be deleted.
ids   Specifies an array of query objects to be deleted.

Description

glDeleteQueries deletes *n* query objects named by the elements of the array *ids*. After a query object is deleted, it has no contents, and its name is free for reuse (for example by glGenQueries).

glDeleteQueries silently ignores 0's and names that do not correspond to existing query objects.

Notes

glDeleteQueries is available only if the GL version is 1.5 or greater.

Errors

GL_INVALID_VALUE is generated if *n* is negative.

GL_INVALID_OPERATION is generated if glDeleteQueries is executed between the execution of glBeginQuery and the corresponding execution of glEndQuery.

GL_INVALID_OPERATION is generated if glDeleteQueries is executed between the execution of glBegin and the corresponding execution of glEnd.

Associated Gets

glIsQuery

See Also

glBeginQuery, glEndQuery, glGenQueries, glGetQueryiv, glGetQueryObject

glDeleteShader

Delete a shader object

C Specification

void **glDeleteShader**(GLuint *shader*);

Parameters

shader   Specifies the shader object to be deleted.

Description

glDeleteShader frees the memory and invalidates the name associated with the shader object specified by *shader*. This command effectively undoes the effects of a call to glCreateShader.

If a shader object to be deleted is attached to a program object, it will be flagged for deletion, but it will not be deleted until it is no longer attached to any program object, for any rendering context (i.e., it must be detached from wherever it was attached before it will be deleted). A value of 0 for *shader* will be silently ignored.

To determine whether an object has been flagged for deletion, call glGetShader with arguments shader and GL_DELETE_STATUS.

Notes

glDeleteShader is available only if the GL version is 2.0 or greater.

Errors

GL_INVALID_VALUE is generated if *shader* is not a value generated by OpenGL.

GL_INVALID_OPERATION is generated if glDeleteShader is executed between the execution of glBegin and the corresponding execution of glEnd.

Associated Gets

glGetAttachedShaders with the program object to be queried
glGetShader with arguments *shader* and GL_DELETE_STATUS
glIsShader

See Also

glCreateProgram, glCreateShader, glDetachShader, glUseProgram

glDeleteTextures

Delete named textures

C Specification

void **glDeleteTextures**(GLsizei   *n*,
                       const GLuint * *textures*);

Parameters

n   Specifies the number of textures to be deleted.
textures   Specifies an array of textures to be deleted.

Description

glDeleteTextures deletes *n* textures named by the elements of the array *textures*. After a texture is deleted, it has no contents or dimensionality, and its name is free for reuse (for example by glGenTextures). If a texture that is currently bound is deleted, the binding reverts to 0 (the default texture).

glDeleteTextures silently ignores 0's and names that do not correspond to existing textures.

Notes

glDeleteTextures is available only if the GL version is 1.1 or greater.

Errors

GL_INVALID_VALUE is generated if *n* is negative.

GL_INVALID_OPERATION is generated if glDeleteTextures is executed between the execution of glBegin and the corresponding execution of glEnd.

Associated Gets

glIsTexture

See Also

glAreTexturesResident, glBindTexture, glCopyTexImage1D, glCopyTexImage2D, glGenTextures, glGet, glGetTexParameter, glPrioritizeTextures, glTexImage1D, glTexImage2D, glTexParameter

glDepthFunc

Specify the value used for depth buffer comparisons

C Specification

```
void glDepthFunc(GLenum func);
```

Parameters

func   Specifies the depth comparison function. Symbolic constants GL_NEVER, GL_LESS, GL_EQUAL, GL_LEQUAL, GL_GREATER, GL_NOTEQUAL, GL_GEQUAL, and GL_ALWAYS are accepted. The initial value is GL_LESS.

Description

glDepthFunc specifies the function used to compare each incoming pixel depth value with the depth value present in the depth buffer. The comparison is performed only if depth testing is enabled. (See glEnable and glDisable of GL_DEPTH_TEST.)

func specifies the conditions under which the pixel will be drawn. The comparison functions are as follows:

GL_NEVER
Never passes.
GL_LESS
Passes if the incoming depth value is less than the stored depth value.
GL_EQUAL
Passes if the incoming depth value is equal to the stored depth value.
GL_LEQUAL
Passes if the incoming depth value is less than or equal to the stored depth value.
GL_GREATER
Passes if the incoming depth value is greater than the stored depth value.
GL_NOTEQUAL
Passes if the incoming depth value is not equal to the stored depth value.

GL_GEQUAL
Passes if the incoming depth value is greater than or equal to the stored depth value.
GL_ALWAYS
Always passes.
The initial value of func is GL_LESS. Initially, depth testing is disabled.

Notes

Even if the depth buffer exists and the depth mask is nonzero, the depth buffer is not updated if the depth test is disabled.

Errors

GL_INVALID_ENUM is generated if *func* is not an accepted value.

GL_INVALID_OPERATION is generated if glDepthFunc is executed between the execution of glBegin and the corresponding execution of glEnd.

Associated Gets

glGet with argument GL_DEPTH_FUNC
glIsEnabled with argument GL_DEPTH_TEST

See Also

glDepthRange, glEnable, glPolygonOffset

glDepthMask

Enable or disable writing into the depth buffer

C Specification

void **glDepthMask**(GLboolean *flag*);

Parameters

flag   Specifies whether the depth buffer is enabled for writing. If *flag* is GL_FALSE, depth buffer writing is disabled. Otherwise, it is enabled. Initially, depth buffer writing is enabled.

Description

glDepthMask specifies whether the depth buffer is enabled for writing. If *flag* is GL_FALSE, depth buffer writing is disabled. Otherwise, it is enabled. Initially, depth buffer writing is enabled.

Errors

GL_INVALID_OPERATION is generated if glDepthMask is executed between the execution of glBegin and the corresponding execution of glEnd.

Associated Gets

glGet with argument GL_DEPTH_WRITEMASK

See Also

glColorMask, glDepthFunc, glDepthRange, glIndexMask, glStencilMask

glDepthRange

Specify mapping of depth values from normalized device coordinates to window coordinates

C Specification

void **glDepthRange**(GLclampd *nearVal*,
                    GLclampd *farVal*);

Parameters

nearVal   Specifies the mapping of the near clipping plane to window coordinates. The initial value is 0.

farVal   Specifies the mapping of the far clipping plane to window coordinates. The initial value is 1.

Description

After clipping and division by *w*, depth coordinates range from -1 to 1, corresponding to the near and far clipping planes. glDepthRange specifies a linear mapping of the normalized depth coordinates in this range to window depth coordinates. Regardless of the actual depth buffer implementation, window coordinate depth values are treated as though they range from 0 through 1 (like color components). Thus, the values accepted by glDepthRange are both clamped to this range before they are accepted.

The setting of (0,1) maps the near plane to 0 and the far plane to 1. With this mapping, the depth buffer range is fully utilized.

Notes

It is not necessary that *nearVal* be less than *farVal*. Reverse mappings such as *nearVal* = 1, and *farVal* = 0 are acceptable.

Errors

GL_INVALID_OPERATION is generated if glDepthRange is executed between the execution of glBegin and the corresponding execution of glEnd.

Associated Gets

glGet with argument GL_DEPTH_RANGE

See Also

glDepthFunc, glPolygonOffset, glViewport

---

glDetachShader

Detach a shader object from a program object to which it is attached

C Specification

void **glDetachShader**(GLuint *program*,
                     GLuint *shader*);

Parameters

program   Specifies the program object from which to detach the shader object.
shader   Specifies the shader object to be detached.

Description

glDetachShader detaches the shader object specified by *shader* from the program object specified by *program*. This command can be used to undo the effect of the command glAttachShader.

If *shader* has already been flagged for deletion by a call to glDeleteShader and it is not attached to any other program object, it will be deleted after it has been detached.

Notes

glDetachShader is available only if the GL version is 2.0 or greater.

Errors

GL_INVALID_VALUE is generated if either *program* or *shader* is a value that was not generated by OpenGL.

GL_INVALID_OPERATION is generated if *program* is not a program object.

GL_INVALID_OPERATION is generated if *shader* is not a shader object.

GL_INVALID_OPERATION is generated if *shader* is not attached to *program*.

GL_INVALID_OPERATION is generated if glDetachShader is executed between the execution of glBegin and the corresponding execution of glEnd.

Associated Gets

glGetAttachedShaders with the handle of a valid program object
glGetShader with arguments *shader* and GL_DELETE_STATUS

```
glIsProgram
glIsShader
```

See Also

glAttachShader

glDrawArrays

Render primitives from array data

C Specification

```
void glDrawArrays(GLenum   mode,
                  GLint    first,
                  GLsizei  count);
```

Parameters

mode   Specifies what kind of primitives to render. Symbolic constants GL_POINTS,
            GL_LINE_STRIP, GL_LINE_LOOP, GL_LINES, GL_TRIANGLE_STRIP,
            GL_TRIANGLE_FAN, GL_TRIANGLES, GL_QUAD_STRIP, GL_QUADS, and GL_POLYGON are
            accepted.

first   Specifies the starting index in the enabled arrays.

count   Specifies the number of indices to be rendered.

Description

glDrawArrays specifies multiple geometric primitives with very few subroutine calls. Instead of
calling a GL procedure to pass each individual vertex, normal, texture coordinate, edge flag, or color,
you can prespecify separate arrays of vertices, normals, and colors and use them to construct a
sequence of primitives with a single call to glDrawArrays.

When glDrawArrays is called, it uses *count* sequential elements from each enabled array to
construct a sequence of geometric primitives, beginning with element *first*. *mode* specifies what
kind of primitives are constructed and how the array elements construct those primitives. If
GL_VERTEX_ARRAY is not enabled, no geometric primitives are generated.

Vertex attributes that are modified by glDrawArrays have an unspecified value after
glDrawArrays returns. For example, if GL_COLOR_ARRAY is enabled, the value of the current color is
undefined after glDrawArrays executes. Attributes that aren't modified remain well defined.

Notes

glDrawArrays is available only if the GL version is 1.1 or greater.

glDrawArrays is included in display lists. If glDrawArrays is entered into a display list, the
necessary array data (determined by the array pointers and enables) is also entered into the display
list. Because the array pointers and enables are client-side state, their values affect display lists when
the lists are created, not when the lists are executed.

Errors

GL_INVALID_ENUM is generated if *mode* is not an accepted value.

GL_INVALID_VALUE is generated if *count* is negative.

GL_INVALID_OPERATION is generated if a nonzero buffer object name is bound to an enabled
array and the buffer object's data store is currently mapped.

GL_INVALID_OPERATION is generated if glDrawArrays is executed between the execution of
glBegin and the corresponding glEnd.

See Also

glArrayElement, glColorPointer, glDrawElements, glDrawRangeElements,
glEdgeFlagPointer, glFogCoordPointer, glGetPointerv, glIndexPointer,
glInterleavedArrays, glNormalPointer, glSecondaryColorPointer, glTexCoordPointer,
glVertexPointer

glDrawBuffer

Specify which color buffers are to be drawn into

C Specification

```
void glDrawBuffer(GLenum mode);
```

Parameters

mode   Specifies up to four color buffers to be drawn into. Symbolic constants GL_NONE, GL_FRONT_LEFT, GL_FRONT_RIGHT, GL_BACK_LEFT, GL_BACK_RIGHT, GL_FRONT, GL_BACK, GL_LEFT, GL_RIGHT, GL_FRONT_AND_BACK, and GL_AUX*i*, where *i* is between 0 and the value of GL_AUX_BUFFERS minus 1, are accepted. (GL_AUX_BUFFERS is not the upper limit; use glGet to query the number of available aux buffers.) The initial value is GL_FRONT for single-buffered contexts, and GL_BACK for double-buffered contexts.

Description

When colors are written to the frame buffer, they are written into the color buffers specified by glDrawBuffer. The specifications are as follows:

GL_NONE
No color buffers are written.

GL_FRONT_LEFT
Only the front left color buffer is written.

GL_FRONT_RIGHT
Only the front right color buffer is written.

GL_BACK_LEFT
Only the back left color buffer is written.

GL_BACK_RIGHT
Only the back right color buffer is written.

GL_FRONT
Only the front left and front right color buffers are written. If there is no front right color buffer, only the front left color buffer is written.

GL_BACK
Only the back left and back right color buffers are written. If there is no back right color buffer, only the back left color buffer is written.

GL_LEFT
Only the front left and back left color buffers are written. If there is no back left color buffer, only the front left color buffer is written.

GL_RIGHT
Only the front right and back right color buffers are written. If there is no back right color buffer, only the front right color buffer is written.

GL_FRONT_AND_BACK
All the front and back color buffers (front left, front right, back left, back right) are written. If there are no back color buffers, only the front left and front right color buffers are written. If there are no right color buffers, only the front left and back left color buffers are written. If there are no right or back color buffers, only the front left color buffer is written.

GL_AUX*i*
Only auxiliary color buffer *i* is written.

If more than one color buffer is selected for drawing, then blending or logical operations are computed and applied independently for each color buffer and can produce different results in each buffer.

Monoscopic contexts include only *left* buffers, and stereoscopic contexts include both *left* and *right* buffers. Likewise, single-buffered contexts include only *front* buffers, and double-buffered contexts include both *front* and *back* buffers. The context is selected at GL initialization.

Notes

It is always the case that GL_AUX*i* = GL_AUX0 + *i*.

Errors

GL_INVALID_ENUM is generated if *mode* is not an accepted value.

GL_INVALID_OPERATION is generated if none of the buffers indicated by *mode* exists.

GL_INVALID_OPERATION is generated if glDrawBuffer is executed between the execution of glBegin and the corresponding execution of glEnd.

Associated Gets

glGet with argument GL_DRAW_BUFFER

glGet with argument GL_AUX_BUFFERS

See Also

glBlendFunc, glColorMask, glIndexMask, glLogicOp, glReadBuffer

glDrawBuffers

Specify a list of color buffers to be drawn into

C Specification

void **glDrawBuffers**(GLsizei   n,
                        const GLenum * bufs);

Parameters

n   Specifies the number of buffers in *bufs*.

bufs   Points to an array of symbolic constants specifying the buffers into which fragment colors or data values will be written.

Description

glDrawBuffers defines an array of buffers into which fragment color values or fragment data will be written. If no fragment shader is active, rendering operations will generate only one fragment color per fragment and it will be written into each of the buffers specified by *bufs*. If a fragment shader is active and it writes a value to the output variable gl_FragColor, then that value will be written into each of the buffers specified by *bufs*. If a fragment shader is active and it writes a value to one or more elements of the output array variable gl_FragData[], then the value of gl_FragData[0] will be written into the first buffer specified by *bufs*, the value of gl_FragData[1] will be written into the second buffer specified by *bufs*, and so on up to gl_FragData[n-1]. The draw buffer used for gl_FragData[n] and beyond is implicitly set to be GL_NONE.

The symbolic constants contained in *bufs* may be any of the following:

GL_NONE

The fragment color/data value is not written into any color buffer.

GL_FRONT_LEFT

The fragment color/data value is written into the front left color buffer.

GL_FRONT_RIGHT

The fragment color/data value is written into the front right color buffer.

GL_BACK_LEFT

The fragment color/data value is written into the back left color buffer.

GL_BACK_RIGHT

The fragment color/data value is written into the back right color buffer.

GL_AUX*i*

The fragment color/data value is written into auxiliary buffer *i*.

Except for GL_NONE, the preceding symbolic constants may not appear more than once in *bufs*. The maximum number of draw buffers supported is implementation dependent and can be queried by calling glGet with the argument GL_MAX_DRAW_BUFFERS. The number of auxiliary buffers can be queried by calling glGet with the argument GL_AUX_BUFFERS.

Notes

glDrawBuffers is available only if the GL version is 2.0 or greater.

It is always the case that GL_AUXi = GL_AUX0 + i.

The symbolic constants GL_FRONT, GL_BACK, GL_LEFT, GL_RIGHT, and GL_FRONT_AND_BACK are not allowed in the *bufs* array since they may refer to multiple buffers.

If a fragment shader writes to neither gl_FragColor nor gl_FragData, the values of the fragment colors following shader execution are undefined. For each fragment generated in this situation, a different value may be written into each of the buffers specified by *bufs*.

Errors

GL_INVALID_ENUM is generated if one of the values in *bufs* is not an accepted value.

GL_INVALID_ENUM is generated if *n* is less than 0.

GL_INVALID_OPERATION is generated if a symbolic constant other than GL_NONE appears more than once in *bufs*.

GL_INVALID_OPERATION is generated if any of the entries in *bufs* (other than GL_NONE) indicates a color buffer that does not exist in the current GL context.

GL_INVALID_VALUE is generated if *n* is greater than GL_MAX_DRAW_BUFFERS.

GL_INVALID_OPERATION is generated if glDrawBuffers is executed between the execution of glBegin and the corresponding execution of glEnd.

Associated Gets

glGet with argument GL_MAX_DRAW_BUFFERS

glGet with argument GL_DRAW_BUFFERS*i* where *i* indicates the number of the draw buffer whose value is to be queried

See Also

glBlendFunc, glColorMask, glDrawBuffers, glIndexMask, glLogicOp, glReadBuffer

glDrawElements

Render primitives from array data

C Specification

```
void glDrawElements(GLenum          mode,
                    GLsizei         count,
                    GLenum          type,
                    const GLvoid *  indices);
```

Parameters

mode   Specifies what kind of primitives to render. Symbolic constants GL_POINTS,
            GL_LINE_STRIP, GL_LINE_LOOP, GL_LINES, GL_TRIANGLE_STRIP,
            GL_TRIANGLE_FAN, GL_TRIANGLES, GL_QUAD_STRIP, GL_QUADS, and
            GL_POLYGON are accepted.

count   Specifies the number of elements to be rendered.

type   Specifies the type of the values in *indices*. Must be one of GL_UNSIGNED_BYTE,
            GL_UNSIGNED_SHORT, or GL_UNSIGNED_INT.

indices   Specifies a pointer to the location where the indices are stored.

Description

glDrawElements specifies multiple geometric primitives with very few subroutine calls. Instead of calling a GL function to pass each individual vertex, normal, texture coordinate, edge flag, or color, you can prespecify separate arrays of vertices, normals, and so on, and use them to construct a sequence of primitives with a single call to glDrawElements.

When glDrawElements is called, it uses *count* sequential elements from an enabled array, starting at *indices* to construct a sequence of geometric primitives. *mode* specifies what kind of primitives are constructed and how the array elements construct these primitives. If more than one array is enabled, each is used. If GL_VERTEX_ARRAY is not enabled, no geometric primitives are constructed.

Vertex attributes that are modified by glDrawElements have an unspecified value after glDrawElements returns. For example, if GL_COLOR_ARRAY is enabled, the value of the current color is undefined after glDrawElements executes. Attributes that aren't modified maintain their previous values.

Notes

glDrawElements is available only if the GL version is 1.1 or greater.

glDrawElements is included in display lists. If glDrawElements is entered into a display list, the necessary array data (determined by the array pointers and enables) is also entered into the display list. Because the array pointers and enables are client-side state, their values affect display lists when the lists are created, not when the lists are executed.

Errors

GL_INVALID_ENUM is generated if *mode* is not an accepted value.

GL_INVALID_VALUE is generated if *count* is negative.

GL_INVALID_OPERATION is generated if a nonzero buffer object name is bound to an enabled array or the element array and the buffer object's data store is currently mapped.

GL_INVALID_OPERATION is generated if glDrawElements is executed between the execution of glBegin and the corresponding glEnd.

See Also

glArrayElement, glColorPointer, glDrawArrays, glDrawRangeElements, glEdgeFlagPointer, glFogCoordPointer, glGetPointerv, glIndexPointer, glInterleavedArrays, glNormalPointer, glSecondaryColorPointer, glTexCoordPointer, glVertexPointer

glDrawPixels

Write a block of pixels to the frame buffer

C Specification

```
void glDrawPixels(GLsizei        width,
                  GLsizei        height,
                  GLenum         format,
                  GLenum         type,
                  const GLvoid * data);
```

Parameters

width, *height* Specify the dimensions of the pixel rectangle to be written into the frame buffer.

format Specifies the format of the pixel data. Symbolic constants GL_COLOR_INDEX, GL_STENCIL_INDEX, GL_DEPTH_COMPONENT, GL_RGB, GL_BGR, GL_RGBA, GL_BGRA, GL_RED, GL_GREEN, GL_BLUE, GL_ALPHA, GL_LUMINANCE, and GL_LUMINANCE_ALPHA are accepted.

type Specifies the data type for *data*. Symbolic constants GL_UNSIGNED_BYTE, GL_BYTE, GL_BITMAP, GL_UNSIGNED_SHORT, GL_SHORT, GL_UNSIGNED_INT, GL_INT, GL_FLOAT, GL_UNSIGNED_BYTE_3_3_2, GL_UNSIGNED_BYTE_2_3_3_REV, GL_UNSIGNED_SHORT_5_6_5, GL_UNSIGNED_SHORT_5_6_5_REV, GL_UNSIGNED_SHORT_4_4_4_4, GL_UNSIGNED_SHORT_4_4_4_4_REV, GL_UNSIGNED_SHORT_5_5_5_1, GL_UNSIGNED_SHORT_1_5_5_5_REV, GL_UNSIGNED_INT_8_8_8_8, GL_UNSIGNED_INT_8_8_8_8_REV, GL_UNSIGNED_INT_10_10_10_2, and GL_UNSIGNED_INT_2_10_10_10_REV are accepted.

data Specifies a pointer to the pixel data.

Description

glDrawPixels reads pixel data from memory and writes it into the frame buffer relative to the current raster position, provided that the raster position is valid. Use glRasterPos or glWindowPos to set the current raster position; use glGet with argument GL_CURRENT_RASTER_POSITION_VALID to determine if the specified raster position is valid, and glGet with argument GL_CURRENT_RASTER_POSITION to query the raster position.

Several parameters define the encoding of pixel data in memory and control the processing of the pixel data before it is placed in the frame buffer. These parameters are set with four commands: glPixelStore, glPixelTransfer, glPixelMap, and glPixelZoom. This reference page describes the effects on glDrawPixels of many, but not all, of the parameters specified by these four commands.

Data is read from *data* as a sequence of signed or unsigned bytes, signed or unsigned shorts, signed or unsigned integers, or single-precision floating-point values, depending on *type*. When *type* is one of GL_UNSIGNED_BYTE, GL_BYTE, GL_UNSIGNED_SHORT, GL_SHORT, GL_UNSIGNED_INT, GL_INT, or GL_FLOAT, each of these bytes, shorts, integers, or floating-point values is interpreted as one color or depth component, or one index, depending on *format*. When *type* is one of GL_UNSIGNED_BYTE_3_3_2, GL_UNSIGNED_SHORT_5_6_5, GL_UNSIGNED_SHORT_4_4_4_4, GL_UNSIGNED_SHORT_5_5_5_1, GL_UNSIGNED_INT_8_8_8_8, or GL_UNSIGNED_INT_10_10_10_2, each unsigned value is interpreted as containing all the components for a single pixel, with the color components arranged according to *format*. When *type* is one of GL_UNSIGNED_BYTE_2_3_3_REV, GL_UNSIGNED_SHORT_5_6_5_REV, GL_UNSIGNED_SHORT_4_4_4_4_REV, GL_UNSIGNED_SHORT_1_5_5_5_REV, GL_UNSIGNED_INT_8_8_8_8_REV, or GL_UNSIGNED_INT_2_10_10_10_REV, each unsigned value is interpreted as containing all color components, specified by *format*, for a single pixel in a reversed order. Indices are always treated individually. Color components are treated as groups of one, two, three, or four values, again based on *format*. Both individual indices and groups of components are referred to as pixels. If *type* is GL_BITMAP, the data must be unsigned bytes, and *format* must be either GL_COLOR_INDEX or GL_STENCIL_INDEX. Each unsigned byte is treated as eight 1-bit pixels, with bit ordering determined by GL_UNPACK_LSB_FIRST (see glPixelStore).

width × *height* pixels are read from memory, starting at location *data*. By default, these pixels are taken from adjacent memory locations, except that after all *width* pixels are read, the read pointer is advanced to the next four-byte boundary. The four-byte row alignment is specified by glPixelStore with argument GL_UNPACK_ALIGNMENT, and it can be set to one, two, four, or eight bytes. Other pixel store parameters specify different read pointer advancements, both before the first pixel is read and after all *width* pixels are read. See the glPixelStore reference page for details on these options.

If a nonzero named buffer object is bound to the GL_PIXEL_UNPACK_BUFFER target (see glBindBuffer) while a block of pixels is specified, *data* is treated as a byte offset into the buffer object's data store.

The *width* × *height* pixels that are read from memory are each operated on in the same way, based on the values of several parameters specified by glPixelTransfer and glPixelMap. The details of these operations, as well as the target buffer into which the pixels are drawn, are specific to the format of the pixels, as specified by *format*. *format* can assume one of 13 symbolic values:

GL_COLOR_INDEX

Each pixel is a single value, a color index. It is converted to fixed-point format, with an unspecified number of bits to the right of the binary point, regardless of the memory data type. Floating-point values convert to true fixed-point values. Signed and unsigned integer data is converted with all fraction bits set to 0. Bitmap data convert to either 0 or 1.

Each fixed-point index is then shifted left by GL_INDEX_SHIFT bits and added to GL_INDEX_OFFSET. If GL_INDEX_SHIFT is negative, the shift is to the right. In either case, zero bits fill otherwise unspecified bit locations in the result.

If the GL is in RGBA mode, the resulting index is converted to an RGBA pixel with the help of the GL_PIXEL_MAP_I_TO_R, GL_PIXEL_MAP_I_TO_G, GL_PIXEL_MAP_I_TO_B, and GL_PIXEL_MAP_I_TO_A tables. If the GL is in color index mode, and if GL_MAP_COLOR is true, the index is replaced with the value that it references in lookup table GL_PIXEL_MAP_I_TO_I. Whether the lookup replacement of the index is done or not, the integer part of the index is then ANDed with $2^b - 1$, where b is the number of bits in a color index buffer.

The GL then converts the resulting indices or RGBA colors to fragments by attaching the current raster position z coordinate and texture coordinates to each pixel, then assigning x and y window coordinates to the nth fragment such that

$$x_n = x_r + n \% width$$

$$y_n = y_r + \left\lfloor \frac{n}{width} \right\rfloor$$

where (x_r, y_r) is the current raster position. These pixel fragments are then treated just like the fragments generated by rasterizing points, lines, or polygons. Texture mapping, fog, and all the fragment operations are applied before the fragments are written to the frame buffer.

GL_STENCIL_INDEX

Each pixel is a single value, a stencil index. It is converted to fixed-point format, with an unspecified number of bits to the right of the binary point, regardless of the memory data type. Floating-point values convert to true fixed-point values. Signed and unsigned integer data is converted with all fraction bits set to 0. Bitmap data convert to either 0 or 1.

Each fixed-point index is then shifted left by GL_INDEX_SHIFT bits, and added to GL_INDEX_OFFSET. If GL_INDEX_SHIFT is negative, the shift is to the right. In either case, zero bits fill otherwise unspecified bit locations in the result. If GL_MAP_STENCIL is true, the index is replaced with the value that it references in lookup table GL_PIXEL_MAP_S_TO_S. Whether the lookup replacement of the index is done or not, the integer part of the index is then ANDed with $2^b - 1$, where b is the number of bits in the stencil buffer. The resulting stencil indices are then written to the stencil buffer such that the nth index is written to location

$$x_n = x_r + n \% width$$

$$y_n = y_r + \left\lfloor \frac{n}{width} \right\rfloor$$

where (x_r, y_r) is the current raster position. Only the pixel ownership test, the scissor test, and the stencil writemask affect these write operations.

GL_DEPTH_COMPONENT

Each pixel is a single-depth component. Floating-point data is converted directly to an internal floating-point format with unspecified precision. Signed integer data is mapped linearly to the internal floating-point format such that the most positive representable integer value maps to 1.0, and the most negative representable value maps to -1.0. Unsigned integer data is mapped similarly: the largest integer value maps to 1.0, and 0 maps to 0.0. The resulting floating-point depth value is then multiplied by GL_DEPTH_SCALE and added to GL_DEPTH_BIAS. The result is clamped to the range [0,1] .

The GL then converts the resulting depth components to fragments by attaching the current raster position color or color index and texture coordinates to each pixel, then assigning x and y window coordinates to the nth fragment such that

$$x_n = x_r + n \% width$$

$$y_n = y_r + \left\lfloor \frac{n}{width} \right\rfloor$$

where (x_r, y_r) is the current raster position. These pixel fragments are then treated just like the fragments generated by rasterizing points, lines, or polygons. Texture mapping, fog, and all the fragment operations are applied before the fragments are written to the frame buffer.

GL_RGBA
GL_BGRA

Each pixel is a four-component group: For GL_RGBA, the red component is first, followed by green, followed by blue, followed by alpha; for GL_BGRA the order is blue, green, red and then alpha. Floating-point values are converted directly to an internal floating-point format with unspecified precision. Signed integer values are mapped linearly to the internal floating-point format such that the most positive representable integer value maps to 1.0, and the most negative representable value maps to -1.0. (Note that this mapping does not convert 0 precisely to 0.0.) Unsigned integer data is mapped similarly: The largest integer value maps to 1.0, and 0 maps to 0.0. The resulting floating-point color values are then multiplied by GL_c_SCALE and added to GL_c_BIAS, where c is RED, GREEN, BLUE, and ALPHA for the respective color components. The results are clamped to the range $[0,1]$.

If GL_MAP_COLOR is true, each color component is scaled by the size of lookup table GL_PIXEL_MAP_c_TO_c, then replaced by the value that it references in that table. c is R, G, B, or A respectively.

The GL then converts the resulting RGBA colors to fragments by attaching the current raster position z coordinate and texture coordinates to each pixel, then assigning x and y window coordinates to the nth fragment such that

$$x_n = x_r + n \% width$$

$$y_n = y_r + \left\lfloor \frac{n}{width} \right\rfloor$$

where (x_r, y_r) is the current raster position. These pixel fragments are then treated just like the fragments generated by rasterizing points, lines, or polygons. Texture mapping, fog, and all the fragment operations are applied before the fragments are written to the frame buffer.

GL_RED

Each pixel is a single red component. This component is converted to the internal floating-point format in the same way the red component of an RGBA pixel is. It is then converted to an RGBA pixel with green and blue set to 0, and alpha set to 1. After this conversion, the pixel is treated as if it had been read as an RGBA pixel.

GL_GREEN

Each pixel is a single green component. This component is converted to the internal floating-point format in the same way the green component of an RGBA pixel is. It is then converted to an RGBA pixel with red and blue set to 0, and alpha set to 1. After this conversion, the pixel is treated as if it had been read as an RGBA pixel.

GL_BLUE

Each pixel is a single blue component. This component is converted to the internal floating-point format in the same way the blue component of an RGBA pixel is. It is then converted to an RGBA pixel with red and green set to 0, and alpha set to 1. After this conversion, the pixel is treated as if it had been read as an RGBA pixel.

GL_ALPHA

Each pixel is a single alpha component. This component is converted to the internal floating-point format in the same way the alpha component of an RGBA pixel is. It is then converted to an RGBA pixel with red, green, and blue set to 0. After this conversion, the pixel is treated as if it had been read as an RGBA pixel.

GL_RGB
GL_BGR

Each pixel is a three-component group: red first, followed by green, followed by blue; for GL_BGR, the first component is blue, followed by green and then red. Each component is converted to the internal floating-point format in the same way the red, green, and blue components of an RGBA pixel are. The color triple is converted to an RGBA pixel with alpha set to 1. After this conversion, the pixel is treated as if it had been read as an RGBA pixel.

`GL_LUMINANCE`

Each pixel is a single luminance component. This component is converted to the internal floating-point format in the same way the red component of an RGBA pixel is. It is then converted to an RGBA pixel with red, green, and blue set to the converted luminance value, and alpha set to 1. After this conversion, the pixel is treated as if it had been read as an RGBA pixel.

`GL_LUMINANCE_ALPHA`

Each pixel is a two-component group: luminance first, followed by alpha. The two components are converted to the internal floating-point format in the same way the red component of an RGBA pixel is. They are then converted to an RGBA pixel with red, green, and blue set to the converted luminance value, and alpha set to the converted alpha value. After this conversion, the pixel is treated as if it had been read as an RGBA pixel. The following table summarizes the meaning of the valid constants for the *type* parameter:

Type	Corresponding Type
GL_UNSIGNED_BYTE	unsigned 8-bit integer
GL_BYTE	signed 8-bit integer
GL_BITMAP	single bits in unsigned 8-bit integers
GL_UNSIGNED_SHORT	unsigned 16-bit integer
GL_SHORT	signed 16-bit integer
GL_UNSIGNED_INT	unsigned 32-bit integer
GL_INT	32-bit integer
GL_FLOAT	single-precision floating-point
GL_UNSIGNED_BYTE_3_3_2	unsigned 8-bit integer
GL_UNSIGNED_BYTE_2_3_3_REV	unsigned 8-bit integer with reversed component ordering
GL_UNSIGNED_SHORT_5_6_5	unsigned 16-bit integer
GL_UNSIGNED_SHORT_5_6_5_REV	unsigned 16-bit integer with reversed component ordering
GL_UNSIGNED_SHORT_4_4_4_4	unsigned 16-bit integer
GL_UNSIGNED_SHORT_4_4_4_4_REV	unsigned 16-bit integer with reversed component ordering
GL_UNSIGNED_SHORT_5_5_5_1	unsigned 16-bit integer
GL_UNSIGNED_SHORT_1_5_5_5_REV	unsigned 16-bit integer with reversed component ordering
GL_UNSIGNED_INT_8_8_8_8	unsigned 32-bit integer
GL_UNSIGNED_INT_8_8_8_8_REV	unsigned 32-bit integer with reversed component ordering
GL_UNSIGNED_INT_10_10_10_2	unsigned 32-bit integer
GL_UNSIGNED_INT_2_10_10_10_REV	unsigned 32-bit integer with reversed component ordering

The rasterization described so far assumes pixel zoom factors of 1. If `glPixelZoom` is used to change the x and y pixel zoom factors, pixels are converted to fragments as follows. If (x_r, y_r) is the current raster position, and a given pixel is in the nth column and mth row of the pixel rectangle, then fragments are generated for pixels whose centers are in the rectangle with corners at

$(x_r + zoom_x\ n, y_r + zoom_y\ m)$

$(x_r + zoom_x\ (n + 1), y_r + zoom_y\ (m + 1))$

where $zoom_x$ is the value of `GL_ZOOM_X` and $zoom_y$ is the value of `GL_ZOOM_Y`.

Notes

`GL_BGR` and `GL_BGRA` are only valid for *format* if the GL version is 1.2 or greater.

`GL_UNSIGNED_BYTE_3_3_2`, `GL_UNSIGNED_BYTE_2_3_3_REV`, `GL_UNSIGNED_SHORT_5_6_5`, `GL_UNSIGNED_SHORT_5_6_5_REV`, `GL_UNSIGNED_SHORT_4_4_4_4`, `GL_UNSIGNED_SHORT_4_4_4_4_REV`, `GL_UNSIGNED_SHORT_5_5_5_1`, `GL_UNSIGNED_SHORT_1_5_5_5_REV`, `GL_UNSIGNED_INT_8_8_8_8`,

GL_UNSIGNED_INT_8_8_8_8_REV, GL_UNSIGNED_INT_10_10_10_2, and
GL_UNSIGNED_INT_2_10_10_10_REV are only valid for *type* if the GL version is 1.2 or greater.

Errors

GL_INVALID_ENUM is generated if *format* or *type* is not one of the accepted values.

GL_INVALID_ENUM is generated if *type* is GL_BITMAP and *format* is not either GL_COLOR_INDEX or GL_STENCIL_INDEX.

GL_INVALID_VALUE is generated if either *width* or *height* is negative.

GL_INVALID_OPERATION is generated if *format* is GL_STENCIL_INDEX and there is no stencil buffer.

GL_INVALID_OPERATION is generated if *format* is GL_RED, GL_GREEN, GL_BLUE, GL_ALPHA, GL_RGB, GL_RGBA, GL_BGR, GL_BGRA, GL_LUMINANCE, or GL_LUMINANCE_ALPHA, and the GL is in color index mode.

GL_INVALID_OPERATION is generated if *format* is one of GL_UNSIGNED_BYTE_3_3_2, GL_UNSIGNED_BYTE_2_3_3_REV, GL_UNSIGNED_SHORT_5_6_5, or GL_UNSIGNED_SHORT_5_6_5_REV and *format* is not GL_RGB.

GL_INVALID_OPERATION is generated if *format* is one of GL_UNSIGNED_SHORT_4_4_4_4, GL_UNSIGNED_SHORT_4_4_4_4_REV, GL_UNSIGNED_SHORT_5_5_5_1, GL_UNSIGNED_SHORT_1_5_5_5_REV, GL_UNSIGNED_INT_8_8_8_8, GL_UNSIGNED_INT_8_8_8_8_REV, GL_UNSIGNED_INT_10_10_10_2, or GL_UNSIGNED_INT_2_10_10_10_REV and *format* is neither GL_RGBA nor GL_BGRA.

GL_INVALID_OPERATION is generated if a nonzero buffer object name is bound to the GL_PIXEL_UNPACK_BUFFER target and the buffer object's data store is currently mapped.

GL_INVALID_OPERATION is generated if a nonzero buffer object name is bound to the GL_PIXEL_UNPACK_BUFFER target and the data would be unpacked from the buffer object such that the memory reads required would exceed the data store size.

GL_INVALID_OPERATION is generated if a nonzero buffer object name is bound to the GL_PIXEL_UNPACK_BUFFER target and *data* is not evenly divisible into the number of bytes needed to store in memory a datum indicated by *type*.

GL_INVALID_OPERATION is generated if glDrawPixels is executed between the execution of glBegin and the corresponding execution of glEnd.

Associated Gets

glGet with argument GL_CURRENT_RASTER_POSITION

glGet with argument GL_CURRENT_RASTER_POSITION_VALID

glGet with argument GL_PIXEL_UNPACK_BUFFER_BINDING

See Also

glAlphaFunc, glBlendFunc, glCopyPixels, glDepthFunc, glLogicOp, glPixelMap, glPixelStore, glPixelTransfer, glPixelZoom, glRasterPos, glReadPixels, glScissor, glStencilFunc, glWindowPos

glDrawRangeElements

Render primitives from array data

C Specification

```
void glDrawRangeElements(GLenum          mode,
                         GLuint          start,
                         GLuint          end,
                         GLsizei         count,
                         GLenum          type,
                         const GLvoid *  indices);
```

Parameters

mode   Specifies what kind of primitives to render. Symbolic constants GL_POINTS, GL_LINE_STRIP, GL_LINE_LOOP, GL_LINES, GL_TRIANGLE_STRIP, GL_TRIANGLE_FAN, GL_TRIANGLES, GL_QUAD_STRIP, GL_QUADS, and GL_POLYGON are accepted.

start   Specifies the minimum array index contained in *indices*.

end   Specifies the maximum array index contained in *indices*.

count   Specifies the number of elements to be rendered.

type   Specifies the type of the values in *count*. Must be one of GL_UNSIGNED_BYTE, GL_UNSIGNED_SHORT, or GL_UNSIGNED_INT.

indices   Specifies a pointer to the location where the indices are stored.

Description

glDrawRangeElements is a restricted form of glDrawElements. *mode*, *start*, *end*, and *count* match the corresponding arguments to glDrawElements, with the additional constraint that all values in the arrays *count* must lie between *start* and *end*, inclusive.

Implementations denote recommended maximum amounts of vertex and index data, which may be queried by calling glGet with argument GL_MAX_ELEMENTS_VERTICES and GL_MAX_ELEMENTS_INDICES. If *end* – *start* + 1 is greater than the value of GL_MAX_ELEMENTS_VERTICES, or if *count* is greater than the value of GL_MAX_ELEMENTS_INDICES, then the call may operate at reduced performance. There is no requirement that all vertices in the range [*start*,*end*] be referenced. However, the implementation may partially process unused vertices, reducing performance from what could be achieved with an optimal index set.

When glDrawRangeElements is called, it uses *count* sequential elements from an enabled array, starting at *start* to construct a sequence of geometric primitives. *mode* specifies what kind of primitives are constructed, and how the array elements construct these primitives. If more than one array is enabled, each is used. If GL_VERTEX_ARRAY is not enabled, no geometric primitives are constructed.

Vertex attributes that are modified by glDrawRangeElements have an unspecified value after glDrawRangeElements returns. For example, if GL_COLOR_ARRAY is enabled, the value of the current color is undefined after glDrawRangeElements executes. Attributes that aren't modified maintain their previous values.

Notes

glDrawRangeElements is available only if the GL version is 1.2 or greater.

glDrawRangeElements is included in display lists. If glDrawRangeElements is entered into a display list, the necessary array data (determined by the array pointers and enables) is also entered into the display list. Because the array pointers and enables are client-side state, their values affect display lists when the lists are created, not when the lists are executed.

Errors

It is an error for indices to lie outside the range [*start*,*end*], but implementations may not check for this situation. Such indices cause implementation-dependent behavior.

GL_INVALID_ENUM is generated if *mode* is not an accepted value.

GL_INVALID_VALUE is generated if *count* is negative.

GL_INVALID_VALUE is generated if *end* < *start*.

GL_INVALID_OPERATION is generated if a nonzero buffer object name is bound to an enabled array or the element array and the buffer object's data store is currently mapped.

GL_INVALID_OPERATION is generated if glDrawRangeElements is executed between the execution of glBegin and the corresponding glEnd.

Associated Gets

glGet with argument GL_MAX_ELEMENTS_VERTICES

glGet with argument GL_MAX_ELEMENTS_INDICES

See Also

glArrayElement, glColorPointer, glDrawArrays, glDrawElements, glEdgeFlagPointer, glGetPointerv, glIndexPointer, glInterleavedArrays, glNormalPointer, glSecondaryColorPointer, glTexCoordPointer, glVertexPointer

glEdgeFlag

Flag edges as either boundary or nonboundary

C Specification

void **glEdgeFlag**(GLboolean *flag*);

Parameters

flag   Specifies the current edge flag value, either GL_TRUE or GL_FALSE. The initial value is GL_TRUE.

C Specification

void **glEdgeFlagv**(const GLboolean * *flag*);

Parameters

flag   Specifies a pointer to an array that contains a single boolean element, which replaces the current edge flag value.

Description

Each vertex of a polygon, separate triangle, or separate quadrilateral specified between a glBegin/glEnd pair is marked as the start of either a boundary or nonboundary edge. If the current edge flag is true when the vertex is specified, the vertex is marked as the start of a boundary edge. Otherwise, the vertex is marked as the start of a nonboundary edge. glEdgeFlag sets the edge flag bit to GL_TRUE if *flag* is GL_TRUE and to GL_FALSE otherwise.

The vertices of connected triangles and connected quadrilaterals are always marked as boundary, regardless of the value of the edge flag.

Boundary and nonboundary edge flags on vertices are significant only if GL_POLYGON_MODE is set to GL_POINT or GL_LINE. See glPolygonMode.

Notes

The current edge flag can be updated at any time. In particular, glEdgeFlag can be called between a call to glBegin and the corresponding call to glEnd.

Associated Gets

glGet with argument GL_EDGE_FLAG

See Also

glBegin, glEdgeFlagPointer, glPolygonMode

glEdgeFlagPointer

Define an array of edge flags

C Specification

void **glEdgeFlagPointer**(GLsizei   *stride*,
                         const GLvoid * *pointer*);

Parameters

stride   Specifies the byte offset between consecutive edge flags. If *stride* is 0, the edge flags are understood to be tightly packed in the array. The initial value is 0.
pointer   Specifies a pointer to the first edge flag in the array. The initial value is 0.

Description

glEdgeFlagPointer specifies the location and data format of an array of boolean edge flags to use when rendering. *stride* specifies the byte *stride* from one edge flag to the next, allowing vertices and attributes to be packed into a single array or stored in separate arrays.

If a nonzero named buffer object is bound to the GL_ARRAY_BUFFER target (see glBindBuffer) while an edge flag array is specified, *pointer* is treated as a byte offset into the buffer object's data store. Also, the buffer object binding (GL_ARRAY_BUFFER_BINDING) is saved as edge flag vertex array client-side state (GL_EDGE_FLAG_ARRAY_BUFFER_BINDING).

When an edge flag array is specified, *stride* and *pointer* are saved as client-side state, in addition to the current vertex array buffer object binding.

To enable and disable the edge flag array, call glEnableClientState and glDisableClientState with the argument GL_EDGE_FLAG_ARRAY. If enabled, the edge flag array is used when glDrawArrays, glMultiDrawArrays, glDrawElements, glMultiDrawElements, glDrawRangeElements, or glArrayElement is called.

Notes

glEdgeFlagPointer is available only if the GL version is 1.1 or greater.

Edge flags are not supported for interleaved vertex array formats (see glInterleavedArrays).

The edge flag array is initially disabled and isn't accessed when glArrayElement, glDrawElements, glDrawRangeElements, glDrawArrays, glMultiDrawArrays, or glMultiDrawElements is called.

Execution of glEdgeFlagPointer is not allowed between the execution of glBegin and the corresponding execution of glEnd, but an error may or may not be generated. If no error is generated, the operation is undefined.

glEdgeFlagPointer is typically implemented on the client side.

Edge flag array parameters are client-side state and are therefore not saved or restored by glPushAttrib and glPopAttrib. Use glPushClientAttrib and glPopClientAttrib instead.

Errors

GL_INVALID_ENUM is generated if *stride* is negative.

Associated Gets

glIsEnabled with argument GL_EDGE_FLAG_ARRAY

glGet with argument GL_EDGE_FLAG_ARRAY_STRIDE

glGet with argument GL_EDGE_FLAG_ARRAY_BUFFER_BINDING

glGet with argument GL_ARRAY_BUFFER_BINDING

glGetPointerv with argument GL_EDGE_FLAG_ARRAY_POINTER

See Also

glArrayElement, glBindBuffer, glColorPointer, glDisableClientState, glDrawArrays, glDrawElements, glDrawRangeElements, glEdgeFlag, glEnableClientState, glFogCoordPointer, glIndexPointer, glInterleavedArrays, glMultiDrawArrays, glMultiDrawElements, glNormalPointer, glPopClientAttrib, glPushClientAttrib, glSecondaryColorPointer, glTexCoordPointer, glVertexAttribPointer, glVertexPointer

glEnable

Enable or disable server-side GL capabilities

C Specification

void **glEnable**(GLenum *cap*);

Parameters

cap   Specifies a symbolic constant indicating a GL capability.

C Specification
    void **glDisable**(GLenum *cap*);

Parameters
cap   Specifies a symbolic constant indicating a GL capability.

Description
    glEnable and glDisable enable and disable various capabilities. Use glIsEnabled or glGet to determine the current setting of any capability. The initial value for each capability with the exception of GL_DITHER is GL_FALSE. The initial value for GL_DITHER is GL_TRUE.
    Both glEnable and glDisable take a single argument, *cap*, which can assume one of the following values:
    GL_ALPHA_TEST
    If enabled, do alpha testing. See glAlphaFunc.
    GL_AUTO_NORMAL
    If enabled, generate normal vectors when either GL_MAP2_VERTEX_3 or GL_MAP2_VERTEX_4 is used to generate vertices. See glMap2.
    GL_BLEND
    If enabled, blend the incoming RGBA color values with the values in the color buffers. See glBlendFunc.
    GL_CLIP_PLANEi
    If enabled, clip geometry against user-defined clipping plane i. See glClipPlane.
    GL_COLOR_LOGIC_OP
    If enabled, apply the currently selected logical operation to the incoming RGBA color and color buffer values. See glLogicOp.
    GL_COLOR_MATERIAL
    If enabled, have one or more material parameters track the current color. See glColorMaterial.
    GL_COLOR_SUM
    If enabled, add the secondary color value to the computed fragment color. See glSecondaryColor.
    GL_COLOR_TABLE
    If enabled, perform a color table lookup on the incoming RGBA color values. See glColorTable.
    GL_CONVOLUTION_1D
    If enabled, perform a 1D convolution operation on incoming RGBA color values. See glConvolutionFilter1D.
    GL_CONVOLUTION_2D
    If enabled, perform a 2D convolution operation on incoming RGBA color values. See glConvolutionFilter2D.
    GL_CULL_FACE
    If enabled, cull polygons based on their winding in window coordinates. See glCullFace.
    GL_DEPTH_TEST
    If enabled, do depth comparisons and update the depth buffer. Note that even if the depth buffer exists and the depth mask is nonzero, the depth buffer is not updated if the depth test is disabled. See glDepthFunc and glDepthRange.
    GL_DITHER
    If enabled, dither color components or indices before they are written to the color buffer.
    GL_FOG
    If enabled, blend a fog color into the post-texturing color. See glFog.
    GL_HISTOGRAM
    If enabled, histogram incoming RGBA color values. See glHistogram.
    GL_INDEX_LOGIC_OP
    If enabled, apply the currently selected logical operation to the incoming index and color buffer indices. See glLogicOp.

GL_LIGHTi

If enabled, include light i in the evaluation of the lighting equation. See glLightModel and glLight.

GL_LIGHTING

If enabled, use the current lighting parameters to compute the vertex color or index. Otherwise, simply associate the current color or index with each vertex. See glMaterial, glLightModel, and glLight.

GL_LINE_SMOOTH

If enabled, draw lines with correct filtering. Otherwise, draw aliased lines. See glLineWidth.

GL_LINE_STIPPLE

If enabled, use the current line stipple pattern when drawing lines. See glLineStipple.

GL_MAP1_COLOR_4

If enabled, calls to glEvalCoord1, glEvalMesh1, and glEvalPoint1 generate RGBA values. See glMap1.

GL_MAP1_INDEX

If enabled, calls to glEvalCoord1, glEvalMesh1, and glEvalPoint1 generate color indices. See glMap1.

GL_MAP1_NORMAL

If enabled, calls to glEvalCoord1, glEvalMesh1, and glEvalPoint1 generate normals. See glMap1.

GL_MAP1_TEXTURE_COORD_1

If enabled, calls to glEvalCoord1, glEvalMesh1, and glEvalPoint1 generate s texture coordinates. See glMap1.

GL_MAP1_TEXTURE_COORD_2

If enabled, calls to glEvalCoord1, glEvalMesh1, and glEvalPoint1 generate s and t texture coordinates. See glMap1.

GL_MAP1_TEXTURE_COORD_3

If enabled, calls to glEvalCoord1, glEvalMesh1, and glEvalPoint1 generate s, t, and r texture coordinates. See glMap1.

GL_MAP1_TEXTURE_COORD_4

If enabled, calls to glEvalCoord1, glEvalMesh1, and glEvalPoint1 generate s, t, r, and q texture coordinates. See glMap1.

GL_MAP1_VERTEX_3

If enabled, calls to glEvalCoord1, glEvalMesh1, and glEvalPoint1 generate x, y, and z vertex coordinates. See glMap1.

GL_MAP1_VERTEX_4

If enabled, calls to glEvalCoord1, glEvalMesh1, and glEvalPoint1 generate homogeneous x, y, z, and w vertex coordinates. See glMap1.

GL_MAP2_COLOR_4

If enabled, calls to glEvalCoord2, glEvalMesh2, and glEvalPoint2 generate RGBA values. See glMap2.

GL_MAP2_INDEX

If enabled, calls to glEvalCoord2, glEvalMesh2, and glEvalPoint2 generate color indices. See glMap2.

GL_MAP2_NORMAL

If enabled, calls to glEvalCoord2, glEvalMesh2, and glEvalPoint2 generate normals. See glMap2.

GL_MAP2_TEXTURE_COORD_1

If enabled, calls to glEvalCoord2, glEvalMesh2, and glEvalPoint2 generate s texture coordinates. See glMap2.

GL_MAP2_TEXTURE_COORD_2

If enabled, calls to glEvalCoord2, glEvalMesh2, and glEvalPoint2 generate s and t texture coordinates. See glMap2.

GL_MAP2_TEXTURE_COORD_3

If enabled, calls to glEvalCoord2, glEvalMesh2, and glEvalPoint2 generate s, t, and r texture coordinates. See glMap2.

GL_MAP2_TEXTURE_COORD_4

If enabled, calls to glEvalCoord2, glEvalMesh2, and glEvalPoint2 generate s, t, r, and q texture coordinates. See glMap2.

GL_MAP2_VERTEX_3

If enabled, calls to glEvalCoord2, glEvalMesh2, and glEvalPoint2 generate x, y, and z vertex coordinates. See glMap2.

GL_MAP2_VERTEX_4

If enabled, calls to glEvalCoord2, glEvalMesh2, and glEvalPoint2 generate homogeneous x, y, z, and w vertex coordinates. See glMap2.

GL_MINMAX

If enabled, compute the minimum and maximum values of incoming RGBA color values. See glMinmax.

GL_MULTISAMPLE

If enabled, use multiple fragment samples in computing the final color of a pixel. See glSampleCoverage.

GL_NORMALIZE

If enabled, normal vectors specified with glNormal are scaled to unit length after transformation. See glNormal.

GL_POINT_SMOOTH

If enabled, draw points with proper filtering. Otherwise, draw aliased points. See glPointSize.

GL_POINT_SPRITE

If enabled, calculate texture coordinates for points based on texture environment and point parameter settings. Otherwise texture coordinates are constant across points.

GL_POLYGON_OFFSET_FILL

If enabled, and if the polygon is rendered in GL_FILL mode, an offset is added to depth values of a polygon's fragments before the depth comparison is performed. See glPolygonOffset.

GL_POLYGON_OFFSET_LINE

If enabled, and if the polygon is rendered in GL_LINE mode, an offset is added to depth values of a polygon's fragments before the depth comparison is performed. See glPolygonOffset.

GL_POLYGON_OFFSET_POINT

If enabled, an offset is added to depth values of a polygon's fragments before the depth comparison is performed, if the polygon is rendered in GL_POINT mode. See glPolygonOffset.

GL_POLYGON_SMOOTH

If enabled, draw polygons with proper filtering. Otherwise, draw aliased polygons. For correct antialiased polygons, an alpha buffer is needed and the polygons must be sorted front to back.

GL_POLYGON_STIPPLE

If enabled, use the current polygon stipple pattern when rendering polygons. See glPolygonStipple.

GL_POST_COLOR_MATRIX_COLOR_TABLE

If enabled, perform a color table lookup on RGBA color values after color matrix transformation. See glColorTable.

GL_POST_CONVOLUTION_COLOR_TABLE

If enabled, perform a color table lookup on RGBA color values after convolution. See glColorTable.

GL_RESCALE_NORMAL

If enabled, normal vectors specified with glNormal are scaled to unit length after transformation. See glNormal.

GL_SAMPLE_ALPHA_TO_COVERAGE

If enabled, compute a temporary coverage value where each bit is determined by the alpha value at the corresponding sample location. The temporary coverage value is then ANDed with the fragment coverage value.

GL_SAMPLE_ALPHA_TO_ONE

If enabled, each sample alpha value is replaced by the maximum representable alpha value.

GL_SAMPLE_COVERAGE

If enabled, the fragment's coverage is ANDed with the temporary coverage value. If GL_SAMPLE_COVERAGE_INVERT is set to GL_TRUE, invert the coverage value. See glSampleCoverage.

GL_SEPARABLE_2D

If enabled, perform a two-dimensional convolution operation using a separable convolution filter on incoming RGBA color values. See glSeparableFilter2D.

GL_SCISSOR_TEST

If enabled, discard fragments that are outside the scissor rectangle. See glScissor.

GL_STENCIL_TEST

If enabled, do stencil testing and update the stencil buffer. See glStencilFunc and glStencilOp.

GL_TEXTURE_1D

If enabled, one-dimensional texturing is performed (unless two- or three-dimensional or cube-mapped texturing is also enabled). See glTexImage1D.

GL_TEXTURE_2D

If enabled, two-dimensional texturing is performed (unless three-dimensional or cube-mapped texturing is also enabled). See glTexImage2D.

GL_TEXTURE_3D

If enabled, three-dimensional texturing is performed (unless cube-mapped texturing is also enabled). See glTexImage3D.

GL_TEXTURE_CUBE_MAP

If enabled, cube-mapped texturing is performed. See glTexImage2D.

GL_TEXTURE_GEN_Q

If enabled, the q texture coordinate is computed using the texture generation function defined with glTexGen. Otherwise, the current q texture coordinate is used. See glTexGen.

GL_TEXTURE_GEN_R

If enabled, the r texture coordinate is computed using the texture generation function defined with glTexGen. Otherwise, the current r texture coordinate is used. See glTexGen.

GL_TEXTURE_GEN_S

If enabled, the s texture coordinate is computed using the texture generation function defined with glTexGen. Otherwise, the current s texture coordinate is used. See glTexGen.

GL_TEXTURE_GEN_T

If enabled, the t texture coordinate is computed using the texture generation function defined with glTexGen. Otherwise, the current t texture coordinate is used. See glTexGen.

GL_VERTEX_PROGRAM_POINT_SIZE

If enabled, and a vertex shader is active, then the derived point size is taken from the (potentially clipped) shader builtin gl_PointSize and clamped to the implementation-dependent point size range.

GL_VERTEX_PROGRAM_TWO_SIDE

If enabled, and a vertex shader is active, it specifies that the GL will choose between front and back colors based on the polygon's face direction of which the vertex being shaded is a part. It has no effect on points or lines.

Notes

GL_POLYGON_OFFSET_FILL, GL_POLYGON_OFFSET_LINE, GL_POLYGON_OFFSET_POINT, GL_COLOR_LOGIC_OP, and GL_INDEX_LOGIC_OP are available only if the GL version is 1.1 or greater.

GL_RESCALE_NORMAL, and GL_TEXTURE_3D are available only if the GL version is 1.2 or greater.

GL_MULTISAMPLE, GL_SAMPLE_ALPHA_TO_COVERAGE, GL_SAMPLE_ALPHA_TO_ONE, GL_SAMPLE_COVERAGE, GL_TEXTURE_CUBE_MAP are available only if the GL version is 1.3 or greater.

GL_POINT_SPRITE, GL_VERTEX_PROGRAM_POINT_SIZE, and GL_VERTEX_PROGRAM_TWO_SIDE is available only if the GL version is 2.0 or greater.

GL_COLOR_TABLE, GL_CONVOLUTION_1D, GL_CONVOLUTION_2D, GL_HISTOGRAM, GL_MINMAX, GL_POST_COLOR_MATRIX_COLOR_TABLE, GL_POST_CONVOLUTION_COLOR_TABLE, and GL_SEPARABLE_2D are available only if ARB_imaging is returned from glGet with an argument of GL_EXTENSIONS.

For OpenGL versions 1.3 and greater, or when ARB_multitexture is supported, GL_TEXTURE_1D, GL_TEXTURE_2D, GL_TEXTURE_3D, GL_TEXTURE_GEN_S, GL_TEXTURE_GEN_T, GL_TEXTURE_GEN_R, and GL_TEXTURE_GEN_Q enable or disable the respective state for the active texture unit specified with glActiveTexture.

Errors

GL_INVALID_ENUM is generated if *cap* is not one of the values listed previously.

GL_INVALID_OPERATION is generated if glEnable or glDisable is executed between the execution of glBegin and the corresponding execution of glEnd.

See Also

glActiveTexture, glAlphaFunc, glBlendFunc, glClipPlane, glColorMaterial, glCullFace, glDepthFunc, glDepthRange, glEnableClientState, glFog, glGet, glIsEnabled, glLight, glLightModel, glLineWidth, glLineStipple, glLogicOp, glMap1, glMap2, glMaterial, glNormal, glPointSize, glPolygonMode, glPolygonOffset, glPolygonStipple, glScissor, glStencilFunc, glStencilOp, glTexGen, glTexImage1D, glTexImage2D, glTexImage3D

glEnableClientState

Enable or disable client-side capability

C Specification

void **glEnableClientState**(GLenum *cap*);

Parameters

cap   Specifies the capability to enable. Symbolic constants GL_COLOR_ARRAY
GL_EDGE_FLAG_ARRAY, GL_FOG_COORD_ARRAY, GL_INDEX_ARRAY, GL_NORMAL_ARRAY, GL_SECONDARY_COLOR_ARRAY, GL_TEXTURE_COORD_ARRAY, and GL_VERTEX_ARRAY are accepted.

C Specification

void **glDisableClientState**(GLenum *cap*);

Parameters

cap   Specifies the capability to disable.

Description

glEnableClientState and glDisableClientState enable or disable individual client-side capabilities. By default, all client-side capabilities are disabled. Both glEnableClientState and glDisableClientState take a single argument, *cap*, which can assume one of the following values:

GL_COLOR_ARRAY

If enabled, the color array is enabled for writing and used during rendering when glArrayElement, glDrawArrays, glDrawElements, glDrawRangeElementsglMultiDrawArrays, or glMultiDrawElements is called. See glColorPointer.

GL_EDGE_FLAG_ARRAY

If enabled, the edge flag array is enabled for writing and used during rendering when glArrayElement, glDrawArrays, glDrawElements, glDrawRangeElementsglMultiDrawArrays, or glMultiDrawElements is called. See glEdgeFlagPointer.

GL_FOG_COORD_ARRAY

If enabled, the fog coordinate array is enabled for writing and used during rendering when glArrayElement, glDrawArrays, glDrawElements, glDrawRangeElementsglMultiDrawArrays, or glMultiDrawElements is called. See glFogCoordPointer.

GL_INDEX_ARRAY

If enabled, the index array is enabled for writing and used during rendering when glArrayElement, glDrawArrays, glDrawElements, glDrawRangeElementsglMultiDrawArrays, or glMultiDrawElements is called. See glIndexPointer.

GL_NORMAL_ARRAY

If enabled, the normal array is enabled for writing and used during rendering when glArrayElement, glDrawArrays, glDrawElements, glDrawRangeElementsglMultiDrawArrays, or glMultiDrawElements is called. See glNormalPointer.

GL_SECONDARY_COLOR_ARRAY

If enabled, the secondary color array is enabled for writing and used during rendering when glArrayElement, glDrawArrays, glDrawElements, glDrawRangeElementsglMultiDrawArrays, or glMultiDrawElements is called. See glColorPointer.

GL_TEXTURE_COORD_ARRAY

If enabled, the texture coordinate array is enabled for writing and used during rendering when glArrayElement, glDrawArrays, glDrawElements, glDrawRangeElementsglMultiDrawArrays, or glMultiDrawElements is called. See glTexCoordPointer.

GL_VERTEX_ARRAY

If enabled, the vertex array is enabled for writing and used during rendering when glArrayElement, glDrawArrays, glDrawElements, glDrawRangeElementsglMultiDrawArrays, or glMultiDrawElements is called. See glVertexPointer.

Notes

glEnableClientState is available only if the GL version is 1.1 or greater.

GL_FOG_COORD_ARRAY and GL_SECONDARY_COLOR_ARRAY are available only if the GL version is 1.4 or greater.

For OpenGL versions 1.3 and greater, or when ARB_multitexture is supported, enabling and disabling GL_TEXTURE_COORD_ARRAY affects the active client texture unit. The active client texture unit is controlled with glClientActiveTexture.

Errors

GL_INVALID_ENUM is generated if *cap* is not an accepted value.

glEnableClientState is not allowed between the execution of glBegin and the corresponding glEnd, but an error may or may not be generated. If no error is generated, the behavior is undefined.

See Also

glArrayElement, glClientActiveTexture, glColorPointer, glDrawArrays, glDrawElements, glEdgeFlagPointer, glFogCoordPointer, glEnable, glGetPointerv, glIndexPointer, glInterleavedArrays, glNormalPointer, glSecondaryColorPointer, glTexCoordPointer, glVertexPointer

glEnableVertexAttribArray

Enable or disable a generic vertex attribute array

C Specification

```
void glEnableVertexAttribArray(GLuint index);
void glDisableVertexAttribArray(GLuint index);
```

Parameters

index   Specifies the index of the generic vertex attribute to be enabled or disabled.

Description

glEnableVertexAttribArray enables the generic vertex attribute array specified by *index*. glDisableVertexAttribArray disables the generic vertex attribute array specified by *index*. By default, all client-side capabilities are disabled, including all generic vertex attribute arrays. If enabled, the values in the generic vertex attribute array will be accessed and used for rendering when calls are made to vertex array commands such as glDrawArrays, glDrawElements, glDrawRangeElements, glArrayElement, glMultiDrawElements, or glMultiDrawArrays.

Notes

glEnableVertexAttribArray and glDisableVertexAttribArray are available only if the GL version is 2.0 or greater.

Errors

GL_INVALID_VALUE is generated if index is greater than or equal to GL_MAX_VERTEX_ATTRIBS.

GL_INVALID_OPERATION is generated if either glEnableVertexAttribArray or glDisableVertexAttribArray is executed between the execution of glBegin and the corresponding execution of glEnd.

Associated Gets

glGet with argument GL_MAX_VERTEX_ATTRIBS
glGetVertexAttrib with arguments index and GL_VERTEX_ATTRIB_ARRAY_ENABLED
glGetVertexAttribPointerv with arguments index and GL_VERTEX_ATTRIB_ARRAY_POINTER

See Also

glArrayElement, glBindAttribLocation, glDrawArrays, glDrawElements, glDrawRangeElements, glMultiDrawElements, glPopClientAttrib, glPushClientAttrib, glVertexAttrib, glVertexAttribPointer

glEvalCoord

Evaluate enabled one- and two-dimensional maps

C Specification

```
void glEvalCoord1f(GLfloat u);
void glEvalCoord1d(GLdouble u);
void glEvalCoord2f(GLfloat u, GLfloat v);
void glEvalCoord2d(GLdouble u, GLdouble v);
```

Parameters

u   Specifies a value that is the domain coordinate *u* to the basis function defined in a previous glMap1 or glMap2 command.

v   Specifies a value that is the domain coordinate *v* to the basis function defined in a previous glMap2 command. This argument is not present in a glEvalCoord1 command.

C Specification

```
void glEvalCoord1fv(const GLfloat * u);
void glEvalCoord1dv(const GLdouble * u);
void glEvalCoord2fv(const GLfloat * u);
void glEvalCoord2dv(const GLdouble * u);
```

Parameters

u   Specifies a pointer to an array containing either one or two domain coordinates. The first coordinate is *u*. The second coordinate is *v*, which is present only in glEvalCoord2 versions.

Description

glEvalCoord1 evaluates enabled one-dimensional maps at argument *u*. glEvalCoord2 does the same for two-dimensional maps using two domain values, *u* and *v*. To define a map, call glMap1 and glMap2; to enable and disable it, call glEnable and glDisable.

When one of the glEvalCoord commands is issued, all currently enabled maps of the indicated dimension are evaluated. Then, for each enabled map, it is as if the corresponding GL command had been issued with the computed value. That is, if GL_MAP1_INDEX or GL_MAP2_INDEX is enabled, a glIndex command is simulated. If GL_MAP1_COLOR_4 or GL_MAP2_COLOR_4 is enabled, a glColor command is simulated. If GL_MAP1_NORMAL or GL_MAP2_NORMAL is enabled, a normal vector is produced, and if any of GL_MAP1_TEXTURE_COORD_1, GL_MAP1_TEXTURE_COORD_2, GL_MAP1_TEXTURE_COORD_3, GL_MAP1_TEXTURE_COORD_4, GL_MAP2_TEXTURE_COORD_1, GL_MAP2_TEXTURE_COORD_2, GL_MAP2_TEXTURE_COORD_3, or GL_MAP2_TEXTURE_COORD_4 is enabled, then an appropriate glTexCoord command is simulated.

For color, color index, normal, and texture coordinates the GL uses evaluated values instead of current values for those evaluations that are enabled, and current values otherwise, However, the evaluated values do not update the current values. Thus, if glVertex commands are interspersed with glEvalCoord commands, the color, normal, and texture coordinates associated with the glVertex commands are not affected by the values generated by the glEvalCoord commands, but only by the most recent glColor, glIndex, glNormal, and glTexCoord commands.

No commands are issued for maps that are not enabled. If more than one texture evaluation is enabled for a particular dimension (for example, GL_MAP2_TEXTURE_COORD_1 and GL_MAP2_TEXTURE_COORD_2), then only the evaluation of the map that produces the larger number of coordinates (in this case, GL_MAP2_TEXTURE_COORD_2) is carried out. GL_MAP1_VERTEX_4 overrides GL_MAP1_VERTEX_3, and GL_MAP2_VERTEX_4 overrides GL_MAP2_VERTEX_3, in the same manner. If neither a three- nor a four-component vertex map is enabled for the specified dimension, the glEvalCoord command is ignored.

If you have enabled automatic normal generation, by calling glEnable with argument GL_AUTO_NORMAL, glEvalCoord2 generates surface normals analytically, regardless of the contents or enabling of the GL_MAP2_NORMAL map. Let

$$m = \frac{\partial p}{\partial u} \times \frac{\partial p}{\partial v}$$

then the generated normal *n* is $n = \frac{m}{\|m\|}$

If automatic normal generation is disabled, the corresponding normal map GL_MAP2_NORMAL, if enabled, is used to produce a normal. If neither automatic normal generation nor a normal map is enabled, no normal is generated for glEvalCoord2 commands.

Associated Gets

glIsEnabled with argument GL_MAP1_VERTEX_3
glIsEnabled with argument GL_MAP1_VERTEX_4

glIsEnabled with argument GL_MAP1_INDEX
glIsEnabled with argument GL_MAP1_COLOR_4
glIsEnabled with argument GL_MAP1_NORMAL
glIsEnabled with argument GL_MAP1_TEXTURE_COORD_1
glIsEnabled with argument GL_MAP1_TEXTURE_COORD_2
glIsEnabled with argument GL_MAP1_TEXTURE_COORD_3
glIsEnabled with argument GL_MAP1_TEXTURE_COORD_4
glIsEnabled with argument GL_MAP2_VERTEX_3
glIsEnabled with argument GL_MAP2_VERTEX_4
glIsEnabled with argument GL_MAP2_INDEX
glIsEnabled with argument GL_MAP2_COLOR_4
glIsEnabled with argument GL_MAP2_NORMAL
glIsEnabled with argument GL_MAP2_TEXTURE_COORD_1
glIsEnabled with argument GL_MAP2_TEXTURE_COORD_2
glIsEnabled with argument GL_MAP2_TEXTURE_COORD_3
glIsEnabled with argument GL_MAP2_TEXTURE_COORD_4
glIsEnabled with argument GL_AUTO_NORMAL
glGetMap

See Also

glBegin, glColor, glEnable, glEvalMesh, glEvalPoint, glIndex, glMap1, glMap2, glMapGrid, glNormal, glTexCoord, glVertex

glEvalMesh

Compute a one- or two-dimensional grid of points or lines

C Specification

void **glEvalMesh1**(GLenum *mode*,
                GLint *i1*,
                GLint *i2*);

Parameters

mode   In glEvalMesh1, specifies whether to compute a one-dimensional mesh of points or lines. Symbolic constants GL_POINT and GL_LINE are accepted.

i1, i2 Specify the first and last integer values for grid domain variable *i*.

C Specification

void **glEvalMesh2**(GLenum *mode*,
                GLint *i1*,
                GLint *i2*,
                GLint *j1*,
                GLint *j2*);

Parameters

mode   In glEvalMesh2, specifies whether to compute a two-dimensional mesh of points, lines, or polygons. Symbolic constants GL_POINT, GL_LINE, and GL_FILL are accepted.

i1, i2 Specify the first and last integer values for grid domain variable *i*.

j1, j2 Specify the first and last integer values for grid domain variable *j*.

Description

glMapGrid and glEvalMesh are used in tandem to efficiently generate and evaluate a series of evenly-spaced map domain values. glEvalMesh steps through the integer domain of a one- or two-dimensional grid, whose range is the domain of the evaluation maps specified by glMap1 and glMap2. *mode* determines whether the resulting vertices are connected as points, lines, or filled polygons.

In the one-dimensional case, glEvalMesh1, the mesh is generated as if the following code fragment were executed:

```
glBegin( type );
for ( i = i1; i <= i2; i += 1 )
    glEvalCoord1( i · Δ u + u₁ );
glEnd();
```

where

$$\Delta u = \frac{(u_2 - u_1)}{n}$$

and n, u_1, and u_2 are the arguments to the most recent glMapGrid1 command. *type* is GL_POINTS if *mode* is GL_POINT, or GL_LINES if *mode* is GL_LINE.

The one absolute numeric requirement is that if $i = n$, then the value computed from $i \cdot \Delta u + u_1$ is exactly u_2.

In the two-dimensional case, glEvalMesh2, let .cp

$$\Delta u = \frac{(u_2 - u_1)}{n}$$

$$\Delta v = \frac{(v_2 - v_1)}{m}$$

where n, u_1, u_2, m, v_1, and v_2 are the arguments to the most recent glMapGrid2 command. Then, if *mode* is GL_FILL, the glEvalMesh2 command is equivalent to:

```
for ( j = j1; j < j2; j += 1 ) {
    glBegin( GL_QUAD_STRIP );
    for ( i = i1; i <= i2; i += 1 ) {
        glEvalCoord2( i · Δu + u1, j · Δv + v₁ );
        glEvalCoord2( i · Δu + u1, (j + 1) · Δv + v₁ );
    }
    glEnd();
}
```

If *mode* is GL_LINE, then a call to glEvalMesh2 is equivalent to:

```
for ( j = j1; j <= j2; j += 1 ) {
    glBegin( GL_LINE_STRIP );
    for ( i = i1; i <= i2; i += 1 )
        glEvalCoord2( i · Δu + u1, j · Δv + v₁ );
    glEnd();
}

for ( i = i1;  i <= i2; i += 1 ) {
    glBegin( GL_LINE_STRIP );
    for ( j = j1; j <= j1; j += 1 )
        glEvalCoord2( i · Δu + u1, j · Δv + v₁ );
    glEnd();
}
```

And finally, if *mode* is GL_POINT, then a call to glEvalMesh2 is equivalent to:

```
glBegin( GL_POINTS );
for ( j = j1; j <= j2; j += 1 )
    for ( i = i1; i <= i2; i += 1 )
        glEvalCoord2( i · Δu + u1, j · Δv + v₁ );
glEnd();
```

In all three cases, the only absolute numeric requirements are that if $i = n$, then the value computed from $i \bullet \Delta u + u_1$ is exactly u_2, and if $j = m$, then the value computed from $j \bullet \Delta v + v_1$ is exactly v_2.

Errors

GL_INVALID_ENUM is generated if *mode* is not an accepted value.

GL_INVALID_OPERATION is generated if glEvalMesh is executed between the execution of glBegin and the corresponding execution of glEnd.

Associated Gets

glGet with argument GL_MAP1_GRID_DOMAIN
glGet with argument GL_MAP2_GRID_DOMAIN
glGet with argument GL_MAP1_GRID_SEGMENTS
glGet with argument GL_MAP2_GRID_SEGMENTS

See Also

glBegin, glEvalCoord, glEvalPoint, glMap1, glMap2, glMapGrid

glEvalPoint

Generate and evaluate a single point in a mesh

C Specification

```
void glEvalPoint1(GLint i);
void glEvalPoint2(GLint i, GLint j);
```

Parameters

i   Specifies the integer value for grid domain variable i.
j   Specifies the integer value for grid domain variable j (glEvalPoint2 only).

Description

glMapGrid and glEvalMesh are used in tandem to efficiently generate and evaluate a series of evenly spaced map domain values. glEvalPoint can be used to evaluate a single grid point in the same gridspace that is traversed by glEvalMesh. Calling glEvalPoint1 is equivalent to calling glEvalCoord1($i \cdot \Delta u + u_1$);

where

$$\Delta u = \frac{(u_2 - u_1)}{n}$$

and n, u_1, and u_2 are the arguments to the most recent glMapGrid1 command. The one absolute numeric requirement is that if $i = n$, then the value computed from $i \bullet \Delta u + u_1$ is exactly u_2.

In the two-dimensional case, glEvalPoint2, let

$$\Delta u = \frac{(u_2 - u_1)}{n}$$

$$\Delta v = \frac{(v_2 - v_1)}{m}$$

where n, u_1, u_2, m, v_1, and v_2 are the arguments to the most recent glMapGrid2 command. Then the glEvalPoint2 command is equivalent to calling

glEvalCoord2 ($i \cdot \Delta u + u1$, $j \cdot \Delta v + v_1$);

The only absolute numeric requirements are that if $i = n$, then the value computed from $i \cdot \Delta u + u_1$ is exactly u_2, and if $j = m$, then the value computed from $j \cdot \Delta v + v_1$ is exactly v_2.

Associated Gets

glGet with argument GL_MAP1_GRID_DOMAIN
glGet with argument GL_MAP2_GRID_DOMAIN
glGet with argument GL_MAP1_GRID_SEGMENTS
glGet with argument GL_MAP2_GRID_SEGMENTS

See Also

glEvalCoord, glEvalMesh, glMap1, glMap2, glMapGrid

glFeedbackBuffer

Controls feedback mode

C Specification

```
void glFeedbackBuffer(GLsizei   size,
                      GLenum    type,
                      GLfloat * buffer);
```

Parameters

size   Specifies the maximum number of values that can be written into *buffer*.
type   Specifies a symbolic constant that describes the information that will be returned
           for each vertex. GL_2D, GL_3D, GL_3D_COLOR, GL_3D_COLOR_TEXTURE, and
           GL_4D_COLOR_TEXTURE are accepted.
buffer   Returns the feedback data.

Description

The glFeedbackBuffer function controls feedback. Feedback, like selection, is a GL mode. The
mode is selected by calling glRenderMode with GL_FEEDBACK. When the GL is in feedback mode, no
pixels are produced by rasterization. Instead, information about primitives that would have been
rasterized is fed back to the application using the GL.

glFeedbackBuffer has three arguments: *buffer* is a pointer to an array of floating-point values
into which feedback information is placed. *size* indicates the size of the array. *type* is a symbolic
constant describing the information that is fed back for each vertex. glFeedbackBuffer must be
issued before feedback mode is enabled (by calling glRenderMode with argument GL_FEEDBACK).
Setting GL_FEEDBACK without establishing the feedback buffer, or calling glFeedbackBuffer while
the GL is in feedback mode, is an error.

When glRenderMode is called while in feedback mode, it returns the number of entries placed in
the feedback array and resets the feedback array pointer to the base of the feedback buffer. The
returned value never exceeds *size*. If the feedback data required more room than was available in
buffer, glRenderMode returns a negative value. To take the GL out of feedback mode, call
glRenderMode with a parameter value other than GL_FEEDBACK.

While in feedback mode, each primitive, bitmap, or pixel rectangle that would be rasterized
generates a block of values that are copied into the feedback array. If doing so would cause the
number of entries to exceed the maximum, the block is partially written so as to fill the array (if there
is any room left at all), and an overflow flag is set. Each block begins with a code indicating the primitive type, followed by values that describe the primitive's vertices and associated data. Entries are also
written for bitmaps and pixel rectangles. Feedback occurs after polygon culling and glPolygonMode
interpretation of polygons has taken place, so polygons that are culled are not returned in the feedback buffer. It can also occur after polygons with more than three edges are broken up into triangles,
if the GL implementation renders polygons by performing this decomposition.

The glPassThrough command can be used to insert a marker into the feedback buffer.
See glPassThrough.

Following is the grammar for the blocks of values written into the feedback buffer. Each primitive is indicated with a unique identifying value followed by some number of vertices. Polygon entries include an integer value indicating how many vertices follow. A vertex is fed back as some number of floating-point values, as determined by *type*. Colors are fed back as four values in RGBA mode and one value in color index mode.

feedbackList ← feedbackItem feedbackList | feedbackItem

feedbackItem ← point | lineSegment | polygon | bitmap | pixelRectangle | passThru

point ← GL_POINT_TOKEN vertex

lineSegment ← GL_LINE_TOKEN vertex vertex | GL_LINE_RESET_TOKEN vertex vertex

polygon ← GL_POLYGON_TOKEN n polySpec

polySpec ← polySpec vertex | vertex vertex vertex

bitmap ← GL_BITMAP_TOKEN vertex

pixelRectangle ← GL_DRAW_PIXEL_TOKEN vertex | GL_COPY_PIXEL_TOKEN vertex

passThru ← GL_PASS_THROUGH_TOKEN value

vertex ← 2d | 3d | 3dColor | 3dColorTexture | 4dColorTexture

2d ← value value

3d ← value value value

3dColor ← value value value color

3dColorTexture ← value value value color tex

4dColorTexture ← value value value value color tex

color ← rgba | index

rgba ← value value value value

index ← value

tex ← value value value value

value is a floating-point number, and *n* is a floating-point integer giving the number of vertices in the polygon. GL_POINT_TOKEN, GL_LINE_TOKEN, GL_LINE_RESET_TOKEN, GL_POLYGON_TOKEN, GL_BITMAP_TOKEN, GL_DRAW_PIXEL_TOKEN, GL_COPY_PIXEL_TOKEN and GL_PASS_THROUGH_TOKEN are symbolic floating-point constants. GL_LINE_RESET_TOKEN is returned whenever the line stipple pattern is reset. The data returned as a vertex depends on the feedback *type*.

The following table gives the correspondence between *type* and the number of values per vertex. *k* is 1 in color index mode and 4 in RGBA mode.

Type	Coordinates	Color	Texture	Total Number of Values
GL_2D	x, y			2
GL_3D	x, y, z			3
GL_3D_COLOR	x, y, z	k		3 + k
GL_3D_COLOR_TEXTURE	x, y, z,	k	4	7 + k
GL_4D_COLOR_TEXTURE	x, y, z, w	k	4	8 + k

Feedback vertex coordinates are in window coordinates, except *w*, which is in clip coordinates. Feedback colors are lighted, if lighting is enabled. Feedback texture coordinates are generated, if texture coordinate generation is enabled. They are always transformed by the texture matrix.

Notes

glFeedbackBuffer, when used in a display list, is not compiled into the display list but is executed immediately.

glFeedbackBuffer returns only the texture coordinate of texture unit GL_TEXTURE0.

Errors

GL_INVALID_ENUM is generated if *type* is not an accepted value.

GL_INVALID_VALUE is generated if *size* is negative.

GL_INVALID_OPERATION is generated if glFeedbackBuffer is called while the render mode is GL_FEEDBACK, or if glRenderMode is called with argument GL_FEEDBACK before glFeedbackBuffer is called at least once.

GL_INVALID_OPERATION is generated if glFeedbackBuffer is executed between the execution of glBegin and the corresponding execution of glEnd.

Associated Gets

glGet with argument GL_RENDER_MODE

glGet with argument GL_FEEDBACK_BUFFER_POINTER

glGet with argument GL_FEEDBACK_BUFFER_SIZE

glGet with argument GL_FEEDBACK_BUFFER_TYPE

See Also

glBegin, glLineStipple, glPassThrough, glPolygonMode, glRenderMode, glSelectBuffer

glFinish

Block until all GL execution is complete

C Specification

void **glFinish**(*void*);

Description

glFinish does not return until the effects of all previously called GL commands are complete. Such effects include all changes to GL state, all changes to connection state, and all changes to the frame buffer contents.

Notes

glFinish requires a round trip to the server.

Errors

GL_INVALID_OPERATION is generated if glFinish is executed between the execution of glBegin and the corresponding execution of glEnd.

See Also

glFlush

glFlush

Force execution of GL commands in finite time

C Specification

void **glFlush**(*void*);

Description

Different GL implementations buffer commands in several different locations, including network buffers and the graphics accelerator itself. glFlush empties all of these buffers, causing all issued commands to be executed as quickly as they are accepted by the actual rendering engine. Though this execution may not be completed in any particular time period, it does complete in finite time.

Because any GL program might be executed over a network, or on an accelerator that buffers commands, all programs should call glFlush whenever they count on having all of their previously issued commands completed. For example, call glFlush before waiting for user input that depends on the generated image.

Notes

glFlush can return at any time. It does not wait until the execution of all previously issued GL commands is complete.

Errors

GL_INVALID_OPERATION is generated if glFlush is executed between the execution of glBegin and the corresponding execution of glEnd.

See Also

glFinish

glFog

Specify fog parameters

C Specification

```
void glFogf(GLenum pname, GLfloat param);
void glFogi(GLenum pname, GLint param);
```

Parameters

pname   Specifies a single-valued fog parameter. GL_FOG_MODE, GL_FOG_DENSITY, GL_FOG_START, GL_FOG_END, GL_FOG_INDEX, and GL_FOG_COORD_SRC are accepted.

param   Specifies the value that *pname* will be set to.

C Specification

```
void glFogfv(GLenum       pname,
             const GLfloat * params);
void glFogiv(GLenum       pname,
             const GLint *  params);
```

Parameters

pname   Specifies a fog parameter. GL_FOG_MODE, GL_FOG_DENSITY, GL_FOG_START, GL_FOG_END, GL_FOG_INDEX, GL_FOG_COLOR, and GL_FOG_COORD_SRC are accepted.

params   Specifies the value or values to be assigned to *pname*. GL_FOG_COLOR requires an array of four values. All other parameters accept an array containing only a single value.

Description

Fog is initially disabled. While enabled, fog affects rasterized geometry, bitmaps, and pixel blocks, but not buffer clear operations. To enable and disable fog, call glEnable and glDisable with argument GL_FOG.

glFog assigns the value or values in *params* to the fog parameter specified by *pname*. The following values are accepted for *pname*:

GL_FOG_MODE

params is a single integer or floating-point value that specifies the equation to be used to compute the fog blend factor, *f*. Three symbolic constants are accepted: GL_LINEAR, GL_EXP, and GL_EXP2. The equations corresponding to these symbolic constants are defined below. The initial fog mode is GL_EXP.

GL_FOG_DENSITY

params is a single integer or floating-point value that specifies *density*, the fog density used in both exponential fog equations. Only nonnegative densities are accepted. The initial fog density is 1.

GL_FOG_START

params is a single integer or floating-point value that specifies *start*, the near distance used in the linear fog equation. The initial near distance is 0.

GL_FOG_END

params is a single integer or floating-point value that specifies *end*, the far distance used in the linear fog equation. The initial far distance is 1.

GL_FOG_INDEX

params is a single integer or floating-point value that specifies i_f, the fog color index. The initial fog index is 0.

GL_FOG_COLOR

params contains four integer or floating-point values that specify C_f, the fog color. Integer values are mapped linearly such that the most positive representable value maps to 1.0, and the most negative representable value maps to -1.0. Floating-point values are mapped directly. After conversion, all color components are clamped to the range [0,1]. The initial fog color is (0, 0, 0, 0).

GL_FOG_COORD_SRC

params contains either of the following symbolic constants: GL_FOG_COORD or GL_FRAGMENT_DEPTH. GL_FOG_COORD specifies that the current fog coordinate should be used as distance value in the fog color computation. GL_FRAGMENT_DEPTH specifies that the current fragment depth should be used as distance value in the fog computation.

Fog blends a fog color with each rasterized pixel fragment's post-texturing color using a blending factor f. Factor f is computed in one of three ways, depending on the fog mode. Let c be either the distance in eye coordinate from the origin (in the case that the GL_FOG_COORD_SRC is GL_FRAGMENT_DEPTH) or the current fog coordinate (in the case that GL_FOG_COORD_SRC is GL_FOG_COORD). The equation for GL_LINEAR fog is

$$f = \frac{end - c}{end - start}$$

The equation for GL_EXP fog is

$$f = e^{-(density \cdot c)}$$

The equation for GL_EXP2 fog is

$$f = e^{-(density \cdot c)^2}$$

Regardless of the fog mode, f is clamped to the range [0,1] after it is computed. Then, if the GL is in RGBA color mode, the fragment's red, green, and blue colors, represented by C_r, are replaced by

$$C_r" = f \times C_r + (1 - f) \times C_f$$

Fog does not affect a fragment's alpha component.

In color index mode, the fragment's color index i_r is replaced by

$$i_r" = i_r + (1 - f) \times i_f$$

Notes

GL_FOG_COORD_SRC is available only if the GL version is 1.4 or greater.

Errors

GL_INVALID_ENUM is generated if *pname* is not an accepted value, or if *pname* is GL_FOG_MODE and *params* is not an accepted value.

GL_INVALID_VALUE is generated if *pname* is GL_FOG_DENSITY and *params* is negative.

GL_INVALID_OPERATION is generated if glFog is executed between the execution of glBegin and the corresponding execution of glEnd.

Associated Gets

glIsEnabled with argument GL_FOG
glGet with argument GL_FOG_COLOR
glGet with argument GL_FOG_INDEX
glGet with argument GL_FOG_DENSITY
glGet with argument GL_FOG_START
glGet with argument GL_FOG_END
glGet with argument GL_FOG_MODE

See Also

glEnable

glFogCoord

Set the current fog coordinates

C Specification

```
void glFogCoordd(GLfloat coord);
void glFogCoordf(GLfloat coord);
```

Parameters

coord   Specify the fog distance.

C Specification

```
void glFogCoorddv(GLfloat * coord);
void glFogCoordfv(GLfloat * coord);
```

Parameters

coord   Specifies a pointer to an array containing a single value representing the fog distance.

Description

glFogCoord specifies the fog coordinate that is associated with each vertex and the current raster position. The value specified is interpolated and used in computing the fog color (see glFog).

Notes

glFogCoord is available only if the GL version is 1.4 or greater.
The current fog coordinate can be updated at any time. In particular, glFogCoord can be called between a call to glBegin and the corresponding call to glEnd.

Associated Gets

glGet with argument GL_CURRENT_FOG_COORD

See Also

glFog, glFogCoordPointer, glVertex

glFogCoordPointer

Define an array of fog coordinates

C Specification

```
void glFogCoordPointer(GLenum    type,
                       GLsizei   stride,
                       GLvoid *  pointer);
```

Parameters

type   Specifies the data type of each fog coordinate. Symbolic constants GL_FLOAT, or
           GL_DOUBLE are accepted. The initial value is GL_FLOAT.
stride   Specifies the byte offset between consecutive fog coordinates. If *stride* is 0, the array
           elements are understood to be tightly packed. The initial value is 0.
pointer Specifies a pointer to the first coordinate of the first fog coordinate in the array. The
           initial value is 0.

Description

glFogCoordPointer specifies the location and data format of an array of fog coordinates to use when rendering. *type* specifies the data type of each fog coordinate, and *stride* specifies the byte stride from one fog coordinate to the next, allowing vertices and attributes to be packed into a single array or stored in separate arrays.

If a nonzero named buffer object is bound to the GL_ARRAY_BUFFER target (see glBindBuffer) while a fog coordinate array is specified, *pointer* is treated as a byte offset into the buffer object's data store. Also, the buffer object binding (GL_ARRAY_BUFFER_BINDING) is saved as fog coordinate vertex array client-side state (GL_FOG_COORD_ARRAY_BUFFER_BINDING).

When a fog coordinate array is specified, *type*, *stride*, and *pointer* are saved as client-side state, in addition to the current vertex array buffer object binding.

To enable and disable the fog coordinate array, call glEnableClientState and glDisableClientState with the argument GL_FOG_COORD_ARRAY. If enabled, the fog coordinate array is used when glDrawArrays, glMultiDrawArrays, glDrawElements, glMultiDrawElements, glDrawRangeElements, or glArrayElement is called.

Notes

glFogCoordPointer is available only if the GL version is 1.4 or greater.

Fog coordinates are not supported for interleaved vertex array formats (see glInterleavedArrays).

The fog coordinate array is initially disabled and isn't accessed when glArrayElement, glDrawElements, glDrawRangeElements, glDrawArrays, glMultiDrawArrays, or glMultiDrawElements is called.

Execution of glFogCoordPointer is not allowed between the execution of glBegin and the corresponding execution of glEnd, but an error may or may not be generated. If no error is generated, the operation is undefined.

glFogCoordPointer is typically implemented on the client side with no protocol.

Fog coordinate array parameters are client-side state and are therefore not saved or restored by glPushAttrib and glPopAttrib. Use glPushClientAttrib and glPopClientAttrib instead.

Errors

GL_INVALID_ENUM is generated if *type* is not either GL_FLOAT or GL_DOUBLE.
GL_INVALID_VALUE is generated if *stride* is negative.

Associated Gets

glIsEnabled with argument GL_FOG_COORD_ARRAY
glGet with argument GL_FOG_COORD_ARRAY_STRIDE
glGet with argument GL_FOG_COORD_ARRAY_TYPE
glGet with argument GL_FOG_COORD_ARRAY_BUFFER_BINDING
glGet with argument GL_ARRAY_BUFFER_BINDING
glGetPointerv with argument GL_FOG_COORD_ARRAY_POINTER

See Also

glArrayElement, glBindBuffer, glColorPointer, glDisableClientState, glDrawArrays, glDrawElements, glDrawRangeElements, glEdgeFlagPointer, glEnableClientState, glFogCoord, glIndexPointer, glInterleavedArrays, glMultiDrawArrays, glMultiDrawElements, glNormalPointer, glPopClientAttrib, glPushClientAttrib, glSecondaryColorPointer, glTexCoordPointer, glVertexAttribPointer, glVertexPointer

glFrontFace

Define front- and back-facing polygons

C Specification

void **glFrontFace**(GLenum *mode*);

Parameters

mode   Specifies the orientation of front-facing polygons. GL_CW and GL_CCW are accepted. The initial value is GL_CCW.

Description

In a scene composed entirely of opaque closed surfaces, back-facing polygons are never visible. Eliminating these invisible polygons has the obvious benefit of speeding up the rendering of the image. To enable and disable elimination of back-facing polygons, call glEnable and glDisable with argument GL_CULL_FACE.

The projection of a polygon to window coordinates is said to have clockwise winding if an imaginary object following the path from its first vertex, its second vertex, and so on, to its last vertex, and finally back to its first vertex, moves in a clockwise direction about the interior of the polygon. The polygon's winding is said to be counterclockwise if the imaginary object following the same path moves in a counterclockwise direction about the interior of the polygon. glFrontFace specifies whether polygons with clockwise winding in window coordinates, or counterclockwise winding in window coordinates, are taken to be front-facing. Passing GL_CCW to *mode* selects counterclockwise polygons as front-facing; GL_CW selects clockwise polygons as front-facing. By default, counterclockwise polygons are taken to be front-facing.

Errors

GL_INVALID_ENUM is generated if *mode* is not an accepted value.

GL_INVALID_OPERATION is generated if glFrontFace is executed between the execution of glBegin and the corresponding execution of glEnd.

Associated Gets

glGet with argument GL_FRONT_FACE

See Also

glCullFace, glLightModel

glFrustum

Multiply the current matrix by a perspective matrix

C Specification

void **glFrustum**(GLdouble *left*,
                GLdouble *right*,
                GLdouble *bottom*,
                GLdouble *top*,
                GLdouble *nearVal*,
                GLdouble *farVal*);

Parameters

left, *right*	Specify the coordinates for the left and right vertical clipping planes.
bottom, *top*	Specify the coordinates for the bottom and top horizontal clipping planes.
nearVal, *farVal*	Specify the distances to the near and far depth clipping planes. Both distances must be positive.

Description

glFrustum describes a perspective matrix that produces a perspective projection. The current matrix (see glMatrixMode) is multiplied by this matrix and the result replaces the current matrix, as if glMultMatrix were called with the following matrix as its argument:

$$
\begin{bmatrix}
\dfrac{2\,nearVal}{right-left} & 0 & A & 0 \\[2ex]
0 & \dfrac{2\,nearVal}{top-bottom} & B & 0 \\[2ex]
0 & 0 & C & D \\[1ex]
0 & 0 & -1 & 0
\end{bmatrix}
$$

$$A = \frac{right+left}{right-left}$$

$$B = \frac{top+bottom}{top-bottom}$$

$$C = -\frac{farVal+nearVal}{farVal-nearVal}$$

$$D = -\frac{2\,farVal\ nearVal}{farVal-nearVal}$$

Typically, the matrix mode is GL_PROJECTION, and (*left*, *bottom*, *-nearVal*) and (*right*, *top*, *-nearVal*) specify the points on the near clipping plane that are mapped to the lower left and upper-right corners of the window, assuming that the eye is located at (0, 0, 0). *-farVal* specifies the location of the far clipping plane. Both *nearVal* and *farVal* must be positive.

Use glPushMatrix and glPopMatrix to save and restore the current matrix stack.

Notes

Depth buffer precision is affected by the values specified for *nearVal* and *farVal*. The greater the ratio of *farVal* to *nearVal* is, the less effective the depth buffer will be at distinguishing between surfaces that are near each other. If

$$r = \frac{farVal}{nearVal}$$

roughly $log_2(r)$ bits of depth buffer precision are lost. Because r approaches infinity as *nearVal* approaches 0, *nearVal* must never be set to 0.

Errors

GL_INVALID_VALUE is generated if *nearVal* or *farVal* is not positive, or if *left* = *right*, or *bottom* = *top*.

GL_INVALID_OPERATION is generated if glFrustum is executed between the execution of glBegin and the corresponding execution of glEnd.

Associated Gets

glGet with argument GL_MATRIX_MODE
glGet with argument GL_MODELVIEW_MATRIX

glGet with argument GL_PROJECTION_MATRIX
glGet with argument GL_TEXTURE_MATRIX
glGet with argument GL_COLOR_MATRIX

See Also

glOrtho, glMatrixMode, glMultMatrix, glPushMatrix, glViewport

glGenBuffers

Generate buffer object names

C Specification

void **glGenBuffers**(GLsizei   n,
                      GLuint * buffers);

Parameters

n   Specifies the number of buffer object names to be generated.
buffers   Specifies an array in which the generated buffer object names are stored.

Description

glGenBuffers returns n buffer object names in buffers. There is no guarantee that the names form a contiguous set of integers; however, it is guaranteed that none of the returned names was in use immediately before the call to glGenBuffers.

Buffer object names returned by a call to glGenBuffers are not returned by subsequent calls, unless they are first deleted with glDeleteBuffers.

No buffer objects are associated with the returned buffer object names until they are first bound by calling glBindBuffer.

Notes

glGenBuffers is available only if the GL version is 1.5 or greater.

Errors

GL_INVALID_VALUE is generated if n is negative.

GL_INVALID_OPERATION is generated if glGenBuffers is executed between the execution of glBegin and the corresponding execution of glEnd.

Associated Gets

glIsBuffer

See Also

glBindBuffer, glDeleteBuffers, glGet

glGenLists

Generate a contiguous set of empty display lists

C Specification

GLuint **glGenLists**(GLsizei range);

Parameters

range   Specifies the number of contiguous empty display lists to be generated.

Description

glGenLists has one argument, *range*. It returns an integer *n* such that *range* contiguous empty display lists, named *n*, *n* + 1,..., *n* + *range* − 1, are created. If *range* is 0, if there is no group of *range* contiguous names available, or if any error is generated, no display lists are generated, and 0 is returned.

Errors

GL_INVALID_VALUE
is generated if *range* is negative.
GL_INVALID_OPERATION is generated if glGenLists is executed between the execution of glBegin and the corresponding execution of glEnd.

Associated Gets

glIsList

See Also

glCallList, glCallLists, glDeleteLists, glNewList

glGenQueries

Generate query object names

C Specification

void **glGenQueries**(GLsizei *n*, GLuint * *ids*);

Parameters

n   Specifies the number of query object names to be generated.
ids   Specifies an array in which the generated query object names are stored.

Description

glGenQueries returns *n* query object names in *ids*. There is no guarantee that the names form a contiguous set of integers; however, it is guaranteed that none of the returned names was in use immediately before the call to glGenQueries.

Query object names returned by a call to glGenQueries are not returned by subsequent calls, unless they are first deleted with glDeleteQueries.

No query objects are associated with the returned query object names until they are first used by calling glBeginQuery.

Notes

glGenQueries is available only if the GL version is 1.5 or greater.

Errors

GL_INVALID_VALUE is generated if *n* is negative.
GL_INVALID_OPERATION is generated if glGenQueries is executed between the execution of glBeginQuery and the corresponding execution of glEndQuery.
GL_INVALID_OPERATION is generated if glGenQueries is executed between the execution of glBegin and the corresponding execution of glEnd.

Associated Gets

glIsQuery

See Also

glBeginQuery, glDeleteQueries, glEndQuery

glGenTextures

Generate texture names

C Specification

```
void glGenTextures(GLsizei   n,
                   GLuint * textures);
```

Parameters

n   Specifies the number of texture names to be generated.
textures   Specifies an array in which the generated texture names are stored.

Description

glGenTextures returns *n* texture names in *textures*. There is no guarantee that the names form a contiguous set of integers; however, it is guaranteed that none of the returned names was in use immediately before the call to glGenTextures.

The generated textures have no dimensionality; they assume the dimensionality of the texture target to which they are first bound (see glBindTexture).

Texture names returned by a call to glGenTextures are not returned by subsequent calls, unless they are first deleted with glDeleteTextures.

Notes

glGenTextures is available only if the GL version is 1.1 or greater.

Errors

GL_INVALID_VALUE is generated if *n* is negative.

GL_INVALID_OPERATION is generated if glGenTextures is executed between the execution of glBegin and the corresponding execution of glEnd.

Associated Gets

glIsTexture

See Also

glBindTexture, glCopyTexImage1D, glCopyTexImage2D, glDeleteTextures, glGet, glGetTexParameter, glTexImage1D, glTexImage2D, glTexImage3D, glTexParameter

glGet

Return the value or values of a selected parameter

C Specification

```
void glGetBooleanv(GLenum      pname,
                   GLboolean * params);
```

C Specification

```
void glGetDoublev(GLenum      pname,
                  GLdouble * params);
```

C Specification

```
void glGetFloatv(GLenum      pname,
                 GLfloat * params);
```

C Specification

```
void glGetIntegerv(GLenum   pname,
                   GLint * params);
```

Parameters

pname   Specifies the parameter value to be returned. The symbolic constants in the list below are accepted.

params   Returns the value or values of the specified parameter.

Description

These four commands return values for simple state variables in GL. *pname* is a symbolic constant indicating the state variable to be returned, and *params* is a pointer to an array of the indicated type in which to place the returned data.

Type conversion is performed if *params* has a different type than the state variable value being requested. If glGetBooleanv is called, a floating-point (or integer) value is converted to GL_FALSE if and only if it is 0.0 (or 0). Otherwise, it is converted to GL_TRUE. If glGetIntegerv is called, boolean values are returned as GL_TRUE or GL_FALSE, and most floating-point values are rounded to the nearest integer value. Floating-point colors and normals, however, are returned with a linear mapping that maps 1.0 to the most positive representable integer value and -1.0 to the most negative representable integer value. If glGetFloatv or glGetDoublev is called, boolean values are returned as GL_TRUE or GL_FALSE, and integer values are converted to floating-point values.

The following symbolic constants are accepted by *pname*:

GL_ACCUM_ALPHA_BITS

params returns one value, the number of alpha bitplanes in the accumulation buffer.

GL_ACCUM_BLUE_BITS

params returns one value, the number of blue bitplanes in the accumulation buffer.

GL_ACCUM_CLEAR_VALUE

params returns four values: the red, green, blue, and alpha values used to clear the accumulation buffer. Integer values, if requested, are linearly mapped from the internal floating-point representation such that 1.0 returns the most positive representable integer value, and -1.0 returns the most negative representable integer value. The initial value is (0, 0, 0, 0). See glClearAccum.

GL_ACCUM_GREEN_BITS

params returns one value, the number of green bitplanes in the accumulation buffer.

GL_ACCUM_RED_BITS

params returns one value, the number of red bitplanes in the accumulation buffer.

GL_ACTIVE_TEXTURE

params returns a single value indicating the active multitexture unit. The initial value is GL_TEXTURE0. See glActiveTexture.

GL_ALIASED_POINT_SIZE_RANGE

params returns two values, the smallest and largest supported sizes for aliased points.

GL_ALIASED_LINE_WIDTH_RANGE

params returns two values, the smallest and largest supported widths for aliased lines.

GL_ALPHA_BIAS

params returns one value, the alpha bias factor used during pixel transfers. The initial value is 0. See glPixelTransfer.

GL_ALPHA_BITS

params returns one value, the number of alpha bitplanes in each color buffer.

GL_ALPHA_SCALE

params returns one value, the alpha scale factor used during pixel transfers. The initial value is 1. See glPixelTransfer.

GL_ALPHA_TEST

params returns a single boolean value indicating whether alpha testing of fragments is enabled. The initial value is GL_FALSE. See glAlphaFunc.

GL_ALPHA_TEST_FUNC

params returns one value, the symbolic name of the alpha test function. The initial value is GL_ALWAYS. See glAlphaFunc.

`GL_ALPHA_TEST_REF`

params returns one value, the reference value for the alpha test. The initial value is 0. See `glAlphaFunc`. An integer value, if requested, is linearly mapped from the internal floating-point representation such that 1.0 returns the most positive representable integer value, and -1.0 returns the most negative representable integer value.

`GL_ARRAY_BUFFER_BINDING`

params returns a single value, the name of the buffer object currently bound to the target `GL_ARRAY_BUFFER`. If no buffer object is bound to this target, 0 is returned. The initial value is 0. See `glBindBuffer`.

`GL_ATTRIB_STACK_DEPTH`

params returns one value, the depth of the attribute stack. If the stack is empty, 0 is returned. The initial value is 0. See `glPushAttrib`.

`GL_AUTO_NORMAL`

params returns a single boolean value indicating whether 2D map evaluation automatically generates surface normals. The initial value is `GL_FALSE`. See `glMap2`.

`GL_AUX_BUFFERS`

params returns one value, the number of auxiliary color buffers available.

`GL_BLEND`

params returns a single boolean value indicating whether blending is enabled. The initial value is `GL_FALSE`. See `glBlendFunc`.

`GL_BLEND_COLOR`

params returns four values, the red, green, blue, and alpha values which are the components of the blend color. See `glBlendColor`.

`GL_BLEND_DST_ALPHA`

params returns one value, the symbolic constant identifying the alpha destination blend function. The initial value is `GL_ZERO`. See `glBlendFunc` and `glBlendFuncSeparate`.

`GL_BLEND_DST_RGB`

params returns one value, the symbolic constant identifying the RGB destination blend function. The initial value is `GL_ZERO`. See `glBlendFunc` and `glBlendFuncSeparate`.

`GL_BLEND_EQUATION_RGB`

params returns one value, a symbolic constant indicating whether the RGB blend equation is `GL_FUNC_ADD`, `GL_FUNC_SUBTRACT`, `GL_FUNC_REVERSE_SUBTRACT`, `GL_MIN` or `GL_MAX`. See `glBlendEquationSeparate`.

`GL_BLEND_EQUATION_ALPHA`

params returns one value, a symbolic constant indicating whether the Alpha blend equation is `GL_FUNC_ADD`, `GL_FUNC_SUBTRACT`, `GL_FUNC_REVERSE_SUBTRACT`, `GL_MIN` or `GL_MAX`. See `glBlendEquationSeparate`.

`GL_BLEND_SRC_ALPHA`

params returns one value, the symbolic constant identifying the alpha source blend function. The initial value is `GL_ONE`. See `glBlendFunc` and `glBlendFuncSeparate`.

`GL_BLEND_SRC_RGB`

params returns one value, the symbolic constant identifying the RGB source blend function. The initial value is `GL_ONE`. See `glBlendFunc` and `glBlendFuncSeparate`.

`GL_BLUE_BIAS`

params returns one value, the blue bias factor used during pixel transfers. The initial value is 0. See `glPixelTransfer`.

`GL_BLUE_BITS`

params returns one value, the number of blue bitplanes in each color buffer.

`GL_BLUE_SCALE`

params returns one value, the blue scale factor used during pixel transfers. The initial value is 1. See `glPixelTransfer`.

GL_CLIENT_ACTIVE_TEXTURE

params returns a single integer value indicating the current client active multitexture unit. The initial value is GL_TEXTURE0. See glClientActiveTexture.

GL_CLIENT_ATTRIB_STACK_DEPTH

params returns one value indicating the depth of the attribute stack. The initial value is 0. See glPushClientAttrib.

GL_CLIP_PLANE*i*

params returns a single boolean value indicating whether the specified clipping plane is enabled. The initial value is GL_FALSE. See glClipPlane.

GL_COLOR_ARRAY

params returns a single boolean value indicating whether the color array is enabled. The initial value is GL_FALSE. See glColorPointer.

GL_COLOR_ARRAY_BUFFER_BINDING

params returns a single value, the name of the buffer object associated with the color array. This buffer object would have been bound to the target GL_ARRAY_BUFFER at the time of the most recent call to glColorPointer. If no buffer object was bound to this target, 0 is returned. The initial value is 0. See glBindBuffer.

GL_COLOR_ARRAY_SIZE

params returns one value, the number of components per color in the color array. The initial value is 4. See glColorPointer.

GL_COLOR_ARRAY_STRIDE

params returns one value, the byte offset between consecutive colors in the color array. The initial value is 0. See glColorPointer.

GL_COLOR_ARRAY_TYPE

params returns one value, the data type of each component in the color array. The initial value is GL_FLOAT. See glColorPointer.

GL_COLOR_CLEAR_VALUE

params returns four values: the red, green, blue, and alpha values used to clear the color buffers. Integer values, if requested, are linearly mapped from the internal floating-point representation such that 1.0 returns the most positive representable integer value, and -1.0 returns the most negative representable integer value. The initial value is (0, 0, 0, 0). See glClearColor.

GL_COLOR_LOGIC_OP

params returns a single boolean value indicating whether a fragment's RGBA color values are merged into the framebuffer using a logical operation. The initial value is GL_FALSE. See glLogicOp.

GL_COLOR_MATERIAL

params returns a single boolean value indicating whether one or more material parameters are tracking the current color. The initial value is GL_FALSE. See glColorMaterial.

GL_COLOR_MATERIAL_FACE

params returns one value, a symbolic constant indicating which materials have a parameter that is tracking the current color. The initial value is GL_FRONT_AND_BACK. See glColorMaterial.

GL_COLOR_MATERIAL_PARAMETER

params returns one value, a symbolic constant indicating which material parameters are tracking the current color. The initial value is GL_AMBIENT_AND_DIFFUSE. See glColorMaterial.

GL_COLOR_MATRIX

params returns sixteen values: the color matrix on the top of the color matrix stack. Initially this matrix is the identity matrix. See glPushMatrix.

GL_COLOR_MATRIX_STACK_DEPTH

params returns one value, the maximum supported depth of the projection matrix stack. The value must be at least 2. See glPushMatrix.

GL_COLOR_SUM

params returns a single boolean value indicating whether primary and secondary color sum is enabled. See glSecondaryColor.

GL_COLOR_TABLE

params returns a single boolean value indicating whether the color table lookup is enabled. See glColorTable.

GL_COLOR_WRITEMASK

params returns four boolean values: the red, green, blue, and alpha write enables for the color buffers. The initial value is (GL_TRUE, GL_TRUE, GL_TRUE, GL_TRUE). See glColorMask.

GL_COMPRESSED_TEXTURE_FORMATS

params returns a GL_NUM_COMPRESSED_TEXTURE_FORMATS of symbolic constants indicating which compressed texture formats are available. See glCompressedTexImage2D.

GL_CONVOLUTION_1D

params returns a single boolean value indicating whether 1D convolution is enabled. The initial value is GL_FALSE. See glConvolutionFilter1D.

GL_CONVOLUTION_2D

params returns a single boolean value indicating whether 2D convolution is enabled. The initial value is GL_FALSE. See glConvolutionFilter2D.

GL_CULL_FACE

params returns a single boolean value indicating whether polygon culling is enabled. The initial value is GL_FALSE. See glCullFace.

GL_CULL_FACE_MODE

params returns one value, a symbolic constant indicating which polygon faces are to be culled. The initial value is GL_BACK. See glCullFace.

GL_CURRENT_COLOR

params returns four values: the red, green, blue, and alpha values of the current color. Integer values, if requested, are linearly mapped from the internal floating-point representation such that 1.0 returns the most positive representable integer value, and -1.0 returns the most negative representable integer value. The initial value is (1, 1, 1, 1). See glColor.

GL_CURRENT_FOG_COORD

params returns one value, the current fog coordinate. The initial value is 0. See glFogCoord.

GL_CURRENT_INDEX

params returns one value, the current color index. The initial value is 1. See glIndex.

GL_CURRENT_NORMAL

params returns three values: the x, y, and z values of the current normal. Integer values, if requested, are linearly mapped from the internal floating-point representation such that 1.0 returns the most positive representable integer value, and -1.0 returns the most negative representable integer value. The initial value is (0, 0, 1). See glNormal.

GL_CURRENT_PROGRAM

params returns one value, the name of the program object that is currently active, or 0 if no program object is active. See glUseProgram.

GL_CURRENT_RASTER_COLOR

params returns four values: the red, green, blue, and alpha color values of the current raster position. Integer values, if requested, are linearly mapped from the internal floating-point representation such that 1.0 returns the most positive representable integer value, and -1.0 returns the most negative representable integer value. The initial value is (1, 1, 1, 1). See glRasterPos.

GL_CURRENT_RASTER_DISTANCE

params returns one value, the distance from the eye to the current raster position. The initial value is 0. See glRasterPos.

GL_CURRENT_RASTER_INDEX

params returns one value, the color index of the current raster position. The initial value is 1. See glRasterPos.

GL_CURRENT_RASTER_POSITION

params returns four values: the x, y, z, and w components of the current raster position. x, y, and z are in window coordinates, and w is in clip coordinates. The initial value is (0, 0, 0, 1). See glRasterPos.

GL_CURRENT_RASTER_POSITION_VALID

params returns a single boolean value indicating whether the current raster position is valid. The initial value is GL_TRUE. See glRasterPos.

GL_CURRENT_RASTER_SECONDARY_COLOR

params returns four values: the red, green, blue, and alpha secondary color values of the current raster position. Integer values, if requested, are linearly mapped from the internal floating-point representation such that 1.0 returns the most positive representable integer value, and -1.0 returns the most negative representable integer value. The initial value is (1, 1, 1, 1). See glRasterPos.

GL_CURRENT_RASTER_TEXTURE_COORDS

params returns four values: the *s*, *t*, *r*, and *q* texture coordinates of the current raster position. The initial value is (0, 0, 0, 1). See glRasterPos and glMultiTexCoord.

GL_CURRENT_SECONDARY_COLOR

params returns four values: the red, green, blue, and alpha values of the current secondary color. Integer values, if requested, are linearly mapped from the internal floating-point representation such that 1.0 returns the most positive representable integer value, and -1.0 returns the most negative representable integer value. The initial value is (0, 0, 0, 0). See glSecondaryColor.

GL_CURRENT_TEXTURE_COORDS

params returns four values: the *s*, *t*, *r*, and *q* current texture coordinates. The initial value is (0, 0, 0, 1). See glMultiTexCoord.

GL_DEPTH_BIAS

params returns one value, the depth bias factor used during pixel transfers. The initial value is 0. See glPixelTransfer.

GL_DEPTH_BITS

params returns one value, the number of bitplanes in the depth buffer.

GL_DEPTH_CLEAR_VALUE

params returns one value, the value that is used to clear the depth buffer. Integer values, if requested, are linearly mapped from the internal floating-point representation such that 1.0 returns the most positive representable integer value, and -1.0 returns the most negative representable integer value. The initial value is 1. See glClearDepth.

GL_DEPTH_FUNC

params returns one value, the symbolic constant that indicates the depth comparison function. The initial value is GL_LESS. See glDepthFunc.

GL_DEPTH_RANGE

params returns two values: the near and far mapping limits for the depth buffer. Integer values, if requested, are linearly mapped from the internal floating-point representation such that 1.0 returns the most positive representable integer value, and -1.0 returns the most negative representable integer value. The initial value is (0, 1). See glDepthRange.

GL_DEPTH_SCALE

params returns one value, the depth scale factor used during pixel transfers. The initial value is 1. See glPixelTransfer.

GL_DEPTH_TEST

params returns a single boolean value indicating whether depth testing of fragments is enabled. The initial value is GL_FALSE. See glDepthFunc and glDepthRange.

GL_DEPTH_WRITEMASK

params returns a single boolean value indicating if the depth buffer is enabled for writing. The initial value is GL_TRUE. See glDepthMask.

GL_DITHER

params returns a single boolean value indicating whether dithering of fragment colors and indices is enabled. The initial value is GL_TRUE.

GL_DOUBLEBUFFER

params returns a single boolean value indicating whether double buffering is supported.

GL_DRAW_BUFFER

params returns one value, a symbolic constant indicating which buffers are being drawn to. See glDrawBuffer. The initial value is GL_BACK if there are back buffers, otherwise it is GL_FRONT.

GL_DRAW_BUFFER*i*

params returns one value, a symbolic constant indicating which buffers are being drawn to by the corresponding output color. See glDrawBuffers. The initial value of GL_DRAW_BUFFER0 is GL_BACK if there are back buffers, otherwise it is GL_FRONT. The initial values of draw buffers for all other output colors is GL_NONE.

GL_EDGE_FLAG

params returns a single boolean value indicating whether the current edge flag is GL_TRUE or GL_FALSE. The initial value is GL_TRUE. See glEdgeFlag.

GL_EDGE_FLAG_ARRAY

params returns a single boolean value indicating whether the edge flag array is enabled. The initial value is GL_FALSE. See glEdgeFlagPointer.

GL_EDGE_FLAG_ARRAY_BUFFER_BINDING

params returns a single value, the name of the buffer object associated with the edge flag array. This buffer object would have been bound to the target GL_ARRAY_BUFFER at the time of the most recent call to glEdgeFlagPointer. If no buffer object was bound to this target, 0 is returned. The initial value is 0. See glBindBuffer.

GL_EDGE_FLAG_ARRAY_STRIDE

params returns one value, the byte offset between consecutive edge flags in the edge flag array. The initial value is 0. See glEdgeFlagPointer.

GL_ELEMENT_ARRAY_BUFFER_BINDING

params returns a single value, the name of the buffer object currently bound to the target GL_ELEMENT_ARRAY_BUFFER. If no buffer object is bound to this target, 0 is returned. The initial value is 0. See glBindBuffer.

GL_FEEDBACK_BUFFER_SIZE

params returns one value, the size of the feedback buffer. See glFeedbackBuffer.

GL_FEEDBACK_BUFFER_TYPE

params returns one value, the type of the feedback buffer. See glFeedbackBuffer.

GL_FOG

params returns a single boolean value indicating whether fogging is enabled. The initial value is GL_FALSE. See glFog.

GL_FOG_COORD_ARRAY

params returns a single boolean value indicating whether the fog coordinate array is enabled. The initial value is GL_FALSE. See glFogCoordPointer.

GL_FOG_COORD_ARRAY_BUFFER_BINDING

params returns a single value, the name of the buffer object associated with the fog coordinate array. This buffer object would have been bound to the target GL_ARRAY_BUFFER at the time of the most recent call to glFogCoordPointer. If no buffer object was bound to this target, 0 is returned. The initial value is 0. See glBindBuffer.

GL_FOG_COORD_ARRAY_STRIDE

params returns one value, the byte offset between consecutive fog coordinates in the fog coordinate array. The initial value is 0. See glFogCoordPointer.

GL_FOG_COORD_ARRAY_TYPE

params returns one value, the type of the fog coordinate array. The initial value is GL_FLOAT. See glFogCoordPointer.

GL_FOG_COORD_SRC

params returns one value, a symbolic constant indicating the source of the fog coordinate. The initial value is GL_FRAGMENT_DEPTH. See glFog.

GL_FOG_COLOR

params returns four values: the red, green, blue, and alpha components of the fog color. Integer values, if requested, are linearly mapped from the internal floating-point representation such that 1.0 returns the most positive representable integer value, and -1.0 returns the most negative representable integer value. The initial value is (0, 0, 0, 0). See glFog.

GL_FOG_DENSITY

params returns one value, the fog density parameter. The initial value is 1. See glFog.

GL_FOG_END

params returns one value, the end factor for the linear fog equation. The initial value is 1. See glFog.

GL_FOG_HINT

params returns one value, a symbolic constant indicating the mode of the fog hint. The initial value is GL_DONT_CARE. See glHint.

GL_FOG_INDEX

params returns one value, the fog color index. The initial value is 0. See glFog.

GL_FOG_MODE

params returns one value, a symbolic constant indicating which fog equation is selected. The initial value is GL_EXP. See glFog.

GL_FOG_START

params returns one value, the start factor for the linear fog equation. The initial value is 0. See glFog.

GL_FRAGMENT_SHADER_DERIVATIVE_HINT

params returns one value, a symbolic constant indicating the mode of the derivative accuracy hint for fragment shaders. The initial value is GL_DONT_CARE. See glHint.

GL_FRONT_FACE

params returns one value, a symbolic constant indicating whether clockwise or counterclockwise polygon winding is treated as front-facing. The initial value is GL_CCW. See glFrontFace.

GL_GENERATE_MIPMAP_HINT

params returns one value, a symbolic constant indicating the mode of the mipmap generation filtering hint. The initial value is GL_DONT_CARE. See glHint.

GL_GREEN_BIAS

params returns one value, the green bias factor used during pixel transfers. The initial value is 0.

GL_GREEN_BITS

params returns one value, the number of green bitplanes in each color buffer.

GL_GREEN_SCALE

params returns one value, the green scale factor used during pixel transfers. The initial value is 1. See glPixelTransfer.

GL_HISTOGRAM

params returns a single boolean value indicating whether histogram is enabled. The initial value is GL_FALSE. See glHistogram.

GL_INDEX_ARRAY

params returns a single boolean value indicating whether the color index array is enabled. The initial value is GL_FALSE. See glIndexPointer.

GL_INDEX_ARRAY_BUFFER_BINDING

params returns a single value, the name of the buffer object associated with the color index array. This buffer object would have been bound to the target GL_ARRAY_BUFFER at the time of the most recent call to glIndexPointer. If no buffer object was bound to this target, 0 is returned. The initial value is 0. See glBindBuffer.

GL_INDEX_ARRAY_STRIDE

params returns one value, the byte offset between consecutive color indexes in the color index array. The initial value is 0. See glIndexPointer.

GL_INDEX_ARRAY_TYPE

params returns one value, the data type of indexes in the color index array. The initial value is GL_FLOAT. See glIndexPointer.

GL_INDEX_BITS

params returns one value, the number of bitplanes in each color index buffer.

GL_INDEX_CLEAR_VALUE

params returns one value, the color index used to clear the color index buffers. The initial value is 0. See glClearIndex.

GL_INDEX_LOGIC_OP

params returns a single boolean value indicating whether a fragment's index values are merged into the framebuffer using a logical operation. The initial value is GL_FALSE. See glLogicOp.

GL_INDEX_MODE

params returns a single boolean value indicating whether the GL is in color index mode (GL_TRUE) or RGBA mode (GL_FALSE).

GL_INDEX_OFFSET

params returns one value, the offset added to color and stencil indices during pixel transfers. The initial value is 0. See glPixelTransfer.

GL_INDEX_SHIFT

params returns one value, the amount that color and stencil indices are shifted during pixel transfers. The initial value is 0. See glPixelTransfer.

GL_INDEX_WRITEMASK

params returns one value, a mask indicating which bitplanes of each color index buffer can be written. The initial value is all 1's. See glIndexMask.

GL_LIGHT*i*

params returns a single boolean value indicating whether the specified light is enabled. The initial value is GL_FALSE. See glLight and glLightModel.

GL_LIGHTING

params returns a single boolean value indicating whether lighting is enabled. The initial value is GL_FALSE. See glLightModel.

GL_LIGHT_MODEL_AMBIENT

params returns four values: the red, green, blue, and alpha components of the ambient intensity of the entire scene. Integer values, if requested, are linearly mapped from the internal floating-point representation such that 1.0 returns the most positive representable integer value, and -1.0 returns the most negative representable integer value. The initial value is (0.2, 0.2, 0.2, 1.0). See glLightModel.

GL_LIGHT_MODEL_COLOR_CONTROL

params returns single enumerated value indicating whether specular reflection calculations are separated from normal lighting computations. The initial value is GL_SINGLE_COLOR.

GL_LIGHT_MODEL_LOCAL_VIEWER

params returns a single boolean value indicating whether specular reflection calculations treat the viewer as being local to the scene. The initial value is GL_FALSE. See glLightModel.

GL_LIGHT_MODEL_TWO_SIDE

params returns a single boolean value indicating whether separate materials are used to compute lighting for front- and back-facing polygons. The initial value is GL_FALSE. See glLightModel.

GL_LINE_SMOOTH

params returns a single boolean value indicating whether antialiasing of lines is enabled. The initial value is GL_FALSE. See glLineWidth.

GL_LINE_SMOOTH_HINT

params returns one value, a symbolic constant indicating the mode of the line antialiasing hint. The initial value is GL_DONT_CARE. See glHint.

GL_LINE_STIPPLE

params returns a single boolean value indicating whether stippling of lines is enabled. The initial value is GL_FALSE. See glLineStipple.

GL_LINE_STIPPLE_PATTERN

params returns one value, the 16-bit line stipple pattern. The initial value is all 1's.
See glLineStipple.

GL_LINE_STIPPLE_REPEAT

params returns one value, the line stipple repeat factor. The initial value is 1.
See glLineStipple.

GL_LINE_WIDTH

params returns one value, the line width as specified with glLineWidth. The initial value is 1.

GL_LINE_WIDTH_GRANULARITY

params returns one value, the width difference between adjacent supported widths for antialiased
lines. See glLineWidth.

GL_LINE_WIDTH_RANGE

params returns two values: the smallest and largest supported widths for antialiased lines. See
glLineWidth.

GL_LIST_BASE

params returns one value, the base offset added to all names in arrays presented to
glCallLists. The initial value is 0. See glListBase.

GL_LIST_INDEX

params returns one value, the name of the display list currently under construction. 0 is returned
if no display list is currently under construction. The initial value is 0. See glNewList.

GL_LIST_MODE

params returns one value, a symbolic constant indicating the construction mode of the display
list currently under construction. The initial value is 0. See glNewList.

GL_LOGIC_OP_MODE

params returns one value, a symbolic constant indicating the selected logic operation mode. The
initial value is GL_COPY. See glLogicOp.

GL_MAP1_COLOR_4

params returns a single boolean value indicating whether 1D evaluation generates colors. The
initial value is GL_FALSE. See glMap1.

GL_MAP1_GRID_DOMAIN

params returns two values: the endpoints of the 1D map's grid domain. The initial value is (0, 1).
See glMapGrid.

GL_MAP1_GRID_SEGMENTS

params returns one value, the number of partitions in the 1D map's grid domain. The initial
value is 1. See glMapGrid.

GL_MAP1_INDEX

params returns a single boolean value indicating whether 1D evaluation generates color indices.
The initial value is GL_FALSE. See glMap1.

GL_MAP1_NORMAL

params returns a single boolean value indicating whether 1D evaluation generates normals. The
initial value is GL_FALSE. See glMap1.

GL_MAP1_TEXTURE_COORD_1

params returns a single boolean value indicating whether 1D evaluation generates 1D texture
coordinates. The initial value is GL_FALSE. See glMap1.

GL_MAP1_TEXTURE_COORD_2

params returns a single boolean value indicating whether 1D evaluation generates 2D texture
coordinates. The initial value is GL_FALSE. See glMap1.

GL_MAP1_TEXTURE_COORD_3

params returns a single boolean value indicating whether 1D evaluation generates 3D texture
coordinates. The initial value is GL_FALSE. See glMap1.

GL_MAP1_TEXTURE_COORD_4

params returns a single boolean value indicating whether 1D evaluation generates 4D texture
coordinates. The initial value is GL_FALSE. See glMap1.

GL_MAP1_VERTEX_3

params returns a single boolean value indicating whether 1D evaluation generates 3D vertex coordinates. The initial value is GL_FALSE. See glMap1.

GL_MAP1_VERTEX_4

params returns a single boolean value indicating whether 1D evaluation generates 4D vertex coordinates. The initial value is GL_FALSE. See glMap1.

GL_MAP2_COLOR_4

params returns a single boolean value indicating whether 2D evaluation generates colors. The initial value is GL_FALSE. See glMap2.

GL_MAP2_GRID_DOMAIN

params returns four values: the endpoints of the 2D map's *i* and *j* grid domains. The initial value is (0,1; 0,1). See glMapGrid.

GL_MAP2_GRID_SEGMENTS

params returns two values: the number of partitions in the 2D map's *i* and *j* grid domains. The initial value is (1,1). See glMapGrid.

GL_MAP2_INDEX

params returns a single boolean value indicating whether 2D evaluation generates color indices. The initial value is GL_FALSE. See glMap2.

GL_MAP2_NORMAL

params returns a single boolean value indicating whether 2D evaluation generates normals. The initial value is GL_FALSE. See glMap2.

GL_MAP2_TEXTURE_COORD_1

params returns a single boolean value indicating whether 2D evaluation generates 1D texture coordinates. The initial value is GL_FALSE. See glMap2.

GL_MAP2_TEXTURE_COORD_2

params returns a single boolean value indicating whether 2D evaluation generates 2D texture coordinates. The initial value is GL_FALSE. See glMap2.

GL_MAP2_TEXTURE_COORD_3

params returns a single boolean value indicating whether 2D evaluation generates 3D texture coordinates. The initial value is GL_FALSE. See glMap2.

GL_MAP2_TEXTURE_COORD_4

params returns a single boolean value indicating whether 2D evaluation generates 4D texture coordinates. The initial value is GL_FALSE. See glMap2.

GL_MAP2_VERTEX_3

params returns a single boolean value indicating whether 2D evaluation generates 3D vertex coordinates. The initial value is GL_FALSE. See glMap2.

GL_MAP2_VERTEX_4

params returns a single boolean value indicating whether 2D evaluation generates 4D vertex coordinates. The initial value is GL_FALSE. See glMap2.

GL_MAP_COLOR

params returns a single boolean value indicating if colors and color indices are to be replaced by table lookup during pixel transfers. The initial value is GL_FALSE. See glPixelTransfer.

GL_MAP_STENCIL

params returns a single boolean value indicating if stencil indices are to be replaced by table lookup during pixel transfers. The initial value is GL_FALSE. See glPixelTransfer.

GL_MATRIX_MODE

params returns one value, a symbolic constant indicating which matrix stack is currently the target of all matrix operations. The initial value is GL_MODELVIEW. See glMatrixMode.

GL_MAX_3D_TEXTURE_SIZE

params returns one value, a rough estimate of the largest 3D texture that the GL can handle. If the GL version is 1.2 or greater, use GL_PROXY_TEXTURE_3D to determine if a texture is too large. See glTexImage3D.

GL_MAX_CLIENT_ATTRIB_STACK_DEPTH

params returns one value indicating the maximum supported depth of the client attribute stack. See glPushClientAttrib.

GL_MAX_ATTRIB_STACK_DEPTH

params returns one value, the maximum supported depth of the attribute stack. The value must be at least 16. See glPushAttrib.

GL_MAX_CLIP_PLANES

params returns one value, the maximum number of application-defined clipping planes. The value must be at least 6. See glClipPlane.

GL_MAX_COLOR_MATRIX_STACK_DEPTH

params returns one value, the maximum supported depth of the color matrix stack. The value must be at least 2. See glPushMatrix.

GL_MAX_COMBINED_TEXTURE_IMAGE_UNITS

params returns one value, the maximum supported texture image units that can be used to access texture maps from the vertex shader and the fragment processor combined. If both the vertex shader and the fragment processing stage access the same texture image unit, then that counts as using two texture image units against this limit. The value must be at least 2. See glActiveTexture.

GL_MAX_CUBE_MAP_TEXTURE_SIZE

params returns one value. The value gives a rough estimate of the largest cube-map texture that the GL can handle. If the GL version is 1.3 or greater, use GL_PROXY_TEXTURE_CUBE_MAP to determine if a texture is too large. See glTexImage2D.

GL_MAX_DRAW_BUFFERS

params returns one value, the maximum number of simultaneous output colors allowed from a fragment shader using the gl_FragData built-in array. The value must be at least 1. See glDrawBuffers.

GL_MAX_ELEMENTS_INDICES

params returns one value, the recommended maximum number of vertex array indices. See glDrawRangeElements.

GL_MAX_ELEMENTS_VERTICES

params returns one value, the recommended maximum number of vertex array vertices. See glDrawRangeElements.

GL_MAX_EVAL_ORDER

params returns one value, the maximum equation order supported by 1D and 2D evaluators. The value must be at least 8. See glMap1 and glMap2.

GL_MAX_FRAGMENT_UNIFORM_COMPONENTS

params returns one value, the maximum number of individual floating-point, integer, or boolean values that can be held in uniform variable storage for a fragment shader. The value must be at least 64. See glUniform.

GL_MAX_LIGHTS

params returns one value, the maximum number of lights. The value must be at least 8. See glLight.

GL_MAX_LIST_NESTING

params returns one value, the maximum recursion depth allowed during display-list traversal. The value must be at least 64. See glCallList.

GL_MAX_MODELVIEW_STACK_DEPTH

params returns one value, the maximum supported depth of the modelview matrix stack. The value must be at least 32. See glPushMatrix.

GL_MAX_NAME_STACK_DEPTH

params returns one value, the maximum supported depth of the selection name stack. The value must be at least 64. See glPushName.

GL_MAX_PIXEL_MAP_TABLE

params returns one value, the maximum supported size of a glPixelMap lookup table. The value must be at least 32. See glPixelMap.

GL_MAX_PROJECTION_STACK_DEPTH

params returns one value, the maximum supported depth of the projection matrix stack. The value must be at least 2. See glPushMatrix.

GL_MAX_TEXTURE_COORDS

params returns one value, the maximum number of texture coordinate sets available to vertex and fragment shaders. The value must be at least 2. See glActiveTexture and glClientActiveTexture.

GL_MAX_TEXTURE_IMAGE_UNITS

params returns one value, the maximum supported texture image units that can be used to access texture maps from the fragment shader. The value must be at least 2. See glActiveTexture.

GL_MAX_TEXTURE_LOD_BIAS

params returns one value, the maximum, absolute value of the texture level-of-detail bias. The value must be at least 4.

GL_MAX_TEXTURE_SIZE

params returns one value. The value gives a rough estimate of the largest texture that the GL can handle. If the GL version is 1.1 or greater, use GL_PROXY_TEXTURE_1D or GL_PROXY_TEXTURE_2D to determine if a texture is too large. See glTexImage1D and glTexImage2D.

GL_MAX_TEXTURE_STACK_DEPTH

params returns one value, the maximum supported depth of the texture matrix stack. The value must be at least 2. See glPushMatrix.

GL_MAX_TEXTURE_UNITS

params returns a single value indicating the number of conventional texture units supported. Each conventional texture unit includes both a texture coordinate set and a texture image unit. Conventional texture units may be used for fixed-function (non-shader) rendering. The value must be at least 2. Additional texture coordinate sets and texture image units may be accessed from vertex and fragment shaders. See glActiveTexture and glClientActiveTexture.

GL_MAX_VARYING_FLOATS

params returns one value, the maximum number of interpolators available for processing varying variables used by vertex and fragment shaders. This value represents the number of individual floating-point values that can be interpolated; varying variables declared as vectors, matrices, and arrays will all consume multiple interpolators. The value must be at least 32.

GL_MAX_VERTEX_ATTRIBS

params returns one value, the maximum number of 4-component generic vertex attributes accessible to a vertex shader. The value must be at least 16. See glVertexAttrib.

GL_MAX_VERTEX_TEXTURE_IMAGE_UNITS

params returns one value, the maximum supported texture image units that can be used to access texture maps from the vertex shader. The value may be 0. See glActiveTexture.

GL_MAX_VERTEX_UNIFORM_COMPONENTS

params returns one value, the maximum number of individual floating-point, integer, or boolean values that can be held in uniform variable storage for a vertex shader. The value must be at least 512. See glUniform.

GL_MAX_VIEWPORT_DIMS

params returns two values: the maximum supported width and height of the viewport. These must be at least as large as the visible dimensions of the display being rendered to. See glViewport.

GL_MINMAX

params returns a single boolean value indicating whether pixel minmax values are computed. The initial value is GL_FALSE. See glMinmax.

GL_MODELVIEW_MATRIX

params returns sixteen values: the modelview matrix on the top of the modelview matrix stack. Initially this matrix is the identity matrix. See glPushMatrix.

GL_MODELVIEW_STACK_DEPTH

params returns one value, the number of matrices on the modelview matrix stack. The initial value is 1. See glPushMatrix.

GL_NAME_STACK_DEPTH

params returns one value, the number of names on the selection name stack. The initial value is 0. See glPushName.

GL_NORMAL_ARRAY

params returns a single boolean value, indicating whether the normal array is enabled. The initial value is GL_FALSE. See glNormalPointer.

GL_NORMAL_ARRAY_BUFFER_BINDING

params returns a single value, the name of the buffer object associated with the normal array. This buffer object would have been bound to the target GL_ARRAY_BUFFER at the time of the most recent call to glNormalPointer. If no buffer object was bound to this target, 0 is returned. The initial value is 0. See glBindBuffer.

GL_NORMAL_ARRAY_STRIDE

params returns one value, the byte offset between consecutive normals in the normal array. The initial value is 0. See glNormalPointer.

GL_NORMAL_ARRAY_TYPE

params returns one value, the data type of each coordinate in the normal array. The initial value is GL_FLOAT. See glNormalPointer.

GL_NORMALIZE

params returns a single boolean value indicating whether normals are automatically scaled to unit length after they have been transformed to eye coordinates. The initial value is GL_FALSE. See glNormal.

GL_NUM_COMPRESSED_TEXTURE_FORMATS

params returns a single integer value indicating the number of available compressed texture formats. The minimum value is 0. See glCompressedTexImage2D.

GL_PACK_ALIGNMENT

params returns one value, the byte alignment used for writing pixel data to memory. The initial value is 4. See glPixelStore.

GL_PACK_IMAGE_HEIGHT

params returns one value, the image height used for writing pixel data to memory. The initial value is 0. See glPixelStore.

GL_PACK_LSB_FIRST

params returns a single boolean value indicating whether single-bit pixels being written to memory are written first to the least significant bit of each unsigned byte. The initial value is GL_FALSE. See glPixelStore.

GL_PACK_ROW_LENGTH

params returns one value, the row length used for writing pixel data to memory. The initial value is 0. See glPixelStore.

GL_PACK_SKIP_IMAGES

params returns one value, the number of pixel images skipped before the first pixel is written into memory. The initial value is 0. See glPixelStore.

GL_PACK_SKIP_PIXELS

params returns one value, the number of pixel locations skipped before the first pixel is written into memory. The initial value is 0. See glPixelStore.

GL_PACK_SKIP_ROWS

params returns one value, the number of rows of pixel locations skipped before the first pixel is written into memory. The initial value is 0. See glPixelStore.

GL_PACK_SWAP_BYTES

params returns a single boolean value indicating whether the bytes of two-byte and four-byte pixel indices and components are swapped before being written to memory. The initial value is GL_FALSE. See glPixelStore.

GL_PERSPECTIVE_CORRECTION_HINT

params returns one value, a symbolic constant indicating the mode of the perspective correction hint. The initial value is GL_DONT_CARE. See glHint.

GL_PIXEL_MAP_A_TO_A_SIZE

params returns one value, the size of the alpha-to-alpha pixel translation table. The initial value is 1. See glPixelMap.

GL_PIXEL_MAP_B_TO_B_SIZE

params returns one value, the size of the blue-to-blue pixel translation table. The initial value is 1. See glPixelMap.

GL_PIXEL_MAP_G_TO_G_SIZE

params returns one value, the size of the green-to-green pixel translation table. The initial value is 1. See glPixelMap.

GL_PIXEL_MAP_I_TO_A_SIZE

params returns one value, the size of the index-to-alpha pixel translation table. The initial value is 1. See glPixelMap.

GL_PIXEL_MAP_I_TO_B_SIZE

params returns one value, the size of the index-to-blue pixel translation table. The initial value is 1. See glPixelMap.

GL_PIXEL_MAP_I_TO_G_SIZE

params returns one value, the size of the index-to-green pixel translation table. The initial value is 1. See glPixelMap.

GL_PIXEL_MAP_I_TO_I_SIZE

params returns one value, the size of the index-to-index pixel translation table. The initial value is 1. See glPixelMap.

GL_PIXEL_MAP_I_TO_R_SIZE

params returns one value, the size of the index-to-red pixel translation table. The initial value is 1. See glPixelMap.

GL_PIXEL_MAP_R_TO_R_SIZE

params returns one value, the size of the red-to-red pixel translation table. The initial value is 1. See glPixelMap.

GL_PIXEL_MAP_S_TO_S_SIZE

params returns one value, the size of the stencil to stencil pixel translation table. The initial value is 1. See glPixelMap.

GL_PIXEL_PACK_BUFFER_BINDING

params returns a single value, the name of the buffer object currently bound to the target GL_PIXEL_PACK_BUFFER. If no buffer object is bound to this target, 0 is returned. The initial value is 0. See glBindBuffer.

GL_PIXEL_UNPACK_BUFFER_BINDING

params returns a single value, the name of the buffer object currently bound to the target GL_PIXEL_UNPACK_BUFFER. If no buffer object is bound to this target, 0 is returned. The initial value is 0. See glBindBuffer.

GL_POINT_DISTANCE_ATTENUATION

params returns three values, the coefficients for computing the attenuation value for points. See glPointParameter.

GL_POINT_FADE_THRESHOLD_SIZE

params returns one value, the point size threshold for determining the point size. See glPointParameter.

GL_POINT_SIZE

params returns one value, the point size as specified by glPointSize. The initial value is 1.

GL_POINT_SIZE_GRANULARITY

params returns one value, the size difference between adjacent supported sizes for antialiased points. See glPointSize.

GL_POINT_SIZE_MAX

params returns one value, the upper bound for the attenuated point sizes. The initial value is 0.0. See glPointParameter.

GL_POINT_SIZE_MIN

params returns one value, the lower bound for the attenuated point sizes. The initial value is 1.0. See glPointParameter.

GL_POINT_SIZE_RANGE

params returns two values: the smallest and largest supported sizes for antialiased points. The smallest size must be at most 1, and the largest size must be at least 1. See glPointSize.

GL_POINT_SMOOTH

params returns a single boolean value indicating whether antialiasing of points is enabled. The initial value is GL_FALSE. See glPointSize.

GL_POINT_SMOOTH_HINT

params returns one value, a symbolic constant indicating the mode of the point antialiasing hint. The initial value is GL_DONT_CARE. See glHint.

GL_POINT_SPRITE

params returns a single boolean value indicating whether point sprite is enabled. The initial value is GL_FALSE.

GL_POLYGON_MODE

params returns two values: symbolic constants indicating whether front-facing and back-facing polygons are rasterized as points, lines, or filled polygons. The initial value is GL_FILL. See glPolygonMode.

GL_POLYGON_OFFSET_FACTOR

params returns one value, the scaling factor used to determine the variable offset that is added to the depth value of each fragment generated when a polygon is rasterized. The initial value is 0. See glPolygonOffset.

GL_POLYGON_OFFSET_UNITS

params returns one value. This value is multiplied by an implementation-specific value and then added to the depth value of each fragment generated when a polygon is rasterized. The initial value is 0. See glPolygonOffset.

GL_POLYGON_OFFSET_FILL

params returns a single boolean value indicating whether polygon offset is enabled for polygons in fill mode. The initial value is GL_FALSE. See glPolygonOffset.

GL_POLYGON_OFFSET_LINE

params returns a single boolean value indicating whether polygon offset is enabled for polygons in line mode. The initial value is GL_FALSE. See glPolygonOffset.

GL_POLYGON_OFFSET_POINT

params returns a single boolean value indicating whether polygon offset is enabled for polygons in point mode. The initial value is GL_FALSE. See glPolygonOffset.

GL_POLYGON_SMOOTH

params returns a single boolean value indicating whether antialiasing of polygons is enabled. The initial value is GL_FALSE. See glPolygonMode.

GL_POLYGON_SMOOTH_HINT

params returns one value, a symbolic constant indicating the mode of the polygon antialiasing hint. The initial value is GL_DONT_CARE. See glHint.

GL_POLYGON_STIPPLE

params returns a single boolean value indicating whether polygon stippling is enabled. The initial value is GL_FALSE. See glPolygonStipple.

GL_POST_COLOR_MATRIX_COLOR_TABLE

params returns a single boolean value indicating whether post color matrix transformation lookup is enabled. The initial value is GL_FALSE. See glColorTable.

GL_POST_COLOR_MATRIX_RED_BIAS

params returns one value, the red bias factor applied to RGBA fragments after color matrix transformations. The initial value is 0. See glPixelTransfer.

GL_POST_COLOR_MATRIX_GREEN_BIAS

params returns one value, the green bias factor applied to RGBA fragments after color matrix transformations. The initial value is 0. See glPixelTransfer.

GL_POST_COLOR_MATRIX_BLUE_BIAS

params returns one value, the blue bias factor applied to RGBA fragments after color matrix transformations. The initial value is 0. See glPixelTransfer.

GL_POST_COLOR_MATRIX_ALPHA_BIAS

params returns one value, the alpha bias factor applied to RGBA fragments after color matrix transformations. The initial value is 0. See glPixelTransfer.

GL_POST_COLOR_MATRIX_RED_SCALE

params returns one value, the red scale factor applied to RGBA fragments after color matrix transformations. The initial value is 1. See glPixelTransfer.

GL_POST_COLOR_MATRIX_GREEN_SCALE

params returns one value, the green scale factor applied to RGBA fragments after color matrix transformations. The initial value is 1. See glPixelTransfer.

GL_POST_COLOR_MATRIX_BLUE_SCALE

params returns one value, the blue scale factor applied to RGBA fragments after color matrix transformations. The initial value is 1. See glPixelTransfer.

GL_POST_COLOR_MATRIX_ALPHA_SCALE

params returns one value, the alpha scale factor applied to RGBA fragments after color matrix transformations. The initial value is 1. See glPixelTransfer.

GL_POST_CONVOLUTION_COLOR_TABLE

params returns a single boolean value indicating whether post convolution lookup is enabled. The initial value is GL_FALSE. See glColorTable.

GL_POST_CONVOLUTION_RED_BIAS

params returns one value, the red bias factor applied to RGBA fragments after convolution. The initial value is 0. See glPixelTransfer.

GL_POST_CONVOLUTION_GREEN_BIAS

params returns one value, the green bias factor applied to RGBA fragments after convolution. The initial value is 0. See glPixelTransfer.

GL_POST_CONVOLUTION_BLUE_BIAS

params returns one value, the blue bias factor applied to RGBA fragments after convolution. The initial value is 0. See glPixelTransfer.

GL_POST_CONVOLUTION_ALPHA_BIAS

params returns one value, the alpha bias factor applied to RGBA fragments after convolution. The initial value is 0. See glPixelTransfer.

GL_POST_CONVOLUTION_RED_SCALE

params returns one value, the red scale factor applied to RGBA fragments after convolution. The initial value is 1. See glPixelTransfer.

GL_POST_CONVOLUTION_GREEN_SCALE

params returns one value, the green scale factor applied to RGBA fragments after convolution. The initial value is 1. See glPixelTransfer.

GL_POST_CONVOLUTION_BLUE_SCALE

params returns one value, the blue scale factor applied to RGBA fragments after convolution. The initial value is 1. See glPixelTransfer.

GL_POST_CONVOLUTION_ALPHA_SCALE

params returns one value, the alpha scale factor applied to RGBA fragments after convolution. The initial value is 1. See glPixelTransfer.

GL_PROJECTION_MATRIX

params returns sixteen values: the projection matrix on the top of the projection matrix stack. Initially this matrix is the identity matrix. See glPushMatrix.

GL_PROJECTION_STACK_DEPTH

params returns one value, the number of matrices on the projection matrix stack. The initial value is 1. See glPushMatrix.

GL_READ_BUFFER

params returns one value, a symbolic constant indicating which color buffer is selected for reading. The initial value is GL_BACK if there is a back buffer, otherwise it is GL_FRONT. See glReadPixels and glAccum.

GL_RED_BIAS

params returns one value, the red bias factor used during pixel transfers. The initial value is 0.

GL_RED_BITS

params returns one value, the number of red bitplanes in each color buffer.

GL_RED_SCALE

params returns one value, the red scale factor used during pixel transfers. The initial value is 1. See glPixelTransfer.

GL_RENDER_MODE

params returns one value, a symbolic constant indicating whether the GL is in render, select, or feedback mode. The initial value is GL_RENDER. See glRenderMode.

GL_RESCALE_NORMAL

params returns single boolean value indicating whether normal rescaling is enabled. See glEnable.

GL_RGBA_MODE

params returns a single boolean value indicating whether the GL is in RGBA mode (true) or color index mode (false). See glColor.

GL_SAMPLE_BUFFERS

params returns a single integer value indicating the number of sample buffers associated with the framebuffer. See glSampleCoverage.

GL_SAMPLE_COVERAGE_VALUE

params returns a single positive floating-point value indicating the current sample coverage value. See glSampleCoverage.

GL_SAMPLE_COVERAGE_INVERT

params returns a single boolean value indicating if the temporary coverage value should be inverted. See glSampleCoverage.

GL_SAMPLES

params returns a single integer value indicating the coverage mask size. See glSampleCoverage.

GL_SCISSOR_BOX

params returns four values: the *x* and *y* window coordinates of the scissor box, followed by its width and height. Initially the *x* and *y* window coordinates are both 0 and the width and height are set to the size of the window. See glScissor.

GL_SCISSOR_TEST

params returns a single boolean value indicating whether scissoring is enabled. The initial value is GL_FALSE. See glScissor.

GL_SECONDARY_COLOR_ARRAY

params returns a single boolean value indicating whether the secondary color array is enabled. The initial value is GL_FALSE. See glSecondaryColorPointer.

GL_SECONDARY_COLOR_ARRAY_BUFFER_BINDING

params returns a single value, the name of the buffer object associated with the secondary color array. This buffer object would have been bound to the target GL_ARRAY_BUFFER at the time of the most recent call to glSecondaryColorPointer. If no buffer object was bound to this target, 0 is returned. The initial value is 0. See glBindBuffer.

GL_SECONDARY_COLOR_ARRAY_SIZE

params returns one value, the number of components per color in the secondary color array. The initial value is 3. See glSecondaryColorPointer.

GL_SECONDARY_COLOR_ARRAY_STRIDE

params returns one value, the byte offset between consecutive colors in the secondary color array. The initial value is 0. See glSecondaryColorPointer.

GL_SECONDARY_COLOR_ARRAY_TYPE

params returns one value, the data type of each component in the secondary color array. The initial value is GL_FLOAT. See glSecondaryColorPointer.

GL_SELECTION_BUFFER_SIZE

params return one value, the size of the selection buffer. See glSelectBuffer.

GL_SEPARABLE_2D

params returns a single boolean value indicating whether 2D separable convolution is enabled. The initial value is GL_FALSE. See glSeparableFilter2D.

GL_SHADE_MODEL

params returns one value, a symbolic constant indicating whether the shading mode is flat or smooth. The initial value is GL_SMOOTH. See glShadeModel.

GL_SMOOTH_LINE_WIDTH_RANGE

params returns two values, the smallest and largest supported widths for antialiased lines. See glLineWidth.

GL_SMOOTH_LINE_WIDTH_GRANULARITY

params returns one value, the granularity of widths for antialiased lines. See glLineWidth.

GL_SMOOTH_POINT_SIZE_RANGE

params returns two values, the smallest and largest supported widths for antialiased points. See glPointSize.

GL_SMOOTH_POINT_SIZE_GRANULARITY

params returns one value, the granularity of sizes for antialiased points. See glPointSize.

GL_STENCIL_BACK_FAIL

params returns one value, a symbolic constant indicating what action is taken for back-facing polygons when the stencil test fails. The initial value is GL_KEEP. See glStencilOpSeparate.

GL_STENCIL_BACK_FUNC

params returns one value, a symbolic constant indicating what function is used for back-facing polygons to compare the stencil reference value with the stencil buffer value. The initial value is GL_ALWAYS. See glStencilFuncSeparate.

GL_STENCIL_BACK_PASS_DEPTH_FAIL

params returns one value, a symbolic constant indicating what action is taken for back-facing polygons when the stencil test passes, but the depth test fails. The initial value is GL_KEEP. See glStencilOpSeparate.

GL_STENCIL_BACK_PASS_DEPTH_PASS

params returns one value, a symbolic constant indicating what action is taken for back-facing polygons when the stencil test passes and the depth test passes. The initial value is GL_KEEP. See glStencilOpSeparate.

GL_STENCIL_BACK_REF

params returns one value, the reference value that is compared with the contents of the stencil buffer for back-facing polygons. The initial value is 0. See glStencilFuncSeparate.

GL_STENCIL_BACK_VALUE_MASK

params returns one value, the mask that is used for back-facing polygons to mask both the stencil reference value and the stencil buffer value before they are compared. The initial value is all 1's. See glStencilFuncSeparate.

GL_STENCIL_BACK_WRITEMASK

params returns one value, the mask that controls writing of the stencil bitplanes for back-facing polygons. The initial value is all 1's. See glStencilMaskSeparate.

GL_STENCIL_BITS

params returns one value, the number of bitplanes in the stencil buffer.

GL_STENCIL_CLEAR_VALUE

params returns one value, the index to which the stencil bitplanes are cleared. The initial value is 0. See glClearStencil.

GL_STENCIL_FAIL

params returns one value, a symbolic constant indicating what action is taken when the stencil test fails. The initial value is GL_KEEP. See glStencilOp. If the GL version is 2.0 or greater, this stencil state only affects non-polygons and front-facing polygons. Back-facing polygons use separate stencil state. See glStencilOpSeparate.

GL_STENCIL_FUNC

params returns one value, a symbolic constant indicating what function is used to compare the stencil reference value with the stencil buffer value. The initial value is GL_ALWAYS. See glStencilFunc. If the GL version is 2.0 or greater, this stencil state only affects non-polygons and front-facing polygons. Back-facing polygons use separate stencil state. See glStencilFuncSeparate.

GL_STENCIL_PASS_DEPTH_FAIL

params returns one value, a symbolic constant indicating what action is taken when the stencil test passes, but the depth test fails. The initial value is GL_KEEP. See glStencilOp. If the GL version is 2.0 or greater, this stencil state only affects non-polygons and front-facing polygons. Back-facing polygons use separate stencil state. See glStencilOpSeparate.

GL_STENCIL_PASS_DEPTH_PASS

params returns one value, a symbolic constant indicating what action is taken when the stencil test passes and the depth test passes. The initial value is GL_KEEP. See glStencilOp. If the GL version is 2.0 or greater, this stencil state only affects non-polygons and front-facing polygons. Back-facing polygons use separate stencil state. See glStencilOpSeparate.

GL_STENCIL_REF

params returns one value, the reference value that is compared with the contents of the stencil buffer. The initial value is 0. See glStencilFunc. If the GL version is 2.0 or greater, this stencil state only affects non-polygons and front-facing polygons. Back-facing polygons use separate stencil state. See glStencilFuncSeparate.

GL_STENCIL_TEST

params returns a single boolean value indicating whether stencil testing of fragments is enabled. The initial value is GL_FALSE. See glStencilFunc and glStencilOp.

GL_STENCIL_VALUE_MASK

params returns one value, the mask that is used to mask both the stencil reference value and the stencil buffer value before they are compared. The initial value is all 1's. See glStencilFunc. If the GL version is 2.0 or greater, this stencil state only affects non-polygons and front-facing polygons. Back-facing polygons use separate stencil state. See glStencilFuncSeparate.

GL_STENCIL_WRITEMASK

params returns one value, the mask that controls writing of the stencil bitplanes. The initial value is all 1's. See glStencilMask. If the GL version is 2.0 or greater, this stencil state only affects non-polygons and front-facing polygons. Back-facing polygons use separate stencil state. See glStencilMaskSeparate.

GL_STEREO

params returns a single boolean value indicating whether stereo buffers (left and right) are supported.

GL_SUBPIXEL_BITS

params returns one value, an estimate of the number of bits of subpixel resolution that are used to position rasterized geometry in window coordinates. The initial value is 4.

GL_TEXTURE_1D

params returns a single boolean value indicating whether 1D texture mapping is enabled. The initial value is GL_FALSE. See glTexImage1D.

GL_TEXTURE_BINDING_1D

params returns a single value, the name of the texture currently bound to the target GL_TEXTURE_1D. The initial value is 0. See glBindTexture.

GL_TEXTURE_2D

params returns a single boolean value indicating whether 2D texture mapping is enabled. The initial value is GL_FALSE. See glTexImage2D.

GL_TEXTURE_BINDING_2D

params returns a single value, the name of the texture currently bound to the target GL_TEXTURE_2D. The initial value is 0. See glBindTexture.

GL_TEXTURE_3D

params returns a single boolean value indicating whether 3D texture mapping is enabled. The initial value is GL_FALSE. See glTexImage3D.

GL_TEXTURE_BINDING_3D

params returns a single value, the name of the texture currently bound to the target GL_TEXTURE_3D. The initial value is 0. See glBindTexture.

GL_TEXTURE_BINDING_CUBE_MAP

params returns a single value, the name of the texture currently bound to the target GL_TEXTURE_CUBE_MAP. The initial value is 0. See glBindTexture.

GL_TEXTURE_COMPRESSION_HINT

params returns a single value indicating the mode of the texture compression hint. The initial value is GL_DONT_CARE.

GL_TEXTURE_COORD_ARRAY

params returns a single boolean value indicating whether the texture coordinate array is enabled. The initial value is GL_FALSE. See glTexCoordPointer.

GL_TEXTURE_COORD_ARRAY_BUFFER_BINDING

params returns a single value, the name of the buffer object associated with the texture coordinate array. This buffer object would have been bound to the target GL_ARRAY_BUFFER at the time of the most recent call to glTexCoordPointer. If no buffer object was bound to this target, 0 is returned. The initial value is 0. See glBindBuffer.

GL_TEXTURE_COORD_ARRAY_SIZE

params returns one value, the number of coordinates per element in the texture coordinate array. The initial value is 4. See glTexCoordPointer.

GL_TEXTURE_COORD_ARRAY_STRIDE

params returns one value, the byte offset between consecutive elements in the texture coordinate array. The initial value is 0. See glTexCoordPointer.

GL_TEXTURE_COORD_ARRAY_TYPE

params returns one value, the data type of the coordinates in the texture coordinate array. The initial value is GL_FLOAT. See glTexCoordPointer.

GL_TEXTURE_CUBE_MAP

params returns a single boolean value indicating whether cube-mapped texture coordinate generation is enabled. The initial value is GL_FALSE. See glTexGen.

GL_TEXTURE_GEN_Q

params returns a single boolean value indicating whether automatic generation of the q texture coordinate is enabled. The initial value is GL_FALSE. See glTexGen.

GL_TEXTURE_GEN_R

params returns a single boolean value indicating whether automatic generation of the r texture coordinate is enabled. The initial value is GL_FALSE. See glTexGen.

GL_TEXTURE_GEN_S

params returns a single boolean value indicating whether automatic generation of the S texture coordinate is enabled. The initial value is GL_FALSE. See glTexGen.

GL_TEXTURE_GEN_T

params returns a single boolean value indicating whether automatic generation of the T texture coordinate is enabled. The initial value is GL_FALSE. See glTexGen.

GL_TEXTURE_MATRIX

params returns sixteen values: the texture matrix on the top of the texture matrix stack. Initially this matrix is the identity matrix. See glPushMatrix.

GL_TEXTURE_STACK_DEPTH

params returns one value, the number of matrices on the texture matrix stack. The initial value is 1. See glPushMatrix.

GL_TRANSPOSE_COLOR_MATRIX

params returns 16 values, the elements of the color matrix in row-major order. See glLoadTransposeMatrix.

GL_TRANSPOSE_MODELVIEW_MATRIX

params returns 16 values, the elements of the modelview matrix in row-major order. See glLoadTransposeMatrix.

GL_TRANSPOSE_PROJECTION_MATRIX

params returns 16 values, the elements of the projection matrix in row-major order. See glLoadTransposeMatrix.

GL_TRANSPOSE_TEXTURE_MATRIX

params returns 16 values, the elements of the texture matrix in row-major order. See glLoadTransposeMatrix.

GL_UNPACK_ALIGNMENT

params returns one value, the byte alignment used for reading pixel data from memory. The initial value is 4. See glPixelStore.

GL_UNPACK_IMAGE_HEIGHT

params returns one value, the image height used for reading pixel data from memory. The initial is 0. See glPixelStore.

GL_UNPACK_LSB_FIRST

params returns a single boolean value indicating whether single-bit pixels being read from memory are read first from the least significant bit of each unsigned byte. The initial value is GL_FALSE. See glPixelStore.

GL_UNPACK_ROW_LENGTH

params returns one value, the row length used for reading pixel data from memory. The initial value is 0. See glPixelStore.

GL_UNPACK_SKIP_IMAGES

params returns one value, the number of pixel images skipped before the first pixel is read from memory. The initial value is 0. See glPixelStore.

GL_UNPACK_SKIP_PIXELS

params returns one value, the number of pixel locations skipped before the first pixel is read from memory. The initial value is 0. See glPixelStore.

GL_UNPACK_SKIP_ROWS

params returns one value, the number of rows of pixel locations skipped before the first pixel is read from memory. The initial value is 0. See glPixelStore.

GL_UNPACK_SWAP_BYTES

params returns a single boolean value indicating whether the bytes of two-byte and four-byte pixel indices and components are swapped after being read from memory. The initial value is GL_FALSE. See glPixelStore.

GL_VERTEX_ARRAY

params returns a single boolean value indicating whether the vertex array is enabled. The initial value is GL_FALSE. See glVertexPointer.

GL_VERTEX_ARRAY_BUFFER_BINDING

params returns a single value, the name of the buffer object associated with the vertex array. This buffer object would have been bound to the target GL_ARRAY_BUFFER at the time of the most recent call to glVertexPointer. If no buffer object was bound to this target, 0 is returned. The initial value is 0. See glBindBuffer.

GL_VERTEX_ARRAY_SIZE

params returns one value, the number of coordinates per vertex in the vertex array. The initial value is 4. See glVertexPointer.

GL_VERTEX_ARRAY_STRIDE

params returns one value, the byte offset between consecutive vertices in the vertex array. The initial value is 0. See glVertexPointer.

GL_VERTEX_ARRAY_TYPE

params returns one value, the data type of each coordinate in the vertex array. The initial value is GL_FLOAT. See glVertexPointer.

GL_VERTEX_PROGRAM_POINT_SIZE

params returns a single boolean value indicating whether vertex program point size mode is enabled. If enabled, and a vertex shader is active, then the point size is taken from the shader built-in gl_PointSize. If disabled, and a vertex shader is active, then the point size is taken from the point state as specified by glPointSize. The initial value is GL_FALSE.

GL_VERTEX_PROGRAM_TWO_SIDE

params returns a single boolean value indicating whether vertex program two-sided color mode is enabled. If enabled, and a vertex shader is active, then the GL chooses the back color output for back-facing polygons, and the front color output for non-polygons and front-facing polygons. If disabled, and a vertex shader is active, then the front color output is always selected. The initial value is GL_FALSE.

GL_VIEWPORT

params returns four values: the *x* and *y* window coordinates of the viewport, followed by its width and height. Initially the *x* and *y* window coordinates are both set to 0, and the width and height are set to the width and height of the window into which the GL will do its rendering. See glViewport.

GL_ZOOM_X

params returns one value, the *x* pixel zoom factor. The initial value is 1. See glPixelZoom.

GL_ZOOM_Y

params returns one value, the *y* pixel zoom factor. The initial value is 1. See glPixelZoom.

Many of the boolean parameters can also be queried more easily using glIsEnabled.

Notes

GL_COLOR_LOGIC_OP, GL_COLOR_ARRAY, GL_COLOR_ARRAY_SIZE, GL_COLOR_ARRAY_STRIDE, GL_COLOR_ARRAY_TYPE, GL_EDGE_FLAG_ARRAY, GL_EDGE_FLAG_ARRAY_STRIDE, GL_INDEX_ARRAY, GL_INDEX_ARRAY_STRIDE, GL_INDEX_ARRAY_TYPE, GL_INDEX_LOGIC_OP, GL_NORMAL_ARRAY, GL_NORMAL_ARRAY_STRIDE, GL_NORMAL_ARRAY_TYPE, GL_POLYGON_OFFSET_UNITS, GL_POLYGON_OFFSET_FACTOR, GL_POLYGON_OFFSET_FILL, GL_POLYGON_OFFSET_LINE, GL_POLYGON_OFFSET_POINT, GL_TEXTURE_COORD_ARRAY, GL_TEXTURE_COORD_ARRAY_SIZE, GL_TEXTURE_COORD_ARRAY_STRIDE, GL_TEXTURE_COORD_ARRAY_TYPE, GL_VERTEX_ARRAY, GL_VERTEX_ARRAY_SIZE, GL_VERTEX_ARRAY_STRIDE, and GL_VERTEX_ARRAY_TYPE are available only if the GL version is 1.1 or greater.

GL_ALIASED_POINT_SIZE_RANGE, GL_FEEDBACK_BUFFER_SIZE, GL_FEEDBACK_BUFFER_TYPE, GL_LIGHT_MODEL_AMBIENT, GL_LIGHT_MODEL_COLOR_CONTROL, GL_MAX_3D_TEXTURE_SIZE, GL_MAX_ELEMENTS_INDICES, GL_MAX_ELEMENTS_VERTICES, GL_PACK_IMAGE_HEIGHT, GL_PACK_SKIP_IMAGES, GL_RESCALE_NORMAL, GL_SELECTION_BUFFER_SIZE, GL_SMOOTH_LINE_WIDTH_GRANULARITY, GL_SMOOTH_LINE_WIDTH_RANGE, GL_SMOOTH_POINT_SIZE_GRANULARITY, GL_SMOOTH_POINT_SIZE_RANGE, GL_TEXTURE_3D, GL_TEXTURE_BINDING_3D, GL_UNPACK_IMAGE_HEIGHT, and GL_UNPACK_SKIP_IMAGES are available only if the GL version is 1.2 or greater.

GL_COMPRESSED_TEXTURE_FORMATS, GL_NUM_COMPRESSED_TEXTURE_FORMATS, GL_TEXTURE_BINDING_CUBE_MAP, and GL_TEXTURE_COMPRESSION_HINT are available only if the GL version is 1.3 or greater.

GL_BLEND_DST_ALPHA, GL_BLEND_DST_RGB, GL_BLEND_SRC_ALPHA, GL_BLEND_SRC_RGB, GL_CURRENT_FOG_COORD, GL_CURRENT_SECONDARY_COLOR, GL_FOG_COORD_ARRAY_STRIDE, GL_FOG_COORD_ARRAY_TYPE, GL_FOG_COORD_SRC, GL_MAX_TEXTURE_LOD_BIAS,

GL_POINT_SIZE_MIN, GL_POINT_SIZE_MAX, GL_POINT_FADE_THRESHOLD_SIZE, GL_POINT_DISTANCE_ATTENUATION, GL_SECONDARY_COLOR_ARRAY_SIZE, GL_SECONDARY_COLOR_ARRAY_STRIDE, and GL_SECONDARY_COLOR_ARRAY_TYPE are available only if the GL version is 1.4 or greater.

GL_ARRAY_BUFFER_BINDING, GL_COLOR_ARRAY_BUFFER_BINDING, GL_EDGE_FLAG_ARRAY_BUFFER_BINDING, GL_ELEMENT_ARRAY_BUFFER_BINDING, GL_FOG_COORD_ARRAY_BUFFER_BINDING, GL_INDEX_ARRAY_BUFFER_BINDING, GL_NORMAL_ARRAY_BUFFER_BINDING, GL_SECONDARY_COLOR_ARRAY_BUFFER_BINDING, GL_TEXTURE_COORD_ARRAY_BUFFER_BINDING, and GL_VERTEX_ARRAY_BUFFER_BINDING are available only if the GL version is 1.5 or greater.

GL_BLEND_EQUATION_ALPHA, GL_BLEND_EQUATION_RGB, GL_DRAW_BUFFER*i*, GL_FRAGMENT_SHADER_DERIVATIVE_HINT, GL_MAX_COMBINED_TEXTURE_IMAGE_UNITS, GL_MAX_DRAW_BUFFERS, GL_MAX_FRAGMENT_UNIFORM_COMPONENTS, GL_MAX_TEXTURE_COORDS, GL_MAX_TEXTURE_IMAGE_UNITS, GL_MAX_VARYING_FLOATS, GL_MAX_VERTEX_ATTRIBS, GL_MAX_VERTEX_TEXTURE_IMAGE_UNITS, GL_MAX_VERTEX_UNIFORM_COMPONENTS, GL_POINT_SPRITE, GL_STENCIL_BACK_FAIL, GL_STENCIL_BACK_FUNC, GL_STENCIL_BACK_PASS_DEPTH_FAIL, GL_STENCIL_BACK_PASS_DEPTH_PASS, GL_STENCIL_BACK_REF, GL_STENCIL_BACK_VALUE_MASK, GL_STENCIL_BACK_WRITEMASK, GL_VERTEX_PROGRAM_POINT_SIZE, and GL_VERTEX_PROGRAM_TWO_SIDE are available only if the GL version is 2.0 or greater.

GL_CURRENT_RASTER_SECONDARY_COLOR, GL_PIXEL_PACK_BUFFER_BINDING and GL_PIXEL_UNPACK_BUFFER_BINDING are available only if the GL version is 2.1 or greater.

GL_LINE_WIDTH_GRANULARITY was deprecated in GL version 1.2. Its functionality was replaced by GL_SMOOTH_LINE_WIDTH_GRANULARITY.

GL_LINE_WIDTH_RANGE was deprecated in GL version 1.2. Its functionality was replaced by GL_SMOOTH_LINE_WIDTH_RANGE.

GL_POINT_SIZE_GRANULARITY was deprecated in GL version 1.2. Its functionality was replaced by GL_SMOOTH_POINT_SIZE_GRANULARITY.

GL_POINT_SIZE_RANGE was deprecated in GL version 1.2. Its functionality was replaced by GL_SMOOTH_POINT_SIZE_RANGE.

GL_BLEND_EQUATION was deprecated in GL version 2.0. Its functionality was replaced by GL_BLEND_EQUATION_RGB and GL_BLEND_EQUATION_ALPHA.

GL_COLOR_MATRIX, GL_COLOR_MATRIX_STACK_DEPTH, GL_COLOR_TABLE, GL_CONVOLUTION_1D, GL_CONVOLUTION_2D, GL_HISTOGRAM, GL_MAX_COLOR_MATRIX_STACK_DEPTH, GL_MINMAX, GL_POST_COLOR_MATRIX_COLOR_TABLE, GL_POST_COLOR_MATRIX_RED_BIAS, GL_POST_COLOR_MATRIX_GREEN_BIAS, GL_POST_COLOR_MATRIX_BLUE_BIAS, GL_POST_COLOR_MATRIX_ALPHA_BIAS, GL_POST_COLOR_MATRIX_RED_SCALE, GL_POST_COLOR_MATRIX_GREEN_SCALE, GL_POST_COLOR_MATRIX_BLUE_SCALE, GL_POST_COLOR_MATRIX_ALPHA_SCALE, GL_POST_CONVOLUTION_COLOR_TABLE, GL_POST_CONVOLUTION_RED_BIAS, GL_POST_CONVOLUTION_GREEN_BIAS, GL_POST_CONVOLUTION_BLUE_BIAS, GL_POST_CONVOLUTION_ALPHA_BIAS, GL_POST_CONVOLUTION_RED_SCALE, GL_POST_CONVOLUTION_GREEN_SCALE, GL_POST_CONVOLUTION_BLUE_SCALE, GL_POST_CONVOLUTION_ALPHA_SCALE, and GL_SEPARABLE_2D are available only if ARB_imaging is returned from glGet when called with the argument GL_EXTENSIONS.

When the ARB_multitexture extension is supported, or the GL version is 1.3 or greater, the following parameters return the associated value for the active texture unit: GL_CURRENT_RASTER_TEXTURE_COORDS, GL_TEXTURE_1D, GL_TEXTURE_BINDING_1D, GL_TEXTURE_2D, GL_TEXTURE_BINDING_2D, GL_TEXTURE_3D, GL_TEXTURE_BINDING_3D, GL_TEXTURE_GEN_S, GL_TEXTURE_GEN_T, GL_TEXTURE_GEN_R, GL_TEXTURE_GEN_Q, GL_TEXTURE_MATRIX, and GL_TEXTURE_STACK_DEPTH. Likewise, the following parameters return the associated value for the active client texture unit: GL_TEXTURE_COORD_ARRAY,

GL_TEXTURE_COORD_ARRAY_BUFFER_BINDING, GL_TEXTURE_COORD_ARRAY_SIZE, GL_TEXTURE_COORD_ARRAY_STRIDE, GL_TEXTURE_COORD_ARRAY_TYPE.

Errors

GL_INVALID_ENUM is generated if *pname* is not an accepted value.

GL_INVALID_OPERATION is generated if glGet is executed between the execution of glBegin and the corresponding execution of glEnd.

See Also

glGetActiveAttrib, glGetActiveUniform, glGetAttachedShaders, glGetAttribLocation, glGetBufferParameteriv, glGetBufferPointerv, glGetBufferSubData, glGetClipPlane, glGetColorTable, glGetColorTableParameter, glGetCompressedTexImage, glGetConvolutionFilter, glGetConvolutionParameter, glGetError, glGetHistogram, glGetHistogramParameter, glGetLight, glGetMap, glGetMaterial, glGetMinmax, glGetMinmaxParameter, glGetPixelMap, glGetPointerv, glGetPolygonStipple, glGetProgram, glGetProgramInfoLog, glGetQueryiv, glGetQueryObject, glGetSeparableFilter, glGetShader, glGetShaderInfoLog, glGetShaderSource, glGetString, glGetTexEnv, glGetTexGen, glGetTexImage, glGetTexLevelParameter, glGetTexParameter, glGetUniform, glGetUniformLocation, glGetVertexAttrib, glGetVertexAttribPointerv, glIsEnabled

glGetActiveAttrib

Return information about an active attribute variable for the specified program object

C Specification

```
void glGetActiveAttrib(GLuint      program,
                       GLuint      index,
                       GLsizei     bufSize,
                       GLsizei *   length,
                       GLint *     size,
                       GLenum *    type,
                       GLchar *    name);
```

Parameters

program   Specifies the program object to be queried.

index   Specifies the index of the attribute variable to be queried.

bufSize   Specifies the maximum number of characters OpenGL is allowed to write in the character buffer indicated by *name*.

length   Returns the number of characters actually written by OpenGL in the string indicated by *name* (excluding the null terminator) if a value other than NULL is passed.

size   Returns the size of the attribute variable.

type   Returns the data type of the attribute variable.

name   Returns a null terminated string containing the name of the attribute variable.

Description

glGetActiveAttrib returns information about an active attribute variable in the program object specified by *program*. The number of active attributes can be obtained by calling glGetProgram with the value GL_ACTIVE_ATTRIBUTES. A value of 0 for *index* selects the first active attribute variable. Permissible values for *index* range from 0 to the number of active attribute variables minus 1.

A vertex shader may use either built-in attribute variables, user-defined attribute variables, or both. Built-in attribute variables have a prefix of "gl_" and reference conventional OpenGL vertex attribtes (e.g., `gl_Vertex`, `gl_Normal`, etc., see the OpenGL Shading Language specification for a complete list.) User-defined attribute variables have arbitrary names and obtain their values through numbered generic vertex attributes. An attribute variable (either built-in or user-defined) is considered active if it is determined during the link operation that it may be accessed during program execution. Therefore, *program* should have previously been the target of a call to `glLinkProgram`, but it is not necessary for it to have been linked successfully.

The size of the character buffer required to store the longest attribute variable name in *program* can be obtained by calling `glGetProgram` with the value `GL_ACTIVE_ATTRIBUTE_MAX_LENGTH`. This value should be used to allocate a buffer of sufficient size to store the returned attribute name. The size of this character buffer is passed in *bufSize*, and a pointer to this character buffer is passed in *name*.

`glGetActiveAttrib` returns the name of the attribute variable indicated by *index*, storing it in the character buffer specified by *name*. The string returned will be null terminated. The actual number of characters written into this buffer is returned in *length*, and this count does not include the null termination character. If the length of the returned string is not required, a value of NULL can be passed in the *length* argument.

The *type* argument will return a pointer to the attribute variable's data type. The symbolic constants `GL_FLOAT`, `GL_FLOAT_VEC2`, `GL_FLOAT_VEC3`, `GL_FLOAT_VEC4`, `GL_FLOAT_MAT2`, `GL_FLOAT_MAT3`, `GL_FLOAT_MAT4`, `GL_FLOAT_MAT2x3`, `GL_FLOAT_MAT2x4`, `GL_FLOAT_MAT3x2`, `GL_FLOAT_MAT3x4`, `GL_FLOAT_MAT4x2`, or `GL_FLOAT_MAT4x3` may be returned. The *size* argument will return the size of the attribute, in units of the type returned in *type*.

The list of active attribute variables may include both built-in attribute variables (which begin with the prefix "gl_") as well as user-defined attribute variable names.

This function will return as much information as it can about the specified active attribute variable. If no information is available, *length* will be 0, and *name* will be an empty string. This situation could occur if this function is called after a link operation that failed. If an error occurs, the return values *length*, *size*, *type*, and *name* will be unmodified.

Notes

`glGetActiveAttrib` is available only if the GL version is 2.0 or greater.

`GL_FLOAT_MAT2x3`, `GL_FLOAT_MAT2x4`, `GL_FLOAT_MAT3x2`, `GL_FLOAT_MAT3x4`, `GL_FLOAT_MAT4x2`, and `GL_FLOAT_MAT4x3` will only be returned as a *type* if the GL version is 2.1 or greater.

Errors

`GL_INVALID_VALUE` is generated if *program* is not a value generated by OpenGL.

`GL_INVALID_OPERATION` is generated if *program* is not a program object.

`GL_INVALID_VALUE` is generated if *index* is greater than or equal to the number of active attribute variables in *program*.

`GL_INVALID_OPERATION` is generated if `glGetActiveAttrib` is executed between the execution of `glBegin` and the corresponding execution of `glEnd`.

`GL_INVALID_VALUE` is generated if *bufSize* is less than 0.

Associated Gets

`glGet` with argument `GL_MAX_VERTEX_ATTRIBS`.

`glGetProgram` with argument `GL_ACTIVE_ATTRIBUTES` or `GL_ACTIVE_ATTRIBUTE_MAX_LENGTH`.

`glIsProgram`

See Also

`glBindAttribLocation`, `glLinkProgram`, `glVertexAttrib`, `glVertexAttribPointer`

glGetActiveUniform

Return information about an active uniform variable for the specified program object

C Specification

```
void glGetActiveUniform(GLuint    program,
                        GLuint    index,
                        GLsizei   bufSize,
                        GLsizei * length,
                        GLint *   size,
                        GLenum *  type,
                        GLchar *  name);
```

Parameters

program   Specifies the program object to be queried.

index   Specifies the index of the uniform variable to be queried.

bufSize   Specifies the maximum number of characters OpenGL is allowed to write in the character buffer indicated by *name*.

length   Returns the number of characters actually written by OpenGL in the string indicated by *name* (excluding the null terminator) if a value other than NULL is passed.

size   Returns the size of the uniform variable.

type   Returns the data type of the uniform variable.

name   Returns a null terminated string containing the name of the uniform variable.

Description

glGetActiveUniform returns information about an active uniform variable in the program object specified by *program*. The number of active uniform variables can be obtained by calling glGetProgram with the value GL_ACTIVE_UNIFORMS. A value of 0 for *index* selects the first active uniform variable. Permissible values for *index* range from 0 to the number of active uniform variables minus 1.

Shaders may use either built-in uniform variables, user-defined uniform variables, or both. Built-in uniform variables have a prefix of "gl_" and reference existing OpenGL state or values derived from such state (e.g., gl_Fog, gl_ModelViewMatrix, etc., see the OpenGL Shading Language specification for a complete list.) User-defined uniform variables have arbitrary names and obtain their values from the application through calls to glUniform. A uniform variable (either built-in or user-defined) is considered active if it is determined during the link operation that it may be accessed during program execution. Therefore, *program* should have previously been the target of a call to glLinkProgram, but it is not necessary for it to have been linked successfully.

The size of the character buffer required to store the longest uniform variable name in *program* can be obtained by calling glGetProgram with the value GL_ACTIVE_UNIFORM_MAX_LENGTH. This value should be used to allocate a buffer of sufficient size to store the returned uniform variable name. The size of this character buffer is passed in *bufSize*, and a pointer to this character buffer is passed in *name*.

glGetActiveUniform returns the name of the uniform variable indicated by *index*, storing it in the character buffer specified by *name*. The string returned will be null terminated. The actual number of characters written into this buffer is returned in *length*, and this count does not include the null termination character. If the length of the returned string is not required, a value of NULL can be passed in the *length* argument.

The *type* argument will return a pointer to the uniform variable's data type. The symbolic constants GL_FLOAT, GL_FLOAT_VEC2, GL_FLOAT_VEC3, GL_FLOAT_VEC4, GL_INT, GL_INT_VEC2, GL_INT_VEC3, GL_INT_VEC4, GL_BOOL, GL_BOOL_VEC2, GL_BOOL_VEC3, GL_BOOL_VEC4, GL_FLOAT_MAT2, GL_FLOAT_MAT3, GL_FLOAT_MAT4, GL_FLOAT_MAT2x3, GL_FLOAT_MAT2x4, GL_FLOAT_MAT3x2, GL_FLOAT_MAT3x4, GL_FLOAT_MAT4x2, GL_FLOAT_MAT4x3, GL_SAMPLER_1D, GL_SAMPLER_2D, GL_SAMPLER_3D, GL_SAMPLER_CUBE, GL_SAMPLER_1D_SHADOW, or GL_SAMPLER_2D_SHADOW may be returned.

If one or more elements of an array are active, the name of the array is returned in *name*, the type is returned in *type*, and the *size* parameter returns the highest array element index used, plus one, as determined by the compiler and/or linker. Only one active uniform variable will be reported for a uniform array.

Uniform variables that are declared as structures or arrays of structures will not be returned directly by this function. Instead, each of these uniform variables will be reduced to its fundamental components containing the "." and "[]" operators such that each of the names is valid as an argument to glGetUniformLocation. Each of these reduced uniform variables is counted as one active uniform variable and is assigned an index. A valid name cannot be a structure, an array of structures, or a subcomponent of a vector or matrix.

The size of the uniform variable will be returned in *size*. Uniform variables other than arrays will have a size of 1. Structures and arrays of structures will be reduced as described earlier, such that each of the names returned will be a data type in the earlier list. If this reduction results in an array, the size returned will be as described for uniform arrays; otherwise, the size returned will be 1.

The list of active uniform variables may include both built-in uniform variables (which begin with the prefix "gl_") as well as user-defined uniform variable names.

This function will return as much information as it can about the specified active uniform variable. If no information is available, *length* will be 0, and *name* will be an empty string. This situation could occur if this function is called after a link operation that failed. If an error occurs, the return values *length*, *size*, *type*, and *name* will be unmodified.

Notes

glGetActiveUniform is available only if the GL version is 2.0 or greater.

GL_FLOAT_MAT2x3, GL_FLOAT_MAT2x4, GL_FLOAT_MAT3x2, GL_FLOAT_MAT3x4, GL_FLOAT_MAT4x2, and GL_FLOAT_MAT4x3 will only be returned as a *type* if the GL version is 2.1 or greater.

Errors

GL_INVALID_VALUE is generated if *program* is not a value generated by OpenGL.

GL_INVALID_OPERATION is generated if *program* is not a program object.

GL_INVALID_VALUE is generated if *index* is greater than or equal to the number of active uniform variables in *program*.

GL_INVALID_OPERATION is generated if glGetActiveUniform is executed between the execution of glBegin and the corresponding execution of glEnd.

GL_INVALID_VALUE is generated if *bufSize* is less than 0.

Associated Gets

glGet with argument GL_MAX_VERTEX_UNIFORM_COMPONENTS or GL_MAX_FRAGMENT_UNIFORM_COMPONENTS.

glGetProgram with argument GL_ACTIVE_UNIFORMS or GL_ACTIVE_UNIFORM_MAX_LENGTH.

glIsProgram

See Also

glGetUniform, glGetUniformLocation, glLinkProgram, glUniform, glUseProgram

glGetAttachedShaders

Return the handles of the shader objects attached to a program object

C Specification

```
void glGetAttachedShaders(GLuint    program,
                          GLsizei   maxCount,
                          GLsizei * count,
                          GLuint *  shaders);
```

Parameters

program	Specifies the program object to be queried.
maxCount	Specifies the size of the array for storing the returned object names.
count	Returns the number of names actually returned in *objects*.
shaders	Specifies an array that is used to return the names of attached shader objects.

Description

glGetAttachedShaders returns the names of the shader objects attached to *program*. The names of shader objects that are attached to *program* will be returned in *shaders*. The actual number of shader names written into *shaders* is returned in *count*. If no shader objects are attached to *program*, *count* is set to 0. The maximum number of shader names that may be returned in *shaders* is specified by *maxCount*.

If the number of names actually returned is not required (for instance, if it has just been obtained by calling glGetProgram), a value of NULL may be passed for count. If no shader objects are attached to *program*, a value of 0 will be returned in *count*. The actual number of attached shaders can be obtained by calling glGetProgram with the value GL_ATTACHED_SHADERS.

Notes

glGetAttachedShaders is available only if the GL version is 2.0 or greater.

Errors

GL_INVALID_VALUE is generated if *program* is not a value generated by OpenGL.

GL_INVALID_OPERATION is generated if *program* is not a program object.

GL_INVALID_VALUE is generated if *maxCount* is less than 0.

GL_INVALID_OPERATION is generated if glGetAttachedShaders is executed between the execution of glBegin and the corresponding execution of glEnd.

Associated Gets

glGetProgram with argument GL_ATTACHED_SHADERS

glIsProgram

See Also

glAttachShader, glDetachShader

glGetAttribLocation

Return the location of an attribute variable

C Specification

```
GLint glGetAttribLocation(GLuint        program,
                          const GLchar * name);
```

Parameters

program	Specifies the program object to be queried.
name	Points to a null terminated string containing the name of the attribute variable whose location is to be queried.

Description

glGetAttribLocation queries the previously linked program object specified by *program* for the attribute variable specified by *name* and returns the index of the generic vertex attribute that is bound to that attribute variable. If *name* is a matrix attribute variable, the index of the first column of the matrix is returned. If the named attribute variable is not an active attribute in the specified program object or if *name* starts with the reserved prefix "gl_", a value of -1 is returned.

The association between an attribute variable name and a generic attribute index can be specified at any time by calling glBindAttribLocation. Attribute bindings do not go into effect until glLinkProgram is called. After a program object has been linked successfully, the index values for attribute variables remain fixed until the next link command occurs. The attribute values can only be queried after a link if the link was successful. glGetAttribLocation returns the binding that actually went into effect the last time glLinkProgram was called for the specified program object. Attribute bindings that have been specified since the last link operation are not returned by glGetAttribLocation.

Notes

glGetAttribLocation is available only if the GL version is 2.0 or greater.

Errors

GL_INVALID_OPERATION is generated if *program* is not a value generated by OpenGL.
GL_INVALID_OPERATION is generated if *program* is not a program object.
GL_INVALID_OPERATION is generated if *program* has not been successfully linked.
GL_INVALID_OPERATION is generated if glGetAttribLocation is executed between the execution of glBegin and the corresponding execution of glEnd.

Associated Gets

glGetActiveAttrib with argument *program* and the index of an active attribute
glIsProgram

See Also

glBindAttribLocation, glLinkProgram, glVertexAttrib, glVertexAttribPointer

glGetBufferParameteriv

Return parameters of a buffer object

C Specification

```
void glGetBufferParameteriv(GLenum    target,
                            GLenum    value,
                            GLint *   data);
```

Parameters

target   Specifies the target buffer object. The symbolic constant must be GL_ARRAY_BUFFER, GL_ELEMENT_ARRAY_BUFFER, GL_PIXEL_PACK_BUFFER, or GL_PIXEL_UNPACK_BUFFER.

value   Specifies the symbolic name of a buffer object parameter. Accepted values are GL_BUFFER_ACCESS, GL_BUFFER_MAPPED, GL_BUFFER_SIZE, or GL_BUFFER_USAGE.

data   Returns the requested parameter.

Description

glGetBufferParameteriv returns in *data* a selected parameter of the buffer object specified by *target*.

value names a specific buffer object parameter, as follows:
GL_BUFFER_ACCESS
params returns the access policy set while mapping the buffer object. The initial value is GL_READ_WRITE.
GL_BUFFER_MAPPED
params returns a flag indicating whether the buffer object is currently mapped. The initial value is GL_FALSE.

GL_BUFFER_SIZE
params returns the size of the buffer object, measured in bytes. The initial value is 0.
GL_BUFFER_USAGE
params returns the buffer object's usage pattern. The initial value is GL_STATIC_DRAW.

Notes

If an error is generated, no change is made to the contents of *data*.
glGetBufferParameteriv is available only if the GL version is 1.5 or greater.
Targets GL_PIXEL_PACK_BUFFER and GL_PIXEL_UNPACK_BUFFER are available only if the GL version is 2.1 or greater.

Errors

GL_INVALID_ENUM is generated if *target* or *value* is not an accepted value.
GL_INVALID_OPERATION is generated if the reserved buffer object name 0 is bound to *target*.
GL_INVALID_OPERATION is generated if glGetBufferParameteriv is executed between the execution of glBegin and the corresponding execution of glEnd.

See Also

glBindBuffer, glBufferData, glMapBuffer, glUnmapBuffer

glGetBufferPointerv

Return the pointer to a mapped buffer object's data store

C Specification

```
void glGetBufferPointerv(GLenum      target,
                         GLenum      pname,
                         GLvoid **   params);
```

Parameters

target   Specifies the target buffer object. The symbolic constant must be GL_ARRAY_BUFFER, GL_ELEMENT_ARRAY_BUFFER, GL_PIXEL_PACK_BUFFER, or GL_PIXEL_UNPACK_BUFFER.

pname   Specifies the pointer to be returned. The symbolic constant must be GL_BUFFER_MAP_POINTER.

params   Returns the pointer value specified by *pname*.

Description

glGetBufferPointerv returns pointer information. *pname* is a symbolic constant indicating the pointer to be returned, which must be GL_BUFFER_MAP_POINTER, the pointer to which the buffer object's data store is mapped. If the data store is not currently mapped, NULL is returned. *params* is a pointer to a location in which to place the returned pointer value.

Notes

If an error is generated, no change is made to the contents of *params*.
glGetBufferPointerv is available only if the GL version is 1.5 or greater.
Targets GL_PIXEL_PACK_BUFFER and GL_PIXEL_UNPACK_BUFFER are available only if the GL version is 2.1 or greater.
The initial value for the pointer is NULL.

Errors

GL_INVALID_ENUM is generated if *target* or *pname* is not an accepted value.
GL_INVALID_OPERATION is generated if the reserved buffer object name 0 is bound to *target*.

GL_INVALID_OPERATION is generated if glGetBufferParameteriv is executed between the execution of glBegin and the corresponding execution of glEnd.

See Also

glBindBuffer, glMapBuffer

glGetBufferSubData

Return a subset of a buffer object's data store

C Specification

```
void glGetBufferSubData(GLenum      target,
                        GLintptr    offset,
                        GLsizeiptr  size,
                        GLvoid *    data);
```

Parameters

target   Specifies the target buffer object. The symbolic constant must be GL_ARRAY_BUFFER, GL_ELEMENT_ARRAY_BUFFER, GL_PIXEL_PACK_BUFFER, or GL_PIXEL_UNPACK_BUFFER.

offset   Specifies the offset into the buffer object's data store from which data will be returned, measured in bytes.

size   Specifies the size in bytes of the data store region being returned.

data   Specifies a pointer to the location where buffer object data is returned.

Description

glGetBufferSubData returns some or all of the data from the buffer object currently bound to target. Data starting at byte offset offset and extending for size bytes is copied from the data store to the memory pointed to by data. An error is thrown if the buffer object is currently mapped, or if offset and size together define a range beyond the bounds of the buffer object's data store.

Notes

If an error is generated, no change is made to the contents of data.

glGetBufferSubData is available only if the GL version is 1.5 or greater.

Targets GL_PIXEL_PACK_BUFFER and GL_PIXEL_UNPACK_BUFFER are available only if the GL version is 2.1 or greater.

Errors

GL_INVALID_ENUM is generated if target is not GL_ARRAY_BUFFER, GL_ELEMENT_ARRAY_BUFFER, GL_PIXEL_PACK_BUFFER, or GL_PIXEL_UNPACK_BUFFER.

GL_INVALID_VALUE is generated if offset or size is negative, or if together they define a region of memory that extends beyond the buffer object's allocated data store.

GL_INVALID_OPERATION is generated if the reserved buffer object name 0 is bound to target.

GL_INVALID_OPERATION is generated if the buffer object being queried is mapped.

GL_INVALID_OPERATION is generated if glGetBufferSubData is executed between the execution of glBegin and the corresponding execution of glEnd.

See Also

glBindBuffer, glBufferData, glBufferSubData, glMapBuffer, glUnmapBuffer

glGetClipPlane

Return the coefficients of the specified clipping plane

C Specification

```
void glGetClipPlane(GLenum      plane,
                    GLdouble * equation);
```

Parameters

plane	Specifies a clipping plane. The number of clipping planes depends on the implementation, but at least six clipping planes are supported. They are identified by symbolic names of the form GL_CLIP_PLANE*i* where *i* ranges from 0 to the value of GL_MAX_CLIP_PLANES - 1.
equation	Returns four double-precision values that are the coefficients of the plane equation of *plane* in eye coordinates. The initial value is (0, 0, 0, 0).

Description

glGetClipPlane returns in *equation* the four coefficients of the plane equation for *plane*.

Notes

It is always the case that GL_CLIP_PLANE*i* = GL_CLIP_PLANE0 + *i*.

If an error is generated, no change is made to the contents of *equation*.

Errors

GL_INVALID_ENUM is generated if *plane* is not an accepted value.

GL_INVALID_OPERATION is generated if glGetClipPlane is executed between the execution of glBegin and the corresponding execution of glEnd.

See Also

glClipPlane

glGetColorTable

Retrieve contents of a color lookup table

C Specification

```
void glGetColorTable(GLenum      target,
                     GLenum      format,
                     GLenum      type,
                     GLvoid * table);
```

Parameters

target	Must be GL_COLOR_TABLE, GL_POST_CONVOLUTION_COLOR_TABLE, or GL_POST_COLOR_MATRIX_COLOR_TABLE.
format	The format of the pixel data in *table*. The possible values are GL_RED, GL_GREEN, GL_BLUE, GL_ALPHA, GL_LUMINANCE, GL_LUMINANCE_ALPHA, GL_RGB, GL_BGR, GL_RGBA, and GL_BGRA.
type	The type of the pixel data in *table*. Symbolic constants GL_UNSIGNED_BYTE, GL_BYTE, GL_BITMAP, GL_UNSIGNED_SHORT, GL_SHORT, GL_UNSIGNED_INT, GL_INT, GL_FLOAT, GL_UNSIGNED_BYTE_3_3_2, GL_UNSIGNED_BYTE_2_3_3_REV, GL_UNSIGNED_SHORT_5_6_5, GL_UNSIGNED_SHORT_5_6_5_REV, GL_UNSIGNED_SHORT_4_4_4_4, GL_UNSIGNED_SHORT_4_4_4_4_REV, GL_UNSIGNED_SHORT_5_5_5_1, GL_UNSIGNED_SHORT_1_5_5_5_REV,

GL_UNSIGNED_INT_8_8_8_8, GL_UNSIGNED_INT_8_8_8_8_REV, GL_UNSIGNED_INT_10_10_10_2, and GL_UNSIGNED_INT_2_10_10_10_REV are accepted.

table   Pointer to a one-dimensional array of pixel data containing the contents of the color table.

Description

glGetColorTable returns in *table* the contents of the color table specified by *target*. No pixel transfer operations are performed, but pixel storage modes that are applicable to glReadPixels are performed.

If a nonzero named buffer object is bound to the GL_PIXEL_PACK_BUFFER target (see glBindBuffer) while a histogram table is requested, *table* is treated as a byte offset into the buffer object's data store.

Color components that are requested in the specified *format*, but which are not included in the internal format of the color lookup table, are returned as zero. The assignments of internal color components to the components requested by *format* are

Internal Component	Resulting Component
Red	Red
Green	Green
Blue	Blue
Alpha	Alpha
Luminance	Red
Intensity	Red

Notes

glGetColorTable is present only if ARB_imaging is returned when glGetString is called with an argument of GL_EXTENSIONS.

Errors

GL_INVALID_ENUM is generated if *target* is not one of the allowable values.

GL_INVALID_ENUM is generated if *format* is not one of the allowable values.

GL_INVALID_ENUM is generated if *type* is not one of the allowable values.

GL_INVALID_OPERATION is generated if *type* is one of GL_UNSIGNED_BYTE_3_3_2, GL_UNSIGNED_BYTE_2_3_3_REV, GL_UNSIGNED_SHORT_5_6_5, or GL_UNSIGNED_SHORT_5_6_5_REV and *format* is not GL_RGB.

GL_INVALID_OPERATION is generated if *type* is one of GL_UNSIGNED_SHORT_4_4_4_4, GL_UNSIGNED_SHORT_4_4_4_4_REV, GL_UNSIGNED_SHORT_5_5_5_1, GL_UNSIGNED_SHORT_1_5_5_5_REV, GL_UNSIGNED_INT_8_8_8_8, GL_UNSIGNED_INT_8_8_8_8_REV, GL_UNSIGNED_INT_10_10_10_2, or GL_UNSIGNED_INT_2_10_10_10_REV and *format* is neither GL_RGBA nor GL_BGRA.

GL_INVALID_OPERATION is generated if a nonzero buffer object name is bound to the GL_PIXEL_PACK_BUFFER target and the buffer object's data store is currently mapped.

GL_INVALID_OPERATION is generated if a nonzero buffer object name is bound to the GL_PIXEL_PACK_BUFFER target and the data would be packed to the buffer object such that the memory writes required would exceed the data store size.

GL_INVALID_OPERATION is generated if a nonzero buffer object name is bound to the GL_PIXEL_PACK_BUFFER target and *table* is not evenly divisible into the number of bytes needed to store in memory a datum indicated by *type*.

GL_INVALID_OPERATION is generated if glGetColorTable is executed between the execution of glBegin and the corresponding execution of glEnd.

Associated Gets

glGetColorTableParameter
glGet with argument GL_PIXEL_PACK_BUFFER_BINDING

See Also

glColorTable, glColorTableParameter

glGetColorTableParameter

Get color lookup table parameters

C Specification

```
void glGetColorTableParameterfv(GLenum      target,
                                GLenum      pname,
                                GLfloat *   params);
void glGetColorTableParameteriv(GLenum      target,
                                GLenum      pname,
                                GLint *     params);
```

Parameters

target   The target color table. Must be GL_COLOR_TABLE,
            GL_POST_CONVOLUTION_COLOR_TABLE, GL_POST_COLOR_MATRIX_COLOR_TABLE,
            GL_PROXY_COLOR_TABLE, GL_PROXY_POST_CONVOLUTION_COLOR_TABLE, or
            GL_PROXY_POST_COLOR_MATRIX_COLOR_TABLE.

pname   The symbolic name of a color lookup table parameter. Must be one of
            GL_COLOR_TABLE_BIAS, GL_COLOR_TABLE_SCALE, GL_COLOR_TABLE_FORMAT,
            GL_COLOR_TABLE_WIDTH, GL_COLOR_TABLE_RED_SIZE, GL_COLOR_TABLE_GREEN_SIZE,
            GL_COLOR_TABLE_BLUE_SIZE, GL_COLOR_TABLE_ALPHA_SIZE,
            GL_COLOR_TABLE_LUMINANCE_SIZE, or GL_COLOR_TABLE_INTENSITY_SIZE.

params   A pointer to an array where the values of the parameter will be stored.

Description

Returns parameters specific to color table *target*.

When *pname* is set to GL_COLOR_TABLE_SCALE or GL_COLOR_TABLE_BIAS,
glGetColorTableParameter returns the color table scale or bias parameters for the table specified
by *target*. For these queries, *target* must be set to GL_COLOR_TABLE,
GL_POST_CONVOLUTION_COLOR_TABLE, or GL_POST_COLOR_MATRIX_COLOR_TABLE and *params*
points to an array of four elements, which receive the scale or bias factors for red, green, blue, and
alpha, in that order.

glGetColorTableParameter can also be used to retrieve the format and size parameters for a
color table. For these queries, set *target* to either the color table target or the proxy color table
target. The format and size parameters are set by glColorTable.

The following table lists the format and size parameters that may be queried. For each symbolic
constant listed below for *pname*, *params* must point to an array of the given length and receive the
values indicated.

Parameter	N	Meaning
GL_COLOR_TABLE_FORMAT	1	Internal format (e.g., GL_RGBA)
GL_COLOR_TABLE_WIDTH	1	Number of elements in table
GL_COLOR_TABLE_RED_SIZE	1	Size of red component, in bits
GL_COLOR_TABLE_GREEN_SIZE	1	Size of green component
GL_COLOR_TABLE_BLUE_SIZE	1	Size of blue component

Parameter	N	Meaning
GL_COLOR_TABLE_ALPHA_SIZE	1	Size of alpha component
GL_COLOR_TABLE_LUMINANCE_SIZE	1	Size of luminance component
GL_COLOR_TABLE_INTENSITY_SIZE	1	Size of intensity component

Notes

glGetColorTableParameter is present only if ARB_imaging is returned when glGetString is called with an argument of GL_EXTENSIONS.

Errors

GL_INVALID_ENUM is generated if *target* or *pname* is not an acceptable value.

GL_INVALID_OPERATION is generated if glGetColorTableParameter is executed between the execution of glBegin and the corresponding execution of glEnd.

See Also

glColorTable, glTexParameter, glColorTableParameter

glGetCompressedTexImage

Return a compressed texture image

C Specification

```
void glGetCompressedTexImage(GLenum   target,
                             GLint    lod,
                             GLvoid * img);
```

Parameters

target   Specifies which texture is to be obtained. GL_TEXTURE_1D, GL_TEXTURE_2D, and GL_TEXTURE_3DGL_TEXTURE_CUBE_MAP_POSITIVE_X, GL_TEXTURE_CUBE_MAP_NEGA-TIVE_X, GL_TEXTURE_CUBE_MAP_POSITIVE_Y, GL_TEXTURE_CUBE_MAP_NEGATIVE_Y, GL_TEXTURE_CUBE_MAP_POSITIVE_Z, and GL_TEXTURE_CUBE_MAP_NEGATIVE_Z are accepted.

lod   Specifies the level-of-detail number of the desired image. Level 0 is the base image level. Level *n* is the *n*th mipmap reduction image.

img   Returns the compressed texture image.

Description

glGetCompressedTexImage returns the compressed texture image associated with *target* and *lod* into *img*. *img* should be an array of GL_TEXTURE_COMPRESSED_IMAGE_SIZE bytes. *target* specifies whether the desired texture image was one specified by glTexImage1D (GL_TEXTURE_1D), glTexImage2D (GL_TEXTURE_2D or any of GL_TEXTURE_CUBE_MAP_*), or glTexImage3D (GL_TEXTURE_3D). *lod* specifies the level-of-detail number of the desired image.

If a nonzero named buffer object is bound to the GL_PIXEL_PACK_BUFFER target (see glBindBuffer) while a texture image is requested, *img* is treated as a byte offset into the buffer object's data store.

To minimize errors, first verify that the texture is compressed by calling glGetTexLevelParameter with argument GL_TEXTURE_COMPRESSED. If the texture is compressed, then determine the amount of memory required to store the compressed texture by calling glGetTexLevelParameter with argument GL_TEXTURE_COMPRESSED_IMAGE_SIZE. Finally, retrieve the internal format of the texture by calling glGetTexLevelParameter with argument GL_TEXTURE_INTERNAL_FORMAT. To store the texture for later use, associate the internal format and size with the retrieved texture image. These data can be used by the respective texture or subtexture loading routine used for loading *target* textures.

Notes

glGetCompressedTexImage is available only if the GL version is 1.3 or greater.

Errors

GL_INVALID_VALUE is generated if *lod* is less than zero or greater than the maximum number of LODs permitted by the implementation.

GL_INVALID_OPERATION is generated if glGetCompressedTexImage is used to retrieve a texture that is in an uncompressed internal format.

GL_INVALID_OPERATION is generated if a nonzero buffer object name is bound to the GL_PIXEL_PACK_BUFFER target and the buffer object's data store is currently mapped.

GL_INVALID_OPERATION is generated if a nonzero buffer object name is bound to the GL_PIXEL_PACK_BUFFER target and the data would be packed to the buffer object such that the memory writes required would exceed the data store size.

GL_INVALID_OPERATION is generated if glGetCompressedTexImage is executed between the execution of glBegin and the corresponding execution of glEnd.

Associated Gets

glGetTexLevelParameter with argument GL_TEXTURE_COMPRESSED
glGetTexLevelParameter with argument GL_TEXTURE_COMPRESSED_IMAGE_SIZE
glGetTexLevelParameter with argument GL_TEXTURE_INTERNAL_FORMAT
glGet with argument GL_PIXEL_PACK_BUFFER_BINDING

See Also

glActiveTexture, glCompressedTexImage1D, glCompressedTexImage2D, glCompressedTexImage3D, glCompressedTexSubImage1D, glCompressedTexSubImage2D, glCompressedTexSubImage3D, glDrawPixels, glReadPixels, glTexEnv, glTexGen, glTexImage1D, glTexImage2D, glTexImage3D, glTexParameter, glTexSubImage1D, glTexSubImage2D, glTexSubImage3D

glGetConvolutionFilter

Get current 1D or 2D convolution filter kernel

C Specification

```
void glGetConvolutionFilter(GLenum    target,
                            GLenum    format,
                            GLenum    type,
                            GLvoid * image);
```

Parameters

target   The filter to be retrieved. Must be one of GL_CONVOLUTION_1D or
            GL_CONVOLUTION_2D.
format   Format of the output image. Must be one of GL_RED, GL_GREEN, GL_BLUE, GL_ALPHA,
            GL_RGB, GL_BGR, GL_RGBA, GL_BGRA, GL_LUMINANCE, or GL_LUMINANCE_ALPHA.
type   Data type of components in the output image. Symbolic constants
            GL_UNSIGNED_BYTE, GL_BYTE, GL_BITMAP, GL_UNSIGNED_SHORT, GL_SHORT,
            GL_UNSIGNED_INT, GL_INT, GL_FLOAT, GL_UNSIGNED_BYTE_3_3_2,
            GL_UNSIGNED_BYTE_2_3_3_REV, GL_UNSIGNED_SHORT_5_6_5,
            GL_UNSIGNED_SHORT_5_6_5_REV, GL_UNSIGNED_SHORT_4_4_4_4,
            GL_UNSIGNED_SHORT_4_4_4_4_REV, GL_UNSIGNED_SHORT_5_5_5_1,

GL_UNSIGNED_SHORT_1_5_5_5_REV, GL_UNSIGNED_INT_8_8_8_8,
GL_UNSIGNED_INT_8_8_8_8_REV, GL_UNSIGNED_INT_10_10_10_2, and
GL_UNSIGNED_INT_2_10_10_10_REV are accepted.

image   Pointer to storage for the output image.

Description

glGetConvolutionFilter returns the current 1D or 2D convolution filter kernel as an image. The one- or two-dimensional image is placed in *image* according to the specifications in *format* and *type*. No pixel transfer operations are performed on this image, but the relevant pixel storage modes are applied.

If a nonzero named buffer object is bound to the GL_PIXEL_PACK_BUFFER target (see glBindBuffer) while a convolution filter is requested, *image* is treated as a byte offset into the buffer object's data store.

Color components that are present in *format* but not included in the internal format of the filter are returned as zero. The assignments of internal color components to the components of *format* are as follows.

Internal Component	Resulting Component
Red	Red
Green	Green
Blue	Blue
Alpha	Alpha
Luminance	Red
Intensity	Red

Notes

glGetConvolutionFilter is present only if ARB_imaging is returned when glGetString is called with an argument of GL_EXTENSIONS.

The current separable 2D filter must be retrieved with glGetSeparableFilter rather than glGetConvolutionFilter.

Errors

GL_INVALID_ENUM is generated if *target* is not one of the allowable values.

GL_INVALID_ENUM is generated if *format* is not one of the allowable values.

GL_INVALID_ENUM is generated if *type* is not one of the allowable values.

GL_INVALID_OPERATION is generated if *type* is one of GL_UNSIGNED_BYTE_3_3_2, GL_UNSIGNED_BYTE_2_3_3_REV, GL_UNSIGNED_SHORT_5_6_5, or GL_UNSIGNED_SHORT_5_6_5_REV and *format* is not GL_RGB.

GL_INVALID_OPERATION is generated if *type* is one of GL_UNSIGNED_SHORT_4_4_4_4, GL_UNSIGNED_SHORT_4_4_4_4_REV, GL_UNSIGNED_SHORT_5_5_5_1, GL_UNSIGNED_SHORT_1_5_5_5_REV, GL_UNSIGNED_INT_8_8_8_8, GL_UNSIGNED_INT_8_8_8_8_REV, GL_UNSIGNED_INT_10_10_10_2, or GL_UNSIGNED_INT_2_10_10_10_REV and *format* is neither GL_RGBA nor GL_BGRA.

GL_INVALID_OPERATION is generated if a nonzero buffer object name is bound to the GL_PIXEL_PACK_BUFFER target and the buffer object's data store is currently mapped.

GL_INVALID_OPERATION is generated if a nonzero buffer object name is bound to the GL_PIXEL_PACK_BUFFER target and the data would be packed to the buffer object such that the memory writes required would exceed the data store size.

GL_INVALID_OPERATION is generated if a nonzero buffer object name is bound to the GL_PIXEL_PACK_BUFFER target and *image* is not evenly divisible into the number of bytes needed to store in memory a datum indicated by *type*.

GL_INVALID_OPERATION is generated if glGetConvolutionFilter is executed between the execution of glBegin and the corresponding execution of glEnd.

Associated Gets

glGetConvolutionParameter
glGet with argument GL_PIXEL_PACK_BUFFER_BINDING

See Also

glGetSeparableFilter, glConvolutionParameter, glConvolutionFilter1D, glConvolutionFilter2D

glGetConvolutionParameter

Get convolution parameters

C Specification

```
void glGetConvolutionParameterfv(GLenum    target,
                                 GLenum    pname,
                                 GLfloat * params);
void glGetConvolutionParameteriv(GLenum    target,
                                 GLenum    pname,
                                 GLint * params);
```

Parameters

target   The filter whose parameters are to be retrieved. Must be one of GL_CONVOLUTION_1D, GL_CONVOLUTION_2D, or GL_SEPARABLE_2D.

pname   The parameter to be retrieved. Must be one of GL_CONVOLUTION_BORDER_MODE, GL_CONVOLUTION_BORDER_COLOR, GL_CONVOLUTION_FILTER_SCALE, GL_CONVOLUTION_FILTER_BIAS, GL_CONVOLUTION_FORMAT, GL_CONVOLUTION_WIDTH, GL_CONVOLUTION_HEIGHT, GL_MAX_CONVOLUTION_WIDTH, or GL_MAX_CONVOLUTION_HEIGHT.

params   Pointer to storage for the parameters to be retrieved.

Description

glGetConvolutionParameter retrieves convolution parameters. *target* determines which convolution filter is queried. *pname* determines which parameter is returned:

GL_CONVOLUTION_BORDER_MODE

The convolution border mode. See glConvolutionParameter for a list of border modes.

GL_CONVOLUTION_BORDER_COLOR

The current convolution border color. *params* must be a pointer to an array of four elements, which will receive the red, green, blue, and alpha border colors.

GL_CONVOLUTION_FILTER_SCALE

The current filter scale factors. *params* must be a pointer to an array of four elements, which will receive the red, green, blue, and alpha filter scale factors in that order.

GL_CONVOLUTION_FILTER_BIAS

The current filter bias factors. *params* must be a pointer to an array of four elements, which will receive the red, green, blue, and alpha filter bias terms in that order.

GL_CONVOLUTION_FORMAT

The current internal format. See glConvolutionFilter1D, glConvolutionFilter2D, and glSeparableFilter2D for lists of allowable formats.

GL_CONVOLUTION_WIDTH

The current filter image width.

GL_CONVOLUTION_HEIGHT

The current filter image height.

GL_MAX_CONVOLUTION_WIDTH

The maximum acceptable filter image width.

GL_MAX_CONVOLUTION_HEIGHT

The maximum acceptable filter image height.

Errors

GL_INVALID_ENUM is generated if *target* is not one of the allowable values.

GL_INVALID_ENUM is generated if *pname* is not one of the allowable values.

GL_INVALID_ENUM is generated if *target* is GL_CONVOLUTION_1D and *pname* is GL_CONVOLUTION_HEIGHT or GL_MAX_CONVOLUTION_HEIGHT.

GL_INVALID_OPERATION is generated if glGetConvolutionParameter is executed between the execution of glBegin and the corresponding execution of glEnd.

See Also

glGetConvolutionFilter, glGetSeparableFilter, glConvolutionParameter

glGetError

Return error information

C Specification

GLenum **glGetError**(*void*);

Description

glGetError returns the value of the error flag. Each detectable error is assigned a numeric code and symbolic name. When an error occurs, the error flag is set to the appropriate error code value. No other errors are recorded until glGetError is called, the error code is returned, and the flag is reset to GL_NO_ERROR. If a call to glGetError returns GL_NO_ERROR, there has been no detectable error since the last call to glGetError, or since the GL was initialized.

To allow for distributed implementations, there may be several error flags. If any single error flag has recorded an error, the value of that flag is returned and that flag is reset to GL_NO_ERROR when glGetError is called. If more than one flag has recorded an error, glGetError returns and clears an arbitrary error flag value. Thus, glGetError should always be called in a loop, until it returns GL_NO_ERROR, if all error flags are to be reset.

Initially, all error flags are set to GL_NO_ERROR.

The following errors are currently defined:

GL_NO_ERROR

No error has been recorded. The value of this symbolic constant is guaranteed to be 0.

GL_INVALID_ENUM

An unacceptable value is specified for an enumerated argument. The offending command is ignored and has no other side effect than to set the error flag.

GL_INVALID_VALUE

A numeric argument is out of range. The offending command is ignored and has no other side effect than to set the error flag.

GL_INVALID_OPERATION

The specified operation is not allowed in the current state. The offending command is ignored and has no other side effect than to set the error flag.

GL_STACK_OVERFLOW

This command would cause a stack overflow. The offending command is ignored and has no other side effect than to set the error flag.

GL_STACK_UNDERFLOW

This command would cause a stack underflow. The offending command is ignored and has no other side effect than to set the error flag.

GL_OUT_OF_MEMORY

There is not enough memory left to execute the command. The state of the GL is undefined, except for the state of the error flags, after this error is recorded.

GL_TABLE_TOO_LARGE

The specified table exceeds the implementation's maximum supported table size. The offending command is ignored and has no other side effect than to set the error flag.

When an error flag is set, results of a GL operation are undefined only if GL_OUT_OF_MEMORY has occurred. In all other cases, the command generating the error is ignored and has no effect on the GL state or frame buffer contents. If the generating command returns a value, it returns 0. If glGetError itself generates an error, it returns 0.

Notes

GL_TABLE_TOO_LARGE was introduced in GL version 1.2.

Errors

GL_INVALID_OPERATION is generated if glGetError is executed between the execution of glBegin and the corresponding execution of glEnd. In this case, glGetError returns 0.

glGetHistogram

Get histogram table

C Specification

```
void glGetHistogram(GLenum    target,
                    GLboolean reset,
                    GLenum    format,
                    GLenum    type,
                    GLvoid *  values);
```

Parameters

target   Must be GL_HISTOGRAM.

reset   If GL_TRUE, each component counter that is actually returned is reset to zero. (Other counters are unaffected.) If GL_FALSE, none of the counters in the histogram table is modified.

format   The format of values to be returned in *values*. Must be one of GL_RED, GL_GREEN, GL_BLUE, GL_ALPHA, GL_RGB, GL_BGR, GL_RGBA, GL_BGRA, GL_LUMINANCE, or GL_LUMINANCE_ALPHA.

type   The type of values to be returned in *values*. Symbolic constants GL_UNSIGNED_BYTE, GL_BYTE, GL_BITMAP, GL_UNSIGNED_SHORT, GL_SHORT, GL_UNSIGNED_INT, GL_INT, GL_FLOAT, GL_UNSIGNED_BYTE_3_3_2, GL_UNSIGNED_BYTE_2_3_3_REV, GL_UNSIGNED_SHORT_5_6_5, GL_UNSIGNED_SHORT_5_6_5_REV, GL_UNSIGNED_SHORT_4_4_4_4, GL_UNSIGNED_SHORT_4_4_4_4_REV, GL_UNSIGNED_SHORT_5_5_5_1, GL_UNSIGNED_SHORT_1_5_5_5_REV, GL_UNSIGNED_INT_8_8_8_8, GL_UNSIGNED_INT_8_8_8_8_REV, GL_UNSIGNED_INT_10_10_10_2, and GL_UNSIGNED_INT_2_10_10_10_REV are accepted.

values   A pointer to storage for the returned histogram table.

Description

glGetHistogram returns the current histogram table as a one-dimensional image with the same width as the histogram. No pixel transfer operations are performed on this image, but pixel storage modes that are applicable to 1D images are honored.

If a nonzero named buffer object is bound to the GL_PIXEL_PACK_BUFFER target (see glBindBuffer) while a histogram table is requested, *values* is treated as a byte offset into the buffer object's data store.

Color components that are requested in the specified *format*, but which are not included in the internal format of the histogram, are returned as zero. The assignments of internal color components to the components requested by *format* are:

Internal Component	Resulting Component
Red	Red
Green	Green
Blue	Blue
Alpha	Alpha
Luminance	Red

Notes

glGetHistogram is present only if ARB_imaging is returned when glGetString is called with an argument of GL_EXTENSIONS.

Errors

GL_INVALID_ENUM is generated if *target* is not GL_HISTOGRAM.

GL_INVALID_ENUM is generated if *format* is not one of the allowable values.

GL_INVALID_ENUM is generated if *type* is not one of the allowable values.

GL_INVALID_OPERATION is generated if *type* is one of GL_UNSIGNED_BYTE_3_3_2, GL_UNSIGNED_BYTE_2_3_3_REV, GL_UNSIGNED_SHORT_5_6_5, or GL_UNSIGNED_SHORT_5_6_5_REV and *format* is not GL_RGB.

GL_INVALID_OPERATION is generated if *type* is one of GL_UNSIGNED_SHORT_4_4_4_4, GL_UNSIGNED_SHORT_4_4_4_4_REV, GL_UNSIGNED_SHORT_5_5_5_1, GL_UNSIGNED_SHORT_1_5_5_5_REV, GL_UNSIGNED_INT_8_8_8_8, GL_UNSIGNED_INT_8_8_8_8_REV, GL_UNSIGNED_INT_10_10_10_2, or GL_UNSIGNED_INT_2_10_10_10_REV and *format* is neither GL_RGBA nor GL_BGRA.

GL_INVALID_OPERATION is generated if a nonzero buffer object name is bound to the GL_PIXEL_PACK_BUFFER target and the buffer object's data store is currently mapped.

GL_INVALID_OPERATION is generated if a nonzero buffer object name is bound to the GL_PIXEL_PACK_BUFFER target and the data would be packed to the buffer object such that the memory writes required would exceed the data store size.

GL_INVALID_OPERATION is generated if a nonzero buffer object name is bound to the GL_PIXEL_PACK_BUFFER target and *values* is not evenly divisible into the number of bytes needed to store in memory a datum indicated by *type*.

GL_INVALID_OPERATION is generated if glGetHistogram is executed between the execution of glBegin and the corresponding execution of glEnd.

Associated Gets

glGetHistogramParameter

glGet with argument GL_PIXEL_PACK_BUFFER_BINDING

See Also

glHistogram, glResetHistogram,

glGetHistogramParameter

Get histogram parameters

C Specification

```
void glGetHistogramParameterfv(GLenum    target,
                                GLenum    pname,
                                GLfloat * params);
void glGetHistogramParameteriv(GLenum    target,
                                GLenum    pname,
                                GLint * params);
```

Parameters

target   Must be one of GL_HISTOGRAM or GL_PROXY_HISTOGRAM.

pname   The name of the parameter to be retrieved. Must be one of GL_HISTOGRAM_WIDTH, GL_HISTOGRAM_FORMAT, GL_HISTOGRAM_RED_SIZE, GL_HISTOGRAM_GREEN_SIZE, GL_HISTOGRAM_BLUE_SIZE, GL_HISTOGRAM_ALPHA_SIZE, GL_HISTOGRAM_LUMINANCE_SIZE, or GL_HISTOGRAM_SINK.

params   Pointer to storage for the returned values.

Description

glGetHistogramParameter is used to query parameter values for the current histogram or for a proxy. The histogram state information may be queried by calling glGetHistogramParameter with a *target* of GL_HISTOGRAM (to obtain information for the current histogram table) or GL_PROXY_HISTOGRAM (to obtain information from the most recent proxy request) and one of the following values for the *pname* argument:

Parameter	Description
GL_HISTOGRAM_WIDTH	Histogram table width
GL_HISTOGRAM_FORMAT	Internal format
GL_HISTOGRAM_RED_SIZE	Red component counter size, in bits
GL_HISTOGRAM_GREEN_SIZE	Green component counter size, in bits
GL_HISTOGRAM_BLUE_SIZE	Blue component counter size, in bits
GL_HISTOGRAM_ALPHA_SIZE	Alpha component counter size, in bits
GL_HISTOGRAM_LUMINANCE_SIZE	Luminance component counter size, in bits
GL_HISTOGRAM_SINK	Value of the *sink* parameter

Notes

glGetHistogramParameter is present only if ARB_imaging is returned when glGetString is called with an argument of GL_EXTENSIONS.

Errors

GL_INVALID_ENUM is generated if *target* is not one of the allowable values.

GL_INVALID_ENUM is generated if *pname* is not one of the allowable values.

GL_INVALID_OPERATION is generated if glGetHistogramParameter is executed between the execution of glBegin and the corresponding execution of glEnd.

See Also

glGetHistogram, glHistogram

glGetLight

Return light source parameter values

C Specification

```
void glGetLightfv(GLenum    light,
                  GLenum    pname,
                  GLfloat * params);
void glGetLightiv(GLenum    light,
                  GLenum    pname,
                  GLint   * params);
```

Parameters

light   Specifies a light source. The number of possible lights depends on the implementation, but at least eight lights are supported. They are identified by symbolic names of the form GL_LIGHT*i* where *i* ranges from 0 to the value of GL_MAX_LIGHTS - 1.

pname   Specifies a light source parameter for *light*. Accepted symbolic names are GL_AMBIENT, GL_DIFFUSE, GL_SPECULAR, GL_POSITION, GL_SPOT_DIRECTION, GL_SPOT_EXPONENT, GL_SPOT_CUTOFF, GL_CONSTANT_ATTENUATION, GL_LINEAR_ATTENUATION, and GL_QUADRATIC_ATTENUATION.

params   Returns the requested data.

Description

glGetLight returns in *params* the value or values of a light source parameter. *light* names the light and is a symbolic name of the form GL_LIGHT*i* where *i* ranges from 0 to the value of GL_MAX_LIGHTS - 1. GL_MAX_LIGHTS is an implementation dependent constant that is greater than or equal to eight. *pname* specifies one of ten light source parameters, again by symbolic name.

The following parameters are defined:

GL_AMBIENT

params returns four integer or floating-point values representing the ambient intensity of the light source. Integer values, when requested, are linearly mapped from the internal floating-point representation such that 1.0 maps to the most positive representable integer value, and -1.0 maps to the most negative representable integer value. If the internal value is outside the range [-1,1], the corresponding integer return value is undefined. The initial value is (0, 0, 0, 1).

GL_DIFFUSE

params returns four integer or floating-point values representing the diffuse intensity of the light source. Integer values, when requested, are linearly mapped from the internal floating-point representation such that 1.0 maps to the most positive representable integer value, and -1.0 maps to the most negative representable integer value. If the internal value is outside the range [-1,1], the corresponding integer return value is undefined. The initial value for GL_LIGHT0 is (1, 1, 1, 1); for other lights, the initial value is (0, 0, 0, 0).

GL_SPECULAR

params returns four integer or floating-point values representing the specular intensity of the light source. Integer values, when requested, are linearly mapped from the internal floating-point representation such that 1.0 maps to the most positive representable integer value, and -1.0 maps to the most negative representable integer value. If the internal value is outside the range [-1,1], the corresponding integer return value is undefined. The initial value for GL_LIGHT0 is (1, 1, 1, 1); for other lights, the initial value is (0, 0, 0, 0).

GL_POSITION

params returns four integer or floating-point values representing the position of the light source. Integer values, when requested, are computed by rounding the internal floating-point values to the nearest integer value. The returned values are those maintained in eye coordinates. They will not be equal to the values specified using glLight, unless the modelview matrix was identity at the time glLight was called. The initial value is (0, 0, 1, 0).

GL_SPOT_DIRECTION

params returns three integer or floating-point values representing the direction of the light source. Integer values, when requested, are computed by rounding the internal floating-point values to the nearest integer value. The returned values are those maintained in eye coordinates. They will not be equal to the values specified using glLight, unless the modelview matrix was identity at the time glLight was called. Although spot direction is normalized before being used in the lighting equation, the returned values are the transformed versions of the specified values prior to normalization. The initial value is (0,0,-1).

GL_SPOT_EXPONENT

params returns a single integer or floating-point value representing the spot exponent of the light. An integer value, when requested, is computed by rounding the internal floating-point representation to the nearest integer. The initial value is 0.

GL_SPOT_CUTOFF

params returns a single integer or floating-point value representing the spot cutoff angle of the light. An integer value, when requested, is computed by rounding the internal floating-point representation to the nearest integer. The initial value is 180.

GL_CONSTANT_ATTENUATION

params returns a single integer or floating-point value representing the constant (not distance-related) attenuation of the light. An integer value, when requested, is computed by rounding the internal floating-point representation to the nearest integer. The initial value is 1.

GL_LINEAR_ATTENUATION

params returns a single integer or floating-point value representing the linear attenuation of the light. An integer value, when requested, is computed by rounding the internal floating-point representation to the nearest integer. The initial value is 0.

GL_QUADRATIC_ATTENUATION

params returns a single integer or floating-point value representing the quadratic attenuation of the light. An integer value, when requested, is computed by rounding the internal floating-point representation to the nearest integer. The initial value is 0.

Notes

It is always the case that GL_LIGHTi = GL_LIGHT0 + i.

If an error is generated, no change is made to the contents of *params*.

Errors

GL_INVALID_ENUM is generated if *light* or *pname* is not an accepted value.

GL_INVALID_OPERATION is generated if glGetLight is executed between the execution of glBegin and the corresponding execution of glEnd.

See Also

glLight

glGetMap

Return evaluator parameters

C Specification

```
void glGetMapdv(GLenum      target,
                GLenum      query,
                GLdouble *  v);
```

```
void glGetMapfv(GLenum   target,
                GLenum   query,
                GLfloat * v);
void glGetMapiv(GLenum   target,
                GLenum   query,
                GLint * v);
```

Parameters

target   Specifies the symbolic name of a map. Accepted values are GL_MAP1_COLOR_4,
             GL_MAP1_INDEX, GL_MAP1_NORMAL, GL_MAP1_TEXTURE_COORD_1,
             GL_MAP1_TEXTURE_COORD_2, GL_MAP1_TEXTURE_COORD_3,
             GL_MAP1_TEXTURE_COORD_4, GL_MAP1_VERTEX_3, GL_MAP1_VERTEX_4,
             GL_MAP2_COLOR_4, GL_MAP2_INDEX, GL_MAP2_NORMAL, GL_MAP2_TEXTURE_COORD_1,
             GL_MAP2_TEXTURE_COORD_2, GL_MAP2_TEXTURE_COORD_3,
             GL_MAP2_TEXTURE_COORD_4, GL_MAP2_VERTEX_3, and GL_MAP2_VERTEX_4.

query   Specifies which parameter to return. Symbolic names GL_COEFF, GL_ORDER, and
             GL_DOMAIN are accepted.

v   Returns the requested data.

Description

glMap1 and glMap2 define evaluators. glGetMap returns evaluator parameters. *target* chooses a map, *query* selects a specific parameter, and *v* points to storage where the values will be returned.

The acceptable values for the target parameter are described in the glMap1 and glMap2 reference pages.

query can assume the following values:

GL_COEFF

v returns the control points for the evaluator function. One-dimensional evaluators return order control points, and two-dimensional evaluators return uorder×vorder control points. Each control point consists of one, two, three, or four integer, single-precision floating-point, or double-precision floating-point values, depending on the type of the evaluator. The GL returns two-dimensional control points in row-major order, incrementing the uorder index quickly and the vorder index after each row. Integer values, when requested, are computed by rounding the internal floating-point values to the nearest integer values.

GL_ORDER

v returns the order of the evaluator function. One-dimensional evaluators return a single value, order. The initial value is 1. Two-dimensional evaluators return two values, uorder and vorder. The initial value is 1,1.

GL_DOMAIN

v returns the linear *u* and *v* mapping parameters. One-dimensional evaluators return two values, u1 and u2, as specified by glMap1. Two-dimensional evaluators return four values (u1, u2, v1, and v2) as specified by glMap2. Integer values, when requested, are computed by rounding the internal floating-point values to the nearest integer values.

Notes

If an error is generated, no change is made to the contents of *v*.

Errors

GL_INVALID_ENUM is generated if either *target* or *query* is not an accepted value.

GL_INVALID_OPERATION is generated if glGetMap is executed between the execution of glBegin and the corresponding execution of glEnd.

See Also

glEvalCoord, glMap1, glMap2

glGetMaterial

Return material parameters

C Specification

```
void glGetMaterialfv(GLenum    face,
                     GLenum    pname,
                     GLfloat * params);
void glGetMaterialiv(GLenum    face,
                     GLenum    pname,
                     GLint *   params);
```

Parameters

face   Specifies which of the two materials is being queried. GL_FRONT or GL_BACK are accepted, representing the front and back materials, respectively.

pname   Specifies the material parameter to return. GL_AMBIENT, GL_DIFFUSE, GL_SPECULAR, GL_EMISSION, GL_SHININESS, and GL_COLOR_INDEXES are accepted.

params   Returns the requested data.

Description

glGetMaterial returns in *params* the value or values of parameter *pname* of material *face*. Six parameters are defined:

GL_AMBIENT

params returns four integer or floating-point values representing the ambient reflectance of the material. Integer values, when requested, are linearly mapped from the internal floating-point representation such that 1.0 maps to the most positive representable integer value, and -1.0 maps to the most negative representable integer value. If the internal value is outside the range [-1,1], the corresponding integer return value is undefined. The initial value is (0.2, 0.2, 0.2, 1.0).

GL_DIFFUSE

params returns four integer or floating-point values representing the diffuse reflectance of the material. Integer values, when requested, are linearly mapped from the internal floating-point representation such that 1.0 maps to the most positive representable integer value, and -1.0 maps to the most negative representable integer value. If the internal value is outside the range [-1,1], the corresponding integer return value is undefined. The initial value is (0.8, 0.8, 0.8, 1.0).

GL_SPECULAR

params returns four integer or floating-point values representing the specular reflectance of the material. Integer values, when requested, are linearly mapped from the internal floating-point representation such that 1.0 maps to the most positive representable integer value, and -1.0 maps to the most negative representable integer value. If the internal value is outside the range [-1,1], the corresponding integer return value is undefined. The initial value is (0, 0, 0, 1).

GL_EMISSION

params returns four integer or floating-point values representing the emitted light intensity of the material. Integer values, when requested, are linearly mapped from the internal floating-point representation such that 1.0 maps to the most positive representable integer value, and -1.0 maps to the most negative representable integer value. If the internal value is outside the range [-1,1], the corresponding integer return value is undefined. The initial value is (0, 0, 0, 1).

GL_SHININESS

params returns one integer or floating-point value representing the specular exponent of the material. Integer values, when requested, are computed by rounding the internal floating-point value to the nearest integer value. The initial value is 0.

GL_COLOR_INDEXES

params returns three integer or floating-point values representing the ambient, diffuse, and specular indices of the material. These indices are used only for color index lighting. (All the other parameters are used only for RGBA lighting.) Integer values, when requested, are computed by rounding the internal floating-point values to the nearest integer values.

Notes

If an error is generated, no change is made to the contents of *params*.

Errors

GL_INVALID_ENUM is generated if *face* or *pname* is not an accepted value.

GL_INVALID_OPERATION is generated if glGetMaterial is executed between the execution of glBegin and the corresponding execution of glEnd.

See Also

glMaterial

glGetMinmax

Get minimum and maximum pixel values

C Specification

```
void glGetMinmax(GLenum      target,
                 GLboolean   reset,
                 GLenum      format,
                 GLenum      types,
                 GLvoid *    values);
```

Parameters

target   Must be GL_MINMAX.

reset   If GL_TRUE, all entries in the minmax table that are actually returned are reset to their initial values. (Other entries are unaltered.) If GL_FALSE, the minmax table is unaltered.

format   The format of the data to be returned in *values*. Must be one of GL_RED, GL_GREEN, GL_BLUE, GL_ALPHA, GL_RGB, GL_BGR, GL_RGBA, GL_BGRA, GL_LUMINANCE, or GL_LUMINANCE_ALPHA.

types   The type of the data to be returned in *values*. Symbolic constants GL_UNSIGNED_BYTE, GL_BYTE, GL_BITMAP, GL_UNSIGNED_SHORT, GL_SHORT, GL_UNSIGNED_INT, GL_INT, GL_FLOAT, GL_UNSIGNED_BYTE_3_3_2, GL_UNSIGNED_BYTE_2_3_3_REV, GL_UNSIGNED_SHORT_5_6_5, GL_UNSIGNED_SHORT_5_6_5_REV, GL_UNSIGNED_SHORT_4_4_4_4, GL_UNSIGNED_SHORT_4_4_4_4_REV, GL_UNSIGNED_SHORT_5_5_5_1, GL_UNSIGNED_SHORT_1_5_5_5_REV, GL_UNSIGNED_INT_8_8_8_8, GL_UNSIGNED_INT_8_8_8_8_REV, GL_UNSIGNED_INT_10_10_10_2, and GL_UNSIGNED_INT_2_10_10_10_REV are accepted.

values   A pointer to storage for the returned values.

Description

glGetMinmax returns the accumulated minimum and maximum pixel values (computed on a per-component basis) in a one-dimensional image of width 2. The first set of return values are the minima, and the second set of return values are the maxima. The format of the return values is determined by *format*, and their type is determined by *types*.

If a nonzero named buffer object is bound to the GL_PIXEL_PACK_BUFFER target (see glBindBuffer) while minimum and maximum pixel values are requested, *values* is treated as a byte offset into the buffer object's data store.

No pixel transfer operations are performed on the return values, but pixel storage modes that are applicable to one-dimensional images are performed. Color components that are requested in the specified *format*, but that are not included in the internal format of the minmax table, are returned as zero. The assignment of internal color components to the components requested by *format* are as follows:

Internal Component	Resulting Component
Red	Red
Green	Green
Blue	Blue
Alpha	Alpha
Luminance	Red

If *reset* is GL_TRUE, the minmax table entries corresponding to the return values are reset to their initial values. Minimum and maximum values that are not returned are not modified, even if *reset* is GL_TRUE.

Notes

glGetMinmax is present only if ARB_imaging is returned when glGetString is called with an argument of GL_EXTENSIONS.

Errors

GL_INVALID_ENUM is generated if *target* is not GL_MINMAX.

GL_INVALID_ENUM is generated if *format* is not one of the allowable values.

GL_INVALID_ENUM is generated if *types* is not one of the allowable values.

GL_INVALID_OPERATION is generated if *types* is one of GL_UNSIGNED_BYTE_3_3_2, GL_UNSIGNED_BYTE_2_3_3_REV, GL_UNSIGNED_SHORT_5_6_5, or GL_UNSIGNED_SHORT_5_6_5_REV and *format* is not GL_RGB.

GL_INVALID_OPERATION is generated if *types* is one of GL_UNSIGNED_SHORT_4_4_4_4, GL_UNSIGNED_SHORT_4_4_4_4_REV, GL_UNSIGNED_SHORT_5_5_5_1, GL_UNSIGNED_SHORT_1_5_5_5_REV, GL_UNSIGNED_INT_8_8_8_8, GL_UNSIGNED_INT_8_8_8_8_REV, GL_UNSIGNED_INT_10_10_10_2, or GL_UNSIGNED_INT_2_10_10_10_REV and *format* is neither GL_RGBA nor GL_BGRA.

GL_INVALID_OPERATION is generated if a nonzero buffer object name is bound to the GL_PIXEL_PACK_BUFFER target and the buffer object's data store is currently mapped.

GL_INVALID_OPERATION is generated if a nonzero buffer object name is bound to the GL_PIXEL_PACK_BUFFER target and the data would be packed to the buffer object such that the memory writes required would exceed the data store size.

GL_INVALID_OPERATION is generated if a nonzero buffer object name is bound to the GL_PIXEL_PACK_BUFFER target and *values* is not evenly divisible into the number of bytes needed to store in memory a datum indicated by *type*.

GL_INVALID_OPERATION is generated if glGetMinmax is executed between the execution of glBegin and the corresponding execution of glEnd.

Associated Gets

glGetMinmaxParameter

glGet with argument GL_PIXEL_PACK_BUFFER_BINDING

See Also

glMinmax, glResetMinmax

glGetMinmaxParameter

Get minmax parameters

C Specification

```
void glGetMinmaxParameterfv(GLenum    target,
                            GLenum    pname,
                            GLfloat * params);
void glGetMinmaxParameteriv(GLenum    target,
                            GLenum    pname,
                            GLint *   params);
```

Parameters

target	Must be GL_MINMAX.
pname	The parameter to be retrieved. Must be one of GL_MINMAX_FORMAT or GL_MINMAX_SINK.
params	A pointer to storage for the retrieved parameters.

Description

glGetMinmaxParameter retrieves parameters for the current minmax table by setting *pname* to one of the following values:

Parameter	Description
GL_MINMAX_FORMAT	Internal format of minmax table
GL_MINMAX_SINK	Value of the sink parameter

Notes

glGetMinmaxParameter is present only if ARB_imaging is returned when glGetString is called with an argument of GL_EXTENSIONS.

Errors

GL_INVALID_ENUM is generated if *target* is not GL_MINMAX.

GL_INVALID_ENUM is generated if *pname* is not one of the allowable values.

GL_INVALID_OPERATION is generated if glGetMinmaxParameter is executed between the execution of glBegin and the corresponding execution of glEnd.

See Also

glMinmax, glGetMinmax

glGetPixelMap

Return the specified pixel map

C Specification

```
void glGetPixelMapfv(GLenum    map,
                     GLfloat * data);
void glGetPixelMapuiv(GLenum    map,
                      GLuint *  data);
void glGetPixelMapusv(GLenum     map,
                      GLushort * data);
```

Parameters

map   Specifies the name of the pixel map to return. Accepted values are
             GL_PIXEL_MAP_I_TO_I, GL_PIXEL_MAP_S_TO_S, GL_PIXEL_MAP_I_TO_R,
             GL_PIXEL_MAP_I_TO_G, GL_PIXEL_MAP_I_TO_B, GL_PIXEL_MAP_I_TO_A,
             GL_PIXEL_MAP_R_TO_R, GL_PIXEL_MAP_G_TO_G, GL_PIXEL_MAP_B_TO_B, and
             GL_PIXEL_MAP_A_TO_A.

data   Returns the pixel map contents.

Description

See the glPixelMap reference page for a description of the acceptable values for the *map* parameter. glGetPixelMap returns in *data* the contents of the pixel map specified in map. Pixel maps are used during the execution of glReadPixels, glDrawPixels, glCopyPixels, glTexImage1D, glTexImage2D, glTexImage3D, glTexSubImage1D, glTexSubImage2D, glTexSubImage3D, glCopyTexImage1D, glCopyTexImage2D, glCopyTexSubImage1D, glCopyTexSubImage2D, and glCopyTexSubImage3D. to map color indices, stencil indices, color components, and depth components to other values.

If a nonzero named buffer object is bound to the GL_PIXEL_PACK_BUFFER target (see glBindBuffer) while a pixel map is requested, *data* is treated as a byte offset into the buffer object's data store.

Unsigned integer values, if requested, are linearly mapped from the internal fixed or floating-point representation such that 1.0 maps to the largest representable integer value, and 0.0 maps to 0. Return unsigned integer values are undefined if the map value was not in the range [0,1].

To determine the required size of *map*, call glGet with the appropriate symbolic constant.

Notes

If an error is generated, no change is made to the contents of *data*.

Errors

GL_INVALID_ENUM is generated if *map* is not an accepted value.

GL_INVALID_OPERATION is generated if a nonzero buffer object name is bound to the GL_PIXEL_PACK_BUFFER target and the buffer object's data store is currently mapped.

GL_INVALID_OPERATION is generated if a nonzero buffer object name is bound to the GL_PIXEL_PACK_BUFFER target and the data would be packed to the buffer object such that the memory writes required would exceed the data store size.

GL_INVALID_OPERATION is generated by glGetPixelMapfv if a nonzero buffer object name is bound to the GL_PIXEL_PACK_BUFFER target and *data* is not evenly divisible into the number of bytes needed to store in memory a GLfloat datum.

GL_INVALID_OPERATION is generated by glGetPixelMapuiv if a nonzero buffer object name is bound to the GL_PIXEL_PACK_BUFFER target and *data* is not evenly divisible into the number of bytes needed to store in memory a GLuint datum.

GL_INVALID_OPERATION is generated by glGetPixelMapusv if a nonzero buffer object name is bound to the GL_PIXEL_PACK_BUFFER target and *data* is not evenly divisible into the number of bytes needed to store in memory a GLushort datum.

GL_INVALID_OPERATION is generated if glGetPixelMap is executed between the execution of glBegin and the corresponding execution of glEnd.

Associated Gets

glGet with argument GL_PIXEL_MAP_I_TO_I_SIZE
glGet with argument GL_PIXEL_MAP_S_TO_S_SIZE
glGet with argument GL_PIXEL_MAP_I_TO_R_SIZE
glGet with argument GL_PIXEL_MAP_I_TO_G_SIZE
glGet with argument GL_PIXEL_MAP_I_TO_B_SIZE

glGet with argument GL_PIXEL_MAP_I_TO_A_SIZE
glGet with argument GL_PIXEL_MAP_R_TO_R_SIZE
glGet with argument GL_PIXEL_MAP_G_TO_G_SIZE
glGet with argument GL_PIXEL_MAP_B_TO_B_SIZE
glGet with argument GL_PIXEL_MAP_A_TO_A_SIZE
glGet with argument GL_MAX_PIXEL_MAP_TABLE
glGet with argument GL_PIXEL_PACK_BUFFER_BINDING

See Also

glColorSubTable, glColorTable, glConvolutionFilter1D, glConvolutionFilter2D,
glCopyColorSubTable, glCopyColorTable, glCopyPixels, glCopyTexImage1D,
glCopyTexImage2D, glCopyTexSubImage1D, glCopyTexSubImage2D, glCopyTexSubImage3D,
glDrawPixels, glGetHistogram, glGetMinmax, glGetTexImage, glPixelMap,
glPixelTransfer, glReadPixels, glSeparableFilter2D, glTexImage1D, glTexImage1D,
glTexImage2DglTexImage2D, glTexImage3D, glTexSubImage1D, glTexSubImage2D,
glTexSubImage3D

glGetPointerv

Return the address of the specified pointer

C Specification

void **glGetPointerv**(GLenum   *pname*,
                       GLvoid ** *params*);

Parameters

pname   Specifies the array or buffer pointer to be returned. Symbolic constants
            GL_COLOR_ARRAY_POINTER, GL_EDGE_FLAG_ARRAY_POINTER,
            GL_FOG_COORD_ARRAY_POINTER, GL_FEEDBACK_BUFFER_POINTER,
            GL_INDEX_ARRAY_POINTER, GL_NORMAL_ARRAY_POINTER,
            GL_SECONDARY_COLOR_ARRAY_POINTER, GL_SELECTION_BUFFER_POINTER,
            GL_TEXTURE_COORD_ARRAY_POINTER, or GL_VERTEX_ARRAY_POINTER are accepted.

params   Returns the pointer value specified by *pname*.

Description

glGetPointerv returns pointer information. *pname* is a symbolic constant indicating the pointer
to be returned, and *params* is a pointer to a location in which to place the returned data.

For all *pname* arguments except GL_FEEDBACK_BUFFER_POINTER and
GL_SELECTION_BUFFER_POINTER, if a nonzero named buffer object was bound to the
GL_ARRAY_BUFFER target (see glBindBuffer) when the desired pointer was previously specified, the
pointer returned is a byte offset into the buffer object's data store. Buffer objects are only available in
OpenGL versions 1.5 and greater.

Notes

glGetPointerv is available only if the GL version is 1.1 or greater.
GL_FOG_COORD_ARRAY_POINTER and GL_SECONDARY_COLOR_ARRAY_POINTER are available only
if the GL version is 1.4 or greater.
The pointers are all client-side state.
The initial value for each pointer is 0.
For OpenGL versions 1.3 and greater, or when the ARB_multitexture extension is supported,
querying the GL_TEXTURE_COORD_ARRAY_POINTER returns the value for the active client texture unit.

Errors

GL_INVALID_ENUM is generated if *pname* is not an accepted value.

See Also

glBindBuffer, glClientActiveTexture, glColorPointer, glEdgeFlagPointer, glFogCoordPointer, glFeedbackBuffer, glGetVertexAttribPointerv, glIndexPointer, glNormalPointer, glSecondaryColorPointer, glSelectBuffer, glTexCoordPointer, glVertexAttribPointer, glVertexPointer

glGetPolygonStipple

Return the polygon stipple pattern

C Specification

void **glGetPolygonStipple**(GLubyte * *pattern*);

Parameters

pattern   Returns the stipple pattern. The initial value is all 1's.

Description

glGetPolygonStipple returns to pattern a 32×32 polygon stipple pattern. The pattern is packed into memory as if glReadPixels with both height and width of 32, type of GL_BITMAP, and format of GL_COLOR_INDEX were called, and the stipple pattern were stored in an internal 32×32 color index buffer. Unlike glReadPixels, however, pixel transfer operations (shift, offset, pixel map) are not applied to the returned stipple image.

If a nonzero named buffer object is bound to the GL_PIXEL_PACK_BUFFER target (see glBindBuffer) while a polygon stipple pattern is requested, pattern is treated as a byte offset into the buffer object's data store.

Notes

If an error is generated, no change is made to the contents of *pattern*.

Errors

GL_INVALID_OPERATION is generated if a nonzero buffer object name is bound to the GL_PIXEL_PACK_BUFFER target and the buffer object's data store is currently mapped.

GL_INVALID_OPERATION is generated if a nonzero buffer object name is bound to the GL_PIXEL_PACK_BUFFER target and the data would be packed to the buffer object such that the memory writes required would exceed the data store size.

GL_INVALID_OPERATION is generated if glGetPolygonStipple is executed between the execution of glBegin and the corresponding execution of glEnd.

Associated Gets

glGet with argument GL_PIXEL_PACK_BUFFER_BINDING

See Also

glPixelStore, glPixelTransfer, glPolygonStipple, glReadPixels

glGetProgramiv

Return a parameter from a program object

C Specification

void **glGetProgramiv**(GLuint   *program*,
                    GLenum   *pname*,
                    GLint * *params*);

Parameters

program	Specifies the program object to be queried.
pname	Specifies the object parameter. Accepted symbolic names are GL_DELETE_STATUS, GL_LINK_STATUS, GL_VALIDATE_STATUS, GL_INFO_LOG_LENGTH, GL_ATTACHED_SHADERS, GL_ACTIVE_ATTRIBUTES, GL_ACTIVE_ATTRIBUTE_MAX_LENGTH, GL_ACTIVE_UNIFORMS, GL_ACTIVE_UNIFORM_MAX_LENGTH.
params	Returns the requested object parameter.

Description

glGetProgram returns in *params* the value of a parameter for a specific program object. The following parameters are defined:

GL_DELETE_STATUS

params returns GL_TRUE if *program* is currently flagged for deletion, and GL_FALSE otherwise.

GL_LINK_STATUS

params returns GL_TRUE if the last link operation on *program* was successful, and GL_FALSE otherwise.

GL_VALIDATE_STATUS

params returns GL_TRUE or if the last validation operation on *program* was successful, and GL_FALSE otherwise.

GL_INFO_LOG_LENGTH

params returns the number of characters in the information log for *program* including the null termination character (i.e., the size of the character buffer required to store the information log). If *program* has no information log, a value of 0 is returned.

GL_ATTACHED_SHADERS

params returns the number of shader objects attached to *program*.

GL_ACTIVE_ATTRIBUTES

params returns the number of active attribute variables for *program*.

GL_ACTIVE_ATTRIBUTE_MAX_LENGTH

params returns the length of the longest active attribute name for *program*, including the null termination character (i.e., the size of the character buffer required to store the longest attribute name). If no active attributes exist, 0 is returned.

GL_ACTIVE_UNIFORMS

params returns the number of active uniform variables for *program*.

GL_ACTIVE_UNIFORM_MAX_LENGTH

params returns the length of the longest active uniform variable name for *program*, including the null termination character (i.e., the size of the character buffer required to store the longest uniform variable name). If no active uniform variables exist, 0 is returned.

Notes

glGetProgram is available only if the GL version is 2.0 or greater.

If an error is generated, no change is made to the contents of *params*.

Errors

GL_INVALID_VALUE is generated if *program* is not a value generated by OpenGL.

GL_INVALID_OPERATION is generated if *program* does not refer to a program object.

GL_INVALID_ENUM is generated if *pname* is not an accepted value.

GL_INVALID_OPERATION is generated if glGetProgram is executed between the execution of glBegin and the corresponding execution of glEnd.

Associated Gets

glGetActiveAttrib with argument *program*

glGetActiveUniform with argument *program*
glGetAttachedShaders with argument *program*
glGetProgramInfoLog with argument *program*
glIsProgram

See Also

glAttachShader, glCreateProgram, glDeleteProgram, glGetShader, glLinkProgram, glValidateProgram

glGetProgramInfoLog

Return the information log for a program object

C Specification

```
void glGetProgramInfoLog(GLuint      program,
                         GLsizei     maxLength,
                         GLsizei *   length,
                         GLchar *    infoLog);
```

Parameters

program	Specifies the program object whose information log is to be queried.
maxLength	Specifies the size of the character buffer for storing the returned information log.
length	Returns the length of the string returned in infoLog (excluding the null terminator).
infoLog	Specifies an array of characters that is used to return the information log.

Description

glGetProgramInfoLog returns the information log for the specified program object. The information log for a program object is modified when the program object is linked or validated. The string that is returned will be null terminated.

glGetProgramInfoLog returns in *infoLog* as much of the information log as it can, up to a maximum of *maxLength* characters. The number of characters actually returned, excluding the null termination character, is specified by *length*. If the length of the returned string is not required, a value of NULL can be passed in the *length* argument. The size of the buffer required to store the returned information log can be obtained by calling glGetProgram with the value GL_INFO_LOG_LENGTH.

The information log for a program object is either an empty string, or a string containing information about the last link operation, or a string containing information about the last validation operation. It may contain diagnostic messages, warning messages, and other information. When a program object is created, its information log will be a string of length 0.

Notes

glGetProgramInfoLog is available only if the GL version is 2.0 or greater.

The information log for a program object is the OpenGL implementer's primary mechanism for conveying information about linking and validating. Therefore, the information log can be helpful to application developers during the development process, even when these operations are successful. Application developers should not expect different OpenGL implementations to produce identical information logs.

Errors

GL_INVALID_VALUE is generated if *program* is not a value generated by OpenGL.
GL_INVALID_OPERATION is generated if *program* is not a program object.

GL_INVALID_VALUE is generated if *maxLength* is less than 0.

GL_INVALID_OPERATION is generated if glGetProgramInfoLog is executed between the execution of glBegin and the corresponding execution of glEnd.

Associated Gets

glGetProgram with argument GL_INFO_LOG_LENGTH
glIsProgram

See Also

glCompileShader, glGetShaderInfoLog, glLinkProgram, glValidateProgram

glGetQueryiv

Return parameters of a query object target

C Specification

```
void glGetQueryiv(GLenum   target,
                  GLenum   pname,
                  GLint * params);
```

Parameters

target	Specifies a query object target. Must be GL_SAMPLES_PASSED.
pname	Specifies the symbolic name of a query object target parameter. Accepted values are GL_CURRENT_QUERY or GL_QUERY_COUNTER_BITS.
params	Returns the requested data.

Description

glGetQueryiv returns in *params* a selected parameter of the query object target specified by *target*.

pname names a specific query object target parameter. When *target* is GL_SAMPLES_PASSED, *pname* can be as follows:

GL_CURRENT_QUERY

params returns the name of the currently active occlusion query object. If no occlusion query is active, 0 is returned. The initial value is 0.

GL_QUERY_COUNTER_BITS

params returns the number of bits in the query counter used to accumulate passing samples. If the number of bits returned is 0, the implementation does not support a query counter, and the results obtained from glGetQueryObject are useless.

Notes

If an error is generated, no change is made to the contents of *params*.

glGetQueryiv is available only if the GL version is 1.5 or greater.

Errors

GL_INVALID_ENUM is generated if *target* or *pname* is not an accepted value.

GL_INVALID_OPERATION is generated if glGetQueryiv is executed between the execution of glBegin and the corresponding execution of glEnd.

See Also

glGetQueryObject, glIsQuery

glGetQueryObject

Return parameters of a query object

C Specification

```
void glGetQueryObjectiv(GLuint    id,
                        GLenum    pname,
                        GLint *   params);
void glGetQueryObjectuiv(GLuint    id,
                         GLenum    pname,
                         GLuint *  params);
```

Parameters

id   Specifies the name of a query object.

pname   Specifies the symbolic name of a query object parameter. Accepted values are
            GL_QUERY_RESULT or GL_QUERY_RESULT_AVAILABLE.

params   Returns the requested data.

Description

glGetQueryObject returns in *params* a selected parameter of the query object specified by *id*.
pname names a specific query object parameter. *pname* can be as follows:
GL_QUERY_RESULT
params returns the value of the query object's passed samples counter. The initial value is 0.
GL_QUERY_RESULT_AVAILABLE
params returns whether the passed samples counter is immediately available. If a delay would
occur waiting for the query result, GL_FALSE is returned. Otherwise, GL_TRUE is returned, which also
indicates that the results of all previous queries are available as well.

Notes

If an error is generated, no change is made to the contents of *params*.

glGetQueryObject implicitly flushes the GL pipeline so that any incomplete rendering delimited by the occlusion query completes in finite time.

If multiple queries are issued using the same query object *id* before calling glGetQueryObject,
the results of the most recent query will be returned. In this case, when issuing a new query, the
results of the previous query are discarded.

glGetQueryObject is available only if the GL version is 1.5 or greater.

Errors

GL_INVALID_ENUM is generated if *pname* is not an accepted value.

GL_INVALID_OPERATION is generated if *id* is not the name of a query object.

GL_INVALID_OPERATION is generated if *id* is the name of a currently active query object.

GL_INVALID_OPERATION is generated if glGetQueryObject is executed between the execution
of glBegin and the corresponding execution of glEnd.

See Also

glBeginQuery, glEndQuery, glGetQueryiv, glIsQuery

glGetSeparableFilter

Get separable convolution filter kernel images

C Specification

```
void glGetSeparableFilter(GLenum    target,
                          GLenum    format,
                          GLenum    type,
                          GLvoid * row,
                          GLvoid * column,
                          GLvoid * span);
```

Parameters

target   The separable filter to be retrieved. Must be GL_SEPARABLE_2D.

format   Format of the output images. Must be one of GL_RED, GL_GREEN, GL_BLUE, GL_ALPHA, GL_RGB, GL_BGRGL_RGBA, GL_BGRA, GL_LUMINANCE, or GL_LUMINANCE_ALPHA.

type   Data type of components in the output images. Symbolic constants GL_UNSIGNED_BYTE, GL_BYTE, GL_BITMAP, GL_UNSIGNED_SHORT, GL_SHORT, GL_UNSIGNED_INT, GL_INT, GL_FLOAT, GL_UNSIGNED_BYTE_3_3_2, GL_UNSIGNED_BYTE_2_3_3_REV, GL_UNSIGNED_SHORT_5_6_5, GL_UNSIGNED_SHORT_5_6_5_REV, GL_UNSIGNED_SHORT_4_4_4_4, GL_UNSIGNED_SHORT_4_4_4_4_REV, GL_UNSIGNED_SHORT_5_5_5_1, GL_UNSIGNED_SHORT_1_5_5_5_REV, GL_UNSIGNED_INT_8_8_8_8, GL_UNSIGNED_INT_8_8_8_8_REV, GL_UNSIGNED_INT_10_10_10_2, and GL_UNSIGNED_INT_2_10_10_10_REV are accepted.

row   Pointer to storage for the row filter image.

column   Pointer to storage for the column filter image.

span   Pointer to storage for the span filter image (currently unused).

Description

glGetSeparableFilter returns the two one-dimensional filter kernel images for the current separable 2D convolution filter. The row image is placed in *row* and the column image is placed in *column* according to the specifications in *format* and *type*. (In the current implementation, *span* is not affected in any way.) No pixel transfer operations are performed on the images, but the relevant pixel storage modes are applied.

If a nonzero named buffer object is bound to the GL_PIXEL_PACK_BUFFER target (see glBindBuffer) while a separable convolution filter is requested, *row*, *column*, and *span* are treated as a byte offset into the buffer object's data store.

Color components that are present in *format* but not included in the internal format of the filters are returned as zero. The assignments of internal color components to the components of *format* are as follows:

Internal Component	Resulting Component
Red	Red
Green	Green
Blue	Blue
Alpha	Alpha
Luminance	Red
Intensity	Red

Notes

glGetSeparableFilter is present only if ARB_imaging is returned when glGetString is called with an argument of GL_EXTENSIONS.

Non-separable 2D filters must be retrieved with glGetConvolutionFilter.

Errors

GL_INVALID_ENUM is generated if *target* is not GL_SEPARABLE_2D.

GL_INVALID_ENUM is generated if *format* is not one of the allowable values.

GL_INVALID_ENUM is generated if *type* is not one of the allowable values.

GL_INVALID_OPERATION is generated if *type* is one of GL_UNSIGNED_BYTE_3_3_2, GL_UNSIGNED_BYTE_2_3_3_REV, GL_UNSIGNED_SHORT_5_6_5, or GL_UNSIGNED_SHORT_5_6_5_REV and *format* is not GL_RGB.

GL_INVALID_OPERATION is generated if *type* is one of GL_UNSIGNED_SHORT_4_4_4_4, GL_UNSIGNED_SHORT_4_4_4_4_REV, GL_UNSIGNED_SHORT_5_5_5_1, GL_UNSIGNED_SHORT_1_5_5_5_REV, GL_UNSIGNED_INT_8_8_8_8, GL_UNSIGNED_INT_8_8_8_8_REV, GL_UNSIGNED_INT_10_10_10_2, or GL_UNSIGNED_INT_2_10_10_10_REV and *format* is neither GL_RGBA nor GL_BGRA.

GL_INVALID_OPERATION is generated if a nonzero buffer object name is bound to the GL_PIXEL_PACK_BUFFER target and the buffer object's data store is currently mapped.

GL_INVALID_OPERATION is generated if a nonzero buffer object name is bound to the GL_PIXEL_PACK_BUFFER target and the data would be packed to the buffer object such that the memory writes required would exceed the data store size.

GL_INVALID_OPERATION is generated if a nonzero buffer object name is bound to the GL_PIXEL_PACK_BUFFER target and *row* or *column* is not evenly divisible into the number of bytes needed to store in memory a datum indicated by type.

GL_INVALID_OPERATION is generated if glGetSeparableFilter is executed between the execution of glBegin and the corresponding execution of glEnd.

Associated Gets

glGetConvolutionParameter

glGet with argument GL_PIXEL_PACK_BUFFER_BINDING

See Also

glGetConvolutionFilter, glConvolutionParameter, glSeparableFilter2D

glGetShaderiv

Return a parameter from a shader object

C Specification

```
void glGetShaderiv(GLuint    shader,
                   GLenum    pname,
                   GLint *   params);
```

Parameters

shader	Specifies the shader object to be queried.
pname	Specifies the object parameter. Accepted symbolic names are GL_SHADER_TYPE, GL_DELETE_STATUS, GL_COMPILE_STATUS, GL_INFO_LOG_LENGTH, GL_SHADER_SOURCE_LENGTH.
params	Returns the requested object parameter.

Description

glGetShader returns in *params* the value of a parameter for a specific shader object. The following parameters are defined:

GL_SHADER_TYPE

params returns GL_VERTEX_SHADER if *shader* is a vertex shader object, and GL_FRAGMENT_SHADER if shader is a fragment shader object.

GL_DELETE_STATUS

params returns GL_TRUE if *shader* is currently flagged for deletion, and GL_FALSE otherwise.

GL_COMPILE_STATUS

params returns GL_TRUE if the last compile operation on *shader* was successful, and GL_FALSE otherwise.

GL_INFO_LOG_LENGTH

params returns the number of characters in the information log for *shader* including the null termination character (i.e., the size of the character buffer required to store the information log). If *shader* has no information log, a value of 0 is returned.

GL_SHADER_SOURCE_LENGTH

params returns the length of the concatenation of the source strings that make up the shader source for the *shader*, including the null termination character. (i.e., the size of the character buffer required to store the shader source). If no source code exists, 0 is returned.

Notes

glGetShader is available only if the GL version is 2.0 or greater.

If an error is generated, no change is made to the contents of *params*.

Errors

GL_INVALID_VALUE is generated if *shader* is not a value generated by OpenGL.

GL_INVALID_OPERATION is generated if *shader* does not refer to a shader object.

GL_INVALID_ENUM is generated if *pname* is not an accepted value.

GL_INVALID_OPERATION is generated if glGetShader is executed between the execution of glBegin and the corresponding execution of glEnd.

Associated Gets

glGetShaderInfoLog with argument *shader*
glGetShaderSource with argument *shader*
glIsShader

See Also

glCompileShader, glCreateShader, glDeleteShader, glGetProgram, glShaderSource

glGetShaderInfoLog

Return the information log for a shader object

C Specification

```
void glGetShaderInfoLog(GLuint     shader,
                        GLsizei    maxLength,
                        GLsizei * length,
                        GLchar * infoLog);
```

Parameters

shader   Specifies the shader object whose information log is to be queried.
maxLength   Specifies the size of the character buffer for storing the returned information log.

length	Returns the length of the string returned in `infoLog` (excluding the null terminator).
infoLog	Specifies an array of characters that is used to return the information log.

Description

`glGetShaderInfoLog` returns the information log for the specified shader object. The information log for a shader object is modified when the shader is compiled. The string that is returned will be null terminated.

`glGetShaderInfoLog` returns in *infoLog* as much of the information log as it can, up to a maximum of *maxLength* characters. The number of characters actually returned, excluding the null termination character, is specified by *length*. If the length of the returned string is not required, a value of NULL can be passed in the *length* argument. The size of the buffer required to store the returned information log can be obtained by calling `glGetShader` with the value GL_INFO_LOG_LENGTH.

The information log for a shader object is a string that may contain diagnostic messages, warning messages, and other information about the last compile operation. When a shader object is created, its information log will be a string of length 0.

Notes

`glGetShaderInfoLog` is available only if the GL version is 2.0 or greater.

The information log for a shader object is the OpenGL implementer's primary mechanism for conveying information about the compilation process. Therefore, the information log can be helpful to application developers during the development process, even when compilation is successful. Application developers should not expect different OpenGL implementations to produce identical information logs.

Errors

GL_INVALID_VALUE is generated if *shader* is not a value generated by OpenGL.

GL_INVALID_OPERATION is generated if *shader* is not a shader object.

GL_INVALID_VALUE is generated if *maxLength* is less than 0.

GL_INVALID_OPERATION is generated if `glGetShaderInfoLog` is executed between the execution of glBegin and the corresponding execution of glEnd.

Associated Gets

`glGetShader` with argument GL_INFO_LOG_LENGTH

`glIsShader`

See Also

`glCompileShader`, `glGetProgramInfoLog`, `glLinkProgram`, `glValidateProgram`

glGetShaderSource

Return the source code string from a shader object

C Specification

```
void glGetShaderSource(GLuint      shader,
                       GLsizei     bufSize,
                       GLsizei *   length,
                       GLchar *    source);
```

Parameters

Shader	Specifies the shader object to be queried.
bufSize	Specifies the size of the character buffer for storing the returned source code string.

Length   Returns the length of the string returned in *source* (excluding the null terminator).
Source   Specifies an array of characters that is used to return the source code string.

Description

glGetShaderSource returns the concatenation of the source code strings from the shader object specified by *shader*. The source code strings for a shader object are the result of a previous call to glShaderSource. The string returned by the function will be null terminated.

glGetShaderSource returns in *source* as much of the source code string as it can, up to a maximum of *bufSize* characters. The number of characters actually returned, excluding the null termination character, is specified by *length*. If the length of the returned string is not required, a value of NULL can be passed in the *length* argument. The size of the buffer required to store the returned source code string can be obtained by calling glGetShader with the value GL_SHADER_SOURCE_LENGTH.

Notes

glGetShaderSource is available only if the GL version is 2.0 or greater.

Errors

GL_INVALID_VALUE is generated if *shader* is not a value generated by OpenGL.
GL_INVALID_OPERATION is generated if *shader* is not a shader object.
GL_INVALID_VALUE is generated if *bufSize* is less than 0.
GL_INVALID_OPERATION is generated if glGetShaderSource is executed between the execution of glBegin and the corresponding execution of glEnd.

Associated Gets

glGetShader with argument GL_SHADER_SOURCE_LENGTH
glIsShader

See Also

glCreateShader, glShaderSource

glGetString

Return a string describing the current GL connection

C Specification

const GLubyte* **glGetString**(GLenum *name*);

Parameters

name   Specifies a symbolic constant, one of GL_VENDOR, GL_RENDERER, GL_VERSION, GL_SHADING_LANGUAGE_VERSION, or GL_EXTENSIONS.

Description

glGetString returns a pointer to a static string describing some aspect of the current GL connection. *name* can be one of the following:
GL_VENDOR
Returns the company responsible for this GL implementation. This name does not change from release to release.
GL_RENDERER
Returns the name of the renderer. This name is typically specific to a particular configuration of a hardware platform. It does not change from release to release.
GL_VERSION
Returns a version or release number.

GL_SHADING_LANGUAGE_VERSION
Returns a version or release number for the shading language.
GL_EXTENSIONS
Returns a space-separated list of supported extensions to GL.

Because the GL does not include queries for the performance characteristics of an implementation, some applications are written to recognize known platforms and modify their GL usage based on known performance characteristics of these platforms. Strings GL_VENDOR and GL_RENDERER together uniquely specify a platform. They do not change from release to release and should be used by platform-recognition algorithms.

Some applications want to make use of features that are not part of the standard GL. These features may be implemented as extensions to the standard GL. The GL_EXTENSIONS string is a space-separated list of supported GL extensions. (Extension names never contain a space character.)

The GL_VERSION and GL_SHADING_LANGUAGE_VERSION strings begin with a version number. The version number uses one of these forms:

*major_number.minor_number*major_number.minor_number.release_number

Vendor-specific information may follow the version number. Its format depends on the implementation, but a space always separates the version number and the vendor-specific information.

All strings are null-terminated.

Notes

If an error is generated, glGetString returns 0.

The client and server may support different versions or extensions. glGetString always returns a compatible version number or list of extensions. The release number always describes the server.

GL_SHADING_LANGUAGE_VERSION is available only if the GL version is 2.0 or greater.

Errors

GL_INVALID_ENUM is generated if *name* is not an accepted value.

GL_INVALID_OPERATION is generated if glGetString is executed between the execution of glDogin and the corresponding execution of glEnd.

glGetTexEnv

Return texture environment parameters

C Specification

```
void glGetTexEnvfv(GLenum    target,
                   GLenum    pname,
                   GLfloat * params);
void glGetTexEnviv(GLenum    target,
                   GLenum    pname,
                   GLint * params);
```

Parameters

target   Specifies a texture environment. May be GL_TEXTURE_ENV, GL_TEXTURE_FILTER_CONTROL, or GL_POINT_SPRITE.

pname   Specifies the symbolic name of a texture environment parameter. Accepted values are GL_TEXTURE_ENV_MODE, GL_TEXTURE_ENV_COLOR, GL_TEXTURE_LOD_BIAS, GL_COMBINE_RGB, GL_COMBINE_ALPHA, GL_SRC0_RGB, GL_SRC1_RGB, GL_SRC2_RGB, GL_SRC0_ALPHA, GL_SRC1_ALPHA, GL_SRC2_ALPHA, GL_OPERAND0_RGB, GL_OPERAND1_RGB, GL_OPERAND2_RGB, GL_OPERAND0_ALPHA, GL_OPERAND1_ALPHA, GL_OPERAND2_ALPHA, GL_RGB_SCALE, GL_ALPHA_SCALE, or GL_COORD_REPLACE.

params   Returns the requested data.

Description

glGetTexEnv returns in *params* selected values of a texture environment that was specified with glTexEnv. *target* specifies a texture environment.

When *target* is GL_TEXTURE_FILTER_CONTROL, *pname* must be GL_TEXTURE_LOD_BIAS. When *target* is GL_POINT_SPRITE, *pname* must be GL_COORD_REPLACE. When *target* is GL_TEXTURE_ENV, *pname* can be GL_TEXTURE_ENV_MODE, GL_TEXTURE_ENV_COLOR, GL_COMBINE_RGB, GL_COMBINE_ALPHA, RGB_SCALE, ALPHA_SCALE, SRC0_RGB, SRC1_RGB, SRC2_RGB, SRC0_ALPHA, SRC1_ALPHA, or SRC2_ALPHA.

pname names a specific texture environment parameter, as follows:

GL_TEXTURE_ENV_MODE

params returns the single-valued texture environment mode, a symbolic constant. The initial value is GL_MODULATE.

GL_TEXTURE_ENV_COLOR

params returns four integer or floating-point values that are the texture environment color. Integer values, when requested, are linearly mapped from the internal floating-point representation such that 1.0 maps to the most positive representable integer, and -1.0 maps to the most negative representable integer. The initial value is (0, 0, 0, 0).

GL_TEXTURE_LOD_BIAS

params returns a single floating-point value that is the texture level-of-detail bias. The initial value is 0.

GL_COMBINE_RGB

params returns a single symbolic constant value representing the current RGB combine mode. The initial value is GL_MODULATE.

GL_COMBINE_ALPHA

params returns a single symbolic constant value representing the current alpha combine mode. The initial value is GL_MODULATE.

GL_SRC0_RGB

params returns a single symbolic constant value representing the texture combiner zero's RGB source. The initial value is GL_TEXTURE.

GL_SRC1_RGB

params returns a single symbolic constant value representing the texture combiner one's RGB source. The initial value is GL_PREVIOUS.

GL_SRC2_RGB

params returns a single symbolic constant value representing the texture combiner two's RGB source. The initial value is GL_CONSTANT.

GL_SRC0_ALPHA

params returns a single symbolic constant value representing the texture combiner zero's alpha source. The initial value is GL_TEXTURE.

GL_SRC1_ALPHA

params returns a single symbolic constant value representing the texture combiner one's alpha source. The initial value is GL_PREVIOUS.

GL_SRC2_ALPHA

params returns a single symbolic constant value representing the texture combiner two's alpha source. The initial value is GL_CONSTANT.

GL_OPERAND0_RGB

params returns a single symbolic constant value representing the texture combiner zero's RGB operand. The initial value is GL_SRC_COLOR.

GL_OPERAND1_RGB

params returns a single symbolic constant value representing the texture combiner one's RGB operand. The initial value is GL_SRC_COLOR.

GL_OPERAND2_RGB

params returns a single symbolic constant value representing the texture combiner two's RGB operand. The initial value is GL_SRC_ALPHA.

GL_OPERAND0_ALPHA

params returns a single symbolic constant value representing the texture combiner zero's alpha operand. The initial value is GL_SRC_ALPHA.

GL_OPERAND1_ALPHA

params returns a single symbolic constant value representing the texture combiner one's alpha operand. The initial value is GL_SRC_ALPHA.

GL_OPERAND2_ALPHA

params returns a single symbolic constant value representing the texture combiner two's alpha operand. The initial value is GL_SRC_ALPHA.

GL_RGB_SCALE

params returns a single floating-point value representing the current RGB texture combiner scaling factor. The initial value is 1.0.

GL_ALPHA_SCALE

params returns a single floating-point value representing the current alpha texture combiner scaling factor. The initial value is 1.0.

GL_COORD_REPLACE

params returns a single boolean value representing the current point sprite texture coordinate replacement enable state. The initial value is GL_FALSE.

Notes

If an error is generated, no change is made to the contents of *params*.

For OpenGL versions 1.3 and greater, or when the ARB_multitexture extension is supported, glGetTexEnv returns the texture environment parameters for the active texture unit.

GL_COMBINE_RGB, GL_COMBINE_ALPHA, GL_SRC0_RGB, GL_SRC1_RGB, GL_SRC2_RGB, GL_SRC0_ALPHA, GL_SRC1_ALPHA, GL_SRC2_ALPHA, GL_OPERAND0_RGB, GL_OPERAND1_RGB, GL_OPERAND2_RGB, GL_OPERAND0_ALPHA, GL_OPERAND1_ALPHA, GL_OPERAND2_ALPHA, GL_RGB_SCALE, and GL_ALPHA_SCALE are available only if the GL version is 1.3 or greater.

GL_TEXTURE_FILTER_CONTROL and GL_TEXTURE_LOD_BIAS are available only if the GL version is 1.4 or greater.

GL_POINT_SPRITE and GL_COORD_REPLACE are available only if the GL version is 2.0 or greater.

Errors

GL_INVALID_ENUM is generated if *target* or *pname* is not an accepted value.

GL_INVALID_OPERATION is generated if glGetTexEnv is executed between the execution of glBegin and the corresponding execution of glEnd.

See Also

glActiveTexture, glTexEnv

glGetTexGen

Return texture coordinate generation parameters

C Specification

```
void glGetTexGendv(GLenum     coord,
                   GLenum     pname,
                   GLdouble * params);
void glGetTexGenfv(GLenum     coord,
                   GLenum     pname,
                   GLfloat *  params);
```

```
void glGetTexGeniv(GLenum   coord,
                   GLenum   pname,
                   GLint * params);
```

Parameters

coord   Specifies a texture coordinate. Must be GL_S, GL_T, GL_R, or GL_Q.

pname   Specifies the symbolic name of the value(s) to be returned. Must be either
             GL_TEXTURE_GEN_MODE or the name of one of the texture generation plane equations:
             GL_OBJECT_PLANE or GL_EYE_PLANE.

params   Returns the requested data.

Description

glGetTexGen returns in *params* selected parameters of a texture coordinate generation function
that was specified using glTexGen. *coord* names one of the (*s, t, r, q*) texture coordinates, using the
symbolic constant GL_S, GL_T, GL_R, or GL_Q.

pname specifies one of three symbolic names:

GL_TEXTURE_GEN_MODE

params returns the single-valued texture generation function, a symbolic constant. The initial
value is GL_EYE_LINEAR.

GL_OBJECT_PLANE

params returns the four plane equation coefficients that specify object linear-coordinate generation. Integer values, when requested, are mapped directly from the internal floating-point representation.

GL_EYE_PLANE

params returns the four plane equation coefficients that specify eye linear-coordinate generation.
Integer values, when requested, are mapped directly from the internal floating-point representation.
The returned values are those maintained in eye coordinates. They are not equal to the values speci-
fied using glTexGen, unless the modelview matrix was identity when glTexGen was called.

Notes

If an error is generated, no change is made to the contents of *params*.

For OpenGL versions 1.3 and greater, or when the ARB_multitexture extension is supported,
glGetTexGen returns the texture coordinate generation parameters for the active texture unit.

Errors

GL_INVALID_ENUM is generated if *coord* or *pname* is not an accepted value.

GL_INVALID_OPERATION is generated if glGetTexGen is executed between the execution of
glBegin and the corresponding execution of glEnd.

See Also

glActiveTexture, glTexGen

glGetTexImage

Return a texture image

C Specification

```
void glGetTexImage(GLenum   target,
                   GLint    level,
                   GLenum   format,
                   GLenum   type,
                   GLvoid * img);
```

Parameters

target	Specifies which texture is to be obtained. GL_TEXTURE_1D, GL_TEXTURE_2D, GL_TEXTURE_3D, GL_TEXTURE_CUBE_MAP_POSITIVE_X, GL_TEXTURE_CUBE_MAP_NEGATIVE_X, GL_TEXTURE_CUBE_MAP_POSITIVE_Y, GL_TEXTURE_CUBE_MAP_NEGATIVE_Y, GL_TEXTURE_CUBE_MAP_POSITIVE_Z, and GL_TEXTURE_CUBE_MAP_NEGATIVE_Z are accepted.
level	Specifies the level-of-detail number of the desired image. Level 0 is the base image level. Level n is the nth mipmap reduction image.
format	Specifies a pixel format for the returned data. The supported formats are GL_RED, GL_GREEN, GL_BLUE, GL_ALPHA, GL_RGB, GL_BGR, GL_RGBA, GL_BGRA, GL_LUMINANCE, and GL_LUMINANCE_ALPHA.
type	Specifies a pixel type for the returned data. The supported types are GL_UNSIGNED_BYTE, GL_BYTE, GL_UNSIGNED_SHORT, GL_SHORT, GL_UNSIGNED_INT, GL_INT, GL_FLOAT, GL_UNSIGNED_BYTE_3_3_2, GL_UNSIGNED_BYTE_2_3_3_REV, GL_UNSIGNED_SHORT_5_6_5, GL_UNSIGNED_SHORT_5_6_5_REV, GL_UNSIGNED_SHORT_4_4_4_4, GL_UNSIGNED_SHORT_4_4_4_4_REV, GL_UNSIGNED_SHORT_5_5_5_1, GL_UNSIGNED_SHORT_1_5_5_5_REV, GL_UNSIGNED_INT_8_8_8_8, GL_UNSIGNED_INT_8_8_8_8_REV, GL_UNSIGNED_INT_10_10_10_2, and GL_UNSIGNED_INT_2_10_10_10_REV.
img	Returns the texture image. Should be a pointer to an array of the type specified by *type*.

Description

glGetTexImage returns a texture image into *img*. *target* specifies whether the desired texture image is one specified by glTexImage1D (GL_TEXTURE_1D), glTexImage2D (GL_TEXTURE_2D or any of GL_TEXTURE_CUBE_MAP_*), or glTexImage3D (GL_TEXTURE_3D). *level* specifies the level-of-detail number of the desired image. *format* and *type* specify the format and type of the desired image array. See the reference pages glTexImage1D and glDrawPixels for a description of the acceptable values for the *format* and *type* parameters, respectively.

If a nonzero named buffer object is bound to the GL_PIXEL_PACK_BUFFER target (see glBindBuffer) while a texture image is requested, *img* is treated as a byte offset into the buffer object's data store.

To understand the operation of glGetTexImage, consider the selected internal four-component texture image to be an RGBA color buffer the size of the image. The semantics of glGetTexImage are then identical to those of glReadPixels, with the exception that no pixel transfer operations are performed, when called with the same *format* and *type*, with x and y set to 0, *width* set to the width of the texture image (including border if one was specified), and *height* set to 1 for 1D images, or to the height of the texture image (including border if one was specified) for 2D images. Because the internal texture image is an RGBA image, pixel formats GL_COLOR_INDEX, GL_STENCIL_INDEX, and GL_DEPTH_COMPONENT are not accepted, and pixel type GL_BITMAP is not accepted.

If the selected texture image does not contain four components, the following mappings are applied. Single-component textures are treated as RGBA buffers with red set to the single-component value, green set to 0, blue set to 0, and alpha set to 1. Two-component textures are treated as RGBA buffers with red set to the value of component zero, alpha set to the value of component one, and green and blue set to 0. Finally, three-component textures are treated as RGBA buffers with red set to component zero, green set to component one, blue set to component two, and alpha set to 1.

To determine the required size of *img*, use glGetTexLevelParameter to determine the dimensions of the internal texture image, then scale the required number of pixels by the storage required for each pixel, based on *format* and *type*. Be sure to take the pixel storage parameters into account, especially GL_PACK_ALIGNMENT.

Notes

If an error is generated, no change is made to the contents of *img*.

The types GL_UNSIGNED_BYTE_3_3_2, GL_UNSIGNED_BYTE_2_3_3_REV, GL_UNSIGNED_SHORT_5_6_5, GL_UNSIGNED_SHORT_5_6_5_REV, GL_UNSIGNED_SHORT_4_4_4_4, GL_UNSIGNED_SHORT_4_4_4_4_REV, GL_UNSIGNED_SHORT_5_5_5_1, GL_UNSIGNED_SHORT_1_5_5_5_REV, GL_UNSIGNED_INT_8_8_8_8, GL_UNSIGNED_INT_8_8_8_8_REV, GL_UNSIGNED_INT_10_10_10_2, GL_UNSIGNED_INT_2_10_10_10_REV, and the formats GL_BGR, and GL_BGRA are available only if the GL version is 1.2 or greater.

For OpenGL versions 1.3 and greater, or when the ARB_multitexture extension is supported, glGetTexImage returns the texture image for the active texture unit.

Errors

GL_INVALID_ENUM is generated if *target*, *format*, or *type* is not an accepted value.

GL_INVALID_VALUE is generated if *level* is less than 0.

GL_INVALID_VALUE may be generated if *level* is greater than $\log_2$ (max), where max is the returned value of GL_MAX_TEXTURE_SIZE.

GL_INVALID_OPERATION is returned if *type* is one of GL_UNSIGNED_BYTE_3_3_2, GL_UNSIGNED_BYTE_2_3_3_REV, GL_UNSIGNED_SHORT_5_6_5, or GL_UNSIGNED_SHORT_5_6_5_REV and *format* is not GL_RGB.

GL_INVALID_OPERATION is returned if *type* is one of GL_UNSIGNED_SHORT_4_4_4_4, GL_UNSIGNED_SHORT_4_4_4_4_REV, GL_UNSIGNED_SHORT_5_5_5_1, GL_UNSIGNED_SHORT_1_5_5_5_REV, GL_UNSIGNED_INT_8_8_8_8, GL_UNSIGNED_INT_8_8_8_8_REV, GL_UNSIGNED_INT_10_10_10_2, or GL_UNSIGNED_INT_2_10_10_10_REV, and *format* is neither GL_RGBA or GL_BGRA.

GL_INVALID_OPERATION is generated if a nonzero buffer object name is bound to the GL_PIXEL_PACK_BUFFER target and the buffer object's data store is currently mapped.

GL_INVALID_OPERATION is generated if a nonzero buffer object name is bound to the GL_PIXEL_PACK_BUFFER target and the data would be packed to the buffer object such that the memory writes required would exceed the data store size.

GL_INVALID_OPERATION is generated if a nonzero buffer object name is bound to the GL_PIXEL_PACK_BUFFER target and *img* is not evenly divisible into the number of bytes needed to store in memory a datum indicated by *type*.

GL_INVALID_OPERATION is generated if glGetTexImage is executed between the execution of glBegin and the corresponding execution of glEnd.

Associated Gets

glGetTexLevelParameter with argument GL_TEXTURE_WIDTH
glGetTexLevelParameter with argument GL_TEXTURE_HEIGHT
glGetTexLevelParameter with argument GL_TEXTURE_BORDER
glGetTexLevelParameter with argument GL_TEXTURE_INTERNAL_FORMAT
glGet with arguments GL_PACK_ALIGNMENT and others
glGet with argument GL_PIXEL_PACK_BUFFER_BINDING

See Also

glActiveTexture, glDrawPixels, glReadPixels, glTexEnv, glTexGen, glTexImage1D, glTexImage2D, glTexImage3D, glTexSubImage1D, glTexSubImage2D, glTexSubImage3D, glTexParameter

glGetTexLevelParameter

Return texture parameter values for a specific level of detail

C Specification

```
void glGetTexLevelParameterfv(GLenum    target,
                              GLint     level,
                              GLenum    pname,
                              GLfloat * params);
void glGetTexLevelParameteriv(GLenum    target,
                              GLint     level,
                              GLenum    pname,
                              GLint * params);
```

Parameters

target   Specifies the symbolic name of the target texture, either GL_TEXTURE_1D,
              GL_TEXTURE_2D, GL_TEXTURE_3D, GL_PROXY_TEXTURE_1D, GL_PROXY_TEXTURE_2D,
              GL_PROXY_TEXTURE_3D, GL_TEXTURE_CUBE_MAP_POSITIVE_X,
              GL_TEXTURE_CUBE_MAP_NEGATIVE_X, GL_TEXTURE_CUBE_MAP_POSITIVE_Y,
              GL_TEXTURE_CUBE_MAP_NEGATIVE_Y, GL_TEXTURE_CUBE_MAP_POSITIVE_Z,
              GL_TEXTURE_CUBE_MAP_NEGATIVE_Z, or GL_PROXY_TEXTURE_CUBE_MAP.

level   Specifies the level-of-detail number of the desired image. Level 0 is the base image level.
              Level n is the nth mipmap reduction image.

pname   Specifies the symbolic name of a texture parameter. GL_TEXTURE_WIDTH,
              GL_TEXTURE_HEIGHT, GL_TEXTURE_DEPTH, GL_TEXTURE_INTERNAL_FORMAT,
              GL_TEXTURE_BORDER, GL_TEXTURE_RED_SIZE, GL_TEXTURE_GREEN_SIZE,
              GL_TEXTURE_BLUE_SIZE, GL_TEXTURE_ALPHA_SIZE, GL_TEXTURE_LUMINANCE_SIZE,
              GL_TEXTURE_INTENSITY_SIZE, GL_TEXTURE_DEPTH_SIZE,
              GL_TEXTURE_COMPRESSED, and GL_TEXTURE_COMPRESSED_IMAGE_SIZE are accepted.

params   Returns the requested data.

Description

glGetTexLevelParameter returns in *params* texture parameter values for a specific level-of-
detail value, specified as *level*. *target* defines the target texture, either GL_TEXTURE_1D,
GL_TEXTURE_2D, GL_TEXTURE_3D, GL_PROXY_TEXTURE_1D, GL_PROXY_TEXTURE_2D,
GL_PROXY_TEXTURE_3D, GL_TEXTURE_CUBE_MAP_POSITIVE_X, GL_TEXTURE_CUBE_MAP_NEGA-
TIVE_X, GL_TEXTURE_CUBE_MAP_POSITIVE_Y, GL_TEXTURE_CUBE_MAP_NEGATIVE_Y,
GL_TEXTURE_CUBE_MAP_POSITIVE_Z, GL_TEXTURE_CUBE_MAP_NEGATIVE_Z, or
GL_PROXY_TEXTURE_CUBE_MAP.

GL_MAX_TEXTURE_SIZE, and GL_MAX_3D_TEXTURE_SIZE are not really descriptive enough. It
has to report the largest square texture image that can be accommodated with mipmaps and borders,
but a long skinny texture, or a texture without mipmaps and borders, may easily fit in texture
memory. The proxy targets allow the user to more accurately query whether the GL can accommodate
a texture of a given configuration. If the texture cannot be accommodated, the texture state variables,
which may be queried with glGetTexLevelParameter, are set to 0. If the texture can be accommodated, the texture state values will be set as they would be set for a non-proxy target.

pname specifies the texture parameter whose value or values will be returned.

The accepted parameter names are as follows:

GL_TEXTURE_WIDTH

params returns a single value, the width of the texture image. This value includes the border of
the texture image. The initial value is 0.

`GL_TEXTURE_HEIGHT`

params returns a single value, the height of the texture image. This value includes the border of the texture image. The initial value is 0.

`GL_TEXTURE_DEPTH`

params returns a single value, the depth of the texture image. This value includes the border of the texture image. The initial value is 0.

`GL_TEXTURE_INTERNAL_FORMAT`

params returns a single value, the internal format of the texture image.

`GL_TEXTURE_BORDER`

params returns a single value, the width in pixels of the border of the texture image. The initial value is 0.

`GL_TEXTURE_RED_SIZE`,
`GL_TEXTURE_GREEN_SIZE`,
`GL_TEXTURE_BLUE_SIZE`,
`GL_TEXTURE_ALPHA_SIZE`,
`GL_TEXTURE_LUMINANCE_SIZE`,
`GL_TEXTURE_INTENSITY_SIZE`,
`GL_TEXTURE_DEPTH_SIZE`

The internal storage resolution of an individual component. The resolution chosen by the GL will be a close match for the resolution requested by the user with the component argument of `glTexImage1D`, `glTexImage2D`, `glTexImage3D`, `glCopyTexImage1D`, and `glCopyTexImage2D`. The initial value is 0.

`GL_TEXTURE_COMPRESSED`

params returns a single boolean value indicating if the texture image is stored in a compressed internal format. The initiali value is `GL_FALSE`.

`GL_TEXTURE_COMPRESSED_IMAGE_SIZE`

params returns a single integer value, the number of unsigned bytes of the compressed texture image that would be returned from `glGetCompressedTexImage`.

Notes

If an error is generated, no change is made to the contents of *params*.

`GL_TEXTURE_INTERNAL_FORMAT` is available only if the GL version is 1.1 or greater. In version 1.0, use `GL_TEXTURE_COMPONENTS` instead.

`GL_PROXY_TEXTURE_1D` and `GL_PROXY_TEXTURE_2D` are available only if the GL version is 1.1 or greater.

`GL_TEXTURE_3D`, `GL_PROXY_TEXTURE_3D`, and `GL_TEXTURE_DEPTH` are available only if the GL version is 1.2 or greater.

`GL_TEXTURE_COMPRESSED`, `GL_TEXTURE_COMPRESSED_IMAGE_SIZE`, `GL_TEXTURE_CUBE_MAP_POSITIVE_X`, `GL_TEXTURE_CUBE_MAP_NEGATIVE_X`, `GL_TEXTURE_CUBE_MAP_POSITIVE_Y`, `GL_TEXTURE_CUBE_MAP_NEGATIVE_Y`, `GL_TEXTURE_CUBE_MAP_POSITIVE_Z`, `GL_TEXTURE_CUBE_MAP_NEGATIVE_Z`, and `GL_PROXY_TEXTURE_CUBE_MAP` are available only if the GL version is 1.3 or greater.

For OpenGL versions 1.3 and greater, or when the `ARB_multitexture` extension is supported, `glGetTexLevelParameter` returns the texture level parameters for the active texture unit.

Errors

`GL_INVALID_ENUM` is generated if *target* or *pname* is not an accepted value.

`GL_INVALID_VALUE` is generated if *level* is less than 0.

`GL_INVALID_VALUE` may be generated if *level* is greater than $\log_2$max, where max is the returned value of `GL_MAX_TEXTURE_SIZE`.

`GL_INVALID_OPERATION` is generated if `glGetTexLevelParameter` is executed between the execution of `glBegin` and the corresponding execution of `glEnd`.

GL_INVALID_OPERATION is generated if GL_TEXTURE_COMPRESSED_IMAGE_SIZE is queried on texture images with an uncompressed internal format or on proxy targets.

See Also

glActiveTexture, glGetTexParameter, glCopyTexImage1D, glCopyTexImage2D, glCopyTexSubImage1D, glCopyTexSubImage2D, glCopyTexSubImage3D, glTexEnv, glTexGen, glTexImage1D, glTexImage2D, glTexImage3D, glTexSubImage1D, glTexSubImage2D, glTexSubImage3D, glTexParameter

glGetTexParameter

Return texture parameter values

C Specification

```
void glGetTexParameterfv(GLenum    target,
                         GLenum    pname,
                         GLfloat * params);
void glGetTexParameteriv(GLenum    target,
                         GLenum    pname,
                         GLint   * params);
```

Parameters

target   Specifies the symbolic name of the target texture. GL_TEXTURE_1D, GL_TEXTURE_2D, GL_TEXTURE_3D, and GL_TEXTURE_CUBE_MAP are accepted.

pname   Specifies the symbolic name of a texture parameter. GL_TEXTURE_MAG_FILTER, GL_TEXTURE_MIN_FILTER, GL_TEXTURE_MIN_LOD, GL_TEXTURE_MAX_LOD, GL_TEXTURE_BASE_LEVEL, GL_TEXTURE_MAX_LEVEL, GL_TEXTURE_WRAP_S, GL_TEXTURE_WRAP_T, GL_TEXTURE_WRAP_R, GL_TEXTURE_BORDER_COLOR, GL_TEXTURE_PRIORITY, GL_TEXTURE_RESIDENT, GL_TEXTURE_COMPARE_MODE, GL_TEXTURE_COMPARE_FUNC, GL_DEPTH_TEXTURE_MODE, and GL_GENERATE_MIPMAP are accepted.

params   Returns the texture parameters.

Description

glGetTexParameter returns in *params* the value or values of the texture parameter specified as *pname*. *target* defines the target texture, either GL_TEXTURE_1D, GL_TEXTURE_2D, or GL_TEXTURE_3D, to specify one-, two-, or three-dimensional texturing. pname accepts the same symbols as glTexParameter, with the same interpretations:

GL_TEXTURE_MAG_FILTER

Returns the single-valued texture magnification filter, a symbolic constant. The initial value is GL_LINEAR.

GL_TEXTURE_MIN_FILTER

Returns the single-valued texture minification filter, a symbolic constant. The initial value is GL_NEAREST_MIPMAP_LINEAR.

GL_TEXTURE_MIN_LOD

Returns the single-valued texture minimum level-of-detail value. The initial value is -1000.

GL_TEXTURE_MAX_LOD

Returns the single-valued texture maximum level-of-detail value. The initial value is 1000.

GL_TEXTURE_BASE_LEVEL

Returns the single-valued base texture mipmap level. The initial value is 0.

GL_TEXTURE_MAX_LEVEL

Returns the single-valued maximum texture mipmap array level. The initial value is 1000.

GL_TEXTURE_WRAP_S

Returns the single-valued wrapping function for texture coordinate *s*, a symbolic constant. The initial value is GL_REPEAT.

GL_TEXTURE_WRAP_T

Returns the single-valued wrapping function for texture coordinate *t*, a symbolic constant. The initial value is GL_REPEAT.

GL_TEXTURE_WRAP_R

Returns the single-valued wrapping function for texture coordinate *r*, a symbolic constant. The initial value is GL_REPEAT.

GL_TEXTURE_BORDER_COLOR

Returns four integer or floating-point numbers that comprise the RGBA color of the texture border. Floating-point values are returned in the range [0,1]. Integer values are returned as a linear mapping of the internal floating-point representation such that 1.0 maps to the most positive representable integer and –1.0 maps to the most negative representable integer. The initial value is (0, 0, 0, 0).

GL_TEXTURE_PRIORITY

Returns the residence priority of the target texture (or the named texture bound to it). The initial value is 1. See glPrioritizeTextures.

GL_TEXTURE_RESIDENT

Returns the residence status of the target texture. If the value returned in *params* is GL_TRUE, the texture is resident in texture memory. See glAreTexturesResident.

GL_TEXTURE_COMPARE_MODE

Returns a single-valued texture comparison mode, a symbolic constant. The initial value is GL_NONE. See glTexParameter.

GL_TEXTURE_COMPARE_FUNC

Returns a single-valued texture comparison function, a symbolic constant. The initial value is GL_LEQUAL. See glTexParameter.

GL_DEPTH_TEXTURE_MODE

Returns a single-valued texture format indicating how the depth values should be converted into color components. The initial value is GL_LUMINANCE. See glTexParameter.

GL_GENERATE_MIPMAP

Returns a single boolean value indicating if automatic mipmap level updates are enabled. See glTexParameter.

Notes

GL_TEXTURE_PRIORITY and GL_TEXTURE_RESIDENT are available only if the GL version is 1.1 or greater.

GL_TEXTURE_3D, GL_TEXTURE_MIN_LOD, GL_TEXTURE_MAX_LOD, GL_TEXTURE_BASE_LEVEL, GL_TEXTURE_MAX_LEVEL, and GL_TEXTURE_WRAP_R are available only if the GL version is 1.2 or greater.

GL_TEXTURE_COMPARE_MODE, GL_TEXTURE_COMPARE_FUNC, and GL_GENERATE_MIPMAP is available only if the GL version is 1.4 or greater.

If an error is generated, no change is made to the contents of *params*.

Errors

GL_INVALID_ENUM is generated if *target* or *pname* is not an accepted value.

GL_INVALID_OPERATION is generated if glGetTexParameter is executed between the execution of glBegin and the corresponding execution of glEnd.

See Also

glAreTexturesResident, glPrioritizeTextures, glTexParameter

glGetUniform

Return the value of a uniform variable

C Specification

```
void glGetUniformfv(GLuint    program,
                    GLint     location,
                    GLfloat * params);
void glGetUniformiv(GLuint   program,
                    GLint    location,
                    GLint *  params);
```

Parameters

program	Specifies the program object to be queried.
location	Specifies the location of the uniform variable to be queried.
params	Returns the value of the specified uniform variable.

Description

glGetUniform returns in *params* the value(s) of the specified uniform variable. The type of the uniform variable specified by *location* determines the number of values returned. If the uniform variable is defined in the shader as a boolean, int, or float, a single value will be returned. If it is defined as a vec2, ivec2, or bvec2, two values will be returned. If it is defined as a vec3, ivec3, or bvec3, three values will be returned, and so on. To query values stored in uniform variables declared as arrays, call glGetUniform for each element of the array. To query values stored in uniform variables declared as structures, call glGetUniform for each field in the structure. The values for uniform variables declared as a matrix will be returned in column major order.

The locations assigned to uniform variables are not known until the program object is linked. After linking has occurred, the command glGetUniformLocation can be used to obtain the location of a uniform variable. This location value can then be passed to glGetUniform in order to query the current value of the uniform variable. After a program object has been linked successfully, the index values for uniform variables remain fixed until the next link command occurs. The uniform variable values can only be queried after a link if the link was successful.

Notes

glGetUniform is available only if the GL version is 2.0 or greater.

If an error is generated, no change is made to the contents of *params*.

Errors

GL_INVALID_VALUE is generated if *program* is not a value generated by OpenGL.

GL_INVALID_OPERATION is generated if *program* is not a program object.

GL_INVALID_OPERATION is generated if *program* has not been successfully linked.

GL_INVALID_OPERATION is generated if *location* does not correspond to a valid uniform variable location for the specified program object.

GL_INVALID_OPERATION is generated if glGetUniform is executed between the execution of glBegin and the corresponding execution of glEnd.

Associated Gets

glGetActiveUniform with arguments *program* and the index of an active uniform variable

glGetProgram with arguments *program* and GL_ACTIVE_UNIFORMS or GL_ACTIVE_UNIFORM_MAX_LENGTH

glGetUniformLocation with arguments *program* and the name of a uniform variable

glIsProgram

See Also

glCreateProgram, glLinkProgram, glUniform

glGetUniformLocation

Return the location of a uniform variable

C Specification

```
GLint glGetUniformLocation(GLuint         program,
                           const GLchar * name);
```

Parameters

program   Specifies the program object to be queried.

name   Points to a null terminated string containing the name of the uniform variable
              whose location is to be queried.

Description

glGetUniformLocation returns an integer that represents the location of a specific uniform variable within a program object. *name* must be a null terminated string that contains no white space. *name* must be an active uniform variable name in *program* that is not a structure, an array of structures, or a subcomponent of a vector or a matrix. This function returns -1 if *name* does not correspond to an active uniform variable in *program* or if *name* starts with the reserved prefix "gl_".

Uniform variables that are structures or arrays of structures may be queried by calling glGetUniformLocation for each field within the structure. The array element operator "[ ]" and the structure field operator "." may be used in name in order to select elements within an array or fields within a structure. The result of using these operators is not allowed to be another structure, an array of structures, or a subcomponent of a vector or a matrix. Except if the last part of name indicates a uniform variable array, the location of the first element of an array can be retrieved by using the name of the array, or by using the name appended by "[0]".

The actual locations assigned to uniform variables are not known until the program object is linked successfully. After linking has occurred, the command glGetUniformLocation can be used to obtain the location of a uniform variable. This location value can then be passed to glUniform to set the value of the uniform variable or to glGetUniform in order to query the current value of the uniform variable. After a program object has been linked successfully, the index values for uniform variables remain fixed until the next link command occurs. Uniform variable locations and values can only be queried after a link if the link was successful.

Notes

glGetUniformLocation is available only if the GL version is 2.0 or greater.

Errors

GL_INVALID_VALUE is generated if *program* is not a value generated by OpenGL.

GL_INVALID_OPERATION is generated if *program* is not a program object.

GL_INVALID_OPERATION is generated if *program* has not been successfully linked.

GL_INVALID_OPERATION is generated if glGetUniformLocation is executed between the execution of glBegin and the corresponding execution of glEnd.

Associated Gets

glGetActiveUniform with arguments *program* and the index of an active uniform variable

glGetProgram with arguments *program* and GL_ACTIVE_UNIFORMS or GL_ACTIVE_UNIFORM_MAX_LENGTH

glGetUniform with arguments *program* and the name of a uniform variable

glIsProgram

See Also

glLinkProgram, glUniform

glGetVertexAttrib

Return a generic vertex attribute parameter

C Specification

```
void glGetVertexAttribdv(GLuint      index,
                         GLenum      pname,
                         GLdouble *  params);
void glGetVertexAttribfv(GLuint      index,
                         GLenum      pname,
                         GLfloat *   params);
void glGetVertexAttribiv(GLuint      index,
                         GLenum      pname,
                         GLint *     params);
```

Parameters

index   Specifies the generic vertex attribute parameter to be queried.

pname   Specifies the symbolic name of the vertex attribute parameter to be queried. Accepted
             values are GL_VERTEX_ATTRIB_ARRAY_BUFFER_BINDING,
             GL_VERTEX_ATTRIB_ARRAY_ENABLED, GL_VERTEX_ATTRIB_ARRAY_SIZE,
             GL_VERTEX_ATTRIB_ARRAY_STRIDE, GL_VERTEX_ATTRIB_ARRAY_TYPE,
             GL_VERTEX_ATTRIB_ARRAY_NORMALIZED, or GL_CURRENT_VERTEX_ATTRIB.

params   Returns the requested data.

Description

glGetVertexAttrib returns in *params* the value of a generic vertex attribute parameter. The
generic vertex attribute to be queried is specified by *index*, and the parameter to be queried is specified by *pname*.

The accepted parameter names are as follows:

GL_VERTEX_ATTRIB_ARRAY_BUFFER_BINDING

params returns a single value, the name of the buffer object currently bound to the binding point
corresponding to generic vertex attribute array *index*. If no buffer object is bound, 0 is returned. The
initial value is 0.

GL_VERTEX_ATTRIB_ARRAY_ENABLED

params returns a single value that is nonzero (true) if the vertex attribute array for *index* is
enabled and 0 (false) if it is disabled. The initial value is GL_FALSE.

GL_VERTEX_ATTRIB_ARRAY_SIZE

params returns a single value, the size of the vertex attribute array for *index*. The size is the
number of values for each element of the vertex attribute array, and it will be 1, 2, 3, or 4. The initial
value is 4.

GL_VERTEX_ATTRIB_ARRAY_STRIDE

params returns a single value, the array stride for (number of bytes between successive elements
in) the vertex attribute array for *index*. A value of 0 indicates that the array elements are stored
sequentially in memory. The initial value is 0.

GL_VERTEX_ATTRIB_ARRAY_TYPE

params returns a single value, a symbolic constant indicating the array type for the vertex
attribute array for *index*. Possible values are GL_BYTE, GL_UNSIGNED_BYTE, GL_SHORT,
GL_UNSIGNED_SHORT, GL_INT, GL_UNSIGNED_INT, GL_FLOAT, and GL_DOUBLE. The initial value is
GL_FLOAT.

GL_VERTEX_ATTRIB_ARRAY_NORMALIZED

params returns a single value that is nonzero (true) if fixed-point data types for the vertex
attribute array indicated by *index* are normalized when they are converted to floating point, and 0
(false) otherwise. The initial value is GL_FALSE.

GL_CURRENT_VERTEX_ATTRIB

params returns four values that represent the current value for the generic vertex attribute specified by index. Generic vertex attribute 0 is unique in that it has no current state, so an error will be generated if *index* is 0. The initial value for all other generic vertex attributes is (0,0,0,1).

All of the parameters except GL_CURRENT_VERTEX_ATTRIB represent client-side state.

Notes

glGetVertexAttrib is available only if the GL version is 2.0 or greater.

If an error is generated, no change is made to the contents of *params*.

Errors

GL_INVALID_VALUE is generated if *index* is greater than or equal to GL_MAX_VERTEX_ATTRIBS.

GL_INVALID_ENUM is generated if *pname* is not an accepted value.

GL_INVALID_OPERATION is generated if *index* is 0 and *pname* is GL_CURRENT_VERTEX_ATTRIB.

Associated Gets

glGet with argument GL_MAX_VERTEX_ATTRIBS

glGetVertexAttribPointerv with arguments *index* and GL_VERTEX_ATTRIB_ARRAY_POINTER

See Also

glBindAttribLocation, glBindBuffer, glDisableVertexAttribArray, glEnableVertexAttribArray, glVertexAttrib, glVertexAttribPointer

glGetVertexAttribPointerv

Return the address of the specified generic vertex attribute pointer

C Specification

```
void glGetVertexAttribPointerv(GLuint     index,
                               GLenum     pname,
                               GLvoid ** pointer);
```

Parameters

index   Specifies the generic vertex attribute parameter to be returned.

pname   Specifies the symbolic name of the generic vertex attribute parameter to be returned. Must be GL_VERTEX_ATTRIB_ARRAY_POINTER.

pointer   Returns the pointer value.

Description

glGetVertexAttribPointerv returns pointer information. *index* is the generic vertex attribute to be queried, *pname* is a symbolic constant indicating the pointer to be returned, and *params* is a pointer to a location in which to place the returned data.

If a nonzero named buffer object was bound to the GL_ARRAY_BUFFER target (see glBindBuffer) when the desired pointer was previously specified, the *pointer* returned is a byte offset into the buffer object's data store.

Notes

glGetVertexAttribPointerv is available only if the GL version is 2.0 or greater.

The pointer returned is client-side state.

The initial value for each pointer is 0.

Errors

GL_INVALID_VALUE is generated if *index* is greater than or equal to GL_MAX_VERTEX_ATTRIBS. GL_INVALID_ENUM is generated if *pname* is not an accepted value.

Associated Gets

glGet with argument GL_MAX_VERTEX_ATTRIBS

See Also

glGetVertexAttrib, glVertexAttribPointer

glHint

Specify implementation-specific hints

C Specification

void **glHint**(GLenum *target*, GLenum *mode*);

Parameters

target   Specifies a symbolic constant indicating the behavior to be controlled. GL_FOG_HINT, GL_GENERATE_MIPMAP_HINT, GL_LINE_SMOOTH_HINT, GL_PERSPECTIVE_CORRECTION_HINT, GL_POINT_SMOOTH_HINT, GL_POLYGON_SMOOTH_HINT, GL_TEXTURE_COMPRESSION_HINT, and GL_FRAGMENT_SHADER_DERIVATIVE_HINT are accepted.

mode   Specifies a symbolic constant indicating the desired behavior. GL_FASTEST, GL_NICEST, and GL_DONT_CARE are accepted.

Description

Certain aspects of GL behavior, when there is room for interpretation, can be controlled with hints. A hint is specified with two arguments. *target* is a symbolic constant indicating the behavior to be controlled, and *mode* is another symbolic constant indicating the desired behavior. The initial value for each *target* is GL_DONT_CARE. *mode* can be one of the following:

GL_FASTEST

The most efficient option should be chosen.

GL_NICEST

The most correct, or highest quality, option should be chosen.

GL_DONT_CARE

No preference.

Though the implementation aspects that can be hinted are well defined, the interpretation of the hints depends on the implementation. The hint aspects that can be specified with *target*, along with suggested semantics, are as follows:

GL_FOG_HINT

Indicates the accuracy of fog calculation. If per-pixel fog calculation is not efficiently supported by the GL implementation, hinting GL_DONT_CARE or GL_FASTEST can result in per-vertex calculation of fog effects.

GL_FRAGMENT_SHADER_DERIVATIVE_HINT

Indicates the accuracy of the derivative calculation for the GL shading language fragment processing built-in functions: dFdx, dFdy, and fwidth.

GL_GENERATE_MIPMAP_HINT

Indicates the quality of filtering when generating mipmap images.

GL_LINE_SMOOTH_HINT

Indicates the sampling quality of antialiased lines. If a larger filter function is applied, hinting GL_NICEST can result in more pixel fragments being generated during rasterization.

GL_PERSPECTIVE_CORRECTION_HINT

Indicates the quality of color, texture coordinate, and fog coordinate interpolation. If perspective-corrected parameter interpolation is not efficiently supported by the GL implementation, hinting GL_DONT_CARE or GL_FASTEST can result in simple linear interpolation of colors and/or texture coordinates.

GL_POINT_SMOOTH_HINT

Indicates the sampling quality of antialiased points. If a larger filter function is applied, hinting GL_NICEST can result in more pixel fragments being generated during rasterization.

GL_POLYGON_SMOOTH_HINT

Indicates the sampling quality of antialiased polygons. Hinting GL_NICEST can result in more pixel fragments being generated during rasterization, if a larger filter function is applied.

GL_TEXTURE_COMPRESSION_HINT

Indicates the quality and performance of the compressing texture images. Hinting GL_FASTEST indicates that texture images should be compressed as quickly as possible, while GL_NICEST indicates that texture images should be compressed with as little image quality loss as possible. GL_NICEST should be selected if the texture is to be retrieved by glGetCompressedTexImage for reuse.

Notes

The interpretation of hints depends on the implementation. Some implementations ignore glHint settings.

GL_TEXTURE_COMPRESSION_HINT is available only if the GL version is 1.3 or greater.

GL_GENERATE_MIPMAP_HINT is available only if the GL version is 1.4 or greater.

GL_FRAGMENT_SHADER_DERIVATIVE_HINT is available only if the GL version is 2.0 or greater.

Errors

GL_INVALID_ENUM is generated if either *target* or *mode* is not an accepted value.

GL_INVALID_OPERATION is generated if glHint is executed between the execution of glBegin and the corresponding execution of glEnd.

glHistogram

Define histogram table

C Specification

```
void glHistogram(GLenum    target,
                 GLsizei   width,
                 GLenum    internalformat,
                 GLboolean sink);
```

Parameters

target   The histogram whose parameters are to be set. Must be one of GL_HISTOGRAM or GL_PROXY_HISTOGRAM.

width   The number of entries in the histogram table. Must be a power of 2.

internalformat   The format of entries in the histogram table. Must be one of GL_ALPHA, GL_ALPHA4, GL_ALPHA8, GL_ALPHA12, GL_ALPHA16, GL_LUMINANCE, GL_LUMINANCE4, GL_LUMINANCE8, GL_LUMINANCE12, GL_LUMINANCE16, GL_LUMINANCE_ALPHA, GL_LUMINANCE4_ALPHA4, GL_LUMINANCE6_ALPHA2, GL_LUMINANCE8_ALPHA8, GL_LUMINANCE12_ALPHA4, GL_LUMINANCE12_ALPHA12, GL_LUMINANCE16_ALPHA16, GL_R3_G3_B2, GL_RGB, GL_RGB4, GL_RGB5, GL_RGB8, GL_RGB10, GL_RGB12, GL_RGB16, GL_RGBA, GL_RGBA2, GL_RGBA4, GL_RGB5_A1, GL_RGBA8, GL_RGB10_A2, GL_RGBA12, or GL_RGBA16.

sink   If GL_TRUE, pixels will be consumed by the histogramming process and no
                          drawing or texture loading will take place. If GL_FALSE, pixels will proceed to
                          the minmax process after histogramming.

Description

When GL_HISTOGRAM is enabled, RGBA color components are converted to histogram table
indices by clamping to the range [0,1], multiplying by the width of the histogram table, and rounding
to the nearest integer. The table entries selected by the RGBA indices are then incremented. (If the
internal format of the histogram table includes luminance, then the index derived from the R color
component determines the luminance table entry to be incremented.) If a histogram table entry is
incremented beyond its maximum value, then its value becomes undefined. (This is not an error.)

Histogramming is performed only for RGBA pixels (though these may be specified originally as
color indices and converted to RGBA by index table lookup). Histogramming is enabled with
glEnable and disabled with glDisable.

When *target* is GL_HISTOGRAM, glHistogram redefines the current histogram table to have
width entries of the format specified by *internalformat*. The entries are indexed 0 through *width*
– 1, and all entries are initialized to zero. The values in the previous histogram table, if any, are lost. If
sink is GL_TRUE, then pixels are discarded after histogramming; no further processing of the pixels
takes place, and no drawing, texture loading, or pixel readback will result.

When *target* is GL_PROXY_HISTOGRAM, glHistogram computes all state information as if the
histogram table were to be redefined, but does not actually define the new table. If the requested
histogram table is too large to be supported, then the state information will be set to zero. This
provides a way to determine if a histogram table with the given parameters can be supported.

Notes

glHistogram is present only if ARB_imaging is returned when glGetString is called with an
argument of GL_EXTENSIONS.

Errors

GL_INVALID_ENUM is generated if *target* is not one of the allowable values.
GL_INVALID_VALUE is generated if *width* is less than zero or is not a power of 2.
GL_INVALID_ENUM is generated if *internalformat* is not one of the allowable values.
GL_TABLE_TOO_LARGE is generated if *target* is GL_HISTOGRAM and the histogram table specified
is too large for the implementation.
GL_INVALID_OPERATION is generated if glHistogram is executed between the execution of
glBegin and the corresponding execution of glEnd.

Associated Gets

glGetHistogramParameter

See Also

glGetHistogram, glResetHistogram

glIndex

Set the current color index

C Specification

```
void glIndexs(GLshort c);
void glIndexi(GLint c);
void glIndexf(GLfloat c);
void glIndexd(GLdouble c);
void glIndexub(GLubyte c);
```

Parameters

c   Specifies the new value for the current color index.

C Specification

```
void glIndexsv(const GLshort * c);
void glIndexiv(const GLint * c);
void glIndexfv(const GLfloat * c);
void glIndexdv(const GLdouble * c);
void glIndexubv(const GLubyte * c);
```

Parameters

c   Specifies a pointer to a one-element array that contains the new value for the current color index.

Description

glIndex updates the current (single-valued) color index. It takes one argument, the new value for the current color index.

The current index is stored as a floating-point value. Integer values are converted directly to floating-point values, with no special mapping. The initial value is 1.

Index values outside the representable range of the color index buffer are not clamped. However, before an index is dithered (if enabled) and written to the frame buffer, it is converted to fixed-point format. Any bits in the integer portion of the resulting fixed-point value that do not correspond to bits in the frame buffer are masked out.

Notes

glIndexub and glIndexubv are available only if the GL version is 1.1 or greater.

The current index can be updated at any time. In particular, glIndex can be called between a call to glBegin and the corresponding call to glEnd.

Associated Gets

glGet with argument GL_CURRENT_INDEX

See Also

glColor, glIndexPointer

glIndexMask

Control the writing of individual bits in the color index buffers

C Specification

```
void glIndexMask(GLuint mask);
```

Parameters

mask   Specifies a bit mask to enable and disable the writing of individual bits in the color index buffers. Initially, the mask is all 1's.

Description

glIndexMask controls the writing of individual bits in the color index buffers. The least significant *n* bits of *mask*, where *n* is the number of bits in a color index buffer, specify a mask. Where a 1 (one) appears in the mask, it's possible to write to the corresponding bit in the color index buffer (or buffers). Where a 0 (zero) appears, the corresponding bit is write-protected.

This mask is used only in color index mode, and it affects only the buffers currently selected for writing (see glDrawBuffer). Initially, all bits are enabled for writing.

Errors

GL_INVALID_OPERATION is generated if glIndexMask is executed between the execution of glBegin and the corresponding execution of glEnd.

Associated Gets

glGet with argument GL_INDEX_WRITEMASK

See Also

glColorMask, glDepthMask, glDrawBuffer, glIndex, glIndexPointer, glStencilMask

glIndexPointer

Define an array of color indexes

C Specification

```
void glIndexPointer(GLenum        type,
                    GLsizei       stride,
                    const GLvoid * pointer);
```

Parameters

type   Specifies the data type of each color index in the array. Symbolic constants GL_UNSIGNED_BYTE, GL_SHORT, GL_INT, GL_FLOAT, and GL_DOUBLE are accepted. The initial value is GL_FLOAT.

stride   Specifies the byte offset between consecutive color indexes. If stride is 0, the color indexes are understood to be tightly packed in the array. The initial value is 0.

pointer   Specifies a pointer to the first index in the array. The initial value is 0.

Description

glIndexPointer specifies the location and data format of an array of color indexes to use when rendering. *type* specifies the data type of each color index and *stride* specifies the byte stride from one color index to the next, allowing vertices and attributes to be packed into a single array or stored in separate arrays.

If a nonzero named buffer object is bound to the GL_ARRAY_BUFFER target (see glBindBuffer) while a color index array is specified, *pointer* is treated as a byte offset into the buffer object's data store. Also, the buffer object binding (GL_ARRAY_BUFFER_BINDING) is saved as color index vertex array client-side state (GL_INDEX_ARRAY_BUFFER_BINDING).

When a color index array is specified, *type*, *stride*, and *pointer* are saved as client-side state, in addition to the current vertex array buffer object binding.

To enable and disable the color index array, call glEnableClientState and glDisableClientState with the argument GL_INDEX_ARRAY. If enabled, the color index array is used when glDrawArrays, glMultiDrawArrays, glDrawElements, glMultiDrawElements, glDrawRangeElements, or glArrayElement is called.

Notes

glIndexPointer is available only if the GL version is 1.1 or greater.

Color indexes are not supported for interleaved vertex array formats (see glInterleavedArrays).

The color index array is initially disabled and isn't accessed when glArrayElement, glDrawElements, glDrawRangeElements, glDrawArrays, glMultiDrawArrays, or glMultiDrawElements is called.

Execution of glIndexPointer is not allowed between glBegin and the corresponding glEnd, but an error may or may not be generated. If an error is not generated, the operation is undefined.

glIndexPointer is typically implemented on the client side.

Color index array parameters are client-side state and are therefore not saved or restored by glPushAttrib and glPopAttrib. Use glPushClientAttrib and glPopClientAttrib instead.

Errors

GL_INVALID_ENUM is generated if *type* is not an accepted value.

GL_INVALID_VALUE is generated if *stride* is negative.

Associated Gets

glIsEnabled with argument GL_INDEX_ARRAY

glGet with argument GL_INDEX_ARRAY_TYPE

glGet with argument GL_INDEX_ARRAY_STRIDE

glGet with argument GL_INDEX_ARRAY_BUFFER_BINDING

glGet with argument GL_ARRAY_BUFFER_BINDING

glGetPointerv with argument GL_INDEX_ARRAY_POINTER

See Also

glArrayElement, glBindBuffer, glColorPointer, glDisableClientState, glDrawArrays, glDrawElements, glDrawRangeElements, glEdgeFlagPointer, glEnableClientState, glFogCoordPointer, glIndex, glInterleavedArrays, glMultiDrawArrays, glMultiDrawElements, glNormalPointer, glPopClientAttrib, glPushClientAttrib, glSecondaryColorPointer, glTexCoordPointer, glVertexAttribPointer, glVertexPointer

glInitNames

Initialize the name stack

C Specification

void **glInitNames**(*void*);

Description

The name stack is used during selection mode to allow sets of rendering commands to be uniquely identified. It consists of an ordered set of unsigned integers. glInitNames causes the name stack to be initialized to its default empty state.

The name stack is always empty while the render mode is not GL_SELECT. Calls to glInitNames while the render mode is not GL_SELECT are ignored.

Errors

GL_INVALID_OPERATION is generated if glInitNames is executed between the execution of glBegin and the corresponding execution of glEnd.

Associated Gets

glGet with argument GL_NAME_STACK_DEPTH

glGet with argument GL_MAX_NAME_STACK_DEPTH

See Also

glLoadName, glPushName, glRenderMode, glSelectBuffer

glInterleavedArrays

Simultaneously specify and enable several interleaved arrays

C Specification

```
void glInterleavedArrays(GLenum          format,
                         GLsizei         stride,
                         const GLvoid *  pointer);
```

Parameters

format   Specifies the type of array to enable. Symbolic constants GL_V2F, GL_V3F, GL_C4UB_V2F, GL_C4UB_V3F, GL_C3F_V3F, GL_N3F_V3F, GL_C4F_N3F_V3F, GL_T2F_V3F, GL_T4F_V4F, GL_T2F_C4UB_V3F, GL_T2F_C3F_V3F, GL_T2F_N3F_V3F, GL_T2F_C4F_N3F_V3F, and GL_T4F_C4F_N3F_V4F are accepted.

stride   Specifies the offset in bytes between each aggregate array element.

Description

glInterleavedArrays lets you specify and enable individual color, normal, texture and vertex arrays whose elements are part of a larger aggregate array element. For some implementations, this is more efficient than specifying the arrays separately.

If *stride* is 0, the aggregate elements are stored consecutively. Otherwise, *stride* bytes occur between the beginning of one aggregate array element and the beginning of the next aggregate array element.

format serves as a "key" describing the extraction of individual arrays from the aggregate array. If *format* contains a T, then texture coordinates are extracted from the interleaved array. If C is present, color values are extracted. If N is present, normal coordinates are extracted. Vertex coordinates are always extracted.

The digits 2, 3, and 4 denote how many values are extracted. F indicates that values are extracted as floating-point values. Colors may also be extracted as 4 unsigned bytes if 4UB follows the C. If a color is extracted as 4 unsigned bytes, the vertex array element which follows is located at the first possible floating-point aligned address.

Notes

glInterleavedArrays is available only if the GL version is 1.1 or greater.

If glInterleavedArrays is called while compiling a display list, it is not compiled into the list, and it is executed immediately.

Execution of glInterleavedArrays is not allowed between the execution of glBegin and the corresponding execution of glEnd, but an error may or may not be generated. If no error is generated, the operation is undefined.

glInterleavedArrays is typically implemented on the client side.

Vertex array parameters are client-side state and are therefore not saved or restored by glPushAttrib and glPopAttrib. Use glPushClientAttrib and glPopClientAttrib instead.

For OpenGL versions 1.3 and greater, or when the ARB_multitexture extension is supported, glInterleavedArrays only updates the texture coordinate array for the client active texture unit. The texture coordinate state for other client texture units is not updated, regardless of whether the client texture unit is enabled or not.

Secondary color values are not supported in interleaved vertex array formats.

Errors

GL_INVALID_ENUM is generated if *format* is not an accepted value.

GL_INVALID_VALUE is generated if *stride* is negative.

See Also

glArrayElement, glClientActiveTexture, glColorPointer, glDrawArrays, glDrawElements, glEdgeFlagPointer, glEnableClientState, glGetPointerv, glIndexPointer, glNormalPointer, glSecondaryColorPointer, glTexCoordPointer, glVertexPointer

glIsBuffer

Determine if a name corresponds to a buffer object

C Specification

GLboolean **glIsBuffer**(GLuint *buffer*);

Parameters

buffer   Specifies a value that may be the name of a buffer object.

Description

glIsBuffer returns GL_TRUE if *buffer* is currently the name of a buffer object. If *buffer* is zero, or is a nonzero value that is not currently the name of a buffer object, or if an error occurs, glIsBuffer returns GL_FALSE.

A name returned by glGenBuffers, but not yet associated with a buffer object by calling glBindBuffer, is not the name of a buffer object.

Notes

glIsBuffer is available only if the GL version is 1.5 or greater.

Errors

GL_INVALID_OPERATION is generated if glIsBuffer is executed between the execution of glBegin and the corresponding execution of glEnd.

See Also

glBindBuffer, glDeleteBuffers, glGenBuffers, glGet

glIsEnabled

Test whether a capability is enabled

C Specification

GLboolean **glIsEnabled**(GLenum *cap*);

Parameters

cap   Specifies a symbolic constant indicating a GL capability.

Description

glIsEnabled returns GL_TRUE if *cap* is an enabled capability and returns GL_FALSE otherwise. Initially all capabilities except GL_DITHER are disabled; GL_DITHER is initially enabled.

The following capabilities are accepted for *cap*:

Constant	See
GL_ALPHA_TEST	glAlphaFunc
GL_AUTO_NORMAL	glEvalCoord
GL_BLEND	glBlendFunc, glLogicOp
GL_CLIP_PLANEi	glClipPlane

GL_COLOR_ARRAY	glColorPointer
GL_COLOR_LOGIC_OP	glLogicOp
GL_COLOR_MATERIAL	glColorMaterial
GL_COLOR_SUM	glSecondaryColor
GL_COLOR_TABLE	glColorTable
GL_CONVOLUTION_1D	glConvolutionFilter1D
GL_CONVOLUTION_2D	glConvolutionFilter2D
GL_CULL_FACE	glCullFace
GL_DEPTH_TEST	glDepthFunc, glDepthRange
GL_DITHER	glEnable
GL_EDGE_FLAG_ARRAY	glEdgeFlagPointer
GL_FOG	glFog
GL_FOG_COORD_ARRAY	glFogCoordPointer
GL_HISTOGRAM	glHistogram
GL_INDEX_ARRAY	glIndexPointer
GL_INDEX_LOGIC_OP	glLogicOp
GL_LIGHT*i*	glLightModel, glLight
GL_LIGHTING	glMaterial, glLightModel, glLight
GL_LINE_SMOOTH	glLineWidth
GL_LINE_STIPPLE	glLineStipple
GL_MAP1_COLOR_4	glMap1
GL_MAP1_INDEX	glMap1
GL_MAP1_NORMAL	glMap1
GL_MAP1_TEXTURE_COORD_1	glMap1
GL_MAP1_TEXTURE_COORD_2	glMap1
GL_MAP1_TEXTURE_COORD_3	glMap1
GL_MAP1_TEXTURE_COORD_4	glMap1
GL_MAP2_COLOR_4	glMap2
GL_MAP2_INDEX	glMap2
GL_MAP2_NORMAL	glMap2
GL_MAP2_TEXTURE_COORD_1	glMap2
GL_MAP2_TEXTURE_COORD_2	glMap2
GL_MAP2_TEXTURE_COORD_3	glMap2
GL_MAP2_TEXTURE_COORD_4	glMap2
GL_MAP2_VERTEX_3	glMap2
GL_MAP2_VERTEX_4	glMap2
GL_MINMAX	glMinmax
GL_MULTISAMPLE	glSampleCoverage
GL_NORMAL_ARRAY	glNormalPointer
GL_NORMALIZE	glNormal
GL_POINT_SMOOTH	glPointSize
GL_POINT_SPRITE	glEnable
GL_POLYGON_SMOOTH	glPolygonMode

Constant	See
GL_POLYGON_OFFSET_FILL	glPolygonOffset
GL_POLYGON_OFFSET_LINE	glPolygonOffset
GL_POLYGON_OFFSET_POINT	glPolygonOffset
GL_POLYGON_STIPPLE	glPolygonStipple
GL_POST_COLOR_MATRIX_COLOR_TABLE	glColorTable
GL_POST_CONVOLUTION_COLOR_TABLE	glColorTable
GL_RESCALE_NORMAL	glNormal
GL_SAMPLE_ALPHA_TO_COVERAGE	glSampleCoverage
GL_SAMPLE_ALPHA_TO_ONE	glSampleCoverage
GL_SAMPLE_COVERAGE	glSampleCoverage
GL_SCISSOR_TEST	glScissor
GL_SECONDARY_COLOR_ARRAY	glSecondaryColorPointer
GL_SEPARABLE_2D	glSeparableFilter2D
GL_STENCIL_TEST	glStencilFunc, glStencilOp
GL_TEXTURE_1D	glTexImage1D
GL_TEXTURE_2D	glTexImage2D
GL_TEXTURE_3D	glTexImage3D
GL_TEXTURE_COORD_ARRAY	glTexCoordPointer
GL_TEXTURE_CUBE_MAP	glTexGen
GL_TEXTURE_GEN_Q	glTexGen
GL_TEXTURE_GEN_R	glTexGen
GL_TEXTURE_GEN_S	glTexGen
GL_TEXTURE_GEN_T	glTexGen
GL_VERTEX_ARRAY	glVertexPointer
GL_VERTEX_PROGRAM_POINT_SIZE	glEnable
GL_VERTEX_PROGRAM_TWO_SIDE	glEnable

Notes

If an error is generated, glIsEnabled returns 0.

GL_COLOR_LOGIC_OP, GL_COLOR_ARRAY, GL_EDGE_FLAG_ARRAY, GL_INDEX_ARRAY, GL_INDEX_LOGIC_OP, GL_NORMAL_ARRAY, GL_POLYGON_OFFSET_FILL, GL_POLYGON_OFFSET_LINE, GL_POLYGON_OFFSET_POINT, GL_TEXTURE_COORD_ARRAY, and GL_VERTEX_ARRAY are available only if the GL version is 1.1 or greater.

GL_RESCALE_NORMAL, and GL_TEXTURE_3D are available only if the GL version is 1.2 or greater.

GL_MULTISAMPLE, GL_SAMPLE_ALPHA_TO_COVERAGE, GL_SAMPLE_ALPHA_TO_ONE, GL_SAMPLE_COVERAGE, GL_TEXTURE_CUBE_MAP are available only if the GL version is 1.3 or greater.

GL_FOG_COORD_ARRAY and GL_SECONDARY_COLOR_ARRAY are available only if the GL version is 1.4 or greater.

GL_POINT_SPRITE, GL_VERTEX_PROGRAM_POINT_SIZE, and GL_VERTEX_PROGRAM_TWO_SIDE are available only if the GL version is 2.0 or greater.

GL_COLOR_TABLE, GL_CONVOLUTION_1D, GL_CONVOLUTION_2D, GL_HISTOGRAM, GL_MINMAX, GL_POST_COLOR_MATRIX_COLOR_TABLE, GL_POST_CONVOLUTION_COLOR_TABLE, and GL_SEPARABLE_2D are available only if ARB_imaging is returned when glGet is called with GL_EXTENSIONS.

For OpenGL versions 1.3 and greater, or when the ARB_multitexture extension is supported, the following parameters return the associated value for the active texture unit: GL_TEXTURE_1D, GL_TEXTURE_BINDING_1D, GL_TEXTURE_2D, GL_TEXTURE_BINDING_2D, GL_TEXTURE_3D, GL_TEXTURE_BINDING_3D, GL_TEXTURE_GEN_S, GL_TEXTURE_GEN_T, GL_TEXTURE_GEN_R, GL_TEXTURE_GEN_Q, GL_TEXTURE_MATRIX, and GL_TEXTURE_STACK_DEPTH. Likewise, the following parameters return the associated value for the active client texture unit: GL_TEXTURE_COORD_ARRAY, GL_TEXTURE_COORD_ARRAY_SIZE, GL_TEXTURE_COORD_ARRAY_STRIDE, GL_TEXTURE_COORD_ARRAY_TYPE.

Errors

GL_INVALID_ENUM is generated if *cap* is not an accepted value.

GL_INVALID_OPERATION is generated if glIsEnabled is executed between the execution of glBegin and the corresponding execution of glEnd.

See Also

glEnable, glEnableClientState, glGet

glIsList

Determine if a name corresponds to a display list

C Specification

GLboolean **glIsList**(GLuint *list*);

Parameters

list   Specifies a potential display list name.

Description

glIsList returns GL_TRUE if *list* is the name of a display list and returns GL_FALSE if it is not, or if an error occurs.

A name returned by glGenLists, but not yet associated with a display list by calling glNewList, is not the name of a display list.

Errors

GL_INVALID_OPERATION is generated if glIsList is executed between the execution of glBegin and the corresponding execution of glEnd.

See Also

glCallList, glCallLists, glDeleteLists, glGenLists, glNewList

glIsProgram

Determine if a name corresponds to a program object

C Specification

GLboolean **glIsProgram**(GLuint *program*);

Parameters

program   Specifies a potential program object.

Description

glIsProgram returns GL_TRUE if *program* is the name of a program object previously created with glCreateProgram and not yet deleted with glDeleteProgram. If *program* is zero or a nonzero value that is not the name of a program object, or if an error occurs, glIsProgram returns GL_FALSE.

Notes

glIsProgram is available only if the GL version is 2.0 or greater.

No error is generated if *program* is not a valid program object name.

A program object marked for deletion with glDeleteProgram but still in use as part of current rendering state is still considered a program object and glIsProgram will return GL_TRUE.

Errors

GL_INVALID_OPERATION is generated if glIsProgram is executed between the execution of glBegin and the corresponding execution of glEnd.

Associated Gets

glGet with the argument GL_CURRENT_PROGRAM

glGetActiveAttrib with arguments *program* and the index of an active attribute variable

glGetActiveUniform with arguments *program* and the index of an active uniform variable

glGetAttachedShaders with argument *program*

glGetAttribLocation with arguments *program* and the name of an attribute variable

glGetProgram with arguments *program* and the parameter to be queried

glGetProgramInfoLog with argument *program*

glGetUniform with arguments *program* and the location of a uniform variable

glGetUniformLocation with arguments program and the name of a uniform variable

See Also

glAttachShader, glBindAttribLocation, glCreateProgram, glDeleteProgram, glDetachShader, glLinkProgram, glUniform, glUseProgram, glValidateProgram

gIIsQuery

Determine if a name corresponds to a query object

C Specification

GLboolean **glIsQuery**(GLuint *id*);

Parameters

id   Specifies a value that may be the name of a query object.

Description

glIsQuery returns GL_TRUE if *id* is currently the name of a query object. If *id* is zero, or is a nonzero value that is not currently the name of a query object, or if an error occurs, glIsQuery returns GL_FALSE.

A name returned by glGenQueries, but not yet associated with a query object by calling glBeginQuery, is not the name of a query object.

Notes

glIsQuery is available only if the GL version is 1.5 or greater.

Errors

GL_INVALID_OPERATION is generated if glIsQuery is executed between the execution of glBegin and the corresponding execution of glEnd.

See Also

glBeginQuery, glDeleteQueries, glEndQuery, glGenQueries

glIsShader

Determine if a name corresponds to a shader object

C Specification

GLboolean **glIsShader**(GLuint *shader*);

Parameters

shader   Specifies a potential shader object.

Description

glIsShader returns GL_TRUE if *shader* is the name of a shader object previously created with glCreateShader and not yet deleted with glDeleteShader. If *shader* is zero or a nonzero value that is not the name of a shader object, or if an error occurs, glIsShader returns GL_FALSE.

Notes

glIsShader is available only if the GL version is 2.0 or greater.

No error is generated if *shader* is not a valid shader object name.

A shader object marked for deletion with glDeleteShader but still attached to a program object is still considered a shader object and glIsShader will return GL_TRUE.

Errors

GL_INVALID_OPERATION is generated if glIsShader is executed between the execution of glBegin and the corresponding execution of glEnd.

Associated Gets

glGetAttachedShaders with a valid program object

glGetShader with arguments *shader* and a parameter to be queried

glGetShaderInfoLog with argument object

glGetShaderSource with argument object

See Also

glAttachShader, glCompileShader, glCreateShader, glDeleteShader, glDetachShader, glLinkProgram, glShaderSource

glIsTexture

Determine if a name corresponds to a texture

C Specification

GLboolean **glIsTexture**(GLuint *texture*);

Parameters

texture   Specifies a value that may be the name of a texture.

Description

glIsTexture returns GL_TRUE if *texture* is currently the name of a texture. If *texture* is zero, or is a nonzero value that is not currently the name of a texture, or if an error occurs, glIsTexture returns GL_FALSE.

A name returned by glGenTextures, but not yet associated with a texture by calling glBindTexture, is not the name of a texture.

Notes

glIsTexture is available only if the GL version is 1.1 or greater.

Errors

GL_INVALID_OPERATION is generated if glIsTexture is executed between the execution of glBegin and the corresponding execution of glEnd.

See Also

glBindTexture, glCopyTexImage1D, glCopyTexImage2D, glDeleteTextures, glGenTextures, glGet, glGetTexParameter, glTexImage1D, glTexImage2D, glTexImage3D, glTexParameter

glLight

Set light source parameters

C Specification

```
void glLightf(GLenum  light,
              GLenum  pname,
              GLfloat param);
void glLighti(GLenum  light,
              GLenum  pname,
              GLint   param);
```

Parameters

light Specifies a light. The number of lights depends on the implementation, but at least eight lights are supported. They are identified by symbolic names of the form GL_LIGHT*i*, where *i* ranges from 0 to the value of GL_MAX_LIGHTS - 1.

pname Specifies a single-valued light source parameter for *light*. GL_SPOT_EXPONENT, GL_SPOT_CUTOFF, GL_CONSTANT_ATTENUATION, GL_LINEAR_ATTENUATION, and GL_QUADRATIC_ATTENUATION are accepted.

param Specifies the value that parameter *pname* of light source *light* will be set to.

C Specification

```
void glLightfv(GLenum        light,
               GLenum        pname,
               const GLfloat * params);
void glLightiv(GLenum        light,
               GLenum        pname,
               const GLint * params);
```

Parameters

light Specifies a light. The number of lights depends on the implementation, but at least eight lights are supported. They are identified by symbolic names of the form GL_LIGHT*i*, where *i* ranges from 0 to the value of GL_MAX_LIGHTS - 1.

pname Specifies a light source parameter for *light*. GL_AMBIENT, GL_DIFFUSE, GL_SPECULAR, GL_POSITION, GL_SPOT_CUTOFF, GL_SPOT_DIRECTION, GL_SPOT_EXPONENT, GL_CONSTANT_ATTENUATION, GL_LINEAR_ATTENUATION, and GL_QUADRATIC_ATTENUA-TION are accepted.

params Specifies a pointer to the value or values that parameter *pname* of light source *light* will be set to.

Description

glLight sets the values of individual light source parameters. *light* names the light and is a symbolic name of the form GL_LIGHT*i*, where *i* ranges from 0 to the value of GL_MAX_LIGHTS - 1. *pname* specifies one of ten light source parameters, again by symbolic name. *params* is either a single value or a pointer to an array that contains the new values.

To enable and disable lighting calculation, call glEnable and glDisable with argument GL_LIGHTING. Lighting is initially disabled. When it is enabled, light sources that are enabled contribute to the lighting calculation. Light source *i* is enabled and disabled using glEnable and glDisable with argument GL_LIGHT*i*.

The ten light parameters are as follows:

GL_AMBIENT

params contains four integer or floating-point values that specify the ambient RGBA intensity of the light. Integer values are mapped linearly such that the most positive representable value maps to 1.0, and the most negative representable value maps to -1.0. Floating-point values are mapped directly. Neither integer nor floating-point values are clamped. The initial ambient light intensity is (0, 0, 0, 1).

GL_DIFFUSE

params contains four integer or floating-point values that specify the diffuse RGBA intensity of the light. Integer values are mapped linearly such that the most positive representable value maps to 1.0, and the most negative representable value maps to -1.0. Floating-point values are mapped directly. Neither integer nor floating-point values are clamped. The initial value for GL_LIGHT0 is (1, 1, 1, 1); for other lights, the initial value is (0, 0, 0, 1).

GL_SPECULAR

params contains four integer or floating-point values that specify the specular RGBA intensity of the light. Integer values are mapped linearly such that the most positive representable value maps to 1.0, and the most negative representable value maps to -1.0. Floating-point values are mapped directly. Neither integer nor floating-point values are clamped. The initial value for GL_LIGHT0 is (1, 1, 1, 1); for other lights, the initial value is (0, 0, 0, 1).

GL_POSITION

params contains four integer or floating-point values that specify the position of the light in homogeneous object coordinates. Both integer and floating-point values are mapped directly. Neither integer nor floating-point values are clamped.

The position is transformed by the modelview matrix when glLight is called (just as if it were a point), and it is stored in eye coordinates. If the *w* component of the position is 0, the light is treated as a directional source. Diffuse and specular lighting calculations take the light's direction, but not its actual position, into account, and attenuation is disabled. Otherwise, diffuse and specular lighting calculations are based on the actual location of the light in eye coordinates, and attenuation is enabled. The initial position is (0, 0, 1, 0); thus, the initial light source is directional, parallel to, and in the direction of the −*z* axis.

GL_SPOT_DIRECTION

params contains three integer or floating-point values that specify the direction of the light in homogeneous object coordinates. Both integer and floating-point values are mapped directly. Neither integer nor floating-point values are clamped.

The spot direction is transformed by the inverse of the modelview matrix when glLight is called (just as if it were a normal), and it is stored in eye coordinates. It is significant only when GL_SPOT_CUTOFF is not 180, which it is initially. The initial direction is (0,0,-1).

GL_SPOT_EXPONENT

params is a single integer or floating-point value that specifies the intensity distribution of the light. Integer and floating-point values are mapped directly. Only values in the range [0,128] are accepted.

Effective light intensity is attenuated by the cosine of the angle between the direction of the light and the direction from the light to the vertex being lighted, raised to the power of the spot exponent. Thus, higher spot exponents result in a more focused light source, regardless of the spot cutoff angle (see GL_SPOT_CUTOFF, next paragraph). The initial spot exponent is 0, resulting in uniform light distribution.

GL_SPOT_CUTOFF

params is a single integer or floating-point value that specifies the maximum spread angle of a light source. Integer and floating-point values are mapped directly. Only values in the range [0,90] and the special value 180 are accepted. If the angle between the direction of the light and the direction from the light to the vertex being lighted is greater than the spot cutoff angle, the light is completely masked. Otherwise, its intensity is controlled by the spot exponent and the attenuation factors. The initial spot cutoff is 180, resulting in uniform light distribution.

GL_CONSTANT_ATTENUATION
GL_LINEAR_ATTENUATION
GL_QUADRATIC_ATTENUATION

params is a single integer or floating-point value that specifies one of the three light attenuation factors. Integer and floating-point values are mapped directly. Only nonnegative values are accepted. If the light is positional, rather than directional, its intensity is attenuated by the reciprocal of the sum of the constant factor, the linear factor times the distance between the light and the vertex being lighted, and the quadratic factor times the square of the same distance. The initial attenuation factors are (1, 0, 0), resulting in no attenuation.

Notes

It is always the case that GL_LIGHT*i* = GL_LIGHT0 + *i*.

Errors

GL_INVALID_ENUM is generated if either *light* or *pname* is not an accepted value.

GL_INVALID_VALUE is generated if a spot exponent value is specified outside the range [0,128], or if spot cutoff is specified outside the range [0,90] (except for the special value 180), or if a negative attenuation factor is specified.

GL_INVALID_OPERATION is generated if glLight is executed between the execution of glBegin and the corresponding execution of glEnd.

Associated Gets

glGetLight
glIsEnabled with argument GL_LIGHTING

See Also

glColorMaterial, glLightModel, glMaterial

glLightModel

Set the lighting model parameters

C Specification

```
void glLightModelf(GLenum  pname,
                   GLfloat param);
void glLightModeli(GLenum  pname,
                   GLint   param);
```

Parameters

pname   Specifies a single-valued lighting model parameter. GL_LIGHT_MODEL_LOCAL_VIEWER, GL_LIGHT_MODEL_COLOR_CONTROL, and GL_LIGHT_MODEL_TWO_SIDE are accepted.

param   Specifies the value that *param* will be set to.

C Specification

```
void glLightModelfv(GLenum           pname,
                    const GLfloat *  params);
void glLightModeliv(GLenum           pname,
                    const GLint *    params);
```

Parameters

pname   Specifies a lighting model parameter. GL_LIGHT_MODEL_AMBIENT,
GL_LIGHT_MODEL_COLOR_CONTROL, GL_LIGHT_MODEL_LOCAL_VIEWER, and
GL_LIGHT_MODEL_TWO_SIDE are accepted.

params   Specifies a pointer to the value or values that *params* will be set to.

Description

glLightModel sets the lighting model parameter. *pname* names a parameter and *params* gives the new value. There are three lighting model parameters:

GL_LIGHT_MODEL_AMBIENT

params contains four integer or floating-point values that specify the ambient RGBA intensity of the entire scene. Integer values are mapped linearly such that the most positive representable value maps to 1.0, and the most negative representable value maps to -1.0. Floating-point values are mapped directly. Neither integer nor floating-point values are clamped. The initial ambient scene intensity is (0.2, 0.2, 0.2, 1.0).

GL_LIGHT_MODEL_COLOR_CONTROL

params must be either GL_SEPARATE_SPECULAR_COLOR or GL_SINGLE_COLOR.
GL_SINGLE_COLOR specifies that a single color is generated from the lighting computation for a vertex. GL_SEPARATE_SPECULAR_COLOR specifies that the specular color computation of lighting be stored separately from the remainder of the lighting computation. The specular color is summed into the generated fragment's color after the application of texture mapping (if enabled). The initial value is GL_SINGLE_COLOR.

GL_LIGHT_MODEL_LOCAL_VIEWER

params is a single integer or floating-point value that specifies how specular reflection angles are computed. If *params* is 0 (or 0.0), specular reflection angles take the view direction to be parallel to and in the direction of the -*z* axis, regardless of the location of the vertex in eye coordinates. Otherwise, specular reflections are computed from the origin of the eye coordinate system. The initial value is 0.

GL_LIGHT_MODEL_TWO_SIDE

params is a single integer or floating-point value that specifies whether one- or two-sided lighting calculations are done for polygons. It has no effect on the lighting calculations for points, lines, or bitmaps. If *params* is 0 (or 0.0), one-sided lighting is specified, and only the *front* material parameters are used in the lighting equation. Otherwise, two-sided lighting is specified. In this case, vertices of back-facing polygons are lighted using the *back* material parameters and have their normals reversed before the lighting equation is evaluated. Vertices of front-facing polygons are always lighted using the *front* material parameters, with no change to their normals. The initial value is 0.

In RGBA mode, the lighted color of a vertex is the sum of the material emission intensity, the product of the material ambient reflectance and the lighting model full-scene ambient intensity, and the contribution of each enabled light source. Each light source contributes the sum of three terms: ambient, diffuse, and specular. The ambient light source contribution is the product of the material ambient reflectance and the light's ambient intensity. The diffuse light source contribution is the product of the material diffuse reflectance, the light's diffuse intensity, and the dot product of the vertex's normal with the normalized vector from the vertex to the light source. The specular light source contribution is the product of the material specular reflectance, the light's specular intensity, and the dot product of the normalized vertex-to-eye and vertex-to-light vectors, raised to the power of the shininess of the material. All three light source contributions are attenuated equally based on the distance from the vertex to the light source and on light source direction, spread exponent, and spread cutoff angle. All dot products are replaced with 0 if they evaluate to a negative value.

The alpha component of the resulting lighted color is set to the alpha value of the material diffuse reflectance.

In color index mode, the value of the lighted index of a vertex ranges from the ambient to the specular values passed to glMaterial using GL_COLOR_INDEXES. Diffuse and specular coefficients, computed with a (.30, .59, .11) weighting of the lights' colors, the shininess of the material, and the same reflection and attenuation equations as in the RGBA case, determine how much above ambient the resulting index is.

Notes

GL_LIGHT_MODEL_COLOR_CONTROL is available only if the GL version is 1.2 or greater.

Errors

GL_INVALID_ENUM is generated if *pname* is not an accepted value.

GL_INVALID_ENUM is generated if *pname* is GL_LIGHT_MODEL_COLOR_CONTROL and *params* is not one of GL_SINGLE_COLOR or GL_SEPARATE_SPECULAR_COLOR.

GL_INVALID_OPERATION is generated if glLightModel is executed between the execution of glBegin and the corresponding execution of glEnd.

Associated Gets

glGet with argument GL_LIGHT_MODEL_AMBIENT
glGet with argument GL_LIGHT_MODEL_COLOR_CONTROL
glGet with argument GL_LIGHT_MODEL_LOCAL_VIEWER
glGet with argument GL_LIGHT_MODEL_TWO_SIDE
glIsEnabled with argument GL_LIGHTING

See Also

glLight, glMaterial

glLineStipple

Specify the line stipple pattern

C Specification

```
void glLineStipple(GLint    factor,
                   GLushort pattern);
```

Parameters

factor   Specifies a multiplier for each bit in the line stipple pattern. If *factor* is 3, for
            example, each bit in the pattern is used three times before the next bit in the pattern is
            used. *factor* is clamped to the range [1, 256] and defaults to 1.

pattern   Specifies a 16-bit integer whose bit pattern determines which fragments of a line will be
            drawn when the line is rasterized. Bit zero is used first; the default pattern is all 1's.

Description

Line stippling masks out certain fragments produced by rasterization; those fragments will not be drawn. The masking is achieved by using three parameters: the 16-bit line stipple pattern *pattern*, the repeat count *factor*, and an integer stipple counter s.

Counter s is reset to 0 whenever glBegin is called and before each line segment of a glBegin(GL_LINES)/glEnd sequence is generated. It is incremented after each fragment of a unit width aliased line segment is generated or after each i fragments of an i width line segment are generated. The i fragments associated with count s are masked out if

$$pattern \, bit \left(\frac{s}{factor} \right) \% \, 16$$

is 0, otherwise these fragments are sent to the frame buffer. Bit zero of *pattern* is the least significant bit.

Antialiased lines are treated as a sequence of $1 \times$ width rectangles for purposes of stippling. Whether rectangle *s* is rasterized or not depends on the fragment rule described for aliased lines, counting rectangles rather than groups of fragments.

To enable and disable line stippling, call glEnable and glDisable with argument GL_LINE_STIPPLE. When enabled, the line stipple pattern is applied as described above. When disabled, it is as if the pattern were all 1's. Initially, line stippling is disabled.

Errors

GL_INVALID_OPERATION is generated if glLineStipple is executed between the execution of glBegin and the corresponding execution of glEnd.

Associated Gets

glGet with argument GL_LINE_STIPPLE_PATTERN
glGet with argument GL_LINE_STIPPLE_REPEAT
glIsEnabled with argument GL_LINE_STIPPLE

See Also

glLineWidth, glPolygonStipple

glLineWidth

Specify the width of rasterized lines

C Specification

void **glLineWidth**(GLfloat *width*);

Parameters

width   Specifies the width of rasterized lines. The initial value is 1.

Description

glLineWidth specifies the rasterized width of both aliased and antialiased lines. Using a line width other than 1 has different effects, depending on whether line antialiasing is enabled. To enable and disable line antialiasing, call glEnable and glDisable with argument GL_LINE_SMOOTH. Line antialiasing is initially disabled.

If line antialiasing is disabled, the actual width is determined by rounding the supplied width to the nearest integer. (If the rounding results in the value 0, it is as if the line width were 1.) If $|\Delta x| >= |\Delta y|$, *i* pixels are filled in each column that is rasterized, where *i* is the rounded value of *width*. Otherwise, *i* pixels are filled in each row that is rasterized.

If antialiasing is enabled, line rasterization produces a fragment for each pixel square that intersects the region lying within the rectangle having width equal to the current line width, length equal to the actual length of the line, and centered on the mathematical line segment. The coverage value for each fragment is the window coordinate area of the intersection of the rectangular region with the corresponding pixel square. This value is saved and used in the final rasterization step.

Not all widths can be supported when line antialiasing is enabled. If an unsupported width is requested, the nearest supported width is used. Only width 1 is guaranteed to be supported; others depend on the implementation. Likewise, there is a range for aliased line widths as well. To query the range of supported widths and the size difference between supported widths within the range, call glGet with arguments GL_ALIASED_LINE_WIDTH_RANGE, GL_SMOOTH_LINE_WIDTH_RANGE, and GL_SMOOTH_LINE_WIDTH_GRANULARITY.

Notes

The line width specified by glLineWidth is always returned when GL_LINE_WIDTH is queried. Clamping and rounding for aliased and antialiased lines have no effect on the specified value.

Nonantialiased line width may be clamped to an implementation-dependent maximum. Call glGet with GL_ALIASED_LINE_WIDTH_RANGE to determine the maximum width.

In OpenGL 1.2, the tokens GL_LINE_WIDTH_RANGE and GL_LINE_WIDTH_GRANULARITY were replaced by GL_ALIASED_LINE_WIDTH_RANGE, GL_SMOOTH_LINE_WIDTH_RANGE, and GL_SMOOTH_LINE_WIDTH_GRANULARITY. The old names are retained for backward compatibility, but should not be used in new code.

Errors

GL_INVALID_VALUE is generated if *width* is less than or equal to 0.

GL_INVALID_OPERATION is generated if glLineWidth is executed between the execution of glBegin and the corresponding execution of glEnd.

Associated Gets

glGet with argument GL_LINE_WIDTH
glGet with argument GL_ALIASED_LINE_WIDTH_RANGE
glGet with argument GL_SMOOTH_LINE_WIDTH_RANGE
glGet with argument GL_SMOOTH_LINE_WIDTH_GRANULARITY
glIsEnabled with argument GL_LINE_SMOOTH

See Also

glEnable

glLinkProgram

Link a program object

C Specification

void **glLinkProgram**(GLuint *program*);

Parameters

program   Specifies the handle of the program object to be linked.

Description

glLinkProgram links the program object specified by *program*. If any shader objects of type GL_VERTEX_SHADER are attached to *program*, they will be used to create an executable that will run on the programmable vertex processor. If any shader objects of type GL_FRAGMENT_SHADER are attached to *program*, they will be used to create an executable that will run on the programmable fragment processor.

The status of the link operation will be stored as part of the program object's state. This value will be set to GL_TRUE if the program object was linked without errors and is ready for use, and GL_FALSE otherwise. It can be queried by calling glGetProgram with arguments *program* and GL_LINK_STATUS.

As a result of a successful link operation, all active user-defined uniform variables belonging to *program* will be initialized to 0, and each of the program object's active uniform variables will be assigned a location that can be queried by calling glGetUniformLocation. Also, any active user-defined attribute variables that have not been bound to a generic vertex attribute index will be bound to one at this time.

Linking of a program object can fail for a number of reasons as specified in the *OpenGL Shading Language Specification*. The following lists some of the conditions that will cause a link error.

- The number of active attribute variables supported by the implementation has been exceeded.
- The storage limit for uniform variables has been exceeded.
- The number of active uniform variables supported by the implementation has been exceeded.
- The main function is missing for the vertex shader or the fragment shader.

- A varying variable actually used in the fragment shader is not declared in the same way (or is not declared at all) in the vertex shader.
- A reference to a function or variable name is unresolved.
- A shared global is declared with two different types or two different initial values.
- One or more of the attached shader objects has not been successfully compiled.
- Binding a generic attribute matrix caused some rows of the matrix to fall outside the allowed maximum of GL_MAX_VERTEX_ATTRIBS.
- Not enough contiguous vertex attribute slots could be found to bind attribute matrices.

When a program object has been successfully linked, the program object can be made part of current state by calling glUseProgram. Whether or not the link operation was successful, the program object's information log will be overwritten. The information log can be retrieved by calling glGetProgramInfoLog.

glLinkProgram will also install the generated executables as part of the current rendering state if the link operation was successful and the specified program object is already currently in use as a result of a previous call to glUseProgram. If the program object currently in use is relinked unsuccessfully, its link status will be set to GL_FALSE , but the executables and associated state will remain part of the current state until a subsequent call to glUseProgram removes it from use. After it is removed from use, it cannot be made part of current state until it has been successfully relinked.

If *program* contains shader objects of type GL_VERTEX_SHADER but does not contain shader objects of type GL_FRAGMENT_SHADER, the vertex shader will be linked against the implicit interface for fixed functionality fragment processing. Similarly, if *program* contains shader objects of type GL_FRAGMENT_SHADER but it does not contain shader objects of type GL_VERTEX_SHADER, the fragment shader will be linked against the implicit interface for fixed functionality vertex processing.

The program object's information log is updated and the program is generated at the time of the link operation. After the link operation, applications are free to modify attached shader objects, compile attached shader objects, detach shader objects, delete shader objects, and attach additional shader objects. None of these operations affects the information log or the program that is part of the program object.

Notes

glLinkProgram is available only if the GL version is 2.0 or greater.

If the link operation is unsuccessful, any information about a previous link operation on *program* is lost (i.e., a failed link does not restore the old state of *program*). Certain information can still be retrieved from *program* even after an unsuccessful link operation. See for instance glGetActiveAttrib and glGetActiveUniform.

Errors

GL_INVALID_VALUE is generated if *program* is not a value generated by OpenGL.

GL_INVALID_OPERATION is generated if *program* is not a program object.

GL_INVALID_OPERATION is generated if glLinkProgram is executed between the execution of glBegin and the corresponding execution of glEnd.

Associated Gets

glGet with the argument GL_CURRENT_PROGRAM
glGetActiveAttrib with argument *program* and the index of an active attribute variable
glGetActiveUniform with argument *program* and the index of an active uniform variable
glGetAttachedShaders with argument *program*
glGetAttribLocation with argument *program* and an attribute variable name
glGetProgram with arguments *program* and GL_LINK_STATUS
glGetProgramInfoLog with argument *program*
glGetUniform with argument *program* and a uniform variable location

glGetUniformLocation with argument *program* and a uniform variable name
glIsProgram

See Also

glAttachShader, glBindAttribLocation, glCompileShader, glCreateProgram,
glDeleteProgram, glDetachShader, glUniform, glUseProgram, glValidateProgram

glListBase

Set the display-list base for glCallLists

C Specification

void **glListBase**(GLuint *base*);

Parameters

base   Specifies an integer offset that will be added to glCallLists offsets to generate display-
list names. The initial value is 0.

Description

glCallLists specifies an array of offsets. Display-list names are generated by adding *base* to
each offset. Names that reference valid display lists are executed; the others are ignored.

Errors

GL_INVALID_OPERATION is generated if glListBase is executed between the execution of
glBegin and the corresponding execution of glEnd.

Associated Gets

glGet with argument GL_LIST_BASE

See Also

glCallLists

glLoadIdentity

Replace the current matrix with the identity matrix

C Specification

void **glLoadIdentity**(*void*);

Description

glLoadIdentity replaces the current matrix with the identity matrix. It is semantically
equivalent to calling glLoadMatrix with the identity matrix

$$\begin{bmatrix} 1 & 0 & 0 & 0 \\ 0 & 1 & 0 & 0 \\ 0 & 0 & 1 & 0 \\ 0 & 0 & 0 & 1 \end{bmatrix}$$

but in some cases it is more efficient.

Errors

GL_INVALID_OPERATION is generated if glLoadIdentity is executed between the execution of
glBegin and the corresponding execution of glEnd.

Associated Gets

glGet with argument GL_MATRIX_MODE
glGet with argument GL_COLOR_MATRIX
glGet with argument GL_MODELVIEW_MATRIX
glGet with argument GL_PROJECTION_MATRIX
glGet with argument GL_TEXTURE_MATRIX

See Also

glLoadMatrix, glLoadTransposeMatrix, glMatrixMode, glMultMatrix, glMultTransposeMatrix, glPushMatrix

---

glLoadMatrix

Replace the current matrix with the specified matrix

C Specification

```
void glLoadMatrixd(const GLdouble * m);
void glLoadMatrixf(const GLfloat * m);
```

Parameters

m   Specifies a pointer to 16 consecutive values, which are used as the elements of a 4 × 4 column-major matrix.

Description

glLoadMatrix replaces the current matrix with the one whose elements are specified by *m*. The current matrix is the projection matrix, modelview matrix, or texture matrix, depending on the current matrix mode (see glMatrixMode).

The current matrix, M, defines a transformation of coordinates. For instance, assume M refers to the modelview matrix. If $v = (v[0], v[1], v[2], v[3])$ is the set of object coordinates of a vertex, and *m* points to an array of 16 single- or double-precision floating-point values $m = \{m[0], m[1], \ldots, m[15]\}$, then the modelview transformation $M(v)$ does the following:

$$
M(v) = \begin{bmatrix} m[0] & m[4] & m[8] & m[12] \\ m[1] & m[5] & m[9] & m[13] \\ m[2] & m[?] & m[10] & m[14] \\ m[3] & m[7] & m[11] & m[15] \end{bmatrix} \times \begin{bmatrix} v[0] \\ v[1] \\ v[2] \\ v[3] \end{bmatrix}
$$

Projection and texture transformations are similarly defined.

Notes

While the elements of the matrix may be specified with single or double precision, the GL implementation may store or operate on these values in less than single precision.

Errors

GL_INVALID_OPERATION is generated if glLoadMatrix is executed between the execution of glBegin and the corresponding execution of glEnd.

Associated Gets

glGet with argument GL_MATRIX_MODE
glGet with argument GL_COLOR_MATRIX
glGet with argument GL_MODELVIEW_MATRIX
glGet with argument GL_PROJECTION_MATRIX
glGet with argument GL_TEXTURE_MATRIX

See Also

glLoadIdentity, glMatrixMode, glMultMatrix, glMultTransposeMatrix, glPushMatrix

glLoadName

Load a name onto the name stack

C Specification

void **glLoadName**(GLuint *name*);

Parameters

name   Specifies a name that will replace the top value on the name stack.

Description

The name stack is used during selection mode to allow sets of rendering commands to be uniquely identified. It consists of an ordered set of unsigned integers and is initially empty.

glLoadName causes *name* to replace the value on the top of the name stack.

The name stack is always empty while the render mode is not GL_SELECT. Calls to glLoadName while the render mode is not GL_SELECT are ignored.

Errors

GL_INVALID_OPERATION is generated if glLoadName is called while the name stack is empty.

GL_INVALID_OPERATION is generated if glLoadName is executed between the execution of glBegin and the corresponding execution of glEnd.

Associated Gets

glGet with argument GL_NAME_STACK_DEPTH
glGet with argument GL_MAX_NAME_STACK_DEPTH

See Also

glInitNames, glPushName, glRenderMode, glSelectBuffer

glLoadTransposeMatrix

Replace the current matrix with the specified row-major ordered matrix

C Specification

void **glLoadTransposeMatrixd**(const GLdouble * *m[16]*);
void **glLoadTransposeMatrixf**(const GLfloat * *m[16]*);

Parameters

m[16]   Specifies a pointer to 16 consecutive values, which are used as the elements of a 4×4 row-major matrix.

Description

glLoadTransposeMatrix replaces the current matrix with the one whose elements are specified by *m[16]*. The current matrix is the projection matrix, modelview matrix, or texture matrix, depending on the current matrix mode (see glMatrixMode).

The current matrix, M, defines a transformation of coordinates. For instance, assume M refers to the modelview matrix. If $v = (v[0], v[1], v[2], v[3])$ is the set of object coordinates of a vertex, and *m[16]* points to an array of 16 single- or double-precision floating-point values $m = \{m[0], m[1],..., m[15]\}$, then the modelview transformation $M(v)$ does the following:

$$M\ (v)\ =\ \begin{bmatrix} m\ [0] & m\ [1] & m\ [2] & m\ [3] \\ m\ [4] & m\ [5] & m\ [6] & m\ [7] \\ m\ [8] & m\ [9] & m\ [10] & m\ [11] \\ m\ [12] & m\ [13] & m\ [14] & m\ [15] \end{bmatrix} \times \begin{bmatrix} v\ [0] \\ v\ [1] \\ v\ [2] \\ v\ [3] \end{bmatrix}$$

Projection and texture transformations are similarly defined.

Calling glLoadTransposeMatrix with matrix M is identical in operation to glLoadMatrix with M^T, where T represents the transpose.

Notes

glLoadTransposeMatrix is available only if the GL version is 1.3 or greater.

While the elements of the matrix may be specified with single or double precision, the GL implementation may store or operate on these values in less than single precision.

Errors

GL_INVALID_OPERATION is generated if glLoadTransposeMatrix is executed between the execution of glBegin and the corresponding execution of glEnd.

Associated Gets

glGet with argument GL_MATRIX_MODE
glGet with argument GL_COLOR_MATRIX
glGet with argument GL_MODELVIEW_MATRIX
glGet with argument GL_PROJECTION_MATRIX
glGet with argument GL_TEXTURE_MATRIX

See Also

glLoadIdentity, glLoadMatrix, glMatrixMode, glMultMatrix, glMultTransposeMatrix, glPushMatrix

glLogicOp

Specify a logical pixel operation for color index rendering

C Specification

void **glLogicOp**(GLenum *opcode*);

Parameters

opcode   Specifies a symbolic constant that selects a logical operation. The following symbols are accepted: GL_CLEAR, GL_SET, GL_COPY, GL_COPY_INVERTED, GL_NOOP, GL_INVERT, GL_AND, GL_NAND, GL_OR, GL_NOR, GL_XOR, GL_EQUIV, GL_AND_REVERSE, GL_AND_INVERTED, GL_OR_REVERSE, and GL_OR_INVERTED. The initial value is GL_COPY.

Description

glLogicOp specifies a logical operation that, when enabled, is applied between the incoming color index or RGBA color and the color index or RGBA color at the corresponding location in the frame buffer. To enable or disable the logical operation, call glEnable and glDisable using the symbolic constant GL_COLOR_LOGIC_OP for RGBA mode or GL_INDEX_LOGIC_OP for color index mode. The initial value is disabled for both operations.

Opcode	Resulting Operation
GL_CLEAR	0
GL_SET	1
GL_COPY	s

Opcode	Resulting Operation
GL_COPY_INVERTED	~s
GL_NOOP	d
GL_INVERT	~d
GL_AND	s & d
GL_NAND	~(s & d)
GL_OR	s | d
GL_NOR	~(s | d)
GL_XOR	s ^ d
GL_EQUIV	~(s ^ d)
GL_AND_REVERSE	s & ~d
GL_AND_INVERTED	~s & d
GL_OR_REVERSE	s | ~d
GL_OR_INVERTED	~s | d

opcode is a symbolic constant chosen from the list above. In the explanation of the logical operations, *s* represents the incoming color index and *d* represents the index in the frame buffer. Standard C-language operators are used. As these bitwise operators suggest, the logical operation is applied independently to each bit pair of the source and destination indices or colors.

Notes

Color index logical operations are always supported. RGBA logical operations are supported only if the GL version is 1.1 or greater.

When more than one RGBA color or index buffer is enabled for drawing, logical operations are performed separately for each enabled buffer, using for the destination value the contents of that buffer (see glDrawBuffer).

Errors

GL_INVALID_ENUM is generated if *opcode* is not an accepted value.

GL_INVALID_OPERATION is generated if glLogicOp is executed between the execution of glBegin and the corresponding execution of glEnd.

Associated Gets

glGet with argument GL_LOGIC_OP_MODE.

glIsEnabled with argument GL_COLOR_LOGIC_OP or GL_INDEX_LOGIC_OP.

See Also

glAlphaFunc, glBlendFunc, glDrawBuffer, glEnable, glStencilOp

glMap1

Define a one-dimensional evaluator

C Specification

```
void glMap1f(GLenum          target,
             GLfloat         u1,
             GLfloat         u2,
             GLint           stride,
             GLint           order,
             const GLfloat * points);
```

```
void glMap1d(GLenum              target,
             GLdouble            u1,
             GLdouble            u2,
             GLint               stride,
             GLint               order,
             const GLdouble *    points);
```

Parameters

target Specifies the kind of values that are generated by the evaluator. Symbolic constants GL_MAP1_VERTEX_3, GL_MAP1_VERTEX_4, GL_MAP1_INDEX, GL_MAP1_COLOR_4, GL_MAP1_NORMAL, GL_MAP1_TEXTURE_COORD_1, GL_MAP1_TEXTURE_COORD_2, GL_MAP1_TEXTURE_COORD_3, and GL_MAP1_TEXTURE_COORD_4 are accepted.

u1, u2 Specify a linear mapping of *u*, as presented to glEvalCoord1, to $\hat{u}$, the variable that is evaluated by the equations specified by this command.

stride Specifies the number of floats or doubles between the beginning of one control point and the beginning of the next one in the data structure referenced in *points*. This allows control points to be embedded in arbitrary data structures. The only constraint is that the values for a particular control point must occupy contiguous memory locations.

order Specifies the number of control points. Must be positive.

points Specifies a pointer to the array of control points.

Description

Evaluators provide a way to use polynomial or rational polynomial mapping to produce vertices, normals, texture coordinates, and colors. The values produced by an evaluator are sent to further stages of GL processing just as if they had been presented using glVertex, glNormal, glTexCoord, and glColor commands, except that the generated values do not update the current normal, texture coordinates, or color.

All polynomial or rational polynomial splines of any degree (up to the maximum degree supported by the GL implementation) can be described using evaluators. These include almost all splines used in computer graphics: B-splines, Bezier curves, Hermite splines, and so on.

Evaluators define curves based on Bernstein polynomials. Define $p(\hat{u})$ as

$$p(\hat{u}) = \sum_{i=0}^{n} B_i^n(\hat{u}) R_i$$

where R_i is a control point and $B_i^n(\hat{u})$ is the *i*th Bernstein polynomial of degree *n* (*order* = *n* + 1):

$$B_i^n(\hat{u}) = \begin{bmatrix} n \\ i \end{bmatrix} \hat{u}^i (1 - \hat{u})^{n-i}$$

Recall that

$$0^0 == 1 \text{ and } \begin{bmatrix} n \\ 0 \end{bmatrix} == 1$$

glMap1 is used to define the basis and to specify what kind of values are produced. Once defined, a map can be enabled and disabled by calling glEnable and glDisable with the map name, one of the nine predefined values for *target* described below. glEvalCoord1 evaluates the one-dimensional maps that are enabled. When glEvalCoord1 presents a value *u*, the Bernstein functions are evaluated using $\hat{u}$, where

$$u = \frac{\hat{u} - u1}{u2 - u1}$$

target is a symbolic constant that indicates what kind of control points are provided in *points*, and what output is generated when the map is evaluated. It can assume one of nine predefined values:

GL_MAP1_VERTEX_3

Each control point is three floating-point values representing *x*, *y*, and *z*. Internal glVertex3 commands are generated when the map is evaluated.

GL_MAP1_VERTEX_4

Each control point is four floating-point values representing *x*, *y*, *z*, and *w*. Internal glVertex4 commands are generated when the map is evaluated.

GL_MAP1_INDEX

Each control point is a single floating-point value representing a color index. Internal glIndex commands are generated when the map is evaluated but the current index is not updated with the value of these glIndex commands.

GL_MAP1_COLOR_4

Each control point is four floating-point values representing red, green, blue, and alpha. Internal glColor4 commands are generated when the map is evaluated but the current color is not updated with the value of these glColor4 commands.

GL_MAP1_NORMAL

Each control point is three floating-point values representing the *x*, *y*, and *z* components of a normal vector. Internal glNormal commands are generated when the map is evaluated but the current normal is not updated with the value of these glNormal commands.

GL_MAP1_TEXTURE_COORD_1

Each control point is a single floating-point value representing the *s* texture coordinate. Internal glTexCoord1 commands are generated when the map is evaluated but the current texture coordinates are not updated with the value of these glTexCoord commands.

GL_MAP1_TEXTURE_COORD_2

Each control point is two floating-point values representing the *s* and *t* texture coordinates. Internal glTexCoord2 commands are generated when the map is evaluated but the current texture coordinates are not updated with the value of these glTexCoord commands.

GL_MAP1_TEXTURE_COORD_3

Each control point is three floating-point values representing the *s*, *t*, and *r* texture coordinates. Internal glTexCoord3 commands are generated when the map is evaluated but the current texture coordinates are not updated with the value of these glTexCoord commands.

GL_MAP1_TEXTURE_COORD_4

Each control point is four floating-point values representing the *s*, *t*, *r*, and *q* texture coordinates. Internal glTexCoord4 commands are generated when the map is evaluated but the current texture coordinates are not updated with the value of these glTexCoord commands.

stride, *order*, and *points* define the array addressing for accessing the control points. *points* is the location of the first control point, which occupies one, two, three, or four contiguous memory locations, depending on which map is being defined. *order* is the number of control points in the array. *stride* specifies how many float or double locations to advance the internal memory pointer to reach the next control point.

Notes

As is the case with all GL commands that accept pointers to data, it is as if the contents of *points* were copied by glMap1 before glMap1 returns. Changes to the contents of *points* have no effect after glMap1 is called.

Errors

GL_INVALID_ENUM is generated if *target* is not an accepted value.

GL_INVALID_VALUE is generated if *u1* is equal to *u2*.

GL_INVALID_VALUE is generated if *stride* is less than the number of values in a control point.

GL_INVALID_VALUE is generated if *order* is less than 1 or greater than the return value of GL_MAX_EVAL_ORDER.

GL_INVALID_OPERATION is generated if glMap1 is executed between the execution of glBegin and the corresponding execution of glEnd.

GL_INVALID_OPERATION is generated if glMap1 is called and the value of GL_ACTIVE_TEXTURE is not GL_TEXTURE0.

Associated Gets

glGetMap
glGet with argument GL_MAX_EVAL_ORDER
glIsEnabled with argument GL_MAP1_VERTEX_3
glIsEnabled with argument GL_MAP1_VERTEX_4
glIsEnabled with argument GL_MAP1_INDEX
glIsEnabled with argument GL_MAP1_COLOR_4
glIsEnabled with argument GL_MAP1_NORMAL
glIsEnabled with argument GL_MAP1_TEXTURE_COORD_1
glIsEnabled with argument GL_MAP1_TEXTURE_COORD_2
glIsEnabled with argument GL_MAP1_TEXTURE_COORD_3
glIsEnabled with argument GL_MAP1_TEXTURE_COORD_4

See Also

glBegin, glColor, glEnable, glEvalCoord, glEvalMesh, glEvalPoint, glMap2, glMapGrid,
glNormal, glTexCoord, glVertex

glMap2

Define a two-dimensional evaluator

C Specification

```
void glMap2f(GLenum         target,
             GLfloat        u1,
             GLfloat        u2,
             GLint          ustride,
             GLint          uorder,
             GLfloat        v1,
             GLfloat        v2,
             GLint          vstride,
             GLint          vorder,
             const GLfloat * points);
void glMap2d(GLenum         target,
             GLdouble       u1,
             GLdouble       u2,
             GLint          ustride,
             GLint          uorder,
             GLdouble       v1,
             GLdouble       v2,
             GLint          vstride,
             GLint          vorder,
             const GLdouble * points);
```

Parameters

target   Specifies the kind of values that are generated by the evaluator. Symbolic constants
GL_MAP2_VERTEX_3, GL_MAP2_VERTEX_4, GL_MAP2_INDEX, GL_MAP2_COLOR_4,
GL_MAP2_NORMAL, GL_MAP2_TEXTURE_COORD_1, GL_MAP2_TEXTURE_COORD_2,
GL_MAP2_TEXTURE_COORD_3, and GL_MAP2_TEXTURE_COORD_4 are accepted.

u1, u2   Specify a linear mapping of u, as presented to glEvalCoord2, to $\hat{u}$, one of the two
variables that are evaluated by the equations specified by this command. Initially, *u1* is
0 and *u2* is 1.

ustride	Specifies the number of floats or doubles between the beginning of control point R_{ij} and the beginning of control point $R_{(i+1)j}$, where i and j are the u and v control point indices, respectively. This allows control points to be embedded in arbitrary data structures. The only constraint is that the values for a particular control point must occupy contiguous memory locations. The initial value of *ustride* is 0.
uorder	Specifies the dimension of the control point array in the u axis. Must be positive. The initial value is 1.
v1, v2	Specify a linear mapping of v, as presented to glEvalCoord2, to $\hat{v}$, one of the two variables that are evaluated by the equations specified by this command. Initially, *v1* is 0 and *v2* is 1.
vstride	Specifies the number of floats or doubles between the beginning of control point R_{ij} and the beginning of control point $R_{i(j+1)}$, where i and j are the u and v control point indices, respectively. This allows control points to be embedded in arbitrary data structures. The only constraint is that the values for a particular control point must occupy contiguous memory locations. The initial value of *vstride* is 0.
vorder	Specifies the dimension of the control point array in the v axis. Must be positive. The initial value is 1.
points	Specifies a pointer to the array of control points.

Description

Evaluators provide a way to use polynomial or rational polynomial mapping to produce vertices, normals, texture coordinates, and colors. The values produced by an evaluator are sent on to further stages of GL processing just as if they had been presented using glVertex, glNormal, glTexCoord, and glColor commands, except that the generated values do not update the current normal, texture coordinates, or color.

All polynomial or rational polynomial splines of any degree (up to the maximum degree supported by the GL implementation) can be described using evaluators. These include almost all surfaces used in computer graphics, including B-spline surfaces, NURBS surfaces, Bezier surfaces, and so on.

Evaluators define surfaces based on bivariate Bernstein polynomials. Define $p\,(\hat{u}, \hat{v})$ as

$$p\,(\hat{u},\hat{v}) = \sum_{i=0}^{n} \sum_{j=0}^{m} B_i^n\,(\hat{u})\; B_j^m\,(\hat{v})\; R_{ij}$$

where R_{ij} is a control point, $B_i^{\,n}(\hat{u})$ is the ith Bernstein polynomial of degree n (*uorder* = $n + 1$)

$$B_i^n\,(\hat{u}) = \begin{bmatrix} n \\ i \end{bmatrix} \hat{u}^i\,(1 - \hat{u})^{n-i}$$

and $B_j^{\,m}(\hat{v})$ is the jth Bernstein polynomial of degree m (*vorder* = $m + 1$)

$$B_j^m\,(\hat{v}) = \begin{bmatrix} m \\ j \end{bmatrix} \hat{v}^j\,(1 - \hat{v})^{m-j}$$

Recall that $0^0 == 1$ and $\begin{bmatrix} n \\ 0 \end{bmatrix} == 1$

glMap2 is used to define the basis and to specify what kind of values are produced. Once defined, a map can be enabled and disabled by calling glEnable and glDisable with the map name, one of the nine predefined values for *target*, described below. When glEvalCoord2 presents values u and v, the bivariate Bernstein polynomials are evaluated using $\hat{u}$ and $\hat{v}$, where

$$\hat{u} = \frac{u - ul}{u2 - ul}$$

$$\hat{v} = \frac{v - vl}{v2 - vl}$$

target is a symbolic constant that indicates what kind of control points are provided in *points*, and what output is generated when the map is evaluated. It can assume one of nine predefined values:

GL_MAP2_VERTEX_3

Each control point is three floating-point values representing *x*, *y*, and *z*. Internal `glVertex3` commands are generated when the map is evaluated.

GL_MAP2_VERTEX_4

Each control point is four floating-point values representing *x*, *y*, *z*, and *w*. Internal `glVertex4` commands are generated when the map is evaluated.

GL_MAP2_INDEX

Each control point is a single floating-point value representing a color index. Internal `glIndex` commands are generated when the map is evaluated but the current index is not updated with the value of these `glIndex` commands.

GL_MAP2_COLOR_4

Each control point is four floating-point values representing red, green, blue, and alpha. Internal `glColor4` commands are generated when the map is evaluated but the current color is not updated with the value of these `glColor4` commands.

GL_MAP2_NORMAL

Each control point is three floating-point values representing the *x*, *y*, and *z* components of a normal vector. Internal `glNormal` commands are generated when the map is evaluated but the current normal is not updated with the value of these `glNormal` commands.

GL_MAP2_TEXTURE_COORD_1

Each control point is a single floating-point value representing the *s* texture coordinate. Internal `glTexCoord1` commands are generated when the map is evaluated but the current texture coordinates are not updated with the value of these `glTexCoord` commands.

GL_MAP2_TEXTURE_COORD_2

Each control point is two floating-point values representing the *s* and *t* texture coordinates. Internal `glTexCoord2` commands are generated when the map is evaluated but the current texture coordinates are not updated with the value of these `glTexCoord` commands.

GL_MAP2_TEXTURE_COORD_3

Each control point is three floating-point values representing the *s*, *t*, and *r* texture coordinates. Internal `glTexCoord3` commands are generated when the map is evaluated but the current texture coordinates are not updated with the value of these `glTexCoord` commands.

GL_MAP2_TEXTURE_COORD_4

Each control point is four floating-point values representing the *s*, *t*, *r*, and *q* texture coordinates. Internal `glTexCoord4` commands are generated when the map is evaluated but the current texture coordinates are not updated with the value of these `glTexCoord` commands.

ustride, *uorder*, *vstride*, *vorder*, and *points* define the array addressing for accessing the control points. *points* is the location of the first control point, which occupies one, two, three, or four contiguous memory locations, depending on which map is being defined. There are *uorder* × *vorder* control points in the array. *ustride* specifies how many float or double locations are skipped to advance the internal memory pointer from control point R_{ij} to control point $R_{(i+1)j}$. *vstride* specifies how many float or double locations are skipped to advance the internal memory pointer from control point R_{ij} to control point $R_{i(j+1)}$.

Notes

As is the case with all GL commands that accept pointers to data, it is as if the contents of *points* were copied by `glMap2` before `glMap2` returns. Changes to the contents of *points* have no effect after `glMap2` is called.

Initially, `GL_AUTO_NORMAL` is enabled. If `GL_AUTO_NORMAL` is enabled, normal vectors are generated when either `GL_MAP2_VERTEX_3` or `GL_MAP2_VERTEX_4` is used to generate vertices.

Errors

`GL_INVALID_ENUM` is generated if *target* is not an accepted value.
`GL_INVALID_VALUE` is generated if *u1* is equal to *u2*, or if *v1* is equal to *v2*.

GL_INVALID_VALUE is generated if either *ustride* or *vstride* is less than the number of values in a control point.

GL_INVALID_VALUE is generated if either *uorder* or *vorder* is less than 1 or greater than the return value of GL_MAX_EVAL_ORDER.

GL_INVALID_OPERATION is generated if glMap2 is executed between the execution of glBegin and the corresponding execution of glEnd.

GL_INVALID_OPERATION is generated if glMap2 is called and the value of GL_ACTIVE_TEXTURE is not GL_TEXTURE0.

Associated Gets

glGetMap

glGet with argument GL_MAX_EVAL_ORDER
glIsEnabled with argument GL_MAP2_VERTEX_3
glIsEnabled with argument GL_MAP2_VERTEX_4
glIsEnabled with argument GL_MAP2_INDEX
glIsEnabled with argument GL_MAP2_COLOR_4
glIsEnabled with argument GL_MAP2_NORMAL
glIsEnabled with argument GL_MAP2_TEXTURE_COORD_1
glIsEnabled with argument GL_MAP2_TEXTURE_COORD_2
glIsEnabled with argument GL_MAP2_TEXTURE_COORD_3
glIsEnabled with argument GL_MAP2_TEXTURE_COORD_4

See Also

glBegin, glColor, glEnable, glEvalCoord, glEvalMesh, glEvalPoint, glMap1, glMapGrid, glNormal, glTexCoord, glVertex

glMapBuffer

Map a buffer object's data store

C Specification

```
void * glMapBuffer(GLenum target,
                   GLenum access);
```

Parameters

target   Specifies the target buffer object being mapped. The symbolic constant must be GL_ARRAY_BUFFER, GL_ELEMENT_ARRAY_BUFFER, GL_PIXEL_PACK_BUFFER, or GL_PIXEL_UNPACK_BUFFER.

access   Specifies the access policy, indicating whether it will be possible to read from, write to, or both read from and write to the buffer object's mapped data store. The symbolic constant must be GL_READ_ONLY, GL_WRITE_ONLY, or GL_READ_WRITE.

C Specification

```
GLboolean glUnmapBuffer(GLenum target);
```

Parameters

target   Specifies the target buffer object being unmapped. The symbolic constant must be GL_ARRAY_BUFFER, GL_ELEMENT_ARRAY_BUFFER, GL_PIXEL_PACK_BUFFER, or GL_PIXEL_UNPACK_BUFFER.

Description

glMapBuffer maps to the client's address space the entire data store of the buffer object currently bound to *target*. The data can then be directly read and/or written relative to the returned pointer, depending on the specified *access* policy. If the GL is unable to map the buffer object's data store, glMapBuffer generates an error and returns NULL. This may occur for system-specific reasons, such as low virtual memory availability.

If a mapped data store is accessed in a way inconsistent with the specified *access* policy, no error is generated, but performance may be negatively impacted and system errors, including program termination, may result. Unlike the *usage* parameter of glBufferData, *access* is not a hint, and does in fact constrain the usage of the mapped data store on some GL implementations. In order to achieve the highest performance available, a buffer object's data store should be used in ways consistent with both its specified *usage* and *access* parameters.

A mapped data store must be unmapped with glUnmapBuffer before its buffer object is used. Otherwise an error will be generated by any GL command that attempts to dereference the buffer object's data store. When a data store is unmapped, the pointer to its data store becomes invalid. glUnmapBuffer returns GL_TRUE unless the data store contents have become corrupt during the time the data store was mapped. This can occur for system-specific reasons that affect the availability of graphics memory, such as screen mode changes. In such situations, GL_FALSE is returned and the data store contents are undefined. An application must detect this rare condition and reinitialize the data store.

A buffer object's mapped data store is automatically unmapped when the buffer object is deleted or its data store is recreated with glBufferData.

Notes

If an error is generated, glMapBuffer returns NULL, and glUnmapBuffer returns GL_FALSE. glMapBuffer and glUnmapBuffer are available only if the GL version is 1.5 or greater. GL_PIXEL_PACK_BUFFER and GL_PIXEL_UNPACK_BUFFER are available only if the GL version is 2.1 or greater.

Parameter values passed to GL commands may not be sourced from the returned pointer. No error will be generated, but results will be undefined and will likely vary across GL implementations.

Errors

GL_INVALID_ENUM is generated if *target* is not GL_ARRAY_BUFFER, GL_ELEMENT_ARRAY_BUFFER, GL_PIXEL_PACK_BUFFER, or GL_PIXEL_UNPACK_BUFFER.

GL_INVALID_ENUM is generated if *access* is not GL_READ_ONLY, GL_WRITE_ONLY, or GL_READ_WRITE.

GL_OUT_OF_MEMORY is generated when glMapBuffer is executed if the GL is unable to map the buffer object's data store. This may occur for a variety of system-specific reasons, such as the absence of sufficient remaining virtual memory.

GL_INVALID_OPERATION is generated if the reserved buffer object name 0 is bound to *target*.

GL_INVALID_OPERATION is generated if glMapBuffer is executed for a buffer object whose data store is already mapped.

GL_INVALID_OPERATION is generated if glUnmapBuffer is executed for a buffer object whose data store is not currently mapped.

GL_INVALID_OPERATION is generated if glMapBuffer or glUnmapBuffer is executed between the execution of glBegin and the corresponding execution of glEnd.

Associated Gets

glGetBufferPointerv with argument GL_BUFFER_MAP_POINTER

glGetBufferParameteriv with argument GL_BUFFER_MAPPED, GL_BUFFER_ACCESS, or GL_BUFFER_USAGE

See Also

glBindBuffer, glBufferData, glBufferSubData, glDeleteBuffers

glMapGrid

Define a one- or two-dimensional mesh

C Specification

```
void glMapGrid1d(GLint    un,
                 GLdouble u1,
                 GLdouble u2);
void glMapGrid1f(GLint    un,
                 GLfloat  u1,
                 GLfloat  u2);
void glMapGrid2d(GLint    un,
                 GLdouble u1,
                 GLdouble u2,
                 GLint    vn,
                 GLdouble v1,
                 GLdouble v2);
void glMapGrid2f(GLint    un,
                 GLfloat  u1,
                 GLfloat  u2,
                 GLint    vn,
                 GLfloat  v1,
                 GLfloat  v2);
```

Parameters

un	Specifies the number of partitions in the grid range interval [*u1*, *u2*]. Must be positive.
u1, u2	Specify the mappings for integer grid domain values $i = 0$ and $i = un$.
vn	Specifies the number of partitions in the grid range interval [*v1*, *v2*] (glMapGrid2 only).
v1, v2	Specify the mappings for integer grid domain values $j = 0$ and $j = vn$ (glMapGrid2 only).

Description

glMapGrid and glEvalMesh are used together to efficiently generate and evaluate a series of evenly-spaced map domain values. glEvalMesh steps through the integer domain of a one- or two-dimensional grid, whose range is the domain of the evaluation maps specified by glMap1 and glMap2.

glMapGrid1 and glMapGrid2 specify the linear grid mappings between the *i* (or *i* and *j*) integer grid coordinates, to the *u* (or *u* and *v*) floating-point evaluation map coordinates. See glMap1 and glMap2 for details of how *u* and *v* coordinates are evaluated.

glMapGrid1 specifies a single linear mapping such that integer grid coordinate 0 maps exactly to u1, and integer grid coordinate un maps exactly to u2. All other integer grid coordinates *i* are mapped so that

$$u = \frac{i\,(u2 - ul)}{un} + ul$$

glMapGrid2 specifies two such linear mappings. One maps integer grid coordinate $i = 0$ exactly to u1, and integer grid coordinate $i = un$ exactly to u2. The other maps integer grid coordinate $j = 0$ exactly to v1, and integer grid coordinate $j = vn$ exactly to v2. Other integer grid coordinates *i* and *j* are mapped such that

$$u = \frac{i\,(u2 - ul)}{un} + ul$$

$$v = \frac{j\,(v2 - vl)}{vn} + vl$$

The mappings specified by glMapGrid are used identically by glEvalMesh and glEvalPoint.

Errors

GL_INVALID_VALUE is generated if either *un* or *vn* is not positive.

GL_INVALID_OPERATION is generated if glMapGrid is executed between the execution of glBegin and the corresponding execution of glEnd.

Associated Gets

glGet with argument GL_MAP1_GRID_DOMAIN
glGet with argument GL_MAP2_GRID_DOMAIN
glGet with argument GL_MAP1_GRID_SEGMENTS
glGet with argument GL_MAP2_GRID_SEGMENTS

See Also

glEvalCoord, glEvalMesh, glEvalPoint, glMap1, glMap2

glMaterial

Specify material parameters for the lighting model

C Specification

```
void glMaterialf(GLenum   face,
                 GLenum   pname,
                 GLfloat  param);
void glMateriali(GLenum   face,
                 GLenum   pname,
                 GLint    param);
```

Parameters

face   Specifies which face or faces are being updated. Must be one of GL_FRONT, GL_BACK, or GL_FRONT_AND_BACK.

pname   Specifies the single-valued material parameter of the face or faces that is being updated. Must be GL_SHININESS.

param   Specifies the value that parameter GL_SHININESS will be set to.

C Specification

```
void glMaterialfv(GLenum         face,
                  GLenum         pname,
                  const GLfloat * params);
void glMaterialiv(GLenum         face,
                  GLenum         pname,
                  const GLint * params);
```

Parameters

face   Specifies which face or faces are being updated. Must be one of GL_FRONT, GL_BACK, or GL_FRONT_AND_BACK.

pname   Specifies the material parameter of the face or faces that is being updated. Must be one of GL_AMBIENT, GL_DIFFUSE, GL_SPECULAR, GL_EMISSION, GL_SHININESS, GL_AMBIENT_AND_DIFFUSE, or GL_COLOR_INDEXES.

params   Specifies a pointer to the value or values that *pname* will be set to.

Description

glMaterial assigns values to material parameters. There are two matched sets of material parameters. One, the *front-facing* set, is used to shade points, lines, bitmaps, and all polygons (when two-sided lighting is disabled), or just front-facing polygons (when two-sided lighting is enabled). The other set, *back-facing*, is used to shade back-facing polygons only when two-sided lighting is enabled. Refer to the glLightModel reference page for details concerning one- and two-sided lighting calculations.

glMaterial takes three arguments. The first, face, specifies whether the GL_FRONT materials, the GL_BACK materials, or both GL_FRONT_AND_BACK materials will be modified. The second, *pname*, specifies which of several parameters in one or both sets will be modified. The third, *params*, specifies what value or values will be assigned to the specified parameter.

Material parameters are used in the lighting equation that is optionally applied to each vertex. The equation is discussed in the glLightModel reference page. The parameters that can be specified using glMaterial, and their interpretations by the lighting equation, are as follows:

GL_AMBIENT

params contains four integer or floating-point values that specify the ambient RGBA reflectance of the material. Integer values are mapped linearly such that the most positive representable value maps to 1.0, and the most negative representable value maps to -1.0. Floating-point values are mapped directly. Neither integer nor floating-point values are clamped. The initial ambient reflectance for both front- and back-facing materials is (0.2, 0.2, 0.2, 1.0).

GL_DIFFUSE

params contains four integer or floating-point values that specify the diffuse RGBA reflectance of the material. Integer values are mapped linearly such that the most positive representable value maps to 1.0, and the most negative representable value maps to -1.0. Floating-point values are mapped directly. Neither integer nor floating-point values are clamped. The initial diffuse reflectance for both front- and back-facing materials is (0.8, 0.8, 0.8, 1.0).

GL_SPECULAR

params contains four integer or floating-point values that specify the specular RGBA reflectance of the material. Integer values are mapped linearly such that the most positive representable value maps to 1.0, and the most negative representable value maps to -1.0. Floating-point values are mapped directly. Neither integer nor floating-point values are clamped. The initial specular reflectance for both front- and back-facing materials is (0, 0, 0, 1).

GL_EMISSION

params contains four integer or floating-point values that specify the RGBA emitted light intensity of the material. Integer values are mapped linearly such that the most positive representable value maps to 1.0, and the most negative representable value maps to -1.0. Floating-point values are mapped directly. Neither integer nor floating-point values are clamped. The initial emission intensity for both front- and back-facing materials is (0, 0, 0, 1).

GL_SHININESS

params is a single integer or floating-point value that specifies the RGBA specular exponent of the material. Integer and floating-point values are mapped directly. Only values in the range [0,128] are accepted. The initial specular exponent for both front- and back-facing materials is 0.

GL_AMBIENT_AND_DIFFUSE

Equivalent to calling glMaterial twice with the same parameter values, once with GL_AMBIENT and once with GL_DIFFUSE.

GL_COLOR_INDEXES

params contains three integer or floating-point values specifying the color indices for ambient, diffuse, and specular lighting. These three values, and GL_SHININESS, are the only material values used by the color index mode lighting equation. Refer to the glLightModel reference page for a discussion of color index lighting.

Notes

The material parameters can be updated at any time. In particular, glMaterial can be called between a call to glBegin and the corresponding call to glEnd. If only a single material parameter is to be changed per vertex, however, glColorMaterial is preferred over glMaterial (see glColorMaterial).

While the ambient, diffuse, specular and emission material parameters all have alpha components, only the diffuse alpha component is used in the lighting computation.

Errors

GL_INVALID_ENUM is generated if either *face* or *pname* is not an accepted value.

GL_INVALID_VALUE is generated if a specular exponent outside the range [0,128] is specified.

Associated Gets

glGetMaterial

See Also

glColorMaterial, glLight, glLightModel

glMatrixMode

Specify which matrix is the current matrix

C Specification

void **glMatrixMode**(GLenum *mode*);

Parameters

mode   Specifies which matrix stack is the target for subsequent matrix operations. Three values are accepted: GL_MODELVIEW, GL_PROJECTION, and GL_TEXTURE. The initial value is GL_MODELVIEW. Additionally, if the ARB_imaging extension is supported, GL_COLOR is also accepted.

Description

glMatrixMode sets the current matrix mode. *mode* can assume one of four values:
GL_MODELVIEW
Applies subsequent matrix operations to the modelview matrix stack.
GL_PROJECTION
Applies subsequent matrix operations to the projection matrix stack.
GL_TEXTURE
Applies subsequent matrix operations to the texture matrix stack.
GL_COLOR
Applies subsequent matrix operations to the color matrix stack.
To find out which matrix stack is currently the target of all matrix operations, call glGet with argument GL_MATRIX_MODE. The initial value is GL_MODELVIEW.

Errors

GL_INVALID_ENUM is generated if *mode* is not an accepted value.

GL_INVALID_OPERATION is generated if glMatrixMode is executed between the execution of glBegin and the corresponding execution of glEnd.

Associated Gets

glGet with argument GL_MATRIX_MODE

See Also

glLoadMatrix, glLoadTransposeMatrix, glMultMatrix, glMultTransposeMatrix, glPopMatrix, glPushMatrix

glMinmax

Define minmax table

C Specification

```
void glMinmax(GLenum    target,
              GLenum    internalformat,
              GLboolean sink);
```

Parameters

target   The minmax table whose parameters are to be set. Must be GL_MINMAX.

internalformat   The format of entries in the minmax table. Must be one of GL_ALPHA,
                    GL_ALPHA4, GL_ALPHA8, GL_ALPHA12, GL_ALPHA16, GL_LUMINANCE,
                    GL_LUMINANCE4, GL_LUMINANCE8, GL_LUMINANCE12, GL_LUMINANCE16,
                    GL_LUMINANCE_ALPHA, GL_LUMINANCE4_ALPHA4, GL_LUMINANCE6_ALPHA2,
                    GL_LUMINANCE8_ALPHA8, GL_LUMINANCE12_ALPHA4,
                    GL_LUMINANCE12_ALPHA12, GL_LUMINANCE16_ALPHA16, GL_R3_G3_B2,
                    GL_RGB, GL_RGB4, GL_RGB5, GL_RGB8, GL_RGB10, GL_RGB12, GL_RGB16,
                    GL_RGBA, GL_RGBA2, GL_RGBA4, GL_RGB5_A1, GL_RGBA8, GL_RGB10_A2,
                    GL_RGBA12, or GL_RGBA16.

sink   If GL_TRUE, pixels will be consumed by the minmax process and no drawing
                    or texture loading will take place. If GL_FALSE, pixels will proceed to the final
                    conversion process after minmax.

Description

When GL_MINMAX is enabled, the RGBA components of incoming pixels are compared to the
minimum and maximum values for each component, which are stored in the two-element minmax
table. (The first element stores the minima, and the second element stores the maxima.) If a pixel
component is greater than the corresponding component in the maximum element, then the
maximum element is updated with the pixel component value. If a pixel component is less than
the corresponding component in the minimum element, then the minimum element is updated with
the pixel component value. (In both cases, if the internal format of the minmax table includes luminance, then the R color component of incoming pixels is used for comparison.) The contents of the
minmax table may be retrieved at a later time by calling glGetMinmax. The minmax operation is
enabled or disabled by calling glEnable or glDisable, respectively, with an argument of
GL_MINMAX.

glMinmax redefines the current minmax table to have entries of the format specified by *internalformat*. The maximum element is initialized with the smallest possible component values, and
the minimum element is initialized with the largest possible component values. The values in the
previous minmax table, if any, are lost. If *sink* is GL_TRUE, then pixels are discarded after minmax;
no further processing of the pixels takes place, and no drawing, texture loading, or pixel readback will
result.

Notes

glMinmax is present only if ARB_imaging is returned when glGetString is called with an argument of GL_EXTENSIONS.

Errors

GL_INVALID_ENUM is generated if *target* is not one of the allowable values.

GL_INVALID_ENUM is generated if *internalformat* is not one of the allowable values.

GL_INVALID_OPERATION is generated if glMinmax is executed between the execution of
glBegin and the corresponding execution of glEnd.

Associated Gets

glGetMinmaxParameter

See Also

glGetMinmax, glResetMinmax

glMultiDrawArrays

Render multiple sets of primitives from array data

C Specification

```
void glMultiDrawArrays(GLenum     mode,
                       GLint *     first,
                       GLsizei *   count,
                       GLsizei     primcount);
```

Parameters

mode   Specifies what kind of primitives to render. Symbolic constants GL_POINTS, GL_LINE_STRIP, GL_LINE_LOOP, GL_LINES, GL_TRIANGLE_STRIP, GL_TRIANGLE_FAN, GL_TRIANGLES, GL_QUAD_STRIP, GL_QUADS, and GL_POLYGON are accepted.

first   Points to an array of starting indices in the enabled arrays.

count   Points to an array of the number of indices to be rendered.

primcount   Specifies the size of the first and count.

Description

glMultiDrawArrays specifies multiple sets of geometric primitives with very few subroutine calls. Instead of calling a GL procedure to pass each individual vertex, normal, texture coordinate, edge flag, or color, you can prespecify separate arrays of vertices, normals, and colors and use them to construct a sequence of primitives with a single call to glMultiDrawArrays.

glMultiDrawArrays behaves identically to glDrawArrays except that primcount separate ranges of elements are specified instead.

When glMultiDrawArrays is called, it uses *count* sequential elements from each enabled array to construct a sequence of geometric primitives, beginning with element *first*. *mode* specifies what kind of primitives are constructed, and how the array elements construct those primitives. If GL_VERTEX_ARRAY is not enabled, no geometric primitives are generated.

Vertex attributes that are modified by glMultiDrawArrays have an unspecified value after glMultiDrawArrays returns. For example, if GL_COLOR_ARRAY is enabled, the value of the current color is undefined after glMultiDrawArrays executes. Attributes that aren't modified remain well defined.

Notes

glMultiDrawArrays is available only if the GL version is 1.4 or greater.

glMultiDrawArrays is included in display lists. If glMultiDrawArrays is entered into a display list, the necessary array data (determined by the array pointers and enables) is also entered into the display list. Because the array pointers and enables are client-side state, their values affect display lists when the lists are created, not when the lists are executed.

Errors

GL_INVALID_ENUM is generated if *mode* is not an accepted value.

GL_INVALID_VALUE is generated if *primcount* is negative.

GL_INVALID_OPERATION is generated if a nonzero buffer object name is bound to an enabled array and the buffer object's data store is currently mapped.

GL_INVALID_OPERATION is generated if glMultiDrawArrays is executed between the execution of glBegin and the corresponding glEnd.

See Also

glArrayElement, glColorPointer, glDrawElements, glDrawRangeElements, glEdgeFlagPointer, glFogCoordPointer, glGetPointerv, glIndexPointer, glInterleavedArrays, glNormalPointer, glSecondaryColorPointer, glTexCoordPointer, glVertexPointer

glMultiDrawElements

Render multiple sets of primitives by specifying indices of array data elements

C Specification

```
void glMultiDrawElements(GLenum           mode,
                         const GLsizei *  count,
                         GLenum           type,
                         const GLvoid **  indices,
                         GLsizei          primcount);
```

Parameters

mode	Specifies what kind of primitives to render. Symbolic constants GL_POINTS, GL_LINE_STRIP, GL_LINE_LOOP, GL_LINES, GL_TRIANGLE_STRIP, GL_TRIANGLE_FAN, GL_TRIANGLES, GL_QUAD_STRIP, GL_QUADS, and GL_POLYGON are accepted.
count	Points to an array of the elements' counts.
type	Specifies the type of the values in *indices*. Must be one of GL_UNSIGNED_BYTE, GL_UNSIGNED_SHORT, or GL_UNSIGNED_INT.
indices	Specifies a pointer to the location where the indices are stored.
primcount	Specifies the size of the *count* array.

Description

glMultiDrawElements specifies multiple sets of geometric primitives with very few subroutine calls. Instead of calling a GL function to pass each individual vertex, normal, texture coordinate, edge flag, or color, you can prespecify separate arrays of vertices, normals, and so on, and use them to construct a sequence of primitives with a single call to glMultiDrawElements.

glMultiDrawElements is identical in operation to glDrawElements except that *primcount* separate lists of elements are specified.

Vertex attributes that are modified by glMultiDrawElements have an unspecified value after glMultiDrawElements returns. For example, if GL_COLOR_ARRAY is enabled, the value of the current color is undefined after glMultiDrawElements executes. Attributes that aren't modified maintain their previous values.

Notes

glMultiDrawElements is available only if the GL version is 1.4 or greater.

glMultiDrawElements is included in display lists. If glMultiDrawElements is entered into a display list, the necessary array data (determined by the array pointers and enables) is also entered into the display list. Because the array pointers and enables are client-side state, their values affect display lists when the lists are created, not when the lists are executed.

Errors

GL_INVALID_ENUM is generated if *mode* is not an accepted value.

GL_INVALID_VALUE is generated if *primcount* is negative.

GL_INVALID_OPERATION is generated if a nonzero buffer object name is bound to an enabled array or the element array and the buffer object's data store is currently mapped.

GL_INVALID_OPERATION is generated if glMultiDrawElements is executed between the execution of glBegin and the corresponding glEnd.

See Also

glArrayElement, glColorPointer, glDrawArrays, glDrawRangeElements, glEdgeFlagPointer, glFogCoordPointer, glGetPointerv, glIndexPointer, glInterleavedArrays, glNormalPointer, glSecondaryColorPointer, glTexCoordPointer, glVertexPointer

glMultiTexCoord

Set the current texture coordinates

C Specification

```
void glMultiTexCoord1s(GLenum   target,
                       GLshort  s);
void glMultiTexCoord1i(GLenum   target,
                       GLint    s);
void glMultiTexCoord1f(GLenum   target,
                       GLfloat  s);
void glMultiTexCoord1d(GLenum   target,
                       GLdouble s);
void glMultiTexCoord2s(GLenum   target,
                       GLshort  s,
                       GLshort  t);
void glMultiTexCoord2i(GLenum   target,
                       GLint    s,
                       GLint    t);
void glMultiTexCoord2f(GLenum   target,
                       GLfloat  s,
                       GLfloat  t);
void glMultiTexCoord2d(GLenum   target,
                       GLdouble s,
                       GLdouble t);
void glMultiTexCoord3s(GLenum   target,
                       GLshort  s,
                       GLshort  t,
                       GLshort  r);
void glMultiTexCoord3i(GLenum   target,
                       GLint    s,
                       GLint    t,
                       GLint    r);
void glMultiTexCoord3f(GLenum   target,
                       GLfloat  s,
                       GLfloat  t,
                       GLfloat  r);
```

```
void glMultiTexCoord3d(GLenum    target,
                       GLdouble  s,
                       GLdouble  t,
                       GLdouble  r);
void glMultiTexCoord4s(GLenum    target,
                       GLshort   s,
                       GLshort   t,
                       GLshort   r,
                       GLshort   q);
void glMultiTexCoord4i(GLenum    target,
                       GLint     s,
                       GLint     t,
                       GLint     r,
                       GLint     q);
void glMultiTexCoord4f(GLenum    target,
                       GLfloat   s,
                       GLfloat   t,
                       GLfloat   r,
                       GLfloat   q);
void glMultiTexCoord4d(GLenum    target,
                       GLdouble  s,
                       GLdouble  t,
                       GLdouble  r,
                       GLdouble  q);
```

Parameters

target   Specifies the texture unit whose coordinates should be modified. The number of
            texture units is implementation dependent, but must be at least two. Symbolic
            constant must be one of GL_TEXTURE*i*, where *i* ranges from 0 to
            GL_MAX_TEXTURE_COORDS - 1, which is an implementation-dependent value.

s, t, r, q   Specify *s*, *t*, *r*, and *q* texture coordinates for *target* texture unit. Not all parameters
            are present in all forms of the command.

C Specification

```
void glMultiTexCoord1sv(GLenum          target,
                        const GLshort *  v);
void glMultiTexCoord1iv(GLenum          target,
                        const GLint *    v);
void glMultiTexCoord1fv(GLenum          target,
                        const GLfloat *  v);
void glMultiTexCoord1dv(GLenum          target,
                        const GLdouble * v);
void glMultiTexCoord2sv(GLenum          target,
                        const GLshort *  v);
void glMultiTexCoord2iv(GLenum          target,
                        const GLint *    v);
void glMultiTexCoord2fv(GLenum          target,
                        const GLfloat *  v);
void glMultiTexCoord2dv(GLenum          target,
                        const GLdouble * v);
void glMultiTexCoord3sv(GLenum          target,
                        const GLshort *  v);
```

```
void glMultiTexCoord3iv(GLenum          target,
                        const GLint *   v);
void glMultiTexCoord3fv(GLenum          target,
                        const GLfloat * v);
void glMultiTexCoord3dv(GLenum          target,
                        const GLdouble * v);
void glMultiTexCoord4sv(GLenum          target,
                        const GLshort * v);
void glMultiTexCoord4iv(GLenum          target,
                        const GLint *   v);
void glMultiTexCoord4fv(GLenum          target,
                        const GLfloat * v);
void glMultiTexCoord4dv(GLenum          target,
                        const GLdouble * v);
```

Parameters

target   Specifies the texture unit whose coordinates should be modified. The number of texture units is implementation dependent, but must be at least two. Symbolic constant must be one of GL_TEXTURE*i*, where *i* ranges from 0 to GL_MAX_TEXTURE_COORDS - 1, which is an implementation-dependent value.

v   Specifies a pointer to an array of one, two, three, or four elements, which in turn specify the *s*, *t*, *r*, and *q* texture coordinates.

Description

glMultiTexCoord specifies texture coordinates in one, two, three, or four dimensions. glMultiTexCoord1 sets the current texture coordinates to $(s,0,0,1)$; a call to glMultiTexCoord2 sets them to $(s,t,0,1)$. Similarly, glMultiTexCoord3 specifies the texture coordinates as $(s,t,r,1)$, and glMultiTexCoord4 defines all four components explicitly as (s,t,r,q).

The current texture coordinates are part of the data that is associated with each vertex and with the current raster position. Initially, the values for (s,t,r,q) are $(0,0,0,1)$.

Notes

glMultiTexCoord is only supported if the GL version is 1.3 or greater, or if ARB_multitexture is included in the string returned by glGetString when called with the argument GL_EXTENSIONS.

The current texture coordinates can be updated at any time. In particular, glMultiTexCoord can be called between a call to glBegin and the corresponding call to glEnd.

It is always the case that GL_TEXTURE*i* = GL_TEXTURE0 + *i*.

Associated Gets

glGet with argument GL_CURRENT_TEXTURE_COORDS with appropriate texture unit selected.
glGet with argument GL_MAX_TEXTURE_COORDS

See Also

glActiveTexture, glClientActiveTexture, glTexCoord, glTexCoordPointer, glVertex

glMultMatrix

Multiply the current matrix with the specified matrix

C Specification

```
void glMultMatrixd(const GLdouble * m);
void glMultMatrixf(const GLfloat * m);
```

Parameters

m   Points to 16 consecutive values that are used as the elements of a 4×4 column-major matrix.

Description

glMultMatrix multiplies the current matrix with the one specified using *m*, and replaces the current matrix with the product.

The current matrix is determined by the current matrix mode (see glMatrixMode). It is either the projection matrix, modelview matrix, or the texture matrix.

Examples

If the current matrix is *C* and the coordinates to be transformed are $v = (v[0], v[1], v[2], v[3])$, then the current transformation is $C \times v$, or

$$
\begin{bmatrix}
c[0] & c[4] & c[8] & c[12] \\
c[1] & c[5] & c[9] & c[13] \\
c[2] & c[6] & c[10] & c[14] \\
c[3] & c[7] & c[11] & c[15]
\end{bmatrix}
\times
\begin{bmatrix}
v[0] \\
v[1] \\
v[2] \\
v[3]
\end{bmatrix}
$$

Calling glMultMatrix with an argument of $m = \{m[0], m[1], ..., m[15]\}$ replaces the current transformation with $(C \times M) \times v$, or

$$
\begin{bmatrix}
c[0] & c[4] & c[8] & c[12] \\
c[1] & c[5] & c[9] & c[13] \\
c[2] & c[6] & c[10] & c[14] \\
c[3] & c[7] & c[11] & c[15]
\end{bmatrix}
\times
\begin{bmatrix}
m[0] & m[4] & m[8] & m[12] \\
m[1] & m[5] & m[9] & m[13] \\
m[2] & m[6] & m[10] & m[14] \\
m[3] & m[7] & m[11] & m[15]
\end{bmatrix}
\times
\begin{bmatrix}
v[0] \\
v[1] \\
v[2] \\
v[3]
\end{bmatrix}
$$

Where *v* is represented as a 4×1 matrix.

Notes

While the elements of the matrix may be specified with single or double precision, the GL may store or operate on these values in less-than-single precision.

In many computer languages, 4×4 arrays are represented in row-major order. The transformations just described represent these matrices in column-major order. The order of the multiplication is important. For example, if the current transformation is a rotation, and glMultMatrix is called with a translation matrix, the translation is done directly on the coordinates to be transformed, while the rotation is done on the results of that translation.

Errors

GL_INVALID_OPERATION is generated if glMultMatrix is executed between the execution of glBegin and the corresponding execution of glEnd.

Associated Gets

glGet with argument GL_MATRIX_MODE
glGet with argument GL_COLOR_MATRIX
glGet with argument GL_MODELVIEW_MATRIX
glGet with argument GL_PROJECTION_MATRIX
glGet with argument GL_TEXTURE_MATRIX

See Also

glLoadIdentity, glLoadMatrix, glLoadTransposeMatrix, glMatrixMode, glMultTransposeMatrix, glPushMatrix

glMultTransposeMatrix

Multiply the current matrix with the specified row-major ordered matrix

C Specification

```
void glMultTransposeMatrixd(const GLdouble * m);
void glMultTransposeMatrixf(const GLfloat * m);
```

Parameters

$m[16]$ Points to 16 consecutive values that are used as the elements of a 4×4 row-major matrix.

Description

glMultTransposeMatrix multiplies the current matrix with the one specified using $m[16]$, and replaces the current matrix with the product.

The current matrix is determined by the current matrix mode (see glMatrixMode). It is either the projection matrix, modelview matrix, or the texture matrix.

Examples

If the current matrix is C and the coordinates to be transformed are $v = (v[0], v[1], v[2], v[3])$, then the current transformation is $C \times v$, or

$$\begin{bmatrix} c[0] & c[4] & c[8] & c[12] \\ c[1] & c[5] & c[9] & c[13] \\ c[2] & c[6] & c[10] & c[14] \\ c[3] & c[7] & c[11] & c[15] \end{bmatrix} \times \begin{bmatrix} v[0] \\ v[1] \\ v[2] \\ v[3] \end{bmatrix}$$

Calling glMultTransposeMatrix with an argument of $m[16] = \{m[0], m[1], ..., m[15]\}$ replaces the current transformation with $(C \times M) \times v$, or

$$\begin{bmatrix} c[0] & c[4] & c[8] & c[12] \\ c[1] & c[5] & c[9] & c[10] \\ c[2] & c[6] & c[10] & c[14] \\ c[3] & c[7] & c[11] & c[15] \end{bmatrix} \times \begin{bmatrix} m[0] & m[1] & m[2] & m[3] \\ m[1] & m[6] & m[6] & m[7] \\ m[8] & m[9] & m[10] & m[11] \\ m[12] & m[13] & m[14] & m[15] \end{bmatrix} \times \begin{bmatrix} v[0] \\ v[1] \\ v[2] \\ v[3] \end{bmatrix}$$

Where v is represented as a 4×1 matrix.

Calling glMultTransposeMatrix with matrix M is identical in operation to glMultMatrix with M^T, where T represents the transpose.

Notes

glMultTransposeMatrix is available only if the GL version is 1.3 or greater.

While the elements of the matrix may be specified with single or double precision, the GL may store or operate on these values in less-than-single precision.

The order of the multiplication is important. For example, if the current transformation is a rotation, and glMultTransposeMatrix is called with a translation matrix, the translation is done directly on the coordinates to be transformed, while the rotation is done on the results of that translation.

Errors

GL_INVALID_OPERATION is generated if glMultTransposeMatrix is executed between the execution of glBegin and the corresponding execution of glEnd.

Associated Gets

glGet with argument GL_MATRIX_MODE
glGet with argument GL_COLOR_MATRIX
glGet with argument GL_MODELVIEW_MATRIX

glGet with argument GL_PROJECTION_MATRIX
glGet with argument GL_TEXTURE_MATRIX

See Also

glLoadIdentity, glLoadMatrix, glLoadTransposeMatrix, glMatrixMode, glPushMatrix

glNewList

Create or replace a display list

C Specification

void **glNewList**(GLuint *list*, GLenum *mode*);

Parameters

list   Specifies the display-list name.
mode   Specifies the compilation mode, which can be GL_COMPILE or
          GL_COMPILE_AND_EXECUTE.

C Specification

void **glEndList**(*void*);

Description

Display lists are groups of GL commands that have been stored for subsequent execution. Display lists are created with glNewList. All subsequent commands are placed in the display list, in the order issued, until glEndList is called.

glNewList has two arguments. The first argument, *list*, is a positive integer that becomes the unique name for the display list. Names can be created and reserved with glGenLists and tested for uniqueness with glIsList. The second argument, mode, is a symbolic constant that can assume one of two values:

GL_COMPILE
Commands are merely compiled.
GL_COMPILE_AND_EXECUTE
Commands are executed as they are compiled into the display list.

Certain commands are not compiled into the display list but are executed immediately, regardless of the display-list mode. These commands are glAreTexturesResident, glColorPointer, glDeleteLists, glDeleteTextures, glDisableClientState, glEdgeFlagPointer, glEnableClientState, glFeedbackBuffer, glFinish, glFlush, glGenLists, glGenTextures, glIndexPointer, glInterleavedArrays, glIsEnabled, glIsList, glIsTexture, glNormalPointer, glPopClientAttrib, glPixelStore, glPushClientAttrib, glReadPixels, glRenderMode, glSelectBuffer, glTexCoordPointer, glVertexPointer, and all of the glGet commands.

Similarly, glTexImage1D, glTexImage2D, and glTexImage3D are executed immediately and not compiled into the display list when their first argument is GL_PROXY_TEXTURE_1D, GL_PROXY_TEXTURE_1D, or GL_PROXY_TEXTURE_3D, respectively.

When the ARB_imaging extension is supported, glHistogram executes immediately when its argument is GL_PROXY_HISTOGRAM. Similarly, glColorTable executes immediately when its first argument is glPROXY_COLOR_TABLE, glPROXY_POST_CONVOLUTION_COLOR_TABLE, or glPROXY_POST_COLOR_MATRIX_COLOR_TABLE.

For OpenGL versions 1.3 and greater, or when the ARB_multitexture extension is supported, glClientActiveTexture is not compiled into display lists, but executed immediately.

When glEndList is encountered, the display-list definition is completed by associating the list with the unique name *list* (specified in the glNewList command). If a display list with name *list* already exists, it is replaced only when glEndList is called.

Notes

glCallList and glCallLists can be entered into display lists. Commands in the display list or lists executed by glCallList or glCallLists are not included in the display list being created, even if the list creation mode is GL_COMPILE_AND_EXECUTE.

A display list is just a group of commands and arguments, so errors generated by commands in a display list must be generated when the list is executed. If the list is created in GL_COMPILE mode, errors are not generated until the list is executed.

Errors

GL_INVALID_VALUE is generated if *list* is 0.

GL_INVALID_ENUM is generated if *mode* is not an accepted value.

GL_INVALID_OPERATION is generated if glEndList is called without a preceding glNewList, or if glNewList is called while a display list is being defined.

GL_INVALID_OPERATION is generated if glNewList or glEndList is executed between the execution of glBegin and the corresponding execution of glEnd.

GL_OUT_OF_MEMORY is generated if there is insufficient memory to compile the display list. If the GL version is 1.1 or greater, no change is made to the previous contents of the display list, if any, and no other change is made to the GL state. (It is as if no attempt had been made to create the new display list.)

Associated Gets

glIsList

glGet with argument GL_LIST_INDEX

glGet with argument GL_LIST_MODE

See Also

glCallList, glCallLists, glDeleteLists, glGenLists

glNormal

Set the current normal vector

C Specification

```
void glNormal3b(GLbyte    nx,
                GLbyte    ny,
                GLbyte    nz);
void glNormal3d(GLdouble nx,
                GLdouble ny,
                GLdouble nz);
void glNormal3f(GLfloat   nx,
                GLfloat   ny,
                GLfloat   nz);
void glNormal3i(GLint nx, GLint ny, GLint nz);
void glNormal3s(GLshort   nx,
                GLshort   ny,
                GLshort   nz);
```

Parameters

nx, ny, nz   Specify the x, y, and z coordinates of the new current normal. The initial value of the current normal is the unit vector, (0, 0, 1).

C Specification

```
void glNormal3bv(const GLbyte * v);
void glNormal3dv(const GLdouble * v);
void glNormal3fv(const GLfloat * v);
void glNormal3iv(const GLint * v);
void glNormal3sv(const GLshort * v);
```

Parameters

v   Specifies a pointer to an array of three elements: the *x*, *y*, and *z* coordinates of the new
           current normal.

Description

The current normal is set to the given coordinates whenever glNormal is issued. Byte, short, or
integer arguments are converted to floating-point format with a linear mapping that maps the most
positive representable integer value to 1.0 and the most negative representable integer value to -1.0.

Normals specified with glNormal need not have unit length. If GL_NORMALIZE is enabled, then
normals of any length specified with glNormal are normalized after transformation. If
GL_RESCALE_NORMAL is enabled, normals are scaled by a scaling factor derived from the modelview
matrix. GL_RESCALE_NORMAL requires that the originally specified normals were of unit length, and
that the modelview matrix contain only uniform scales for proper results. To enable and disable
normalization, call glEnable and glDisable with either GL_NORMALIZE or GL_RESCALE_NORMAL.
Normalization is initially disabled.

Notes

The current normal can be updated at any time. In particular, glNormal can be called between a
call to glBegin and the corresponding call to glEnd.

Associated Gets

glGet with argument GL_CURRENT_NORMAL
glIsEnabled with argument GL_NORMALIZE
glIsEnabled with argument GL_RESCALE_NORMAL

See Also

glBegin, glColor, glIndex, glMultiTexCoord, glNormalPointer, glTexCoord, glVertex

glNormalPointer

Define an array of normals

C Specification

```
void glNormalPointer(GLenum        type,
                     GLsizei       stride,
                     const GLvoid * pointer);
```

Parameters

type   Specifies the data type of each coordinate in the array. Symbolic constants GL_BYTE,
            GL_SHORT, GL_INT, GL_FLOAT, and GL_DOUBLE are accepted. The initial value is
            GL_FLOAT.
stride   Specifies the byte offset between consecutive normals. If *stride* is 0, the normals are
            understood to be tightly packed in the array. The initial value is 0.
pointer   Specifies a pointer to the first coordinate of the first normal in the array. The initial
            value is 0.

Description

glNormalPointer specifies the location and data format of an array of normals to use when rendering. *type* specifies the data type of each normal coordinate, and *stride* specifies the byte stride from one normal to the next, allowing vertices and attributes to be packed into a single array or stored in separate arrays. (Single-array storage may be more efficient on some implementations; see glInterleavedArrays.)

If a nonzero named buffer object is bound to the GL_ARRAY_BUFFER target (see glBindBuffer) while a normal array is specified, pointer is treated as a byte offset into the buffer object's data store. Also, the buffer object binding (GL_ARRAY_BUFFER_BINDING) is saved as normal vertex array client-side state (GL_NORMAL_ARRAY_BUFFER_BINDING).

When a normal array is specified, *type*, *stride*, and *pointer* are saved as client-side state, in addition to the current vertex array buffer object binding.

To enable and disable the normal array, call glEnableClientState and glDisableClientState with the argument GL_NORMAL_ARRAY. If enabled, the normal array is used when glDrawArrays, glMultiDrawArrays, glDrawElements, glMultiDrawElements, glDrawRangeElements, or glArrayElement is called.

Notes

glNormalPointer is available only if the GL version is 1.1 or greater.

The normal array is initially disabled and isn't accessed when glArrayElement, glDrawElements, glDrawRangeElements, glDrawArrays, glMultiDrawArrays, or glMultiDrawElements is called.

Execution of glNormalPointer is not allowed between glBegin and the corresponding glEnd, but an error may or may not be generated. If an error is not generated, the operation is undefined.

glNormalPointer is typically implemented on the client side.

Normal array parameters are client-side state and are therefore not saved or restored by glPushAttrib and glPopAttrib. Use glPushClientAttrib and glPopClientAttrib instead.

Errors

GL_INVALID_ENUM is generated if *type* is not an accepted value.

GL_INVALID_VALUE is generated if *stride* is negative.

Associated Gets

glIsEnabled with argument GL_NORMAL_ARRAY

glGet with argument GL_NORMAL_ARRAY_TYPE

glGet with argument GL_NORMAL_ARRAY_STRIDE

glGet with argument GL_NORMAL_ARRAY_BUFFER_BINDING

glGet with argument GL_ARRAY_BUFFER_BINDING

glGetPointerv with argument GL_NORMAL_ARRAY_POINTER

See Also

glArrayElement, glBindBuffer, glColorPointer, glDisableClientState, glDrawArrays, glDrawElements, glDrawRangeElements, glEdgeFlagPointer, glEnableClientState, glFogCoordPointer, glIndexPointer, glInterleavedArrays, glMultiDrawArrays, glMultiDrawElements, glNormal, glPopClientAttrib, glPushClientAttrib, glSecondaryColorPointer, glTexCoordPointer, glVertexAttribPointer, glVertexPointer

glOrtho

Multiply the current matrix with an orthographic matrix

C Specification

```
void glOrtho(GLdouble  left,
             GLdouble  right,
             GLdouble  bottom,
             GLdouble  top,
             GLdouble  nearVal,
             GLdouble  farVal);
```

Parameters

left, *right*   Specify the coordinates for the left and right vertical clipping planes.
bottom, *top*   Specify the coordinates for the bottom and top horizontal clipping planes.
nearVal, *farVal*   Specify the distances to the nearer and farther depth clipping planes. These values are negative if the plane is to be behind the viewer.

Description

glOrtho describes a transformation that produces a parallel projection. The current matrix (see glMatrixMode) is multiplied by this matrix and the result replaces the current matrix, as if glMultMatrix were called with the following matrix as its argument:

$$\begin{bmatrix} \frac{2}{right-left} & 0 & 0 & t_x \\ 0 & \frac{2}{top-bottom} & 0 & t_y \\ 0 & 0 & \frac{-2}{farVal-nearVal} & t_z \\ 0 & 0 & 0 & 1 \end{bmatrix}$$

where

$$t_x = -\frac{right+left}{right-left}$$

$$t_y = -\frac{top+bottom}{top-bottom}$$

$$t_z = -\frac{farVal+nearVal}{farVal-nearVal}$$

Typically, the matrix mode is GL_PROJECTION, and (*left*, *bottom*, -*nearVal*) and (*right*, *top*, -*nearVal*) specify the points on the near clipping plane that are mapped to the lower-left and upper-right corners of the window, respectively, assuming that the eye is located at (0, 0, 0). -*farVal* specifies the location of the far clipping plane. Both *nearVal* and *farVal* can be either positive or negative.

Use glPushMatrix and glPopMatrix to save and restore the current matrix stack.

Errors

GL_INVALID_OPERATION is generated if glOrtho is executed between the execution of glBegin and the corresponding execution of glEnd.

Associated Gets

glGet with argument GL_MATRIX_MODE
glGet with argument GL_COLOR_MATRIX

glGet with argument GL_MODELVIEW_MATRIX
glGet with argument GL_PROJECTION_MATRIX
glGet with argument GL_TEXTURE_MATRIX

See Also

glFrustum, glMatrixMode, glMultMatrix, glPushMatrix, glViewport

glPassThrough

Place a marker in the feedback buffer

C Specification

void **glPassThrough**(GLfloat *token*);

Parameters

token   Specifies a marker value to be placed in the feedback buffer following a
GL_PASS_THROUGH_TOKEN.

Description

Feedback is a GL render mode. The mode is selected by calling glRenderMode with
GL_FEEDBACK. When the GL is in feedback mode, no pixels are produced by rasterization. Instead,
information about primitives that would have been rasterized is fed back to the application using the
GL. See the glFeedbackBuffer reference page for a description of the feedback buffer and the values
in it.

glPassThrough inserts a user-defined marker in the feedback buffer when it is executed in feedback mode. *token* is returned as if it were a primitive; it is indicated with its own unique identifying
value: GL_PASS_THROUGH_TOKEN. The order of glPassThrough commands with respect to the specification of graphics primitives is maintained.

Notes

glPassThrough is ignored if the GL is not in feedback mode.

Errors

GL_INVALID_OPERATION is generated if glPassThrough is executed between the execution of
glBegin and the corresponding execution of glEnd.

Associated Gets

glGet with argument GL_RENDER_MODE

See Also

glFeedbackBuffer, glRenderMode

glPixelMap

Set up pixel transfer maps

C Specification

void **glPixelMapfv**(GLenum   *map*,
                GLsizei   *mapsize*,
                const GLfloat * *values*);
void **glPixelMapuiv**(GLenum   *map*,
                GLsizei   *mapsize*,
                const GLuint * *values*);

```
void glPixelMapusv(GLenum           map,
                   GLsizei          mapsize,
                   const GLushort * values);
```

Parameters

map   Specifies a symbolic map name. Must be one of the following: GL_PIXEL_MAP_I_TO_I,
GL_PIXEL_MAP_S_TO_S, GL_PIXEL_MAP_I_TO_R, GL_PIXEL_MAP_I_TO_G,
GL_PIXEL_MAP_I_TO_B, GL_PIXEL_MAP_I_TO_A, GL_PIXEL_MAP_R_TO_R,
GL_PIXEL_MAP_G_TO_G, GL_PIXEL_MAP_B_TO_B, or GL_PIXEL_MAP_A_TO_A.

mapsize   Specifies the size of the map being defined.

values   Specifies an array of *mapsize* values.

Description

glPixelMap sets up translation tables, or *maps*, used by glCopyPixels, glCopyTexImage1D,
glCopyTexImage2D, glCopyTexSubImage1D, glCopyTexSubImage2D, glCopyTexSubImage3D,
glDrawPixels, glReadPixels, glTexImage1D, glTexImage2D, glTexImage3D,
glTexSubImage1D, glTexSubImage2D, and glTexSubImage3D. Additionally, if the ARB_imaging
subset is supported, the routines glColorTable, glColorSubTable, glConvolutionFilter1D,
glConvolutionFilter2D, glHistogram, glMinmax, and glSeparableFilter2D. Use of these
maps is described completely in the glPixelTransfer reference page, and partly in the reference
pages for the pixel and texture image commands. Only the specification of the maps is described in
this reference page.

map is a symbolic map name, indicating one of ten maps to set. mapsize specifies the number of
entries in the map, and values is a pointer to an array of *mapsize* map values.

If a nonzero named buffer object is bound to the GL_PIXEL_UNPACK_BUFFER target (see
glBindBuffer) while a pixel transfer map is specified, *values* is treated as a byte offset into the
buffer object's data store.

The ten maps are as follows:

GL_PIXEL_MAP_I_TO_I
Maps color indices to color indices.

GL_PIXEL_MAP_S_TO_S
Maps stencil indices to stencil indices.

GL_PIXEL_MAP_I_TO_R
Maps color indices to red components.

GL_PIXEL_MAP_I_TO_G
Maps color indices to green components.

GL_PIXEL_MAP_I_TO_B
Maps color indices to blue components.

GL_PIXEL_MAP_I_TO_A
Maps color indices to alpha components.

GL_PIXEL_MAP_R_TO_R
Maps red components to red components.

GL_PIXEL_MAP_G_TO_G
Maps green components to green components.

GL_PIXEL_MAP_B_TO_B
Maps blue components to blue components.

GL_PIXEL_MAP_A_TO_A
Maps alpha components to alpha components.

The entries in a map can be specified as single-precision floating-point numbers, unsigned short
integers, or unsigned int integers. Maps that store color component values (all but
GL_PIXEL_MAP_I_TO_I and GL_PIXEL_MAP_S_TO_S) retain their values in floating-point format,
with unspecified mantissa and exponent sizes. Floating-point values specified by glPixelMapfv are

converted directly to the internal floating-point format of these maps, then clamped to the range [0,1]. Unsigned integer values specified by glPixelMapusv and glPixelMapuiv are converted linearly such that the largest representable integer maps to 1.0, and 0 maps to 0.0.

Maps that store indices, GL_PIXEL_MAP_I_TO_I and GL_PIXEL_MAP_S_TO_S, retain their values in fixed-point format, with an unspecified number of bits to the right of the binary point. Floating-point values specified by glPixelMapfv are converted directly to the internal fixed-point format of these maps. Unsigned integer values specified by glPixelMapusv and glPixelMapuiv specify integer values, with all 0's to the right of the binary point.

The following table shows the initial sizes and values for each of the maps. Maps that are indexed by either color or stencil indices must have *mapsize* = 2^n for some n or the results are undefined. The maximum allowable size for each map depends on the implementation and can be determined by calling glGet with argument GL_MAX_PIXEL_MAP_TABLE. The single maximum applies to all maps; it is at least 32.

map	Lookup Index	Lookup Value	Initial Size	Initial Value
GL_PIXEL_MAP_I_TO_I	color index	color index	1	0
GL_PIXEL_MAP_S_TO_S	stencil index	stencil index	1	0
GL_PIXEL_MAP_I_TO_R	color index	R	1	0
GL_PIXEL_MAP_I_TO_G	color index	G	1	0
GL_PIXEL_MAP_I_TO_B	color index	B	1	0
GL_PIXEL_MAP_I_TO_A	color index	A	1	0
GL_PIXEL_MAP_R_TO_R	R	R	1	0
GL_PIXEL_MAP_G_TO_G	G	G	1	0
GL_PIXEL_MAP_B_TO_B	B	B	1	0
GL_PIXEL_MAP_A_TO_A	A	A	1	0

Errors

GL_INVALID_ENUM is generated if *map* is not an accepted value.

GL_INVALID_VALUE is generated if *mapsize* is less than one or larger than GL_MAX_PIXEL_MAP_TABLE.

GL_INVALID_VALUE is generated if map is GL_PIXEL_MAP_I_TO_I, GL_PIXEL_MAP_S_TO_S, GL_PIXEL_MAP_I_TO_R, GL_PIXEL_MAP_I_TO_G, GL_PIXEL_MAP_I_TO_B, or GL_PIXEL_MAP_I_TO_A, and *mapsize* is not a power of two.

GL_INVALID_OPERATION is generated if a nonzero buffer object name is bound to the GL_PIXEL_UNPACK_BUFFER target and the buffer object's data store is currently mapped.

GL_INVALID_OPERATION is generated if a nonzero buffer object name is bound to the GL_PIXEL_UNPACK_BUFFER target and the data would be unpacked from the buffer object such that the memory reads required would exceed the data store size.

GL_INVALID_OPERATION is generated by glPixelMapfv if a nonzero buffer object name is bound to the GL_PIXEL_UNPACK_BUFFER target and *values* is not evenly divisible into the number of bytes needed to store in memory a GLfloat datum.

GL_INVALID_OPERATION is generated by glPixelMapuiv if a nonzero buffer object name is bound to the GL_PIXEL_UNPACK_BUFFER target and *values* is not evenly divisible into the number of bytes needed to store in memory a GLuint datum.

GL_INVALID_OPERATION is generated by glPixelMapusv if a nonzero buffer object name is bound to the GL_PIXEL_UNPACK_BUFFER target and *values* is not evenly divisible into the number of bytes needed to store in memory a GLushort datum.

GL_INVALID_OPERATION is generated if glPixelMap is executed between the execution of glBegin and the corresponding execution of glEnd.

Associated Gets

glGetPixelMap
glGet with argument GL_PIXEL_MAP_I_TO_I_SIZE
glGet with argument GL_PIXEL_MAP_S_TO_S_SIZE
glGet with argument GL_PIXEL_MAP_I_TO_R_SIZE
glGet with argument GL_PIXEL_MAP_I_TO_G_SIZE
glGet with argument GL_PIXEL_MAP_I_TO_B_SIZE
glGet with argument GL_PIXEL_MAP_I_TO_A_SIZE
glGet with argument GL_PIXEL_MAP_R_TO_R_SIZE
glGet with argument GL_PIXEL_MAP_G_TO_G_SIZE
glGet with argument GL_PIXEL_MAP_B_TO_B_SIZE
glGet with argument GL_PIXEL_MAP_A_TO_A_SIZE
glGet with argument GL_MAX_PIXEL_MAP_TABLE
glGet with argument GL_PIXEL_UNPACK_BUFFER_BINDING

See Also

glColorTable, glColorSubTable, glConvolutionFilter1D, glConvolutionFilter2D, glCopyPixels, glCopyTexImage1D, glCopyTexImage2D, glCopyTexSubImage1D, glCopyTexSubImage2D, glDrawPixels, glHistogram, glMinmax, glPixelStore, glPixelTransfer, glReadPixels, glSeparableFilter2D, glTexImage1D, glTexImage2D, glTexImage3D, glTexSubImage1D, glTexSubImage2D, glTexSubImage3D

glPixelStore

Set pixel storage modes

C Specification

void **glPixelStoref**(GLenum   pname,
                   GLfloat param);
void **glPixelStorei**(GLenum   pname,
                   GLint   param);

Parameters

pname   Specifies the symbolic name of the parameter to be set. Six values affect the packing of
           pixel data into memory: GL_PACK_SWAP_BYTES, GL_PACK_LSB_FIRST,
           GL_PACK_ROW_LENGTH, GL_PACK_IMAGE_HEIGHT, GL_PACK_SKIP_PIXELS,
           GL_PACK_SKIP_ROWS, GL_PACK_SKIP_IMAGES, and GL_PACK_ALIGNMENT. Six more
           affect the unpacking of pixel data *from* memory: GL_UNPACK_SWAP_BYTES,
           GL_UNPACK_LSB_FIRST, GL_UNPACK_ROW_LENGTH, GL_UNPACK_IMAGE_HEIGHT,
           GL_UNPACK_SKIP_PIXELS, GL_UNPACK_SKIP_ROWS, GL_UNPACK_SKIP_IMAGES, and
           GL_UNPACK_ALIGNMENT.

param   Specifies the value that pname is set to.

Description

glPixelStore sets pixel storage modes that affect the operation of subsequent glDrawPixels and glReadPixels as well as the unpacking of polygon stipple patterns (see glPolygonStipple), bitmaps (see glBitmap), texture patterns (see glTexImage1D, glTexImage2D, glTexImage3D, glTexSubImage1D, glTexSubImage2D, glTexSubImage3D). Additionally, if the ARB_imaging extension is supported, pixel storage modes affect convolution filters (see glConvolutionFilter1D, glConvolutionFilter2D, and glSeparableFilter2D, color table (see glColorTable, and glColorSubTable, and unpacking histogram (See glHistogram), and minmax (See glMinmax) data.

pname is a symbolic constant indicating the parameter to be set, and param is the new value. Six of the twelve storage parameters affect how pixel data is returned to client memory. They are as follows:

GL_PACK_SWAP_BYTES

If true, byte ordering for multibyte color components, depth components, color indices, or stencil indices is reversed. That is, if a four-byte component consists of bytes b_0, b_1, b_2, b_3, it is stored in memory as b_3, b_2, b_1, b_0 if GL_PACK_SWAP_BYTES is true. GL_PACK_SWAP_BYTES has no effect on the memory order of components within a pixel, only on the order of bytes within components or indices. For example, the three components of a GL_RGB format pixel are always stored with red first, green second, and blue third, regardless of the value of GL_PACK_SWAP_BYTES.

GL_PACK_LSB_FIRST

If true, bits are ordered within a byte from least significant to most significant; otherwise, the first bit in each byte is the most significant one. This parameter is significant for bitmap data only.

GL_PACK_ROW_LENGTH

If greater than 0, GL_PACK_ROW_LENGTH defines the number of pixels in a row. If the first pixel of a row is placed at location p in memory, then the location of the first pixel of the next row is obtained by skipping

$$k = \begin{cases} n\,l & s >= a \\ \dfrac{a}{s} \left\lceil \dfrac{s\,n\,l}{a} \right\rceil & s < a \end{cases}$$

components or indices, where n is the number of components or indices in a pixel, l is the number of pixels in a row (GL_PACK_ROW_LENGTH if it is greater than 0, the width argument to the pixel routine otherwise), a is the value of GL_PACK_ALIGNMENT, and s is the size, in bytes, of a single component (if $a<s$, then it is as if $a = s$). In the case of 1-bit values, the location of the next row is obtained by skipping

$$k = 8\,a \left\lceil \dfrac{n\,l}{8\,a} \right\rceil$$

components or indices.

The word component in this description refers to the nonindex values red, green, blue, alpha, and depth. Storage format GL_RGB, for example, has three components per pixel: first red, then green, and finally blue.

GL_PACK_IMAGE_HEIGHT

If greater than 0, GL_PACK_IMAGE_HEIGHT defines the number of pixels in an image three-dimensional texture volume, where "image" is defined by all pixels sharing the same third dimension index. If the first pixel of a row is placed at location p in memory, then the location of the first pixel of the next row is obtained by skipping

$$k = \begin{cases} n\,l\,h & s >= a \\ \dfrac{a}{s} \left\lceil \dfrac{s\,n\,l\,h}{a} \right\rceil & s < a \end{cases}$$

components or indices, where n is the number of components or indices in a pixel, l is the number of pixels in a row (GL_PACK_ROW_LENGTH if it is greater than 0, the width argument to glTexImage3d otherwise), h is the number of rows in a pixel image (GL_PACK_IMAGE_HEIGHT if it is greater than 0, the height argument to the glTexImage3D routine otherwise), a is the value of GL_PACK_ALIGNMENT, and s is the size, in bytes, of a single component (if $a<s$, then it is as if $a = s$).

The word component in this description refers to the nonindex values red, green, blue, alpha, and depth. Storage format GL_RGB, for example, has three components per pixel: first red, then green, and finally blue.

GL_PACK_SKIP_PIXELS, GL_PACK_SKIP_ROWS, and GL_PACK_SKIP_IMAGES

These values are provided as a convenience to the programmer; they provide no functionality that cannot be duplicated simply by incrementing the pointer passed to glReadPixels. Setting GL_PACK_SKIP_PIXELS to i is equivalent to incrementing the pointer by in components or indices, where n is the number of components or indices in each pixel. Setting GL_PACK_SKIP_ROWS to j is equivalent to incrementing the pointer by jm components or indices, where m is the number of components or indices per row, as just computed in the GL_PACK_ROW_LENGTH section. Setting GL_PACK_SKIP_IMAGES to k is equivalent to incrementing the pointer by kp, where p is the number of components or indices per image, as computed in the GL_PACK_IMAGE_HEIGHT section.

GL_PACK_ALIGNMENT

Specifies the alignment requirements for the start of each pixel row in memory. The allowable values are 1 (byte-alignment), 2 (rows aligned to even-numbered bytes), 4 (word-alignment), and 8 (rows start on double-word boundaries).

The other six of the twelve storage parameters affect how pixel data is read from client memory. These values are significant for glDrawPixels, glTexImage1D, glTexImage2D, glTexImage3D, glTexSubImage1D, glTexSubImage2D, glTexSubImage3D, glBitmap, and glPolygonStipple.

Additionally, if the ARB_imaging extension is supported, glColorTable, glColorSubTable, glConvolutionFilter1D, glConvolutionFilter2D, and glSeparableFilter2D. They are as follows:

GL_UNPACK_SWAP_BYTES

If true, byte ordering for multibyte color components, depth components, color indices, or stencil indices is reversed. That is, if a four-byte component consists of bytes b_0, b_1, b_2, b_3, it is taken from memory as b_3, b_2, b_1, b_0 if GL_UNPACK_SWAP_BYTES is true. GL_UNPACK_SWAP_BYTES has no effect on the memory order of components within a pixel, only on the order of bytes within components or indices. For example, the three components of a GL_RGB format pixel are always stored with red first, green second, and blue third, regardless of the value of GL_UNPACK_SWAP_BYTES.

GL_UNPACK_LSB_FIRST

If true, bits are ordered within a byte from least significant to most significant; otherwise, the first bit in each byte is the most significant one. This is relevant only for bitmap data.

GL_UNPACK_ROW_LENGTH

If greater than 0, GL_UNPACK_ROW_LENGTH defines the number of pixels in a row. If the first pixel of a row is placed at location p in memory, then the location of the first pixel of the next row is obtained by skipping

$$k = \begin{cases} n\,l & s >= a \\ \dfrac{a}{s}\left\lceil \dfrac{s\,n\,l}{a} \right\rceil & s < a \end{cases}$$

components or indices, where n is the number of components or indices in a pixel, l is the number of pixels in a row (GL_UNPACK_ROW_LENGTH if it is greater than 0, the *width* argument to the pixel routine otherwise), a is the value of GL_UNPACK_ALIGNMENT, and s is the size, in bytes, of a single component (if $a<s$, then it is as if $a = s$). In the case of 1-bit values, the location of the next row is obtained by skipping

$$k = 8\,a \left\lceil \dfrac{n\,l}{8\,a} \right\rceil$$

components or indices.

The word *component* in this description refers to the nonindex values red, green, blue, alpha, and depth. Storage format GL_RGB, for example, has three components per pixel: first red, then green, and finally blue.

GL_UNPACK_IMAGE_HEIGHT

If greater than 0, GL_UNPACK_IMAGE_HEIGHT defines the number of pixels in an image of a three-dimensional texture volume. Where "image" is defined by all pixel sharing the same third dimension index. If the first pixel of a row is placed at location p in memory, then the location of the first pixel of the next row is obtained by skipping

$$k = \begin{cases} n\,l\,h & s >= a \\ \dfrac{a}{s}\left\lceil \dfrac{s\,n\,l\,h}{a} \right\rceil & s < a \end{cases}$$

components or indices, where n is the number of components or indices in a pixel, l is the number of pixels in a row (GL_UNPACK_ROW_LENGTH if it is greater than 0, the *width* argument to glTexImage3D otherwise), h is the number of rows in an image (GL_UNPACK_IMAGE_HEIGHT if it is greater than 0, the *height* argument to glTexImage3D otherwise), a is the value of GL_UNPACK_ALIGNMENT, and s is the size, in bytes, of a single component (if $a<s$, then it is as if $a = s$).

The word *component* in this description refers to the nonindex values red, green, blue, alpha, and depth. Storage format GL_RGB, for example, has three components per pixel: first red, then green, and finally blue.

GL_UNPACK_SKIP_PIXELS and GL_UNPACK_SKIP_ROWS

These values are provided as a convenience to the programmer; they provide no functionality that cannot be duplicated by incrementing the pointer passed to glDrawPixels, glTexImage1D, glTexImage2D, glTexSubImage1D, glTexSubImage2D, glBitmap, or glPolygonStipple. Setting GL_UNPACK_SKIP_PIXELS to i is equivalent to incrementing the pointer by in components or indices, where n is the number of components or indices in each pixel. Setting GL_UNPACK_SKIP_ROWS to j is equivalent to incrementing the pointer by jk components or indices, where k is the number of components or indices per row, as just computed in the GL_UNPACK_ROW_LENGTH section.

GL_UNPACK_ALIGNMENT

Specifies the alignment requirements for the start of each pixel row in memory. The allowable values are 1 (byte-alignment), 2 (rows aligned to even-numbered bytes), 4 (word-alignment), and 8 (rows start on double-word boundaries).

The following table gives the type, initial value, and range of valid values for each storage parameter that can be set with glPixelStore.

pname	Type	Initial Value	Valid Range
GL_PACK_SWAP_BYTES	boolean	false	true or false
GL_PACK_LSB_FIRST	boolean	false	true or false
GL_PACK_ROW_LENGTH	integer	0	$[0, \infty)$
GL_PACK_IMAGE_HEIGHT	integer	0	$[0, \infty)$
GL_PACK_SKIP_ROWS	integer	0	$[0, \infty)$
GL_PACK_SKIP_PIXELS	integer	0	$[0, \infty)$
GL_PACK_SKIP_IMAGES	integer	0	$[0, \infty)$
GL_PACK_ALIGNMENT	integer	4	1, 2, 4, or 8
GL_UNPACK_SWAP_BYTES	boolean	false	true or false
GL_UNPACK_LSB_FIRST	boolean	false	true or false
GL_UNPACK_ROW_LENGTH	integer	0	$[0, \infty)$
GL_UNPACK_IMAGE_HEIGHT	integer	0	$[0, \infty)$
GL_UNPACK_SKIP_ROWS	integer	0	$[0, \infty)$
GL_UNPACK_SKIP_PIXELS	integer	0	$[0, \infty)$
GL_UNPACK_SKIP_IMAGES	integer	0	$[0, \infty)$
GL_UNPACK_ALIGNMENT	integer	4	1, 2, 4, or 8

glPixelStoref can be used to set any pixel store parameter. If the parameter type is boolean, then if *param* is 0, the parameter is false; otherwise it is set to true. If *pname* is a integer type parameter, *param* is rounded to the nearest integer.

Likewise, glPixelStorei can also be used to set any of the pixel store parameters. Boolean parameters are set to false if *param* is 0 and true otherwise.

Notes

The pixel storage modes in effect when glDrawPixels, glReadPixels, glTexImage1D, glTexImage2D, glTexImage3D, glTexSubImage1D, glTexSubImage2D, glTexSubImage3D, glBitmap, or glPolygonStipple is placed in a display list control the interpretation of memory data. Likewise, if the ARB_imaging extension is supported, the pixel storage modes in effect when glColorTable, glColorSubTable, glConvolutionFilter1D, glConvolutionFilter2D, of glSeparableFilter2D is placed in a display list control the interpretation of memory data. The pixel storage modes in effect when a display list is executed are not significant.

Pixel storage modes are client state and must be pushed and restored using glPushClientAttrib and glPopClientAttrib.

Errors

GL_INVALID_ENUM is generated if *pname* is not an accepted value.

GL_INVALID_VALUE is generated if a negative row length, pixel skip, or row skip value is specified, or if alignment is specified as other than 1, 2, 4, or 8.

GL_INVALID_OPERATION is generated if glPixelStore is executed between the execution of glBegin and the corresponding execution of glEnd.

Associated Gets

glGet with argument GL_PACK_SWAP_BYTES
glGet with argument GL_PACK_LSB_FIRST
glGet with argument GL_PACK_ROW_LENGTH
glGet with argument GL_PACK_IMAGE_HEIGHT
glGet with argument GL_PACK_SKIP_ROWS
glGet with argument GL_PACK_SKIP_PIXELS
glGet with argument GL_PACK_SKIP_IMAGES
glGet with argument GL_PACK_ALIGNMENT
glGet with argument GL_UNPACK_SWAP_BYTES
glGet with argument GL_UNPACK_LSB_FIRST
glGet with argument GL_UNPACK_ROW_LENGTH
glGet with argument GL_UNPACK_IMAGE_HEIGHT
glGet with argument GL_UNPACK_SKIP_ROWS
glGet with argument GL_UNPACK_SKIP_PIXELS
glGet with argument GL_UNPACK_SKIP_IMAGES
glGet with argument GL_UNPACK_ALIGNMENT

See Also

glBitmap, glColorTable, glColorSubTable, glConvolutionFilter1D, glConvolutionFilter2D, glSeparableFilter2D, glDrawPixels, glHistogram, glMinmax, glPixelMap, glPixelTransfer, glPixelZoom, glPolygonStipple, glPushClientAttrib, glReadPixels, glTexImage1D, glTexImage2D, glTexImage3D, glTexSubImage1D, glTexSubImage2D, glTexSubImage3D

glPixelTransfer

Set pixel transfer modes

C Specification

```
void glPixelTransferf(GLenum   pname,
                      GLfloat  param);
void glPixelTransferi(GLenum   pname,
                      GLint    param);
```

Parameters

pname   Specifies the symbolic name of the pixel transfer parameter to be set. Must be one of the following: GL_MAP_COLOR, GL_MAP_STENCIL, GL_INDEX_SHIFT, GL_INDEX_OFFSET, GL_RED_SCALE, GL_RED_BIAS, GL_GREEN_SCALE, GL_GREEN_BIAS, GL_BLUE_SCALE, GL_BLUE_BIAS, GL_ALPHA_SCALE, GL_ALPHA_BIAS, GL_DEPTH_SCALE, or GL_DEPTH_BIAS.

Additionally, if the ARB_imaging extension is supported, the following symbolic names are accepted:

GL_POST_COLOR_MATRIX_RED_SCALE, GL_POST_COLOR_MATRIX_GREEN_SCALE, GL_POST_COLOR_MATRIX_BLUE_SCALE, GL_POST_COLOR_MATRIX_ALPHA_SCALE, GL_POST_COLOR_MATRIX_RED_BIAS, GL_POST_COLOR_MATRIX_GREEN_BIAS, GL_POST_COLOR_MATRIX_BLUE_BIAS, GL_POST_COLOR_MATRIX_ALPHA_BIAS, GL_POST_CONVOLUTION_RED_SCALE, GL_POST_CONVOLUTION_GREEN_SCALE, GL_POST_CONVOLUTION_BLUE_SCALE, GL_POST_CONVOLUTION_ALPHA_SCALE, GL_POST_CONVOLUTION_RED_BIAS, GL_POST_CONVOLUTION_GREEN_BIAS, GL_POST_CONVOLUTION_BLUE_BIAS, and GL_POST_CONVOLUTION_ALPHA_BIAS.

param   Specifies the value that *pname* is set to.

Description

glPixelTransfer sets pixel transfer modes that affect the operation of subsequent glCopyPixels, glCopyTexImage1D, glCopyTexImage2D, glCopyTexSubImage1D, glCopyTexSubImage2D, glCopyTexSubImage3D, glDrawPixels, glReadPixels, glTexImage1D, glTexImage2D, glTexImage3D, glTexSubImage1D, glTexSubImage2D, and glTexSubImage3D commands. Additionally, if the ARB_imaging subset is supported, the routines glColorTable, glColorSubTable, glConvolutionFilter1D, glConvolutionFilter2D, glHistogram, glMinmax, and glSeparableFilter2D are also affected. The algorithms that are specified by pixel transfer modes operate on pixels after they are read from the frame buffer (glCopyPixelsglCopyTexImage1D, glCopyTexImage2D, glCopyTexSubImage1D, glCopyTexSubImage2D, glCopyTexSubImage3D, and glReadPixels), or unpacked from client memory (glDrawPixels, glTexImage1D, glTexImage2D, glTexImage3D, glTexSubImage1D, glTexSubImage2D, and glTexSubImage3D). Pixel transfer operations happen in the same order, and in the same manner, regardless of the command that resulted in the pixel operation. Pixel storage modes (see glPixelStore) control the unpacking of pixels being read from client memory and the packing of pixels being written back into client memory.

Pixel transfer operations handle four fundamental pixel types: *color, color index, depth,* and *stencil. Color* pixels consist of four floating-point values with unspecified mantissa and exponent sizes, scaled such that 0 represents zero intensity and 1 represents full intensity. *Color indices* comprise a single fixed-point value, with unspecified precision to the right of the binary point. *Depth* pixels comprise a single floating-point value, with unspecified mantissa and exponent sizes, scaled such that 0.0 represents the minimum depth buffer value, and 1.0 represents the maximum depth buffer value. Finally, *stencil* pixels comprise a single fixed-point value, with unspecified precision to the right of the binary point.

The pixel transfer operations performed on the four basic pixel types are as follows:

Color

Each of the four color components is multiplied by a scale factor, then added to a bias factor. That is, the red component is multiplied by GL_RED_SCALE, then added to GL_RED_BIAS; the green component is multiplied by GL_GREEN_SCALE, then added to GL_GREEN_BIAS; the blue component is multiplied by GL_BLUE_SCALE, then added to GL_BLUE_BIAS; and the alpha component is multiplied by GL_ALPHA_SCALE, then added to GL_ALPHA_BIAS. After all four color components are scaled and biased, each is clamped to the range [0,1]. All color, scale, and bias values are specified with glPixelTransfer.

If GL_MAP_COLOR is true, each color component is scaled by the size of the corresponding color-to-color map, then replaced by the contents of that map indexed by the scaled component. That is, the red component is scaled by GL_PIXEL_MAP_R_TO_R_SIZE, then replaced by the contents of GL_PIXEL_MAP_R_TO_R indexed by itself. The green component is scaled by GL_PIXEL_MAP_G_TO_G_SIZE, then replaced by the contents of GL_PIXEL_MAP_G_TO_G indexed by itself. The blue component is scaled by GL_PIXEL_MAP_B_TO_B_SIZE, then replaced by the contents of GL_PIXEL_MAP_B_TO_B indexed by itself. And the alpha component is scaled by GL_PIXEL_MAP_A_TO_A_SIZE, then replaced by the contents of GL_PIXEL_MAP_A_TO_A indexed by itself. All components taken from the maps are then clamped to the range [0,1]. GL_MAP_COLOR is specified with glPixelTransfer. The contents of the various maps are specified with glPixelMap.

If the ARB_imaging extension is supported, each of the four color components may be scaled and biased after transformation by the color matrix. That is, the red component is multiplied by GL_POST_COLOR_MATRIX_RED_SCALE, then added to GL_POST_COLOR_MATRIX_RED_BIAS; the green component is multiplied by GL_POST_COLOR_MATRIX_GREEN_SCALE, then added to GL_POST_COLOR_MATRIX_GREEN_BIAS; the blue component is multiplied by GL_POST_COLOR_MATRIX_BLUE_SCALE, then added to GL_POST_COLOR_MATRIX_BLUE_BIAS; and the alpha component is multiplied by GL_POST_COLOR_MATRIX_ALPHA_SCALE, then added to GL_POST_COLOR_MATRIX_ALPHA_BIAS. After all four color components are scaled and biased, each is clamped to the range [0,1].

Similarly, if the ARB_imaging extension is supported, each of the four color components may be scaled and biased after processing by the enabled convolution filter. That is, the red component is multiplied by GL_POST_CONVOLUTION_RED_SCALE, then added to GL_POST_CONVOLUTION_RED_BIAS; the green component is multiplied by GL_POST_CONVOLUTION_GREEN_SCALE, then added to GL_POST_CONVOLUTION_GREEN_BIAS; the blue component is multiplied by GL_POST_CONVOLUTION_BLUE_SCALE, then added to GL_POST_CONVOLUTION_BLUE_BIAS; and the alpha component is multiplied by GL_POST_CONVOLUTION_ALPHA_SCALE, then added to GL_POST_CONVOLUTION_ALPHA_BIAS. After all four color components are scaled and biased, each is clamped to the range [0,1].

Color index

Each color index is shifted left by GL_INDEX_SHIFT bits; any bits beyond the number of fraction bits carried by the fixed-point index are filled with zeros. If GL_INDEX_SHIFT is negative, the shift is to the right, again zero filled. Then GL_INDEX_OFFSET is added to the index. GL_INDEX_SHIFT and GL_INDEX_OFFSET are specified with glPixelTransfer.

From this point, operation diverges depending on the required format of the resulting pixels. If the resulting pixels are to be written to a color index buffer, or if they are being read back to client memory in GL_COLOR_INDEX format, the pixels continue to be treated as indices. If GL_MAP_COLOR is true, each index is masked by $2^n - 1$, where n is GL_PIXEL_MAP_I_TO_I_SIZE, then replaced by the contents of GL_PIXEL_MAP_I_TO_I indexed by the masked value. GL_MAP_COLOR is specified with glPixelTransfer. The contents of the index map is specified with glPixelMap.

If the resulting pixels are to be written to an RGBA color buffer, or if they are read back to client memory in a format other than GL_COLOR_INDEX, the pixels are converted from indices to colors by referencing the four maps GL_PIXEL_MAP_I_TO_R, GL_PIXEL_MAP_I_TO_G, GL_PIXEL_MAP_I_TO_B, and GL_PIXEL_MAP_I_TO_A. Before being dereferenced, the index is masked by $2^n - 1$, where n is GL_PIXEL_MAP_I_TO_R_SIZE for the red map, GL_PIXEL_MAP_I_TO_G_SIZE for the green map, GL_PIXEL_MAP_I_TO_B_SIZE for the blue map, and GL_PIXEL_MAP_I_TO_A_SIZE for the alpha map. All components taken from the maps are then clamped to the range [0,1]. The contents of the four maps is specified with glPixelMap.

Depth

Each depth value is multiplied by GL_DEPTH_SCALE, added to GL_DEPTH_BIAS, then clamped to the range [0,1].

Stencil

Each index is shifted GL_INDEX_SHIFT bits just as a color index is, then added to GL_INDEX_OFFSET. If GL_MAP_STENCIL is true, each index is masked by 2^n ? 1, where n is GL_PIXEL_MAP_S_TO_S_SIZE, then replaced by the contents of GL_PIXEL_MAP_S_TO_S indexed by the masked value.

The following table gives the type, initial value, and range of valid values for each of the pixel transfer parameters that are set with glPixelTransfer.

pname	Type	Initial Value	Valid Range
GL_MAP_COLOR	boolean	false	true/false
GL_MAP_STENCIL	boolean	false	true/false
GL_INDEX_SHIFT	integer	0	$(-\infty, \infty)$
GL_INDEX_OFFSET	integer	0	$(-\infty, \infty)$
GL_RED_SCALE	float	1	$(-\infty, \infty)$
GL_GREEN_SCALE	float	1	$(-\infty, \infty)$
GL_BLUE_SCALE	float	1	$(-\infty, \infty)$
GL_ALPHA_SCALE	float	1	$(-\infty, \infty)$
GL_DEPTH_SCALE	float	1	$(-\infty, \infty)$
GL_RED_BIAS	float	0	$(-\infty, \infty)$
GL_GREEN_BIAS	float	0	$(-\infty, \infty)$
GL_BLUE_BIAS	float	0	$(-\infty, \infty)$
GL_ALPHA_BIAS	float	0	$(-\infty, \infty)$
GL_DEPTH_BIAS	float	0	$(-\infty, \infty)$
GL_POST_COLOR_MATRIX_RED_SCALE	float	1	$(-\infty, \infty)$
GL_POST_COLOR_MATRIX_GREEN_SCALE	float	1	$(-\infty, \infty)$
GL_POST_COLOR_MATRIX_BLUE_SCALE	float	1	$(-\infty, \infty)$
GL_POST_COLOR_MATRIX_ALPHA_SCALE	float	1	$(-\infty, \infty)$
GL_POST_COLOR_MATRIX_RED_BIAS	float	0	$(-\infty, \infty)$
GL_POST_COLOR_MATRIX_GREEN_BIAS	float	0	$(-\infty, \infty)$
GL_POST_COLOR_MATRIX_BLUE_BIAS	float	0	$(-\infty, \infty)$
GL_POST_COLOR_MATRIX_ALPHA_BIAS	float	0	$(-\infty, \infty)$
GL_POST_CONVOLUTION_RED_SCALE	float	1	$(-\infty, \infty)$
GL_POST_CONVOLUTION_GREEN_SCALE	float	1	$(-\infty, \infty)$
GL_POST_CONVOLUTION_BLUE_SCALE	float	1	$(-\infty, \infty)$
GL_POST_CONVOLUTION_ALPHA_SCALE	float	1	$(-\infty, \infty)$
GL_POST_CONVOLUTION_RED_BIAS	float	0	$(-\infty, \infty)$
GL_POST_CONVOLUTION_GREEN_BIAS	float	0	$(-\infty, \infty)$
GL_POST_CONVOLUTION_BLUE_BIAS	float	0	$(-\infty, \infty)$
GL_POST_CONVOLUTION_ALPHA_BIAS	float	0	$(-\infty, \infty)$

glPixelTransferf can be used to set any pixel transfer parameter. If the parameter type is boolean, 0 implies false and any other value implies true. If *pname* is an integer parameter, *param* is rounded to the nearest integer.

Likewise, glPixelTransferi can be used to set any of the pixel transfer parameters. Boolean parameters are set to false if *param* is 0 and to true otherwise. *param* is converted to floating point before being assigned to real-valued parameters.

Notes

If a glColorTable, glColorSubTable, glConvolutionFilter1D, glConvolutionFilter2D, glCopyPixels, glCopyTexImage1D, glCopyTexImage2D, glCopyTexSubImage1D, glCopyTexSubImage2D, glCopyTexSubImage3D, glDrawPixels, glReadPixels, glSeparableFilter2D, glTexImage1D, glTexImage2D, glTexImage3D, glTexSubImage1D, glTexSubImage2D, or glTexSubImage3D command is placed in a display list (see glNewList and glCallList), the pixel transfer mode settings in effect when the display list is *executed* are the ones that are used. They may be different from the settings when the command was compiled into the display list.

Errors

GL_INVALID_ENUM is generated if *pname* is not an accepted value.

GL_INVALID_OPERATION is generated if glPixelTransfer is executed between the execution of glBegin and the corresponding execution of glEnd.

Associated Gets

glGet with argument GL_MAP_COLOR
glGet with argument GL_MAP_STENCIL
glGet with argument GL_INDEX_SHIFT
glGet with argument GL_INDEX_OFFSET
glGet with argument GL_RED_SCALE
glGet with argument GL_RED_BIAS
glGet with argument GL_GREEN_SCALE
glGet with argument GL_GREEN_BIAS
glGet with argument GL_BLUE_SCALE
glGet with argument GL_BLUE_BIAS
glGet with argument GL_ALPHA_SCALE
glGet with argument GL_ALPHA_BIAS
glGet with argument GL_DEPTH_SCALE
glGet with argument GL_DEPTH_BIAS
glGet with argument GL_POST_COLOR_MATRIX_RED_SCALE
glGet with argument GL_POST_COLOR_MATRIX_RED_BIAS
glGet with argument GL_POST_COLOR_MATRIX_GREEN_SCALE
glGet with argument GL_POST_COLOR_MATRIX_GREEN_BIAS
glGet with argument GL_POST_COLOR_MATRIX_BLUE_SCALE
glGet with argument GL_POST_COLOR_MATRIX_BLUE_BIAS
glGet with argument GL_POST_COLOR_MATRIX_ALPHA_SCALE
glGet with argument GL_POST_COLOR_MATRIX_ALPHA_BIAS
glGet with argument GL_POST_CONVOLUTION_RED_SCALE
glGet with argument GL_POST_CONVOLUTION_RED_BIAS
glGet with argument GL_POST_CONVOLUTION_GREEN_SCALE
glGet with argument GL_POST_CONVOLUTION_GREEN_BIAS
glGet with argument GL_POST_CONVOLUTION_BLUE_SCALE
glGet with argument GL_POST_CONVOLUTION_BLUE_BIAS
glGet with argument GL_POST_CONVOLUTION_ALPHA_SCALE
glGet with argument GL_POST_CONVOLUTION_ALPHA_BIAS

See Also

glCallList, glColorTable, glColorSubTable, glConvolutionFilter1D, glConvolutionFilter2D, glCopyPixels, glCopyTexImage1D, glCopyTexImage2D, glCopyTexSubImage1D, glCopyTexSubImage2D, glCopyTexSubImage3D, glDrawPixels, glNewList, glPixelMap, glPixelStore, glPixelZoom, glReadPixels, glTexImage1D, glTexImage2D, glTexImage3D, glTexSubImage1D, glTexSubImage2D, glTexSubImage3D

glPixelZoom

Specify the pixel zoom factors

C Specification

void **glPixelZoom**(GLfloat *xfactor*,
                 GLfloat *yfactor*);

Parameters

xfactor, *yfactor*   Specify the *x* and *y* zoom factors for pixel write operations.

Description

glPixelZoom specifies values for the *x* and *y* zoom factors. During the execution of glDrawPixels or glCopyPixels, if (xr, yr) is the current raster position, and a given element is in the *m*th row and *n*th column of the pixel rectangle, then pixels whose centers are in the rectangle with corners at

$(xr + n \bullet xfactor, yr + m \bullet yfactor)$

$(xr + (n + 1) \bullet xfactor, yr + (m + 1) \bullet yfactor)$

are candidates for replacement. Any pixel whose center lies on the bottom or left edge of this rectangular region is also modified.

Pixel zoom factors are not limited to positive values. Negative zoom factors reflect the resulting image about the current raster position.

Errors

GL_INVALID_OPERATION is generated if glPixelZoom is executed between the execution of glBegin and the corresponding execution of glEnd.

Associated Gets

glGet with argument GL_ZOOM_X
glGet with argument GL_ZOOM_Y

See Also

glCopyPixels, glDrawPixels

glPointParameter

Specify point parameters

C Specification

void **glPointParameterf**(GLenum   *pname*,
                       GLfloat *param*);
void **glPointParameteri**(GLenum   *pname*,
                       GLint   *param*);

Parameters

pname   Specifies a single-valued point parameter. GL_POINT_SIZE_MIN,
                 GL_POINT_SIZE_MAX, GL_POINT_FADE_THRESHOLD_SIZE, and
                 GL_POINT_SPRITE_COORD_ORIGIN are accepted.

param   Specifies the value that *pname* will be set to.

C Specification

```
void glPointParameterfv(GLenum          pname,
                        const GLfloat * params);
void glPointParameteriv(GLenum          pname,
                        const GLint * params);
```

Parameters

pname   Specifies a point parameter. GL_POINT_SIZE_MIN, GL_POINT_SIZE_MAX,
                 GL_POINT_DISTANCE_ATTENUATION, GL_POINT_FADE_THRESHOLD_SIZE, and
                 GL_POINT_SPRITE_COORD_ORIGIN are accepted.

params   Specifies the value or values to be assigned to *pname*. GL_POINT_DISTANCE_ATTENUA-
                 TION requires an array of three values. All other parameters accept an array containing
                 only a single value.

Description

The following values are accepted for *pname*:

GL_POINT_SIZE_MIN

params is a single floating-point value that specifies the minimum point size. The default value is 0.0.

GL_POINT_SIZE_MAX

params is a single floating-point value that specifies the maximum point size. The default value is 1.0.

GL_POINT_FADE_THRESHOLD_SIZE

params is a single floating-point value that specifies the threshold value to which point sizes are clamped if they exceed the specified value. The default value is 1.0.

GL_POINT_DISTANCE_ATTENUATION

params is an array of three floating-point values that specify the coefficients used for scaling the computed point size. The default values are (1,0,0).

GL_POINT_SPRITE_COORD_ORIGIN

params is a single enum specifying the point sprite texture coordinate origin, either GL_LOWER_LEFT or GL_UPPER_LEFT. The default value is GL_UPPER_LEFT.

Notes

glPointParameter is available only if the GL version is 1.4 or greater.

GL_POINT_SPRITE_COORD_ORIGIN is available only if the GL version is 2.0 or greater.

Errors

GL_INVALID_VALUE is generated If the value specified for GL_POINT_SIZE_MIN, GL_POINT_SIZE_MAX, or GL_POINT_FADE_THRESHOLD_SIZE is less than zero.

GL_INVALID_ENUM is generated If the value specified for GL_POINT_SPRITE_COORD_ORIGIN is not GL_LOWER_LEFT or GL_UPPER_LEFT.

If the value for GL_POINT_SIZE_MIN is greater than GL_POINT_SIZE_MAX, the point size after clamping is undefined, but no error is generated.

Associated Gets

glGet with argument GL_POINT_SIZE_MIN
glGet with argument GL_POINT_SIZE_MAX
glGet with argument GL_POINT_FADE_THRESHOLD_SIZE
glGet with argument GL_POINT_DISTANCE_ATTENUATION
glGet with argument GL_POINT_SPRITE_COORD_ORIGIN

See Also

glPointSize

glPointSize

Specify the diameter of rasterized points

C Specification

void **glPointSize**(GLfloat *size*);

Parameters

size   Specifies the diameter of rasterized points. The initial value is 1.

Description

glPointSize specifies the rasterized diameter of both aliased and antialiased points. Using a point size other than 1 has different effects, depending on whether point antialiasing is enabled. To enable and disable point antialiasing, call glEnable and glDisable with argument GL_POINT_SMOOTH. Point antialiasing is initially disabled.

The specified point size is multiplied with a distance attenuation factor and clamped to the specified point size range, and further clamped to the implementation-dependent point size range to produce the derived point size using

$$pointSize = clamp\left[size \times \sqrt{\left(\frac{1}{a + b \times d + c \times d^2} \right)} \right]$$

where *d* is the eye-coordinate distance from the eye to the vertex, and *a*, *b*, and *c* are the distance attenuation coefficients (see glPointParameter).

If multisampling is disabled, the computed point size is used as the point's width.

If multisampling is enabled, the point may be faded by modifying the point alpha value (see glSampleCoverage) instead of allowing the point width to go below a given threshold (see glPointParameter). In this case, the width is further modified in the following manner:

$$pointWidth = \begin{cases} pointSize & pointSize >= threshold \\ threshold & otherwise \end{cases}$$

The point alpha value is modified by computing:

$$pointAlpha = \begin{cases} 1 & pointSize >= threshold \\ \left(\frac{pointSize}{threshold} \right)^2 & otherwise \end{cases}$$

If point antialiasing is disabled, the actual size is determined by rounding the supplied size to the nearest integer. (If the rounding results in the value 0, it is as if the point size were 1.) If the rounded size is odd, then the center point (x, y) of the pixel fragment that represents the point is computed as

$$(\lfloor x_w \rfloor + .5, \lfloor y_w \rfloor + .5)$$

where *w* subscripts indicate window coordinates. All pixels that lie within the square grid of the rounded size centered at (x, y) make up the fragment. If the size is even, the center point is

$$(\lfloor x_w + .5 \rfloor, \lfloor y_w + .5 \rfloor)$$

and the rasterized fragment's centers are the half-integer window coordinates within the square of the rounded size centered at (x,y). All pixel fragments produced in rasterizing a nonantialiased point are assigned the same associated data, that of the vertex corresponding to the point.

If antialiasing is enabled, then point rasterization produces a fragment for each pixel square that intersects the region lying within the circle having diameter equal to the current point size and centered at the point's (x_w, y_w). The coverage value for each fragment is the window coordinate area of the intersection of the circular region with the corresponding pixel square. This value is saved and used in the final rasterization step. The data associated with each fragment is the data associated with the point being rasterized.

Not all sizes are supported when point antialiasing is enabled. If an unsupported size is requested, the nearest supported size is used. Only size 1 is guaranteed to be supported; others depend on the implementation. To query the range of supported sizes and the size difference between supported sizes within the range, call glGet with arguments GL_SMOOTH_POINT_SIZE_RANGE and GL_SMOOTH_POINT_SIZE_GRANULARITY. For aliased points, query the supported ranges and granularity with glGet with arguments GL_ALIASED_POINT_SIZE_RANGE.

Notes

The point size specified by glPointSize is always returned when GL_POINT_SIZE is queried. Clamping and rounding for aliased and antialiased points have no effect on the specified value.

A non-antialiased point size may be clamped to an implementation-dependent maximum. Although this maximum cannot be queried, it must be no less than the maximum value for antialiased points, rounded to the nearest integer value.

GL_POINT_SIZE_RANGE and GL_POINT_SIZE_GRANULARITY are deprecated in GL versions 1.2 and greater. Their functionality has been replaced by GL_SMOOTH_POINT_SIZE_RANGE and GL_SMOOTH_POINT_SIZE_GRANULARITY.

Errors

GL_INVALID_VALUE is generated if *size* is less than or equal to 0.

GL_INVALID_OPERATION is generated if glPointSize is executed between the execution of glBegin and the corresponding execution of glEnd.

Associated Gets

glGet with argument GL_ALIASED_POINT_SIZE_RANGE
glGet with argument GL_POINT_SIZE
glGet with argument GL_POINT_SIZE_MIN
glGet with argument GL_POINT_SIZE_MAX
glGet with argument GL_POINT_FADE_THRESHOLD_SIZE
glGet with argument GL_POINT_DISTANCE_ATTENUATION
glGet with argument GL_SMOOTH_POINT_SIZE_RANGE
glGet with argument GL_SMOOTH_POINT_SIZE_GRANULARITY
glIsEnabled with argument GL_POINT_SMOOTH

See Also

glEnable, glPointParameter

glPolygonMode

Select a polygon rasterization mode

C Specification

void **glPolygonMode**(GLenum *face*, GLenum *mode*);

Parameters

face   Specifies the polygons that *mode* applies to. Must be GL_FRONT for front-facing polygons, GL_BACK for back-facing polygons, or GL_FRONT_AND_BACK for front- and back-facing polygons.

mode   Specifies how polygons will be rasterized. Accepted values are GL_POINT, GL_LINE, and GL_FILL. The initial value is GL_FILL for both front- and back-facing polygons.

Description

glPolygonMode controls the interpretation of polygons for rasterization. *face* describes which polygons *mode* applies to: front-facing polygons (GL_FRONT), back-facing polygons (GL_BACK), or both (GL_FRONT_AND_BACK). The polygon mode affects only the final rasterization of polygons. In particular, a polygon's vertices are lit and the polygon is clipped and possibly culled before these modes are applied.

Three modes are defined and can be specified in *mode*:

GL_POINT

Polygon vertices that are marked as the start of a boundary edge are drawn as points. Point attributes such as GL_POINT_SIZE and GL_POINT_SMOOTH control the rasterization of the points. Polygon rasterization attributes other than GL_POLYGON_MODE have no effect.

GL_LINE

Boundary edges of the polygon are drawn as line segments. They are treated as connected line segments for line stippling; the line stipple counter and pattern are not reset between segments (see glLineStipple). Line attributes such as GL_LINE_WIDTH and GL_LINE_SMOOTH control the rasterization of the lines. Polygon rasterization attributes other than GL_POLYGON_MODE have no effect.

GL_FILL

The interior of the polygon is filled. Polygon attributes such as GL_POLYGON_STIPPLE and GL_POLYGON_SMOOTH control the rasterization of the polygon.

Examples

To draw a surface with filled back-facing polygons and outlined front-facing polygons, call glPolygonMode(GL_FRONT,GL_LINE);

Notes

Vertices are marked as boundary or nonboundary with an edge flag. Edge flags are generated internally by the GL when it decomposes polygons; they can be set explicitly using glEdgeFlag.

Errors

GL_INVALID_ENUM is generated if either *face* or *mode* is not an accepted value.
GL_INVALID_OPERATION is generated if glPolygonMode is executed between the execution of glBegin and the corresponding execution of glEnd.

Associated Gets

glGet with argument GL_POLYGON_MODE

See Also

glBegin, glEdgeFlag, glLineStipple, glLineWidth, glPointSize, glPolygonStipple

glPolygonOffset

Set the scale and units used to calculate depth values

C Specification

```
void glPolygonOffset(GLfloat factor,
                     GLfloat units);
```

Parameters

factor Specifies a scale factor that is used to create a variable depth offset for each polygon. The initial value is 0.

units Is multiplied by an implementation-specific value to create a constant depth offset. The initial value is 0.

Description

When GL_POLYGON_OFFSET_FILL, GL_POLYGON_OFFSET_LINE, or GL_POLYGON_OFFSET_POINT is enabled, each fragment's *depth* value will be offset after it is interpolated from the *depth* values of the appropriate vertices. The value of the offset is $factor \times DZ + r \times units$, where DZ is a measurement of the change in depth relative to the screen area of the polygon, and r is the smallest value that is guaranteed to produce a resolvable offset for a given implementation. The offset is added before the depth test is performed and before the value is written into the depth buffer.

glPolygonOffset is useful for rendering hidden-line images, for applying decals to surfaces, and for rendering solids with highlighted edges.

Notes

glPolygonOffset is available only if the GL version is 1.1 or greater.

glPolygonOffset has no effect on depth coordinates placed in the feedback buffer.

glPolygonOffset has no effect on selection.

Errors

GL_INVALID_OPERATION is generated if glPolygonOffset is executed between the execution of glBegin and the corresponding execution of glEnd.

Associated Gets

glIsEnabled with argument GL_POLYGON_OFFSET_FILL, GL_POLYGON_OFFSET_LINE, or GL_POLYGON_OFFSET_POINT.

glGet with argument GL_POLYGON_OFFSET_FACTOR or GL_POLYGON_OFFSET_UNITS.

See Also

glDepthFunc, glEnable, glGet, glIsEnabled

glPolygonStipple

Set the polygon stippling pattern

C Specification

void **glPolygonStipple**(const GLubyte * *pattern*);

Parameters

pattern Specifies a pointer to a 32 × 32 stipple pattern that will be unpacked from memory in the same way that glDrawPixels unpacks pixels.

Description

Polygon stippling, like line stippling (see glLineStipple), masks out certain fragments produced by rasterization, creating a pattern. Stippling is independent of polygon antialiasing.

pattern is a pointer to a 32 × 32 stipple pattern that is stored in memory just like the pixel data supplied to a glDrawPixels call with height and width both equal to 32, a pixel format of GL_COLOR_INDEX, and data type of GL_BITMAP. That is, the stipple pattern is represented as a 32 × 32 array of 1-bit color indices packed in unsigned bytes. glPixelStore parameters like GL_UNPACK_SWAP_BYTES and GL_UNPACK_LSB_FIRST affect the assembling of the bits into a stipple pattern. Pixel transfer operations (shift, offset, pixel map) are not applied to the stipple image, however.

If a nonzero named buffer object is bound to the GL_PIXEL_UNPACK_BUFFER target (see glBindBuffer) while a stipple pattern is specified, pattern is treated as a byte offset into the buffer object's data store.

To enable and disable polygon stippling, call glEnable and glDisable with argument GL_POLYGON_STIPPLE. Polygon stippling is initially disabled. If it's enabled, a rasterized polygon fragment with window coordinates x_w and y_w is sent to the next stage of the GL if and only if the $(x_w\%32)$th bit in the $(y_w\%32)$th row of the stipple pattern is 1 (one). When polygon stippling is disabled, it is as if the stipple pattern consists of all 1's.

Errors

GL_INVALID_OPERATION is generated if a nonzero buffer object name is bound to the GL_PIXEL_UNPACK_BUFFER target and the buffer object's data store is currently mapped.

GL_INVALID_OPERATION is generated if a nonzero buffer object name is bound to the GL_PIXEL_UNPACK_BUFFER target and the data would be unpacked from the buffer object such that the memory reads required would exceed the data store size.

GL_INVALID_OPERATION is generated if glPolygonStipple is executed between the execution of glBegin and the corresponding execution of glEnd.

Associated Gets

glGetPolygonStipple
glIsEnabled with argument GL_POLYGON_STIPPLE
glGet with argument GL_PIXEL_UNPACK_BUFFER_BINDING

See Also

glDrawPixels, glLineStipple, glPixelStore, glPixelTransfer

glPrioritizeTextures

Set texture residence priority

C Specification

void **glPrioritizeTextures**(GLsizei   n,
                        const GLuint *   textures,
                        const GLclampf * priorities);

Parameters

n   Specifies the number of textures to be prioritized.
textures   Specifies an array containing the names of the textures to be prioritized.
priorities Specifies an array containing the texture priorities. A priority given in an element of priorities applies to the texture named by the corresponding element of textures.

Description

glPrioritizeTextures assigns the n texture priorities given in priorities to the n textures named in textures.

The GL establishes a "working set" of textures that are resident in texture memory. These textures may be bound to a texture target much more efficiently than textures that are not resident. By specifying a priority for each texture, glPrioritizeTextures allows applications to guide the GL implementation in determining which textures should be resident.

The priorities given in priorities are clamped to the range [0,1] before they are assigned. 0 indicates the lowest priority; textures with priority 0 are least likely to be resident. 1 indicates the highest priority; textures with priority 1 are most likely to be resident. However, textures are not guaranteed to be resident until they are used.

glPrioritizeTextures silently ignores attempts to prioritize texture 0 or any texture name that does not correspond to an existing texture.

glPrioritizeTextures does not require that any of the textures named by *textures* be bound to a texture target. glTexParameter may also be used to set a texture's priority, but only if the texture is currently bound. This is the only way to set the priority of a default texture.

Notes

glPrioritizeTextures is available only if the GL version is 1.1 or greater.

Errors

GL_INVALID_VALUE is generated if *n* is negative.

GL_INVALID_OPERATION is generated if glPrioritizeTextures is executed between the execution of glBegin and the corresponding execution of glEnd.

Associated Gets

glGetTexParameter with parameter name GL_TEXTURE_PRIORITY retrieves the priority of a currently bound texture.

See Also

glAreTexturesResident, glBindTexture, glCopyTexImage1D, glCopyTexImage2D, glTexImage1D, glTexImage2D, glTexImage3D, glTexParameter

glPushAttrib

Push and pop the server attribute stack

C Specification

void **glPushAttrib**(GLbitfield *mask*);

Parameters

mask   Specifies a mask that indicates which attributes to save. Values for *mask* are listed below.

C Specification

void **glPopAttrib**(*void*);

Description

glPushAttrib takes one argument, a mask that indicates which groups of state variables to save on the attribute stack. Symbolic constants are used to set bits in the mask. *mask* is typically constructed by specifying the bitwise-or of several of these constants together. The special mask GL_ALL_ATTRIB_BITS can be used to save all stackable states.

The symbolic mask constants and their associated GL state are as follows (the second column lists which attributes are saved):

GL_ACCUM_BUFFER_BIT	Accumulation buffer clear value
GL_COLOR_BUFFER_BIT	GL_ALPHA_TEST enable bit
	Alpha test function and reference value
	GL_BLEND enable bit
	Blending source and destination functions
	Constant blend color
	Blending equation
	GL_DITHER enable bit
	GL_DRAW_BUFFER setting

	GL_COLOR_LOGIC_OP enable bit
	GL_INDEX_LOGIC_OP enable bit
	Logic op function
	Color mode and index mode clear values
	Color mode and index mode writemasks
GL_CURRENT_BIT	Current RGBA color
	Current color index
	Current normal vector
	Current texture coordinates
	Current raster position
	GL_CURRENT_RASTER_POSITION_VALID flag
	RGBA color associated with current raster position
	Color index associated with current raster position
	Texture coordinates associated with current raster position
	GL_EDGE_FLAG flag
GL_DEPTH_BUFFER_BIT	GL_DEPTH_TEST enable bit
	Depth buffer test function
	Depth buffer clear value
	GL_DEPTH_WRITEMASK enable bit
GL_ENABLE_BIT	GL_ALPHA_TEST flag
	GL_AUTO_NORMAL flag
	GL_BLEND flag
	Enable bits for the user-definable clipping planes
	GL_COLOR_MATERIAL
	GL_CULL_FACE flag
	GL_DEPTH_TEST flag
	GL_DITHER flag
	GL_FOG flag
	GL_LIGHTi where $0 \leq i < $ GL_MAX_LIGHTS
	GL_LIGHTING flag
	GL_LINE_SMOOTH flag
	GL_LINE_STIPPLE flag
	GL_COLOR_LOGIC_OP flag
	GL_INDEX_LOGIC_OP flag
	GL_MAP1_x where x is a map type
	GL_MAP2_x where x is a map type
	GL_MULTISAMPLE flag
	GL_NORMALIZE flag
	GL_POINT_SMOOTH flag
	GL_POLYGON_OFFSET_LINE flag
	GL_POLYGON_OFFSET_FILL flag
	GL_POLYGON_OFFSET_POINT flag
	GL_POLYGON_SMOOTH flag

	GL_POLYGON_STIPPLE flag
	GL_SAMPLE_ALPHA_TO_COVERAGE flag
	GL_SAMPLE_ALPHA_TO_ONE flag
	GL_SAMPLE_COVERAGE flag
	GL_SCISSOR_TEST flag
	GL_STENCIL_TEST flag
	GL_TEXTURE_1D flag
	GL_TEXTURE_2D flag
	GL_TEXTURE_3D flag
	Flags GL_TEXTURE_GEN_x where x is S, T, R, or Q
GL_EVAL_BIT	GL_MAP1_x enable bits, where x is a map type
	GL_MAP2_x enable bits, where x is a map type
	1D grid endpoints and divisions
	2D grid endpoints and divisions
	GL_AUTO_NORMAL enable bit
GL_FOG_BIT	GL_FOG enable bit
	Fog color
	Fog density
	Linear fog start
	Linear fog end
	Fog index
	GL_FOG_MODE value
GL_HINT_BIT	GL_PERSPECTIVE_CORRECTION_HINT setting
	GL_POINT_SMOOTH_HINT setting
	GL_LINE_SMOOTH_HINT setting
	GL_POLYGON_SMOOTH_HINT setting
	GL_FOG_HINT setting
	GL_GENERATE_MIPMAP_HINT setting
	GL_TEXTURE_COMPRESSION_HINT setting
GL_LIGHTING_BIT	GL_COLOR_MATERIAL enable bit
	GL_COLOR_MATERIAL_FACE value
	Color material parameters that are tracking the current color
	Ambient scene color
	GL_LIGHT_MODEL_LOCAL_VIEWER value
	GL_LIGHT_MODEL_TWO_SIDE setting
	GL_LIGHTING enable bit
	Enable bit for each light
	Ambient, diffuse, and specular intensity for each light
	Direction, position, exponent, and cutoff angle for each light
	Constant, linear, and quadratic attenuation factors for each light
	Ambient, diffuse, specular, and emissive color for each material
	Ambient, diffuse, and specular color indices for each material
	Specular exponent for each material
	GL_SHADE_MODEL setting

GL_LINE_BIT	GL_LINE_SMOOTH flag
	GL_LINE_STIPPLE enable bit
	Line stipple pattern and repeat counter
	Line width
GL_LIST_BIT	GL_LIST_BASE setting
GL_MULTISAMPLE_BIT	GL_MULTISAMPLE flag
	GL_SAMPLE_ALPHA_TO_COVERAGE flag
	GL_SAMPLE_ALPHA_TO_ONE flag
	GL_SAMPLE_COVERAGE flag
	GL_SAMPLE_COVERAGE_VALUE value
	GL_SAMPLE_COVERAGE_INVERT value
GL_PIXEL_MODE_BIT	GL_RED_BIAS and GL_RED_SCALE settings
	GL_GREEN_BIAS and GL_GREEN_SCALE values
	GL_BLUE_BIAS and GL_BLUE_SCALE
	GL_ALPHA_BIAS and GL_ALPHA_SCALE
	GL_DEPTH_BIAS and GL_DEPTH_SCALE
	GL_INDEX_OFFSET and GL_INDEX_SHIFT values
	GL_MAP_COLOR and GL_MAP_STENCIL flags
	GL_ZOOM_X and GL_ZOOM_Y factors
	GL_READ_BUFFER setting
GL_POINT_BIT	GL_POINT_SMOOTH flag
	Point size
GL_POLYGON_BIT	GL_CULL_FACE enable bit
	GL_CULL_FACE_MODE value
	GL_FRONT_FACE indicator
	GL_POLYGON_MODE setting
	GL_POLYGON_SMOOTH flag
	GL_POLYGON_STIPPLE enable bit
	GL_POLYGON_OFFSET_FILL flag
	GL_POLYGON_OFFSET_LINE flag
	GL_POLYGON_OFFSET_POINT flag
	GL_POLYGON_OFFSET_FACTOR
	GL_POLYGON_OFFSET_UNITS
GL_POLYGON_STIPPLE_BIT	Polygon stipple image
GL_SCISSOR_BIT	GL_SCISSOR_TEST flag
	Scissor box
GL_STENCIL_BUFFER_BIT	GL_STENCIL_TEST enable bit
	Stencil function and reference value
	Stencil value mask
	Stencil fail, pass, and depth buffer pass actions
	Stencil buffer clear value
	Stencil buffer writemask

GL_TEXTURE_BIT	Enable bits for the four texture coordinates
	Border color for each texture image
	Minification function for each texture image
	Magnification function for each texture image
	Texture coordinates and wrap mode for each texture image
	Color and mode for each texture environment
	Enable bits GL_TEXTURE_GEN_*x*, *x* is S, T, R, and Q
	GL_TEXTURE_GEN_MODE setting for S, T, R, and Q
	glTexGen plane equations for S, T, R, and Q
	Current texture bindings (for example, GL_TEXTURE_BINDING_2D)
GL_TRANSFORM_BIT	Coefficients of the six clipping planes
	Enable bits for the user-definable clipping planes
	GL_MATRIX_MODE value
	GL_NORMALIZE flag
	GL_RESCALE_NORMAL flag
GL_VIEWPORT_BIT	Depth range (near and far)
	Viewport origin and extent

glPopAttrib restores the values of the state variables saved with the last glPushAttrib command. Those not saved are left unchanged.

It is an error to push attributes onto a full stack or to pop attributes off an empty stack. In either case, the error flag is set and no other change is made to GL state.

Initially, the attribute stack is empty.

Notes

Not all values for GL state can be saved on the attribute stack. For example, render mode state, and select and feedback state cannot be saved. Client state must be saved with glPushClientAttrib.

The depth of the attribute stack depends on the implementation, but it must be at least 16.

For OpenGL versions 1.3 and greater, or when the ARB_multitexture extension is supported, pushing and popping texture state applies to all supported texture units.

Errors

GL_STACK_OVERFLOW is generated if glPushAttrib is called while the attribute stack is full.

GL_STACK_UNDERFLOW is generated if glPopAttrib is called while the attribute stack is empty.

GL_INVALID_OPERATION is generated if glPushAttrib or glPopAttrib is executed between the execution of glBegin and the corresponding execution of glEnd.

Associated Gets

glGet with argument GL_ATTRIB_STACK_DEPTH
glGet with argument GL_MAX_ATTRIB_STACK_DEPTH

See Also

glGet, glGetClipPlane, glGetError, glGetLight, glGetMap, glGetMaterial, glGetPixelMap, glGetPolygonStipple, glGetString, glGetTexEnv, glGetTexGen, glGetTexImage, glGetTexLevelParameter, glGetTexParameter, glIsEnabled, glPushClientAttrib

glPushClientAttrib

Push and pop the client attribute stack

C Specification

void **glPushClientAttrib**(GLbitfield *mask*);

Parameters

mask   Specifies a mask that indicates which attributes to save. Values for *mask* are listed below.

C Specification

void **glPopClientAttrib**(*void*);

Description

glPushClientAttrib takes one argument, a mask that indicates which groups of client-state variables to save on the client attribute stack. Symbolic constants are used to set bits in the mask. *mask* is typically constructed by specifying the bitwise-or of several of these constants together. The special mask GL_CLIENT_ALL_ATTRIB_BITS can be used to save all stackable client state.

The symbolic mask constants and their associated GL client state are as follows (the second column lists which attributes are saved):

GL_CLIENT_PIXEL_STORE_BIT Pixel storage modes GL_CLIENT_VERTEX_ARRAY_BIT Vertex arrays (and enables)

glPopClientAttrib restores the values of the client-state variables saved with the last glPushClientAttrib. Those not saved are left unchanged.

It is an error to push attributes onto a full client attribute stack or to pop attributes off an empty stack. In either case, the error flag is set, and no other change is made to GL state.

Initially, the client attribute stack is empty.

Notes

glPushClientAttrib is available only if the GL version is 1.1 or greater.

Not all values for GL client state can be saved on the attribute stack. For example, select and feedback state cannot be saved.

The depth of the attribute stack depends on the implementation, but it must be at least 16.

Use glPushAttrib and glPopAttrib to push and restore state that is kept on the server. Only pixel storage modes and vertex array state may be pushed and popped with glPushClientAttrib and glPopClientAttrib.

For OpenGL versions 1.3 and greater, or when the ARB_multitexture extension is supported, pushing and popping client vertex array state applies to all supported texture units, and the active client texture state.

Errors

GL_STACK_OVERFLOW is generated if glPushClientAttrib is called while the attribute stack is full.

GL_STACK_UNDERFLOW is generated if glPopClientAttrib is called while the attribute stack is empty.

Associated Gets

glGet with argument GL_ATTRIB_STACK_DEPTH
glGet with argument GL_MAX_CLIENT_ATTRIB_STACK_DEPTH

See Also

glColorPointer, glDisableClientState, glEdgeFlagPointer, glEnableClientState, glFogCoordPointer, glGet, glGetError, glIndexPointer, glNormalPointer, glNewList, glPixelStore, glPushAttrib, glTexCoordPointer, glVertexPointer

glPushMatrix

Push and pop the current matrix stack

C Specification

void **glPushMatrix**(*void*);

C Specification

void **glPopMatrix**(*void*);

Description

There is a stack of matrices for each of the matrix modes. In GL_MODELVIEW mode, the stack depth is at least 32. In the other modes, GL_COLOR, GL_PROJECTION, and GL_TEXTURE, the depth is at least 2. The current matrix in any mode is the matrix on the top of the stack for that mode.

glPushMatrix pushes the current matrix stack down by one, duplicating the current matrix. That is, after a glPushMatrix call, the matrix on top of the stack is identical to the one below it.

glPopMatrix pops the current matrix stack, replacing the current matrix with the one below it on the stack.

Initially, each of the stacks contains one matrix, an identity matrix.

It is an error to push a full matrix stack or to pop a matrix stack that contains only a single matrix. In either case, the error flag is set and no other change is made to GL state.

Errors

GL_STACK_OVERFLOW is generated if glPushMatrix is called while the current matrix stack is full.

GL_STACK_UNDERFLOW is generated if glPopMatrix is called while the current matrix stack contains only a single matrix.

GL_INVALID_OPERATION is generated if glPushMatrix or glPopMatrix is executed between the execution of glBegin and the corresponding execution of glEnd.

Associated Gets

glGet with argument GL_MATRIX_MODE
glGet with argument GL_COLOR_MATRIX
glGet with argument GL_MODELVIEW_MATRIX
glGet with argument GL_PROJECTION_MATRIX
glGet with argument GL_TEXTURE_MATRIX
glGet with argument GL_COLOR_MATRIX_STACK_DEPTH
glGet with argument GL_MODELVIEW_STACK_DEPTH
glGet with argument GL_PROJECTION_STACK_DEPTH
glGet with argument GL_TEXTURE_STACK_DEPTH
glGet with argument GL_MAX_MODELVIEW_STACK_DEPTH
glGet with argument GL_MAX_PROJECTION_STACK_DEPTH
glGet with argument GL_MAX_TEXTURE_STACK_DEPTH

See Also

glFrustum, glLoadIdentity, glLoadMatrix, glLoadTransposeMatrix, glMatrixMode, glMultMatrix, glMultTransposeMatrix, glOrtho, glRotate, glScale, glTranslate, glViewport

glPushName

Push and pop the name stack

C Specification

    void **glPushName**(GLuint *name*);

Parameters

name   Specifies a name that will be pushed onto the name stack.

C Specification

    void **glPopName**(*void*);

Description

The name stack is used during selection mode to allow sets of rendering commands to be uniquely identified. It consists of an ordered set of unsigned integers and is initially empty.

glPushName causes *name* to be pushed onto the name stack. glPopName pops one name off the top of the stack.

The maximum name stack depth is implementation-dependent; call GL_MAX_NAME_STACK_DEPTH to find out the value for a particular implementation. It is an error to push a name onto a full stack or to pop a name off an empty stack. It is also an error to manipulate the name stack between the execution of glBegin and the corresponding execution of glEnd. In any of these cases, the error flag is set and no other change is made to GL state.

The name stack is always empty while the render mode is not GL_SELECT. Calls to glPushName or glPopName while the render mode is not GL_SELECT are ignored.

Errors

GL_STACK_OVERFLOW is generated if glPushName is called while the name stack is full.

GL_STACK_UNDERFLOW is generated if glPopName is called while the name stack is empty.

GL_INVALID_OPERATION is generated if glPushName or glPopName is executed between a call to glBegin and the corresponding call to glEnd.

Associated Gets

glGet with argument GL_NAME_STACK_DEPTH
glGet with argument GL_MAX_NAME_STACK_DEPTH

See Also

glInitNames, glLoadName, glRenderMode, glSelectBuffer

glRasterPos

Specify the raster position for pixel operations

C Specification

    void **glRasterPos2s**(GLshort *x*, GLshort *y*);
    void **glRasterPos2i**(GLint *x*, GLint *y*);
    void **glRasterPos2f**(GLfloat *x*, GLfloat *y*);
    void **glRasterPos2d**(GLdouble *x*, GLdouble *y*);
    void **glRasterPos3s**(GLshort *x*,
                      GLshort *y*,
                      GLshort *z*);
    void **glRasterPos3i**(GLint *x*, GLint *y*, GLint *z*);

```
void glRasterPos3f(GLfloat x,
                   GLfloat y,
                   GLfloat z);
void glRasterPos3d(GLdouble x,
                   GLdouble y,
                   GLdouble z);
void glRasterPos4s(GLshort x,
                   GLshort y,
                   GLshort z,
                   GLshort w);
void glRasterPos4i(GLint x,
                   GLint y,
                   GLint z,
                   GLint w);
void glRasterPos4f(GLfloat x,
                   GLfloat y,
                   GLfloat z,
                   GLfloat w);
void glRasterPos4d(GLdouble x,
                   GLdouble y,
                   GLdouble z,
                   GLdouble w);
```

Parameters

x, y, z, w
Specify the *x*, *y*, *z*, and *w* object coordinates (if present) for the raster position.

C Specification

```
void glRasterPos2sv(const GLshort * v);
void glRasterPos2iv(const GLint * v);
void glRasterPos2fv(const GLfloat * v);
void glRasterPos2dv(const GLdouble * v);
void glRasterPos3sv(const GLshort * v);
void glRasterPos3iv(const GLint * v);
void glRasterPos3fv(const GLfloat * v);
void glRasterPos3dv(const GLdouble * v);
void glRasterPos4sv(const GLshort * v);
void glRasterPos4iv(const GLint * v);
void glRasterPos4fv(const GLfloat * v);
void glRasterPos4dv(const GLdouble * v);
```

Parameters

v   Specifies a pointer to an array of two, three, or four elements, specifying *x*, *y*, *z*, and *w* coordinates, respectively.

Description

The GL maintains a 3D position in window coordinates. This position, called the raster position, is used to position pixel and bitmap write operations. It is maintained with subpixel accuracy. See glBitmap, glDrawPixels, and glCopyPixels.

The current raster position consists of three window coordinates (*x*, *y*, *z*), a clip coordinate value (*w*), an eye coordinate distance, a valid bit, and associated color data and texture coordinates. The *w* coordinate is a clip coordinate, because *w* is not projected to window coordinates. glRasterPos4 specifies object coordinates *x*, *y*, *z*, and *w* explicitly. glRasterPos3 specifies object coordinate *x*, *y*, and *z* explicitly, while *w* is implicitly set to 1. glRasterPos2 uses the argument values for *x* and *y* while implicitly setting *z* and *w* to 0 and 1.

The object coordinates presented by glRasterPos are treated just like those of a glVertex command: They are transformed by the current modelview and projection matrices and passed to the clipping stage. If the vertex is not culled, then it is projected and scaled to window coordinates, which become the new current raster position, and the GL_CURRENT_RASTER_POSITION_VALID flag is set. If the vertex *is* culled, then the valid bit is cleared and the current raster position and associated color and texture coordinates are undefined.

The current raster position also includes some associated color data and texture coordinates. If lighting is enabled, then GL_CURRENT_RASTER_COLOR (in RGBA mode) or GL_CURRENT_RASTER_INDEX (in color index mode) is set to the color produced by the lighting calculation (see glLight, glLightModel, and glShadeModel). If lighting is disabled, current color (in RGBA mode, state variable GL_CURRENT_COLOR) or color index (in color index mode, state variable GL_CURRENT_INDEX) is used to update the current raster color. GL_CURRENT_RASTER_SECONDARY_COLOR (in RGBA mode) is likewise updated.

Likewise, GL_CURRENT_RASTER_TEXTURE_COORDS is updated as a function of GL_CURRENT_TEXTURE_COORDS, based on the texture matrix and the texture generation functions (see glTexGen). Finally, the distance from the origin of the eye coordinate system to the vertex as transformed by only the modelview matrix replaces GL_CURRENT_RASTER_DISTANCE.

Initially, the current raster position is (0, 0, 0, 1), the current raster distance is 0, the valid bit is set, the associated RGBA color is (1, 1, 1, 1), the associated color index is 1, and the associated texture coordinates are (0, 0, 0, 1). In RGBA mode, GL_CURRENT_RASTER_INDEX is always 1; in color index mode, the current raster RGBA color always maintains its initial value.

Notes

The raster position is modified by glRasterPos, glBitmap, and glWindowPos.

When the raster position coordinates are invalid, drawing commands that are based on the raster position are ignored (that is, they do not result in changes to GL state).

Calling glDrawElements or glDrawRangeElements may leave the current color or index indeterminate. If glRasterPos is executed while the current color or index is indeterminate, the current raster color or current raster index remains indeterminate.

To set a valid raster position outside the viewport, first set a valid raster position, then call glBitmap with NULL as the *bitmap* parameter.

When the ARB_imaging extension is supported, there are distinct raster texture coordinates for each texture unit. Each texture unit's current raster texture coordinates are updated by glRasterPos.

Errors

GL_INVALID_OPERATION is generated if glRasterPos is executed between the execution of glBegin and the corresponding execution of glEnd.

Associated Gets

glGet with argument GL_CURRENT_RASTER_POSITION
glGet with argument GL_CURRENT_RASTER_POSITION_VALID
glGet with argument GL_CURRENT_RASTER_DISTANCE
glGet with argument GL_CURRENT_RASTER_COLOR
glGet with argument GL_CURRENT_RASTER_SECONDARY_COLOR
glGet with argument GL_CURRENT_RASTER_INDEX
glGet with argument GL_CURRENT_RASTER_TEXTURE_COORDS

See Also

glBitmap, glCopyPixels, glDrawArrays, glDrawElements, glDrawRangeElements, glDrawPixels, glMultiTexCoord, glTexCoord, glTexGen, glVertex, glWindowPos

glReadBuffer

Select a color buffer source for pixels

C Specification

```
void glReadBuffer(GLenum mode);
```

Parameters

mode   Specifies a color buffer. Accepted values are GL_FRONT_LEFT, GL_FRONT_RIGHT, GL_BACK_LEFT, GL_BACK_RIGHT, GL_FRONT, GL_BACK, GL_LEFT, GL_RIGHT, and GL_AUX*i*, where *i* is between 0 and the value of GL_AUX_BUFFERS minus 1.

Description

glReadBuffer specifies a color buffer as the source for subsequent glReadPixels, glCopyTexImage1D, glCopyTexImage2D, glCopyTexSubImage1D, glCopyTexSubImage2D, glCopyTexSubImage3D, and glCopyPixels commands. *mode* accepts one of twelve or more predefined values. (GL_AUX0 through GL_AUX3 are always defined.) In a fully configured system, GL_FRONT, GL_LEFT, and GL_FRONT_LEFT all name the front left buffer, GL_FRONT_RIGHT and GL_RIGHT name the front right buffer, and GL_BACK_LEFT and GL_BACK name the back left buffer.

Nonstereo double-buffered configurations have only a front left and a back left buffer. Single-buffered configurations have a front left and a front right buffer if stereo, and only a front left buffer if nonstereo. It is an error to specify a nonexistent buffer to glReadBuffer.

mode is initially GL_FRONT in single-buffered configurations and GL_BACK in double-buffered configurations.

Errors

GL_INVALID_ENUM is generated if *mode* is not one of the twelve (or more) accepted values.

GL_INVALID_OPERATION is generated if *mode* specifies a buffer that does not exist.

GL_INVALID_OPERATION is generated if glReadBuffer is executed between the execution of glBegin and the corresponding execution of glEnd.

Associated Gets

glGet with argument GL_READ_BUFFER

See Also

glCopyPixels, glCopyTexImage1D, glCopyTexImage2D, glCopyTexSubImage1D, glCopyTexSubImage2D, glCopyTexSubImage3D, glDrawBuffer, glReadPixels

glReadPixels

Read a block of pixels from the frame buffer

C Specification

```
void glReadPixels(GLint    x,
                  GLint    y,
                  GLsizei  width,
                  GLsizei  height,
                  GLenum   format,
                  GLenum   type,
                  GLvoid * data);
```

Parameters

x, y   Specify the window coordinates of the first pixel that is read from the frame buffer. This location is the lower-left corner of a rectangular block of pixels.

width, *height*	Specify the dimensions of the pixel rectangle. *width* and *height* of one correspond to a single pixel.
format	Specifies the format of the pixel data. The following symbolic values are accepted: GL_COLOR_INDEX, GL_STENCIL_INDEX, GL_DEPTH_COMPONENT, GL_RED, GL_GREEN, GL_BLUE, GL_ALPHA, GL_RGB, GL_BGR, GL_RGBA, GL_BGRA, GL_LUMINANCE, and GL_LUMINANCE_ALPHA.
type	Specifies the data type of the pixel data. Must be one of GL_UNSIGNED_BYTE, GL_BYTE, GL_BITMAP, GL_UNSIGNED_SHORT, GL_SHORT, GL_UNSIGNED_INT, GL_INT, GL_FLOAT, GL_UNSIGNED_BYTE_3_3_2, GL_UNSIGNED_BYTE_2_3_3_REV, GL_UNSIGNED_SHORT_5_6_5, GL_UNSIGNED_SHORT_5_6_5_REV, GL_UNSIGNED_SHORT_4_4_4_4, GL_UNSIGNED_SHORT_4_4_4_4_REV, GL_UNSIGNED_SHORT_5_5_5_1, GL_UNSIGNED_SHORT_1_5_5_5_REV, GL_UNSIGNED_INT_8_8_8_8, GL_UNSIGNED_INT_8_8_8_8_REV, GL_UNSIGNED_INT_10_10_10_2, or GL_UNSIGNED_INT_2_10_10_10_REV.
data	Returns the pixel data.

Description

glReadPixels returns pixel data from the frame buffer, starting with the pixel whose lower-left corner is at location (*x*, *y*), into client memory starting at location *data*. Several parameters control the processing of the pixel data before it is placed into client memory. These parameters are set with three commands: glPixelStore, glPixelTransfer, and glPixelMap. This reference page describes the effects on glReadPixels of most, but not all of the parameters specified by these three commands.

If a nonzero named buffer object is bound to the GL_PIXEL_PACK_BUFFER target (see glBindBuffer) while a block of pixels is requested, *data* is treated as a byte offset into the buffer object's data store rather than a pointer to client memory.

When the ARB_imaging extension is supported, the pixel data may be processed by additional operations including color table lookup, color matrix transformations, convolutions, histograms, and minimum and maximum pixel value computations.

glReadPixels returns values from each pixel with lower-left corner at ($x + i, y + j$) for $0 <= i < width$ and $0 <= j < height$. This pixel is said to be the ith pixel in the jth row. Pixels are returned in row order from the lowest to the highest row, left to right in each row.

format specifies the format for the returned pixel values; accepted values are:

GL_COLOR_INDEX

Color indices are read from the color buffer selected by glReadBuffer. Each index is converted to fixed point, shifted left or right depending on the value and sign of GL_INDEX_SHIFT, and added to GL_INDEX_OFFSET. If GL_MAP_COLOR is GL_TRUE, indices are replaced by their mappings in the table GL_PIXEL_MAP_I_TO_I.

GL_STENCIL_INDEX

Stencil values are read from the stencil buffer. Each index is converted to fixed point, shifted left or right depending on the value and sign of GL_INDEX_SHIFT, and added to GL_INDEX_OFFSET. If GL_MAP_STENCIL is GL_TRUE, indices are replaced by their mappings in the table GL_PIXEL_MAP_S_TO_S.

GL_DEPTH_COMPONENT

Depth values are read from the depth buffer. Each component is converted to floating point such that the minimum depth value maps to 0 and the maximum value maps to 1. Each component is then multiplied by GL_DEPTH_SCALE, added to GL_DEPTH_BIAS, and finally clamped to the range [0,1].

GL_RED
GL_GREEN
GL_BLUE

```
GL_ALPHA
GL_RGB
GL_BGR
GL_RGBA
GL_BGRA
GL_LUMINANCE
GL_LUMINANCE_ALPHA
```

Processing differs depending on whether color buffers store color indices or RGBA color components. If color indices are stored, they are read from the color buffer selected by `glReadBuffer`. Each index is converted to fixed point, shifted left or right depending on the value and sign of `GL_INDEX_SHIFT`, and added to `GL_INDEX_OFFSET`. Indices are then replaced by the red, green, blue, and alpha values obtained by indexing the tables `GL_PIXEL_MAP_I_TO_R`, `GL_PIXEL_MAP_I_TO_G`, `GL_PIXEL_MAP_I_TO_B`, and `GL_PIXEL_MAP_I_TO_A`. Each table must be of size 2^n, but n may be different for different tables. Before an index is used to look up a value in a table of size 2^n, it must be masked against $2^n - 1$.

If RGBA color components are stored in the color buffers, they are read from the color buffer selected by `glReadBuffer`. Each color component is converted to floating point such that zero intensity maps to 0.0 and full intensity maps to 1.0. Each component is then multiplied by `GL_c_SCALE` and added to `GL_c_BIAS`, where c is RED, GREEN, BLUE, or ALPHA. Finally, if `GL_MAP_COLOR` is `GL_TRUE`, each component is clamped to the range [0,1], scaled to the size of its corresponding table, and is then replaced by its mapping in the table `GL_PIXEL_MAP_c_TO_c`, where c is R, G, B, or A.

Unneeded data is then discarded. For example, `GL_RED` discards the green, blue, and alpha components, while `GL_RGB` discards only the alpha component. `GL_LUMINANCE` computes a single-component value as the sum of the red, green, and blue components, and `GL_LUMINANCE_ALPHA` does the same, while keeping alpha as a second value. The final values are clamped to the range [0,1].

The shift, scale, bias, and lookup factors just described are all specified by `glPixelTransfer`. The lookup table contents themselves are specified by `glPixelMap`.

Finally, the indices or components are converted to the proper format, as specified by *type*. If *format* is GL_COLOR_INDEX or GL_STENCIL_INDEX and *type* is not GL_FLOAT, each index is masked with the mask value given in the following table. If *type* is GL_FLOAT, then each integer index is converted to single-precision floating-point format.

If *format* is GL_RED, GL_GREEN, GL_BLUE, GL_ALPHA, GL_RGB, GL_BGR, GL_RGBA, GL_BGRA, GL_LUMINANCE, or GL_LUMINANCE_ALPHA and *type* is not GL_FLOAT, each component is multiplied by the multiplier shown in the following table. If type is GL_FLOAT, then each component is passed as is (or converted to the client's single-precision floating-point format if it is different from the one used by the GL).

type	Index Mask	Component Conversion
GL_UNSIGNED_BYTE	$2^8 - 1$	$(2^8 - 1)\,c$
GL_BYTE	$2^7 - 1$	$\dfrac{(2^8 - 1)\,c - 1}{2}$
GL_BITMAP	1	1
GL_UNSIGNED_SHORT	$2^{16} - 1$	$(2^{16} - 1)\,c$
GL_SHORT	$2^{15} - 1$	$\dfrac{(2^{16} - 1)\,c - 1}{2}$
GL_UNSIGNED_INT	$2^{32} - 1$	$(2^{32} - 1)\,c$
GL_INT	$2^{31} - 1$	$\dfrac{(2^{32} - 1)\,c - 1}{2}$
GL_FLOAT	none	c

Return values are placed in memory as follows. If *format* is GL_COLOR_INDEX, GL_STENCIL_INDEX, GL_DEPTH_COMPONENT, GL_RED, GL_GREEN, GL_BLUE, GL_ALPHA, or GL_LUMI-NANCE, a single value is returned and the data for the *i*th pixel in the *j*th row is placed in location (*j*) width + *i*. GL_RGB and GL_BGR return three values, GL_RGBA and GL_BGRA return four values, and GL_LUMINANCE_ALPHA returns two values for each pixel, with all values corresponding to a single pixel occupying contiguous space in *data*. Storage parameters set by glPixelStore, such as GL_PACK_LSB_FIRST and GL_PACK_SWAP_BYTES, affect the way that data is written into memory. See glPixelStore for a description.

Notes

Values for pixels that lie outside the window connected to the current GL context are undefined. If an error is generated, no change is made to the contents of *data*.

Errors

GL_INVALID_ENUM is generated if *format* or *type* is not an accepted value.

GL_INVALID_ENUM is generated if *type* is GL_BITMAP and *format* is not GL_COLOR_INDEX or GL_STENCIL_INDEX.

GL_INVALID_VALUE is generated if either *width* or *height* is negative.

GL_INVALID_OPERATION is generated if *format* is GL_COLOR_INDEX and the color buffers store RGBA color components.

GL_INVALID_OPERATION is generated if *format* is GL_STENCIL_INDEX and there is no stencil buffer.

GL_INVALID_OPERATION is generated if *format* is GL_DEPTH_COMPONENT and there is no depth buffer.

GL_INVALID_OPERATION is generated if *type* is one of GL_UNSIGNED_BYTE_3_3_2, GL_UNSIGNED_BYTE_2_3_3_REV, GL_UNSIGNED_SHORT_5_6_5, or GL_UNSIGNED_SHORT_5_6_5_REV and *format* is not GL_RGB.

GL_INVALID_OPERATION is generated if *type* is one of GL_UNSIGNED_SHORT_4_4_4_4, GL_UNSIGNED_SHORT_4_4_4_4_REV, GL_UNSIGNED_SHORT_5_5_5_1, GL_UNSIGNED_SHORT_1_5_5_5_REV, GL_UNSIGNED_INT_8_8_8_8, GL_UNSIGNED_INT_8_8_8_8_REV, GL_UNSIGNED_INT_10_10_10_2, or GL_UNSIGNED_INT_2_10_10_10_REV and *format* is neither GL_RGBA nor GL_BGRA.

The formats GL_BGR, and GL_BGRA and types GL_UNSIGNED_BYTE_3_3_2, GL_UNSIGNED_BYTE_2_3_3_REV, GL_UNSIGNED_SHORT_5_6_5, GL_UNSIGNED_SHORT_5_6_5_REV, GL_UNSIGNED_SHORT_4_4_4_4, GL_UNSIGNED_SHORT_4_4_4_4_REV, GL_UNSIGNED_SHORT_5_5_5_1, GL_UNSIGNED_SHORT_1_5_5_5_REV, GL_UNSIGNED_INT_8_8_8_8, GL_UNSIGNED_INT_8_8_8_8_REV, GL_UNSIGNED_INT_10_10_10_2, and GL_UNSIGNED_INT_2_10_10_10_REV are available only if the GL version is 1.2 or greater.

GL_INVALID_OPERATION is generated if a nonzero buffer object name is bound to the GL_PIXEL_PACK_BUFFER target and the buffer object's data store is currently mapped.

GL_INVALID_OPERATION is generated if a nonzero buffer object name is bound to the GL_PIXEL_PACK_BUFFER target and the data would be packed to the buffer object such that the memory writes required would exceed the data store size.

GL_INVALID_OPERATION is generated if a nonzero buffer object name is bound to the GL_PIXEL_PACK_BUFFER target and *data* is not evenly divisible into the number of bytes needed to store in memory a datum indicated by *type*.

GL_INVALID_OPERATION is generated if glReadPixels is executed between the execution of glBegin and the corresponding execution of glEnd.

Associated Gets

glGet with argument GL_INDEX_MODE
glGet with argument GL_PIXEL_PACK_BUFFER_BINDING

See Also

glCopyPixels, glDrawPixels, glPixelMap, glPixelStore, glPixelTransfer, glReadBuffer

glRect

Draw a rectangle

C Specification

```
void glRectd(GLdouble x1,
             GLdouble y1,
             GLdouble x2,
             GLdouble y2);
void glRectf(GLfloat x1,
             GLfloat y1,
             GLfloat x2,
             GLfloat y2);
void glRecti(GLint x1,
             GLint y1,
             GLint x2,
             GLint y2);
void glRects(GLshort x1,
             GLshort y1,
             GLshort x2,
             GLshort y2);
```

Parameters

x1, y1   Specify one vertex of a rectangle.
x2, y2   Specify the opposite vertex of the rectangle.

C Specification

```
void glRectdv(const GLdouble * v1,
              const GLdouble * v2);
void glRectfv(const GLfloat * v1,
              const GLfloat * v2);
void glRectiv(const GLint * v1,
              const GLint * v2);
void glRectsv(const GLshort * v1,
              const GLshort * v2);
```

Parameters

v1   Specifies a pointer to one vertex of a rectangle.
v2   Specifies a pointer to the opposite vertex of the rectangle.

Description

glRect supports efficient specification of rectangles as two corner points. Each rectangle command takes four arguments, organized either as two consecutive pairs of (x,y) coordinates or as two pointers to arrays, each containing an (x,y) pair. The resulting rectangle is defined in the $z = 0$ plane.

glRect(*x1*, *y1*, *x2*, *y2*) is exactly equivalent to the following sequence:
glBegin(GL_POLYGON);
glVertex2(*x1*, *y1*);
glVertex2(*x2*, *y1*);
glVertex2(*x2*, *y2*);
glVertex2(*x1*, *y2*);
glEnd();

Note that if the second vertex is above and to the right of the first vertex, the rectangle is constructed with a counterclockwise winding.

Errors

GL_INVALID_OPERATION is generated if glRect is executed between the execution of glBegin and the corresponding execution of glEnd.

See Also

glBegin, glVertex

glRenderMode

Set rasterization mode

C Specification

GLint **glRenderMode**(GLenum *mode*);

Parameters

mode   Specifies the rasterization mode. Three values are accepted: GL_RENDER, GL_SELECT, and GL_FEEDBACK. The initial value is GL_RENDER.

Description

glRenderMode sets the rasterization mode. It takes one argument, *mode*, which can assume one of three predefined values:

GL_RENDER

Render mode. Primitives are rasterized, producing pixel fragments, which are written into the frame buffer. This is the normal mode and also the default mode.

GL_SELECT

Selection mode. No pixel fragments are produced, and no change to the frame buffer contents is made. Instead, a record of the names of primitives that would have been drawn if the render mode had been GL_RENDER is returned in a select buffer, which must be created (see glSelectBuffer) before selection mode is entered.

GL_FEEDBACK

Feedback mode. No pixel fragments are produced, and no change to the frame buffer contents is made. Instead, the coordinates and attributes of vertices that would have been drawn if the render mode had been GL_RENDER is returned in a feedback buffer, which must be created (see glFeedbackBuffer) before feedback mode is entered.

The return value of glRenderMode is determined by the render mode at the time glRenderMode is called, rather than by *mode*. The values returned for the three render modes are as follows:

GL_RENDER

0.

GL_SELECT

The number of hit records transferred to the select buffer.

GL_FEEDBACK

The number of values (not vertices) transferred to the feedback buffer.

See the glSelectBuffer and glFeedbackBuffer reference pages for more details concerning selection and feedback operation.

Notes

If an error is generated, glRenderMode returns 0 regardless of the current render mode.

Errors

GL_INVALID_ENUM is generated if *mode* is not one of the three accepted values.

GL_INVALID_OPERATION is generated if glSelectBuffer is called while the render mode is GL_SELECT, or if glRenderMode is called with argument GL_SELECT before glSelectBuffer is called at least once.

GL_INVALID_OPERATION is generated if glFeedbackBuffer is called while the render mode is GL_FEEDBACK, or if glRenderMode is called with argument GL_FEEDBACK before glFeedbackBuffer is called at least once.

GL_INVALID_OPERATION is generated if glRenderMode is executed between the execution of glBegin and the corresponding execution of glEnd.

Associated Gets

glGet with argument GL_RENDER_MODE

See Also

glFeedbackBuffer, glInitNames, glLoadName, glPassThrough, glPushName, glSelectBuffer

glResetHistogram

Reset histogram table entries to zero

C Specification

void **glResetHistogram**(GLenum *target*);

Parameters

target   Must be GL_HISTOGRAM.

Description

glResetHistogram resets all the elements of the current histogram table to zero.

Notes

glResetHistogram is present only if ARB_imaging is returned when glGetString is called with an argument of GL_EXTENSIONS.

Errors

GL_INVALID_ENUM is generated if *target* is not GL_HISTOGRAM.

GL_INVALID_OPERATION is generated if glResetHistogram is executed between the execution of glBegin and the corresponding execution of glEnd.

See Also

glHistogram

glResetMinmax

Reset minmax table entries to initial values

C Specification

void **glResetMinmax**(GLenum *target*);

Parameters

target   Must be GL_MINMAX.

Description

glResetMinmax resets the elements of the current minmax table to their initial values: the "maximum" element receives the minimum possible component values, and the "minimum" element receives the maximum possible component values.

Notes

glResetMinmax is present only if ARB_imaging is returned when glGetString is called with an argument of GL_EXTENSIONS.

Errors

GL_INVALID_ENUM is generated if *target* is not GL_MINMAX.

GL_INVALID_OPERATION is generated if glResetMinmax is executed between the execution of glBegin and the corresponding execution of glEnd.

See Also

glMinmax

glRotate

Multiply the current matrix by a rotation matrix

C Specification

```
void glRotated(GLdouble angle,
               GLdouble x,
               GLdouble y,
               GLdouble z);
void glRotatef(GLfloat  angle,
               GLfloat  x,
               GLfloat  y,
               GLfloat  z);
```

Parameters

angle   Specifies the angle of rotation, in degrees.
x, y, z   Specify the x, y, and z coordinates of a vector, respectively.

Description

glRotate produces a rotation of *angle* degrees around the vector (x,y,z). The current matrix (see glMatrixMode) is multiplied by a rotation matrix with the product replacing the current matrix, as if glMultMatrix were called with the following matrix as its argument:

$$\begin{bmatrix} x^2(1-c)+c & xy(1-c)-zs & xz(1-c)+ys & 0 \\ yx(1-c)+zs & y^2(1-c)+c & yz(1-c)-xs & 0 \\ xz(1-c)-ys & yz(1-c)+xs & z^2(1-c)+c & 0 \\ 0 & 0 & 0 & 1 \end{bmatrix}$$

Where $c = cos(angle)$, $s = sin(angle)$, and $\|(x,y,z)\| = 1$ (if not, the GL will normalize this vector).If the matrix mode is either GL_MODELVIEW or GL_PROJECTION, all objects drawn after glRotate is called are rotated. Use glPushMatrix and glPopMatrix to save and restore the unrotated coordinate system.

Notes

This rotation follows the right-hand rule, so if the vector (x,y,z) points toward the user, the rotation will be counterclockwise.

Errors

GL_INVALID_OPERATION is generated if glRotate is executed between the execution of glBegin and the corresponding execution of glEnd.

Associated Gets

glGet with argument GL_MATRIX_MODE
glGet with argument GL_COLOR_MATRIX
glGet with argument GL_MODELVIEW_MATRIX
glGet with argument GL_PROJECTION_MATRIX
glGet with argument GL_TEXTURE_MATRIX

See Also

glMatrixMode, glMultMatrix, glPushMatrix, glScale, glTranslate

glSampleCoverage

Specify multisample coverage parameters

C Specification

```
void glSampleCoverage(GLclampf  value,
                      GLboolean invert);
```

Parameters

value   Specify a single floating-point sample coverage value. The value is clamped to the range [0,1]. The initial value is 1.0.

invert Specify a single boolean value representing if the coverage masks should be inverted. GL_TRUE and GL_FALSE are accepted. The initial value is GL_FALSE.

Description

Multisampling samples a pixel multiple times at various implementation-dependent subpixel locations to generate antialiasing effects. Multisampling transparently antialiases points, lines, polygons, bitmaps, and images if it is enabled.

value is used in constructing a temporary mask used in determining which samples will be used in resolving the final fragment color. This mask is bitwise-anded with the coverage mask generated from the multisampling computation. If the *invert* flag is set, the temporary mask is inverted (all bits flipped) and then the bitwise-and is computed.

If an implementation does not have any multisample buffers available, or multisampling is disabled, rasterization occurs with only a single sample computing a pixel's final RGB color.

Provided an implementation supports multisample buffers, and multisampling is enabled, then a pixel's final color is generated by combining several samples per pixel. Each sample contains color, depth, and stencil information, allowing those operations to be performed on each sample.

Notes

glSampleCoverage is available only if the GL version is 1.3 or greater.

Errors

GL_INVALID_OPERATION is generated if glSampleCoverage is executed between the execution of glBegin and the corresponding execution of glEnd.

Associated Gets

glGet with argument GL_SAMPLE_COVERAGE_VALUE
glGet with argument GL_SAMPLE_COVERAGE_INVERT
glIsEnabled with argument GL_MULTISAMPLE
glIsEnabled with argument GL_SAMPLE_ALPHA_TO_COVERAGE
glIsEnabled with argument GL_SAMPLE_ALPHA_TO_ONE
glIsEnabled with argument GL_SAMPLE_COVERAGE

See Also

glEnable, glPushAttrib

glScale

Multiply the current matrix by a general scaling matrix

C Specification

```
void glScaled(GLdouble x,
              GLdouble y,
              GLdouble z);
void glScalef(GLfloat x, GLfloat y, GLfloat z);
```

Parameters

x, y, z   Specify scale factors along the *x*, *y*, and *z* axes, respectively.

Description

glScale produces a nonuniform scaling along the *x*, *y*, and *z* axes. The three parameters indicate the desired scale factor along each of the three axes.

The current matrix (see glMatrixMode) is multiplied by this scale matrix, and the product replaces the current matrix as if glMultMatrix were called with the following matrix as its argument:

$$\begin{bmatrix} x & 0 & 0 & 0 \\ 0 & y & 0 & 0 \\ 0 & 0 & z & 0 \\ 0 & 0 & 0 & 1 \end{bmatrix}$$

If the matrix mode is either GL_MODELVIEW or GL_PROJECTION, all objects drawn after glScale is called are scaled.

Use glPushMatrix and glPopMatrix to save and restore the unscaled coordinate system.

Notes

If scale factors other than 1 are applied to the modelview matrix and lighting is enabled, lighting often appears wrong. In that case, enable automatic normalization of normals by calling glEnable with the argument GL_NORMALIZE.

Errors

GL_INVALID_OPERATION is generated if glScale is executed between the execution of glBegin and the corresponding execution of glEnd.

Associated Gets

glGet with argument GL_MATRIX_MODE
glGet with argument GL_COLOR_MATRIX
glGet with argument GL_MODELVIEW_MATRIX
glGet with argument GL_PROJECTION_MATRIX
glGet with argument GL_TEXTURE_MATRIX

See Also

glMatrixMode, glMultMatrix, glPushMatrix, glRotate, glTranslate

glScissor

Define the scissor box

C Specification

```
void glScissor(GLint   x,
               GLint   y,
               GLsizei width,
               GLsizei height);
```

Parameters

x, y   Specify the lower-left corner of the scissor box. Initially (0, 0).
width, *height*   Specify the width and height of the scissor box. When a GL context is first
                    attached to a window, *width* and *height* are set to the dimensions of that
                    window.

Description

glScissor defines a rectangle, called the scissor box, in window coordinates. The first two arguments, x and y, specify the lower-left corner of the box. *width* and *height* specify the width and height of the box.

To enable and disable the scissor test, call glEnable and glDisable with argument GL_-
SCISSOR_TEST. The test is initially disabled. While the test is enabled, only pixels that lie within the scissor box can be modified by drawing commands. Window coordinates have integer values at the shared corners of frame buffer pixels. glScissor(0,0,1,1) allows modification of only the lower-left pixel in the window, and glScissor(0,0,0,0) doesn't allow modification of any pixels in the window.

When the scissor test is disabled, it is as though the scissor box includes the entire window.

Errors

GL_INVALID_VALUE is generated if either *width* or *height* is negative.
GL_INVALID_OPERATION is generated if glScissor is executed between the execution of glBegin and the corresponding execution of glEnd.

Associated Gets

glGet with argument GL_SCISSOR_BOX
glIsEnabled with argument GL_SCISSOR_TEST

See Also

glEnable, glViewport

glSecondaryColor

Set the current secondary color

C Specification

```
void glSecondaryColor3b(GLbyte   red,
                        GLbyte   green,
                        GLbyte   blue);
void glSecondaryColor3s(GLshort  red,
                        GLshort  green,
                        GLshort  blue);
```

```
void glSecondaryColor3i(GLint      red,
                        GLint      green,
                        GLint      blue);
void glSecondaryColor3f(GLfloat    red,
                        GLfloat    green,
                        GLfloat    blue);
void glSecondaryColor3d(GLdouble   red,
                        GLdouble   green,
                        GLdouble   blue);
void glSecondaryColor3ub(GLubyte   red,
                         GLubyte   green,
                         GLubyte   blue);
void glSecondaryColor3us(GLushort  red,
                         GLushort  green,
                         GLushort  blue);
void glSecondaryColor3ui(GLuint    red,
                         GLuint    green,
                         GLuint    blue);
```

Parameters

red, *green*, *blue*   Specify new red, green, and blue values for the current secondary color.

C Specification

```
void glSecondaryColor3bv(const GLbyte * v);
void glSecondaryColor3sv(const GLshort * v);
void glSecondaryColor3iv(const GLint * v);
void glSecondaryColor3fv(const GLfloat * v);
void glSecondaryColor3dv(const GLdouble * v);
void glSecondaryColor3ubv(const GLubyte * v);
void glSecondaryColor3usv(const GLushort * v);
void glSecondaryColor3uiv(const GLuint * v);
```

Parameters

v   Specifies a pointer to an array that contains red, green, blue.

Description

The GL stores both a primary four-valued RGBA color and a secondary four-valued RGBA color (where alpha is always set to 0.0) that is associated with every vertex.

The secondary color is interpolated and applied to each fragment during rasterization when GL_COLOR_SUM is enabled. When lighting is enabled, and GL_SEPARATE_SPECULAR_COLOR is specified, the value of the secondary color is assigned the value computed from the specular term of the lighting computation. Both the primary and secondary current colors are applied to each fragment, regardless of the state of GL_COLOR_SUM, under such conditions. When GL_SEPARATE_SPECULAR_COLOR is specified, the value returned from querying the current secondary color is undefined.

glSecondaryColor3b, glSecondaryColor3s, and glSecondaryColor3i take three signed byte, short, or long integers as arguments. When **v** is appended to the name, the color commands can take a pointer to an array of such values.

Color values are stored in floating-point format, with unspecified mantissa and exponent sizes. Unsigned integer color components, when specified, are linearly mapped to floating-point values such that the largest representable value maps to 1.0 (full intensity), and 0 maps to 0.0 (zero intensity). Signed integer color components, when specified, are linearly mapped to floating-point values such that the most positive representable value maps to 1.0, and the most negative representable value maps to -1.0. (Note that this mapping does not convert 0 precisely to 0.0). Floating-point values are mapped directly.

Neither floating-point nor signed integer values are clamped to the range [0,1] before the current color is updated. However, color components are clamped to this range before they are interpolated or written into a color buffer.

Notes

glSecondaryColor is available only if the GL version is 1.4 or greater.

The initial value for the secondary color is (0, 0, 0, 0).

The secondary color can be updated at any time. In particular, glSecondaryColor can be called between a call to glBegin and the corresponding call to glEnd.

Associated Gets

glGet with argument GL_CURRENT_SECONDARY_COLOR

glGet with argument GL_RGBA_MODE

glIsEnabled with argument GL_COLOR_SUM

See Also

glColor, glIndex, glIsEnabled, glLightModel, glSecondaryColorPointer

glSecondaryColorPointer

Define an array of secondary colors

C Specification

```
void glSecondaryColorPointer(GLint    size,
                             GLenum        type,
                             GLsizei       stride,
                             const GLvoid * pointer);
```

Parameters

size	Specifies the number of components per color. Must be 3.
type	Specifies the data type of each color component in the array. Symbolic constants GL_BYTE, GL_UNSIGNED_BYTE, GL_SHORT, GL_UNSIGNED_SHORT, GL_INT, GL_UNSIGNED_INT, GL_FLOAT, or GL_DOUBLE are accepted. The initial value is GL_FLOAT.
stride	Specifies the byte offset between consecutive colors. If stride is 0, the colors are understood to be tightly packed in the array. The initial value is 0.
pointer	Specifies a pointer to the first component of the first color element in the array. The initial value is 0.

Description

glSecondaryColorPointer specifies the location and data format of an array of color components to use when rendering. size specifies the number of components per color, and must be 3. type specifies the data type of each color component, and stride specifies the byte stride from one color to the next, allowing vertices and attributes to be packed into a single array or stored in separate arrays.

If a nonzero named buffer object is bound to the GL_ARRAY_BUFFER target (see glBindBuffer) while a secondary color array is specified, pointer is treated as a byte offset into the buffer object's data store. Also, the buffer object binding (GL_ARRAY_BUFFER_BINDING) is saved as secondary color vertex array client-side state (GL_SECONDARY_COLOR_ARRAY_BUFFER_BINDING).

When a secondary color array is specified, size, type, stride, and pointer are saved as client-side state, in addition to the current vertex array buffer object binding.

To enable and disable the secondary color array, call `glEnableClientState` and `glDisableClientState` with the argument `GL_SECONDARY_COLOR_ARRAY`. If enabled, the secondary color array is used when `glArrayElement`, `glDrawArrays`, `glMultiDrawArrays`, `glDrawElements`, `glMultiDrawElements`, or `glDrawRangeElements` is called.

Notes

`glSecondaryColorPointer` is available only if the GL version is 1.4 or greater. Secondary colors are not supported for interleaved vertex array formats (see `glInterleavedArrays`).

The secondary color array is initially disabled and isn't accessed when `glArrayElement`, `glDrawElements`, `glDrawRangeElements`, `glDrawArrays`, `glMultiDrawArrays`, or `glMultiDrawElements` is called.

Execution of `glSecondaryColorPointer` is not allowed between the execution of `glBegin` and the corresponding execution of `glEnd`, but an error may or may not be generated. If no error is generated, the operation is undefined.

`glSecondaryColorPointer` is typically implemented on the client side.

Secondary color array parameters are client-side state and are therefore not saved or restored by `glPushAttrib` and `glPopAttrib`. Use `glPushClientAttrib` and `glPopClientAttrib` instead.

Errors

`GL_INVALID_VALUE` is generated if *size* is not 3.
`GL_INVALID_ENUM` is generated if *type* is not an accepted value.
`GL_INVALID_VALUE` is generated if *stride* is negative.

Associated Gets

`glIsEnabled` with argument `GL_SECONDARY_COLOR_ARRAY`
`glGet` with argument `GL_SECONDARY_COLOR_ARRAY_SIZE`
`glGet` with argument `GL_SECONDARY_COLOR_ARRAY_TYPE`
`glGet` with argument `GL_SECONDARY_COLOR_ARRAY_STRIDE`
`glGet` with argument `GL_SECONDARY_COLOR_ARRAY_BUFFER_BINDING`
`glGet` with argument `GL_ARRAY_BUFFER_BINDING`
`glGetPointerv` with argument `GL_SECONDARY_COLOR_ARRAY_POINTER`

See Also

`glArrayElement`, `glBindBuffer`, `glColorPointer`, `glDisableClientState`, `glDrawArrays`, `glDrawElements`, `glDrawRangeElements`, `glEdgeFlagPointer`, `glEnableClientState`, `glFogCoordPointer`, `glIndexPointer`, `glInterleavedArrays`, `glMultiDrawArrays`, `glMultiDrawElements`, `glNormalPointer`, `glPopClientAttrib`, `glPushClientAttrib`, `glSecondaryColor`, `glTexCoordPointer`, `glVertexAttribPointer`, `glVertexPointer`

glSelectBuffer

Establish a buffer for selection mode values

C Specification

```
void glSelectBuffer(GLsizei  size,
                    GLuint * buffer);
```

Parameters

size   Specifies the size of *buffer*.
buffer   Returns the selection data.

Description

glSelectBuffer has two arguments: *buffer* is a pointer to an array of unsigned integers, and *size* indicates the size of the array. *buffer* returns values from the name stack (see glInitNames, glLoadName, glPushName) when the rendering mode is GL_SELECT (see glRenderMode). glSelectBuffer must be issued before selection mode is enabled, and it must not be issued while the rendering mode is GL_SELECT.

A programmer can use selection to determine which primitives are drawn into some region of a window. The region is defined by the current modelview and perspective matrices.

In selection mode, no pixel fragments are produced from rasterization. Instead, if a primitive or a raster position intersects the clipping volume defined by the viewing frustum and the user-defined clipping planes, this primitive causes a selection hit. (With polygons, no hit occurs if the polygon is culled.) When a change is made to the name stack, or when glRenderMode is called, a hit record is copied to *buffer* if any hits have occurred since the last such event (name stack change or glRenderMode call). The hit record consists of the number of names in the name stack at the time of the event, followed by the minimum and maximum depth values of all vertices that hit since the previous event, followed by the name stack contents, bottom name first.

Depth values (which are in the range [0,1]) are multiplied by $2^{32} - 1$, before being placed in the hit record.

An internal index into *buffer* is reset to 0 whenever selection mode is entered. Each time a hit record is copied into *buffer*, the index is incremented to point to the cell just past the end of the block of names\(emthat is, to the next available cell If the hit record is larger than the number of remaining locations in *buffer*, as much data as can fit is copied, and the overflow flag is set. If the name stack is empty when a hit record is copied, that record consists of 0 followed by the minimum and maximum depth values.

To exit selection mode, call glRenderMode with an argument other than GL_SELECT. Whenever glRenderMode is called while the render mode is GL_SELECT, it returns the number of hit records copied to *buffer*, resets the overflow flag and the selection buffer pointer, and initializes the name stack to be empty. If the overflow bit was set when glRenderMode was called, a negative hit record count is returned.

Notes

The contents of buffer is undefined until glRenderMode is called with an argument other than GL_SELECT.

glBegin/glEnd primitives and calls to glRasterPos can result in hits. glWindowPos will always generate a selection hit.

Errors

GL_INVALID_VALUE is generated if *size* is negative.

GL_INVALID_OPERATION is generated if glSelectBuffer is called while the render mode is GL_SELECT, or if glRenderMode is called with argument GL_SELECT before glSelectBuffer is called at least once.

GL_INVALID_OPERATION is generated if glSelectBuffer is executed between the execution of glBegin and the corresponding execution of glEnd.

Associated Gets

glGet with argument GL_NAME_STACK_DEPTH
glGet with argument GL_SELECTION_BUFFER_SIZE
glGetPointerv with argument GL_SELECTION_BUFFER_POINTER

See Also

glFeedbackBuffer, glInitNames, glLoadName, glPushName, glRenderMode

glSeparableFilter2D

Define a separable two-dimensional convolution filter

C Specification

```
void glSeparableFilter2D(GLenum    target,
                         GLenum    internalformat,
                         GLsizei   width,
                         GLsizei   height,
                         GLenum    format,
                         GLenum    type,
                         const     GLvoid * row,
                         const     GLvoid * column);
```

Parameters

target	Must be GL_SEPARABLE_2D.
internalformat	The internal format of the convolution filter kernel. The allowable values are GL_ALPHA, GL_ALPHA4, GL_ALPHA8, GL_ALPHA12, GL_ALPHA16, GL_LUMINANCE, GL_LUMINANCE4, GL_LUMINANCE8, GL_LUMINANCE12, GL_LUMINANCE16, GL_LUMINANCE_ALPHA, GL_LUMINANCE4_ALPHA4, GL_LUMINANCE6_ALPHA2, GL_LUMINANCE8_ALPHA8, GL_LUMINANCE12_ALPHA4, GL_LUMINANCE12_ALPHA12, GL_LUMINANCE16_ALPHA16, GL_INTENSITY, GL_INTENSITY4, GL_INTENSITY8, GL_INTENSITY12, GL_INTENSITY16, GL_R3_G3_B2, GL_RGB, GL_RGB4, GL_RGB5, GL_RGB8, GL_RGB10, GL_RGB12, GL_RGB16, GL_RGBA, GL_RGBA2, GL_RGBA4, GL_RGB5_A1, GL_RGBA8, GL_RGB10_A2, GL_RGBA12, or GL_RGBA16.
width	The number of elements in the pixel array referenced by *row*. (This is the width of the separable filter kernel.)
height	The number of elements in the pixel array referenced by *column*. (This is the height of the separable filter kernel.)
format	The format of the pixel data in *row* and *column*. The allowable values are GL_RED, GL_GREEN, GL_BLUE, GL_ALPHA, GL_RGB, GL_BGR, GL_RGBA, GL_BGRA, GL_INTENSITY, GL_LUMINANCE, and GL_LUMINANCE_ALPHA.
type	The type of the pixel data in *row* and *column*. Symbolic constants GL_UNSIGNED_BYTE, GL_BYTE, GL_BITMAP, GL_UNSIGNED_SHORT, GL_SHORT, GL_UNSIGNED_INT, GL_INT, GL_FLOAT, GL_UNSIGNED_BYTE_3_3_2, GL_UNSIGNED_BYTE_2_3_3_REV, GL_UNSIGNED_SHORT_5_6_5, GL_UNSIGNED_SHORT_5_6_5_REV, GL_UNSIGNED_SHORT_4_4_4_4, GL_UNSIGNED_SHORT_4_4_4_4_REV, GL_UNSIGNED_SHORT_5_5_5_1, GL_UNSIGNED_SHORT_1_5_5_5_REV, GL_UNSIGNED_INT_8_8_8_8, GL_UNSIGNED_INT_8_8_8_8_REV, GL_UNSIGNED_INT_10_10_10_2, and GL_UNSIGNED_INT_2_10_10_10_REV are accepted.
row	Pointer to a one-dimensional array of pixel data that is processed to build the row filter kernel.
column	Pointer to a one-dimensional array of pixel data that is processed to build the column filter kernel.

Description

glSeparableFilter2D builds a two-dimensional separable convolution filter kernel from two arrays of pixels.

The pixel arrays specified by (*width*, *format*, *type*, *row*) and (*height*, *format*, *type*, *column*) are processed just as if they had been passed to glDrawPixels, but processing stops after the final expansion to RGBA is completed.

If a nonzero named buffer object is bound to the GL_PIXEL_UNPACK_BUFFER target (see glBindBuffer) while a convolution filter is specified, *row* and *column* are treated as byte offsets into the buffer object's data store.

Next, the R, G, B, and A components of all pixels in both arrays are scaled by the four separable 2D GL_CONVOLUTION_FILTER_SCALE parameters and biased by the four separable 2D GL_CONVOLUTION_FILTER_BIAS parameters. (The scale and bias parameters are set by glConvolutionParameter using the GL_SEPARABLE_2D target and the names GL_CONVOLUTION_FILTER_SCALE and GL_CONVOLUTION_FILTER_BIAS. The parameters themselves are vectors of four values that are applied to red, green, blue, and alpha, in that order.) The R, G, B, and A values are not clamped to [0,1] at any time during this process.

Each pixel is then converted to the internal format specified by *internalformat*. This conversion simply maps the component values of the pixel (R, G, B, and A) to the values included in the internal format (red, green, blue, alpha, luminance, and intensity). The mapping is as follows:

Internal Format	Red	Green	Blue	Alpha	Luminance	Intensity
GL_LUMINANCE					R	
GL_LUMINANCE_ALPHA				A	R	
GL_INTENSITY						R
GL_RGB	R	G	B			
GL_RGBA	R	G	B	A		

The red, green, blue, alpha, luminance, and/or intensity components of the resulting pixels are stored in floating-point rather than integer format. They form two one-dimensional filter kernel images. The row image is indexed by coordinate *i* starting at zero and increasing from left to right. Each location in the row image is derived from element *i* of *row*. The column image is indexed by coordinate *j* starting at zero and increasing from bottom to top. Each location in the column image is derived from element *j* of *column*.

Note that after a convolution is performed, the resulting color components are also scaled by their corresponding GL_POST_CONVOLUTION_*c*_SCALE parameters and biased by their corresponding GL_POST_CONVOLUTION_*c*_BIAS parameters (where *c* takes on the values RED, GREEN, BLUE, and ALPHA). These parameters are set by glPixelTransfer.

Notes

glSeparableFilter2D is present only if ARB_imaging is returned when glGetString is called with an argument of GL_EXTENSIONS.

Errors

GL_INVALID_ENUM is generated if *target* is not GL_SEPARABLE_2D.

GL_INVALID_ENUM is generated if *internalformat* is not one of the allowable values.

GL_INVALID_ENUM is generated if *format* is not one of the allowable values.

GL_INVALID_ENUM is generated if *type* is not one of the allowable values.

GL_INVALID_VALUE is generated if *width* is less than zero or greater than the maximum supported value. This value may be queried with glGetConvolutionParameter using target GL_SEPARABLE_2D and name GL_MAX_CONVOLUTION_WIDTH.

GL_INVALID_VALUE is generated if *height* is less than zero or greater than the maximum supported value. This value may be queried with glGetConvolutionParameter using target GL_SEPARABLE_2D and name GL_MAX_CONVOLUTION_HEIGHT.

GL_INVALID_OPERATION is generated if *height* is one of GL_UNSIGNED_BYTE_3_3_2, GL_UNSIGNED_BYTE_2_3_3_REV, GL_UNSIGNED_SHORT_5_6_5, or GL_UNSIGNED_SHORT_5_6_5_REV and *format* is not GL_RGB.

GL_INVALID_OPERATION is generated if *height* is one of GL_UNSIGNED_SHORT_4_4_4_4, GL_UNSIGNED_SHORT_4_4_4_4_REV, GL_UNSIGNED_SHORT_5_5_5_1, GL_UNSIGNED_SHORT_1_ 5_5_5_REV, GL_UNSIGNED_INT_8_8_8_8, GL_UNSIGNED_INT_8_8_8_8_REV, GL_UNSIGNED_ INT_10_10_10_2, or GL_UNSIGNED_INT_2_10_10_10_REV and *format* is neither GL_RGBA nor GL_BGRA.

GL_INVALID_OPERATION is generated if a nonzero buffer object name is bound to the GL_PIXEL_UNPACK_BUFFER target and the buffer object's data store is currently mapped.

GL_INVALID_OPERATION is generated if a nonzero buffer object name is bound to the GL_PIXEL_UNPACK_BUFFER target and the data would be unpacked from the buffer object such that the memory reads required would exceed the data store size.

GL_INVALID_OPERATION is generated if a nonzero buffer object name is bound to the GL_PIXEL_UNPACK_BUFFER target and *row* or *column* is not evenly divisible into the number of bytes needed to store in memory a datum indicated by **type**.

GL_INVALID_OPERATION is generated if glSeparableFilter2D is executed between the execution of glBegin and the corresponding execution of glEnd.

Associated Gets

glGetConvolutionParameter, glGetSeparableFilter
glGet with argument GL_PIXEL_UNPACK_BUFFER_BINDING

See Also

glConvolutionFilter1D, glConvolutionFilter2D, glConvolutionParameter, glPixelTransfer

glShadeModel

Select flat or smooth shading

C Specification

void **glShadeModel**(GLenum mode);

Parameters

mode   Specifies a symbolic value representing a shading technique. Accepted values are GL_FLAT and GL_SMOOTH. The initial value is GL_SMOOTH.

Description

GL primitives can have either flat or smooth shading. Smooth shading, the default, causes the computed colors of vertices to be interpolated as the primitive is rasterized, typically assigning different colors to each resulting pixel fragment. Flat shading selects the computed color of just one vertex and assigns it to all the pixel fragments generated by rasterizing a single primitive. In either case, the computed color of a vertex is the result of lighting if lighting is enabled, or it is the current color at the time the vertex was specified if lighting is disabled.

Flat and smooth shading are indistinguishable for points. Starting when glBegin is issued and counting vertices and primitives from 1, the GL gives each flat-shaded line segment *i* the computed color of vertex *i* + 1, its second vertex. Counting similarly from 1, the GL gives each flat-shaded polygon the computed color of the vertex listed in the following table. This is the last vertex to specify the polygon in all cases except single polygons, where the first vertex specifies the flat-shaded color.

Primitive Type of Polygon i	Vertex
Single polygon (i==1)	1
Triangle strip	$i + 2$
Triangle fan	$i + 2$
Independent triangle	$3i$
Quad strip	$2i + 2$
Independent quad	$4i$

Flat and smooth shading are specified by glShadeModel with *mode* set to GL_FLAT and GL_SMOOTH, respectively.

Errors

GL_INVALID_ENUM is generated if *mode* is any value other than GL_FLAT or GL_SMOOTH.

GL_INVALID_OPERATION is generated if glShadeModel is executed between the execution of glBegin and the corresponding execution of glEnd.

Associated Gets

glGet with argument GL_SHADE_MODEL

See Also

glBegin, glColor, glLight, glLightModel

glShaderSource

Replace the source code in a shader object

C Specification

```
void glShaderSource(GLuint          shader,
                    GLsizei         count,
                    const GLchar ** string,
                    const GLint *   length);
```

Parameters

shader   Specifies the handle of the shader object whose source code is to be replaced.
count   Specifies the number of elements in the *string* and *length* arrays.
string   Specifies an array of pointers to strings containing the source code to be loaded into the shader.
length   Specifies an array of string lengths.

Description

glShaderSource sets the source code in *shader* to the source code in the array of strings specified by *string*. Any source code previously stored in the shader object is completely replaced. The number of strings in the array is specified by *count*. If length is NULL, each string is assumed to be null terminated. If *length* is a value other than NULL, it points to an array containing a string length for each of the corresponding elements of *string*. Each element in the *length* array may contain the length of the corresponding string (the null character is not counted as part of the string length) or a value less than 0 to indicate that the string is null terminated. The source code strings are not scanned or parsed at this time; they are simply copied into the specified shader object.

Notes

glShaderSource is available only if the GL version is 2.0 or greater.
OpenGL copies the shader source code strings when glShaderSource is called, so an application may free its copy of the source code strings immediately after the function returns.

Errors

GL_INVALID_VALUE is generated if *shader* is not a value generated by OpenGL.

GL_INVALID_OPERATION is generated if *shader* is not a shader object.

GL_INVALID_VALUE is generated if *count* is less than 0.

GL_INVALID_OPERATION is generated if glShaderSource is executed between the execution of glBegin and the corresponding execution of glEnd.

Associated Gets

glGetShader with arguments *shader* and GL_SHADER_SOURCE_LENGTH

glGetShaderSource with argument *shader*

glIsShader

See Also

glCompileShader, glCreateShader, glDeleteShader

glStencilFunc

Set front and back function and reference value for stencil testing

C Specification

```
void glStencilFunc(GLenum func,
                   GLint  ref,
                   GLuint mask);
```

Parameters

func   Specifies the test function. Eight tokens are valid: GL_NEVER, GL_LESS, GL_LEQUAL, GL_GREATER, GL_GEQUAL, GL_EQUAL, GL_NOTEQUAL, and GL_ALWAYS. The initial value is GL_ALWAYS.

ref   Specifies the reference value for the stencil test. *ref* is clamped to the range $[0, 2^n - 1]$, where n is the number of bitplanes in the stencil buffer. The initial value is 0.

mask   Specifies a mask that is ANDed with both the reference value and the stored stencil value when the test is done. The initial value is all 1's.

Description

Stenciling, like depth-buffering, enables and disables drawing on a per-pixel basis. You draw into the stencil planes using GL drawing primitives, then render geometry and images, using the stencil planes to mask out portions of the screen. Stenciling is typically used in multipass rendering algorithms to achieve special effects, such as decals, outlining, and constructive solid geometry rendering.

The stencil test conditionally eliminates a pixel based on the outcome of a comparison between the reference value and the value in the stencil buffer. To enable and disable the test, call glEnable and glDisable with argument GL_STENCIL_TEST. To specify actions based on the outcome of the stencil test, call glStencilOp or glStencilOpSeparate.

There can be two separate sets of *func*, *ref*, and *mask* parameters; one affects back-facing polygons, and the other affects front-facing polygons as well as other non-polygon primitives. glStencilFunc sets both front and back stencil state to the same values. Use glStencilFuncSeparate to set front and back stencil state to different values.

func is a symbolic constant that determines the stencil comparison function. It accepts one of eight values, shown in the following list. *ref* is an integer reference value that is used in the stencil comparison. It is clamped to the range $[0, 2^n - 1]$, where n is the number of bitplanes in the stencil buffer. *mask* is bitwise ANDed with both the reference value and the stored stencil value, with the ANDed values participating in the comparison.

If *stencil* represents the value stored in the corresponding stencil buffer location, the following list shows the effect of each comparison function that can be specified by *func*. Only if the comparison succeeds is the pixel passed through to the next stage in the rasterization process (see glStencilOp). All tests treat *stencil* values as unsigned integers in the range [0,2^n – 1], where *n* is the number of bitplanes in the stencil buffer.

The following values are accepted by *func*:

GL_NEVER
Always fails.
GL_LESS
Passes if (*ref* & *mask*) < (*stencil* & *mask*).
GL_LEQUAL
Passes if (*ref* & *mask*) <= (*stencil* & *mask*).
GL_GREATER
Passes if (*ref* & *mask*) > (*stencil* & *mask*).
GL_GEQUAL
Passes if (*ref* & *mask*) >= (*stencil* & *mask*).
GL_EQUAL
Passes if (*ref* & *mask*) = (*stencil* & *mask*).
GL_NOTEQUAL
Passes if (*ref* & *mask*) != (*stencil* & *mask*).
GL_ALWAYS
Always passes.

Notes

Initially, the stencil test is disabled. If there is no stencil buffer, no stencil modification can occur and it is as if the stencil test always passes.

glStencilFunc is the same as calling glStencilFuncSeparate with *face* set to GL_FRONT_AND_BACK.

Errors

GL_INVALID_ENUM is generated if *func* is not one of the eight accepted values.

GL_INVALID_OPERATION is generated if glStencilFunc is executed between the execution of glBegin and the corresponding execution of glEnd.

Associated Gets

glGet with argument GL_STENCIL_FUNC, GL_STENCIL_VALUE_MASK, GL_STENCIL_REF, GL_STENCIL_BACK_FUNC, GL_STENCIL_BACK_VALUE_MASK, GL_STENCIL_BACK_REF, or GL_STENCIL_BITS

glIsEnabled with argument GL_STENCIL_TEST

See Also

glAlphaFunc, glBlendFunc, glDepthFunc, glEnable, glLogicOp, glStencilFuncSeparate, glStencilMask, glStencilMaskSeparate, glStencilOp, glStencilOpSeparate

glStencilFuncSeparate

Set front and/or back function and reference value for stencil testing

C Specification

```
void glStencilFuncSeparate(GLenum face,
                           GLenum func,
                           GLint  ref,
                           GLuint mask);
```

Parameters

face   Specifies whether front and/or back stencil state is updated. Three tokens are valid: GL_FRONT, GL_BACK, and GL_FRONT_AND_BACK.

func   Specifies the test function. Eight tokens are valid: GL_NEVER, GL_LESS, GL_LEQUAL, GL_GREATER, GL_GEQUAL, GL_EQUAL, GL_NOTEQUAL, and GL_ALWAYS. The initial value is GL_ALWAYS.

ref   Specifies the reference value for the stencil test. ref is clamped to the range $[0, 2^n - 1]$, where n is the number of bitplanes in the stencil buffer. The initial value is 0.

mask   Specifies a mask that is ANDed with both the reference value and the stored stencil value when the test is done. The initial value is all 1's.

Description

Stenciling, like depth-buffering, enables and disables drawing on a per-pixel basis. You draw into the stencil planes using GL drawing primitives, then render geometry and images, using the stencil planes to mask out portions of the screen. Stenciling is typically used in multipass rendering algorithms to achieve special effects, such as decals, outlining, and constructive solid geometry rendering.

The stencil test conditionally eliminates a pixel based on the outcome of a comparison between the reference value and the value in the stencil buffer. To enable and disable the test, call glEnable and glDisable with argument GL_STENCIL_TEST. To specify actions based on the outcome of the stencil test, call glStencilOp or glStencilOpSeparate.

There can be two separate sets of *func*, *ref*, and *mask* parameters; one affects back-facing polygons, and the other affects front-facing polygons as well as other non-polygon primitives. glStencilFunc sets both front and back stencil state to the same values, as if glStencilFuncSeparate were called with *face* set to GL_FRONT_AND_BACK.

func is a symbolic constant that determines the stencil comparison function. It accepts one of eight values, shown in the following list. *ref* is an integer reference value that is used in the stencil comparison. It is clamped to the range $[0, 2^n - 1]$, where n is the number of bitplanes in the stencil buffer. *mask* is bitwise ANDed with both the reference value and the stored stencil value, with the ANDed values participating in the comparison.

If *stencil* represents the value stored in the corresponding stencil buffer location, the following list shows the effect of each comparison function that can be specified by *func*. Only if the comparison succeeds is the pixel passed through to the next stage in the rasterization process (see glStencilOp). All tests treat *stencil* values as unsigned integers in the range $[0, 2^n - 1]$, where n is the number of bitplanes in the stencil buffer.

The following values are accepted by *func*:

GL_NEVER
Always fails.
GL_LESS
Passes if (ref & mask) < (stencil & mask).
GL_LEQUAL
Passes if (ref & mask) <= (stencil & mask).
GL_GREATER
Passes if (ref & mask) > (stencil & mask).
GL_GEQUAL
Passes if (ref & mask) >= (stencil & mask).
GL_EQUAL
Passes if (ref & mask) = (stencil & mask).
GL_NOTEQUAL
Passes if (ref & mask) != (stencil & mask).
GL_ALWAYS
Always passes.

Notes

glStencilFuncSeparate is available only if the GL version is 2.0 or greater.
Initially, the stencil test is disabled. If there is no stencil buffer, no stencil modification can occur and it is as if the stencil test always passes.

Errors

GL_INVALID_ENUM is generated if *func* is not one of the eight accepted values.
GL_INVALID_OPERATION is generated if glStencilFuncSeparate is executed between the execution of glBegin and the corresponding execution of glEnd.

Associated Gets

glGet with argument GL_STENCIL_FUNC, GL_STENCIL_VALUE_MASK, GL_STENCIL_REF, GL_STENCIL_BACK_FUNC, GL_STENCIL_BACK_VALUE_MASK, GL_STENCIL_BACK_REF, or GL_STENCIL_BITS
glIsEnabled with argument GL_STENCIL_TEST

See Also

glAlphaFunc, glBlendFunc, glDepthFunc, glEnable, glLogicOp, glStencilFunc, glStencilMask, glStencilMaskSeparate, glStencilOp, glStencilOpSeparate

glStencilMask

Control the front and back writing of individual bits in the stencil planes

C Specification

void **glStencilMask**(GLuint *mask*);

Parameters

mask   Specifies a bit mask to enable and disable writing of individual bits in the stencil planes. Initially, the mask is all 1's.

Description

glStencilMask controls the writing of individual bits in the stencil planes. The least significant *n* bits of *mask*, where *n* is the number of bits in the stencil buffer, specify a mask. Where a 1 appears in the mask, it's possible to write to the corresponding bit in the stencil buffer. Where a 0 appears, the corresponding bit is write-protected. Initially, all bits are enabled for writing.

There can be two separate *mask* writemasks; one affects back-facing polygons, and the other affects front-facing polygons as well as other non-polygon primitives. glStencilMask sets both front and back stencil writemasks to the same values. Use glStencilMaskSeparate to set front and back stencil writemasks to different values.

Notes

glStencilMask is the same as calling glStencilMaskSeparate with *face* set to GL_FRONT_AND_BACK.

Errors

GL_INVALID_OPERATION is generated if glStencilMask is executed between the execution of glBegin and the corresponding execution of glEnd.

Associated Gets

glGet with argument GL_STENCIL_WRITEMASK, GL_STENCIL_BACK_WRITEMASK, or GL_STENCIL_BITS

See Also

glColorMask, glDepthMask, glIndexMask, glStencilFunc, glStencilFuncSeparate, glStencilMaskSeparate, glStencilOp, glStencilOpSeparate

glStencilMaskSeparate

Control the front and/or back writing of individual bits in the stencil planes

C Specification

```
void glStencilMaskSeparate(GLenum face,
                           GLuint mask);
```

Parameters

face   Specifies whether the front and/or back stencil writemask is updated. Three tokens are valid: GL_FRONT, GL_BACK, and GL_FRONT_AND_BACK.

mask   Specifies a bit mask to enable and disable writing of individual bits in the stencil planes. Initially, the mask is all 1's.

Description

glStencilMaskSeparate controls the writing of individual bits in the stencil planes. The least significant n bits of *mask*, where n is the number of bits in the stencil buffer, specify a mask. Where a 1 appears in the mask, it's possible to write to the corresponding bit in the stencil buffer. Where a 0 appears, the corresponding bit is write-protected. Initially, all bits are enabled for writing.

There can be two separate *mask* writemasks; one affects back-facing polygons, and the other affects front-facing polygons as well as other non-polygon primitives. glStencilMask sets both front and back stencil writemasks to the same values, as if glStencilMaskSeparate were called with *face* set to GL_FRONT_AND_BACK.

Notes

glStencilMaskSeparate is available only if the GL version is 2.0 or greater.

Errors

GL_INVALID_OPERATION is generated if glStencilMaskSeparate is executed between the execution of glBegin and the corresponding execution of glEnd.

Associated Gets

glGet with argument GL_STENCIL_WRITEMASK, GL_STENCIL_BACK_WRITEMASK, or GL_STENCIL_BITS

See Also

glColorMask, glDepthMask, glIndexMask, glStencilFunc, glStencilFuncSeparate, glStencilMask, glStencilOp, glStencilOpSeparate

glStencilOp

Set front and back stencil test actions

C Specification

```
void glStencilOp(GLenum sfail,
                 GLenum dpfail,
                 GLenum dppass);
```

Parameters

sfail   Specifies the action to take when the stencil test fails. Eight symbolic constants are accepted: GL_KEEP, GL_ZERO, GL_REPLACE, GL_INCR, GL_INCR_WRAP, GL_DECR, GL_DECR_WRAP, and GL_INVERT. The initial value is GL_KEEP.

dpfail   Specifies the stencil action when the stencil test passes, but the depth test fails. *dpfail* accepts the same symbolic constants as *sfail*. The initial value is GL_KEEP.

dppass   Specifies the stencil action when both the stencil test and the depth test pass, or when the stencil test passes and either there is no depth buffer or depth testing is not enabled. *dppass* accepts the same symbolic constants as *sfail*. The initial value is GL_KEEP.

Description

Stenciling, like depth-buffering, enables and disables drawing on a per-pixel basis. You draw into the stencil planes using GL drawing primitives, then render geometry and images, using the stencil planes to mask out portions of the screen. Stenciling is typically used in multipass rendering algorithms to achieve special effects, such as decals, outlining, and constructive solid geometry rendering.

The stencil test conditionally eliminates a pixel based on the outcome of a comparison between the value in the stencil buffer and a reference value. To enable and disable the test, call glEnable and glDisable with argument GL_STENCIL_TEST; to control it, call glStencilFunc or glStencilFuncSeparate.

There can be two separate sets of *sfail, dpfail*, and *dppass* parameters; one affects back-facing polygons, and the other affects front-facing polygons as well as other non-polygon primitives. glStencilOp sets both front and back stencil state to the same values. Use glStencilOpSeparate to set front and back stencil state to different values.

glStencilOp takes three arguments that indicate what happens to the stored stencil value while stenciling is enabled. If the stencil test fails, no change is made to the pixel's color or depth buffers, and *sfail* specifies what happens to the stencil buffer contents. The following eight actions are possible.

GL_KEEP
Keeps the current value.

GL_ZERO
Sets the stencil buffer value to 0.

GL_REPLACE
Sets the stencil buffer value to *ref*, as specified by glStencilFunc.

GL_INCR
Increments the current stencil buffer value. Clamps to the maximum representable unsigned value.

GL_INCR_WRAP
Increments the current stencil buffer value. Wraps stencil buffer value to zero when incrementing the maximum representable unsigned value.

GL_DECR
Decrements the current stencil buffer value. Clamps to 0.

GL_DECR_WRAP
Decrements the current stencil buffer value. Wraps stencil buffer value to the maximum representable unsigned value when decrementing a stencil buffer value of zero.

GL_INVERT
Bitwise inverts the current stencil buffer value.

Stencil buffer values are treated as unsigned integers. When incremented and decremented, values are clamped to 0 and $2^n - 1$, where n is the value returned by querying GL_STENCIL_BITS.

The other two arguments to glStencilOp specify stencil buffer actions that depend on whether subsequent depth buffer tests succeed (*dppass*) or fail (*dpfail*) (see glDepthFunc). The actions are specified using the same eight symbolic constants as *sfail*. Note that *dpfail* is ignored when there is no depth buffer, or when the depth buffer is not enabled. In these cases, *sfail* and *dppass* specify stencil action when the stencil test fails and passes, respectively.

Notes

GL_DECR_WRAP and GL_INCR_WRAP are available only if the GL version is 1.4 or greater.

Initially the stencil test is disabled. If there is no stencil buffer, no stencil modification can occur and it is as if the stencil tests always pass, regardless of any call to glStencilOp.

glStencilOp is the same as calling glStencilOpSeparate with *face* set to GL_FRONT_AND_BACK.

Errors

GL_INVALID_ENUM is generated if *sfail*, *dpfail*, or *dppass* is any value other than the eight defined constant values.

GL_INVALID_OPERATION is generated if glStencilOp is executed between the execution of glBegin and the corresponding execution of glEnd.

Associated Gets

glGet with argument GL_STENCIL_FAIL, GL_STENCIL_PASS_DEPTH_PASS, GL_STENCIL_PASS_DEPTH_FAIL, GL_STENCIL_BACK_FAIL, GL_STENCIL_BACK_PASS_DEPTH_PASS, GL_STENCIL_BACK_PASS_DEPTH_FAIL, or GL_STENCIL_BITS

glIsEnabled with argument GL_STENCIL_TEST

See Also

glAlphaFunc, glBlendFunc, glDepthFunc, glEnable, glLogicOp, glStencilFunc, glStencilFuncSeparate, glStencilMask, glStencilMaskSeparate, glStencilOpSeparate

glStencilOpSeparate

Set front and/or back stencil test actions

C Specification

```
void glStencilOpSeparate(GLenum face,
                         GLenum sfail,
                         GLenum dpfail,
                         GLenum  dppass);
```

Parameters

face   Specifies whether front and/or back stencil state is updated. Three tokens are valid: GL_FRONT, GL_BACK, and GL_FRONT_AND_BACK.

sfail   Specifies the action to take when the stencil test fails. Eight symbolic constants are accepted: GL_KEEP, GL_ZERO, GL_REPLACE, GL_INCR, GL_INCR_WRAP, GL_DECR, GL_DECR_WRAP, and GL_INVERT. The initial value is GL_KEEP.

dpfail   Specifies the stencil action when the stencil test passes, but the depth test fails. dpfail accepts the same symbolic constants as *sfail*. The initial value is GL_KEEP.

dppass   Specifies the stencil action when both the stencil test and the depth test pass, or when the stencil test passes and either there is no depth buffer or depth testing is not enabled. *dppass* accepts the same symbolic constants as *sfail*. The initial value is GL_KEEP.

Description

Stenciling, like depth-buffering, enables and disables drawing on a per-pixel basis. You draw into the stencil planes using GL drawing primitives, then render geometry and images, using the stencil planes to mask out portions of the screen. Stenciling is typically used in multipass rendering algorithms to achieve special effects, such as decals, outlining, and constructive solid geometry rendering.

The stencil test conditionally eliminates a pixel based on the outcome of a comparison between the value in the stencil buffer and a reference value. To enable and disable the test, call glEnable and glDisable with argument GL_STENCIL_TEST; to control it, call glStencilFunc or glStencilFuncSeparate.

There can be two separate sets of *sfail*, *dpfail*, and *dppass* parameters; one affects back-facing polygons, and the other affects front-facing polygons as well as other non-polygon primitives. glStencilOp sets both front and back stencil state to the same values, as if glStencilOpSeparate were called with *face* set to GL_FRONT_AND_BACK.

glStencilOpSeparate takes three arguments that indicate what happens to the stored stencil value while stenciling is enabled. If the stencil test fails, no change is made to the pixel's color or depth buffers, and *sfail* specifies what happens to the stencil buffer contents. The following eight actions are possible.

GL_KEEP

Keeps the current value.

GL_ZERO

Sets the stencil buffer value to 0.

GL_REPLACE

Sets the stencil buffer value to *ref*, as specified by glStencilFunc.

GL_INCR

Increments the current stencil buffer value. Clamps to the maximum representable unsigned value.

GL_INCR_WRAP

Increments the current stencil buffer value. Wraps stencil buffer value to zero when incrementing the maximum representable unsigned value.

GL_DECR

Decrements the current stencil buffer value. Clamps to 0.

GL_DECR_WRAP

Decrements the current stencil buffer value. Wraps stencil buffer value to the maximum representable unsigned value when decrementing a stencil buffer value of zero.

GL_INVERT

Bitwise inverts the current stencil buffer value.

Stencil buffer values are treated as unsigned integers. When incremented and decremented, values are clamped to 0 and $2^n - 1$, where n is the value returned by querying GL_STENCIL_BITS.

The other two arguments to glStencilOpSeparate specify stencil buffer actions that depend on whether subsequent depth buffer tests succeed (*dppass*) or fail (*dpfail*) (see glDepthFunc). The actions are specified using the same eight symbolic constants as *sfail*. Note that *dpfail* is ignored when there is no depth buffer, or when the depth buffer is not enabled. In these cases, *sfail* and *dppass* specify stencil action when the stencil test fails and passes, respectively.

Notes

glStencilOpSeparate is available only if the GL version is 2.0 or greater.

Initially the stencil test is disabled. If there is no stencil buffer, no stencil modification can occur and it is as if the stencil test always passes.

Errors

GL_INVALID_ENUM is generated if *face* is any value other than GL_FRONT, GL_BACK, or GL_FRONT_AND_BACK.

GL_INVALID_ENUM is generated if *sfail*, *dpfail*, or *dppass* is any value other than the eight defined constant values.

GL_INVALID_OPERATION is generated if glStencilOpSeparate is executed between the execution of glBegin and the corresponding execution of glEnd.

Associated Gets

glGet with argument GL_STENCIL_FAIL, GL_STENCIL_PASS_DEPTH_PASS, GL_STENCIL_PASS_DEPTH_FAIL, GL_STENCIL_BACK_FAIL, GL_STENCIL_BACK_PASS_DEPTH_PASS, GL_STENCIL_BACK_PASS_DEPTH_FAIL, or GL_STENCIL_BITS
glIsEnabled with argument GL_STENCIL_TEST

See Also

glAlphaFunc, glBlendFunc, glDepthFunc, glEnable, glLogicOp, glStencilFunc, glStencilFuncSeparate, glStencilMask, glStencilMaskSeparate, glStencilOp

glTexCoord

Set the current texture coordinates

C Specification

```
void glTexCoord1s(GLshort  s);
void glTexCoord1i(GLint    s);
void glTexCoord1f(GLfloat  s);
void glTexCoord1d(GLdouble s);
void glTexCoord2s(GLshort  s, GLshort t);
void glTexCoord2i(GLint    s, GLint t);
void glTexCoord2f(GLfloat  s, GLfloat t);
void glTexCoord2d(GLdouble s, GLdouble t);
void glTexCoord3s(GLshort  s,
                  GLshort  t,
                  GLshort  r);
void glTexCoord3i(GLint    s, GLint t, GLint r);
void glTexCoord3f(GLfloat  s,
                  GLfloat  t,
                  GLfloat  r);
void glTexCoord3d(GLdouble s,
                  GLdouble t,
                  GLdouble r);
void glTexCoord4s(GLshort  s,
                  GLshort  t,
                  GLshort  r,
                  GLshort  q);
void glTexCoord4i(GLint    s,
                  GLint    t,
                  GLint    r,
                  GLint    q);
void glTexCoord4f(GLfloat  s,
                  GLfloat  t,
                  GLfloat  r,
                  GLfloat  q);
void glTexCoord4d(GLdouble s,
                  GLdouble t,
                  GLdouble r,
                  GLdouble q);
```

Parameters

s, t, r, q Specify s, t, r, and q texture coordinates. Not all parameters are present in all forms of the command.

C Specification

```
void glTexCoord1sv(const GLshort * v);
void glTexCoord1iv(const GLint * v);
void glTexCoord1fv(const GLfloat * v);
void glTexCoord1dv(const GLdouble * v);
void glTexCoord2sv(const GLshort * v);
void glTexCoord2iv(const GLint * v);
void glTexCoord2fv(const GLfloat * v);
void glTexCoord2dv(const GLdouble * v);
void glTexCoord3sv(const GLshort * v);
void glTexCoord3iv(const GLint * v);
void glTexCoord3fv(const GLfloat * v);
void glTexCoord3dv(const GLdouble * v);
void glTexCoord4sv(const GLshort * v);
void glTexCoord4iv(const GLint * v);
void glTexCoord4fv(const GLfloat * v);
void glTexCoord4dv(const GLdouble * v);
```

Parameters

v   Specifies a pointer to an array of one, two, three, or four elements, which in turn specify the s, t, r, and q texture coordinates.

Description

glTexCoord specifies texture coordinates in one, two, three, or four dimensions. glTexCoord1 sets the current texture coordinates to $(s,0,0,1)$; a call to glTexCoord2 sets them to $(s,t,0,1)$. Similarly, glTexCoord3 specifies the texture coordinates as $(s,t,r,1)$, and glTexCoord4 defines all four components explicitly as (s,t,r,q).

The current texture coordinates are part of the data that is associated with each vertex and with the current raster position. Initially, the values for s, t, r, and q are $(0, 0, 0, 1)$.

Notes

The current texture coordinates can be updated at any time. In particular, glTexCoord can be called between a call to glBegin and the corresponding call to glEnd.

When the ARB_imaging extension is supported, glTexCoord always updates texture unit GL_TEXTURE0.

Associated Gets

glGet with argument GL_CURRENT_TEXTURE_COORDS

See Also

glMultiTexCoord, glTexCoordPointer, glVertex

glTexCoordPointer

Define an array of texture coordinates

C Specification

```
void glTexCoordPointer(GLint      size,
                       GLenum     type,
                       GLsizei    stride,
                       const GLvoid * pointer);
```

Parameters

size   Specifies the number of coordinates per array element. Must be 1, 2, 3, or 4. The initial value is 4.

type   Specifies the data type of each texture coordinate. Symbolic constants GL_SHORT, GL_INT, GL_FLOAT, or GL_DOUBLE are accepted. The initial value is GL_FLOAT.

stride   Specifies the byte offset between consecutive texture coordinate sets. If *stride* is 0, the array elements are understood to be tightly packed. The initial value is 0.

pointer   Specifies a pointer to the first coordinate of the first texture coordinate set in the array. The initial value is 0.

Description

glTexCoordPointer specifies the location and data format of an array of texture coordinates to use when rendering. *size* specifies the number of coordinates per texture coordinate set, and must be 1, 2, 3, or 4. *type* specifies the data type of each texture coordinate, and *stride* specifies the byte stride from one texture coordinate set to the next, allowing vertices and attributes to be packed into a single array or stored in separate arrays. (Single-array storage may be more efficient on some implementations; see glInterleavedArrays.)

If a nonzero named buffer object is bound to the GL_ARRAY_BUFFER target (see glBindBuffer) while a texture coordinate array is specified, *pointer* is treated as a byte offset into the buffer object's data store. Also, the buffer object binding (GL_ARRAY_BUFFER_BINDING) is saved as texture coordinate vertex array client-side state (GL_TEXTURE_COORD_ARRAY_BUFFER_BINDING).

When a texture coordinate array is specified, *size*, *type*, *stride*, and *pointer* are saved as client-side state, in addition to the current vertex array buffer object binding.

To enable and disable a texture coordinate array, call glEnableClientState and glDisableClientState with the argument GL_TEXTURE_COORD_ARRAY. If enabled, the texture coordinate array is used when glArrayElement, glDrawArrays, glMultiDrawArrays, glDrawElements, glMultiDrawElements, or glDrawRangeElements is called.

Notes

glTexCoordPointer is available only if the GL version is 1.1 or greater.

For OpenGL versions 1.3 and greater, or when the ARB_multitexture extension is supported, glTexCoordPointer updates the texture coordinate array state of the active client texture unit, specified with glClientActiveTexture.

Each texture coordinate array is initially disabled and isn't accessed when glArrayElement, glDrawElements, glDrawRangeElements, glDrawArrays, glMultiDrawArrays, or glMultiDrawElements is called.

Execution of glTexCoordPointer is not allowed between the execution of glBegin and the corresponding execution of glEnd, but an error may or may not be generated. If no error is generated, the operation is undefined.

glTexCoordPointer is typically implemented on the client side.

Texture coordinate array parameters are client-side state and are therefore not saved or restored by glPushAttrib and glPopAttrib. Use glPushClientAttrib and glPopClientAttrib instead.

Errors

GL_INVALID_VALUE is generated if *size* is not 1, 2, 3, or 4.
GL_INVALID_ENUM is generated if *type* is not an accepted value.
GL_INVALID_VALUE is generated if *stride* is negative.

Associated Gets

glIsEnabled with argument GL_TEXTURE_COORD_ARRAY
glGet with argument GL_TEXTURE_COORD_ARRAY_SIZE
glGet with argument GL_TEXTURE_COORD_ARRAY_TYPE

glGet with argument GL_TEXTURE_COORD_ARRAY_STRIDE
glGet with argument GL_TEXTURE_COORD_ARRAY_BUFFER_BINDING
glGet with argument GL_ARRAY_BUFFER_BINDING
glGetPointerv with argument GL_TEXTURE_COORD_ARRAY_POINTER

See Also

glArrayElement, glBindBuffer, glClientActiveTexture, glColorPointer,
glDisableClientState, glDrawArrays, glDrawElements, glDrawRangeElements,
glEdgeFlagPointer, glEnableClientState, glFogCoordPointer, glIndexPointer,
glInterleavedArrays, glMultiDrawArrays, glMultiDrawElements, glMultiTexCoord,
glNormalPointer, glPopClientAttrib, glPushClientAttrib, glSecondaryColorPointer,
glTexCoord, glVertexAttribPointer, glVertexPointer

glTexEnv

Set texture environment parameters

C Specification

```
void glTexEnvf(GLenum   target,
               GLenum   pname,
               GLfloat  param);
void glTexEnvi(GLenum   target,
               GLenum   pname,
               GLint    param);
```

Parameters

target Specifies a texture environment. May be GL_TEXTURE_ENV,
          GL_TEXTURE_FILTER_CONTROL or GL_POINT_SPRITE.

pname   Specifies the symbolic name of a single-valued texture environment parameter. May be
          either GL_TEXTURE_ENV_MODE, GL_TEXTURE_LOD_BIAS, GL_COMBINE_RGB,
          GL_COMBINE_ALPHA, GL_SRC0_RGB, GL_SRC1_RGB, GL_SRC2_RGB, GL_SRC0_ALPHA,
          GL_SRC1_ALPHA, GL_SRC2_ALPHA, GL_OPERAND0_RGB, GL_OPERAND1_RGB,
          GL_OPERAND2_RGB, GL_OPERAND0_ALPHA, GL_OPERAND1_ALPHA, GL_OPERAND2_ALPHA,
          GL_RGB_SCALE, GL_ALPHA_SCALE, or GL_COORD_REPLACE.

param   Specifies a single symbolic constant, one of GL_ADD, GL_ADD_SIGNED, GL_INTERPOLATE,
          GL_MODULATE, GL_DECAL, GL_BLEND, GL_REPLACE, GL_SUBTRACT, GL_COMBINE,
          GL_TEXTURE, GL_CONSTANT, GL_PRIMARY_COLOR, GL_PREVIOUS, GL_SRC_COLOR,
          GL_ONE_MINUS_SRC_COLOR, GL_SRC_ALPHA, GL_ONE_MINUS_SRC_ALPHA, a single
          boolean value for the point sprite texture coordinate replacement, a single floating-point
          value for the texture level-of-detail bias, or 1.0, 2.0, or 4.0 when specifying the
          GL_RGB_SCALE or GL_ALPHA_SCALE.

C Specification

```
void glTexEnvfv(GLenum          target,
                GLenum          pname,
                const GLfloat * params);
void glTexEnviv(GLenum          target,
                GLenum          pname,
                const GLint *   params);
```

Parameters

target Specifies a texture environment. May be either GL_TEXTURE_ENV, or
          GL_TEXTURE_FILTER_CONTROL.

pname   Specifies the symbolic name of a texture environment parameter. Accepted values are
             GL_TEXTURE_ENV_MODE, GL_TEXTURE_ENV_COLOR, or GL_TEXTURE_LOD_BIAS.

params   Specifies a pointer to a parameter array that contains either a single symbolic constant,
             single floating-point number, or an RGBA color.

Description

A texture environment specifies how texture values are interpreted when a fragment is textured.
When *target* is GL_TEXTURE_FILTER_CONTROL, *pname* must be GL_TEXTURE_LOD_BIAS. When
target is GL_TEXTURE_ENV, *pname* can be GL_TEXTURE_ENV_MODE, GL_TEXTURE_ENV_COLOR,
GL_COMBINE_RGB, GL_COMBINE_ALPHA, RGB_SCALE, ALPHA_SCALE, SRC0_RGB, SRC1_RGB,
SRC2_RGB, SRC0_ALPHA, SRC1_ALPHA, or SRC2_ALPHA.

If *pname* is GL_TEXTURE_ENV_MODE, then *params* is (or points to) the symbolic name of a texture
function. Six texture functions may be specified: GL_ADD, GL_MODULATE, GL_DECAL, GL_BLEND,
GL_REPLACE, or GL_COMBINE.

A texture function acts on the fragment to be textured using the texture image value that applies
to the fragment (see glTexParameter) and produces an RGBA color for that fragment. The following
table shows how the RGBA color is produced for each of the three texture functions that can be
chosen. C is a triple of color values (RGB) and A is the associated alpha value. RGBA values extracted
from a texture image are in the range [0,1]. The subscript f refers to the incoming fragment, the
subscript t to the texture image, the subscript c to the texture environment color, and subscript v indicates a value produced by the texture function.

A texture image can have up to four components per texture element (see glTexImage1D,
glTexImage2D, glTexImage3D, glCopyTexImage1D, and glCopyTexImage2D). In a one-
component image, L_t indicates that single component. A two-component image uses L_t and A_t. A
three-component image has only a color value, C_t. A four-component image has both a color value C_t
and an alpha value A_t.

Texture Base Internal Format	GL_MODULATE Function	GL_DECAL Function	GL_BLEND Function
GL_ALPHA	$C_v = C_f$ $A_v = A_f A_t$	undefined	$C_v = C_f$ $A_v = A_f A_t$
GL_LUMINANCE (or 1)	$C_v = L_t C_f$ $A_v = A_f$	undefined	$C_v = (1 - L_t)C_f$ $A_v = A_f$
GL_LUMINANCE_ALPHA (or 2)	$C_v = L_t C_f$ $A_v = A_t A_f$	undefined	$C_v = (1 - L_t)C_f$ $A_v = A_t A_f$
GL_INTENSITY	$C_v = C_f I_t$ $A_v = A_f I_t$	undefined	$C_v = (1 - I_t)C_f$ $A_v = (1 - I_t)A_f$
GL_RGB (or 3)	$C_v = C_t C_f$ $A_v = A_f$	$C_v = C_t$ $A_v = A_f$	$C_v = (1 - C_t)C_f$ $A_v = A_f$
GL_RGBA (or 4)	$C_v = C_t C_f$ $A_v = A_t A_f$	$C_v = (1 - A_t) C_f + A_t C_t$ $A_v = A_f$	$C_v = (1 - C_t)C_f$ $A_v = A_t A_f$

Texture Base Internal Format	GL_REPLACE Function	GL_ADD Function
GL_ALPHA	$C_v = C_f$ $A_v = A_t$	$C_v = C_f$ $A_v = A_f A_t$
GL_LUMINANCE (or 1)	$C_v = L_t$ $A_v = A_f$	$C_v = C_f + L_t$ $A_v = A_f$

Texture Base Internal Format	GL_REPLACE Function	GL_ADD Function
GL_LUMINANCE_ALPHA	$C_v = L_t + L_tC_c$	$C_v = C_f + L_t$
(or 2)	$A_v = A_f$	$A_v = A_fA_t$
GL_INTENSITY	$C_v = I_t + I_tC_c$	$C_v = C_f + I_t$
	$A_v = I_t + I_tA_c$	$A_v = A_f + I_t$
GL_RGB	$C_v = C_t + C_tC_c$	$C_v = C_f + C_t$
(or 3)	$A_v = A_f$	$A_v = A_f$
GL_RGBA	$C_v = C_t + C_tC_c$	$C_v = C_f + C_t$
(or 4)	$A_v = A_t$	$A_v = A_t$

If *pname* is GL_TEXTURE_ENV_MODE, and *params* is GL_COMBINE, the form of the texture function depends on the values of GL_COMBINE_RGB and GL_COMBINE_ALPHA.

The following describes how the texture sources, as specified by GL_SRC0_RGB, GL_SRC1_RGB, GL_SRC2_RGB, GL_SRC0_ALPHA, GL_SRC1_ALPHA, and GL_SRC2_ALPHA, are combined to produce a final texture color. In the following tables, GL_SRC0_c is represented by *Arg0*, GL_SRC1_c is represented by *Arg1*, and GL_SRC2_c is represented by *Arg2*.

GL_COMBINE_RGB accepts any of GL_REPLACE, GL_MODULATE, GL_ADD, GL_ADD_SIGNED, GL_INTERPOLATE, GL_SUBTRACT, GL_DOT3_RGB, or GL_DOT3_RGBA.

GL_COMBINE_RGB	Texture Function
GL_REPLACE	*Arg0*
GL_MODULATE	$Arg0 \times Arg1$
GL_ADD	$Arg0 + Arg1$
GL_ADD_SIGNED	$Arg0 + Arg1 - 0.5$
GL_INTERPOLATE	$Arg0 \times Arg2 + Arg1 \times (1 - Arg2)$
GL_SUBTRACT	$Arg0 - Arg1$
GL_DOT3_RGB	$4 \times ((Arg0_r - 0.5) \times (Arg1_r - 0.5)) +$
or	$((Arg0_g - 0.5) \times (Arg1_g - 0.5)) +$
GL_DOT3_RGBA	$((Arg0_b - 0.5) \times (Arg1_b - 0.5))$

The scalar results for GL_DOT3_RGB and GL_DOT3_RGBA are placed into each of the 3 (RGB) or 4 (RGBA) components on output.

Likewise, GL_COMBINE_ALPHA accepts any of GL_REPLACE, GL_MODULATE, GL_ADD, GL_ADD_SIGNED, GL_INTERPOLATE, or GL_SUBTRACT. The following table describes how alpha values are combined:

GL_COMBINE_ALPHA	Texture Function
GL_REPLACE	*Arg0*
GL_MODULATE	$Arg0 \times Arg1$
GL_ADD	$Arg0 + Arg1$
GL_ADD_SIGNED	$Arg0 + Arg1 - 0.5$
GL_INTERPOLATE	$Arg0 \times Arg2 + Arg1 \times (1 - Arg2)$
GL_SUBTRACT	$Arg0 - Arg1$

In the following tables, the value C_s represents the color sampled from the currently bound texture, C_c represents the constant texture-environment color, C_f represents the primary color of the incoming fragment, and C_p represents the color computed from the previous texture stage, or zero if processing texture stage 0. Likewise, A_s, A_c, A_p and A_p represent the respective alpha values.

The following table describes the values assigned to *Arg0*, *Arg1*, and *Arg2* based upon the RGB sources and operands:

GL_SRCn_RGB	GL_OPERANDn_RGB	Argument Value
GL_TEXTURE	GL_SRC_COLOR	C_s
	GL_ONE_MINUS_SRC_COLOR	$1 - C_s$
	GL_SRC_ALPHA	A_s
	GL_ONE_MINUS_SRC_ALPHA	$1 - A_s$
GL_TEXTUREn	GL_SRC_COLOR	C_s
	GL_ONE_MINUS_SRC_COLOR	$1 - C_s$
	GL_SRC_ALPHA	A_s
	GL_ONE_MINUS_SRC_ALPHA	$1 - A_s$
GL_CONSTANT	GL_SRC_COLOR	C_c
	GL_ONE_MINUS_SRC_COLOR	$1 - C_c$
	GL_SRC_ALPHA	A_c
	GL_ONE_MINUS_SRC_ALPHA	$1 - A_c$
GL_PRIMARY_COLOR	GL_SRC_COLOR	C_f
	GL_ONE_MINUS_SRC_COLOR	$1 - C_f$
	GL_SRC_ALPHA	A_f
	GL_ONE_MINUS_SRC_ALPHA	$1 - A_f$
GL_PREVIOUS	GL_SRC_COLOR	C_p
	GL_ONE_MINUS_SRC_COLOR	$1 - C_p$
	GL_SRC_ALPHA	A_p
	GL_ONE_MINUS_SRC_ALPHA	$1 - A_p$

For GL_TEXTUREn sources, C_s and A_s represent the color and alpha, respectively, produced from texture stage *n*.

The follow table describes the values assigned to *Arg0*, *Arg1*, and *Arg2* based upon the alpha sources and operands:

GL_SRCn_ALPHA	GL_OPERANDn_ALPHA	Argument Value
GL_TEXTURE	GL_SRC_ALPHA	A_s
	GL_ONE_MINUS_SRC_ALPHA	$1 - A_s$
GL_TEXTUREn	GL_SRC_ALPHA	A_s
	GL_ONE_MINUS_SRC_ALPHA	$1 - A_s$
GL_CONSTANT	GL_SRC_ALPHA	A_c
	GL_ONE_MINUS_SRC_ALPHA	$1 - A_c$
GL_PRIMARY_COLOR	GL_SRC_ALPHA	A_f
	GL_ONE_MINUS_SRC_ALPHA	$1 - A_f$
GL_PREVIOUS	GL_SRC_ALPHA	A_p
	GL_ONE_MINUS_SRC_ALPHA	$1 - A_p$

The RGB and alpha results of the texture function are multipled by the values of GL_RGB_SCALE and GL_ALPHA_SCALE, respectively, and clamped to the range [0,1].

If *pname* is GL_TEXTURE_ENV_COLOR, *params* is a pointer to an array that holds an RGBA color consisting of four values. Integer color components are interpreted linearly such that the most positive integer maps to 1.0, and the most negative integer maps to -1.0. The values are clamped to the range [0,1] when they are specified. C_c takes these four values.

If *pname* is GL_TEXTURE_LOD_BIAS, the value specified is added to the texture level-of-detail parameter, that selects which mipmap, or mipmaps depending upon the selected GL_TEXTURE_MIN_FILTER, will be sampled.

GL_TEXTURE_ENV_MODE defaults to GL_MODULATE and GL_TEXTURE_ENV_COLOR defaults to (0, 0, 0, 0).

If *target* is GL_POINT_SPRITE and *pname* is GL_COORD_REPLACE, the boolean value specified is used to either enable or disable point sprite texture coordinate replacement. The default value is GL_FALSE.

Notes

GL_REPLACE may only be used if the GL version is 1.1 or greater.

GL_TEXTURE_FILTER_CONTROL and GL_TEXTURE_LOD_BIAS may only be used if the GL version is 1.4 or greater.

GL_COMBINE mode and its associated constants may only be used if the GL version is 1.3 or greater.

GL_TEXTUREn may only be used if the GL version is 1.4 or greater.

Internal formats other than 1, 2, 3, or 4 may only be used if the GL version is 1.1 or greater.

For OpenGL versions 1.3 and greater, or when the ARB_multitexture extension is supported, glTexEnv controls the texture environment for the current active texture unit, selected by glActiveTexture.

GL_POINT_SPRITE and GL_COORD_REPLACE are available only if the GL version is 2.0 or greater.

Errors

GL_INVALID_ENUM is generated when *target* or *pname* is not one of the accepted defined values, or when *params* should have a defined constant value (based on the value of *pname*) and does not.

GL_INVALID_VALUE is generated if the *params* value for GL_RGB_SCALE is not one of 1.0, 2.0, or 4.0.

GL_INVALID_OPERATION is generated if glTexEnv is executed between the execution of glBegin and the corresponding execution of glEnd.

Associated Gets

glGetTexEnv

See Also

glActiveTexture, glCopyPixels, glCopyTexImage1D, glCopyTexImage2D, glCopyTexSubImage1D, glCopyTexSubImage2D, glCopyTexSubImage3D, glTexImage1D, glTexImage2D, glTexImage3D, glTexParameter, glTexSubImage1D, glTexSubImage2D, glTexSubImage3D

glTexGen

Control the generation of texture coordinates

C Specification

```
void glTexGeni(GLenum    coord,
               GLenum    pname,
               GLint     param);
```

```
void glTexGenf(GLenum    coord,
               GLenum    pname,
               GLfloat   param);
void glTexGend(GLenum    coord,
               GLenum    pname,
               GLdouble  param);
```

Parameters

coord   Specifies a texture coordinate. Must be one of GL_S, GL_T, GL_R, or GL_Q.

pname   Specifies the symbolic name of the texture-coordinate generation function. Must be GL_TEXTURE_GEN_MODE.

param   Specifies a single-valued texture generation parameter, one of GL_OBJECT_LINEAR, GL_EYE_LINEAR, GL_SPHERE_MAP, GL_NORMAL_MAP, or GL_REFLECTION_MAP.

C Specification

```
void glTexGeniv(GLenum          coord,
                GLenum          pname,
                const GLint *   params);
void glTexGenfv(GLenum          coord,
                GLenum          pname,
                const GLfloat * params);
void glTexGendv(GLenum          coord,
                GLenum          pname,
                const GLdouble * params);
```

Parameters

coord   Specifies a texture coordinate. Must be one of GL_S, GL_T, GL_R, or GL_Q.

pname   Specifies the symbolic name of the texture-coordinate generation function or function parameters. Must be GL_TEXTURE_GEN_MODE, GL_OBJECT_PLANE, or GL_EYE_PLANE.

paramo Specifies a pointer to an array of texture generation parameters. If *pname* is GL_TEXTURE_GEN_MODE, then the array must contain a single symbolic constant, one of GL_OBJECT_LINEAR, GL_EYE_LINEAR, GL_SPHERE_MAP, GL_NORMAL_MAP, or GL_REFLECTION_MAP. Otherwise, *params* holds the coefficients for the texture-coordinate generation function specified by *pname*.

Description

glTexGen selects a texture-coordinate generation function or supplies coefficients for one of the functions. *coord* names one of the (s, t, r, q) texture coordinates; it must be one of the symbols GL_S, GL_T, GL_R, or GL_Q. *pname* must be one of three symbolic constants: GL_TEXTURE_GEN_MODE, GL_OBJECT_PLANE, or GL_EYE_PLANE. If pname is GL_TEXTURE_GEN_MODE, then *params* chooses a mode, one of GL_OBJECT_LINEAR, GL_EYE_LINEAR, GL_SPHERE_MAP, GL_NORMAL_MAP, or GL_REFLECTION_MAP. If *pname* is either GL_OBJECT_PLANE or GL_EYE_PLANE, *params* contains coefficients for the corresponding texture generation function.

If the texture generation function is GL_OBJECT_LINEAR, the function

$$g = p_1 \times x_o + p_2 \times y_o + p_3 \times z_o + p_4 \times w_o$$

is used, where g is the value computed for the coordinate named in *coord*, p_1, p_2, p_3, and p_4 are the four values supplied in *params*, and x_o, y_o, z_o, and w_o are the object coordinates of the vertex. This function can be used, for example, to texture-map terrain using sea level as a reference plane (defined by p_1, p_2, p_3, and p_4). The altitude of a terrain vertex is computed by the GL_OBJECT_LINEAR coordinate generation function as its distance from sea level; that altitude can then be used to index the texture image to map white snow onto peaks and green grass onto foothills.

If the texture generation function is GL_EYE_LINEAR, the function

$$g = p_1'' \times x_e + p_2'' \times y_e + p_3'' \times z_e + p_4'' \times w_e$$

is used, where

$$(p_1''\ p_2''\ p_3''\ p_4'') = (p_1 p_2 p_3 p_4)M^{-1}$$

and x_e, y_e, z_e, and w_e are the eye coordinates of the vertex, p_1, p_2, p_3, and p_4 are the values supplied in *params*, and M is the modelview matrix when glTexGen is invoked. If M is poorly conditioned or singular, texture coordinates generated by the resulting function may be inaccurate or undefined.

Note that the values in *params* define a reference plane in eye coordinates. The modelview matrix that is applied to them may not be the same one in effect when the polygon vertices are transformed. This function establishes a field of texture coordinates that can produce dynamic contour lines on moving objects.

If *pname* is GL_SPHERE_MAP and *coord* is either GL_S or GL_T, *s* and *t* texture coordinates are generated as follows. Let *u* be the unit vector pointing from the origin to the polygon vertex (in eye coordinates). Let *n* sup prime be the current normal, after transformation to eye coordinates. Let

$$f = (f_x f_y f_z)^T$$ be the reflection vector such that

$$f = u - 2n''n''^T u$$

Finally, let $2\sqrt{(f_x^2 + f_y^2 + (f_z + 1)^2)}$. Then the values assigned to the *s* and *t* texture coordinates are

$$s = \frac{f_x}{m} + \frac{1}{2}$$

$$t = \frac{f_y}{m} + \frac{1}{2}$$

To enable or disable a texture-coordinate generation function, call glEnable or glDisable with one of the symbolic texture-coordinate names (GL_TEXTURE_GEN_S, GL_TEXTURE_GEN_T, GL_TEXTURE_GEN_R, or GL_TEXTURE_GEN_Q) as the argument. When enabled, the specified texture coordinate is computed according to the generating function associated with that coordinate. When disabled, subsequent vertices take the specified texture coordinate from the current set of texture coordinates. Initially, all texture generation functions are set to GL_EYE_LINEAR and are disabled. Both *s* plane equations are (1, 0, 0, 0), both *t* plane equations are (0, 1, 0, 0), and all *r* and *q* plane equations are (0, 0, 0, 0).

When the ARB_multitexture extension is supported, glTexGen set the texture generation parameters for the currently active texture unit, selected with glActiveTexture.

Errors

GL_INVALID_ENUM is generated when *coord* or *pname* is not an accepted defined value, or when *pname* is GL_TEXTURE_GEN_MODE and *params* is not an accepted defined value.

GL_INVALID_ENUM is generated when *pname* is GL_TEXTURE_GEN_MODE, params is GL_SPHERE_MAP, and *coord* is either GL_R or GL_Q.

GL_INVALID_OPERATION is generated if glTexGen is executed between the execution of glBegin and the corresponding execution of glEnd.

Associated Gets

glGetTexGen
glIsEnabled with argument GL_TEXTURE_GEN_S
glIsEnabled with argument GL_TEXTURE_GEN_T
glIsEnabled with argument GL_TEXTURE_GEN_R
glIsEnabled with argument GL_TEXTURE_GEN_Q

See Also

glActiveTexture, glCopyPixels, glCopyTexImage2D, glCopyTexSubImage1D, glCopyTexSubImage2D, glCopyTexSubImage3D, glTexEnv, glTexImage1D, glTexImage2D, glTexImage3D, glTexParameter, glTexSubImage1D, glTexSubImage2D, glTexSubImage3D

glTexImage1D

Specify a one-dimensional texture image

C Specification

```
void glTexImage1D(GLenum          target,
                  GLint           level,
                  GLint           internalFormat,
                  GLsizei         width,
                  GLint           border,
                  GLenum          format,
                  GLenum          type,
                  const GLvoid *  data);
```

Parameters

target   Specifies the target texture. Must be GL_TEXTURE_1D or GL_PROXY_TEXTURE_1D.

level   Specifies the level-of-detail number. Level 0 is the base image level. Level *n* is the *n*th mipmap reduction image.

internalFormat Specifies the number of color components in the texture. Must be 1, 2, 3, or 4, or one of the following symbolic constants: GL_ALPHA, GL_ALPHA4, GL_ALPHA8, GL_ALPHA12, GL_ALPHA16, GL_COMPRESSED_ALPHA, GL_COMPRESSED_LUMINANCE, GL_COMPRESSED_LUMINANCE_ALPHA, GL_COMPRESSED_INTENSITY, GL_COMPRESSED_RGB, GL_COMPRESSED_RGBA, GL_DEPTH_COMPONENT, GL_DEPTH_COMPONENT16, GL_DEPTH_COMPONENT24, GL_DEPTH_COMPONENT32, GL_LUMINANCE, GL_LUMINANCE4, GL_LUMINANCE8, GL_LUMINANCE12, GL_LUMINANCE16, GL_LUMINANCE_ALPHA, GL_LUMINANCE4_ALPHA4, GL_LUMINANCE6_ALPHA2, GL_LUMINANCE8_ALPHA8, GL_LUMINANCE12_ALPHA4, GL_LUMINANCE12_ALPHA12, GL_LUMINANCE16_ALPHA16, GL_INTENSITY, GL_INTENSITY4, GL_INTENSITY8, GL_INTENSITY12, GL_INTENSITY16, GL_R3_G3_B2, GL_RGB, GL_RGB4, GL_RGB5, GL_RGB8, GL_RGB10, GL_RGB12, GL_RGB16, GL_RGBA, GL_RGBA2, GL_RGBA4, GL_RGB5_A1, GL_RGBA8, GL_RGB10_A2, GL_RGBA12, GL_RGBA16, GL_SLUMINANCE, GL_SLUMINANCE8, GL_SLUMINANCE_ALPHA, GL_SLUMINANCE8_ALPHA8, GL_SRGB, GL_SRGB8, GL_SRGB_ALPHA, or GL_SRGB8_ALPHA8.

width   Specifies the width of the texture image including the border if any. If the GL version does not support non-power-of-two sizes, this value must be 2^n + 2(*border*) for some integer *n*. All implementations support texture images that are at least 64 texels wide. The height of the 1D texture image is 1.

border   Specifies the width of the border. Must be either 0 or 1.

format   Specifies the format of the pixel data. The following symbolic values are accepted: GL_COLOR_INDEX, GL_RED, GL_GREEN, GL_BLUE, GL_ALPHA, GL_RGB, GL_BGR, GL_RGBA, GL_BGRA, GL_LUMINANCE, and GL_LUMINANCE_ALPHA.

type   Specifies the data type of the pixel data. The following symbolic values are accepted: GL_UNSIGNED_BYTE, GL_BYTE, GL_BITMAP, GL_UNSIGNED_SHORT, GL_SHORT, GL_UNSIGNED_INT, GL_INT, GL_FLOAT, GL_UNSIGNED_BYTE_3_3_2, GL_UNSIGNED_BYTE_2_3_3_REV, GL_UNSIGNED_SHORT_5_6_5, GL_UNSIGNED_SHORT_5_6_5_REV, GL_UNSIGNED_SHORT_4_4_4_4, GL_UNSIGNED_SHORT_4_4_4_4_REV, GL_UNSIGNED_SHORT_5_5_5_1, GL_UNSIGNED_SHORT_1_5_5_5_REV, GL_UNSIGNED_INT_8_8_8_8, GL_UNSIGNED_INT_8_8_8_8_REV, GL_UNSIGNED_INT_10_10_10_2, and GL_UNSIGNED_INT_2_10_10_10_REV.

data   Specifies a pointer to the image data in memory.

Description

Texturing maps a portion of a specified texture image onto each graphical primitive for which texturing is enabled. To enable and disable one-dimensional texturing, call glEnable and glDisable with argument GL_TEXTURE_1D.

Texture images are defined with glTexImage1D. The arguments describe the parameters of the texture image, such as width, width of the border, level-of-detail number (see glTexParameter), and the internal resolution and format used to store the image. The last three arguments describe how the image is represented in memory; they are identical to the pixel formats used for glDrawPixels.

If *target* is GL_PROXY_TEXTURE_1D, no data is read from *data*, but all of the texture image state is recalculated, checked for consistency, and checked against the implementation's capabilities. If the implementation cannot handle a texture of the requested texture size, it sets all of the image state to 0, but does not generate an error (see glGetError). To query for an entire mipmap array, use an image array level greater than or equal to 1.

If *target* is GL_TEXTURE_1D, data is read from *data* as a sequence of signed or unsigned bytes, shorts, or longs, or single-precision floating-point values, depending on *type*. These values are grouped into sets of one, two, three, or four values, depending on *format*, to form elements. If *type* is GL_BITMAP, the data is considered as a string of unsigned bytes (and *format* must be GL_COLOR_INDEX). Each data byte is treated as eight 1-bit elements, with bit ordering determined by GL_UNPACK_LSB_FIRST (see glPixelStore).

If a nonzero named buffer object is bound to the GL_PIXEL_UNPACK_BUFFER target (see glBindBuffer) while a texture image is specified, *data* is treated as a byte offset into the buffer object's data store.

The first element corresponds to the left end of the texture array. Subsequent elements progress left-to-right through the remaining texels in the texture array. The final element corresponds to the right end of the texture array.

format determines the composition of each element in *data*. It can assume one of these symbolic values:

GL_COLOR_INDEX

Each element is a single value, a color index. The GL converts it to fixed point (with an unspecified number of zero bits to the right of the binary point), shifted left or right depending on the value and sign of GL_INDEX_SHIFT, and added to GL_INDEX_OFFSET (see glPixelTransfer). The resulting index is converted to a set of color components using the GL_PIXEL_MAP_I_TO_R, GL_PIXEL_MAP_I_TO_G, GL_PIXEL_MAP_I_TO_B, and GL_PIXEL_MAP_I_TO_A tables, and clamped to the range [0,1].

GL_RED

Each element is a single red component. The GL converts it to floating point and assembles it into an RGBA element by attaching 0 for green and blue, and 1 for alpha. Each component is then multiplied by the signed scale factor GL_c_SCALE, added to the signed bias GL_c_BIAS, and clamped to the range [0,1] (see glPixelTransfer).

GL_GREEN

Each element is a single green component. The GL converts it to floating point and assembles it into an RGBA element by attaching 0 for red and blue, and 1 for alpha. Each component is then multiplied by the signed scale factor GL_c_SCALE, added to the signed bias GL_c_BIAS, and clamped to the range [0,1] (see glPixelTransfer).

GL_BLUE

Each element is a single blue component. The GL converts it to floating point and assembles it into an RGBA element by attaching 0 for red and green, and 1 for alpha. Each component is then multiplied by the signed scale factor GL_c_SCALE, added to the signed bias GL_c_BIAS, and clamped to the range [0,1] (see glPixelTransfer).

GL_ALPHA

Each element is a single alpha component. The GL converts it to floating point and assembles it into an RGBA element by attaching 0 for red, green, and blue. Each component is then multiplied by the signed scale factor GL_c_SCALE, added to the signed bias GL_c_BIAS, and clamped to the range [0,1] (see glPixelTransfer).

GL_INTENSITY

Each element is a single intensity value. The GL converts it to floating point, then assembles it into an RGBA element by replicating the intensity value three times for red, green, blue, and alpha. Each component is then multiplied by the signed scale factor GL_c_SCALE, added to the signed bias GL_c_BIAS, and clamped to the range [0,1] (see glPixelTransfer).

GL_RGB

GL_BGR

Each element is an RGB triple. The GL converts it to floating point and assembles it into an RGBA element by attaching 1 for alpha. Each component is then multiplied by the signed scale factor GL_c_SCALE, added to the signed bias GL_c_BIAS, and clamped to the range [0,1] (see glPixelTransfer).

GL_RGBA

GL_BGRA

Each element contains all four components. Each component is multiplied by the signed scale factor GL_c_SCALE, added to the signed bias GL_c_BIAS, and clamped to the range [0,1] (see glPixelTransfer).

GL_LUMINANCE

Each element is a single luminance value. The GL converts it to floating point, then assembles it into an RGBA element by replicating the luminance value three times for red, green, and blue and attaching 1 for alpha. Each component is then multiplied by the signed scale factor GL_c_SCALE, added to the signed bias GL_c_BIAS, and clamped to the range [0,1] (see glPixelTransfer).

GL_LUMINANCE_ALPHA

Each element is a luminance/alpha pair. The GL converts it to floating point, then assembles it into an RGBA element by replicating the luminance value three times for red, green, and blue. Each component is then multiplied by the signed scale factor GL_c_SCALE, added to the signed bias GL_c_BIAS, and clamped to the range [0,1] (see glPixelTransfer).

GL_DEPTH_COMPONENT

Each element is a single depth value. The GL converts it to floating point, multiplies by the signed scale factor GL_DEPTH_SCALE, adds the signed bias GL_DEPTH_BIAS, and clamps to the range [0,1] (see glPixelTransfer).

Refer to the glDrawPixels reference page for a description of the acceptable values for the *type* parameter.

If an application wants to store the texture at a certain resolution or in a certain format, it can request the resolution and format with *internalFormat*. The GL will choose an internal representation that closely approximates that requested by *internalFormat*, but it may not match exactly. (The representations specified by GL_LUMINANCE, GL_LUMINANCE_ALPHA, GL_RGB, and GL_RGBA must match exactly. The numeric values 1, 2, 3, and 4 may also be used to specify the above representations.)

If the *internalFormat* parameter is one of the generic compressed formats, GL_COMPRESSED_ALPHA, GL_COMPRESSED_INTENSITY, GL_COMPRESSED_LUMINANCE, GL_COMPRESSED_LUMINANCE_ALPHA, GL_COMPRESSED_RGB, or GL_COMPRESSED_RGBA, the GL will replace the internal format with the symbolic constant for a specific internal format and compress the texture before storage. If no corresponding internal format is available, or the GL can not compress that image for any reason, the internal format is instead replaced with a corresponding base internal format.

If the *internalFormat* parameter is GL_SRGB, GL_SRGB8, GL_SRGB_ALPHA, GL_SRGB8_ALPHA8, GL_SLUMINANCE, GL_SLUMINANCE8, GL_SLUMINANCE_ALPHA, or GL_SLUMINANCE8_ALPHA8, the texture is treated as if the red, green, blue, or luminance components are encoded in the sRGB color space. Any alpha component is left unchanged. The conversion from the sRGB encoded component c_s to a linear component c_l is:

$$c_l = \begin{cases} \dfrac{c_s}{12.92} & \text{if } c_s <= 0.04045 \\[2ex] (\dfrac{c_s + 0.055}{1.055})\,2.4 & \text{if } c_s > 0.04045 \end{cases}$$

Assume c_s is the sRGB component in the range [0,1].

Use the GL_PROXY_TEXTURE_1D target to try out a resolution and format. The implementation will update and recompute its best match for the requested storage resolution and format. To then query this state, call glGetTexLevelParameter. If the texture cannot be accommodated, texture state is set to 0.

A one-component texture image uses only the red component of the RGBA color from *data*. A two-component image uses the R and A values. A three-component image uses the R, G, and B values. A four-component image uses all of the RGBA components.

Depth textures can be treated as LUMINANCE, INTENSITY or ALPHA textures during texture filtering and application. Image-based shadowing can be enabled by comparing texture r coordinates to depth texture values to generate a boolean result. See glTexParameter for details on texture comparison.

Notes

Texturing has no effect in color index mode.

If the ARB_imaging extension is supported, RGBA elements may also be processed by the imaging pipeline. The following stages may be applied to an RGBA color before color component clamping to the range [0,1]:

1. Color component replacement by the color table specified for GL_COLOR_TABLE, if enabled. See glColorTable.
2. One-dimensional convolution filtering, if enabled. See glConvolutionFilter1D. If a convolution filter changes the *width* of the texture (by processing with a GL_CONVOLUTION_BORDER_MODE of GL_REDUCE, for example), the *width* must $2^n + 2(border)$, for some integer n, after filtering.
3. RGBA components may be multiplied by GL_POST_CONVOLUTION_c_SCALE, and added to GL_POST_CONVOLUTION_c_BIAS, if enabled. See glPixelTransfer.
4. Color component replacement by the color table specified for GL_POST_CONVOLUTION_COLOR_TABLE, if enabled. See glColorTable.
5. Transformation by the color matrix. See glMatrixMode.
6. RGBA components may be multiplied by GL_POST_COLOR_MATRIX_c_SCALE, and added to GL_POST_COLOR_MATRIX_c_BIAS, if enabled. See glPixelTransfer.
7. Color component replacement by the color table specified for GL_POST_COLOR_MATRIX_COLOR_TABLE, if enabled. See glColorTable.

The texture image can be represented by the same data formats as the pixels in a glDrawPixels command, except that GL_STENCIL_INDEX cannot be used. glPixelStore and glPixelTransfer modes affect texture images in exactly the way they affect glDrawPixels.

GL_PROXY_TEXTURE_1D may be used only if the GL version is 1.1 or greater.

Internal formats other than 1, 2, 3, or 4 may be used only if the GL version is 1.1 or greater.

In GL version 1.1 or greater, *data* may be a null pointer. In this case texture memory is allocated to accommodate a texture of width *width*. You can then download subtextures to initialize the texture memory. The image is undefined if the program tries to apply an uninitialized portion of the texture image to a primitive.

Formats GL_BGR, and GL_BGRA and types GL_UNSIGNED_BYTE_3_3_2, GL_UNSIGNED_BYTE_2_3_3_REV, GL_UNSIGNED_SHORT_5_6_5, GL_UNSIGNED_SHORT_5_6_5_REV, GL_UNSIGNED_SHORT_4_4_4_4, GL_UNSIGNED_SHORT_4_4_4_4_REV, GL_UNSIGNED_SHORT_5_5_5_1, GL_UNSIGNED_SHORT_1_5_5_5_REV, GL_UNSIGNED_INT_8_8_8_8, GL_UNSIGNED_INT_8_8_8_8_REV, GL_UNSIGNED_INT_10_10_10_2, and GL_UNSIGNED_INT_2_10_10_10_REV are available only if the GL version is 1.2 or greater.

When the ARB_multitexture extension is supported, or the GL version is 1.3 or greater, glTexImage1D specifies the one-dimensional texture for the current texture unit, specified with glActiveTexture.

GL_DEPTH_COMPONENT, GL_DEPTH_COMPONENT16, GL_DEPTH_COMPONENT24, and GL_DEPTH_COMPONENT32 are available only if the GL version is 1.4 or greater.

Non-power-of-two textures are supported if the GL version is 2.0 or greater, or if the implementation exports the GL_ARB_texture_non_power_of_two extension.

The GL_SRGB, GL_SRGB8, GL_SRGB_ALPHA, GL_SRGB8_ALPHA8, GL_SLUMINANCE, GL_SLUMINANCE8, GL_SLUMINANCE_ALPHA, and GL_SLUMINANCE8_ALPHA8 internal formats are only available if the GL version is 2.1 or greater.

Errors

GL_INVALID_ENUM is generated if *target* is not GL_TEXTURE_1D or GL_PROXY_TEXTURE_1D.

GL_INVALID_ENUM is generated if *format* is not an accepted format constant. Format constants other than GL_STENCIL_INDEX are accepted.

GL_INVALID_ENUM is generated if *type* is not a type constant.

GL_INVALID_ENUM is generated if *type* is GL_BITMAP and *format* is not GL_COLOR_INDEX.

GL_INVALID_VALUE is generated if *level* is less than 0.

GL_INVALID_VALUE may be generated if level is greater than $log_2(max)$, where *max* is the returned value of GL_MAX_TEXTURE_SIZE.

GL_INVALID_VALUE is generated if *internalFormat* is not 1, 2, 3, 4, or one of the accepted resolution and format symbolic constants.

GL_INVALID_VALUE is generated if *width* is less than 0 or greater than 2 + GL_MAX_TEXTURE_SIZE.

GL_INVALID_VALUE is generated if non-power-of-two textures are not supported and the *width* cannot be represented as $2^n + 2(border)$ for some integer value of *n*.

GL_INVALID_VALUE is generated if *border* is not 0 or 1.

GL_INVALID_OPERATION is generated if *type* is one of GL_UNSIGNED_BYTE_3_3_2, GL_UNSIGNED_BYTE_2_3_3_REV, GL_UNSIGNED_SHORT_5_6_5, or GL_UNSIGNED_SHORT_5_6_5_REV and *format* is not GL_RGB.

GL_INVALID_OPERATION is generated if *type* is one of GL_UNSIGNED_SHORT_4_4_4_4, GL_UNSIGNED_SHORT_4_4_4_4_REV, GL_UNSIGNED_SHORT_5_5_5_1, GL_UNSIGNED_SHORT_1_5_5_5_REV, GL_UNSIGNED_INT_8_8_8_8, GL_UNSIGNED_INT_8_8_8_8_REV, GL_UNSIGNED_INT_10_10_10_2, or GL_UNSIGNED_INT_2_10_10_10_REV and *format* is neither GL_RGBA nor GL_BGRA.

GL_INVALID_OPERATION is generated if *format* is GL_DEPTH_COMPONENT and internalFormat is not GL_DEPTH_COMPONENT, GL_DEPTH_COMPONENT16, GL_DEPTH_COMPONENT24, or GL_DEPTH_COMPONENT32.

GL_INVALID_OPERATION is generated if *internalFormat* is GL_DEPTH_COMPONENT, GL_DEPTH_COMPONENT16, GL_DEPTH_COMPONENT24, or GL_DEPTH_COMPONENT32, and *format* is not GL_DEPTH_COMPONENT.

GL_INVALID_OPERATION is generated if a nonzero buffer object name is bound to the GL_PIXEL_UNPACK_BUFFER target and the buffer object's data store is currently mapped.

GL_INVALID_OPERATION is generated if a nonzero buffer object name is bound to the GL_PIXEL_UNPACK_BUFFER target and the data would be unpacked from the buffer object such that the memory reads required would exceed the data store size.

GL_INVALID_OPERATION is generated if a nonzero buffer object name is bound to the GL_PIXEL_UNPACK_BUFFER target and *data* is not evenly divisible into the number of bytes needed to store in memory a datum indicated by type.

GL_INVALID_OPERATION is generated if glTexImage1D is executed between the execution of glBegin and the corresponding execution of glEnd.

Associated Gets

glGetTexImage
glIsEnabled with argument GL_TEXTURE_1D
glGet with argument GL_PIXEL_UNPACK_BUFFER_BINDING

See Also

glActiveTexture, glColorTable, glCompressedTexImage1D, glCompressedTexSubImage1D, glConvolutionFilter1D, glCopyPixels, glCopyTexImage1D, glCopyTexSubImage1D, glDrawPixels, glGetCompressedTexImage, glMatrixMode, glPixelStore, glPixelTransfer, glTexEnv, glTexGen, glTexImage2D, glTexImage3D, glTexSubImage1D, glTexSubImage2D, glTexSubImage3D, glTexParameter

glTexImage2D

Specify a two-dimensional texture image

C Specification

```
void glTexImage2D(GLenum        target,
                  GLint         level,
                  GLint         internalFormat,
                  GLsizei       width,
                  GLsizei       height,
                  GLint         border,
                  GLenum        format,
                  GLenum        type,
                  const GLvoid * data);
```

Parameters

target	Specifies the target texture. Must be GL_TEXTURE_2D, GL_PROXY_TEXTURE_2D, GL_TEXTURE_CUBE_MAP_POSITIVE_X, GL_TEXTURE_CUBE_MAP_NEGATIVE_X, GL_TEXTURE_CUBE_MAP_POSITIVE_Y, GL_TEXTURE_CUBE_MAP_NEGATIVE_Y, GL_TEXTURE_CUBE_MAP_POSITIVE_Z, GL_TEXTURE_CUBE_MAP_NEGATIVE_Z, or GL_PROXY_TEXTURE_CUBE_MAP.
level	Specifies the level-of-detail number. Level 0 is the base image level. Level *n* is the *n*th mipmap reduction image.
internalFormat	Specifies the number of color components in the texture. Must be 1, 2, 3, or 4, or one of the following symbolic constants: GL_ALPHA, GL_ALPHA4, GL_ALPHA8, GL_ALPHA12, GL_ALPHA16, GL_COMPRESSED_ALPHA, GL_COMPRESSED_LUMINANCE, GL_COMPRESSED_LUMINANCE_ALPHA, GL_COMPRESSED_INTENSITY, GL_COMPRESSED_RGB, GL_COMPRESSED_RGBA, GL_DEPTH_COMPONENT, GL_DEPTH_COMPONENT16, GL_DEPTH_COMPONENT24, GL_DEPTH_COMPONENT32, GL_LUMINANCE, GL_LUMINANCE4, GL_LUMINANCE8, GL_LUMINANCE12, GL_LUMINANCE16, GL_LUMINANCE_ALPHA, GL_LUMINANCE4_ALPHA4, GL_LUMINANCE6_ALPHA2,

	GL_LUMINANCE8_ALPHA8, GL_LUMINANCE12_ALPHA4, GL_LUMINANCE12_ALPHA12, GL_LUMINANCE16_ALPHA16, GL_INTENSITY, GL_INTENSITY4, GL_INTENSITY8, GL_INTENSITY12, GL_INTENSITY16, GL_R3_G3_B2, GL_RGB, GL_RGB4, GL_RGB5, GL_RGB8, GL_RGB10, GL_RGB12, GL_RGB16, GL_RGBA, GL_RGBA2, GL_RGBA4, GL_RGB5_A1, GL_RGBA8, GL_RGB10_A2, GL_RGBA12, GL_RGBA16, GL_SLUMINANCE, GL_SLUMINANCE8, GL_SLUMINANCE_ALPHA, GL_SLUMINANCE8_ALPHA8, GL_SRGB, GL_SRGB8, GL_SRGB_ALPHA, or GL_SRGB8_ALPHA8.

width
Specifies the width of the texture image including the border if any. If the GL version does not support non-power-of-two sizes, this value must be $2^n + 2(border)$ for some integer n. All implementations support texture images that are at least 64 texels wide.

height
Specifies the height of the texture image including the border if any. If the GL version does not support non-power-of-two sizes, this value must be $2^m + 2(border)$ for some integer m. All implementations support texture images that are at least 64 texels high.

border
Specifies the width of the border. Must be either 0 or 1.

format
Specifies the format of the pixel data. The following symbolic values are accepted: GL_COLOR_INDEX, GL_RED, GL_GREEN, GL_BLUE, GL_ALPHA, GL_RGB, GL_BGR, GL_RGBA, GL_BGRA, GL_LUMINANCE, and GL_LUMINANCE_ALPHA.

type
Specifies the data type of the pixel data. The following symbolic values are accepted: GL_UNSIGNED_BYTE, GL_BYTE, GL_BITMAP, GL_UNSIGNED_SHORT, GL_SHORT, GL_UNSIGNED_INT, GL_INT, GL_FLOAT, GL_UNSIGNED_BYTE_3_3_2, GL_UNSIGNED_BYTE_2_3_3_REV, GL_UNSIGNED_SHORT_5_6_5, GL_UNSIGNED_SHORT_5_6_5_REV, GL_UNSIGNED_SHORT_4_4_4_4, GL_UNSIGNED_SHORT_4_4_4_4_REV, GL_UNSIGNED_SHORT_5_5_5_1, GL_UNSIGNED_SHORT_1_5_5_5_REV, GL_UNSIGNED_INT_8_8_8_8, GL_UNSIGNED_INT_8_8_8_8_REV, GL_UNSIGNED_INT_10_10_10_2, and GL_UNSIGNED_INT_2_10_10_10_REV.

data
Specifies a pointer to the image data in memory.

Description

Texturing maps a portion of a specified texture image onto each graphical primitive for which texturing is enabled. To enable and disable two-dimensional texturing, call glEnable and glDisable with argument GL_TEXTURE_2D. To enable and disable texturing using cube-mapped texture, call glEnable and glDisable with argument GL_TEXTURE_CUBE_MAP.

To define texture images, call glTexImage2D. The arguments describe the parameters of the texture image, such as height, width, width of the border, level-of-detail number (see glTexParameter), and number of color components provided. The last three arguments describe how the image is represented in memory; they are identical to the pixel formats used for glDrawPixels.

If *target* is GL_PROXY_TEXTURE_2D or GL_PROXY_TEXTURE_CUBE_MAP, no data is read from *data*, but all of the texture image state is recalculated, checked for consistency, and checked against the implementation's capabilities. If the implementation cannot handle a texture of the requested texture size, it sets all of the image state to 0, but does not generate an error (see glGetError). To query for an entire mipmap array, use an image array level greater than or equal to 1.

If *target* is GL_TEXTURE_2D, or one of the GL_TEXTURE_CUBE_MAP targets, data is read from *data* as a sequence of signed or unsigned bytes, shorts, or longs, or single-precision floating-point values, depending on *type*. These values are grouped into sets of one, two, three, or four values, depending on *format*, to form elements. If *type* is GL_BITMAP, the data is considered as a string of unsigned bytes (and *format* must be GL_COLOR_INDEX). Each data byte is treated as eight 1-bit elements, with bit ordering determined by GL_UNPACK_LSB_FIRST (see glPixelStore).

If a nonzero named buffer object is bound to the GL_PIXEL_UNPACK_BUFFER target (see glBindBuffer) while a texture image is specified, data is treated as a byte offset into the buffer object's data store.

The first element corresponds to the lower-left corner of the texture image. Subsequent elements progress left-to-right through the remaining texels in the lowest row of the texture image, and then in successively higher rows of the texture image. The final element corresponds to the upper-right corner of the texture image.

format determines the composition of each element in *data*. It can assume one of these symbolic values:

GL_COLOR_INDEX

Each element is a single value, a color index. The GL converts it to fixed point (with an unspecified number of zero bits to the right of the binary point), shifted left or right depending on the value and sign of GL_INDEX_SHIFT, and added to GL_INDEX_OFFSET (see glPixelTransfer). The resulting index is converted to a set of color components using the GL_PIXEL_MAP_I_TO_R, GL_PIXEL_MAP_I_TO_G, GL_PIXEL_MAP_I_TO_B, and GL_PIXEL_MAP_I_TO_A tables, and clamped to the range [0,1].

GL_RED

Each element is a single red component. The GL converts it to floating point and assembles it into an RGBA element by attaching 0 for green and blue, and 1 for alpha. Each component is then multiplied by the signed scale factor GL_c_SCALE, added to the signed bias GL_c_BIAS, and clamped to the range [0,1] (see glPixelTransfer).

GL_GREEN

Each element is a single green component. The GL converts it to floating point and assembles it into an RGBA element by attaching 0 for red and blue, and 1 for alpha. Each component is then multiplied by the signed scale factor GL_c_SCALE, added to the signed bias GL_c_BIAS, and clamped to the range [0,1] (see glPixelTransfer).

GL_BLUE

Each element is a single blue component. The GL converts it to floating point and assembles it into an RGBA element by attaching 0 for red and green, and 1 for alpha. Each component is then multiplied by the signed scale factor GL_c_SCALE, added to the signed bias GL_c_BIAS, and clamped to the range [0,1] (see glPixelTransfer).

GL_ALPHA

Each element is a single alpha component. The GL converts it to floating point and assembles it into an RGBA element by attaching 0 for red, green, and blue. Each component is then multiplied by the signed scale factor GL_c_SCALE, added to the signed bias GL_c_BIAS, and clamped to the range [0,1] (see glPixelTransfer).

GL_INTENSITY

Each element is a single intensity value. The GL converts it to floating point, then assembles it into an RGBA element by replicating the intensity value three times for red, green, blue, and alpha. Each component is then multiplied by the signed scale factor GL_c_SCALE, added to the signed bias GL_c_BIAS, and clamped to the range [0,1] (see glPixelTransfer).

GL_RGB

GL_BGR

Each element is an RGB triple. The GL converts it to floating point and assembles it into an RGBA element by attaching 1 for alpha. Each component is then multiplied by the signed scale factor GL_c_SCALE, added to the signed bias GL_c_BIAS, and clamped to the range [0,1] (see glPixelTransfer).

GL_RGBA

GL_BGRA

Each element contains all four components. Each component is multiplied by the signed scale factor GL_c_SCALE, added to the signed bias GL_c_BIAS, and clamped to the range [0,1] (see glPixelTransfer).

GL_LUMINANCE

Each element is a single luminance value. The GL converts it to floating point, then assembles it into an RGBA element by replicating the luminance value three times for red, green, and blue and attaching 1 for alpha. Each component is then multiplied by the signed scale factor GL_c_SCALE, added to the signed bias GL_c_BIAS, and clamped to the range [0,1] (see glPixelTransfer).

GL_LUMINANCE_ALPHA

Each element is a luminance/alpha pair. The GL converts it to floating point, then assembles it into an RGBA element by replicating the luminance value three times for red, green, and blue. Each component is then multiplied by the signed scale factor GL_c_SCALE, added to the signed bias GL_c_BIAS, and clamped to the range [0,1] (see glPixelTransfer).

GL_DEPTH_COMPONENT

Each element is a single depth value. The GL converts it to floating point, multiplies by the signed scale factor GL_DEPTH_SCALE, adds the signed bias GL_DEPTH_BIAS, and clamps to the range [0,1] (see glPixelTransfer).

Refer to the glDrawPixels reference page for a description of the acceptable values for the *type* parameter.

If an application wants to store the texture at a certain resolution or in a certain format, it can request the resolution and format with *internalFormat*. The GL will choose an internal representation that closely approximates that requested by *internalFormat*, but it may not match exactly. (The representations specified by GL_LUMINANCE, GL_LUMINANCE_ALPHA, GL_RGB, and GL_RGBA must match exactly. The numeric values 1, 2, 3, and 4 may also be used to specify the above representations.)

If the *internalFormat* parameter is one of the generic compressed formats, GL_COMPRESSED_ALPHA, GL_COMPRESSED_INTENSITY, GL_COMPRESSED_LUMINANCE, GL_COMPRESSED_LUMINANCE_ALPHA, GL_COMPRESSED_RGB, or GL_COMPRESSED_RGBA, the GL will replace the internal format with the symbolic constant for a specific internal format and compress the texture before storage. If no corresponding internal format is available, or the GL can not compress that image for any reason, the internal format is instead replaced with a corresponding base internal format.

If the *internalFormat* parameter is GL_SRGB, GL_SRGB8, GL_SRGB_ALPHA, GL_SRGB8_ALPHA8, GL_SLUMINANCE, GL_SLUMINANCE8, GL_SLUMINANCE_ALPHA, or GL_SLUMINANCE8_ALPHA8, the texture is treated as if the red, green, blue, or luminance components are encoded in the sRGB color space. Any alpha component is left unchanged. The conversion from the sRGB encoded component c_s to a linear component c_l is:

$$c_l = \begin{cases} \dfrac{c_s}{12.92} & \text{if } c_s <= 0.04045 \\[2em] (\dfrac{c_s + 0.055}{1.055})\,2.4 & \text{if } c_s > 0.04045 \end{cases}$$

Assume c_s is the sRGB component in the range [0,1].

Use the GL_PROXY_TEXTURE_2D or GL_PROXY_TEXTURE_CUBE_MAP target to try out a resolution and format. The implementation will update and recompute its best match for the requested storage resolution and format. To then query this state, call glGetTexLevelParameter. If the texture cannot be accommodated, texture state is set to 0.

A one-component texture image uses only the red component of the RGBA color extracted from *data*. A two-component image uses the R and A values. A three-component image uses the R, G, and B values. A four-component image uses all of the RGBA components.

Depth textures can be treated as LUMINANCE, INTENSITY or ALPHA textures during texture filtering and application. Image-based shadowing can be enabled by comparing texture r coordinates to depth texture values to generate a boolean result. See glTexParameter for details on texture comparison.

Notes

Texturing has no effect in color index mode.

If the ARB_imaging extension is supported, RGBA elements may also be processed by the imaging pipeline. The following stages may be applied to an RGBA color before color component clamping to the range [0,1]:

1. Color component replacement by the color table specified for GL_COLOR_TABLE, if enabled. See glColorTable.
2. Two-dimensional Convolution filtering, if enabled.
   See glConvolutionFilter1D.
   If a convolution filter changes the *width* of the texture (by processing with a GL_CONVOLUTION_BORDER_MODE of GL_REDUCE, for example), and the GL does not support non-power-of-two textures, the *width* must $2^n + 2(border)$, for some integer n, and *height* must be $2^m + 2(border)$, for some integer m, after filtering.
3. RGBA components may be multiplied by GL_POST_CONVOLUTION_c_SCALE, and added to GL_POST_CONVOLUTION_c_BIAS, if enabled. See glPixelTransfer.
4. Color component replacement by the color table specified for GL_POST_CONVOLUTION_COLOR_TABLE, if enabled. See glColorTable.
5. Transformation by the color matrix.
   See glMatrixMode.
6. RGBA components may be multiplied by GL_POST_COLOR_MATRIX_c_SCALE, and added to GL_POST_COLOR_MATRIX_c_BIAS, if enabled. See glPixelTransfer.
7. Color component replacement by the color table specified for GL_POST_COLOR_MATRIX_COLOR_TABLE, if enabled. See glColorTable.

The texture image can be represented by the same data formats as the pixels in a glDrawPixels command, except that GL_STENCIL_INDEX cannot be used. glPixelStore and glPixelTransfer modes affect texture images in exactly the way they affect glDrawPixels.

glTexImage2D and GL_PROXY_TEXTURE_2D are available only if the GL version is 1.1 or greater. Internal formats other than 1, 2, 3, or 4 may be used only if the GL version is 1.1 or greater.

In GL version 1.1 or greater, *data* may be a null pointer. In this case, texture memory is allocated to accommodate a texture of width *width* and height *height*. You can then download subtextures to initialize this texture memory. The image is undefined if the user tries to apply an uninitialized portion of the texture image to a primitive.

Formats GL_BGR, and GL_BGRA and types GL_UNSIGNED_BYTE_3_3_2, GL_UNSIGNED_BYTE_2_3_3_REV, GL_UNSIGNED_SHORT_5_6_5, GL_UNSIGNED_SHORT_5_6_5_REV, GL_UNSIGNED_SHORT_4_4_4_4, GL_UNSIGNED_SHORT_4_4_4_4_REV, GL_UNSIGNED_SHORT_5_5_5_1, GL_UNSIGNED_SHORT_1_5_5_5_REV, GL_UNSIGNED_INT_8_8_8_8, GL_UNSIGNED_INT_8_8_8_8_REV, GL_UNSIGNED_INT_10_10_10_2, and GL_UNSIGNED_INT_2_10_10_10_REV are available only if the GL version is 1.2 or greater.

When the ARB_multitexture extension is supported or the GL version is 1.3 or greater, glTexImage2D specifies the two-dimensional texture for the current texture unit, specified with glActiveTexture.

GL_TEXTURE_CUBEMAP and GL_PROXY_TEXTURE_CUBEMAP are available only if the GL version is 1.3 or greater.

GL_DEPTH_COMPONENT, GL_DEPTH_COMPONENT16, GL_DEPTH_COMPONENT24, and GL_DEPTH_COMPONENT32 are available only if the GL version is 1.4 or greater.

Non-power-of-two textures are supported if the GL version is 2.0 or greater, or if the implementation exports the GL_ARB_texture_non_power_of_two extension.

The GL_SRGB, GL_SRGB8, GL_SRGB_ALPHA, GL_SRGB8_ALPHA8, GL_SLUMINANCE, GL_SLUMINANCE8, GL_SLUMINANCE_ALPHA, and GL_SLUMINANCE8_ALPHA8 internal formats are only available if the GL version is 2.1 or greater.

Errors

GL_INVALID_ENUM is generated if *target* is not GL_TEXTURE_2D, GL_PROXY_TEXTURE_2D, GL_PROXY_TEXTURE_CUBE_MAP, GL_TEXTURE_CUBE_MAP_POSITIVE_X, GL_TEXTURE_CUBE_MAP_NEGATIVE_X, GL_TEXTURE_CUBE_MAP_POSITIVE_Y, GL_TEXTURE_CUBE_MAP_NEGATIVE_Y, GL_TEXTURE_CUBE_MAP_POSITIVE_Z, or GL_TEXTURE_CUBE_MAP_NEGATIVE_Z.

GL_INVALID_ENUM is generated if *target* is one of the six cube map 2D image targets and the width and height parameters are not equal.

GL_INVALID_ENUM is generated if *type* is not a type constant.

GL_INVALID_ENUM is generated if *type* is GL_BITMAP and *format* is not GL_COLOR_INDEX.

GL_INVALID_VALUE is generated if *width* or *height* is less than 0 or greater than 2 + GL_MAX_TEXTURE_SIZE.

GL_INVALID_VALUE is generated if *level* is less than 0.

GL_INVALID_VALUE may be generated if *level* is greater than $log_2(max)$, where *max* is the returned value of GL_MAX_TEXTURE_SIZE.

GL_INVALID_VALUE is generated if *internalFormat* is not 1, 2, 3, 4, or one of the accepted resolution and format symbolic constants.

GL_INVALID_VALUE is generated if *width* or *height* is less than 0 or greater than 2 + GL_MAX_TEXTURE_SIZE.

GL_INVALID_VALUE is generated if non-power-of-two textures are not supported and the *width* or *height* cannot be represented as $2^k + 2(border)$ for some integer value of *k*.

GL_INVALID_VALUE is generated if *border* is not 0 or 1.

GL_INVALID_OPERATION is generated if *type* is one of GL_UNSIGNED_BYTE_3_3_2, GL_UNSIGNED_BYTE_2_3_3_REV, GL_UNSIGNED_SHORT_5_6_5, or GL_UNSIGNED_SHORT_5_6_5_REV and *format* is not GL_RGB.

GL_INVALID_OPERATION is generated if *type* is one of GL_UNSIGNED_SHORT_4_4_4_4, GL_UNSIGNED_SHORT_4_4_4_4_REV, GL_UNSIGNED_SHORT_5_5_5_1, GL_UNSIGNED_SHORT_1_5_5_5_REV, GL_UNSIGNED_INT_8_8_8_8, GL_UNSIGNED_INT_8_8_8_8_REV, GL_UNSIGNED_INT_10_10_10_2, or GL_UNSIGNED_INT_2_10_10_10_REV and *format* is neither GL_RGBA nor GL_BGRA.

GL_INVALID_OPERATION is generated if *target* is not GL_TEXTURE_2D or GL_PROXY_TEXTURE_2D and *internalFormat* is GL_DEPTH_COMPONENT, GL_DEPTH_COMPONENT16, GL_DEPTH_COMPONENT24, or GL_DEPTH_COMPONENT32.

GL_INVALID_OPERATION is generated if *format* is GL_DEPTH_COMPONENT and *internalFormat* is not GL_DEPTH_COMPONENT, GL_DEPTH_COMPONENT16, GL_DEPTH_COMPONENT24, or GL_DEPTH_COMPONENT32.

GL_INVALID_OPERATION is generated if *internalFormat* is GL_DEPTH_COMPONENT, GL_DEPTH_COMPONENT16, GL_DEPTH_COMPONENT24, or GL_DEPTH_COMPONENT32, and *format* is not GL_DEPTH_COMPONENT.

GL_INVALID_OPERATION is generated if a nonzero buffer object name is bound to the GL_PIXEL_UNPACK_BUFFER target and the buffer object's data store is currently mapped.

GL_INVALID_OPERATION is generated if a nonzero buffer object name is bound to the GL_PIXEL_UNPACK_BUFFER target and the data would be unpacked from the buffer object such that the memory reads required would exceed the data store size.

GL_INVALID_OPERATION is generated if a nonzero buffer object name is bound to the GL_PIXEL_UNPACK_BUFFER target and *data* is not evenly divisible into the number of bytes needed to store in memory a datum indicated by type.

GL_INVALID_OPERATION is generated if glTexImage2D is executed between the execution of glBegin and the corresponding execution of glEnd.

Associated Gets

glGetTexImage

glIsEnabled with argument GL_TEXTURE_2D or GL_TEXTURE_CUBE_MAP

glGet with argument GL_PIXEL_UNPACK_BUFFER_BINDING

See Also

glActiveTexture, glColorTable, glConvolutionFilter2D, glCopyPixels, glCopyTexImage1D, glCopyTexImage2D, glCopyTexSubImage1D, glCopyTexSubImage2D, glCopyTexSubImage3D, glDrawPixels, glMatrixMode, glPixelStore, glPixelTransfer, glSeparableFilter2D, glTexEnv, glTexGen, glTexImage1D, glTexImage3D, glTexSubImage1D, glTexSubImage2D, glTexSubImage3D, glTexParameter

glTexImage3D

Specify a three-dimensional texture image

C Specification

```
void glTexImage3D(GLenum          target,
                  GLint           level,
                  GLint           internalFormat,
                  GLsizei         width,
                  GLsizei         height,
                  GLsizei         depth,
                  GLint           border,
                  GLenum          format,
                  GLenum          type,
                  const GLvoid * data);
```

Parameters

target	Specifies the target texture. Must be GL_TEXTURE_3D or GL_PROXY_TEXTURE_3D.
level	Specifies the level-of-detail number. Level 0 is the base image level. Level n is the nth mipmap reduction image.
internalFormat	Specifies the number of color components in the texture. Must be 1, 2, 3, or 4, or one of the following symbolic constants: GL_ALPHA, GL_ALPHA4, GL_ALPHA8, GL_ALPHA12, GL_ALPHA16, GL_COMPRESSED_ALPHA, GL_COMPRESSED_LUMINANCE, GL_COMPRESSED_LUMINANCE_ALPHA, GL_COMPRESSED_INTENSITY, GL_COMPRESSED_RGB, GL_COMPRESSED_RGBA, GL_LUMINANCE, GL_LUMINANCE4, GL_LUMINANCE8, GL_LUMINANCE12, GL_LUMINANCE16, GL_LUMINANCE_ALPHA, GL_LUMINANCE4_ALPHA4, GL_LUMINANCE6_ALPHA2, GL_LUMINANCE8_ALPHA8, GL_LUMINANCE12_ALPHA4, GL_LUMINANCE12_ALPHA12, GL_LUMINANCE16_ALPHA16, GL_INTENSITY, GL_INTENSITY4, GL_INTENSITY8, GL_INTENSITY12, GL_INTENSITY16, GL_R3_G3_B2, GL_RGB, GL_RGB4, GL_RGB5, GL_RGB8, GL_RGB10, GL_RGB12, GL_RGB16, GL_RGBA, GL_RGBA2, GL_RGBA4, GL_RGB5_A1, GL_RGBA8, GL_RGB10_A2, GL_RGBA12, GL_RGBA16, GL_SLUMINANCE, GL_SLUMINANCE8, GL_SLUMINANCE_ALPHA, GL_SLUMINANCE8_ALPHA8, GL_SRGB, GL_SRGB8, GL_SRGB_ALPHA, or GL_SRGB8_ALPHA8.
width	Specifies the width of the texture image including the border if any. If the GL version does not support non-power-of-two sizes, this value must be $2^n + 2(border)$ for some integer n. All implementations support texture images that are at least 64 texels wide.

height	Specifies the height of the texture image including the border if any. If the GL version does not support non-power-of-two sizes, this value must be $2^m + 2(border)$ for some integer m. All implementations support texture images that are at least 64 texels high.
depth	Specifies the depth of the texture image including the border if any. If the GL version does not support non-power-of-two sizes, this value must be $2^k + 2^k(border)$ for some integer k. All implementations support texture images that are at least 64 texels deep.
border	Specifies the width of the border. Must be either 0 or 1.
format	Specifies the format of the pixel data. The following symbolic values are accepted: GL_COLOR_INDEX, GL_RED, GL_GREEN, GL_BLUE, GL_ALPHA, GL_RGB, GL_BGR, GL_RGBA, GL_BGRA, GL_LUMINANCE, and GL_LUMINANCE_ALPHA.
type	Specifies the data type of the pixel data. The following symbolic values are accepted: GL_UNSIGNED_BYTE, GL_BYTE, GL_BITMAP, GL_UNSIGNED_SHORT, GL_SHORT, GL_UNSIGNED_INT, GL_INT, GL_FLOAT, GL_UNSIGNED_BYTE_3_3_2, GL_UNSIGNED_BYTE_2_3_3_REV, GL_UNSIGNED_SHORT_5_6_5, GL_UNSIGNED_SHORT_5_6_5_REV, GL_UNSIGNED_SHORT_4_4_4_4, GL_UNSIGNED_SHORT_4_4_4_4_REV, GL_UNSIGNED_SHORT_5_5_5_1, GL_UNSIGNED_SHORT_1_5_5_5_REV, GL_UNSIGNED_INT_8_8_8_8, GL_UNSIGNED_INT_8_8_8_8_REV, GL_UNSIGNED_INT_10_10_10_2, and GL_UNSIGNED_INT_2_10_10_10_REV.
data	Specifies a pointer to the image data in memory.

Description

Texturing maps a portion of a specified texture image onto each graphical primitive for which texturing is enabled. To enable and disable three-dimensional texturing, call glEnable and glDisable with argument GL_TEXTURE_3D.

To define texture images, call glTexImage3D. The arguments describe the parameters of the texture image, such as height, width, depth, width of the border, level-of-detail number (see glTexParameter), and number of color components provided. The last three arguments describe how the image is represented in memory; they are identical to the pixel formats used for glDrawPixels.

If *target* is GL_PROXY_TEXTURE_3D, no data is read from *data*, but all of the texture image state is recalculated, checked for consistency, and checked against the implementation's capabilities. If the implementation cannot handle a texture of the requested texture size, it sets all of the image state to 0, but does not generate an error (see glGetError). To query for an entire mipmap array, use an image array level greater than or equal to 1.

If *target* is GL_TEXTURE_3D, data is read from *data* as a sequence of signed or unsigned bytes, shorts, or longs, or single-precision floating-point values, depending on *type*. These values are grouped into sets of one, two, three, or four values, depending on *format*, to form elements. If *type* is GL_BITMAP, the data is considered as a string of unsigned bytes (and format must be GL_COLOR_INDEX). Each data byte is treated as eight 1-bit elements, with bit ordering determined by GL_UNPACK_LSB_FIRST (see glPixelStore).

If a nonzero named buffer object is bound to the GL_PIXEL_UNPACK_BUFFER target (see glBindBuffer) while a texture image is specified, *data* is treated as a byte offset into the buffer object's data store.

The first element corresponds to the lower-left corner of the texture image. Subsequent elements progress left-to-right through the remaining texels in the lowest row of the texture image, and then in successively higher rows of the texture image. The final element corresponds to the upper-right corner of the texture image.

format determines the composition of each element in *data*. It can assume one of these symbolic values:

GL_COLOR_INDEX

Each element is a single value, a color index. The GL converts it to fixed point (with an unspecified number of zero bits to the right of the binary point), shifted left or right depending on the value and sign of GL_INDEX_SHIFT, and added to GL_INDEX_OFFSET (see glPixelTransfer). The resulting index is converted to a set of color components using the GL_PIXEL_MAP_I_TO_R, GL_PIXEL_MAP_I_TO_G, GL_PIXEL_MAP_I_TO_B, and GL_PIXEL_MAP_I_TO_A tables, and clamped to the range [0,1].

GL_RED

Each element is a single red component. The GL converts it to floating point and assembles it into an RGBA element by attaching 0 for green and blue, and 1 for alpha. Each component is then multiplied by the signed scale factor GL_c_SCALE, added to the signed bias GL_c_BIAS, and clamped to the range [0,1] (see glPixelTransfer).

GL_GREEN

Each element is a single green component. The GL converts it to floating point and assembles it into an RGBA element by attaching 0 for red and blue, and 1 for alpha. Each component is then multiplied by the signed scale factor GL_c_SCALE, added to the signed bias GL_c_BIAS, and clamped to the range [0,1] (see glPixelTransfer).

GL_BLUE

Each element is a single blue component. The GL converts it to floating point and assembles it into an RGBA element by attaching 0 for red and green, and 1 for alpha. Each component is then multiplied by the signed scale factor GL_c_SCALE, added to the signed bias GL_c_BIAS, and clamped to the range [0,1] (see glPixelTransfer).

GL_ALPHA

Each element is a single alpha component. The GL converts it to floating point and assembles it into an RGBA element by attaching 0 for red, green, and blue. Each component is then multiplied by the signed scale factor GL_c_SCALE, added to the signed bias GL_c_BIAS, and clamped to the range [0,1] (see glPixelTransfer).

GL_INTENSITY

Each element is a single intensity value. The GL converts it to floating point, then assembles it into an RGBA element by replicating the intensity value three times for red, green, blue, and alpha. Each component is then multiplied by the signed scale factor GL_c_SCALE, added to the signed bias GL_c_BIAS, and clamped to the range [0,1] (see glPixelTransfer).

GL_RGB
GL_BGR

Each element is an RGB triple. The GL converts it to floating point and assembles it into an RGBA element by attaching 1 for alpha. Each component is then multiplied by the signed scale factor GL_c_SCALE, added to the signed bias GL_c_BIAS, and clamped to the range [0,1] (see glPixelTransfer).

GL_RGBA
GL_BGRA

Each element contains all four components. Each component is multiplied by the signed scale factor GL_c_SCALE, added to the signed bias GL_c_BIAS, and clamped to the range [0,1] (see glPixelTransfer).

GL_LUMINANCE

Each element is a single luminance value. The GL converts it to floating point, then assembles it into an RGBA element by replicating the luminance value three times for red, green, and blue and attaching 1 for alpha. Each component is then multiplied by the signed scale factor GL_c_SCALE, added to the signed bias GL_c_BIAS, and clamped to the range [0,1] (see glPixelTransfer).

GL_LUMINANCE_ALPHA

Each element is a luminance/alpha pair. The GL converts it to floating point, then assembles it into an RGBA element by replicating the luminance value three times for red, green, and blue. Each component is then multiplied by the signed scale factor GL_c_SCALE, added to the signed bias GL_c_BIAS, and clamped to the range [0,1] (see glPixelTransfer).

Refer to the glDrawPixels reference page for a description of the acceptable values for the *type* parameter.

If an application wants to store the texture at a certain resolution or in a certain format, it can request the resolution and format with *internalFormat*. The GL will choose an internal representation that closely approximates that requested by *internalFormat*, but it may not match exactly. (The representations specified by GL_LUMINANCE, GL_LUMINANCE_ALPHA, GL_RGB, and GL_RGBA must match exactly. The numeric values 1, 2, 3, and 4 may also be used to specify the above representations.)

If the *internalFormat* parameter is one of the generic compressed formats, GL_COMPRESSED_ALPHA, GL_COMPRESSED_INTENSITY, GL_COMPRESSED_LUMINANCE, GL_COMPRESSED_LUMINANCE_ALPHA, GL_COMPRESSED_RGB, or GL_COMPRESSED_RGBA, the GL will replace the internal format with the symbolic constant for a specific internal format and compress the texture before storage. If no corresponding internal format is available, or the GL can not compress that image for any reason, the internal format is instead replaced with a corresponding base internal format.

If the *internalFormat* parameter is GL_SRGB, GL_SRGB8, GL_SRGB_ALPHA, GL_SRGB8_ALPHA8, GL_SLUMINANCE, GL_SLUMINANCE8, GL_SLUMINANCE_ALPHA, or GL_SLUMINANCE8_ALPHA8, the texture is treated as if the red, green, blue, or luminance components are encoded in the sRGB color space. Any alpha component is left unchanged. The conversion from the sRGB encoded component c_s to a linear component c_l is:

$$c_l = \begin{cases} \dfrac{c_s}{12.92} & \text{if } c_s <= 0.04045 \\[2ex] \left(\dfrac{c_s + 0.055}{1.055}\right) 2.4 & \text{if } c_s > 0.04045 \end{cases}$$

Assume c_s is the sRGB component in the range [0,1].

Use the GL_PROXY_TEXTURE_3D target to try out a resolution and format. The implementation will update and recompute its best match for the requested storage resolution and format. To then query this state, call glGetTexLevelParameter. If the texture cannot be accommodated, texture state is set to 0.

A one-component texture image uses only the red component of the RGBA color extracted from *data*. A two-component image uses the R and A values. A three-component image uses the R, G, and B values. A four-component image uses all of the RGBA components.

Notes

Texturing has no effect in color index mode.

The texture image can be represented by the same data formats as the pixels in a glDrawPixels command, except that GL_STENCIL_INDEX and GL_DEPTH_COMPONENT cannot be used. glPixelStore and glPixelTransfer modes affect texture images in exactly the way they affect glDrawPixels.

glTexImage3D is available only if the GL version is 1.2 or greater.

Internal formats other than 1, 2, 3, or 4 may be used only if the GL version is 1.1 or greater.

data may be a null pointer. In this case texture memory is allocated to accommodate a texture of width *width*, height *height*, and depth *depth*. You can then download subtextures to initialize this texture memory. The image is undefined if the user tries to apply an uninitialized portion of the texture image to a primitive.

Formats GL_BGR, and GL_BGRA and types GL_UNSIGNED_BYTE_3_3_2, GL_UNSIGNED_BYTE_2_3_3_REV, GL_UNSIGNED_SHORT_5_6_5, GL_UNSIGNED_SHORT_5_6_5_REV, GL_UNSIGNED_SHORT_4_4_4_4, GL_UNSIGNED_SHORT_4_4_4_4_REV,

GL_UNSIGNED_SHORT_5_5_5_1, GL_UNSIGNED_SHORT_1_5_5_5_REV, GL_UNSIGNED_INT_8_8_8_8,
GL_UNSIGNED_INT_8_8_8_8_REV, GL_UNSIGNED_INT_10_10_10_2, and
GL_UNSIGNED_INT_2_10_10_10_REV are available only if the GL version is 1.2 or greater.

For OpenGL versions 1.3 and greater, or when the ARB_multitexture extension is supported,
glTexImage3D specifies the three-dimensional texture for the current texture unit, specified with
glActiveTexture.

If the ARB_imaging extension is supported, RGBA elements may also be processed by the
imaging pipeline. The following stages may be applied to an RGBA color before color component
clamping to the range [0,1]:

1. Color component replacement by the color table specified for GL_COLOR_TABLE, if
   enabled. See glColorTable.
2. Color component replacement by the color table specified for
   GL_POST_CONVOLUTION_COLOR_TABLE, if enabled. See glColorTable.
3. Transformation by the color matrix. See glMatrixMode.
4. RGBA components may be multiplied by GL_POST_COLOR_MATRIX_c_SCALE, and added
   to GL_POST_COLOR_MATRIX_c_BIAS, if enabled. See glPixelTransfer.
5. Color component replacement by the color table specified for
   GL_POST_COLOR_MATRIX_COLOR_TABLE, if enabled. See glColorTable.

Non-power-of-two textures are supported if the GL version is 2.0 or greater, or if the implementation exports the GL_ARB_texture_non_power_of_two extension.

The GL_SRGB, GL_SRGB8, GL_SRGB_ALPHA, GL_SRGB8_ALPHA8, GL_SLUMINANCE, GL_SLUMI-
NANCE8, GL_SLUMINANCE_ALPHA, and GL_SLUMINANCE8_ALPHA8 internal formats are only available
if the GL version is 2.1 or greater.

Errors

GL_INVALID_ENUM is generated if *target* is not GL_TEXTURE_3D or GL_PROXY_TEXTURE_3D.

GL_INVALID_ENUM is generated if *format* is not an accepted format constant. Format constants
other than GL_STENCIL_INDEX and GL_DEPTH_COMPONENT are accepted.

GL_INVALID_ENUM is generated if *type* is not a type constant.

GL_INVALID_ENUM is generated if *type* is GL_BITMAP and *format* is not GL_COLOR_INDEX.

GL_INVALID_VALUE is generated if *level* is less than 0.

GL_INVALID_VALUE may be generated if *level* is greater than $log_2(max)$, where *max* is the
returned value of GL_MAX_TEXTURE_SIZE.

GL_INVALID_VALUE is generated if *internalFormat* is not 1, 2, 3, 4, or one of the accepted
resolution and format symbolic constants.

GL_INVALID_VALUE is generated if *width*, *height*, or *depth* is less than 0 or greater than
2 + GL_MAX_TEXTURE_SIZE.

GL_INVALID_VALUE is generated if non-power-of-two textures are not supported and the *width*,
height, or *depth* cannot be represented as $2^k + 2(border)$ for some integer value of *k*.

GL_INVALID_VALUE is generated if *border* is not 0 or 1.

GL_INVALID_OPERATION is generated if *type* is one of GL_UNSIGNED_BYTE_3_3_2,
GL_UNSIGNED_BYTE_2_3_3_REV, GL_UNSIGNED_SHORT_5_6_5, or
GL_UNSIGNED_SHORT_5_6_5_REV and *format* is not GL_RGB.

GL_INVALID_OPERATION is generated if *type* is one of GL_UNSIGNED_SHORT_4_4_4_4,
GL_UNSIGNED_SHORT_4_4_4_4_REV, GL_UNSIGNED_SHORT_5_5_5_1,
GL_UNSIGNED_SHORT_1_5_5_5_REV, GL_UNSIGNED_INT_8_8_8_8,
GL_UNSIGNED_INT_8_8_8_8_REV, GL_UNSIGNED_INT_10_10_10_2, or
GL_UNSIGNED_INT_2_10_10_10_REV and *format* is neither GL_RGBA nor GL_BGRA.

GL_INVALID_OPERATION is generated if *format* or *internalFormat* is GL_DEPTH_COMPONENT,
GL_DEPTH_COMPONENT16, GL_DEPTH_COMPONENT24, or GL_DEPTH_COMPONENT32.

GL_INVALID_OPERATION is generated if a nonzero buffer object name is bound to the
GL_PIXEL_UNPACK_BUFFER target and the buffer object's data store is currently mapped.

GL_INVALID_OPERATION is generated if a nonzero buffer object name is bound to the GL_PIXEL_UNPACK_BUFFER target and the data would be unpacked from the buffer object such that the memory reads required would exceed the data store size.

GL_INVALID_OPERATION is generated if a nonzero buffer object name is bound to the GL_PIXEL_UNPACK_BUFFER target and *data* is not evenly divisible into the number of bytes needed to store in memory a datum indicated by *type*.

GL_INVALID_OPERATION is generated if glTexImage3D is executed between the execution of glBegin and the corresponding execution of glEnd.

Associated Gets

glGetTexImage
glIsEnabled with argument GL_TEXTURE_3D
glGet with argument GL_PIXEL_UNPACK_BUFFER_BINDING

See Also

glActiveTexture, glColorTable, glCompressedTexImage1D, glCompressedTexImage2D, glCompressedTexImage3D, glCompressedTexSubImage1D, glCompressedTexSubImage2D, glCompressedTexSubImage3D, glCopyPixels, glCopyTexImage1D, glCopyTexImage2D, glCopyTexSubImage1D, glCopyTexSubImage2D, glCopyTexSubImage3D, glDrawPixels, glGetCompressedTexImage, glMatrixMode, glPixelStore, glPixelTransfer, glTexEnv, glTexGen, glTexImage1D, glTexImage2D, glTexSubImage1D, glTexSubImage2D, glTexSubImage3D, glTexParameter

glTexParameter

Set texture parameters

C Specification

```
void glTexParameterf(GLenum   target,
                     GLenum   pname,
                     GLfloat  param);
void glTexParameteri(GLenum   target,
                     GLenum   pname,
                     GLint    param);
```

Parameters

target   Specifies the target texture, which must be either GL_TEXTURE_1D, GL_TEXTURE_2D, GL_TEXTURE_3D, or GL_TEXTURE_CUBE_MAP.

pname   Specifies the symbolic name of a single-valued texture parameter. *pname* can be one of the following: GL_TEXTURE_MIN_FILTER, GL_TEXTURE_MAG_FILTER, GL_TEXTURE_MIN_LOD, GL_TEXTURE_MAX_LOD, GL_TEXTURE_BASE_LEVEL, GL_TEXTURE_MAX_LEVEL, GL_TEXTURE_WRAP_S, GL_TEXTURE_WRAP_T, GL_TEXTURE_WRAP_R, GL_TEXTURE_PRIORITY, GL_TEXTURE_COMPARE_MODE, GL_TEXTURE_COMPARE_FUNC, GL_DEPTH_TEXTURE_MODE, or GL_GENERATE_MIPMAP.

param   Specifies the value of *pname*.

C Specification

```
void glTexParameterfv(GLenum          target,
                      GLenum          pname,
                      const GLfloat * params);
void glTexParameteriv(GLenum          target,
                      GLenum          pname,
                      const GLint *   params);
```

Parameters

target   Specifies the target texture, which must be either GL_TEXTURE_1D, GL_TEXTURE_2D or GL_TEXTURE_3D.

pname   Specifies the symbolic name of a texture parameter. *pname* can be one of the following: GL_TEXTURE_MIN_FILTER, GL_TEXTURE_MAG_FILTER, GL_TEXTURE_MIN_LOD, GL_TEXTURE_MAX_LOD, GL_TEXTURE_BASE_LEVEL, GL_TEXTURE_MAX_LEVEL, GL_TEXTURE_WRAP_S, GL_TEXTURE_WRAP_T, GL_TEXTURE_WRAP_R, GL_TEXTURE_BORDER_COLOR, GL_TEXTURE_PRIORITY, GL_TEXTURE_COMPARE_MODE, GL_TEXTURE_COMPARE_FUNC, GL_DEPTH_TEXTURE_MODE, or GL_GENERATE_MIPMAP.

params   Specifies a pointer to an array where the value or values of *pname* are stored.

Description

Texture mapping is a technique that applies an image onto an object's surface as if the image were a decal or cellophane shrink-wrap. The image is created in texture space, with an (s, t) coordinate system. A texture is a one- or two-dimensional image and a set of parameters that determine how samples are derived from the image.

glTexParameter assigns the value or values in *params* to the texture parameter specified as *pname*. *target* defines the target texture, either GL_TEXTURE_1D, GL_TEXTURE_2D, or GL_TEXTURE_3D. The following symbols are accepted in *pname*:

GL_TEXTURE_MIN_FILTER

The texture minifying function is used whenever the pixel being textured maps to an area greater than one texture element. There are six defined minifying functions. Two of them use the nearest one or nearest four texture elements to compute the texture value. The other four use mipmaps.

A mipmap is an ordered set of arrays representing the same image at progressively lower resolutions. If the texture has dimensions $2^n \times 2^m$, there are $max(n,m) + 1$ mipmaps. The first mipmap is the original texture, with dimensions $2^n \times 2^m$. Each subsequent mipmap has dimensions $2^{k-1} \times 2^{l-1}$, where $2^k \times 2^l$ are the dimensions of the previous mipmap, until either $k = 0$ or $l = 0$. At that point, subsequent mipmaps have dimension $1 \times 2^{l-1}$ or $2^{k-1} \times 1$ until the final mipmap, which has dimension 1×1. To define the mipmaps, call glTexImage1D, glTexImage2D, glTexImage3D, glCopyTexImage1D, or glCopyTexImage2D with the *level* argument indicating the order of the mipmaps. Level 0 is the original texture; level $max(n,m)$ is the final 1×1 mipmap.

params supplies a function for minifying the texture as one of the following:

GL_NEAREST

Returns the value of the texture element that is nearest (in Manhattan distance) to the center of the pixel being textured.

GL_LINEAR

Returns the weighted average of the four texture elements that are closest to the center of the pixel being textured. These can include border texture elements, depending on the values of GL_TEXTURE_WRAP_S and GL_TEXTURE_WRAP_T, and on the exact mapping.

GL_NEAREST_MIPMAP_NEAREST

Chooses the mipmap that most closely matches the size of the pixel being textured and uses the GL_NEAREST criterion (the texture element nearest to the center of the pixel) to produce a texture value.

GL_LINEAR_MIPMAP_NEAREST

Chooses the mipmap that most closely matches the size of the pixel being textured and uses the GL_LINEAR criterion (a weighted average of the four texture elements that are closest to the center of the pixel) to produce a texture value.

GL_NEAREST_MIPMAP_LINEAR

Chooses the two mipmaps that most closely match the size of the pixel being textured and uses the GL_NEAREST criterion (the texture element nearest to the center of the pixel) to produce a texture value from each mipmap. The final texture value is a weighted average of those two values.

GL_LINEAR_MIPMAP_LINEAR

Chooses the two mipmaps that most closely match the size of the pixel being textured and uses the GL_LINEAR criterion (a weighted average of the four texture elements that are closest to the center of the pixel) to produce a texture value from each mipmap. The final texture value is a weighted average of those two values.

As more texture elements are sampled in the minification process, fewer aliasing artifacts will be apparent. While the GL_NEAREST and GL_LINEAR minification functions can be faster than the other four, they sample only one or four texture elements to determine the texture value of the pixel being rendered and can produce moire patterns or ragged transitions. The initial value of GL_TEXTURE_MIN_FILTER is GL_NEAREST_MIPMAP_LINEAR.

GL_TEXTURE_MAG_FILTER

The texture magnification function is used when the pixel being textured maps to an area less than or equal to one texture element. It sets the texture magnification function to either GL_NEAREST or GL_LINEAR (see below). GL_NEAREST is generally faster than GL_LINEAR, but it can produce textured images with sharper edges because the transition between texture elements is not as smooth. The initial value of GL_TEXTURE_MAG_FILTER is GL_LINEAR.

GL_NEAREST

Returns the value of the texture element that is nearest (in Manhattan distance) to the center of the pixel being textured.

GL_LINEAR

Returns the weighted average of the four texture elements that are closest to the center of the pixel being textured. These can include border texture elements, depending on the values of GL_TEXTURE_WRAP_S and GL_TEXTURE_WRAP_T, and on the exact mapping.

GL_TEXTURE_MIN_LOD

Sets the minimum level-of-detail parameter. This floating-point value limits the selection of highest resolution mipmap (lowest mipmap level). The initial value is -1000.

GL_TEXTURE_MAX_LOD

Sets the maximum level-of-detail parameter. This floating-point value limits the selection of the lowest resolution mipmap (highest mipmap level). The initial value is 1000.

GL_TEXTURE_BASE_LEVEL

Specifies the index of the lowest defined mipmap level. This is an integer value. The initial value is 0.

GL_TEXTURE_MAX_LEVEL

Sets the index of the highest defined mipmap level. This is an integer value. The initial value is 1000.

GL_TEXTURE_WRAP_S

Sets the wrap parameter for texture coordinate s to either GL_CLAMP, GL_CLAMP_TO_BORDER, GL_CLAMP_TO_EDGE, GL_MIRRORED_REPEAT, or GL_REPEAT. GL_CLAMP causes s coordinates to be clamped to the range [0,1] and is useful for preventing wrapping artifacts when mapping a single image onto an object. GL_CLAMP_TO_BORDER causes the s coordinate to be clamped to the range $\left[\frac{-1}{2}N, 1 + \frac{1}{2}N\right]$, where N is the size of the texture in the direction of clamping. GL_CLAMP_TO_EDGE causes s coordinates to be clamped to the range $\left[\frac{1}{2}N, 1 - \frac{1}{2}N\right]$, where N is the size of the texture in the direction of clamping.

GL_REPEAT causes the integer part of the s coordinate to be ignored; the GL uses only the fractional part, thereby creating a repeating pattern. GL_MIRRORED_REPEAT causes the s coordinate to be set to the fractional part of the texture coordinate if the integer part of s is even; if the integer part of s is odd, then the s texture coordinate is set to $1 - frac(s)$, where $frac(s)$ represents the fractional part of s. Border texture elements are accessed only if wrapping is set to GL_CLAMP or GL_CLAMP_TO_BORDER. Initially, GL_TEXTURE_WRAP_S is set to GL_REPEAT.

GL_TEXTURE_WRAP_T

Sets the wrap parameter for texture coordinate *t* to either GL_CLAMP, GL_CLAMP_TO_BORDER, GL_CLAMP_TO_EDGE, GL_MIRRORED_REPEAT, or GL_REPEAT. See the discussion under GL_TEXTURE_WRAP_S. Initially, GL_TEXTURE_WRAP_T is set to GL_REPEAT.

GL_TEXTURE_WRAP_R

Sets the wrap parameter for texture coordinate *r* to either GL_CLAMP, GL_CLAMP_TO_BORDER, GL_CLAMP_TO_EDGE, GL_MIRRORED_REPEAT, or GL_REPEAT. See the discussion under GL_TEXTURE_WRAP_S. Initially, GL_TEXTURE_WRAP_R is set to GL_REPEAT.

GL_TEXTURE_BORDER_COLOR

Sets a border color. *params* contains four values that comprise the RGBA color of the texture border. Integer color components are interpreted linearly such that the most positive integer maps to 1.0, and the most negative integer maps to -1.0. The values are clamped to the range [0,1] when they are specified. Initially, the border color is (0, 0, 0, 0).

GL_TEXTURE_PRIORITY

Specifies the texture residence priority of the currently bound texture. Permissible values are in the range [0,1]. See glPrioritizeTextures and glBindTexture for more information.

GL_TEXTURE_COMPARE_MODE

Specifies the texture comparison mode for currently bound depth textures. That is, a texture whose internal format is GL_DEPTH_COMPONENT_*; see glTexImage2D) Permissible values are:

GL_COMPARE_R_TO_TEXTURE

Specifies that the interpolated and clamped *r* texture coordinate should be compared to the value in the currently bound depth texture. See the discussion of GL_TEXTURE_COMPARE_FUNC for details of how the comparison is evaluated. The result of the comparison is assigned to luminance, intensity, or alpha (as specified by GL_DEPTH_TEXTURE_MODE).

GL_NONE

Specifies that the luminance, intensity, or alpha (as specified by GL_DEPTH_TEXTURE_MODE) should be assigned the appropriate value from the currently bound depth texture.

GL_TEXTURE_COMPARE_FUNC

Specifies the comparison operator used when GL_TEXTURE_COMPARE_MODE is set to GL_COMPARE_R_TO_TEXTURE. Permissible values are:

Texture Comparison Function	Computed result
GL_LEQUAL	$result = \begin{cases} 1.0 & r \le D_t \\ 0.0 & r > D_t \end{cases}$
GL_GEQUAL	$result = \begin{cases} 1.0 & r \ge D_t \\ 0.0 & r < D_t \end{cases}$
GL_LESS	$result = \begin{cases} 1.0 & r < D_t \\ 0.0 & r \ge D_t \end{cases}$
GL_GREATER	$result = \begin{cases} 1.0 & r > D_t \\ 0.0 & r \le D_t \end{cases}$
GL_EQUAL	$result = \begin{cases} 1.0 & r = D_t \\ 0.0 & r \ne D_t \end{cases}$
GL_NOTEQUAL	$result = \begin{cases} 1.0 & r \ne D_t \\ 0.0 & r = D_t \end{cases}$
GL_ALWAYS	$result = 1.0$
GL_NEVER	$result = 0.0$

where r is the current interpolated texture coordinate, and D_t is the depth texture value sampled from the currently bound depth texture. *result* is assigned to the either the luminance, intensity, or alpha (as specified by GL_DEPTH_TEXTURE_MODE).

GL_DEPTH_TEXTURE_MODE

Specifies a single symbolic constant indicating how depth values should be treated during filtering and texture application. Accepted values are GL_LUMINANCE, GL_INTENSITY, and GL_ALPHA. The initial value is GL_LUMINANCE.

GL_GENERATE_MIPMAP

Specifies a boolean value that indicates if all levels of a mipmap array should be automatically updated when any modification to the base level mipmap is done. The initial value is GL_FALSE.

Notes

GL_TEXTURE_3D, GL_TEXTURE_MIN_LOD, GL_TEXTURE_MAX_LOD, GL_CLAMP_TO_EDGE, GL_TEXTURE_BASE_LEVEL, and GL_TEXTURE_MAX_LEVEL are available only if the GL version is 1.2 or greater.

GL_CLAMP_TO_BORDER is available only if the GL version is 1.3 or greater.

GL_MIRRORED_REPEAT, GL_TEXTURE_COMPARE_MODE, GL_TEXTURE_COMPARE_FUNC, GL_DEPTH_TEXTURE_MODE, and GL_GENERATE_MIPMAP are available only if the GL version is 1.4 or greater.

GL_TEXTURE_COMPARE_FUNC allows the following additional comparison modes only if the GL version is 1.5 or greater: GL_LESS, GL_GREATER, GL_EQUAL, GL_NOTEQUAL, GL_ALWAYS, and GL_NEVER.

Suppose that a program has enabled texturing (by calling glEnable with argument GL_TEXTURE_1D, GL_TEXTURE_2D, or GL_TEXTURE_3D) and has set GL_TEXTURE_MIN_FILTER to one of the functions that requires a mipmap. If either the dimensions of the texture images currently defined (with previous calls to glTexImage1D, glTexImage2D, glTexImage3D, glCopyTexImage1D, or glCopyTexImage2D) do not follow the proper sequence for mipmaps (described above), or there are fewer texture images defined than are needed, or the set of texture images have differing numbers of texture components, then it is as if texture mapping were disabled.

Linear filtering accesses the four nearest texture elements only in 2D textures. In 1D textures, linear filtering accesses the two nearest texture elements.

For OpenGL versions 1.3 and greater, or when the ARB_multitexture extension is supported, glTexParameter specifies the texture parameters for the active texture unit, specified by calling glActiveTexture.

Errors

GL_INVALID_ENUM is generated if *target* or *pname* is not one of the accepted defined values.

GL_INVALID_ENUM is generated if *params* should have a defined constant value (based on the value of *pname*) and does not.

GL_INVALID_OPERATION is generated if glTexParameter is executed between the execution of glBegin and the corresponding execution of glEnd.

Associated Gets

glGetTexParameter
glGetTexLevelParameter

See Also

glActiveTexture, glBindTexture, glCopyPixels, glCopyTexImage1D, glCopyTexImage2D, glCopyTexSubImage1D, glCopyTexSubImage2D, glCopyTexSubImage3D, glDrawPixels, glPixelStore, glPixelTransfer, glPrioritizeTextures, glTexEnv, glTexGen, glTexImage1D, glTexImage2D, glTexImage3D, glTexSubImage1D, glTexSubImage2D, glTexSubImage3D

glTexSubImage1D

Specify a one-dimensional texture subimage

C Specification

```
void glTexSubImage1D(GLenum          target,
                     GLint           level,
                     GLint           xoffset,
                     GLsizei         width,
                     GLenum          format,
                     GLenum          type,
                     const GLvoid *  data);
```

Parameters

target   Specifies the target texture. Must be GL_TEXTURE_1D.

level   Specifies the level-of-detail number. Level 0 is the base image level. Level *n* is the *n*th mipmap reduction image.

xoffset   Specifies a texel offset in the x direction within the texture array.

width   Specifies the width of the texture subimage.

format   Specifies the format of the pixel data. The following symbolic values are accepted: GL_COLOR_INDEX, GL_RED, GL_GREEN, GL_BLUE, GL_ALPHA, GL_RGB, GL_BGR, GL_RGBA, GL_BGRA, GL_LUMINANCE, and GL_LUMINANCE_ALPHA.

type   Specifies the data type of the pixel data. The following symbolic values are accepted: GL_UNSIGNED_BYTE, GL_BYTE, GL_BITMAP, GL_UNSIGNED_SHORT, GL_SHORT, GL_UNSIGNED_INT, GL_INT, GL_FLOAT, GL_UNSIGNED_BYTE_3_3_2, GL_UNSIGNED_BYTE_2_3_3_REV, GL_UNSIGNED_SHORT_5_6_5, GL_UNSIGNED_SHORT_5_6_5_REV, GL_UNSIGNED_SHORT_4_4_4_4, GL_UNSIGNED_SHORT_4_4_4_4_REV, GL_UNSIGNED_SHORT_5_5_5_1, GL_UNSIGNED_SHORT_1_5_5_5_REV, GL_UNSIGNED_INT_8_8_8_8, GL_UNSIGNED_INT_8_8_8_8_REV, GL_UNSIGNED_INT_10_10_10_2, and GL_UNSIGNED_INT_2_10_10_10_REV.

data   Specifies a pointer to the image data in memory.

Description

Texturing maps a portion of a specified texture image onto each graphical primitive for which texturing is enabled. To enable or disable one-dimensional texturing, call glEnable and glDisable with argument GL_TEXTURE_1D.

glTexSubImage1D redefines a contiguous subregion of an existing one-dimensional texture image. The texels referenced by *data* replace the portion of the existing texture array with x indices *xoffset* and *xoffset* + *width* – 1, inclusive. This region may not include any texels outside the range of the texture array as it was originally specified. It is not an error to specify a subtexture with width of 0, but such a specification has no effect.

If a nonzero named buffer object is bound to the GL_PIXEL_UNPACK_BUFFER target (see glBindBuffer) while a texture image is specified, *data* is treated as a byte offset into the buffer object's data store.

Notes

glTexSubImage1D is available only if the GL version is 1.1 or greater.

Texturing has no effect in color index mode.

glPixelStore and glPixelTransfer modes affect texture images in exactly the way they affect glDrawPixels.

Formats GL_BGR, and GL_BGRA and types GL_UNSIGNED_BYTE_3_3_2, GL_UNSIGNED_BYTE_2_3_3_REV, GL_UNSIGNED_SHORT_5_6_5, GL_UNSIGNED_SHORT_5_6_5_REV,

GL_UNSIGNED_SHORT_4_4_4_4, GL_UNSIGNED_SHORT_4_4_4_4_REV, GL_UNSIGNED_SHORT_5_5_5_1, GL_UNSIGNED_SHORT_1_5_5_5_REV, GL_UNSIGNED_INT_8_8_8_8, GL_UNSIGNED_INT_8_8_8_8_REV, GL_UNSIGNED_INT_10_10_10_2, and GL_UNSIGNED_INT_2_10_10_10_REV are available only if the GL version is 1.2 or greater.

For OpenGL versions 1.3 and greater, or when the ARB_multitexture extension is supported, glTexSubImage1D specifies a one-dimensional subtexture for the current texture unit, specified with glActiveTexture.

When the ARB_imaging extension is supported, the RGBA components specified in data may be processed by the imaging pipeline. See glTexImage1D for specific details.

Errors

GL_INVALID_ENUM is generated if *target* is not one of the allowable values.

GL_INVALID_ENUM is generated if *format* is not an accepted format constant.

GL_INVALID_ENUM is generated if *type* is not a type constant.

GL_INVALID_ENUM is generated if *type* is GL_BITMAP and *format* is not GL_COLOR_INDEX.

GL_INVALID_VALUE is generated if *level* is less than 0.

GL_INVALID_VALUE may be generated if *level* is greater than log_2max, where *max* is the returned value of GL_MAX_TEXTURE_SIZE.

GL_INVALID_VALUE is generated if *xoffset*<–*b*, or if (*xoffset* + *width*) > (*w* – *b*), where *w* is the GL_TEXTURE_WIDTH, and *b* is the width of the GL_TEXTURE_BORDER of the texture image being modified. Note that *w* includes twice the border width.

GL_INVALID_VALUE is generated if *width* is less than 0.

GL_INVALID_OPERATION is generated if the texture array has not been defined by a previous glTexImage1D operation.

GL_INVALID_OPERATION is generated if *type* is one of GL_UNSIGNED_BYTE_3_3_2, GL_UNSIGNED_BYTE_2_3_3_REV, GL_UNSIGNED_SHORT_5_6_5, or GL_UNSIGNED_SHORT_5_6_5_REV and *format* is not GL_RGB.

GL_INVALID_OPERATION is generated if *type* is one of GL_UNSIGNED_SHORT_4_4_4_4, GL_UNSIGNED_SHORT_4_4_4_4_REV, GL_UNSIGNED_SHORT_5_5_5_1, GL_UNSIGNED_SHORT_1_5_5_5_REV, GL_UNSIGNED_INT_8_8_8_8, GL_UNSIGNED_INT_8_8_8_8_REV, GL_UNSIGNED_INT_10_10_10_2, or GL_UNSIGNED_INT_2_10_10_10_REV and *format* is neither GL_RGBA nor GL_BGRA.

GL_INVALID_OPERATION is generated if a nonzero buffer object name is bound to the GL_PIXEL_UNPACK_BUFFER target and the buffer object's data store is currently mapped.

GL_INVALID_OPERATION is generated if a nonzero buffer object name is bound to the GL_PIXEL_UNPACK_BUFFER target and the data would be unpacked from the buffer object such that the memory reads required would exceed the data store size.

GL_INVALID_OPERATION is generated if a nonzero buffer object name is bound to the GL_PIXEL_UNPACK_BUFFER target and *data* is not evenly divisible into the number of bytes needed to store in memory a datum indicated by *type*.

GL_INVALID_OPERATION is generated if glTexSubImage1D is executed between the execution of glBegin and the corresponding execution of glEnd.

Associated Gets

glGetTexImage

glIsEnabled with argument GL_TEXTURE_1D

glGet with argument GL_PIXEL_UNPACK_BUFFER_BINDING

See Also

glActiveTexture, glCopyTexImage1D, glCopyTexImage2D, glCopyTexSubImage1D, glCopyTexSubImage2D, glCopyTexSubImage3D, glDrawPixels, glPixelStore, glPixelTransfer, glTexEnv, glTexGen, glTexImage1D, glTexImage2D, glTexImage3D, glTexParameter, glTexSubImage2D, glTexSubImage3D

glTexSubImage2D

Specify a two-dimensional texture subimage

C Specification

```
void glTexSubImage2D(GLenum          target,
                     GLint           level,
                     GLint           xoffset,
                     GLint           yoffset,
                     GLsizei         width,
                     GLsizei         height,
                     GLenum          format,
                     GLenum          type,
                     const GLvoid *  data);
```

Parameters

target   Specifies the target texture. Must be GL_TEXTURE_2D, GL_TEXTURE_CUBE_MAP_
           POSITIVE_X, GL_TEXTURE_CUBE_MAP_NEGATIVE_X, GL_TEXTURE_CUBE_MAP_
           POSITIVE_Y, GL_TEXTURE_CUBE_MAP_NEGATIVE_Y, GL_TEXTURE_CUBE_
           MAP_POSITIVE_Z, GL_TEXTURE_CUBE_MAP_NEGATIVE_Z, or
           GL_PROXY_TEXTURE_CUBE_MAP.

level   Specifies the level-of-detail number. Level 0 is the base image level. Level n is the nth
           mipmap reduction image.

xoffset Specifies a texel offset in the x direction within the texture array.

yoffset Specifies a texel offset in the y direction within the texture array.

width   Specifies the width of the texture subimage.

height   Specifies the height of the texture subimage.

format   Specifies the format of the pixel data. The following symbolic values are accepted:
           GL_COLOR_INDEX, GL_RED, GL_GREEN, GL_BLUE, GL_ALPHA, GL_RGB, GL_BGR, GL_RGBA,
           GL_BGRA, GL_LUMINANCE, and GL_LUMINANCE_ALPHA.

type   Specifies the data type of the pixel data. The following symbolic values are accepted:
           GL_UNSIGNED_BYTE, GL_BYTE, GL_BITMAP, GL_UNSIGNED_SHORT, GL_SHORT,
           GL_UNSIGNED_INT, GL_INT, GL_FLOAT, GL_UNSIGNED_BYTE_3_3_2,
           GL_UNSIGNED_BYTE_2_3_3_REV, GL_UNSIGNED_SHORT_5_6_5,
           GL_UNSIGNED_SHORT_5_6_5_REV, GL_UNSIGNED_SHORT_4_4_4_4,
           GL_UNSIGNED_SHORT_4_4_4_4_REV, GL_UNSIGNED_SHORT_5_5_5_1,
           GL_UNSIGNED_SHORT_1_5_5_5_REV, GL_UNSIGNED_INT_8_8_8_8,
           GL_UNSIGNED_INT_8_8_8_8_REV, GL_UNSIGNED_INT_10_10_10_2, and
           GL_UNSIGNED_INT_2_10_10_10_REV.

data   Specifies a pointer to the image data in memory.

Description

Texturing maps a portion of a specified texture image onto each graphical primitive for which
texturing is enabled. To enable and disable two-dimensional texturing, call glEnable and glDisable
with argument GL_TEXTURE_2D.

glTexSubImage2D redefines a contiguous subregion of an existing two-dimensional texture
image. The texels referenced by data replace the portion of the existing texture array with x indices
xoffset and *xoffset* + *width* – 1, inclusive, and y indices *yoffset* and *yoffset* + *height* – 1,
inclusive. This region may not include any texels outside the range of the texture array as it was originally specified. It is not an error to specify a subtexture with zero width or height, but such a specification has no effect.

If a nonzero named buffer object is bound to the GL_PIXEL_UNPACK_BUFFER target (see glBindBuffer) while a texture image is specified, data is treated as a byte offset into the buffer object's data store.

Notes

glTexSubImage2D is available only if the GL version is 1.1 or greater.

Texturing has no effect in color index mode.

glPixelStore and glPixelTransfer modes affect texture images in exactly the way they affect glDrawPixels.

Formats GL_BGR, and GL_BGRA and types GL_UNSIGNED_BYTE_3_3_2, GL_UNSIGNED_BYTE_2_3_3_REV, GL_UNSIGNED_SHORT_5_6_5, GL_UNSIGNED_SHORT_5_6_5_REV, GL_UNSIGNED_SHORT_4_4_4_4, GL_UNSIGNED_SHORT_4_4_4_4_REV, GL_UNSIGNED_SHORT_5_5_5_1, GL_UNSIGNED_SHORT_1_5_5_5_REV, GL_UNSIGNED_INT_8_8_8_8, GL_UNSIGNED_INT_8_8_8_8_REV, GL_UNSIGNED_INT_10_10_10_2, and GL_UNSIGNED_INT_2_10_10_10_REV are available only if the GL version is 1.2 or greater.

For OpenGL versions 1.3 and greater, or when the ARB_multitexture extension is supported, glTexSubImage2D specifies a two-dimensional subtexture for the current texture unit, specified with glActiveTexture.

When the ARB_imaging extension is supported, the RGBA components specified in *data* may be processed by the imaging pipeline. See glTexImage1D for specific details.

Errors

GL_INVALID_ENUM is generated if *target* is not GL_TEXTURE_2D.

GL_INVALID_ENUM is generated if *format* is not an accepted format constant.

GL_INVALID_ENUM is generated if *type* is not a type constant.

GL_INVALID_ENUM is generated if *type* is GL_BITMAP and *format* is not GL_COLOR_INDEX.

GL_INVALID_VALUE is generated if *level* is less than 0.

GL_INVALID_VALUE may be generated if *level* is greater than log_2max, where *max* is the returned value of GL_MAX_TEXTURE_SIZE.

GL_INVALID_VALUE is generated if $xoffset < -b$, $(xoffset + width) > (w - b)$, $yoffset < -b$, or $(yoffset + height) > (h - b)$, where w is the GL_TEXTURE_WIDTH, h is the GL_TEXTURE_HEIGHT, and b is the border width of the texture image being modified. Note that w and h include twice the border width.

GL_INVALID_VALUE is generated if *width* or *height* is less than 0.

GL_INVALID_OPERATION is generated if the texture array has not been defined by a previous glTexImage2D operation.

GL_INVALID_OPERATION is generated if *type* is one of GL_UNSIGNED_BYTE_3_3_2, GL_UNSIGNED_BYTE_2_3_3_REV, GL_UNSIGNED_SHORT_5_6_5, or GL_UNSIGNED_SHORT_5_6_5_REV and *format* is not GL_RGB.

GL_INVALID_OPERATION is generated if *type* is one of GL_UNSIGNED_SHORT_4_4_4_4, GL_UNSIGNED_SHORT_4_4_4_4_REV, GL_UNSIGNED_SHORT_5_5_5_1, GL_UNSIGNED_SHORT_1_5_5_5_REV, GL_UNSIGNED_INT_8_8_8_8, GL_UNSIGNED_INT_8_8_8_8_REV, GL_UNSIGNED_INT_10_10_10_2, or GL_UNSIGNED_INT_2_10_10_10_REV and *format* is neither GL_RGBA nor GL_BGRA.

GL_INVALID_OPERATION is generated if a nonzero buffer object name is bound to the GL_PIXEL_UNPACK_BUFFER target and the buffer object's data store is currently mapped.

GL_INVALID_OPERATION is generated if a nonzero buffer object name is bound to the GL_PIXEL_UNPACK_BUFFER target and the data would be unpacked from the buffer object such that the memory reads required would exceed the data store size.

GL_INVALID_OPERATION is generated if a nonzero buffer object name is bound to the GL_PIXEL_UNPACK_BUFFER target and *data* is not evenly divisible into the number of bytes needed to store in memory a datum indicated by *type*.

GL_INVALID_OPERATION is generated if glTexSubImage2D is executed between the execution of glBegin and the corresponding execution of glEnd.

Associated Gets

glGetTexImage
glIsEnabled with argument GL_TEXTURE_2D
glGet with argument GL_PIXEL_UNPACK_BUFFER_BINDING

See Also

glActiveTexture, glCopyTexImage1D, glCopyTexImage2D, glCopyTexSubImage1D, glCopyTexSubImage2D, glCopyTexSubImage3D, glDrawPixels, glPixelStore, glPixelTransfer, glTexEnv, glTexGen, glTexImage1D, glTexImage2D, glTexImage3D, glTexSubImage1D, glTexSubImage3D, glTexParameter

glTexSubImage3D

Specify a three-dimensional texture subimage

C Specification

```
void glTexSubImage3D(GLenum          target,
                     GLint           level,
                     GLint           xoffset,
                     GLint           yoffset,
                     GLint           zoffset,
                     GLsizei         width,
                     GLsizei         height,
                     GLsizei         depth,
                     GLenum          format,
                     GLenum          type,
                     const GLvoid *  data);
```

Parameters

target	Specifies the target texture. Must be GL_TEXTURE_3D.
level	Specifies the level-of-detail number. Level 0 is the base image level. Level n is the nth mipmap reduction image.
xoffset	Specifies a texel offset in the x direction within the texture array.
yoffset	Specifies a texel offset in the y direction within the texture array.
zoffset	Specifies a texel offset in the z direction within the texture array.
width	Specifies the width of the texture subimage.
height	Specifies the height of the texture subimage.
depth	Specifies the depth of the texture subimage.
format	Specifies the format of the pixel data. The following symbolic values are accepted: GL_COLOR_INDEX, GL_RED, GL_GREEN, GL_BLUE, GL_ALPHA, GL_RGB, GL_BGR, GL_RGBA, GL_BGRA, GL_LUMINANCE, and GL_LUMINANCE_ALPHA.
type	Specifies the data type of the pixel data. The following symbolic values are accepted: GL_UNSIGNED_BYTE, GL_BYTE, GL_BITMAP, GL_UNSIGNED_SHORT, GL_SHORT, GL_UNSIGNED_INT, GL_INT, GL_FLOAT, GL_UNSIGNED_BYTE_3_3_2, GL_UNSIGNED_BYTE_2_3_3_REV, GL_UNSIGNED_SHORT_5_6_5, GL_UNSIGNED_SHORT_5_6_5_REV, GL_UNSIGNED_SHORT_4_4_4_4, GL_UNSIGNED_SHORT_4_4_4_4_REV, GL_UNSIGNED_SHORT_5_5_5_1, GL_UNSIGNED_SHORT_1_5_5_5_REV, GL_UNSIGNED_INT_8_8_8_8,

GL_UNSIGNED_INT_8_8_8_8_REV, GL_UNSIGNED_INT_10_10_10_2, and
GL_UNSIGNED_INT_2_10_10_10_REV.

data   Specifies a pointer to the image data in memory.

Description

Texturing maps a portion of a specified texture image onto each graphical primitive for which texturing is enabled. To enable and disable three-dimensional texturing, call glEnable and glDisable with argument GL_TEXTURE_3D.

glTexSubImage3D redefines a contiguous subregion of an existing three-dimensional texture image. The texels referenced by *data* replace the portion of the existing texture array with x indices *xoffset* and *xoffset* + *width* – 1, inclusive, y indices *yoffset* and *yoffset* + *height* – 1, inclusive, and z indices *zoffset* and *zoffset* + *depth* – 1, inclusive. This region may not include any texels outside the range of the texture array as it was originally specified. It is not an error to specify a subtexture with zero width, height, or depth but such a specification has no effect.

If a nonzero named buffer object is bound to the GL_PIXEL_UNPACK_BUFFER target (see glBindBuffer) while a texture image is specified, *data* is treated as a byte offset into the buffer object's data store.

Notes

glTexSubImage3D is available only if the GL version is 1.2 or greater.

Texturing has no effect in color index mode.

glPixelStore and glPixelTransfer modes affect texture images in exactly the way they affect glDrawPixels.

Formats GL_BGR, and GL_BGRA and types GL_UNSIGNED_BYTE_3_3_2, GL_UNSIGNED_BYTE_2_3_3_REV, GL_UNSIGNED_SHORT_5_6_5, GL_UNSIGNED_SHORT_5_6_5_REV, GL_UNSIGNED_SHORT_4_4_4_4, GL_UNSIGNED_SHORT_4_4_4_4_REV, GL_UNSIGNED_SHORT_5_5_5_1, GL_UNSIGNED_SHORT_1_5_5_5_REV, GL_UNSIGNED_INT_8_8_8_8, GL_UNSIGNED_INT_8_8_8_8_REV, GL_UNSIGNED_INT_10_10_10_2, and GL_UNSIGNED_INT_2_10_10_10_REV are available only if the GL version is 1.2 or greater.

For OpenGL versions 1.3 and greater, or which the ARB_multitexture extension is supported, glTexSubImage3D specifies a three-dimensional subtexture for the current texture unit, specified with glActiveTexture.

When the ARB_imaging extension is supported, the RGBA components specified in *data* may be processed by the imaging pipeline. See glTexImage3D for specific details.

Errors

GL_INVALID_ENUM is generated if target is not GL_TEXTURE_3D.

GL_INVALID_ENUM is generated if *format* is not an accepted format constant.

GL_INVALID_ENUM is generated if *type* is not a type constant.

GL_INVALID_ENUM is generated if *type* is GL_BITMAP and *format* is not GL_COLOR_INDEX.

GL_INVALID_VALUE is generated if *level* is less than 0.

GL_INVALID_VALUE may be generated if *level* is greater than $log_2 max$, where *max* is the returned value of GL_MAX_TEXTURE_SIZE.

GL_INVALID_VALUE is generated if *xoffset*<–*b*, (*xoffset* + *width*) > (*w* – *b*), *yoffset*<–*b*, or (*yoffset* + *height*) > (*h* – *b*), or *zoffset*<–*b*, or (*zoffset* + *depth*) > (*d* – *b*), where *w* is the GL_TEXTURE_WIDTH, *h* is the GL_TEXTURE_HEIGHT, *d* is the GL_TEXTURE_DEPTH and *b* is the border width of the texture image being modified. Note that *w*, *h*, and *d* include twice the border width.

GL_INVALID_VALUE is generated if *width*, *height*, or *depth* is less than 0.

GL_INVALID_OPERATION is generated if the texture array has not been defined by a previous glTexImage3D operation.

GL_INVALID_OPERATION is generated if *type* is one of GL_UNSIGNED_BYTE_3_3_2, GL_UNSIGNED_BYTE_2_3_3_REV, GL_UNSIGNED_SHORT_5_6_5, or

GL_UNSIGNED_SHORT_5_6_5_REV and *format* is not GL_RGB.

GL_INVALID_OPERATION is generated if *type* is one of GL_UNSIGNED_SHORT_4_4_4_4,
GL_UNSIGNED_SHORT_4_4_4_4_REV, GL_UNSIGNED_SHORT_5_5_5_1,
GL_UNSIGNED_SHORT_1_5_5_5_REV, GL_UNSIGNED_INT_8_8_8_8,
GL_UNSIGNED_INT_8_8_8_8_REV, GL_UNSIGNED_INT_10_10_10_2, or
GL_UNSIGNED_INT_2_10_10_10_REV and *format* is neither GL_RGBA nor GL_BGRA.

GL_INVALID_OPERATION is generated if a nonzero buffer object name is bound to the
GL_PIXEL_UNPACK_BUFFER target and the buffer object's data store is currently mapped.

GL_INVALID_OPERATION is generated if a nonzero buffer object name is bound to the
GL_PIXEL_UNPACK_BUFFER target and the data would be unpacked from the buffer object such that
the memory reads required would exceed the data store size.

GL_INVALID_OPERATION is generated if a nonzero buffer object name is bound to the
GL_PIXEL_UNPACK_BUFFER target and *data* is not evenly divisible into the number of bytes needed
to store in memory a datum indicated by *type*.

GL_INVALID_OPERATION is generated if glTexSubImage3D is executed between the execution of
glBegin and the corresponding execution of glEnd.

Associated Gets

glGetTexImage
glIsEnabled with argument GL_TEXTURE_3D
glGet with argument GL_PIXEL_UNPACK_BUFFER_BINDING

See Also

glActiveTexture, glCopyTexImage1D, glCopyTexImage2D, glCopyTexSubImage1D,
glCopyTexSubImage2D, glCopyTexSubImage3D, glDrawPixels, glPixelStore,
glPixelTransfer, glTexEnv, glTexGen, glTexImage1D, glTexImage2D, glTexImage3D,
glTexSubImage1D, glTexSubImage2D, glTexParameter

glTranslate

Multiply the current matrix by a translation matrix

C Specification

```
void glTranslated(GLdouble x,
                  GLdouble y,
                  GLdouble z);
void glTranslatef(GLfloat  x,
                  GLfloat  y,
                  GLfloat  z);
```

Parameters

x, y, z   Specify the x, y, and z coordinates of a translation vector.

Description

glTranslate produces a translation by (*x,y,z*). The current matrix (see glMatrixMode) is multiplied by this translation matrix, with the product replacing the current matrix, as if glMultMatrix
were called with the following matrix for its argument:

$$\begin{bmatrix} 1 & 0 & 0 & x \\ 0 & 1 & 0 & y \\ 0 & 0 & 1 & z \\ 0 & 0 & 1 & 0 \\ 0 & 0 & 0 & 1 \end{bmatrix}$$

If the matrix mode is either GL_MODELVIEW or GL_PROJECTION, all objects drawn after a call to glTranslate are translated.

Use glPushMatrix and glPopMatrix to save and restore the untranslated coordinate system.

Errors

GL_INVALID_OPERATION is generated if glTranslate is executed between the execution of glBegin and the corresponding execution of glEnd.

Associated Gets

glGet with argument GL_MATRIX_MODE
glGet with argument GL_COLOR_MATRIX
glGet with argument GL_MODELVIEW_MATRIX
glGet with argument GL_PROJECTION_MATRIX
glGet with argument GL_TEXTURE_MATRIX

See Also

glMatrixMode, glMultMatrix, glPushMatrix, glRotate, glScale

glUniform

Specify the value of a uniform variable for the current program object

C Specification

```
void glUniform1f(GLint location, GLfloat v0);
void glUniform2f(GLint location,
                 GLfloat v0,
                 GLfloat v1);
void glUniform3f(GLint location,
                 GLfloat v0,
                 GLfloat v1,
                 GLfloat v2);
void glUniform4f(GLint location,
                 GLfloat v0,
                 GLfloat v1,
                 GLfloat v2,
                 GLfloat v3);
void glUniform1i(GLint location, GLint v0);
void glUniform2i(GLint location,
                 GLint v0,
                 GLint v1);
void glUniform3i(GLint location,
                 GLint v0,
                 GLint v1,
                 GLint v2);
void glUniform4i(GLint location,
                 GLint v0,
                 GLint v1,
                 GLintv2,
                 GLint v3);
```

Parameters

location   Specifies the location of the uniform variable to be modified.
v0, v1, v2, v3 Specifies the new values to be used for the specified uniform variable.

C Specification

```
void glUniform1fv(GLint location,
                  GLsizei count,
                  const GLfloat * value);
void glUniform2fv(GLint location,
                  GLsizei count,
                  const GLfloat * value);
void glUniform3fv(GLint location,
                  GLsizei count,
                  const GLfloat * value);
void glUniform4fv(GLint location,
                  GLsizei count,
                  const GLfloat * value);
void glUniform1iv(GLint location,
                  GLsizei count,
                  const GLint *   value);
void glUniform2iv(GLint location,
                  GLsizei count,
                  const GLint *   value);
void glUniform3iv(GLint location,
                  GLsizei count,
                  const GLint *   value);
void glUniform4iv(GLint location,
                  GLsizei count,
                  const GLint * value);
```

Parameters

location	Specifies the location of the uniform value to be modified.
count	Specifies the number of elements that are to be modified. This should be 1 if the targeted uniform variable is not an array, and 1 or more if it is an array.
value	Specifies a pointer to an array of *count* values that will be used to update the specified uniform variable.

C Specification

```
void glUniformMatrix2fv(GLint          location,
                        GLsizei        count,
                        GLboolean      transpose,
                        const GLfloat * value);
void glUniformMatrix3fv(GLint          location,
                        GLsizei        count,
                        GLboolean      transpose,
                        const GLfloat * value);
void glUniformMatrix4fv(GLint          location,
                        GLsizei        count,
                        GLboolean      transpose,
                        const GLfloat * value);
void glUniformMatrix2x3fv(GLint          ocation,
                          GLsizei        count,
                          GLboolean      transpose,
                          const GLfloat * value);
```

```
void glUniformMatrix3x2fv(GLint          location,
                          GLsizei         count,
                          GLboolean       transpose,
                          const GLfloat * value);
void glUniformMatrix2x4fv(GLint          location,
                          GLsizei         count,
                          GLboolean       transpose,
                          const GLfloat * value);
void glUniformMatrix4x2fv(GLint          location,
                          GLsizei         count,
                          GLboolean       transpose,
                          const GLfloat * value);
void glUniformMatrix3x4fv(GLint          location,
                          GLsizei         count,
                          GLboolean       transpose,
                          const GLfloat * value);
void glUniformMatrix4x3fv(GLint          location,
                          GLsizei         count,
                          GLboolean       transpose,
                          const GLfloat * value);
```

Parameters

location   Specifies the location of the uniform value to be modified.

count   Specifies the number of matrices that are to be modified. This should be 1 if the targeted uniform variable is not an array of matrices, and 1 or more if it is an array of matrices.

transpose Specifies whether to transpose the matrix as the values are loaded into the uniform variable.

value   Specifies a pointer to an array of *count* values that will be used to update the specified uniform variable.

Description

glUniform modifies the value of a uniform variable or a uniform variable array. The location of the uniform variable to be modified is specified by *location*, which should be a value returned by glGetUniformLocation. glUniform operates on the program object that was made part of current state by calling glUseProgram.

The commands glUniform{1¦2¦3¦4}{f¦i} are used to change the value of the uniform variable specified by *location* using the values passed as arguments. The number specified in the command should match the number of components in the data type of the specified uniform variable (e.g., 1 for float, int, bool; 2 for vec2, ivec2, bvec2, etc.). The suffix f indicates that floating-point values are being passed; the suffix i indicates that integer values are being passed, and this type should also match the data type of the specified uniform variable. The i variants of this function should be used to provide values for uniform variables defined as int, ivec2, ivec3, ivec4, or arrays of these. The f variants should be used to provide values for uniform variables of type float, vec2, vec3, vec4, or arrays of these. Either the i or the f variants may be used to provide values for uniform variables of type bool, bvec2, bvec3, bvec4, or arrays of these. The uniform variable will be set to false if the input value is 0 or 0.0f, and it will be set to true otherwise.

All active uniform variables defined in a program object are initialized to 0 when the program object is linked successfully. They retain the values assigned to them by a call to glUniform until the next successful link operation occurs on the program object, when they are once again initialized to 0.

The commands glUniform{1¦2¦3¦4}{f¦i}v can be used to modify a single uniform variable or a uniform variable array. These commands pass a count and a pointer to the values to be loaded into a uniform variable or a uniform variable array. A count of 1 should be used if modifying the value of a single uniform variable, and a count of 1 or greater can be used to modify an entire array or part of an array. When loading n elements starting at an arbitrary position m in a uniform variable array, elements $m + n$ - 1 in the array will be replaced with the new values. If m + n - 1 is larger than the size of the uniform variable array, values for all array elements beyond the end of the array will be ignored. The number specified in the name of the command indicates the number of components for each element in *value*, and it should match the number of components in the data type of the specified uniform variable (e.g., 1 for float, int, bool; 2 for vec2, ivec2, bvec2, etc.). The data type specified in the name of the command must match the data type for the specified uniform variable as described previously for glUniform{1¦2¦3¦4}{f¦i}.

For uniform variable arrays, each element of the array is considered to be of the type indicated in the name of the command (e.g., glUniform3f or glUniform3fv can be used to load a uniform variable array of type vec3). The number of elements of the uniform variable array to be modified is specified by *count*.

The commands glUniformFloatMatrix{2¦3¦4¦2x3¦3x2¦2x4¦4x2¦3x4¦4x3}fv are used to modify a matrix or an array of matrices. The numbers in the command name are interpreted as the dimensionality of the matrix. The number 2 indicates a 2×2 matrix (i.e., 4 values), the number 3 indicates a 3×3 matrix (i.e., 9 values), and the number 4 indicates a 4×4 matrix (i.e., 16 values). Non-square matrix dimensionality is explicit, with the first number representing the number of columns and the second number representing the number of rows. For example, 2x4 indicates a 2×4 matrix with 2 columns and 4 rows (i.e., 8 values). If *transpose* is GL_FALSE, each matrix is assumed to be supplied in column major order. If *transpose* is GL_TRUE, each matrix is assumed to be supplied in row major order. The *count* argument indicates the number of matrices to be passed. A count of 1 should be used if modifying the value of a single matrix, and a count greater than 1 can be used to modify an array of matrices.

Notes

glUniform is available only if the GL version is 2.0 or greater.

glUniformMatrix{2x3¦3x2¦2x4¦4x2¦3x4¦4x3}fv is available only if the GL version is 2.1 or greater.

glUniform1i and glUniform1iv are the only two functions that may be used to load uniform variables defined as sampler types. Loading samplers with any other function will result in a GL_INVALID_OPERATION error.

If *count* is greater than 1 and the indicated uniform variable is not an array, a GL_INVALID_OPERATION error is generated and the specified uniform variable will remain unchanged.

Other than the preceding exceptions, if the type and size of the uniform variable as defined in the shader do not match the type and size specified in the name of the command used to load its value, a GL_INVALID_OPERATION error will be generated and the specified uniform variable will remain unchanged.

If *location* is a value other than -1 and it does not represent a valid uniform variable location in the current program object, an error will be generated, and no changes will be made to the uniform variable storage of the current program object. If *location* is equal to -1, the data passed in will be silently ignored and the specified uniform variable will not be changed.

Errors

GL_INVALID_OPERATION is generated if there is no current program object.

GL_INVALID_OPERATION is generated if the size of the uniform variable declared in the shader does not match the size indicated by the glUniform command.

GL_INVALID_OPERATION is generated if one of the integer variants of this function is used to load a uniform variable of type float, vec2, vec3, vec4, or an array of these, or if one of the floating-point variants of this function is used to load a uniform variable of type int, ivec2, ivec3, or ivec4, or an array of these.

GL_INVALID_OPERATION is generated if *location* is an invalid uniform location for the current program object and *location* is not equal to -1.

GL_INVALID_VALUE is generated if *count* is less than 0.

GL_INVALID_OPERATION is generated if *count* is greater than 1 and the indicated uniform variable is not an array variable.

GL_INVALID_OPERATION is generated if a sampler is loaded using a command other than glUniform1i and glUniform1iv.

GL_INVALID_OPERATION is generated if glUniform is executed between the execution of glBegin and the corresponding execution of glEnd.

Associated Gets

glGet with the argument GL_CURRENT_PROGRAM

glGetActiveUniform with the handle of a program object and the index of an active uniform variable

glGetUniform with the handle of a program object and the location of a uniform variable

glGetUniformLocation with the handle of a program object and the name of a uniform variable

See Also

glLinkProgram, glUseProgram

glUseProgram

Installs a program object as part of current rendering state

C Specification

void **glUseProgram**(GLuint *program*);

Parameters

program   Specifies the handle of the program object whose executables are to be used as part of current rendering state.

Description

glUseProgram installs the program object specified by *program* as part of current rendering state. One or more executables are created in a program object by successfully attaching shader objects to it with glAttachShader, successfully compiling the shader objects with glCompileShader, and successfully linking the program object with glLinkProgram.

A program object will contain an executable that will run on the vertex processor if it contains one or more shader objects of type GL_VERTEX_SHADER that have been successfully compiled and linked. Similarly, a program object will contain an executable that will run on the fragment processor if it contains one or more shader objects of type GL_FRAGMENT_SHADER that have been successfully compiled and linked.

Successfully installing an executable on a programmable processor will cause the corresponding fixed functionality of OpenGL to be disabled. Specifically, if an executable is installed on the vertex processor, the OpenGL fixed functionality will be disabled as follows.

- The modelview matrix is not applied to vertex coordinates.
- The projection matrix is not applied to vertex coordinates.
- The texture matrices are not applied to texture coordinates.
- Normals are not transformed to eye coordinates.

- Normals are not rescaled or normalized.
- Normalization of GL_AUTO_NORMAL evaluated normals is not performed.
- Texture coordinates are not generated automatically.
- Per-vertex lighting is not performed.
- Color material computations are not performed.
- Color index lighting is not performed.
- This list also applies when setting the current raster position.

The executable that is installed on the vertex processor is expected to implement any or all of the desired functionality from the preceding list. Similarly, if an executable is installed on the fragment processor, the OpenGL fixed functionality will be disabled as follows.

- Texture environment and texture functions are not applied.
- Texture application is not applied.
- Color sum is not applied.
- Fog is not applied.

Again, the fragment shader that is installed is expected to implement any or all of the desired functionality from the preceding list.

While a program object is in use, applications are free to modify attached shader objects, compile attached shader objects, attach additional shader objects, and detach or delete shader objects. None of these operations will affect the executables that are part of the current state. However, relinking the program object that is currently in use will install the program object as part of the current rendering state if the link operation was successful (see glLinkProgram). If the program object currently in use is relinked unsuccessfully, its link status will be set to GL_FALSE, but the executables and associated state will remain part of the current state until a subsequent call to glUseProgram removes it from use. After it is removed from use, it cannot be made part of current state until it has been successfully relinked.

If *program* contains shader objects of type GL_VERTEX_SHADER but it does not contain shader objects of type GL_FRAGMENT_SHADER, an executable will be installed on the vertex processor, but fixed functionality will be used for fragment processing. Similarly, if *program* contains shader objects of type GL_FRAGMENT_SHADER but it does not contain shader objects of type GL_VERTEX_SHADER, an executable will be installed on the fragment processor, but fixed functionality will be used for vertex processing. If *program* is 0, the programmable processors will be disabled, and fixed functionality will be used for both vertex and fragment processing.

Notes

glUseProgram is available only if the GL version is 2.0 or greater.

While a program object is in use, the state that controls the disabled fixed functionality may also be updated using the normal OpenGL calls.

Like display lists and texture objects, the name space for program objects may be shared across a set of contexts, as long as the server sides of the contexts share the same address space. If the name space is shared across contexts, any attached objects and the data associated with those attached objects are shared as well.

Applications are responsible for providing the synchronization across API calls when objects are accessed from different execution threads.

Errors

GL_INVALID_VALUE is generated if *program* is neither 0 nor a value generated by OpenGL.

GL_INVALID_OPERATION is generated if *program* is not a program object.

GL_INVALID_OPERATION is generated if *program* could not be made part of current state.

GL_INVALID_OPERATION is generated if glUseProgram is executed between the execution of glBegin and the corresponding execution of glEnd.

Associated Gets

glGet with the argument GL_CURRENT_PROGRAM
glGetActiveAttrib with a valid program object and the index of an active attribute variable
glGetActiveUniform with a valid program object and the index of an active uniform variable
glGetAttachedShaders with a valid program object
glGetAttribLocation with a valid program object and the name of an attribute variable
glGetProgram with a valid program object and the parameter to be queried
glGetProgramInfoLog with a valid program object
glGetUniform with a valid program object and the location of a uniform variable
glGetUniformLocation with a valid program object and the name of a uniform variable
glIsProgram

See Also

gllAttachShader, glBindAttribLocation, glCompileShader, glCreateProgram, glDeleteProgram, glDetachShader, glLinkProgram, glUniform, glValidateProgram, glVertexAttrib

glValidateProgram

Validates a program object

C Specification

void **glValidateProgram**(GLuint *program*);

Parameters

program   Specifies the handle of the program object to be validated.

Description

glValidateProgram checks to see whether the executables contained in *program* can execute given the current OpenGL state. The information generated by the validation process will be stored in *program*'s information log. The validation information may consist of an empty string, or it may be a string containing information about how the current program object interacts with the rest of current OpenGL state. This provides a way for OpenGL implementers to convey more information about why the current program is inefficient, suboptimal, failing to execute, and so on.

The status of the validation operation will be stored as part of the program object's state. This value will be set to GL_TRUE if the validation succeeded, and GL_FALSE otherwise. It can be queried by calling glGetProgram with arguments *program* and GL_VALIDATE_STATUS. If validation is successful, *program* is guaranteed to execute given the current state. Otherwise, *program* is guaranteed to not execute.

This function is typically useful only during application development. The informational string stored in the information log is completely implementation dependent; therefore, an application should not expect different OpenGL implementations to produce identical information strings.

Notes

glValidateProgram is available only if the GL version is 2.0 or greater.

This function mimics the validation operation that OpenGL implementations must perform when rendering commands are issued while programmable shaders are part of current state. The error GL_INVALID_OPERATION will be generated by glBegin, glRasterPos, or any command that performs an implicit call to glBegin if:

- any two active samplers in the current program object are of different types, but refer to the same texture image unit,
- any active sampler in the current program object refers to a texture image unit where fixed-function fragment processing accesses a texture target that does not match the sampler type, or

- the sum of the number of active samplers in the program and the number of texture image units enabled for fixed-function fragment processing exceeds the combined limit on the total number of texture image units allowed.

It may be difficult or cause a performance degradation for applications to catch these errors when rendering commands are issued. Therefore, applications are advised to make calls to glValidateProgram to detect these issues during application development.

Errors

GL_INVALID_VALUE is generated if *program* is not a value generated by OpenGL.

GL_INVALID_OPERATION is generated if *program* is not a program object.

GL_INVALID_OPERATION is generated if glValidateProgram is executed between the execution of glBegin and the corresponding execution of glEnd.

Associated Gets

glGetProgram with arguments *program* and GL_VALIDATE_STATUS

glGetProgramInfoLog with argument *program*

glIsProgram

See Also

glLinkProgram, glUseProgram

glVertex

Specify a vertex

C Specification

```
void glVertex2s(GLshort x, GLshort y);
void glVertex2i(GLint x, GLint y);
void glVertex2f(GLfloat x, GLfloat y);
void glVertex2d(GLdouble x, GLdouble y);
void glVertex3s(GLshort   x,
                GLshort   y,
                GLshort   z);
void glVertex3i(GLint x, GLint y, GLint z);
void glVertex3f(GLfloat   x,
                GLfloat   y,
                GLfloat   z);
void glVertex3d(GLdouble  x,
                GLdouble  y,
                GLdouble  z);
void glVertex4s(GLshort   x,
                GLshort   y,
                GLshort   z,
                GLshort   w);
void glVertex4i(GLint     x,
                GLint     y,
                GLint     z,
                GLint     w);
void glVertex4f(GLfloat   x,
                GLfloat   y,
                GLfloat   z,
                GLfloat   w);
```

```
void glVertex4d(GLdouble  x,
                GLdouble  y,
                GLdouble  z,
                GLdouble  w);
```

Parameters

x, y, z, w   Specify *x*, *y*, *z*, and *w* coordinates of a vertex. Not all parameters are present in all forms of the command.

C Specification

```
void glVertex2sv(const GLshort * v);
void glVertex2iv(const GLint * v);
void glVertex2fv(const GLfloat * v);
void glVertex2dv(const GLdouble * v);
void glVertex3sv(const GLshort * v);
void glVertex3iv(const GLint * v);
void glVertex3fv(const GLfloat * v);
void glVertex3dv(const GLdouble * v);
void glVertex4sv(const GLshort * v);
void glVertex4iv(const GLint * v);
void glVertex4fv(const GLfloat * v);
void glVertex4dv(const GLdouble * v);
```

Parameters

v   Specifies a pointer to an array of two, three, or four elements. The elements of a two-element array are *x* and *y*; of a three-element array, *x*, *y*, and *z*; and of a four-element array, *x*, *y*, *z*, and *w*.

Description

glVertex commands are used within glBegin/glEnd pairs to specify point, line, and polygon vertices. The current color, normal, texture coordinates, and fog coordinate are associated with the vertex when glVertex is called.

When only *x* and *y* are specified, *z* defaults to 0 and *w* defaults to 1. When *x*, *y*, and *z* are specified, *w* defaults to 1.

Notes

Invoking glVertex outside of a glBegin/glEnd pair results in undefined behavior.

See Also

glBegin, glCallList, glColor, glEdgeFlag, glEvalCoord, glFogCoord, glIndex, glMaterial, glMultiTexCoord, glNormal, glRect, glTexCoord, glVertexPointer

glVertexAttrib

Specifies the value of a generic vertex attribute

C Specification

```
void glVertexAttrib1f(GLuint   index,
                      GLfloat  v0);
void glVertexAttrib1s(GLuint   index,
                      GLshort  v0);
void glVertexAttrib1d(GLuint   index,
                      GLdouble v0);
```

```
void glVertexAttrib2f (GLuint  index,
                       GLfloat v0,
                       GLfloat v1);
void glVertexAttrib2s (GLuint  index,
                       GLshort v0,
                       GLshort v1);
void glVertexAttrib2d (GLuint  index,
                       GLdouble v0,
                       GLdouble v1);
void glVertexAttrib3f (GLuint  index,
                       GLfloat v0,
                       GLfloat v1,
                       GLfloat v2);
void glVertexAttrib3s (GLuint  index,
                       GLshort v0,
                       GLshort v1,
                       GLshort v2);
void glVertexAttrib3d (GLuint  index,
                       GLdouble v0,
                       GLdouble v1,
                       GLdouble v2);
void glVertexAttrib4f (GLuint  index,
                       GLfloat v0,
                       GLfloat v1,
                       GLfloat v2,
                       GLfloat v3);
void glVertexAttrib4s (GLuint  index,
                       GLshort v0,
                       GLshort v1,
                       GLshort v2,
                       GLshort v3);
void glVertexAttrib4d (GLuint  index,
                       GLdouble v0,
                       GLdouble v1,
                       GLdouble v2,
                       GLdouble v3);
void glVertexAttrib4Nub(GLuint index,
                       GLubyte v0,
                       GLubyte v1,
                       GLubyte v2,
                       GLubyte v3);
```

Parameters

index   Specifies the index of the generic vertex attribute to be modified.
v0, v1, v2, v3 Specifies the new values to be used for the specified vertex attribute.

C Specification

```
void glVertexAttrib1fv(GLuint        index,
                       const GLfloat * v);
void glVertexAttrib1sv(GLuint        index,
                       const GLshort * v);
```

```
void glVertexAttrib1dv(GLuint         index,
                 const GLdouble *  v);
void glVertexAttrib2fv(GLuint         index,
                 const GLfloat *   v);
void glVertexAttrib2sv(GLuint         ndex,
                 const GLshort *   v);
void glVertexAttrib2dv(GLuint         index,
                 const GLdouble *  v);
void glVertexAttrib3fv(GLuint         index,
                 const GLfloat *   v);
void glVertexAttrib3sv(GLuint         index,
                 const GLshort *   v);
void glVertexAttrib3dv(GLuint         index,
                 const GLdouble *  v);
void glVertexAttrib4fv(GLuint         index,
                 const GLfloat *   v);
void glVertexAttrib4sv(GLuint         index,
                 const GLshort *   v);
void glVertexAttrib4dv(GLuint         index,
                 const GLdouble *  v);
void glVertexAttrib4iv(GLuint         index,
                 const GLint *     v);
void glVertexAttrib4bv(GLuint         index,
                 const GLbyte *    v);
void glVertexAttrib4ubv(GLuint        index,
                 const GLubyte *   v);
void glVertexAttrib4usv(GLuint        index,
                 const GLushort *  v);
void glVertexAttrib4uiv(GLuint        index,
                 const GLuint *    v);
void glVertexAttrib4Nbv(GLuint        index,
                 const GLbyte *    v);
void glVertexAttrib4Nsv(GLuint        index,
                 const GLshort *   v);
void glVertexAttrib4Niv(GLuint        index,
                 const GLint *     v);
void glVertexAttrib4Nubv(GLuint       index,
                 const GLubyte **  v);
void glVertexAttrib4Nusv(GLuint       index,
                 const GLushort *  v);
void glVertexAttrib4Nuiv(GLuint       index,
                 const GLuint *    v);
```

Parameters

index   Specifies the index of the generic vertex attribute to be modified.

v   Specifies a pointer to an array of values to be used for the generic vertex attribute.

Description

OpenGL defines a number of standard vertex attributes that applications can modify with standard API entry points (color, normal, texture coordinates, etc.). The glVertexAttrib family of entry points allows an application to pass generic vertex attributes in numbered locations.

Generic attributes are defined as four-component values that are organized into an array. The first entry of this array is numbered 0, and the size of the array is specified by the implementation-dependent constant GL_MAX_VERTEX_ATTRIBS. Individual elements of this array can be modified with a glVertexAttrib call that specifies the index of the element to be modified and a value for that element.

These commands can be used to specify one, two, three, or all four components of the generic vertex attribute specified by *index*. A 1 in the name of the command indicates that only one value is passed, and it will be used to modify the first component of the generic vertex attribute. The second and third components will be set to 0, and the fourth component will be set to 1. Similarly, a 2 in the name of the command indicates that values are provided for the first two components, the third component will be set to 0, and the fourth component will be set to 1. A 3 in the name of the command indicates that values are provided for the first three components and the fourth component will be set to 1, whereas a 4 in the name indicates that values are provided for all four components.

The letters s, f, i, d, ub, us, and ui indicate whether the arguments are of type short, float, int, double, unsigned byte, unsigned short, or unsigned int. When v is appended to the name, the commands can take a pointer to an array of such values. The commands containing N indicate that the arguments will be passed as fixed-point values that are scaled to a normalized range according to the component conversion rules defined by the OpenGL specification. Signed values are understood to represent fixed-point values in the range [-1,1], and unsigned values are understood to represent fixed-point values in the range [0,1].

OpenGL Shading Language attribute variables are allowed to be of type mat2, mat3, or mat4. Attributes of these types may be loaded using the glVertexAttrib entry points. Matrices must be loaded into successive generic attribute slots in column major order, with one column of the matrix in each generic attribute slot.

A user-defined attribute variable declared in a vertex shader can be bound to a generic attribute index by calling glBindAttribLocation. This allows an application to use more descriptive variable names in a vertex shader. A subsequent change to the specified generic vertex attribute will be immediately reflected as a change to the corresponding attribute variable in the vertex shader.

The binding between a generic vertex attribute index and a user-defined attribute variable in a vertex shader is part of the state of a program object, but the current value of the generic vertex attribute is not. The value of each generic vertex attribute is part of current state, just like standard vertex attributes, and it is maintained even if a different program object is used.

An application may freely modify generic vertex attributes that are not bound to a named vertex shader attribute variable. These values are simply maintained as part of current state and will not be accessed by the vertex shader. If a generic vertex attribute bound to an attribute variable in a vertex shader is not updated while the vertex shader is executing, the vertex shader will repeatedly use the current value for the generic vertex attribute.

The generic vertex attribute with index 0 is the same as the vertex position attribute previously defined by OpenGL. A glVertex2, glVertex3, or glVertex4 command is completely equivalent to the corresponding glVertexAttrib command with an index argument of 0. A vertex shader can access generic vertex attribute 0 by using the built-in attribute variable gl_Vertex. There are no current values for generic vertex attribute 0. This is the only generic vertex attribute with this property; calls to set other standard vertex attributes can be freely mixed with calls to set any of the other generic vertex attributes.

Notes

glVertexAttrib is available only if the GL version is 2.0 or greater.

Generic vertex attributes can be updated at any time. In particular, glVertexAttrib can be called between a call to glBegin and the corresponding call to glEnd.

It is possible for an application to bind more than one attribute name to the same generic vertex attribute index. This is referred to as aliasing, and it is allowed only if just one of the aliased attribute variables is active in the vertex shader, or if no path through the vertex shader consumes more than one of the attributes aliased to the same location. OpenGL implementations are not required to do error checking to detect aliasing, they are allowed to assume that aliasing will not occur, and they are allowed to employ optimizations that work only in the absence of aliasing.

There is no provision for binding standard vertex attributes; therefore, it is not possible to alias generic attributes with standard attributes.

Errors

GL_INVALID_VALUE is generated if *index* is greater than or equal to GL_MAX_VERTEX_ATTRIBS.

Associated Gets

glGet with the argument GL_CURRENT_PROGRAM
glGetActiveAttrib with argument *program* and the index of an active attribute variable
glGetAttribLocation with argument *program* and an attribute variable name
glGetVertexAttrib with arguments GL_CURRENT_VERTEX_ATTRIB and *index*

See Also

glBindAttribLocation, glVertex, glVertexAttribPointer

glVertexAttribPointer

Define an array of generic vertex attribute data

C Specification

```
void glVertexAttribPointer(GLuint          index,
                           GLint           size,
                           GLenum          type,
                           GLboolean       normalized,
                           GLsizei         stride,
                           const GLvoid *  pointer);
```

Parameters

index	Specifies the index of the generic vertex attribute to be modified.
size	Specifies the number of components per generic vertex attribute. Must be 1, 2, 3, or 4. The initial value is 4.
type	Specifies the data type of each component in the array. Symbolic constants GL_BYTE, GL_UNSIGNED_BYTE, GL_SHORT, GL_UNSIGNED_SHORT, GL_INT, GL_UNSIGNED_INT, GL_FLOAT, or GL_DOUBLE are accepted. The initial value is GL_FLOAT.
normalized	Specifies whether fixed-point data values should be normalized (GL_TRUE) or converted directly as fixed-point values (GL_FALSE) when they are accessed.
stride	Specifies the byte offset between consecutive generic vertex attributes. If *stride* is 0, the generic vertex attributes are understood to be tightly packed in the array. The initial value is 0.
pointer	Specifies a pointer to the first component of the first generic vertex attribute in the array. The initial value is 0.

Description

glVertexAttribPointer specifies the location and data format of the array of generic vertex attributes at index *index* to use when rendering. *size* specifies the number of components per attribute and must be 1, 2, 3, or 4. *type* specifies the data type of each component, and *stride* specifies the byte stride from one attribute to the next, allowing vertices and attributes to be packed into a single array or stored in separate arrays. If set to GL_TRUE, *normalized* indicates that values stored in an integer format are to be mapped to the range [-1,1] (for signed values) or [0,1] (for unsigned values) when they are accessed and converted to floating point. Otherwise, values will be converted to floats directly without normalization.

If a nonzero named buffer object is bound to the `GL_ARRAY_BUFFER` target (see `glBindBuffer`) while a generic vertex attribute array is specified, *pointer* is treated as a byte offset into the buffer object's data store. Also, the buffer object binding (`GL_ARRAY_BUFFER_BINDING`) is saved as generic vertex attribute array client-side state (`GL_VERTEX_ATTRIB_ARRAY_BUFFER_BINDING`) for index *index*.

When a generic vertex attribute array is specified, *size*, *type*, *normalized*, *stride*, and *pointer* are saved as client-side state, in addition to the current vertex array buffer object binding. To enable and disable a generic vertex attribute array, call `glEnableVertexAttribArray` and `glDisableVertexAttribArray` with *index*. If enabled, the generic vertex attribute array is used when `glArrayElement`, `glDrawArrays`, `glMultiDrawArrays`, `glDrawElements`, `glMultiDrawElements`, or `glDrawRangeElements` is called.

Notes

`glVertexAttribPointer` is available only if the GL version is 2.0 or greater.

Each generic vertex attribute array is initially disabled and isn't accessed when `glArrayElement`, `glDrawElements`, `glDrawRangeElements`, `glDrawArrays`, `glMultiDrawArrays`, or `glMultiDrawElements` is called.

Execution of `glVertexAttribPointer` is not allowed between the execution of `glBegin` and the corresponding execution of `glEnd`, but an error may or may not be generated. If no error is generated, the operation is undefined.

`glVertexAttribPointer` is typically implemented on the client side.

Generic vertex attribute array parameters are client-side state and are therefore not saved or restored by `glPushAttrib` and `glPopAttrib`. Use `glPushClientAttrib` and `glPopClientAttrib` instead.

Errors

`GL_INVALID_VALUE` is generated if *index* is greater than or equal to `GL_MAX_VERTEX_ATTRIBS`.
`GL_INVALID_VALUE` is generated if *size* is not 1, 2, 3, or 4.
`GL_INVALID_ENUM` is generated if *type* is not an accepted value.
`GL_INVALID_VALUE` is generated if *stride* is negative.

Associated Gets

`glGet` with argument `GL_MAX_VERTEX_ATTRIBS`
`glGetVertexAttrib` with arguments *index* and `GL_VERTEX_ATTRIB_ARRAY_ENABLED`
`glGetVertexAttrib` with arguments *index* and `GL_VERTEX_ATTRIB_ARRAY_SIZE`
`glGetVertexAttrib` with arguments *index* and `GL_VERTEX_ATTRIB_ARRAY_TYPE`
`glGetVertexAttrib` with arguments *index* and `GL_VERTEX_ATTRIB_ARRAY_NORMALIZED`
`glGetVertexAttrib` with arguments *index* and `GL_VERTEX_ATTRIB_ARRAY_STRIDE`
`glGetVertexAttrib` with arguments *index* and `GL_VERTEX_ATTRIB_ARRAY_BUFFER_BINDING`
`glGet` with argument `GL_ARRAY_BUFFER_BINDING`
`glGetVertexAttribPointerv` with arguments *index* and
`GL_VERTEX_ATTRIB_ARRAY_POINTER`

See Also

`glArrayElement`, `glBindAttribLocation`, `glBindBuffer`, `glColorPointer`, `glDisableVertexAttribArray`, `glDrawArrays`, `glDrawElements`, `glDrawRangeElements`, `glEnableVertexAttribArray`, `glEdgeFlagPointer`, `glFogCoordPointer`, `glIndexPointer`, `glInterleavedArrays`, `glMultiDrawArrays`, `glMultiDrawElements`, `glNormalPointer`, `glPopClientAttrib`, `glPushClientAttrib`, `glSecondaryColorPointer`, `glTexCoordPointer`, `glVertexAttrib`, `glVertexPointer`

glVertexPointer

Define an array of vertex data

C Specification

```
void glVertexPointer(GLint          size,
                     GLenum         type,
                     GLsizei        stride,
                     const GLvoid * pointer);
```

Parameters

size   Specifies the number of coordinates per vertex. Must be 2, 3, or 4. The initial value is 4.

type   Specifies the data type of each coordinate in the array. Symbolic constants GL_SHORT, GL_INT, GL_FLOAT, or GL_DOUBLE are accepted. The initial value is GL_FLOAT.

stride   Specifies the byte offset between consecutive vertices. If *stride* is 0, the vertices are understood to be tightly packed in the array. The initial value is 0.

pointer   Specifies a pointer to the first coordinate of the first vertex in the array. The initial value is 0.

Description

glVertexPointer specifies the location and data format of an array of vertex coordinates to use when rendering. *size* specifies the number of coordinates per vertex, and must be 2, 3, or 4. *type* specifies the data type of each coordinate, and *stride* specifies the byte stride from one vertex to the next, allowing vertices and attributes to be packed into a single array or stored in separate arrays. (Single-array storage may be more efficient on some implementations; see glInterleavedArrays.)

If a nonzero named buffer object is bound to the GL_ARRAY_BUFFER target (see glBindBuffer) while a vertex array is specified, *pointer* is treated as a byte offset into the buffer object's data store. Also, the buffer object binding (GL_ARRAY_BUFFER_BINDING) is saved as vertex array client-side state (GL_VERTEX_ARRAY_BUFFER_BINDING).

When a vertex array is specified, *size*, *type*, *stride*, and *pointer* are saved as client-side state, in addition to the current vertex array buffer object binding.

To enable and disable the vertex array, call glEnableClientState and glDisableClientState with the argument GL_VERTEX_ARRAY. If enabled, the vertex array is used when glArrayElement, glDrawArrays, glMultiDrawArrays, glDrawElements, glMultiDrawElements, or glDrawRangeElements is called.

Notes

glVertexPointer is available only if the GL version is 1.1 or greater.

The vertex array is initially disabled and isn't accessed when glArrayElement, glDrawElements, glDrawRangeElements, glDrawArrays, glMultiDrawArrays, or glMultiDrawElements is called.

Execution of glVertexPointer is not allowed between the execution of glBegin and the corresponding execution of glEnd, but an error may or may not be generated. If no error is generated, the operation is undefined.

glVertexPointer is typically implemented on the client side.

Vertex array parameters are client-side state and are therefore not saved or restored by glPushAttrib and glPopAttrib. Use glPushClientAttrib and glPopClientAttrib instead.

Errors

GL_INVALID_VALUE is generated if *size* is not 2, 3, or 4.

GL_INVALID_ENUM is generated if *type* is not an accepted value.

GL_INVALID_VALUE is generated if *stride* is negative.

Associated Gets

glIsEnabled with argument GL_VERTEX_ARRAY
glGet with argument GL_VERTEX_ARRAY_SIZE
glGet with argument GL_VERTEX_ARRAY_TYPE
glGet with argument GL_VERTEX_ARRAY_STRIDE
glGet with argument GL_VERTEX_ARRAY_BUFFER_BINDING
glGet with argument GL_ARRAY_BUFFER_BINDING
glGetPointerv with argument GL_VERTEX_ARRAY_POINTER

See Also

glArrayElement, glBindBuffer, glColorPointer, glDisableClientState, glDrawArrays, glDrawElements, glDrawRangeElements, glEdgeFlagPointer, glEnableClientState, glFogCoordPointer, glIndexPointer, glInterleavedArrays, glMultiDrawArrays, glMultiDrawElements, glNormalPointer, glPopClientAttrib, glPushClientAttrib, glSecondaryColorPointer, glTexCoordPointer, glVertex, glVertexAttribPointer

glViewport

Set the viewport

C Specification

void **glViewport**(GLint   x,
                   GLint   y,
                   GLsizei width,
                   GLsizei height);

Parameters

x, y   Specify the lower-left corner of the viewport rectangle, in pixels. The initial
                value is (0,0).
width, height   Specify the width and height of the viewport. When a GL context is first
                attached to a window, width and height are set to the dimensions of that
                window.

Description

glViewport specifies the affine transformation of x and y from normalized device coordinates to window coordinates. Let (x_{nd}, y_{nd}) be normalized device coordinates. Then the window coordinates (x_w, y_w) are computed as follows:

$$x_w = (x_{nd} + 1)\left(\frac{width}{2}\right) + x$$

$$y_w = (y_{nd} + 1)\left(\frac{height}{2}\right) + y$$

Viewport width and height are silently clamped to a range that depends on the implementation. To query this range, call glGet with argument GL_MAX_VIEWPORT_DIMS.

Errors

GL_INVALID_VALUE is generated if either width or height is negative.
GL_INVALID_OPE RATION is generated if glViewport is executed between the execution of glBegin and the corresponding execution of glEnd.

Associated Gets

glGet with argument GL_VIEWPORT
glGet with argument GL_MAX_VIEWPORT_DIMS

See Also

glDepthRange

glWindowPos

Specify the raster position in window coordinates for pixel operations

C Specification

```
void glWindowPos2s(GLshort  x, GLshort y);
void glWindowPos2i(GLint    x, GLint y);
void glWindowPos2f(GLfloat  x, GLfloat y);
void glWindowPos2d(GLdouble x, GLdouble y);
void glWindowPos3s(GLshort  x,
                   GLshort  y,
                   GLshort  z);
void glWindowPos3i(GLint    x, GLint y, GLint z);
void glWindowPos3f(GLfloat  x,
                   GLfloat  y,
                   GLfloat  z);
void glWindowPos3d(GLdouble x,
                   GLdouble y,
                   GLdouble z);
```

Parameters

x, y, z   Specify the x, y, z coordinates for the raster position.

C Specification

```
   void glWindowPos2sv(const GLshort * v);
   void glWindowPos2iv(const GLint * v);
   void glWindowPos2fv(const GLfloat * v);
   void glWindowPos2dv(const GLdouble * v);
   void glWindowPos3sv(const GLshort * v);
   void glWindowPos3iv(const GLint * v);
   void glWindowPos3fv(const GLfloat * v);
   void glWindowPos3dv(const GLdouble * v);
```

Parameters

v   Specifies a pointer to an array of two or three elements, specifying x, y, z coordinates, respectively.

Description

The GL maintains a 3D position in window coordinates. This position, called the raster position, is used to position pixel and bitmap write operations. It is maintained with subpixel accuracy. See glBitmap, glDrawPixels, and glCopyPixels.

glWindowPos2 specifies the x and y coordinates, while z is implicitly set to 0. glWindowPos3 specifies all three coordinates. The w coordinate of the current raster position is always set to 1.0.

glWindowPos directly updates the *x* and *y* coordinates of the current raster position with the values specified. That is, the values are neither transformed by the current modelview and projection matrices, nor by the viewport-to-window transform. The *z* coordinate of the current raster position is updated in the following manner:

$$z = \begin{cases} n & \text{if } z <= 0 \\ f & \text{if } z >= 1 \\ n + z \times (f - n) & \text{normal otherwise} \end{cases}$$

where *n* is GL_DEPTH_RANGE's near value, and *f* is GL_DEPTH_RANGE's far value. See glDepthRange. The specified coordinates are not clip-tested, causing the raster position to always be valid.

The current raster position also includes some associated color data and texture coordinates. If lighting is enabled, then GL_CURRENT_RASTER_COLOR (in RGBA mode) or GL_CURRENT_RASTER_INDEX (in color index mode) is set to the color produced by the lighting calculation (see glLight, glLightModel, and glShadeModel). If lighting is disabled, current color (in RGBA mode, state variable GL_CURRENT_COLOR) or color index (in color index mode, state variable GL_CURRENT_INDEX) is used to update the current raster color. GL_CURRENT_RASTER_SECONDARY_COLOR (in RGBA mode) is likewise updated.

Likewise, GL_CURRENT_RASTER_TEXTURE_COORDS is updated as a function of GL_CURRENT_TEXTURE_COORDS, based on the texture matrix and the texture generation functions (see glTexGen). The GL_CURRENT_RASTER_DISTANCE is set to the GL_CURRENT_FOG_COORD.

Notes

glWindowPos is available only if the GL version is 1.4 or greater.

The raster position is modified by glRasterPos, glBitmap, and glWindowPos.

Calling glDrawElements, or glDrawRangeElements may leave the current color or index indeterminate. If glWindowPos is executed while the current color or index is indeterminate, the current raster color or current raster index remains indeterminate.

There are distinct raster texture coordinates for each texture unit. Each texture unit's current raster texture coordinates are updated by glWindowPos.

Errors

GL_INVALID_OPERATION is generated if glWindowPos is executed between the execution of glBegin and the corresponding execution of glEnd.

Associated Gets

glGet with argument GL_CURRENT_RASTER_POSITION
glGet with argument GL_CURRENT_RASTER_POSITION_VALID
glGet with argument GL_CURRENT_RASTER_DISTANCE
glGet with argument GL_CURRENT_RASTER_COLOR
glGet with argument GL_CURRENT_RASTER_SECONDARY_COLOR
glGet with argument GL_CURRENT_RASTER_INDEX
glGet with argument GL_CURRENT_RASTER_TEXTURE_COORDS

See Also

glBitmap, glCopyPixels, glDrawArrays, glDrawElements, glDrawRangeElements, glDrawPixels, glMultiTexCoord, glRasterPos, glTexCoord, glTexGen, glVertex

Index

Numbers

H